The 1995 World Book

YEAR BOOK

The Annual Supplement to The World Book Encyclopedia

▪▪▪ A REVIEW OF THE EVENTS OF 1994 ▪▪▪

World Book, Inc.

a Scott Fetzer company

Chicago ▪ London ▪ Sydney ▪ Toronto

© 1995 World Book, Inc. All rights reserved. This volume may not be reproduced in
whole or in part in any form without prior written permission from the publisher.
Portions of the material contained in this volume are taken from *The World Book
Encyclopedia* © 1995 and from *The World Book Dictionary* © 1995 World Book, Inc.

World Book, Inc.
525 W. Monroe
Chicago, IL 60661

ISBN 0-7166-0495-7
ISSN 0084-1439
Library of Congress Catalog Card Number: 62-4818

Printed in the United States of America.

Staff

Contributors

Contributors not listed on these pages are members of *The World Book Year Book* editorial staff.

- **ALEXIOU, ARTHUR G.**, B.S.E.E., M.S.E.E.; Assistant Secretary, Committee on Climatic Changes and Ocean. [Ocean]

- **ANDERSON, PORTER**, B.A., M.A., M.F.A.; Theater Critic, *Village Voice*. [Theater]

- **ANDREWS, PETER J.**, B.A., M.S.; free-lance writer; biochemist. [Chemistry]

- **APSELOFF, MARILYN FAIN**, B.A., M.A.; Associate Professor of English, Kent State University. [Literature for children]

- **ARNDT, RANDOLPH C.**, Media Relations Director, National League of Cities. [City]

- **BARBER, PEGGY**, B.A., M.L.S.; Associate Executive Director for Communications, American Library Association. [Library]

- **BARNHART, BILL**, B.A., M.S.T., M.B.A.; Financial markets columnist, *Chicago Tribune*. [Stocks and bonds]

- **BERGER, JIM**, B.A., M.P.A.; Editor/Publisher, Trade Reports International Group. [International trade]

- **BESSMAN, JIM**, contributor, *Billboard* magazine; Senior Editor, *Spin* magazine. [Popular music]

- **BLACKADAR, ALFRED K.**, A.B., Ph.D.; Professor Emeritus, Pennsylvania State University. [Weather]

- **BOHANNAN, PAUL**, B.A., B.Sc., M.A., D.Phil.; Professor Emeritus of Anthropology, University of Southern California. [World Book Supplement: Culture]

- **BOWER, BRUCE**, M.A.; Behavioral Sciences Editor, *Science News* magazine. [Psychology]

- **BOYD, JOHN D.**, B.S.; Midwest Bureau Chief, *Journal of Commerce*. [Economics]

- **BRADSHER, HENRY S.**, A.B., B.J.; foreign affairs analyst. [Asia and Asian country articles]

- **BRETT, CARLTON E.**, B.A., M.S., Ph.D.; Professor of Geological Sciences, University of Rochester. [Paleontology]

- **CAMPBELL, GEOFFREY A.**, B.J.; Staff Reporter, *The Bond Buyer*. [Civil rights; Courts; Supreme Court of the United States]

- **CAMPBELL, LINDA P.**, B.A., M.S.L.; National Legal Affairs Correspondent, *Chicago Tribune*. [Civil rights; Courts; Supreme Court of the United States]

- **CARDINALE, DIANE P.**, B.A.; Assistant Communications Director, Toy Manufacturers of America. [Toys and games]

- **CARMODY, DEIRDRE**, Media Reporter, *The New York Times*. [Magazine]

- **CHERTOW, MARIAN R.**, A.B.; M.P.P.M.; Director, Project on Solid Wastes and the Environment, Yale University. [World Book Supplement: Environmental pollution]

- **CORNELL, VINCENT J.**, B.A., M.A., Ph.D.; Andrew W. Mellon Assistant Professor of Religion, Duke University. [Islam]

- **CROMIE, WILLIAM J.**, B.S., M.S.; science writer, Harvard University. [Space exploration]

- **DeFRANK, THOMAS M.**, B.A., M.A.; White House Correspondent, *Newsweek* magazine. [Armed forces]

- **DeLANCEY, MARK W.**, B.A., M.A., Ph.D.; Professor of Government and International Studies, University of South Carolina. [Africa and African country articles]

- **DILLON, DAVID**, B.A., M.A., Ph.D.; Architect Critic, *The Dallas Morning News*. [Architecture]

- **DIRDA, MICHAEL**, B.A., M.A., Ph.D.; writer and editor, *The Washington Post Book World*. [Poetry]

- **EATON, WILLIAM J.**, B.S.J., M.S.J.; Correspondent, *Los Angeles Times*. [U.S. government articles]

- **ELLIS, GAVIN**, Assistant Editor, *New Zealand Herald*. [New Zealand]

- **FARR, DAVID M. L.**, M.A., D.Phil.; Professor Emeritus of History, Carleton University, Ottawa. [Canada; Canadian provinces]

- **FEELY, MARY**, B.A.; free-lance editor and writer. [Nobel Prizes; Pulitzer Prizes]

- **FERRELL, KEITH**, Editor, *Omni* magazine. [Computer]

- **FETTER, BRUCE**, B.A., M.Phil., Ph.D.; Professor of History, University of Wisconsin, Milwaukee. [World Book Supplement: South Africa]

- **FISHER, ROBERT W.**, B.A., M.A.; free-lance writer; formerly a Senior Economist/Editor, U.S. Bureau of Labor Statistics. [Labor]

- **FITZGERALD, MARK**, B.A.; Midwest Editor, *Editor & Publisher* magazine. [Newspaper]

- **FIXICO, DONALD L.**, B.A., M.A., Ph.D.; Professor of History, Western Michigan University. [Indian, American]

- **FOX, THOMAS C.**, B.A., M.A.; Editor, *National Catholic Reporter*. [Roman Catholic Church]

- **FRIEDMAN, EMILY**, B.A.; Contributing Editor, *Hospitals* magazine. [Health care issues]

- **GARVIE, MAUREEN**, B.A., B.Ed., M.A.; Books Editor, *The* (Kingston, Ont.) *Whig-Standard*. [Canadian literature]

- **GATTY, BOB**, Editor, Periodicals News Service. [Food]

- **GOLDEN, CARON**, B.A.; free-lance writer. [San Diego]

- **GOLDNER, NANCY**, B.A.; Dance Critic, *The Philadelphia Inquirer*. [Dancing]

- **HARAKAS, STANLEY SAMUEL**, B.A., B.D., Th.D.; Archbishop Iakovos Professor of Orthodox Theology, Hellenic College, Holy Cross Greek Orthodox School of Theology. [Eastern Orthodox Churches]

- **HAVERSTOCK, NATHAN A.**, A.B.; Affiliate Scholar, Oberlin College. [Latin America and Latin-American country articles]

- **HAYMER, DAVID S.**, B.S., M.A., Ph.D.; Associate Professor, Department of Genetics, University of Hawaii. [Courts Special Report: Guilty or Not Guilty...by a Hair?]

- **HELLMAN, JOEL**, B.A., M.A., Ph.D.; Russian Research Center, Harvard University. [Commonwealth of Independent States and former Soviet republic articles]

- **HELMS, CHRISTINE**, B.A., Ph.D.; foreign affairs analyst; author. [Middle East and Middle Eastern country articles; North Africa country articles]

- **HENDERSON, NELL**, B.S.J.; Staff Writer, *The Washington Post*. [Washington, D.C.]

- **HILLGREN, SONJA**, B.J., M.A.; Washington Editor, *Farm Journal*. [Farm and farming]

- **HOFFMAN, SAUL D.**, B.A., M.A., Ph.D.; Professor of Economics, University of Delaware. [Welfare Special Report: Time to Reform Welfare?]

- **HOWELL, LEON**, A.B., M.Div.; Editor and Publisher, *Christianity and Crisis*. [Religion]

- **JOHANSON, DONALD C.**, B.S., M.A., Ph.D.; President, Institute of Human Origins. [Anthropology]

- **JONES, TIM**, B.A.; Financial Correspondent, *Chicago Tribune*. [Telecommunications]

- **KIM, HYUNG-CHAN**, A.B., M.A., Ph.D.; Professor of Education and Asian American Studies, Western Washington University. [World Book Supplement: Asian Americans]

- **KING, MIKE**, Reporter, *The Montreal Gazette*. [Montreal]

- **KISOR, HENRY**, B.A., M.S.J.; Book Editor, *Chicago Sun-Times*. **[Literature; Literature, American]**

- **KISTE, ROBERT C.**, Ph.D.; Director and Professor, Center for Pacific Islands Studies, University of Hawaii. **[Pacific Islands]**

- **KOLGRAF, RONALD**, B.A., M.A.; Publisher, *Adweek/New England* magazine. **[Manufacturing]**

- **KORMAN, RICHARD**, Associate Editor, *Engineering News-Record*. **[Labor Special Report: Unions in Decline; Building and construction]**

- **KUTLER, STANLEY I.**, B.S., M.A., Ph.D.; E. Gordon Fox Professor of American Institutions and Law, University of Wisconsin. **[Deaths Special Report: Richard M. Nixon: How Will History Judge His Legacy?]**

- **LAWRENCE, AL**, B.A., M.A., M.Ed.; Executive Director, United States Chess Federation. **[Chess]**

- **LEWIS, DAVID C.**, M.D.; Professor of Medicine and Community Health, Brown University. **[Drug abuse]**

- **LEWYN, MARK**, B.S.; Washington Correspondent, *Business Week* magazine. **[Telecommunications Special Report: Regulating the Information Highway]**

- **LITSKY, FRANK**, B.S.; Sportswriter, *The New York Times*. **[Sports articles]**

- **LOVE, JANICE**, B.A., M.A., Ph.D.; Associate Professor and Graduate Director of International Studies, University of South Carolina. **[South Africa Special Report: New Era for South Africa]**

- **MARCH, ROBERT H.**, A.B., S.M., Ph.D.; Professor of Physics, University of Wisconsin at Madison. **[Physics]**

- **MARSCHALL, LAURENCE A.**, Ph.D.; Professor of Physics, Gettysburg College. **[Astronomy]**

- **MARTY, MARTIN E.**, Ph.D.; Fairfax M. Cone Distinguished Service Professor, University of Chicago. **[Protestantism]**

- **MATHER, IAN J.**, B.A., M.A.; Diplomatic Editor, *The European*, London. **[Ireland; Northern Ireland; United Kingdom]**

- **MAUGH, THOMAS H., II**, Ph.D.; Science Writer, *Los Angeles Times*. **[Biology]**

- **MERINA, VICTOR**, A.A., B.A., M.S.; free-lance writer. **[Los Angeles]**

- **MERLINE, JOHN W.**, B.A.; Washington Correspondent, *Investor's Business Daily*. **[Consumerism]**

- **MORITZ, OWEN**, B.A.; free-lance writer. **[New York City]**

- **MORRIS, BERNADINE**, B.A., M.A.; Chief Fashion Writer, *The New York Times*. **[Fashion]**

- **MUCHNIC, SUZANNE**, B.A., M.A.; Art Writer, *Los Angeles Times*. **[Art]**

- **MULLINS, HENRY T.**, B.S., M.S., Ph.D.; Professor of Geology, Syracuse University. **[Geology]**

- **NAUGHTON, KEITH P.**, B.A.; Auto Writer, *The Detroit News*. **[Automobile]**

- **NGUYEN, J. TUYET**, B.A.; Bureau manager, United Nations Correspondent, United Press International. **[United Nations]**

- **NOMANI, ASRA Q.**, B.A., M.A.; Reporter, *The Wall Street Journal*. **[Aviation]**

- **OPPMANN, ANDREW**, B.A.; Metropolitan Editor, *The Houston Post*. **[Houston]**

- **PENNISI, ELIZABETH**, B.S., M.S.; Biomedical Editor, *Science News* magazine. **[Zoology]**

- **PHILLIPS, HERBERT P.**, A.B., Ph.D.; Professor of Anthropology, University of California, Berkeley. **[World Book Supplement: Thailand]**

- **POWERS, THOMAS**, Free-lance writer. **[Espionage Special Report: Why Spy?]**

- **PRIESTAF, IRIS**, B.A., M.A., Ph.D.; Geographer and Vice President, David Keith Todd Consulting Engineers, Incorporated. **[Water]**

- **RALOFF, JANET**, B.S.J., M.S.J.; Senior Editor, *Science News* magazine. **[Environmental pollution]**

- **RAPHAEL, M. L.**, B.A., M.A., Ph.D.; Gimenick Professor of Judaic Studies, College of William and Mary. **[Judaism]**

- **REARDON, PATRICK T.**, B.A.; Urban Affairs Writer, *Chicago Tribune*. **[Chicago]**

- **REVZIN, PHILIP**, B.A., M.A.; Editor, *The Wall Street Journal Europe*. **[Europe and Western European country articles]**

- **ROSE, MARK J.**, M.A.; Managing Editor, *Archaeology* magazine. **[Archaeology]**

- **SAVAGE, IAN**, B.A., M.A., Ph.D.; Assistant Professor of Economics and Transportation, Northwestern University. **[Transportation]**

- **SEGAL, TROY**, B.A.; free-lance writer. **[Television]**

- **SHAPIRO, HOWARD S.**, B.S.; Cultural Arts Editor, *The Philadelphia Inquirer*. **[Philadelphia]**

- **SOLNICK, STEVEN L.**, B.A., M.A., Ph.D.; Professor of Political Science, Columbia University. **[Baltic states and other former Soviet republic articles]**

- **STEIN, DAVID LEWIS**, B.A., M.S.; Urban Affairs Columnist, *The Toronto Star*. **[Toronto]**

- **STOKESBURY, JAMES L.**, B.A., M.A., Ph.D.; Professor of History, Acadia University. **[Armed forces Special Report: The World Remembers D-Day]**

- **STUART, ELAINE**, B.A.; Managing Editor, Council of State Governments. **[State government]**

- **TANNER, JAMES C.**, B.S.J.; Senior Energy Correspondent, *The Wall Street Journal*. **[Petroleum and gas]**

- **TATUM, HENRY K.**, B.A.; Associate Editorial Page Editor, *The Dallas Morning News*. **[Dallas; World Book Supplement: Dallas]**

- **THOMAS, PAULETTE**, B.A.; Staff Writer, *The Wall Street Journal*. **[Bank]**

- **TOCH, THOMAS W.**, B.A., M.A.; Associate Editor and Education Correspondent, *U.S. News & World Report*. **[Education]**

- **TONRY, MICHAEL**, A.B., LL.B.; Sonosky Professor of Law and Public Policy, University of Minnesota Law School. **[Crime Special Report: Fighting Crime in America; Prison]**

- **TOY, VIVIAN S.**, B.A.; Staff Writer, *The Detroit News*. **[Detroit]**

- **VIZARD, FRANK**, B.A.; Electronics Editor, *Popular Mechanics*. **[Electronics]**

- **von RHEIN, JOHN**, B.A., M.A.; Music critic, *Chicago Tribune*. **[Classical music]**

- **WALTER, EUGENE J., Jr.**, B.A.; free-lance writer. **[Zoos Special Report: The New Aquariums; Conservation; Zoos]**

- **WELSOME, EILEEN**, B.S.; Reporter, *The Albuquerque* (N. Mex.) *Tribune*. **[Public health Special Report: The Radiation Experiments]**

- **WILLIAMS, SUSAN G.**, B.A.; free-lance journalist, Sydney, Australia. **[Australia]**

- **WOLCHIK, SHARON L.**, B.A., M.A., Ph.D.; Director, Russian and East European Studies, George Washington University. **[Eastern European country articles]**

- **WOODS, MICHAEL**, B.S.; Science Editor, *The* (Toledo, Ohio) *Blade*. **[AIDS Special Report: The Changing Face of AIDS; Industry articles and health articles]**

- **WUNTCH, PHILIP**, B.A.; Film Critic, *The Dallas Morning News*. **[Motion pictures]**

C ontents

▲ Page 462

Cross-Reference Tabs

A tear-out page of Cross-Reference Tabs for insertion in *The World Book Encyclopedia* appears before page 1.

The Year in Brief   10

A pictorial review of the top stories in the news and where to find information about them.

◄ Page 324

▲ Page 462

The Year's Major News Stories

From the genocidal slaughter of an estimated 500,000 people in the central African nation of Rwanda to the peaceful restoration of democracy in the Caribbean nation of Haiti, 1994 was a year filled with momentous events. On these two pages are the stories that *Year Book* editors picked as the most memorable, exciting, or most important of the year, along with details on where to find information about them in *The World Book Year Book.*   *The Editors*

Peace in the Middle East
Israeli Prime Minister Yitzhak Rabin, left, and Jordan's King Hussein I shake hands as U.S. President Bill Clinton looks on, after reaching a peace accord on July 25, 1994. See **Middle East,** page 302.

▼

IRA cease-fire
The Irish Republican Army declares a cease-fire on Aug. 31, 1994, in its 25-year struggle to end British rule of Northern Ireland. Protestant paramilitary groups, seeking to maintain ties with the United Kingdom, also declare a cease-fire on October 13. See **Northern Ireland,** page 321.

South Africa ▶
Supporters of the African National Congress (ANC) wave a poster of ANC leader Nelson Mandela after the ANC swept South Africa's first all-race elections in April. See **Africa,** page 38; **South Africa,** page 370.

Baseball strike

On Aug. 12, 1994, major league baseball players went on strike, and by year's end, the longest-running walk-out in professional sports was still unsettled. The strike canceled the World Series for the first time since 1904. See **Baseball,** page 92; **Labor,** page 262.

◄ **Mass exodus in Rwanda**

An estimated 1 million Rwandan refugees flee into neighboring Zaire in April to escape ethnic warfare that killed up to 500,000 people. See **Rwanda,** page 361; **United Nations,** page 427.

Los Angeles quake ►

Freeway overpasses crumble from the impact of an earthquake that struck the Los Angeles area on Jan. 17, 1994, killing 57 people. See **Geology,** page 233; **Los Angeles,** page 291.

▲

U.S. troops in Haiti

U.S. troops enter Port-au-Prince, capital of Haiti, on Sept. 19, 1994, to safeguard the return of democratically elected President Jean-Bertrand Aristide on October 15. See **Haiti,** page 239.

U.S. midterm elections

The Republican Party sweeps the Nov. 8, 1994, midterm congressional elections in the United States, winning control of both the House of Representatives and the Senate for the first time since 1954. See **Congress of the United States,** page 141; **Elections,** page 200; **Republican Party,** page 356.

◄ **O. J. Simpson trial**

Ex-football star O. J. Simpson appears in court on charges that he murdered an ex-wife and her friend on June 12, 1994. Simpson's trial was still underway at year's end. See **Courts,** page 150; **Courts** Special Report: **Guilty or Not Guilty . . . by a Hair?** page 152; **Crime,** page 158; **Los Angeles,** page 291.

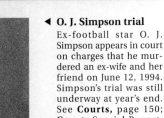

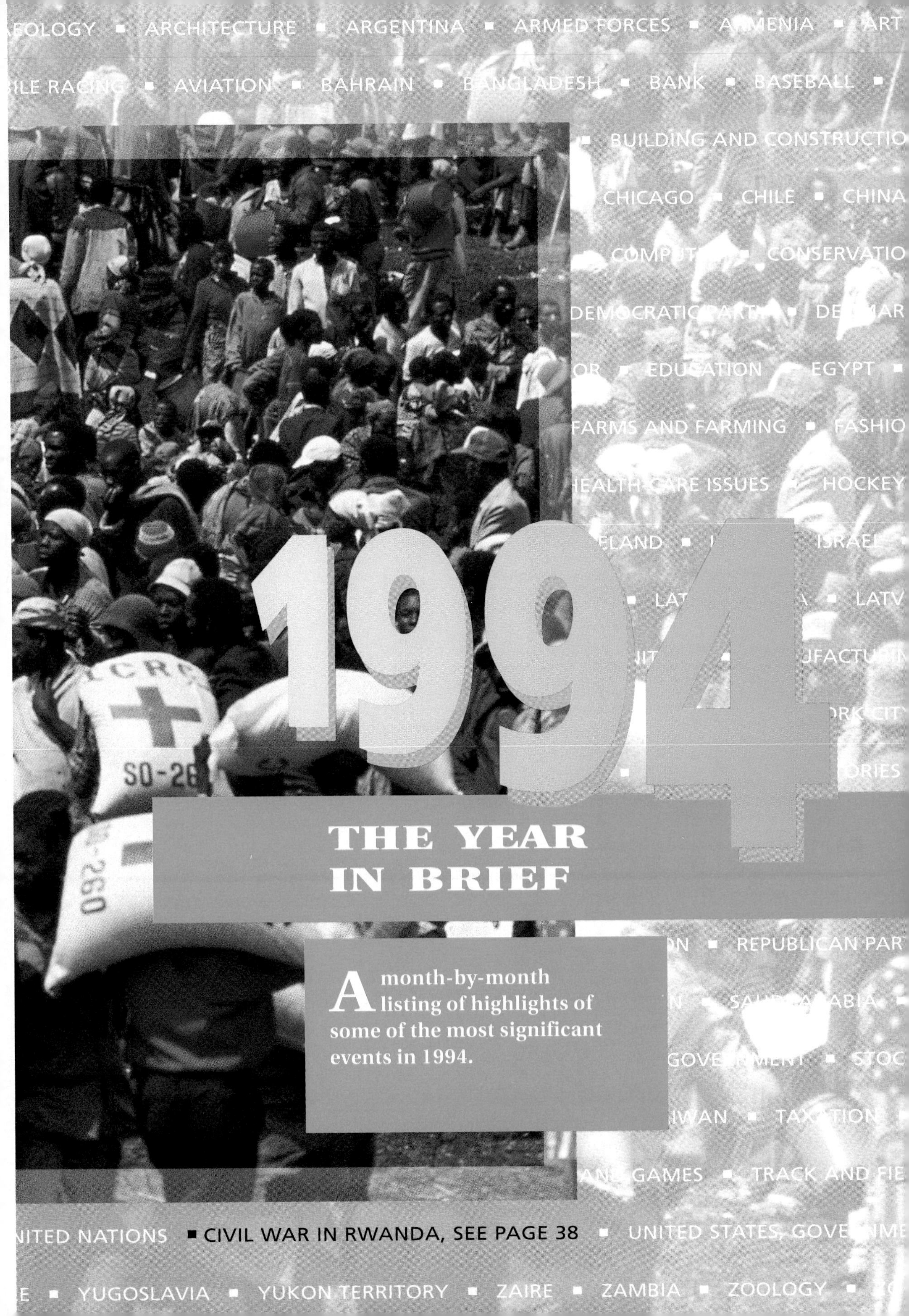

BUILDING AND CONSTRUCTIO

CHICAGO ▪ CHILE ▪ CHINA

COMPUT... ▪ CONSERVATIO

DEMOCRATIC PART... ▪ DE... MAR

OR ▪ EDUCATION ▪ EGYPT ▪

FARMS AND FARMING ▪ FASHIO

HEALTH CARE ISSUES ▪ HOCKEY

ELAND ▪ I... ▪ ISRAEL ▪

▪ LAT... ▪ LATV

...IT ...UFACTU...

...RK CIT

...ORIES

1994

THE YEAR
IN BRIEF

A month-by-month
listing of highlights of
some of the most significant
events in 1994.

...N ▪ REPUBLICAN PAR

...N ▪ SAUDI ARABIA ▪

▪ GOVE...MENT ▪ STOC

...IWAN ▪ TAX...TION

...AND GAMES ▪ TRACK AND FIE

S	M	T	W	TH	F	S
January 1994						1
2	3	4	5	6	7	8
9	10	11	12	13	14	15
16	17	18	19	20	21	22
23	24	25	26	27	28	29
30	31					

Officials inspect a freeway collapse after an earthquake measuring 6.7 on the Richter scale struck the Los Angeles area on January 17.

1 Guerrillas in the Mexican state of Chiapas capture four towns in fighting with government forces. The rebels, who called themselves the Zapatista National Liberation Army, said their attack was timed to coincide with the implementation of the North American Free Trade Agreement, which they decried as a "death sentence" for Mexico's poor.

6 American figure skater Nancy Kerrigan, a gold medal favorite for the 1994 Winter Olympics, is attacked by an unidentified man who struck her on the right knee with a blunt object following a practice at an arena in Detroit. By January 19, rival skater Tonya Harding's ex-husband, her bodyguard, and two other men had been charged with conspiracy to commit assault.

7 The beaches of San Juan, Puerto Rico, are awash with diesel oil after a barge carrying more than 1.5 million gallons (5.7 million liters) of the fuel struck an offshore coral reef and spilled about half its cargo.

8 Wildfires in Australia ravage a 750-mile (1,200-kilometer) stretch of coastline in New South Wales and reach the outskirts of Sydney, Australia's largest city. By January 13, the fires were largely under control, but they had killed four people and had burned about 1.9 million acres (770,000 hectares) of land.

12 United States President Bill Clinton asks Attorney General Janet Reno to appoint a special prosecutor to investigate Clinton's dealings with a former partner in the Whitewater Development Corporation, a failed real estate venture that Clinton helped finance when he was governor of Arkansas.

17 An earthquake strikes the Los Angeles area at 4:31 a.m. local time, killing 57 people and knocking out power and water service for hundreds of thousands of people. About 25,000 people are left homeless, and estimates of damages range up to $20 billion. The quake measures 6.7 on the Richter scale.

24 President Clinton nominates Deputy Defense Secretary William J. Perry for the post of secretary of defense.

25 In his State of the Union address before a joint session of Congress, President Clinton makes an anticrime bill and health care and welfare reform his principal legislative objectives for 1994 and vows to veto any bill that does not guarantee universal health insurance coverage.
Popular music star Michael Jackson reaches an out-of-court settlement with a teen-age boy who charged in a civil lawsuit that Jackson sexually molested him when he was 13 years old. The settlement was reportedly in excess of $10 million.

30 The Dallas Cowboys win Super Bowl XXVIII in Atlanta, Ga., defeating the Buffalo Bills, 30-13, as Dallas running back Emmitt Smith, the regular season and the Super Bowl Most Valuable Player, rushed for two touchdowns. It was the Cowboys' second straight Super Bowl victory and Buffalo's fourth consecutive Super Bowl loss.

◀ Figure skater Nancy Kerrigan grimaces in pain after an assailant struck her on the right knee on January 6 during a practice session in Detroit. By January 19, four associates of rival skater Tonya Harding had been arrested in connection with the assault.

S	M	T	W	TH	F	S
		1	2	3	4	5
6	7	8	9	10	11	12
13	14	15	16	17	18	19
20	21	22	23	24	25	26
27	28					

February 1994

3 **The United States trade embargo against Vietnam,** begun in 1975, is lifted by President Bill Clinton, despite protests by some veterans' groups.
The space shuttle Discovery lifts off from Cape Canaveral, Fla., carrying cosmonaut Sergei K. Krikalev, the first Russian astronaut ever to join a U.S. space shuttle mission.

5 **A mortar shell explodes in Sarajevo's** central market, killing 68 people and wounding more than 200 in the deadliest attack on civilians since the civil war in Bosnia-Herzegovina began in 1992.
White supremacist Byron De La Beckwith is found guilty by a jury in Jackson, Miss., of the 1963 murder of civil rights leader Medgar Evers and is immediately sentenced to life imprisonment. Beckwith had been tried twice in 1964, but all-white juries were deadlocked both times.

9 **Israeli Foreign Minister Shimon Peres** and Palestine Liberation Organization (PLO) Chairman Yasir Arafat initial an accord that settles several issues responsible for delaying implementation of the 1993 peace agreement.

12 **The XVII Winter Olympic Games open** in Lillehammer, Norway, with 1,920 athletes from a record 80 nations and political units. The games come to a close on February 27, with Norway winning 26 medals, Germany 24, and Russia 23.

20 **Air strikes against Bosnian Serb forces** surrounding Sarajevo, capital of Bosnia-Herzegovina, are called off by the United Nations (UN) and the North Atlantic Treaty Organization (NATO). Officials determined that the Serbs had complied sufficiently with a NATO ultimatum to remove all heavy weapons from the hills surrounding Sarajevo or surrender them to UN control.

21 **A major espionage scandal** unfolds as U.S. authorities arrest Aldrich H. Ames, a senior Central Intelligence Agency official, and his wife, Rosario, on charges of spying for the Soviet Union from 1985 to 1991 and of then spying for Russia.

25 **A Jewish settler opens fire on Muslim** worshipers in a mosque in the Israeli-occupied West Bank town of Hebron, killing 29 people and wounding about 170 people before he is beaten to death. Israeli Prime Minister Yitzhak Rabin condemns the attack and urges the PLO to continue peace negotiations. On February 27, Israel releases 1,000 Palestinian prisoners and says it will establish a commission to investigate the massacre.

28 **Four Bosnian Serb light-attack bombers** are shot down by two U.S. F-16 Falcon fighters under NATO command after the Serb aircraft violated a UN no-fly zone over central Bosnia-Herzegovina. It was the first use of NATO military force since the alliance was established in 1949.
Roman Catholic Cardinal Joseph Bernardin is cleared of sexual abuse charges after the man who made the charges, Steven Cook, 34, of Philadelphia, withdraws his lawsuit against the cardinal, saying he no longer believes his memories of the alleged abuse "are true and accurate."

The XVII Winter Olympic Games open in Lillehammer, Norway, on February 12 with 1,920 athletes participating.

S	M	T	W	TH	F	S
		1	2	3	4	5
6	7	8	9	10	11	12
13	14	15	16	17	18	19
20	21	22	23	24	25	26
27	28	29	30	31		

March 1994

Debris is all that remains of a country church outside Piedmont, Ala., after a tornado ripped through the area on March 27, killing 20 people who were attending Palm Sunday services, including 6 children.

2 **The Mexican government** and the Zapatista National Liberation Army reach a tentative agreement to end the Indian uprising in the state of Chiapas, following negotiations in San Cristóbal de las Casas. The accord calls for sweeping political reforms and increased aid to Indian communities in southern Mexico. But on June 2, the rebels reject the accord.

4 **Four defendants in the 1993 World Trade Center** bombing in New York City are convicted of conspiracy. The bombing killed six people and injured more than 1,000.

5 **Antiabortion activist Michael F. Griffin** is convicted by a Pensacola, Fla., jury of first-degree murder in the 1993 killing of David Gunn, a physician who performed abortions.

11 **The president of the South African homeland** of Bophuthatswana, in the face of widespread protests and a mutiny by homeland troops, agrees to allow residents of the homeland to participate in national elections. South African troops enter the homeland to restore order and to expel armed white extremists, at least three of whom are killed by homeland troops.

12 **The Church of England ordains 32 women** as priests, the first female priests since King Henry VIII established the church in 1534.

13 **Israel's cabinet outlaws** two Jewish extremist groups, Kach and Kahane Lives, in the wake of February's Hebron massacre. The gunman in that massacre, Baruch Goldstein, was a follower of the late Rabbi Meir Kahane, who formed the extremist Kach movement.

16 **Ice skater Tonya Harding** pleads guilty to conspiring to hinder the prosecution of an assault on rival skater Nancy Kerrigan. Harding is sentened to three years of probation, fined $100,000, ordered to perform 500 hours of community service, and is forced to resign from the United States Figure Skating Association.

20 **Voters in El Salvador go to the polls** in the first presidential election since the nation's 12-year civil war ended in 1992. The results set up a runoff election between the ruling party and the left wing Democratic Convergence coalition, which includes the guerrilla organization that led the peasant-based rebellion during the civil war.

23 **Mexico's leading presidential candidate,** Luis Donaldo Colosio Murrieta, is assassinated in Tijuana, Mexico, during a campaign rally. Police arrest a 23-year-old suspect with no known political affiliations. On April 4, a special prosecutor says that at least seven people were involved in the assassination, including the head of security for the rally.

27 **A tornado rips through a small country church** outside Piedmont, Ala., during Palm Sunday services, killing 20 people, including 6 children. The same storm system spawned a series of tornadoes in the Southeast that was responsible for at least 43 deaths.

Voters cast their ballots on March 20 in El Salvador's first presidential election since the nation's civil war ended in 1992.

▼

▲

Mexico's leading presidential candidate, Luis Donaldo Colosio Murrieta (circle), is assassinated during a campaign rally in Tijuana on March 23.

PM 7:12
MAR 23 1994

PAPELETAS
ELECCION DE

17

S	M	T	W	TH	F	S
April 1994						
					1	2
3	4	5	6	7	8	9
10	11	12	13	14	15	16
17	18	19	20	21	22	23
24	25	26	27	28	29	30

Hundreds of thousands of Rwandan refugees cross the border into Zaire, fleeing a civil war in April that pitted the Hutu and Tutsi ethnic groups against each other. ▶

North Carolina's women's basketball team erupts in celebration after Charlotte Smith sinks a three-point shot with seven-tenths of a second left on the clock to win the college women's basketball championship on April 3. ▼

3, 4 **The North Carolina women's basketball team** wins the National Collegiate Athletic Association's women's championship by defeating Louisiana Tech, 60-59, on a three-point shot by Charlotte Smith with seven-tenths of a second remaining in the game. On April 4, the Arkansas Razorbacks win the men's national basketball championship, defeating the Duke Blue Devils, 76-72.

6 **The presidents of the central African nations** of Rwanda and Burundi, returning by air from peace talks in Tanzania to Kigali, Rwanda's capital, are assassinated as rocket fire hits their plane. The killings set off a wave of ethnic violence that by June had resulted in the deaths of an estimated 500,000 people.
United States Supreme Court Justice Harry A. Blackmun, author of the *Roe v. Wade* decision that legalized abortion in 1973, announces his intention to retire from the court at the end of its current term.

8 **Japan's Prime Minister** Morihiro Hosokawa, who portrayed himself as a reformer during elections in 1993, unexpectedly announces his resignation after being implicated in a financial scandal.

10 **José María Olazábal of Spain wins** the Masters golf tournament in Augusta, Ga., after a putt for eagle on the 15th hole of the final round put him in the lead.

14 **Two U.S. Air Force fighters,** enforcing a no-flight zone over a Kurdish enclave in northern Iraq, mistakenly shoot down two American Army helicopters, killing 26 U.S. and allied personnel on board.

16 **Bosnian Serb forces** besieging the city of Gorazde in Bosnia-Herzegovina shoot down a British jet fighter in the first downing of a North Atlantic Treaty Organization (NATO) combat plane since NATO began air patrols over Bosnia in 1993.

19 **South Africa's Chief Mangosuthu G. Buthelezi,** leader of the Zulu-based Inkatha Freedom Party, agrees to participate in national elections, canceling a boycott that threatened to plunge the nation into civil war.
A Los Angeles jury awards black motorist Rodney G. King $3.8 million in damages for the beating he suffered at the hands of Los Angeles police officers in 1991.
A jury in Versailles, France, convicts Paul Touvier of crimes against humanity for ordering the execution of seven Jews as a member of a pro-Nazi French militia during World War II (1939-1945). Touvier was the first Frenchman to be tried for persecuting Jews during the German occupation.

24 **Armando Calderón Sol,** the leader of El Salvador's ruling right wing party, wins a presidential runoff election by a 2-to-1 margin, defeating Ruben Zamora, a former guerrilla leader.

26-29 **South Africans participate in the first all-racial** elections in the nation's history, casting an estimated 20 million ballots in voting that was relatively free of violence.

18

S	M	T	W	TH	F	S
May 1994						
1	2	3	4	5	6	7
8	9	10	11	12	13	14
15	16	17	18	19	20	21
22	23	24	25	26	27	28
29	30	31				

2 **South Africa's president,** Frederik Willem de Klerk, leader of the National Party, concedes defeat in South Africa's first all-race parliamentary elections to Nelson Mandela of the African National Congress (ANC), who pronounces South Africa "free at last."

4 **Palestine Liberation Organization Chairman** Yasir Arafat and Israeli Prime Minister Yitzhak Rabin sign an agreement in Cairo, Egypt, that implements Palestinian self-rule in the Gaza Strip and in Jericho, areas occupied by Israel since 1967.

5 **A full-scale civil war erupts in Yemen** between forces loyal to the former North Yemen and forces loyal to the former South Yemen, threatening to end a union that began in 1990.
American teen-ager Michael P. Fay is flogged in Singapore for alleged acts of vandalism, despite protests by the United States government.
The U.S. House of Representatives unexpectedly passes by a vote of 216 to 214 a ban on 19 types of semiautomatic assault weapons, the second congressional defeat for the gun lobby in six months.

10 **ANC leader Nelson Mandela is inaugurated** as South Africa's first black president after the ANC won almost 63 percent of the vote and 252 of the 400 seats in elections for the National Assembly.

11. **Italy's billionaire media tycoon,** Silvio Berlusconi, is sworn in as prime minister after leading a right wing coalition to victory in March parliamentary elections.

13 **Federal appeals court Judge Stephen G. Breyer** is nominated to fill the seat on the U.S. Supreme Court left vacant by the resignation of Justice Harry Blackmun.

23 **Jacqueline Kennedy Onassis** is buried in Arlington National Cemetery in Virginia, next to the grave of her husband John F. Kennedy, following a eulogy by U.S. President Bill Clinton, who said she had borne "great burdens . . . with dignity and grace."

24 **Four Muslim fundamentalists** convicted of bombing the World Trade Center in New York City are each sentenced to 240 years in prison, without the possibility of parole.
Denny's restaurant chain agrees to pay a record $54 million to settle discrimination complaints brought by black patrons who were denied the service given to whites.

29 **Hungary's former Communists,** now known as the Socialist Party, are swept back into power in the final round of parliamentary elections.

31 **United States Representative Dan Rostenkowski** (D., Ill.) is indicted by a federal grand jury on 17 counts of fraud and misconduct, forcing him to resign as chairman of the powerful House Ways and Means Committee. In the November 8 midterm elections, Rostenkowski is defeated by a political neophyte.

▲
Nelson R. Mandela takes the oath of office on May 10 as South Africa's first black head of state, after his party swept the parliamentary elections.

John F. Kennedy, Jr., left foreground, and Caroline Kennedy Schlossberg, at center kneeling, attend the casket of their mother, Jacqueline Kennedy Onassis, during burial services on May 23 at Arlington National Cemetery in Virginia. ▶

S	M	T	W	TH	F	S
June 1994						
			1	2	3	4
5	6	7	8	9	10	11
12	13	14	15	16	17	18
19	20	21	22	23	24	25
26	27	28	29	30		

22   **A United Nations commission,** established to investigate war crimes in Bosnia-Herzegovina, formally accuses Bosnian Serbs of a campaign of genocide directed against Bosnian Croats and Muslims.

6   **The 50th anniversary of D-Day,** the Allied invasion of Europe during World War II (1939-1945), is commemorated on the beaches of Normandy in France by leaders of the Allied nations and thousands of veterans of the largest seaborne invasion in history.

13, 18   **The North Korean government** on June 13 declares its intention to expel international nuclear inspectors, leading to a call for sanctions by the United States government. But on June 18, following an unofficial visit by former U.S. President Jimmy Carter, the leaders of North and South Korea agree to hold a summit meeting to discuss a nuclear-free Korean peninsula.

17   **Former football star O. J. Simpson** is charged with the June 12 murder of his second ex-wife, Nicole Brown Simpson, and her friend Ronald L. Goldman and leads police on a nationally televised 1½-hour chase along an interstate highway before he surrenders to police outside his home in a Los Angeles suburb.

19   **Colombia's Liberal Party leader,** Ernesto Samper Pizano, declares victory in the closest presidential election in Colombian history.

22   **The Houston Rockets win** the National Basketball Association championship, defeating the New York Knicks, 90-84, behind the play of center and Most Valuable Player Hakeem Olajuwon.

23   **French troops arrive in Rwanda** to help protect civilians in that country's bloody civil war, but the Rwandan Patriotic Front, composed mostly of the Tutsi ethnic group, objects because of France's past support of the Hutu-dominated government that has committed most of the war's atrocities.
South Africa, which was suspended from membership in the United Nations in 1974 because of its policy of *apartheid* (racial segregation), is readmitted to the UN General Assembly following the nation's first all-race parliamentary elections in April.

24   **Austria, Sweden, Norway, and Finland** are formally invited to join the European Union (EU), formerly the European Community, at a meeting of the EU in Corfu, a Greek island.

25   **Japan's Prime Minister** Tsutomu Hata resigns after only two months in office, rather than face the likelihood of a no-confidence vote in parliament. On June 29, Tomiichi Murayama is elected prime minister.

26   **Tens of thousands of supporters of homosexual rights** march through the streets of New York City to commemorate the 25th anniversary of the beginning of the gay civil rights movement.

▲
Fans of former football star O. J. Simpson, accused of murdering his ex-wife and her friend, line a section of a highway in the Los Angeles area on June 17 as police cars pursue Simpson's white Ford Bronco.

◄ United States President Bill Clinton, left, and British Prime Minister John Major attend a ceremony in June in Cambridge, England, to commemorate those who died during the Allied invasion of Europe on D-Day, June 6, 1944.

S	M	T	W	TH	F	S
					1	2
3	4	5	6	7	8	9
10	11	12	13	14	15	16
17	18	19	20	21	22	23
24	25	26	27	28	29	30
31						

July 1994

Brazil's Dunga scores the winning goal over Italy's Gianluca Pagliuca in a shootout on July 17, as Brazil wins a record fourth World Cup championship.
▼

4 **Tropical Storm Alberto sweeps** through Florida and southwestern Georgia, causing flooding along the Apalachicola, Flint, and Ocmulgee rivers. The death toll eventually climbed to 31 people.

10 **Runoff presidential elections in two former republics** of the Soviet Union result in victories for candidates who favor closer ties with Russia. In Belarus, Alexander Lukashenko claims victory in the second round of voting, defeating Prime Minister Vyacheslav Kebich by a landslide. In Ukraine, former Prime Minister Leonid Kuchma prevailed over incumbent President Leonid Kravchuk.

11 **Haiti's military regime expels** international human rights monitors. As a result, observers predict a new wave of political killings in Haiti. On July 31, the United Nations Security Council authorizes a United States invasion of Haiti if Haiti's military rulers fail to cede power.

13 **North Korea's state-run radio reports** that Kim Chong-il, son of Kim Il-song who died on July 8, has succeeded his father as president, as commander of the armed forces, and as the head of the Communist Workers' Party.

16 **Fragments from Comet Shoemaker-Levy 9** begin smashing into Jupiter, the solar system's largest planet, with an explosive force 100,000 times greater than a hydrogen bomb, leaving visible spots in the planet's atmosphere.

17 **Hundreds of thousands of refugees from Rwanda,** fleeing the advance of the rebel Rwandan Patriotic Front, pour into the town of Goma in Zaire, raising fears that thousands may die as international relief efforts are overwhelmed. On July 18, the Front claimed victory in the country's civil war, it formed a new government on July 19, and by July 21, an estimated 1 million refugees had entered Zaire.
Brazil wins soccer's World Cup championship at the Rose Bowl in Pasadena, Calif., defeating Italy on penalty kicks, 3-2, after a scoreless tie, the first time a World Cup final was scoreless in regulation time and overtime.

18 **In Buenos Aires, Argentina, a bomb blast** destroys a seven-story building that housed the country's two main Jewish organizations, killing about 100 people and injuring about 230 people.

25 **Jordan's King Hussein I** and Israeli Prime Minister Yitzhak Rabin, meeting at the White House in Washington, D.C., agree to normalize relations, ending 46 years of conflict.

29 **The U.S. Senate confirms Stephen G. Breyer,** a Boston federal court judge, as an associate justice of the U.S. Supreme Court to replace retiring Justice Harry A. Blackmun.
An abortion clinic doctor and a clinic escort are shot to death outside an abortion clinic in Pensacola, Fla. Police charge former minister Paul Hill with two counts of murder and one count of attempted murder.

Jordan's King Hussein I on July 25 signs a declaration ending 46 years of conflict between Jordan and Israel, as U.S. President Bill Clinton, center, and Israeli Prime Minister Yitzhak Rabin, right, look on.

S	M	T	W	TH	F	S
August 1994						
		1	2	3	4	5	6
7	8	9	10	11	12	13
14	15	16	17	18	19	20
21	22	23	24	25	26	27
28	29	30	31			

A crowd celebrates a replay (complete with mud) of the 1969 Woodstock music festival with a 25th anniversary concert in Saugerties, N.Y., on August 13. ▶

5 **Yugoslavia severs political and economic ties** with Serbs in Bosnia-Herzegovina after the Bosnian Serbs rejected an international peace plan to settle the civil war in the former Yugoslav republic.

10 **Strikes shut down Burundi's capital,** Bujumbura, for the second consecutive day as an opposition political group, dominated by the Tutsi ethnic group, steps up its campaign against the Hutu-led government.

11 **A Moscow court acquits** the last defendant in the trials of eight Communist Party leaders accused of treason for their roles in a 1991 coup attempt against Mikhail Gorbachev, leader of the former Soviet Union.

12 **Major league baseball players** in the United States and Canada go on strike, causing the eighth shutdown of the national pastime since 1972. The strike cancels the remainder of the season, the play-offs, and the World Series, the first time a World Series had not been played since 1904.

13 **About 350,000 people flock to Saugerties, N.Y.,** for Woodstock '94, the 25th anniversary celebration of the original Woodstock music festival that defined a generation.

14, 15 **Police in Sudan seize the international terrorist** known as Carlos the Jackal, wanted for terrorist bombings and kidnappings during the 1970's and 1980's. The next day, August 15, he is flown to France to stand trial.

17 **United States Deputy Treasury Secretary** Roger C. Altman submits his resignation after coming under fire for his testimony before a congressional committee investigating President Bill Clinton's Arkansas real estate ventures.

19 **Cuban refugees are picked up at sea** and taken to detention camps in Guantánamo Bay, Cuba, as the Clinton Administration reverses a long-standing policy of admitting Cubans into the United States.

22 **Mexico's Ernesto Zedillo Ponce de León claims victory** in the August 21 presidential election over two rival candidates with 50.03 percent of the vote. The level of voter support for his Institutional Revolutionary Party (PRI) was the lowest since the PRI came to power in 1929, but Zedillo's closest rival received only 27 percent of the vote.

25 **The U.S. Senate passes a $30.2-billion anticrime bill** by a vote of 61 to 39, sparing a measure that earlier seemed certain to be defeated.

31 **The Irish Republican Army declares** an unconditional and unilateral cease-fire in Northern Ireland, saying that after 25 years of warfare it is ready to seek a political solution to a united Ireland.

▲

Residents of Belfast, Northern Ireland, celebrate a cease-fire declared by the Irish Republican Army on August 31.

▲
A member of the grounds crew at Yankee Stadium in New York City strolls off the field after baseball players went on strike on August 12.

27

S	M	T	W	TH	F	S
				1	2	3
4	5	6	7	8	9	10
11	12	13	14	15	16	17
18	19	20	21	22	23	24
25	26	27	28	29	30	

September 1994

8 **The last Allied soldiers leave Berlin, Germany,** ending an occupation that began in 1945 as a result of the end of World War II (1939-1945) and the beginning of the Cold War.

5 **The United Nations'** third International Conference on Population and Development opens in Cairo, Egypt, with delegations representing 179 nations in attendance. Some Islamic countries boycott the conference.

9 **Cuba and the United States** reach an agreement on immigration under which the United States will accept 20,000 Cuban immigrants each year and Cuba will prevent its citizens from fleeing on makeshift rafts.

12 **A two-seat Cessna 150 airplane** crashes on the South Lawn of the White House in Washington, D.C., and comes to rest two stories below President Bill Clinton's bedroom, killing the pilot, Frank E. Corder, a truckdriver with a reported history of drug and alcohol problems.
The separatist Parti Québécois captures 77 of 125 legislative seats in Quebec's provincial elections, setting the stage for a possible referendum on Quebec's separation from Canada.

14 **Baseball's Acting Commissioner Bud Selig** cancels the remainder of the season, the play-offs, and the World Series on the 34th day of the players' strike. It was the first time since 1904 that a World Series would not be played.

18, 19 **Haiti's military rulers avert a U.S. invasion** by agreeing to concede power to democratically elected President Jean-Bertrand Aristide. The agreement follows last-minute negotiations between junta leader Raoul Cédras and former President Jimmy Carter, who was joined by Senator Sam Nunn (D., Ga.) and General Colin Powell, former chairman of the Joint Chiefs of Staff. A multinational peacekeeping force arrives in Haiti on September 19 to enforce the agreement.

22 **Anthropologists report the discovery of fossils** belonging to the oldest human ancestors, a new species known as *Australopithecus ramidus* that lived about 4.4 million years ago. Scientists said it was the closest find yet to the so-called missing link that separated the evolution of humans from that of apes.

26 **Efforts to reform health insurance,** President Clinton's principal legislative goal, are at an end for the second session of the 103rd Congress, declares Senate Majority Leader George J. Mitchell.

28 **A gunman assassinates Mexican political leader** José Francisco Ruiz Massieu, secretary general of the Institutional Revolutionary Party (PRI), on a crowded street in Mexico City, the second murder of a PRI official in a six-month period.

30 **The opening of the National Hockey League** season is delayed by team owners as they negotiate a contract with the players' association. By year-end, an agreement had not been reached, and the 1994-1995 season was in jeopardy.

▲

Jubilant Haitians greet U.S. soldiers as they arrive in Port-au-Prince, Haiti's capital, on September 19 to restore to power Haitian President Jean-Bertrand Aristide, the country's first democratically elected leader.

S	M	T	W	TH	F	S
						1
2	3	4	5	6	7	8
9	10	11	12	13	14	15
16	17	18	19	20	21	22
23	24	25	26	27	28	29
30	31					

October 1994

3   **Exit polls in Brazil's presidential elections** show former Finance Minister Fernando Henrique Cardoso of the Social Democratic Party winning by a large margin.
United States Agriculture Secretary Mike Espy resigns under pressure for alleged ethics violations, becoming the first member of President Bill Clinton's Cabinet to resign.

4-6   **An apparent cult mass murder-suicide** claims the lives of 53 people in Switzerland and Canada. Authorities discovered the charred remains of 48 bodies at three ski chalets in Switzerland on October 5. On October 4 and 6, five bodies were found in adjoining homes in Quebec.

9-11   **In response to a buildup of Iraqi troops** on the border with Kuwait, President Clinton orders 36,000 troops and several hundred combat planes to the Persian Gulf. By October 11, as U.S. forces continued to build, Iraqi President Saddam Hussein pulled back most of his troops from the border.

13   **Protestant paramilitary groups** in Northern Ireland announce a cease-fire in response to an earlier cease-fire pledge by the Irish Republican Army.

14   **The Nobel Committee awards its Peace Prize** to Israeli Prime Minister Yitzhak Rabin, Foreign Minister Shimon Peres, and Palestine Liberation Organization chairman Yasir Arafat for negotiating a 1993 peace accord.

15   **Haiti's President Jean-Bertrand Aristide** returns to the nation's capital, Port-au-Prince, for the first time since he was overthrown in a 1991 military coup.

17   **German Chancellor Helmut Kohl** claims victory for his governing coalition in the October 16 parliamentary elections.
The prime ministers of Israel and Jordan initial a draft peace treaty in Amman, Jordan, clearing the way for greater commerce between the two nations and resolving disputes over borders and water rights. The peace treaty is formally signed on October 26 at a ceremony on the Israeli-Jordan border with President Clinton participating.

19   **A powerful bomb demolishes a crowded bus** in the main commercial district of Tel Aviv, Israel, killing 23 people and wounding at least 46 in one of the worst terrorist attacks in Israeli history.

24   **A suicide bomber assassinates Sri Lanka's** leading opposition presidential candidate, Gamini Dissanayake, and kills 51 other people at a campaign rally on the outskirts of Colombo, the capital.

29   **A gunman opens fire on the West Wing** of the White House, shattering windows in the press briefing room but injuring no one. Officials identified the gunman as Francisco Martin Duran, a 26-year-old native of Albuquerque, N. Mex. On November 17, he was charged with attempting to assassinate the President.

▲
U.S. tanks head for Kuwait's border with Iraq in October after a buildup of Iraqi troops threatened the peace. By October 11, most of the Iraqi troops had withdrawn.

Dignitaries on October 26 attend the formal signing on the Israeli-Jordanian border of a peace treaty between Israel and Jordan, ending 46 years of conflict. ▶

Haiti's President Jean-
Bertrand Aristide, left, returns to the capital, Port-
au-Prince, on October 15
to reclaim his presidency
after three years in exile.

S	M	T	W	TH	F	S
November 1994						
		1	2	3	4	5
6	7	8	9	10	11	12
13	14	15	16	17	18	19
20	21	22	23	24	25	26
27	28	29	30			

Representative Newt Gingrich (R., Ga.), left, and Senator Robert J. Dole (R., Kans.) are all smiles after Republicans swept the November 8 elections, winning control of the U.S. Congress for the first time since 1954. ▶

4   **The United Nations Security Council** votes unanimously to withdraw the remaining 17,000 UN troops in Somalia by mid-March 1995, ending a mission that to date had cost the UN about $1 billion.

6   **George Foreman becomes the oldest boxer,** at age 45, to win a championship fight in any weight class by knocking out Michael Moorer in Las Vegas, Nev., to claim the International Boxing Federation and World Boxing Association heavyweight titles.

8   **The Republican Party (GOP) scores historic gains** in midterm congressional elections in the United States, winning control of both the House of Representatives and the Senate for the first time since 1954. The GOP also gained 11 more governorships, including New York and Texas, giving them 30 governorships, the first Republican majority since 1970.

9   **Sri Lanka's Prime Minister Chandrika Kumaratunga** wins a landslide victory in presidential elections by a margin of 62 percent to 35 percent over her closest rival. On November 15, Kumaratunga appoints her mother, Sirima Bandaranaike, to succeed her as prime minister.

10   **The Administration of United States President** Bill Clinton says it will no longer police the arms embargo on the Muslim-led government of Bosnia-Herzegovina, setting off a protest by French Foreign Minister Alain Juppé.
The only privately owned manuscript of Italian Renaissance artist Leonardo da Vinci is sold at auction at Christie's in New York City for $30.8 million, the highest amount ever paid for a manuscript.

14   **The Channel Tunnel,** a 31-mile (50-kilometer) tunnel under the English Channel that links Folkestone, England, and Calais, France, opens to passenger traffic.

17   **Ireland's Prime Minister Albert Reynolds resigns** his office as lawmakers were about to take a no-confidence vote on his coalition government.

18   **Palestinian police open fire on Islamic militants** outside a mosque in the Gaza Strip, sparking riots that killed at least 14 people and wounded at least 200.

19   **Mozambique President Joaquim A. Chissano** and his Frelimo party claim victory in the country's first multiparty presidential and parliamentary elections.

27   **Bosnian Serbs take 150 United Nations (UN)** peacekeepers as hostages to prevent air strikes by the North Atlantic Treaty Organization (NATO). The UN commander in Bosnia concedes that neither NATO nor the UN can halt the Bosnian Serbs' advance on the UN-designated safe area of Bihac.

29   **Voters in Norway reject a proposal to join** the European Union (EU), formerly the European Community, despite voter approval of EU membership in 1994 in Austria, Finland, and Sweden.

Islamic militants outside a mosque in the Gaza Strip hurl rocks at Palestinian police on November 18.
▼

S	M	T	W	TH	F	S
December 1994				1	2	3
4	5	6	7	8	9	10
11	12	13	14	15	16	17
18	19	20	21	22	23	24
25	26	27	28	29	30	31

6 **United States Treasury Secretary** Lloyd M. Bentsen, Jr., announces his resignation, effective December 22, from the Cabinet of President Bill Clinton. On December 9, Clinton fires Surgeon General Joycelyn Elders for reportedly suggesting that masturbation be taught in the schools.

11 **Up to 40,000 Russian troops invade Chechnya,** a semi-autonomous republic on Russia's border with Georgia, to put down a secessionist rebellion. On December 25, Russia said that its forces had killed about 1,000 Chechen fighters in a major battle near the town of Argun.

17 **North Korea says that it shot down** a U.S. Army helicopter in North Korean airspace, killing one pilot. The helicopter's second pilot was reportedly uninjured but was being held by North Korea. North Korea released the body of the slain pilot on December 22.

20 **Former U.S. President Jimmy Carter** announces that the warring parties in Bosnia-Herzegovina have agreed to begin a four-month cease-fire starting on December 23. Carter arrived in the country's war-torn capital, Sarajevo, to act as a mediator on December 18.

21 **An incendiary device explodes on a crowded subway** in lower Manhattan, a borough of New York City, injuring more than 40 people. Police the same day arrest one of the burn victims in his hospital bed, saying the man had been carrying the firebomb when it accidentally went off.
The Mexican government adopts an emergency economic plan that allows its currency, the peso, to trade freely against the U.S. dollar, and the value of the peso plummets 20 percent on December 22.

22 **Italy's Prime Minister Silvio Berlusconi** resigns after only seven months in office, following corruption charges against him that deepened a split in his coalition government. President Oscar Luigi Scalfaro allowed Berlusconi to stay on as a caretaker while he sought a new government.

23 **The owners of major league baseball teams** in the United States and Canada declare an impasse in their labor negotiations with the players' association and unilaterally impose a salary cap that the players had rejected.

26 **French paramilitary commandos storm** a hijacked Air France Airbus at Marseille's Marignane Airport, killing the four Islamic militants who had seized the plane on December 24 and rescuing the 170 passengers and crew who were being held hostage. The militants, identified as members of Algeria's Armed Islamic Group, had killed three hostages after they took over the plane in Algiers, the capital of Algeria.

28 **U.S. Central Intelligence Agency Director** R. James Woolsey resigns his position, effective December 31, after his relations worsened with the White House and Congress.
President Clinton nominates outgoing Representative Dan Glickman (D., Kans.) as secretary of agriculture.

◄ Russian troops approach the outskirts of a town in the semiautonomous republic of Chechnya. They were part of a force of 40,000 soldiers who invaded Chechnya on December 11 to put down a secessionist rebellion.

French commandos storm a hijacked Air France airliner at Marseille, France, on December 26, killing four Islamic gunmen.
▼

1994
WORLD BOOK
YEAR BOOK UPDATE

The major events of 1994 are summarized in nearly 300 alphabetically arranged articles, from "Africa" to "Zoos." In most cases, the article titles are the same as those of the articles in *The World Book Encyclopedia* that they update. Included are 12 Special Reports that offer in-depth looks at particular subjects, ranging from the use of DNA fingerprints in criminal investigations to the emerging Information Super-highway. The Special Reports can be found on the following pages under their respective Update article titles.

▪ U.S. TROOPS WELCOMED IN HAITI, SEE PAGE 239

Africa

The emergence of democracy in Africa continued in 1994, though falteringly. The greatest success story was South Africa, which ended decades of white-minority rule, but several other nations also made progress. There were also setbacks, however, particularly in Rwanda, which was plunged into a nightmare as old ethnic hatreds led to widespread slaughter. Some improvement was noted in the continent's generally decrepit economies, though experts said the day was still far off when most Africans would enjoy a decent standard of living.

South Africa held its first all-race elections from April 26 to 29. Candidates of the African National Congress (ANC), the oldest and largest organization in the long struggle against *apartheid* (racial separation), collected 62.6 percent of the vote. On May 9, the new National Assembly chose ANC President Nelson R. Mandela as South Africa's first black head of state. Mandela's government immediately set about trying to solve the nation's many problems.

Earlier in the year, it had seemed questionable whether the elections would even be held. One major obstacle was the Inkatha Freedom Party, a Zulu-based organization headed by Chief Mangosuthu Buthelezi. Buthelezi, fearing that Inkatha would not fare well in the balloting and that Zulus would be dominated by Mandela's Xhosa ethnic group in an ANC-led government, said Inkatha would not take part in the elections. But on April 19, after winning concessions that protected Zulu interests, Buthelezi relented and agreed to participate.

The electoral process was also jeopardized by right wing whites outraged at the prospect of black rule. In April, white extremists set off bombs in many areas, killing more than 20 people. To almost everyone's relief, when the elections were finally held, there was little violence. (See **South Africa: New Era for South Africa.** In the World Book Supplement section, see **South Africa.**)

Other progress toward democracy. Malawi, where elections had been promised in 1993, voted for a president on May 17, 1994. Incumbent President Hastings Kamuzu Banda was ousted from office by Muluzi Bakili, a former secretary-general of Banda's Malawi Congress Party. However, Bakili's party, the United Democratic Front, failed to win a majority in Parliament, and the formation of a coalition government was delayed for several weeks.

Elections were held beginning on October 27 in Mozambique, a country that has been torn by civil war since 1975. Afonso Dhlakama, the leader of the major opposition party, the Mozambique Resistance Movement (Renamo), at first threatened to withdraw his name, charging election fraud, but he relented and the elections proceeded peacefully. President Joaquím Alberto Chissano and his party, the Front for the Liberation of Mozambique (Frelimo), won a majority of seats in the legislature, but Renamo captured about 40 percent of the seats.

Uganda also saw significant political progress during 1994. Once one of Africa's political and economic disaster areas, the country has been stabilizing its political system under President Yoweri Kaguta Museveni, whose National Resistance Movement took power in 1986. On March 28, 1994, Uganda held elections for a Constituent Assembly, which was to work out the final form of a constitution. Presidential and parliamentary elections were expected to take place in early 1995.

In Ivory Coast, the death of long-time President Félix Houphouët-Boigny in December 1993 was followed in 1994 by a peaceful and constitutional succession. The new president, Henri Konan Bédié, will hold office until October 1995, when a presidential election is scheduled.

In October, Botswana, one of the democratic success stories in Africa, held its sixth national elections since gaining its independence from British rule in 1966. As expected, the Botswana Democratic Party, the nation's dominant political organization, collected the most votes, but opposition parties made a respectable showing.

The results of elections on February 6 and 20 in Togo surprised many, as the opposition won a majority in the 81-member National Assembly. But in negotiations to form a government, President Gnassingbé Eyadéma was able to place an ally, Edem Kodjo, as prime minister.

In Sierra Leone, Valentine E. M. Strasser, the nation's military ruler, announced a transition plan for a return to civilian rule by January 1996. But the country was in the grip of a civil war, which was sure to hinder the transition to civilian government.

Carnage in Rwanda. The continent's most publicized disaster in 1994 occurred in Rwanda, which was torn apart by an orgy of violence and murder. The turmoil in Rwanda threatened to spread into neighboring Burundi. Both countries face the problem of a division between Hutus and Tutsis, the two main ethnic groups. Burundi experienced savage bloodletting in 1993 between Hutus and Tutsis, but in late 1993 and early 1994 it was in the process of reestablishing democracy.

Rwanda, too, had seemed to be laying its ethnic animosities to rest. A peace treaty signed in August 1993 between the Rwandan government, which is predominantly Hutu, and the mostly Tutsi Rwandan Patriotic Front (RPF) brought joy to much of the pop-

Rwandan refugees, mostly of the Hutu ethnic group, swarm into a relief camp in Goma, Zaire, in July to escape warfare in Rwanda between Hutus and the rival Tutsis.

ulace. But the pact dismayed a small group of Hutus who wished to drive the Tutsis out of the country.

On April 6, 1994, an airplane carrying President Juvénal Habyarimana of Rwanda and President Cyprien Ntaryamira of Burundi—both Hutus—went down as it approached Kigali, Rwanda's capital. The plane had reportedly been hit by gunfire or a rocket, and the Rwandan government blamed the RPF. Almost immediately government troops and civilian gangs unleashed a vicious attack against the Tutsi population and against Hutus who were considered disloyal. By the end of the month, the death toll was estimated at 200,000, and up to 500,000 people had fled, most of them to Tanzania. By June, estimates of the dead ranged as high as 500,000.

But then the military situation reversed, and the RPF gained the upper hand. By July 4, the RPF controlled Kigali. Then began another massive movement of people, mainly Hutus, into Zaire. The horror of the killings inside Rwanda was soon matched by the horror of the conditions in Zairian refugee camps, which were ridden with disease and controlled by brutal Hutu troops.

In Rwanda, the RPF announced on July 19 that it was forming a new broad-based coalition government. The RPF-dominated government ended the year struggling to establish its authority and to prevent retaliation against Hutu citizens.

Conceding failure in Somalia. In March, the United States withdrew its last sizable contingent of troops from Somalia and left the chaotic situation in the hands of a United Nations (UN) peacekeeping force, UNISOM. At year-end, the UN was planning its own withdrawal in March 1995.

The United States and the UN had entered Somalia in 1992 and 1993 in the hope of both feeding victims of a famine and ending a civil war between rival clans, which was one of the major causes of the famine. The intervention saved lives, but neither the United States nor the UN could find a way to resolve the hostilities between the many clan leaders. Attempts to establish a new government for the country were unsuccessful. Most observers predicted that Somalia would again be ravaged by war and starvation once the UNISOM troops departed.

No reform for Nigeria. Nigeria, once viewed as a model for the transition from military to democratic rule, continued in 1994 to be an example of military entrenchment. Head of State Sani Abacha, a general who took control of the country in a bloodless coup in November 1993, faced strong opposition during 1994 from Nigerians desiring a return to democracy. But rather than making concessions, Abacha moved in a more authoritarian direction.

On June 23, Abacha arrested Moshood Abiola, who had been elected president in June 1993 but was never allowed to take office, and charged him with treason. In protest, workers in the petroleum industry and other important sectors of the economy launched a devastating strike. But on September 4, after eight weeks of demonstrations, the workers gave up. The triumphant Abacha proclaimed himself above the law.

Abacha's one nod to democratic reform during the year was to allow the convening in June of a constitutional conference aimed at starting yet another transition to civilian rule. The populace, numbed by a series of such conferences over the many years of military rule in Nigeria, was cynical about the latest alleged move toward democracy. Abacha pledged his support for the resumption of civilian rule, but he refused to set a date for it.

Mobutu holds fast in Zaire. Workers in Zaire called a general strike on January 19 to protest President Mobutu Sese Seko's decision five days earlier to dissolve the legislature and his refusal to recognize Etienne Tshisekedi as prime minister. Mobutu and Tshisekedi were heading rival governments. In late January, Mobutu merged the two governments into one, and in June he named a new prime minister, Kengo wa Dondo. Mobutu eventually won over enough of the opposition to secure his position at the head of a single government.

As a result of the ongoing political crisis, Zaire's economy slowed almost to a standstill, inflation skyrocketed, and roads and other public works fell into decay. Nonetheless, Mobutu seemed to have a firm grasp on power at year-end, helped in large part by his control of the military and the treasury.

Other trouble spots. Democracy also fared badly in several other nations, and in a few—Lesotho in particular—past progress was reversed. Successful elections in Lesotho in 1993 were followed in 1994 by a mutiny in the army on January 14. On April 14, soldiers killed a top government minister, Selometsi Baholo. Three issues were involved in the uprising: a desire by the military for higher pay, the wish by some in the military to overthrow the elected government and replace it with the opposition party, and an attempt by King Letsie III to abolish the government. Conditions remained tense at year-end.

Little progress was made in 1994 in resolving the civil war in Liberia. Agreements reached in 1993 to end the fighting, disarm the several armies, and establish a government did not succeed. Although combat did decrease in 1994, disarmament efforts made no headway, and a proposed National Transition Government never took office. Nigeria, the major member of a west African peacekeeping force dispatched to Liberia in 1990, expressed frustration with the lack of progress. In October 1994, it began reducing its troop commitments to Liberia.

In Angola, fighting intensified between government troops and the rebel forces of the National Union for the Total Liberation of Angola (UNITA), led by Jonas Savimbi, despite peace talks that began in November 1993. Hunger became a major weapon, with both sides preventing the delivery of food re-

Supporters of the African National Congress display a poster of Nelson Mandela, as they celebrate in May the ANC's victory in South Africa's first all-race elections.

lief shipments to cities occupied by opposing forces. At least 3 million people were affected by this tactic, and many died from starvation. Other Angolans died from disease and wounds as the war ground on, and the country's economy was in a shambles.

Proposals for a peace accord in late October and early November wavered as Savimbi changed his mind almost daily on whether or not to sign. Finally, on November 20, the two sides signed a pact pledging to end the war and rebuild the devastated nation. Savimbi, however, did not attend the signing ceremony, saying he feared for his life.

An extended civil war also continued in Sudan, though a government offensive in the spring came close to destroying the rebel forces. Peace talks were held intermittently in 1994 with help from Eritrea, Kenya, Uganda, and Ethiopia but without result.

Another setback to civilian and democratic rule occurred in the tiny west African nation of Gambia. On July 23, a small group of officers, led by 29-year-old Lieutenant Yahya Jammeh, overthrew the government of President Sir Dawda Kairaba Jawara, ending one of Africa's few multiparty governments.

In Congo, ethnic strife that broke out in December 1993 continued through January 1994 and flared up again in June. The violence raised fears that successful elections held in 1992 might be undone by civil unrest. In several African countries, the return to multiparty government has been accompanied by an increase in ethnic tensions and conflicts as politi-

Facts in brief on African political units

Country	Population	Government	Monetary unit*	Foreign trade (million U.S.$) Exports†	Imports†
Algeria	28,581,000	President Liamine Zeroual; Prime Minister Mokdad Sifi	dinar (40.92 = $1)	11,137	8,648
Angola	11,072,000	President José Eduardo dos Santos	new kwanza (140,473.00 = $1)	2,989	1,140
Benin	5,399,000	President Nicephore Soglo	CFA franc (513.29 = $1)	97	207
Botswana	1,433,000	President Sir Ketumile Masire	pula (2.67 = $1)	1,700	1,800
Burkina Faso	10,352,000	Popular Front Chairman, Head of State, & Head of Government Blaise Compaoré	CFA franc (513.29 = $1)	105	536
Burundi	6,343,000	Interim President Sylvestre Ntibantunganya; Prime Minister Anatole Kanyenkiko	franc (243.38 = $1)	69	205
Cameroon	13,275,000	President Paul Biya	CFA franc (513.29 = $1)	1,815	1,175
Cape Verde	419,000	President Antonio Mascarenhas Monteiro; Prime Minister Carlos Alberto Wahnon de Carvalho Veiga	escudo (82.97 = $1)	5	180
Central African Republic	3,429,000	President Ange Patasse	CFA franc (513.29 = $1)	109	159
Chad	6,361,000	President Idriss Deby	CFA franc (513.29 = $1)	194	297
Comoros	653,000	President Said Mohamed Djohar	franc (384.97 = $1)	22	69
Congo	2,590,000	President Pascal Lissouba; Prime Minister Jacques Joachim Yhombi-Opango	CFA franc (513.29 = $1)	975	617
Djibouti	511,000	President Hassan Gouled Aptidon; Prime Minister Barkat Gourad Hamadou	franc (177.72 = $1)	17	214
Egypt	58,519,000	President Hosni Mubarak; Prime Minister Atef Sedky	pound (3.38 = $1)	2,243	8,176
Equatorial Guinea	400,000	President Teodoro Obiang Nguema Mbasogo; Prime Minister Silvestre Siale Bileka	CFA franc (513.29 = $1)	37	64
Eritrea	3,651,000	President Issaias Afeworke	Ethiopian birr	no statistics available	
Ethiopia	53,711,000	President Meles Zenawi	birr (5.59 = $1)	169	707
Gabon	1,367,000	President El Hadj Omar Bongo; Prime Minister Casimir Oye-Mba	CFA franc (513.29 = $1)	2,273	884
Gambia	980,000	Chairman, Armed Forces Provisional Ruling Council, & Head of State Yahya Jammeh	dalasi (9.70 = $1)	42	222
Ghana	17,453,000	President Jerry John Rawlings	cedi (1,025.00 = $1)	1,020	1,277
Guinea	6,700,000	President Lansana Conté	franc (977.74 = $1)	622	768
Guinea-Bissau	1,073,000	President João Bernardo Vieira	peso (12,459.00 = $1)	20	64
Ivory Coast	14,401,000	President Henri Konan Bédié	CFA franc (513.29 = $1)	2,931	2,185
Kenya	27,885,000	President Daniel T. arap Moi	shilling (43.83 = $1)	1,374	1,711
Lesotho	1,977,000	King Letsie III; Prime Minister Ntsu Mokhehle	maloti (3.50 = $1)	109	964
Liberia	3,039,000	Transitional government led by a Council of State	dollar (1 = $1)	396	272
Libya	5,407,000	Leader of the Revolution Muammar Muhammad al-Qadhafi; General People's Committee Secretary (Prime Minister) Abd al Majid al-Qaud	dinar (0.30 = $1)	11,213	5,356

*Exchange rates as of Oct. 28, 1994, or latest available data.   †Latest available data.

Country	Population	Government	Monetary unit*	Foreign trade (million U.S.$) Exports†	Imports†
Madagascar	14,155,000	President Albert Zafy; Prime Minister Francisque Ravony	franc (3,530.00 = $1)	268	453
Malawi	11,304,000	President Muluzi Bakili	kwacha (14.92 = $1)	319	545
Mali	10,797,000	President Alpha Oumar Konare; Prime Minister Ibrahima Boubacar Keita	CFA franc (513.29 = $1)	247	340
Mauritania	2,335,000	President Maaouya Ould Sid Ahmed Taya	ouguiya (126.53 = $1)	437	222
Mauritius	1,130,000	President Sir Cassam Uteem; Prime Minister Sir Anerood Jugnauth	rupee (17.36 = $1)	1,464	1,919
Morocco	28,260,000	King Hassan II; Prime Minister Abdellatif Filali	dirham (8.61 = $1)	3,416	7,153
Mozambique	16,359,000	President Joaquím Alberto Chissano; Prime Minister Mário da Graça Machungo	metical (6,239.00 = $1)	131	938
Namibia	1,688,000	President Sam Nujoma; Prime Minister Hage Geingob	rand (3.50 = $1)	1,289	1,178
Niger	9,102,000	President Mahamane Ousmane; Prime Minister Mahamadou Issoufou	CFA franc (513.29 = $1)	312	355
Nigeria	105,134,000	Head of State Sani Abacha	naira (21.89 = $1)	11,886	8,276
Rwanda	8,000,000	Interim President Theodore Sindikubwabo	franc (135.25 = $1)	68	288
São Tomé and Príncipe	133,000	President Miguel Trovoada	dobra (820.56 = $1)	5	32
Senegal	8,387,000	President Abdou Diouf; Prime Minister Habib Thiam	CFA franc (513.29 = $1)	741	1,292
Seychelles	74,000	President France Albert René	rupee (4.85 = $1)	52	192
Sierra Leone	4,740,000	Supreme Council of State Chairman Valentine E. M. Strasser	leone (575.00 = $1)	115	149
Somalia	7,233,000	No functioning government	shilling (2,620 = $1)	104	132
South Africa	42,741,000	Executive President Nelson Mandela	rand (4.05 = $1)	23,339	19,090
Sudan	28,960,000	President Umar Hasan Ahmad al-Bashir	pound (311.00 = $1)	509	1,060
Swaziland	859,000	King Mswati III; Prime Minister Prince Jameson Mbilini Dlamini	lilangeni (3.50 = $1)	632	734
Tanzania	30,742,000	President Ali Hassan Mwinyi; Prime Minister John Malecela	shilling (538.00 = $1)	349	1,127
Togo	4,138,000	President Gnassingbé Eyadéma	CFA franc (513.29 = $1)	253	444
Tunisia	8,933,000	President Zine El Abidine Ben Ali; Prime Minister Hamed Karoui	dinar (0.96 = $1)	3,804	6,215
Uganda	18,764,000	President Yoweri Kaguta Museveni; Prime Minister George Cosmas Adyebo	shilling (917.00 = $1)	143	516
Zaire	43,814,000	President Mobutu Sese Seko	zaire (2,019.95 = $1)	429	438
Zambia	9,381,000	President Frederick Chiluba	kwacha (670.00 = $1)	1,095	908
Zimbabwe	11,536,000	Executive President Robert Mugabe	dollar (8.31 = $1)	1,530	2,037

The U.S.S. *Spartanburg County,* carrying the last major contingent of U.S. troops serving in Somalia, departs from Mogadishu, the capital, in March.

cal parties have become dominated by one ethnic group or another.

Conflicts between African nations were at a minimum in 1994. The most serious clash was a border dispute between Nigeria and Cameroon over the petroleum-rich Bakassi area in the Gulf of Guinea. The incident began on January 3 when Nigeria sent troops into the area. The Organization of African Unity, an association of more than 50 African nations, said it would try to help mediate a solution to the crisis.

A long-standing dispute between Chad and Libya over Aouzou Strip, a 45,000-square-mile (115,000-square-kilometer) uranium-rich area, was settled in 1994. On February 3, the International Court of Justice at The Hague in the Netherlands ruled that the land belonged to Chad.

Economic conditions in Africa showed a small improvement during 1994, though the reason for it was disputed. The World Bank, a UN agency, claimed that its reform plans, the Structural Adjustment Programs, were an important factor. Some experts credited rising prices for various export commodities, such as cocoa and coffee. Coffee prices, for example, rose steeply during the year because of a severe freeze in Brazil, a major coffee producer.

Currency devaluation. But overall, economic conditions on the continent remained far from satisfactory in 1994. That fact was illustrated by the de-

valuation of the currency by 50 percent in 14 African countries. All but one of the countries—Equatorial Guinea—are former colonies of France and are referred to as the franc zone because they tie their currency, the CFA franc, to the value of the French franc. On January 11, the French government announced that it would now cost twice as many African francs to buy a French franc. The devaluation took effect in the franc zone the next day. The action was taken to bolster the African countries' faltering economies by making their exports more competitive on the international market. But it also had the effect of making imports more expensive.

The franc zone countries depend heavily on the purchase of industrial and agricultural products from France. The immediate result of devaluation was a 100 percent increase in price for such imports. Even though there had been warnings that a devaluation might occur, the citizens of the affected nations were shocked. A wave of political instability swept through the franc zone countries. Gabon and Senegal were rocked by violence as people protested the decreased buying power of their currency for imported products.

AIDS continued to expand in Africa in 1994. In Uganda and Zimbabwe, the governments estimated that 10 percent of the population was infected with HIV, the virus that causes the disease.

Those and other African countries where AIDS

has become a serious problem were finding that the epidemic was having severe side effects on their societies. Money that might have been spent for disease prevention was going instead for the treatment of AIDS patients. And because AIDS seemed to be especially prevalent among the middle class, it was killing many of the skilled and educated leaders that Africa so desperately needs. Moreover, as families were hit by AIDS deaths, large numbers of children were being orphaned, overburdening already weakened social-service agencies. Countries wracked by political instability, such as Zaire, were finding it impossible to keep up their AIDS prevention campaigns. (See **AIDS: The Changing Face of AIDS.**)

Protecting the natural world continued to be an issue of great concern in 1994. With deserts spreading and forests being cut down, African leaders debated how to protect the environment.

How best to save big-game animals from extinction—the elephant, in particular—was another concern. The international ban on the sale of ivory has greatly reduced the slaughter of elephants, but it has also cut off a needed source of income for some poor nations. Ironically, the legitimate, controlled sale of ivory and other elephant products had provided revenue that those countries used to protect elephant herds. □ Mark DeLancey

See also the various African country articles. In *World Book,* see **Africa.**

AIDS. Researchers in the United States and France reported on Feb. 21, 1994, that the drug AZT can greatly reduce the risk that a pregnant woman infected with the AIDS virus will transmit the virus to her unborn child. The National Institute of Allergy and Infectious Diseases (NIAID), an agency of the National Institutes of Health in Bethesda, Md., co-sponsored the research.

In the study, pregnant women infected with HIV, the AIDS-causing human immunodeficiency virus, were given AZT during pregnancy and labor, and their infants received the drug from birth until 6 weeks of age. Another group of HIV-infected women got no medication. Only 8.3 percent of the infants treated with AZT were infected with HIV, compared with 25.5 percent of infants in the untreated group. AZT has been widely used to delay the onset of other illnesses brought on by AIDS.

The researchers said AZT seemed to cause no serious short-term side effects in mothers or infants, though the long-term effects were unknown. The benefits were so dramatic that a special monitoring panel recommended that the study, begun in 1991, be halted early so that AZT could be offered to all HIV-infected women. On Aug. 9, 1994, the U.S. Food and Drug Administration (FDA) approved AZT for use by pregnant women.

AIDS vaccines. NIAID on June 17, 1994, decided against beginning full-scale clinical trials of the ef-

fectiveness of the two most promising AIDS vaccines. Anthony S. Fauci, NIAID director, made the decision after an advisory panel found inadequate evidence that the vaccines could protect against AIDS.

The genetically engineered vaccines, produced from a protein on the surface of HIV, had undergone small-scale safety tests on human volunteers. Fauci said these limited studies of the vaccines would continue but large-scale tests, which would involve thousands of volunteers at high risk for AIDS, probably would not begin for two years.

AIDS worldwide. The World Health Organization (WHO), an agency of the United Nations, on July 1 reported a 60 percent increase from the previous year in the estimated number of AIDS cases. The global number of cases rose from 2.5 million in July 1993 to about 4 million in July 1994. The number of adults infected with HIV rose by about 23 percent, from 13 million in 1993 to 16 million in 1994.

Michael H. Merson, executive director of WHO's Global Program on AIDS, said that the disease is spreading more rapidly in Asia than anywhere else. He added that Asia could have the largest number of AIDS cases in the world by the late 1990's unless new prevention programs are put into effect. AIDS cases in Asia rose eightfold, from about 30,000 cases in 1993 to more than 250,000 in 1994. (See **AIDS** Special Report: **The Changing Face of AIDS.**)

New drug. The FDA on June 27 approved a fourth drug for treating AIDS and HIV infection. The medication, stavudine or D4T, interferes with the reproduction of HIV. It was approved for use in patients who no longer respond to other AIDS-fighting drugs. The FDA said stavudine may delay the onset of AIDS symptoms in people infected with HIV and extend their survival. Bristol-Myers Squibb Company, based in New York City, manufactures stavudine and sells it under the trade name Zerit. The drug joins AZT, didanosine, and zalcitabine.

A dispute over royalties from the patent on a blood test to detect the AIDS virus ended on July 11, when the U.S. government agreed to give France's Pasteur Institute a bigger share of the money. The National Institutes of Health formally acknowledged that Robert C. Gallo, a virologist at the National Cancer Institute, had used an AIDS virus supplied by Pasteur scientists in developing the test. Gallo previously maintained that he had independently discovered the virus and developed the test, which he patented in 1985.

U.S. AIDS cases. The Centers for Disease Control and Prevention in Atlanta, Ga., reported that a total of 361,164 cases of AIDS and 220,736 deaths had occurred in the United States as of Dec. 31, 1993.

□ Michael Woods

See also **Drugs.** In *World Book,* see **AIDS.**

Air pollution. See Environmental pollution.

Alabama. See State government.

Alaska. See State government.

Formerly seen mainly in Africa and among homosexual men in the West, the AIDS epidemic has spread to parts of Asia and among women and intravenous drug users.

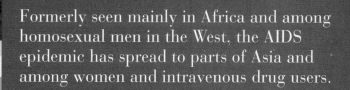

Janice
HIV Positive

The Changing Face of AIDS

By Michael Woods

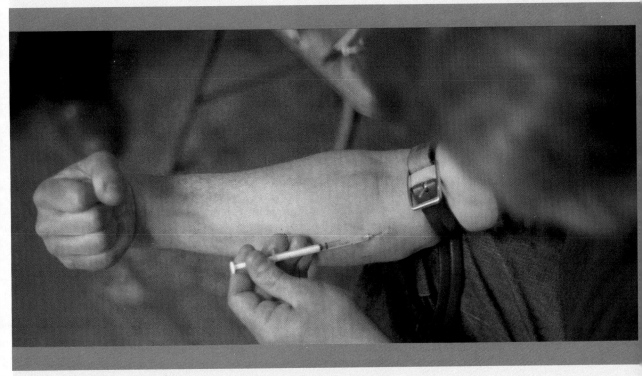

T he face of AIDS in North America is changing, and the world-wide epidemic, far from easing, is spreading aggressively. These developments in the course of a disease that by September 1994 had infected about 16 million people and killed more than 2 million worldwide were reflected in two announcements.

In March 1994, the United States Centers for Disease Control and Prevention (CDC) in Atlanta, Ga., reported that U.S. cases of hetero-sexual transmission of AIDS—passing the virus between males and females through sexual contact—had risen by a larger percentage in 1993 than cases in any other risk category. And in August, experts with the World Health Organization (WHO), an agency of the United Nations (UN), warned that AIDS in Asia, where nearly two-thirds of the world's people reside, ultimately may kill more people there than anywhere else.

Glossary

AIDS: *A*cquired *immu*no*d*eficiency *s*yndrome is the final stage of HIV infection and is characterized by a severely damaged immune system leading to death.

HIV: *H*uman *immuno*deficiency *v*irus, which causes AIDS. People may be infected with HIV for several years before developing AIDS.

Immune system: The body's disease-fighting cells and antibodies that work together in a complex response against disease and infection.

IV drug abuser: Someone who injects illegal drugs, often heroin, using intravenous needles.

■ **The author**

Michael Woods is Science Editor for *The* (Toledo, Ohio) *Blade.*

The face of AIDS in America

Since the AIDS epidemic was first recorded in North America in the early 1980's, most Americans have known only one demographic face of this public health menace. AIDS first appeared mainly among homosexual or bisexual men and later spread among intravenous (IV) drug abusers. These two groups accounted for most cases in the United States, Canada, Western Europe, Australia, North Africa, and parts of South America. In those areas, they still account for the majority of people infected with the human immunodeficiency virus (HIV) that causes AIDS. In 1993, for instance, only 9 percent of AIDS cases in the United States resulted from heterosexual contact.

The number of adolescent and adult Americans who contracted AIDS by heterosexual contact, however, increased by 130 percent, from 4,114 cases in 1992 to 9,570 cases in 1993. In contrast, cases due to male homosexual contact, IV drug use, and all other forms of transmission increased by 125 percent. This overall jump in numbers, however, occurred partly because physicians in the United States began in 1993 to diagnose a person with AIDS at the earliest stages of infection with HIV. Previously, patients who were infected but did not have full-blown AIDS were simply known as HIV-infected. Under the new definition, the total number of AIDS cases more than doubled, from about 46,000 in 1992 to about 106,000 in 1993.

AIDS cases contracted homosexually for the first time dropped below 50 percent of the total number of new AIDS cases in 1993, to 47 percent. Experts credited the adoption of safe sexual practices, such as use of latex condoms, for the decrease among homosexual men. However, the number of cases transmitted among IV drug abusers, usually due to sharing unsterilized needles, alarmed experts. In 1985, those cases made up about 18 percent of the total. In 1993, they rose to about 28 percent. Cases of HIV infection due to blood transfusions and hemophilia accounted for only about 2 percent of the total, and about 8 percent of the cases reported to the CDC had unspecified causes. A combined category of homosexual and bisexual males who also inject drugs made up 6 percent of total cases.

More women were becoming infected with HIV in the early 1990's. The infection of women carries the high risk of mother-to-child transmission of AIDS during pregnancy and childbirth. About 900 American children under the age of 13 were reported to be HIV-infected from their mothers in 1993, accounting for less than 1 percent of the total. Women accounted for nearly twice as many of the heterosexual AIDS cases than men in 1993. About 45 percent of these women had sexual relations with male IV drug abusers.

AIDS increased among heterosexuals in the United States mainly because many adolescents and adults failed to adopt safer sexual behaviors, the CDC reported. Safer behaviors include postponing sexual

AIDS in the United States

AIDS cases due to homosexual contact accounted for less than 50 percent of new AIDS cases reported in the United States in 1993, while AIDS cases among other groups continued to rise. In 1993, the public health definition of AIDS was broadened to include all people who are HIV-infected, thus accounting for a large jump in the number of new cases from 1992 to 1993.

The rise of AIDS in the United States

Year	Cases
1982	827
1983	2,952
1984	7,504
1985	15,719
1986	12,910
1987	20,303
1988	34,601
1989	34,598
1990	42,557
1991	44,823
1992	46,335
1993	105,990

AIDS cases from injected drug use in the United States

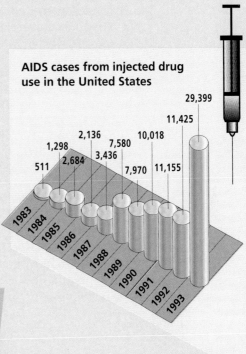

Year	Cases
1983	511
1984	1,298
1985	2,684
1986	2,136
1987	3,436
1988	7,580
1989	7,970
1990	10,018
1991	11,155
1992	11,425
1993	29,399

AIDS cases from heterosexual contact in the United States

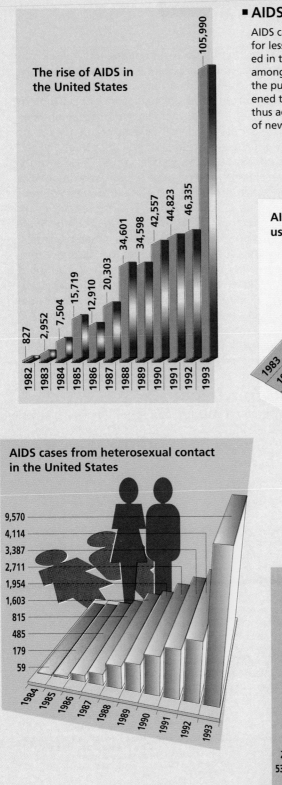

Year	Cases
1984	59
1985	179
1986	485
1987	815
1988	1,603
1989	1,954
1990	2,711
1991	3,387
1992	4,114
1993	9,570

Source: Centers for Disease Control and Prevention.

AIDS cases from male homosexual contact in the United States

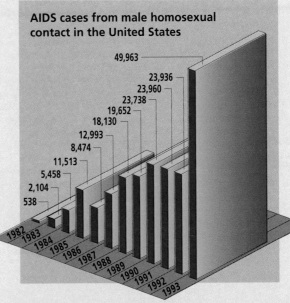

Year	Cases
1982	538
1983	2,104
1984	5,458
1985	11,513
1986	8,474
1987	12,993
1988	18,130
1989	19,652
1990	23,738
1991	23,960
1992	23,936
1993	49,963

activity until marriage, restricting sex to a monogamous relationship with an uninfected partner, and using a latex condom during every instance of sexual intercourse outside of such a relationship.

Among heterosexuals, groups with the highest risk of getting AIDS, according to the CDC, include people who have more than one sex partner, sexually active people who live in heavily populated urban areas with many HIV-infected drug abusers, and people who have sexually transmitted diseases (STD's). People with STD's are vulnerable to HIV infection because they tend to be people who do not practice safe sexual behaviors and also because their immune systems may be weakened from the STD. In addition, HIV can enter the bloodstream directly through the open sores that accompany some STD's.

Young people were one of the largest segments of heterosexuals who are contracting AIDS. Close to 30 percent of the 1993 cases occurred among people aged 13 to 29. Public health experts caution that sexually active teen-age girls may be at high risk for AIDS, especially because they tend to have intercourse with older teen-agers or men, who are more likely to have had multiple sexual partners. In teen-age girls, the cells of the *cervix* (the opening of the uterus) are immature and more easily infected with HIV. Also, the vaginal walls of teen-age girls produce little of the secretions that act as a barrier to viruses.

- AIDS has been most devastating in sub-Saharan Africa. World health experts have warned that the spread of AIDS in Asia, where about two-thirds of the world's people live, may kill more people there than anywhere else.

AIDS impact on Africa

In other parts of the world, the AIDS epidemic has long had a different demographic profile than that in the United States. In these areas, especially countries of sub-Saharan Africa, AIDS always has been a dis-

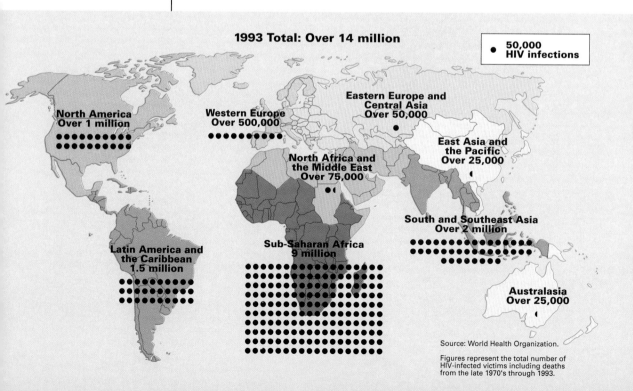

1993 Total: Over 14 million

● **50,000 HIV infections**

North America Over 1 million

Western Europe Over 500,000

Eastern Europe and Central Asia Over 50,000

East Asia and the Pacific Over 25,000

North Africa and the Middle East Over 75,000

South and Southeast Asia Over 2 million

Latin America and the Caribbean 1.5 million

Sub-Saharan Africa 9 million

Australasia Over 25,000

Source: World Health Organization.

Figures represent the total number of HIV-infected victims including deaths from the late 1970's through 1993.

ease that mainly existed among heterosexuals. WHO estimated in April 1994 that more than half of the nearly 16 million HIV infections worldwide resulted from heterosexual contact.

AIDS has had a devastating impact in some African countries that are too poor to provide even basic health-care services, let alone the sophisticated care needed to treat AIDS. The AIDS epidemic reversed many of the improvements in health status that had occurred during the previous several decades, the U.S. Bureau of the Census reported in April 1994 in its annual report on the world's population. In Zambia, for example, infant and child mortality rates have increased by 15 percent since 1980. The report said that increasing numbers of pregnant women were infected with HIV and were at risk for transmitting the virus to their babies. Studies have shown that at least 20 percent of pregnant women in the capital cities of Kampala, Uganda; Lusaka, Zambia; and Lilongwe, Malawi, were HIV positive.

Prostitutes and their clients have been significant factors in the spread of AIDS in Africa. The Census Bureau report estimated that at least 50 percent of the prostitutes in Kenya and Rwanda were infected with HIV. In many other countries, infection rates among prostitutes approached or exceeded 40 percent.

■ A truck driver in India consorts with a prostitute, *above*. Truckers often engage prostitutes along their routes, spreading AIDS nationwide. In Thailand, health officials use posters, *below*, to promote awareness that IV drug use can lead to AIDS.

AIDS growth in Asia

By late 1994, the areas where AIDS was newest and spreading most rapidly were Thailand, India, Burma, and other countries of Asia. HIV began to spread in Asia later than anywhere else, with the first big outbreaks reported in the middle to late 1980's. By 1994, more than 2 million people in Asia had been infected. Experts predict that HIV will infect more than 1 million Asians each year during the rest of the 1990's.

Heterosexual contact has been responsible for about 75 percent of the cases in the Asian epidemic. Most of the remaining cases resulted from sharing contaminated needles among IV drug abusers. Sex between men has been only a minor factor.

Most of the Asian AIDS infections are in India and Thailand. The story of how AIDS spread in

■ A public health volunteer offers free condoms to a prostitute in Bangkok, Thailand, where a large commercial sex industry has fueled an AIDS epidemic. Latex condoms provide an effective barrier against HIV infection.

Thailand has been well documented. Thailand's first HIV infections surfaced among IV drug abusers in 1984. The epidemic then spread from IV drug abusers to female prostitutes, who are part of the country's large commercial sex industry. Its next victims were young heterosexual men who visit prostitutes. Although sex outside of marriage for Thai women is frowned upon, Thai men face no such taboo, and millions of them visit prostitutes each week.

Experts have been surprised at how rapidly AIDS spread in Thailand. In 1989, for instance, the HIV-positive rate was less than 1 percent even in studies of high-risk men—those with other sexually transmitted diseases. By 1993, studies reported that an alarming 15 percent of young men in some parts of the country were HIV positive. Experts anticipate that many of these men, who were infected by prostitutes, will pass the disease to their wives and girlfriends, who will become the next victims of AIDS's march through the country.

Ignorance of the threat of AIDS has fed the Thai epidemic. Thai people and other Asians have tended to view AIDS as a disease of foreigners. They believed that infection came from having sex with foreigners or sharing hypodermic needles with foreigners. Thus, they saw little need to use condoms or take other precautions among themselves. In addition, many people live in severe poverty and cannot afford condoms, which have been scarce and expensive in Asian countries.

AIDS in India

In India, an estimated 1 million cases of HIV infection have resulted from some of these same factors. Indian public health officials estimated that the proportion of Bombay prostitutes infected with HIV shot from 1 percent in 1987 to more than 40 percent by 1992. Similarly rapid increases have occurred in other Indian cities.

By the year 2000, India may have more HIV-positive people than any other country in the world, according to WHO projections. The president of the Indian Medical Association, P. K. Choudhuri, reported at the 10th international conference on AIDS in Yokohama, Japan, in August 1994 that only 728 full-blown AIDS cases were reported in India as of May 1994. But he predicted that India will have 1 million AIDS cases by the year 2000. A large proportion of the new cases may occur among women.

Studies conducted in the southeastern Indian state of Tamil Nadu identified a number of reasons why HIV is expected to spread among women at large. Indian traditions value chastity before marriage and sexual relations only within marriage, but sex with prostitutes has become increasingly common among young Tamil men, who visit commercial sex establishments that abound in big cities. Many prostitution clients are men who have temporarily left wives or girlfriends behind in their villages to find jobs in the cities. The men become infected with HIV when they have sex with prostitutes and, when these men return to their villages, they are likely to infect their wives or girlfriends. Public health specialists term this tendency to have sex with two or more women sexual networking, and it contributes heavily to the heterosexual spread of AIDS throughout Asia.

Other social factors have contributed to the frequenting of prostitutes in India, according to a 1994 report by Family Health International, a nonprofit organization based in Arlington, Va., that works with AIDS-prevention and family-planning programs. In the past, for instance, many Indian men married as teen-agers. But men today frequently delay marriage until their late 20's or 30's in order to complete their education, find a job, and save money. While doing so, some turn to prostitutes for sex. Also, men who are about to marry but who have not had sexual intercourse often visit commercial sex establishments to gain experience. All too often, they also gain HIV.

Growing concern in Latin America

In Latin America, the AIDS problem has not yet generated the level of concern that the Asian and African epidemics have. However, WHO reported in 1994 that increases in the number of IV drug abusers has contributed to the spread of AIDS among heterosexuals in Argentina, Brazil, Chile, Guatemala, and Mexico. In all of Latin America, includ-

■ IV drug users in Seattle are given clean hypodermic needles in exchange for old ones. Needle exchange programs aim to prevent HIV transmission between addicts who share needles.

AMERICA RESPONDS TO AIDS

Christina
HIV Positive

Ric
HIV Positive

■ In January 1994, the United States Centers for Disease Control and Prevention launched an HIV-prevention program, which included televised public service announcements featuring people with AIDS. The ads targeted young people and promoted two main HIV-prevention strategies: Either refrain from sexual activity or use condoms.

ing the West Indies, most HIV infections first occurred among homosexual and bisexual men. But since the mid-1980's, heterosexual transmission in these areas has increased, especially among bisexual men and their female sex partners and among female prostitutes and their clients. In Brazil, for instance, the percentage of AIDS cases due to heterosexual transmission jumped from 7.5 percent in 1987 to 23 percent in 1992. WHO says that in most of the West Indies, heterosexual contact has been the main way that AIDS has been transmitted since the early 1980's.

The public health response

In response to the worldwide AIDS epidemic, WHO has developed a public health program to halt its spread. Measures shown to be highly effective in preventing HIV transmission include promoting and distributing condoms to the general population; encouraging condom use by prostitutes and their clients; creating AIDS information and education programs in the mass media and in schools; providing clean needles for IV drug users; and expanding treatment programs for conventional sexually transmitted diseases such as gonorrhea and syphilis. These diseases, if left untreated, make people far more likely to acquire HIV infection and thus pass the virus on to sexual partners.

Experts cite many instances of the effectiveness of such measures.

Condom sales in Africa, for instance, rose from less than 2 million per year in 1986 to 70 million in 1993 due to AIDS awareness programs. In Zaire alone, WHO estimated that 20 million condoms sold at subsidized prices in 1991 prevented 25,000 cases of AIDS. Condom use in Thailand among men visiting prostitutes rose dramatically in the early 1990's after the government began an anti-AIDS program.

The Indian government has responded to the spread of AIDS with programs to educate the public and physicians about HIV. Efforts also are underway to encourage condom use at commercial sex establishments and at highway stops where truckers visit prostitutes. Long-distance truck drivers were one of the chief reasons HIV spread so quickly from one region of India to another. Choudhuri said many Indian men still are unaware of the risk of getting HIV from prostitutes. Myths that washing or urinating after sex can prevent infection still are prevalent, he said.

Overcoming obstacles to fight AIDS

Health experts would like to see women have more power to protect themselves from HIV infection. To this end, researchers began a major effort to develop a prevention technique that women could use without the consent or knowledge of men. Experts at WHO say such a method is needed because women in many parts of the world have little control over the circumstances of sexual intercourse. A woman can ask a partner to use a condom, but may be powerless if he refuses. Researchers are seeking to create a medication, similar to contraceptive foams or gels, to be inserted into the vagina before sexual intercourse. Called a microbicide, it would kill HIV and perhaps microbes that cause other STD's.

Cultural and religious beliefs and other social factors sometimes make implementation of prevention programs controversial. The governments of some developing countries, for instance, are reluctant to acknowledge a serious AIDS problem. They fear the international stigma and a possible loss of income from tourism. Some citizens are concerned that promoting the use of condoms, especially in school-based programs, may encourage sexual activity outside of marriage. Others fear that needle exchange programs, which provide IV drug abusers with free, sterilized needles, will encourage illicit activity. Debate on these issues is likely to intensify as AIDS continues its worldwide rampage. ■ ■ ■

For further information:

National AIDS Hot Line (800-342-AIDS), operated by the Centers for Disease Control and Prevention, provides information and referrals 24 hours a day, 7 days a week. Spanish-language information is available at 800-344-7432. People who are hearing impaired can call 800-243-7889.

Albania. Conflict between President Sali Berisha's ruling Democratic Party and the Albanian Socialist Party continued to dominate Albanian politics in 1994. On April 3, Fatos Nano, leader of the Socialist Party and Berisha's chief opponent, was sentenced to 12 years in prison for misappropriating state funds and falsifying government documents. On July 2, past President Ramiz Alia and nine other officials of Albania's former Communist government were also sentenced to prison terms for misappropriating state property and violating citizens' rights.

Economy. The Albanian government reported economic improvement in 1994 under Berisha's reform program. Officials predicted continued growth of the *gross domestic product* (the total value of goods and services produced in a country) for 1994 and reported a significant drop in inflation.

In April, the International Monetary Fund, an agency of the United Nations, loaned Albania more than $12 million to encourage economic reform. The United States contributed $30 million to support private industry and foreign investment. In September, the World Bank, an international lending agency, granted $10 million in credit to Albania for improvement of farmland irrigation.

Nevertheless, Albania's economy carried a high level of foreign debt—about $1.1 billion in early 1994. Albania remained heavily dependent on the import of foreign goods. Albanian leaders also had little success in attracting foreign investors during the year.

Many Albanians continued to suffer financial hardship in 1994. Food shortages plagued many areas, and the nation continued to rely on foreign food aid. The number of homeless Albanians also continued to rise, leading the government to finance the construction of 10,000 public housing units in 1994.

Foreign relations. In January, Albania joined the Partnership for Peace, a new North Atlantic Treaty Organization program of cooperation with nations that had belonged to the Warsaw Pact, the military alliance led by the former Soviet Union. Albanian leaders also applied for associate membership in the European Union (EU), formerly the European Community.

Tensions between Albania and Greece worsened in 1994, particularly over the treatment of ethnic Greeks in Albania. In August, five Albanian Greeks were convicted of espionage and illegal possession of firearms. Greek officials retaliated by expelling many ethnic Albanians and by blocking a loan from the EU intended for Albania. Tensions were heightened further when Greece recalled its ambassador to Albania and tightened control along the Albanian border. □ Sharon L. Wolchik

See also **Europe** (Facts in brief table); **Greece.** In *World Book,* see **Albania.**

Alberta. See **Canadian provinces.**

Algeria. A three-year-old civil struggle in Algeria erupted onto the world stage when four young Algerians, saying they were members of the Armed Islamic Group, hijacked an Air France airplane at Algiers, the capital, on Dec. 24, 1994. The hijackers killed three passengers before forcing the pilot to fly to Marseille, France. French commandos stormed the plane on December 26, killing the hijackers and freeing those onboard. On December 27, Islamic militants killed four Roman Catholic priests in Algeria, presumably to revenge the hijackers' deaths.

Algerian officials had said in August that more than 10,000 people had been killed in the violence that began in January 1992, when the military seized power to keep the fundamentalist Islamic Salvation Front (FIS) from winning parliamentary elections. Independent estimates of the deaths, however, reached as high as 30,000 by the end of 1994.

To stem political violence, government officials had begun negotiations in August with members of FIS. But in early October, they declared that their attempts had failed. In September 1994, Algerian President Liamine Zeroual had sought to ease friction by transferring two FIS leaders—Abassi Madani and his militant aide Ali Belhaj—from jail to house arrest. By early November, though, they had been returned to jail and the government had launched a massive offensive against the FIS.

Zeroual, a former general, was appointed president by the military-backed High Security Council on January 30. On April 11, Zeroual named Mokdad Sifi to replace Redha Malek as prime minister.

More political violence. On March 10, about 900 prisoners, aided by Muslim militants and prison guards, escaped from a prison 215 miles (346 kilometers) east of the capital, Algiers. An estimated several hundred people died later as security forces rounded up prisoners and suspected militants. More than 120 soldiers died in July in an ambush on their convoy 240 miles (386 kilometers) east of Algiers.

Revenge slayings became common in 1994. On March 30, two teen-aged women without veils were shot to death at a bus station, presumably by fundamentalists who disapproved of women not wearing veils. The militants also added students and teachers to their list of civilian targets, which already included artists, journalists, and heads of state companies.

Violence against foreigners. Many embassies in Algeria decided to close or reduce their staffs after Muslim extremists attacked a French diplomatic complex in Algiers, killing five people on August 3. By late October, 68 foreigners had been murdered since Muslim militants began to target foreigners in October 1993. Among other attacks, five Eastern Europeans, who were working for the Algerian government, were slain in Algiers after being forced off a bus on July 11, 1994. A week earlier, seven Italian seamen had their throats slit aboard their vessel 160 miles (260 kilometers) east of Algiers.

Algerian women march in their capital, Algiers, in May to protest Islamic fundamentalist terrorism that has wracked the nation.

International strains. The United States urged Zeroual to open talks with FIS, but France argued that concessions led to more violence. Fearing terrorism and a mass immigration of North Africans to Europe if Islamic extremists took over Algeria, France deported some 25 suspected militants to Burkina Faso after the attack on their Algiers complex. Algeria's instability prompted Morocco on August 28 to impose visa restrictions on Algerians. Algeria retaliated by closing its Moroccan border.

Economy. Algeria agreed in April to devalue its monetary unit, the dinar, in order to qualify for $1-billion in loans from the International Monetary Fund, an agency of the United Nations. The government also rescheduled payments on some of its $26-billion foreign debt. Falling oil prices led to estimates that 1994 oil revenues might drop from $9 billion to $7 billion. Oil revenues provide more than 90 percent of Algeria's foreign earnings.

Natural disasters. An earthquake 250 miles (400 kilometers) west of Algiers on August 18 killed at least 171 people and left 15,000 homeless. The worst drought in 50 years was expected to halve 1994 wheat production and increase food import bills. □ Christine Helms

See also **Africa** (Facts in brief table). In *World Book,* see **Algeria.**

Angola. See Africa.

Animal. See Conservation; Zoology; Zoos.

Anthropology. Fossils of an apelike human ancestor that lived more than 4 million years ago were discovered in Ethiopia, according to a September 1994 report by anthropologists Tim D. White of the University of California at Berkeley, Gen Suwa of the University of Tokyo, and Berhane Asfaw of Addis Ababa, Ethiopia. The fossils represent a new species of *hominid,* a group that includes human beings and their close prehuman ancestors.

The anthropologists found fragmentary remains of 17 hominid fossils in Aramis, Ethiopia, 50 miles (80 kilometers) south of Hadar, Ethiopia, where the skeleton dubbed "Lucy" was found in 1974. The Aramis remains consist of teeth, parts of an arm, skull fragments, and part of a youngster's lower jaw. Scientists dated a layer of volcanic ash below the hominid fossils to 4.4 million years ago. That date indicated that the fossils were about 500,000 years older than the most ancient remains of the oldest previously known hominid species, *Australopithecus afarensis.*

The skull and tooth fragments from Aramis suggest that the creature had a more apelike anatomy than *A. afarensis.* Because the Aramis fossils had primitive features—such as an apelike milk molar in the youngster's jaw—the anthropologists decided to categorize the newly discovered fossils as a new species, which they called *Australopithecus ramidus.*

The apelike features of *A. ramidus* are consistent with the view that living African apes and human

Anthropology

A step closer to the "missing link"

A fossil dig in Ethiopia produced bones of the oldest known *hominid* (a group of species that includes human beings and their apelike human ancestors), according to a September report. Anthropologists discovered the fossils at a site called Aramis, *below*.

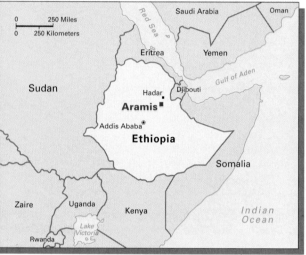

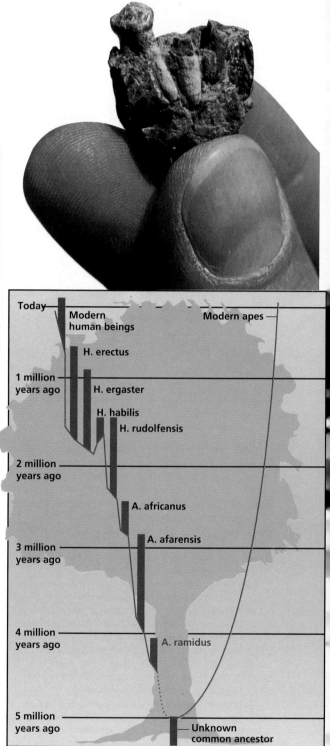

beings descended from a common ancestor. The Aramis discovery brings scientists one step closer to the common ancestor, but because that animal is thought to have lived from 5 million to 8 million years ago, early hominids that are even more primitive than *A. ramidus* may one day be found.

Lucy-era skull found. Scientists working at Hadar discovered 53 new hominid specimens, according to a March 1994 report by anthropologists William H. Kimbel and Donald C. Johanson of the Institute of Human Origins in Berkeley, Calif., and Yoel Rak of Tel Aviv University in Israel. Teeth, jaws, and some limb bones were among the finds, but the most significant discovery was a nearly complete skull.

The skull, as well as the other fossils, are assigned to Lucy's species, *A. afarensis*. The species is known from several sites in eastern Africa and hundreds of fossil specimens, but no other complete skull had ever been found. Robert C. Walter, a geochronologist at the Institute of Human Origins, dated the skull to about 3 million years ago. The skull, pieced together from more than 200 rock-encrusted fragments, has a small brain case, an apelike jutting jaw, and thick protruding ridges over the eye sockets. Its large size, in comparison with Lucy, and other features suggest that the skull is of a male.

The skull confirms, in large part, an earlier reconstruction of an *A. afarensis* skull, which had been assembled from the bones of several different individ-

The fragmentary fossils included several teeth, *top*. The fossils were dated to about 4.4 million years ago, making them 500,000 years older than the oldest previously known hominid species. A proposed hominid family tree, *above*, shows the species named for the new fossils, *A. ramidus*, to be close to the common ancestor of human beings and apes, which is thought to have lived from 5 million to 8 million years ago.

uals. Furthermore, the Hadar skull is very similar to fragments of a skull dated to approximately 3.9 million years ago. This suggests that *A. afarensis* was a stable species exhibiting no obvious sign of evolutionary change for almost 1 million years.

Java *Homo erectus*. *Homo erectus* lived in Java, Indonesia, some 800,000 years earlier than previously believed, according to a February 1994 report by paleontologist Carl C. Swisher III of the Berkeley Geochronology Center in Berkeley, Calif. Swisher and his colleagues made the finding by redating skull fossils discovered in 1936 and in the 1970's.

Previous attempts to date Java fossils relied on estimates of the age of rocks and animal remains near the fossil bones. That method indicated that the fossils were roughly 1 million years old. In comparison, the most ancient remains of *H. erectus* in Africa are about 1.8 million years old.

Swisher and his co-workers established more precise dates by determining the age of pumice and other volcanic rock in the layer of earth in which the specimens were found. The scientists were able to date one set of fossils to approximately 1.8 million years ago and others to about 1.6 million years ago. The authors concluded that because the earliest dates for *H. erectus* are roughly equivalent in Africa and Java, it is possible that *Homo erectus* may have evolved outside Africa. □ Donald C. Johanson

In *World Book*, see **Anthropology.**

Arafat, Yasir (1929-   ), chairman of the Palestine Liberation Organization (PLO) since 1969, shared the Nobel Peace Prize in October 1994 with Israeli Prime Minister Yitzhak Rabin and Foreign Minister Shimon Peres for their role in negotiating a 1993 agreement for limited Palestinian self-rule. The selection of Arafat drew controversy, however, because of the PLO's past sponsorship of terrorism.

Arafat was sworn in on July 5, 1994, as head of the Palestine National Authority, formed in 1994 to administer Palestinian self-rule in the West Bank town of Jericho and the Gaza Strip. On May 4, Israel and the PLO had signed an accord to implement Palestinian self-rule in the West Bank and Gaza, occupied by Israel since 1967. (See **Middle East.**)

Arafat claims to have been born in Jerusalem, in what was then Palestine, but a birth certificate indicates that he was born in Cairo, Egypt. He earned a degree in civil engineering at Cairo University, but left his career to organize guerrilla groups. Starting in the 1960's, he helped plan raids against Israel. In 1974, Arafat addressed the United Nations General Assembly, which subsequently recognized the PLO as the representative of Palestinian Arabs. Secret peace talks between Israel and the PLO began in January 1993. In September, Arafat and Rabin met in Washington, D.C., to sign the self-rule accord.

In 1990, Arafat married Suha Tawil, a Palestinian Christian. □ Mary Carvlin

Archaeology. In 1994, DNA testing helped solve archaeological mysteries ranging from the colonization of the Pacific and the Americas to the spread of disease in the ancient world. (DNA is deoxyribonucleic acid, the molecule of which genes are made.)

Triumphs for DNA testing. In May 1994, an international team of scientists reported that analyzing the DNA of ancient skeletons excavated on Easter Island revealed the origins of the island's first inhabitants. The DNA testing confirmed the theory that the original inhabitants, who erected the colossal stone heads for which Easter Island is famous, were of Polynesian descent.

Another long-standing archaeological mystery is the date, or dates, when human beings came to the Americas. Scientists at Emory University in Atlanta, Ga., compared the DNA of 544 Native Americans with the genes of 411 east Asians. Certain types of genetic mutations occur in a population at a steady rate, and scientists can use those mutations to determine how long groups of related people have been isolated from one another. The results of the DNA tests, publicized in January 1994, indicate that human beings may have come to the New World from Asia 23,000 to 29,000 years ago, more than 10,000 years earlier than widely believed.

In June 1994, scientists reported the completion of DNA testing on the celebrated Ice Man, a 5,300-year-old shepherd found frozen in the Alps in 1991. Tests showed that the shepherd is most closely related to central and northern Europeans. The result silenced doubters who thought the Ice Man might have been an Egyptian mummy planted as a hoax.

Finally, scientists with the University of Minnesota in Duluth in March 1994 found DNA of the bacterium that causes tuberculosis in a 900-year-old mummy discovered in Peru. The discovery indicated that tuberculosis was present in the New World centuries before the arrival of Christopher Columbus.

Huge cache of Maya jade. Archaeologists working at Blue Creek, a Maya site in northwestern Belize, discovered a cache of more than 890 jade beads, pendants, and other artifacts, according to an August 1994 report. It was the largest collection of jade deposited at one time that was ever found in the Maya world. Jade was prized by the Maya, according to archaeologist Thomas H. Guderjan, who has directed excavations at the site for St. Mary's University in San Antonio since 1992.

The Maya settlement at Blue Creek, which flourished from A.D. 600 to 750, was apparently a trading center linking inland regions with the coastal plain. More than 80 buildings have survived at the site, including a temple containing a man's tomb, a ball court, and a 20-foot-tall (6-meter-tall) structure, probably an administrative center, in which the cache was discovered. The jade, along with numerous shells, obsidian blades, stone and bone beads, pottery, and a scattering of human bones, had been

Archaeology

The 3,000-year-old corpse of a light-haired woman is one of more than 100 such bodies found in China since 1978 that show features of Caucasians, an American archaeologist reported in April 1994. The finds suggest that Europeans and Asians had earlier contact than once believed.

placed in a stone-lined shaft extending from the building's summit to its foundation.

Egyptian finds. Geologists Thomas M. Bown, of the U.S. Geological Survey, and James A. Harrell, of the University of Toledo in Ohio, identified 16 segments of what they believe to be the oldest known stone-paved road, the researchers announced in May 1994. The road starts at a landing on the former shoreline of Lake Moeris, southwest of Cairo, and leads more than 6 miles (10 kilometers) to basalt quarries and a miner's camp at Gebel Qatrani. The road, quarries, and camp date to Dynasties V and VI of Egypt's Old Kingdom (2686-2181 B.C.).

Construction workers digging at Giza, site of the Great Pyramids and Sphinx, discovered remains of an Old Kingdom harbor in February 1994. The find, a 231-foot-long (70-meter-long) section of stone wall, suggests that each pyramid had a harbor linked to the Nile River by a canal. The harbor is believed to date to Dynasty IV of the Old Kingdom of King Khufu, who built the largest of the pyramids.

Frozen mummy. Russian archaeologist Natalya Polosmak discovered a 2,500-year-old frozen mummy of a noblewoman near the town of Ukok in the Altai Mountains of southern Siberia in 1993. The mummy became known to the West when it was flown to Moscow in early 1994. The noblewoman, about 20 years old, was a Pazyryk. The Pazyryks were an ancient seminomadic people who lived in the region from 600 to 200 B.C.

The young woman had been buried in a log tomb. As part of the mummification process, her internal organs had been removed and replaced with fur and moss. A hollow larch trunk decorated with carvings of snow leopards and geese served as a sarcophagus. In the tomb were six horses, which had been ritually sacrificed by being speared in the head, and other evidence of the young woman's high status, such as a silver mirror and carved figurines of winged snow leopards. The woman wore a long white dress with two red stripes, a blouse, gold earrings, and a wooden hair ornament with a tall plume of felt decorated with abstract patterns and animals. Her arms and hands bore tattoos of snow leopards and a mythical horse-eagle.

Because the body had frozen, it was in an excellent state of preservation when it was found. It took more than four weeks to arrange for a helicopter to remove the body from the site, however, and high temperatures in the interim caused the olive-toned skin to blacken. Experts said that much of the mummy's value to science had been lost as a result.

Nicknamed "the lady," the mummy was being restored in 1994. After treatment, the mummy will be displayed at a museum in southern Siberia.

□ Mark Rose

In the World Book Supplement section, see **Culture.** In *World Book*, see **Archaeology.**

Architecture.

Architecture. The surge that lifted the American economy in 1994 lifted architecture as well. Home construction was up, new museums and theaters opened, and sports facilities emerged as a new growth industry.

Sports facilities. About half of American professional sports teams were planning, building, or opening new facilities in 1994. In April, the Texas Rangers and the Cleveland Indians inaugurated new ball parks in dramatically different settings.

The $189-million Ballpark in Arlington, home of the Rangers, is the quintessential suburban field, adjacent to a freeway and barely a pop fly from a gigantic amusement park. Washington, D.C., architect David Schwarz designed an eclectic exterior of brick arches and vaguely Moorish towers, decorated with longhorns and Lone Stars, and enclosing a grass field that evokes New York's Yankee and Detroit's Tiger stadiums. Nostalgia for old-time ball parks is mixed with economics, in the form of luxury suites (leasing for up to $90,000 per season), 50 restaurants and concession stands, a jumbo electronic scoreboard, and an office building beyond center field.

The Cleveland Indians, on the other hand, built Jacobs Field on the edge of the city's downtown as part of the $425-million Gateway Center project. Designed by HOK Sports Facilities, the ball park recalls Cleveland's industrial past with its massive steel trusses and rugged stone base. Inside it is a purist's dream: grass playing surface, asymmetrical outfield, and mostly unobstructed views of the downtown skyline for 42,000 fans. In October, Gund Arena, home of the Cleveland Cavaliers basketball team and the last piece of the Gateway complex, opened next door.

French openings. In Paris, I. M. Pei's renovation of the Louvre, begun in the mid-1980's, was completed. The museum's maze of galleries and offices was reconfigured, with the architect's glistening glass pyramid standing as the symbol of its renewal.

A few miles away, architect Frank Gehry's $40-million American Center building opened in June 1994 after two years of turmoil over programs and personnel. The center has been home to expatriate artists and the international avant-garde for more than 30 years, and its new building expresses that adventurous spirit. Its jutting angles and sweeping curves suit the energy of the work produced inside, while its limestone walls and galvanized roofs recall the more traditional architecture of Paris. In addition to theaters, studios, and classrooms, the center contains 26 apartments for visiting artists.

In the United States, The Virginia Opera took up residence in the $10-million Harrison Opera House in Norfolk. American architect Graham Gund transformed a 1940's United Service Organizations auditorium into a 1,700-seat showpiece, taking his stylistic cues from the Italianate Chrysler Museum of Art next door but giving them a contemporary spin.

The American Center, a base for expatriate artists designed by American architect Frank Gehry, opened in Paris in June.

Awards. French architect Christian de Portzamparc won the $100,000 Pritzker Prize, given annually to a living architect who has contributed significantly to the art of design. A modernist with a strong lyrical flair, Portzamparc is best known for the City of Music, a studio, classroom, and recital hall complex in Paris.

The American Institute of Architects awarded its gold medal to English architect Norman Foster, whose dramatic high-tech buildings are crafted with the same care and delicacy as those made of wood and stone. Foster is best known for the 60-story Hong Kong and Shanghai Banking Corporation building in Hong Kong, completed in 1985 and indisputably one of the most innovative skyscrapers.

Two major international airports were completed in 1994. The $15-billion Kansai International Airport in Osaka, Japan, made its debut in September—50 percent over budget and two years late because the reclaimed land on which it sits kept sinking. Designed by Noriaki Okabe and Renzo Piano, who made his reputation with the Pompidou Center in Paris, the airport is a vast structure of steel and glass reminiscent of train stations of the 1800's.

In America, the $4.9-billion Denver International Airport remained inoperative because of problems with its baggage handling system. Promoted as the most advanced and efficient airport in the world, it has cost the city hundreds of millions of dollars in bond interest and imperiled the city's credit rating. The airport was scheduled to open early in 1995.

Exhibits. Two major architecture exhibits of 1994 provided a clash of opposites. In April, Peter Eisenman's "Cities of Artificial Excavation" opened at the Canadian Center for Architecture in Montreal. The show featured 11 projects from 1978 to 1988, only one of which—The Wexner Center for the Arts in Columbus, Ohio—was actually built. Eisenman has described his work as a sustained critique of what the rest of the profession is doing. His goal is to make viewers question conventional notions of clarity, function, comfort, and context. The critical response was polite bafflement.

One of the most important 1994 exhibits was of the works of the late American architect Frank Lloyd Wright, whose style is the antithesis of Eisenman's intensely cerebral and theoretical work. "Frank Lloyd Wright: Architect" at New York's Museum of Modern Art contained more than 500 pieces: plans, drawings, models, furniture, stained glass, even mock-ups of rooms and walls. Wright's every period was represented, from the early prairie houses to the sculptural bravura of the Guggenheim Museum in the late 1950's. Although the exhibit offered few fresh insights into Wright's work, it confirmed once again why Wright is often considered America's greatest architect. □ David Dillon

See also **Art.** In *World Book,* see **Architecture.**

Argentina. Argentina's first substantially new Constitution since 1853 took effect on Aug. 24, 1994. The document was drafted by a special assembly, which was elected in April and comprised 305 delegates from the country's major political parties.

In a major change, the new Constitution allows Argentina's president to be reelected. Presidents can now serve two consecutive, four-year terms instead of just one six-year term. It also drops the requirement that the president be Roman Catholic. In addition, a new Cabinet post was created—a chief of staff to be appointed by the president. The new position will resemble that of a prime minister.

A potentially troublesome clause in the new Constitution reasserts Argentine claims to sovereignty over the Falkland Islands, which lie about 320 miles (515 kilometers) off Argentina in the South Atlantic Ocean. Argentina lost a 74-day war in 1982 with the United Kingdom over control of the islands.

The provision to allow presidential reelection was a personal victory for President Carlos Saúl Menem, who had pressed strongly for the right to seek a second term. But despite this triumph, there were signs that support for the once popular Menem was eroding. In polls taken between April and July 1994, Menem's approval rating fell from 42 percent to 32 percent, and the approval rating for his administration fell from 38 percent to 27 percent, giving opposition parties hope of winning national elec-

Rescue workers search the ruins of a Jewish center in Buenos Aires, Argentina, after a bomb destroyed the building, killing about 100 people in July.

tions scheduled for May 1995. Public anger over continuing revelations of government corruption contributed to Menem's falling popularity. One scandal that preoccupied the country for much of 1994 involved payoffs that the head of a $2-billion government health fund for retirees allegedly demanded from psychiatric centers in return for business contracts.

Jewish center bombing. A terrorist bomb hidden in a truck exploded outside Argentina's main Jewish center in Buenos Aires on July 18, killing about 100 people and wounding more than 200. On July 21, 150,000 people demonstrated in Buenos Aires against the bombing and demanded that the police find and arrest those responsible for the act. The attack resembled one that demolished the Israeli Embassy in Buenos Aires in 1992, killing more than 32 people. No arrests had been made in that attack by the end of 1994.

On August 9, an Argentine judge issued arrest warrants for four Iranian diplomats in conjunction with the bombing. But Argentine officials later admitted the evidence for the diplomats' involvement in the bombing was slim. Police arrested an Argentine automobile mechanic as an accessory to the bombing, but authorities had not charged anyone with planning the attack by the end of the year.

The day after the blast, Menem created a central security agency to combat terrorism. The move was an attempt to counter criticism that Argentina's federal security forces were poorly trained and unresponsive to terrorist threats. The new Ministry of Security and Community Protection would control the federal police, the Coast Guard, and the nation's border patrol. Menem named an Air Force brigadier general to head the new agency, though some critics expressed fears that increased central police authority might lead to a revival of past repression. In the late 1970's, some 10,000 people disappeared in Argentina after the military seized control of the government and began a severe crackdown on leftists and other government opponents.

Workers protest. On July 6, 1994, between 30,000 and 60,000 people gathered in Buenos Aires to protest poor economic conditions in the nation's provinces. Fearing violence, 20,000 police officers lined the streets. The protest was the largest against Menem since he took office in 1989 and countered the president's popular international image as an economic savior. Menem's policies helped revitalize the Argentine economy in the early 1990's by taming runaway inflation and attracting billions of dollars in foreign investment. But critics claim those policies also increased unemployment and drove down wages among scores of poorer provincial workers. ☐ Nathan A. Haverstock

In *World Book,* see **Argentina.**
Arizona. See **State government.**
Arkansas. See **State government.**

Armed forces. The United States military strained in 1994 to help keep order in a variety of trouble spots around the world. During the year, U.S. troops performed peacekeeping and humanitarian roles in Bosnia-Herzegovina, Somalia, Macedonia, and Rwanda. In the fall of 1994, however, these activities were dwarfed by massive U.S. troop deployments in the Persian Gulf and Haiti.

Persian Gulf. In an eerie replay of events that led to the 1991 Persian Gulf War, U.S. military forces returned to Saudi Arabia and Kuwait in October 1994 to confront a buildup of tens of thousands of Iraqi troops near the border with Kuwait. President Bill Clinton ordered 4,000 Army troops from the 24th Mechanized Infantry Division to Kuwait on October 8 and moved 2,000 Marine troops in amphibious ships to Kuwaiti waters. Clinton also dispatched the aircraft carrier U.S.S. *George Washington* to the Red Sea and sent two Patriot missile batteries to Saudi Arabia. Within 48 hours, an additional 18,000 Marines and 16,000 Army troops were ordered to the Gulf, along with several hundred more combat aircraft. With the moves, the Clinton Administration hoped to prevent further warlike actions by Iraq, whose 1990 invasion triggered Operation Desert Storm, in which a U.S.-led military coalition drove Iraqi President Saddam Hussein's forces from Kuwait. (See **Iraq; Kuwait; Middle East.**)

By Oct. 11, 1994, Iraq had begun withdrawing its troops, but the United States continued its buildup. The crisis eased, and the deployment peaked at 17,000 troops in November. The United States had stationed more than 12,000 troops in the region prior to the buildup.

Haiti. United States military forces launched a peaceful invasion of Haiti on Sept. 19, 1994, to restore ousted Haitian President Jean-Bertrand Aristide to power. More than 20,000 troops arrived in Haiti for what was expected to be a stay of several months. A U.S. delegation headed by former President Jimmy Carter negotiated a last-minute political settlement with Haiti's military leaders to avert a full-scale attack by U.S. forces. Troops from the Army's 82nd Airborne Division were already en route to Haiti when the agreement was reached. Operation Restore Democracy was controversial. A majority of Americans opposed it, according to public opinion polls, and many members of Congress believed that restoring democracy in Haiti was not a proper use of U.S. military forces. But the peaceful outcome of the intervention took the edge off much of the opposition. (See **Haiti.**)

Helicopter downing brings charges. The Pentagon charged an Air Force F-15 pilot with dereliction of duty and negligent homicide on September 8 in association with an April 14 incident in which two F-15's shot down two U.S. Army helicopters over northern Iraq, killing all 26 persons onboard. Also charged with dereliction were five crew members of

Armed forces

An infantryman displays futuristic battle gear at Fort Irwin, Calif., in March. Equipment includes a minicamera, a computer, and a heat-sensing gunsight.

an Air Force Airborne Warning and Control System (AWACS) radar plane monitoring Iraqi airspace during the incident. The helicopters were engaged in a United Nations (UN) humanitarian mission in the "no-fly zone" established after the 1991 Gulf War to protect Kurds from repression by the Iraqi government. The fighter pilots had mistakenly identified the U.S. helicopters as Iraqi Soviet-made helicopters flying in restricted airspace. Fifteen Americans, along with UN peacekeepers, died in the accident.

On Dec. 19, 1994, charges against four of the AWACS crew members were dismissed. The AWAC officer in charge of the crew, however, was ordered to face a court-martial. On December 20, charges against the F-15 pilot were dropped.

Somalia. The United States ended its ill-fated military involvement in Somalia on March 25, 1994, when the last contingent of more than 25,000 American troops left the capital of Mogadishu. Former President George Bush had ordered forces to Somalia in December 1992 to help distribute food to thousands of starving Somalis. But U.S. troops were drawn into bitter tribal disputes, culminating in an October 1993 firefight in which 18 U.S. soldiers died. Forty-four American soldiers died during the Somalia operation, 30 of them in combat.

Tailhook scandal closed. On Feb. 8, 1994, military judges dismissed the last four cases remaining from the Tailhook affair, in which naval aviators al-

legedly sexually assaulted or molested at least 83 women during a convention in Las Vegas, Nev., in September 1991. Citing lack of evidence, a naval judge in Norfolk, Va., dismissed sexual misconduct charges against three Navy officers stemming from the affair. Another military judge in Quantico, Va., also dismissed charges stemming from the scandal against a Marine aviator in early February.

Navy Lieutenant Paula Coughlin ignited the Tailhook controversy by publicly alleging that she had been sexually assaulted during the convention. Although 140 officers were implicated in misconduct during the convention, none were court-martialed. The February dismissals meant that none of the aviators would stand trial.

Fallout from Tailhook forced Chief of Naval Operations Frank B. Kelso II to quit on April 30, 1994, two months earlier than expected. On February 8, a Navy judge alleged that Kelso lied when he claimed not to have observed sexual harassment at the Tailhook convention. Kelso denied the charges.

Strategic developments. On Jan. 10, 1994, the United States, Ukraine, and Russia signed an agreement to eliminate the Ukraine's arsenal of nuclear weapons. The agreement calls for the Ukraine to ship its 175 nuclear missiles containing about 1,640 warheads to Russia, where the weapons would be dismantled. Russian technicians would convert the weapons-grade nuclear material in the warheads to the kind used in nuclear energy plants. The converted fuel would then be sold, with proceeds to be shared among Russia and the three other former Soviet republics—including Ukraine—that maintained nuclear weapons. The other two republics—Kazakhstan and Belarus—agreed to disarm their nuclear weapons in 1993. The United States had agreed to provide about $175 million to help dismantle the weapons.

A shrinking military. Declining budgets in the wake of the Cold War's end forced the Pentagon to accelerate plans in 1994 for sharp reductions. On September 8, the U.S. Army deactivated its Berlin Brigade, marking the end of an American military presence that began in the once-divided German city in 1945. By the end of the year, U.S. troop presence in Europe had been slashed to 140,000—a decline of 200,000 from 1990.

A new round of base closings was scheduled for 1995, and troop levels continued to drop. The Pentagon's budget for the 1995 fiscal year emphasized funds for readiness and training rather than for new weapons systems. Cuts in the defense budget also affected training activities. In September, the Navy canceled training for about 20,000 reservists after running out of money.

Conventional weapons. Despite the defense drawdown, the Pentagon continued development of a few new weapons systems at reduced levels of procurement. The largest such program was the Air Force's F-22 jet fighter, which was expected to cost $72 billion despite cutbacks.

The Army chose a new air-defense missile system on February 17, rejecting the controversial Patriot missile currently in use. Defense officials had sharply criticized the Patriots' performance in defending Saudi Arabia and Israel from Iraqi SCUD missiles during the 1991 Persian Gulf War. The Navy commissioned a new Trident missile submarine and five other warships in 1994.

Defense mergers. The decline in military spending triggered a wave of mergers within the defense industry. The second- and third-largest U.S. defense contractors, Lockheed and Martin Marietta, agreed to a $10-billion merger on August 30. The new company, to be called Lockheed Martin Corporation, had nearly $12 billion in military contracts in fiscal year 1993. On April 4, Northrop Corporation outbid Martin Marietta and acquired Grumman Aircraft Corporation for $2.1 billion.

Women in the military. Barriers against women in the military continued to fall in 1994. In January, the Pentagon ordered all the services to open more assignments to women. The aircraft carrier U.S.S. *Eisenhower* became the first Navy warship to receive women crew members on March 7, when the first of 500 women joined the crew of 5,000. By the end of 1994, women were serving as combat pilots in all three branches of the military. The Army

opened more combat support positions to women but said in July that it would retain the prohibition against women in positions that would place them in direct ground combat. Lieutenant Kara Hultgreen, the first female Navy combat pilot, died on October 25 when her F-14 jet crashed into the Pacific Ocean.

A federal judge reinstated a highly decorated Army nurse in July who had been discharged from the military because she is a lesbian. The judge denied a government request to delay the reinstatement of Colonel Margarethe Cammermeyer to her position in the Washington state National Guard. A lower court had ruled on June 1 that Cammermeyer's ouster was unconstitutional.

On July 22, a federal judge ordered The Citadel, an all-male, public military college in Charleston, S.C., to fully admit its first female student—19-year-old Shannon Faulkner. A previous court order had permitted Faulkner to attend day classes. The July order permitted Faulkner to join the cadet corps and live on campus. But on August 12, a federal appeals court blocked Faulkner's entry into the corps, saying she must remain a day student while the college appealed. (See **Civil rights.**)

Cheating scandal. Secretary of the Navy John H. Dalton expelled 24 midshipmen from the U.S. Naval Academy on April 28 in the culmination of the worst cheating scandal in the history of the institution. A naval board of inquiry claimed that 134 midshipmen received advanced information concerning a December 1992 electrical engineering examination. In an effort to repair the damage to the academy's reputation, President Clinton nominated Admiral Charles R. Larson, the commander of U.S naval forces in the Pacific, to be superintendent of the academy.

Defense budget. The Clinton Administration's defense budget for the 1995 fiscal year, released on Feb. 7, 1994, requested spending authority of $263.7 billion, an increase of $2.8 billion from the previous year's projected spending. On Sept. 29, 1994, Congress authorized the Pentagon to spend $243.7 billion for fiscal year 1995, a decrease of $17.1 billion from the previous year.

Command changes. On Feb. 3, 1994, the Senate confirmed William J. Perry as secretary of defense. Perry replaced Les Aspin, Jr. Retired Admiral Bobby Ray Inman was nominated for the position in December 1993 but withdrew from consideration on January 18, saying that critics were conspiring to hurt his reputation.

On April 23, Admiral Jeremy M. Boorda succeeded Admiral Frank B. Kelso II as chief of naval operations. General Ronald R. Fogleman was named Air Force chief of staff, succeeding General Merrill M. McPeak. Brigadier General Carol A. Mutter became the first woman promoted to the rank of major general by the Marine Corps. □ Thomas M. DeFrank

In *World Book*, see the articles on the branches of the armed forces.

The World Remembers
D-Day

Fifty years after the historic World War II invasion that liberated France from the Germans, the Allies gather once again on the beaches of Normandy.

By James L. Stokesbury

D-Day—June 6, 1944—the invasion of Nazi-occupied Europe, was the dramatic high point of World War II (1939-1945) and the beginning of the end for Germany's Adolf Hitler and his Third Reich. The epic assault, across the English Channel and onto the heavily defended beaches of Normandy, on the northern coast of France, was the largest seaborne invasion in history. For the millions of men and women who planned and carried out the operation—soldiers, sailors, airmen, and civilians—it was the single most important public event of their lives.

On June 6, 1994, thousands of D-Day veterans gathered in France to commemorate the 50th anniversary of D-Day. The ceremonies were an emotional celebration of sacrifice and survival and eventual triumph. The visiting celebrants were from the United States, the senior partner in the Allied forces on D-Day; the two other nations playing leading roles in the invasion, Canada and the United Kingdom; and veterans of the French and Polish armies who also confronted the Germans on D-Day. In addition, France played host to all the official and private visitors to the battlegrounds and towns of Normandy.

Germany, to the dismay of many Germans, was excluded from the ceremonies. Several arguments were put forth in favor of German participation: that the hatreds of World War II are long past, that thousands of German soldiers killed during the D-Day assault are buried in Normandy, and that many Germans who lived during the Nazi era feel that they, too, were victims of Hitler's tyranny. Nonethe-

Opposite page: United States President Bill Clinton speaks at a D-Day commemoration ceremony in June 1994 at an Allied cemetery in Cambridge, England. Clinton made several appearances at the various D-Day observances, which culminated on June 6 in Normandy, France—the site of the June 6, 1944, invasion.

less, the French government decided to invite only the Allied nations that were involved in the invasion.

Using that criterion, France also declined to invite representatives from Russia, part of the former Soviet Union. Although the Soviet Union was one of the Allies in 1944, it did not take part in D-Day. It was, however, an important factor in the success of the invasion. At the time, the Soviet army was fighting a huge German force that had invaded Russia in 1941. If the hundreds of thousands of German soldiers in Russia had been available for the defense of Normandy, the D-Day invasion would have been much harder for the Western Allies.

But controversies over who was included in the ceremonies and who was excluded paled before the sheer emotional power of the thousands of men and women who gathered to remember D-Day. Some had returned to Normandy for the first time since the war.

The commemoration, spread over several days and culminating on June 6, included a series of reenactments of D-Day events. The main ceremonies were held on June 6 at the invasion beaches. The American cemetery overlooking Omaha Beach, the most storied of those battlegrounds, was the site of the day's largest gathering. French President François Mitterrand presided over the program, and speakers included U.S. President Bill Clinton. Standing in sunlight that broke through overcast skies and illuminated the many rows of white headstones, Clinton said, "When they were young, these men saved the world. . . . We are the children of your sacrifice."

Fifty years before, when the battle of D-Day had yet to be decided, those men had jumped out of airplanes in the dark, hurtled into the night-shrouded French countryside in rickety gliders, or staggered onto beaches under heavy enemy fire. Despite the many medals that were awarded after the battle, almost every veteran attending the ceremonies denied having exhibited any special heroism, insisting that they were just doing a job that needed to be done. But it was a monumental job. The liberation of "Fortress Europe" from Nazi domination was one of the greatest military achievements of this century.

The epic invasion takes shape

Nazi Germany had ruled nearly all of Western Europe since June 1940, when its forces conquered France and drove the British army into the sea. The Germans anticipated that the Western Allies would eventually strike back from their stronghold in Britain. But even after the United States entered the war in December 1941, the Allies were too weak to challenge German power directly in a cross-channel invasion. Instead, they were forced to fight a long diversionary campaign against German forces in North Africa and then, from 1943 on, in Italy. Meanwhile, the Soviet Union grappled with the Germans on the huge Eastern Front, dealing several crushing defeats to Hitler's armies.

For all that time, the Western Allies sought to assemble an invasion force in England that would be strong enough to land in France—and to stay there. In January 1944, American General Dwight D. Eisenhower, who had been named supreme commander of the Allied Ex-

■ **The author**

James L. Stokesbury is a professor of history at Acadia University in Canada.

peditionary Force in Europe, arrived in London to head the immense undertaking. The Normandy invasion would be the largest and probably the most dangerous operation of the entire war.

The buildup had begun in 1942, and by the spring of 1944 people joked that if the invasion did not come soon, southern England would tilt and sink under the weight of personnel and war material. Altogether there were more than 2.5 million men in uniform, tens of thousands of trucks and tanks, more than 10,000 planes, and 5,300 vessels, ranging from battleships and cruisers to landing craft.

On the far side of the channel, some 50,000 German troops, under the command of Field Marshal Erwin Rommel, manned the beach defenses and waited. Under Rommel's direction, the Germans had spent much of the year fortifying the defenses of the so-called Atlantic Wall. The French coastline bristled with landing-craft obstacles, concrete bunkers, guns of every caliber, and 6 million explosive mines. Rommel's plan for defeating the expected invasion force was to pin the Allies down on the beaches and then drive them into the sea with his armored divisions. But the Germans were kept guessing about where the invasion would come. An elaborate Allied deception plan, complete with dummy tanks and imaginary armies sending out radio messages, convinced the Germans that the landings would be farther to the north, near Calais, where the channel is narrowest.

But the Allies had decided to strike at Normandy. Eisenhower's invasion plan, dubbed Operation Overlord, called for a force of more than 176,000 men in nine divisions to land in France on the first day. During the night prior to D-Day, British and American paratroopers and glider-borne soldiers would land behind German lines to protect

■ **The great assault**
The June 6, 1944, invasion plan called for a large force of American, British, and Canadian troops to land in Normandy at five beaches. They were to be preceded by glider-borne soldiers and paratroopers who would be flown behind enemy lines during the night to protect the Allied flanks from German counterattacks and to capture bridges and other objectives. By the end of the day, the Allies had secured the beaches and moved inland.

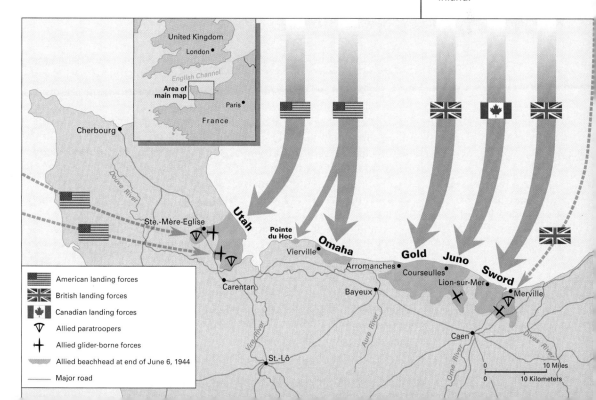

United Kingdom
London ●

English Channel

Area of
main map

Paris ●

France

Cherbourg ●

Douve River

Ste.-Mère-Eglise

Utah

Pointe
du Hoc

Vierville ●

Omaha

Gold Juno

Sword

Arromanches ● Courseulles ●

Lion-sur-Mer ●

Merville ●

Carentan

Bayeux ●

Vire River

Aure River

Caen ●

Dives River

St.-Lô ●

Orne River

American landing forces

British landing forces

Canadian landing forces

▽ Allied paratroopers

✝ Allied glider-borne forces

〜 Allied beachhead at end of June 6, 1944

── Major road

0   10 Miles
0   10 Kilometers

■ **On to Normandy**
Just before the invasion, General Dwight D. Eisenhower, the commander of Allied forces in Europe, talks with U.S. paratroopers, *above*. At Omaha Beach the next morning, *top*, troops take cover from withering German fire behind a landing craft obstacle.

the flanks of the invasion force from German counterattacks and to capture bridges and other important targets. In the morning, after a heavy shore bombardment by planes and ships to soften German defenses, the landing forces would come ashore at five beaches, code-named Gold, Sword, Juno, Omaha, and Utah. Gold and Sword were British; Juno, Canadian; and Omaha and Utah, American.

By early June, all the pieces of Operation Overlord were in place, and Eisenhower was faced with the decision of when to launch the invasion. The schedule of tides in the English Channel indicated that June 5, 6, and 7 would be the best days for the landings. On those days, there would be a low tide near dawn on the French coast and bright moonlight. On June 5, the channel was whipped up by a storm, but weather forecasters issued a cautious prediction for calm seas on June 6. Rather than delay the invasion for two weeks until the desired conditions recurred and risk losing the element of surprise, Eisenhower gave the order for the invasion to proceed. By nightfall, the great armada was on its way.

During the night, the glider and parachute forces landed at a number of sites in Normandy. These advance troops suffered high casualties, particularly the American paratroopers, who came down in widely scattered groups and had difficulty regrouping. Some paratroopers ran into heavy enemy resistance, while others drowned in areas that the Germans had flooded. Nonetheless, the airborne troops managed to carry out most of their objectives.

In the predawn hours of D-Day, Allied ships and planes pounded German positions along the coast. Then, as the sky turned light, the bombardment was lifted and swarms of landing craft headed for shore. Now, for the first time, the German defenders could see the immensity of what was bearing down on them from the sea. But even then, the German high command in Berlin was still so convinced that Calais was the Allied target that they dismissed the Normandy landings as a diversionary action. For hours, the Germans held back their armored divisions as they waited in vain for the "real" invasion.

Onto the beaches and into France

While the Germans delayed, the Allies were gaining a foothold on the beaches. The British and Canadian landings went more or less as planned, though resistance was heavy. At Utah Beach, where thin German defenses had been torn up by naval guns, American troops landed with no difficulty. But the landing at Omaha Beach was nearly a disaster. The first wave of troops, wading through neck-deep water full of mines and obstacles and swept by intense German fire, was almost wiped out. Many of the men who were not shot, drowned. But those who made it to shore finally took control of the beach. They were helped by Army Rangers, who destroyed a major gun emplacement at a coastal overlook called Pointe du Hoc, and by U.S. Navy destroyers that came in close to shore to blast German positions.

By the end of the day, more than 155,000 Allied troops were securely ashore at the five landing sites and were moving inland. Allied dead, wounded, and missing amounted to nearly 5,000. German casualties, though hard to determine, were apparently slightly lower.

After June 6, the Allies built up their forces rapidly—by the end of the month, they had more than 1 million troops in France. In the weeks after the invasion, Allied divisions waged a series of fierce battles with the Germans, and British and American planes by the thousands bombed and strafed German positions at every opportunity. But the Germans fought back stubbornly, stalling the Allied advance. Finally, beginning in August, the Allies broke out of Normandy, liberated all of France, and pressed on toward the German frontier.

Although much bitter combat was still to come—most notably a desperate December 1944 German counterattack remembered as the Battle of the Bulge—the outcome of the war was no longer in doubt. Pummeled on the west by the Allies and on the east by the advancing Soviet army, Germany's fate was sealed. On April 30, 1945, with his "Thousand-Year Reich" in ruins, Hitler committed suicide in his underground bunker in Berlin. On May 7, Germany surrendered.

Hitler had clung to impossible visions of victory almost to the last, but a prediction by Rommel as he prepared for the cross-channel invasion—"The war will be won or lost on the beaches"—had proved correct. Once they had overrun the coastal defenses, the Allies could be bloodied but not beaten. D-Day thus signaled the ultimate end of Nazi Germany. ■ ■ ■

Armenia agreed to a cease-fire with neighboring Azerbaijan on May 16, 1994, raising hopes for an end to their ongoing war over Nagorno-Karabakh, an ethnic Armenian enclave in Azerbaijan. By the end of 1993, Armenian forces occupied about 20 percent of Azerbaijani territory and had gained control over the enclave. Hopes for a lasting settlement received a boost on July 27, 1994, as Armenia agreed to extend the cease-fire while negotiations for a permanent settlement continued. Armenia's refusal to withdraw from Azerbaijani territory prior to a settlement remained a major obstacle to final peace.

Despite the nation's military success in 1994, Armenia's economy continued to be crippled by the war. Severe food and energy shortages remained, and thousands of Armenians immigrated to Russia during the year to escape economic hardship. In July, former Prime Minister Vazgen Manukyan led a rally of about 50,000 people in Yerevan, the nation's capital, to protest Armenia's economic situation. Manukyan was ousted in 1993 as part of President Levon Ter-Petrosyan's plan to attack the nation's economic crisis. In October 1994, the United Nations' International Monetary Fund granted Armenia a loan of $500 million. The loan was approved after Ter-Petrosyan pledged that his government would initiate stricter financial policies.   □ Steven L. Solnick

See also **Asia** (Facts in brief table); **Azerbaijan**. In *World Book*, see **Armenia**.

Art. Andy Warhol, the pop artist who became as famous as the celebrities he depicted, was a media star in 1994—seven years after his death. The primary reason was a museum established in his honor in his hometown of Pittsburgh, Pa. Billed as the nation's largest institution dedicated to a single artist, the Andy Warhol Museum opened in May under the direction of Thomas N. Armstrong III, former director of the Whitney Museum of American Art in New York City.

Housed in a seven-floor former warehouse renovated by New York architect Richard Gluckman, the museum displays about 500 Warhol works from a collection of 900 paintings, 70 sculptures, 1,500 drawings, 500 prints, 400 photographs, and exhibition prints of all his films and videotapes. The new showcase is a joint venture of Pittsburgh's Carnegie Institute, which manages the museum and raised about $15 million to buy, renovate, and staff the building; the Andy Warhol Foundation for the Visual Arts in New York, which supplied $2 million in seed money and most of the art; and New York's Dia Center, which donated additional artworks.

Warhol value debated. The opening came in the wake of a legal feud over the value of Warhol's estate. Pitting the foundation against Edward W. Hayes, its former attorney, the affair raised questions about prices of Warhol's art and pointed to the volatility of the entire contemporary art market. Following Warhol's death in 1987, the foundation valued Warhol's estate at $220 million based on an appraisal by Christie's auction house. Hayes, who claimed that he was entitled to 2 percent of the estate's value, contended that it was actually worth $827 million. A Manhattan Surrogate Court judge split the difference, ruling in April that Warhol's estate was worth about $510 million when he died.

The market value of Warhol's artwork came under public scrutiny again in November, when his portrait of actress Marilyn Monroe, *Shot Red Marilyn* (1964), went up for auction at Christie's New York. The painting was sold for the record price of $4.07-million in 1989, but Christie's estimated the 1994 selling price at $2.5 million to $3.5 million. Dealers, collectors, and officials of Warhol's museum and foundation watched nervously to see if the artist's luster had faded. The painting was sold on November 2 for about $3.5 million.

Museum openings. Despite the volatility of the art market and reduced government funding, new museums and expansion projects were completed. The George Gustav Heye Center of the Smithsonian Institution's National Museum of the American Indian opened on October 30 at the Alexander Hamilton United States Custom House in New York City. The $24-million center is the first of three planned branches of the museum, which has more than 1 million objects in its collection. The central facility is scheduled to open in 2001 on the Mall in Washington, D.C., and a research center is expected to be complete in 1997 in Suitland, Md.

The Baltimore Museum of Art opened a new 50,000-square-foot (4,600-square meter) wing for modern and contemporary art in October. The following month, the Joslyn Art Museum in Omaha, Nebr., christened a 58,000-square-foot (5,400-square-meter) expansion and renovation project.

In Paris, the Cartier Foundation for Contemporary Art in May opened an adventurous glass and steel building designed by French architect Jean Nouvel. The American Center, which had been housed on the same site, moved to a new flamboyant structure designed by American architect Frank Gehry.

Swiss advocates of contemporary art heaved a sigh of relief when Geneva opened its Museum of Modern and Contemporary Art in September after a 20-year effort. The museum is housed in a 1930's factory renovated by Swiss architect Erwin Oberwiller.

In Moscow, the historic Tretyakov Gallery announced plans for a December unveiling of a nine-year renovation and expansion project. A preview introduced 10 new rooms, galleries dedicated to Russian symbolist Mikhail Vrubel and the Russian avant-garde, a sculpture hall, and an administrative building. The Tretyakov, which has a collection of 42,000 pieces of Russian art ranging from 11th-century icons to early 20th-century paintings, is expected to expand during the next two years.

New museum

Marc Chagall's *Composition* (1912), *left,* is one of more than 180 works of art featured in The Kreeger Museum, *below,* which opened in June in Washington, D.C. Designed by architect Philip Johnson in 1967, the museum is the converted home of insurance magnate and art collector David Lloyd Kreeger, whose collection includes works by Joan Miró, Piet Mondrian, and Pablo Picasso, among others.

Pope John Paul II in April unveils the restoration of *The Last Judgment,* the fresco painted by Michelangelo for the altar wall of the Vatican's Sistine Chapel in Rome.

The National Endowment for the Arts (NEA) came under attack again in 1994, when the endowment's National Council on the Arts rejected grant applications from three photographers whose work was endorsed by a panel of their peers. Applicants Andres Serrano, Merry Alpern, and Barbara De Genevieve are known for subject matter that tends to offend conservative members of the United States Congress. Council members' claims that the decision was based on artistic quality were questioned because their action followed the U.S. Senate's recommendation of a 5 percent cut in the NEA's $170.2-million budget. (In September, however, congressional subcommittees agreed to cut the NEA budget by only 2 percent.)

The proposed 5 percent cut came in response to an uproar over $150 in NEA funding for a March performance in which HIV-positive artist Ron Athey drew blood from himself and a colleague, blotted the blood on towels, and hung the towels above the audience. No blood dripped on the audience, but the event provided Congress with more doubts over the propriety of arts funding.

Technology. Several museums, including the National Gallery in London, the Frick Collection in New York, the Seattle Art Museum, and the San Diego Museum of Art, introduced CD-ROM's and other interactive devices designed to provide easy access to their collections. Even as these technological aids to art education were being developed, museum officials expressed concern about attempts by outside vendors to purchase reproduction rights to museum-owned artworks for undetermined uses. At issue were the protection of the art's integrity and the museums' potential loss of income from the sale of reproduction rights. The Association of Art Museum Directors focused on these issues at a June meeting in Seattle, but found few answers on how to deal with the digital age.

Theft. The theft of Norwegian expressionist Edvard Munch's best-known painting, *The Scream* (1893), from Norway's National Art Museum in Oslo on February 12 set off fears that the work of art would be lost or seriously damaged. But the painting was recovered in relatively good condition on May 7, and two suspects were arrested while attempting to collect a ransom.

The U.S. Congress made stealing artworks from museums a federal crime, punishable by up to 10 years in prison, in an omnibus crime bill passed in August. The legislation authorized the Federal Bureau of Investigation to begin immediate investigation of thefts of cultural objects that either are valued at more than $100,000 or are more than 100 years old and worth over $5,000. Knowingly trafficking in such stolen objects is also a federal offense.

Tussle over *Graces*. The J. Paul Getty Museum's five-year battle to buy and export from England *The Three Graces,* a neoclassical marble sculpture by Italian artist Antonio Canova, ended in defeat for the wealthy Malibu, Calif., institution. The sculpture was commissioned in 1814 for Woburn Abbey in Bedfordshire, England, and sold in 1984 to a Cayman Islands holding company. The Getty agreed to buy the piece for about $12 million in 1989, after the British government declined to buy the sculpture for a much smaller sum. But the museum's attempts to obtain the necessary export license were thwarted.

London's Victoria and Albert Museum and the National Galleries of Scotland mounted a fund-raising campaign to match the Getty's price, and British cultural authorities repeatedly extended deadlines. Three days after the supposedly final deadline had passed, the Victoria and Albert announced that John Paul Getty II, son of the Getty's founder, had promised $1.5 million to the campaign. Swiss industrialist Baron Hans Heinrich von Thyssen-Bornemisza agreed to pay the balance of $1.2 million. The Getty said that the British broke their own export laws, but its court appeals were in vain. The sculpture, which has long been in storage, is expected to rotate among the two British museums and a Madrid museum that houses the baron's art collection.

Reichstag wrap-up. Another art-world saga that ended in 1994 featured Christo, an artist known for wrapping massive buildings in fabric. After a 20-year struggle, Christo won the German parliament's permission to wrap Berlin's historic Reichstag (parliament building), which was left in ruin after World War II (1939-1945) but is now being renovated. Christo planned to drape the building with 1 million square feet (93,000 square meters) of recyclable silver cloth for two weeks in May 1995.

Sistine Chapel restoration. The controversial cleaning and restoration of Michelangelo's frescoes in the Vatican's Sistine Chapel came to an end in 1994 with the April unveiling of *The Last Judgment* (1541), a painting covering one wall. Michelangelo populated the fresco with virile male nudes whose genitals were later covered with painted breeches by other artists. Conservators removed breeches from 17 figures but left them on 23 others. Critics of the entire project charged that the restoration destroyed subtleties of Michelangelo's shading, but most scholars approved of the work.

Exhibits. Abstract expressionist Willem de Kooning and Bruce Nauman, a master of many mediums, dominated the 1994 exhibition circuit. De Kooning's traveling retrospective, which opened at the National Gallery of Art in Washington, D.C., traced the career of a consummate painter who hit his stride in the 1950's. Nauman's show, which made its debut at the Reina Sofia in Madrid, Spain, was a midcareer survey of an influential artist whose works in video, neon, and sculpture address issues of psychological manipulation and frustration.   □ Suzanne Muchnic

See also **Architecture.** In *World Book,* see **Art and the arts; Painting; Sculpture.**

Asia

Asia overcame a variety of natural disasters in 1994 to make uneven progress toward improving the lives of its diverse people. Civil wars disrupted life in areas of Afghanistan, Burma, Cambodia, India, Indonesia, the Philippines, and Sri Lanka. Nevertheless, most of the continent remained peaceful.

Nuclear weapons in Asia caused worldwide concern throughout 1994, particularly North Korea's refusal to allow inspections of its nuclear facilities. The United States Central Intelligence Agency believed that North Korea had already produced nuclear weapons. Just as the United States and North Korea were to open talks in July on North Korea's nuclear program, its leader, Kim Il-song, died. However, on October 21, the two nations signed an agreement under which North Korea would comply with the terms of the Nuclear Nonproliferation Treaty. (See **Korea, North.**)

But U.S. officials were unsuccessful in getting India and Pakistan to agree not to compete with each other in manufacturing nuclear weapons. Both nations claimed to have the technology, and tensions between them were high due to a territorial dispute over Kashmir. China also continued to defy international opinion by testing nuclear devices underground on June 10 and October 7.

Afghanistan. The largest civil conflict in Asia in 1994 was the ongoing struggle for control of Afghanistan, which had begun with the 1992 collapse of a Communist regime. Burhanuddin Rabbani had become president in 1992 with the support of a northern warlord, Abdul Rashid Dostam. They were opposed by Gulbuddin Hikmatyar, said to be the most ruthless of the factional leaders who had fought the Communists. Hikmatyar's troops had killed thousands of civilians in indiscriminate rocket and artillery attacks on Kabul, the capital.

On Jan. 1, 1994, Dostam, who had fought for the Communists before switching sides in 1992, switched sides again and joined Hikmatyar in an attempt to defeat Rabbani. Intensified fighting failed to alter the political situation. The estimated death toll since the Communists fell was at least 12,000 people.

Rabbani's term as president under an agreement among the factions was due to end on June 28, 1994, but Afghanistan's Supreme Court extended his term an additional six months. Thus, he retained the post's limited power in the absence of an agreed procedure to select a new leadership.

Economic progress in Asia was tied to industrial development, but many Asian countries continued to produce goods requiring only basic skills that paid workers low wages. Educational systems in Asia could not train enough workers with adequate skills for high-wage technologies. Not only were engineers and technicians in short supply in many coun-

tries, but also workers who could read and understand mathematics. Governments in such countries as India and Pakistan, where most children receive only a few years of schooling, recognized the problem, but still failed to find money in already strained budgets to improve education significantly.

The Asian Development Bank predicted in October that, despite problems across the continent, economic growth would remain strong for at least two years. It expected Asia's growth rate of 7.8 percent in 1994 to fall only slightly to 7.3 percent for 1995, a rate more than twice the estimated worldwide rate.

Social changes long evident in Western cultures became apparent in Asia in 1994. For example, in many countries where prosperity was rising, the divorce rate also was rising. The rate had doubled in South Korea and Taiwan from 1980 to 1990, a peri-

Vietnamese pedestrians hustle past a wall of headlines proclaiming the end in February of the 19-year U.S. trade embargo against Vietnam.

od of strong economic growth there. The number of divorces in China more than tripled from 1990 to 1994. The Ministry of Civil Affairs reported in May that a record 909,000 Chinese couples had divorced in 1993. In most Asian nations, women were having fewer babies. In fact, women in the more industrialized nations, such as Singapore and South Korea, had on average fewer babies than U.S. women.

These changes were partly explained by the changing status of women. More women became wage earners in addition to being farm wives. But social tensions in many countries also increased as a result of the growing contributions of women to the economy. Traditionalist Muslim religious leaders in Bangladesh's villages, for example, resisted giving

women a larger voice in local affairs, though they had a vital economic role.

Environmental problems. Summer floods in 1994 in south and southeastern China killed an estimated 3,000 people, while some central provinces suffered the worst drought in more than 45 years. An August typhoon killed more than 710 people in Zhejiang Province on China's east coast. Vietnam also suffered prolonged flooding in the Mekong River Delta. The swollen river killed nearly 300 people and devastated the summer rice crop.

From August until late into 1994, four Southeast Asian nations suffered from smoky haze caused by forest fires. Smoke from fires in Indonesian Kalimantan and Sumatra Island trapped car exhaust and in-

Country	Population	Government	Monetary unit*	Foreign trade (million U.S.$)	
				Exports†	Imports†
Afghanistan	18,828,000	President Burhanuddin Rabbani; Prime Minister Gulbuddin Hikmatyar	afghani (2,602.81 = $1)	243	737
Armenia	3,730,000	President Levon Ter-Petrosyan	C.I.S. ruble (3,055.00 = $1)	29	85
Australia	17,820,000	Governor General Bill Hayden; Prime Minister Paul Keating	dollar (1.35 = $1)	42,710	45,556
Azerbaijan	7,447,000	President Heydar A. Aliyev	C.I.S. ruble (3,055.00 = $1)	351	241
Bangladesh	118,786,000	President Abdur Rahman Biswas; Prime Minister Khaleda Ziaur Rahman	taka (40.38 = $1)	2,273	3,989
Bhutan	1,729,000	King Jigme Singye Wangchuck	ngultrum (31.39 = $1)	66	125
Brunei	288,000	Sultan Sir Hassanal Bolkiah	dollar (1.47 = $1)	2,370	1,176
Burma (Myanmar)	46,548,000	State Law and Order Restoration Council Chairman Than Shwe	kyat (5.70 = $1)	585	814
Cambodia (Kampuchea)	9,447,000	King Norodom Sihanouk; Prime Minister Norodom Ranariddh	riel (2,582 = $1)	70	360
China	1,238,319,000	Communist Party General Secretary and President Jiang Zemin; Premier Li Peng	yuan (8.53 = $1)	91,737	103,881
Georgia	5,473,000	Parliament Chairman Eduard Shevardnadze	C.I.S. ruble (3,055.00 = $1)	176	1,500
India	931,044,000	President Shankar Dayal Sharma; Prime Minister P. V. Narasimha Rao	rupee (31.39 = $1)	21,432	22,035
Indonesia	201,477,000	President Suharto; Vice President Try Sutrisno	rupiah (2,172.00 = $1)	33,861	27,311
Iran	66,720,000	Leader of the Islamic Revolution Ali Hoseini Khamenei; President Ali Akbar Hashemi Rafsanjani	rial (1,749.00 = $1)	15,500	23,700
Japan	125,879,000	Emperor Akihito; Prime Minister Tomiichi Murayama	yen (97.02 = $1)	362,286	241,652
Kazakhstan	17,436,000	President Nursultan Nazarbayev	C.I.S. ruble (3,055.00 = $1)	1,271	358
Korea, North	23,922,000	President Kim Chong-il; Premier Kang Song-San	won (2.15 = $1)	1,300	1,900
Korea, South	45,182,000	President Kim Yong-Sam; Prime Minister Lee Hong-koo	won (797.30 = $1)	82,189	83,784
Kyrgyzstan	4,693,000	President Askar Akayev	C.I.S. ruble (3,055.00 = $1)	112	112

dustrial fumes as it drifted over Malaysia, Singapore, and Brunei. Indonesia's forestry minister blamed the fires on small-scale slash-and-burn farming, but environmentalists charged that large plantations had set fire to drought-dry vegetation to clear land for agriculture and loggers had started fires to cover up their illegal cutting of trees.

Throughout Asia, the rate at which forests were being cut or burned had tripled from 1960 to 1994 and was still rising. Deforestation was driven by growing populations that required more farmland and increasing demand for tropical timber that drove up the price more than 50 percent from 1991 to 1994.

Vietnamese refugees. The United Nations (UN) high commissioner for refugees, Sadako Ogata, said on February 14 that Vietnamese who had fled by boat after the Communist take-over of Vietnam in 1975, so-called boat people, no longer would be automatically granted asylum as political refugees. The UN said the Vietnamese would be treated the same as economic refugees from other nations.

Nations of Southeast Asia, who had taken in most of the Vietnamese, found that most of the 60,000 Vietnamese living in Southeast Asian camps were jobseekers rather than political refugees. The countries decided they could no longer provide free food, housing, and other care for them. The nations

Country	Population	Government	Monetary unit*	Foreign trade (million U.S.$)	
				Exports†	Imports†
Laos	4,882,000	President Nouhak Phoumsavan; Prime Minister Khamtai Siphandon	kip (720.00 = $1)	81	162
Malaysia	20,125,000	Paramount Ruler Tuanku Ja'afar ibni Al-Marhum Tuanku Abdul Rahman; Prime Minister Mahathir bin Mohamad	ringgit (2.55 = $1)	47,122	45,657
Maldives	248,000	President Maumoon Abdul Gayoom	rufiyaa (11.94 = $1)	35	191
Mongolia	2,498,000	President Punsalmaagiyn Ochirbat; Prime Minister Puntsagiyn Jasray	tughrik (400.00 = $1)	355	501
Nepal	22,124,000	King Birendra Bir Bikram Shah Dev; Prime Minister Mana Mohan Adhikari	rupee (49.40 = $1)	374	792
New Zealand	3,552,000	Governor General Dame Catherine Tizard; Prime Minister James B. Bolger	dollar (1.63 = $1)	10,537	9,636
Pakistan	134,974,000	President Farooq Leghari; Prime Minister Benazir Bhutto	rupee (30.73 = $1)	6,672	9,481
Papua New Guinea	4,344,000	Governor General Sir Wiwa Korowi; Prime Minister Sir Julius Chan	kina (1.14 = $1)	2,452	1,297
Philippines	67,078,000	President Fidel Ramos	peso (26.05 = $1)	9,752	15,459
Russia	149,740,000	President Boris Yeltsin	C.I.S. ruble (3,055.00 = $1)	44,297	26,807
Singapore	2,853,000	President Ong Teng Cheong; Prime Minister Goh Chok Tong	dollar (1.47= $1)	74,008	85,229
Sri Lanka	18,346,000	President Chandrika Kumaratunga; Prime Minister Sirimavo Bandaranaike	rupee (48.94 = $1)	2,443	3,410
Taiwan	21,512,000	President Li Teng-hui; Premier Lien Chan	dollar (26.04 = $1)	85,000	77,100
Tajikistan	6,005,000	Acting President Emomili Rakhmonov	C.I.S. ruble (3,055.00 = $1)	374	263
Thailand	58,265,000	King Phumiphon Adunyadet; Prime Minister Chuan Likphai	baht (24.90 = $1)	36,741	46,058
Turkmenistan	4,156,000	President Saparmurad Niyazov	C.I.S. ruble (3,055.00 = $1)	1,049	501
Uzbekistan	22,829,000	President Islam Karimov	C.I.S. ruble (3,055.00 = $1)	707	947
Vietnam	73,811,000	Communist Party General Secretary Do Muoi; President Le Duc Anh; Prime Minister Vo Van Kiet	dong (10,860.00 = $1)	2,600	3,100

*Exchange rates as of Oct. 28, 1994, or latest available data.
†Latest available data.

planned to send the Vietnamese back home and close the camps by the end of 1995. But some boat people refused to leave. Many of the 24,000 Vietnamese in Hong Kong fought riot police trying to put them on planes for home. And since the number of Vietnamese who volunteered to return home had dropped in 1994, Hong Kong officials said in November that the deadline date for closing camps there would be postponed beyond 1995.

Territorial dispute. China claimed to have jurisdiction over much of the South China Sea in the most contentious Asian territorial dispute of 1994. China's claims overlapped those of Brunei, Indonesia, Malaysia, the Philippines, Taiwan, and Vietnam.

At stake were the Spratly Islands, a cluster of barren atolls and rocks jutting from a seabed potentially rich in oil and natural gas.

Acting on its jurisdictional claim, China granted a drilling concession to an oil company about 900 miles (1,500 kilometers) from mainland China and 200 miles (320 kilometers) from the coast of Vietnam. But in April, when a Chinese seismic research vessel entered the disputed area, Vietnamese gunboats chased it out. Then, when Vietnam sent a rig to drill there, China sent warships to block it. On July 22, the two nations agreed not to fight, but tensions remained. The Philippines on May 8 granted an oil exploration permit in the disputed region.

Singapore maintained its economic momentum by establishing factories with more sophisticated production technologies. These factories required greater skills and thus paid higher wages to workers. Factories shipped simpler work to less-developed countries with lower wage scales. The result was an economic growth rate of 9 to 10 percent in 1994.

But what attracted international attention to the island state was its legal system. On May 5, an 18-year-old American, Michael P. Fay, was given four lashes on his bare buttocks with a rattan cane as punishment for a 10-day vandalism spree, which he had confessed to but later recanted. The caning, part of Singapore's tough criminal code based on British colonial practice, was denounced by many Americans as barbaric. Fay returned to the United States after serving a four-month prison sentence.

On September 23, Singapore hanged a Dutch engineer, the first Westerner among 78 people who have been executed there for drug offenses. In 1991, officials had found 9.5 pounds (4.3 kilograms) of heroin hidden in his suitcase.

Nepal held parliamentary elections on Nov. 15, 1994, after feuding within the Nepali Congress Party caused it to split and lose its majority in parliament. The Nepal Communist Party-United Marxist Leninist (UML) won 88 of the 205 seats in parliament, while the Congress Party won only 83.

After negotiations failed to produce a majority coalition, King Birendra Bir Bikram Shah Dev named the UML chairman, Mana Mohan Adhikari, as prime minister. Adhikari was sworn in on November 30 at the head of a minority government. He said his party would follow pragmatic policies in trying to overcome Nepal's poverty rather than seek to implement traditional Communist policies.

The Association of Southeast Asian Nations (ASEAN), consisting of Brunei, Indonesia, Malaysia, the Philippines, Singapore, and Thailand, agreed in 1994 to add Vietnam to its membership in 1995. The group was formed in 1967 to promote economic cooperation as the Vietnam War (1957-1975) increasingly affected the region. ASEAN inaugurated a new organization, called the Regional Forum, in Bangkok, Thailand, on July 25, 1994. It brought the United States, the European Union, and 10 Asian-Pacific countries together with ASEAN to discuss ways of maintaining regional stability and building post-Cold War institutions for peace.

Laos opened on July 2 its first permanent bridge across the Mekong River, which forms most of its border with Thailand. The bridge, located near the capital, Vientiane, was built with Australian aid to improve access to the landlocked Communist nation. A former acting president of Laos, Phoumi Vongvichit, died January 7. He was 85.   □ Henry S. Bradsher

See also the articles on the individual Asian nations. In *World Book,* see **Asia.**

Residents of a town near Kabul, the capital of Afghanistan, try to put out fires touched off by a bombing attack as civil war intensified in January.

The atmosphere of Jupiter glows on July 20 after several pieces of Comet Shoemaker-Levy 9 struck the planet, creating huge explosions.

Astronomy. The most spectacular astronomical event of 1994, if not of the entire century, occurred in July as pieces of a disintegrated comet plunged into the atmosphere of Jupiter. The impacts caused huge, fiery explosions on the giant planet.

Astronomers had been keeping an eye on the comet, named Shoemaker-Levy 9 (SL9), since it was discovered in 1993. SL9 had passed so close to Jupiter in July 1992 that it was torn into at least 21 fragments by the planet's immense gravity. Jupiter's gravity also bent SL9's orbit, ensuring that when the comet returned from its next trip around the sun, in July 1994, the fragments would hit the planet.

Although no one had ever before seen a comet smash into a planet, many astronomers tried to downplay the coming event. They explained that all the collisions would occur out of sight of Earth, just around the curve of the planet, and that the impacts might not be very dramatic, in any case.

But when the first piece of the comet hit on July 16, it was clear that the collisions would create a dazzling show. The impact sent a bright plume of glowing gases more than 600 miles (1,000 kilometers) above Jupiter, easily visible above the rim of the planet. When the impact site rotated into view just a few minutes later, it appeared as a dark spot against Jupiter's clouds.

The collisions continued until July 22, with one fragment after another plunging into Jupiter's at-mosphere, creating enormous fireballs that turned into dark spots. One collision left a dark blotch more than twice the diameter of the Earth. The dark impact sites lined up across the southern hemisphere of the planet and were visible for months.

Astronomers expect to spend years analyzing the data on the collisions from telescope observations on Earth and from the Galileo space probe. Galileo, headed for a 1995 rendezvous with Jupiter, obtained direct views of several impacts. Investigators will try to determine what the comet was made of, what Jupiter's atmosphere consists of, and what effects cometary impacts have on planets.

The Hubble gets new glasses. In December 1993, after repairs by space shuttle astronauts, the flawed Hubble Space Telescope finally began to see the universe as clearly as it had been designed to. Since its launch in 1990, the orbiting telescope had been troubled by an improperly ground primary mirror. The defect caused the Hubble to produce fuzzy images and made it difficult for the telescope to record light from very faint or very distant objects.

In five spacewalks, astronauts aboard the space shuttle Endeavour installed a set of special mirrors to compensate for the imperfections in the primary mirror and made several other changes to the telescope to improve its operation. In January 1994, the National Aeronautics and Space Administration announced that the repair mission had been a complete success. Throughout the year, the repaired telescope performed superbly, producing many new astronomical findings.

A younger universe? The universe may be considerably younger than most astronomers had believed, three research teams reported in 1994. Although the universe's age had been calculated to be as old as 20 billion years, the new findings indicate that its true age may be in the range of 7 billion to 14 billion years. The findings were announced in September by astronomers at Harvard University in Cambridge, Mass., and Indiana University in Bloomington and in October by a group using the Hubble telescope.

The astronomers arrived at the new estimates by making improved measurements of the distance of faraway galaxies and the speed at which those galaxies are moving away from our own Milky Way. By determining those two factors, investigators can calculate how long it took the galaxies to reach their present positions since the *big bang.* The big bang was an explosion of matter and energy that astronomers believe gave birth to the universe.

One problem with putting the age of the universe at 14 billion years or less is that the oldest stars seem to be 15 billion to 16 billion years old. Because of this discrepancy, some astronomers expressed doubts about the new age estimates of the universe. The 1994 findings are sure to stimulate further studies of both the structure and life cycle of stars and the evolution of the universe.

Solid evidence for a black hole. One of the most dramatic images produced by the Hubble telescope in 1994 was of a probable *black hole* in another galaxy. Black holes, objects so dense that not even light can escape from their gravity, may lurk within many galaxies, but until 1994 astronomers had only scanty evidence of their existence.

In May, astronomers at the Space Telescope Science Institute in Baltimore saw strong indications of a huge black hole at the center of a galaxy known as M87, about 50 million *light-years* from Earth. (A light-year is the distance light travels in one year, about 5.9 trillion miles [9.5 trillion kilometers].) The space telescope returned a sharp picture of M87 showing a small, intense point of light at the center of the galaxy. The point of light is surrounded by a disk of matter and has a jet of gas emerging from it.

Although the black hole itself cannot be seen in the Hubble image, astronomers believe the intense light comes from gas and other material that is being sucked into the black hole by its powerful gravity. As it is drawn toward the hole, the matter is heated to a very high temperature, causing it to emit large amounts of X rays and other forms of energy. Matter farther away from the hole, swirling around like water going down a drain, is visible as the disk. The jet, astronomers think, is formed by

Mysterious rings of glowing gas surround supernova 1987A, an exploding star whose light reached Earth in 1987, in a February 1994 Hubble telescope image.

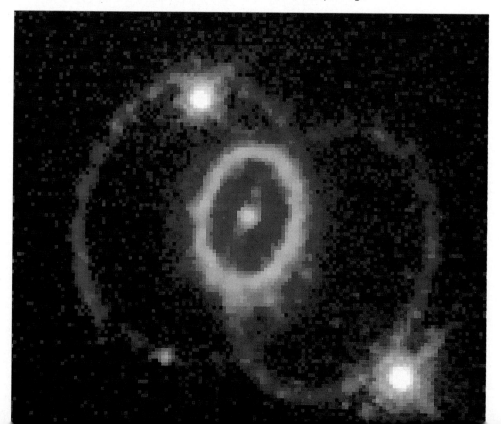

matter that misses being drawn into the hole and is ejected into space, like water from a fire hose.

Analysis of the disk showed that it is rotating at a speed of about 1.2 million miles (1.9 million kilometers) an hour. That finding means that it must be circling an object containing as much mass as 3 billion suns. The only known body that could contain so much matter in so small a volume is a black hole.

An asteroid with its own moon. In March 1994, astronomers announced the discovery of a tiny moon orbiting the asteroid Ida, the first moon of an asteroid ever detected. Ida is a potato-shaped hunk of rock about 37 miles (60 kilometers) long. It is part of the asteroid belt, a ring of rocky debris between Mars and Jupiter. The moon appeared in images taken in August 1993 by the Galileo spacecraft.

In the Galileo images, the moon appears as a tiny blob of light near the asteroid, indicating that it is about 1 mile (1.6 kilometers) in diameter and is orbiting Ida at a distance of about 60 miles (100 kilometers). The moon may be a fragment of Ida that was produced when Ida collided with another asteroid. Alternatively, both Ida and its moon may be remnants of an even larger body that broke up into many pieces. The tiny moon has been named Dactyl, after mythological beings said to live on Mount Ida in ancient Greece. □ Laurence A. Marschall

See also **Space exploration.** In *World Book,* see **Astronomy.**

Australia.

Australia. The Australian economy boomed in 1994, growing faster than it had for nine years. Unemployment fell to 9.5 percent of the work force in July 1994, its lowest level in three years. The rate had topped 11 percent during the depth of the recession, which began in 1990 and ended in 1993.

Boosting employment. On May 4, Labor Prime Minister Paul Keating released a policy paper on employment and growth. The paper outlined a plan, called Working Nation, in which the government pledged to spend $6.5 billion over four years on programs to reduce the unemployment rate to 5 percent by the year 2000. (All monetary figures in this article are in Australian dollars.) The report included programs to help the long-term jobless (those unemployed for 18 months or more) find work, subsidies to employers who would hire the long-term jobless, and job training for teen-agers and adults.

Deregulating wages was central to Keating's goal of reducing unemployment. In 1993, he had promised to deregulate Australia's tightly controlled industrial relations system, which is administered by the Industrial Relations Commission (IRC). Thus, on March 30, 1994, labor reform laws went into effect that allowed employers and employees to bypass unions and negotiate wages between themselves. The IRC still had to approve such agreements.

Responding to the improving economy, the IRC in September decided that by July 1996, about 3 million low-paid workers would receive a minimum pay increase of $24 a week, their first raise in three years. This raise would affect mainly union workers who had failed to negotiate pay increases during regular bargaining with their employers. The IRC expected all employers to honor the decision.

Monetary issues. On May 10, 1994, Treasurer Ralph Willis handed down a budget aimed at reducing the $16-billion federal deficit to about $5 billion in four years. By September, the deficit was lowered to about $11.7 billion.

The Australian Reserve Bank raised interest rates three times in 1994 to prevent inflation from eroding economic progress. The rates went up from 2.75 percent to 7.5 percent. Inflation was running at 1.9 percent by year end.

Alexander Downer, leader of the opposition Liberal Party, criticized the rate increase, calling it the price Australians must pay for a government that spends too much and runs too big a deficit. Downer had ousted John Hewson as party leader in a May 23 vote of Liberal senators and other party leaders.

Drought continued to plague Australia in 1994, particularly in the eastern states, where rain had not fallen in some places for four years. More than 90 percent of New South Wales was suffering from the worst drought in the state's history, and more than a third of Queensland was declared drought-stricken.

As a result, many farmers did not plant crops in 1994. By September, a national appeal for farm relief, called Farm Hand, had raised $1.5 million through donations and proceeds from a rock concert. In an attempt to ensure the survival of family farms, the federal government approved $164 million in drought relief funds on September 21. More than 14,000 farms were eligible for state and federal government assistance.

By late September, the drought had caused $2-billion in agricultural losses. Overall, agricultural production fell 6 percent in 1994 from 1993. Wheat production was down 65 percent (the smallest crop since 1957), barley was down 50 percent, and oats down 53 percent. Australia is the world's largest exporter of wool, but production was down 28 percent. Feed grain prices for livestock skyrocketed 353 percent and rose almost daily.

Political assassination. In New South Wales, state legislator John Newman of the Labor Party was shot to death in the driveway of his home on Sept. 5, 1994. He was believed to be the first politician to be assassinated in Australia. By November, police still had no suspects. However, some officials speculated that his killing was related to his campaign against Asian gangs in his district. The gangs reportedly intimidate other Asian nationals living in Cabramatta, a suburb of Sydney. Newman had fought for tougher penalties against the gangs, which have been accused of breaking into homes and torturing the occupants until they gave up their valuables.

A resident of suburban Sydney, Australia, hoses down his roof as wind-driven fires, the worst in 200 years, burn out of control in January.

State news. The parliament of New South Wales in May awarded preferred status to a joint Australian-American venture to build and operate a gambling casino in Sydney Harbor. The license was to be awarded in November. But in September, the government began public hearings into the American company, Showboat, Inc., after state opposition leader Robert Carr alleged that Showboat had links to organized crime. Carr's allegations raised concern that organized crime could penetrate the Sydney casino. Adding to the uncertainty of the venture, the proposed casino design was widely criticized as being ugly, too big, and out of character with the residential nature of the chosen site. The Sydney city council then proposed to move the site, but that prompted the joint venture to threaten to delay payment of the $376-million license fee to the state government. New South Wales has been trying to establish a casino for more than 10 years.

In April, the government of Tasmania voted to retain laws that criminalize homosexual sex, despite a March ruling by the United Nations Human Rights Commission that Tasmania's laws violated an international civil rights covenant that Australia had signed. The federal government tried to override the Tasmanian law with a national law ensuring the sexual privacy of consenting adults. Some members of the conservative opposition claimed the federal authorities were attempting to trample state sovereignty. In August, the federal Cabinet endorsed the privacy bill, and in October, Australia's House of Representatives passed it.

Telecommunications. The government established in February an expert group to determine how telecommunication services, such as pay television and interactive home banking and shopping, can best be delivered to Australian industry and consumers. The government wanted to avoid another embarrassment such as occurred in 1993, when it awarded licenses to pay television companies only to have them renege on paying licensing fees.

Australia dominated the Commonwealth Games held in Vancouver, Canada, in August 1994, winning 87 gold medals, 52 silver, and 43 bronze. The only world records broken were by freestyle swimmer Kieren Perkins, who bettered both the 800-meter and 1,500-meter records. Australian swimmer Samantha Riley also set a record in the 100-meter breaststroke in September in Rome.

New Zealanders were required for the first time to obtain a visa before entering Australia under new regulations that took effect on September 1. The changes were designed to simplify Australia's complex immigration procedures and to make it more difficult for illegal immigrants to challenge deportation decisions in the civil courts. □ Susan G. Williams

See also **Asia** (Facts in brief table). In *World Book,* see **Australia.**

Austria voted to join the European Union (EU) in a nationwide referendum held June 12, 1994. Membership in the EU, formerly known as the European Community, started Jan. 1, 1995. About 66 percent of the voters approved membership in the union. The Austrian government signed the formal EU membership treaty on June 24, 1994, during an EU summit on the Greek island of Corfu.

Austria became the 13th EU member, joining Belgium, Denmark, France, Germany, Greece, Ireland, Italy, Luxembourg, the Netherlands, Portugal, Spain, and the United Kingdom. Finland and Sweden were also expected to join the EU on Jan. 1, 1995. The decision to join the EU marked the first time since the end of World War II (1939-1945) that Austria had opted to give up its position of neutrality and link itself politically and economically with neighboring European nations. Austria had been occupied by Nazi Germany during the war.

Austrian opponents of EU membership, led by right wing politician Jörg Haider, leader of the Freedom Party, argued that the country would have to give up too much control of internal affairs to EU officials. Opponents also believed that the country might face unlimited immigration from neighboring countries and that Austria might even be forced to build nuclear power plants to supply electricity to its neighbors. During the hotly fought referendum campaign, government officials countered that such fears were exaggerated and said that Austria would suffer economically if it stayed outside the EU.

Parliamentary election results. The ruling coalition of the leftist Social Democratic Party and the conservative People's Party retained a legislative majority in parliamentary elections on October 9, despite a strong showing from the nationalist Freedom Party. The Social Democrats won 35.2 percent of the vote, taking 66 seats in the 183-seat parliament. The People's Party, winning 52 seats, garnered 28 percent of the vote. And the Freedom Party won 22.8 percent of the vote and 42 seats. The Greens environmental party and the Liberal Forum won 13 and 10 seats respectively. Voter turnout in the election was at 78 percent, the lowest since World War II.

Presidential breakup. Austrian President Thomas Klestil announced on Jan. 25, 1994, that he had separated from his wife, Edith, to whom he had been married for 37 years. Edith Klestil had publicly confirmed rumors of her husband's long-running love affair with an aide, Margot Löffler. Klestil had been elected president in 1992, following the controversial term of Kurt Waldheim, who was alleged to have been involved in Nazi war crimes during World War II. Edith Klestil's disclosures damaged the president's image as a proponent of traditional family values. ☐ Philip Revzin

See also **Europe** (Facts in brief table). In *World Book,* see **Austria; European Union.**

Automobile. Consumers grew weary of their old models in 1994 as the average age of cars and trucks in the United States reached eight years. Demand for new cars and trucks soared, overwhelming dealers and auto factories. Sales of cars and light trucks in the United States surged to an estimated 15.3 million vehicles, up 10.1 percent from 1993 and the best sales figures since 1988. Some analysts believed sales would have approached 16 million vehicles if automakers had kept pace with consumer demand. Several analysts predicted that 1995 sales would top the 1986 record of 16.3 million vehicles.

Detroit's Big Three automakers—General Motors Corporation (GM), Ford Motor Company, and Chrysler Corporation—pressed their factories to squeeze out extra cars and trucks. Overtime in the auto industry reached a record of more than eight hours per week per worker in 1994, and the Big Three automakers began running assembly plants around the clock. Detroit's automakers separately announced plans throughout 1994 to spend $3 billion and increase factory output by 1.5 million cars and trucks by 1996.

Trucks powered the boom in auto sales in 1994 as consumers increasingly stepped out of cars and into minivans, pickups, and sport-utility vehicles. Trucks accounted for 4 in 10 new vehicle sales, a rate double that of a decade earlier. New trucks, such as the restyled Dodge Ram pickup and Chevrolet Blazer, received a strong welcome from buyers. And old favorites, such as the Ford Explorer and Dodge Caravan, continued to sell well. The Big Three continued to enjoy a decided edge in the truck market with designs that consumers preferred and a price advantage over imports. Tariffs added 25 percent to the price of most trucks imported from Asia and Europe in 1994. The German automaker Daimler-Benz, maker of the Mercedes-Benz, hoped to get in on the booming truck market and avoid the stiff tariff by breaking ground in May on a sport-utility vehicle plant in Vance, Ala., scheduled to open in 1997.

Japanese sales off. The strong yen, which traded at around 100 to the U.S. dollar in 1994, continued to hurt Japanese automakers' sales in the United States. A strong yen gave Big Three cars an average $2,000 price advantage over Japanese cars and trucks. To overcome that price difference, Japanese automakers said that they would expand their factories in the United States and Canada. Toyota said it would double production of the Camry at its Kentucky factory and added the new Avalon car to that assembly line. Avalon production began in September. Toyota also said that it would double its output of Corollas in Ontario, Canada. Honda said it would expand Accord and Civic production and add two Acura models to its plants in Ohio and Ontario. Honda's moves came after the company announced in May 1994 that total earnings for its 1994 fiscal year, which ended in March, fell 36 percent to $230 mil-

Mercedes-Benz and the Swiss watchmaker Swatch display their jointly produced
Swatchmobile in March. The vehicle was to debut in 1997.

lion. The automaker launched a global reorganization to put greater emphasis on building cars where they are sold. Toyota overhauled its U.S. sales organization after turning in its worst financial performance since 1987, with 1993 U.S. pretax profits dropping nearly 50 percent to $756 million. Still, Asian automakers managed to increase their share of the U.S. vehicle market to 24.5 percent for the first 10 months of 1994, up from 24.1 percent dur-ing the same period in 1993. Detroit, unable to keep automobile dealers stocked with enough vehicles, saw its 1994 slice of the U.S. car and truck market narrow to 72.8 percent, compared with 73.7 percent a year earlier.

GM truck safety settlement. A two-year government investigation of alleged safety problems in certain GM trucks ended on December 9 when the company agreed to spend $51 million over five years on safety research. The Transportation Department had considered a recall of GM trucks built from 1973 to 1987 on the grounds that the position of the fuel tanks outside the trucks' internal frame made them vulnerable to explosion in side-impact collisions.

New models. The Big Three rolled out a parade of new models in 1994. GM overhauled its factories to begin producing restyled versions of the Chevrolet Lumina, Monte Carlo, Cavalier, Pontiac Sunfire (formerly the Sunbird), and Oldsmobile Aurora. The number-one automaker also had high expectations

for its new sport-utility vehicles—the Chevy Blazer and GMC Jimmy, which added driver's airbags, luxury car amenities, and rounded exterior styling. In the fall, Ford launched the Contour and Mercury Mystique, the U.S. versions of a global line of compact cars Ford developed in 1993 for $6 billion. Chrysler began building its new Chrysler Cirrus compact in September 1994, to be followed by the Dodge Stratus in spring 1995. Plymouth was to begin building a version of the Cirrus in the fall of 1995.

Chrysler's new compact lineup featured the automaker's cab-forward design theme that enlarges the passenger compartment by moving the wheels toward the corners of the car. Chrysler featured the cab forward design in its Neon small car, which debuted in January 1994 and became a runaway sales hit. Despite several recalls, dealers complained they could not get enough of the bug-eyed little car.

The minivan market heated up in 1994, after a decade of dominance by Chrysler's Dodge Caravan and Plymouth Voyager. In spring 1994, Ford introduced its Windstar minivan and reversed plans to discontinue its older Aerostar. Those two models, combined with Ford's popular Mercury Villager, tightened the race for the most popular minivan maker by year's end. Chrysler hoped to reclaim its undisputed hold on the minivan market with a revolutionary restyling of the Caravan and Voyager in the spring of 1995.

Top sellers. The Ford Taurus and Honda Accord battled for the title of America's top selling car in 1994. The Accord, with sportier looks for the 1994 model, was close to unseating the Taurus by year's end, despite new incentives from Ford dealers.

Ford did not have to resort to such tactics to keep its F-series pickup as the top selling truck in America as it enjoyed its best sales since 1979. Ford announced plans to hire a third shift of workers at its Wayne, Mich., F-series factory to run the assembly plant around the clock.

Labor woes. The breakneck pace at GM took a toll on labor relations in 1994 as the automaker suffered short strikes In Shreveport, La.; Anderson, Ind.; and Flint, Mich. Workers walked out to protest unrelenting overtime. GM settled the strikes and avoided others by hiring hundreds of extra workers. The strikes cost GM the production of 44,000 vehicles and about $150 million in the third quarter.

Despite shortages and strife, the Big Three's profits surged in 1994. For the first nine months of the year, GM, Ford, and Chrysler earned $9.6 billion, more than double the $4.7 billion they made during the same period in 1993. Big Three sales rose 15 percent to $245.2 billion. Chrysler and Ford were on track for record profits for 1994, but GM continued to struggle following huge losses in the early 1990's.

□ Keith Naughton

In *World Book,* see **Automobile.**

Automobile racing. Tragedy and turmoil marred auto racing competition in 1994 in the United States and abroad. In the Grand Prix international series for the sleek Formula One cars, a three-time world champion, 34-year-old Ayrton Senna of Brazil, was killed in a race on May 1. In America, two stock-car drivers were killed, and another miraculously survived a crash. And in the richest race in history, the $7.86-million Indianapolis 500, the best team found a loophole in the rules and won.

Crashes. On April 30 in Imola, Italy, a 31-year-old Austrian driver, Roland Ratzenberger, was killed in a crash while trying to qualify for the Grand Prix of San Marino. Senna was so shaken that he stopped racing for the day. The next day, in the race itself, Senna was killed when his Williams-Renault, while leading, hit a concrete wall almost head on at 185 miles (300 kilometers) per hour.

The International Automobile Federation, the world governing body for the sport, ordered quick safety measures. Minimum weights of cars were increased, downforce was reduced about 15 percent, and the drivers' cockpit protection was improved.

In the National Association for Stock Car Racing's (NASCAR) Winston Cup series for late-model sedans, Neil Bonnett, from Hueytown, Ala., was killed on February 11 during practice for the Daytona 500 at Daytona Beach, Fla. Three days later, Rodney Orr of Palm Coast, Fla., died in a crash on the same track.

Ayrton Senna's car shatters after hitting the wall in a Formula One race in Imola, Italy, in May. Senna died from injuries he suffered in the crash.

Automobile racing

On August 20 in Brooklyn, Mich., Ernie Irvan of Concord, N.C., was critically injured and placed on life support when he hit a wall in practice for the Goodwrench Dealers 400 at about 180 miles (290 kilometers) per hour. He slowly recovered.

Indianapolis 500. Cars owned by Roger Penske had won 9 of the 25 previous Indianapolis 500's. This time, the Penske team won again because it capitalized on a loophole intended to encourage smaller teams to design less-expensive engines based on passenger-car parts. The rule allowed Penske to have Mercedes-Benz build him a new-type stock-block, push-rod, V-8 engine rather than a conventional double overhead-cam V-8. The new engine was lighter, allowed more turbocharger boost, and developed 150 more horsepower.

The only cars with that engine were the three entered by Penske. One, with his new driver, Al Unser, Jr., of Albuquerque, N. Mex., won the pole position. In the race itself, on May 29 at the Indianapolis Motor Speedway, either Unser or his teammate and defending champion, Emerson Fittipaldi of Brazil, led for 193 of the 200 laps. Fittipaldi was leading when he crashed on the 185th lap, and Unser won. It was Unser's second Indianapolis victory to go with four for his father and three for his uncle, Bobby Unser.

The Indianapolis 500 was the feature of the Indy-Car Series from March to October. Penske cars won 12 of the 16 races. Unser won 8 races himself and became the series champion.

Formula One. Michael Schumacher, driving a Bennetton-Ford, won the title in the last of the season's 16 races, the Australian Grand Prix on November 13 in Adelaide. He became the first German to win the World Drivers' Championship since it was established in 1950. Schumacher won the first 4 races and 6 of the first 8.

Andretti retires. Mario Andretti, 54, competed in his 407th—and last—Indy Car race on October 9 in the Monterey (Calif.) Grand Prix. Andretti began Indy Car racing in 1963. He won the Indianapolis 500 in 1969 and finished his career with 52 Indy Car victories, second to A. J. Foyt's record of 67.

Other. Dale Earnhardt won his seventh NASCAR series title, equaling Richard Petty's record. In the richest races, Sterling Marlin won the $2,756,845 Daytona 500 on February 20, and Jeff Gordon won the inaugural $3.2-million Brickyard 400 on August 6 at the Indianapolis Motor Speedway.

In the National Hot Rod Association's drag-racing series, Scott Kalitta won his First Top Fuel season title and John Force his fourth Funny Car title. In one race, Kalitta set two records—fastest elapsed time for a quarter-mile (4.726 seconds) and fastest time through a speed trap (308.95 miles [497.2 kilometers] per hour). Later, Kenny Bernstein raised the speed record to 314.46 miles (506 kilometers) per hour. □ Frank Litsky

In *World Book,* see **Automobile racing.**

Aviation. U.S. airlines pared down to essentials and restructured their finances in 1994, often turning to employees for bailouts. But hopes for a major airline recovery soured as the price of fares fell an average of 3 percent, largely due to the pressure put on the industry by low-cost, low-fare carriers. Financial experts predicted U.S. carriers would post a net loss of at least $300 million in 1994, down from the $1.2-billion loss posted in 1993. Airline analysts expected an upswing in profits for 1995.

Economic rebound. Indications of an industry revival were slow to surface in 1994. But by the second quarter, a number of airlines had shown signs of a turnaround. AMR Corporation's American Airlines, Delta Air Lines, and Northwest Airlines, a unit of Wings Holdings Incorporated, all posted strong second- and third-quarter earnings. UAL Corporation's United Airlines did well in the second quarter but saw third-quarter profit fall 45 percent, reflecting costs associated with an employee buy-out of the airline. Southwest's low-cost system allowed it to continue to earn good profits throughout the year.

Northwest, which skirted near-bankruptcy in 1993, concentrated on making customers happy through better service in 1994. Among its notable changes were improved baggage handling, on-time flight performance, and new food choices, including gourmet brand names and regional food items.

The aviation casualties of 1994 were USAir Group Incorporated's USAir and Trans World Airlines (TWA), both saddled with huge debts. Analysts expected the anemic TWA to become the next airline to collapse, yet another symbol of the decline of the industry during the 1990's. From 1990 to 1993, airlines lost a staggering $12 billion.

Employee bailouts and cutbacks. Snubbed by banks and investors, airline financial planners turned to employees to bail them out of financial trouble in 1994. On July 12, UAL shareholders agreed to a $4.8-billion employee buy-out plan in which United employees took a 55 percent stake in the company in return for wage cuts and other cost-saving measures.

The buy-out made United one of the largest employee-owned companies in the United States. This effort was the fifth buy-out attempt at UAL since 1987, and it succeeded because investors considered it the best way to avoid otherwise likely asset sales, layoffs, and labor strife.

Other companies that were kept afloat only after employees paid with wage concessions and lost jobs included Continental Airlines Holdings Incorporated, which gave workers stock in exchange for pay cuts. USAir executives also negotiated with the airline's unions to exchange stock for contract concessions in 1994. American Airlines also encouraged its employees to accept stock in exchange for pay cuts.

Airline employees continued to suffer job loss in 1994. As part of its April 28 cost-cutting announcement, Delta shirked its tradition of job security and

The tragic crash of USAir Flight 427 in a ravine outside the Greater Pittsburgh International Airport killed all 132 people on board in September.

said it would lay off up to 15,000 workers, or 20 percent of its work force, over the next three years. On August 3, TWA said it would lay off as many as 3,000 workers, or 8 percent of its employees. American has eliminated about 5,000 jobs since 1992. United went against the trend, however, when on August 16, it announced that it would hire about 1,700 employees by the end of the year.

No-frills flying. Major airlines continued to mimic Southwest Airlines' strategy of offering low-cost, low-fare, short flights in 1994. USAir started a no-frills strategy called "Project High Ground" on February 16 in 18 Eastern city-pairs separated by fewer than 500 miles (805 kilometers). On March 9, Continental tripled the number of flights it offered through its low-fare "CALite" service. United also launched a no-frills carrier called Shuttle by United.

With the growth of such low-cost carriers as Southwest, MarkAir, Private Jet, American Trans Air, and CALite, the U.S. airline industry expanded slightly in 1994. A number of other upstart regional carriers have also emerged in recent years. Among them are Reno Air and the newly incarnated Frontier Airlines and Midway Airlines, which opened powder rooms for women aboard all flights.

Delta became the last of the industry's major carriers to overhaul its operations as a result of fierce competition from start-up and low-fare operators. On April 28, it announced plans to cut $2 billion in

costs through a program called "Project Leadership 7.5," a reference to the airline's goal of reducing its operating cost of flying one seat 1 mile from 9.26 cents to 7.5 cents by the summer of 1997.

Pricing reform. In a sweeping reform of airline pricing practices, the major airlines resolved a federal antitrust suit by agreeing not to announce price increases in advance. The suit, the second price-fixing lawsuit brought against the airline industry, was based on allegations that the airlines had conspired to use computer reservations systems to boost ticket prices. On October 11, in a pact reached with 10 state attorneys general, major airlines announced their agreement to pay $40 million in discounts to state and local governments to settle a third price-fixing lawsuit.

A fear of flying spread through the traveling public after USAir Flight 427 crashed September 8 in a ravine 5 miles (8 kilometers) from the Greater Pittsburgh International Airport, killing all 132 passengers and crew members aboard. The crash marked the fifth USAir crash in five years and the second in 1994, dampening the airline's bookings. Earlier, on July 2, 37 people were killed when a USAir flight attempted to abort a landing at Charlotte, N.C.

Concern also rose over the accident rate in the small commuter plane industry, which specializes in planes with fewer than 31 seats. The Federal Aviation Administration agreed to tighten regulations over the commuter industry after the National Transportation Safety Board issued a preliminary report in November that widely criticized the industry's safety standards. The board recommended that airlines adopt the strict standards governing large planes for their small commuter planes.

FAA ban on ATR's. On December 9, the Federal Aviation Administration announced a ban on the flying of ATR *(Avion de Transport Régional)* commuter aircraft when icy conditions are present or forecast. The ban came after the French-Italian maker of ATR's reported that icing could sometimes destabilize a plane. Testing on ATR's came after a commuter plane crash on October 31 in Indiana during icy weather killed all 68 people aboard. The ban marked the first time the FAA has not allowed a plane to fly in such conditions.

White House crash. On September 12, a small, low-flying Cessna 150 plane crashed into the White House lawn and then skidded into the White House, two stories below the presidential bedroom, killing its pilot on impact. The plane was flown by Frank E. Corder, who was reportedly depressed and on a suicide mission. No one was injured in the crash. The Clinton family was spending the night at a residence across the street while workers repaired faulty ducting. The crash exposed the vulnerability of the White House to sneak air attacks. □ Asra Q. Nomani

In *World Book,* see **Aviation.**

Azerbaijan agreed to a cease-fire in its war with Armenia on May 11, 1994. The two former Soviet republics had fought since 1988 over the status of Nagorno-Karabakh, an ethnic Armenian enclave in Azerbaijan. Azerbaijani President Heydar A. Aliyev signed the truce despite objections from opposition leaders in parliament, who complained that the agreement left 20 percent of Azerbaijani territory in Armenian hands. At the end of the year, the nations were still negotiating a permanent settlement.

In September, Azerbaijan signed a major oil development contract with an international consortium of oil companies. The partners will develop three large oil fields near the coast in the Caspian Sea. Azerbaijani officials predicted a gain of $34 billion in oil revenues over the next 30 years.

The nation continued to suffer from political instability in 1994. On September 29, two government officials were assassinated. In October, renegade special police forces mounted an abortive coup against Aliyev after three special police were arrested for the assassinations. Soon after, Aliyev imposed a state of emergency and initiated a shakeup of the government. □ Steven L. Solnick

See also **Armenia; Asia** (Facts in brief table). In *World Book,* see **Azerbaijan.**

Bahamas. See **West Indies.**

Bahrain. See **Middle East.**

Ballet. See **Dancing.**

Bangladesh. Agitation by an opposition political party, the Awami League, challenged parliamentary democracy and hindered Bangladesh's economic development in 1994. The league's action stemmed from the 1991 parliamentary elections, in which it had won only 88 of the 330 seats. The Bangladesh Nationalist Party (BNP), led by Khaleda Ziaur Rahman (known as Zia), and its allies won an absolute majority, and Zia became prime minister. But the league leader, Hasina Wajed, never accepted the election results. Many observers saw the unrest in the country as arising from personal hostility between the two political leaders.

Election turmoil. In January 1994, the league won mayoral elections in the nation's two main cities, Chittagong and Dhaka. But on March 20, the BNP won a parliamentary by-election. The league immediately accused the BNP of election-rigging and, on March 23, called for nationwide protest strikes. When Parliament reconvened on May 5, the league boycotted it, charging that Zia had lost her election mandate because of "official corruption and administrative inefficiency." It demanded that the Constitution be amended so that parliamentary elections, due by 1996, would be held under a caretaker government, not the BNP. Zia rejected the demand, insisting that her government had full constitutional rights to stay in power. The league then organized more demonstrations, despite strong criticism from the business community. Businesses and schools were repeatedly closed by demonstrations.

Islamic militants supported the league's agitation in a move to increase their authority. Militants attacked foreign aid organizations and local self-help groups for women, whose work reduced the influence of village religious leaders.

In May, the militants renewed their death sentence, first made in October 1993, against feminist writer Taslima Nasrin, who advocated changing strict Islamic rules that limit women's activities. The threat was made after an Indian newspaper quoted her as saying Islam's holy book, the Koran, should be "revised thoroughly." She denied the quote, insisting that she had only called for revision of Islamic traditions that were not based on the Koran. She was forced to go into hiding on June 5, 1994, and fled to Sweden on August 9.

Economic progress. The World Bank, an international lending agency, said at an April meeting that Bangladesh "currently enjoys an unprecedented window of opportunity" for reforms to speed up economic growth. The government's budget emphasized incentives for more export-led growth.

Some refugees of a Buddhist minority returned to Bangladesh in February from camps in India. But in May, the group's militant leader sought greater autonomy for his group. □ Henry S. Bradsher

See also **Asia** (Facts in brief table). In *World Book,* see **Bangladesh.**

Bank. A strong economy helped bolster bank profits in the United States in 1994 even as interest rates, which had sunk to a 25-year low in 1993, rose steadily through the year. In the first half of the year, the nation's 11,000 banks posted record profits of $22.3 billion. The 2,300 savings and loans earned $2.46 billion in the first half of 1994. Only four banks and two thrifts failed in the first half of 1994, compared with 23 banks during the same period in 1993.

Fighting off inflation. Strong economic expansion in the United States led to fears of inflation in 1994. In a strong economy, the demand for goods and services increases and pushes prices higher. The higher prices, in turn, can cause inflation. From mid-1992 through 1993, the Federal Reserve Bank (commonly known as the Fed), the nation's central bank and top banking regulator, had held interest rates low and steady. But on Feb. 4, 1994, the Fed began the first of a series of rate hikes designed to slow the economy and ward off inflation. It raised the federal funds rate—that is, the interest rate that member banks of the Federal Reserve charge each other for short-term loans—from 3 percent to 3.25 percent.

By early November, the economy had been so strong that the Fed had lifted rates five times. Then, on November 15, the Fed raised the rate for the sixth time, up three-quarters of a percentage point, the largest single rate increase since 1981.

The rising Fed rates soon affected consumers. Those who deposited money in banks' certificates of deposit to earn interest profited from the increased rates. For example, interest rates on three-month certificates of deposit rose to 4.75 percent in November, up two whole points from 2.75 percent a year earlier. But businesses and homeowners who borrowed from banks had to face higher interest rates as banks charged customers more for loans to make up for the increase in interest paid to depositers. Many leading banks boosted their prime interest rate, the rate they charge on business loans to their best customers, to keep pace with the Fed's interest rate hikes. By the end of 1994, many of the largest banks, including Citicorp, BankAmerica Corporation, Chemical Banking Corporation, and Chase Manhattan Corporation, had increased their prime lending rates to 8.75 percent, up from 5.75 percent in early 1994. Rates on 30-year mortgages, which were about 7.2 percent in late 1993, were above 9 percent by the end of 1994.

Fed sheds mystique. On February 4, Federal Reserve Chairman Alan Greenspan announced that the Fed was increasing its federal funds rate, marking the first time that the Fed had announced a rate shift. In the past, the Fed had let the financial markets determine on their own whether the rates would change. The move came in part to calm the stocks and bonds markets, which were fluctuating wildly. The Fed continued to announce rate hikes throughout the year.

Interstate banking approved. On September 29, President Clinton signed the Interstate Banking and Branching Efficiency Act, which permits banks to establish branches across state lines as of Sept. 29, 1995. Banks had been restricted from expanding across state lines since the 1920's.

Small bankers and other opponents of the law said the bill would lead to a wave of consolidation in the banking industry. Some worried that it would remove lending decisions from local bankers and make it difficult for local businesses and homeowners to get loans.

Many bankers liked the idea, because some states already allow out-of-state bank-holding companies to own banks in their states. Also, the new law could reduce the cost of expanding across states because the banks would not need separate banking officials to run the out-of-state banks. The law might also lead to more stabilized loan operations because it allows banks to lend in many regions. For example, if the economy soured in one region, profitable loans in another region could keep a bank strong. The new law would also allow a greater variety of interstate banking service on automated teller machines. Such services would greatly benefit people who commute to work across state lines.

Loans to the poor. In an attempt to strengthen Clinton's pledge to strengthen the Community Rein-

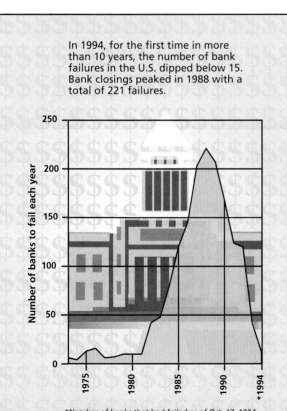

In 1994, for the first time in more than 10 years, the number of bank failures in the U.S. dipped below 15. Bank closings peaked in 1988 with a total of 221 failures.

Number of banks to fail each year

*Number of banks that had failed as of Oct. 17, 1994.
Source: Federal Deposit Insurance Corporation.

vestment Act (CRA), on Sept. 29, 1994, federal bank regulators issued the first rules in 17 years to require banks and thrifts to offer better service to poor people.The proposed rules would have allowed federal banking regulators to issue strong sanctions, such as monetary penalties, against banks and thrifts that did not lend throughout their communities.

But on December 16, the U.S. Justice Department ruled that the regulatory agencies involved lacked the legal authority to impose the sanctions. The decision means that the only way federal regulators can enforce the CRA is by denying merger applications or applications to open new branches to banks with too few branches in poor communities.

Woman heads FDIC. On October 4, the Senate confirmed Ricki Rhodarmer Tigert as chairman of the Federal Deposit Insurance Corporation (FDIC), the government institution that insures $2.5 trillion in deposits in banks and thrifts. Tigert, a former Federal Reserve board lawyer, became the first woman to head a federal banking agency. The FDIC had been without a confirmed chairman since the death in August 1992 of FDIC Chairman William Taylor.

New York Republican Senator Alphonse D'Amato blocked the nomination of Tigert until after the Senate held hearings to investigate President Clinton's involvement with the controversial Whitewater Development Company, an Arkansas company linked to a failed savings and loan. Senator D'Amato said that Tigert was a close friend of President Clinton and his wife, Hillary Rodham Clinton, and argued that it was inappropriate for a friend of the President to head a regulatory agency that was looking into the Whitewater affair. Earlier in the year, Tigert agreed to step aside from Whitewater-related decisions if she were confirmed.

New threat to banks. Federal banking regulators grew concerned in 1994 over so-called exotic instruments, such as interest rate swap contracts that some large investment banks began to buy and sell during the year. The instruments are often called derivatives because their value is derived from other securities (stocks and bonds). Banks own an estimated $120-billion of such contracts, which banks and others buy and hold in case interest rates or currencies swing in one direction or another. Several big companies lost hundreds of millions of dollars on swap contracts sold to them by Bankers Trust Company Incorporated of New York City.

The Securities and Exchange Commission (SEC), which regulates the securities of publicly traded companies, said in October that it was investigating sales practices at Bankers Trust. The SEC also said it was considering changes in how banks and others account for their holdings of the derivatives.

□ Paulette Thomas

In *World Book,* see **Bank.**

Baseball. The longest work stoppage in the history of professional sports ended the 1994 regular season 52 days early. There were no play-offs and no World Series. And as the year ended, negotiations between club owners and players were still stalled, and the 1995 season was in danger.

Strike. Bud Selig, the owner of the Milwaukee Brewers and baseball's acting commissioner, said 19 of the 28 teams were losing money in 1994. He later claimed that only 12 to 14 teams were losing money, however. To help poorer teams from struggling markets, the owners asked the players to agree to a salary cap, combined with a revenue-sharing program among clubs. The owners also wanted to end salary arbitration, which had raised many salaries to dizzying heights.

In 1994, player salaries accounted for 58 percent of club expenses. The owners wanted to split certain income equally with the players and said they would guarantee the players a minimum of $1 billion in 1995. If the players agreed to these proposals, the owners said they would institute revenue sharing, in which richer clubs would help subsidize poorer clubs.

The players wanted nothing to do with a salary cap. They said the problem was among owners and not between players and owners. When neither side would yield, the players struck on Aug. 12, 1994, creating the major leagues' eighth work stoppage since 1972.

On Sept. 8, 1994, the players proposed a variation of the owners' plan. The players' plan would require the 16 clubs with the highest revenues to pay a tax of 1.6 percent on their revenues. The same percentage tax would apply to the 16 teams with the highest payrolls. The 10 clubs with the lowest revenues would then share the tax money.

The owners rejected the tax proposal, and on September 14 they called off the rest of the season. The cancellation affected 669 regular-season games and the entire postseason. The 28 teams stood to lose as much as $500 million to $600 million, including $140 million from national television revenue.

The cancellation of the World Series was nearly unprecedented in the 1900's. With the exception of 1904, the World Series had been played every year since 1903. The series had survived two world wars, the Great Depression, and an earthquake in 1989.

On October 14, Labor Secretary Robert B. Reich appointed William J. Usery, Jr., a highly regarded labor negotiator, to mediate the dispute. Negotiations resumed and John Harrington, the Boston Red Sox' chief executive, assumed the role of owners' spokesman and chief labor negotiator from Richard Ravitch in November. Ravitch later resigned.

After further talks failed, the owners imposed the salary cap and eliminated salary arbitration on December 23. On December 27, both sides filed protests with the National Labor Relations Board

Final standings in major league baseball

American League*

Eastern Division	W.	L.	Pct.	G.B.
New York Yankees	70	43	.619	
Baltimore Orioles	63	49	.563	6½
Toronto Blue Jays	55	60	.478	16
Boston Red Sox	54	61	.470	17
Detroit Tigers	53	62	.465	18

Central Division	W.	L.	Pct.	G.B.
Chicago White Sox	67	46	.593	
Cleveland Indians	66	47	.584	1
Kansas City Royals	64	51	.557	4
Minnesota Twins	53	60	.469	14
Milwaukee Brewers	53	62	.461	15

Western Division	W.	L.	Pct.	G.B.
Texas Rangers	52	62	.456	
Oakland Athletics	51	63	.447	1
Seattle Mariners	49	63	.438	2
California Angels	47	68	.409	5½

American League champion—No champion due to strike.

World Series champion—No World Series due to strike.

Offensive leaders

Batting average—Paul O'Neill, New York	.359
Runs scored—Frank Thomas, Chicago	106
Home runs—Ken Griffey, Jr., Seattle	40
Runs batted in—Kirby Puckett, Minnesota	112
Hits—Kenny Lofton, Cleveland	160
Stolen bases—Kenny Lofton, Cleveland	60
Slugging percentage—Frank Thomas, Chicago	.729

Leading pitchers

Games won—Jimmy Key, New York	17
Win average (10 decisions or more)—Jason Bere, Chicago (12-2)	.857
Earned run average (113 or more innings)— Steve Ontiveros, Oakland	2.65
Strikeouts—Randy Johnson, Seattle	204
Saves—Lee Smith, Baltimore	33
Shut-outs—Randy Johnson, Seattle	4

Awards[†]

Most Valuable Player—Frank Thomas, Chicago
Cy Young—David Cone, Kansas City
Rookie of the Year—Bob Hamelin, Kansas City
Manager of the Year—Buck Showalter, New York

*The regular season was not completed due to a players' strike that began on August 12.
[†]Selected by the Baseball Writers Association of America.

National League*

Eastern Division	W.	L.	Pct.	G.B.
Montreal Expos	74	40	.649	
Atlanta Braves	68	46	.596	6
New York Mets	55	58	.487	18½
Philadelphia Phillies	54	61	.470	20½
Florida Marlins	51	64	.443	23½

Central Division	W.	L.	Pct.	G.B.
Cincinnati Reds	66	48	.579	
Houston Astros	66	49	.574	½
Pittsburgh Pirates	53	61	.465	13
St. Louis Cardinals	53	61	.465	13
Chicago Cubs	49	64	.434	16½

Western Division	W.	L.	Pct.	G.B.
Los Angeles Dodgers	58	56	.509	
San Francisco Giants	55	60	.478	3½
Colorado Rockies	53	64	.453	6½
San Diego Padres	47	70	.402	12½

National League champion—No champion due to strike.

Offensive leaders

Batting average—Tony Gwynn, San Diego	.394
Runs scored—Jeff Bagwell, Houston	104
Home runs—Matt Williams, San Francisco	43
Runs batted in—Jeff Bagwell, Houston	116
Hits—Tony Gwynn, San Diego	165
Stolen bases—Craig Biggio, Houston	39
Slugging percentage—Jeff Bagwell, Houston	.750

Leading pitchers

Games won—Ken Hill, Montreal; Greg Maddux, Atlanta (tie)	16
Win average (10 decisions or more)— Marvin Freeman, Colorado (10-2)	.833
Earned run average (113 or more innings)— Greg Maddux, Atlanta	1.56
Strikeouts—Andy Benes, San Diego	189
Saves—John Franco, New York	30
Shut-outs—Ramon Martinez, Los Angeles; Greg Maddux, Atlanta (tie)	3

Awards[†]

Most Valuable Player—Jeff Bagwell, Houston
Cy Young—Greg Maddux, Atlanta
Rookie of the Year—Raul Mondesi, Los Angeles
Manager of the Year—Felipe Alou, Montreal

(NLRB) in New York City, each charging that the other side engaged in unfair labor practices by negotiating in bad faith.

Commissioner. The owners, who forced out Francis (Fay) Vincent, Jr., as commissioner in 1992, still had not chosen a replacement, and they did not intend to choose a permanent replacement until they had achieved labor peace.

In 1994, they diluted the powers of the commissioner so he could not use the "best interests of baseball" clause to go against their wishes. They also restructured the office and duties, making the commissioner their prime negotiator in labor disputes.

They paid Selig $1 million per year as a temporary commissioner with limited powers. The leading candidate for the permanent job appeared to be George J. Mitchell, a Democrat from Maine and the majority leader in the United States Senate until he declined to run for reelection in November 1994.

Standings. For the first time ever, each major league split into three divisions. The plan was to advance to the play-offs each league's three division winners plus the remaining team with the best record. That created an extra round of play-offs, making the national television package more attractive. Due to the short season, the owners decided to call the six division leaders winners and not champions.

In the National League, the Montreal Expos won the Eastern Division with a 74-40 record, the best in the major leagues. The Expos finished six games

Baseball

ahead of the Atlanta Braves. The Cincinnati Reds (66-48) won the Central Division by a half-game over the Houston Astros. The Los Angeles Dodgers (58-56) were the Western Division leaders, 3½ games ahead of the San Francisco Giants.

In the American League, the New York Yankees (70-43) finished 6½ games ahead of the Baltimore Orioles in the Eastern Division, and the Chicago White Sox (67-46) finished one game ahead of the Cleveland Indians in the Central Division. In the Western Division, the Texas Rangers (52-62), despite a winning percentage of only .456, finished a game ahead of the Oakland Athletics.

Stars. The unanimous choice of baseball writers as the National League's Most Valuable Player (MVP) was first baseman Jeff Bagwell of Houston. Bagwell batted .368, hit 39 home runs, and led the major leagues with 116 runs batted in. Two days before the strike began, he broke his left hand.

For the second consecutive year, the American League's MVP was first baseman Frank Thomas of Chicago. He batted .353 with 38 home runs and 101 runs batted in. He led the league in slugging percentage (.729), on-base percentage (.487), walks (109), and runs (106), and tied for first in extra-base hits (73).

Greg Maddux of Atlanta, for the third consecutive year, and David Cone of the Kansas City Royals won the Cy Young Awards as the pitchers of the year. The managers of the year were Felipe Alou of Montreal and Buck Showalter of the Yankees.

On August 1, shortstop Cal Ripken, Jr., of Baltimore became the second player in major league history to play in 2,000 consecutive games, and he was on target to break Lou Gehrig's record of 2,130 late in the 1995 season. On July 8, 1994, shortstop John Valentin of Boston became the 10th player in major league history to make an unassisted triple play. On July 28, Kenny Rogers of Texas pitched the 12th perfect game in major league history.

Hall of Fame. Steve Carlton, a left-handed pitcher who won 329 games in 24 years, mostly for the St. Louis Cardinals and Philadelphia Phillies, was elected on January 12 to the National Baseball Hall of Fame. The veterans committee elected Phil Rizzuto, the Yankees' shortstop for all but three years from 1941 to 1956, and the late Leo Durocher, who won 2,008 games as the manager of the Brooklyn Dodgers, New York Giants, Chicago Cubs, and Houston.

New league. Organizers announced the formation of the United Baseball League on Nov. 1, 1994, the first new major league since the Federal League in 1914 and 1915. The new league planned to start in the 1996 season with eight teams in the United States, one in Canada, and one in Mexico. Possible team locations included Long Island, New York, and Washington, D.C. ☐ Frank Litsky

In *World Book,* see **Baseball.**

Baseball fans in New York City hold a sign in August expressing their opinion of the cause of labor difficulties that led to a baseball strike that month.

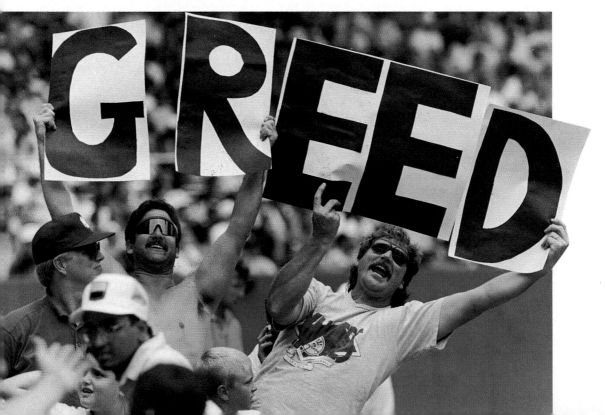

Basketball. Partly because Michael Jordan, their star player, had given up the sport and become a minor league baseball player, the Chicago Bulls failed in 1994 to win a fourth consecutive National Basketball Association (NBA) championship. Instead, the Houston Rockets won their first, defeating the New York Knicks in a tense seven-game final series.

College basketball also produced two first-time champions—the Arkansas men and North Carolina women. The United States, with a team of NBA stars, easily won the world championship.

Professional. During the regular season, the NBA's 27 teams played 82 games each from November 1993 to April 1994. The division champions were the Seattle SuperSonics (63-19), Houston (58-24), New York (57-25), and the Atlanta Hawks (57-25).

In the first round of the play-offs, the Denver Nuggets, after losing the first two games, surprisingly eliminated Seattle, 3 games to 2. In the next round, New York defeated Chicago, 4 games to 3, in a rough series in which 17 players were fined and 2 suspended for an on-court fight.

In the finals, New York took a 3-2 lead in games over Houston. Then the series moved back to Houston, where the Rockets won Game 6. On June 22, the Rockets won the decisive Game 7, 90-84, as center Hakeem Olajuwon of Houston helped harass John Starks, New York's best marksman, into 2-for-18 shooting. Olajuwon was voted the Most Valuable Player (MVP) in the play-offs after receiving the MVP award for the regular season.

Honors. Center David Robinson of the San Antonio Spurs won the regular-season scoring title, averaging 29.8 points per game to 29.3 for center Shaquille O'Neal of the Orlando Magic. On the last day of the season, Robinson scored 71 points against the Los Angeles Clippers to clinch the title. Jordan, the scoring champion the seven previous seasons, quit basketball at age 30 to play baseball. He struggled with the Chicago White Sox' Birmingham (Ala.) Barons AA farm team, batting .202 for the season.

The NBA all-star team consisted of Karl Malone of the Utah Jazz and Scottie Pippen of Chicago at forward, Olajuwon at center, and John Stockton of Utah and Latrell Sprewell of the Golden State Warriors at guard. Lenny Wilkens of Atlanta was voted Coach of the Year.

College men. North Carolina, the defending national champion, started the season ranked first and led again in the Associated Press (AP) postseason poll of writers and broadcasters. Arkansas led the final *USA Today*/CNN poll of coaches.

In the NCAA's 64-team championship tournament, the top-seeded teams in the four regions were North Carolina (27-6), Arkansas (25-3), Purdue (26-4), and Missouri (25-3). Loyola of Maryland made the tournament with a 17-12 record after finishing at 2-25 the year before.

In the first weekend of the tournament, North

Carolina was eliminated by Boston College, 75-72, the first time in 13 years the Tar Heels had failed to reach the final 16. In the regional finals, Arkansas defeated Michigan, 76-68; Duke eliminated Purdue, 69-60; Arizona whipped Missouri, 92-72, and outsider Florida beat Boston College, 74-66.

The Final Four on April 2 and 4 in Charlotte, N.C., began with Arkansas defeating Arizona, 91-82, and Duke rallying to beat Florida, 70-65. In the championship game, with President Bill Clinton, the former Arkansas governor, on hand, Arkansas defeated

National Basketball Association standings

Eastern Conference

Atlantic Division	W.	L.	Pct.	G.B.
New York Knicks*	57	25	.695	
Orlando Magic*	50	32	.610	7
New Jersey Nets*	45	37	.549	12
Miami Heat*	42	40	.512	15
Boston Celtics	32	50	.390	25
Philadelphia 76ers	25	57	.305	32
Washington Bullets	24	58	.293	33

Central Division	W.	L.	Pct.	G.B.
Atlanta Hawks*	57	25	.695	
Chicago Bulls*	55	27	.671	2
Indiana Pacers*	47	35	.573	10
Cleveland Cavaliers*	47	35	.573	10
Charlotte Hornets	41	41	.500	16
Detroit Pistons	20	62	.244	37
Milwaukee Bucks	20	62	.244	37

Western Conference

Midwest Division	W.	L.	Pct.	G.B.
Houston Rockets*	58	24	.707	
San Antonio Spurs*	55	27	.671	3
Utah Jazz*	53	29	.646	5
Denver Nuggets*	42	40	.512	16
Minnesota Timberwolves	20	62	.244	38
Dallas Mavericks	13	69	.159	45

Pacific Division	W.	L.	Pct.	G.B.
Seattle SuperSonics*	63	19	.768	
Phoenix Suns*	56	26	.683	7
Golden State Warriors*	50	32	.610	13
Portland Trail Blazers*	47	35	.573	16
Los Angeles Lakers	33	49	.402	30
Sacramento Kings	28	54	.341	35
Los Angeles Clippers	27	55	.329	36

*Made play-off.

NBA champions—Houston Rockets (defeated New York Knicks, 4 games to 3)

Individual leaders

Scoring	G.	F.G.	F.T.	Pts.	Avg.
David Robinson, San Antonio	80	840	693	2,383	29.8
Shaquille O'Neal, Orlando	81	953	471	2,377	29.3
Hakeem Olajuwon, Houston	80	894	388	2,184	27.3
Dominique Wilkins, Atl./LA-C	74	698	442	1,923	26.0
Karl Malone, Utah	82	772	511	2,063	25.2
Patrick Ewing, New York	79	745	445	1,939	24.5
Mitch Richmond, Sacramento	78	635	426	1,823	23.4
Scottie Pippen, Chicago	72	627	270	1,587	22.0
Charles Barkley, Phoenix	65	518	318	1,402	21.6

Rebounding	G.	Tot.	Avg.
Dennis Rodman, San Antonio	79	1,367	17.3
Shaquille O'Neal, Orlando	81	1,072	13.2
Kevin Willis, Atlanta	80	963	12.0
Hakeem Olajuwon, Houston	80	955	11.9
Olden Polynice, Det./Sac.	68	809	11.9

The 1993-1994 college basketball season

College tournament champions

NCAA	(Men)	Division I: Arkansas
		Division II: California State (Bakersfield)
		Division III: Lebanon Valley (Pa.)
NCAA	(Women)	Division I: North Carolina
		Division II: North Dakota State
		Division III: Capital (Ohio)
NAIA	(Men)	Division I: Oklahoma City
		Division II: Eureka (Ill.)
	(Women)	Division I: Southern Nazarene (Okla.)
		Division II: Northern State (S. Dak.)
NIT	(Men)	Villanova
Junior College	(Men)	Division I: Hutchison (Kans.)
		Division II: Joliet (Ill.)
		Division III: Gloucester County (N.J.)
	(Women)	Division I: Trinity Valley (Tex.)
		Division II: Southwestern Michigan
		Division III: Anoka-Ramsey (Minn.)

Men's college champions

Conference	School
Atlantic Coast	Duke (reg. season)
	North Carolina (tournament)
Atlantic Ten	Massachusetts*
Big East	Connecticut (reg. season)
	Providence (tournament)
Big Eight	Missouri (reg. season)
	Nebraska (tournament)
Big Sky	Weber State—Idaho State (tie; reg. season)
	Boise State (tournament)
Big South	Towson State (reg. season)
	Liberty (tournament)
Big Ten	Purdue (reg. season)
Big West	New Mexico State*
Colonial A.A.	Old Dominion—James Madison (tie; reg. season)
	James Madison (tournament)
East Coast	Troy State (reg. season)
	Hofstra (tournament)
Great Midwest	Marquette (reg. season)
	Cincinnati (tournament)
Ivy League	Pennsylvania (reg. season)
Metro Atlantic	Canisius (reg. season)
	Loyola (Md.) (tournament)
Metropolitan	Louisville*
Mid-American	Ohio*
Mid-Continent	Wisconsin-Green Bay*
Mid-Eastern	Coppin State (reg. season)
	North Carolina A&T (tournament)
Midwestern	Xavier (Ohio)
	Detroit Mercy (tournament)
Missouri Valley	Southern Illinois—Tulsa (tie; reg. season)
	Southern Illinois (tournament)
North Atlantic	Drexel*
Northeast	Rider*
Ohio Valley	Murray State (reg. season)
	Tennessee State (tournament)
Pacific Ten	Arizona (reg. season)
Patriot League	Navy—Fordham—Colgate—Holy Cross (tie; reg. season)
	Navy (tournament)
Southeastern	Kentucky (tournament)
Eastern Division	Florida—Kentucky (tie; reg. season)
Western Division	Arkansas (reg. season)
Southern	Tennessee-Chattanooga*
Southland	Northeast Louisiana (reg. season)
	Southwest Texas State (tournament)
Southwest	Texas*
Southwestern	Texas Southern*
Sun Belt	Western Kentucky (reg. season)
	Southwestern Louisiana (tournament)
Trans America	Charleston (S.C.) (reg. season)
	Central Florida (tournament)
West Coast	Gonzaga (reg. season)
	Pepperdine (tournament)
Western Athletic	New Mexico (reg. season)
	Hawaii (tournament)

*Regular season and conference tournament champions.

Arkansas guard Scotty Thurman launches the three-point shot that put the Razorbacks ahead to stay in their championship game against Duke on April 4.

Duke, 76-72. Corliss Williamson, Arkansas's burly forward, scored 29 points against Arizona and 23 in the final to win MVP honors in the Final Four.

Glenn Robinson, Purdue's junior forward, was the regular-season scoring champion, averaging 30.3 points per game. He was a widespread choice as Player of the Year.

The consensus All-America team consisted of Donyell Marshall of Connecticut and Robinson at forward, Clifford Rozier of Louisville at center, and Grant Hill of Duke and Jason Kidd of California at guard. In the NBA draft, Robinson was chosen first, Kidd second, Hill third, and Marshall fourth. Robinson later signed with Milwaukee for $68.1 million over 10 years.

College women. The best regular-season records belonged to Tennessee (29-1), North Carolina and Connecticut (both 27-2), Penn State (25-2), and Louisiana Tech and Bowling Green (both 26-3). Tennessee led the final AP poll.

For the first time, the NCAA tournament involved 64 teams rather than 48. The top-seeded teams in the regional eliminations were Tennessee, Connecticut, Penn State, and Purdue (25-4).

In a regional semifinal, Louisiana Tech eliminated Tennessee, 71-68. In regional finals, North Carolina beat Connecticut, 81-69, and Penn State lost to Alabama, 96-82.

The Final Four on April 2 and 3 in Richmond, Va.,

involved North Carolina, Alabama, and Purdue, all for the first time, and Louisiana Tech for the eighth time in 13 years. In the semifinals, North Carolina whipped Purdue, 89-74, and Louisiana Tech got by Alabama, 69-66, for its 25th consecutive victory. In the final, North Carolina beat Louisiana Tech, 60-59, when Charlotte Smith sank a 3-point shot with seven-tenths of a second left. Smith also made 23 rebounds in the final, a tournament record, and was voted the MVP in the Final Four.

The Player of the Year was Lisa Leslie, Southern California's 6-foot-5-inch (196-centimeter) center. She averaged 21.9 points and 12.3 rebounds per game in leading the Trojans to a regional final.

International. In the men's world championship from August 4 to 14 in Toronto, professional stars such as Shaquille O'Neal, Reggie Miller, Dominique Wilkins, and Larry Johnson, and Alonzo Mourning led the United States. This so-called Dream Team II won every game comfortably, and in the final it routed Russia, 137-91.

In the women's world championship in June in Sydney, Australia, Brazil defeated China, 96-87, in the final, and the United States beat Australia, 100-95, for third place. Brazil's 110-107 victory over the United States in the semifinals was the first loss in 11 years for the Americans in these championships.

☐ Frank Litsky

In *World Book,* see **Basketball.**

Belarus. Alexander Lukashenko, a former collective farm manager, was elected the first president of Belarus on July 10, 1994. Since Belarus split from the Soviet Union in 1991, the head of state had been the chairman of parliament. Lukashenko won a surprising 80 percent of the votes in a runoff election against Prime Minister Vyacheslav Kebich, who resigned after the election. Lukashenko ran a flamboyant campaign directed against corruption and the return of Communism and marked by sweeping promises to restore a strong national economy.

Lukashenko's message became more attractive as the Belarus economy neared collapse in 1994. By midsummer, the average monthly wage had fallen below $25, and the inflation rate had grown to more than 500 percent. In April, Belarus and Russia announced an agreement to merge the Belarus economy with Russia's. The union faced opposition in both countries, however, as many Belarusians feared Russian domination and many Russians considered the costs of stabilizing Belarusian currency as too high. Russian leaders supported Kebich in the presidential election, though both candidates favored strong ties with Russia. In October, the economic union was postponed indefinitely, and the Belarusian parliament outlawed using the Russian ruble for domestic transactions. ☐ Steven L. Solnick

See also **Europe** (Facts in brief table). In *World Book,* see **Belarus.**

Belgium. Belgian Prime Minister Jean-Luc Dehaene narrowly missed becoming president of the European Commission, the nearest equivalent to being president of Europe, when his nomination was vetoed by British Prime Minister John Major during a meeting of the European Union (EU), formerly the European Community, on the Greek island of Corfu on June 25, 1994. Major believed Dehaene was too strongly in favor of a federal Europe, in which member countries would cede powers in many areas to a strong central European government. Dehaene, a member of the Christian Democratic Party of Flanders, the Dutch-speaking part of Belgium, was known as a pragmatic deal-maker, admired for his ability to keep his often fractious coalition government in power. Dehaene remained Belgian prime minister while Jacques Santer, prime minister of Luxembourg, was chosen president of the European Commission on July 21.

3 Guys resign. Dehaene's coalition government was shaken by scandal early in 1994. Three leading members of the Wallonian, or French-speaking, Socialist Party, Deputy Prime Minister and Telecommunications Minister Guy Coeme, Wallonia regional President Guy Spitaels, and Wallonian Interior Minister Guy Mathot, were all forced to resign on January 21. The "3 Guys," as the officials came to be known, were accused of accepting bribes from Italian helicopter maker Agusta in the award of an 8-billion Belgian franc (U.S. $259-million) government contract from 1988. The three politicians and Agusta all denied they had committed any crimes. Coeme was succeeded by Elio di Rupo, also a French-speaking Socialist Party member.

French businessman jailed. Belgian investigating judge Jean-Claude Van Espen shocked European business circles when he ordered French businessman Didier Pineau-Valencienne, the chairman of French electronics company Schneider SA, jailed for 12 days, beginning May 27. The judge was investigating allegations of possible illegal payments at Schneider's Belgian subsidiary. French officials strongly protested the detention.

Liberation celebration. On September 3, Belgium celebrated the 50th anniversary of its liberation from Nazi occupation during World War II (1939-1945). The day was marked by special demonstrations of thanks to British soldiers, who were the first Allied troops to enter Brussels on Sept. 3, 1944.

Leading fascist dies. Leon Degrelle, 87, who had been a leading Belgian fascist and Nazi sympathizer during the occupation of Belgium by Germany in World War II, died in Malaga, Spain, on March 31. Degrelle had fled to Spain in 1944 after being sentenced to death by a Belgian court. ☐ Philip Revzin

See also **Europe** (Facts in brief table). In *World Book,* see **Belgium; European Union.**

Belize. See Latin America.

Benin. See Africa.

Berlusconi, Silvio (1936-), billionaire media and real estate tycoon, had a short-lived reign as prime minister of Italy. He was named to the post on May 11, 1994, after the right wing coalition he led won a majority of seats in Italy's March 27 and 28 parliamentary elections. But Berlusconi resigned on December 22, after corruption charges precipitated the collapse of his government. (See **Italy.**)

Berlusconi was born in Milan, Italy, on Sept. 29, 1936. He graduated from Milan's Catholic University with a law degree. He began his business career in real estate development at the age of 23. In the 1970's, Berlusconi began building a private television network. In 1994, his television operations held a monopoly on private programming in Italy.

In the 1980's, Berlusconi expanded his business empire to include advertising, publishing, supermarkets, a soccer team, and other ventures. His holding company, Fininvest SpA, is Italy's third largest private enterprise.

In January 1994, Berlusconi created the political party, Forza Italia (Go Italy), with a probusiness platform. As prime minister, he pledged to reduce taxes, create jobs, and curb the influence of the Mafia.

Over the years, Berlusconi has been implicated in a number of scandals. In December 1994, concerns over Berlusconi's involvement with corruption at Fininvest destabilized the government, leading to Berlusconi's resignation. □ Patricia Ohlenroth

Biology. A biological research project in July 1994 raised questions about a long-standing belief in sociology—that overcrowding in America's inner cities contributes substantially to stress and aggressiveness and thus to crime. That conclusion was based primarily on studies in the 1960's in which rats kept in crowded cages became unusually aggressive and combative. The 1994 study, conducted at the Yerkes Regional Primate Research Center in Atlanta, Ga., suggests that the early studies may not be relevant to primates—the group of animals that includes apes, monkeys, and human beings.

The Yerkes researchers studied the behavior of 413 rhesus monkeys. After comparing monkeys confined to crowded enclosures with monkeys given plenty of room, the researchers reported that the confined monkeys showed no significant increase in aggressiveness. In fact, the animals displayed an increase in coping behaviors, such as grooming each other, making submissive gestures, and avoiding dominant animals.

Lactating males. American researchers discovered the first male animals in the wild that *lactate* (produce milk from mammary glands), according to a February report. Only highly inbred males in captivity had previously been observed to lactate. Biologists discovered the animals, a species of fruit bat, in Malaysia. The research team speculated that the bats may represent an unusually monogamous species in which both parents participate in feeding offspring. Another possibility is that the bats consume a plant that produces a hormonelike substance, which causes the mammary glands to grow.

How bees orient themselves. Researchers at the University of Sussex in Brighton, England, reported in March that they had learned how honey bees get their bearings when looking for food sources. The scientists had known that bees memorize a shape by looking at it with one part of the eye. Later, bees will recognize the shape only if viewing it with the same portion of the eye. The bees thus have to find a way to orient themselves properly when looking for familiar landmarks.

The Brighton researchers reported that bees get their bearings by orienting their bodies in Earth's magnetic field. The scientists found that the bees tended to face magnetic south when homing in on a source of nectar. And when the researchers placed the bees in an altered magnetic field, the insects became disoriented.

Deep-dwelling bacteria. Earth's "biosphere," the portion of the planet capable of sustaining life, may extend farther into the Earth than had been thought. Researchers with the University of Bristol in England reported in September that they had discovered bacteria living at least 1,600 feet (500 meters) below the ocean floor.

Researchers had previously reported the presence of small quantities of bacteria in deep holes, but many skeptics believed the microbes had been carried below the surface on drilling instruments. The British scientists reported finding bacteria present in large numbers, however, indicating that the microbes originated below the surface of the ocean floor.

Cystic fibrosis and cholera. The symptoms of cholera may help explain the prevalence of cystic fibrosis, researchers at the University of North Carolina in Chapel Hill announced in October. Cystic fibrosis is a fatal genetic disease that causes certain cells of the body to produce abnormally thick mucus.

The persistence of cystic fibrosis and other fatal genetic defects in the human population is puzzling, because the adverse effects of the disorders should serve to weed them out of the population. But genetic defects may persist if they have some beneficial effect in addition to the harmful ones. Scientists have found, for example, that the gene for sickle cell disease provides protection against malaria.

The North Carolina researchers reported that studies in mice show that the cystic fibrosis gene partially blocks the activity of the *toxin* (poison) produced by the bacterium that causes cholera. The gene prevents the secretion of fluids from cells in response to cholera toxin, limiting diarrhea. The gene may thus have helped prevent the fatal dehydration typical of cholera. □ Thomas H. Maugh II

See also **Medicine.** In *World Book,* see **Biology.**

Boating. Women have traditionally sailed against women in racing sloops and have infrequently competed with and against men. But in 1994, a yacht with an all-female crew completed the 32,000-mile (51,500-kilometer) Whitbread Round the World race for only the second time, and an all-female crew prepared for the 1995 America's Cup competition.

The Whitbread race began on Sept. 25, 1993, and ended when the yacht *Heineken,* with a 12-woman crew, finished on June 8, 1994. It attracted ten 60-foot (18-meter) boats, including *Heineken,* from the new Whitbread 60 class and 5 from the older 80-foot (24-meter) maxiclass.

The boats fought pounding gales, icebergs, and bitter cold as they sailed from Southampton, United Kingdom, to Punta del Este, Uruguay, to Fremantle, Australia, to Auckland, New Zealand, to Punta del Este to Fort Lauderdale, Fla., and back to Southampton. The winners were *Endeavour* of New Zealand in the maxiclass in 120 days 5 hours and *Yamaha* in the Whitbread 60 class in 120 days 14 hours. *Heineken* finished 6 days after the final-leg leader, a remarkable achievement for a boat that broke two rudders during the final week and could barely move.

America's Cup. Dawn Riley, *Heineken*'s skipper, was also named skipper of the first all-female crew in the 143-year history of the America's Cup, the world's most prestigious yacht competition. Riley was the only woman who sailed in 1992 in the last America's Cup competition. In the 1992 eliminations to pick an American defender, she worked in the pit, helping raise and lower headsails.

Bill Koch, the industrialist who financed the winning U.S. yacht in 1992, provided start-up money for the women's boat. Two other U.S. syndicates were also preparing for the elimination races, starting in January 1995, to choose a defender.

America's Cup officials also set dates for the eliminations and challenge round, all off San Diego. The three American groups and eight foreign syndicates were scheduled for separate first rounds from January to March. Elimination finals were planned for April, with a best-of-11 race series for the Americans and a best-of-9 series for the foreign challengers. The survivors would meet for the cup in a best-of-9 series rather than the previous best-of-7 format.

Powerboats. Unlimited hydroplanes, equipped with modified helicopter engines, raced eight times from June to October 1994. Although the new fuel-flow restrictor valves saved engine parts, as intended, speeds still reached 200 miles (320 kilometers) per hour. As usual, Chip Hanauer of Seattle won the series with the boat *Miss Budweiser.*

□ Frank Litsky

In *World Book,* see **Boating; Sailing.**

Bolivia. See **Latin America.**

Books. See **Canadian literature; Literature; Literature, American; Literature for children.**

The first all-female crew to challenge men in an America's Cup race gather in New York City in March 1994. The women's team will race in 1995.

Bosnia-Herzegovina. Civil war continued in 1994 to ravage Bosnia (as the nation is often called), despite international efforts to end the hostilities. When the nation declared its independence from the Yugoslav federation in March 1992, the government intended to maintain Bosnia as a multiethnic state. But soon after, fighting broke out between the Muslim-dominated government forces and Bosnian Serbs and Croats, who called for separate ethnic states. By late 1994, Bosnian Serb forces still held more than 70 percent of Bosnian territory.

Croat agreement. Bosnian officials signed a cease-fire agreement with the nation's Croat leaders on Feb. 23, 1994. In March, both sides met in Washington, D.C., and agreed to form a Croat-Muslim federation in Bosnia. According to the plan, the two groups would rule the federation jointly, sharing such responsibilities as national defense, foreign affairs, and commerce. Plans to eventually link the federation with Croatia were also outlined. But Serb occupation of Bosnian territory made it impossible to proceed with the plans.

Bosnian Serbs agreed in February to hand over their heavy weapons to United Nations (UN) troops and begin withdrawing their forces from Sarajevo, Bosnia's capital. Under threat of air strikes by the North Atlantic Treaty Organization (NATO), the Bosnian Serb troops withdrew beyond a 12-mile (19-kilometer) "exclusion zone" around Sarajevo. In the months that followed, however, Serb forces reportedly violated the agreement. Heavy weapons remained hidden within the exclusion zone, and Serbs continued to strike Sarajevo with mortar fire. They also continued shelling other Bosnian cities, particularly Gorazde, Tuzla, and Prijedor. In September, Serb forces cut off Sarajevo's water, gas, and power for more than 10 days, provoking a retaliation by Bosnian forces.

Bosnian Serbs also carried on their policy of "ethnic cleansing" in 1994 by forcing Muslims from their homes in Serb-controlled areas of Bosnia. From July to September, an estimated 10,000 Muslims were driven from their homes.

Serb forces clashed repeatedly with UN peacekeeping forces in Bosnia in 1994, interrupting UN efforts to bring relief to civilians. In March, Serb forces highjacked 10 UN trucks carrying food and medicine to Bosnia's Muslims. UN officials voted in March to send an additional 3,500 peacekeeping troops to Bosnia. The UN Security Council imposed additional sanctions against the Serbs in September.

International pressure on the Bosnian Serbs to help end the war increased in 1994. In July, Serb leaders rejected a peace plan drafted by the United States, Russia, the United Kingdom, France, and Germany. The plan, which had been accepted by Bosnian leaders, would have given 49 percent of Bosnian territory to the Serbs and 51 percent to Bosnian Muslims and Croats.

A wounded woman in Sarajevo gets help after mortar fire struck a crowded marketplace in February, killing more than 60 people.

In response to the Bosnian Serbs' rejection of the plan, Serbian President Slobodan Milošević—Yugoslavia's most powerful leader—cut off most support for Bosnian Serb forces, who had relied on supplies from Serbia, a Yugoslav republic. Milošević had been under pressure from the UN, which had imposed a trade embargo against Yugoslavia, but due to his action, the UN eased some sanctions.

In late 1994, disagreement arose between the United States and other nations over lifting the arms embargo for the Bosnian Muslims and between the UN and NATO over further NATO air strikes on Bosnian Serb positions. In December, France and the United Kingdom discussed withdrawing their peacekeeping troops in light of Bosnian Serb military gains and the increased vulnerability of peacekeeping forces. A number of UN soldiers were taken hostage by Bosnian Serbs. Also, in late December, former U.S. President Jimmy Carter met with Bosnian Serbs in an attempt to negotiate a cease-fire.

Carter succeeded in negotiating a seven-day cease-fire. As it was due to expire, the UN commander in Bosnia negotiated on December 31 a four-month cease-fire agreement with Bosnian Serb leaders and the Bosnian government. □ Sharon L. Wolchik

See also **Croatia; Europe** (Facts in brief table); **United Nations; Yugoslavia.** In *World Book,* see **Bosnia-Herzegovina.**

Botswana. See Africa.

Bowling. Norm Duke and Walter Ray Williams, Jr., dominated the Professional Bowlers Association (PBA) 1994 tour. The same situation prevailed on the Ladies Pro Bowlers Tour (LPBT), where Aleta Sill and Anne Marie Duggan swept most of the honors.

Men. The PBA conducted 30 tournaments worth more than $9 million in prize money. Duke, from Edmond, Okla., won five tournaments; Bryan Goebel of Merriam, Kans., four, and Williams, from Stockton, Calif., two. Williams also won the world archery championship.

In prize money, Duke ranked first with $273,753, Williams a distant second with $189,745. In scoring average, Duke was first with 222.83, Williams second with 222.59. Duke won the year's richest tournament, the $325,000 General Tire Tournament of Champions from April 18 to 23 in Fairlawn, Ohio, by beating Eric Forkel of Chatsworth, Calif., in the final, 217-184. Duke also broke a tour record with a 255 average for 12 games.

In the first-ever tour title match between brothers, 31-year-old David Traber of Woodstock, Ill., won the $175,000 PBA national championship, held from February 25 to March 5 in Toledo, Ohio. In the last match of the stepladder finals, he defeated 36-year-old Dale Traber of Cedarburg, Wis., 196-187.

Justin Hromek of Andover, Kans., captured his first tour victory when he won the $250,000 United States Open held from April 3 to 9 in Troy, Mich. In the final, he beat Parker Bohn III of Jackson, N.J., 267-230, finishing with nine strikes.

In 1993, Steve Fehr of Cincinnati, at age 38, became the youngest man inducted into the American Bowling Congress (ABC) Hall of Fame. From May 3 to 7, 1994, he won the $235,000 ABC Masters in Mobile, Ala., defeating Steve Anderson of Colorado Springs, Colo., 224-206, in the final.

The PBA senior tour comprised 13 tournaments with $1.5 million in prize money. Gary Dickinson of Edmond, Okla., won the PBA seniors title and Delano Boothe of Canoga Park, Calif., the ABC Seniors Masters. Dickinson led in earnings with $54,096. John Handegard of Las Vegas, Nev., led in average with 222.12.

Women. The LPBT's 21 tournaments were worth $2.5 million. Sill, a lefthander from Dearborn, Mich., won four tournaments and Duggan, a righthander from Edmond, Okla., won three.

Sill led in prize money with earnings of $126,325, a LPBT record, to Duggan's $124,722. Duggan's average of 213.47 led the tour. In the finals of the two most important competitions, Duggan defeated Sill, 238-218, in the Women's International Bowling Congress Queens tournament held from May 8 to 12 in Salt Lake City, Utah, and Sill defeated Duggan, 229-170, in the United States Open, held from September 27 to October 1 in Wichita, Kans.

☐ Frank Litsky

In *World Book,* see **Bowling.**

Boxing. The two widely recognized world heavyweight champions lost their titles to underdogs in 1994, and one of the new champions lost his title six months later. After all the ups and downs, one of the new champions was the oldest heavyweight champion ever, 45-year-old George Foreman of Houston.

Heavyweights. On Nov. 6, 1993, Evander Holyfield of Atlanta, Ga., regained the World Boxing Association (WBA) and International Boxing Federation (IBF) titles by stopping Riddick Bowe of Brooklyn, N.Y. Holyfield's first title defense came on April 22, 1994, in Las Vegas, Nev., against Michael Moorer of Monessen, Pa. Moorer won a majority decision and became history's first left-handed heavyweight champion. Six days before that fight, Holyfield had agreed to a November bout against Lennox Lewis of England, the World Boxing Council (WBC) champion, to unify the title. But with Holyfield no longer a champion, Holyfield was out of the picture, and Lewis would soon be, too.

Instead of fighting, Holyfield was hospitalized because his heart was not pumping enough blood to his muscles, leaving him fatigued. He retired from boxing in April, then said he intended to fight again because, he said, medication had made him sound once more. He received medical clearance in November to return to the ring.

Moorer made his first defense on November 5 in

World champion boxers

World Boxing Association

Division	Champion	Country	Date won
Heavyweight	Evander Holyfield	U.S.A.	1993
	Michael Moorer	U.S.A.	April '94
	George Foreman	U.S.A.	Nov. '94
Light heavyweight	Virgil Hill	U.S.A.	1992
Middleweight	John David Jackson	U.S.A.	1993
	Vacant		
	Jorge Castro	Argentina	Aug. '94
Welterweight	Cristano Espana	Venezuela	1992
	Ike Quartey	Ghana	June '94
Lightweight	Orzubek Nazarov	Russia	1993
Featherweight	Eloy Rojas	Venezuela	1993
Bantamweight	Junior Jones	U.S.A.	1993
	John Michael Johnson	U.S.A.	April '94
	Daorung Chuwatana	Thailand	July '94
Flyweight	David Griman	Venezuela	1992
	Saen Sor Ploenchit	Thailand	Feb. '94

World Boxing Council

Division	Champion	Country	Date won
Heavyweight	Lennox Lewis	United Kingdom	1992
	Oliver McCall	U.S.A.	Sept. '94
Light heavyweight	Jeff Harding	Australia	1991
	Mike McCallum	U.S.A.	July '94
Middleweight	Gerald McClellan	U.S.A.	1993
Welterweight	Pernell Whitaker	U.S.A.	1993
Lightweight	Miguel Gonzalez	Mexico	1992
Featherweight	Kevin Kelley	U.S.A.	1993
Bantamweight	Yasuei Yakushiji	Japan	1993
Flyweight	Yuri Arbachakov	Russia	1992

Boxing

Las Vegas against Foreman, a bout many regarded as simply a final payday for Foreman. Moorer, who had never lost as a professional, was clearly winning until Foreman knocked him out in the 10th round with a straight right to the chin. Foreman was wearing the trunks he wore 20 years earlier when he lost the title to Muhammad Ali in Zaire.

Lewis defended the WBC title twice. On May 6 in Atlantic City, N.J., he stopped Phil Jackson of Miami, Fla., in eight rounds. On September 25 in London, Oliver McCall of Chicago floored Lewis in the second round to win the title. Lewis, like Moorer, had never lost as a pro and had never been knocked down.

McCall planned his first defense in January 1995 against Larry Holmes, like Foreman a 45-year-old recycled former champion. McCall's promoter, Don King, was indicted by a federal grand jury in New York City on nine counts of wire fraud. He pleaded not guilty in July to all counts.

Chávez. The legendary Julio César Chávez of Mexico, undefeated in 90 professional fights, lost the WBC super lightweight title to an American, Frankie Randall, a 15-1 underdog, on January 29 in Las Vegas. Chávez regained the title in May when a head butt by Randall opened a huge gash over Chávez's right eye. Randall was penalized a point for the butt, and that was the margin as Chávez won on points. ☐ Frank Litsky

In *World Book,* see **Boxing.**

Brazil. On Oct. 3, 1994, Brazilians elected Fernando Henrique Cardoso, 63, to be the nation's next president. Cardoso was a member of the Social Democratic Party, and he was to begin a four-year term on Jan. 1, 1995. Cardoso was a former sociology professor who suffered exile, imprisonment, and blacklisting under the Brazilian military government in the late 1960's and through much of the 1970's. Cardoso served as a senator from the state of São Paulo from 1983 to 1992 and subsequently became Brazil's foreign minister. (See **Cardoso, Fernando.**)

Stabilization plan. But Cardoso may have exerted his most influential role as Brazil's finance minister, a position he held from May 1993 to March 1994. In early 1994 he forged an economic stabilization plan, which the Brazilian Congress approved on February 8. The plan involved establishing a Social Emergency Fund financed with $16 billion from increased taxes and funds that otherwise would have gone to federal agencies and the states.

The creation of the stabilization plan helped reduce Brazil's deficit and made it possible to introduce a stable new currency on July 1—one whose value was pegged to the dollar. Many economists also credited the plan with reducing inflation from 45 percent a month in June to about 1.5 percent a month in September.

Common market. Brazil played a leading role in hammering out an August agreement with its part-

Super lightweight champion Julio César Chávez hits the canvas in January during his first defeat, losing to Frankie Randall. But he regained the title in May.

Fernando Henrique Cardoso of the Social Democratic Party waves to supporters while casting his ballot in Brazil's October presidential elections. Cardoso won.

ners in a regional market—Argentina, Paraguay, and Uruguay—whereby 85 percent of the goods traded between the four nations will be duty-free beginning Jan. 1, 1995. The combined population of the four nations was about 200 million people. Their total *gross domestic product* (the value of all goods and services produced within a country) in 1994 was $800 billion—two-thirds of South America's total.

Corruption. On Jan. 7, 1994, the mastermind of a kickback scheme that toppled former Brazilian President Fernando Collor de Mello was sentenced to four years in prison for tax evasion. Paulo César Farias, Collor's former campaign treasurer, was accused of an elaborate scheme to steal public monies through kickbacks on public works projects. Revelation of his activities led to Collor's impeachment on charges of corruption in September 1992.

On Dec. 12, 1994, the Brazilian Supreme Court acquitted Collor of corruption charges, citing lack of evidence. The court said that much of the strongest evidence against Collor had been obtained illegally.

On April 13 and 14, the Chamber of Deputies, the lower house of Brazil's Congress, voted to expel three members of Congress allegedly involved in a corruption scandal in the budget committee. The three were among 18 Congress members that a congressional investigative panel had recommended be expelled in January for taking kickbacks and stealing from the public treasury. Four other Congress mem-

bers accused in the scheme had resigned in March.

Amazon surveillance. A consortium led by the Raytheon Corporation of the United States won a contract in excess of $1 billion on July 21 to build a sophisticated system to monitor the rate of deforestation and other activities in the Amazon River Basin. Using satellites, aircraft, ground-based sensors, and computers, the system will record the rate of deforestation and operations of drug traffickers.

Coffee bean shortage. Two severe frosts damaged Brazil's coffee crop in late June and early July. Brazil is the world's largest coffee producer. The frosts sent prices for coffee commodities to their highest levels since 1986.

Brazil takes fourth World Cup. Brazil won the World Cup—the world championship of soccer held every four years—on July 17, 1994, in Pasadena, Calif. The tie-breaking shoot-out victory over Italy made Brazil the only team to have won four World Cups. (See **Soccer.**)

The largest funeral in Brazilian history occurred on May 5 when hundreds of thousands of people turned out in the city of São Paulo to mourn the loss of 34-year-old Ayrton Senna. The three-time champion of the Formula One race car circuit died in an accident while competing in a Grand Prix race at Imola, Italy, on May 1.   □ Nathan A. Haverstock

See also **Latin America** (Facts in brief table). In *World Book,* see **Brazil.**

Breyer, Stephen G. (1938-   ), formerly the chief judge of the United States Court of Appeals for the First Circuit, in Boston, was formally sworn in as an associate justice of the Supreme Court of the United States on Aug. 12, 1994. Breyer is considered a moderate who is likely to take a centrist stance on most issues facing the high court.

Breyer was born on Aug. 15, 1938, in San Francisco. He graduated from Stanford University in Stanford, Calif., in 1959 and then attended Oxford University in England for two years as a Marshall scholar. He earned a law degree at the Harvard University Law School in Cambridge, Mass., in 1964.

After clerking for one year for Supreme Court Justice Arthur J. Goldberg, Breyer taught at the Harvard Law School until 1980, when he joined the First Circuit Court of Appeals. He had been nominated to the post in the waning days of the Administration of President Jimmy Carter after serving as counsel to the Senate Judiciary Committee.

Breyer became the chief judge of the Court of Appeals in 1990. During his tenure at the appeals court, he gained a reputation as a protector of the environment, and his nomination to the Supreme Court was hailed by conservationists.

Breyer is married to the former Joanna Hare. They have three children.   □ David Dreier

British Columbia. See **Canadian provinces.**
Brunei. See **Asia.**

Building and construction. Just as the United States construction industry gained momentum leading into 1994, the Federal Reserve System, known as the *central bank*, cooled the economy with a series of interest rate hikes aimed at preventing inflation. As a result, U.S. residential construction gained only 5 percent, with 1.27 million units built, according to DRI/McGraw-Hill, Inc., a New York City economic forecasting firm.

Most nonresidential construction grew but remained below levels reached in the late 1980's. Office buildings showed a 10 percent increase, factory construction went up 6 percent, and commercial building grew by 13 percent. Along with quickening demand came the first signs of inflation. Prices of gypsum (plaster) board shot up 15 percent, according to a 20-city survey reported in *ENR* magazine. Prices of portland cement, which is used to make concrete, shot up about 6 percent during the first six months of 1994 but then leveled off.

Global boom. The rest of the world continued what some described as a full-fledged building boom. Developing countries in particular worked on infrastructures that would be needed to support more advanced economies. The single busiest region in the world was Southeast Asia, said George E. Fischer in August 1994. Fischer publishes *The Fischer Report*, a newsletter that tracks major projects around the world. Indonesia, Malaysia, the Philip-

pines, Singapore, and Thailand were among the most active, said Fischer. Vietnam encouraged foreign investment and launched many projects.

Cement consumption, a strong indicator of building activity, had been increasing by 3.6 percent annually worldwide, according to the July 18 *Forbes* magazine. By August, the price of cement had increased by 6.8 percent over 1993, reported the U.S. Bureau of Labor Statistics. The growing overseas demand helped drive the price higher.

Infrastructures. In a report released June 19, 1994, the World Bank, an agency of the United Nations, estimated that 1 billion people in the world do not have access to clean water, almost 2 billion lack acceptable sanitation, and 2 billion people do not have electricity. To pay for the construction of these infrastructure systems, developing nations mainly borrow from banks and international lending agencies. But private companies increasingly have provided financing to pay for the projects in addition to doing the work. In exchange, these companies operate the facilities and collect tolls and fees for their use. This process is known as privatization.

Brokerage firms in 1994 tracked an increased number of stocks in overseas companies engaged in private infrastructure development. Also, investors and finance companies launched several new funds designed to tap into this development, especially the construction of power plants in China and other parts of Asia.

California earthquake. Near dawn on January 17, an earthquake measuring 6.7 on the Richter scale struck the Los Angeles area, damaging about 60,000 buildings. By late 1994, insurance claims had reached $7.2 billion, according to the Insurance Information Institute in New York City.

Five damaged segments of three freeways were among the most visible effects of the quake. Engineers studied the damage for clues to safer construction and found that short concrete columns supporting highways and bridges appeared to suffer more damage than long columns. The long ones seemed able to sway and return to their original alignment but short, inflexible columns cracked. Contractors working for the California Department of Transportation collected incentives for repairing the damaged roads quickly. For example, C. C. Myers, Inc., of Rancho Cordova, Calif., earned a $200,000-per-day bonus, or $14.8 million total, for completing repairs to the Santa Monica Freeway 74 days early.

The earthquake proved again the vulnerability of buildings made of unreinforced masonry, which is bricks or blocks that are not held together with steel rods or wire. However, some engineering solutions proved their value. Many medium-sized buildings had devices called *base isolators* that act like shock absorbers between a building and its foundation. These devices are usually bearings made of alternate layers of steel and an elastic material, such as syn-

A parking garage at the Northridge campus of California State University lies badly crumpled after a major earthquake that struck in January.

thetic rubber. Base isolators absorb some of the sideways motion so the building sways more slowly, thus reducing damage.

Steel-frame structures perform better than concrete or masonry structures in a quake, because steel frames are more flexible. But on March 3, earthquake engineers told California's Seismic Safety Commission that after the quake, many steel-frame buildings bore cracks at welded connections. Engineers and inspectors worked on solutions to mend the breaks and examine the welds on steel frames in more buildings.

The English Channel Tunnel, the long-awaited, underground, underwater link between England and France, officially opened on May 6. Passenger service began on November 14. The 31-mile (50-kilometer) tunnel connects Folkestone, England, and Calais, France.

Other projects. The world's longest cable-stayed bridge, crossing the Seine Estuary in Normandy, France, neared completion in 1994. The deck of the bridge was 2,808 feet (856 meters) in length. In a cable-stayed bridge, the cables that support the roadway connect directly to the bridge's towers.

Work continued on Petronas Towers in Kuala Lumpur, Malaysia. These twin office buildings will be the world's tallest structures at 1,476 feet (450 meters), rising 22 feet (6.7 meters) higher than the Sears Tower in Chicago. □ Richard Korman

In *World Book,* see **Building construction.**

Bulgaria. Bulgaria's former Communists returned to power following parliamentary elections on Dec. 18, 1994. The Bulgarian Socialist Party, formerly the Communist Party, won an absolute majority of 124 seats in the 240-seat parliament, taking 43.7 percent of the popular vote. Their main rivals, the Union of Democratic Forces, won 68 seats. Bulgaria was politically unstable throughout the year. On October 17, President Zhelyu Zhelev dissolved parliament after legislators failed to create a new cabinet. Zhelev appointed economist Reneta Indjova prime minister of an interim government and called for the December 18 elections.

Bulgaria's troubled economy showed few signs of improvement. Unemployment remained at about 16 percent. In April, the government levied an additional tax on goods and services, which increased already high levels of inflation. Real wages dropped during the year, and the cost of living increased.

In August, the government introduced a plan to privatize about 340 state-owned businesses. Berov also managed to reduce Bulgaria's debt by refinancing loans from two commercial banking organizations. In September, the United Nations' International Monetary Fund approved a loan to Bulgaria of $102 million. □ Sharon L. Wolchik

See also **Europe** (Facts in brief table). In *World Book,* see Bulgaria.

Burkina Faso. See Africa.

Burma. On Sept. 20, 1994, leaders of the ruling military junta of Burma (officially named Myanmar) held talks for the first time with democracy leader Aung San Suu Kyi. The junta had been keeping Suu Kyi under house arrest since July 1989. She headed the National League for Democracy that had won 82 percent of the popular vote in 1990 elections, but the junta, which seized power in 1988 after killing prodemocracy demonstrators, had refused to give up control of the government. Junta leaders also had kept Suu Kyi from personally accepting the Nobel Peace Prize in 1991, despite worldwide protests.

The first sign that the junta's defiance might be weakening came in February 1994, when Suu Kyi was allowed to see United States Representative Bill Richardson (D., N.M.) at her home. It was the first time she was allowed to see nonfamily, foreign visitors since her incarceration. Richardson had asked Khin Nyunt, the junta's military intelligence chief, for permission to see Suu Kyi in August 1993 and had urged him to negotiate with her on some plan to move Burma toward democracy. At their February meetings, Suu Kyi told Richardson she was ready to negotiate with the junta, but that she would never leave Burma for exile abroad, as the junta wanted. She said the junta had granted the visit to ease world pressure on it to end civil rights abuses.

Junta meeting. Suu Kyi's September 20 meeting with Khin Nyunt and the junta's titular head, Than Shwe, was officially described as "cordial." The junta provided no details regarding the talks, only a brief television report. However, in the first photographs of her published since 1988, Suu Kyi appeared to be healthy. After the meeting, the junta continued to work slowly on a new constitution that barred Suu Kyi from politics and guaranteed continued military control of the country.

On October 28, Khin Nyunt and several other junta leaders held a second meeting with Suu Kyi. Although described as both "frank and cordial," the meeting did not lead to immediate changes.

Isolation ends. Most foreign countries had ostracized Burma since the junta seized power, but this began to change in 1994. Prime Minister Goh Chok Tong of Singapore visited Burma on March 28 to look into investment opportunities. On July 26, a meeting in Bangkok, Thailand, of Southeast Asian and Western foreign ministers endorsed a new policy of "constructive engagement" with Burma, though the United States opposed this change.

Guerrilla wars between the junta and some ethnic minorities seeking autonomy or independence continued in 1994. Most groups refused to accept compromise terms offered by the junta. But one of the largest forces, the Kachin Independence Army, ended hostilities in February. □ Henry S. Bradsher

See also **Asia** (Facts in brief table). In *World Book,* see **Burma.**

Burundi. People in Burundi watched anxiously in 1994 as neighboring Rwanda became a killing ground, with the majority ethnic group, the Hutus, murdering the minority Tutsis by the tens of thousands. Because Burundi has the same division as Rwanda between Hutus and Tutsis, there were fears that Burundi would also be consumed by violence.

Burundi had already experienced much Hutu-Tutsi warfare, most recently in late 1993, following the assassination of Burundi's newly elected Hutu president, Melchior Ndadaye, by Tutsi soldiers. In the following weeks, more than 150,000 people, mostly Tutsis, were murdered.

On Jan. 13, 1994, another Hutu, Cyprien Ntaryamira, was elected president of Burundi. But on April 6, Ntaryamira and Rwandan President Juvénal Habyarimana, also a Hutu, died in a plane crash. When the Rwandan government charged that a Tutsi rebel group shot the plane down, Hutus in Rwanda began systematically slaughtering Tutsis.

In Burundi, an interim Hutu president, Sylvestre Ntibantunganya, came to power immediately, and on September 30 he was confirmed in his office by the National Assembly. Nonetheless, at year-end the nation remained tense. □ Mark DeLancey

See also **Africa** (Facts in brief table). In *World Book,* see Burundi.

Bus. See Transit.

Business. See Bank; Economics; Manufacturing.

Cabinet, U.S.

Cabinet, U.S. Facing serious ethics charges, Secretary of Agriculture Mike Espy announced on Oct. 3, 1994, that he would resign from President Bill Clinton's Cabinet at the end of the year. Espy, who was accused of accepting gifts from companies subject to regulation by his department, apparently quit under pressure from the White House.

On September 9, a special panel of appeals court judges appointed an independent counsel, Los Angeles lawyer Donald C. Smaltz, to decide if Espy had broken the law. At issue was whether Espy violated a strict 1906 law that prohibits Agriculture Department officials from accepting gifts from companies subject to meat and poultry regulations.

Espy also came under fire for charging the government for the lease of a car that he used on trips to his home state. Pressure on Espy intensified after it was reported that his girlfriend had received a $1,200 scholarship from a foundation affiliated with Tyson Foods Inc., an Arkansas poultry producer.

On December 28, Clinton nominated outgoing Representative Dan Glickman (D., Kans.) to succeed Espy as agriculture secretary.

Cisneros under investigation. The Department of Justice announced on September 22 that it had begun an investigation of Henry G. Cisneros, the secretary of Housing and Urban Development (HUD). The Justice Department was seeking to determine whether Cisneros had misled federal agents about the amount of money he gave Linda Medlar, a woman with whom he had an extramarital affair in the late 1980's while he was mayor of San Antonio. The revelation of Cisneros' relationship with Medlar in 1988 resulted in a scandal that, she claimed, made it impossible for her to find a job. As a result, she said, Cisneros agreed to help her financially.

In early 1993, while undergoing a routine background check prior to his confirmation as HUD secretary, Cisneros reportedly told the Federal Bureau of Investigation that his payments to Medlar from 1990 to 1992 totaled about $60,000. But Medlar claimed in September 1994 that Cisneros had actually given her more than $150,000 during that period. Medlar said she received an additional $50,000 from Cisneros in 1993 after he became HUD secretary.

Ron Brown cleared. On February 2, Secretary of Commerce Ronald H. Brown was cleared of charges that he accepted a $700,000 bribe to help end the U.S. trade embargo against Vietnam. The Justice Department said it had found no evidence of wrongdoing on Brown's part.

Bentsen grilled on Whitewater. Secretary of the Treasury Lloyd M. Bentsen, Jr., was questioned by Senate and House investigators on August 3 regarding his knowledge of contacts between Treasury officials and the White House in the so-called Whitewater affair. Whitewater concerns a land development company and a failed savings and loan (S&L) institution in Arkansas that Bill and Hillary Rodham

Secretary of Agriculture Mike Espy, facing an investigation of possible ethics violations in office, announces his resignation in October.

Clinton were involved with while Clinton was governor of Arkansas.

Bentsen said he could not recall being told by aides that the Resolution Trust Company (RTC), the federal agency that has overseen the bailout of bankrupt S&L's, had sent documents to the Justice Department listing the Clintons as possible beneficiaries of illegal financial dealings at the Arkansas S&L. Two Treasury officials, Deputy Secretary Roger C. Altman and General Counsel Jean Hanson, also testified. Hanson said that she had held meetings with White House officials in late 1993 to discuss the RTC probe. Altman said he knew of just one contact, in February 1994. Hanson and Altman later resigned.

Bentsen resigns. Bentsen announced on December 6 that he was resigning, effective December 22. Clinton nominated Robert Rubin, the White House economic-policy adviser, to succeed Bentsen.

New defense secretary, chief of staff. On January 24, Clinton nominated William J. Perry, a Defense Department official, to succeed Les Aspin, Jr., as secretary of defense. Perry received unanimous confirmation from the Senate and was sworn in on February 3. On June 27, Clinton picked Leon E. Panetta, director of the Office of Management and Budget, to replace Thomas F. McLarty III as his chief of staff. □ William J. Eaton

See also **Perry, William J.** In *World Book*, see **Cabinet.**

Calderón Sol, Armando

Calderón Sol, Armando (1948-), was elected president of El Salvador in a runoff election on April 24, 1994. He was a member of the ruling right wing National Republican Alliance. He was inaugurated on June 1.

With 68.2 percent of the vote, Calderón Sol defeated Rubén Zamora Rivas of the Democratic Convergence, the left wing coalition led by the former rebel group known as the Farabundo Martí National Liberation Front. Calderón Sol won 49 percent of the vote in El Salvador's March 20 presidential election, just short of the 50 percent margin he needed to avoid the April runoff. (See **El Salvador.**)

Calderón Sol was born on June 24, 1948, in San Salvador, the capital, and attended the University of El Salvador. He earned a doctorate in law and social sciences in 1977. In 1988, Calderón Sol was elected mayor of San Salvador. He was reelected in 1991. He also served in El Salvador's Legislative Assembly.

As mayor, Calderón Sol was known as a conciliator between members of his party and rebels who fought a civil war against the government from 1981 to January 1992, when the two sides signed a peace treaty. Calderón Sol promised to uphold provisions of the peace treaty during his campaign.

Calderón Sol is married. The family has three children and lives in San Salvador. ☐ Mark Dunbar

California. See **Los Angeles; San Diego; State government.**

Cambodia. Despite a $2-billion United Nations (UN) effort to bring peace and a popularly elected government to Cambodia, the country was mired in warfare, bureaucratic inefficiency, and official corruption in 1994. The UN had finally organized elections in May 1993, after years of fighting among the Vietnam-backed government of the Communist Cambodian People's Party (CPP); the radical Communist Khmer Rouge (KR); and non-Communist groups, particularly the National United Front for an Independent, Neutral, Peaceful, and Cooperative Cambodia (known as FUNCINPEC), the party of King Norodom Sihanouk. But the KR had boycotted the elections. FUNCINPEC, headed by Sihanouk's son, Norodom Ranariddh, and the CPP then formed a coalition government with Ranariddh as first premier and CPP leader Hun Sen as second premier.

Sihanouk was restored as king with vaguely defined powers. He spent most of the year in China undergoing treatment for cancer. During the year, he made several unsuccessful efforts to reconcile Cambodian factions in a national unity government.

KR troops, under the same leaders responsible for the deaths of hundreds of thousands of Cambodians in the 1970's, resumed the war against the Cambodian government. In January and March 1994, the Cambodian army seized KR strongholds near the border with Thailand, where the KR over the years has openly obtained weapons and other support in

Cambodians with ties to Communist Khmer Rouge (KR) guerrillas flee to Thailand after the Cambodian army captured KR headquarters in March.

return for millions of dollars in logs, gems, and other Cambodian resources. But in April, KR forces regained their strongholds, and in early May, they briefly threatened Cambodia's second largest city, Battambang. KR guerrilla units won support both by opposing government corruption and terrorizing unsympathetic farmers.

Sihanouk arranged for a peace conference, which began on June 15 in Phnom Penh, the capital. But talks collapsed the next day because the KR demanded that negotiations for sharing government power had to begin before it would agree to a cease-fire. The government then expelled KR officials from the country, and on July 7, the parliament outlawed the KR. Three days later, the KR established a rival provi-

port said military intelligence units in western Cambodia were torturing and executing civilians to extort money. Civilian officials, unwilling to give up military patronage and profit, ignored the report.

Coup attempt. On July 2, some 300 troops slowly moved toward Phnom Penh in what was later labeled an attempt to overthrow the government. Blame was put on two CPP leaders, Sin Song and Prince Chakrapong, a dissident son of Sihanouk's. They had briefly rebelled against FUNCINPEC's 1993 election victory. But many Cambodians believed that senior CPP members of the government were also involved. Chakrapong was allowed to go into exile in Malaysia, and Sin Song later escaped house arrest. Thailand denied any involvement, though 14 Thai citizens were accused by Phnom Penh of a role.

CPP in charge. The government's limited authority was exercised by CPP officials who had clung to office despite the party's second-place finish in the 1993 elections. FUNCINPEC was too weak and disorganized to formulate or enforce its own policies or to offer a weary, abused public a non-Communist alternative to the KR and CPP. On Oct. 20, 1994, the government fired Finance Minister Sam Rainsy, who had crusaded against corruption and the bloated bureaucracy, and Foreign Minister, Prince Norodom Sirivut, resigned. □ Henry S. Bradsher

See also **Asia** (Facts in brief table). In **World Book,** see **Cambodia.**

Cameroon. The citizens of Cameroon and other Francophone countries in Africa—the former African colonies of France—were shocked on Jan. 12. 1994, when their currency, the CFA franc, was devalued by 50 percent. The devaluation, aimed at strengthening the nations' faltering economies by boosting exports, caused hardship for many Cameroonians.

During the year, some of Cameroon's foreign creditors agreed to reduce Cameroon's large debt load. And on March 15, the International Monetary Fund, an agency of the United Nations, said it would give Cameroon a loan of about $114 million. The loan was contingent upon the government of President Paul Biya making large cuts in the civil service.

On January 3, a border crisis with Nigeria erupted as Nigeria sent troops to a disputed sector of the petroleum-rich Bakassi area in the Gulf of Guinea. Loss of the Bakassi petroleum reserves would compound Cameroon's economic crisis. The Organization of African Unity—an association of more than 50 African nations—agreed to investigate the dispute.

The Biya regime continued to resist pressure for greater democratic reforms, and the year was marked by continued widespread discontent with the government. At year-end, Biya remained in power, but no resolution of the many problems facing the nation was in sight. □ Mark DeLancey

See also **Africa** (Facts in brief table). In **World Book,** see **Cameroon.**

sional government, based in an unspecified part of Preah Vihear, a northern province.

On July 26, the KR kidnapped a number of passengers from a train, including three young tourists from Australia, France, and England. The attack was organized in cooperation with corrupt local officials. The KR said it would not release the tourists until their countries quit aiding the Cambodian government. But in November, the KR admitted to executing the tourists in October, saying they were spies.

Inept army. Soldiers from the United States, Australia, and France gave military training to the Cambodian army, but the 90,000 Cambodian soldiers still had very limited effectiveness against fewer than 10,000 KR fighters. Government officials admitted the main reason was corruption. Poorly paid, unmotivated soldiers and police were more interested in money-making rackets than in fighting. A UN re-

Canada's team captain Luc Robitaille lets out a yell after Canada won the world hockey championships in Milan, Italy, in May, its first title since 1961.

Canada

Canada in 1994 again faced the possibility of losing Quebec, one of its largest provinces, when Quebecers voted the separatist Parti Québécois (PQ) into provincial office on September 12. Immediately following the election, PQ leader and Quebec's new premier, Jacques Parizeau, announced that the question of the province's independence from Canada would be placed before the people in a referendum by the end of 1995. The PQ victory had thus set the nation's political agenda for the next year.

The Quebec election was preceded by a campaign of 50 days. During this time, the PQ attacked the Liberal Party—which had governed the province since 1985—for failing to secure a more autonomous position for Quebec within Canada. In his campaign, the 64-year-old Parizeau stated that the PQ would focus on problems of concern to Quebec and would not cooperate with the national government in Ottawa in maintaining a "dysfunctional" federation. And he made no bones about the PQ's primary objective to win independence for Quebec. If elected, he noted, the PQ would ask the provincial legislature to approve a "solemn declaration" affirming Quebec's desire to break from Canada. Quebecers would then be asked to vote for either the status quo under the current federation or outright separation. No compromise would be offered. Parizeau

Quebec's National Assembly, won 77 seats in the election, while the Liberals dropped from 78 to 47 seats. A splinter party, which had advocated a more gradual move toward Quebec's separation, elected 1 member.

The PQ's victory was somewhat dampened by the election's failure to give Parizeau the sweeping majority he wanted. The Liberals retained a substantial presence in the Assembly, and Johnson had clearly gained the authority to lead federalist forces in the 1995 referendum on independence. More important, the popular vote was almost equally divided, with the Liberals winning 44.7 percent and the PQ capturing 44.3 percent.

This outcome did not bode well for the PQ's separatist goal and, following the election, Parizeau began to tone down his promise that the referendum in 1995 would be a straight choice between independence or the status quo. Polls showed that support for sovereignty in 1994 was at virtually the same level—about 40 percent—as it had been during 1980, when Quebecers turned down the first referendum on independence. Thus, the 1994 election results may have indicated only that Quebecers had cast their ballots for a change in government, not for independence. However, recent changes in the composition of the federal government created a political climate that differed significantly from that in 1980 and put the sovereignty issue on more volatile ground.

Grappling with separatism. A federal election in 1993 had brought 54 members of the separatist Bloc Québécois (BQ) to Canada's House of Commons and made the BQ the largest opposition party in the House. During 1994, the BQ was regarded as a provocative force in Parliament, continually sniping at Prime Minister Jean Chrétien and his federalist government. BQ leader Lucien Bouchard was expected to join Parizeau in promoting Quebec's separation.

In addition, the mood in the provinces outside Quebec did not appear to support a unified Canada at any cost. Many members of the provincial governments expressed the belief that Canada should make no more concessions to Quebec, and that the time for changing the Constitution to satisfy Quebec had passed. Thus, no prospect of a revised federal system was on the horizon.

The Western-based Reform Party expressed these views most strongly. Its 52 House members were convinced that the central government's agenda was too strongly influenced by the concerns of Quebec. Thus, Reformers indicated that they would most likely oppose any effort the Chrétien government made to accommodate Quebec's wishes.

These competing attitudes set up a difficult predicament for Canada's Liberal government. On the one hand, it had to combat separatism and avoid being drawn into conflicts with the Quebec government, which the PQ could now use to gain

also promised that the PQ would focus on stimulating the economy and creating jobs. In 1994, Quebec had an unemployment rate of about 10 percent.

The Liberal Party had been led by Daniel Johnson since Jan. 11, 1994, when Premier Robert Bourassa retired for personal reasons. The 49-year-old Johnson was the son of a former premier and the brother of another. Johnson differed from Bourassa by putting aside nationalist ideology and committing himself and his party to a strong federalist stance. Economically, the federal union had greatly benefited Quebec, he stated, while allowing it to fully exercise its language and culture. Like Parizeau, Johnson stressed economic improvement as a main objective.

The PQ, which had held 33 of the 125 seats in

Prime Minister Jean Chrétien, left, reviews Canadian troops in Quebec in June and thanks them for serving in United Nations peacekeeping missions.

support for the separatist cause. On the other hand, it needed to carry out an economic and social agenda for the nation that Quebec might oppose.

But Canada's government possessed a strong leader in Chrétien. At 60, he was a vigorous political figure who had energetically campaigned to defeat sovereignty in the 1980 referendum. Chrétien was an experienced minister, having held most of the major positions in previous Liberal Cabinets. He regularly pointed out that separatism for Quebec had to prove itself, to demonstrate its advantages over membership in a federated Canada.

Although Chrétien did not have a large group of French-speaking supporters in Parliament, the popularity of his government, even in Quebec, had grown quickly among the populace after it assumed office. In April 1994, polls revealed that 54 percent of Canadians supported Chrétien and his government, a gain of 13 percentage points from the 41 percent of the popular vote won in the 1993 election.

Party standings in the 295-seat House of Commons reflected the Liberal party's solid majority. In September 1994, the Liberals held 176 seats, the BQ 53, the Reform Party 52, the New Democratic Party 9, the Progressive Conservative Party 2, and there were 2 independents. (The death of a BQ member on September 1 resulted in 1 vacancy.)

The new government moved cautiously in its first year in office, with Parliament approving only

35 bills, most of them noncontroversial. The government devoted much attention to review possible changes to the social welfare system, unemployment assistance, health care, foreign affairs, and defense. In accordance with campaign promises, the government allocated $2 billion (all monetary figures are in Canadian dollars)—which the provinces were to match—to improve roads and public buildings. The government's most far-reaching achievement was an agreement reached with the provinces on July 18 to reduce interprovincial trade barriers after July 1, 1995. Five hundred regulations hindering internal trade were estimated to cost Canadians about $6.5-billion annually.

Canada, provinces, and territories population estimates

	1994 estimates
Alberta	2,716,200
British Columbia	3,668,400
Manitoba	1,131,100
New Brunswick	759,300
Newfoundland	582,400
Northwest Territories	64,300
Nova Scotia	936,700
Ontario	10,927,800
Prince Edward Island	134,500
Quebec	7,281,100
Saskatchewan	1,016,200
Yukon Territory	30,100
Canada	29,248,100

City and metropolitan populations

	Metropolitan area 1993 estimates	City 1991 census
Toronto, Ont.	4,127,900	635,395
Montreal, Que.	3,260,100	1,017,666
Vancouver, B.C.	1,709,800	471,844
Ottawa-Hull	994,300	
Ottawa, Ont.		313,987
Hull, Que.		60,707
Edmonton, Alta.	874,200	616,741
Calgary, Alta.	792,200	710,677
Winnipeg, Man.	667,500	616,790
Quebec, Que.	680,600	167,517
Hamilton, Ont.	629,400	318,499
London, Ont.	406,600	303,165
St. Catharines-Niagara	384,700	
St. Catharines, Ont.		129,300
Niagara Falls, Ont.		75,399
Kitchener, Ont.	382,100	168,282
Halifax, N.S.	329,700	114,455
Victoria, B.C.	305,000	71,228
Windsor, Ont.	276,800	191,435
Oshawa, Ont.	266,300	129,344
Saskatoon, Sask.	214,800	186,058
Regina, Sask.	195,900	179,178
St. John's, Nfld.	176,000	95,770
Sudbury, Ont.	168,000	92,884
Chicoutimi-Jonquière	165,900	
Chicoutimi, Que.		62,670
Jonquière, Que.		57,933
Sherbrooke, Que.	144,600	76,429
Trois-Rivières, Que.	141,800	49,426
Thunder Bay, Ont.	130,400	113,946
Saint John, N.B.	129,400	74,969

Source: Statistics Canada.

The Canadian economy continued its slow climb out of the recession that had gripped the country since 1990. The recovery was spurred by exports, which produced a record trade surplus in July 1994. Forest products, fertilizers, and manufactured goods—many going to the United States—led export figures.

The International Monetary Fund, an agency of the United Nations (UN), in September forecast an overall growth rate of 4.1 percent. At the end of June, economists estimated that the gross domestic product—the total value of all goods and services produced within a country—was $739.6 billion.

The economy did not suffer from inflationary pressures, as was evident in May, when the consumer price index was down 0.2 percent from the previous May, the first such decline in 40 years. The elimination of tobacco taxes in five provinces had caused most of the decrease. In September 1994, economists predicted that the rate of increase in the consumer price index would average only 0.2 percent for the entire year.

The country also saw encouraging growth in employment, especially in full-time jobs. In October, 10 percent of the labor force was unemployed, the lowest level since January 1991. Almost all the growth in new jobs occurred in Ontario and in the Western provinces.

Budget targets defense. Finance Minister Paul Martin introduced his first budget on Feb. 22, 1994. Based on extensive consultations with economists and interest groups, the budget imposed no new or increased taxes. It offered a modest reduction in the deficit from $45.7 billion recorded in fiscal year 1993-1994 to $39.7 billion for fiscal 1994-1995. Federal spending was set at $163.6 billion, an increase of 2 percent from the previous year.

Despite the increase in expenditures, Martin announced reductions in defense spending totaling $7 billion during the next five years. The trimming would close four major bases and two military colleges during the next three years. Sixteen smaller installations would also close or be pared down. The plan would also terminate more than 16,500 military and civilian employees of the defense department, leaving an armed force and civilian support staff of 91,900 men and women by 1998.

The budget further called for an extension of a salary freeze for 381,000 public servants until 1997. Members of Parliament also became targets of a salary freeze. And funding for a space station program with the United States was to be reduced after negotiations with the United States.

Smoker's delight. A substantial cut in federal tobacco taxes, announced on Feb. 8, 1994, was designed to check the flood of illegal cigarettes into Canada. The traffic in contraband cigarettes had cost the federal government and some provincial governments large amounts of tax revenue and led to smuggling through the Akwesasne Indian reservation along the international section of the St. Lawrence River near Cornwall, Ontario. In response to pleas from Quebec, the federal government cut its cigarette tax by $5 a carton and then matched provincial tax cuts exceeding this amount, up to another $5 a carton. As a result, the price of a carton of cigarettes in Quebec fell from near $47 to about $23. Neighboring provinces reluctantly followed suit because of their desire to deter smoking by keeping tobacco prices high. The measure successfully reduced smuggling, which, according to police, dropped by as much as 90 percent during the first month it became effective.

Foreign affairs. Chrétien sought to follow a more independent approach to dealing with the United States than had his predecessor, Brian Mulroney. For example, despite U.S. objections, Chrétien decided on June 20 to allow aid shipments to Cuba. The aid included $500,000 in emergency food supplies for children and another $1 million from nongovernmental organizations. Although Canada had never suspended diplomatic ties with Cuba, it had banned aid in 1978 to protest Cuban involvement in Angola's civil war.

Chrétien also declined to take part in the initial phase of the U.S. intervention in Haiti in September 1994. But he announced that Canada would later send 100 Royal Canadian Mounted Police and 500 soldiers to Haiti to help restore law and order.

Chrétien agreed reluctantly with the North Atlantic Treaty Organization (NATO) decision to use air strikes in Bosnia-Herzegovina (usually referred to as Bosnia) to compel ethnic Serbian forces to withdraw heavy artillery from around the capital, Sarajevo. Chrétien expressed concern that air strikes could escalate the conflict and compromise the safety of Canadian peacekeepers in the area. He insisted that air attacks be used only as a last resort, and that any operation be authorized by the UN commander in Bosnia. Canadian soldiers guarded 40,000 Muslim refugees gathered around Srebrenica, Bosnia, for a year before they were relieved by troops from the Netherlands.

Canada's peacekeepers served throughout the brutal civil war in Rwanda before UN forces were increased during the summer. Commanded by a Canadian general, the original small UN force operated a hazardous air link between Rwanda and neighboring Kenya, carrying out 305 missions in six months. Altogether, Canada had 3,825 personnel serving under the UN flag in the Balkans, the Middle East, Africa, and Asia.

Canada-U.S. relations. Canada and the United States experienced more than their share of disputes in 1994. The most serious concerned durum wheat. Farmers in the U.S. Midwest alleged that Canadian wheat was being sold in the United States at unfairly subsidized prices. Canadian durum wheat sales in

Federal spending in Canada
Estimated budget for fiscal 1994-1995*

Department or agency	Millions of dollars†
Agriculture and agri-food	2,073
Atlantic Canada Opportunities Agency	386
Canadian heritage	2,993
Citizenship and immigration	663
Environment	737
Finance	50,383
Fisheries and oceans	775
Foreign affairs and international trade	3,739
Governor general	10
Health	8,431
Human resources development	32,840
Indian affairs and northern development	4,954
Industry	2,983
Justice	724
National defence	11,563
National revenue	2,207
Natural resources	1,259
Parliament	297
Privy Council	173
Public works and government services	4,464
Solicitor general	2,541
Transport	2,851
Treasury board	1,239
Veterans affairs	2,088
Western economic diversification	452
Total	**140,825**

* April 1, 1994, to March 31, 1995.
† Canadian dollars; $1 = U.S. $0.74 as of Oct. 28, 1994.

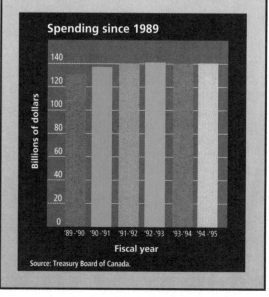

Spending since 1989

Source: Treasury Board of Canada.

the United States had risen to capture nearly 30 percent of the U.S. market. Canadians claimed that this growth occurred because U.S. durum wheat was being sent abroad under the generous provisions of the Export Enhancement Program. A last-minute effort to avert an agricultural trade war resulted in an agreement on August 1. Under a one-year plan, Canada is allowed to export 300,000 tons of durum wheat to the United States, after which punitive tariffs take effect. The countries also agreed not to impose trade sanctions during the year and to appoint an independent commission to study the dispute.

Lumber. An Extraordinary Challenge Panel that had been arranged for through the Canada-United States Free Trade Agreement settled on August 3 a long-standing dispute over a U.S. tariff on softwood lumber from Canada. The panel affirmed a 1993 decision in ruling that U.S. border tariffs on Canadian lumber were not justified. The panel directed that some $800 million, collected for two years under a U.S. tariff, be refunded to Canadian lumber exporters. The United States had justified the tariff by claiming that the stumpage fees of certain Canadian provinces constituted a form of subsidy. The panel was the third of its kind to settle such disputes. In each case, the panel had ruled in favor of Canada.

Fish stories. Another dispute, involving salmon fishing, erupted on the Pacific coasts of Canada and the United States. Canada claimed that too many salmon that had spawned in British Columbia rivers were being taken at sea by fishermen from the United States. Evidence compiled by the United States-Canada Pacific Salmon Commission revealed that in 1993 U.S. fishermen caught 9 million salmon that had originated in Canadian rivers, wheras Canadians had caught only 3.7 million salmon from U.S. rivers. The two countries were unable to reach a new agreement specifying quotas for catches from one another's waters. But to assert its position, Canada in June levied a $1,500 license fee on U.S. fishermen using the sheltered inside waters off the coast of British Columbia. Canadians also increased their catch in open waters, hoping to reduce the number of Canadian salmon available to U.S. fishermen.

Unfortunately for both Canada and the United States, initial estimates of the number of salmon in the northwest Pacific Ocean were highly inaccurate. In September 1994, the commission downgraded its estimate of the size of the summer salmon run in the lower reaches of the Fraser River, a major British Columbia salmon river. The commission's estimate of 10.3 million salmon declined to between 5 million and 7 million. The reason for the initial misestimate was unclear, but because fewer salmon were available to spawn, the fisheries could not expect to be replenished in the near future.   □ David M. L. Farr

See also **Canadian provinces; Canadian territories; Chrétien, Jean; Montreal; Toronto; United Nations.** In *World Book,* see **Canada; Quebec.**

Canadian literature. Two of Canada's foremost authors, Robertson Davies and Alice Munro, led a strong showing by the nation's fiction writers in 1994. Davies, who turned 81 during the year, showed no signs of flagging as a storyteller. In his new novel, *The Cunning Man,* the hero looks back on an expansive life of miracles and an unusual death. Munro once again demonstrated her mastery of vision and craft with *Open Secrets,* eight long, polished stories that span centuries and blur the boundaries of reality.

Other highlights of the year included Paul Quarrington's new comic novel, *Civilization,* set in Hollywood during the early 1900's. M. J. Vassanji won the $25,000 Giller Prize for *The Book of Secrets,* which dealt with a clash of cultures in Tanzania, the writer's former home. Rudy Wiebe's *The Discovery of Strangers* dramatized the first contact between native people and members of Sir John Franklin's Arctic expedition in 1821. (See also **Canadian territories.**)

Brian Fawcett defied classification again with *Gender Wars,* exploring the dynamics of sexual politics through fiction and essay. *In the Language of Love* extended Diane Schoemperlen's experiments with form. Steve Weiner's *In the Museum of Love* brought magic realism to the Great Lakes region.

Promising new writers contributed to the year's good crop of fiction. Shyam Selvadurai made an impressive debut with six linked stories about a young man's homosexual awakening amidst political turmoil in Sri Lanka. Russell Smith's *How Insensitive* portrayed the "generation X" of Toronto. In *Division of Surgery,* Donna McFarlane explored medical process and physical pain.

Fine story collections included *Bellydancer,* by young Vancouver writer Sky Lee; *Lives of the Mind Slaves,* by Matt Cohen; *Around the Mountain: Scenes from Montreal Life* by Hugh Hood; and Katherine Govier's *The Immaculate Conception Photography Gallery.* Ann Diamond was praised for *Evil Eye* and Gayla Reid brought an Australian perspective to Canadian life in *To Be There with You.*

Political subjects remained popular in Canadian nonfiction in 1994. Journalist Stevie Cameron brought on a public furor with *On the Take,* an account of corruption in the Progressive Conservative Party during the leadership of recent Prime Minister Brian Mulroney. Christina Newman and Stephen Clarkson released the second volume *Trudeau and Our Time,* a biography of former Prime Minister Pierre Trudeau.

Right Honourable Men, Michael Bliss's popular history of 10 Canadian prime ministers, from Sir John Macdonald to Mulroney, charted Canada's development into a unique North American democracy. *Poisoned Chalice—How the Tories Self-Destructed,* by David McLaughlin, followed the campaign of Canada's first woman prime minister, Kim Campbell, up to her defeat in November 1993.

Analysis of culture also influenced new nonfiction in 1994. Neil Bissoondath took a critical look at Canada's multicultural movement in *Selling Illusions: The Cult of Multiculturalism.* Maggie Siggins reassessed the controversial métis leader Louis Riel in *Riel: A Life of Revolution.* Both Denise Chong's *The Concubine's Children: Portrait of a Family Divided* and Joan Haggerty's *The Invitation: A Memoir of Family Love and Reconciliation* explored family history and culture.

Other nonfiction. Sharon Butala captured the public's imagination with her first nonfiction work, *The Perfection of the Morning,* about her evolving relationship with the natural world on a high-country Albertan farm. John Livingston's *Rogue Primate: An Exploration of Human Domestication* argued that human beings must make room for other species on Earth. *True North,* by feminist historian Jill Conway, continued the story of *The Road from Coorain* (1989). In *Microphone Wars,* Canada's veteran anchorman Knowlton Nash gave an insider's view of the Canadian Broadcasting Corporation.

In *This Year in Jerusalem,* Mordecai Richler compared a recent journey to Israel with a visit 30 years earlier, illuminating his experience as a Jew growing up in Montreal. Journalist Bronwen Drainie offered another reaction to the Holy City and the complexities of the region in *My Jerusalem.*

Biographies. Elspeth Cameron, a well-known editor and writer of author biographies, sparked a scandal in 1994 with *Earle Birney: A Life,* an intimate look at the late poet's life. Judith Skelton Grant chronicled the life of Robertson Davies, and Ezra Schabas filled a gap in Canada's musical history with his biography of Sir Ernest MacMillan, conductor of the Toronto Symphony Orchestra for 25 years.

Poetry. Several of Canada's established poets released new works in 1994. They included Christopher Dewdney's *Demon Pond,* Susan Musgrave's *Forcing the Narcissus,* and Al Purdy's *Naked with Summer in Your Mouth.* Purdy also produced an autobiography, *Reaching for the Beaufort Sea.* Robin Blaser's *The Holy Forest* collected work from a more-than-30-year career. *Cantos from a Small Room* by Robert Hilles chronicled the slow dying of the poet's mother-in-law. Monty Reid's *Dog Sleeps: Irritated Texts* included five prose pieces on identity and escape.

Children's literature. Nick Bantock's *Griffin and Sabine* trilogy, completed in 1993, maintained its popularity in 1994, as did Robert Munsch's phenomenal *Love You Forever* (1986). Jim McGugan's *Josepha: A Prairie Boy's Story* followed an immigrant boy's life in the early 1900's. *The Burning Time,* by Carol Matas, described witch hunts in France. Kit Pearson completed her wartime trilogy with *The Lights Go On Again. Out of the Blue* by Sarah Ellis dealt with the legacy of adoption, and Julie Johnston's *Adam and Eve and Pinch Me* featured a rejected illegitimate child. Michael Coren's *The Man Who Created Narnia: The Story of C. S. Lewis* brought a beloved author to life.

Awards. Winners of the 1994 Governor-General's Literary Award for books in English included Rudy Wiebe for *A Discovery of Strangers* (fiction); Robert Hilles for *Cantos from a Small Room* (poetry); Morris Panych for *The Ends of the Earth* (drama); John Livingston for *Rogue Primate* (nonfiction); Julie Johnston for *Adam and Eve and Pinch Me* (children's literature—text); Murray Kimber for *Josepha: A Prairie Boy's Adventure* (children's literature—illustration); and Donald Winkler for *The Lyric Generation: The Life and Times of the Baby Boomers* (translation).

Winners for French language books were Robert Lalonde for *Le Petite Aigle à tête blanche* (fiction); Fulvio Caccia for *Aknos* (poetry); Michel Ouellette for *French Town* (drama); Chantal Saint-Jarre for *Du sida* (nonfiction); Suzanne Martel for *Une belle journée pour mourir* (children's literature—text); Pierre Pratt for *Mon chien est un éléphant* (children's literature—illustration); and Jude Des Chenes, for *Le mythe du sauvage* (translation).

The 1994 Stephen Leacock Medal for Humour went to Bill Richardson for *Bachelor Brothers Bed and Breakfast.* Deborah Joy Corey won the 1993 Smith Books/Books in Canada First Novel Award for *Losing Eddie.* ☐ Maureen McCallum Garvie

In **World Book,** see **Canadian literature.**

Canadian provinces faced growing financial pressure in 1994. Many provincial governments initiated tough spending cuts to reduce their budget deficits. Several provinces also took advantage of a federal government program offering funds to support improvements in infrastructure.

Alberta. In a televised address on Jan. 17, 1994, Premier Ralph Klein introduced a program of spending cuts designed to balance Alberta's budget by 1997. Klein told Albertans that his Progressive Conservative Party would reduce government spending by 20 percent over the next three years. Funds for the province's three largest programs—education, health care, and social services—would be cut by 16 percent. Other programs would face cuts of up to 30 percent. The budget, released on February 24, showed that Alberta had the highest per capita budget deficit of any Canadian province.

Critics of the spending cuts demanded that the government raise taxes rather than reduce social services. But Klein refused to raise existing taxes or institute a sales tax, which Alberta, unlike the other provinces, does not have. Instead, the budget increased the fees for many goods and services provided by the government. Health care premiums, for example, were projected to rise by about 20 percent over the next three years.

The deficit reduction program was considered most extreme in its approach toward welfare. Klein sought to eliminate "welfare shoppers," who he accused of moving to locations where welfare benefits are the highest. The budget slashed welfare allowances in Alberta to some of the lowest levels in the country, and Klein encouraged recipients to undertake education and skill-training courses.

British Columbia. The management of British Columbia's rich forests remained a crucial issue in the Pacific coastal province's affairs in 1994. Premier Michael Harcourt and the ruling New Democratic Party sought to balance the interests of environmentalists and the logging industry, which accounts for about one of every six jobs in British Columbia.

In February, the government's Commission on Resources and Environment (CORE) released a plan for the use of Vancouver Island's heavily forested land. It recommended that the amount of land protected from logging be raised from 10 to 13 percent of the island. Reports estimated that the plan would reduce logging operations by about 6 percent and would eliminate about 900 jobs.

Despite fierce protests from forestry workers, Harcourt's government accepted most of the CORE recommendations in June and established 23 new parks on Vancouver Island. Harcourt pledged that new jobs in conservation would replace jobs lost in the logging industry. Workers would be trained to plant, prune, and fertilize reforested areas and maintain the forest environment. The program would be financed by new logging fees, expected to raise $2 billion over the next five years.

In July, CORE proposed similar logging restrictions for the Cariboo-Chilcotin region in central British Columbia. The government accepted the recommendations in October, setting aside about 12 percent of the region as parkland and promising forestry jobs for unemployed lumber workers. Both environmentalists and loggers hailed the Cariboo-Chilcotin forestry plan as "a watershed agreement." The government continued its promotion of reforestation and laid down a strict forest practice code that places heavy fines on logging companies convicted of harming the environment.

Manitoba became in 1994 the first province in Canada to abolish tax-free benefits for its legislators. An independent commission determined that a tax-exempt portion of the salaries of legislators should be eliminated after the next provincial election. However, the commission also approved a pay increase for members of the legislature. In the future, members' salaries will be adjusted in relation to changes in the province's average weekly wage.

Manitoba's budget, released on April 20, reflected the government's caution as it heads toward elections to be held no later than early 1995. The budget contained no new taxes and no increase in income, corporate, or sales taxes. A $296-million budget deficit was forecast for fiscal 1994-1995, a substan-

Jacques Parizeau, right, whose Parti Québécois won control of Quebec's government in September elections, greets the press after voting in Montreal.

Police officers guide Nova Scotia Finance Minister Bernie Boudreau to safety after angry construction workers crashed a legislative session in April.

tial improvement over the 1993-1994 budget deficit of $461 million.

New Brunswick. Premier Frank J. McKenna established a new cabinet position in January by appointing engineer George Corriveau New Brunswick's minister for the information highway. The minister will be charged with exploring the possibilities of electronic communications. Corriveau was directed to examine whether the new technology might be applied to improving education and cutting the cost of delivering government services such as Medicare.

The first World Congress of Acadians was held in southeastern New Brunswick for two weeks in August. More than 70,000 Acadians and their descendants gathered to celebrate their survival as a distinct national group. Acadia was the name of a region in eastern Canada that now includes New Brunswick. Settled during the early 1600's, it was the first permanent French colony in North America. The Acadians were expelled from their territory by the British, starting in 1755. In time, many returned to the region. About 340,000 people of Acadian descent now live in Canada's Atlantic provinces.

Newfoundland. The year 1994 brought more bad news for Newfoundland's fishing industry, as scientists reported that fish stocks continued to decline. In spite of a two-year fishing ban, declared in 1992, on cod, haddock, and flatfish, stocks of north-

ern cod in 1994 were estimated to be only 5 percent of what they had been in 1990. Increased harvesting of turbot, pollock, and redfish reduced their numbers to a precarious level in 1994 as well. Factors identified as contributing to the decline were overfishing in the 1980's, gill netting, a dramatic rise in the seal population, and colder Atlantic waters.

The Canadian government introduced a revised federal assistance package on April 19 for the 30,000 people forced out of work by the 1992 fishing ban. About 80 percent of the fisherfolk affected by the package live in Newfoundland. The new plan reduced weekly payments to fisherfolk and plant workers by 6 percent. Individuals receiving aid will be required to upgrade their education in order to take on new jobs. In October, the government initiated a buy-out plan, offering to buy back fishing licenses issued to full-time fisherfolk. The federal government plans to cut the capacity of the Newfoundland fishery by 50 percent over the next five years.

Nova Scotia enacted tough measures to reduce its deficit in 1994. The budget imposed a 3 percent wage cut on public employees who earn more than $25,000 a year. The reduced wages will be frozen for the next three years. Budget cuts in health care will bring about the closing of three hospitals and will scale back services at more than half of the province's other medical institutions. Legislators planned to reduce the deficit from $372 million in 1993-1994 to about $297 million in 1994-1995.

Finance Minister Bernie Boudreau's formal reading of the budget on April 29 was disrupted by angry construction workers protesting a government measure to make traditionally union jobs available to nonunion workers. The protestors stormed into the legislative chambers, forcing officials to suspend the session. Premier John Savage was assaulted but not seriously injured in the incident. In its 235-year history, Nova Scotia's legislature had never before been canceled because of a protest.

The proposed budget cuts brought about other less violent objections from labor groups. Seventeen public service unions threatened a provincewide strike, but the move was voted down by union members. The province's teachers' union also backed down from a strike threat, accepting the wage cuts and pay freeze in return for offers of early retirement to as many as 2,400 teachers.

Ontario. The ruling New Democratic Party, led by Premier Robert K. Rae, sponsored a series of landmark bills that came to a vote in June 1994, during the spring session of the Ontario legislature. The legislature passed a law that prohibits the sale of ammunition to anyone under age 18. The law also demands photo identification for ammunition purchases and requires gun shop owners to keep a register of all ammunition sales. The bill won quick support after a Toronto police officer was fatally shot on June 17.

Legislators also passed one of the toughest tobacco-control measures in North America. The law prohibits tobacco sales to anyone under 19 and forbids smoking on school grounds. It also bans the sale of cigarettes in pharmacies and vending machines.

Rae's government failed, however, to win legislative approval for a controversial bill that would provide homosexual couples with the same rights and obligations as legally married heterosexual couples. Although the government dropped the bill's most controversial clause, which would give homosexual couples the right to adopt a child, it was defeated 68-59 after a bitter debate in the legislature.

On May 5, Finance Minister Floyd Laughren presented the province's budget, which contained no tax increases for the first time in four years. The budget introduced a 12-month exemption from the payroll tax for companies that expand their work force. Companies that invest in research and development are also eligible for a 10 percent tax credit. Laughren estimated a budget deficit of $8.5 billion for fiscal 1994-1995, a 9 percent reduction from the previous year. But some reports described his estimate as overly optimistic and predicted an even greater economic burden in the coming year.

The path to establish a National Basketball Association (NBA) team in Toronto was finally cleared in February, when the Ontario government and the

NBA reached an agreement over sports gambling in the province. The NBA, which granted a franchise to a group of Toronto business people in November 1993, insisted that Ontario withdraw basketball betting from its sports lottery. Ontario officials argued that such a move would cost the province millions of dollars in tax revenues every year. Under the deal, Ontario's government agreed to drop basketball gambling in return for an estimated $12 million in compensation from the NBA over the next five years.

In other sports news, the Ontario government sold the SkyDome, home of major league baseball's champion Toronto Blue Jays, to a group of private investors for $151 million. The 50,000-seat stadium, which features a retractable roof and adjoining hotel, cost about $600 million to build in the mid-1980's.

Prince Edward Island. The provincial budget, released in April, included broad spending cuts intended to reduce Prince Edward Island's budget deficit. One of the budget's most dramatic measures involved the Public Sector Pay Reduction Act, which reduced the wages of civil servants by 7.5 percent. According to the act, workers were allowed to negotiate with the government how the cut would be taken—in salary or in benefits.

An unusual issue related to the act surfaced in September when the province's chief justice ruled that judges of the Provincial Court could not be considered independent if they were subject to the government wage cut. The court determined that "a reasonable person" may perceive the government's action in salary negotiations as influencing the independence of a judge. Prince Edward Island's three Provincial Court judges refused to hear cases for a week in late September, following the chief justice's ruling. They returned to work when the government announced that it would change its regulations to bar Provincial Court judges from negotiating how the pay cut would affect them.

Quebec faced two changes in leadership in 1994, and Quebecers continued to demonstrate their desire for reform in the province's government. On January 11, Daniel Johnson succeeded retiring Robert Bourassa as premier and head of the Liberal Party, which had governed Quebec for nine years. Johnson promised to create new jobs and cut back on government spending. But the new administration was short-lived. In elections held on September 12, the Parti Québécois won the majority of government seats and party leader Jacques Parizeau became premier. The Liberal Party, however, retained more than one-third of the legislative seats—a stronger showing than expected.

The Parti Québécois has promoted Quebec's independence from Canada, while the Liberal Party has remained committed to national unity. However, opinion polls revealed that most Quebecers did not support the new government's separatist policies.

Canadian provinces

Most observers agreed that voters supported the Parti Québécois because they wanted change in their government and believed the Liberal Party had been in power too long.

The Johnson administration presented a budget on May 12 that provided income tax cuts for low- and middle-income earners, who make up 92 percent of the Quebec electorate. The sales tax on goods was lowered from 8 to 6.5 percent but raised on services from 4 to 6.5 percent. Public employee salaries were left untouched, but new spending was limited to a 1.7 percent increase.

Premier Jacques Parizeau made the dramatic announcement on November 18 that the $13-billion Great Whale hydroelectric project in northern Quebec would be canceled. International opposition to the plan, the result of protests by Cree Indians in the region, combined with energy surpluses in North America, damaged the project in the eyes of the new Parti Québécois government.

Quebec and Ontario signed a trade agreement on May 3 eliminating barriers against Ontario residents who wished to work in Quebec. Ontario, which traditionally maintained an open border with Quebec, had threatened to impose restrictions if Quebec's leaders did not agree to negotiate. Under the May 3 accord, the provinces also agreed to allow their public institutions to purchase goods and services from businesses in either province.

Saskatchewan. The New Democratic Party government of Premier Roy Romanow continued in 1994 on its course to balance Saskatchewan's budget by the 1996-1997 fiscal year. Facing a projected deficit of $1.3 billion when it came to power in 1991, the Romanow government had reduced the deficit to $294 million by 1993-1994. In her budget introduction on February 17, Finance Minister Janice MacKinnon predicted that the deficit would fall to about $189 million the following year, making Saskatchewan's deficit reduction program the most successful among the provinces. The new budget included no new taxes, no tax increases, and no major spending cuts. Major spending cuts and tax increases in the previous year's budget received some credit for the province's financial turnaround. MacKinnon also predicted that the province would gain increased revenue from legalized gambling and support from the federal government.

On June 2, legislators passed a bill making Saskatchewan the first province in Canada to require companies with more than 20 employees to pay medical, dental, and life insurance benefits to part-time workers. Benefits will be calculated according to the number of hours worked each week. Health reform remained a priority in Saskatchewan in 1994, as the government pressed ahead with measures to establish a system based on wellness and preventive treatment. □ David M. L. Farr

In *World Book,* see the various province articles.

Canadian territories. In a report released on July 13, 1994, Canada's Royal Commission on Aboriginal Peoples concluded that the federal government showed negligence when it relocated 17 *Inuit* (Eskimo) families to the Northwest Territories, far north of the Arctic Circle, during the 1950's. The government, concerned about a rising population and a declining food supply at the Inuits' traditional home in northern Quebec, moved about 90 Inuit to the barren coast of Ellesmere Island. In later years, critics claimed that the move was intended to assert Canada's sovereignty over the Arctic islands. In its 1994 report, the Royal Commission rejected this criticism but blamed the government of that time for not explaining to the natives why they were being moved. The commission recommended that the federal government offer an apology and pay compensation to the original group's descendants, some of whom still reside on Ellesmere Island.

Indians of the Yukon Territory moved closer to autonomy on June 22, when the Canadian Parliament approved two bills granting them land ownership and limited self-government. Passage of the bills was held up for a time by the western-based Reform Party, which believed the sweeping nature of the measures required further study.

Under the measures, the government will transfer to four native *bands* (groups) in the Yukon part of a 16,000-square-mile (41,439-square-kilometer) region and $242.6 million over the next 15 years. The bands also gained jurisdiction over taxation, justice, hunting practices, and health care. Under a pending bill, the remaining land and similar rights would be granted to the rest of the Yukon native population, which consists of 10 other bands.

Arctic voyage reexamined. New light was shed on one of the great mysteries of Arctic exploration in June 1994, when Canadian anthropologist Anne Keenleyside completed a study of the remains of an expedition begun by Sir John Franklin in 1845. Franklin's party perished without explanation while searching for the Northwest Passage. The remains consisted of 400 bone fragments, found on King William Island in the Northwest Territories. The study revealed that the party suffered from scurvy, arthritis, and lead poisoning from food containers. Knife marks on the bones indicated that members of the crew may have resorted to cannibalism.

Mine to reopen. Anvil Range Mining Corporation of Toronto announced in May a bid to purchase the Faro lead and zinc mine for $27 million. The mine, once the Yukon's largest employer, was shut down in September 1993 after metal prices dropped. Under the agreement, Anvil will be required to fund an environmental cleanup and negotiate an agreement ensuring economic benefits to the Ross River Indian band. □ David M. L. Farr

In *World Book,* see **Northwest Territories; Yukon Territory.**

Cardoso, Fernando Henrique (1931-   ), was elected president of Brazil on Oct. 3, 1994. Cardoso was the leader of Brazil's Social Democratic Party. He succeeded Itamar Franco. His most recent government post was as minister of finance from May 1993 to March 1994. He had also served as Brazil's foreign minister.

Cardoso was born on June 18, 1931, in Rio de Janiero. He earned a degree in sociology from the University of São Paulo and completed graduate studies at the University of Paris. He taught sociology at universities in the United Kingdom, France, Chile, and the United States for much of the 1970's.

Cardoso was arrested by Brazil's military government in 1969 and banned from teaching in Brazil. In response, he formed the Brazilian Analysis and Research Center in São Paulo as a haven for other blacklisted professors. In 1974, right wing terrorists bombed the center.

Cardoso entered the Brazilian Senate in 1983. In 1988, he helped found the Social Democratic Party, and he was the Senate leader of that party when he was elected president.

Brazilians expected Cardoso to continue fighting inflation. As finance minister, he introduced measures that later helped reduce inflation in Brazil from about 45 percent per month to 1.5 percent.

Cardoso is married to anthropologist Ruth Corrêa Leite. They have three children.   □ Mark Dunbar

Census. The number of workers in the United States with full-time jobs whose earnings fell below the poverty line for a family of four increased by 50 percent from 1979 to 1992. That statistic was reported on March 30, 1994, by the U.S. Bureau of the Census, which called the finding "astounding."

The Census Bureau said 18 percent of the full-time work force, or 14.6 million people, had earnings below the poverty line in 1992, compared with 12 percent of all full-time workers in 1979. The report defined the poverty line as less than $13,091 in 1992 dollars, equal to a year of full-time work at a wage of $6.50 an hour. The Census Bureau's figure differs from the official U.S. poverty level for a family of four in 1992—$14,335—because the bureau used a different formula to adjust for inflation.

Analysts attributed the apparent increase in the numbers of "working poor" to the decline in labor unions, rising global competition, and the failure of the U.S. minimum wage to keep pace with inflation.

Overall poverty rate up in 1993. On Oct. 6, 1994, the Census Bureau released poverty figures for all U.S. households in 1993. The statistics showed that 39.3 million Americans were living in poverty, an increase of 1.3 million from 1992. The bureau said 15.1 percent of the population was living below the poverty line in 1993, compared with 14.8 percent in 1992. The bureau was using the official U.S. poverty level for 1993—$14,763 for a family of four.

The bureau said the disparity between the richest and poorest U.S. households reached a record level in 1993. The wealthiest one-fifth of households received 48.2 percent of household income, compared with just 3.6 percent for the poorest fifth.

Americans' net worth declines. In another report, issued on Jan. 25, 1994, the Census Bureau said the net worth of the typical American household fell by 12 percent from 1988 to 1991. The bureau said the decline was caused by a drop in real estate values and the effects of the 1990-1991 recession.

According to the report, the *median* (midpoint) net worth of U.S. households in 1991 was $36,623, down from $41,472 in 1988. Half of the households in the nation had a net worth greater than the median figure, while the other half had a lower net worth. Median net worth for white families was $44,408 in 1991, compared with $4,604 for black households and $5,345 for Hispanic households.

Booming Nevada. In a March 1994 report, the Census Bureau said Nevada was the fastest-growing state from 1990 to 1993, increasing its population by 15.6 percent. Las Vegas, Nev., which grew 13.9 percent in the same period, was the fastest-growing metropolitan area.   □ William J. Eaton

See also **City; Population.** In *World Book,* see **Census; Population.**

Central African Republic. See Africa.
Chad. See Africa.

Chemistry. A new coating material is a loner in the world of materials: Paints, marker inks, dirt, tar, adhesive tape, and even water hold no attraction for it. Chemist Donald L. Schmidt and his colleagues at Dow Chemical Company of Midland, Mich., described the surprising properties of the hard, clear coating in March 1994.

The material, made up of *polymers* (long chains of molecules) that are linked together, forms a nonstick coating on walls and other surfaces. One reason the material is so effective is that it is extraordinarily smooth, denying paints and inks the crevices they lock into. As the coating is applied, the material crowds fluorine groups, the same chemical groups that make Teflon nonstick, along its outer surface.

An obvious application of the new material is to frustrate graffiti artists. Other potential applications include easy-clean coatings for surfaces in bathrooms, kitchens, and operating rooms.

Toxic shock block. In July, medical researcher Roy A. Black and his co-workers at Immunex Research and Development Corporation of Seattle reported a major step toward fighting toxic shock syndrome, blood poisoning caused by staphylococcus and streptococcus bacterial infections. Toxic shock and septic shock, a more general condition, occur when the body releases tumor necrosis factor (TNF) into the bloodstream in large amounts. TNF destroys cells throughout the body, causing bleeding, organ failure, shock, and even death. Each year, 250,000 people in the United States are afflicted with septic shock, and almost half of them die as a result.

Black and his colleagues demonstrated that a hydroxamic acid compound can block the release of TNF into the bloodstream. The compound works by inhibiting an *enzyme* (natural catalyst) that releases TNF from the surface of cells. In tests on mice, 85 percent of treated animals survived bouts with septic shock. Although more animal testing must be done before a decision is made about beginning human trials with the inhibitor, researchers say the compound appears to have potential as an oral medication. The inhibitor may also lead to new drugs for other illnesses associated with high levels of TNF, including arthritis, multiple sclerosis, and asthma.

Chain of successes. Chemists love to make molecules with familiar shapes, including cubes, soccer balls, and even butterflies. Creating the shapes is challenging in itself, and often a molecule with an interesting shape will have equally interesting chemical properties. One long-sought molecular shape is a long chain of freely moving rings, and in June 1994, David B. Amabilino, J. Fraser Stoddart, and their colleagues at the University of Birmingham in England reported a major step toward that goal.

The team synthesized a linear chain of five interlocked rings, which they called *olympiadane* because the molecule resembles the symbol for the Olympic Games. The scientists created the compound in large enough quantities to isolate and analyze. The synthesis of a ring chain was once considered almost impossible, but the new work has encouraged chemists to predict that long chains of rings will be created before the end of the decade.

Outdoing the yew. The race to synthesize taxol ended in a photo finish in 1994, but the real winners may be cancer patients. In February, two groups of chemists announced that they had successfully formulated taxol, a drug being used to treat ovarian and certain other cancers. Taxol was isolated from the bark of the Pacific yew tree in the 1960's. Since the 1970's, chemists have been trying to create the complex molecule in the lab.

The two groups pursued different strategies for the synthesis. Robert A. Holton and his colleagues at Florida State University in Tallahassee started with a ring of camphor and built the taxol molecule upon it. A group of scientists at Scripps Research Institute in La Jolla, Calif., and the University of California, San Diego, approached the problem differently. This group, led by Kyriacou C. Nicolaou, created two distinct, ring-shaped molecules that ultimately were joined and manipulated to form taxol.

Because the amount of taxol that can be produced by these methods is very small, the most practical source of taxol is still the yew tree. But not enough taxol can be extracted from the yew to meet the amounts needed for drugs. To make up the shortfall, the Florida scientists had created an effective method for the partial synthesis of taxol, starting with a similar compound isolated from the yew's needles and twigs. The complete syntheses, however, give scientists the ability to create compounds similar to taxol. Those derivatives are likely to help scientists gain a better understanding of how taxol works, and these compounds may be more effective or less toxic.

Catching rays. Solar energy is free and nonpolluting, but gathering it cheaply has been a problem. A promising solution, thin-film solar technology, was announced in January 1994 by materials scientist Subhendu Guha of United Solar Systems Corporation of Troy, Mich. Guha's work culminated a three-year project sponsored by United Solar Systems and the United States Department of Energy.

In the new approach, three layers of silicon alloy are applied to stainless steel to create a panel that captures energy from blue, green, and infrared wavelengths of light. The result is a thin-film technology with better than 10 percent efficiency—a new record for a thin-film solar panel. Solar energy currently costs 25 to 50 cents per kilowatt-hour, but the new method should cost 16, and eventually as little as 12, cents per kilowatt-hour. United Solar planned to manufacture solar panels using the new technology as early as 1995.   □ Peter J. Andrews

In *World Book*, see **Chemistry**.

Chess. For the first time, a computer defeated a reigning world chess champion in a tournament game. *Chess Genius*, a software program running on a computer with an Intel Pentium chip, beat Professional Chess Association (PCA) world champion Garry Kasparov of Russia in London on Aug. 31, 1994.

The world championship remained split in 1994. Anatoly Karpov of Russia reigned as world champion of the International Chess Federation (FIDE). Kasparov, widely regarded as the strongest player in the world, held the crown of the PCA. Kasparov helped found the PCA in 1993 while he was FIDE world champion, forfeiting the FIDE title. In 1994, the rival groups held elimination matches to determine who would play for their titles in 1995.

FIDE qualifiers. In January, 12 contenders played in Wijk ann Zee, the Netherlands, to qualify for the quarterfinals later held in Nagar, India. From the quarterfinals three semifinalists emerged: Gata Kamsky of the United States, Valery Salov of Russia, and Boris Gelfand of Belarus. In February 1995, Karpov will play Salov and Kamsky will play Gelfand. The winner of each match will play for the FIDE world crown.

PCA qualifiers. In June, eight PCA quarterfinalists played knockout matches in New York City. The surviving four were paired in such matches in Linares, Spain. The victorious players, Kamsky and In-

Seventeen mammoth bronze sculptures by Colombian artist Fernando Botero were on display in Chicago's Grant Park during summer 1994.

dia's Viswanathan Anand, will meet to determine who will play Kasparov for the title.

Tournaments. On May 1, six-time U.S. champion Walter Browne of Berkeley, Calif., won the National Open in Las Vegas, Nev. On July 4, Artashes Minasian of Armenia won the World Open in Philadelphia. On August 5, Elena Donaldson of Federal Way, Wash., won the U.S. Women's Championship in Blooming-ton, Ill. On August 19, Georgi Orlov of Federal Way, Wash., won the U.S. Open in Chicago. On November 25, Boris Gulko of Fairlawn, N.J., won the U.S. Inter-play Invitational Championship held in Key West, Fla. In the Chess Olympiad in Moscow from Novem-ber 30 to December 18, Russia I won the gold, Bosnia won the silver, and Russia II won the bronze.

School players. The 1994 U.S. Chessathon, held on June 11 in New York City's Grand Central Station, matched more than 2,000 youngsters against the world's top players. The event drew a record 400,000 spectators. On May 6, New York City's Hunter School won the National Elementary School Championship in San Jose, Calif. On April 17, Dalton School of New York City won the National Junior High School Championship for the fifth time in Rye Brook, N.Y. On May 1, Edward R. Murrow High School of New York City won its third consec-utive national high school championship in Dear-born, Mich. □ Al Lawrence

In *World Book,* see **Chess.**

Chicago. Crime was a major concern in Chicago in 1994 as drive-by shootings and gang warfare escalat-ed. By December 12, when 881 homicides had been recorded, it appeared that the murder total for the year would approach the record of 970, set in 1974.

One of the most disturbing cases in 1994 involved an 11-year-old boy, Robert Sandifer, Jr. In late Au-gust, the police were searching for Sandifer, who be-longed to a local gang, in connection with the fatal shooting of a 14-year-old girl and the wounding of a rival gang member in two incidents in a far South Side neighborhood. But before the boy could be captured, he was killed. His body was found shortly after midnight on September 1 in a pedestrian un-derpass. Investigators said Sandifer had been shot in the back of the head, execution-style. Two fellow gang members were charged with the slaying.

In another chilling incident, a 5-year-old boy was dropped to his death from the 14th floor of a high-rise by two older boys on October 13. The child was killed for refusing to steal candy for the other boys.

Despite an overall decline in the number of vio-lent crimes, Chicago remained one of the most dan-gerous cities in the nation. Figures released in May 1994 by the Federal Bureau of Investigation showed that, based on 1993 data, Chicago ranked fifth in vi-olent crime. The only American cities with higher rates of violent crime were Atlanta, Ga.; Miami, Fla.; St. Louis, Mo.; and Baltimore.

Chicago gets next Democratic convention.
On August 4, Democratic Party officials announced
that the party would hold its 1996 national convention in Chicago. The site of the convention will be
the new United Center arena near downtown.

The announcement came 26 years after the disastrous 1968 Democratic National Convention in Chicago. During that convention, which nominated Vice
President Hubert Humphrey as the party's presidential candidate, the Chicago police and youthful demonstrators against the Vietnam War clashed in the
city's Grant Park, besmirching the image of the city
and the Democrats. Since then, both major parties
had avoided Chicago as a convention site.

The economy revives. After two years of being
mired in an economic recession, the economy of the
Chicago metropolitan region was on the rebound in
1994. An Illinois state report issued in February indicated that the region had added more than 41,000
jobs in 1993. That increase amounted to a modest
1.4 percent, but it was a sharp turnabout from 1991
and 1992, when the metropolitan area lost a total of
more than 77,000 jobs. Although all of the job gains
in 1993 were in the suburbs, the chronic job losses in
the city itself appeared to be slowing down.

Trouble for Chicago congressmen. United
States Representative Dan Rostenkowski, a Democrat from the Northwest Side of Chicago, was indicted on May 31 on charges of corruption in office.
Rostenkowski denied any wrongdoing and said he
would fight the charges in court. Meanwhile, he was
forced to step down as chairman of the powerful
House Ways and Means Committee. And on November 8, he was defeated for reelection by Republican Michael P. Flanagan, a political newcomer.

Rostenkowski was accused of misusing more than
$600,000 in federal funds over a 20-year period and
of trying to obstruct an investigation into his conduct. A key charge was that the congressman illegally received about $50,000 in cash from the House of
Representatives Post Office in exchange for stamp
vouchers given to lawmakers to reimburse them for
official mailings. He was also accused of hiring at
least 14 "ghost payrollers"—people who were paid
from government funds but who did no work except
personal errands and services for Rostenkowski.

On August 19, Illinois state prosecutors made
public the indictment of Representative Mel Reynolds, a first-term Democrat from Chicago's South
Side, on 20 charges, including statutory rape and solicitation of child pornography. Reynolds was accused of having begun a sexual relationship with a
16-year-old girl during his 1992 election campaign
and also of asking the girl to provide him with
"lewd photographs" of a 15-year-old friend of hers.
Reynolds, who is black, claimed the charges were
racially motivated.   □ Patrick T. Reardon

See also **City.** In *World Book,* see **Chicago.**
Children's books. See **Literature for children.**

Chile. Eduardo Frei Ruíz-Tagle of the center-left
Coalition for Democracy was sworn in to a six-year
term as president on March 11, 1994. Frei, the son of
a former Chilean president, promised to fight poverty and double the nation's economic output.

Frei vowed to continue the free-market economic
policies that have given the country one of the highest rates of economic growth in Latin America. Frei
also pledged to honor the provision of the 1980
Constitution that permits Chile's top military commander and former dictator, General Augusto Pino-
chet Ugarte, to stay in his post until 1997. But Frei
said that elected authorities would exercise ultimate
power in his administration.

Chile to join NAFTA. In a widely anticipated
move, the United States, Canada, and Mexico on
Dec. 11, 1994, invited Chile to join the North American Free Trade Agreement (NAFTA). The pact would
eliminate tariffs on trade between Chile and the
other three NAFTA members.

Human rights. On March 31, a civilian judge
sentenced nine military policemen to long jail terms
for their involvement in the 1985 slayings of three
Communists. Three defendants received life sentences. It was only the second time that members of
Chile's military had been tried and sentenced for human rights violations.   □ Nathan A. Haverstock

See also **Latin America** (Facts in brief table). In
World Book, see **Chile.**

China. The ruling Communist Party made minor
leadership changes in 1994 as it anticipated the
death of Deng Xiaoping, China's dominant leader
since 1978. Deng turned 90 on Aug. 22, 1994, and
other aging Communists opposed to his policies
seemed poised to challenge his political legacy.
Deng had ended the disruptive political campaigns
of the late Mao Zedong and modified Mao's rigid
Marxist ideas by decentralizing economic decisions.
Deng had introduced "socialism with Chinese characteristics," which had created an economic boom
and raised living standards for most of China's 1.2
billion people. But economic growth was uneven in
1994, and inflation was rampant, intensifying the
public's uneasiness over the future.

Deng's health was a subject of constant speculation. His relatives repeatedly described him as being
alert and active. But unofficial reports said he was
extremely feeble and nearly blind. Deng made a rare
public appearance on February 9, when he was televised in Shanghai having difficulty walking. He
missed the customary gathering of Communist leaders at a resort in August, as well as the Communist
regime's 45th anniversary celebrations in Beijing, the
capital, on October 1. Nevertheless, Deng still guided
government policy through a daughter. The officially controlled media praised him, and the people
were urged to study his old speeches.

Chen Yun, 89 years old, and Peng Zhen, 92, both

China's aging leader, Deng Xiaoping, accompanied by his nurses, makes a
rare public appearance during a walk in a Shanghai park in February.

survivors from the party's rise to power, had the authority to replace Deng's followers with more conservative figures. Observers thought that their first
target after Deng's death probably would be Jiang
Zemin. Jiang, 68, a Soviet-trained electrical engineer,
had come up through the Shanghai party organization. After assuming leadership of the national party
and becoming chairman of the powerful Central Military Commission, he also became president of China
in 1993.

At a meeting in September 1994, the Communist
Party's Central Committee promoted Jiang's two
protégés from Shanghai to party positions at the national level. Wu Bangguo gave up the job of Shanghai party boss to become a national party secretary,
and Huang Ju was promoted to the Politburo. This
meant that 7 of the Politburo's 21 members had
strong ties to Shanghai.

Although these promotions added reformers
to the party's national leadership, the September
meeting also recognized concerns of the old-guard
conservatives, namely lax discipline and a worsening
party image due to growing corruption. Members
called for improvements in these areas, but earlier
anticorruption drives had achieved little.

Social upheaval. Premier Li Peng warned of
the danger of public disorder stemming from corruption and pockets of poverty amid China's economic boom. On March 10, Li told China's parlia-

ment, the National People's Congress (NPC), of a
need to fight "money-worship, ultraindividualism,
and decadent life styles."

A book of uncertain authorship, which circulated
during the summer before being banned, blamed
Deng's reforms for upsetting the social order. His reforms had released rural workers from bondage to
Communist-run farms. The workers who stayed on
the farms boosted farm productivity, only to have local officials buy farm produce with bogus promises
for future payment. And displaced rural workers—
an estimated 100 million to 150 million people—
moved about the country seeking jobs. In booming
cities along the east coast, they turned into a volatile
underclass. Moreover, with so many people seeking
jobs, private entrepreneurs could keep wages low
without fear of losing workers.

China's Academy of Social Sciences said the country needed to create 17 million or 18 million new
jobs a year. It called for small-town development
programs because of overcrowding in cities. Beijing
tried to limit new residents there by imposing a residence fee equivalent to $11,600. The NPC was told
that nearly 750,000 Chinese had gone abroad illegally to seek jobs, with some 200,000 living illegally in
the United States.

Crime. Many Chinese reportedly regarded the
police as corrupt and ineffectual at combating crime.
Released from old Communist orders to deny any so-

Troops heavily guard Beijing's Tiananmen Square in June to prevent any observances of the fifth anniversary of prodemocracy protests there.

cial ills, the media reported a rising crime problem in China. Two cases attracted special attention in 1994. First, on March 31, tourists from Taiwan taking a scenic boat ride on Qiandao Lake in eastern Zhejiang Province were robbed by bandits, who then burned the boat, killing all 32 people aboard. After Taiwan accused China of trying to cover up the crime, Chinese authorities caught and in June executed three men who, officials said, admitted to committing the crime. The second case occurred on September 20, when an army lieutenant, angry over being disciplined and expelled from the army, fired his automatic rifle into a bus and several cars in downtown Beijing. Before police shot him dead, he killed 8 people, including 2 foreigners, and 22 others died later.

Inflation rages. Officials reintroduced price controls on basic foods in July as part of an economic stabilization program. They feared that rising prices would produce even greater public unrest. But late in 1994, inflation topped 27 percent in big cities, and the price of basic grains rose more than 60 percent in a year.

Living standards fell as a result of high inflation, and inflation was fed by official subsidies. About half the 100,000 government-owned businesses, which included most heavy industries essential to the economy, operated at a loss, mainly because they employed too many workers. While recognizing the need to quit helping failing enterprises, officials were unwilling to allow these businesses to shrink their payrolls. They feared fired workers would riot. But trouble festered anyway because many workers were not paid regularly.

Stuck halfway between a Communist economy and a free enterprise system, China continued on its path to greater wealth in 1994. Officials expected the economy to grow by 11.5 percent for the year and overall inflation to average 19.5 percent.

Hong Kong played a key role in the Chinese economy as China's 1997 take-over of the British colony neared. But Beijing and London continued to disagree. China opposed Hong Kong's first fully democratic elections, held Sept. 18, 1994, for district boards. Beijing rejected the idea of elected government, which did not exist in China, and promised to abolish the boards after it took over. Meanwhile, China's supporters in Hong Kong contested the election results. They won only 66 board seats, while their democratic opponents won 104 seats, and independents and others took 169 seats.

Human rights talks between China and the United States halted in March. Nevertheless, on May 26, U.S. President Bill Clinton renewed China's most-favored-nation status, a status that allowed China to pay relatively low tariff rates on exports to the United States. In 1993, Clinton had extended China's status only on the condition that political freedoms and human rights improve within a year, but they did not. Clinton said that the United States would no longer link human rights issues with trade in future decisions on China's trading status.

Within hours of Clinton's decision, China arrested three leading Chinese advocates of democratic reforms. China also broke off talks with the International Committee of the Red Cross regarding opening Chinese prisons to Red Cross inspections. An international human rights group, known as Asia Watch, reported on August 28 that China was transplanting organs from condemned prisoners without their permission to foreigners who paid for the organs. On August 30, during his trip to China, U.S. Commerce Secretary Ronald H. Brown announced human rights talks between the two nations would resume in September.

Military affairs. The United States agreed on October 4 to remove a 1993 ban on the export of high-technology satellite systems to China in return for Beijing's promise to begin observing international restrictions on providing other countries with surface-to-surface missiles. On October 18, U.S. Defense Secretary William Perry said in Beijing that the two nations would increase military consultations.

Russia and China agreed on September 3 not to aim nuclear missiles at each other. However, China continued to defy international pressure to adhere to a nuclear test ban moratorium. China tested nuclear weapons on June 10 and October 7, saying it was testing the reliability of warheads designed in the 1980's and would finish tests by 1996.

Meanwhile, China's armed forces earned money in 1994 by selling weapons to other countries. Some profits were plowed back into expansion of the military's civilian industrial activities, but defense spending also rose rapidly. Officials explained to worried neighboring countries that the increased spending was needed to make up for years of neglect.

Chinese gunboats periodically stole the cargo from ships they captured in international waters. Navy personnel also smuggled stolen cars into China.

In Tibet and Xinjiang province of western China, unrest continued. Responding to U.S. inquiries, Beijing conceded in June that 56 Tibetans had been imprisoned in the first eight months of 1993, implying that they were political prisoners. In August 1994, China announced jail terms of up to 15 years for five Tibetans who had put up posters calling for independence and had smashed a Communist Party symbol. In Xinjiang, Muslims seeking independence bombed a bridge in June and distributed leaflets for their cause.

Natural disasters. Floods killed some 3,000 people and affected more than 65 million people in six southern and eastern provinces in June and in the northeast in July. Drought hit the central provinces, and a typhoon killed at least 710 people around Wenzhou on August 20 and 21. □ Henry S. Bradsher

See also **Asia** (Facts in brief table); **Taiwan.** In *World Book*, see **China.**

Chrétien, Jean (1934-). Sworn in as Canada's 20th prime minister on Nov. 4, 1993, Jean Chrétien enjoyed wide personal popularity during 1994, his first full year in office. With 66 percent of Canadians approving Chrétien's handling of his job, the prime minister's personal standing ran ahead of the Liberal Party he headed. Chrétien's frugal approach to public business included obtaining furniture for his official residence at government warehouses.

Chrétien remained on the sidelines during provincial elections in Quebec in September, which were swept by the separatist Parti Québécois. He was convinced that the Parti Québécois could not win a referendum on Quebec's independence from Canada, which is expected in 1995. He also refused to put forward new initiatives for changing the Constitution, believing that Canadians had tired of such proposals. Instead, Chrétien favored incremental administrative changes as a way to improve federalism.

Chrétien spent 1994 seeking Canadian views on how to change policies regarding unemployment assistance and health care. He also prepared for 1995, when he would have to reduce the deficit and face the issue of Quebec sovereignty. □ David M. L. Farr

See also **Canada.** In *World Book*, see **Chrétien, Jean.**

Churches. See Eastern Orthodox Churches; Islam; Judaism; Protestantism; Religion; Roman Catholic Church.

City. Fresh ideas and a surge of energy helped to generate a renewed confidence in 1994 that the cities of the United States could begin to make progress against stubborn problems. At the same time, America's urban centers remained gripped by the fear of crime.

The spirit and the challenges facing cities were dramatized by two monuments, one permanent and the other temporary, unveiled within weeks of each other in New York City and Washington, D.C. One of those monuments was a statue honoring one of the most beloved mayors of New York City, Fiorello La Guardia. The statue of a striding, buoyant, hand-clapping La Guardia captured the energy and humanity he brought to the city while serving as mayor from 1934 to 1945.

A new array of city leaders in 1994 were emulating La Guardia's devotion to improving urban life. Mayor Edward G. Rendell of Philadelphia, for example, was praised by many urban experts for showing the same vigorous and innovative approach to problem solving. Rendell's accomplishments included ending several years of budget deficits, improving relations between the city government and state and local political leaders, and drawing up a "New Urban Agenda" that called for federal policies and local actions that could strengthen cities.

The other "monument," a collection of nearly 40,000 pairs of shoes assembled near the Capitol in Washington, D.C., in September, provided a graphic reminder of the greatest challenges facing city leaders today: crime and violence. The shoes had been gathered from the families or friends of victims of gun violence. The personal reminders of those victims formed a powerful image capturing the appalling impact of crime and violence on U.S. cities.

Concern about crime was the top local issue among city dwellers in 1994, according to the annual opinion survey of municipal leaders by the National League of Cities, a Washington, D.C.-based organization representing U.S. cities. Urban leaders pressed hard in 1994 for passage of a comprehensive federal anticrime bill, and such a bill was enacted by Congress in August.

One factor fueling public anxiety over crime was the extreme youth of many criminals and their victims. In one episode that made national headlines, an 11-year-old Chicago boy was found shot to death, allegedly by fellow gang members, on September 1, just four days after he had shot and killed a 14-year-old girl, apparently while aiming at another youth. In another incident in Chicago, a 5-year-old boy was dropped to his death from a 14th-floor window on October 13 by two older boys when he refused to steal candy for them. (See also **Chicago.**)

Both those tragic events occurred in public-housing projects, which have been widely condemned for trapping people in hopeless conditions that foster

Chicago Mayor Richard M. Daley, hosting the U.S. Conference of Mayors in August, blasts Congress for failing to pass a crime bill. The legislation was later approved.

50 largest cities in the United States

Rank	City	Population*	Percent change in population since 1990	Unemployment rate†	Mayor‡
1.	New York City	7,311,966	-0.1	8.3%	Rudolph W. Giuliani (R, 1/98)
2.	Los Angeles	3,489,779	+0.1	10.0	Richard J. Riordan (R, 6/97)
3.	Chicago	2,768,483	-0.5	5.6	Richard M. Daley (D, 4/95)
4.	Houston	1,690,180	+3.7	6.9	Bob Lanier (NP, 12/95)
5.	Philadelphia	1,552,572	-2.1	6.5	Edward G. Rendell (D, 1/96)
6.	San Diego	1,148,851	+3.4	8.3	Susan Golding (NP, 12/96)
7.	Dallas	1,022,497	+1.6	5.6	Steve Bartlett (NP, 5/95)
8.	Phoenix	1,012,230	+2.9	4.9	Skip Rimsza (NP, 1/96)
9.	Detroit	1,012,110	-1.5	6.8	Dennis Archer (D, 1/98)
10.	San Antonio	966,437	+3.3	5.6	Nelson W. Wolff (D, 6/95)
11.	San Jose	801,331	+2.4	7.1	Susan Hammer (NP, 12/98)
12.	Indianapolis	746,538	+2.1	4.4	Stephen Goldsmith (R, 12/95)
13.	San Francisco	728,921	+0.7	6.5	Frank M. Jordan (D, 1/96)
14.	Baltimore	726,096	-1.3	6.3	Kurt L. Schmoke (D, 12/95)
15.	Jacksonville, Fla.	661,177	+4.1	5.1	T. Ed Austin (D, 7/95)
16.	Columbus, Ohio	642,987	+1.6	4.1	Gregory S. Lashutka (R, 1/96)
17.	Milwaukee	617,043	-1.8	4.5	John O. Norquist (D, 4/96)
18.	Memphis	610,275	0.0	4.4	W. W. Herenton (D, 12/95)
19.	Washington, D.C.	585,221	-3.6	4.2	Marion S. Barry, Jr. (D, 1/99)
20.	Boston	551,675	-3.9	5.3	Thomas M. Menino (D, 1/97)
21.	El Paso	543,813	+5.5	10.4	Larry Francis (NP, 5/95)
22.	Seattle	519,598	+0.6	5.0	Norman B. Rice (NP, 12/97)
23.	Cleveland	502,539	-0.6	5.9	Michael R. White (D, 12/97)
24.	Nashville	495,012	+1.4	3.1	Philip Bredesen (D, 9/95)
25.	Austin	492,329	+5.7	3.9	Bruce Todd (NP, 6/97)
26.	New Orleans, La.	489,595	-1.5	7.6	Marc Morial (D, 5/98)
27.	Denver, Colo.	483,852	+3.5	4.2	Wellington E. Webb (D, 6/95)
28.	Fort Worth, Tex.	454,430	+1.5	5.8	Kay Granger (NP, 5/95)
29.	Oklahoma City, Okla.	453,995	+2.1	4.4	Ronald J. Norick (NP, 4/98)
30.	Portland, Ore.	445,458	+1.9	4.2	Vera Katz (NP, 12/96)
31.	Long Beach, Calif.	438,771	+2.2	10.0	Beverly O'Neill (D, 6/98)
32.	Kansas City, Mo.	431,553	-0.8	4.5	Emanuel Cleaver II (D, 4/95)
33.	Virginia Beach, Va.	417,061	+6.1	5.7	Meyera E. Oberndorf (NP, 6/96)
34.	Charlotte, N.C.	416,294	+5.1	4.2	Richard Vinroot (R, 11/95)
35.	Tucson, Ariz.	415,079	+2.4	4.5	George Miller (D, 12/95)
36.	Albuquerque, N. Mex.	398,492	+3.6	4.7	Martin J. Chavez (D, 11/97)
37.	Atlanta, Ga.	394,848	+0.2	4.9	Bill Campbell (D, 1/98)
38.	St. Louis, Mo.	383,733	-3.3	4.7	Freeman R. Bosley, Jr. (D, 4/97)
39.	Sacramento, Calif.	382,816	+3.6	7.9	Joe Serna, Jr. (D, 11/96)
40.	Fresno, Calif.	376,130	+6.2	13.1	Jim Patterson (NP, 3/97)
41.	Tulsa, Okla.	375,307	+2.2	5.5	M. Susan Savage (D, 5/98)
42.	Oakland, Calif.	373,219	+0.3	7.3	Elihu Mason Harris (NP, 12/98)
43.	Honolulu, Hawaii	371,320	+1.7	4.7	Jeremy Harris (D, 1/97)
44.	Miami, Fla.	367,016	+2.4	7.9	Stephen P. Clark (D, 11/97)
45.	Pittsburgh, Pa.	366,852	-0.8	6.6	Thomas Murphy (D, 12/97)
46.	Cincinnati, Ohio	364,278	+0.1	4.8	Roxanne Qualls (D, 11/95)
47.	Minneapolis, Minn.	362,696	-1.5	2.7	Sharon Sayles Belton (D, 12/97)
48.	Omaha, Nebr.	339,671	+1.2	2.9	Subby Anzaldo (D, 12/94)
49.	Toledo, Ohio	329,325	-1.1	5.8	Carlton Finkbeiner (D, 12/97)
50.	Buffalo, N.Y.	323,284	-1.5	6.3	Anthony Masiello (D, 12/97)

*1992 estimates (source: U.S. Bureau of the Census).
†July 1994 unemployment figures are for metropolitan areas (source: U.S. Bureau of Labor Statistics).
‡The letters in parentheses represent the mayor's party, with *D* meaning Democrat, *R* Republican, *I* Independent, and *NP* nonpartisan. The date is when the term of office ends (source: mayors' offices).

crime. In April, the Carnegie Corporation of New York, a philanthropic organization in New York City, issued a report on the distressing conditions confronting many children in America. The study found that one-quarter of the infants and young children in the United States live in poverty. Most of that group live in cities, often in deteriorating and unsafe public housing.

In March, Newark, N.J., followed a course of action taken by a number of other communities when it demolished an abandoned high-rise project. But in San Francisco, a study showed that strict controls can restore safety to troubled projects. In June 1991, the U.S. Department of Housing and Urban Development (HUD) took control of a crime-infested housing development and turned it over to a private contractor. The new managers installed fences and strict security at entrances and hired a full-time security staff with authority to conduct weapons searches. The strategy virtually eliminated crime from the 576-unit complex. Still, the city, with HUD's approval, was planning in late 1994 to tear down the complex and replace it with low-income town houses.

Other communities were developing other strategies to deal with crime. Dozens of cities and towns, including Hartford, Conn., and Baltimore, enacted curfew ordinances in an effort to get young people off the streets and away from criminal activity. Some cities, including Fort Worth, Tex., and San Diego, organized and trained volunteer citizen patrols to monitor neighborhoods and alert the police to any suspicious activity. (See **Crime: Fighting Crime in America.**)

Violence in the schools. Crime and violence in schools also continued to be a serious problem in 1994. A survey of 700 cities and towns by the National League of Cities, reported in November, found that school violence and gangs and efforts to deal with those problems had become a growing concern nationwide during the previous five years. Most of the communities included in the survey were suburbs, rural towns, and small cities. Although school violence has long plagued schools in large central cities, by the 1990's it had become a growing problem in cities of all sizes and types.

Thirty-eight percent of the communities reported that violence in their school districts had increased noticeably during that time, and nearly 40 percent said student or neighborhood gangs were a significant factor in school violence. Only 6 percent of the communities said the problem had decreased, and 11 percent said school violence was not a problem for them.

Some communities have tried to deal with the situation by assigning police officers to patrol duty in the schools. Seventy percent of the communities in the survey said they had taken such action. Twenty percent of the cities said metal detectors were used regularly at some local schools. More than half of

that group had begun the use of metal detectors within the previous two years, and nearly 90 percent had adopted the policy within the past five years.

Other school policies. In an effort to keep children in school as well as to keep them safe, some cities were taking steps to prevent truancy. Judges in Hamilton, Ohio, and Abilene, Tex., for example, regularly scheduled court sessions to deal with truancy, often requiring parents or guardians to post a bond of $100, which would be returned if the child's attendance at school was maintained. In Los Angeles, the juvenile department of the city's district attorney's office developed procedures to ensure school attendance that were used with nearly 2,000 chronically truant students and their families.

Cities also continued to experiment with privately operated schools and community-based alternatives to public education. Hartford turned the operation of all its 32 public schools over to a private firm, Education Alternatives, Incorporated, which was also operating nine schools in Baltimore. Another enterprise, the Edison Project, was running six schools in Kansas and was selected as one of 13 groups to operate 15 schools in Massachusetts.

The charter school movement also gained momentum in 1994. This system, begun in Minnesota in 1991, allows community groups or other organizations to apply for a city charter to operate a public school. The charter groups have more flexibility in teacher standards, duties, and pay but must meet specific educational goals. (See also **Education.**)

Seeking new revenue sources. Faced with tight budgets and taxpayer anger, many cities were experimenting with new ways of raising money in 1994. In Michigan, voters overwhelmingly approved a tax reform plan in March to substitute a statewide sales tax and a cigarette tax in place of local property taxes to support schools. The plan was designed to equalize funding for all schools and to relieve the burden of local property taxes.

In many communities in Alabama, California, and Texas, prosecutors were helping business owners collect on bad checks and unpaid bills. The fees for the service were comparable to those charged by private collection agencies. South Orange, N.J., put itself into the credit card business by sponsoring a South Orange bank credit card and marketing it to the 17,500 residents of the city. A portion of the transaction fee for each sale goes to the city.

Census debate. The long-running controversy over the 1990 census and its effect on cities was reopened in 1994. In August, a federal appeals court in New York City ruled that the federal government must give a good reason for certifying population counts for various cities that were known to have undercounted populations. Whether and how adjustments would be made to those inaccurate censuses remained unresolved at year-end. This was a vital issue for cities because much federal funding for

50 largest cities in the world

Rank	Urban center	Population
1.	Tokyo-Yokohama, Japan	28,447,000
2.	Mexico City, Mexico	23,913,000
3.	São Paulo, Brazil	21,539,000
4.	Seoul, South Korea	19,065,000
5.	New York City, U.S.	14,638,000
6.	Osaka-Kobe-Kyoto, Japan	14,060,000
7.	Bombay, India	13,532,000
8.	Calcutta, India	12,885,000
9.	Rio de Janeiro, Brazil	12,786,000
10.	Buenos Aires, Argentina	12,232,000
11.	Teheran, Iran	11,681,000
12	Manila, Philippines	11,342,000
13.	Cairo, Egypt	11,155,000
14.	Jakarta, Indonesia	11,151,000
15.	Moscow, Russia	10,769,000
16.	Los Angeles, U.S.	10,414,000
17.	Delhi, India	10,105,000
18.	Lagos, Nigeria	9,799,000
19.	Karachi, Pakistan	9,350,000
20.	London, U.K.	8,897,000
21.	Paris, France	8,764,000
22.	Lima, Peru	7,853,000
23.	Istanbul, Turkey	7,624,000
24.	Taipei, Taiwan	7,477,000
25.	Essen, Germany	7,364,000
26.	Shanghai, China	7,194,000
27.	Bogotá, Colombia	6,801,000
28.	Bangkok, Thailand	6,657,000
29.	Madras, India	6,550,000
30.	Chicago, U.S.	6,541,000
31.	Beijing, China	5,865,000
32.	Hong Kong	5,841,000
33.	Santiago, Chile	5,812,000
34.	Pusan, South Korea	5,748,000
35.	Bangalore, India	5,644,000
36.	Dhaka, Bangladesh	5,296,000
37.	Tianjin, China	5,041,000
38.	Nagoya, Japan	5,017,000
39.	Lahore, Pakistan	4,986,000
40.	Milan, Italy	4,795,000
41.	Madrid, Spain	4,772,000
42.	St. Petersburg, Russia	4,694,000
43.	Baghdad, Iraq	4,566,000
44.	Kinshasa, Zaire	4,520,000
45.	Barcelona, Spain	4,492,000
46.	Shenyang, China	4,457,000
47.	Belo Horizonte, Brazil	4,373,000
48.	Ahmadabad, India	4,200,000
49.	Hyderabad, India	4,149,000
50.	San Francisco Bay Area, U.S.	4,104,000

*An urban center is a continuous built-up area, similar to a metropolitan area, having a population density of at least 5,000 persons per square mile (1,900 per square kilometer). Source: 1995 estimates from the U.S. Bureau of the Census.

urban programs is based on census figures. In May, the U.S. Bureau of the Census announced that it was developing new techniques and strategies for the next census, in the year 2000, to get a more accurate population count.

Telecommuting. A growing trend toward *telecommuting* in 1994 offered the possibility that commuter rush hours and automobile-choked city streets may someday be just a memory. Telecommuting is the use of computers and telephone lines to work at a remote location while staying in communication with a central office. Already in 1994, a growing number of Americans were choosing to work on their own as independent contract workers, and the downtown offices of many companies had shrunk as employees spent more time working at home or in other locations.

Nature's fury. On January 17, Los Angeles was struck by a major earthquake. The quake caused 57 deaths and at least 7,000 injuries and caused serious damage to several expressway overpasses and thousands of other structures. (See also **Los Angeles**.)

Also in January, cities on the East Coast endured some of the worst storms in decades. Record-low temperatures paralyzed a four-state area around Washington, D.C., causing D.C. businesses and the federal government to shut down for a full day on January 20 to conserve energy.   □ Randolph C. Arndt

In *World Book,* see **City**.

Civil rights. The National Association for the Advancement of Colored People (NAACP), founded in 1909 to end discrimination against African Americans, fired its executive director of 16 months, Benjamin F. Chavis, Jr., on Aug. 20, 1994. The group's board of directors decided at a special meeting in Baltimore to fire Chavis after learning that he had agreed to pay a former assistant $332,400 out of NAACP funds in an out-of-court settlement. The assistant, Mary E. Stansel, had threatened to sue Chavis for sexual harassment and sex discrimination after he had fired her. The settlement became public when Stansel sued Chavis for breach of contract on June 30, claiming he broke the agreement after paying her only $82,400.

Chavis's problems with the board had been building prior to the lawsuit disclosure. Chavis was held responsible for a $2.7-million budget deficit reported in May, and some members disagreed with his overtures to Nation of Islam leader Louis Farrakhan and others with controversial racial views. Chavis sued the NAACP on August 22 to get his job back. The group responded by suing him and Stansel to recover the money. On October 10, the NAACP said that it would pay $12,300 to settle with Chavis. He agreed to pay back a loan from the group and some personal charges on an NAACP credit card.

Police brutality. A federal jury on April 19 ordered the city of Los Angeles to pay $3.8 million in

Marchers carry a banner in a New York City parade in June celebrating the 25th anniversary of the birth of the gay rights movement.

damages to Rodney King, a black motorist who was beaten by white police officers during an arrest in 1991. A witness had videotaped the incident and the tape was seen nationwide. The jury awarded the damages to King as compensation for medical expenses, pain, and suffering resulting from the assault. On June 1, 1994, the same jury decided that officers involved in the beating did not have to pay King punitive damages. Punitive damages are designed to punish a wrongdoer.

In 1993, a different federal jury had found officers Stacey C. Koon and Laurence M. Powell guilty of violating King's rights. A judge sentenced each to 30 months in prison. A state court jury on April 29, 1992, had acquitted Koon, Powell, and two other of-

ficers on charges stemming from the beating. That verdict touched off five days of rioting in Los Angeles that killed more than 50 people and caused more than $1 billion in property damage.

Restaurant settlement. Flagstar Companies, parent of the Denny's restaurant chain, agreed on May 24 to pay $45.7 million to African-American patrons who claimed that Denny's discriminated against them because of their race and another $8.7-million to their lawyers. The settlement was based on class-action lawsuits that represented 4,300 racial bias complaints nationwide. Among these complaints, black customers in California said that Denny's required them to pay cover charges and pay for their food in advance, while white customers were not required to do the same. In Maryland, six black Secret Service agents had said they were refused service because of their race in May 1993. Although they admitted to no wrongdoing, Denny's agreed as part of the settlement to hire an outside lawyer to monitor the company's civil rights compliance.

Justice Department. After more than a year of searching, the Administration of President Bill Clinton got a chief for the Civil Rights Division of the U.S. Department of Justice. On Feb. 1, 1994, President Clinton nominated Boston lawyer Deval L. Patrick, who easily won Senate confirmation and was sworn in on April 14. The job had remained empty for an unusually long time due to controversy surrounding Clinton's first nominee, law professor Lani Guinier, and Clinton's withdrawal of her name. The Administration was unable for some time to find another noncontroversial candidate.

The U.S. Supreme Court ruled 8 to 1 on April 26 that the Civil Rights Act of 1991 did not cover thousands of lawsuits that had yet to be decided by the federal courts when the statute took effect. The act made it easier for workers to win job discrimination suits and allowed workers to sue for monetary awards if they could show that they suffered bias due to their sex, religion, or national origin. Previously, only victims of race discrimination could sue.

On April 19, 1994, the justices extended a series of rulings that banned unfair discrimination in jury selection. Voting 6 to 3 in an Alabama case, the court said lawyers cannot exclude people from juries based strictly on their gender. Since 1986, the court has made several decisions, based on the Constitution's equal-protection guarantees, that bar lawyers from excluding potential jurors based on their race. The April 1994 ruling was the first time the justices applied that reasoning to sex discrimination.

In two June 30 rulings, the court limited the scope of the federal Voting Rights Act of 1965, which prohibited state and local governments from restricting the voting rights of racial or ethnic minorities. The justices ruled 7 to 2 in a Florida case that when state legislatures draw voting districts they do not have to create as many minority districts as possible. In a 5 to 4 vote on a Georgia case, the court said the act could not be used to challenge the size of governing bodies such as county boards. They ruled that a Georgia county governed by a single commissioner did not have to create a multimember board to give minorities a chance to serve.

Reverse discrimination. A federal judge on Aug. 19, 1994, ruled that the University of Texas School of Law, in Austin, violated the U.S. Constitution and federal civil rights law with its method of screening black, Hispanic, and white students for admission. The judge said the school illegally discriminated against four white students who were either denied admission or had their acceptance delayed in 1992.

The judge agreed that law schools need affirmative action programs aimed at enrolling more students from racial and ethnic minority groups. However, he said that the University of Texas had wrongly used separate evaluations for some white applicants and minorities applying to the law school. The judge ordered the school to allow the four people who sued to reapply without paying more fees.

Sex and the Citadel. On July 22, a federal judge said the Citadel, an all-male public military college in Charleston, S.C., must admit a female student. Judge Weston Houck said that the 151-year-old school violated the Constitution's equal protection guarantees by excluding women. The woman, Shannon Faulkner, age 19, had won admission to the school by omitting her gender from the application. When school officials discovered her sex, they refused to admit her. Houck had ordered the Citadel to let Faulkner attend day classes as a civilian beginning in January 1994. His July order meant she could enter the cadet corps. He also gave the school until fall of 1995 to decide how to deal with other female applicants. On Aug. 12, 1994, the Fourth U.S. Circuit Court of Appeals blocked Faulkner's entry into the corps, saying she had to remain a civilian student while the court considered the school's appeal.

Sexual harassment. In a San Francisco case, a jury decided on September 1 that Baker & McKenzie, the world's largest law firm, and one of its former partners must pay a former secretary $7.1 million in punitive damages for sexual harassment. The jury found that lawyer Martin R. Greenstein had violated the rights of Rena Weeks by fondling her and making suggestive comments in 1991.

The firm did not properly deal with Greenstein's behavior or protect Weeks's rights, the jury said. Greenstein denied Weeks's claims but admitted improper conduct toward two other secretaries. The jury awarded Weeks $50,000 in general compensation. The firm was ordered to pay her another $6.9-million as punishment, and Greenstein was ordered to pay $225,000.

Amnesty International, a London-based human rights organization, highlighted rights violations in 151 countries in its 1994 annual report that covered events of 1993. The report said that thousands of men and women were persecuted, assassinated, jailed, and tortured for their beliefs despite "a crescendo" of official pronouncements in support of human rights, especially during a June United Nations World Conference on Human Rights.

Amnesty International, which opposes the death penalty under all circumstances, reported that there were more than 2,750 people on death row in 34 of the United States in 1994. Thirty-eight inmates died by execution in 1993, more than in any year since executions resumed in the United States in 1977.

☐ Linda P. Campbell and Geoffrey A. Campbell

In *World Book*, see **Civil rights.**

Classical music

Classical music. The Bastille Opera of Paris, plagued by administrative strife and mounting deficits, in September 1994 dismissed Myung-Whun Chung, the South Korean-born conductor and pianist, as its music director. The opera's management claimed Chung refused to renegotiate his contract, amounting to a salary of some $650,000 a year. Chung replied that artistic control, not money, was the real issue. In an interview published in the Paris newspaper *Le Monde* the day before his dismissal, he insisted on his right to maintain a voice in the Bastille's artistic decisions.

At the height of the dispute, Chung showed up at the theater to conduct rehearsals for the opening production of the season, Italian composer Giuseppe Verdi's *Simon Boccanegra* (1881), but was barred from entering. The issue finally went to court, where a judge ruled that Chung be allowed to conduct only the *Boccanegra* and then be relieved of his contract. The opera company, in turn, was ordered to pay Chung fines and two years of his salary. Chung, widely credited for raising the Bastille Opera Orchestra to an international level in his five years as chief conductor, emerged the hero of the sometimes grotesque *opera buffa* (comic opera) in which the main actors exchanged insults while the audience watched with perplexed amusement.

In another highly publicized firing, the Metropolitan Opera in New York City dismissed temperamental soprano Kathleen Battle. She displayed "unprofessional actions . . . profoundly detrimental . . . to artistic collaboration," according to general manager Joseph Volpe.

American operatic premieres in 1994 included composer Conrad Susa's *The Dangerous Liaisons* with a *libretto* (text) written by Philip Littell and based on the French novel *Les Liaisons Dangéreuses* (1782) by Choderlos de Laclos. The San Francisco Opera commissioned and gave the first performance of the work on Sept. 10, 1994, with an all-star cast headed by mezzo-soprano Frederica von Stade, baritone Thomas Hampson, and soprano Renee Fleming.

The Opera Theatre of St. Louis (Mo.) presented a revised version of Susa's *Black River* in June. The original had premiered in 1975. *The Dream of Valentino,* an opera by Pulitzer-winning composer Dominick Argento based on the life of Rudolph Valentino, had its world premiere by the Washington (D.C.) Opera on Jan. 15, 1994. The Santa Fe (N. Mex.) Opera gave the first U.S. performance of Scottish composer Judith Weir's *Blond Eckbert* on July 30.

The Lyric Opera Center for American Artists, the apprentice wing of the Lyric Opera of Chicago, premiered resident composer Bruce Saylor's adaptation of Tennessee Williams' *Orpheus Descending,* with a libretto by J. D. McClatchy, in June. The San Francisco Opera Center presented the U.S. premiere of Michael Tippett's *King Priam* on July 1. The work had premiered at London's Covent Garden in 1962.

Robert Moran's chamber opera *The Dracula Diaries* opened at the Houston Grand Opera on March 18.

Contemporary orchestral music. The Chicago Symphony Orchestra (CSO), conducted by Daniel Barenboim, premiered Elliott Carter's *Partita* in Chicago on February 17. Commissioned by the CSO, the work presented, in the American composer's words, "the many changes and oppositions of mood that make up our experience of life." John Adams composed a violin concerto for the Minnesota Orchestra and soloist Jorja Fleezanis, which they premiered on January 19. Adams is a leader in American *minimalism,* a style that uses repeated short patterns of music and complex rhythmic variations.

The choruses of the CSO and Lyric Opera of Chicago joined forces on April 24 to give the first U.S. performance of *Miserere* by Polish composer Henryk Górecki, whose Symphony No. 3 (1976) topped recording charts in 1993. The National Symphony Orchestra, in Washington, D.C., conducted by Mstislav Rostropovich, played the U.S. premiere of Russian composer Alfred Schnittke's Symphony No. 6, on Feb. 3, 1994. British composer Nicholas Maw's *Odyssey,* a full-evening orchestral work, had its first U.S. performance by the St. Louis Symphony, with Leonard Slatkin conducting, on September 23.

The Next Wave Festival, held annually at the Brooklyn Academy of Music in New York City, on December 7 presented the first performance of *La Belle*

Grammy Award winners in 1994

Classical Album, Béla Bartók, *The Wooden Prince* and *Cantata Profana*, Chicago Symphony Orchestra, Pierre Boulez, conductor.

Orchestral Performance, Béla Bartók, *The Wooden Prince*, Chicago Symphony Orchestra, Pierre Boulez, conductor.

Opera Recording, George Frideric Handel, *Semele*, English Chamber Orchestra and Ambrosian Opera Chorus, John Nelson, conductor.

Choral Performance, Béla Bartók, *Cantata Profana*, Chicago Symphony Orchestra and Chorus, Pierre Boulez, conductor, and Margaret Hillis, choral director.

Classical Performance, Instrumental Solo with Orchestra, Alban Berg, *Violin Concerto/RIHM: Time Chant*, Anne-Sophie Mutter, violin, with Chicago Symphony Orchestra, James Levine, conductor.

Classical Performance, Instrumental Solo Without Orchestra, *Samuel Barber: The Complete Solo Piano Music,* John Browning, piano.

Chamber Music Performance, Charles Ives, String Quartets Nos. 1 and 2; Samuel Barber, String Quartet Opus 11; Emerson String Quartet.

Classical Vocal Performance, *The Art of Arleen Auger*, Arleen Auger, soprano.

Contemporary Composition, Violin Concerto, Elliott Carter, composer.

Placido Domingo, left, Jose Carreras, and Luciano Pavarotti, right, sing to an audience of 56,000 at Dodger Stadium in Los Angeles in July.

et la Bête, the latest in a series of stage works by the American minimalist composer Philip Glass. The work incorporated singers, instrumentalists, and a landmark film by French filmmaker Jean Cocteau.

Van Cliburn. Amid much fanfare, pianist Van Cliburn announced he would make a comeback tour during the summer of 1994 with the Moscow Philharmonic orchestra. The nine-city jaunt ended his 16 years of scarcely interrupted retirement. But the tour floundered on July 11 at the Hollywood Bowl in Los Angeles when Cliburn, obviously not in top form, canceled the scheduled Third Piano Concerto (1909) of Russian composer Sergei Rachmaninoff midway through the concert. Cliburn told the audience he felt too faint to perform. The remainder of the tour concerts turned out to be largely disappointing. Cliburn had become an American cultural hero in 1958 after winning the International Tchaikovsky Piano Competition in Moscow at the age of 24.

Three great tenors—Jose Carreras, Placido Domingo, and Luciano Pavarotti—reunited for a hugely promoted, $10-million vocal extravaganza at Los Angeles' Dodger Stadium on July 16, 1994, the eve of the World Cup soccer finals. The event drew an audience of 56,000 and was broadcast to a television audience estimated at more than 1 billion people worldwide. Compact disc and video versions of the concert promptly soared to first place on *Billboard* magazine's record sales chart. The trio had also performed in Rome before the 1990 Cup finals.

The Tanglewood Festival, which runs from late June to early September in Lenox, Mass., opened its new $9.7-million, 1,180-seat Seiji Ozawa Hall, named after the Boston Symphony's music director, on July 7, 1994. Composer Oliver Knussen wrote a fanfare especially for the occasion. Ozawa had launched his career at Tanglewood as a 24-year-old conducting fellow in 1960. In 1994, he celebrated his 20th anniversary season as the Boston Symphony's music director. On July 23 at Tanglewood, pianist Leon Fleisher premiered the Piano Concerto for the Left Hand written for him by Lukas Foss, with Ozawa conducting the Tanglewood Music Center Orchestra.

Prizes. Composer Gunther Schuller won the 1994 Pulitzer Prize in music for his *Of Reminiscences and Reflections* (1993), a work which he described as "basically a lyrical, reflective piece," written in memory of his late wife. Pianist Garrick Ohlsson won the year's $25,000, 1994 Avery Fisher Prize. Finnish pianist Ralf Gothoni won the 1994 Gilmore Music Prize awarded by the Irving S. Gilmore International Keyboard Competition. This award, believed to be the largest prize in music, totaled more than $500,000. Gothoni received $115,000 in financial assistance, plus at least four years of concert engagements and promotional services. Toru Takemitsu won the year's $150,000 Grawemeyer Award for music composition for his *Fantasma/Cantos,* commissioned and premiered by the Welsh Orchestra of the British Broadcasting Company (BBC) in 1991.

Deaths. A giant of contemporary music, Polish composer Witold Lutoslawski, died on Feb. 7, 1994, at the age of 81. Lutoslawski drew on traditional and modern techniques to create works in a voice distinctively his own. In 1956, he and several other major Polish composers founded the Warsaw (Poland) Autumn Festival, a contemporary music festival that quickly established Warsaw as an important center for new music. Lutoslawski was known for demonstrating a highly original use of orchestral structure, serial techniques, and chance elements without subscribing to one system, style, or musical ideology.

Lejaren Hiller, the first composer to write music with a computer, passed away on Jan. 26, 1994, at the age of 69. Hungarian pianist Gyorgy Cziffra, age 72, best known for his performances of Franz Liszt's keyboard works, died on January 15. Another eminent pianist, the Czech-born Rudolf Firkusny, passed away on July 19 at the age of 82. Jarmila Novotna, a Czech-born lyric soprano widely considered one of the finest singing actresses of her time, who sang leading roles at New York City's Metropolitan Opera from 1940 to 1956, died on February 9 at the age of 86. □ John von Rhein

See also **Popular Music.** In *World Book,* see **Classical music; Opera.**

Clinton, Bill. President Bill Clinton suffered enormous political setbacks in 1994. He failed to get a health care reform bill enacted, and Republicans won control of both houses of Congress for the first time since 1954 in the November 8 midterm elections. Clinton was also bedeviled by sexual harassment charges and a long-running investigation of his past financial dealings. Although the President offered to cooperate with the new Republican leaders of the Senate and House of Representatives, his powers to influence legislation promised to be sharply limited by the loss of Democratic dominance in Congress. (See **Elections.**)

Democratic rout. The Democrats' disastrous showing in the November elections was widely interpreted as a national vote of no confidence in Clinton. Despite an improved economy and some foreign policy successes, the President suffered from a perceived lack of decisive leadership on many important issues. But Clinton was constantly being tugged in opposite directions by two major Democratic factions in Congress—the liberals and the centrists.

The two groups gave Clinton conflicting advice, with the centrists urging that he govern along "New Democrat" themes, particularly aid to the middle class. The liberals urged him to stick by traditional Democratic policies supported by organized labor, African Americans and other minorities, and big-city voters. Some observers remarked that Clinton tried to please everyone and ended up pleasing almost no one. Clinton responded to the Democratic debacle by outlining a proposal for a middle-class tax cut in a nationally televised speech on December 15.

Whitewater woes. The so-called Whitewater affair haunted Clinton and his wife, Hillary, throughout the year. The Whitewater affair concerned financial dealings that the Clintons were involved with in Arkansas while Clinton was governor of that state. At issue was whether the Clintons benefited improperly from their partnership with James B. McDougal, owner of the Madison Guaranty Savings and Loan in Little Rock, Ark., in a real estate venture, the Whitewater Development Corporation.

Faced with mounting public criticism, the President on January 12 asked Attorney General Janet Reno to appoint an independent counsel to investigate the matter. She named Robert B. Fiske, Jr., a New York City attorney and former federal prosecutor. In a precedent-setting move, Fiske on June 12 questioned Bill and Hillary Clinton under oath at the White House. It was the first time that a sitting President had submitted to direct questions in a legal case involving his own conduct.

Fiske reported on June 30 that White House officials had not broken the law by meeting with Treasury Department aides in late 1993 to discuss an allegation that the Clintons may have benefited from illegal actions taken by the Madison Guaranty firm. Those meetings were the focus of Senate and House hearings in late July and early August 1994. Fiske also concluded that the July 1993 death of Vincent W. Foster, Jr., a White House counsel who was a friend of the Clintons', was a suicide, as the police had reported at the time.

In a surprise move, a panel of federal judges on August 5 replaced Fiske and named Kenneth W. Starr, a former federal appeals court judge, to take over the Whitewater investigation. The choice of Starr, a conservative Republican, drew criticism from some Democrats.

Sexual harassment charges. More legal troubles for the President emerged on May 6 when Paula Corbin Jones, a former Arkansas state employee, filed a civil suit accusing Clinton of making unwanted sexual advances to her in May 1991. Jones asked for a public apology and $700,000 in damages in what was reported to be the first such legal action filed against a sitting President. Clinton, who denied her charges, had hired Robert S. Bennett, a prominent Washington lawyer, to defend him. On December 28, a federal judge set aside the suit for the duration of Clinton's presidency.

Health care reform dies. Clinton began the year with high hopes for his comprehensive plan to overhaul the nation's health care system and provide universal coverage through the private insurance system. The plan, however, was fiercely attacked by Republicans and the health insurance industry. Dem-

President Bill Clinton speaks in July at the Brandenburg Gate in Berlin, Germany, becoming the first U.S. President to visit the city's eastern sector since 1945.

ocrats split over whether to back its main provision, a requirement that employers pay 80 percent of their workers' insurance costs. Because the legislators could find so little common ground, no bill ever made it past the talking stage.

Crime bill passes. The President had better luck with anticrime legislation, as Congress on August 25 approved a $30.2-billion measure to pay for more police, build more prisons, ban some combat-style assault weapons, and impose life sentences on three-time violent offenders. Earlier in the month, the bill had appeared to be dead, but it was placed back on the agenda at Clinton's insistence. The long battle over the legislation was so partisan and bitter, however, that it tarnished the President's victory.

On the foreign-policy front, Clinton was able to achieve more in 1994 than in his first year in office. On January 14, he reached a nuclear-missile agreement with Russian President Boris N. Yeltsin. They pledged that their nations' strategic nuclear missiles would no longer be aimed at any other country but rather targeted on the oceans.

The President on February 3 lifted the 19-year-old trade embargo against Vietnam, opening the way for normalization of relations with the former enemy. And in a policy reversal, Clinton on May 26 renewed China's most-favored-nation (MFN) trading status for another year and declared that the United States would no longer link trade with China to human rights conditions in that country. MFN status allows a country to export products to the United States under the lowest tariff rate being charged.

In another turnabout, Clinton announced on August 19 that the United States would end its 28-year policy of accepting all Cuban refugees who arrive on U.S. shores or are rescued in American waters. He acted after Cuban leader Fidel Castro said his government would not interfere with the departures of thousands of Cubans who boarded makeshift rafts for the 90-mile (145-kilometer) trip to Florida. A compromise was reached that would allow 20,000 Cubans to enter the United States each year.

Military action. Clinton claimed a success in Haiti by restoring ousted President Jean-Bertrand Aristide to power on October 15 with the aid of about 20,000 U.S. troops. The American force landed in Haiti after the military dictators who seized power in 1991 were persuaded to step down by a team of mediators led by former President Jimmy Carter.

In a showdown with Iraq's leader Saddam Hussein, the United States dispatched troops to Kuwait on October 8 after Iraqi forces massed near Kuwait's northern border. In response to the American action, Iraq pulled back its troops.

Staff changes. White House counsel Bernard W. Nussbaum resigned on March 5 under criticism for arranging White House briefings on bank regulators' actions in the Whitewater affair. On August 11, Abner J. Mikva, chief judge of the U.S. Court of Appeals in the District of Columbia, was named White House counsel to succeed Lloyd N. Cutler on October 1. Cutler took Nussbaum's position. And on May 26, Clinton fired David Watkins, White House director of administration, for using a government helicopter to fly to and from a golf outing in nearby Maryland.

Stung by criticism of White House mismanagement, the President removed his old friend, Thomas F. (Mack) McLarty III, as chief of staff on June 27. Clinton appointed Leon E. Panetta, his budget director, to the top job and made McLarty a senior counselor. At the same time, media expert David R. Gergen was transferred from the White House to the State Department to advise on foreign policy.

White House attacks. On September 12, a man crashed a small plane on the South Lawn of the White House. The pilot—Frank E. Corder of Aberdeen, Md., an unemployed truckdriver—was killed. Clinton was not present at the time.

On October 29, a gunman fired 27 shots at the north side of the White House with a semiautomatic rifle. Clinton was in the White House when the attack occurred, but he was not hurt. A Colorado man, Francisco Martin Duran, was charged on November 17 with attempting to assassinate the President. Police said someone may have fired shots at the White House on December 17. □ William J. Eaton

See also **Congress of the United States; United States, Government of the.** In *World Book*, see **Clinton, Bill.**

Coal. The National Coal Association (NCA) predicted in July that 1994 coal production in the United States would increase by more than 9 percent, reaching a record 1 billion tons (907 million metric tons). NCA, a coal industry organization based in Washington, D.C., said that 1993 production totaled about 944 million tons (856 million metric tons).

Part of the increased production resulted from efforts by electric utility companies and other coal consumers to replenish coal stockpiles depleted during a long 1993 strike by the United Mine Workers of America (UMWA) union. The rest of the increase resulted from the improved economy which brought increased demand for electricity, much of which is produced with coal. Coal exports, however, were expected to decline from 74 million tons (67 million metric tons) in 1993 to 67 million tons (61 million metric tons) in 1994.

Mine workers victory. The U.S. Supreme Court on June 30 ruled that the UMWA did not have to pay $52 million in civil contempt-of-court fines imposed by a Virginia state judge during UMWA's 1989 strike against two Virginia coal companies. The fines were believed to be the largest civil contempt fines ever levied in America.

The fines were for blocking roads and other activities that the judge tried to restrict. He issued detailed guidelines on how many pickets could appear at a given time, how many union supervisors had to be present, and other matters. The Supreme Court ruled that violations of civil court orders that are extensive and occur outside a courtroom should be regarded as criminal contempt of court and tried before a jury. UMWA President Richard L. Trumka said the high court's decision saved the union from possible bankruptcy.

New processing techniques will allow the American coal industry to recover and market a valuable resinous material from coal mined in Western states, a researcher reported on Aug. 21, 1994. Jan D. Miller, a professor of metallurgy at the University of Utah in Salt Lake City, said the material, fossil resin, is found in coal mined in Arizona, Colorado, Utah, and other Western states. Fossil resin is an amberlike material that can be used in the manufacture of inks, adhesives, rubber, varnish, and other coatings. If extracted and refined, fossil resin could be sold for 50 cents per pound, Miller said. Yet most fossil resin now is burned as fuel with coal, which is worth about 1 cent per pound. Miller estimated that in one Utah coal field alone, 200 million pounds (91 million kilograms) of resin, worth $100 million, are wasted in this way each year.

New advances in technology for separating fossil resin from coal now make it practical to extract and sell large quantities of the material. Miller said that the coal industry has the technology needed to begin recovering fossil resin. □ Michael Woods

In *World Book*, see **Coal.**

Colombia. Ernesto Samper Pizano of the Liberal Party was inaugurated as president of Colombia on Aug. 7, 1994. Samper defeated Conservative Party candidate Andrés Pastrana Arango in a June 19 run-off in the closest election in Colombian history.

Samper carried four bullets in his body from a 1989 assassination attempt by drug traffickers. Although he pledged to fight drug corruption and make the money-laundering of drug profits a crime, he faced allegations that his own campaign had accepted hefty contributions from a drug cartel based in the city of Cali.

The Colombian government itself seemed to lose heart in the struggle against the nation's powerful drug traffickers in 1994. On May 6, Colombia's top law enforcement official, Prosecutor General Gustavo de Greiff, suggested that the world turn from fighting drugs to legalizing them. His comment followed a decision by Colombia's Constitutional Court to legalize the possession of drugs for personal use. Colombia's outgoing president, César Gaviría Trujillo, issued a decree on May 31 that curtailed the public possession and use of drugs but did not abolish the right to use them.

Controversy. In remarks aired on national television in Colombia on September 29, the day after he retired as chief of the United States Drug Enforcement Administration's office in Colombia, Joe Toft called Colombia a "narco-democracy" and said that he could not think of a single political or judicial institution that drug traffickers had not penetrated. President Samper accused the DEA agent of insulting Colombia's dignity and straining U.S.-Colombian relations.

Rebels. On January 23, gunmen thought to belong to the Revolutionary Forces of Colombia (FARC) attacked rivals in Apartado, killing 35 people. On July 30, FARC attacked government forces around the country, leaving about 100 rebels and 50 government soldiers dead. The rebels timed the attacks to coincide with the departure of President Gaviria.

But on February 16, some 400 urban guerrillas in Medellín disarmed in return for amnesty. Another 400 rebels, belonging to the Socialist Renewal Movement, accepted a similar deal on April 9. The agreement entitled each former rebel to receive $215 per month for one year, a $4,000 low-interest loan, and a pardon for past crimes.

Soccer tragedy. A gunman shot Colombian soccer star Andrés Escobar to death near Medellín on July 2. Escobar had kicked the ball into his own net and accidentally scored a goal against Colombia in a 2-1 World Cup loss to the United States on June 22. The loss eliminated Colombia from the tournament. (See **Soccer.**) □ Nathan A. Haverstock

See also **Latin America** (Facts in brief table). In *World Book,* see **Colombia.**

Colorado. See **State government.**

Common Market. See **Europe.**

Commonwealth of Independent States.
The 12 former Soviet republics that make up the Commonwealth of Independent States (C.I.S.) strengthened their economic ties at an October 1994 summit in Moscow. The members agreed to establish the commonwealth's first executive body, the Interstate Economic Committee (I.E.C.). Under the direction of a permanent staff in Moscow, the I.E.C. is intended to manage and coordinate the economic union formed by the member states. The committee's powers were not clearly defined, however, raising doubts about its effectiveness. The states rejected a proposal to give the I.E.C. authority to punish members that do not follow its decisions.

The C.I.S. also established a payments union to monitor the compatibility of the independent currencies issued by member states. Ukraine, Azerbaijan, and Turkmenistan refused to join the union and several states expressed their intention to retain control over their own monetary policy.

National security and military issues also marked the C.I.S. agenda in 1994. In April, Russia and Ukraine made progress in negotiations over the status of the Black Sea fleet, a central part of the former Soviet navy based in the Ukrainian port of Sevastopol. The two nations agreed again to divide the ships between their navies. By year's end, however, they had not determined how the fleet would be divided or who would control the port.

In June, eight member states signed a draft of a collective security plan. The plan was revised in October and described a C.I.S. alliance to jointly defend national borders, engage in peacekeeping operations, cooperate in the production of military equipment, and maintain a common strategic headquarters. The plan also called for the formation of a C.I.S. rapid deployment force.

The C.I.S. authorized the deployment of Russian peacekeeping forces in May to protect a cease-fire pact between Armenia and Azerbaijan in the disputed territory of Nagorno-Karabakh. The C.I.S. also backed Russian mediation of the conflict between Georgia and the separatist region of Abkhazia.

Broader membership. In March, Kazakh President Nursultan Nazarbayev proposed that the C.I.S. create a "Eurasian Union," whose membership would not be limited to the current C.I.S. members. In later months, Kazakhstan, Uzbekistan, and Kyrgyzstan moved toward its creation by forming an economic and military union. Other C.I.S. members expressed fears that it might too closely resemble the old Russian-dominated Soviet Union.

The parliaments of Georgia and Moldova ratified their nations' C.I.S. membership in 1994.

□ Joel S. Hellman

See also **Armenia; Azerbaijan; Georgia; Russia; Ukraine.** In *World Book,* see **Commonwealth of Independent States.**

Comoros. See **Africa.**

Computer

Computer. Rapid growth in traffic on the "information superhighway" dominated personal computer news during 1994. By year's end some sources estimated that as many as 30 million individuals were using *modems* (devices that connect computers to telephone lines) to tap into global networks connecting individual, university, government, and corporate computers. Via telephone lines, computer users can gain access to government archives, university libraries, and private message and electronic bulletin boards. Perhaps the most popular use of such networks was electronic mail, which allows messages to be sent virtually instantly from one computer to another.

The heart of the growing information superhighway was the Internet, a computer network that links most colleges and universities as well as many businesses and government offices. During 1994, the Internet became a popular destination for home computer users as well as a source of much speculation for businesses and advertisers hoping to exploit the system's commercial potential.

The popularity of commercial on-line services also grew dramatically during 1994. These services—including Prodigy, based in White Plains, N.Y., and America Online of Vienna, Va.—are designed to be easier to use than the often-complex Internet. They are aimed primarily at home users, who pay a fee for the services. A typical on-line service offers electronic mail, current news and financial information, and specialized databases. In 1994, America Online more than doubled its customer base, to over 1 million.

Many on-line services offered Internet access to subscribers. Internet users arriving by way of on-line services accounted for some of the congestion on the Internet and were viewed with annoyance by some experienced Internet users. (See also **Telecommunications**.)

Microsoft going on-line. In November, Bill Gates, chief executive officer of Microsoft Corporation of Redmond, Wash., the world's largest software company, announced his company was developing an on-line service, tentatively named the Microsoft Network. Microsoft's new service will be included as part of its Windows 95 software program, scheduled for introduction in mid-1995. Microsoft Windows is currently the most popular software program in the world, with millions of users. The software uses pictures called icons to make personal computers easier to use.

By including the new on-line service as part of its next Windows upgrade, Microsoft expects its network to become one of the leading telecommunications services almost instantly. Some existing on-line services felt that the Microsoft strategy took unfair advantage of the popularity of the company's Windows software.

Microsoft also made news in October, when it announced plans to acquire Intuit, Inc., of Menlo Park, Calif., for approximately $1.5 billion. Intuit is the developer and publisher of Quicken, the leading personal finance software. Personal finance software is used to manage household and small business bank accounts, transactions, and assets. With the software and a computer equipped with a modem, an individual can track investments, monitor bank accounts, transfer funds, and pay bills electronically.

The combination of Microsoft Windows, Quicken, and the Microsoft Network could potentially allow Microsoft to become involved in much of the nation's banking transactions. For this reason, as well as Microsoft's dominance in personal computer software, the Intuit acquisition was subjected to intense governmental scrutiny, with the completion of the deal dependent upon government approval.

PowerPC and Pentium chips. Makers of a new microprocessor introduced in March 1994 hoped to challenge the computer chip leadership of the Intel Corporation of Santa Clara, Calif. Microprocessors—the "brains" of computers—made by Intel are the chips on which Windows and many other popular software programs run. Intel processors are used in up to 85 percent of all personal computers.

The new processor, called the PowerPC, was developed by Apple Computer Incorporated of Cupertino, Calif.; International Business Machines Corporation (IBM) of Armonk, N.Y.; and Motorola Incorporated of Schaumburg, Ill. The partnership re-

Computer scientist Matthew Blaze in May reported a flaw in the Clipper coding technology designed to allow government wiretaps of encoded data.

sulted in a processor that can run Intel-compatible software as well as software designed for Apple's Macintosh series of personal computers.

PowerPCs take advantage of RISC (*reduced instruction set computing*) technology, a new approach to computing that lets microprocessors perform more than one function at a time. Using more than 2.5 million transistors on a chip the size of a small fingernail, PowerPC processors are smaller and run some software faster than traditional processors. Initial sales of PowerPC-based computers were good but not spectacular.

Problems with its popular Pentium chip plagued Intel during late 1994 and may have boosted sales of PowerPC computers. In November, Intel announced that a *bug* (mistake) had been found in the Pentium, causing the microprocessor to make errors while performing complex mathematical functions. Intel said such errors were rare and infinitesimal, but in December, IBM announced that it was halting shipment of its Pentium-based personal computers.

Aptiva. In September, IBM introduced a new line of personal computers called Aptiva, aimed specifically at home consumers. The computers' entire inventory was spoken for within a month, an indication of just how popular home computers had become. IBM planned to increase production of Aptiva computers in early 1995. ☐ Keith Ferrell

See also **Electronics**. In *World Book,* see **Computer**.

Congress of the United States. The

Democratic-controlled 103rd Congress tried but failed in 1994 to pass a health care bill, the number-one item on President Bill Clinton's priority list. Nor did Clinton manage to get a welfare-reform bill passed. The President waited until late in the session to unveil his plan for "ending welfare as we know it," and Congress took no action on the highly controversial issue in an election year. The entire legislative session was marked by bitter partisanship, with Senate Republicans blocking passage of other key reform measures in the final days before adjournment on October 8.

To make matters worse—much worse—for the Democrats, the November 8 midterm elections resulted in a Republican landslide. The GOP (Grand Old Party) gained majorities in both the Senate and House of Representatives for the first time in 40 years. Democrats frustrated with their lack of legislative success in 1994 could only look forward to 1995 with foreboding.

The deadlock during 1994, however, overshadowed some important achievements, including passage of a comprehensive crime-fighting measure. (See **Crime: Fighting Crime in America.**)

Voters reward Republicans. Sensing the angry mood of the public in the months leading up to the November elections, more than 300 Republican candidates for Congress on September 27 signed a "Contract with America." The contract held out hope for fast approval of several popular measures in 1995, including a middle-class tax cut, spending reductions, and constitutional amendments to impose term limits in Congress and require a balanced federal budget. GOP leaders also attempted to make the midterm elections a referendum on Clinton's first two years in office.

The two strategies apparently worked, because voters on November 8 handed the Republicans a bigger victory than almost anyone had predicted. While Democrats lost in droves, not a single Republican incumbent was beaten. Among the Democratic stalwarts who went down to defeat was House Speaker Thomas S. Foley of Washington state. Foley's loss marked the first time since 1862 that a Speaker was spurned by voters.

The GOP gained 52 seats in the House, changing the lineup from 258-176 in the Democrats' favor to a 230-204 margin for the Republicans. (In each Congress, a lone independent in the House rounded out the 435-seat total.) In the Senate, Republicans picked up eight seats in the election and widened their majority still further when, the day after the election, Democratic Senator Richard C. Shelby of Alabama switched parties. The nine-seat gain gave the GOP a 53-47 edge in the new Congress, compared with a 56-44 Democratic advantage in 1994.

Health care reform. The President and Democratic leaders were never able to get enough support for a health care reform measure during the year to bring a bill to the floor of either the House or the Senate. Clinton's original proposal—a 1,400-page bill that was denounced by Republican opponents as a government take-over of the health care industry—was dead on arrival on Capitol Hill.

The main provision of the bill, a requirement that employers pick up 80 percent of the cost of private health insurance for their workers, drew fierce opposition from business groups, who lobbied hard against it. Insurance companies also spent hundreds of millions of dollars on television advertising to oppose key elements of the President's plan. The basic approach of the Clinton plan was approved by a margin of one vote in the House Ways and Means Committee but clearly lacked sufficient support for passage in the House.

Democratic leaders in Congress tried to draft a compromise bill that could win bipartisan support but were unable to do so. As the months went by, it looked less and less likely that consensus would be reached. Clinton, who originally had insisted that any health care legislation would have to cover all Americans, offered to modify his proposal and accept less than universal coverage. But the President's compromise failed to win Republican converts. As autumn approached, Republicans retreated from some of their original proposals, making it nearly impossible to produce a bipartisan bill.

Members of the United States Senate

The Senate of the first session of the 104th Congress consisted of 47 Democrats and 53 Republicans when it convened on Jan. 4, 1995. James M. Inhofe of Oklahoma was elected Nov. 8, 1994, to fill the seat left vacant after David L. Boren resigned to become president of the University of Oklahoma. The first date in each listing shows when the senator's term began. The second date in each listing shows when the senator's term expires.

State	Term	State	Term	State	Term
Alabama		**Louisiana**		**Ohio**	
Howell T. Heflin, D.	1979-1997	J. Bennett Johnston, Jr., D.	1972-1997	John H. Glenn, Jr., D.	1974-1999
Richard C. Shelby, R.	1987-1999	John B. Breaux, D.	1987-1999	Mike DeWine, R.	1995-2001
Alaska		**Maine**		**Oklahoma**	
Theodore F. Stevens, R.	1968-1997	William S. Cohen, R.	1979-1997	Don Nickles, R.	1981-1999
Frank H. Murkowski, R.	1981-1999	Olympia Snowe, R.	1995-2001	James M. Inhofe, R.	1994-1997
Arizona		**Maryland**		**Oregon**	
John McCain III, R.	1987-1999	Paul S. Sarbanes, D.	1977-2001	Mark O. Hatfield, R.	1967-1997
Jon Kyl, R.	1995-2001	Barbara A. Mikulski, D.	1987-1999	Bob Packwood, R.	1969-1999
Arkansas		**Massachusetts**		**Pennsylvania**	
Dale Bumpers, D.	1975-1999	Edward M. Kennedy, D.	1962-2001	Arlen Specter, R.	1981-1999
David H. Pryor, D.	1979-1997	John F. Kerry, D.	1985-1997	Rick Santorum, R.	1995-2001
California		**Michigan**		**Rhode Island**	
Barbara Boxer, D.	1993-1999	Carl Levin, D.	1979-1999	Claiborne Pell, D.	1961-1997
Dianne Feinstein, D.	1993-2001	Spencer Abraham, R.	1995-2001	John H. Chafee, R.	1976-2001
Colorado		**Minnesota**		**South Carolina**	
Hank Brown, R.	1991-1997	Paul D. Wellstone, D.	1991-1997	Strom Thurmond, R.	1955-1997
Ben N. Campbell, D.	1993-1999	Rod Grams, R.	1995-2001	Ernest F. Hollings, D.	1967-1999
Connecticut		**Mississippi**		**South Dakota**	
Christopher J. Dodd, D.	1981-1999	Thad Cochran, R.	1978-1997	Larry Pressler, R.	1979-1997
Joseph I. Lieberman, D.	1989-2001	Trent Lott, R.	1989-2001	Thomas A. Daschle, D.	1987-1999
Delaware		**Missouri**		**Tennessee**	
William V. Roth, Jr., R.	1971-2001	Christopher S. (Kit) Bond, R.	1987-1999	Bill Frist, R.	1995-2001
Joseph R. Biden, Jr., D.	1973-1997	John Ashcroft, R.	1995-2001	Fred Thompson, R.	1995-2001
Florida		**Montana**		**Texas**	
Bob Graham, D.	1987-1999	Max Baucus, D.	1978-1997	Phil Gramm, R.	1985-1997
Connie Mack III, R.	1989-2001	Conrad Burns, R.	1989-2001	Kay Bailey Hutchison, R.	1993-2001
Georgia		**Nebraska**		**Utah**	
Sam Nunn, D.	1972-1997	J. James Exon, D.	1979-1997	Orrin G. Hatch, R.	1977-2001
Paul Coverdell, R.	1993-1999	J. Robert Kerrey, D.	1989-2001	Robert F. Bennett, R.	1993-1999
Hawaii		**Nevada**		**Vermont**	
Daniel K. Inouye, D.	1963-1999	Harry M. Reid, D.	1987-1999	Patrick J. Leahy, D.	1975-1999
Daniel K. Akaka, D.	1990-2001	Richard H. Bryan, D.	1989-2001	James M. Jeffords, R.	1989-2001
Idaho		**New Hampshire**		**Virginia**	
Larry E. Craig, R.	1991-1997	Robert C. Smith, R.	1990-1997	John W. Warner, R.	1979-1997
Dirk Kempthorne, R.	1993-1999	Judd Gregg, R.	1993-1999	Charles S. Robb, D.	1989-2001
Illinois		**New Jersey**		**Washington**	
Paul Simon, D.	1985-1997	Bill Bradley, D.	1979-1997	Slade Gorton, R.	1989-2001
Carol Moseley-Braun, D.	1993-1999	Frank R. Lautenberg, D.	1982-2001	Patty Murray, D.	1993-1999
Indiana		**New Mexico**		**West Virginia**	
Richard G. Lugar, R.	1977-2001	Pete V. Domenici, R.	1973-1997	Robert C. Byrd, D.	1959-2001
Dan R. Coats, R.	1989-1999	Jeff Bingaman, D.	1983-2001	John D. Rockefeller IV, D.	1985-1997
Iowa		**New York**		**Wisconsin**	
Charles E. Grassley, R.	1981-1999	Daniel P. Moynihan, D.	1977-2001	Herbert Kohl, D.	1989-2001
Tom Harkin, D.	1985-1997	Alfonse M. D'Amato, R.	1981-1999	Russell D. Feingold, D.	1993-1999
Kansas		**North Carolina**		**Wyoming**	
Robert J. Dole, R.	1969-1999	Jesse A. Helms, R.	1973-1997	Alan K. Simpson, R.	1979-1997
Nancy Landon Kassebaum, R.	1979-1997	Lauch Faircloth, R.	1993-1999	Craig Thomas, R.	1995-2001
Kentucky		**North Dakota**			
Wendell H. Ford, D.	1974-1999	Kent Conrad, D.	1987-2001		
Mitch McConnell, R.	1985-1997	Byron L. Dorgan, D.	1992-1999		

Senate Majority Leader George J. Mitchell (D., Me.) tried for weeks to reach agreement with a group of moderate Republicans, but he finally admitted failure on September 26 and declared health care reform dead for 1994. Mitchell, who had decided not to run for reelection in November, passed up a chance for a seat on the Supreme Court of the United States in order to work on health care legislation. He blamed GOP obstructionism for the failure to pass a bill, but Republicans countered that Democrats were unwilling to accept a package of modest changes that could get widespread backing.

Money and the political process. Congress also failed in 1994 to deliver on two major political-reform bills endorsed by the President and Democratic leaders. One bill would have barred most gifts from lobbyists to lawmakers and required detailed public disclosures of lobbying activities. It was killed on October 8 by a Republican-led *filibuster* (extended debate used as a delaying tactic).

The other measure provided for some public financing of congressional campaigns for candidates who voluntarily complied with spending limits. It also would have limited donations by special interest groups, especially political action committees (PAC's) representing corporations, labor unions, and other groups. The bill was defeated on September 20 when supporters failed to get the 60 votes needed to break a Republican filibuster against it.

Crime bill. One of Clinton's major triumphs in 1994 came in August, when Congress approved a $30.2-billion anticrime bill after weeks of partisan bickering had delayed its final passage. The legislation, aimed at putting an additional 100,000 police officers on city streets, building more prisons, and imposing tougher sentences on three-time violent offenders, had been strongly endorsed by the President. But inclusion of a ban on combat-style assault weapons and a vast expansion of the death penalty for federal crimes caused defections by both conservatives and liberals. As a result, an early version of the bill was blocked in the House, forcing changes to reduce spending on crime-prevention programs.

The bill finally was approved, 235 to 195, in the House on August 21. It cleared the Senate, 61 to 38, on August 25 after its supporters overcame a filibuster by Senate Republicans. Clinton signed it into law on September 13, and the Department of Justice immediately began allocating funds for additional police officers and anticrime efforts.

The final days of the 103rd Congress were marked more by the death of major bills than by the usual end-of-session flurry of legislation getting final approval. Using the filibuster effectively, Republicans stopped passage of the bills to restrict the activities of lobbyists and overhaul the financing of congressional campaigns.

The Republicans' delaying tactics also torpedoed chances for several pieces of environmental legislation, including a program to clean up toxic waste and revisions of federal laws to provide safe drinking water. But Democrats on October 8 broke a GOP filibuster to give final approval to a bill placing 7 million acres (2.8 million hectares) of fragile desert lands in California under federal protection. It was considered the single most significant environmental achievement of the Clinton Administration.

The Senate also halted another filibuster before approving, on October 5, a five-year extension of the Elementary and Secondary Education Act, the government's major school-aid program. And in rare bipartisan accord, Congress on October 4 agreed to a sweeping reorganization of the Department of Agriculture that would reduce its payroll by 7,500 and close 1,274 of the agency's 3,700 field offices. In addition, the bill overhauled the federal crop insurance program in hopes of saving $151 million over five years.

Another measure passed on September 20 with bipartisan backing revised the federal government's purchasing system to cut down on paperwork and delays in acquiring equipment costing less than $100,000. On October 6, Congress also revised the so-called "nanny tax"—social security withholding tax for household workers. The wage threshold per worker for paying the tax was increased from $50 a quarter to $1,000 a year.

In other actions, Congress on October 8 authorized compensation for victims of the so-called "Persian Gulf syndrome," a mysterious condition that has caused a variety of ailments in more than 3,000 American veterans of the 1991 Persian Gulf War against Iraq. Sufferers of the syndrome have complained of nausea, hair loss, respiratory problems, and other symptoms.

GATT approved. Congress decided to put off a vote on a new world trade pact, the General Agreement on Tariffs and Trade (GATT), until after the midterm elections. GATT called for the lowering of tariffs around the globe and the creation of an international body, the World Trade Organization, to govern commerce among nations. Congress reconvened in late November to vote on the accord. The House approved it, 288 to 146, on November 29, and the Senate passed it, 76 to 24, on December 1.

Investigating Whitewater. Republicans succeeded during the year in forcing Senate and House hearings on the so-called Whitewater case. This involved an investment that Clinton and his wife, Hillary, made in an Arkansas real estate concern, the Whitewater Development Corporation, while Clinton was governor of Arkansas.

Because an independent prosecutor was looking into the transactions to see if any laws were violated, the congressional investigations were limited in scope. The televised Senate and House hearings, in late July and early August, focused on conflicting testimony by Treasury Department officials about

Members of the United States House of Representatives

The House of Representatives of the first session of the 104th Congress consisted of 204 Democrats, 230 Republicans, and 1 independent (not including representatives from American Samoa, the District of Columbia, Guam, Puerto Rico, and the Virgin Islands), when it convened on Jan. 4, 1995. There were 258 Democrats, 176 Republicans, and 1 independent when the second session of the 103rd Congress convened. This table shows congressional district, legislator, and party affiliation. Asterisk (*) denotes those who served in the 103rd Congress; dagger (†) denotes "at large."

Alabama
1. Sonny Callahan, R.*
2. Terry Everett, R.*
3. Glen Browder, D.*
4. Tom Bevill, D.*
5. Bud Cramer, D.*
6. Spencer Bachus, R.*
7. Earl Hilliard, D.

Alaska
† Donald E. Young, R.*

Arizona
1. Matt Salmon, R.
2. Ed Pastor, D.*
3. Bob Stump, R.*
4. John Shadegg, R.
5. Jim Kolbe, R.*
6. J. D. Hayworth, R.

Arkansas
1. Blanche Lambert, D.*
2. Ray Thornton, D.*
3. Tim Hutchinson, R.*
4. Jay Dickey, R.*

California
1. Frank Riggs, R.
2. Wally Herger, R.*
3. Vic Fazio, D.*
4. John Doolittle, R.*
5. Robert T. Matsui, D.*
6. Lynn Woolsey, D.*
7. George E. Miller, D.*
8. Nancy Pelosi, D.*
9. Ronald V. Dellums, D.*
10. Bill Baker, R.*
11. Richard Pombo, R.*
12. Tom Lantos, D.*
13. Fortney H. (Peter) Stark, D.*
14. Anna Eshoo, D.*
15. Norman Mineta, D.*
16. Zoe Lofgren, D.*
17. Sam Farr, D.*
18. Gary Condit, D.*
19. George Radanovich, R.
20. Calvin Dooley, D.*
21. William M. Thomas, R.*
22. Andrea Seastrand, R.
23. Elton Gallegly, R.*
24. Anthony Beilenson, D.*
25. Howard McKeon, R.*
26. Howard L. Berman, D.*
27. Carlos J. Moorhead, R.*
28. David Dreier, R.*
29. Henry A. Waxman, D.*
30. Xavier Becerra, D.*
31. Matthew Martinez, D.*
32. Julian C. Dixon, D.*
33. Lucille Roybal-Allard, D.*
34. Esteban E. Torres, D.*
35. Maxine Waters, D.*
36. Jane Harman, D.*
37. Walter Tucker, D.*
38. Steve Horn, R.
39. Edward Royce, R.*
40. Jerry Lewis, R.*
41. Jay Kim, R.*
42. George E. Brown, Jr., D.*
43. Kenneth Calvert, R.*
44. Sonny Bono, R.
45. Dana Rohrabacher, R.*
46. Robert K. Dornan, R.*
47. C. Christopher Cox, R.*
48. Ronald C. Packard, R.*
49. Brian Bilbray, R.
50. Bob Filner, D.*
51. Randy (Duke) Cunningham, R.*
52. Duncan L. Hunter, R.*

Colorado
1. Patricia Schroeder, D.*
2. David E. Skaggs, D.*
3. Scott McInnis, R.*
4. Wayne Allard, R.*
5. Joel Hefley, R.*
6. Daniel Schaefer, R.*

Connecticut
1. Barbara B. Kennelly, D.*
2. Sam Gejdenson, D.*
3. Rosa DeLauro, D.*
4. Christopher Shays, R.*
5. Gary Franks, R.*
6. Nancy L. Johnson, R.*

Delaware
†Michael Castle, R.*

Florida
1. Joe Scarborough, R.
2. Pete Peterson, D.*
3. Corrine Brown, D.*
4. Tillie Fowler, R.*
5. Karen Thurman, D.*
6. Clifford B. Stearns, R.*
7. John Mica, R.*
8. Bill McCollum, R.*
9. Michael Bilirakis, R.*
10. C. W. Bill Young, R.*
11. Sam M. Gibbons, D.*
12. Charles Canady, R.*
13. Dan Miller, R.*
14. Porter J. Goss, R.*
15. Dave Weldon, R.
16. Mark Foley, R.
17. Carrie Meek, D.*
18. Ileana Ros-Lehtinen, R.*
19. Harry A. Johnston II, D.*
20. Peter Deutsch, D.*
21. Lincoln Diaz-Balart, R.*
22. E. Clay Shaw, Jr., R.*
23. Alcee Hastings, D.*

Georgia
1. Jack Kingston, R.*
2. Sanford Bishop, D.*
3. Mac Collins, R.*
4. John Linder, R.*
5. John Lewis, D.*
6. Newt Gingrich, R.*
7. Bob Barr, R.
8. Saxby Chambliss, R.
9. Nathan Deal, D.*
10. Charlie Norwood, R.
11. Cynthia McKinney, D.*

Hawaii
1. Neil Abercrombie, D.*
2. Patsy T. Mink, D.*

Idaho
1. Helen Chenoweth, R.
2. Michael Crapo, R.*

Illinois
1. Bobby Rush, D.*
2. Mel Reynolds, D.*
3. William O. Lipinski, D.*
4. Luis Gutierrez, D.*
5. Michael Flanagan, R.
6. Henry J. Hyde, R.*
7. Cardiss Collins, D.*
8. Philip M. Crane, R.*
9. Sidney R. Yates, D.*
10. John Edward Porter, R.*
11. Gerald Weller, R.
12. Jerry F. Costello, D.*
13. Harris W. Fawell, R.*
14. J. Dennis Hastert, R.*
15. Thomas W. Ewing, R.*
16. Donald Manzullo, R.*
17. Lane A. Evans, D.*
18. Ray LaHood, R.
19. Glenn Poshard, D.*
20. Richard J. Durbin, D.*

Indiana
1. Peter J. Visclosky, D.*
2. David McIntosh, R.
3. Tim Roemer, D.*
4. Mark Souder, R.
5. Steve Buyer, R.*
6. Danny L. Burton, R.*
7. John T. Myers, R.*
8. John Hostettler, R.
9. Lee H. Hamilton, D.*
10. Andrew Jacobs, Jr., D.*

Iowa
1. Jim Leach, R.*
2. Jim Nussle, R.*
3. Jim Ross Lightfoot, R.*
4. Greg Ganske, R.
5. Tom Latham, R.

Kansas
1. Pat Roberts, R.*
2. Sam Brownback, R.
3. Jan Meyers, R.*
4. Todd Tiahrt, R.

Kentucky
1. Edward Whitfield, R.
2. Ron Lewis, R.*
3. Mike Ward, D.
4. Jim Bunning, R.*
5. Harold (Hal) Rogers, R.*
6. Scotty Baesler, D.*

Louisiana
1. Robert L. Livingston, Jr., R.*
2. William J. Jefferson, D.*
3. W. J. (Billy) Tauzin, D.*
4. Cleo Fields, D.*
5. Jim McCrery, R.*
6. Richard Hugh Baker, R.*
7. James A. (Jimmy) Hayes, D.*

Maine
1. James Longley, R.
2. John Baldacci, D.

Maryland
1. Wayne T. Gilchrest, R.*
2. Robert Ehrlich, Jr., R.
3. Benjamin L. Cardin, D.*
4. Albert Wynn, D.*
5. Steny H. Hoyer, D.*
6. Roscoe Bartlett, R.*
7. Kweisi Mfume, D.*
8. Constance A. Morella, R.*

Massachusetts
1. John W. Olver, D.*
2. Richard E. Neal, D.*
3. Peter Blute, R.*
4. Barney Frank, D.*
5. Martin Meehan, D.*
6. Peter Torkildsen, R.*
7. Edward J. Markey, D.*
8. Joseph P. Kennedy II, D.*
9. John Joseph Moakley, D.*
10. Gerry E. Studds, D.*

Michigan
1. Bart Stupak, D.*
2. Peter Hoekstra, R.*
3. Vernon Ehlers, R.*
4. Dave Camp, R.*
5. James Barcia, D.*
6. Frederick S. Upton, R.*
7. Nick Smith, R.*
8. Dick Chrysler, R.
9. Dale E. Kildee, D.*
10. David E. Bonior, D.*
11. Joseph Knollenberg, R.*
12. Sander M. Levin, D.*
13. Lynn Rivers, D.
14. John Conyers, Jr., D.*
15. Barbara-Rose Collins, D.*
16. John D. Dingell, D.*

Minnesota
1. Gil Gutknecht, R.
2. David Minge, D.*
3. Jim Ramstad, R.*
4. Bruce F. Vento, D.*
5. Martin O. Sabo, D.*
6. William P. Luther, D.
7. Collin C. Peterson, D.*
8. James L. Oberstar, D.*

Mississippi
1. Roger Wicker, R.
2. Bennie Thompson, D.*
3. G. V. (Sonny) Montgomery, D.*
4. Mike Parker, D.*
5. Gene Taylor, D.*

Missouri
1. William L. (Bill) Clay, D.*
2. James Talent, R.*
3. Richard A. Gephardt, D.*
4. Ike Skelton, D.*
5. Karen McCarthy, D.
6. Pat Danner, D.*
7. Mel Hancock, R.*
8. Bill Emerson, R.*
9. Harold L. Volkmer, D.*

Montana
† Pat Williams, D.*

Nebraska
1. Doug Bereuter, R.*
2. Jon Christensen, R.
3. Bill Barrett, R.*

Nevada
1. John Ensign, R.
2. Barbara F. Vucanovich, R.*

New Hampshire
1. Bill Zeliff, R.*
2. Charles Bass, R.

New Jersey
1. Robert E. Andrews, D.*
2. Frank LoBiondo, R.
3. H. James Saxton, R.*
4. Christopher H. Smith, R.*
5. Marge Roukema, R.*
6. Frank Pallone, Jr., D.*
7. Bob Franks, R.*
8. Bill Martini, R.
9. Robert G. Torricelli, D.*
10. Donald M. Payne, D.*
11. Rodney Frelinghuysen, R.
12. Richard A. Zimmer, R.*
13. Robert Menendez, D.*

New Mexico
1. Steven H. Schiff, R.*
2. Joe Skeen, R.*
3. William B. Richardson, D.*

New York
1. Michael Forbes, R.
2. Rick Lazio, R.*
3. Peter King, R.*
4. Daniel Frisa, R.
5. Gary L. Ackerman, D.*
6. Floyd H. Flake, D.*
7. Thomas J. Manton, D.*
8. Jerrold Nadler, D.*
9. Charles E. Schumer, D.*
10. Edolphus Towns, D.*
11. Major R. Owens, D.*
12. Nydia Velazquez, D.*
13. Susan Molinari, R.*
14. Carolyn Maloney, D.*
15. Charles B. Rangel, D.*
16. Jose E. Serrano, D.*
17. Eliot L. Engel, D.*
18. Nita M. Lowey, D.*
19. Sue Kelly, R.
20. Benjamin A. Gilman, R.*
21. Michael R. McNulty, D.*
22. Gerald B. Solomon, R.*
23. Sherwood L. Boehlert, R.*
24. John McHugh, R.*
25. James Walsh, R.*
26. Maurice Hinchey, D.*
27. William Paxon, R.*
28. Louise M. Slaughter, D.*
29. John J. LaFalce, D.*
30. Jack Quinn, R.*
31. Amory Houghton, Jr., R.*

North Carolina
1. Eva Clayton, D.*
2. David Funderburk, R.
3. Walter Jones, Jr., R.
4. Frederick Heineman, R.
5. Richard Burr, R.
6. Howard Coble, R.*
7. Charles Rose III, D.*
8. W. G. (Bill) Hefner, D.*
9. Sue Myrick, R.
10. Cass Ballenger, R.*
11. Charles H. Taylor, R.*
12. Melvin Watt, D.

North Dakota
† Earl Pomeroy, D.*

Ohio
1. Steve Chabot, R.
2. Rob Portman, R.*
3. Tony P. Hall, D.*
4. Michael G. Oxley, R.*
5. Paul E. Gillmor, R.*
6. Frank Cremeans, R.
7. David L. Hobson, R.*
8. John A. Boehner, R.*
9. Marcy Kaptur, D.*
10. Martin Hoke, R.*
11. Louis Stokes, D.*
12. John R. Kasich, R.*
13. Sherrod Brown, D.*
14. Thomas C. Sawyer, D.*
15. Deborah Pryce, R.*
16. Ralph Regula, R.*
17. James A. Traficant, Jr., D.*
18. Bob Ney, R.
19. Steven LaTourette, R.

Oklahoma
1. Steve Largent, R.
2. Tom Coburn, R.
3. Bill Brewster, D.*
4. J. C. Watts, R.
5. Ernest Jim Istook, R.*
6. Frank Lucas, R.*

Oregon
1. Elizabeth Furse, D.*
2. Wes Cooley, R.
3. Ron Wyden, D.*
4. Peter A. DeFazio, D.*
5. Jim Bunn, R.

Pennsylvania
1. Thomas M. Foglietta, D.*
2. Chaka Fattah, D.
3. Robert A. Borski, Jr., D.*
4. Ron Klink, D.*
5. William F. Clinger, Jr., R.*
6. Tim Holden, D.*
7. W. Curtis Weldon, R.*
8. Jim Greenwood, R.*
9. E. G. (Bud) Shuster, R.*
10. Joseph M. McDade, R.*
11. Paul E. Kanjorski, D.*
12. John P. Murtha, D.*
13. Jon Fox, R.
14. William J. Coyne, D.*
15. Paul McHale, D.*
16. Robert S. Walker, R.*
17. George W. Gekas, R.*
18. Michael Doyle, D.
19. William F. Goodling, R.*
20. Frank Mascara, D.
21. Philip English, R.

Rhode Island
1. Patrick Kennedy, D.
2. John F. Reed, D.*

South Carolina
1. Mark Sanford, R.
2. Floyd Spence, R.*
3. Lindsey Graham, R.
4. Bob Inglis, R.*
5. John M. Spratt, Jr., D.*
6. James Clyburn, D.*

South Dakota
† Tim Johnson, D.*

Tennessee
1. James H. Quillen, R.*
2. John J. Duncan, Jr., R.*
3. Zach Wamp, R.
4. Van Hilleary, R.
5. Bob Clement, D.*
6. Bart Gordon, D.*
7. Ed Bryant, R.
8. John S. Tanner, D.*
9. Harold E. Ford, D.*

Texas
1. Jim Chapman, D.*
2. Charles Wilson, D.*
3. Sam Johnson, R.*
4. Ralph M. Hall, D.*
5. John W. Bryant, D.*
6. Joe Barton, R.*
7. Bill Archer, R.*
8. Jack Fields, Jr., R.*
9. Steve Stockman, R.
10. Lloyd Doggett, D.
11. Chet Edwards, D.*
12. Preston P. (Pete) Geren, D.*
13. William Thornberry, R.
14. Greg Laughlin, D.*
15. Eligio (Kika) de la Garza, D.*
16. Ronald D. Coleman, D.*
17. Charles W. Stenholm, D.*
18. Sheila Lee, D.
19. Larry Combest, R.*
20. Henry B. Gonzalez, D.*
21. Lamar S. Smith, R.*
22. Tom DeLay, R.*
23. Henry Bonilla, R.*
24. Martin Frost, D.*
25. Ken Bentsen, D.
26. Richard K. Armey, R.*
27. Solomon P. Ortiz, D.*
28. Frank Tejeda, D.*
29. Gene Green, D.*
30. Eddie Bernice Johnson, D.*

Utah
1. James V. Hansen, R.*
2. Enid Waldholtz, R.
3. William Orton, D.*

Vermont
† Bernard Sanders, Ind.*

Virginia
1. Herbert H. Bateman, R.*
2. Owen B. Pickett, D.*
3. Robert Scott, D.*
4. Norman Sisisky, D.*
5. Lewis F. Payne, Jr., D.*
6. Robert Goodlatte, R.*
7. Thomas J. (Tom) Bliley, Jr., R.*
8. James P. Moran, Jr., D.*
9. Frederick C. Boucher, D.*
10. Frank R. Wolf, R.*
11. Thomas Davis III, R.

Washington
1. Rick White, R.
2. Jack Metcalf, R.
3. Linda Smith, R.
4. Doc Hastings, R.
5. George Nethercutt, R.
6. Norman D. Dicks, D.*
7. Jim McDermott, D.*
8. Jennifer Dunn, R.*
9. Randy Tate, R.

West Virginia
1. Alan B. Mollohan, D.*
2. Robert E. Wise, Jr., D.*
3. Nick J. Rahall II, D.*

Wisconsin
1. Mark Neumann, R.
2. Scott Klug, R.*
3. Steven Gunderson, R.*
4. Gerald D. Kleczka, D.*
5. Thomas Barrett, D.*
6. Thomas E. Petri, R.*
7. David R. Obey, D.*
8. Toby Roth, R.*
9. F. James Sensenbrenner, Jr., R.*

Wyoming
† Barbara Cubin, R.

Nonvoting representatives
American Samoa
Eni F. H. Faleomavaega, D.*

District of Columbia
Eleanor Holmes Norton, D.*

Guam
Robert Underwood, D.*

Puerto Rico
Carlos Romero-Barceló, D.*

Virgin Islands
Victor O. Frazer, Ind.

Newt Gingrich (R., Ga.), *above,* greets reporters after the results of November's midterm elections made Gingrich Speaker of the House, replacing Thomas S. Foley (D. Wash.), *above right.*

White House briefings on federal action planned against the Madison Guaranty Savings and Loan Association. Madison Guaranty was an Arkansas firm whose owner was a partner with the Clintons in the Whitewater venture. White House officials said they sought the information to respond to press inquiries about the case. Robert S. Fiske, Jr., the first independent counsel named to investigate the case, had concluded in June that there was nothing improper about the briefings.

Republicans, who will head Senate and House committees in the 104th Congress, said they would conduct additional hearings in 1995.

Leadership changes. In addition to the departure of Speaker Foley, there were other leadership changes in Congress—mostly stemming from the Republican victory in November. Long-time House Republican leader Robert H. Michel of Illinois had announced in 1993 that he would retire at the end of the 1994 session. The new House Republican leader, Newt Gingrich of Georgia, was chosen by his fellow House Republicans on December 5 to become Speaker of the House in the 104th Congress.

Representative Richard K. Armey of Texas was the choice for House majority leader. Representative Richard A. Gephardt of Missouri, the House majority leader in the 103rd Congress, was chosen on November 30 to continue as leader of the Democrats when they become the minority party.

In the Senate, Republican Robert J. Dole of Kansas was in line to succeed Mitchell as majority leader. Democratic Senator Thomas A. Daschle of South Dakota was due to be minority-party leader.

Ethics. Representative Dan Rostenkowski (D., Ill.), chairman of the House Ways and Means Committee, was indicted May 31 on charges of embezzlement and obstruction of justice. He pleaded innocent. Although the Chicago congressman had won renomination in March, he had to resign as chairman. He was defeated in the November election after serving 36 years in Congress.

Two other Democratic members of the House were indicted in 1994. Representative Mel Reynolds, also of Chicago, was indicted August 19 on state charges of statutory rape and solicitation of child pornography. Representative Walter Tucker of California was indicted August 11 on federal charges of extortion and tax evasion. Both pleaded innocent.

In the Senate, Republican Bob Packwood of Oregon turned over his personal diaries to the Select Committee on Ethics in early 1994 for its inquiry into sexual harassment charges against him. Congress held no hearings on the Packwood case in 1994 but was expected to in 1995.   □ William J. Eaton

See also **Elections; United States, Government of the.** In *World Book,* see **Congress of the United States.**

Connecticut. See State government.

Conservation. The United States Congress approved the California Desert Protection Act on Oct. 8, 1994, designating about 7 million acres (2.8 million hectares) of arid but scenic landscape as national parks and preserves. The act was the largest land-preservation law passed since approval of the Alaska National Interest Lands Conservation Act in 1980.

The act elevated Death Valley and Joshua Tree national monuments to the more-protected national park status and enlarged both. The legislation added about 1.2 million acres (500,000 hectares) to Death Valley and about 234,000 acres (100,000 hectares) to Joshua Tree. At about 3.3 million acres (1.3 million hectares), Death Valley National Park became the largest national park in the lower 48 states.

The act also created the East Mojave National Preserve near the town of Needles, Calif. Preserves allow some hunting and trapping, but national parks do not. The act also created extra wilderness area in Joshua Tree National Park and Death Valley. Visitors to wilderness areas are prohibited from operating motorized vehicles.

The boundaries of this desert realm contain enormous, sweeping sand dunes, some of which rise 700 feet (210 meters); 90 mountain ranges; the world's largest forest of Joshua trees; and the only dinosaur tracks found in California. The lands are home to more than 2,000 species of plants and animals, including the endangered desert tortoise. Ancient rock paintings also exist in the new parks. President Bill Clinton, who strongly favored the law, signed the act on Oct. 31, 1994.

Smog in national parks. The results of a 10-year study of air quality in national parks released in May 1994 showed that visible smog increased significantly in 2 Southeastern parks but remained steady or fell in 10 Western parks. Physicist Thomas Cahill of the University of California at Davis and his colleagues conducted the study by taking air samples each week from the parks.

The study showed that atmospheric haze, often called smog, had increased 39 percent at Great Smoky Mountains National Park in Tennessee and North Carolina and 37 percent at Shenandoah Park in Virginia. In 1950, visibility in Great Smoky Mountains National Park was about 70 miles (110 kilometers). But by 1992, it had declined to 12 miles (19 kilometers), worse than summer visibility in Los Angeles, the scientists said.

The smog formed mainly as a result of emissions of sulfur dioxide from power plants. Sulfur dioxide particles combined with moisture in the air in the presence of sunlight to create the smog.

At the same time, the study reported that smog remained at about the same level or declined in 10 Western parks. At the Chiricahua National Monument in Arizona, haze decreased 33 percent, and Mesa Verde National Park in Colorado recorded a 25 percent reduction.

Scientists could not fully explain the worsening air quality in the Southeastern parks. Monitoring by the U.S. Environmental Protection Agency showed that sulfur dioxide emissions either remained steady or fell in the Southeast during the study years. But the scientists said that fewer power plants in the West, stricter emissions controls, and lower humidity, which contributes to smog formation, probably helped improve air quality in the West.

Everglades protection. Florida Governor Lawton M. Chiles signed the Everglades Forever Act into law on May 3, 1994. The law was designed to help restore the Everglades to a more natural condition by creating marshes around Lake Okeechobee. The marshes filter polluted water as it enters the Everglades from the north. Agricultural runoff, mostly phosphorus used in fertilizer on sugar plantations around Lake Okeechobee, has polluted the Everglades for decades. The phosphorus has encouraged the growth of cattails—not a natural component of the ecosystem—wiping out much of the region's natural saw grass, disrupting fish breeding, and harming other wildlife.

The restoration will create 40,000 acres (16,200 hectares) of filtration marshes around Lake Okeechobee, a project estimated to cost $685 million. Sugar companies in the area will contribute about 30 percent of that cost. Many conservationists were unhappy with the agreement, however, claiming that it allows the sugar industry too much time—as many as 10 years—to achieve the new clean water standards.

Lower logging limits. On April 21, a federal judge in Seattle approved the Clinton Administration's plan to allow limited logging in 24 million acres (9.7 million hectares) of public forests in the Pacific Northwest. The new logging limits are part of a broader forest management program that the Clinton Administration has proposed for the Pacific Northwest that is aimed at protecting the area's giant trees (some of which are hundreds of years old), as well as more than 1,000 plant and animal species that depend on the ancient forests for survival. Such plants and animals include northern spotted owls, marbled murrelets, and salmon.

The Clinton plan permits logging on 4 million acres (1.6 million hectares). Much of this area is second growth forest or is already fragmented by highways. No-logging zones will also be increased to 100 feet (30 meters) on each side of streams, doubling the previous requirement. Forests along streams help salmon populations by reducing damaging silt from runoff.

On June 6, the judge formally removed the three-year ban on logging in the Pacific Northwest. Since the Clinton plan offered significant protection for the area, the ban was no longer necessary, the judge said. However, conservationists complained that the plan still did not provide sufficient protection for an-

California's Death Valley, *background,* became a national park in October when Congress passed the California Desert Protection Act, creating two new national parks— Death Valley and Joshua Tree National Park. Besides elevating the two areas from the less-protected status of national monuments, the act enlarged both areas, *above,* and also created the East Mojave National Preserve.

cient forests, and loggers were angry because the projected number of job losses rose to 9,500, nearly doubling previous estimates.

Wildlife comebacks. On June 16, Interior Secretary Bruce Babbitt announced that gray wolves would be reintroduced into Yellowstone National Park and locations in central Idaho. Wolves were common in the northern Rocky Mountains until early in the 1900's. By the 1920's, ranchers and government agents had exterminated the species there because of the perceived threat to domestic livestock. To appease ranchers, the Clinton Administration withdrew protection for wolves under the Endangered Species Act, which covers wolves elsewhere in the United States. Wolves caught attacking livestock on private land outside the park or other protected areas can be shot.

Wildlife managers planned to begin importing wolves from Canada in late 1994 and release them in early 1995. On Nov. 15, 1994, the American Farm Bureau Federation sued in federal court to halt the reintroduction, and the situation remained unresolved at year's end.

The Interior Department proposed changing the status of the bald eagle from endangered to threatened over most of its range on June 29. The move meant that America's national symbol was no longer on the verge of extinction, but its existence still remained precarious. Under the new status, the federal government will still review activities such as logging and development that threaten bald eagle habitats, but the process will be less stringent.

Bald eagles and other birds of prey were devastated by DDT, a pesticide that interfered with their ability to reproduce. Only 417 bald eagle pairs were found in the lower 48 states by 1963. Regulators banned DDT in 1972, and in 1973 the Endangered Species Act, which protects threatened animals, took effect. These measures, followed by captive breeding and reintroduction programs, increased bald eagle populations to more than 4,000 pairs by 1993.

Survival in the mist. Only some 650 mountain gorillas remain in Africa, a third of them in the Virunga Mountains of Rwanda. Scientists at the Karisoke Research Station have studied a large group of the gorillas since the mid-1970's. The late naturalist Dian Fossey made these animals famous through her research on them, which she described in her book *Gorillas in the Mist* (1983).

When a bloody civil war broke out in April 1994, researchers and park wardens had to be evacuated, and many feared for the rare primates' survival. In late August, as fighting subsided, a few scientists managed to return to Karisoke. The study group of 60 gorillas had only 2 missing, and 1 of those was believed to be alive. A second group of 60 also appeared to be intact.   □ Eugene J. Walter, Jr.

See also **Environmental pollution.** In *World Book,* see **Conservation.**

Consumerism. The United States economy grew strongly in 1994. Economists expected the *gross domestic product (GDP)* to have grown 3.8 percent by the year's end. The GDP is the value of all goods and services produced in a country and is one of the most widely used measures of a nation's total economic performance in a single year.

Inflation, measured by the Consumer Price Index (CPI), remained at low levels in 1994. Prices rose only 2.7 percent over a 12-month period that began in November 1993, barely above the rate from the year before. The CPI is the standard measure of the cost of living compiled by the Bureau of Labor Statistics.

Nevertheless, U.S. interest rates climbed in 1994 due to fears of inflation. By mid-November, the Federal Reserve board, which controls the nation's money supply, had raised short-term interest rates six times in 1994 to keep inflation under control.

Consumer confidence in the economy rose steadily throughout most of 1994. Consumer confidence is measured by the Consumer Confidence Index, a monthly survey that asks consumers about their confidence in their financial status for the next six months. As of November, the Index stood at 101, much higher than it was the same month in 1993. An index of 100 represents the level of consumer confidence in 1985, when the U.S. economy was growing steadily.

Legislation. The U.S. Congress failed to pass health care reform in 1994. Various proposals sought to reform the health insurance market to lower costs and guarantee coverage. Critics complained that the reform proposals relied too heavily on government and would lower quality of care. Supporters vowed to take up the issue again in 1995.

A bill to deregulate the local telephone industry also died in Congress in 1994. The bill would have allowed local phone companies to offer long-distance service and cable television services.

In August 1994, Congress did pass a measure to eliminate state and local regulations on the trucking industry that affected trucking rates and services when shipping within a state. Studies showed that the regulations ultimately added to the cost of consumer products. The Administration of President Bill Clinton calculated that the total cost of the regulations to the industry was $10 billion a year.

Congress passed a bill in the spring allowing banks to open branches in any state starting in 1997. Previously, banks were restricted in their power to open branches in different states. Supporters said the new law would lower banking costs for consumers and increase consumer convenience. Opponents of the bill were concerned about the increased power of large banks and the possibility of inadequate government oversight. Some small banks also feared extinction.

The U.S. Environmental Protection Agency on May 4, 1994, proposed emissions standards for newly manufactured lawn mowers, golf carts, and other products with gasoline-burning engines. The standards were scheduled to take effect in 1996.

The National Highway Traffic Safety Administration warned on Feb. 18, 1994, that children in rear-facing safety seats should not be placed in the front passenger seat because they could be killed if the passenger-side airbag deployed. The report suggested placing baby seats in the rear seat.

Antilock brakes failed to reduce accidents, according to a study released on January 27 by the Highway Loss Data Institute, an auto insurance industry group. Although controlled tests had shown that the brakes help avoid accidents by preventing skidding, accident data and insurance claims showed that cars equipped with antilock brakes had the same accident record as those without. The institute suggested that many drivers do not properly use antilock brakes, which require the driver to hold down the brake pedal in a skid rather than pump it.

Cable TV. The Federal Communications Commission ordered a 7 percent cut in basic cable TV rates in 1994. A 10 percent cut had been ordered in 1993. Increasing competition from direct broadcast satellites was also expected to lower cable TV rates. This new technology enables subscribers to receive as many as 175 channels. ☐ John Merline

In *World Book,* see **Consumerism; Economics.**
Costa Rica. See **Latin America.**

Courts. The most sensational trial of 1994 involved former professional football star O. J. Simpson, who was accused of stabbing to death his second ex-wife, Nicole Brown Simpson, and a friend of hers, Ronald L. Goldman, outside her home in Brentwood, a subdivision of Los Angeles. Prosecutors used sophisticated genetic testing in an attempt to link Simpson to the June 12 killings. On June 17, Simpson was arrested at his home after he and a friend led police on a freeway chase that was televised live across the United States. Simpson pleaded not guilty.

The case drew extensive publicity because of Simpson's celebrity and the gravity of the charges. In 1968, he won the Heisman Trophy, college football's most prestigious award, as a running back for the University of Southern California in Los Angeles. Simpson later played professional football for the Buffalo Bills. In 1989, Simpson was sentenced to two years' probation and 120 hours of community service for physically abusing Nicole Simpson. The couple married in 1985, had two children, and divorced in 1992. Simpson's murder trial started on Sept. 26, 1994, and continued into 1995. (See **Courts** Special Report: **Guilty or Not Guilty . . . by a Hair?**)

***Exxon Valdez* settlements.** A federal jury on Sept. 16, 1994, ordered Exxon Corporation to pay $5 billion to Alaskans in compensation for damages stemming from a massive 1989 oil spill off the coast of Alaska. The oil spill, which occurred after the

Former football star O. J. Simpson confers with one of his attorneys during pretrial hearings in July on charges that he murdered his ex-wife and her friend.

tanker *Exxon Valdez* ran aground, poured nearly 11 million gallons (42 million liters) of crude oil into Prince William Sound. The jury also ordered the ship's captain, Joseph J. Hazelwood, who was fired after the incident, to pay $5,000 in punitive damages. On June 13, 1994, the jury found that Exxon had acted recklessly in letting Hazelwood, who was known to have a drinking problem, serve as captain of the *Valdez*. Hazelwood admitted having several drinks before the accident.

During the year, juries also awarded commercial fishermen $287 million for economic losses caused by the spill and Alaskan natives $9.7 million for damage to their hunting and fishing grounds. Exxon settled with another group of natives for $20 million.

Coffee burns. On August 17, a New Mexico jury awarded nearly $2.9 million to an 81-year-old woman who had been severely burned at a McDonald's fast-food restaurant in 1992 when she spilled a cup of coffee in her lap. The award included $160,000 in compensation for her medical expenses and $2.7 million in punitive damages against the McDonald's Corporation for serving its coffee too hot. The judge later reduced the punitive damages to $480,000, and the parties later settled for an undisclosed amount.

Smoking liability? On May 23, 1994, Mississippi became the first state to sue tobacco companies for reimbursement of millions of tax dollars spent on medical treatment for smoking-related illnesses through such programs as Medicaid. West Virginia filed a similar suit on September 20. Minnesota sued cigarette makers on August 18, claiming they violated antitrust laws by conspiring to mislead consumers about the dangers of smoking. Those cases were still pending at year's end. Florida Governor Lawton M. Chiles, Jr., signed a law on May 26 allowing the state to file class-action lawsuits against cigarette companies, using statistics to demonstrate a connection between smoking and certain illnesses.

Immigration payments. Five states sued the federal government in 1994, seeking more than $4-billion to cover the costs of providing social services to immigrants who were in the United States illegally. The states—Arizona, California, Florida, New Jersey, and Texas—claimed the federal government should reimburse them for providing emergency medical care to illegal aliens, educating their children, and imprisoning those convicted of crimes.

The states argued that most of the taxes paid by illegal immigrants go to the federal government, which, they said, does not adequately control immigration. A study released on September 14 by the Urban Institute, a think tank in Washington, D.C., said that the seven states with the largest numbers of illegal immigrants—the five bringing suits plus New York and Illinois—spend nearly $4 billion a year on services for those immigrants.

Gun control. Federal judges in Arizona, Mississippi, Montana, and Vermont struck down a new federal requirement that local law officers check the backgrounds of gun purchasers. The background checks are a key part of a federal gun-control law that took effect February 28. The law also imposes a five-day waiting period before the completion of a handgun sale. The judges said that under the Constitution, Congress cannot force state officials to carry out a federal program. The judges all upheld the waiting-period provision, however. On June 21, a federal judge in Texas ruled that both provisions of the law are permissible under the Constitution. The Mississippi and Texas rulings were appealed, but no decision had been reached by year's end.

Abortion shooting. Outspoken abortion opponent and former minister Paul Hill was found guilty on November 2 of two counts of murder. Hill had been charged with first-degree murder in the deaths of abortion doctor John B. Britton and his security escort, James H. Barrett, on July 29 outside a Pensacola, Fla., abortion clinic. Barrett's wife, June, was wounded in the shootings. On December 6, Hill was sentenced to death. Hill also was convicted on October 5 of violating a new federal law making it a crime to block access to a facility offering abortions.

Assisted suicide. On May 3, a federal judge in Seattle struck down a 1975 Washington state law that banned assisted suicide, saying it violated constitutional guarantees of privacy. On May 10, 1994, Michigan's Court of Appeals struck down a 1993 state law banning assisted suicide, on a technicality involving the law's phrasing. At the same time, the Michigan court ruled that the Constitution does not protect the right to commit suicide.

The Michigan appeals court also reinstated murder charges against physician Jack Kevorkian for helping two terminally ill women die in 1991, before the enactment of the law. And in a separate case, a Michigan jury on May 2, 1994, concluded that Kevorkian had not violated the assisted-suicide ban in aiding the 1993 death of a man suffering from a fatal disorder of the nervous system. Kevorkian's lawyer had argued that the law allows doctors to administer drugs that ultimately hasten death if the intention is to ease pain and not to cause death.

Bombing sentences. Four men convicted in the 1993 bombing of the World Trade Center in New York City were sentenced on May 24 to 240 years in prison without parole and fined $250,000 each. Mohammed Salameh, Nidal Ayyad, Mahmud Abouhalima, and Ahmad Ajaj were the first of seven men charged in the terrorist bombing to be sentenced. The charges ranged from conspiracy to destruction of government property. A fifth man, Bilal Alkaisi, pleaded guilty to a minor charge and awaited sentencing. Two other suspects remained at large. Six people died and more than 1,000 were injured in the blast. ☐ Geoffrey A. Campbell and Linda P. Campbell

See also **Crime; Supreme Court of the United States.** In *World Book,* see **Court.**

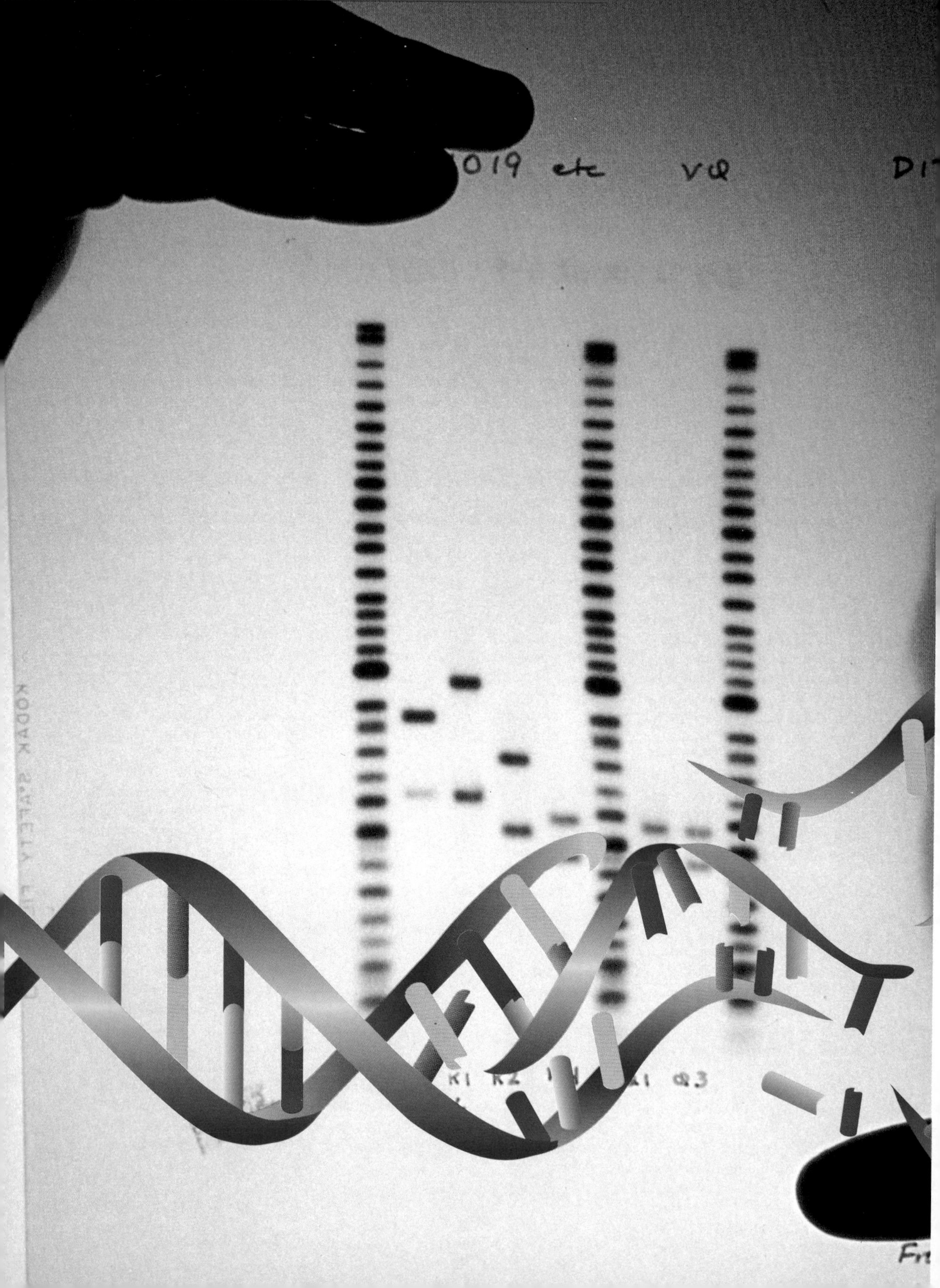

The terms DNA fingerprinting and DNA testing became household words in the summer of 1994, the result of a media blitz surrounding the trial of O. J. Simpson. The former football star, sportscaster, and actor was accused of murdering his second ex-wife, Nicole Brown Simpson, and her friend Ronald L. Goldman on June 12. Among the items found at the crime scene outside Nicole Simpson's home were bloodstains and hair, both of which were hotly contested items of evidence because they can be used for DNA testing. And such tests have recently revolutionized criminal investigations.

DNA testing can be used to help prove the guilt or innocence of crime suspects through analysis of genetic material called deoxyribonucleic acid (DNA). DNA is the molecule of which genes are made. It is carried on threadlike structures called chromosomes in every cell of the body, except red blood cells. Genes are the basic units of heredity and carry the instructions that determine a person's inherited characteristics. With the exception of identical twins, no two individuals have the same genetic makeup. The unique quality of a person's genetic makeup is what makes DNA testing so valuable in criminal investigations.

There are two DNA tests commonly used in criminal investigations: the restriction fragment length polymorphism (RFLP) test (also called DNA fingerprinting) and the polymerase chain reaction (PCR) test. RFLP testing involves comparing the pattern of chemical subunits in DNA from different people. The PCR test compares certain forms of one or more genes that can vary from person to person.

The RFLP test is considered the more discerning DNA test because it can identify a DNA pattern unique to an individual if certain stand-

Guilty
or
Not Guilty . . .
by a Hair?

By David S. Haymer

The widely publicized murder trial of O. J. Simpson focused the public's attention in 1994 on the use of DNA testing in criminal investigations.

Glossary

DNA: Deoxyribonucleic acid, the molecule of which genes are made. It carries the coded information for inherited characteristics.

DNA fingerprinting: Popular term for restriction fragment length polymorphism (RFLP) test. Also known as DNA profiling.

Genes: The basic units of heredity. They are located in all cells, except red blood cells, on threadlike structures called chromosomes.

PCR: Polymerase chain reaction, a method used to produce millions of copies of certain genes.

RFLP: Restriction fragment length polymorphism, a method used to look at DNA chopped up into fragments of different length.

■ The author

David S. Haymer is professor of genetics at the University of Hawaii in Honolulu.

ards are met. However, RFLP can only be done if enough samples of genetic material are collected and the samples are handled properly. If samples are scarce, the PCR test has some important advantages over RFLP. Whereas an RFLP test requires several hairs or a drop of blood the size of a dime, the PCR test can be performed on only a single hair or a tiny drop of blood. An RFLP test also requires DNA that has not been extensively damaged or degraded because of age. PCR, however, can work with very old or deteriorated DNA. So the choice between whether to run an RFLP test or a PCR test depends upon how much evidence is available and what kind of condition it is in.

Producing a DNA test

The RFLP test was developed in 1985 by British geneticist Alec Jeffreys of Leicester University in England. It is based on the theory that, with the exception of identical twins, it is highly unlikely that the DNA fingerprint of one person would match that of another.

To produce a DNA fingerprint, also known as a DNA profile, DNA is first isolated from the biological material available as evidence. Typically, such evidence could be blood, hair, saliva, semen, or skin found at the crime scene. Once the DNA is isolated, it is chopped up into pieces by restriction enzymes. The resulting fragments vary in length from person to person, and each fragment contains a certain pattern of chemical subunits of DNA. The fragments are then separated according to size by a technique called electrophoresis, in which an electric current moves the fragments through a gel. The fragments separate into a pattern of discrete bands. The fragments marked by radioactive tags show up on X-ray film and resemble a crude supermarket bar code.

Forensic technicians then obtain a DNA fingerprint from a suspect, typically using a blood sample, and compare it with the profile from the evidence. If the two fingerprints match, many juries consider such a match powerful evidence that the suspect was at the crime scene.

PCR is a method used to produce millions of copies of certain genes. This ability to replicate genes makes PCR useful in criminal investigations where only a tiny amount of biological evidence is available or the DNA in the evidence is damaged. PCR was developed in the 1980's by biochemist Kary Mullis, while employed by the Cetus Corporation, a biotechnology company based in Emeryville, Calif. Mullis won the 1993 Nobel Prize in chemistry for developing PCR.

The PCR test is based on the fact that in human populations, many different forms of some genes exist. Different forms of the same gene are called alleles. The PCR test determines which allele or alleles—people can have a pair of alleles—can be

■ DNA tests used in criminal investigations

DNA testing has been widely hailed as one of the greatest advances in criminal investigations in recent history. By comparing DNA found in evidence from a crime scene with that of a suspect, DNA tests can help show who is innocent and who is guilty. The two most common types of DNA tests are the restriction fragment length polymorphism (RFLP) test, also known as DNA fingerprinting, and the polymerase chain reaction (PCR) test.

Some characteristics of RFLP test

- Compares the pattern of chemical subunits in DNA from different people.
- Considered the more discerning type of DNA test for criminal investigations because it identifies a pattern in DNA with a high probability of being unique to one individual.
- A match between the DNA fingerprints of the suspect and material found at the crime scene can be proof that both came from the same person.
- A mismatch between the suspect's profile and that of the material found at the crime scene can be considered proof of a suspect's innocence.
- Requires many cells—for example, the DNA from several strands of hair or a drop of blood the size of a dime.
- Requires DNA that is fresh and in good condition. Strands of DNA cannot be extensively damaged.
- Requires five weeks to three months before test results are available.

Some characteristics of PCR test

- Compares certain forms of genes that can vary from person to person.
- A DNA match between biological evidence from the crime scene and a suspect means that the suspect might be guilty.
- A mismatch between the test samples means the suspect is innocent. If both do not contain the same form of gene, they do not come from the same source.
- Requires only a few cells—for example, a single hair or a tiny drop of blood—because millions of copies of the genes can be made from the limited supply.
- Can be performed on old and damaged DNA because only a small fragment of the DNA strand is used.
- Requires a few days to a week to complete.

■ Technicians visually analyze DNA fingerprints at a commercial laboratory. To help standardize the analysis of DNA testing, the federal government has established an advisory board to recommend testing standards for crime laboratories.

■ Glen Woodall was released from prison and cleared of rape charges after DNA evidence in 1992 showed he had not committed the crime.

found in biological material from the scene of a crime.

The gene most commonly used for the PCR test is called the HLA DQ alpha gene. This gene plays an important role in the body's *immune system* (the body's means of fighting off infections). To determine which allele is present in a crime sample, experts first use the PCR method to make multiple copies of a gene from the sample.

The form of the HLA DQ alpha gene found in the crime evidence is then compared with that of the suspect. If the suspect has the same allele, this is not conclusive proof of identity because other people may also have the same form of the gene. Certain forms of the HLA DQ alpha gene may appear more frequently in certain ethnic groups. However, if there is no match at all between the genes of the suspect and those found in the evidence from the crime scene, that suspect can certainly be excluded from possible guilt.

DNA testing and the courts

DNA testing has been admitted as evidence in state and federal courts in the United States as well as other countries around the world since the first landmark cases in 1987. Some states have passed legislation permitting DNA evidence to be introduced in trials. Other states require that the courts rule on its admissibility on a case-by-case basis. California, for example, uses the Frye rule to determine admissibility. This standard, based on a 1923 federal court decision, requires judges to accept evidence only if it is based on principles generally accepted by the scientific community.

In a federal courtroom, DNA evidence must pass a set of guidelines known as the Federal Rules of Evidence before it can be introduced. These rules state that scientific information should be admitted if it will be helpful to the jury in deciding what happened in the case. Under a 1993 United States Supreme Court ruling, federal judges became responsible for deciding what scientific evidence is admissible. The trial judge may consider many factors related to scientific validity, such as whether a scientific procedure has been tested and verified as accurate and is generally accepted by scientists. In addition, the court may exclude the evidence if the risk that the jury will misunderstand or misinterpret it outweighs its value as proof of what happened.

Objections to DNA evidence

In recent years, trial judges have come to expect the presentation of DNA evidence in many cases. However, defense attorneys often contest the reliability of DNA tests if the results are unfavorable to their client. Some critics of the technique have argued that different results have been obtained by different testing laboratories.

The statistical interpretations of the RFLP test have also been called into question. In 1991, two prominent geneticists, Richard C. Lewontin of Harvard University in Cambridge, Mass., and Daniel L. Hartl, then of Washington University School of Medicine in St. Louis, Mo., published a report challenging the method used to find the likelihood of a chance match between two DNA samples. They argued that not enough was known about DNA patterns within ethnic groups. Certain patterns, they said, might occur more frequently within certain ethnic groups, making the possibility of a chance match more likely. Since their report was published, however, other scientists have concluded that by comparing a sufficient number of fragments from the RFLP test, the odds of a random match can be reduced significantly.

DNA testing procedures have also been called into question. In some cases, courts rejected DNA test results because mistakes were made in handling the sample evidence or because tests were not performed correctly. In these instances, the courts did not dispute the validity of DNA tests, but found that the laboratory did not conduct the tests fairly and accurately.

One potential problem in DNA testing, for example, is that a drop of blood from the scene of a crime may in fact be a mixture of several people's blood. It is also easy for samples to become contaminated with DNA from mold or a variety of other nonhuman sources. Finally, improperly handled evidence can lead to damaged or degraded DNA and poor test results. To address concerns such as these, the Federal Bureau of Investigation (FBI) has established a Forensic Science Research and Training Center (FSRTC) in Quantico, Va. It has also been working with other government agencies and private organizations to establish uniform standards that all laboratories must meet.

To strengthen and standardize the use of DNA testing in the courts, U.S. President Bill Clinton signed into law on Sept. 13, 1994, the DNA Identification Act, part of the federal crime bill. The act would provide grants to states for developing their forensic DNA research laboratories. It also authorized the establishment of an FBI-run national DNA identification index to allow for the exchange of DNA records among states. Finally, it established a DNA standards advisory board to recommend testing standards for crime laboratories.

DNA tests have been a tremendous aid in solving crimes, both in showing who is innocent and in helping prove who is guilty. In recent years, they have even helped release from prison people falsely convicted of crimes. As scientists learn more about the unique genetic information that everyone carries in their chromosomes, DNA tests could become one of the most powerful tools science has to offer in settling questions of innocence or guilt. ■ ■ ■

■ Former football star O. J. Simpson, charged with the murder of his ex-wife and her friend, appears in a Los Angeles courtroom at a preliminary hearing in June 1994. DNA tests were a key component of Simpson's pretrial hearings.

Crime. Crime captivated the public during 1994, from the sensational trial of former football star O. J. Simpson on murder charges to the passage of a major federal anticrime bill. Regardless of statistics that showed that most violent crime rates dropped during the previous year, Americans regarded crime as the nation's most serious problem.

Elected officials scrambled to convince voters that they favored strong anticrime measures. In late August, the United States Congress passed a $30.2-billion anticrime bill that would authorize federal spending for six years.

The bill provided $13.5 billion for law enforcement, including $8.8 billion to state and local authorities to add about 100,000 new police officers. The bill also provided $6.1 billion for crime prevention and inmate rehabilitation programs and $7.9-billion for state prison construction. Other measures included a ban on the sale and possession of 19 types of semiautomatic assault weapons and an extension of the death penalty to more than 50 federal crimes, including carjacking. (See **Crime** Special Report: **Fighting Crime in America.**)

O. J. Simpson, whom many believed to be the greatest running back in the history of football, was charged on June 17 with the brutal stabbing murders of his former wife, Nicole Brown Simpson, and a male friend, Ronald L. Goldman, on June 12 in the Brentwood section of Los Angeles. Simpson alleged-

ly killed the two outside his former wife's residence. Simpson forcefully denied committing the killings and hired the most celebrated group of criminal defense lawyers ever assembled for one defendant. His trial began in September 1994 and was expected to continue into 1995. (See **Courts.**)

Cult deaths. Police in Switzerland and Canada said that 52 people in the same religious cult died in early October 1994 from incidents that combined elements of mass suicide and ritual execution. A 3-month-old child also died in Canada in connection with the cult deaths.

Most of the deaths occurred in Switzerland. Police said 48 members of the Order of the Solar Temple died on October 5 in two towns in Switzerland. Police discovered the bodies after the residences in which the victims were living were set ablaze.

Police said that 23 of the Swiss cult members died in the basement of a burned farmhouse in Cheiry, Switzerland, about 50 miles (80 kilometers) north of Geneva. Many of the Cheiry victims had been shot in the head. Police also found 25 bodies in three chalets in Granges-sur-Salvan, near Geneva.

In Canada, police found the bodies of 4 other cult members and the child on October 4 and 6 in adjoining houses in Morin Heights, about 50 miles north of Montreal. Two of the victims were parents of the child. Two other cult members had arranged for the couple and the child to be killed because one of the

Police hold Paul Hill for the killing of a Pensacola, Fla., abortion doctor and his security escort in July. Hill was convicted of murder in the case in November.

cult leaders thought the child was the Antichrist, police said. The two cult members who had arranged the killing committed suicide, police said.

The cult leaders, Luc Jouret, 46, a Belgian physician, and Joseph DiMambro, 70, a French-Canadian, died in Switzerland. Police said the cult blended elements of Roman Catholicism, astrology, and New Age spiritualism. Police in three regions of France arrested 42 people in December in connection with the cult murders. Police believed that the cult and those arrested in December may have been buying and selling illegal arms.

Mother drowns children. Susan V. Smith of Union, S.C., told police that an armed carjacker forced her out of her car on October 25 and drove off with her two young sons, aged 3 years and 14 months. Along with her estranged husband, Smith pleaded several times on television for the carjacker, whom she described as an African-American man, to return her children safely. Scores of people helped search for the children, and the case of the missing boys drew sympathy from the entire nation.

But Smith's story fell apart, and police arrested her on November 3 and charged her with killing the boys. Smith had confessed that she put the children in the back seat of her car and let it roll into a lake. She told investigators that she had been depressed over a recent breakup with her boyfriend.

Clinic attacks. A gunman killed physician John B. Britton, 69, and his security escort, James H. Barrett, 74, in a shotgun attack outside an abortion clinic in Pensacola, Fla., on July 29. Police arrested Paul J. Hill, 40, a former Presbyterian minister, and charged him with the murders. On October 5, Hill was the first person convicted under a new federal law prohibiting violence at abortion clinics or interfering with visitors to clinics. A state court also found Hill guilty on November 2 of first-degree murder in the shooting. On December 6, Hill was sentenced to die in the electric chair. Hill had advocated killing physicians who perform abortions.

On December 30, a gunman attacked two abortion clinics in Brookline, Mass., killing two people and wounding five others. Police said the alleged gunman, John C. Salvi III, also attacked a Norfolk, Va., abortion clinic the next day, though no one was injured there. Police arrested Salvi outside the Norfolk clinic. He faced first-degree murder charges in Massachusetts.

White House shootings. On October 29, a man fired 27 shots from a semiautomatic weapon at the White House in Washington, D.C. Some shots struck the front pillars of the White House and shattered a window. President Bill Clinton was in the White House during the shooting but was unharmed.

Police arrested Francisco M. Duran in the shooting. Duran, a dishonorably discharged Army medic from Colorado Springs, Colo., had allegedly told acquaintances that he intended to "take out" Clinton.

Duran was indicted on 15 felonies, including trying to kill the President.

Police said that someone also may have fired several shots at the White House on December 17. No one was injured, but police found one bullet just inside a dining room window and another on a driveway. Police had no suspects by the end of the year.

Kerrigan saga. Nancy Kerrigan, 24, the top U.S. female figure skater, was clubbed on the right knee in Detroit on January 6, forcing her out of the U.S. figure skating championships. The competition served as the qualifier for the 1994 Winter Olympics in Lillehammer, Norway.

Between January 12 and 19, federal authorities arrested four men in connection with the attack. One of the men, Jeff Gillooly, was the former husband of Tonya Harding, Kerrigan's main rival. Police arrested Gillooly on January 19 in Portland, Ore., Harding's hometown. Gillooly told police that Harding had helped plan the attack, but Harding denied it. On February 1, Gillooly pleaded guilty to racketeering in connection with planning the assault and was sentenced in July to two years' imprisonment.

On March 16, Harding pleaded guilty to a conspiracy charge of hindering the investigation of the attack. The charge resulted from her admission that she discovered the plot to attack Kerrigan after it happened but conspired with Gillooly to cover it up. She denied prior knowledge of the attack.

Mail bomber strikes again. A mail bomb killed advertising executive Thomas J. Mosser, 50, on December 10 in North Caldwell, N.J. The Federal Bureau of Investigation (FBI) said that the bombing strongly resembled 14 others that had occurred since 1978 around the United States. The bombing victims had included airline executives and scholars involved in computer sciences and genetics.

Crime rates down. According to the FBI, crime rates fell during the first six months of 1994 compared with the same period in 1993. FBI figures released in December 1994 showed that the number of crimes reported to police in the first six months of the year fell 3 percent compared with the first six months of 1993.

The December figures demonstrated a long-term pattern of declining crime rates. Although rates for most crimes rose steadily from the mid-1960's to 1980, rates in the 1990's for most crimes were at or below 1980 levels. The National Crime Victimization Survey (NCVS), which the U.S. Bureau of the Census has conducted annually since 1973, also showed a decline in crime rates. Researchers compile the NCVS by interviewing 80,000 to 100,000 Americans about crimes committed against them or their family members. In the March 1994 victimization survey, which recorded crime rates for 1992, robbery, rape, theft, and burglary rates were lower in 1992 than in 1973.

□ Michael Tonry

In *World Book,* see **Crime.**

Fighting Crime in America

New approaches to fighting crime were part of federal crime legislation enacted in 1994, but will the new law be effective in deterring crime?

By Michael Tonry

M any Americans have become increasingly alarmed by what they see as an epidemic of lawlessness in the United States. In early 1994, according to a Gallup Poll, most Americans named crime as the most important problem facing the country. Sensing the public's concern, President Bill Clinton made toughness on crime a major element of his January State of the Union address. Congress, too, heard the call to action and spent weeks during the summer of 1994 hotly debating proposals for a new crime bill.

Paradoxically, the intensified concern over crime came at a time when overall crime rates were falling. The U.S. Department of Justice's Bureau of Justice Statistics (BJS) reported in November 1993 that the nation's crime rate, based on victims' reports of crime happening to them or to family members, had reached a 20-year low in 1992. The Federal Bureau of Investigation likewise reported that official police records of crime for 1992 showed overall rates were about the same as in 1980. However, within those declining overall statistics were rising numbers of murders, robberies, and assaults involving handguns. Such violent crimes outraged and shocked most Americans, leading to a belief that crime in general was rampant.

Many elected officials, especially those who were up for reelection in the fall of 1994, decided they could not afford to appear "soft on crime" to their constituencies. Thus, in August, after weeks of heated debate, Congress enacted the Violent Crime Control and Law Enforcement Act of 1994.

Among its many provisions, the new $30.2-billion act provided for mandatory life sentences for those convicted of three serious felonies, the so-called three-strikes-and-you're-out provision. It also called for the establishment of boot camps for young offenders, support for a program known as Community Oriented Policing Services (COPS), and an increase in the number of federal crimes. All are newly popular approaches to the effort to control crime. The three-strikes-and-you're-out provision addresses the issue of what many people regard as lenient treatment for repeat offenders. The military discipline of a boot camp is supposed to raise the self-esteem of young nonviolent offenders who are thought to benefit from the rigid structure of the camps. And the COPS program sends officers to work closely with citizens and local businesses to prevent crime and help people feel safer.

But none of these provisions are without controversy, and as with most controversies, the opposing sides generally divide along conservative and liberal lines. Reflecting the "get-tough-on-crime" mood in Congress, most of the act's major provisions stiffen penalties or encourage states to impose harsher sentences than in previous laws.

Three-strikes laws

The 1994 act requires federal judges to impose life sentences on offenders convicted for a third time of violent or other serious crimes. Such habitual offender laws have existed since the 1920's, but the concept began to attract renewed attention in 1993, when Washington state voters approved a crime initiative mandating a life sentence

■ **The author**
Michael Tonry is a professor of law and public policy at the University of Minnesota Law School in Minneapolis.

for a third violent felony. The measure was quickly dubbed a three-strikes-and-you're-out law. Since 1993, 16 states have passed three-strikes laws, and in 1994 another 14 states were considering them.

Proponents of three-strikes laws argue that people who repeatedly commit serious violent crimes have shown that they are indifferent to the well-being of others and deserve to be severely punished. Confining them for life prevents them from repeating their crimes in society at large. Advocates also claim that such laws will serve as deterrents to crime and reduce crime rates.

Critics say that three-strikes laws seldom deter violent crimes. Furthermore, they say, many of the laws at the state level are drafted too broadly and include offenders who are not chronically violent. For example, California's three-strikes law, which the governor signed in March 1994, includes burglaries. Most burglaries do not involve violence. In 1993, 427,000 burglaries were committed in California. This means that the number of convicted burglars who could face a life sentence is potentially enormous.

Some California judges say that the law takes away their power to evaluate cases individually. In 1994, for example, a man already convicted of several felonies faced the possibility of a life sentence for stealing pizza. Another man faced life in prison for the theft of two bicycles.

It was this inability of the state law to differentiate between property crimes and violent felonies that made a California superior court judge rule the law unconstitutional. In July, the judge refused to sentence a convict to life for smuggling $\frac{3}{10}$ of an ounce (8 grams) of marijuana into his cell, his third felony conviction. The judge's ruling, however, could be overturned by the state supreme court.

Major provisions of the 1994 crime act

- Expands the death penalty to more than 50 federal crimes.
- Bans the manufacture, sale, and possession of 19 models of semi-automatic weapons.
- Provides grants to local governments to hire more police.
- Mandates life in prison for those convicted in federal court of three violent felonies or serious drug offenses.
- Provides grants to states to build and operate new prisons.
- Orders sexual offenders to be registered with state law-enforcement officials for 10 years.
- Allows previous sex offenses to be used as evidence in federal trials.
- Allows adult treatment of 13-year-olds charged with some violent crimes, including murder, armed robbery, and rape.
- Provides funds for boot camps and other alternatives to prison for young offenders.

An expanded inmate population under three-strikes laws could place an enormously costly burden on state and federal budgets, say the critics. Construction of prison space for one inmate runs from $50,000 to $150,000, depending on the location of the prison and its level of security. Operating the prison typically costs from $15,000 to $35,000 per prisoner annually. In California, the Department of Corrections estimated that the state's new law would add 267,000 more inmates to the state prison population by the year 2027 at an annual cost of $5.7 billion. Building the needed prisons would cost an additional $21 billion. The department estimated that its budget would double from 9 to 18 percent of state spending by the year 2002.

Even laws drafted to include only the most violent crimes carry an expensive price tag and may not significantly improve public safety,

▪ Crime in America

The Federal Bureau of Investigation receives crime reports from law enforcement agencies nationwide. It tracks seven serious offenses that would most likely be reported accurately to the police, categorizing them as violent or property crimes.

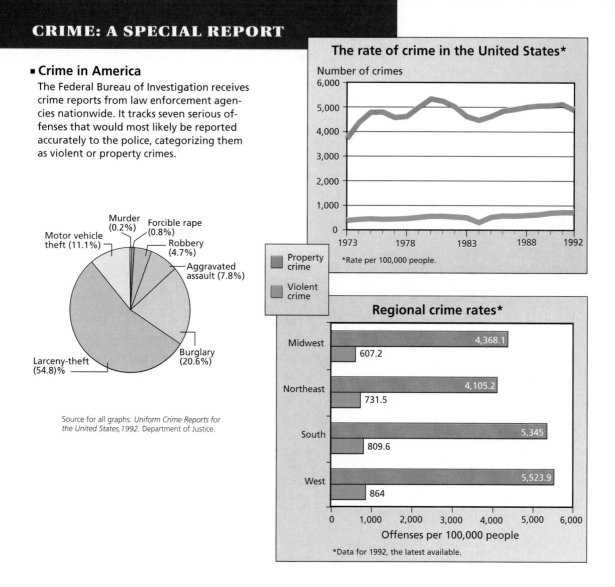

The rate of crime in the United States*

Number of crimes

*Rate per 100,000 people.

Murder (0.2%)
Forcible rape (0.8%)
Motor vehicle theft (11.1%)
Robbery (4.7%)
Aggravated assault (7.8%)
Burglary (20.6%)
Larceny-theft (54.8)%

Property crime
Violent crime

Source for all graphs: *Uniform Crime Reports for the United States, 1992.* Department of Justice.

Regional crime rates*

Region	Property crime	Violent crime
Midwest	4,368.1	607.2
Northeast	4,105.2	731.5
South	5,345	809.6
West	5,523.9	864

Offenses per 100,000 people

*Data for 1992, the latest available.

say critics. Most violent offenders cease being violent by the time they reach their middle to late 30's, according to the BJS. Therefore, holding them in prison into their 50's, 60's, and beyond does little to prevent violent crime. However, the cost of incarceration rises, fueled for one thing by increased medical care that usually accompanies aging.

Finally, critics of three-strikes laws and other harsh sentencing measures argue that there is little evidence these measures deter crime. The Administration of President Ronald Reagan asked the National Academy of Sciences (NAS) in Washington, D.C., to survey the effects of criminal penalties on crime rates in the United States. The NAS Panel on the Understanding and Control of Violence found that the average prison sentences for committing violent crimes tripled from the mid-1970's to the late 1980's. The NAS report, issued in 1993, noted that "if tripling the average length of sentence of incarceration per crime had a strong preventive effect, then violent crime rates

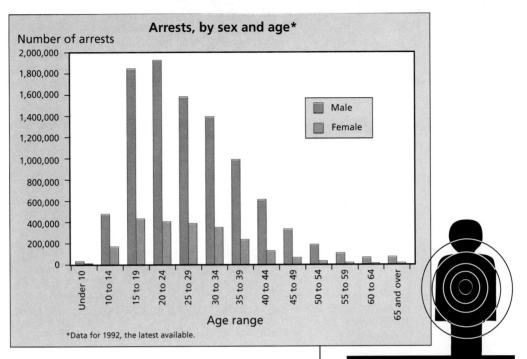

Arrests, by sex and age*

Number of arrests

Legend:
- Male
- Female

Age range

*Data for 1992, the latest available.

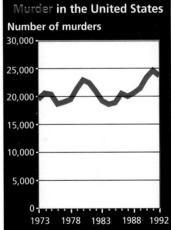

Murder in the United States

Number of murders

1973 1978 1983 1988 1992

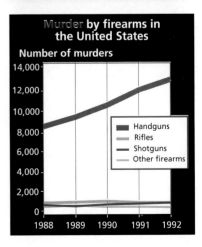

Murder by firearms in the United States

Number of murders

Legend:
- Handguns
- Rifles
- Shotguns
- Other firearms

1988 1989 1990 1991 1992

should have declined." Overall, the panel found they did not.

Similar conclusions have been reached by commissions in other countries. In the United Kingdom, a government study on sentencing laws and their effects, issued in 1990, found that "it is unrealistic to construct sentencing arrangements on the assumption that most offenders will weigh up the possibilities in advance and base their conduct on rational calculation." In Canada, the Canadian Sentencing Commission in 1987 concluded from their study that there was no justification for using deterrence as a guide in imposing sentences.

Boot camps

Another provision of the 1994 crime act that won widespread support among lawmakers and the public is the establishment of more boot camps for young, nonviolent offenders. The first boot camp opened in November 1983 in Oklahoma, and by 1994, the concept had spread to 30 states and the federal correction system. In 1994, there were about 8,000 inmates in 50 camps. Offenders serve from three- to six-month terms at hard labor under constant military discipline, after which they "graduate" into an intensely monitored probation. The discipline and long hours of hard work are intended to shock them into quitting their criminal behavior for

■ Combating crime

The 1994 crime bill authorized funds for more boot camps for youthful first offenders and for community policing programs. It also provided for stiffer prison sentences.

Officers shout at new arrivals to line up in a Florida boot camp, *below*. Military discipline and hours of hard work are supposed to shock young offenders into giving up crime. But, experts say, once released, boot camp inmates are no less likely to commit crimes than inmates from conventional prisons.

A new state prison goes up in Texas, *left.* Under the 1994 crime bill, anyone convicted of a third violent crime or a federal drug charge will be sentenced to life in prison. The new law and similar laws at the state levels, experts say, could place enormous pressures on state and federal budgets as inmate populations grow and new prisons are built.

Officers in a community policing program ride bicycles on a routine visit to a New York City park, *above.* Although people feel safer when police are highly visible, expert studies show that their presence does not necessarily deter crime.

good, which for most offenders in boot camps means giving up burglary or drug dealing. Boot camps are also supposed to reduce prison overcrowding.

But critics of the camps say they have fallen far short of these goals. In 1994, criminologist Doris L. MacKenzie of the University of Maryland in College Park studied boot camps in eight states for the U.S. Justice Department. MacKenzie found that boot camp inmates were no less likely to commit new crimes once returned to society than were comparable offenders in other types of facilities. In most states, boot camps actually increased prison crowding and costs, rather than reducing them. This occurred because judges often sentenced to boot camp offenders who otherwise would have been given probation. Thus, the existence of boot camps increased the inmate population.

Many convicts are also returned to the prison population because they flunk out of the boot camps. MacKenzie and others found that on average about 40 percent of boot camp inmates cannot, or will not, finish their sentences, even though in many cases their sentences had been reduced by entering the camp. As punishment, they were reassigned to regular prisons for longer terms.

Many corrections officials oppose the use of boot camps for nonviolent first offenders. They say that boot camps save money only when used for prisoners who otherwise would have received long sentences in regular prisons. The MacKenzie report agreed with that viewpoint and also recommended that prison managers, not judges, select inmates who are appropriate for boot camp.

Community policing

The centerpiece of the federal crime act, according to many analysts, is the COPS program. COPS would enable cities to qualify for federal grants to hire more police officers, up to 100,000 nationwide, by setting up programs in which the police work with social service agencies at the local level.

COPS is not a new concept. So-called "community policing" began in various cities in the mid-1970's. Police departments in Newark, N.J., Houston, and elsewhere, for example, began pilot projects to test the effectiveness of making police officers more visible to citizens. They set up small neighborhood police offices and assigned officers to foot patrol, rather than riding in vehicles. The officers also attempted to work closely with social service agencies and neighborhood groups to identify potential trouble-spots or troublemakers. The main goal was to intervene before a crime occurred. Evaluations in Newark and Houston by the Police Foundation, a Washington, D.C.-based organization that seeks to increase police effectiveness to control crime, showed that the pilot projects had little effect on crime rates, but that residents felt safer and preferred the new approach. For these reasons, other cities soon began community policing as well.

Many police officials, however, are skeptical about COPS because of the way federal funding is structured. The 1994 law authorizes funding that gradually decreases over a six-year period. Thereafter, cities that have received the grants must find ways to support the new officers. With many cities strapped for revenue, they could be hard-pressed to keep the program going.

Critics say that the Clinton Administration's claim of 100,000 new police officers is misleading in any event. A city could decide to use the money for overtime pay, not new officers, or to buy equipment. The money, critics say, is only a short-term subsidy that will never cover more than 75 percent of an officer's salary, and at that, only for a few years. Thus, the effect is that a total of as few as 20,000 officers may be added to police forces. Furthermore, the law states that half the total sum for COPS must be spent in cities of less than 150,000 inhabitants, though most crime is committed in much larger cities.

Constitutional questions

Finally, the 1994 crime act raises important constitutional issues concerning relations between the federal government and state governments. Some of the provisions of the 1994 act "federalize" crimes that had been prosecuted in state courts, and other provisions set federal requirements that states must meet to use federally funded prisons. Both sets of provisions may be construed as federal interference with state sovereignty.

The states have long had the primary authority over local law enforcement. The new law, however, gives federal courts jurisdiction to handle any violent crime involving a gun and many sex crimes. This could result in a drastic reorganization of the federal court system as potentially tens of thousands of cases are transferred from state to federal courts. The federal court system would then need more money to hire additional federal judges and other judicial employees.

The new law also requires states to change their sentencing laws in order to qualify for federal funds to build new prisons for violent state offenders. Currently, most violent criminals serve about 55 percent of their sentences. The new law requires that prisoners serve at least 85 percent of their sentences. To be able to use federal funds to relieve overcrowding in state prisons, most states would have to fundamentally overhaul their existing sentencing and corrections systems.

The constitutional question to be decided is whether the federal government, by controlling funding, has the power to coerce states into changing their laws. Proponents argue that crime is a serious problem and federal lawmakers should do everything they can to control it. Opponents counter that such laws undermine the states' sovereignty and are a radical departure from well-established divisions of authority between federal and state governments.

The value of the new law

In scrutinizing the entire 1994 crime act, many critics say the new laws do not form a coherent program. They are instead, these critics say, a conglomeration of pet projects of lawmakers whose votes were needed for passage. Moreover, they say, funding for all the programs may be illusory. The money is supposed to come from reductions in other government spending, mainly through reduced federal payrolls as more than 270,000 federal employees retire over the next six years and are not replaced.

On the other hand, defenders of the crime act say it is an important symbol, representing government's determination to combat the pestilence of violent crime infesting cities from coast to coast. They say it will make Americans feel that the federal government is responsive to their fears and concerns. The next few years' experience will test the validity of each of these views. ■ ■ ■

For further reading:

Containing Crime: Community Based Approaches. Ed. by John McNeill and Bryan Williams. Macmillan, 1991.

Moore, Mark H. "Problem Solving and Community Policing." In *Modern Policing.* Ed. by Michael Tonry and Norval Morris. University of Chicago Press, 1992.

Stenson, Kevin and Cowell, D. *The Politics of Crime Control.* Sage, 1992.

Croatia

Croatia agreed on Jan. 19, 1994, to establish low-level diplomatic relations with Serbia, the dominant republic of Yugoslavia, ending fighting that had erupted sporadically since Croatia split from Yugoslavia in June 1991. But Croatian leaders continued to protest the presence of a self-proclaimed Serbian republic in the Krajina region, a part of Croatian territory. In September 1994, Croatian President Franjo Tudjman called for international sanctions against Yugoslavia for its support of Serb forces in Krajina, but his call was not answered.

Bosnian agreement. In 1994, tensions eased between Croatia and Bosnia-Herzegovina (often called Bosnia), which had fought over Croat claims to Bosnian territory. In March, Croatian officials endorsed an agreement between the Muslim-dominated Bosnian government and Croat leaders in Bosnia. The agreement outlined the formation of a Croat-Muslim federation in Bosnia, which the two groups would rule jointly. Under a separate plan, Croatian officials agreed to an eventual merger between the new federation and Croatia. Implementation of the plan was held up by Serb occupation of Bosnian territory. Croatian leaders expressed hope that their cooperation with Bosnia would diffuse the threat of economic sanctions from the United Nations and would lead to foreign financial assistance. New Bosnian Serb offensives in Bosnia in late 1994, however, raised fears of new conflicts in Croatia.

Economy. Croatian leaders remained committed in 1994 to an economic stabilization program initiated in October 1993. The government continued to control wages and took steps to maintain low inflation levels achieved in late 1993. However, industrial production continued to decline, and the unemployment level remained high at about 17 percent in March 1994.

Croatia harbored an estimated 380,000 Bosnian refugees—nearly one-tenth of Croatia's total population. Most had no income and had to rely on government aid. But the government was forced to cut back on social welfare spending, increasing the burden on the nation's poor population.

In 1994, Croatian officials sought to revive privatization of industry. Regulations were eased on the use of foreign currency to purchase shares in state businesses. Sales of shares began in March. Workers held several strikes in early 1994 to protest privatization, which they claimed would reduce wages and eliminate jobs. Teachers and university professors also struck to protest national budget cuts.

A border dispute between Croatia and Slovenia arose in 1994, when Slovenian officials included four Croatian villages on Slovenian voting rolls. Croatia and its northern neighbor carried on discussions regarding various border issues during the year.

□ Sharon L. Wolchik

See also **Bosnia-Herzegovina; Europe** (Facts in brief table); **Yugoslavia.** In *World Book,* see **Croatia.**

Cuba. Amid growing unrest over a seemingly endless string of hardships, Cubans fled their island nation by the thousands during 1994. Some 30,000 Cubans struck out for Florida during the year, often aboard fragile, unseaworthy craft. The exodus was the largest since the 1980 Mariel boatlift carried about 125,000 Cubans to the United States, and it caused a political crisis in Washington, D.C., as the Administration of President Bill Clinton attempted to halt the flow of refugees.

The situation reached crisis proportions in late July and early August after hijackers seized several ferries near Havana, the capital, and attempted to flee the island. The hijackers clashed with Cuban Coast Guard vessels, and further confrontations led to antigovernment riots on August 5 in Havana in which two police died, and hundreds were arrested.

Cuban President Fidel Castro blamed his nation's hardships on the U.S.-led trade embargo against Cuba that had been in effect since 1962. Many observers believed that Castro encouraged the exodus in an effort to persuade Washington to loosen or cancel the embargo.

On Aug. 19, 1994, Clinton reversed a 28-year-old U.S. policy that granted asylum to any Cuban who reached the United States or its waters. Most refugees picked up at sea were taken to the U.S. naval base at Guantánamo Bay, Cuba.

Refugee agreement. On September 9, the Clinton Administration reached an agreement in New York City with the Cuban regime to resolve the crisis. Castro promised to halt the exodus in return for a U.S. pledge to provide visas to 20,000 Cubans annually to immigrate to the United States. The United States had agreed to grant a maximum of 20,000 visas annually to Cubans in 1984.

Increased austerity. Castro streamlined Cuba's government and instituted broad austerity programs in April. His moves were in anticipation of a poor sugar harvest, the mainstay of the Cuban economy. The Cuban sugar crop was worse in 1994 than in 1993, when it fell to a 30-year low. The reorganization cut spending on the armed forces in half, cut subsidies for food and medicine, and increased the cost of water and electricity. In a frantic effort to feed the Cuban people, Castro permitted farmers, beginning in September 1994, to sell surplus production on the open market.

Castro, meanwhile, continued to call on the United States to lift its trade embargo. He found a sympathetic hearing among most of the region's leaders. On June 20, Canada announced the restoration of its aid program, which it had suspended in 1978. It was "time to turn the page on Cuba," said Canada's foreign minister, in releasing emergency food aid worth $500,000, in Canadian dollars, the amount to be doubled in 1995. □ Nathan A. Haverstock

See also **Latin America** (Facts in brief table). In *World Book,* see **Cuba.**

A U.S. Navy warship steams forward to intercept two rafts carrying Cuban refugees in August as Cubans fled their island by the thousands.

Czech Republic remained politically stable in 1994, the nation's second year of independence since splitting from the former Czechoslovak federation in January 1993. The Czech economy also continued to show promise, in contrast to the troubles faced by most other former Communist countries. The Czech system became widely regarded as one of the most successful efforts toward establishing a democratic government and a market economy.

Prime Minister Václav Klaus's government continued to enjoy public confidence, despite growing reports of corruption among government and business leaders. In November 1994 municipal elections, Klaus's Civic Democratic Party won a majority of seats in most major cities, including Prague.

Property rights dominated much of the public debate in 1994. Controversy erupted over whether property should be returned to people who had lost it during World War II (1939-1945) and the Communist take-over in the late 1940's. In 1994, the Czech government voted to return to Jews property in Bohemia and Moravia taken from them during that time. A related conflict arose over the rights of Sudeten Germans, who were expelled from Czechoslovakia after World War II. Leaders also argued over treatment of the country's large Romany (Gypsy) population. Fueled by widespread anti-Romany sentiment, many Czech officials tried unsuccessfully to restrict the residence rights of Romanies.

The Czech economy continued its recovery in 1994. Production increased slightly during the first half of the year. Contrary to expectations, unemployment remained low—from 3 to 4 percent. Inflation, however, increased gradually.

The nation's privatization program advanced, as the government continued to distribute to citizens vouchers that could be exchanged for stock in state-owned assets. By the end of the year, about 70 percent of Czech industry had been privatized.

Confidence in the Czech leadership led to continued foreign investment in 1994. The United States and Germany ranked as the leading investors. In August, the Czech government elected to repay ahead of schedule a $471-million loan from the United Nations' International Monetary Fund.

International alliance remained a high priority among Czech leaders in 1994. In February, the nation joined the Partnership for Peace, a new North Atlantic Treaty Organization (NATO) program of cooperation with nations that had belonged to the former Soviet Union-led Warsaw Pact. Czech officials also continued to lobby for membership in the European Union (formerly European Community).

A nuclear power plant, planned for construction near the Austrian border, sparked protests from environmentalists and Austrian officials in 1994.

◻ Sharon L. Wolchik

See also **Europe** (Facts in brief table). In *World Book,* see **Czech Republic.**

Dallas. A $112-million expansion of the Dallas Convention Center opened on Jan. 8, 1994, heralding a year of major revitalization for the downtown area. A $7-million face-lift of Main Street was completed in March, and a new downtown park, Pegasus Plaza, was dedicated in October. City officials hoped the improvements would halt a business exodus from downtown that has left 10 million square feet (929,000 square meters) of vacant office space.

Mayor calls it quits. In July, Mayor Steve Bartlett announced that he would not seek a second term in 1995. Bartlett gave up a seat in Congress to run for mayor in 1991. During his mayoral term, violent crime in Dallas was reduced by 34 percent, and the city's economy improved. But Bartlett frequently clashed with members of the City Council.

Education lawsuit dropped. After 24 years, a federal desegregation lawsuit against the Dallas Independent School District was dismissed by a United States District Court judge on July 26, 1994. When the lawsuit was filed in 1970, 42 percent of public school students were minorities. In 1994, more than 85 percent of the students were minorities.

SMU says farewell to its president. Suffering from terminal cancer, Southern Methodist University (SMU) President A. Kenneth Pye resigned on June 22. He died less than three weeks later. During his seven-year tenure at SMU, Pye increased the university's minority enrollment from 9.4 percent to 15.7 percent and doubled student financial aid to $62-million. James Kirby, former dean of the SMU theology school, was named interim president.

Airport turns 20. On January 13, the Dallas/Fort Worth International Airport observed its 20th anniversary and announced that it is now the second busiest airport in the world. The airport recorded 803,902 take-offs and landings in 1993, compared with about 844,000 at O'Hare International Airport in Chicago.

Youth curfew. A curfew that prohibited youths under the age of 17 from being out after 11 p.m. on weeknights and midnight on weekends went into effect on May 1. The curfew and an expanded gang task force in the police department were credited with reducing juvenile crime in Dallas by year-end.

Sports. The Dallas Cowboys football team won its second straight Super Bowl game on January 30 with a decisive 30-13 victory over the Buffalo Bills. In March, Cowboys owner Jerry Jones and coach Jimmy Johnson argued at a National Football League meeting. Less than a week later, Johnson agreed to step down, and former University of Oklahoma coach Barry Switzer was named as the new Cowboys coach.

Dallas hosted six World Cup '94 soccer matches at the Cotton Bowl stadium during June and July. The games attracted more than 350,000 visitors and generated an estimated $144 million in tourist business.

S&L tycoon ordered to prison. Real estate developer D. L. "Danny" Faulkner lost a final appeal of a 20-year federal jail sentence in October after being convicted in 1991 of embezzling more than $100-million from Dallas area savings and loans (S&L's). Faulkner was one of the first major Texas developers charged with looting S&L's during the 1980's.

Nobel Prize. On Oct. 10, Alfred G. Gilman, a researcher at the University of Texas Southwestern Medical Center in Dallas, shared the Nobel Prize for physiology or medicine. Gilman was honored for his discovery of cellular master molecules called G proteins. He was the fourth faculty member at the medical center to become a Nobel laureate in the last 10 years.

Rail line progressing. More than 85 percent of the tunnel work for a new Dallas Area Rapid Transit passenger rail line was completed in 1994. When finished in 1997, the first phase of the light-rail system will transport riders from the Oak Cliff section of South Dallas through downtown to North Dallas.

Dallas Plan is finalized. In October, the City Council received the final draft of the Dallas Plan, a long-range project for the city. The plan is the most ambitious effort since the early 1900's to chart the city's growth and development. The plan called for expansion of the downtown area, revitalization of older neighborhoods, and the construction of more recreation and arts facilities.   □ Henry K. Tatum

See also **City.** In the World Book Supplement section, see **Dallas.** In *World Book,* see **Dallas.**

Dancing. An ever-present tension between artistic leaders of dance companies, who seek growth, and the companies' boards of directors, who desire financial restraint, escalated in 1994 as dance funding continued a downward trend. In the spring, at least four regional ballet companies lost their artistic directors as a result of these conflicting interests.

The most shocking upheaval occurred within BalletMet of Columbus, Ohio, when the board of trustees fired John McFall. Director of the troupe since 1986, McFall had transformed the semiamateur group into a nationally recognized, professional organization. A budget dispute between McFall and the board came to a head when McFall accused several key people on his staff of not doing enough fund-raising. The trustees asked him to resign. He responded that he would have to be fired. In spite of public demonstrations in support of McFall, the trustees announced in March that his contract would not be renewed in August.

The artistic head of the Atlanta (Ga.) Ballet for 31 years, Robert Barnett, said in March that he would step down in June, a year earlier than he planned. The final straw, Barnett said, was board decisions to cut the dancers' contracts by four weeks and not to seek funding for a new production of *The Nutcracker* (1892). These were artistic decisions, Barnett said, and were made without his approval.

In May, Christopher d'Amboise resigned as director of the Pennsylvania Ballet, headquartered in Philadelphia. D'Amboise's budget had been cut from about $8 million to about $6 million during his four-year tenure, and the board wanted to make a further cut for the 1994-1995 season.

In the spring, the board of the Indianapolis Ballet Theater decided that the company needed a stronger administrator. The trustees then fired Dace Dindonis, artistic director since 1988.

Although the need for artistic directors to be more financially conservative was not disputed, many dance observers saw an alarming trend in these boards' actions. Trustees increasingly come from the corporate world, rather than from *philanthropic* (charitable) backgrounds. Perhaps, observers said, corporate standards of management were mistakenly being applied to arts organizations, which are nonprofit and traditionally have been supported mainly by donations rather than earned income.

Two major ballet companies, American Ballet Theater (ABT) and The Joffrey Ballet, operated in 1994 under reduced budgets imposed in 1993. ABT performed infrequently, and artistic director Kevin McKenzie kept new ballets to a minimum. ABT's major novelty, which premiered in April 1994 at the Metropolitan Opera in New York City, was the *Red Shoes* (1993). Of more artistic significance was a revival of Antony Tudor's *Echoing of Trumpets* (1963). Based on a historical event—a massacre of Czech citizens by Nazi soldiers—this ballet was praised for the truth of its psychology. The Joffrey Ballet survived financially in 1994 on the tremendous box-office success of *Billboards*, a rock music-based ballet that had debuted in 1993.

The New York City Ballet remained financially solvent but was artistically thin in 1994. In May, during its annual spring season at the New York State Theater at Lincoln Center in New York City, the second round of an effort called the Diamond Project introduced a dozen new ballets by both experienced and emerging *choreographers* (creators of dances). Some critics, however, said they lacked originality.

New creations. Exciting choreography came from Jerome Robbins, who had not created a new ballet since leaving the City Ballet in 1990. Robbins made a comeback with two new works. He created a solo, *A Suite of Dances*, for dancer Mikhail Baryshnikov, who premiered it on March 3, 1994, during a weeklong run in New York City of the troupe he founded, the White Oak Dance Project. The simplicity of the solo gave it a theatrical flair.

Robbins created a more ambitious dance for students of the School of American Ballet, the school affiliated with the City Ballet, for their annual workshop performance on June 4. City Ballet director Peter Martins regarded Robbins' tribute to pristine classicism as so beautiful that he announced that it would enter the repertory in 1995.

Mark Morris created an outstanding dance for

Zivili, a folk-dance troupe based in Columbus, Ohio, that specialized in preserving the dance heritage of the Balkans. Morris' dance, *The Office,* followed the modern-dance style, but the subject matter referred to the civil war in Bosnia-Herzegovina. It opened with five dancers onstage. After each dance section ended, a woman with a clipboard entered and called out a name of a dancer, who then exited. At the end of the dance, only one person was left. Critics marveled at the chilling, ominous atmosphere created by the dance, which premiered on April 22, 1994.

The Martha Graham Dance Company celebrated the 100th birthday of the late Martha Graham, an American choreographer who pioneered modern dance. The troupe performed a selection of Graham's works during the Next Wave Festival at the Brooklyn Academy of Music in New York City, September 28 through October 6. Later in October, the troupe danced with the St. Paul Chamber Orchestra in St. Paul, Minn., in a program featuring music commissioned by Graham. During the last week of the month, the company was in residency in Ann Arbor, Mich., where dance performances, photo exhibitions, and *symposia* (meetings and discussions) dealing with Graham's art took place. Also in 1994, for the first time, the company gave permission to other dance institutions to perform Graham's work.

Netherlands Dance 3 made its United States debut in August at the Jacob's Pillow Dance Festival in Lee, Mass., and returned in October to the Next Wave Festival. The dance troupe was the brainchild of Jiri Kylian, director of Netherlands Dance Company, who wanted to form a troupe of ballet veterans 40 years and older. These dancers perform in works tailored to the talents of first-rate dancers who were too old to dance in standard repertory but were still exciting performers.

The Royal Ballet of England made the unusual move of premiering *The Sleeping Beauty* on April 6 at the Kennedy Center for Performing Arts in Washington, D.C., rather than at home in London. Most notable about the new production of an old favorite was massive, nightmarish decor by Maria Bjornson, designer for *The Phantom of the Opera* (1986).

The Bolshoi Theater Ballet of Moscow, one of the world's most famous troupes and an important source of foreign currency for Russia, canceled most of a 1994 summer tour in England because of poor ticket sales. This scandalous turn of events was one factor leading to an entire reorganization of the Bolshoi. Artistic director Yuri Grigorovich, who had dictatorial control of the Bolshoi, was held most responsible for the troupe's 10-year decline. The new arrangement, ratified by President Boris Yeltsin in September, was more democratic and emphasized merit, not seniority. All Bolshoi artists would be required to sign yearly contracts, with no one assured of permanent status. □ Nancy Goldner

In *World Book*, see **Ballet; Dancing.**

Deaths

Deaths in 1994 included those listed below, who were Americans unless otherwise indicated.

Acton, Sir Harold (1904-February 27), British author and scholar known for *The Last Medici* (1932) and *The Memoirs of an Esthete* (1948).

Ball, George W. (1909-May 26), diplomat and author known for his opposition to the Vietnam War (1957-1975).

Beery, Noah, Jr. (1916-November 1), character actor best known for his role as the father in the television series "The Rockford Files."

Belluschi, Pietro (1899-February 14), Italian-born architect known for his modernist designs and his contributions to a Pacific Northwest regional style.

Benson, Ezra Taft (1899-May 30), president of The Church of Jesus Christ of Latter-day Saints since 1985 and former secretary of agriculture during the Administration of President Dwight D. Eisenhower.

Bich, Baron Marcel (1914-May 30), French industrialist who founded the company that made Bic pens and disposable razors household words around the world.

Borotra, Jean (1898-June 17), French tennis player known as one of the "Four Musketeers," the French team that won five Davis Cups in the late 1920's and early 1930's.

Boulle, Pierre (1912-January 30), French novelist who wrote *The Bridge over the River Kwai* (1954) and *Planet of the Apes* (1963), both of which were made into motion pictures.

Bukowski, Charles (1920-March 9), poet, novelist, and screenwriter whose younger days were portrayed in the motion picture *Barfly* (1987).

Calloway, Cab (1907-November 18), bandleader, songwriter, and singer who led one of the most popular bands of the 1930's and became known for his "hi-de-hi-de-ho" scat lyrics to his song "Minnie the Moocher."

Candy, John (1950-March 4), Canadian actor known mostly for his comic roles in such films as *Planes, Trains and Automobiles* (1987) and *Cool Runnings* (1993).

Canetti, Elias (1905-August 14), Bulgarian-born writer who won the Nobel Prize in literature in 1981 for his fiction and nonfiction, including the 1935 novel *Auto-da-fe* and the 1960 study *Crowds and Power.*

Carey, Macdonald (1913-March 21), actor who appeared as a leading man in a number of motion pictures in the 1940's and 1950's and then became a fixture on the television soap opera "Days of Our Lives."

Childress, Alice (1916-August 14), actress, playwright, and novelist known for her fiction for young readers, including *A Hero Ain't Nothin' but a Sandwich* (1973).

Clampitt, Amy (1920-September 10), poet whose first full-length book of poetry in 1983, *The Kingfisher,* catapulted her into the front ranks of American poets.

Clavell, James (1924-September 6), Australian-born novelist and naturalized U.S. citizen best known for his historical novels—*Tai-Pan* (1966) and *Shogun* (1975)—set in the Far East.

Cobain, Kurt (1967-April 8), lead singer and songwriter for the rock group Nirvana.

Collins, Dorothy (1926-July 21), Canadian-born singer who was a fixture on the television series "Your Hit Parade" in the 1950's.

Conrad, William (1920-February 11), actor who began his career as the original Matt Dillon of the "Gunsmoke" radio series and later gained fame as the narrator of the TV series

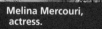

Melina Mercouri, actress.

John Candy, motion-picture actor.

Henry Mancini, composer.

Wilma Rudolph, track and field Olympian.

"Rocky & His Friends" and the district attorney in "Jake and the Fatman."

Cormier, Frank (1927-February 9), journalist who was the White House correspondent for the Associated Press for almost 20 years, covering the Administrations of President John F. Kennedy through Jimmy Carter; contributor to *The World Book Year Book* from 1982 to 1993.

Cotten, Joseph (1905-February 6), motion-picture actor who starred in several film classics, including *Citizen Kane* (1941), *Shadow of a Doubt* (1943), and *The Third Man* (1949).

Curry, John (1949-April 15), English figure skater who won the men's world championship and the men's Olympic gold medal in 1976.

Cushing, Peter (1913-August 11), British motion-picture actor known for his film roles as the mad scientist Baron Frankenstein.

Damita, Lili (Liliane Carré) (1904?-March 21), French-born actress who starred in the early years of talking motion pictures in such films as *Bridge of San Luis Rey* (1929) and *Frisco Kid* (1935).

Dandridge, Ray (1914?-February 12), baseball player who starred in the Negro Leagues as a third baseman and was inducted into the National Baseball Hall of Fame in 1987.

Raul Julia, stage and motion-picture actor.

Kurt Cobain, rock singer and songwriter.

Dixy Lee Ray, scientist and politician.

Carmen McRae, jazz singer.

Diego, Eliseo (1920-March 1), Cuban poet regarded by some as one of the greatest modern poets in the Spanish language.

Doisneau, Robert (1912-April 1), French photographer who documented Parisian life in such famous photographs as *The Kiss by the Hôtel de Ville, Paris* (1950).

Ellison, Ralph (1914-April 16), African-American writer best known for his influential novel *Invisible Man* (1952).

Erikson, Erik H. (1902-May 12), German-born psychoanalyst who coined the term, "identity crisis," and whose theories of ego development joined psychoanalysis with the social sciences.

Ewell, Tom (Yewell Tompkins) (1909-September 12), character actor best known for his role in *The Seven Year Itch* (1955).

Feather, Leonard (1914-September 22), jazz critic and composer known as an early advocate of the bebop style.

Feeney, Charles S. "Chub" (1921-January 10), baseball executive with the New York and San Francisco Giants and National League president from 1970 to 1986.

Furness, Betty (1916-April 2), consumer advocate and broadcast reporter on consumer issues.

Gerulaitis, Vitas (1954-September 18), tennis star who won the Australian Open in 1977.

Haukelid, Knut Anders (1911-March 8), American-born Norwegian resistance hero who helped sabotage Nazi Germany's atomic weapons program in Norway, a feat chronicled in several books and the motion picture *Heroes of Telemark* (1965).

Hodgkin, Dorothy Crowfoot (1910-July 29), British biochemist and crystallographer who won the Nobel Prize in chemistry in 1964 for using X rays to determine the structure of complex biochemical compounds, such as penicillin and vitamin B_{12}.

Honecker, Erich (1912-May 29), Communist leader of East Germany from 1971 until 1989.

Ionesco, Eugène (1912-March 28), Romanian-born French playwright known as a surrealist for such plays as *The Chairs* (1952) and *Rhinoceros* (1959).

Ish Kabibble (Merwyn Bogue) (1908?-June 5), comedian and cornet player who performed with the Kay Kyser orchestra in the 1930's and 1940's.

Jobim, António Carlos (1927-December 8), Brazilian composer who inspired the bossa-nova craze of

Thomas P. "Tip" O'Neill, congressman.

George Peppard, motion-picture actor.

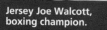

Jersey Joe Walcott, boxing champion.

Harriet Nelson, television actress.

the 1960's with his song "The Girl from Ipanema."

John, Fritz (1910-February 10), German-born mathematician regarded as a leading expert on partial differential equations.

Judd, Donald (1928-February 12), artist who became a major figure in the minimalist art movement.

Julia, Raul (Raúl Rafael Carlos Julia y Arcelay) (1940-October 24), Puerto Rican-born stage and motion-picture actor acclaimed for his roles with the New York Shakespeare Festival and in the 1985 movie *The Kiss of the Spider Woman.*

Kelley, Virginia Clinton (born Virginia Cassidy) (1923-January 6), mother of United States President Bill Clinton.

Kienholz, Edward (1927-June 9), sculptor who blended expressionism and pop art to create macabre scenes of everyday life.

Kim Il-song (Kim Sung-ju) (1912-July 8), president of North Korea from its founding in 1948 until his death.

Kirby, Jack (Jacob Kurtzberg) (1917-February 6), comic-book artist who created the characters Captain America and the Incredible Hulk.

La Fontaine, Harry (1913?-April 12), Danish resistance leader during World War II who helped smug-

gle 8,000 Jews from Nazi-occupied Denmark to neutral Sweden.

Lancaster, Burt (1913-October 20), motion-picture actor who starred in more than 70 movies, received four Academy Award nominations, won the Academy Award for best actor for his role in *Elmer Gantry* (1960), and left many enduring film images with his performances in *From Here to Eternity* (1953), *Birdman of Alcatraz* (1962), and *Atlantic City* (1980).

Lantz, Walter (1900-March 22), animator known for his creation of the cartoon character Woody Woodpecker.

Lasch, Christopher (1932-February 14), historian and social scientist best known for his 1979 study *The Culture of Narcissism.*

Levitt, William J. (1907-January 28), real estate developer who created Levittown, N.Y., and helped spur a mass migration to the suburbs after World War II (1939-1945).

Lutoslawski, Witold (1913-February 7), Polish composer and conductor regarded as a leading figure in contemporary music.

Maier, Ulrike (1968?-January 29), Austrian skier and two-time world skiing champion.

Mancini, Henry (1924-June 14), composer for motion-picture and television sound tracks and winner of four Academy Awards for his film scores and songs, including the song "Moon River" and the entire score for the 1961 film *Breakfast at Tiffany's.*

Masina, Giulietta (1921-March 23), Italian actress known for her leading roles in such motion pictures as *La Strada* (1954) and *Juliet of the Spirits* (1965), which were directed by her husband Federico Fellini.

May, Rollo (1909-October 22), psychotherapist who helped pioneer the field of humanistic psychology in such works as *Love and Will* (1969) and *The Courage to Create* (1975).

McGuire, Frank (1913-October 11), basketball coach who led two different colleges to the National Collegiate Athletic Association final—St. John's in 1952 and North Carolina in 1957.

McRae, Carmen (1922-November 10), jazz singer regarded as "the last great stylist of her time."

Mercouri, Melina (1925-March 6), Greek actress and political activist best known for her leading role in the 1960 motion picture *Never on Sunday* and for her opposition to the junta that ruled Greece from 1967 to 1974.

Mitchell, Cameron (1918-July 6), character actor

who appeared in more than 90 motion pictures and the television series "High Chaparral."

Morgan, Henry (1915-May 19), radio broadcaster and television quiz show panelist known for his acerbic wit.

Morgan, William W. (1906-June 21), astronomer who discovered the spiral shape of the Milky Way galaxy.

Nelson, Harriet (Peggy Lou Snyder) (1909-October 2), actress who starred in the television series "The Adventures of Ozzie & Harriet" from 1952 to 1966.

Nilsson, Harry (Harry E. Nelson III) (1941-January 15), popular music composer and singer.

Nixon, Richard M. (1913-April 22), 37th President of the United States and the only President ever to resign from the office; Vice President of the United States under the Administrations of Dwight D. Eisenhower; and a former member of the U.S. House of Representatives and the U.S. Senate whose political career spanned almost 30 years. (See **Deaths: Richard Nixon: How Will History Judge His Legacy?**)

Onassis, Jacqueline Bouvier Kennedy (1929-May 19), former First Lady and wife of President John F. Kennedy who later married Greek shipping magnate Aristotle Onassis.

O' Neill, Thomas P. "Tip," Jr. (1912-January 5), a Massachusetts congressman for 17 terms and a powerful, pivotal figure as Speaker of the House of Representatives from 1977 until 1987, when he retired.

Onetti, Juan Carlos (1909-May 30), Uruguayan novelist and poet considered one of Latin America's most distinguished writers.

Osborne, John (1929-December 24), British playwright whose *Look Back in Anger* (1956) ushered in a new era in British theater.

Pass, Joe (Joseph Anthony Jacobi Passalaqua) (1929-May 23), jazz drummer who played with such outstanding artists as Duke Ellington, Ella Fitzgerald, and Oscar Peterson.

Pauling, Linus C. (1901-August 19), chemist and political activist who won the Nobel Prize in chemistry in 1954 for his research on the nature of the chemical bond and who won the Nobel Peace Prize in 1962 for his efforts to ban nuclear weapons, including a campaign against the testing of nuclear weapons that helped lead to a test ban in 1963. Pauling was also noted for his advocacy of the health benefits of vitamin C.

Peppard, George (1928-May 8), mo-tion-picture and television actor best known for his role in *Breakfast at Tiffany's* (1961) and in the 1980's television series "The A-Team."

Phoumi Vongvichit (1909-January 7), Laotian Communist leader who held several positions in the government, including acting president and acting prime minister.

Primus, Pearl (1920?-October 29), Trinidad-born dancer, choreographer, and dance teacher who helped introduce African and Caribbean dances to dance companies in the United States.

Puller, Lewis B., Jr. (1945?-May 11), author who won the Pulitzer Prize in 1992 for his 1991 book *Fortunate Son,* an account of his recovery from alcoholism and wounds suffered in the Vietnam War (1957-1975).

Ray, Dixy Lee (1914-January 2), first chairwoman of the United States Atomic Energy Commission and governor of Washington from 1977 to 1981.

Raye, Martha (Margaret Teresa Yvonne Reed) (1916-October 19), comedian and singer known for her role in entertaining American troops during World War II (1939-1945), the Korean War (1950-1953), and the Vietnam War (1957-1975).

Rewald, John (1912-February 2), art historian

Cab Calloway, band leader, singer, and songwriter.

Joseph Cotten, motion-picture actor.

Burt Lancaster, motion-picture actor.

Dinah Shore, singer and TV show host.

Deaths

known for his studies of impressionist and postimpressionist art.

Rey, Fernando (Fernando Casado Arambillet) (1917-March 9), Spanish motion-picture actor known mostly for his roles in the films of director Luis Buñuel and for his role as the drug lord in *The French Connection* (1971).

Rodney, Red (Robert Chudnick) (1927-May 27), jazz trumpeter who won renown as a bebop musician after joining Charlie Parker's quintet in 1949.

Roland, Gilbert (Luis Antonio Dámaso de Alonso) (1905-May 15), Mexican-born motion-picture actor who was known mostly as a character actor and appeared in more than 100 films.

Romero, Cesar (1907-January 1), motion-picture and television actor who was typecast as a Latin lover in his film roles but played The Joker in the "Batman" television series of the 1960's.

Roueché, Berton (1911-April 28), journalist who wrote for *The New Yorker* magazine for almost 50 years, narrating medical case histories in the style of a detective story.

Rubin, Jerry (1938-November 28), radical activist who opposed the U.S. role in the Vietnam War and was prosecuted as a member of the Chicago 7, a group of antiwar protesters who organized demonstrations at the 1968 Democratic Party convention in Chicago.

Rudolph, Wilma (1940-November 12), track and field star who won three gold medals at the 1960 Olympic Games in Rome and who set world records during her career in the 100-meter and 200-meter races.

Rusk, Dean (1909-December 20), U.S. secretary of state during the Administrations of John F. Kennedy and Lyndon B. Johnson, known for his defense of U.S. involvement in the Vietnam War.

Savalas, Telly (Aristotle Savalas) (1924-January 22), motion-picture and television actor best known for his role as a tough-talking New York City police detective in the TV series "Kojak."

Scarry, Richard (1919-April 30), author and illustrator of children's books, known for his humorous and detailed sketches.

Schneerson, Menachem M. (1902-June 12), rebbe, or grand rabbi, of the Lubavitcher sect of Hasidic Orthodox Judaism.

Schwinger, Julian (1918-July 16), theoretical physicist who shared the Nobel Prize in physics in 1965 for his pioneering contributions to the field of quantum electrodynamics.

Scott, Hugh, Jr. (1900-July 21), Pennsylvania congressman for 34 years and former minority leader of the U.S. Senate.

Senna de Silva, Ayrton (1960-May 1), Brazilian automobile race car driver who won the Formula One world championship three times.

Sharkey, Jack (Joseph Paul Cukoschay) (1902-August 17), former heavyweight boxing champion who unexpectedly defeated Max Schmeling in 1932.

Shilts, Randy (1951-February 17), journalist who chronicled the beginnings of the AIDS epidemic; best known for his 1987 book *And the Band Played On: Politics, People and the AIDS Epidemic.*

Shore, Dinah (Frances Rose Shore) (1917-February 24), popular singer, motion-picture actress, and television show host.

Smith, John (1938-May 12), Scottish attorney and leader of the United Kingdom's Labour Party.

Smith, Willie Mae Ford (1904?-February 2), pioneering gospel singer.

Sperry, Roger W. (1913-April 17), neurobiologist who shared the Nobel Prize in physiology or medicine in 1981 for his discoveries regarding the

Cesar Romero, motion-picture and TV actor.

Betty Furness, consumer advocate.

Jacqueline Kennedy Onassis, former first lady.

Eugène Ionesco, playwright.

cognitive functions of the human brain.

Spivak, Lawrence E. (1900-March 9), broadcast journalist who originated the television program "Meet the Press."

Strom, Earl (1928?-July 10), referee for the National Basketball Association for more than three decades.

Styne, Jule (Julius Stein) (1905-September 20), composer and lyricist who wrote the music for many popular Broadway shows, including *Gypsy* (1959) and *Funny Girl* (1964), and won an Academy Award for best song with "Three Coins in the Fountain" in the 1954 movie of the same name.

Sullivan, Barry (Patrick Barry) (1912-June 6), motion-picture actor who starred in *Lady in the Dark* (1944).

Tandy, Jessica (1909-September 11), British-born American actress whose career on the stage and in motion pictures spanned five decades, including her performance as Blanche DuBois in the 1947 Broadway premiere of *A Streetcar Named Desire* and as the title character in the 1989 film *Driving Miss Daisy,* for which she won the Academy Award for best actress.

Ralph Ellison, novelist.

Linus Pauling, Nobel Prize-winning chemist.

Jessica Tandy, stage and film actress.

Telly Savalas, TV and film actor.

Taylor, Peter (1917-November 2), novelist and short-story writer who won the Pulitzer Prize for fiction in 1986 for his novel *A Summons to Memphis.*

Temin, Howard M. (1934-February 9), cancer researcher who shared the Nobel Prize in physiology or medicine in 1975 for his discovery of an enzyme found in certain viruses that cause cancer by changing the genetic makeup of the cells that they infect.

Thomas, Caitlin (1913-July 31), British writer and widow of the Welsh poet Dylan Thomas.

Tinbergen, Jan (1903-June 9) Dutch economist who shared the first Nobel Prize in economics in 1969.

Vines, Ellsworth (1911-March 17), grand slam tennis champion of the 1930's.

Wain, John B. (1925-May 24), British novelist, poet, and critic who was considered part of the "angry young men," a literary group that included John Osborne, Kingsley Amis, and Philip Larkin.

Walcott, Jersey Joe (Arnold Raymond Cream) (1914-February 25), boxing champion who was once the oldest fighter ever to hold the world heavyweight title.

Warren, Earle (1914-June 4), jazz saxophonist and singer best known as the lead alto for the original Count Basie Orchestra that rose to fame in the late 1930's.

Watts, James W. (1904-November 7), neurosurgeon who performed the first frontal lobotomy in 1936.

Weisner, Jerome B. (1915-October 21), former president of the Massachusetts Institute of Technology in Cambridge and former science adviser to the Administration of President John F. Kennedy.

Williams, Marion (1927-July 2), gospel singer known for her influence on popular music.

Wilkinson, Bud (1916-February 9), football coach known for his tenure at the University of Oklahoma, where his teams won three national championships in the 1950's and a record 47 consecutive games over a five-season span.

Wolfberg, Dennis (1945?-October 3), stand-up comedian who appeared frequently on television's "The Tonight Show."

Youskevitch, Igor (1912-June 13), Ukrainian-born ballet dancer known for his legendary partnership with the Cuban-born dancer Alicia Alonso.

Zola, Irving Kenneth (1935?-December 1), sociologist who championed the rights of people with disabilities.
　　　　　　　　　　　　　　　　□ Rod Such

Richard Nixon:
How Will History
Judge His Legacy?

By Stanley I. Kutler

Richard M. Nixon, the 37th President of the United States, died in April 1994, but controversies about his political career live on and probably will be revisited by historians for years to come.

R ichard Milhous Nixon, 37th President of the United States, died on April 22, 1994, after suffering a stroke. He was elected President in 1968, reelected in 1972, and resigned in 1974, just prior to his likely impeachment by the U.S. House of Representatives. For nearly 20 years thereafter, Nixon labored to recover his reputation and establish his claim to historical greatness. But the obituaries noted the most distinctive event of his career: Nixon was the first President of the United States to resign his office. His resignation followed the uncovering of evidence that indicated his personal involvement in criminal activity and abuse of power.

Nixon was a commanding presence in American public life for nearly a half century. But controversy lingers over his achievements and reputation, and judgments of Nixon today are as intense as they were while he was in office. In time, perhaps passions will cool.

Nixon was born on Jan. 9, 1913, in Yorba Linda, Calif. He attended elementary schools in several California towns and went to Whittier High School. He graduated from Whittier College in 1934, ranked second in his class, and won a scholarship to the Duke University School of Law in Durham, N.C. At Duke, he was elected president of the student law association and graduated third out of a class of 44 students in 1937. After graduation, Nixon returned to Whittier, where he joined a law firm, and in 1940 married Thelma Catharine (Pat) Ryan.

During World War II (1939-1945), Nixon served in the Navy, and at his discharge, had attained the rank of lieutenant commander. In 1946, Nixon ran as the Republican candidate against Democrat Jerry Voorhis for the U.S. House of Representatives in the November elections. In a year when Communism was beginning to be seen as a serious threat to America's security, Nixon repeatedly suggested that Voorhis was a Communist, though there was no evidence to prove the charge. Nixon won the election.

Nixon's path to the White House

In the House, Nixon worked on a committee that laid the groundwork for the Marshall Plan to rebuild Europe after the war's devastation. He also served on the controversial House Committee on Un-American Activities, which investigated Communist influence inside and outside of government. In 1948, he played a key role in the committee's highly publicized investigation of Alger Hiss, who was accused of passing secrets to the Soviet Union. Hiss denied the charges, and many members of the committee wanted to end the hearings. Nixon, however, insisted that the investigation proceed, and in 1949, Hiss was brought to trial on perjury charges and ultimately convicted.

Nixon's aggressive anti-Communist stance won him a seat in the Senate in 1950. He ran against Democratic U.S. Representative Helen Gahagan Douglas. Nixon called Douglas a "Pink Lady," which implied that she sympathized with Communism. She in turn labeled him "Tricky Dick." Nixon defeated Douglas by nearly 700,000 votes.

Nixon's victory put him in great demand to speak at Republican Party affairs nationwide. This exposure helped earn him the party's nomination as General Dwight D. Eisenhower's vice presidential running mate in the 1952 election. They won two terms in office.

In 1960, Nixon won the Republican nomination for President. For the first time, presidential candidates debated each other before a live television audience. But Nixon's nervous presence could not overcome Democrat John F. Kennedy's charisma. Nixon lost the election by one of the narrowest margins in U.S. history.

■ **The author**

Stanley I. Kutler is
E. Gordon Fox professor
of American Institutions and Law
at the University of
Wisconsin in Madison.

Nixon then ran for governor of California in 1962 and lost again. He vowed he would leave politics, telling reporters they would not have "Nixon to kick around anymore." But after the defeat in 1964 of Republican presidential candidate Barry Goldwater, Nixon once again came to the forefront of the Republican Party. He narrowly defeated Democratic Vice President Hubert H. Humphrey in the 1968 election.

During the campaign, Nixon hinted that he had a plan to end the Vietnam War (1957-1975), which had sharply divided Americans. Once in office, he increasingly turned the conduct of the war over to the South Vietnamese and began a gradual withdrawal of U.S. troops. But in 1970, Nixon ordered U.S. and South Vietnamese forces into Cambodia to cap-

▪ Twists and turns on a political road

Richard Nixon's political career spanned much of the 20th century, from the "Red scare" of the late 1940's to the opening of relations with Communist China in the early 1970's.

▪ Nixon talks to the press in 1948 about the congressional investigation of accused Communist spy Alger Hiss, which brought Nixon national recognition, *left.*

▪ Nixon, alongside Republican presidential candidate Dwight D. Eisenhower and his wife, Mamie, accepts the Republican nomination for Vice President at the party's national convention in Chicago in 1952, *right.*

▪ Nixon debates the Democratic presidential candidate, John F. Kennedy, in 1960, *left,* in the first televised presidential debate.

▪ Nixon tours China's Great Wall in 1972, *right,* during a visit that reopened relations between the United States and China, a major foreign policy achievement of Nixon's first term as President.

ture North Vietnamese weapons supplies. The invasion aroused protests in the United States that led to the shooting deaths of four students at Kent State University in Ohio. Finally, in January 1973, the United States reached a cease-fire agreement with North Vietnam, and in March the last U.S. troops left South Vietnam.

Nixon's first term was noted for two foreign policy achievements. First, he reopened trade with China. American trade with China had ceased during the Korean War (1950-1953) because China had entered the Korean conflict in opposition to United Nations forces led by the United States. Second, he signed agreements in Moscow with the Soviet Union to limit nuclear weapons production.

In the November 1972 election, Nixon won a landslide victory over Democratic Senator George S. McGovern of South Dakota for a second term. But Nixon's voter mandate was soon overshadowed by the Watergate scandal, the biggest political scandal in U.S. history.

The Watergate scandal

The name arose from a burglary at the headquarters of the Democratic National Committee in the Watergate building complex in Washington, D.C., in June 1972. Police arrested five men at the scene. They and two others were subsequently indicted, and in January 1973, five of the seven men pleaded guilty to a number of crimes, including burglary and wiretapping. A jury found the other two guilty. The motive for the break-in still remains unclear, but investigations revealed that Nixon's official campaign committee, the Committee for the Re-election of the President, authorized the burglary.

For nearly two years after the trial, various congressional inquiries and investigations by the Watergate Special Prosecutor Force uncovered numerous criminal activities by White House and campaign staff. The activities had been designed to help Nixon win reelection in 1972. Most notable was the creation of an extra-legal group, known as the Plumbers, who used criminal methods to obtain information to discredit political opponents of the Nixon Administration. About 70 people were charged with crimes, including Attorney General John N. Mitchell and Nixon's top aides, John D. Ehrlichman and H. R. Haldeman. Watergate involved more high-level officials than any previous scandal in U.S. history. Most were convicted or pleaded guilty.

In July 1973, investigators learned that Nixon had secretly taped conversations with his aides in the White House. Nixon insisted that executive privilege protected the privacy of the tapes, but in July 1974, the U.S. Supreme Court ruled that Nixon had to surrender them.

The tapes proved fatal to his presidency. They indicated that six days after the break-in Nixon had ordered a cover-up of his staff's attempts to destroy evidence, thwart probes by the Federal Bureau of Investigation, and make "hush money" payments to the burglars. The House Judiciary Committee adopted three articles of impeachment against Nixon: obstruction of justice, abuses of power, and illegally withholding evidence from the committee. Most historians agree that the House would have voted to impeach Nixon if he had not resigned on Aug. 9, 1974. The outcome of a Senate trial is less certain.

Assessing Nixon's legacy

Twenty years after the resignation, historians were still assessing Nixon's presidency. Many historians consider Nixon's accomplishments on his trips to China and the Soviet Union his greatest achievements. Some historians consider Nixon's finest moment in foreign policy to be his mediation at the end of the Yom Kippur War between Israel and its opponents, Syria and Egypt, in 1973. Nixon's insistence that neither side be allowed to attain a total victory laid the basis for a process that culminated in the Camp David peace accords in 1978.

But detractors of Nixon's foreign policy record cite what they consider his failures. They point to his support of repressive military regimes in Greece and Chile, for example, though chiefly they argue that Nixon needlessly prolonged the war in Vietnam, bargaining only for a "decent interval" for American troop withdrawal.

As for his domestic policies, most historians agree that Nixon was not an innovator. Some admirers emphasize the gains made in Southern school desegregation during his Administration. They cite his welfare proposal for a guaranteed income for the poor. But memoranda discovered in his presidential papers and the diaries of his chief of staff, H. R. Haldeman, published after Nixon's death, show that Nixon privately opposed most of these policies. Nixon's critics say these revelations point to a long thread of deception that began with unfounded accusations against political opponents and continued into the White House with attempts to use government agencies, such as the Central Intelligence Agency, against a list of political enemies.

In September 1974, President Gerald Ford pardoned Nixon for all federal crimes he may have committed. For the next 20 years, Nixon sought to reestablish himself as a national figure by writing numerous books and offering his views on a variety of political issues.

But for many Americans, Nixon shattered the fragile bond of trust that must exist between rulers and the people and in doing so damaged the integrity of the presidency. The founders of the nation had firm views on standards of political morality. In his Farewell Address in 1796, George Washington said that "virtue" and "morality" formed the "necessary spring of government" and were "indispensable supports" for political well-being. Washington insisted that "the mere politician . . . ought to respect and cherish them." Nixon once said, however, that "virtue is not what lifts great leaders above others." That belief might have cost him the presidency. ■ ■ ■

■ Nixon bids farewell to his staff, and the presidency, before boarding a helicopter in 1974, after investigations uncovered his role in the worst political scandal in U.S. history.

For further reading:

Ambrose, Stephen E. *Nixon.* 3 vols. Simon & Schuster, 1987-1992.

Kutler, Stanley I. *The Wars of Watergate.* Norton, 1992.

Democratic Party. The Democrats suffered a crushing defeat in the Nov. 8, 1994, midterm elections, losing control of both houses of Congress for the first time since 1954. In addition, Republicans took away governorships in New York, Pennsylvania, Texas, and several other states while retaining control of the state houses in a dozen states, including California, Illinois, Michigan, and Ohio. Many political analysts saw the outcome as a massive vote of no confidence in President Bill Clinton even though his name was not on the ballot.

Shaken Democrats pondered how to respond to the election. Meanwhile, Clinton offered to work with the new Republican leadership in the House of Representatives and Senate on issues where they could find agreement. Party leaders such as House Speaker Thomas S. Foley of Washington state and three-term Senator James Sasser of Tennessee lost their seats to first-time candidates in the debacle. Not a single Republican incumbent governor or member of the House or Senate was defeated.

Many analysts said voters were angry because Clinton and the Democratic leadership in Congress failed to deliver on promises to reform health care, welfare, and campaign finance. Republicans, who effectively blocked action on some of these issues, were not blamed because they were not in charge, the analysts concluded. Allies of Clinton said he did not receive enough credit for the sharply improved economy or for passage of a comprehensive anti-crime bill. Nonetheless, Republicans capitalized on the President's low approval ratings and linked Democratic candidates to Clinton.

Partial casualties list. The new House lineup showed a Republican pickup of 52 seats, giving Republicans a 230-to-204 advantage, with one independent. Republican gains were most notable in the South, where the party has become dominant in recent years, but there were Republican victories in every region of the country. In Washington state, for example, six Democratic members of the House, including Foley—the first Speaker to be defeated since 1862—were ousted.

In other races, veteran Democratic Representative Jack Brooks of Texas, chairman of the House Judiciary committee, lost his race, as did 18-term Representative Dan Rostenkowski of Chicago, the former chairman of the House Ways and Means committee. Rostenkowski lost to a young Republican lawyer who had never held public office. In Pennsylvania, Senator Harris L. Wofford, who was swept into office in a special election in 1991 after campaigning on a health care platform, also was defeated.

The day after the election, Democratic Senator Richard C. Shelby compounded the damage by switching parties. Shelby's defection gave the Republicans a 53-to-47 advantage in the Senate, compared with the Democrats' 56-to-44 edge in the Senate of the expiring 103rd Congress.

In state house races, three-term New York Governor Mario M. Cuomo was beaten by George E. Pataki, a Republican newcomer to statewide politics. In Texas, George W. Bush, the eldest son of former President George Bush, defeated popular Democratic Governor Ann W. Richards.

A few wins. Not all Democratic incumbents went down to defeat. Florida Governor Lawton M. Chiles, Jr., won reelection in a hard-fought race against Jeb Bush, another son of the former President. In Virginia, Senator Charles S. Robb eked out a victory over former Marine Lieutenant Colonel Oliver L. North. And in Massachusetts, Senator Edward M. Kennedy won a sixth term.

A foretaste of November. The outcome of the November elections was foreshadowed on May 24 in a special congressional election in Kentucky to fill the seat vacated by the death of Democratic Representative William H. Natcher. Republican Ron Lewis, owner of a Christian bookstore, defeated the Democratic candidate, former State Senator Joe Prather. Lewis became the first Republican elected from that district since the end of the Civil War in 1865.

House Democrats face charges. Several Democrats in the House faced criminal charges in 1994. Rostenkowski was indicted on May 31 on 17 felony counts, including embezzlement, fraud, and obstruction of justice. Representative Mel Reynolds, another Chicago congressman, was indicted on August 19 on charges of statutory rape, solicitation of child pornography, and obstruction of justice. And Representative Walter R. Tucker III of California was indicted on August 11 on charges of extortion and tax evasion. All three men pleaded innocent.

Ron Brown exonerated. On February 2, the Department of Justice cleared Secretary of Commerce Ronald H. Brown of charges that he had accepted a $700,000 bribe from Vietnamese government officials for help in ending the United States trade embargo against Vietnam. The Justice Department said it had found no evidence of wrongdoing on Brown's part.

Wilhelm resigns. Democratic National Committee Chairman David Wilhelm announced on August 9 that he would be leaving his post at the end of 1994. At the same time, Tony Coelho, a former House member from California, was named as the Democrats' chief political strategist in hopes of reviving Democratic prospects before the 1996 campaign.

Chicago gets next Democratic Convention. The Democratic National Committee announced on August 4 that the party would hold its 1996 presidential nominating convention in Chicago. Neither major party has held its national convention in Chicago since the tumultuous Democratic meeting in 1968 when the police clashed with thousands of antiwar demonstrators. ☐ William J. Eaton

See also **Clinton, Bill; Congress; Elections; Republican Party.** In *World Book,* see **Democratic Party.**

Denmark. Danish voters in 1994 kept Social Democratic Party Prime Minister Poul Nyrup Rasmussen in office, though his four-party coalition government suffered major losses in the general election on September 21. Rasmussen, whose coalition won only 75 seats in the 179-seat Folketing (parliament), was forced to govern with the tacit support of the left wing Socialist People's Party and Unity List party. Prior to the election, Rasmussen's coalition had a 1-seat majority in the Folketing.

Within the ruling coalition, Rasmussen's Social Democrats won 62 seats in the Folketing, down from the 69 seats they had won in the 1990 election, whereas the Radical Liberal Party won 8 seats, up from 7 four years earlier; the Center Democratic Party won 5 seats compared to 9 in 1990; and the Christian People's Party lost all 4 of its seats. The main opposition party, the Liberal Party, gained the most in the election, rising to 42 seats in the Folketing from 29. But the Conservative Party, a former coalition partner of the Liberals, lost 3 seats, giving them 27.

Liberal Party leader Uffe Ellemann-Jensen, the center-right's losing candidate for prime minister, predicted that Rasmussen would have to call an election in 1996 because his coalition members disagreed on many issues among themselves. Rasmussen became prime minister without an election in January 1993, after Conservative Party head Poul Schlüter resigned for covering up a 1987 scandal concerning Tamil refugees from Sri Lanka.

Key issues in the election were unemployment and the high cost of the welfare state. After the election, Rasmussen maintained his government's policies of attempting to revive the Danish economy by keeping interest rates tied to those of Germany, and keeping government spending under control.

Among Rasmussen's main social initiatives in 1994 was a welfare program under which parents of young children or employees wishing retraining can take up to six months off work, while still being paid by the state, and then return to their old jobs.

European Union issues. Rasmussen's need for the support of the Socialist People's Party and the Unity List party could affect Denmark's dealings with the European Union (EU), formerly called the European Community. Both of those parties opposed broader unity within the EU and Denmark's ratification of the EU's Maastricht Treaty on European Union. Denmark finally approved the treaty on May 18, 1993, after having rejected it in 1992. Denmark won for itself the right to stay out of certain EU programs, such as a common defense policy or a single European currency, which the EU may adopt in the late 1990's. Because some EU policies need to be adopted by unanimous vote, strong Danish opposition could slow down the course of European unity.

☐ Philip Revzin

See also **Europe** (Facts in brief table). In *World Book,* see **Denmark; European Union.**

Detroit got its first new mayor in 20 years when Dennis W. Archer, 52, was sworn in on Jan. 3, 1994. Archer, a former Michigan Supreme Court judge, succeeded Mayor Coleman A. Young, 76, who decided not to run for a sixth term because of health problems and advancing age.

Archer immediately set out to make good on his promises to upgrade city services and improve the city's relations with suburban communities and the state and federal governments. He said that forging ties with people and institutions outside of Detroit would be the best way to attract new economic development to the city.

Economic summit. Archer, a Democrat, developed a close relationship with President Bill Clinton and members of Clinton's Administration in 1994. One of the earliest benefits from those ties came on March 14 and 15, when Clinton hosted an international jobs summit in Detroit. The meeting brought together top officials from the Group of Seven (G-7), the world's largest industrialized nations. The group consists of Canada, France, Germany, Italy, Japan, the United Kingdom, and the United States. The international leaders gathered in Detroit to discuss ways to stem rising unemployment worldwide.

Empowerment zone. On December 21, Clinton chose Detroit as one of six cities to qualify for a federal empowerment zone. Under Clinton's urban program, the city was to receive $100 million in social service grants and $225 million in tax breaks.

Civil rights icon becomes a crime victim. On August 30, Rosa L. Parks, a pioneer in the civil rights movement of the 1950's and 1960's, was robbed and beaten in her Detroit home. Neighbors helped capture her alleged attacker, Joseph Skipper, the next day. Skipper, 28, a reputed crack cocaine addict who lived in abandoned buildings in Parks's neighborhood, was charged with the attack and was awaiting trial at year-end.

Parks, 81, is known as the mother of the modern civil rights movement because of her refusal in 1955 to give up her bus seat to a white man in Montgomery, Ala. Her action, a violation of a city ordinance, resulted in her arrest and set off a yearlong bus boycott led by Martin Luther King, Jr., and a revolution against racial segregation and inequality in the United States.

Beating death still making waves. Legal maneuvering continued in the controversial case involving four Detroit police officers tried for the 1992 beating death of a black motorist, Malice W. Green. Green was killed on November 5, after the officers—three of whom are white—confronted him outside a house where crack cocaine was being sold.

Two officers convicted of second-degree murder in August 1993, Larry Nevers and Walter Budzyn, continued to serve lengthy prison sentences in 1994 as their attorneys appealed to the Michigan Court of Appeals. The attorneys claimed that the officers did not get fair trials because the prosecutors in the case improperly suppressed evidence.

On July 1, Freddie Douglas, the supervising sergeant at the scene, was found guilty of willful neglect of duty. A fourth officer, Robert Lessnau, who was found not guilty of an assault charge in August 1993, was reinstated to the police department in March 1994. He subsequently sued two emergency medical service workers for libel for their court testimony against him.

Also during the year, a federal judge approved a $5.25-million settlement the city had negotiated with the Green family.

Casino gambling for Detroit? On Aug. 2, 1994, Detroit voters approved two plans for casinos in the city. One plan called for riverboat gambling on the Detroit River, and the other was for a downtown casino that would be partially owned and run by one of Michigan's Indian tribes. On September 8, however, Michigan Governor John Engler rejected the land-based casino plan, saying that the proposal was not part of an overall economic development plan for Detroit. Instead, he formed a commission to study the future of gaming throughout Michigan. The riverboat gambling proposal, too, was on hold at year-end. Both plans require the approval of the state legislature.   □ Vivian S. Toy

See also **City.** In *World Book,* see **Detroit.**

Dinosaur. See Paleontology.

Disabled. The final phase of the Americans with Disabilities Act (ADA) of 1990 went into effect on July 26, 1994. As of that date, some 400,000 private businesses in the United States that employ 15 to 24 people had to have made reasonable efforts to remove structures on their premises that might be barriers to the disabled, according to Tony Coelho, chairman of the President's Committee on Employment of People with Disabilities. Firms employing fewer than 15 workers were exempt from the law. In addition to making structural changes to accommodate the disabled, ADA prohibits discrimination against a disabled person in workplace promotions, pay, or training. As of July 26, an estimated 86 percent of American workers were covered by the ADA.

Nevertheless, many experts on discrimination believed that ADA was too slow in alleviating joblessness among the 43 million people that the President's Committee defined as disabled. A July Harris poll found that two-thirds of disabled Americans of working age were unemployed, about the same as in 1986.

The Empire State Building in New York City was to undergo changes to make it accessible to the disabled under a settlement reached on March 3, 1994, by the U.S. Department of Justice and the building owners. A disability-rights group had filed a claim against the building in January 1992 in one of the first cases charging a violation of ADA. Under

London police pull a woman out of the path of a bus during demonstrations in May over the defeat of an antidiscrimination bill to protect the disabled.

the settlement, the owners agreed to build ramps, lower counters, and add new restrooms to bring the building into compliance with ADA. The observation deck on the 86th floor and other areas of the building also would be made accessible to the disabled. Many of the changes, expected to cost about $2 million, had to be approved by an historic preservations group, given the building's historic landmark status.

SAT settlement. On March 31, the Justice Department settled another dispute involving ADA that gave disabled students a second chance at taking a revised Scholastic Aptitude Test (SAT). The SAT measures verbal and mathematical skills and is used by many colleges and universities nationwide as admissions criteria. The Educational Testing Service of Princeton, N.J., which administers the SAT, was phasing in a revised test with the old version. Disabled students who required extra time or special accommodations, such as large type, could take the revised SAT only in mid-March or the old SAT on later dates. But other students could take the revised SAT as late as June 4. About 50 families with disabled students complained to the Justice Department that by limiting the time their children could take the revised test, their rights under ADA had been violated. Under the settlement, the disabled students could cancel their March test scores and retake the test in May or June.   □ Carol L. Hanson

In *World Book,* see **Disabled.**

Disasters. The natural disaster that claimed the most lives in 1994 was an earthquake that struck southwestern Colombia near the border with Ecuador, killing more than 1,000 people. The quake measured 6.4 on the Richter scale and caused mudslides that buried entire villages.

Disasters that resulted in 25 or more deaths in 1994 included the following:

Aircraft crashes

January 3—Near Irkutsk, Russia. A Russian airliner crashed and exploded after taking off from Irkutsk, a city in Siberia, killing 125 people, including all passengers and crew on board and another person on the ground. According to TASS, a Russian news agency, the plane was more than 20 tons (18 metric tons) above the weight limit, and one of the plane's three engines had recently been under repair.

February 25—Near Huanuco, Peru. A Russian-built passenger airplane en route to Lima, capital of Peru, from the Peruvian jungle town of Tingo Maria disappeared after passing over the highland city of Huanuco. Twenty-nine people were reportedly killed, including two Russian crew members.

March 22—Near Mezhdurechensk, Russia. A Russian Aeroflot airliner crashed near the town of Mezhdurechensk in Siberia, and all 75 people aboard were killed. The airplane disappeared from radar without sending a distress signal. A Russian government commission that investigated the crash revealed on April 5 that a member of the crew was showing his children how to pilot the aircraft minutes before it crashed. According to Western aviation experts who heard tapes recovered from the aircraft's flight recorder, one or more of the children disengaged the automatic controls and sent the plane into a dive.

April 26—Nagoya, Japan. A China Airlines jetliner that took off from Taipei, Taiwan, crashed as it approached the runway at Nagoya, Japan. The plane burst into flames, killing 264 passengers and crew members. Seven people reportedly survived the crash.

June 2—Southwestern Scotland. A helicopter carrying the head of Northern Ireland's Special Branch, an antiterrorist security force, and nine of his senior colleagues, crashed in heavy fog in a remote region of southwestern Scotland. The helicopter was en route from Aldergrove Airport in Northern Ireland to an antiterrorist conference near Inverness in northern Scotland. All 29 passengers and crew, including nine British Army intelligence officers, were killed.

June 6—Xian, China. In the worst single air disaster in China's history, all 160 passengers and crew perished when their Russian-built Chinese provincial airline crashed minutes after take-off from Xian.

July 1—Central Mauritania. An Air Mauritania passenger airliner crashed while attempting to land during a sandstorm at an airport in central Mauritania, killing 94 of the 101 people on board.

July 2—Charlotte, N.C. USAir Flight 1016 crashed as the pilot attempted to abort a landing at the airport in Charlotte, N.C., because of bad weather. The crash killed 37 people and injured about 20 others.

August 21—Near Agadir, Morocco. All 44 passengers and crew aboard a Royal Air Maroc passenger plane were killed when the plane crashed into the Atlas Mountains shortly after take-off from Agadir, Morocco. The plane was en route to Casablanca. Among the passengers was Ali al Mahmoud al Jaber as Sabah, a Kuwaiti prince and the brother of Kuwait's defense minister. Investigators said the crash was deliberately caused by a suicidal pilot.

September 8—Pittsburgh, Pa. A USAir Boeing 737 crashed as it approached Greater Pittsburgh International Airport, killing all 132 people on board. The plane, en route from Chicago, went down near Hopewell Township, Pa. Witnesses said that the plane's engines appeared to quit,

A rescue worker from a Swedish Navy helicopter examines corpses found in a life raft after the ferry *Estonia* sank in the Baltic Sea in September, killing more than 900 people.

and it went into a sudden descent.

September 26—Siberia, Russia. A Russian passenger plane, forced to divert from its flight plan because of bad weather, crashed in a forest near the remote village of Vanavara in Siberia, killing all 27 people on board. The turbojet was flying from the Siberian city of Krasnoyarsk to the town of Tura.

October 12—Near Natanz, Iran. A commuter plane en route from Isfahan, Iran, to the capital, Teheran, crashed in the Karkas Mountains near Natanz, killing all 66 people aboard.

October 31—Near Roselawn, Ind. An American Eagle turboprop commuter plane en route to Chicago crashed into a soybean field near Roselawn, Ind., during a rainstorm. All 68 passengers and crew aboard were killed. The plane was an ATR commuter aircraft, owned and operated by American Eagle, a commuter airline specializing in short routes. The plane's manufacturer later said that ATR's could become unstable in icy weather. The Federal Aviation Administration on December 9 grounded all ATR's when icy conditions were present or forecast.

Earthquakes

January 17—Los Angeles. An earthquake measuring 6.7 on the Richter scale struck the Los Angeles area at 4:31 a.m., killing 57 people and disrupting power and water service for hundreds of thousands of people. The quake was centered in the Northridge area of the San Fernando Valley. In the worst single incident, a three-story apartment complex near California State University at Northridge collapsed. At least 16 residents there were crushed to death.

February 16—Sumatra, Indonesia. An earthquake struck the island of Sumatra in Indonesia just after midnight, killing about 184 people and seriously injuring about 550 others. The hardest hit area was the province of Lampung in southeastern Sumatra. The United States Geological Survey estimated the strength of the quake at 7.2 on the Richter scale.

June 3—Java and Bali islands, Indonesia. An offshore earthquake triggered tidal waves that swept through coastal villages of Indonesia's main island of Java and the island of Bali, killing at least 218 people. The U.S. Geological Survey said the quake had a *surface-wave magnitude* (a measurement of seismic waves) of 7.2.

June 7—Toez, Colombia. An earthquake measuring 6.4 on the Richter scale caused an avalanche of mud and rocks to descend on several villages in a river valley near the border with Ecuador. Authorities said that more than 1,000 people may

190

have been killed, mostly in the villages of Toez and Irlanda, which were completely destroyed. It was the strongest quake to hit Colombia since a May 1957 quake that registered 6.8 on the Richter scale.

August 18—Northwest Algeria. An earthquake struck several cities and villages in northwest Algeria, killing at least 171 people and leaving about 15,000 people homeless. The quake registered 5.6 on the Richter scale.

November 15—Mindoro Island, Philippines. An earthquake measuring 7.0 on the Richter scale, according to Philippine government seismologists, struck the central Philippine island of Mindoro. More than 60 people were killed in the quake and from the tidal wave it spawned.

Explosions and fires

January 23—Puerto Madryn, Argentina. An all-volunteer fire brigade consisting of 25 young apprentices, most of them teen-agers, was encircled by flames as firefighters sought to extinguish a brush fire. All 25 youths perished.

November 2—Dronka, Egypt. After torrential rains loosened railroad tracks, a train carrying fuel oil derailed, causing an oil spill. The oil was carried by floodwaters into the town of Dronka in southern Egypt, where electrical fires ignited the oil. The fires spread quickly, killing at least 475 people.

December 8—Karamay, China. A fire broke out in a cinema crowded with primary and high school students who were watching a variety show in the town of Karamay in the northwest region of Xinjiang in China. Officials said that as many as 300 children were killed in the fire, most from smoke inhalation.

Shipwrecks

January 1—Off Newfoundland in the Atlantic Ocean. A Liberian-registered iron ore carrier, the *Marika 7,* sank in high seas in the North Atlantic Ocean 930 miles (1,500 kilometers) east of Newfoundland. A search for the crew, which consisted of 30 Filipino sailors and six Greek officers, was called off on January 6 after officials said there was no hope of finding survivors.

February 13—Off Bangkok, Thailand. A boat carrying about 200 Burmese workers capsized off Bangkok, Thailand. Police and rescue workers said that all aboard were feared dead.

March 7—Near Sikri Island, Kenya. A passenger ferry capsized during a storm on Lake Victoria, drowning at least 40 people.

June 13—Gulf of Aden. An estimated 50 Somalis, returning to their homeland to escape a civil war in Yemen, perished when their ship sank in the Gulf of Aden.

July 13—Off Havana, Cuba. Thirty-two Cuban refugees drowned after a tugboat they had reportedly stolen in Havana, the capital, collided with a government ship that had pursued it.

August 20—Near Chandpur, Bangladesh. A double-decker passenger ferry capsized and sank in choppy waters as it approached the port of Chandpur in Bangladesh, killing about 350 people. The ferry was carrying more than 400 people, twice its authorized passenger limit.

September 28—Off Finland's southwest coast. More than 900 people died when a ferry capsized and sank in the Baltic Sea during a storm off Finland's southwest coast. It was one of the worst ferry disasters in history. The ferry, called the *Estonia,* was traveling from Talinn, capital of Estonia, to Stockholm, Sweden. The *Estonia* sent out an emergency call at 1:24 a.m. local time, after flooding through a cargo door in the bow overwhelmed the ferry's pumps. Rescuers were able to save about 140 people. Investigators reported on October 3 that the cargo door had become completely detached from the ferry.

December 2—Manila Bay, Philippines. An interisland ferry collided with a freighter in Manila Bay in the Philippines, drowning more than 140 passengers and crew. Ships in the area rescued about 450 people.

Storms and floods

March 27—Southeastern United States. A storm system spawned dozens of tornadoes that swept through the Southeastern United States, killing 22 people in Alabama, 17 in Georgia, 2 in Tennessee, and 2 in North Carolina. One of the tornadoes hit the Goshen United Methodist Church outside Piedmont, Ala., killing 20 people, including 6 children, who were attending Palm Sunday services.

May 3—Near Cox's Bazar, Bangladesh. A cyclone that swept along the southeastern coast of Bangladesh killed at least 120 people, many of them refugees from Burma. The storm damaged 16 of 18 Burmese refugee camps near the city of Cox's Bazar and left more than 500,000 people homeless.

July 4—Southwestern Georgia. Tropical storm Alberto swept through southwestern Georgia, causing flooding along several rivers that led to the deaths of 31 people.

August 20, 21—Zhejiang Province, China. Typhoon Fred pounded the coastal region of Zhejiang Province in China, killing more than 700 people and causing damage estimated at $1.6-billion. Officials said most of the casualties occurred in the city of Wenzhou. About 700,000 houses throughout the province were damaged, and flooding from the storm affected more than

A young boy views the rubble left by a tornado that struck the Goshen United Methodist Church near Piedmont, Ala., in March, killing 20 people.

42 million people, government officials reported.

November 5 and 6—Northern Italy. Heavy rains caused flooding along the Po and Tanaro rivers in the Piedmont region of northwestern Italy, killing at least 54 people. Officials said the death toll rose to as many as 100 people in Italy's worst flooding since 1913.

November 12 and 13—Haiti. Tropical Storm Gordon spawned torrential rains that battered Haiti, causing landslides and floods. More than 800 people were killed, and Haiti declared a state of emergency.

Train wrecks

March 8—Near Durban, South Africa. A commuter train derailed and plunged down a wooded hillside, killing at least 64 passengers and injuring about 370. The cause of the derailment was unknown, and the possibility that it was the work of terrorists was not ruled out. The train was carrying more than 800 black passengers. It was the worst train accident in South Africa since 1965 when a train derailment killed 91 people.

September 22—Near Tolunda, Angola. A train derailed and plunged into a ravine near Tolunda in the Huila province of Angola, killing about 300 people and injuring 147 others.

December 2—Near Szajol, Hungary. Hungary's worst train disaster in 26 years took the lives of 29 people and injured 52 others after an express train derailed near Szajol station.

Other disasters

February 10—Sumatra, Indonesia. A bus went into a ravine near Gulbong in north Sumatra, killing at least 36 people and injuring 11 others.

May 23—Mina, Saudi Arabia. At least 250 Muslim pilgrims were trampled to death at Mina, just outside Mecca, Islam's holiest city, when a stampede broke out during a religious ritual.

October 21—Seoul, South Korea. A section of the Songsu Bridge spanning the Han River in Seoul, the capital of South Korea, collapsed during the morning rush hour, killing 32 people. Those killed were passengers in automobiles and a commuter bus. Officials blamed the accident on poor maintenance of the bridge. □ Rod Such

Djibouti. See Africa.

Drug abuse. The suicide in April of rock star Kurt Cobain, 27, an alleged heroin user, drew attention to drug abuse in the United States in 1994. Various news sources reported that heroin had become popular among affluent people and that its use had increased in the inner cities as well.

Increased drug use. Based on its annual survey, the U.S. Substance Abuse and Mental Health Services Administration estimated in July that 7.5 million Americans over age 35 used drugs in 1993, significantly more than the 6 million users in 1992. Teenagers also showed higher rates, with 2.1 million teens using marijuana in 1993, compared with 1.7 million in 1992.

The federal government's Drug Abuse Warning Network reported a 9 percent increase in drug-related emergency hospital visits in early 1993. Many of these were heroin-related as stronger, purer forms of heroin became available. One potent blend released in New York City, called China Cat, was tied to the deaths of several people in August 1994.

Reassessing the war on drugs. In March, the Rand Corporation reported that state and federal governments had spent nearly $13 billion on law enforcement to combat drug use. About 1.4 million inmates occupied local jails and state and federal prisons for drug crimes in 1994. The Rand study said that trying to stop drug abuse with legal action cost seven times as much as treatment programs.

The California Drug and Alcohol Treatment Assessment, a study released in August, tracked more then 1,800 people in drug treatment programs. The study found that for every $1 invested in treatment there was a $7 return, measured in reductions in criminal activity, increases in worker productivity, and savings in health care.

Nicotine as drug. In February, U.S. Food and Drug Administration (FDA) Commissioner David Kessler said the FDA was considering whether to designate nicotine, an active ingredient in cigarette tobacco, as a drug subject to FDA regulation. In March, a congressional committee began hearings in which experts debated the addictive nature of nicotine. Cigarette manufacturers denied nicotine's addictive potential as well as accusations that they intentionally increased nicotine content in cigarettes to create addicts to their products. Scientists and medical experts provided data showing nicotine as one of the most addictive drugs available. In a 1989 survey, done by the Addiction Research Foundation in Toronto, Canada, 45 percent of cocaine addicts who also smoked cigarettes said that the urge to smoke was stronger than their cravings for cocaine.

About 3 million people worldwide die from smoking-related illnesses each year, according to a September 1994 study by the World Health Organization, the American Cancer Society, and the Imperial Cancer Research Fund.   □ David C. Lewis

In *World Book,* see **Drug abuse.**

Drugs. The United States Food and Drug Administration (FDA) on Jan. 11, 1994, approved the first new nonprescription pain reliever since 1984. The drug, naproxen sodium, has been available since 1976 as the prescription medications Naprosyn and Anaprox used in treating arthritis and other conditions associated with mild to moderate pain. The FDA said naproxen sodium had proved safe enough to be sold over-the-counter in a dosage lower than that of the prescription form.

Naproxen sodium belongs to a family of medicines termed nonsteroidal anti-inflammatory agents that includes such familiar pain relievers as Advil and Motrin. The Procter & Gamble Company sells the product under the trade name Aleve. The FDA said Aleve is suitable for relief of minor pain associated with arthritis, headache, menstrual cramps, muscle aches, and similar conditions.

Tamoxifen risks. The FDA in April 1994 announced that the manufacturer of tamoxifen would send a warning letter that presented new data about the drug's cancer risk to some 380,000 physicians who might prescribe the medication. Tamoxifen is a synthetic hormone used in treating breast cancer and is manufactured by Zeneca Pharmaceuticals. Physicians prescribe the drug following breast cancer surgery to reduce the risk that the cancer will recur. A major government-sponsored study was underway in 1994 to determine whether tamoxifen can prevent breast cancer altogether in women at high risk for the disease.

Zeneca's letter alerted physicians to a Swedish study showing that breast cancer patients on tamoxifen were six times more likely to develop cancer of the *endometrium,* the lining of the uterus, than were patients not taking the drug. The FDA advised women taking tamoxifen to get regular gynecologic examinations and to report any unusual symptoms to their physician. Women also were warned to avoid becoming pregnant while taking the drug because of evidence that it can harm the fetus.

RU-486. Roussel Uclaf, the French manufacturer of the abortion pill RU-486, on May 16 announced an agreement that would make the controversial drug available in the United States by 1996. The firm gave patent rights to RU-486, free of charge, to the Population Council, a nonprofit research agency based in New York City. The Council said it would conduct clinical trials on the safety and effectiveness of RU-486 and then select an American firm to manufacture and market the drug.

RU-486 is intended to induce abortion during the first seven weeks after conception. The Population Council estimated that RU-486 could be used in 25 percent to 40 percent of the estimated 1.6 million abortions performed in the United States each year. Although the drug has been available in France, Sweden, and the United Kingdom, Roussel Uclaf chose not to market it in the United States because

Drugs

of the controversy surrounding abortion. Abortion-rights groups hailed the agreement, and opponents of abortion denounced it.

Drugs approved. The FDA on April 12 approved the marketing of a drug that helps prevent rejection of a transplanted organ. Rejection occurs when the body's immune system identifies transplanted tissue as foreign and attacks it. The drug tacrolimus, which suppresses immune system activity, is derived from a soil fungus found near the headquarters of its developer, Fujisawa Pharmaceutical Company Limited of Osaka, Japan. In October, U.S. teams studying tacrolimus reported that the drug had side effects so severe that some patients had to be taken off it.

Bristol-Myers Squibb Company on February 7 obtained FDA approval to market the drug Capoten as a treatment for kidney disease in people with Type I (insulin-dependent) diabetes. Studies have shown that Capoten can cut by half the number of diabetics who develop kidney failure and need *dialysis* or a kidney transplant. (Dialysis is a mechanical means of filtering wastes from the bloodstream, a job normally performed by the kidneys.) Experts said Capoten could substantially reduce the cost of caring for patients with kidney failure. Capoten is already used to reduce high blood pressure and treat heart failure.

Are cigarettes drugs? The FDA moved closer toward regulating cigarettes as drugs when a scientific advisory panel concluded on August 2 that the nicotine in cigarettes is addictive. Federal law defines a drug as any product intended to have an effect on the structure or function of the body.

Experts told the panel that nicotine has such an effect and that 85 to 90 percent of America's 45 million smokers are addicted to nicotine. (Smoking five cigarettes a day is sufficient to cause addiction, the panel was told.) Some scientists suggested an FDA policy of gradually lowering the nicotine content of cigarettes over a period of 10 to 15 years to the point where cigarettes no longer contained enough nicotine to be addictive. But no decision had been reached by year's end. Cigarette manufacturers argued that smoking is a habit, not an addiction.

Cholera vaccine. The Swiss Serum and Vaccine Institute in Bern announced on May 27 that it had received approval to market in Switzerland a new oral vaccine to protect against cholera. Cholera is a potentially deadly intestinal disease spread by contaminated water. An injectable cholera vaccine has been available for years, but the World Health Organization does not recommend that vaccine because it offers only partial protection. The new vaccine is a genetically engineered product that is taken in a single dose. It was developed in collaboration with scientists at the University of Maryland in College Park. The institute expects the vaccine, Orochol Berna, to become available in other European countries and in the United States.   □ Michael Woods

See also **Medicine.** In *World Book,* see **Drugs.**

Eastern Orthodox Churches. Ecumenical Patriarch Bartholomew I of Constantinople (Istanbul, Turkey) reinstated three repentant clergymen of the Jerusalem patriarchate at a synod meeting in Istanbul in April 1994. The clergy had been deposed in 1993 because of their activities in setting up dioceses in Australia that were in competition with established Orthodox churches there. Diorodos, patriarch of Jerusalem, whose policy the clergy were attempting to carry out, agreed at the meeting to halt such activities in Australia.

On April 19, 1994, Bartholomew I also called for a spiritual basis for strengthening European unity when he addressed the European Parliament in Strasbourg, France, at the invitation of then parliament President Egon Klepsch. It was the first time an Orthodox clergyman had been asked to address the parliament, an advisory body to the 12-nation European Union, formerly the European Community.

In Zagreb, Croatia, on January 27, Metropolitan Jovan held the first Orthodox liturgy since September 1991, when he left the region because of full-scale civil war. Croatia had declared its independence from Yugoslavia in June 1991. Croatian officials and a representative of the Roman Catholic Church attended the liturgy. This act and the granting of Croatian citizenship to Jovan were seen as efforts to improve relations between the Orthodox minority and the Roman Catholic majority who fought each other in the civil war.

In Russia, Alexei II, patriarch of Moscow, entered into agreements on March 1, 1994, with Russian Defense Minister Pavel Grachev to provide Orthodox chaplains to the Russian army, the first since Russia had become a Communist nation in 1917. After the Soviet Union dissolved and Communist rule ended in 1991, the Orthodox Church, the nation's largest religious body, began to function freely.

In April, Alexis II spoke to the Hungarian parliament. He asked forgiveness for the Soviet invasion of Hungary in 1956 and stressed his desire for ecumenical relationships with the Hungarian Roman Catholic and Protestant churches.

Albania. On April 10, 1994, Archbishop Anastasios, head of the Autocephalous (self-governing) Albanian Orthodox Church, called for peace between Albania and Greece. The Albanian government had banned the Orthodox Easter procession in Tirana, the capital, after ethnic Greeks came under suspicion in the deaths of two Albanian border guards. The Greek government then pressured Albania to lift the ban. Tensions rose on May 6, when Albania charged six ethnic Greeks with fomenting separatism, and Greece accused Albania of trying to terrorize its ethnic Greek population.

Celebrations in Washington, D.C., in September ended a year's observance of Orthodoxy's 200th anniversary in North America.   □ Stanley S. Harakas

In *World Book,* see **Eastern Orthodox Churches.**

Economics. The United States economy was so strong in 1994 that the Federal Reserve System, a government agency that helps oversee the nation's money supply and banks, began raising interest rates early in the year to slow the economy down and prevent a binge of rising prices. The Federal Reserve, known as the *Fed* or the *central bank,* kept raising rates into the fall. These actions represented a policy shift reversing years of the Fed cutting interest rates, first done to combat the 1990-1991 recession and then to assist the slow recovery from that recession. By the end of 1993, the economy had gained considerable strength, and it continued growing solidly through 1994.

As a result of the Fed's policy shift, all other types of interest rates surged in 1994. The prime rate, which commercial banks reserve for their best business customers, rose to 8.5 percent on November 15 from 5.5 percent when the year began. Interest on long-term, fixed-rate home mortgages started 1994 at 7.2 percent and inched up to 9.25 percent by the year's end. The rate surge curbed a boom in home mortgage refinancing and dampened home sales and new housing construction. In reaction to rising interest rates, the stock and bond markets tumbled sharply in late winter and spring (See **Bank; Stocks and bonds.**)

The best overall measure of economic growth is the government's report on quarterly *gross domestic product (GDP),* the total value of all goods and services produced within a country. The U.S. GDP had risen at a bristling annual rate of 6.3 percent in the final three months of 1993, before the Fed started pushing interest rates higher. For 1994, the GDP grew a solid 3.3 percent in the first quarter, then sped up to 4.1 percent in the second three months, and was unexpectedly strong at 3.9 percent in the third quarter.

Economists, however, summed up 1994's economic expansion as weaker than previous growth periods following recessions since World War II (1939-1945), with only modest gains in the average living standard. But economists also said the Fed's attempts to hold growth to a slower rate could pay off in a long-term, low-inflation recovery.

Inflation contained. The interest rate hikes through 1994 were meant to brake the surging economy enough to avoid a chain reaction of higher and higher prices known as an *inflation spiral*. If such a spiral were to occur, the Federal Reserve would have to "tighten" money and credit severely, which could trigger another recession.

By fall, the best-known inflation measures still showed a fairly tame rate of price increases. The U.S. Consumer Price Index, which measures cost changes for average household goods, was up only 2.6 percent for a 12-month-period ending in October, slightly below the pace for all of 1993. The Producer

Leaders of the Group of Seven—seven major industrial nations—gather in Naples, Italy, in July to discuss economic issues.

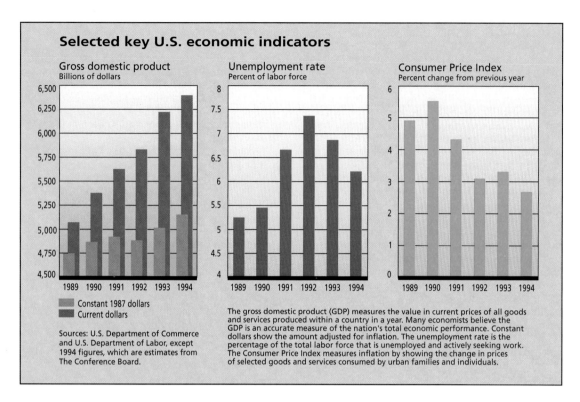

Selected key U.S. economic indicators

Gross domestic product
Billions of dollars

6,500
6,250
6,000
5,750
5,500
5,250
5,000
4,750
4,500

1989 1990 1991 1992 1993 1994

■ Constant 1987 dollars
■ Current dollars

Sources: U.S. Department of Commerce
and U.S. Department of Labor, except
1994 figures, which are estimates from
The Conference Board.

Unemployment rate
Percent of labor force

8
7.5
7
6.5
6
5.5
5
4.5
4

1989 1990 1991 1992 1993 1994

Consumer Price Index
Percent change from previous year

6
5
4
3
2
1
0

1989 1990 1991 1992 1993 1994

The gross domestic product (GDP) measures the value in current prices of all goods and services produced within a country in a year. Many economists believe the GDP is an accurate measure of the nation's total economic performance. Constant dollars show the amount adjusted for inflation. The unemployment rate is the percentage of the total labor force that is unemployed and actively seeking work. The Consumer Price Index measures inflation by showing the change in prices of selected goods and services consumed by urban families and individuals.

Price Index, which tracks prices at the wholesale level before they reach consumers, actually declined in September and October 1994 and had risen just 1 percent since October 1993. (See also **Consumerism.**)

But policymakers at the Federal Reserve remained concerned about more basic and predictive signals, such as rising prices of commodities used by industry, rising freight rates, tightening labor markets that might force companies to bid up wages to fill jobs, and other signs that inflation could speed up. The Fed took action in a Nov. 15, 1994, meeting. For the sixth time in 1994, it boosted the most basic market interest rate—the so-called Fed funds rate that banks charge each other for overnight loans between commercial banks—by three-fourths of a percent to 5.5 percent. Before the Fed first raised interest charges on February 4, that rate was just 3 percent, its lowest level since the 1960's.

Americans remained worried in 1994, however, about their basic economic health and the future. The rising interest rates came just as many people thought the economy was moving on a solid track, which added to people's worries and thus to frustration with the ruling Democratic Party. In 1992, voters had ended 12 years of Republican domination of the White House by electing Democrat Bill Clinton as President, but in 1994 people voted against Clinton's party. In a pivotal November 8 election, Republicans swept into control of the House of Representatives

for the first time since 1954, took over the Senate for the first time since 1986, and gained a majority of state governorships for the first time since 1970.

Voter frustration was linked to a range of economic issues. Some felt left out of the economic recovery, and some were concerned that Democrats under Clinton had tried to bring about radical changes in the nation's health insurance industry—a huge part of the economy that affects everyone's standard of living. Newly empowered Republican leaders pledged after the elections to cut taxes for the middle class, add a balanced-budget amendment to the Constitution of the United States, and make tax changes aimed at boosting business.

Employment. Economic growth put people to work throughout 1994. The unemployment rate among those looking for work fell from 6.7 percent as the year began to 5.6 percent in November. That was good news for families. But economists and Fed officials worried that the labor pool had tightened so much that additional shrinkage of the jobless rate might only come about by bidding up wages—producing what economists call *wage inflation*.

In spite of the growing economy and shrinking unemployment, many major corporations announced large cuts in their work forces in 1994, adding to the feeling of economic insecurity among many workers. Also, average earnings showed little net gain after adjusting for inflation, indicating that many households were making little headway financially and that wage inflation had not taken hold.

Foreign economies. Other major industrial nations saw their economies improve from the recession level or very slow growth they experienced in 1993, though none matched the U.S. pace. France, Germany, and the United Kingdom grew about 1 percent in the 1994 second quarter, compared with the 4.1 percent U.S. rate. Japan, undergoing political upheaval after the 1993 ouster of the party that had run its government for decades, at year's end appeared to be finally emerging from a recession. Growth continued at a stronger pace for China and other Asian nations and for Latin America.

GATT. President Clinton worked in 1994 to erase barriers to international trade. Clinton pressed the U.S. Congress to approve a global trade agreement, called the GATT Treaty because it would install new rules for the existing General Agreement on Tariffs and Trade. The GATT Treaty became controversial. Some people worried about the cost to implement the treaty. Critics complained it might hurt some U.S. industries or could cede U.S. power to an envisioned World Trade Organization. On November 29, the House of Representatives approved the agreement, and on December 1, the Senate also approved it. (See also **International trade.**) □ John Boyd

In *World Book,* see Economics.

Ecuador. See Latin America.

Education. Troubled by the nation's slow pace of education reform, states and school systems took bold steps in 1994 to improve schools in the United States. For many years, local school systems have run public schools with public monies. But in 1994, education officials began permitting other institutions to educate students with public funding. Supporting this so-called privatization movement was President Bill Clinton, who during his State of the Union address in January, urged school systems to "experiment with ideas like chartering their schools to be run by private corporations." In May, the President signed legislation that permitted local educators to spend federal education funds on exploring the possibility of privatization.

Privatization projects. In August, the Hartford, Conn., school board agreed to let Educational Alternatives, Incorporated (EAI) run the city's public schools, making Hartford the nation's first city to hire a private company to manage its entire school system. Opponents of the privatization, including the American Federation of Teachers, fear that the company's profit motive may adversely impact the quality of education at Hartford schools.

Also in 1994, nearly a dozen school systems from around the nation entered negotiations with the Edison Project of New York City to manage public schools for profit. The Edison Project, headed by former Yale University President Benno Schmidt, Jr.,

proposes to educate students to a far higher standard than EAI, using a longer school year and school day, a new curriculum, and new ways of staffing schools and of using technology in teaching. But by the end of 1994, Edison's future was in doubt, as the company needed at least $25 million in additional funding to open its first schools in 1995.

Edison's problems did not stop educators from turning to other alternative school programs in 1994. In May, the school board in Osceola County, Florida, approved a plan to have the Walt Disney Company build a nonprofit public school as part of a planned community that the company is building near Walt Disney World outside Orlando. The $36-million Celebration School and Teaching Academy is scheduled to open in 1996 with 1,400 students in high-tech classrooms that stress hands-on learning methods designed by the Disney company.

In October 1994, New Jersey education officials proposed a five-year school voucher experiment in the Jersey City school system, the state's second largest, which has been controlled by the state since 1989. Parents of students entering the first and ninth grades in the Jersey City school system would be permitted to spend tuition vouchers at local private or parochial schools. In the past, public school officials had strongly opposed vouchers.

Goals 2000. While some reformers sought alternatives to traditional public schooling in 1994, others tried to upgrade the nation's public schools by promoting higher academic standards. In March, President Clinton signed the Goals 2000: Educate America Act, a law that offers $400 million in federal grants over a five-year period to states and local school districts that create a rigorous curriculum and set high academic standards for their students. The law codifies eight voluntary education goals to be met by the year 2000. They are as follows:

- All children will start school ready to learn.
- The high school graduation rate will increase to at least 90 percent.
- All students will leave grades 4, 8, and 12 having grasped challenging subject matter in English, science, math, foreign languages, civics and government, economics, the arts, history, and geography.
- Teachers will have the opportunity to continue their own education in rigorous programs.
- American students will rank first in the world in math and science.
- Every adult American will be literate and have the knowledge and skills needed to compete in a global economy and to fulfill the rights and responsibilities of citizenship.
- Every school in the United States will be free of drugs, violence, and illegal guns.
- Every school will increase parental involvement in its educational programs.

Other academic standards. Also in 1994, experts drafted tough new standards in a number

197

of academic fields. In March, a consortium of national arts groups released the nation's first set of national standards in art education. It recommended that by the end of high school, all students be able to compose music, demonstrate acting techniques, or write a play.

In October, the National Center on History in the Schools at the University of California at Los Angeles released a 271-page report outlining the history that the nation's students should master. Proponents have argued that national curriculum standards are needed because local educators have failed to establish high expectations for students. But critics of the standards charge that they impinge on the long-standing tradition of local control in U.S. public education. The history standards also came under fire from conservatives for failing to include a number of famous male figures in U.S. history and for emphasizing negative events. One critic noted that the standards cite Joseph McCarthy or McCarthyism 19 times but never mention Thomas Edison, Albert Einstein, or Robert E. Lee.

Extended school day? In May, the National Education Commission on Time and Learning, a congressionally funded commission, recommended another solution to the nation's educational woes: a longer school day and a longer school year. The commission recommended in a report that schools in the United States should spend five and a half hours a day teaching core academic subjects, a block of time equivalent to that given to academics in Japan and many European countries and nearly double the amount of time U.S. schools presently spend teaching academics.

The race to meet global standards. The need for more rigor in U.S. classrooms was brought to light in a congressionally sponsored report card on American education released in September. The report of the National Education Goals Panel, which was based on academic achievement tests from 1992, revealed that only 18 percent of 4th graders, 25 percent of 8th graders, and 16 percent of 12th graders meet "world class standards" in mathematics. Twenty-five percent of 4th graders, 28 percent of 8th graders, and 37 percent of 12th graders meet international standards in reading, the panel reported.

Cutting costs of higher education. Higher education in the United States also was under the gun in 1994, as it struggled to cut costs in the face of a shrinking pool of applicants and a mounting public backlash against rising tuition. The College Board, an organization of schools and colleges, reported in September that tuition at the nation's colleges and universities rose at a slower pace than in previous years. But tuition increases at both private and public institutions outpaced the inflation rate, as they have for many consecutive years, the board reported. Tuition at four-year public and private institutions rose an average of 6 percent

for the 1994-1995 school year, twice the rate of inflation.

Worried about pricing themselves out of business, a number of colleges and universities took dramatic steps to make themselves more affordable. Bennington College, a small liberal arts school in Bennington, Vt., and one of the nation's most expensive colleges, announced in June that it would cut its faculty by one-third, abolish tenure for professors, and slash tuition by 10 percent.

Vermont's Middlebury College, one of the nation's highest ranked liberal arts schools, announced in February that it would permit a limited number of students to earn bachelor's degrees in three rather than four years, a move that will cut the cost of an education at the college.

The University of Montana in September announced it would guarantee graduation in four years to students taking a full course load, or pay the students' additional tuition and fees if they were unable to take the courses they needed to graduate in four years. The university also pledged to cancel highly specialized courses with low enrollments and increase faculty teaching loads by 20 percent. Like students at many other U.S. colleges and universities, Montana students have often been unable to enroll in courses they need to graduate as a result of budget cuts and declining teaching loads.

Race-based scholarships. A federal appellate court rocked higher education in October, when it struck down a University of Maryland policy to offer scholarships only to high-achieving African-American students. The university offered the scholarships to attract talented black students to its campus. But the federal court ruled that the university had failed to demonstrate that the race-based scholarships were designed specifically to overcome present consequences of past discrimination against black students, as required by the U.S. Supreme Court's interpretation of "affirmative action." Affirmative action is aimed at creating equity among different social groups in employment, education, and other areas. If the court's ruling is not overturned on appeal to the Supreme Court, many colleges and universities that award scholarships similar to Maryland's will have to change their scholarship policies.

Scholar defends "dead white men." The renowned Yale literary scholar Harold Bloom in October added his voice to the "culture wars" raging on the nation's campuses. In recent years, women, minorities, and homosexuals, among others, have urged that colleges and universities expose their students to a broader cultural range of writers, artists, and thinkers. In the past, schools disproportionately taught the works of European intellectuals. Bloom, in a new book titled *The Western Canon: The Books and School of the Ages,* staunchly defends the greatness of Shakespeare, Dante, Milton and many other "dead white European men."

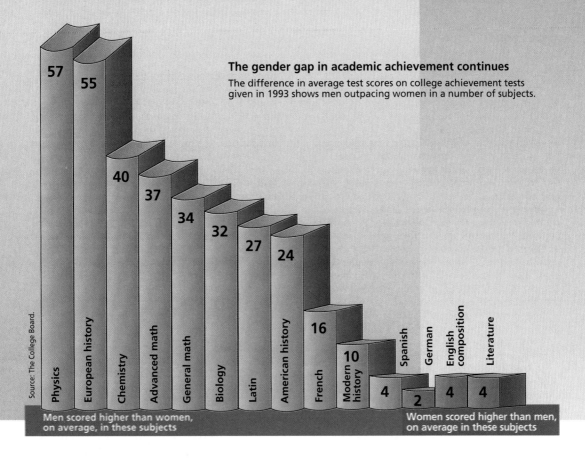

The gender gap in academic achievement continues
The difference in average test scores on college achievement tests given in 1993 shows men outpacing women in a number of subjects.

Source: The College Board.

Physics 57
European history 55
Chemistry 40
Advanced math 37
General math 34
Biology 32
Latin 27
American history 24
French 16
Modern history 10
Spanish 4
German 2
English composition 4
Literature 4

Men scored higher than women, on average, in these subjects

Women scored higher than men, on average in these subjects

Enrollment and costs. According to a report released in August by the United States Department of Education, the nation spent $506.5 billion on education during the 1994-1995 school year, an increase of 4.6 percent from the previous year. The report stated that public elementary and secondary schooling consumed nearly $300 million of the total. Over the past decade, spending on public education increased by more than 40 percent, after adjusting for inflation. The department also reported that the average public-school teacher's salary was $37,200 in the 1994-1995 school year.

The federal report also revealed that increasing numbers of Americans were attending school at all levels. Nearly 7 million students were attending preschool in the fall of 1994, up 33 percent in a decade. Elementary and secondary schools enrolled nearly 50 million students, an increase of about 1 million students from a year earlier. The department noted that the complexion of the nation's students was changing. Thirty-two percent of elementary and secondary children were minorities in 1994, up from about 27 percent a decade earlier. The department also reported that a record 14.7 million Americans were enrolled in higher education. In all, more than one in four Americans were part of the nation's education system in 1994, either as employees of the system or as students. □ Thomas Toch

In *World Book*, see **Education.**

Egypt. President Hosni Mubarak's campaign to curb violence by militant Islamic fundamentalists seeking to establish an Islamic state had mixed results in 1994. Deadly clashes between government security forces and militants occurred often. But attacks against high government officials, such as those seen in 1993, were rare.

However, on April 9, 1994, Major General Raouf Khayrat, a senior antiterrorist official, was assassinated, raising fears that militants had penetrated Egypt's intelligence services. Police later that month killed a leader of the militant Gamaa al-Islamiya, or Islamic Group, which is blamed for much of the violence. On April 11, the government extended until May 1997 an emergency law that gave its security forces broad powers. Also, the government outlined plans in July to appoint mayors, rather than allow mayoral elections, in order to curb the power of Islamic militants in rural areas. Since the spring of 1992, the government had executed 42 militants.

Islamic fervor. The death on April 27, 1994, of a jailed Islamic militant lawyer, Abdel Harith Madani, led to a clash of the Egyptian Bar Association with the government. Police prevented a May 17 protest march of 2,000 lawyers and arrested 30, prompting a hunger strike by another 33. A coroner had reportedly concluded that Madani died of torture.

A controversial 1994 decree by Egypt's education minister that schoolgirls could wear head scarves

199

only if their parents approved was rescinded in September in favor of one requiring schools to notify parents if their daughters did so. Wearing scarves had become a symbol of support for Islamic ideals.

Floods killed some 600 people and left thousands homeless in southern Egypt in early November. More than 490 people died in Dronka near Asyut when fuel at a storage depot ignited and was carried throughout the village by floodwater, setting homes on fire.

Tourism. In early February, Islamic militants warned foreigners to leave the country. Five attacks occurred that month against trains and cruise ships, and bombs were planted at six banks. Violence let up until August 26, when a Spanish teen-ager died in an attack on a bus. Another tourist was killed on October 23. In March, Egypt announced a $42-million publicity campaign to win back tourists.

Economy. In November, the International Monetary Fund was stalled in negotiations with Egypt over the exchange rate for the Egyptian pound. Until the issue was resolved, Egypt would not be forgiven a $4-billion debt to the Paris Club, a group of Western creditors. In 1991, the group had agreed to write off $10 billion if Egypt met financial reform targets. The $4 billion was the last of three installments on the debt.   □ Christine Helms

See also **Middle East** (Facts in brief table). In *World Book*, see **Egypt.**

El Salvador. Armando Calderón Sol of the incumbent National Republican Alliance (ARENA) was sworn in for a five-year term as president on June 1, 1994. Calderón Sol had won a runoff election on April 24. The national election was the first since a 1992 peace agreement ended a bitter 12-year civil war in El Salvador. A former mayor of San Salvador, the nation's capital, Calderón Sol pledged to uphold the peace agreement and serve all the people of El Salvador. (See **Calderón Sol, Armando.**)

Security plan. Yet old animosities surfaced almost immediately after the inauguration in the form of death threats against judges, prelates, and members of Calderón Sol's administration. In response to the threats and a sudden surge in crime, Calderón Sol announced a new national security plan on June 22. The plan would rely heavily on the military and the ARENA-dominated national police.

The opposition Farabundo Martí National Liberation Front (FMLN), which consisted mostly of former rebels, opposed the new security plan. FMLN members complained that the security plan assigned only a nominal role to the new national civilian police. This force was created in June 1993 to allow former rebels to participate in a nonpartisan police force that would eventually replace the national police.
                                    □ Nathan A. Haverstock

See also **Latin America** (Facts in brief table). In *World Book,* see **El Salvador.**

Elections. Republicans scored a smashing victory in the Nov. 8, 1994, midterm elections, seizing control of both houses of Congress for the first time since 1954 and taking governorships in a number of states. The outcome was seen by many observers as a dramatic rebuke for President Bill Clinton, who had tried without much success to convince voters to vote for Democratic candidates. Making the victory for the GOP (Grand Old Party) even more remarkable, not a single Republican incumbent in Congress or a governor's office was defeated.

Republicans picked up eight Senate seats at the polls. Then, the day after the elections, Senator Richard C. Shelby of Alabama switched from the Democratic Party to the GOP to give the Republicans a 53-47 advantage in the 104th Congress. In the House, Republicans picked up 52 seats to gain a 230-204 edge over Democrats, with one independent.

Republican strategy. During the countdown to the elections, Republicans took advantage of Clinton's low standing in the polls, particularly in the South. Their strategy, apparently successful, was to make the midterm balloting a national referendum on Clinton's first two years in office.

On September 27, House Republican Whip Newt Gingrich of Georgia, (who in December was chosen by his fellow Republicans to become the next Speaker of the House) persuaded about 300 Republican House candidates to sign a "Contract with America." The document held out the promise of swift action on a variety of legislation within the first 100 days of the 104th Congress in early 1995. Among the contract provisions were balanced-budget and term-limits amendments to the Constitution, a $500-a-child tax cut, a reduction in House committee staffs, and a hike in defense spending. Gingrich also proposed making radical reforms in the welfare system, including replacing federal welfare programs with cash grants to the states.

Foreshadow. Earlier in 1994 in special elections in Kentucky and Oklahoma, Republican take-overs of House seats previously held by Democrats foreshadowed the GOP sweep in November. Also in Oklahoma, Representative Mike Synar, a liberal Democrat, lost a September primary battle, sending shock waves through the Democratic Party.

In the November elections, such leading Democratic figures as Speaker of the House Thomas S. Foley of Washington state, who had served in the House for 30 years, and three-term Senator James Sasser of Tennessee lost to relatively unknown opponents. Representative Dan Rostenkowski of Illinois, the long-time chairman of the House Ways and Means Committee, who was indicted May 31 on corruption charges, also was defeated.

Despite the debacle for their party, some leading Democrats survived after difficult races. In one of the most controversial contests, Senator Charles S. Robb of Virginia was reelected over Republican

The Republicans take control

In a sweeping election day triumph in November, Republicans won control of both houses of Congress for the first time since 1954. Republican victories in state races gave the party 30 governorships, a net gain of 11. (The Republicans picked up 12 new governorships in the elections, but they lost Maine, whose newly elected governor, Angus King, is an independent.)

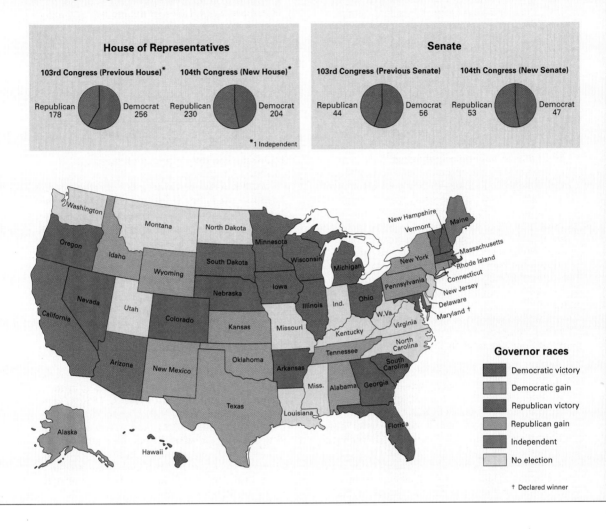

House of Representatives

103rd Congress (Previous House)* — Republican 178 | Democrat 256

104th Congress (New House)* — Republican 230 | Democrat 204

*1 Independent

Senate

103rd Congress (Previous Senate) — Republican 44 | Democrat 56

104th Congress (New Senate) — Republican 53 | Democrat 47

Governor races

- Democratic victory
- Democratic gain
- Republican victory
- Republican gain
- Independent
- No election

† Declared winner

Oliver L. North, a former Marine lieutenant colonel. In 1989, North was convicted of lying to Congress in connection with secret arms deliveries to Iran during the Administration of President Ronald Reagan. Although North's conviction was later reversed on appeal, his nomination split the Virginia GOP and another Republican, J. Marshall Coleman, entered the race as an independent. Robb, whose image was tarnished by confessions of sexual misconduct, won by a narrow margin.

In Massachusetts, 32-year veteran Democratic Senator Edward M. (Ted) Kennedy faced a strong challenge from Republican businessman Mitt Romney but fought back to win a sixth term by a wide margin. California Democratic Senator Dianne Fein-

stein won a narrow victory over Republican Representative Michael Huffington, who put up more than $28 million of his own money in the race. Together, the two candidates spent almost $40 million, the most of any Senate campaign in history.

In Tennessee, home of Vice President Albert Gore, Jr., and usually a Democratic stronghold, the Republicans picked up two seats. Senator Sasser, chairman of the Senate Budget Committee, lost to a political novice, Nashville surgeon Bill Frist. In the race to fill Gore's unexpired term, Fred Thompson, a lawyer turned actor, easily defeated Democratic Representative James H. Cooper.

Governors' races. Republicans made a net gain of 11 governorships in November, giving them a total of 30. New Republican governors included George E. Pataki in New York, who defeated Democratic Governor Mario M. Cuomo, and George W. Bush, the oldest son of former President George Bush, who bested Democratic Governor Ann W. Richards. But in Florida, Democratic Governor Lawton M. Chiles, Jr., defeated Jeb Bush, another son of the ex-President, in a close race. Governorships in several other states, including California and Illinois, remained in GOP hands, giving the GOP control in seven of the nation's eight most populous states.

Referendums. Ballot initiatives generally favored by Republicans also enjoyed success. Seven states and the District of Columbia voted to impose term limits on political officeholders.

In California, a measure to deny most public services to illegal immigrants, including education, welfare benefits, and nonemergency medical care, was approved by a 3 to 2 margin. Opponents, however, mounted a legal challenge in an effort to cancel the result. South Dakota and Missouri voted in favor of gambling casinos, but Florida and five areas in Rhode Island rejected the idea. Efforts to restrict laws that protect homosexuals from discrimination were voted down by narrow margins in Oregon and Idaho.   □ William J. Eaton

See also **Congress of the United States; Democratic Party; Republican Party; State government.** In *World Book,* see **Election; Election campaign.**

Electronics. A highlight of 1994 was the long-awaited first direct broadcast satellite television system in the United States. Called Digital Satellite System (DSS) and introduced by RCA Corporation, the device consisted of an 18-inch (46-centimeter) dish antenna and a receiver. DSS captured 175 channels beamed directly from a pair of orbiting satellites owned by two companies. The picture quality delivered by the system was akin to standard-setting laserdiscs, and the sound was comparable to that produced by compact discs. Consumer costs included the device itself, at about $700; installation; and programming costs similar to those of cable TV.

The introduction of DSS in September came amid strong television sales, generally a benchmark of health in the electronics industry. Particularly popular were large-screen TV's and combined television and video cassette recorders (VCR's).

The year was one of increasing convergences of consumer electronics, computer, and telecommunications products. For example, Compaq Computer's Presario 520 incorporated a computer, telephone, fax machine, and television. It was billed as a *desktop information appliance.* Toshiba introduced a color TV with inputs for a computer connection.

Small but capable. Sony Corporation debuted Magic Link personal communicator in 1994. Early entries in this field, such as the Newton personal digital assistant (PDA) from Apple Computer Incorporated,

had met consumer and industry resistance. But by late 1994, industry acceptance of the operating software used in Magic Link had grown. Launched in September, Magic Link sold for about $1,000 and was the size of a paperback book. The handheld device, in addition to serving as a personal organizer, could send and receive messages—via a phone connection—by e-mail, fax, or voice.

Communicating with a computer became easier as well when Timex Corporation introduced the Data Link watch. The watch used built-in software to transfer information from an owner's computer to the watch. No wires were required—the user pointed the watch at the computer screen and the watch could scan and store information typed on the screen.

HMD's. A new consumer product category was head-mounted displays (HMD's), devices used in *virtual reality* (computer-created simulations). A company called Virtual I/O offered $600 "i-glasses," personal head-mounted displays. The device featured a small liquid crystal display screen, and the images appeared as if they were being shown on a large-screen TV. The headset could display two- or three-dimensional video.   □ Frank Vizard

See also **Computer.** In *World Book,* see **Computer; Electronics; Television.**

Employment. See Economics; Labor.

Endangered species. See Conservation.

Energy supply. The prospect of producing vast amounts of energy through nuclear fusion attracted attention through much of 1994. The United States Department of Energy (DOE) announced plans on October 21 to spend $1.8 billion on a new fusion device. The machine would be part of a huge laboratory, called the National Ignition Facility (NIF), at the Lawrence Livermore National Laboratory in Livermore, Calif. The NIF's fusion reactor would work by means of lasers.

Nuclear fusion is the process that fuels the sun and other stars. Fusion occurs when *nuclei* (cores) of atoms combine under extremely high temperatures and pressures to create energy. The NIF will fuse two *isotopes* (forms) of hydrogen. Fusion differs from the standard method of producing nuclear energy—fission—which works by splitting atomic nuclei. For decades, researchers have pursued fusion as a safer and cheaper way of producing energy.

The NIF's fusion machine would be the size of two football fields and would include an array of 192 lasers focused onto a tiny pellet containing the hydrogen isotopes. Energy from the lasers would be enough to overcome the natural repulsive forces that keep atomic nuclei apart, forcing hydrogen isotopes to fuse. The reaction would create a helium nucleus, a neutron, and energy.

Experts hope the fusion reactions will become self-sustaining, continuing without any further addition of energy from outside. Such a demonstration of self-sustaining fusion reactions would be a major advance toward development of commercial fusion reactors, DOE officials said.

Fusion record. Scientists at Princeton University in New Jersey set a record for fusion energy on May 27, when they produced 9 million watts in the Toka-mak Fusion Test Reactor. The previous record was 6.2 million watts. Unlike the planned Livermore reactor, the Princeton reactor used magnets and a strong electric current to fuse hydrogen isotopes.

The Princeton reactor consists of graphite-lined magnets constructed in the shape of a large dough-nut. Scientists circulate gas containing the hydrogen isotopes through the reactor and heat the gas with tremendous amounts of electricity. The electric current creates a magnetic field within the gas. The magnets repel the field, keeping the hot gas away from the reactor walls. The isotopes in the heated gas fuse to produce energy. As with all fusion experiments to date, however, the Princeton reactor consumed far more energy than it produced.

New light bulb. On October 20, the DOE announced development of a sulfur light bulb that produces hundreds of times more light than high-intensity mercury vapor lamps—while consuming only a fraction of the electricity. According to the DOE, the sulfur lamp represented "a major technological breakthrough in lighting." The new lighting system consists of a clear quartz bulb about the size of a golfball filled with inert gas and a small amount of sulfur. A small microwave generator bombards the bulb with microwaves, which cause the bulb to glow with an intense white light.

The DOE said initial versions of the bulb, expected to go on sale in 1995, are not intended for home lighting. Rather, they will be used in illuminating outdoor areas such as parking lots and sports fields, as well as factories, office lobbies, aircraft hangars, and factories. DOE said the bulb could substantially reduce costs for lighting such areas, which now total about $8 billion per year.

In such places, the sulfur bulb may be used in "light pipe" systems, in which reflectors in long plastic tubes transmit light from a high-intensity source to outlets along the pipe's course. The lack of a suitable high-intensity light source had been a major barrier to light-pipe systems. DOE said tests of such a system in the lobby of its Washington, D.C., headquarters used two sulfur bulbs shining into a light pipe 240 feet (70 meters) long by 10 inches (25 centimeters) in diameter. The two bulbs replaced 240 mercury vapor bulbs, each with 175-watts, and produced four times as much light while consuming only one-third as much electricity.

Weather boosts energy use. Unusually cold winter temperatures helped to boost U.S. consumption of energy by about 3.6 percent during the first half of 1994. The DOE reported in September 1994

that Americans consumed 43.5 quadrillion British thermal units (Btu's), or "quads," of energy during the first six months of the year compared with 42.0 quads during the same period in 1993. (A Btu is the amount of heat needed to raise the temperature of 1 pound [0.45 kilogram] of water by 1 Fahrenheit degree [0.56 Celsius degree].) The United States produced about 33.4 quads of energy during the first half of 1994, compared with 32.9 quads during the same period in 1993.

Nuclear plant performance. The performance of the 109 nuclear power plants operating in the United States improved during 1993, the Institute of Nuclear Power Operations (INPO) reported on April 18, 1994. INPO is an industry organization, based in Atlanta, Ga., that was formed in 1979 to improve standards at nuclear plants.

INPO found that the *capability factor* at nuclear plants increased for the seventh straight year, reaching a median of 77.3 percent. The capability factor is the percentage of time during which plants were able to operate at maximum power output. In 1992, the median capability factor was 76.5 percent. In 1993, the plants produced 641 billion kilowatt-hours of electricity, enough to supply 65 million average homes for one year. Output fell slightly from 650 billion kilowatt-hours in 1992, because one nuclear plant was out of operation during 1993, INPO said.

Practical electric cars? On June 29, 1994, the German auto manufacturer BMW demonstrated the first working model of an energy storage device that could help make electric cars practical. The device, a flywheel battery, stores energy in a rapidly spinning wheel and then uses the wheel's momentum to supply energy for increased range and surges of power during acceleration.

United Technologies Corporation, a major manufacturer of automotive electrical parts based in Hartford, Conn., developed the device. It consists of a 55-pound (25-kilogram) doughnut-shaped device made of a carbon composite about the size of a motorcycle tire. Energy to spin the flywheel comes from the conventional chemical batteries in an electric car and from energy recaptured from the car's wheels during braking. Special bearings and computerized controls allow the flywheel to float in a magnetic field as it spins at 35,000 revolutions per minute. Friction does not slow the wheel, which continues to spin even after the car has stopped.

United Technologies' engineers claimed that energy can be stored and removed from the wheel much like a conventional battery. Although the flywheel stores only as much energy as a conventional automobile battery, engineers envision electric cars that use flywheels to supplement power supplied by conventional batteries. □ Michael Woods

In *World Book,* see **Energy supply.**
Engineering. See Building and construction.
England. See United Kingdom.

Environmental pollution

Environmental pollution. Since 1985, scientists have observed an annual thinning of ozone high above Antarctica from August to October—the Southern Hemisphere's spring. So scientists were not surprised to find that this thinning, called an *ozone hole,* appeared again above Antarctica in 1994. But they did not anticipate the hole's size, which equaled the record-breaking hole of 1993.

Ozone is a molecule made up of three oxygen atoms. In the *stratosphere* (upper portion of Earth's atmosphere), ozone protects life on Earth by absorbing much of the sun's damaging ultraviolet radiation. Certain chemicals called *chlorofluorocarbons* (CFC's), which contain chlorine, break down and take part in chemical reactions that destroy ozone. Refrigerant gases commonly contain CFC's. Other pollutants, however, can increase the effect of CFC's. Among these are airborne droplets of sulfuric acid formed from sulfur dioxide emitted during volcanic eruptions.

Scientists had expected the ozone thinning to be less than in 1993 as the effects of the June 1991 volcanic eruption of Mount Pinatubo, in the Philippines, diminished. But this year's hole again encompassed an area about the size of North America. And within the hole's region of peak loss, some 70 percent of the ozone temporarily vanished.

Climate change treaty. On March 21, 1994, a new international treaty on climate change took effect. First roughed out in negotiations in 1991, its details were finally resolved during the June 1992 Earth Summit in Rio de Janeiro, Brazil.

Signed by more than 60 countries, the treaty requires the world's poorer nations to inventory their sources of *greenhouse gases.* Such gases trap heat in the atmosphere, much like a greenhouse traps solar radiation. Greenhouse gases are released into the atmosphere as a result of burning *fossil fuels* (coal, oil, and natural gas). The most common greenhouse gas is carbon dioxide, and the most common human activities that release carbon dioxide are operating automobiles, coal-fired power plants, and burning forests. Some scientists fear that Earth's atmosphere could warm to dangerous levels if current levels of carbon dioxide emissions continue. Scientists refer to the possibility of such a scenario as global warming.

Because the richer, industrialized countries emit most of those greenhouse gases, however, they must do more than create a greenhouse gas inventory. The treaty requires them to outline how they plan to reduce greenhouse gas releases by the year 2000 to 1990 levels.

Gender-bending pollutants. At a January 1994 meeting in Washington, D.C., sponsored by the National Institute of Environmental Health Sciences, several research teams presented new data suggesting that pollution may have begun feminizing male animals in some wildlife populations.

A huge oil spill burns near Usinsk, Russia, in November. The spill, which began in August, was estimated to be at least 10 times bigger than the 1989 *Exxon Valdez* spill in Alaska.

Biologist Louis J. Guillette, Jr., of the University of Florida in Gainesville described problems he had witnessed in alligator eggs in a lake heavily contaminated with dicofol, a pesticide resembling DDT. DDT is banned in the United States because of its ill effects on bird eggshells. The vast majority of the gator eggs at Lake Apopka, Florida's fourth largest freshwater lake, did not hatch, Guillette said. By examining their contents, the researchers established that these eggs contained excessive levels of estrogen, the animal kingdom's primary female sex hormone. Moreover, male eggs contained almost no testosterone, the primary male sex hormone.

When Florida biologists examined juvenile alligators at the same lake, they found that the females contained *ovaries*—an egg-nurturing organ—but that the egg cells inside them were abnormal and more numerous than usual. Males appeared excessively feminized, possessing a smaller than normal *phallus* (male sex organ) and a ratio of hormones typical of females.

Other scientists reported that birds in areas that had been polluted with DDT and polychlorinated biphenyls (PCB's), an insulating fluid once commonly used in transformers, frequently experience reproductive problems. In particular, males exhibit signs of partially developed female sex organs. Biologists in England and Canada have noted similar changes in male fish swimming in polluted waterways.

Many of the researchers attending the NIH meeting reported in late 1994 the results of other experiments which showed that dozens of common pollutants possess the ability to mimic natural female sex hormones. Such pollutants include pesticides, the ingredients in many plastics and spermicidal contraceptives, and some PCB's.

Human exposure to these substances may underlie several troubling reproductive trends affecting men throughout the industrial world, Danish endocrinologist Niels E. Skakkebaek of University Hospital in Copenhagen, Denmark, noted at the NIH meeting. These trends include a fall in the normal amount of sperm that men produce, increased rates of testicular cancer, and increasing numbers of boys born with undescended testicles.

Pollution settlements. On June 21, Occidental Chemical Corporation agreed to pay $98 million toward the cleanup of a Niagara Falls, N.Y., community known as Love Canal. From 1942 to 1953, Occidental's predecessor—Hooker Chemicals and Plastics Corporation—buried about 22,000 short tons (20,000 metric tons) of toxic chemicals at its Love Canal site. Developers later converted this land into a residential neighborhood with schools.

In the late 1970's, many Love Canal residents reported unusual rates of disease and miscarriage that they attributed to the toxic chemicals migrating through the soils of their community and into their homes. The settlement ended a 14-year-old lawsuit brought by the state against Occidental to recover money it had already spent to clean up the area and resettle some 900 former residents.

On Sept. 16, 1994, a federal jury ordered the Exxon Corporation to pay $5 billion in punitive damages to commercial fishermen and other Alaska residents who could show economic injury from the nation's worst oil spill, the 1989 *Exxon Valdez* accident in Prince William Sound in Alaska. This reward came in addition to some $3.4 billion Exxon had already paid for activities relating to the accident and its cleanup. If upheld, the award would be the largest pollution settlement in history. Exxon said it would appeal the verdict.

Dioxin still dangerous. On Sept. 13, 1994, the Environmental Protection Agency (EPA) released a report reaffirming that the group of synthetic chemicals known as dioxins are probable cancer-causing substances. Dioxins are a group of chemicals produced as by-products in papermaking and other industrial processes. The EPA reviewed the known or suspected risks associated with exposure to dioxins and surveyed industrial activities that release dioxins into the air and water. The government had determined in the mid-1970's that dioxin was a probable cause of cancer in humans and animals, but in the mid-1980's, some industry leaders had questioned whether the chemicals were as deadly as perceived.

The report indicated that throughout the United States, perhaps only 30 pounds (13.6 kilograms) of these chemicals enter the environment each year. However, even these tiny amounts are unacceptable, according to the EPA's toxic substance division.

Aside from the claim that dioxins probably cause cancer, the EPA reported new data on the chemicals' other effects. These showed that dioxin can cause immune-system abnormalities and foster hormone-related disorders in animals—ranging from malformed reproductive organs in male animals to diabetes. The EPA's data also indicate that hospitals and other operators of medical-waste incinerators constitute the biggest—and as-yet-unregulated—source of airborne dioxin and dioxinlike pollutants.

Cleaner auto fuels. To comply with a smog-limiting provision of the 1990 U.S. Clean Air Act, refiners were required to reformulate gasoline they produced for sale in all or parts of 11 states by Dec. 1, 1994. Refiners had to reduce the amount of toxic gases their gasolines emit into the air by 15 percent, compared with 1990 levels. The law did not specify what recipe must be used to achieve the cleaner fuels. However, specific limits were set for a few individual toxic agents—such as benzene, a cancer-causing component.   □ Janet Raloff

In the World Book Supplement section, see **Environmental pollution.** In *World Book,* see **Environmental pollution.**

Equatorial Guinea. See Africa.

Eritrea. See Africa.

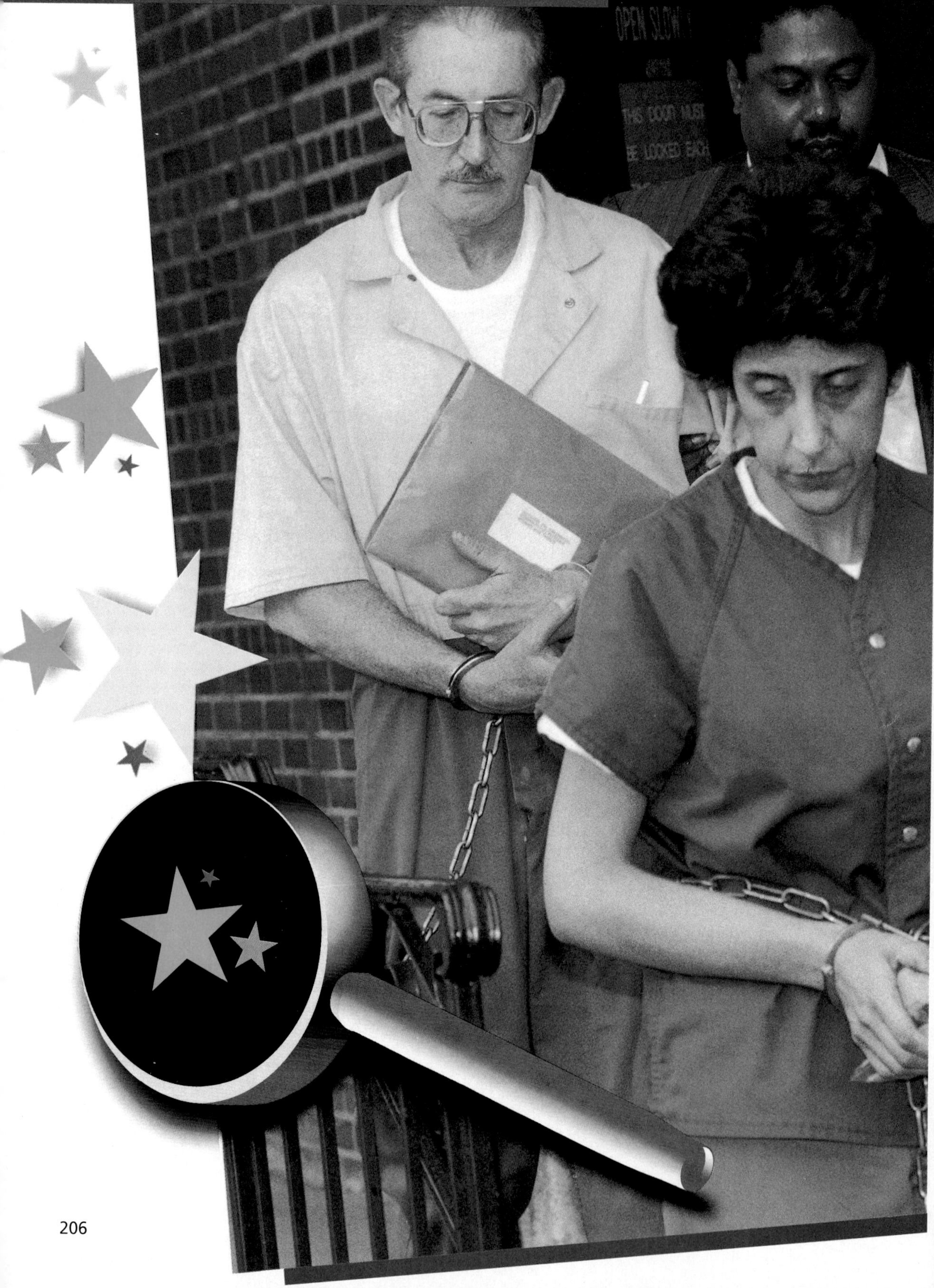

Why Spy?

By Thomas Powers

The Soviet Union no longer exists.

The Cold War is over. Yet the United States

still spies on other countries and maintains

a vast espionage network.

Aldrich H. Ames liked to live well, it seemed. The 52-year-old, 31-year veteran of the Central Intelligence Agency (CIA) drove a fancy sports car, lived in an expensive house, and bought large amounts of stock. Some people, including the Federal Bureau of Investigation (FBI), began to wonder how Ames did so well on his relatively modest government salary. The FBI began to keep an eye on him. On Feb. 21, 1994, FBI agents arrested Ames and his wife, Rosario, near their home in Arlington, Va., on charges of spying for the Soviet Union from 1985 to 1991 and then spying for Russia.

The FBI alleged that Ames revealed the identities of Soviet and Russian citizens working as CIA spies to Soviet and later Russian intelligence, causing many of the spies to be executed. For his treachery, Ames received more than $2 million. Ames was the highest-ranking CIA employee ever to be charged with espionage. He was convicted on April 28, 1994, and sentenced to life imprisonment.

The arrest shocked the American public and intelligence officials, but for very different reasons. The general public found it hard to understand why Russia would risk American friendship and financial support for the dubious benefit of having an agent inside the American intelligence community. The intelligence professionals, on the other hand—understanding the Russian motives completely—were shocked by their own failure to discover Ames's treachery for nine years, despite numerous clues.

The Ames case illustrates that espionage remains a fact of life in the post-Cold War world. The end of the Cold War and the collapse of the Soviet Union, however, has forced U.S. intelligence-gathering agencies to reevaluate their purpose. Many believe that although the danger of large-scale nuclear war has subsided, other threats have emerged. These include acts of state-sponsored terrorism, efforts by nonnuclear nations to acquire nuclear weapons, and the danger that regional conflicts, such as those in the Balkans and the former Soviet republics, could erupt into larger wars.

This reevaluation of purpose is further complicated by the fact that some influential people think the CIA and other intelligence-gathering agencies are ineffective and should be reorganized. Some government leaders even believe that the CIA has outlived its usefulness and should be disbanded.

Much of the structure and methods of U.S. intelligence-gathering agencies grew out of espionage activities undertaken during World War II (1939-1945). The U.S. government established its first intelligence agency, the Office of Strategic Services, in 1942 but disbanded it at the end of the war. In 1947, largely in order to prepare for a long political struggle with the Soviet Union, Congress replaced the War Department with the Department of Defense, and almost as an afterthought created the CIA.

After its formation, the CIA quickly began the traditional tasks of intelligence services. Such tasks included recruiting spies, defending itself against other countries' spies (counterintelligence), and gathering and analyzing both secret and public information in order to estimate the military strength and intentions of other nations. Well before the end of the Korean War in 1953, the CIA had become one of the world's biggest, best financed, and most ambitious intelligence organizations. In 1994, the CIA reportedly employed about 20,000 people and had an annual budget estimated at $2 billion to $3 billion.

The U.S. intelligence community

Many other organizations within the U.S. government have full- or part-time intelligence duties. The responsibility for overseeing all intelligence-gathering activities in the government lies with the director of central intelligence (DCI). The President appoints the DCI, who is in charge of the day-to-day operations of the CIA. Although the DCI does not oversee daily operations of other intelligence agencies, the DCI does set their goals, coordinate their activities, and exercises some control over determining the size of their budgets.

The principal sister organizations of the CIA in the intelligence community are the Defense Intelligence Agency (DIA), the FBI, the National Reconnaissance Office (NRO), and the National Security Agency (NSA). Together these organizations provide the intelligence needs of the United States.

The DIA acquired its present form during the Administration of

■ **Previous pages:** Aldrich Ames and his wife, Rosario, leave a federal courthouse in Alexandria, Va., in March 1994 after being charged with spying for Russia and the former Soviet Union. Ames was the highest-ranking U.S. Central Intelligence Agency officer ever to be charged with spying for another country.

■ **The author**

Thomas Powers is a Pulitzer Prize-winning author who has written widely on the subject of espionage.

President John F. Kennedy (1961-1963), when Congress created an intelligence organization above the separate intelligence-gathering arms of the Army, Air Force, Navy, and Marine Corps. Although the separate branches of the armed forces maintain their own intelligence-gathering services, the DIA also collects intelligence. The DIA provides its intelligence to the armed services to help them devise military strategies in the face of changing political and military conditions in the world. The DIA reportedly also helps minimize interservice bickering and forces the Pentagon to speak with one voice on foreign security threats and the development of new weapons. The DIA employs between 5,000 and 6,000 people and operates on a budget of about $622 million.

President Harry S. Truman established the NSA in 1952. Some of its main duties include making and breaking codes and collecting all types of radio transmissions (called "signals intelligence," or SIGINT). The NSA has also been one of the main forces behind the invention and development of computers. Government documents based on information provided by the NSA are top secret in order to prevent foreign intelligence organizations from learning the full range of codes the NSA can read and the electronic transmissions it can collect. The NSA employs about 25,000 people, and its annual budget is about $3.5 billion.

The primary intelligence responsibility of the FBI is to investigate treason, sabotage, and espionage within the United States. Since the other intelligence organizations are common targets for foreign espionage, the FBI is closely involved in counterintelligence cases that affect the security of those organizations. Counterintelligence investigations can lead to friction with other agencies, however. Such investigations usually require gathering detailed information about how other agencies operate, and other agencies do not always relish giving away their secrets. Some intelligence professionals say, for instance, that the CIA's reluctance to share information with the FBI contributed to the long delay in uncovering Ames's spying.

Spying from space

The largest and the least known of American intelligence organizations is the NRO. The NRO is responsible for satellite reconnaissance of friendly and adversarial nations. The agency's satellites monitor both human activity and natural events, such as droughts and floods that could alter the balance of power in a region by affecting the economies of target nations. The NRO's budget is about $6.5 billion, and the agency employs about 3,000 people directly. Experts believe that number, however, may be as high as 70,000 if employees of companies working for the NRO were included.

Since the 1960's, the U.S. government has used photographic images taken from space as an espionage tool. In the mid-1990's, photographic images still provided the majority of intelligence gathered from satellites. But in recent years, the NRO has also used radar, as well as infrared cameras, on satellites. Infrared cameras record heat cast off by human bodies, aircraft or missile engines, factory smoke-stacks, and electronic equipment. Infrared sensing provides continuous coverage of human and industrial activity, even at night and during cloud-covered days. Although satellites have been a principal American intelligence tool since the early 1960's, the U.S. government did not officially admit they existed until 1978. The government did not admit the existence of the NRO until 1992.

Before the U.S. intelligence community developed its present far-reaching capacities, the main problem facing intelligence analysts was a lack of information. Useful information concerning the former Soviet Union was difficult to collect, due to the country's sealed borders and highly effective security police. But the growth of U.S. intelligence agencies and their technical skills, especially those of the NRO, allowed massive amounts of information to be gathered.

Reconnaissance satellites and intercepted radio signals and other forms of electronic snooping soon resolved the problem of too little information and replaced it with another one—too much information. For example, CIA analysts watching the Soviet Union in the

The U.S. intelligence community consists of many agencies and governmental units that report their intelligence activities to the director of central intelligence (DCI). These agencies collect secret and public information pertaining to U.S. national security. The DCI's staff uses such information to prepare reports on vital national security matters to the National Security Council.

National Security Council

The National Security Council (NSC) is part of the Executive Office of the President. It includes the President, Vice President, and the secretaries of state and defense and is assisted by a staff headed by the assistant to the President for national security affairs. The council advises the President on national security issues and supervises the Central Intelligence Agency (CIA). The head of the CIA, the director of central intelligence (DCI), reports to the council.

Defense Intelligence Agency

The DIA collects intelligence on potential military threats and provides it to all branches of the armed forces, as well as to other branches of the intelligence community.

Central Imagery Office

Coordinates all intelligence-related photography from satellites, spy planes, or more conventional means.

Department of Energy

The intelligence function of the Department of Energy is to track the manufacturing and transport of nuclear fuel around the world. It also monitors foreign nuclear programs and assesses the vulnerability of U.S. nuclear facilities to attack.

Director of central intelligence

The DCI oversees and coordinates the activities of all federal intelligence agencies and receives information from some Cabinet-level departments and some law-enforcement agencies.

State Department

The intelligence arm of the State Department produces daily reports on various aspects of foreign governments and their leaders.

National Reconnaissance Office

The NRO acquires and operates spy satellites and, occasionally, spy planes.

1970's and 1980's received transcripts of every radio broadcast in the Soviet Union each day and obtained photographs of nearly every major construction project in the country. These *national technical means*—an official term used to avoid admitting the existence of spy planes and satellites—told analysts everything they wanted to know, except the secret plans of the Soviet leadership.

The value of spies

Human spies are often necessary to learn the hidden plans of other governments. In espionage terminology, the information spies provide is known as HUMINT (human intelligence). Regardless of the amount of information available from technical means, however sophisticated, intelligence officials acknowledge that nothing can replace the reports of well-placed spies. This was the case during the Cuban missile crisis that developed in 1962, when photographs from spy planes uncovered preparations for Soviet atomic missile installations in Cuba. The photographs enabled the United States to confront

National Security Agency

The NSA collects foreign intelligence by intercepting electronic communications from military and civilian sources. The NSA also protects the secrecy of U.S. intelligence communications and those between government agencies.

Treasury Department

The intelligence function of this Cabinet-level department is to provide unclassified economic information concerning foreign countries to the CIA and other intelligence agencies.

Central Intelligence Agency

The CIA gathers and analyzes intelligence on a wide array of foreign activities. It also attempts to support U.S. foreign policy by secretly influencing foreign governments and other organizations.

Federal Bureau of Investigation

The FBI, a unit of the Department of Justice, protects against foreign agents and Americans spying for other countries in the United States.

Drug Enforcement Administration

This Justice Department agency reports to the DCI about illegal drug manufacturing and trafficking originating in foreign countries.

Army, Navy, Air Force, and Marine Corps intelligence

These separate branches of the armed forces collect and analyze information that may affect their operations against enemies.

■ How intelligence is gathered

United States intelligence organizations gather information on foreign governments, individuals, and organizations that may pose a threat to national security. Intercepted electronic messages, spy plane photographs and satellite images, and reports by human agents in the field are the most common means of gathering intelligence.

■ Advanced technology plays a vital role in gathering intelligence. Spy ships such as the U.S.S. *Pueblo, above,* carry sophisticated electronic listening equipment to intercept telephone conversations, radio signals, and other electronic messages. Aircraft such as the U.S. Blackbird spy plane, *left,* are equipped with powerful cameras to record activities in target countries. An intelligence analyst, *below,* at the CIA's Digital Image Processing Facility manipulates images taken from aircraft and satellites in order to determine their significance.

the Soviets about their plans to place nuclear weapons 90 miles (145 kilometers) from the U.S. mainland, but not until circumstances had reached a crisis. A similar situation resulted in 1968, when satellites failed to provide enough information to predict the Soviet Union's sudden invasion of Czechoslovakia. In both cases, CIA analysts misjudged Soviet actions, and in both cases, the error resulted from the lack of a well-placed spy who actually knew Moscow's plans.

Informants in foreign governments, militaries, labor unions, intelligence agencies, or industries often provide the most valuable information available to the CIA. These informants, or agents, are citizens of foreign countries who betray their governments by giving secret information to the United States, or other countries. If agents work for the United States, they deliver their findings to case officers, professional employees of the CIA who work in the U.S. embassy or in other jobs in the target country. Case officers collect information gathered in the field and send it to Washington, D.C., for interpretation by intelligence analysts in the CIA. Contrary to the glamorous image of spies in motion pictures, television, and books, collecting reliable information and analyzing it correctly is slow, difficult, expensive, and dangerous. Nearly all countries execute agents or give them long jail terms if they are captured. An unwritten international code protects professional CIA personnel and those of other secret-service organizations from physical retaliation, however.

Why do we still need spies?

But with the Cold War over and the Russians preoccupied with economic recovery after the stagnation of Communism, no other great power threatens the peace of the world. Since that is the case, why do the United States and other countries continue to gather secret information by all available means, including espionage?

The answer to that question lies in the emergence of new threats to U.S. security. These new dangers include efforts by several countries, notably Libya, Iraq, and North Korea, to acquire nuclear weapons. The CIA first learned of some of these efforts from Israel, a U.S. ally that closely monitors the military programs of Arab neighbors, and from contacts within the nuclear technology industry. After the Persian Gulf War of 1991, the CIA found that it had underestimated Iraq's progress toward making nuclear materials for missile warheads. The result was a more serious effort to monitor North Korea's nuclear research program, which in turn led to a United Nations effort to force North Korea to abide by international inspections under the 1968 Treaty on the Non-Proliferation of Nuclear Weapons. The death of North Korea's leader, Kim Il-song, in July 1994 has left unclear the status and direction of that country's nuclear weapons program.

But manufacturing nuclear weapons is not the only way to acquire them. The collapse of the Soviet Union, and the weakening of central authority in Russia itself, have raised fears over possible threats from terrorists or criminal gangs. Fears exist that such groups might steal some of the former Soviet Union's nuclear warheads or the nuclear

■ Spying technology may tell intelligence officials what an enemy country is doing but not why. For that, intelligence agencies need spies, such as Rudolph Abel, a Soviet spy who was captured in New York City in 1957.

material to make a nuclear bomb. Beginning in May 1994, German police seized several shipments of uranium and plutonium, some of which were of the type used in making nuclear weapons. German police believed that the shipments were from a Russian nuclear reactor, but Russia denied it.

Terrorists do not have to be nuclear engineers to cause extensive damage with nuclear material, however. Just a small amount of plutonium could poison a city's water supply. Terrorists could also pollute the atmosphere by detonating a conventional bomb containing radioactive material. Monitoring the obvious dangers of this trade requires close liaison with foreign intelligence services and maintaining a close watch over international commerce.

Political instability and terrorism

The Soviet Union's demise and the breakup of Communist control in Eastern Europe have also created a new danger of local wars by rival national, ethnic, and religious groups. Continual armed conflict has occurred since 1991 in the former Soviet republics of Armenia, Azerbaijan, and Georgia, and in the former republics of Yugoslavia. Such regional instability could drag other countries in at any time.

When the Soviet Union broke up, new countries formed, such as Georgia and Ukraine, that have a long history of hostility with Russia. Many observers fear that leaders in Moscow, angered by the treatment of ethnic Russians in the breakaway countries, may attempt to intervene militarily. Poland and the Czech Republic, which separated from Slovakia in 1993, have both asked for membership in the North Atlantic Treaty Organization (NATO), obviously fearing for their independence. Russian military officials have insisted that an expansion of NATO would be considered a direct military threat to Russia.

All of these factors have created a degree of political instability in Europe and western Asia unknown since before World War I (1914-1918). Keeping track of developments has required a vast expansion of intelligence efforts in these areas.

Another danger to world stability is terrorism, which has been the tool of choice for certain political movements and for certain countries, such as Syria, Iraq, and Libya, which are too weak to challenge their opponents openly. Terrorist attacks tend to be small and local, but their economic and psychological effects often extend throughout the world. The explosion of terrorist bombs on commercial aircraft, for example, has frightened travelers and led to huge expenditures on airport security in many countries. A powerful blast in London's financial district caused an estimated $1 billion in damage and loss of business in April 1993. A terrorist car-bomb that detonated in a basement parking garage beneath the World Trade Center in New York City in February 1993 killed six people. But perhaps more importantly, the blast convinced Americans that the political violence of the Middle East was about to become a feature of life in the United States.

Terrorist organizations tend to be small and difficult to penetrate with spies, because their members share a common national back-

■ Threats to security

Terrorist activity, such as the bombing of the World Trade Center in New York City, *left,* remains a threat to international security, despite the end of the Cold War.

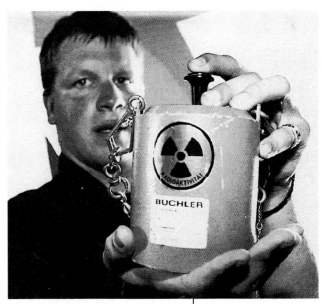

■ A German police officer holds a container of plutonium confiscated from a smuggler in August 1994. The smuggler had reportedly offered to obtain enough plutonium to make a nuclear bomb. Intelligence officials are increasingly worried that nuclear material from Russia and other former republics of the Soviet Union might fall into the hands of terrorist groups or such countries as Libya and Iraq.

ground and passionate political convictions. But intelligence agencies can monitor terrorists through their communications, travel, and financial transactions. Local authorities can help carry out these efforts, but when their help is insufficient, specially trained intelligence professionals may need to take over.

Is the CIA still necessary?

The U.S. Congress has attempted to cut the CIA's budget and that of other U.S. intelligence organizations since the fall of the Soviet Union. The intelligence organizations have resisted the cuts. At the same time, American political leaders, such as Senator Daniel P. Moynihan, (D., N.Y.) have called for radical reform of U.S. intelligence gathering. Such critics most often focus on the CIA in proposing changes, claiming that the CIA is an obsolete relic of the Cold War. Despite the CIA's massive resources, critics say it has provided flawed or irrelevant information to U.S. government and military leaders in critical matters of national interest. Critics frequently point to the CIA's failure to predict the fall of the Soviet Union as evidence that the agency needs reform. Although the CIA collected nearly every fact possible about life in the Soviet Union in the 1980's, it failed to detect the most important fact—that the nation was about to collapse as a political unit.

Largely because of this failure, Moynihan has proposed drastically reducing the size of the CIA and placing a new intelligence-collection effort under control of the State Department. The pared-down CIA would still collect intelligence but through more public sources and contacts established through U.S. embassies. The diminished CIA would collect less information but still satisfy post-Cold War intelligence requirements, supporters of reorganization claim. Since Russia and the other former Soviet states are no longer enemies, they should require less observation, reorganization backers claim.

Others, such as Admiral Stansfield Turner, the DCI under President Jimmy Carter, have called for creation of a new organization that would control all U.S. intelligence efforts yet work as a separate unit. The new organization would act as a watchdog to prevent major lapses in intelligence gathering and analysis.

Such radical changes in the organization of American intelligence would require broad support in Congress. That support appeared to grow as 1994 ended. In September 1994, Congress agreed to form a committee to review the role and necessity of the CIA. The review committee stemmed from Congress's desire for better political intelligence. It has little patience for mistakes, and it seeks an end to spy scandals such as the Ames case. Currently, the CIA collects only foreign intelligence and is responsible for protecting itself against spies within its midst. The FBI's duties also include uncovering American spies working for other countries. This leaves a gray area concerning spies like Ames—an American working for the Russians, but inside the CIA. When such cases occur, federal law is unclear as to when—or even if—the FBI should take over. Some members of Congress would like to abolish this gray area by giving more authority to the FBI.

Despite congressional dissatisfaction with the CIA's recent record, however, the U.S. intelligence community as a whole remains central to the conduct of American foreign policy. It is likely to continue receiving generous financial support, currently at the rate of about $28-billion per year, according to unofficial estimates.

In many ways, the world was safer in 1994 than at the height of the Cold War, when two hostile superpowers threatened each other with arsenals of nuclear weapons. Yet new, serious conflicts and grievances between nations and among ethnic groups have arisen, and old ones have become more prominent. Focusing on new threats to national security will require changes within intelligence services, say expert observers, and those changes will, in turn, determine how well the intelligence community meets the new challenges. ■ ■ ■

For further reading:

Kurland, Michael. *Encyclopedia of World Espionage.* Facts on File, 1993.

Powers, Thomas. *The Man Who Kept the Secrets: Richard Helms and the CIA.* Knopf, 1979.

Ranelagh, John. *The Agency: The Rise and Decline of the CIA.* Simon and Schuster, 1987.

Richelson, Jeffrey. *American Espionage and the Soviet Target.* Morrow, 1988.

Estonia sought to strengthen its ties to Western nations in 1994, as relations with Russia continued to be strained. In February, Estonia joined the Partnership for Peace, a new North Atlantic Treaty Organization (NATO) program of cooperation with nations that had belonged to the Warsaw Pact, the military alliance led by the former Soviet Union. In July, Estonia signed a free trade agreement with the European Union (formerly the European Community).

Border disputes and the presence of Russian troops in Estonia contributed to the conflict between the two nations in 1994. In June, Russian officials began unilaterally redrawing Russia's border with Estonia, reclaiming territory ceded to Estonia in the 1920 Treaty of Tartu. The Estonian government angrily protested the action. Tensions persisted even after Russia completed its withdrawal of troops from Estonia on August 31.

Estonian Prime Minister Mart Laar resigned in September after losing a parliamentary vote of no confidence. Laar's ruling coalition broke apart after he was connected to a scandal involving misappropriated government funds. Laar was replaced by former Environment Minister Andres Tarand, who retained many of Laar's cabinet ministers. Parliamentary elections were scheduled for March 1995.

□ Steven L. Solnick

See also **Europe** (Facts in brief table). In *World Book,* see **Estonia**.

Ethiopia in 1994 continued its slow recovery from a long civil war that ended in 1991, but the process was hindered by some serious setbacks.

On June 5, 1994, national elections were held for a Constituent Assembly charged with writing a new constitution. The election was peaceful, and 90 percent of the country's registered voters took part. The major opposition parties boycotted it, however. Thus, the ruling party, the Ethiopian People's Revolutionary Democratic Front (EPRDF), won 484 of the 547 seats in the Assembly. Elections for a new government based on the new constitution were planned for late 1995.

Opponents accused the EPRDF of establishing front groups—allies posing as adversaries—to take part in the election, thereby creating an appearance of democratic reform where none really existed. The main opposition group, the Oromo Liberation Front, began armed resistance against the government. A threat to do likewise came from a group that demanded independence for the Ogaden region.

Ethiopia was again hit with famine in 1994. By June, at least 5,000 people had died as a result of dwindling food supplies due to drought, cattle disease, and the inability of the government to transport food from regions producing agricultural surpluses to areas of shortage.

□ Mark DeLancey

See also **Africa** (Facts in brief table). In *World Book,* see **Ethiopia**.

Estonia's President Lennart Meri, left, exchanges documents in August with Russian President Boris Yeltsin that called for the withdrawal of Russian troops by August 31.

Europe

The year 1994 saw Europe emerge unevenly from a long, deep economic recession and continue to adjust to the changing political climate of the post-Communist era. The European Union (EU) and the North Atlantic Treaty Organization (NATO), the Western defense alliance, both chose new leaders and formed new missions in 1994. The EU, formerly the European Community, also prepared in 1994 to expand its membership from 12 to 15 countries. And NATO established a sweeping new peace program, which more closely associates NATO member nations with Eastern and Central European countries, whose defense was previously controlled by the former Soviet Union.

EU membership grows. The EU prepared in 1994 to admit new members on Jan. 1, 1995. Austria, Finland, and Sweden, all signed treaties of accession to the EU on June 24, 1994, during an EU summit meeting on the Greek island of Corfu. Citizens of the countries later approved EU membership in national referendums. Norway had also signed a treaty of accession on Corfu, but Norwegians voted against membership on November 28. The European Community's last expansion was on Jan. 1, 1986, when Spain and Portugal joined. Other EU members are Belgium, Denmark, France, Germany, Greece, Ireland, Italy, Luxembourg, the Netherlands, and the United Kingdom.

Austria, Finland, Norway, and Sweden were all members of the European Free Trade Association (EFTA), along with Iceland, Liechtenstein, and Switzerland. All of the EFTA countries except Switzerland had joined with the EU to form the European Economic Area, a free trade zone, on Jan. 1, 1994. But the four countries also felt they had to join the EU in order to reap the full benefits of the EU's open borders for trade and travel.

Debates over EU membership generally centered on whether national governments would have to give up too much decision-making power to the central European Union government, based in Brussels, Belgium. Opponents of membership, especially in the Scandinavian countries, argued that farmers might suffer under the EU's agricultural programs, and that rich countries would have to subsidize farming and social programs in poorer EU countries such as Greece and Portugal. Opponents also argued that wealthier countries would suffer economically if former Soviet bloc countries were eventually admitted to the EU.

East seeks EU membership. Four members of the former Soviet bloc—Hungary, Poland, the Czech Republic, and Slovakia—all applied in 1994 for membership in the EU. All four countries, in addition to Romania and Bulgaria, signed special trade and political agreements with the EU that could lead to

membership when certain legal and economic conditions are met. However, most EU experts doubted the Union would expand again before the end of the decade. On October 4, EU foreign ministers decided to invite ministers from these six countries to attend certain EU ministerial meetings, the first of which was held on October 31 in Luxembourg.

New EU president. After an embarrassing internal fight, the 12 EU member nations on July 15 appointed Jacques Santer, prime minister of Luxembourg, to be the next president of the EU's Commission, an executive body. Santer, whose five-year term began Jan. 1, 1995, succeeds Jacques Delors, a French Socialist Party member, who had been commission president since 1984. Delors' term as president was marked by a number of notable achievements, including the adoption of the Maastricht Treaty on European Union, which called for tighter economic and political integration among EU nations, possibly leading to a single European currency by the year 2000.

Santer, little known in Europe outside his own country, was seen as a compromise choice for the powerful job after British Prime Minister John Major vetoed Belgian Prime Minister Jean-Luc Dehaene for the post on June 25 at the EU summit on Corfu. Dehaene had been the first choice of French President François Mitterrand and German Chancellor Helmut Kohl and was preferred at that summit to two other candidates, Ruud Lubbers, former prime minister of the Netherlands, and Sir Leon Brittan, the EU's trade commissioner. But Major refused to back Dehaene, because he thought the Belgian would too quickly transfer political power away from the national governments of EU member states and funnel it into the central EU government.

On July 21, the European Parliament approved Santer's appointment by a relatively close vote of 260 in favor to 238 against, with 23 members abstaining. Many members said they voted against Santer to protest the secretive manner in which EU heads of government chose him without consulting parliament.

New NATO chief. Belgian Foreign Minister Willy Claes was named secretary general of NATO on September 29. He succeeded Manfred Wörner of Germany, who died of cancer on August 13.

Elections to European Parliament. Elections were held in the United Kingdom on June 9 and across the rest of Europe on June 12 to elect the new 567-member European Parliament. Right wing parties increased their representation in the parliament to about 270 seats, compared with about 250 seats held by left wing parties. The remaining seats were taken by nationalist parties. German and Italian voters gave heavy backing to candidates from ruling right wing parties, the Christian Democratic Union of German Chancellor Kohl, and Forza Italia (Go Italy) of Italian Prime Minister Silvio Berlusconi.

Thousands of youths march down the Champs Élysées in Paris in August to celebrate the liberation of France from Nazi control 50 years earlier.

Facts in brief on European countries

Country	Population	Government	Monetary unit*	Foreign trade (million U.S.$)	
				Exports†	Imports†
Albania	3,390,000	President Sali Berisha; Prime Minister Aleksander Gabriel Meksi	lek (100.00 = $1)	70	524
Andorra	59,000	The bishop of Urgel, Spain, and the president of France	French franc & Spanish peseta	1	531
Austria	7,861,000	President Thomas Klestil; Chancellor Franz Vranitzky	schilling (10.56 = $1)	40,200	48,616
Belarus	10,310,000	President Alexander Lukashenko	C.I.S. ruble (3,055.00 = $)	715	747
Belgium	10,031,000	King Albert II; Prime Minister Jean-Luc Dehaene	franc (30.85 = $1)	123,564	125,153
				(includes Luxembourg)	
Bosnia-Herzegovina	4,454,000	President Alija Izetbegovic	dinar (25.9 = $1)	no statistics available	
Bulgaria	8,887,000	President Zhelyu Zhelev; Prime Minister Lyuben Berov	lev (64.88 = $1)	4,071	4,239
Croatia	4,803,000	President Franjo Tudjman	kuna (5.46 = $1)	3,903	4,667
Czech Republic	10,407,000	President Václav Havel; Premier Václav Klaus	koruna (27.28 = $1)	12,784	12,559
Denmark	5,192,000	Queen Margrethe II; Prime Minister Nyrup Rasmussen	krone (5.87 = $1)	36,707	30,448
Estonia	1,571,000	President Lennart Meri	kroon (11.96 = $1)	473	438
Finland	5,046,000	President Martti Ahtisaari; Prime Minister Andres Tarand	markka (4.57 = $1)	23,291	18,059
France	57,769,000	President François Mitterrand; Prime Minister Edouard Balladur	franc (5.13 = $1)	206,275	200,797
Germany	81,264,000	President Roman Herzog; Chancellor Helmut Kohl	mark (1.50 = $1)	368,620	332,663
Greece	10,322,000	President Konstandinos Karamanlis; Prime Minister Andreas Papandreou	drachma (231.12 = $1)	9,509	23,232
Hungary	10,542,000	President Arpad Goncz; Prime Minister Gyula Horn	forint (106.71 = $1)	8,604	12,520
Iceland	268,000	President Vigdis Finnbogadóttir; Prime Minister David Oddsson	krona (66.07 = $1)	1,400	1,342
Ireland	3,469,000	President Mary Robinson; Prime Minister John Bruton	pound (punt) (0.62 = $1)	28,336	22,483
Italy	57,910,000	President Oscar Scalfaro	lira (1,533.25 = $1)	178,164	188,521
				(includes San Marino)	
Latvia	2,650,000	President Guntis Ulmanis; Prime Minister Maris Gailis	lat (0.54 = $1)	896	843
Liechtenstein	28,000	Prince Hans Adam II; Prime Minister Mario Frick	Swiss franc	no statistics available	

In Spain, the Socialist Party of Prime Minister Felipe González Márquez suffered a heavy defeat, as right wing parties advanced. In France, the right wing parties led by Prime Minister Edouard Balladur won the vast majority of seats, as support for the Socialist Party of President Mitterrand crumbled. L'Autre Europe (The Other Europe), a French party opposed to the Maastricht Treaty and led by financier Sir James Goldsmith, won 13 seats. In the United Kingdom, however, the left wing Labour Party increased its parliamentary delegation as support for the Conservative Party headed by Prime Minister Major continued to slide.

War and strife. Civil war and political tensions continued in the former Yugoslavia and surrounding areas of Europe throughout 1994, despite diplomatic and military efforts by the European Union, the United Nations (UN), and NATO. Greece continued to oppose international recognition of Macedonia, a former republic of Yugoslavia, disputing the republic's use of the name Macedonia, which is also the name of a region in Greece. Greece charged that the republic had made claims on its territory. The ex-Yugoslav republic denied any such claims. Nonetheless, Greece imposed a trade embargo on the republic on February 16 by blocking shipments of goods to Macedonia through Greek ports, the republic's only access to the sea. Greece refused to lift the embargo despite criticism from other EU countries. The European Court of Justice delayed a ruling

| Country | Population | Government | Monetary unit* | Foreign trade (million U.S.$) | |
				Exports†	Imports†
Lithuania	3,771,000	President Algirdas Brazauskas	litas (4.00 = $1)	700	2,200
Luxembourg	386,000	Grand Duke Jean; Prime Minister Jacques Santer	franc (30.85 = $1)	123,564	125,153 (includes Belgium)
Macedonia	2,117,000	President Kiro Gligorov	denar (47.5 = $1)	1,055	1,199
Malta	367,000	President Ugo Mifsud Bonnici; Prime Minister Eddie Fenech Adami	lira (0.36 = $1)	1,349	2,166
Moldova	4,350,000	President Mircea Ivanovich Snegur; Prime Minister Andrei Sangheli	C.I.S. ruble (3,055.00 = $1)	174	181
Monaco	30,000	Prince Rainier III	French franc	no statistics available	
Netherlands	15,499,000	Queen Beatrix; Prime Minister Willem Kok	guilder (1.68 = $1)	139,601	129,896
Norway	4,357,000	King Harald V; Prime Minister Gro Harlem Brundtland	krone (6.52 = $1)	31,886	23,970
Poland	38,736,000	President Lech Walesa; Prime Minister Waldemar Pawlak	zloty (23,077.00 = $1)	14,143	18,834
Portugal	9,884,000	President Mário Alberto Soares; Prime Minister Aníbal Cavaço Silva	escudo (153.15 = $1)	15,403	24,319
Romania	23,505,000	President Ion Iliescu; Prime Minister Nicolae Vacaroíu	leu (1,752 = $1)	4,536	5,683
Russia	149,740,000	President Boris Yeltsin	C.I.S. ruble (3,055.00 = $1)	44,297	26,807
San Marino	23,000	2 captains regent appointed by Grand Council every 6 months	Italian lira	178,164	188,521 (includes Italy)
Slovakia	5,353,000	President Michal Kovac; Prime Minister Jozef Moravčik	koruna (30.61 = $1)	5,130	5,950
Slovenia	2,012,000	President Milan Kucan; Prime Minister Janez Drnovsek	tolar (119.25 = $1)	5,100	5,300
Spain	39,276,000	King Juan Carlos I; Prime Minister Felipe González Márquez	peseta (124.75 = $1)	62,872	81,876
Sweden	8,773,000	King Carl XVI Gustaf; Prime Minister Ingvar Carlsson	krona (7.13 = $1)	49,864	42,687
Switzerland	6,955,000	President Otto Stich	franc (1.25 = $1)	58,694	56,722
Turkey	62,032,000	President Süleyman Demirel; Prime Minister Tansu Ciller	lira (35,859.00 = $1)	14,878	22,579
Ukraine	52,393,000	President Leonid Kuchma	karbovanet (43,000.00 = $1)	3,116	2,431
United Kingdom	57,988,000	Queen Elizabeth II; Prime Minister John Major	pound (0.61 = $1)	181,559	206,321
Yugoslavia	9,898,000	President Zoran Lilic; Prime Minister Radoje Kontic	new dinar (1.49 = $1)	4,400	6,400

*Exchange rates as of Oct. 28, 1994, or latest available data.   †Latest available data.

on the legality of Greece's trade embargo until 1995.

Peace partnership with East. On Jan. 10, 1994, NATO adopted a historic plan called "Partnership for Peace," which offered countries of the former Soviet bloc and republics of the former Soviet Union participation in certain military exercises, peace-keeping missions, and information exchanges. The offer, however, stopped short of extending full NATO membership to the new partners. The partnership plan, proposed by the United States, also did not guarantee that full NATO members would defend the new partners, a security enjoyed by nations with full NATO membership.

NATO was formed by most Western European countries, the United States, and Canada after World War II (1939-1945) to guard Europe against any military threat from the Soviet bloc. The Partnership for Peace was seen as a compromise plan that would form an alliance with former Cold War enemies without intimidating Russia by expanding NATO territory to Russia's western border.

Russian President Boris Yeltsin initially opposed the partnership plan and also opposed NATO membership for any former Soviet bloc nation. But after months of diplomatic talks, a special agreement was signed with Russia on June 22, making it the 21st nation to join the partnership program. The agreement recognized Russia's "weight and responsibility as a major European, international and nuclear power," but did not grant Russia any special con-

The United Kingdom's Queen Elizabeth II, left, and French President François Mitterrand, right, pose before a huge drill at the Channel Tunnel's May opening.

cessions. Russia on June 22 also indicated it would not oppose future NATO membership for its former satellite countries.

Planning for monetary union. With most European economies coming out of recession in 1994, talk of possible economic and monetary union in Europe was revived. An important issue on the EU economic agenda is the creation of a single currency for some or all EU members by 1999. The European Monetary Institute, the forerunner of a possible European Central Bank, opened Jan. 1, 1994. It is based in Frankfurt, Germany. Its president, Belgian Alexandre Lamfallusy, predicted in 1994 that at least some European nations might be ready to unite their currencies by the end of the decade. Under the Maastricht Treaty, EU members will meet in 1996 to decide which member states, if any, will form a single currency. EU countries would have to meet a strict set of economic guidelines laid down by the Maastricht Treaty before they could join the single currency. Denmark and the United Kingdom have both indicated they probably will not join.

On September 1, politicians in Germany and France proposed that the initial members of a single currency group be those two countries plus Belgium, Luxembourg, and the Netherlands. This proposal worried politicians in other EU member states, who feared that a "two-speed" Europe might leave their countries behind economically.

Economic recovery. As 1994 went on, Belgium, France, Germany, Italy, the Scandinavian countries, and the United Kingdom all made strong economic recoveries from the recession. Growth rates climbed above 2 percent in many countries, after two or three years of declines. But because many European companies were reducing their employment levels by restructuring or using more automation to improve productivity, unemployment rates in Europe remained high.

The International Monetary Fund, an agency of the UN, estimated on October 2 that the EU countries' *gross domestic product* (a measure of the amount of goods and services produced within a country) would grow by 2.1 percent in 1994 and by 2.9 percent in 1995.

France and England linked. The Channel Tunnel, a 31-mile (50-kilometer) long link under the English Channel between Folkestone, England, and Calais, France, was formally inaugurated on May 6 by Queen Elizabeth II of the United Kingdom and President François Mitterrand of France. Freight service, which transports goods between the United Kingdom and the European mainland on special trains, began in August. Passenger service began on November 14 after several months delay. The tunnel, actually two train tunnels with a smaller service tunnel between them, cost more than $15 billion to build and opened about two years behind schedule.

Ferry sinks in Baltic. European ferry operators reviewed and changed safety procedures after more than 900 people died when the car ferry *Estonia* sank in the Baltic Sea on September 28 during a voyage from Tallinn, the capital of Estonia, to Stockholm, Sweden. Officials investigating the tragedy said water appeared to enter the ferry through a cargo door in the bow, causing the ship to sink rapidly. Only 140 people survived the sinking. Maritime officials in several European countries ordered their ferry operators to permanently seal the doors in the bows of large ferries.

Forging competiveness. The EU's Commission issued a report on June 5 that called for Europe to open up its markets to international competition, and for governments to privatize their telephone companies and other monopolies. The report also said European companies should move quickly to build "information superhighways" and to introduce multimedia technology in order to compete globally. Europe's high-technology industries, led by government-owned monopoly telephone companies, formed European and international alliances in 1994 as part of an effort to prepare for global competition in information services.   □ Philip Revzin

See also the various European country articles. In *World Book,* see **Europe; European Union;** and the various country articles.

Explosion. See Disasters.

Farm and farming. Farmers in the Midwestern United States in 1994 managed to clear enough debris, silt, and sand left by the 1993 floods of the Mississippi and Missouri rivers and their tributaries to plant crops of unparalleled bounty. The U.S. Congress, responding to the flood damage, reformed federal crop insurance to assure farmers financial protection in future disasters. Reforms included the first major reorganization of the U.S. Department of Agriculture (USDA) in 60 years. Finally, in December 1994, Congress approved the global General Agreement on Tariffs and Trade (GATT) that set in motion reforms that experts believed would increase U.S. agricultural exports for years to come.

U.S. farm production. A record 1994 corn harvest of 10 billion bushels was 58 percent larger than the water-logged 1993 crop. Soybean production rose by 35 percent to reach 2.52 billion bushels, breaking a 15-year-old record set in 1979. Spring-planted durum wheat rebounded from floods with a 33.5 percent increase to 94 million bushels. The record cotton crop of 19.5 million bales was 21 percent larger than the 1993 harvest. Oats rose by 11 percent and rice by 2 percent.

Beef production rose 5 percent, pork production increased 2 percent, and poultry production was up 5 percent over 1993. The large supplies depressed prices, placing especially intense financial pressure on hog farmers. But the USDA said those low prices

fueled an 18 percent increase in U.S. exports of beef, 15 percent for pork, and 37 percent for chickens.

However, U.S. wheat production fell by 3.5 percent to 2.3 billion bushels. Winter wheat, which was not dramatically affected by the 1993 floods, declined by 6 percent to 1.67 billion bushels in 1994.

World production of wheat also declined in 1994, falling 6 percent from last year's harvests. But world rice production rose 1 percent, corn production rose 19 percent, and soybean production was up 14 percent. Cotton increased 13 percent. World beef production rose 1 percent, pork rose 2 percent, and poultry was up 6 percent.

Fewer U.S. farms. The overall rise in U.S. farm production occurred despite a declining number of farms. The number fell below 2 million for the first time since 1850, according to a November report by the U.S. Bureau of the Census. The average farm had 491 acres (198.7 hectares). Of the 1.9 million farms operating in 1994, only 333,865—17 percent—produced 83 percent of the total sales of farm products.

Shrinking the USDA. Fewer farms was a major reason that Congress reduced the size of the USDA for the first time since the 1930's, when many of its agencies were created to aid farmers struggling through the Great Depression. Signed into law on Oct. 13, 1994, the reform legislation folded the oversight of farm subsidies, farm loans, and crop insurance into one new organization, called the Farm Service Agency. This reorganization would pave the way for closing 1,274 of the USDA's 3,700 field offices currently operating in every county nationwide and reducing the number of USDA employees by 7,500 by fiscal 1999.

The new federal crop insurance program requires farmers to buy federally subsidized catastrophic crop insurance in order to qualify for other government benefits, including commodity price supports. The program was designed to replace billions of dollars in federal disaster payments made to farmers after a natural disaster ruined crops, such as the Midwest floods and drought in the South in 1993. The near certainty of receiving disaster payments had kept many farmers from buying adequate crop insurance, and the disaster payments subsidized farmers without coming out of the USDA budget.

The reform law also replaced the Soil Conservation Service with the Natural Resources Conservation Service to run most conservation programs. A new food safety and inspection division reflected greater emphasis on meat inspection and food safety.

USDA secretary resigns. Secretary of Agriculture Mike Espy announced his resignation on Oct. 3, 1994, the same day the House of Representatives approved the USDA reorganization bill and a day before the Senate passed it. Espy was credited with shepherding the bill through Congress. Espy's resignation, effective December 31, came as a result of an investigation by an independent counsel appointed

Sand and silt surround grain storage bins on a Missouri farm in 1994, after being pushed over in 1993 by Missouri River floodwaters 12 feet (3.7 meters) deep.

by the U.S. Department of Justice into possible misconduct. The independent counsel said a 1906 law barring meat inspectors from accepting "anything of value" also applied to the USDA's chief official.

The investigation revealed that Espy had used government-paid travel to the Super Bowl and had received free sports tickets from several companies, especially Tyson Foods Inc., an Arkansas-based company whose meat and poultry products are inspected by the USDA. Espy also had the government lease a vehicle for his personal use when he traveled to his Mississippi home. He repaid the firms and the government more than $7,500, but after it was revealed that his girlfriend received a $1,200 scholarship from a Tyson foundation, Espy resigned.

New regulations. As of May 27, the USDA required that raw ground beef and poultry products be sold with safe cooking and handling labels. Such labeling had been blocked by a federal court in 1993. The USDA mandated labels for other raw meat and poultry products on July 6. Espy pressed for the new labeling after more than 500 people became ill and four died as a result of eating hamburgers in fast-food restaurants in the Pacific Northwest in 1993. The outbreak was traced to the presence of a virulent form of *Escherichia coli* bacteria found in undercooked ground meat.

On July 11, 1994, Espy proposed regulations requiring stricter federal inspection of poultry products, including a "zero tolerance" for disease and contamination on birds leaving the slaughterhouse. On September 14, Espy proposed legislation to Congress that would require a scientific test for disease-causing microbes in meat and poultry. The test would replace an inspection system dating to 1907 that relied on sight and feel. (See also **Food.**)

Ethanol in gasoline. The U.S. Environmental Protection Agency (EPA) announced on June 30, 1994, a regulation mandating that beginning Jan. 1, 1995, cleaner-burning gasoline be sold in the nine U.S. cities with the worst pollution problems. The reformulated gasoline would contain ethanol, usually made from corn, and ETBE, a derivative of ethanol as the oxygen additives that make gasoline burn cleaner. The EPA said that for 1995 ethanol and ETBE must make up 15 percent of the oxygen additives. Thereafter, 30 percent of the additives must be ethanol and ETBE. Farmers hoped the regulation would boost the market for their bumper corn crop.

But on Sept. 13, 1994, the U.S. Court of Appeals for the District of Columbia blocked the rule until the court could hear arguments in a lawsuit challenging the ethanol rule. The lawsuit was brought by the American Petroleum Institute and the National Petroleum Refiners Association, representing oil companies who prefer to use petroleum-based methanol as an oxygen additive.

International trade. A wheat war nearly erupted between the United States and Canada over an increase in Canadian wheat shipments to the United States. In 1994, U.S. pasta makers looked to Canada for wheat because the 1993 floods had reduced the quality and quantity of spring wheat grown in the northern Midwest. On Aug. 2, 1994, over the opposition of U.S. pasta manufacturers, both nations announced an agreement to cap Canadian wheat shipments to the United States at 55.1 million bushels for 12 months beginning August 1. They also agreed to establish a Joint Commission on Grains to examine each other's grain marketing and price support systems and to refrain from pursuing any trade action against each other for a year.

Farmers fared better in trade with Mexico. During the first seven months of the North American Free Trade Agreement (NAFTA) with Canada and Mexico, which went into effect on January 1, U.S. agricultural shipments to Mexico rose by 11 percent. There was a 10 percent increase in grains, an 11 percent increase in poultry, a 50 percent increase in fruits and vegetables, and a 60 percent increase in beef and veal.

GATT passes. More than 300 food and agricultural groups formed the largest agricultural coalition ever created to push for congressional ratification of GATT. The House approved GATT on November 29, and the Senate on December 1. With strong rules to discipline agricultural trade, GATT called for the reduction of agricultural export subsidies over six years and the lowering of trade barriers.

In exchange for their support, farmer organizations won agreement from the Administration of President Bill Clinton to change the focus of a U.S. export subsidy program, the Export Enhancement Program, which faced reductions under GATT. The program's new focus would be to expand foreign markets, not just combat unfair trade practices. The Administration also promised to spend $600 million over five years on programs permitted under GATT to promote U.S. agricultural exports, which reached $42.5 billion in fiscal year 1994. On March 16, Espy told the House Agriculture Committee that GATT would increase U.S. agricultural exports by $4.7 billion to $8.7 billion by the year 2005, with almost half the increase coming from grain.

Soil erosion slows. On July 13, 1994, the USDA issued a comprehensive U.S. soil inventory based on a sampling of 800,000 sites. The inventory indicated that the rate of soil erosion had declined by one-third from 1982 to 1992, which translated into a savings of more than 1 billion short tons (907 million metric tons) of soil per year, largely due to the Conservation Reserve Program (CRP). The CRP required participants with highly erodible soils to reduce tillage in order to leave more crop residue on fields. The residue helped prevent the soil from being washed away or blown away. □ Sonja Hillgren

See also **Weather.** In *World Book,* see **Agriculture; Farm and farming.**

Fashion. "Glamour" replaced "grunge" as the fashion catchword during 1994. Grunge, a style derived from clothes worn by rock musicians and their fans in the Seattle area, was an assortment of jackets, vests, sweaters, skirts in all lengths, scarves, and footwear resembling hiking boots or high-buttoned shoes. New York City designers, including Marc Jacobs and Anna Sui, developed grunge collections. Kate Moss and other young-and-vulnerable-looking models walked down runways in 1994 and peered from magazine pages in outfits that resembled an assemblage of found objects.

Although European designers, such as Gianni Versace, picked up on grunge as an expression of Americana, the styles never caught on. Most women refused to pay designer prices for what they thought resembled second-hand clothes.

Simple clothes with hemlines ending at the knee had more success. Calvin Klein was a major promoter of this look, but other sportswear designers, such as Donna Karan, Ralph Lauren, and Isaac Mizrahi, also presented it in their collections. Working women found these clothes appealing.

Glamour takes over. But by autumn, when fashion collections for spring and summer of 1995 were introduced, glamour took over in Europe and the United States. Shoes had high, spindly heels. Dresses were made of satin, metallic, or other high-shine fabrics. Feathers and fringe, beads and sequins

Yves Saint Laurent's dark suit with its very short skirt and tall mock-crocodile boots opened the designer's comeback show in Paris in July.

adorned clothes that hugged the body, echoing the glamorous styles of the 1950's and 1970's.

The distinctive fit of these styles brought about a revival of incorporating undergarments into the bodice of dresses, a look Jean-Paul Gaultier had introduced in Paris in the early 1980's. In 1994, Karl Lagerfeld, the Parisian designer of the Chanel collection, had his models wear lightly padded, waist-length bras under his jackets.

However, comfort persisted in the clothes worn by women in their leisure hours. Tights made of stretchy spandex, T-shirts, and loose sweaters dominated weekend wear and were closely related in design to exercise clothes.

The suitable suit. Although designers tried to call attention to their dresses, women generally found the suit to be the most useful and economical way to dress for the fast-paced modern world. The unconstructed styles of Giorgio Armani, the Milan, Italy, tailor of both men's and women's clothes, or Lagerfeld's Chanel cardigan jacket influenced the design of most suits in any price range.

The year's newest suit style had minimal padding on the shoulders, a long jacket that stopped at the knuckle or fingertips, and a slender fit. It was the versatile workhorse of a woman's wardrobe, one reason being that a variety of sweaters and blouses could change the look. When women had to dress up a bit, they generally chose a suit with a short, softly flared skirt, though pants were an acceptable alternative. For more formal occasions, jackets tended to match the shirt or pants, but different colors, patterns, and fabrics could be mixed in the same outfit. A vest in silk or leather added more variety.

Yves Saint Laurent, the French couturier, appeared at Saks Fifth Avenue in New York City in September, his first visit to the United States in 12 years. He helped celebrate the introduction of his new perfume, called Champagne. In his honor, the store showed some of his styles in its Fifth Avenue store windows.

However, animal rights activists picketed the store during the perfume celebration because three jackets among the Saint Laurent designs displayed in the windows featured borders trimmed with fox fur. In May, activists also had picketed stores on Seventh Avenue during the showing of fur collections for the winter of 1994-1995.

Since the 1980's, animal rights activists have put a severe dent in the fur business in the United States. Some designers, including Bill Blass, Calvin Klein, and Carolina Herrera, have given up making fur collections. Instead, they and other designers have turned to creating styles made of fabrics that resemble fur, often indistinguishable from the real thing. In 1994, popular fakes included glamorous long-haired "fox," crinkled "Mongolian lamb," and thick, richly colored "mink." □ Bernadine Morris

In *World Book,* see **Clothing; Fashion.**

Finland voted to join the European Union (EU), formerly known as the European Community, in a national referendum held on Oct. 16, 1994. The vote, which was 57 percent in favor of membership, made Finland part of the EU on Jan. 1, 1995. Opposition to EU membership during the referendum campaign was based on Finland's policy of political neutrality, which it had maintained since World War II (1939-1945), and its role as a buffer state between Western Europe and neighboring Russia.

Election results. Martti Ahtisaari, a member of the Social Democratic Party and a former United Nations diplomat, was elected president of Finland in a runoff election on Feb. 6, 1994. It was Finland's second direct presidential vote, but the first in which the electoral college did not decide the outcome. In the 1988 elections, the electoral college voted after no candidate received 50 percent of the direct vote.

Ahtisaari succeeded fellow Social Democrat Mauno Koivisto, who retired after two six-year terms in office. Ahtisaari defeated Defense Minister Elisabeth Rehn, a member of the small Swedish People's Party, taking 54 percent of the vote. Both candidates had backed Finland's EU membership.   □ Philip Revzin

See also **Europe** (Facts in brief table). In *World Book,* see **European Union; Finland.**

Fire. See **Disasters.**

Flood. See **Disasters.**

Florida. See **State government.**

Food. The United States Food and Drug Administration (FDA) and the U.S. Department of Agriculture (USDA) shifted in 1994 to emphasizing science-based, state-of-the-art programs to prevent the contamination of food. Traditionally, the food safety programs of both agencies have relied on visual inspections and end-product testing to detect the presence of contamination.

The new approach, called Hazard Analysis Critical Control Points (HACCP), requires food producers to develop a safety plan that reflects the uniqueness of the food, its method of processing, and the facility in which it is prepared. The producer identifies points in the process where safety problems are likely to occur, installs preventive measures at those points, and strictly monitors and records the results.

The FDA brought the seafood industry under HACCP regulations in January. In August, it asked the food industry for comments on further implementation of HACCP. The USDA's Food Safety and Inspection Service (FSIS) planned to replace its meat and poultry inspection system with HACCP plans.

Testing ground beef. In October 1994, the FSIS announced a new policy for the testing of raw ground beef for the presence of *Escherichia coli* bacteria, which were responsible for four deaths and hundreds of illnesses in the Pacific Northwest in 1993. The USDA planned to conduct 5,000 tests annually, half at retail outlets and half at meat-packing

Finnish President-elect Martti Ahtisaari receives a hug from his opponent, Elisabeth Rehn, after a runoff election in February.

plants. Retail outlets would have to condemn contaminated raw ground meat. Production facilities would have to either cook contaminated meat to kill the bacteria or condemn it. If suspect meat were already sold, it would have to be recalled.

The FSIS said it was unlikely that the service's sampling program would detect a significant number of lots contaminated with *E. coli,* which is found in about 4 percent of the beef supply. Nor would the program significantly reduce outbreaks of foodborne illness caused by *E. coli.* But the FSIS believed the program would provide an incentive for companies that handle raw ground beef to control processes and conduct their own tests.

What is "fresh" poultry? Several congressional representatives "bowled" with frozen chickens in June 1994 in Washington, D.C., to dramatize why the USDA should change its laws on fresh and frozen labeling for poultry. The policy allowed a bird to be labeled fresh if its internal temperature was 1 °F (–17.2 °C) or higher and it had never been kept at or below 0 °F (–17.7 °C). Poultry labeled fresh commanded higher prices than frozen birds.

The "bowlers" were from California, which had passed a law in 1993 that prohibited a fresh label for any poultry product chilled to temperatures of 25 °F (–3.9 °C) or lower at its center or that had been held at or below that level for at least 24 hours. But the Arkansas Poultry Federation, the National Broiler Council, and the American Meat Institute brought a suit against California to block the implementation of the labeling law. Both California and Arkansas have large poultry industries that ship products nationwide. The poultry organizations said that besides temperature, other factors, such as taste, aroma, bacteria quality, and nutritional characteristics must be taken into account in determining freshness. Their suit also argued that federal law took precedence over state law. A California federal judge ruled in their favor, and California was appealing the case. Meanwhile, Congress was considering legislation that would require the USDA to change its labeling policy.

"Healthy" labeling. As of May 8, 1994, any new food product coming on the market with "healthy" in its name or on its label had to comply with specific criteria, according to new FDA and USDA standards. To be called "healthy," a product must contain at least 10 percent of the recommended daily requirement of vitamin A, vitamin C, iron, calcium, protein, or fiber. The product's fat, sodium, and cholesterol levels also must be low. Products already on the market by May 8 would have until January 1996 to comply or change their labels.

Milk hormone for cows. Some dairy farmers began treating their herds in 1994 with a synthetic version of *bovine somatotropin,* a hormone that increases milk production in dairy cows. The FDA had approved the synthetic product, bovine growth hor-

mone (BGH), in November 1993. But Congress then approved a 90-day moratorium on sales to allow for further study. The ban ended on Feb. 4, 1994.

The FDA said no special labeling was necessary for milk from BGH-treated cows, because all milk contains small amounts of the hormone. The American Dietetic Association, the American Medical Association, the National Institutes of Health, and the World Health Organization stated that milk from treated cows was the same as milk from nontreated cows in safety, composition, taste, and nutrition. Still, some 20 states in 1994 considered legislation requiring BGH labeling.

School lunches. The USDA announced on June 8 that it had updated the National School Lunch Program for the first time since it was established in 1946. The old lunch program required each meal to include a meat or meat substitute, milk, a fruit and a vegetable, and bread or a bread substitute. The new, more flexible School Meals Initiative required schools to analyze the nutrient content of an entire week's menu to ensure that no more than 30 percent of the calories come from fat and no more than 10 percent from saturated fat. Lunches must continue to provide one-third of the recommended daily requirement of vitamins and minerals and must meet the recommendations of the 1990 Dietary Guidelines for Americans by July 1998. ☐ Bob Gatty

In *World Book,* see **Food; Food supply.**

Football. In a professional season in which National Football League (NFL) teams produced more touchdowns and more points because of new rules favoring the offense, the teams with the best records were the San Francisco 49ers, the Dallas Cowboys, and the Pittsburgh Steelers. In a college season in which Nebraska and Penn State finished undefeated, untied, and then won bowl games, Nebraska was voted the unofficial national champion.

Pro. In March, the NFL club owners, hoping to make the game more appealing to the public and more attractive to television, made the most sweeping rule changes in 20 years. A team, previously limited to a one-point conversion attempt after a touchdown, could now try for one point by a kick or two points by a run or a pass, an option that college teams had enjoyed for years.

That change lessened the impact of field goals. So did another new rule that, on a missed field goal, gave the ball to the other team at the point where it had been spotted for the kick, rather than at the line of scrimmage, a difference of 7 or 8 yards.

Kickoffs were now made from the 30-yard line, rather than the 35-yard line, allowing more kicks to be run back. Another change reduced the 3-inch (7.6-centimeter) kickoff tees to 1 inch (2.5 centimeters), leading to shorter kickoffs and thus more returns. Game officials were also ordered to enforce the rule more tightly that bars defenders from

National Football League final standings

American Conference

Eastern Division	W.	L.	T.	Pct.
Miami Dolphins*	10	6	0	.625
New England Patriots*	10	6	0	.625
Indianapolis Colts	8	8	0	.500
Buffalo Bills	7	9	0	.438
New York Jets	6	10	0	.375

Central Division	W.	L.	T.	Pct.
Pittsburgh Steelers*	12	4	0	.750
Cleveland Browns*	11	5	0	.688
Cincinnati Bengals	3	13	0	.188
Houston Oilers	2	14	0	.125

Western Division	W.	L.	T.	Pct.
San Diego Chargers*	11	5	0	.688
Kansas City Chiefs*	9	7	0	.563
Los Angeles Raiders	9	7	0	.563
Denver Broncos	7	9	0	.438
Seattle Seahawks	6	10	0	.375

*Made play-off.

National Conference

Eastern Division	W.	L.	T.	Pct.
Dallas Cowboys*	12	4	0	.750
New York Giants	9	7	0	.563
Arizona Cardinals	8	8	0	.500
Philadelphia Eagles	7	9	0	.438
Washington Redskins	3	13	0	.188

Central Division	W.	L.	T.	Pct.
Minnesota Vikings*	10	6	0	.625
Green Bay Packers*	9	7	0	.563
Detroit Lions*	9	7	0	.563
Chicago Bears*	9	7	0	.563
Tampa Bay Buccaneers	6	10	0	.375

Western Division	W.	L.	T.	Pct.
San Francisco 49ers*	13	3	0	.813
New Orleans Saints	7	9	0	.438
Atlanta Falcons	7	9	0	.438
Los Angeles Rams	4	12	0	.250

Individual statistics

Leading scorers, touchdowns	TD's	Rush	Rec.	Ret.	Pts.
Marshall Faulk, Indianapolis	12	11	1	0	72
Natrone Means, San Diego	12	12	0	0	72
Chris Warren, Seattle	11	9	2	0	68
Carl Pickens, Cincinnati	11	0	11	0	66
Tim Brown, L.A. Raiders	9	0	9	0	54
Leroy Hoard, Cleveland	9	5	4	0	54
Leonard Russell, Denver	9	9	0	0	54
Thurman Thomas, Buffalo	9	7	2	0	54
Marion Butts, New England	8	8	0	0	48
Andre Reed, Buffalo	8	0	8	0	48

Leading scorers, kicking	PAT	FG	Longest	Pts
John Carney, San Diego	33/33	34/38	50	135
Jason Elam, Denver	29/29	30/37	54	119
Matt Bahr, New England	36/36	27/34	48	117
Steve Christie, Buffalo	38/38	24/28	52	110
Matt Stover, Cleveland	32/32	26/28	45	110

Leading quarterbacks	Att.	Comp.	Yds.	TD's	Int.
Dan Marino, Miami	615	385	4,453	30	17
John Elway, Denver	494	307	3,490	16	10
Jim Kelly, Buffalo	448	285	3,114	22	17
Joe Montana, Kansas City	493	299	3,283	16	9
Stan Humphries, San Diego	453	264	3,209	17	12
Jeff Hostetler, L.A. Raiders	454	263	3,334	20	16
Neil O'Donnell, Pittsburgh	370	212	2,443	13	9
Boomer Esiason, N.Y. Jets	440	255	2,782	17	13
Jeff Blake, Cincinnati	306	156	2,154	14	9
Drew Bledsoe, New England	691	400	4,555	25	27

Leading receivers	Number caught	Total yards	Avg. gain	TD's
Ben Coates, New England	96	1,174	12.2	7
Andre Reed, Buffalo	90	1,303	14.5	8
Tim Brown, L.A. Raiders	89	1,309	14.7	9
Shannon Sharpe, Denver	87	1,010	11.6	4
Brian Blades, Seattle	81	1,086	13.4	4
Rob Moore, N.Y. Jets	78	1,010	12.9	6
Glyn Milburn, Denver	77	549	7.1	3
Michael Timpson, New England	74	941	12.7	3
Irving Fryar, Miami	73	1,270	17.4	7
Carl Pickens, Cincinnati	71	1,127	15.9	11

Leading rushers	No.	Yards	Avg.	TD's
Chris Warren, Seattle	333	1,545	4.6	9
Natrone Means, San Diego	343	1,350	3.9	12
Marshall Faulk, Indianapolis	314	1,282	4.1	11
Thurman Thomas, Buffalo	287	1,093	3.8	7
Harvey Williams, L.A. Raiders	282	983	3.5	4
Johnny Johnson, N.Y. Jets	240	931	3.9	3
Leroy Hoard, Cleveland	209	890	4.3	5
Bernie Parmalee, Miami	216	868	4.0	6
Barry Foster, Pittsburgh	216	851	3.9	5
Byron Morris, Pittsburgh	198	836	4.2	7

Leading punters	No.	Yards	Avg.	Longest
Jeff Gossett, L.A. Raiders	77	3,377	43.9	65
Lee Johnson, Cincinnati	79	3,461	43.8	64
Rick Tuten, Seattle	91	3,905	42.9	64
Tom Rouen, Denver	76	3,258	42.9	59
Rich Camarillo, Houston	96	4,115	42.9	58

Individual statistics

Leading scorers, touchdowns	TD's	Rush	Rec.	Ret.	Pts.
Emmitt Smith, Dallas	22	21	1	0	132
Sterling Sharpe, Green Bay	18	0	18	0	108
Jerry Rice, San Francisco	15	2	13	0	92
Terance Mathis, Atlanta	11	0	11	0	70
Herman Moore, Detroit	11	0	11	0	66
Ricky Watters, San Francisco	11	6	5	0	66
Brent Jones, San Francisco	9	0	9	0	56
Edgar Bennett, Green Bay	9	5	4	0	54
Terry Allen, Minnesota	8	8	0	0	50
Andre Rison, Atlanta	8	0	8	0	50

Leading scorers, kicking	PAT	FG	Longest	Pts
Fuad Reveiz, Minnesota	30/30	34/39	51	132
Morten Andersen, New Orleans	32/32	28/39	48	116
Chris Boniol, Dallas	48/48	22/29	47	114
Doug Brien, San Francisco	60/62	15/20	48	105
Chris Jacke, Green Bay	41/43	19/26	50	98

Leading quarterbacks	Att.	Comp.	Yds.	TD's	Int.
Steve Young, San Francisco	461	324	3,969	35	10
Brett Favre, Green Bay	582	363	3,882	33	14
Jim Everett, New Orleans	540	346	3,855	22	18
Troy Aikman, Dallas	361	233	2,676	13	12
Jeff George, Atlanta	524	322	3,734	23	18
Craig Erickson, Tampa Bay	399	225	2,919	16	10
Warren Moon, Minnesota	601	371	4,264	18	19
Steve Walsh, Chicago	343	208	2,078	10	8
Randall Cunningham, Philadelphia	490	265	3,229	16	13
Chris Miller, L.A. Rams	317	173	2,104	16	14

Leading receivers	Number caught	Total yards	Avg. gain	TD's
Cris Carter, Minnesota	122	1,256	10.3	7
Jerry Rice, San Francisco	112	1,499	13.4	13
Terance Mathis, Atlanta	111	1,342	12.1	11
Sterling Sharpe, Green Bay	94	1,119	11.9	18
Jake Reed, Minnesota	85	1,175	13.8	4
Quinn Early, New Orleans	82	894	10.9	4
Andre Rison, Atlanta	81	1,088	13.4	8
Michael Irvin, Dallas	79	1,241	15.7	6
Fred Barnett, Philadelphia	78	1,127	14.4	5
Edgar Bennett, Green Bay	78	546	7.0	4

Leading rushers	No.	Yards	Avg.	TD's
Barry Sanders, Detroit	331	1,883	5.7	7
Emmitt Smith, Dallas	368	1,484	4.0	21
Rodney Hampton, N.Y. Giants	327	1,075	3.3	6
Terry Allen, Minnesota	255	1,031	4.0	8
Jerome Bettis, L.A. Rams	319	1,025	3.2	3
Errict Rhett, Tampa Bay	284	1,011	3.6	7
Lewis Tillman, Chicago	275	899	3.3	7
Ricky Watters, San Francisco	239	877	3.7	6
Ron Moore, Arizona	232	780	3.4	4
Craig Heyward, Atlanta	183	779	4.3	7

Leading punters	No.	Yards	Avg.	Longest
Sean Landeta, L.A. Rams	78	3,494	44.8	62
Reggie Roby, Washington	82	3,639	44.4	65
Greg Montgomery, Detroit	63	2,782	44.2	64
Tommy Barnhardt, New Orleans	67	2,920	43.6	57

Running back Rashaan Salaam (19) of the University of Colorado, who won the Heisman Trophy in December 1994, carries the ball in a 1993 game against Nebraska.

bumping receivers more than five yards downfield.

As the NFL entered the second year of unrestricted free agency, accompanied by a salary cap, parity continued to exist among the teams. With three weeks left in the regular season, 13 of the 28 teams had records of 7-6 or 6-7, and only three teams had been eliminated from play-off contention. A week later, only three more teams had fallen.

The winners. San Francisco won 11 consecutive games before losing a meaningless regular-season finale to the Minnesota Vikings, and the 49ers' 13-3 record was the best in the league. The other division winners in the National Conference were Dallas (12-4) and Minnesota (10-6). The conference's three wild-card teams that advanced to the play-offs were the Green Bay Packers (9-7), the Chicago Bears (9-7), and the Detroit Lions (9-7).

Minnesota, Green Bay, Chicago, and Detroit played in the Central Division, the first time any division had sent four teams to the play-offs. The New York Giants (9-7) finished with six consecutive victories, but lost seven straight games before that.

In the American Conference, the Pittsburgh Steelers (12-4), the San Diego Chargers (11-5), and the Miami Dolphins (10-6) won the division titles. The wild-card teams were the Cleveland Browns (11-5), the New England Patriots (10-6), and the Kansas City Chiefs (9-7).

The Los Angeles Raiders (9-7) missed the play-offs

The 1994 college football season

College conference champions

Conference	School
Atlantic Coast	Florida State
Big East	Miami (Fla.)
Big Eight	Nebraska
Big Sky	Boise State
Big Ten	Penn State
Big West	Nevada—Nevada-Las Vegas—Southwestern Louisiana (tie)
Gateway	Northern Iowa
Ivy League	Pennsylvania
Mid-American	Central Michigan
Mid-Eastern	South Carolina State
Ohio Valley	Eastern Kentucky
Pacific Ten	Oregon
Patriot	Lafayette
Southeastern	Florida
Southern	Marshall
Southland	North Texas
Southwest	Baylor—Rice—Texas—Texas Christian—Texas Tech (tie)
Southwestern	Alcorn State—Grambling (tie)
Western Athletic	Colorado State
Yankee	New Hampshire

Major bowl games

Bowl	Winner	Loser
Alamo	Washington State 10	Baylor 3
Aloha	Boston College 12	Kansas State 7
Amos Alonzo Stagg (Div. III)	Albion (Mich.) 38	Washington & Jefferson 15
Blue-Gray	Blue 38	Gray 27
Carquest	South Carolina 24	West Virginia 21
Copper	Brigham Young 31	Oklahoma 6
Cotton	Southern California 55	Texas Tech 14
Fiesta	Colorado 41	Notre Dame 24
Florida Citrus	Alabama 24	Ohio State 17
Freedom	Utah 16	Arizona 13
Gator	Tennessee 45	Virginia Tech 23
Hall of Fame	Wisconsin 34	Duke 20
Heritage	South Carolina State 31	Grambling 27
Holiday	Michigan 24	Colorado State 14
Independence	Virginia 20	Texas Christian 10
Las Vegas	University of Nevada-Las Vegas 52	Central Michigan 24
Liberty	Illinois 30	East Carolina 0
Orange	Nebraska 24	Miami 17
Peach	North Carolina State 28	Mississippi State 24
Rose	Penn State 38	Oregon 20
Sugar	Florida State 23	Florida 17
Sun Bowl	Texas 35	North Carolina 31
NCAA Div. I-AA	Youngstown State 28	Boise State 14
NCAA Div. II	North Alabama 16	Texas A&M-Kingsville 10
NAIA Div. I	Northeastern State (Okla.) 13	Arkansas-Pine Bluff 12
NAIA Div. II	Westminster (Pa.) 27	Pacific Lutheran 7

All-America team (as picked by AP)

Offense
Quarterback—Kerry Collins, Penn State
Running backs—Rashaan Salaam, Colorado; Ki-Jana Carter, Penn State
Wide receivers—Frank Sanders, Auburn; Jack Jackson, Florida
Tight end—Pete Mitchell, Boston College
Center—Cory Raymer, Wisconsin
Other linemen—Tony Boselli, Southern California; Jeff Hartings, Penn State; Korey Stringer, Ohio State; Zach Wiegert, Nebraska
All-purpose—Brian Pruitt, Central Michigan
Place-kicker—Brian Leaver, Bowling Green

Defense
Linemen—Derrick Alexander, Florida State; Tedy Bruschi, Arizona; Luther Elliss, Utah; Warren Sapp, Miami
Linebackers—Antonio Armstrong, Texas A&M; Dana Howard, Illinois; Ed Stewart, Nebraska
Backs—Clifton Abraham, Florida State; Chris Hudson, Colorado; C. J. Richardson, Miami; Brian Robinson, Auburn
Punter—Todd Sauerbrun, West Virginia

Player awards
Heisman Trophy (best player)—Rashaan Salaam, Colorado
Lombardi Award (best lineman)—Warren Sapp, Miami
Outland Trophy (best interior lineman)—Zach Wiegert, Nebraska

when they lost to Kansas City in their final game. The Buffalo Bills, beaten in the Super Bowl the four previous seasons, slipped to a 7-9 record. New England was the surprise team of the season, finishing with seven consecutive victories.

Dallas achieved its success under a new coach, Barry Switzer. A personality clash between Jerry Jones, the team's owner and general manager, and Jimmy Johnson, who had coached the team to the two previous Super Bowl championships, led to Johnson's departure on March 29. The next day, Johnson was replaced by Switzer, who had been out of football for 5 years after a highly successful 16-year reign as a college coach at the University of Oklahoma.

Stars. Steve Young of San Francisco, with a quarterback efficiency rating of 112.8, broke the NFL record of 112.4 by Joe Montana in 1989. Young completed 324 of 461 passes (70.3 percent accuracy) for 3,969 yards, with 35 touchdowns and only 10 interceptions. Jerry Rice, led the league with 1,499 yards in receptions and broke Jim Brown's NFL record of 126 career touchdowns on September 5. Cris Carter of Minnesota caught 122 passes, an NFL single-season record, and Ben Coates of New England caught 96, an NFL record for tight ends.

Barry Sanders of Detroit, often facing massed defenses, led the league with 1,883 yards rushing, ending the three-year reign of Emmitt Smith of Dallas. Sanders was a unanimous choice of the 98 writers and sportscasters who chose the Associated Press all-NFL team.

Canadian. The Canadian Football League (CFL) expanded to 12 teams–8 in Canada and 4 (Baltimore; Shreveport, La.; Las Vegas, Nev; and Sacramento, Calif.) in the United States. The Baltimore team was successful on the field (12-6) and the box office (37,347 spectators per home game). Its greatest battle was with the NFL, which went to court to block it from calling itself the Baltimore Colts, the name of an NFL team before it became the Indianapolis Colts. The new team finally called itself the Baltimore Football Club.

The Winnipeg Blue Bombers (13-5) and the Calgary Stampeders (15-3) won the division titles. In the Grey Cup championship game on November 27, in Vancouver, the British Columbia Lions defeated Baltimore, 26-23, on Lui Passaglia's 38-yard field goal on the last play of the game.

For the fourth consecutive year, Doug Flutie, the Calgary Stampeders' quarterback, was voted the league's outstanding player. His 48 touchdown passes broke the league record.

Hall of Fame. Five players were voted to the Pro Football Hall of Fame: running backs Tony Dorsett and Leroy Kelly, tight end Jackie Smith, defensive tackle Randy White, and cornerback Jimmy Johnson. They were joined by Bud Grant, who led Minnesota to the Super Bowl in 4 of his 18 years as coach.

College. The best regular-season records among major colleges belonged to Nebraska (12-0), Penn State (11-0), Alabama (11-1), Texas A&M (10-0-1), Florida (10-1-1), Miami (10-1), Colorado (10-1), Colorado State (10-1), Florida State (9-1-1), and Auburn (9-1-1). The Associated Press postseason poll of reporters and sportscasters and the *USA Today*/CNN poll of coaches had the same leaders—Nebraska first, Penn State second, and Miami of Florida third.

Then came the bowl games that would decide the unofficial national champion. Under guidelines from the bowl coalition, which allowed some of the best-known bowls to get the best teams, the Orange Bowl matched Nebraska against Miami on Jan. 1, 1995, in Miami. The only other game affecting the championship was the Rose Bowl on January 2, in Pasadena, Calif. The Rose Bowl was not part of the coalition, but it matched the champions of the Big Ten (Penn State) and the Pacific Ten (Oregon).

In the bowl games, Nebraska defeated Miami, 24-17, and Penn State beat Oregon, 38-20. A day later, the two polls crowned Nebraska as the national champion, with Penn State second, and Colorado third.

Bowl alliance. For years, many college athletic directors and coaches had wanted to stage postseason play-offs to crown a national champion on the field rather than in the polls. There was widespread opposition from university presidents, who felt play-offs would further diminish classroom time for football players for three or four additional weeks.

Although the National Collegiate Athletic Association (NCAA) rejected play-off proposals again, it did move in that direction. The bowl coalition expired after the 1994 season, but a new six-year alliance was formed to begin after the 1995 season.

The new system provided the Fiesta, Orange, and Sugar Bowls with six teams: the champions of the Southeastern, Atlantic Coast, Big 12 (formerly Big Eight), and Big East Conferences, plus two at-large teams, one almost sure to be Notre Dame.

Stars. Rashaan Salaam, a junior tailback from Colorado, easily won the voting for the Heisman Trophy as the outstanding college player. Tailback Ki-Jana Carter of Penn State finished second and quarterback Steve McNair of Alcorn State third. Salaam led major-college running backs with 2,055 yards, 24 touchdowns, and four 200-yard rushing games.

McNair became the NCAA's career leader in total offense with a four-year total of 16,823 yards. His 1994 passing statistics were staggering—304 completions in 530 attempts for 4,863 yards and 44 touchdowns. He also rushed 119 times for 936 yards and 9 touchdowns. However, he was handicapped in the Heisman voting because he played in Division I-AA against teams that were not national powers.

□ Frank Litsky

In *World Book*, see **Football**.

Student protesters in Paris overturn cars during demonstrations in March against a law to lower the minimum wage for workers under 25 years old.

France. Politics in France heated up in 1994 as candidates jockeyed to succeed President François Mitterrand in the May 1995 presidential election. In the meantime, Mitterrand continued his battle with prostate cancer and on July 18, underwent surgery to remove scar tissue left from a 1992 operation.

On Dec. 11, 1994, Jacques Delors, president of the executive commission of the European Union (EU), announced that he would not seek the French presidency in the 1995 election. Delors, a Socialist, had been favored to win. He feared France's conservative cabinet and parliament would undermine his political program.

EU elections. France's Socialist Party fared poorly in elections on June 12, 1994, to the 567-member European Parliament. The Socialists won only 14.5 percent of the vote and 16 seats. Socialist Party leader Michel Rocard resigned on June 19 after he failed to win support from the party's national council.

Youth protests. Young people staged widespread protests in March after the government implemented a law to lower the minimum wage for workers under the age of 25. Protesters charged that the law discriminated against young people. The law sought to lower the nation's high unemployment by encouraging businesses to hire youths. After nearly a month of protests, Prime Minister Edouard Balladur formally revoked the law on March 30.

The Jackal is snared. French counterintelligence agents made one of their biggest arrests in years on August 15, when they arrested Illich Ramirez Sanchez, a Venezuelan-born terrorist also known as "Carlos" and "the Jackal." Carlos was seized on August 14 in the African nation of Sudan by Sudanese police at the request of the French.

French authorities charged Carlos with planting a car bomb in Paris in 1982, which killed 1 person and wounded 70. He had previously been convicted in absentia of killing two French intelligence officers and wounding a third in 1975. The terrorist's most notorious act was the kidnapping of 11 oil ministers at a meeting of the Organization of Petroleum Exporting Countries in Vienna, Austria, in 1975.

Failed hijacking. French security forces stormed a hijacked Air France jetliner in Marseille on December 26, rescuing all 170 hostages on board and killing all four Islamic militants. The plane had been hijacked from Algiers, Algeria, on December 24.

Franglais ban. A law that would ban the use of languages other than French in most official and public writings and announcements in France was passed on July 1. However, the Constitutional Council on July 31 struck down major provisions, ruling that the new law would not apply to private companies, private citizens, and the news media. The ``Toubon Law,'' named after French Culture Minister Jacques Toubon, its sponsor, was the latest step in France's effort to protect itself against an invasion of foreign words and expressions, especially in English. Opponents of the new law feared it would inhibit foreign investment.

Rwandan aid. More than 2,500 French marines and soldiers of the Foreign Legion entered the troubled African nation of Rwanda on June 23 to help restore order and give humanitarian aid. A civil war between Rwanda's minority Tutsi and ruling Hutu ethnic groups had cost hundreds of thousands of lives. The Tutsi-led Rwandan Patriotic Front, however, opposed the presence of French troops because France had supported the Hutu government for many years. The troops withdrew on August 22.

War crimes conviction. Paul Touvier, intelligence chief of a pro-Nazi militia in Lyons during World War II (1939-1945), was convicted of crimes against humanity on April 19 and sentenced to life imprisonment. Touvier was the first Frenchman to be tried for persecuting Jews during the Nazi occupation of France.

Channel Tunnel opens. The 31-mile (50-kilometer) Channel Tunnel, a railroad tunnel that links France and the United Kingdom under the English Channel, was inaugurated on May 6 by Mitterrand and Queen Elizabeth II. □ Philip Revzin

See also **Europe** (Facts in brief table). In *World Book,* see **European Union; France.**

Gabon. See Africa.

Gambia. See Africa.

Gas and gasoline. See Petroleum and gas.

Genetic engineering. See Medicine.

Geology. Geological research during 1994 ranged from the traditional to the highly innovative, with particular emphasis on studies of the geologic record of global environmental change. Earth scientists are keenly interested in learning how the climate varied in the past, because such studies may help improve understanding of the potential impact of *global warming*. Global warming is a predicted temperature increase due to an atmospheric build-up of heat-trapping gases, particularly carbon dioxide pollution from the burning of coal, oil, and gas.

Tree studies. Regional droughts may result if a global warming occurs, according to a June analysis of ancient tree stumps rooted in modern wetlands in California and the Patagonia region of Argentina. Environmental scientist Scott Stine of California State University at Hayward documented severe droughts that occurred 600 to 900 years ago, during a period known as the Medieval Warm Epoch. Stine theorized that the warming caused changes in global atmospheric circulation, resulting in the droughts.

In August, geologists analyzed tree rings of bristlecone pines, the longest living tree species, to create an 8,000-year record of temperatures in the White Mountains of California. Xiahong Feng and Samuel Epstein of the California Institute of Technology in Pasadena compiled the data, which indicated that global temperatures 6,800 years ago were as much as 9 Fahrenheit degrees (5 Celsius degrees) warmer than today. That warm period has been followed by continuous cooling.

Ancient volcanic eruptions that sent ash and gas into the atmosphere may have contributed to the global cooling trend of the past 11,000 years, according to a May report by Earth scientist Gregory A. Zielinski and his colleagues at the University of New Hampshire in Durham and at Pennsylvania State University in University Park. The researchers examined volcanic compounds trapped in ice in Greenland to provide a 9,000-year record of severe volcanic eruptions. The scientists found that such eruptions were much more frequent 7,000 to 9,000 years ago than during the past 2,000 years.

Glacier studies. In May and June, researchers working on two continents overturned old ideas about a geological event of 10,000 to 11,000 years ago called the Younger Dryas. The Younger Dryas was an abrupt, short-lived cooling that interrupted a much longer period of climate warming. The event is best known from studies of fossil pollen in Europe. Scientists had thought the brief cooling occurred only in the North Atlantic.

The new research was conducted by two groups of geologists. Mel A. Reasoner and his colleagues at the University of Alberta and the University of Calgary in Canada studied *moraines* (ridges of debris deposited by glaciers) in the Canadian Rockies.

Geology

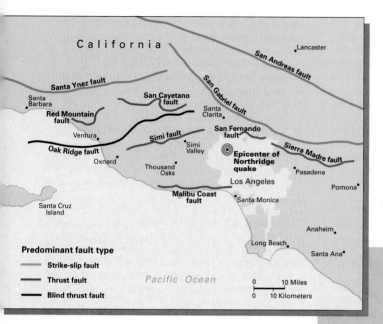

C a l i f o r n i a

Lancaster

San Andreas fault

Santa Ynez fault

San Cayetano fault

San Gabriel fault

Santa Barbara

Red Mountain fault

Santa Clarita

Ventura

Simi fault

San Fernando fault

Oak Ridge fault

Oxnard

Simi Valley

Sierra Madre fault

Epicenter of Northridge quake

Thousand Oaks

Pasadena

Los Angeles

Pomona

Malibu Coast fault

Santa Monica

Santa Cruz Island

Anaheim

Long Beach

Santa Ana

Predominant fault type

Strike-slip fault

Thrust fault

Blind thrust fault

Pacific Ocean

0   10 Miles
0   10 Kilometers

Devastating earthquake

On Jan. 17, 1994, an earthquake measuring 6.7 on the Richter scale rocked southern California, killing at least 57 people and causing up to $20 billion in damage. The quake, centered in the town of Northridge, occurred on a previously unmapped blind thrust fault, *left.* Unlike the two other major types of faults, blind thrust faults do not cause a break in the rock at the surface, *bottom.*

George H. Denton of the University of Maine in Orono and C. H. Hendy of the University of Waikato in Hamilton, New Zealand, studied moraines in the Southern Alps of New Zealand. The scientists found that alpine glaciers in both hemispheres advanced during the Younger Dryas. The discoveries suggest that the cold interval was a worldwide event, perhaps driven by global atmospheric changes.

New findings may have resolved a paradox concerning the period when the glaciers reached their greatest extent, about 20,000 years ago. Estimates had indicated that tropical continents were about 10 Fahrenheit degrees (5.6 Celsius degrees) cooler than today, but ocean temperatures changed little. By studying the chemistry of ancient Barbados corals, scientists with the Lamont-Doherty Earth Observatory in Palisades, N.Y., showed in February that tropical sea surface temperatures were also 10 Fahrenheit degrees cooler 20,000 years ago.

Mild ancient climates. What was the climate like 50 million years ago? Data compiled from fossil plants suggest that land areas were warm throughout the year, but computer simulations have indicated dramatic seasonal changes. A University of Chicago scientist helped solve the riddle by studying how the fossils of reptiles that thrive in warm zones were distributed. His July report suggested that continental temperatures millions of years ago were more uniformly warm than today.

☐ Henry T. Mullins

See also **Disasters; Los Angeles.** In *World Book,* see **Geology.**

Three types of faults

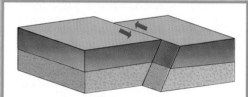

In a strike-slip fault, two rock surfaces slide sideways past each other.

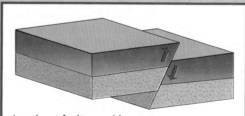

In a thrust fault, one side moves up and over the other.

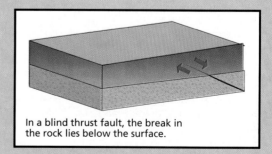

In a blind thrust fault, the break in the rock lies below the surface.

Georgia in 1994 remained politically unstable and under a national state of emergency. In May, Parliament Chairman Eduard Shevardnadze persuaded party leaders to sign a Declaration of National Unity and Accord. But the agreement quickly unraveled in July when government police forcibly dispersed a massive opposition-led demonstration in Tbilisi, the capital. In September, opposition deputies failed in an attempt to force Shevardnadze's resignation.

In February, the separatist region of Abkhazia declared independence from Georgia. Georgian troops attacked in March, but were repelled. The two sides remained at odds over the status of the region and whether some 250,000 Georgians who had fled from Abkhazia when fighting began in 1993 could return. But on April 4 the two sides agreed to a cease-fire, to be monitored by Russian peacekeeping troops.

Former President Zviad K. Gamsakhurdia died in January, when government militia cornered the rebel forces he was leading. Some reports said his death was a suicide, but officials reported that he was killed by the militia.

Tensions with the border region of South Ossetia increased when Georgian officials refused to recognize elections held in March for a regional parliament in South Ossetia. □ Steven L. Solnick

See also **Asia** (Facts in brief table). In *World Book,* see **Georgia.**

Georgia. See **State government.**

Germany. German Chancellor Helmut Kohl was narrowly named to a fourth four-year term on Oct. 16, 1994, despite a drop in popularity for his Christian Democratic Union (CDU) party.

Kohl's coalition of the CDU, its sister party, the Christian Democrats, and the Free Democratic Party, led by Foreign Minister Klaus Kinkel, narrowly maintained their majority in the Bundestag (lower house of parliament), winning 48.4 percent of the vote and 341 of 672 house seats. The opposition coalition of the Social Democratic Party, the environmentalist Green Party, and the reformed Communist Party won 48.1 percent and 331 seats. The right wing Republican Party failed to win any seats.

During the campaign, Social Democratic leader Rudolf Scharping had argued that Kohl's policies toward German reunification had proven too costly and that although Kohl had promised not to raise taxes to fund reunification, taxes had increased for virtually everyone. Despite these strong challenges to Kohl's leadership, his coalition government remained in power, in part due to the significant economic recovery that occurred in 1994.

Presidential elections. Roman Herzog, the president of the Federal Constitutional Court, the country's highest court, was elected president of Germany on May 23 by an electoral college made up of federal and state legislators. Herzog, who succeeded Richard von Weizsäcker in the mainly

ceremonial post, became Kohl's choice following the 1993 withdrawal from the race of Steffen Heitmann, the justice minister of Saxony in eastern Germany. Heitmann's views on the role of the Nazis in World War II (1939-1945) and other topics proved too controversial. Herzog defeated Johannes Rau, the candidate of the Social Democratic Party, by 696 votes to 605.

Economic news. The German economy began to recover during the spring of 1994 after nearly two years of economic recession. Throughout the year, the German central bank, the Deutsche Bundesbank, was able to gradually lower interest rates, making it easier for consumers and businesses to borrow money to spend or invest.

The International Monetary Fund on October 2 estimated that, after nearly two years of decline, the German economy would grow by 2.3 percent in 1994 and by 2.8 percent in 1995. Some international organizations estimated that growth in the six former Communist East German states would far exceed that in the Western part of the country, at a rate of nearly 10 percent in both 1994 and 1995.

EU news. Germany continued to join France in seeking a more unified European Union (EU), formerly known as the European Community. On September 1, the CDU called for a core group made up of Germany, France, Belgium, Luxembourg, and the Netherlands to move toward a single European currency and to coordinate their foreign, domestic, and defense policies, even if other EU members wanted to move more slowly.

Germany brought itself in line with EU regulations and joined most other industrial nations when it enacted on August 1 a law making insider trading of stocks illegal. Under the law, which had been passed by the Bundestag on June 17 and the upper house of parliament, the Bundesrat, on July 8, it became a crime punishable by up to five years in prison for officials to trade financial information before it was made public.

Right wing and neo-Nazi violence against foreigners and immigrants continued to worry Germans in 1994, despite official statistics indicating that such attacks had fallen off. Federal officials said that violence in 1994 was less frequent than in 1993, when 1,322 such incidents were reported.

Corporate intrigue. Controversy continued to swirl in Germany in 1994 over Jose Ignacio Lopez de Arriortua, the top purchasing manager for Volkswagen AG, the large German car and truck manufacturer. Lopez joined Volkswagen in March 1993 from Adam Opel AG, a subsidiary of General Motors Corporation (GM) of the United States. After he left, GM accused him of taking various secret GM documents with him. Lopez denied showing any secret documents to his new employers. On May 4, 1994, he agreed to pay 75,000 German marks ($45,000 U.S.) to charity after German prosecutors agreed not

German Chancellor Helmut Kohl waves to supporters in October after election returns showed his coalition government would remain in power.

to charge him with lying about certain aspects of the case. In August, Germany's Justice Ministry said it would aid a U.S. probe of the accusations.

Juergen Schneider, one of Germany's largest real estate developers, disappeared on April 8, leaving behind him a trail of debts. His disappearance and insolvency forced his company, Juergen Schneider AG, to file for bankruptcy on April 15. The disappearance of Schneider and his wife, Claudia, who together owned the company, also left many of Germany's biggest banks holding about $3 billion in probably worthless loans to the company.

Metallgesellschaft AG, a large German metals company, reorganized in 1994 under a $1.9-billion rescue package assembled by German banks. The company's chief executive, Heinz Schimmelbusch, and other officials were fired on Dec. 17, 1993, after the company lost more than $1 billion in trading oil futures contracts in the United States.

Nuclear weapons material confiscated. German police confiscated plutonium and enriched uranium, materials used in making nuclear weapons, in four separate incidents in 1994. German authorities said the plutonium and uranium were smuggled out of nuclear weapons plants in the former Soviet Union, though Russian officials denied it.

On August 22, Russia and Germany reached an agreement aimed at halting illegal smuggling of nuclear material out of the former Soviet Union. Nucle-

ar weapons experts feared that lax controls at nuclear weapons factories and storehouses in Russia and other former Soviet republics could enable other countries to obtain the materials necessary to make nuclear weapons. (See also **Espionage: Why Spy?**)

Military role. The Federal Constitutional Court ruled on July 12 that German troops could take part in military action outside Germany, provided that the action was first approved by the Bundestag and that it was part of an international action under the control of an organization such as the North Atlantic Treaty Organization (NATO) or the United Nations (UN). The West German Constitution, which was drawn up by the victorious Allied powers after World War II, banned any German military action, except that of defending Germany under NATO control. The new court ruling will allow Germany to participate in UN peacekeeping missions and other international activities.

Deaths. Erich Honecker, former president of East Germany, died of liver cancer at the age of 81 in Santiago, Chile, on May 29. Honecker had been freed from house arrest in Germany to go to Chile in 1993, after his trial in Germany on charges of treason and manslaughter was halted due to his failing health.   □ Philip Revzin

See also **Europe** (Facts in brief table). In *World Book,* see European Union; Germany.
Ghana. See Africa.

Golf. The professional tours were more successful than ever in 1994, with purse money reaching an all-time high. The Professional Golfers' Association (PGA) Tour comprised 51 tournaments worth $55-million, the PGA Senior Tour held 43 tournaments worth $32 million, and the Ladies Professional Golf Association (LPGA) Tour's 37 tournaments were worth $22 million.

The most sucessful pros were Nick Price of Zimbabwe and Greg Norman of Australia on the PGA Tour; Dave Stockton, Raymond Floyd, and Lee Trevino of the United States on the PGA Senior Tour, and Beth Daniel of the United States and Laura Davies of England on the LPGA Tour.

PGA. The umbrella organization for touring male pros underwent a change in leadership. At age 56, PGA Commissioner Deane Beman resigned after 20 years of tour growth and prosperity to design courses and play on the senior tour. He was replaced by Deputy Commissioner Tim Finchem.

A proposed World Golf Tour challenged the PGA's control of the sport. With financing from the Fox television network, this tour planned to start in 1995 with eight tournaments worth $3 million each. Tournaments would include the top 30 players in the world rankings, plus 10 invitees. Winners would receive $600,000 per tournament.

Some of the tournaments would conflict with those on the PGA Tour, and Finchem said the PGA would bar its players from conflicting tournaments. Norman was the leader of the new tour, but when no other member of the PGA Tour said he would break away, the prospects of a 1995 start for the new tour seemed slim.

PGA Tour. For the first time ever, the four grand-slam tournaments for men were won by non-Americans, the last two by Price a month apart. In the British Open, held from July 14 to 17 in Turnberry, Scotland, Price sank a 50-foot (15-meter) eagle putt on the 17th hole, and his 72-hole score of 268 defeated Jesper Parnevik of Sweden by a stroke. In the PGA championship, held from August 11 to 14 in Tulsa, Okla., Price's record 269 beat Corey Pavin by six strokes. Price became the first to win successive grand-slam tournaments since Tom Watson won the United States Open and the British Open in 1982.

In the Masters from April 7 to 10 in Augusta, Ga., José María Olazábal of Spain sank a 30-foot (9-meter) eagle putt on the 69th hole, and his 279 beat Tom Lehman by two strokes. In the United States Open from June 16 to 20 in Oakmont, Pa., Ernie Els of South Africa, Colin Montgomerie of Scotland, and Loren Roberts of the United States tied for first at 279. In an 18-hole play-off the next day, Els and Roberts shot 74's and Montgomerie 78. Els then won a sudden-death play-off on the second hole.

Price led in tour earnings with $1,499,927, with Norman second with $1,330,307. Norman won the Vardon Trophy for low stroke average (68.81 per

Nick Price of Zimbabwe kisses the victor's trophy after he won the PGA Championship in August.

round), with Price third with 69.39. During the year, the 37-year-old Price won five PGA tour tournaments plus the British Open. In a 24-month period, he won three major titles, 16 tournaments worldwide, and $6 million in purses.

Senior. Stockton ($1,402,519) and Floyd were the leading money-winners on the senior tour. Floyd's earnings of $1,382,762 surpassed Norman's. Trevino won six tournaments, Floyd four, and Stockton three. Trevino won the PGA Seniors Championship, Stockton the Senior Players Championship, and Simon Hobday of South Africa the United States Senior Open.

On the LPGA Tour, Laura Davies led in earnings ($687,201 to Daniel's $659,426) and Daniel in scoring (70.90 to Davies' 70.91). Daniel won the Rolex Player of the Year title with 48 points to Davies' 47. Daniel won four tournaments, Davies three, and Liselotte Neumann of Sweden three. In the majors, Donna Andrews captured the Dinah Shore, Davies the LPGA championship, Patty Sheehan the United States Open, and Martha Nause the du Maurier Classic.

Amateur. Eldrick (Tiger) Woods won the United States men's amateur title by defeating Trip Kuehne, 1 up, in the 36-hole final August 28 in Ponte Vedra Beach, Fla. The 18-year-old Woods became the first African American and the youngest champion in the tournament's 99-year history. □ Frank Litsky

In *World Book,* see **Golf.**

Gore, Albert, Jr. Vice President Albert Gore, Jr., in 1994 continued to play a prominent role in the Administration of President Bill Clinton, taking the chief responsibility for encouraging the development of a national "information superhighway" for electronic communications. The Vice President challenged large telecommunications companies to link all the nation's hospitals, clinics, libraries, and classrooms into a unified communications system based on a single set of standards by the year 2000. (See **Telecommunications: Regulating the Information Highway.**)

In a follow-up to Gore's 1993 report on reinventing government, Congress on March 24, 1994, passed a bill to reduce the federal payroll. The bill called for cash payments to many government workers to encourage them to resign or retire early.

During the year, Gore handled the usual chores assigned to the Vice President, such as raising funds for Democratic candidates for Congress. He also attended the May 10 inauguration of South African President Nelson R. Mandela and in September was the chief U.S. spokesman at the United Nations' International Conference on Population and Development in Cairo, Egypt.

On August 20, Gore tore his Achilles' tendon while playing basketball. He underwent surgery the same day. □ William J. Eaton

In *World Book,* see **Gore, Al.**

Greece came into disfavor in the European Union (EU), formerly the European Community, on Feb. 16, 1994, when it unilaterally imposed a trade embargo on Macedonia, a former republic of the federal state of Yugoslavia. Since the breakup of Yugoslavia in 1991, Greece has disputed the former republic's use of the name Macedonia because a region of Greece bears the same name. Greece also charged that the ex-Yugoslav republic, which it refuses to recognize, had made claims on Greek territory.

The embargo angered EU members because it violated EU treaties, which forbid most unilateral efforts on external trade matters. On April 13, the European Commission, a legislative arm of the European Union, took unprecedented legal action when it asked the European Court of Justice, the EU's supreme court, to force Greece to lift the embargo. A temporary ruling on June 29 left the embargo in place. A final ruling was expected in 1995.

Despite Greece's objections to the former Yugoslav republic, the United States recognized Macedonia as an independent state on February 9. The move sparked widespread protest in Greece, and on February 15, tens of thousands of Greeks marched in the port city of Salonika to protest the decision.

EU presidency. On January 1, Greece assumed the six-month seat of the EU's rotating presidency.

Although somewhat marred by the dispute over Macedonia, the Greek presidency was praised for its efforts in helping Austria, Finland, and Sweden to join the EU on Jan. 1, 1995. The issue raised controversy within Greece because some government officials, including Theodoros Pangalos, minister for European affairs, opposed the expansion. Because of his opposition, Pangalos was reassigned on July 7, 1994, to the post of transport minister in the Greek government. During its presidency, Greece continued to block EU membership for its long-time rival, Turkey.

Economic news. The Greek economy continued to struggle behind that of its EU partners. On June 22, the government submitted to the EU a five-year plan aimed at cutting government spending, privatizing more state-owned enterprises, and curbing rampant income tax evasion.

Ex-king loses citizenship. Parliament passed a law on April 14, depriving exiled former King Constantine II and his family of citizenship. The monarchy was abolished in 1973, six years after a military coup sent Constantine into exile. Constantine's property in Greece was taken over by the government. The former king lives in London.

□ Philip Revzin

See also **Europe** (Facts in brief table). In *World Book,* see **European Union; Greece.**

Grenada. See **Latin America.**

Griffey, Ken, Jr. (1969-), was recognized as one of the most popular stars in baseball in 1994, receiving more votes than any player in history in balloting for major league baseball's All-Star Game in July. Griffey collected 6,079,688 votes, surpassing Rod Carew's 1977 record of 4,292,740.

George Kenneth Griffey, Jr., was born on Nov. 21, 1969, in Donora, Pa., the son of baseball star Ken Griffey, Sr. In 1973, Griffey's family moved to Cincinnati, Ohio, where Ken, Sr., played outfield for the Cincinnati Reds. Ken, Jr., excelled at baseball at Moeller High School in Cincinnati and turned professional at age 17 when the Seattle Mariners drafted him.

In 1989, at 19 years of age, Griffey became the youngest player in the major leagues when he debuted with the Mariners. The Griffeys became the first father-son duo to play in the major leagues at the same time in 1989, and on Aug. 31, 1990, the two became the first father-son duo to be on the same major league team at the same time.

From July 20 to 28, 1993, Griffey tied a major league record by hitting at least one home run in eight consecutive games. On June 15, 1993, at age 23 years, 6 months, and 25 days, Griffey became the sixth-youngest major league player to hit 100 home runs.

Griffey lives in Issaquah, Wash. He and his wife, Melissa, have a son. □ Mark Dunbar

Guatemala. On Jan. 30, 1994, Guatemalans voted "yes" in a referendum to approve reforms proposed by President Ramiro de León Carpio. The reform measures aimed to combat political corruption by making government officials more accountable for how they managed and spent public funds.

On April 11, the president transferred authority for controlling rising violence from the army, which had been accused of brutality in the past, to the national police force. His action helped pave the way for an accord between the government and the leftist rebel National Revolutionary Union. The accord, signed in Oslo, Norway, on June 23, provided for investigation of past human-rights abuses, resettlement of some 40,000 Guatemalans who had fled oppression, and for the United Nations to monitor the peace process in Guatemala. The accord was a step toward ending a more than 30-year-old civil war.

On August 14, the Guatemalan Republican Front (FRG) of former dictator General Efraín Ríos Montt won 32 of 80 seats in the new Congress. Ríos Montt had seized power in a 1982 coup and was known for his brutal suppression of dissidents.

In March 1994, rumors flew that foreigners were stealing Guatemalan children. An Alaskan woman was severely stabbed and beaten by a village mob on March 29 after a peasant had falsely accused her of stealing her child. ☐ Nathan A. Haverstock

In *World Book*, see **Guatemala.**

Haiti. On Oct. 15, 1994, Jean-Bertrand Aristide reclaimed the presidency of Haiti, as some 20,000 United States troops guarded the peace of the troubled, bankrupt nation. Behind a bullet-proof glass enclosure outside the National Palace in Port-au-Prince, the capital, Aristide threw a dove into the air and urged the nation to say "No to violence, no to vengeance, yes to reconciliation."

End to exile. It was an extraordinary personal triumph for Aristide. He had become Haiti's first democratically elected president in December 1990 with nearly 71 percent of the vote. But in September 1991, he was overthrown in a military coup led by Brigadier General Raoul Cédras. Despite repeated calls by international leaders for Aristide's return and a near-total United Nations (UN) trade embargo against Haiti, the country's military leaders refused to allow the deposed president to return.

Cédras had reneged on a July 1993 agreement that called for Aristide's return by the end of October that year. As it became apparent that U.S. diplomatic efforts had failed and that Haiti's ruling elite would suffer few serious consequences as a result of its defiance, military leaders grew bolder in the repression of Aristide supporters. Paramilitary squads killed hundreds of Aristide backers in Port-au-Prince in the first half of 1994, according to UN observers. As many as 20,000 Haitian refugees took to the sea in flimsy rafts and boats in an attempt to reach Flori-

Haitian President Jean-Bertrand Aristide waves to supporters in Port-au-Prince, Haiti, in October after returning from three years in exile.

da during 1994, overwhelming the U.S. Coast Guard.

UN agrees to invasion. On July 31, the UN Security Council voted unanimously to authorize a U.S.-led invasion of Haiti. President Bill Clinton delivered an ultimatum to Cédras on September 15, saying "Leave now, or we will force you from power."

Carter mission. In a last attempt to avoid a military confrontation, Clinton sent former President Jimmy Carter, Senator Sam Nunn (D., Ga.), and retired General Colin L. Powell as special envoys to Haiti. They held tense negotiations with Cédras and other top Haitian officials. On September 18, as a U.S. invasion force was en route, Cédras agreed to give up power.

The agreement called for the Haitian military to work with U.S. forces to achieve a peaceful transfer of power. It also called for the lifting of the UN embargo against Haiti. Although the agreement allowed Cédras to remain on the island, he later left to live in exile in Panama.

U.S. occupation. On September 19, U.S. infantry troops began arriving in Haiti, and they soon outnumbered the Haitian military. When 20,000 troops were on the ground, U.S. forces began searching out suspected arms caches and raiding facilities used by paramilitary and police operatives loyal to the former military rulers.   □ Nathan A. Haverstock

See also **Latin America** (Facts in brief table). In *World Book*, see **Haiti**.

Hanks, Tom (1956-), won the Academy Award for best actor in March 1994 for his performance as a homosexual lawyer dying of AIDS in the motion picture *Philadelphia* (1993). Hanks went on in 1994 to achieve success with his lead role in the popular movie *Forrest Gump*, the saga of a simple-minded man's journey through modern times.

Hanks was born on July 9, 1956, in Concord, Calif. His parents divorced when he was 5 years old, and Hanks and two of his three siblings lived with his father, a cook, who moved often. Hanks attended a junior college and then studied acting and technical theater at California State University in Sacramento in 1976 and 1977.

Hanks first became well known as a lead character in a television series, "Bosom Buddies" (1980-1982). In 1984, first-time director Ron Howard cast Hanks in the romantic comedy hit *Splash*, after which Hanks's career took off. He received an Academy Award nomination for best actor for *Big* (1988), the story of an adolescent boy trapped in a man's body. In 1993, he costarred with Meg Ryan in a popular romance, *Sleepless in Seattle*.

Hanks married actress Samantha Lewes in 1978. The couple had a son and daughter but divorced in 1987. In 1988, Hanks wed actress Rita Wilson, and they have a son.   □ Mary Carvlin

Harness racing. See Horse racing.

Hawaii. See State government.

Health care issues. United States President Bill Clinton's promise of "health care that can never be taken away" for all Americans hit a wall in 1994. A deeply divided Congress failed to pass any legislation to reform health care, let alone Clinton's sweeping proposal. Some states that had been pursuing their own reforms also found their way blocked.

The Clinton proposal. In late 1993, Clinton had proposed a comprehensive program under which all Americans, including the estimated 40 million who are uninsured, would receive health care coverage through plans subsidized largely by employers. The program called for employers to cover 80 percent of the premiums, with employees paying the rest. The cost to small businesses would have been softened by federal subsidies. Additional funds, for covering the uninsured, were to be raised through cigarette taxes and reduced federal spending on Medicare (government health insurance for retirees) and Medicaid (government-funded health care for the poor).

The proposal would have required most people to join large purchasing pools, called health alliances, that would negotiate rates with insurance companies. The insurers would then negotiate with organized health plans, such as health maintenance organizations, for the provision of services. Premium increases would have been capped, with the goal of cutting health care cost increases in half—to less than 4 percent per year—by 1999.

In his State of the Union speech on Jan. 25, 1994, Clinton waved a pen and vowed to veto any legislation that did not include coverage for all Americans. But his proposal never really had a chance.

Insurance companies opposed premium caps, health alliances, and in some cases, provisions that would have prohibited them from excluding from coverage people with existing health problems. Some health care providers feared the cost-containment provisions would affect the quality of health care and set caps on earnings. And representatives of small business, notably the National Federation of Independent Business, bitterly opposed the idea of forcing employers to pay for most of the program. Other opponents resented the leadership role that First Lady Hillary Rodham Clinton played in the creation of the plan. Most serious, however, was an absence of support for the proposal among Republican members of Congress and a lack of enthusiasm among many Democrats.

Congressional alternatives. Over the course of the year, several alternative health care proposals were put forward. Representative James H. Cooper (D., Tenn.) offered a plan that relied heavily on market competition to control costs and expand coverage. Representative Jim McDermott (D., Wash.) and Senator Paul D. Wellstone (D., Minn.) led a group that supported a "single-payer" plan, under which one government agency would pay all health care bills and control health care spending. Senator

Robert J. Dole (R., Kans.), then the Senate minority leader, favored milder action that would make insurance easier to acquire but did not address the issue of cost containment. A bipartisan group of senators proposed elements of several plans.

The debate raged all year. A subcommittee in the House of Representatives passed a bill that included some elements of the President's plan. In the Senate, Dole threatened to block any bill that required employers to pay for health insurance. Senator George J. Mitchell (D., Me.), then the majority leader, conceded he did not have the votes to override a filibuster. A new bill from Mitchell and a proposal from the bipartisan group briefly raised hopes late in the congressional session. But on September 26, Mitchell declared health care reform dead for the year.

States working on reform programs of their own had a mixed year. Hawaii and Minnesota went ahead with efforts to expand coverage. But in Vermont, where the legislature had approved sweeping reform, no funding mechanism could be agreed upon, and the program was put on hold. The same thing happened in Florida. As many as 20 states continued to streamline Medicaid, in many cases by requiring families with dependent children to enroll in health maintenance organizations or similar systems.

☐ Emily Friedman

See also **Medicine.** In *World Book,* see **Health.**

Hobbies. See Toys and games.

Hockey. The New York Rangers, who last won the National Hockey League's (NHL) Stanley Cup in 1940, captured it again in 1994. Then they endured a bitter dispute when their coach, Mike Keenan, quit a month after the season ended, citing a contract technicality. The NHL's referees and linesmen struck for 17 days at the start of the 1993-1994 season, and a labor dispute between club owners and players threatened the 1994-1995 season.

Season and play-offs. In the 1993-1994 season, two teams were new (the Florida Panthers in Miami, Fla., and the Mighty Ducks in Anaheim, Calif.) and one had been relocated (the Dallas Stars, formerly the Minnesota North Stars). The best regular-season records belonged to the Rangers (112 points) and the New Jersey Devils (106 points).

In the play-offs, the Rangers defeated the New York Islanders (4 games to 0); the Washington Capitals (4 games to 1); and New Jersey (4 games to 3). The surprising Vancouver Canucks eliminated the Calgary Flames (4 games to 3); Dallas (4 games to 1); and the Toronto Maple Leafs (4 games to 1). Vancouver forced the finals to a seventh game, which the Rangers won, 3-2, on Mark Messier's goal.

That game was played on June 14. On July 15, Keenan said the Rangers had broken his contract because they were a day late in paying a play-off bonus. Within 48 hours, Keenan had signed with the St. Louis Blues as coach and general manager. The

Wayne Gretzky of the Los Angeles Kings, far right, releases the shot that scored his 802nd career goal, breaking Gordie Howe's NHL record, in March.

National Hockey League standings

Western Conference

Central Division

	W.	L.	T.	Pts.
Detroit Red Wings*	46	30	8	100
Toronto Maple Leafs*	43	29	12	98
Dallas Stars*	42	29	13	97
St. Louis Blues*	40	33	11	91
Chicago Blackhawks*	39	36	9	87
Winnipeg Jets	24	51	9	57

Pacific Division

Calgary Flames*	42	29	13	97
Vancouver Canucks*	41	40	3	85
San Jose Sharks*	33	35	16	82
Anaheim Mighty Ducks	33	46	5	71
Los Angeles Kings	27	45	12	66
Edmonton Oilers	25	45	14	64

Eastern Conference

Northeast Division

Pittsburgh Penguins*	44	27	13	101
Boston Bruins*	42	29	13	97
Montreal Canadiens*	41	29	14	96
Buffalo Sabres*	43	32	9	95
Quebec Nordiques	34	42	8	76
Hartford Whalers	27	48	9	63
Ottawa Senators	14	61	9	37

Atlantic Division

New York Rangers*	52	24	8	112
New Jersey Devils*	47	25	12	106
Washington Capitals*	39	35	10	88
New York Islanders*	36	36	12	84
Florida Panthers	33	34	17	83
Philadelphia Flyers	35	39	10	80
Tampa Bay Lightning	30	43	11	71

*Made play-off.

Stanley Cup winner—
New York Rangers (defeated Vancouver Canucks, 4 games to 3)

Scoring leaders	Games	Goals	Assists	Pts.
Wayne Gretzky, Los Angeles	81	38	92	130
Sergei Fedorov, Detroit	82	56	64	120
Adam Oates, Boston	77	32	80	112
Doug Gilmour, Toronto	83	27	84	111
Pavel Bure, Vancouver	76	60	47	107
Jeremy Roenick, Chicago	84	46	61	107
Mark Recchi, Philadelphia	84	40	67	107
Brendan Shanahan, St. Louis	81	52	50	102
Dave Andreychuk, Toronto	83	53	46	99
Jaromir Jagr, Pittsburgh	80	32	67	99

Leading goalies (27 or more games)	Games	Goals against	Avg.
Dominik Hasek, Buffalo	58	109	1.95
Martin Brodeur, New Jersey	47	105	2.40
Patrick Roy, Montreal	68	161	2.50
John Vanbiesbrouck, Florida	57	145	2.53
Mike Richter, N.Y. Rangers	68	159	2.57

Awards

Calder Trophy (best rookie)—Martin Brodeur, New Jersey
Hart Trophy (most valuable player)—Sergei Fedorov, Detroit
Lady Byng Trophy (sportsmanship)—Wayne Gretzky, Los Angeles
Masterton Trophy (perseverance, dedication to hockey)—
  Cam Neely, Boston
Norris Trophy (best defenseman)—Ray Bourque, Boston
Ross Trophy (leading scorer)—Wayne Gretzky, Los Angeles
Selke Trophy (best defensive forward)—Sergei Fedorov, Detroit
Smythe Trophy (most valuable player in Stanley Cup)—
  Brian Leetch, New York Rangers
Vezina Trophy (most valuable goalie)—Dominik Hasek, Buffalo

Rangers appealed to NHL Commissioner Gary Bettman, who suspended Keenan for 60 days.

The stars. Center Sergei Fedorov of Detroit, a 24-year-old Russian, won the Hart Trophy as the NHL's Most Valuable Player. Wayne Gretzky of Los Angeles won his fourth Lady Byng Trophy for gentlemanly play, Ray Bourque of the Boston Bruins won his fifth Norris Trophy as the best defenseman, and Dominik Hasek of the Buffalo Sabres won the Vezina Trophy for goaltending.

On March 23, Gretzky's 802nd career goal broke Gordie Howe's NHL record. Center Mario Lemieux of the Pittsburgh Penguins, another premier player, was weakened by anemia, a result of radiation treatment for cancer, and at age 28 he decided to sit out the 1994-1995 season.

International. In the Olympic Winter Games in February in Norway, Sweden defeated Canada for the gold medal, 3-2, after a 10-minute overtime and subsequent shoot-out. The United States finished eighth, its poorest ever in an Olympics. Canada won the world men's championships on May 8 in Milan, Italy, over Finland. The United States finished fourth. In the final of the women's world championships, Canada defeated the United States, 6-3, on April 17 in Lake Placid, N.Y. ☐ Frank Litsky

See also **Olympic Games.** In *World Book*, see **Hockey.**

Honduras. See Latin America.

Horse racing. At the climax of the 1994 racing season—November's Breeders' Cup races—Holy Bull, the year's best thoroughbred, stayed home in his barn. His owners rested him for the season after he won nearly every race he entered during the year.

Holy Bull ran in only the first of the Triple Crown races for 3-year-olds, the Kentucky Derby on May 7 at Churchill Downs in Louisville, Ky. On a rainy day, over a sloppy track in a race with much bumping, he finished 12th in a field of 14. He was 20 lengths behind the winner, Go for Gin, a sad fate for a 2-1 favorite.

Tabasco Cat won both of the other Triple Crown races—the Preakness on May 21 at Pimlico in Baltimore and the Belmont Stakes on June 11 at Belmont Park in Elmont, N.Y. Tabasco Cat was trained by D. Wayne Lukas. In December 1993, the colt trampled Lukas' son and assistant trainer, Jeff. The son recovered and spent 1994 rehabilitating.

Once Holy Bull overcame a minor leg injury, he was overwhelming. Of his 10 races during the year, he won 8—the Hutcheson Stakes, Florida Derby, Blue Grass, Metropolitan Mile, Dwyer, Haskell, Travers Stakes, and Woodward. He was owned and trained by Jimmy Croll and ridden by Mike Smith.

The Breeders' Cup races on November 5 at Churchill Downs attracted 65 American and 27 foreign horses. In the richest of the seven races, the $3-million Classic, a 3-year-old American colt, Concern, closed strongly and defeated Tabasco Cat by a neck. Favored Cherokee Run won the $1-million Sprint, and Tikkanen of France upset Paradise Creek in the $2-million Turf, giving Smith his 63rd stakes victory of the year, a record for a jockey.

Harness. Cam's Card Shark was the best harness horse of the year. Before the Triple Crown series for 3-year-old pacers, he won the $1-million North American Cup and the $1-million Meadowlands Pace. In the Triple Crown races, he won the Messenger Stakes and finished fifth in the Cane. But he was scratched two minutes before the start of the Little Brown Jug because of a lame leg. He was then retired to stud.

Cam's Card Shark was harness racing's top money-winner for the year with $2,264,714, breaking Presidential Ball's one-year record of $2,222,166. In the year's 18 races for Cam's Card Shark, he won 15.

Falcons Future won the Cane and Magical Mike the Little Brown Jug. In the Triple Crown races for 3-year-old trotters, Victory Dream won the $1.2-million Hambletonian, and Bullville Victory the Yonkers Trot and the Kentucky Futurity. The world record for a 1-mile trot was broken twice by 4-year-olds—1 minute 51⅗ seconds by the mare Beat the Wheel on July 8 in East Rutherford, N.J., and 1:51 by the colt Pine Chip in a time trial October 1 in Lexington, Ky.

☐ Frank Litsky

In *World Book,* see **Horse racing.**

Houston was elated in 1994 by its first-ever major professional sports championship, a seventh-game victory on June 22 by the Houston Rockets over the New York Knicks in the National Basketball Association finals. The win erased years of frustration among Houston sports fans, many of whom had longed for a major sports title for decades.

On June 24, an estimated 500,000 screaming fans jammed the downtown area to attend a victory parade for the Rockets. Unlike victory celebrations in some other major cities in recent years, where celebrating turned to violence, the Houston event was noted for its civility. Only four arrests were made, all for fairly minor offenses.

Education. On January 20, school board trustee Rod Paige, dean of education at Texas Southern University in Houston, was named superintendent of the Houston Independent School District. He replaced Frank Petruzielo, who left in January to lead the school system in Broward County, Fla.

The board's 5-to-3 vote naming Paige was a surprise move and raised concerns about the sudden and unusual selection process. The biggest protests came from the Hispanic community. Hispanics made up nearly 50 percent of the school district's students, compared with 36 percent who were African American, and many Hispanics thought that a Hispanic American should be the next superintendent. Some people said the selection process may have violated

Jockey Chris McCarron tosses his crop after winning the Kentucky Derby aboard Go for Gin in May.

Major horse races of 1994

Race	Winner	Value to winner
Arlington Million	Paradise Creek	$600,000
Belmont Stakes	Tabasco Cat	$392,280
Breeders' Cup Classic	Concern	$1,560,000
Breeders' Cup Distaff	One Dreamer	$520,000
Breeders' Cup Juvenile	Timber Country	$520,000
Breeders' Cup Juvenile Fillies	Flanders	$520,000
Breeders' Cup Mile	Barathea	$520,000
Breeders' Cup Sprint	Cherokee Run	$520,000
Breeders' Cup Turf	Tikkanen	$1,040,000
Derby Stakes (England)	Erhaab	$698,219
Hollywood Gold Cup Handicap	Slew of Damascus	$412,500
Irish Derby (Ireland)	Balanchine	$488,627
Japan Cup (Japan)	Marvelous Crown	$1,123,000
Jockey Club Gold Cup	Colonial Affair	$450,000
Kentucky Derby	Go for Gin	$628,800
King George VI and Queen Elizabeth Diamond Stakes (England)	King's Theatre	$392,306
Molson Export Million	Dramatic Gold	$600,000
Oaklawn Handicap	The Wicked North	$450,000
Pacific Classic Stakes	Tinners Way	$550,000
Pimlico Special Handicap	As Indicated	$360,000
Preakness Stakes	Tabasco Cat	$447,720
Prix de l'Arc de Triomphe (France)	Carnegie	$674,240
Rothmans International (Canada)	Raintrap	$606,900
Santa Anita Handicap	Stuka*	$550,000
Super Derby	Soul of the Matter	$450,000
Travers Stakes	Holy Bull	$450,000

*Stuka won due to disqualification of The Wicked North.

Major U.S. harness races of 1994

Race	Winner	Value to winner
Cane Pace	Falcons Future	$195,890
Hambletonian	Victory Dream	$550,000
Little Brown Jug	Magical Mike	$203,592
Meadowlands Pace	Cam's Card Shark	$500,000
Messenger Stakes	Cam's Card Shark	$171,297
Woodrow Wilson	Dontgetinmyway	$387,375

Sources: *The Blood-Horse* magazine and U.S. Trotting Association.

the state's Open Meeting Act, but the Harris County district attorney said on April 6 that he saw no evidence of that.

Space Center. Houston, home of the Lyndon B. Johnson Space Center, in July honored the center's role in Apollo 11, the first manned moon landing, with ceremonies and events marking the 25th anniversary of the 1969 lunar mission. On Jan. 6, 1994, the space center announced sweeping management changes, including the appointment of its first female director, Carolyn Huntoon.

Crime. The Harris County courthouse in late September ended a record two weeks of trials in which prosecutors had sought the death penalty. Four of six defendants received death sentences, and the other two were sentenced to life in prison.

Three of the four sentenced to die by lethal injection were involved in the June 1993 rape and murder of Jennifer Lee Ertman, 14, and Elizabeth Peña, 16. The brutal slaying of the two girls, who inadvertently came upon a youth gang initiation and were attacked by the gang members, focused Houston's attention on juvenile crime problems. From Jan. 1 to Sept. 19, 1994, 100 youths were certified in Harris County to stand trial as adults—three times as many as in the same period the year before.

Violent crime, in general, however, had declined since 1991. Figures released by the city in September showed that all violent crimes except aggravated assault had decreased in Houston from January 1991 to August 1994.

No downtown stadium. An ambitious push by Bud Adams, owner of the Houston Oilers football team, to get a downtown domed stadium for his team ended in August. Adams had contended that the Oilers' existing home, the Astrodome, did not offer enough prime seating and was too small to lure a Super Bowl to Houston. He envisioned a stadium that would accommodate both the Oilers and the Rockets. But that idea was dashed on August 29 when Rockets owner Les Alexander announced that he had no interest in participating in the deal. After failing to win Alexander's support, Adams withdrew his proposal for a new stadium.

Flooding. About 10,000 people in Houston and southeast Texas were forced from their homes in mid-October during a relentless stretch of rainstorms that caused widespread flooding. Seven deaths were attributed to the floods, which were punctuated by a series of pipeline ruptures that spilled thousands of gallons of gasoline and fuel oil into the San Jacinto River.

Reviving Main Street. Houstonians in 1994 considered an initiative to revitalize Main Street, a major artery running through the center of the city.

Thoroughbred horse racing returned to Texas on April 29 with the opening of the Sam Houston Race Park in Houston. ☐ Andrew Oppmann

See also **City.** In *World Book,* see **Houston.**

Hungary. In parliamentary elections held in May 1994, Hungarians rejected the government of former Prime Minister Jozsef Antall, who died in office in December 1993. Antall's Hungarian Democratic Forum (HDF), led by Acting Prime Minister Peter Boross, lost nearly one-third of its seats in the election. Antall's death had accelerated the loss of public support for the HDF.

The Hungarian Socialist Party (HSP)—the successor to the Communist Party—won more than 50 percent of the vote in the second round of elections on May 29. The HSP formed a coalition government with the Alliance of Free Democrats (AFD), who won about 20 percent of the vote. The election results reflected public dissatisfaction with the programs of reform carried out by the government since Communist rule ended in 1989. Many Hungarians expressed hope that the new government would increase attention to social programs and economic security.

The Alliance of Young Democrats (AYF), whose popularity was rising in mid-1993, fared poorly in the elections. The AYF suffered a major blow when one of its influential leaders, Gabor Fodor, defected to the AFD. Leaders of the Young Democrats also rejected a possible alliance with the HSP.

Prime Minister Gyula Horn of the HSP headed Hungary's new government. Gabor Kunze, leader of the AFD, became minister of internal affairs and was appointed to the newly created post of deputy premier. The new leaders pledged to continue Hungary's transition to a free market economy.

Foreign policy. Hungary continued to strengthen its ties with other democratic European nations in 1994. On February 8, Hungary joined the Partnership for Peace, a new North American Treaty Organization (NATO) program of cooperation with nations that had belonged to the Warsaw Pact, the military alliance led by the former Soviet Union. On April 1, Hungary became the first post-Communist nation to apply for membership in the European Union (formerly European Community). After the election, Horn and other leaders of the new government pledged their continued commitment to these relationships with the West.

Hungary's leaders continued to express concern over the treatment of ethnic Hungarians in Slovakia and Romania. The issue has soured Hungary's relations with the bordering nations in recent years. Horn's government responded positively in June, when a new Slovakian government repealed certain laws that discriminated against ethnic Hungarians. Horn also met with Romanian officials in Bucharest, the capital of Romania, on September 5 to discuss a treaty between the two nations. But Horn asserted that such an agreement would only be possible if conflicts were settled between Romanians and Hungarians living in Romania. Nevertheless, nationalist leaders in Hungary criticized Horn's overtures to the bordering nations.

Economic affairs in 1994 were dominated by concern over Hungary's increasing national debt, estimated at nearly $2 billion by mid-year. In August, the Hungarian central bank devalued its currency, the forint, by 8 percent in an attempt to reduce the country's debt and increase exports, which dropped during the first half of the year. It was the fifth time in 1994 that the central bank had devalued Hungary's currency. The forint lost nearly 14 percent of its value from January to October.

The nation also continued to carry a massive budget deficit in 1994. In September, Horn's government introduced an emergency program to reduce the deficit and began negotiations with leaders of trade unions and industries to establish guidelines for wage increases.

Despite the growing debt, Hungary's economy in 1994 remained one of the strongest among post-Communist nations. Industrial production grew during the first half of 1994. Unemployment continued to drop—by June, it had fallen to about 11 percent. Investment from foreign nations also remained steady, and Hungary's trade with Western nations continued to expand. But privatization of large state enterprises proceeded slowly in 1994, and government-owned businesses still dominated Hungary's economy. □ Sharon L. Wolchik

See also **Europe** (Facts in brief table). In *World Book,* see **Hungary.**

Hunter, Holly (1958-   ), won the Academy Award for best actress in March 1994 for her role as a mute woman who communicates through her music in the motion picture *The Piano* (1993). The film also earned Hunter the best-actress award at the 1993 Cannes International Film Festival in France.

Hunter was born on March 20, 1958, in Atlanta, Ga., and raised on a farm nearby. By age 10, she was an ardent piano student, and at 16 she was invited to act in a professional summer troupe. She graduated from Carnegie Mellon University in Pittsburgh, Pa., in 1980, with a major in acting. She made her Broadway debut a year later in Beth Henley's Pulitzer Prize-winning Southern drama *Crimes of the Heart* (1981).

Hunter's first major film role was in a wacky comedy, *Raising Arizona* (1987). She won an Academy Award nomination for best actress for her role as a television news producer in *Broadcast News* (1987). Hunter won Emmys for her roles in two television movies, *Roe vs. Wade* (1989) and *The Positively True Adventures of the Alleged Texas Cheerleader-Murdering Mom* (1993). Hunter also earned an Academy Award nomination in 1994 for best supporting actress for her role in *The Firm* (1993).

Hunter is said to be intensely energetic, hardworking, and innovative. She plays diverse roles, often defying Hollywood stereotypes both personally and professionally. □ Mary Carvlin

Ice skating. In 1994, former professional figure skaters participated in the Olympic Winter Games for the first time. The season also saw exceptional performances in the Olympics and a scandal involving the clubbing of Nancy Kerrigan, the top United States female skater. The most dynamic star was Johann Olav Koss, a 25-year-old Norwegian speed skater and medical student.

Figure. In 1993, the International Skating Union, the world governing body, reinstated professionals to amateur status so that they could skate in the 1994 Olympics. They included such former Olympic champions as Jayne Torvill and Christopher Dean of the United Kingdom and Ekaterina Gordeeva and Sergei Grinkov of Russia. Of that group, only Gordeeva and Grinkov won gold medals at the 1994 Olympics in Lillehammer, Norway. Soon after the Olympics, they all became professionals again.

On January 6, during the U.S. Olympic qualifying championships in Detroit, an associate of Tonya Harding, Kerrigan's rival for supremacy among U.S. female skaters, clubbed Kerrigan on the right knee. Although Kerrigan was unable to compete in the qualifying trials, U.S. Olympic officials placed her on the Olympic team anyway.

Russia's Sergei Grinkov lifts Ekaterina Gordeeva during the Olympic pairs competition in February. The pair won the gold medal.

In the Olympics, Oksana Baiul, a 16-year-old Ukrainian, narrowly won the gold medal. Kerrigan finished second, the only American medalist in figure skating. Russians won the other gold medals— Aleksei Urmanov in men's singles, Gordeeva and Grinkov in pairs, and Oksana Grichtchuk and Yevgeny Platov in ice dancing. Torvill and Dean, with the avant-garde style that won the Olympic gold medal in 1984, took the bronze in ice dancing.

Speed. In the Olympics, Koss won the three longest races (1,500, 5,000, and 10,000 meters) for men, all in world-record time. He won the World Cup season combined title for 5,000/10,000 meters. He also won the world all-around title March 12 and 13 in Göteborg, Sweden, and then retired from skating.

Bonnie Blair won the Olympic title in the women's 500 meters for the third consecutive time and the 1,000 meters for the second consecutive time. Dan Jansen, often an Olympic favorite but never before a winner, won the men's 1,000 meters in world-record time. Blair and Jansen also captured the World Cup titles at 500 and 1,000 meters. In August, Jansen retired from skating. □ Frank Litsky

See also **Olympics; Sports.** In *World Book,* see **Ice skating.**

Iceland. See Europe.

Idaho. See State government.

Illinois. See State government.

Immigration. Reacting to rising public concern, federal and state governments moved in 1994 to halt illegal immigration and restrict benefits to people residing in the United States without permission.

Quota on Cubans. On August 19, President Bill Clinton reversed a 28-year-old policy of accepting all Cuban refugees. Clinton acted after Cuban President Fidel Castro halted his pursuit of Cubans trying to leave their island homeland, and thousands of Cubans attempted the hazardous 90-mile (145-kilometer) sea crossing to Florida on makeshift rafts. By July 1, a total of 3,854 Cuban refugees had arrived in the United States, more than the total for all of 1993. With the change of policy, Cuban refugees picked up at sea were taken to camps in Panama or at the U.S. Naval Base in Guantánamo Bay, Cuba. On Sept. 9, 1994, Cuba and the United States reached an agreement whereby 20,000 Cubans would be allowed to enter the United States each year.

New policy on Haiti. Clinton announced on May 8 a change in the U.S. policy of returning any refugee from Haiti who was intercepted at sea while trying to reach the United States. The new policy allowed Haitians to be granted political asylum interviews aboard U.S. ships. After the announcement, a surge of Haitians attempted the 500-mile (800-kilometer) sea journey to the United States. Hundreds attempting the crossing were drowned at sea. Thousands of Haitians were confined at Guantánamo.

Battling illegal immigration. On March 29, Clinton announced a set of rules on political asylum cases, designed to discourage immigrants from filing false claims. The new rules imposed a $130 fee on each person filing an asylum claim and gave immigration officials the ability to quickly identify and deport people with doubtful claims. The former investigative process took an average of 18 months.

Proposition 187, a controversial California initiative aimed at curbing illegal immigration, was approved by voters on November 8 by a 59 percent to 41 percent margin. The initiative would deny schooling, nonemergency health care, and other social services to undocumented aliens. It would also require teachers, doctors, and government officials to report to immigration authorities anyone suspected of being an illegal immigrant.

Proponents of the initiative said the law would save California taxpayers billions of dollars. Critics called the measure racist. On December 14, a federal district judge in Los Angeles barred California from carrying out most provisions of Proposition 187, delaying enforcement of the measure and casting doubt on its legality. The judge ruled that the initiative conflicted with federal law on health and social services and with the federal government's authority to regulate immigration. □ William J. Eaton

In *World Book,* see **Immigration.**

Income tax. See Taxation.

India suffered from an outbreak of pneumonic plague that began in September 1994 in Surat, a city of 1.6 million in western India. The plague, an airborne infection originally harbored in rats, spread panic, causing hundreds of thousands of people to flee the city. A plague during the 1300's, known as the Black Death, killed almost a quarter of Europe's population. The epidemic in Surat subsided after several weeks, but not before it was carried to other parts of India. Almost 6,000 people were infected. The official death toll was 56, mainly in Surat.

Politics and religion. Prime Minister P. V. Narasimha Rao, who had taken office in 1991 with only a minority in Parliament, gained political strength early in 1994. Defections from small political parties to his Congress Party gave him a parliamentary majority. His reforms overcame a financial crisis and aided the nation's economic growth, further consolidating his support. In what was considered an endorsement of Rao's rule, his Congress Party retained five parliamentary seats in May 26 by-elections.

Rao's main opposition, the Bharatiya Janata Party (BJP), which is based on Hindu revivalism, also retained its seat in the by-election. But the BJP's ability to use militant Hinduism for political purposes was declared unconstitutional by India's Supreme Court on March 11. In what was considered a landmark judgment, the court said secularism is a basic feature of India's Constitution, and that any state govern-

A father carries the body of his young son from a hospital in Surat, India, where an epidemic of pneumonic plague broke out in September.

ment that pursued "unsecular policies" did so in violation of the Constitution. The court ruled that the national government could oust such a state government.

Rao's political fortunes turned around in December, however. The Congress Party suffered overwhelming defeats in elections for three state legislatures. In Rao's home state, Andhra Pradesh, a local populist group won 224 out of 292 legislative seats. In Karnataka, the leftist Janata Dal won control of the legislature, and the Congress Party fell to third place. And in Sikkim, Congress, by winning only 2 of the 32 seats, lost control to a local political group.

The election results were widely interpreted as a rejection of Rao's efforts to stimulate the economy by introducing more competition. Poor people felt they had suffered from his economic reforms.

Election reform. During 1994, the chief election commissioner, T. N. Seshan, campaigned for a clean-up of elections. Buying votes, exceeding spending limits in campaigns, and using armed gangs to seize and stuff ballot boxes had become common, as had voter impersonation at the polls. Thus, on January 20, Seshan declared that no elections would be held after 1994 unless all voters had photo identity cards. He also delayed some 1994 elections because incumbent candidates abused government powers in their campaigns. Alarmed politicians tried to restrict his authority, but they were unsuccessful.

Insurgencies flared in several parts of India in 1994. In Assam state in the northeast, militants of the Bodo tribe, who are mainly farmers, attacked Muslims from Bangladesh and Hindus from India's state of West Bengal who were seeking farmland in Assam. The Bodos said the settlers threatened their culture. In July, after a 1993 agreement for Bodo autonomy broke down, militants killed an estimated 100 villagers and others who had fled from earlier fighting to relief camps.

In the state of Jammu and Kashmir, the four-year fight between government security forces and Muslims seeking independence there became more complex. Both government and guerrilla factions were torn between seeking a military victory or a political compromise. On June 19, a Kashmiri leader and Muslim scholar, who advocated a political settlement without independence for Kashmir, was murdered. The unsolved killing raised questions about whether the most militant Kashmiri guerrillas were killing their own leaders, because they were willing to compromise with India. Then, on August 8, the government again delayed Kashmir elections by extending for six months its emergency powers to control the state. The government said that ongoing violence would taint elections, though the overall level of violence had declined from recent years.

Still, India did not allow international human rights groups to visit Kashmir. India has been accused of brutality in dealing with the insurgents. The international human rights group Amnesty International also accused the government of complacency in responding to reports of illegal detention and torture in Maharashtra state. The judge who headed India's National Human Rights Commission called for the abolition or drastic amendment of the 1985 Terrorist and Disruptive Activities Act, which the government admitted in August had been misused in jailing people.

Nuclear arms race. India rebuffed efforts led by the United States to restrict the arms race between India and neighboring Pakistan. A former Pakistani prime minister claimed that his country had nuclear weapons, and a former chairman of India's Atomic Energy Commission said on September 18 that India had a nuclear arms capability. India's defense minister said that the nation's Prithvi missile will be ready for mass production by mid-1995.

The economy. India's central bank predicted a 3 percent growth in agricultural output in the year ending March 31, 1995. The bank also expected a 7 percent increase in industrial production. But critics blamed the government for high inflation and failure to reduce the budget deficit. Critics also opposed government ownership of 75 percent of the nation's industrial assets.   □ Henry S. Bradsher

See also **Asia** (Facts in brief table). In *World Book,* see **India.**

Indian, American. On April 29, 1994, United States President Bill Clinton, Vice President Al Gore, and all but one member of the Cabinet met at the White House with 300 elected Native-American leaders of 547 federally recognized tribes. The White House said the meeting was historic because it was the first time all tribes were invited to meet with the President. Past Presidents have met with one or several tribes at a time. The purpose of the meeting was to discuss tribal self-determination and relations between American-Indian tribal governments.

Native Americans had expressed concern about a 13 percent appropriations cut in the 1995 federal budget for the Indian Health Service (IHS), an agency of the national Public Health Service. The IHS is an important source of care for many Indians, whose health is among the poorest in the nation. At an earlier meeting on April 29, 1994, then Office of Management and Budget Director Leon E. Panetta informed tribal representatives that a budget amendment would restore the $125-million cut.

Chief Wilma Mankiller of the Oklahoma Cherokee announced on April 4 that she would not seek reelection in 1995, because it was "time to make a change." In 1985, Mankiller became the first woman to lead a major Native-American tribe. She has been credited with revitalizing the Oklahoma Cherokee, who claimed a 1994 population of 163,740, one of the largest Indian tribes in the United States.

American Indian tribal leaders perform a ceremony at the White House where Indian leaders met with President Bill Clinton in April.

White buffalo. On the morning of August 20, a white, female buffalo calf was born at the farm of Dave and Valerie Heider near Janesville, Wis. The birth was seen as a miracle by many Plains Indians, whose prophecies say a white buffalo is a sign of global peace. Sioux medicine man Floyd Hand said, "The legend is she [the white buffalo] would return and unify the nations of the four colors—the black, red, yellow, and white." Thousands of people visited the farm to see the calf, which was reportedly not an albino. Buffalo experts said the genuinely white buffalo is extremely rare.

Banishment. On September 3, Tlingit judges of the Kuye'di Kuiu Kwaan Tribal Court in Kiawock, Alaska, sentenced two teen-aged boys to yearlong banishment on separate, uninhabited islands. They were to live off the land and reflect on the shame they had brought to their people. The boys had been found guilty by a state court of robbing and severely beating a pizza deliveryman in Everett, Wash. The Washington judge had agreed to the request of a Tlingit tribesman to return the boys to their own people for judgment. The boys were scheduled to return to the Washington court in March 1996.

Mascots barred. The athletic board of the University of Iowa in Iowa City announced in April 1994 that Iowa would not play against nonconference teams that used "offensive" Indian mascots. The school would continue to play the University of Illinois, which has a mascot called Chief Illiniwek, because of Big Ten conference rules, but such mascots would be barred from Iowa's campus.

Larry EchoHawk, attorney general of Idaho and Pawnee tribe member, won the Democratic gubernatorial nomination by an overwhelming margin in a primary election on May 24. EchoHawk ran against former Lieutenant Governor Phil Batt, a Republican, who defeated him by a narrow margin in the election on November 8. If he had been elected, Echo-Hawk would have become the first Native-American state governor.

Supreme Court tax ruling. On June 13, the U.S. Supreme Court unanimously ruled in favor of restrictions by New York on vendors who sold untaxed cigarettes on Indian reservations. Federal law had prevented states from taxing products sold on Indian reservations. New York said that the state had lost about $65 million due to non-Indians buying untaxed cigarettes on reservations.

Protest walk. A five-month, cross-country protest walk ended on July 15 with a rally in Washington, D.C., to seek clemency for imprisoned Indian activist Leonard Peltier. Peltier was serving two life sentences for the deaths of two FBI agents on a reservation in South Dakota in 1975. About 700 protesters gathered, some 20 of whom had walked from San Francisco. □ Donald L. Fixico

In *World Book,* see **Indian, American.**

Indiana. See State government.

Indonesia. President Suharto said on March 12, 1994, that he would retire in 1998 at the end of his current five-year term, when he will be 77 years old. He was first elected president in 1968.

Suharto's political control remained strong in 1994. But after a small opposition party, the Indonesian Democratic Party, chose its new leader on Dec. 23, 1993, observers began to speculate on the country's future political course. The new leader was Megawati Sukarnoputri, a daughter of the late President Sukarno, the founder of Indonesian independence. Some observers thought she had the backing of certain army leaders, which might indicate erosion of Suharto's own traditional military support.

Labor troubles. Tensions over low wages exploded in 1994. The government had long supported industrialization, in part to provide jobs for those squeezed off farms by population growth. As new industries opened and the economy grew, the average annual income per person had risen from $70 to $700 over the last 25 years. But most new industries were based on cheap labor. Many manufacturers paid less than the legal minimum wage, which in 1994 was $1.80 a day in the main industrial area around Jakarta, the capital and largest city.

Labor unrest turned into 10 days of rioting beginning on April 14 in Medan, the second-largest city. Factory workers complained they were not paid the minimum wage, and labor leaders charged that police had killed a worker for taking part in a strike at a rubber factory. Workers from 42 factories marched on the regional governor's office to demand an investigation into the death and into low wage practices. Ultimately, the workers turned against prosperous ethnic Chinese, looting 150 of their shops. A Chinese businessman was killed.

Media crackdown. The media reported on the riots, labor unrest, and other problems, including internal government disputes over the purchase of former East German warships. Suharto said that three weekly publications had threatened national unity by such reporting, and on June 21, he closed them down. Many Indonesians then took part in protests against the government, seeing Suharto's action as the end of his promised policy of political openness. Human rights groups worldwide voiced criticism of the government's actions.

On East Timor, a former Portuguese colony seized by Indonesia in 1975, the predominantly Roman Catholic population clashed with Muslim Indonesian troops. But on Oct. 6, 1994, Indonesian officials held talks for the first time with exiled spokesmen for guerrillas seeking East Timor independence.

Earthquakes hit southern Sumatra island on February 16, killing more than 180 people. On June 3, earthquakes struck Java and Bali islands, killing more than 200 people. □ Henry S. Bradsher

See also **Asia** (Facts in brief table). In *World Book,* see **Indonesia.**

International trade

International trade. The United States Congress in 1994 passed legislation approving a broad expansion of the General Agreement on Tariffs and Trade (GATT), one of the most sweeping trade liberalization agreements in history. The expansion lowered tariffs—taxes on imported goods—by an average of 30 to 40 percent. GATT is the main international agreement on world trade, with 125 member nations. Talks to expand GATT, the so-called Uruguay Round of negotiations, had begun in 1986 and were finally concluded in December 1993. The agreement was formally signed on April 15, 1994, at a ceremony in Marrakech, Morocco.

It took nearly a year for the U.S. Congress to pass the legislation needed to implement the U.S. role in the agreement. After much debate and in a special session, the House of Representatives passed a 641-page bill on November 29 by a vote of 288 to 146. A companion bill cleared the Senate on December 1 by a vote of 76 to 24. United States President Bill Clinton had said failure to pass the bill would signal a return to the isolationism of the 1930's.

The agreement replaced the GATT organization with a new oversight body called the World Trade Organization (WTO), which would enforce the new trade accord and penalize nations that violate it. Each of the signing members agreed to reduce tariffs, including agricultural tariffs. In addition, certain import quotas were prohibited by the agreement. For example, Japan, a major rice producer, had banned rice imports from other nations. That ban will no longer be allowed. The GATT agreement also provided for the protection of patents, trademarks, and copyrights.

The debate. Final passage of the U.S. legislation was delayed through 1994 by Clinton Administration attempts to tack on to the bill future negotiating powers for the President and by Republican objections to including environmental and labor issues. Delay also was caused by a congressional procedure that forced the Administration to find federal revenues to make up for the nearly $12 billion expected to be lost because of lower tariffs. Both Congress and the Administration were intent, however, on not raising taxes to pay for the accord, and as a result other revenues were found.

Concerns continued to surface over the power of the WTO. A coalition of U.S. state tax and financing officials viewed the WTO as a threat to their own taxing powers. The U.S. Trade Representative's office, however, successfully stifled concerns over sovereignty by writing into the implementing bill that no GATT or WTO action alone could force a change in federal, state, or local law. In addition, states were promised an active role in dealing with any disputed WTO decisions that may involve state officials.

That guarantee, however, was not enough for some members of Congress who insisted that the WTO was a serious threat to U.S. sovereignty. Conservative Republicans late in the congressional debate wrung further assurances from the Administration. One such assurance allowed Congress to review U.S. participation in the WTO after the first five years of the agreement and guaranteed members of Congress the right to introduce legislation to pull out of the WTO. Further, within a week of the final vote, Senate Republican leader Robert Dole of Kansas obtained a promise from Clinton to create a five-member commission to review WTO rulings adverse to the United States. If three of those rulings over a first-year period were found to be "capricious" or outside the WTO panel's legal authority, the commission could suggest that the United States quit the WTO. Dole's decision to back GATT clinched victory in the Senate.

Japan. Another major effort for the Clinton Administration in 1994 was convincing Japan to open its markets to foreign goods. A trade team, led by U.S. Trade Representative Mickey Kantor, focused on opening up specific sectors that were important for U.S. companies and U.S. export growth. Japanese distrust of the Clinton Administration caused delay in reaching agreement as did three changes in the Japanese government in the span of a year.

By the end of 1994, however, the United States and Japan settled disputes over the construction market and flat glass sales and came to an understanding on purchases of telecommunications and medical equipment. Both sides also came to an understanding on reforms in Japan's insurance market, primarily by streamlining and reducing many regulations. The largest of U.S. insurance companies had had only tiny shares of Japan's insurance market.

However, the market that comprised the major portion of the more than $60 billion U.S.-Japan trade imbalance—automobiles and auto parts—went unresolved in 1994. American attempts to have Japan guarantee more purchases of auto parts and increased access for U.S. cars in Japan fell through.

China. On May 26, 1994, President Clinton extended most-favored-nation (MFN) status to China. MFN status offers a nation's lowest regular tariff rates to the trading partner. The President had extended the MFN for China in May 1993, but had pledged not to renew it in 1994 if China's human rights record did not improve. In May 1994, the President admitted China had made little progress on human rights. But despite harsh congressional criticism, he extended MFN to China again and said future trade decisions would not be tied to the human rights issue. Clinton proposed that closer ties with China would encourage China's rulers to treat their citizens better.

The Clinton Administration in 1994 regarded China as one of the top 10 developing markets for U.S. exports. United States Secretary of Commerce Ronald H. Brown went to China in August, bringing with him two dozen top U.S. executives and signing at least $5 billion worth of business contracts. The United States also loosened controls on high-technology exports to China.

The United States and other nations refused China's entry into the WTO in 1994. Negotiators insisted that China had not done enough to change its restrictive regulations and practices to warrant entry into the group of mostly free market economies.

APEC. At the fifth annual meeting of the Asia-Pacific Economic Cooperation (APEC) forum, held in Indonesia in early November, the 18 member nations, including the United States, set a target date of 2020 for complete free trade among nations on the Pacific Ocean. The advanced nations would drop barriers to trade and investment by 2010, giving developing countries until 2020 to meet that goal.

Summit of the Americas. In December 1994, a summit meeting took place in Miami, Fla., for all the nations of Latin America and the Caribbean except Cuba. The 34 attending nations agreed to create a mutual free trade zone within 10 years. The summit concluded with an announcement by Canada, Mexico, and the United States that they had agreed to include Chile as a fourth partner in the North American Free Trade Agreement (NAFTA). ☐ Jim Berger

In *World Book,* see **General Agreement on Tariffs and Trade; International trade.**

Iowa. See State government.

Iran. The political fortunes of Iranian President Ali Akbar Hashemi Rafsanjani and Iran's economy were hurt when some $9 billion in national debt fell due in 1994. Rafsanjani rescheduled some $10 billion in debt payments, but outsiders guessed that Iran's total debt was twice the $17 billion Iran said it was. Another $5 billion was to come due in March 1995. Iran was cash-strapped because of a steep drop in world oil prices in late 1993 and early 1994. This caused oil revenues to fall to $13 billion in the fiscal year ending in March from $17 billion for the previous fiscal year. Iran's oil revenues usually account for about 80 percent of total revenues.

The Iranian parliament in November approved a $136-billion, five-year budget that would begin March 21, 1995. It called for the doubling of fuel prices. But the parliament, fearing a negative reaction from the public, opposed easing subsidies on food. Rafsanjani, forced to cut imports by 17 percent in 1994, also had to reestablish in May a multilevel exchange rate for many imports. This led to the devaluation of the Iranian rial by nearly 33 percent against the United States dollar.

The population growth rate in Iran, as high as 4 percent in urban areas by some 1989 estimates, dropped to 3.1 percent in 1994. But Iran faced staggering new problems because about 44 percent of its 66 million people were under 15 years old. Iran's education minister said in August that the student

population had doubled to nearly 18 million since the 1979 Iranian revolution, creating a need for 120,000 new classrooms and 65,000 new teachers.

Refugees. Iran's varied refugee population, which fell from 4.1 million in 1993 to only 2.4 million in 1994 in a repatriation drive, remained one of the world's largest and an economic drain. Some of the nearly 1.8 million Afghans who fled Afghanistan after the Soviet Union invaded in 1979 were implicated in drug trafficking. Iranian police seized 74 tons (67 metric tons) of illegal drugs in a six-month period beginning March 21, 1994. Over 60 percent of those drugs were confiscated in a region bordering Afghanistan and Pakistan. Some 100 Iranian policemen died fighting drug traffickers in the year ending March 21.

Violence. Iran blamed the opposition group Mujahideen al-Khalq (MKO) for such acts of violence during 1994 as the January murder in Teheran of Protestant Bishop Haik Hovsepian Mehr, who opposed persecution of Christians. A June 20 bombing at a mosque in Meshed killed at least 24 people and wounded 70 others. Bombs were discovered before they could explode on June 24 at a Sunni mosque in Zahedan and also on July 5 at the tomb of Muslim leader Ayatollah Ruhollah Khomeini in Teheran and at a Shiite shrine in Qom. The MKO denied responsibility for the attacks.

Terrorism. Argentina blamed Iran for a July 18 bombing of a building in Buenos Aires that housed Argentina's two main Jewish organizations. The blast killed nearly 100 people and wounded 200. Argentine officials implicated four former Iranian diplomats in the incident but in August admitted that their evidence was insufficient. Venezuela expelled four Iranian diplomats in July for attempting to kidnap an Iranian exile in that country. Iran denied the allegations. In August, Thailand arrested an Iranian suspect for plotting to bomb the Israeli Embassy in a suicide mission in March. The United Kingdom accused Iran in April of having secret contacts with the outlawed Irish Republican Army.

Island dispute. Iran rejected a renewed plea by the Arab Gulf states in September that it accept international arbitration to resolve a sovereignty dispute over the Persian Gulf islands of Abu Musa and the Greater and Lesser Tunbs. The dispute flared in 1992 when Iran extended its control over Abu Musa, which Iran and the United Arab Emirates had jointly controlled since 1971.

Grand Ayatollah Mohammad Ali Araki, the last Shiite grand ayatollah, which is the highest authority in the Shiite Muslim sect, died Nov. 29, 1994, at the age of 100. Iran declared a week of mourning, and it remained unclear who would replace the grand ayatollah. Shiites make up about 10 percent of Muslims worldwide. ☐ Christine Helms

See also **Middle East** (Facts in brief table). In *World Book,* see **Iran.**

Iraq. Iraqi President Saddam Hussein's deployment of military forces near the Kuwaiti border in early October 1994 raised fears of another military confrontation between Iraq and the United States. The action also hurt Iraqi chances for a lifting of United Nations (UN) sanctions that prevented Iraq from selling oil, its main revenue source, since it invaded Kuwait in 1990. The October crisis receded when Hussein, fearing a military response, pulled back two elite troop divisions to central Iraq after a U.S. airlift of troops to the region.

Reaction. Hussein's ill-timed action stunned even Iraq's key UN sympathizers, France and Russia, who voted with a UN resolution on October 15 warning Iraq not to reinforce its troops on the border. Many observers were also puzzled because monitoring of Iraqi weapons programs, which most UN Security Council members saw as the sole requirement for lifting sanctions, was to begin October 10. Analysts speculated that Hussein was frustrated by the UN failure to set a specific deadline for lifting sanctions.

Russia proposed to the Security Council on October 20 that Iraq recognize Kuwait in return for a guaranteed six-month deadline for lifting the sanctions. However, the United States and the United Kingdom dismissed the proposal and warned Iraq that they would use military force to stop any build-up of forces in a zone south of Iraq's 32nd parallel. The United States wanted sanctions kept against Iraq until it recognized Kuwaiti sovereignty, provided information about 600 Kuwaitis missing since the 1991 Gulf War, and improved its human rights record. The United States has hoped that harsh sanctions would lead to the overthrow of Hussein.

On Nov. 10, 1994, Iraq officially recognized Kuwait. The Council acknowledged Iraq's move as a "significant step" toward dropping the sanctions.

Internal problems. Iraq blamed sanctions for some 460,000 deaths by July, including those of about 165,000 children under age 5. Typhoid and pneumonia cases had risen sharply. Once-rare diseases, such as cholera, measles, and malaria, reappeared. Malnutrition increased 300 percent.

The government began stringent measures to curb rising crime and unrest, announcing June 5 that serious theft would be punished by amputating hands. In July, new restrictions were imposed on public entertainment, liquor sales, and imports. Iraq clamped down in August on black market currency exchanges after its dinar dropped very low against the U.S. dollar on the black market. The government more than doubled a travel tax, required to exit Iraq, in order to increase revenues and slow an exodus of Iraqis. Iraq also cut by half subsidies for food and other supplies in September.

Kurds. Conditions in mainly Kurdish northern Iraq began deteriorating rapidly in May. Supporters of Jalal Talabani, leader of the Patriotic Union of Kurdistan, and Massoud Barzani of the Kurdistan

Democratic Party, who had agreed to a power sharing arrangement in July 1992, fought for dominance. At least 600 Kurds had died in the struggle by mid-1994, and Iranian sources reported another 600 dead in August. Although the United States and the United Kingdom attempted to broker an agreement between Talabani and Barzani, unrest continued.

Oil. Iraq continued to refuse a $1.6 billion, one-time, UN-sponsored oil sale that would provide humanitarian aid to Iraqis. Iraq disliked UN terms for distributing the aid, claiming they infringed on Iraqi sovereignty and might lead to more conditions being imposed prior to lifting sanctions. Iraq also refused in 1994 to accept UN conditions allowing the removal and sale of Iraqi oil sitting in a pipeline that transits Turkey to the Mediterranean Sea. Idle since 1990, the pipeline has deteriorated.

Aircraft down. Two U.S. Air Force jets shot down two U.S. helicopters, believing they were Iraqi aircraft on April 14, 1994, in northern Iraq. The accident killed 26 people from four allied nations who were headed for a meeting with Kurdish leaders.

Lebanon broke ties with Iraq in April. The break came after Lebanon blamed three Iraqi diplomats and an Iraqi Embassy guard for murdering an Iraqi opposition figure in Beirut, Lebanon, on April 12.

□ Christine Helms

See also **Middle East** (Facts in brief table). In *World Book,* see **Iraq.**

Ireland. Strains developed within the ruling coalition of Fianna Fáil (also known as the Republican Party) and the Labour Party in 1994. Disagreements over actions taken by Irish Prime Minister Albert Reynolds finally led to a collapse of the government in November and the installation of a new coalition in December led by new Prime Minister John Bruton.

Renewed relations with Sinn Fein. On September 6, Reynolds met with Gerry Adams, president of the outlawed Irish Republican Army's (IRA) political wing, Sinn Fein, marking the first time that an Irish prime minister had met officially with the Sinn Fein since the 1920's. The meeting came after Reynolds helped negotiate a historic cease-fire by the IRA, which was announced on Aug. 31, 1994.

Beef scandal. Pressure on the coalition mounted in August following the publication of an official report into irregularities in the Irish beef industry. Reynolds had been criticized for providing government insurance on Irish meat sales to Iraq six years earlier during a previous administration. The decision exposed Irish taxpayers to a potential 100-million-Irish-pound ($62-million) liability when Iraq failed to pay for the beef.

Appointment shakes government. On November 11, Reynolds announced his nomination of Attorney General Harry Whelehan to the presidency of the High Court. Whelehan, a conservative

Catholic, was known for his opposition to divorce and abortion rights, which Labour supported.

Dick Spring, deputy prime minister, foreign minister and Labour leader, objected to the nomination because Whelehan had reportedly delayed for seven months the extradition of a Catholic priest accused of child molestation in Northern Ireland. Despite the objection, Whelehan was sworn in, infuriating Spring, who maintained that government appointments should be made by the entire coalition and not by the dominant government partner alone. Reports later surfaced that Whelehan had lied when he tried to defend his actions.

On November 16, Spring resigned, saying that Reynolds knew of Whelehan's false claims and swore him in anyway. The resignation effectively collapsed the government. To avoid a no-confidence vote, Reynolds resigned on November 17. Whelehan also resigned on that day.

Crisis ends. After one month of scrambling to put together a government, John Bruton, leader of the Fine Gael party, was elected to head a new government comprised of the Fine Gael, the Labour Party, and the small, far-left leaning Democratic Left. Spring, who was heavily involved in affairs with Northern Ireland, was reappointed to the post of foreign minister.   □ Ian J. Mather

See also **Northern Ireland.** In *World Book,* see **Ireland.**

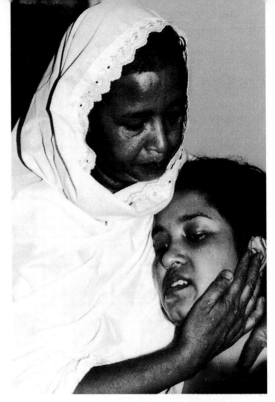

Feminist author Taslima Nasrin is consoled by her mother in August, as she emerged from hiding to face charges in a Bangladesh court for defaming Islam.

Islam. Political events, often accompanied by violence, continued to dominate the world of Islam in 1994. Algerian officials said in August that about 10,000 people had been killed in political violence since January 1992, when the military seized power to prevent the fundamentalist Islamic Salvation Front from winning a parliamentary majority. The fundamentalists wanted Algeria to become an Islamic state. Muslim radicals of the fundamentalist Islamic Jihad and the Islamic Resistance Movement, known as Hamas, opposed Yasir Arafat's Palestine Liberation Organization as the sole authority in the Gaza Strip after Israel withdrew in May 1994. And the terrorist Gemaa al-Islamiya (Islamic Group) continued to disrupt tourism in Egypt, after its military leader was killed in a police shoot-out on April 25.

Malaysian sect. On August 26, the government of Malaysia outlawed Al Arqam, a missionary movement founded in 1968 by Ashaari Muhammad. Malaysian officials accused Al Arqam, which was said to have 100,000 followers, of wanting to turn the country into an Islamic state modeled on Iran. Brunei, Indonesia, Singapore, and Thailand also had banned the movement. In October, Ashaari publicly disbanded Al Arqam. He called for the followers of Al Arqam to return to traditional Islamic principles.

Some Muslim and Roman Catholic leaders joined forces in September to call for delegates to the United Nations International Conference on Population and Development in Cairo, Egypt, to reject abortion. Three Islamic nations—Lebanon, Saudi Arabia, and Sudan—boycotted the conference on the grounds that its positions would undermine Islamic values, such as Islam's prohibition of both extramarital sex and abortion on demand. Some Muslim authorities allow abortion in cases of incest or rape or to save the life of the mother. Contraception is widely practiced in the Islamic world.

Prime Minister Benazir Bhutto of Pakistan, who attended the conference, condemned abortion. However, she endorsed the conference's goals of promoting education and improving the status of women. (See also **Population; Religion.**)

In Bangladesh, the feminist writer Taslima Nasrin emerged on August 3 from two months of hiding to appear before a Bangladesh court on charges that she had defamed Islam in an Indian newspaper interview. Nasrin strongly advocated women's rights and openly discussed female sexuality in her poems and novels. Her latest novel, *Lajja* (Shame), told from the perspective of a Bangladesh Hindu minority, denounced religious extremism. She was accused of advocating abolishing the Koran, Islam's holy book, but she claimed only to have criticized the *sharia,* the Islamic code of law. In May, Islamic militants had renewed their death threat against her. On August 9, Nasrin fled to Sweden.   □ Vincent J. Cornell

In *World Book,* see **Muslims; Islam.**

Israel

Israel. Israeli Prime Minister Yitzhak Rabin, Foreign Minister Shimon Peres, and Palestine Liberation Organization (PLO) head Yasir Arafat all received the Nobel Peace Prize in 1994 in recognition of a 1993 accord between the PLO and Israel that could lead to Palestinian self-rule in the Israeli-occupied Gaza Strip and the West Bank town of Jericho. However, peace was buffeted in 1994 by the bloodiest acts of terrorism by both Jewish and Arab extremists since the 1967 Arab-Israeli war.

Massacre. A Jewish settler intent on stopping the peace process fired an automatic weapon into a group of Muslims kneeling in prayer at the Tomb of the Patriarchs in the West Bank town of Hebron on Feb. 25, 1994. The settler killed at least 29 people and wounded another 150 before worshipers killed him. News of the incident ignited rioting in which 65 people died and some 360 were wounded. Israeli leaders denounced the settler's action, which occurred at a shrine of both Muslims and Jews. Israeli President Ezer Weizman called it "the worst thing that has happened to us in the history of Zionism."

Presumably to keep Arafat at the peace table, Rabin said two days after the massacre that Israel would begin releasing some of its 9,000 Arab prisoners. An Israeli commission investigated the massacre and reported on June 26 that only one gunman had been involved. However, testimony revealed that Israeli security at the shrine had been lax. The settler

had freely entered the Muslim section and was not disarmed because Jews were allowed to carry weapons. Israeli soldiers also had orders not to shoot settlers even if they fired on Palestinians.

Peace. In spite of tensions, Israel and the PLO signed an autonomy pact on May 4 in Cairo, Egypt, giving Palestinians a first taste of self-rule in Gaza and Jericho, occupied by Israel since 1967. A six-year-old evening curfew was lifted in Gaza in June, one month after a newly trained Palestinian police force assumed duties and Israeli troops left. An Aug. 24, 1994, agreement allowed greater Arab control over education, tax collection, and social services.

Israel and Jordan exchanged ratified copies of a peace treaty between their countries on October 26. On July 25, they had signed a nonaggression pact in Washington, D.C. On August 8, Rabin became the first Israeli prime minister to visit Jordan as he and King Hussein I celebrated the establishment of phone links between their countries and the opening of a mutual border crossing. On December 11, Jordan opened an embassy in Tel Aviv, Israel, and Israel opened an embassy in Amman, Jordan.

Syria kept open the doors to peace with Israel, though it resisted making concessions without an Israeli pledge to withdraw from the Golan Heights—Syrian land occupied by Israel in 1967 and annexed in 1981. Israel advocated a gradual withdrawal and wanted Syria to state publicly its terms for peace. In

A family mourns the death of one of 23 people who died in October when an Islamic militant suicide bomber blew up a bus in Tel Aviv, Israel.

August 1994, Israel credited Syria for helping to stop rocket attacks by pro-Iranian groups into Israel.

Diplomacy. Peace paid a string of dividends for Israel beginning on June 15 when Israel and the Vatican opened full diplomatic relations after centuries of tension between Catholics and Jews. On September 1, Morocco became the second Arab state other than Egypt to establish ties with Israel, though at a low level. On September 30, Bahrain, Kuwait, Oman, Qatar, Saudi Arabia, and the United Arab Emirates agreed to a partial lifting of their economic boycott of Israel. A day later, Israel and Tunisia announced the exchange of economic liaison officers.

Jewish settlers. After the Hebron massacre, some people viewed the 115,000 Jewish settlers in the occupied territories as a threat to peace. Rabin agreed in February to the establishment of security zones around the Jewish settlements. Israeli officials also ordered five leaders of two radical Jewish groups, Kach and Kahane Chai, detained and 18 leaders disarmed in March. On March 13, Israel banned the groups and arrested Kach's leader on April 3. By September 21, Israeli authorities also had arrested some 10 men, including 4 Israeli soldiers, for allegedly belonging to an underground right wing Jewish group that had been killing Arabs.

Arab violence. On October 9, the radical, pro-Islamic group Hamas kidnapped Israeli soldier Nahshon Waxman and demanded the release of their leader, Sheik Ahmed Yassin, and 200 jailed Hamas members. Rabin demanded that the PLO assume responsibility for controlling Hamas. But on October 14, an Israeli officer, three kidnappers, and Waxman died in a failed Israeli rescue attempt at a location in the West Bank outside of Jerusalem.

Although the PLO rounded up some 150 suspected Hamas sympathizers, fears grew that a split between Hamas and the more moderate PLO could lead to a Gazan civil war. Fears grew on October 19 when 23 people were killed and more than 50 wounded when a Hamas suicide bomber blew up an Israeli bus in Tel Aviv. Officials believed the attack signaled a campaign of violence by Iranian-sponsored terrorists. In April, two pro-Islamic suicide bombers had killed 13 people and wounded some 74 near heavily traveled civilian areas.

Abduction. Israeli commandos abducted guerrilla leader Mustafa Dirani from his home inside of Lebanon on May 21. Dirani was to be questioned on the fate of Israeli Air Force pilot Ron Arad, captured in 1986 and believed to be the only one of six captured Israeli airmen still alive.

The United Nations Human Rights Commission on March 9 condemned *anti-Semitism* (prejudice against Jews) as a violation of human rights. It also called upon Israel on April 25 to ban the mistreatment of Arab prisoners. ☐ Christine Helms

See also **Jordan; Middle East** (Facts in brief table). In *World Book,* see **Israel.**

Italy. Italy faced a tumultuous year politically in 1994. It began when Italian voters broke up the political order that had ruled their country through a succession of unstable governments for nearly 50 years by choosing a coalition of parties led by conservative businessman Silvio Berlusconi. But soon after his selection as prime minister, Berlusconi became entangled in a controversy surrounding one of his businesses. And the corruption charges that he had thrown at political leaders during his campaign came back to haunt him and undermined the stability of his government at year's end.

Election results. The Freedom Alliance, the three-party coalition led by Berlusconi, won 366 seats in the 630-seat Chamber of Deputies, the lower house of parliament, and 155 seats in the 315-seat Senate, the upper house, in the election held on March 27 and 28. Berlusconi's party, Forza Italia (Go Italy), was allied with the Northern League, led by Umberto Bossi, and the National Alliance, a neo-Fascist party led by Gianfranco Fini.

The Berlusconi government. Berlusconi became prime minister on May 11, naming a 25-member Cabinet that included ministers from each of his coalition partners, including five neo-Fascists. This marked the first time since the end of World War II (1939-1945) that Fascists had served in the Italian government. Their inclusion sparked immediate controversy, especially after Fini said in an interview published on April 1 that former Fascist dictator Benito Mussolini was Italy's greatest statesman of the 1900's. In response to the election of the neo-Fascists, the European Parliament passed an anti-Fascist resolution on May 5 to remind Italy to remain faithful to the values held by the European Union.

The Berlusconi government was also the first post-war government not to contain members of the Christian Democratic Party, whose members had renamed themselves the Italian Popular Party on January 18. Berlusconi pledged to fight crime, cut taxes and the government budget deficit, and improve Italy's economy.

Corruption investigations. Although Berlusconi had campaigned against the corruption uncovered by a two-year-long investigation into Italian politicians and businessmen, which was dubbed "Bribe City," he became embroiled in the affair shortly after taking office. On July 13, Berlusconi issued a decree that would end preventive detention in most of the bribe cases, and freed more than 2,000 suspects in the ongoing probe and other investigations. But a public outcry, including the threatened resignation of most of the investigating magistrates, and the opposition of his own coalition partners, forced Berlusconi to rescind the decree on July 19.

Meanwhile, the corruption investigation began to focus on Berlusconi's company, Fininvest SpA, which was Italy's third largest private enterprise in

Italian Prime Minister Silvio Berlusconi pauses for reflection after a debate in May over the competency of his government. He resigned in December.

1994. Several Fininvest executives, as well as Berlusconi's younger brother Paolo, were arrested in July and charged with bribery. Berlusconi had been forced to give up direct control of Fininvest after he became prime minister, because he was in a position to determine national business policies in his favor, but by December, he had not sold his interests in the company.

Government in jeopardy. On November 22, Berlusconi was informed that he was suspected of bribing tax inspectors as head of Fininvest. Soon after, on December 6, Italy's most respected magistrate, Antonio Di Pietro, resigned to protest political pressure he said was aimed at limiting his corruption inquiries. On December 13, magistrates questioned Berlusconi about bribes his company allegedly paid to government tax agents in return for favorable tax audits. Berlusconi continued to deny any wrongdoing. But concerns over the corruption charges began to destabilize the Alliance. On December 14, the Northern League joined the ranks of the opposition. After three no-confidence motions were presented on December 21 in the lower house, including one from the Northern League, Berlusconi resigned on December 22.   □ Philip Revzin

See also **Berlusconi, Silvio; Europe** (Facts in brief table). In *World Book,* see **European Union; Italy.**
Ivory Coast. See **Africa.**
Jamaica. See **West Indies.**

Japan had three different prime ministers in 1994 as its political system continued to change and its economy struggled out of a long recession. Political change had begun in 1993, when the conservative Liberal-Democratic Party (LDP), which had governed since 1955, split and lost power. Morihiro Hosokawa then became prime minister at the head of a seven-party coalition that was in power as 1994 began. However, in April, he resigned, and his foreign minister, Tsutomu Hata, became prime minister. Hata, a former LDP member, lasted until June, when he also resigned, and Socialist Tomiichi Murayama was named prime minister. (See **Murayama, Tomiichi.**)

Electoral reform. On Jan. 29, 1994, Hosokawa pushed through the Diet (the lower house of Japan's parliament) legislation to reform the electoral system. Under the old system, multiseat constituencies pitted party members against each other. Politicians usually sought election by spending huge amounts of money on favors to voters. The money came from corporations seeking political favors. The reforms were expected to shift power in the next parliamentary elections from big business and agricultural interests, which had long dominated Japan's government, to urban and rural consumers.

The reform law also reduced the total seats in the Diet from 511 to 500. Of these, 300 seats went to single-member constituencies, and 200 seats went to 11 regions with proportional representation, where a party had to win at least 2 percent of the vote to get a seat. An independent body was to draw new constituency boundaries. As for campaign financing, each corporation was now limited to giving 500,000 yen (about $5,000) to each candidate, and the government was to give each party a limited subsidy.

Hosokawa's downfall. In February, Hosokawa turned to reforming the tax system. He proposed lower income taxes and higher consumption taxes. The Social Democratic Party (SDP), the largest element in his coalition, and another coalition party opposed his plan and withdrew their support, virtually paralyzing the government. Hosokawa then was accused of taking money years earlier from a delivery company and of involvement in some questionable stock dealings. Denying any impropriety, he abruptly resigned on April 8.

Hata's rise and fall. Hata became prime minister on April 25. He was a former LDP minister of agriculture and finance and Hosokawa's foreign minister. He also shared leadership of the Japan Renewal Party with former LDP boss Ichiro Ozawa, who was widely regarded as the main power behind the Japanese political scene. Hata was elected with support from the SDP, but the SDP left his coalition later the same day, charging that Ozawa had organized other coalition members into a reformist group, known as Kaishin, that ignored SDP interests. Without the SDP, Hata was backed by only a minority in the Diet.

Nevertheless, with tacit support from the LDP and the SDP, Hata was able to get a long-overdue budget through the Diet on June 23. But immediately thereafter, the LDP submitted a motion of no-confidence. Thus, facing a showdown on his weak parliamentary support, Hata resigned on June 25.

Murayama elected. The Diet named Tomiichi Murayama of the leftist SDP as the new prime minister on June 29. Murayama had the backing of the LDP and a small third party. Thus, his government formed an unprecedented union of leftists with their ideological enemies on the right. The LDP, taking most of the Cabinet posts, dominated the new government.

The SDP had a record of supporting the Soviet Union and North Korea, criticizing the United States, claiming Japan's armed forces were illegal, and opposing most of Japan's international involvements. But popular support for these positions was in decline, reflected in the fact the SDP held 70 Diet seats.

On July 18, in his first policy statement, Murayama promised to firmly maintain the security treaty between Japan and the United States and to continue economic and political reforms. Abandoning the SDP's pacifist position to align himself with the LDP, Murayama said on July 20 that the Japanese armed forces were constitutional. He also reversed SDP doctrine by accepting the national flag and anthem as legal. Later, the SDP formally adopted his views.

The governing coalition disagreed on tax reform. The SDP objected to reforms that raised sales taxes, which hit its main supporters, poor people. However, on September 22, the Cabinet agreed to extend a temporary income tax cut and raise the 3 percent sales tax to 5 percent in 1997.

The coalition also disagreed over foreign policy. Murayama resisted pressure from the foreign ministry for Japan to seek a permanent seat on the United Nations (UN) Security Council. Professional diplomats wanted Japan to join the Council as a symbol of its world importance and to reflect the fact that Japan was second only to the United States in paying UN costs. But Murayama was afraid this would involve Japan in UN peacekeeping conflicts, which he argued would be against the constitutional ban on military operations. A compromise was reached, and on Sept. 27, 1994, Foreign Minister Yohei Kono told the UN General Assembly that Japan sought the seat but would not play a combat role in peacekeeping. Forty nations endorsed Japan's bid.

Test of strength fails. In September, Murayama's coalition backed one candidate for a vacant seat in the upper house of parliament in a contest viewed as a test of the government's strength. The campaign was virtually an unprecedented battle between two main candidates over issues, not the traditional fuzzy contests based on local influence and gifts to voters. In a low turnout in the industrial city

Tokyo shoppers stop to watch Morihiro Hosokawa on a giant television screen as he announces his resignation as prime minister on April 8.

of Nagoya, the coalition's man got only 25 percent of the vote and lost to the candidate backed by the opposition parties led by Ozawa and Hata.

New coalition. The election spurred Ozawa to unite the opposition against the governing coalition. On December 10, he became the secretary-general of the New Frontier Party, composed of nine non-Communist parties. Ozawa's party planned to challenge the LDP-led coalition in the next parliamentary elections.

Recession's slow recovery. Japan's economy had slipped to almost no growth in 1992. A slight upturn was noticeable in 1994, but the long recession continued to affect the way Japan did business. Consumers were less willing to pay prices significantly higher than in most other developed countries. Mom-and-pop stores, which had dominated retail sales before the recession, suffered as the government's relaxed rules allowed for more discount merchandising. Companies that had overinvested in new factories in the 1980's closed some factories in 1994. A rise in the value of the Japanese currency, the yen, in relation to the U.S. dollar made it more difficult to sell exports from high-cost factories, so more production was moved to countries with cheaper labor. Labor unions worried about this loss of jobs, though unemployment was only about 3 percent.

Trade controversies. Nevertheless, Japan continued to sell far more products abroad than it bought. Its trade surplus had almost tripled since 1990, totaling more than $120 billion in 1994. The surplus hurt its relations with trading partners, particularly the United States. For almost a quarter-century, U.S. leaders had complained that Japan protected its markets from foreign competition, while taking advantage of free trade elsewhere. Washington intensified pressure in 1994 to get Japan to end trade restrictions. Finally, after 15 months of contentious talks, the two countries agreed on October 1 on steps for more open competition in Japan's insurance market and in government purchases of telecommunications and medical equipment. They also agreed on principles for opening up Japan's glass market. But negotiators were unable to agree on opening Japan's market for automobiles and auto parts, which represented two-thirds of Japan's $60-billion trade surplus with the United States.

World War II (1939-1945) issue. Justice Minister Shigeto Nagano was forced to resign on May 7, 1994, for denying that the Japanese Army massacred Chinese civilians at Nanjing in 1937 and that Japan was an aggressor in World War II. On August 12, Environment Minister Shin Sakurai also denied Japan's aggression in the war, and he too had to resign. On August 14, Murayama apologized for the "tragic sacrifices" that Japan inflicted on other countries during the war. □ Henry S. Bradsher

See also **Asia** (Facts in brief table). In *World Book,* see **Japan.**

Jordan. Braving a road of peace, King Hussein I of Jordan and Israel's Prime Minister Yitzhak Rabin exchanged peace treaties on Oct. 26, 1994. They had agreed on July 25 to end the state of war that had existed between their countries since 1948. That historic pledge was embodied in "The Washington Declaration," signed at the United States White House before U.S. President Bill Clinton and many guests.

The peace was a personal triumph for Hussein, ruler of Jordan since 1953. After Hussein had expressed sympathy for Iraq in the 1991 Persian Gulf War, Jordan was politically isolated and in financial straits. However, the July 1994 agreement gave Jordan a role in administering the Dome of the Rock in Jerusalem, one of Islam's holiest sites, and promises of international fiscal aid. Both Hussein and Rabin, who it was later revealed had met secretly for 20 years, also made a historic joint address to the U.S. Congress. Returning home on August 3, Hussein's airplane traveled through Israeli airspace, circling Jerusalem as Hussein conversed by radio with Rabin.

The agreement. On August 8, Rabin paid the first official visit to Jordan by an Israeli leader. The two leaders met at Hussein's palace in Aqaba and then opened a border crossing between Aqaba and the Israeli city of Elat. Telephone links between the countries opened on August 7.

Other cooperative endeavors were announced in early October. They included plans for a northern border crossing, opened later in 1994, and developing the Jordan River Valley, which separates the two countries. Also being considered were free-trade zones, funding of business ventures and development, and cooperation in environmental problems. Israel also released to Jordan 141 million cubic feet (4 million cubic meters) of water between early August and November to ease a water shortage.

Jordanian businesspeople looked to benefit from the peace. Several launched projects to take advantage of a predicted jump in tourism from 500,000 tourists a year to 5 million. Others speculated that shipping goods through Israel's port cities on the Mediterranean Sea could save millions of dollars.

Peace dividends. President Clinton promised to forgive Jordan some $700 million in debt for participating in the nonaggression pact. Up to $220 million of that was approved by the U.S. Congress in August. The same month, Clinton appealed to 13 nations to ease Jordan's debt burden. The United Kingdom had already converted some $90 million in Jordanian debt to grants. Jordan's debt in late 1994 was about $6.7 billion.

Blockade. The U.S.-led sea-based inspections of ships headed for Jordan's Aqaba port ceased on August 25, after the United States agreed to land-based inspections by Lloyd's Register, a private London firm. Jordan had bitterly complained that the sea searches, which were intended to find material headed for Iraq, had cost their economy $1 billion in revenues. Also, Aqaba lost business as ships unloaded elsewhere to avoid the searches. Hussein had threatened in March to withdraw from the peace process if the issue was not addressed.

Violence. Jordan ordered 21 of Iran's 26 diplomats to leave the country five days after a January 29 slaying of Jordan's second-ranking diplomat in Beirut, Lebanon. Jordan feared Iranian links to Islamic extremist groups opposed to Jordan's peace talks with Israel. However, Jordan later blamed the murder of its diplomat on the Palestinian Fatah Revolutionary Council (FRC), headed by terrorist Abu Nidal. At least 28 FRC members were arrested during February and March and others were sought. FRC, which opposes the Arab-Israeli peace talks, denied responsibility for the murder.

Jordan blamed Islamic terrorists for the bombings of two cinemas in early February. Officials announced in June that 25 Islamic extremists would be tried for the bombings and for plotting to assassinate prominent Jordanians. On December 21, eleven of the extremists were sentenced to death.

Diplomacy. Jordan, which has 62,000 Roman Catholics, and the Vatican established diplomatic ties on March 3. Hussein also improved relations with Arab nations that resented Jordan's position in the 1991 Gulf War. □ Christine Helms

See also **Middle East** (Facts in brief table). In *World Book,* see **Jordan.**

Judaism. Five major issues in 1994 dominated American Judaism's threee main branches—Orthodox, Conservative, and Reform. The issues were interfaith marriage, homosexuality, spirituality, *anti-Semitism* (prejudice againt Jews), and peace in the Middle East.

Interfaith marriages. The religious wings of the American Jewish community struggled to decrease the rate of marriages between Jews and Gentiles, citing intermarriage as a cause of the decline in the number of religious Jews. Since 1985, one in two Jews who marry has married a Gentile, and most of the Gentiles did not convert to Judaism, according to the 1990 National Jewish Population Survey. Only 28 percent of the children of these mixed marriages were being raised as Jews, according to the survey. Orthodox congregations in 1994 sought ways to encourage marriage only within the faith. Reform synagogues of the Union of American Hebrew Congregations encouraged interfaith married couples to join in synagogue life. And congregations within the United Synagogue of Conservative Judaism encouraged the conversion to Judaism of a spouse without religious ties.

Sexual issues. The 1,400-member Rabbinical Assembly, an organization of rabbis serving Conservative congregations, debated a seventh version of a controversial "Jewish Pastoral Letter on Human Sexuality." The letter dealt with such issues as sex without marriage, homosexuality, AIDS, masturbation, and abortion. The letter said that in cases where couples form "committed loving relationships between mature people," sex between unmarried adults "can embody a measure of holiness." However, on October 23, the executive council decided to have the Assembly's Jewish law committee review such issues as gay and lesbian union rites and ordaining homosexuals to the rabbinate. The council was to vote on the revised letter in January 1995.

The Rabbinical Council of America, an organization of Orthodox rabbis, reaffirmed in 1994 its position that homosexual acts are "immoral and repugnant." Reform synagogues continued to welcome gay and lesbian couples, but their leaders also struggled over whether to perform public ceremonies for homosexual unions and whether to allow sexually active homosexuals to be rabbis or cantors.

Spirituality was a major issue for American Judaism in 1994. Some scholars defined it as inner peace, others as a relationship to something greater than oneself. Congregations that sought to make worship more spiritual redesigned their pulpits, enhanced prayers, rewrote liturgies, and encouraged retreats. Spirituality drew the national spotlight in June, when an independent Cincinnati, Ohio, congregation, which was "committed to spiritual exploration" but rejected references to God in its liturgy, applied for admission to the Reform movement's 865-member Union of American Hebrew Congregations (UAHC). The UAHC constitution does not mention specific tests of belief, but other local synagogues, the Reform movement's regional board, the national rabbinical organization, and the Union all rejected the application.

Anti-Semitism. Some leaders of the Nation of Islam, a Muslim sect for African Americans, toured black colleges and universities in 1994 and delivered lectures that many in the Jewish community regarded as anti-Semitic. Throughout the year, Jews sought ways to build better relationships with blacks.

The Middle East and the quest for peace there reportedly appeared in rabbinical sermons in 1994 more frequently than any other topic. Rabbis expressed concern for Jews in the occupied territories and the threat that Islamic militants posed in the newly independent Palestinian regions of Gaza and Jericho. Tensions rose in February, when an Israeli Jew opened fire in a Hebron mosque, killing 29 Muslims, and in October, when a militant Muslim set off a bomb in a Tel Aviv bus, killing 22 Jews and himself. But hopes also rose in October, when Israel signed a peace treaty with Jordan. □ Marc Lee Raphael

In *World Book,* see **Jews; Judaism.**

Kampuchea. See Cambodia.

Kansas. See State government.

Kazakhstan. See Commonwealth of Independent States.

Kentucky. See State government.

Kerrigan, Nancy

Kerrigan, Nancy (1969-   ), overcame an assault to her right knee to win, on Feb. 25, 1994, the silver medal for women's figure skating at the Winter Olympic Games in Lillehammer, Norway. Kerrigan had been attacked on January 6, while competing for the United States Figure Skating Championships in Detroit, a qualifying event for the Olympics. (See **Ice skating; Olympic Games; Sports.**)

Kerrigan was born Oct. 13, 1969, in Woburn, Mass. Her father, Dan, a welder, and her mother, Brenda, who became blind when Kerrigan was a baby, already had two sons, Mark and Michael. Kerrigan took her first skating lessons at age 6, and as coaches and judges began recognizing her athletic ability, her father worked extra jobs to pay for advanced lessons.

Kerrigan began skating competitively in 1987, when she placed third in the New England junior championships. In 1989, she won the bronze medal at the World University Games and at the U.S. Olympic Festival. She won the gold medal at the 1990 U.S. Olympic Festival. In 1991, she was the bronze medalist at the U.S. championships and the world championships. Kerrigan was the silver medalist at both of these events in 1992, and she won the bronze medal at the 1992 Winter Olympics in Albertville, France. In January 1993, she won the U.S. championships, and in October placed first at the Piruetten competition in Norway.   □ Carol L. Hanson

Kim Chong-il (1942-   ), reportedly became the new leader of North Korea following the death of his father, Kim Il-song, on July 8, 1994. His father had ruled with absolute power since 1948, but began grooming his son for leadership in the early 1970's. Young Kim was rumored to have been the actual leader since 1992 because of his father's ill health. (See **Korea, North.**)

Kim Chong-il was born on Feb. 16, 1942, in Khabarovsk, a city in Siberia on the border of northeastern China. His mother died in childbirth when he was 7 years old. His father remarried in 1963.

Kim Chong-il lived in China during the Korean War (1950-1953). Later, he attended schools in North Korea and in 1960 entered Kim Il-song University in Pyongyang, the capital of North Korea. He graduated in 1964 with a degree in political economy and joined the Communist party, called the Korean Workers' Party.

In 1977, North Korea announced that Kim was the designated successor to his father. The younger Kim then began to be called "Dear Leader," while his father remained the "Great Leader." In 1990, Kim was elected first vice chairman of the National Defense Committee, his first state post. In December 1991, he became supreme commander of the People's Army.

Kim reportedly has three, possibly four, children and is married to Kim Yong Suk.   □ Carol L. Hanson

Korea, North. Kim Il-song, the ruler of North Korea since the state was created in 1948, died on July 8, 1994, of a heart attack at the age of 82, his government announced. His son Kim Chong-il reportedly took over as president as well as general secretary of the Communist Party in Communism's first family succession. (See **Kim Chong-il.**)

Kim Il-song had dominated a police state that taught he was one of history's greatest men. Newly uncovered historical records revealed that he had persuaded the Soviet Union to help him start the Korean War (1950-1953) in an attempt to take over South Korea. After failing, he turned the North into an isolated land that defied international rules.

Kim Il-song focused on building the nation's military strength, presumably to try again to seize the South. Kim's emphasis on military spending reportedly ruined the economy. By the time of his death, many North Koreans were said to be starving.

Kim, called "the Great Leader" in the most intense personality cult of modern times, packed the national leadership with his relatives. He designated Kim Chong-il as "the Dear Leader" and turned over many government and military roles to him in the 1980's. But beginning in 1989, signs of disagreement between father and son appeared, including a rift over the nation's nuclear arms policy. However, at Kim's funeral on July 20 in Pyongyang, the capital, officials publicly vowed their loyalty to the son.

A curious delay occurred in Kim Chong-il's formal assumption of power. Information trickling out of the closed country suggested that the son was in control, but there had long been reports that military leaders and others opposed his succession.

Nuclear negotiations. North Korea stalled throughout 1994 on allowing inspections of its nuclear facilities. The delaying tactics heightened fears that North Korea was perfecting a nuclear arsenal in violation of the Nuclear Nonproliferation Treaty, which North Korea had signed in 1985. The United States intelligence community believed that North Korea already had one or two nuclear weapons in 1993. A high-level North Korean defector said on July 27, 1994, that it had five such weapons and was making missiles to deliver them. A missile had been tested, but North Korea denied having the weapons.

In February 1994, North Korea agreed to permit the International Atomic Energy Agency (IAEA), an affiliate of the United Nations (UN), to inspect its facilities. But in March, it refused to allow complete inspections, including sampling radioactivity at one site. As a result, the United States stepped up planning for military exercises with South Korea, where American troops stood guard over the border. North Korea said the U.S. action pushed the situation to the "brink of war," and on June 13, North Korea threatened to withdraw from the IAEA. On June 15, the U.S. government proposed that the UN Security Council impose economic sanctions on North Korea.

North Koreans mourn the death of their leader, Kim Il-song, in July, *left*. Kim's son and heir to power, Kim Chong-il, poses for a portrait issued as part of his 52nd birthday celebration in February, *below*.

Carter visit. The same day, former U.S. President Jimmy Carter entered North Korea to meet with Kim Il-song. Carter said Kim was prepared to halt the nuclear program and meet with South Korean President Kim Yong-sam to discuss North-South tensions. The Carter visit paved the way for North Korean-U.S. talks in Geneva, Switzerland, on July 8, but Kim Il-song's death delayed the meeting.

The Geneva talks resumed in August and resulted in a preliminary agreement on August 13 that said North Korea would cease producing weapons-grade plutonium and the United States would arrange for North Korea to get $4 billion worth of nuclear power plants incapable of producing plutonium. North Korea rejected Kim Yong-sam's August 15 offer to supply the power plants, saying it would deal only with the United States. On October 21, after weeks of negotiations, North Korea signed an accord committing to inspections only after a significant completion of the new nuclear plants. This meant that IAEA inspections could be delayed up to five years. But relations were tense after December 17, when North Korea said it shot down a U.S. helicopter that had crossed the border from the South. North Korea on December 22 returned the body of a U.S. pilot killed in the incident and released the surviving pilot on December 30. □ Henry S. Bradsher

See also **Asia** (Facts in brief table). In *World Book*, see **Korea.**

Korea, South. President Kim Yong-sam maintained his reform momentum of 1993, his first year in office, by pushing three electoral reform laws through parliament in March 1994. One of these laws ended the practice of uncontrolled spending by political candidates on their election campaigns. In the past, tightly regulated corporations had bribed candidates with campaign donations in order to obtain favorable treatment from them once they were elected. The new law fixed spending limits, created a Central Election Management Committee to monitor the spending, and provided for government subsidies to political parties for campaign expenses.

The second reform law established new electoral procedures, and the third returned local control over elections to cities and provinces. Local control had been suspended after a military take-over of the government in 1961.

Political changes. Lee Hoi Chang resigned on April 22, 1994, after only four months as prime minister, a weak position in the national government. South Korean newspapers said Lee was frustrated with President Kim's domination in making policy decisions, particularly those regarding North Korea and its continued refusal to allow international inspections of its nuclear facilities. Kim took a strong stand toward the North, charging that it was insincere in talks with the United States.

Government officials said that Lee tried to extend

261

the scope of the prime minister's authority, and upon failing, he quit. But the opposition Democratic Party alleged that Lee, who had become popular for his uncompromising stand against corruption in government, was forced out for trying to investigate illicit funding of Kim's ruling Democratic Liberal Party.

Lee was succeeded on April 28 by Lee Yong-duk. The new prime minister had been deputy prime minister and unification affairs minister. He had fled North Korea years before and was noted for his tough attitudes toward the North. But on December 17, he, too, was replaced. The president named Lee Hong-koo as the new prime minister.

Radical student demonstrations for reunification with the Communist North erupted in the South after North Korean dictator Kim Il-song died on July 8. Unification demonstrations are banned in South Korea, and those following Kim's death were widely viewed as being manipulated by the North.

Economic cooperation between the North and South would soon begin, however, Kim said on November 7. South Korean plans to build resorts and factories in North Korea had been announced before the nuclear inspections issue arose in 1993. Kim said the time had come to reexamine restrictions and that he would take "step-by-step measures" to promote joint projects.   □ Henry S. Bradsher

See also **Asia** (Facts in brief table). In *World Book,* see **Korea.**

Kuchma, Leonid D.

Kuchma, Leonid D. (1938-   ), took the oath of office as president of the Ukraine on July 19, 1994. He succeeded Leonid M. Kravchuk, who had become president in 1991 after Ukraine declared its independence from the Soviet Union.

Kuchma was born Aug. 9, 1938, to a farming family in the Chernigov region of northern Ukraine. In 1960, he graduated from Dnepropetrovsk State University with a degree in mechanical engineering. He held various positions in the Soviet aerospace industry until becoming director in 1986 of the Soviet Union's largest missile factory.

From October 1992 to September 1993, Kuchma served as prime minister in Kravchuk's Cabinet. He resigned that position after his effort to introduce economic reforms were blocked in parliament and he received little support from Kravchuk.

During the campaign of 1994, Kuchma promised to boost Ukraine's ailing economy by establishing a free trade agreement with Russia. He also pledged to make Russian an official language. Ethnic Russians make up about one-fifth of Ukraine's population.

After no candidate received at least 50 percent of the vote in the first round of voting on June 26, a runoff election was held July 10. In the election, Kuchma defeated Kravchuk, taking more than 52 percent of the vote. Most of his support came from the industrialized east and south, areas heavily populated by ethnic Russians.   □ Patricia Ohlenroth

Kuwait. Still traumatized by Iraq's 1990 invasion, Kuwait again felt threatened in early October 1994 when Iraq massed forces along their mutual border. The threat receded when the United States and other Western allies swiftly sent forces to Kuwait. But the Kuwaitis remained anxious and foreign forces stayed on. Iraq recognized Kuwaiti sovereignty and their mutual border in November, but Kuwait wanted United Nations sanctions against Iraq kept up as long as Saddam Hussein remained Iraq's president.

Kuwait signed a major weapons deal with Russia in August. Since 1991, Kuwait had also signed defense pacts and made weapons purchases from four major powers. Those countries were France, United Kingdom, United States, and Russia.

Islamic ideals were said to have taken deeper root in Kuwait after Iraq's invasion. On July 21, 1994, Kuwait's prime minister rejected a motion to make Islam the sole source of Kuwaiti law even though 39 of 50 elected parliamentary deputies had signed the motion.

Bomb plot. A Kuwaiti court sentenced five Iraqis and a Kuwaiti to death on June 4 on charges they planned a bomb attack on former U.S. President George Bush during his 1993 visit to Kuwait. Another six Iraqis and a Kuwaiti were sentenced to prison in the plot.   □ Christine Helms

In *World Book,* see Kuwait.

Kyrgyzstan. See Asia.

Labor. The thriving United States economy created more than 3 million jobs in 1994. However, the threat of job loss continued to haunt Americans throughout the year. Medium-sized and small firms created new jobs, but large multinational corporations continued to cut staff and merge operations, which improved profits for corporations but worsened employee job security. Also, serious budget shortfalls in federal, state, and local governments led to staff eliminations. The federal government in 1994 planned to eliminate about 250,000 jobs.

Companies in 1994 sought a competitive edge in a rapidly changing national and world economy by demanding that employees give up previously negotiated wage and benefit increases, accept bonuses and profit-sharing instead of fixed wage and benefit increases, or agree to less costly health care plans. Unions fought these trends, though they showed willingness to reach accommodation with some troubled companies by accepting employee ownership plans and delaying scheduled wage and benefit increases.

Employment and compensation. Unemployment fell from 6.7 percent of the labor force—more than 8 million workers—at the beginning of the year to 5.6 percent—about 7 million workers—in November. The labor force also grew by more than 1.3 million workers.

Compensation for all civilian workers climbed

moderately in 1994. Wages and benefits for all U.S. workers rose 3.2 percent in the year ended in September 1994; wages and salaries alone, 2.9 percent. Wage increases negotiated in 1994 for union workers alone averaged 2.1 percent over the life of the contract. Wage increases have been trending downward since 1992, according to the Labor Department's Bureau of Labor Statistics.

Sports bargaining provided a microcosm of 1994's themes of employers attempting to contain payrolls and workers searching for security. Baseball owners wanted to impose a salary cap on players, which the Major League Baseball Players' Association opposed. Compromise between the owners and the players proved impossible, and the players struck on August 12. Fruitless bargaining then continued until September 14, when the owners declared the season over. And for the first time since 1904 there was no World Series. In December, the owners imposed the salary cap, and both sides filed charges with the National Labor Relations Board.

Hockey feud. The National Hockey League (NHL) attempted to avoid major league baseball's truncated season in 1994. On September 30, NHL Commissioner Gary Bettman ruled out starting the season on October 1 if a new agreement was not reached. But even tough tactics and the lure of playing without competition from baseball's World Series did not break the player-owner deadlock. Issues under debate included many of the same issues being discussed in other sports: salary caps, free agency, and arbitration. Of concern for many was finding ways to prevent small-market teams from losing money. At year-end, the deadlock continued, casting doubt on the likelihood of a 1994-1995 hockey season. (See also **Baseball; Hockey.**)

Insurance industry. In January, the Prudential Insurance Company of America and the United Food and Commercial Workers International Union, representing Prudential's 16,000 agents in 36 states and the District of Columbia, finally reached an agreement on a two-year contract after two earlier union rejections. Weekly wages for workers were improved by almost $21, and benefits were increased by just over $5 a week. The company's control over the introduction and use of computer technology was also confirmed in the new contract.

Freight industry. On April 6, the International Brotherhood of Teamsters struck 22 companies belonging to the umbrella group Trucking Management, Incorporated. Soon after the start of the strike, some of the companies broke away from Trucking Management, agreeing in advance to abide by whatever terms were eventually agreed upon. However, the "big four" companies—Roadway Services Incorporated, Yellow Freight System Incorporated of Delaware, Consolidated Freightways Incorporated, and ABF Systems—which employed

Members of the United Auto Workers union hold a massive rally in May in Peoria, Ill., to pressure Caterpillar Incorporated for a new contract.

the majority of the 70,000 strikers who initially went on strike, could not reach interim agreements.

The main sticking point in the disagreement was that companies were trying to replace full-time workers with part-time workers, who receive little in the way of benefits and compensation. At issue also was the companies' desire to increase the permissible amount of freight they could move by rail.

The agreement, reached on May 6 with the help of the Federal Mediation and Conciliation Service, gave workers an increase of $3.20 an hour over four years. It also prevented companies from replacing full-time workers with part-time workers. In return, the companies were permitted to ship up to 28 percent of their freight by rail. However, if the amount of freight shipped by trucks was reduced, the amount shipped by rail also had to be reduced.

Food industry. In Chicago, the United Food and Commercial Workers International Union ratified in January a 34-month contract retroactive to September 1993 that covered 8,000 employees of Dominick's Finer Foods. The contract called for a wage freeze in the first year, but bonuses of 3 percent scheduled for December 1994 and December 1995. According to the terms of the agreement, Dominick's would also increase its contribution to the joint health and welfare trust fund from $1.48 to $2.10 an hour over the life of the contract.

Keebler Company of Elmhurst, Ill., and the Bakery, Confectionery and Tobacco Workers International Union reached agreement in 1994 on a three-year contract. The agreement provided wage increases and substituted a managed health care plan for a major medical health plan.

In February, Anheuser-Busch Companies of St. Louis, Mo., and the Teamsters agreed on a four-year contract calling for a lump sum payment of $1,250 in the first year, and $1,000 in each of the last three years, together with 40-cent hourly wage increases in the second and third years, and a 45-cent increase in the fourth year. Job security and health care changes were also negotiated.

Garment industry. The International Ladies' Garment Workers' Union reached a three-year agreement with 45 employer associations covering some 90,000 workers in the outerwear industry. Wages were boosted 4 percent in the first year and 3 percent in the second and third years. Employer contributions to the health care fund rose from 7.5 to 11 percent of payroll by 1996.

Electronics industry. The International Union of Electronic, Electrical, Salaried, Machine, and Furniture Workers and the United Electrical Workers, a small group of workers at the General Electric Company (GE), on July 6 ratified a three-year pact with GE, covering more than 51,000 workers. The pact provided 8.5 percent wage increases over the contract's life and six cost-of-living reviews. Part of any increase from the cost-of-living adjustments would go to help cover health costs. The bargainers improved pensions and provided a $10,000 bonus for workers who retire voluntarily in the event of a future reduction in force.

Communications industry. Nynex Corporation, one of the nation's seven regional Bell telephone companies, reached agreement with the Communications Workers of America on a three-year extension of their 1991 contract. The extension gave workers two 4.0 and one 3.5 percent annual pay increases, bonuses for meeting public service standards, early retirement, educational leave, and protection from layoffs and pay cuts. In return, the company planned to cut 16,800 jobs over three years, including 12,800 jobs in two union bargaining units. However, in 1994, Nynex added 700 jobs.

Airline industry. Airlines continued to seek concessions from employees to stay in business. Trans World Airlines (TWA) won the approval in late August of 13,800 employees for a scheduled 5 percent wage boost and the furloughing of 400 food service workers.

In late September, TWA also reached agreement with the Air Line Pilots Association on work rule changes intended to save $30 million for the airline. The airline has lost more than $150 million since emerging from bankruptcy in November 1993 with employees owning a 45 percent stake in the company in exchange for $660 million in concessions.

Changes in the United States labor force

	1993	1994
Civilian labor force	128,040,000	130,679,750
Total employment	119,306,000	122,440,500
Unemployment	8,734,000	8,239,000
Unemployment rate	6.8%	6.3%
Changes in real weekly earnings of production and nonsupervisory workers (private nonfarm sector)*	0.7%	1.5%
Change in output per employee hour (private nonfarm sector)†	1.5%	2.1%

*Constant (1982) dollars. 1993 change from December 1992 to December 1993; 1994 change from October 1993 to October 1994 (preliminary data).

†Annual rate for 1993; for 1994, change is from third quarter 1993 to third quarter 1994 (preliminary data).

Source: U.S. Bureau of Labor Statistics.

Occupations with greatest projected growth

The following 25 occupations will account for more than half of the total employment growth in the United States from 1992 to 2005, according to the United States Labor Department.

Projected number of jobs (in thousands)

Cooks, restaurant	276
Clerical supervisors	301
Accountants	304
Receptionists	305
Food counter workers	308
Teachers, elementary	311
Gardeners	311
Maintenance workers	319
Top executives	380
Teacher aides	381
Marketing, sales supervisors	407
Guards	408
Child-care workers	450
Teachers, secondary school	462
Home health aides	479
Systems analysts	501
Food preparation workers	524
Janitors and cleaners	548
Nursing aides, orderlies, and attendants	594
Waiters and waitresses	637
Truckdrivers, light and heavy	648
General office clerks	654
Cashiers	670
Registered nurses	765
Retail salespeople	786

Source: U.S. Department of Labor.

After more than three years of bargaining, the Association of Flight Attendants reached an agreement with Alaska Airlines in early January on a three-year pact that increased pay but reduced the airline's contribution to workers' pensions. The contract also introduced work-rule changes to increase productivity.

Automobile industry. Although auto workers reached a labor agreement in 1993, the United Automobile Workers and auto manufacturers continued to fence over staffing and the issue of purchasing labor services outside the union. The situation boiled into a strike at the General Motors Corporation (GM) complex in Flint, Mich., on September 27. Workers complained of too much overtime, assembly line speed-up to meet soaring demand, and other related issues. The company also wanted to hire temporary workers, which the union opposed. As the strike began to have ripple effects on other GM plants, the sides reached an agreement that permitted production at the Flint complex to resume.

Union membership. Data released in February 1994 showed that after a 14-year free fall, the number of union workers rose from 16.6 million in 1993 to 16.8 million members in 1994. Almost all of the increase occurred among government employees, as the number of private sector members continued to slide. Overall, membership held steady at 15.8 percent of the work force. More than 37 percent of public employees belong to unions, compared with 11.2 percent in private industry.

Government policy for workers emphasized training funds for young workers entering the labor force and older workers displaced by reduced defense spending, corporate downsizing, or global competition. The federal budget approved in 1994 included $1.5 billion to help laidoff workers train for new careers and $3 billion for training unemployed workers.

Legislation that unions have supported since the 1980's failed again to pass in the U.S. Senate in 1994. The legislation, which would prohibit companies from hiring permanent replacements for striking employees, fell before a filibuster by Senate Republicans. After two attempts in mid-July to end the filibuster, the Democratic Senate leadership withdrew the bill from consideration.

The Administration of President Bill Clinton also declared its support for a thorough reform of the Comprehensive Occupational Safety and Health Reform Act. But the proposals that called for expanding coverage of the act to state and local government workers and for establishment of labor-management safety committees did not get beyond committee. ☐ Robert W. Fisher

See also **Economics; Labor: Unions in Decline; Manufacturing.** In *World Book*, see **Labor force; Labor movement.**

y Job

Mexico

$4 a Day?
NO
WAY!

TEAMSTERS
for Fair Trade

SERVICE
EMPLOYEES
UNION

Send
Job

Tell Congress
NO NAFTA

■ Despite union-led protests, *above,* and major lobbying efforts, organized labor failed in its attempt to block passage of the North American Free Trade Agreement (NAFTA) in 1993. Labor had much greater clout during the 1930's and 1940's, when the nation rumbled with union activity. The 1937 sit-down·strike against Chrysler Corporation, *top right,* broke out amid a wave of union organizing in auto manufacturing and other industries.

266

Unions in Decline

By Richard Korman

Recent legislative defeats for the labor movement underscore a long-term slide in union membership and influence.

United States labor leaders were furious when President Bill Clinton won congressional approval of the North American Free Trade Agreement (NAFTA) in late 1993. The leaders of organized labor, who bitterly opposed the agreement, had supported Clinton in his successful election campaign of 1992. Union leaders attempted to convince Clinton and members of Congress that by removing trade barriers between Canada, the United States, and Mexico, NAFTA would shift scores of U.S. jobs to Mexico, where wages are lower. But despite their protests and political threats, Clinton pushed hard for the trade agreement.

Labor's defeat in the free trade issue and its inability to influence the President and Congress illustrates how much has changed since organized labor's political glory days of the mid-1900's. During the presidential election campaign of 1944, opponents of Franklin D. Roosevelt claimed that he had to consult with union leader Sidney Hillman before selecting a running mate. Organized labor was so powerful that the public and the press had little difficulty believing that Roosevelt had to "clear it with Sidney" before choosing Harry S. Truman as the candidate for Vice President.

Whether Roosevelt consulted Hillman or not, organized labor during the 1940's enjoyed a broad and growing membership. About 33 percent of workers in private business belonged to a union. During the following decades, however, union membership and influence gradually declined, and the decline has gained momentum. The share of nonagricultural workers in unions fell by more than 10 percentage points—from 27 percent in 1970 to 16 percent in 1993. In 1994, only about 10 percent of workers in private business belonged to a union.

What went wrong for unions is a subject of some disagreement. Labor scholars say a variety of factors are behind the decline of organized labor. These include the shift from a manufacturing to a service economy, the failure of union organizing campaigns, more aggressive opposition to unions by employers, and changes in labor laws.

The development of unions

By many measures, American workers have made great progress since the early 1800's, when the first local labor unions were formed. During that time, laborers commonly worked 12-hour days at wages that barely covered the cost of living. Many workers had difficulty feeding their families and saw little hope of ever owning a home.

During the 1820's, skilled-craft workers such as carpenters and tailors banded together to form the first local unions, seeking higher wages, shorter hours, and better working conditions. Most of these early unions were restricted to a single profession within a particular city. The first national labor unions formed during the mid-1800's. Among the most successful was the Noble Order of the Knights of Labor, established in 1869 by a group of Philadelphia garment workers. The organization was founded on the principle of equality among all workers and accepted merchants, farmers, and workers from many trades. In 1885, the Knights won a strike against railroads owned by the American mil-

■ The author

Richard Korman is Associate Editor at *Engineering News-Record* magazine in New York City. His work has also appeared in *Business Week* magazine.

lionaire Jay Gould. After this important and widely publicized victory, the Knights grew rapidly in membership and power.

The leaders of the Knights sought broad social reform, such as improving the treatment of women and blacks in the workplace. The organization also contended that workers would not be treated fairly until the American economic system was radically changed. But most workers were more concerned with basic changes in working conditions, such as the establishment of an eight-hour workday. Differences such as these brought about the gradual breakup of the Knights of Labor.

As the Knights dissolved, however, another national labor organization emerged. In 1881, Samuel Gompers, leader of a cigar makers union in New York City, and other skilled-craft leaders formed the Federation of Organized Trades and Labor Unions. In 1886, several unions from the federation joined with a few Knights of Labor unions and became the American Federation of Labor (AFL).

Unlike the Knights of Labor, leaders of the AFL rejected the notion that social reform was needed to improve the status of workers. Instead, the major AFL unions chose to work within the economic system. Their approach, known as business unionism, simply called for better wages and working conditions and emphasized respect for the independence of local unions. In particular, business unionism became characteristic of skilled-craft unions, which made up most of the AFL. By the early 1900's, the AFL had become the nation's dominant labor organization.

From the early days of the labor movement, unions had suffered from a vague legal status—even the basic right to organize a union had never been established. Under these conditions, the AFL struggled with fierce attacks from employers. In 1919, for example, the AFL attempted to organize the steel industry and called for a massive strike against United States Steel, the world's largest steel producer. U.S. Steel accused the union leaders of promoting Communism and quickly won the support of local police and elected officials. The company fired thousands of union sympathizers and the AFL called off the strike. Labor then went into a steep decline, losing nearly a quarter of its members during the 1920's.

The tide slowly turned in favor of organized labor, however, during the Great Depression, the nation's worst economic slump, which began in 1929. As millions of Americans lost their jobs and unemployment reached an unprecedented 25 percent, many people also lost their confidence in business leaders. People began to see labor unions as a positive force for improving the nation's economy. This change in public sentiment helped elect members of Congress who were sympathetic to workers.

Key labor laws

During the 1930's, Congress enacted two laws that were particularly important in securing basic rights for workers and labor unions. The Norris-La Guardia Act, passed in 1932, limited the power of federal courts to interfere in labor disputes. Prior to the law, courts had regu-

Glossary

Craft union: A labor union made up of skilled workers in a particular trade, such as carpentry or plumbing.

Industrial union: A labor union made up of skilled and unskilled workers in the same industry.

Labor union: An association of workers who aim to improve their working conditions and economic position.

Local union: The smallest unit of labor organization, which represents workers in a specific plant, city, or other area.

National union: An association of local unions with common interests.

Organized labor: Any association of workers or all labor unions collectively.

Organizing campaign: The process of bringing workers together into a labor union.

Strike: A protest in which employees refuse to work until their employer meets certain demands, such as higher wages.

The Rise and Fall of Organized Labor

Union membership grew rapidly during the 1930's and 1940's. At its peak in the mid-1940's, about 36 percent of U.S. workers belonged to a union. During those years, Congress passed legislation that favored organized labor. Since the late 1940's, the percentage of the work force represented by unions has steadily dropped as labor suffered under changing economic and political conditions.

Percentage of the work force in unions

1947 The Taft-Hartley Act placed broad restrictions on union activities and increased the rights of employers in labor disputes.

1935 The Wagner Act guaranteed the right of workers to organize unions and established the National Labor Relations Board.

1939–1945 World War II brought increased industrial growth and new cooperation between unions and the U.S. government.

1932 The Norris-La Guardia Act established new protection for unions by limiting the power of federal courts in labor union disputes.

1938 Dynamic labor leader John L. Lewis left the AFL to create the independent CIO with other former AFL union leaders.

1955 The AFL and CIO merged, and George Meany, *left*, with arm raised, became the first AFL-CIO president.

1930   1935   1940   1945   1950   1955

1962 President John F. Kennedy granted federal employees the right to organize and bargain collectively, but not to strike.

1981 President Ronald Reagan fired most of the nation's federal air traffic controllers for striking illegally.

1994 A bill to prohibit employers from permanently replacing striking workers was blocked in Congress by a Republican-led filibuster.

1993 The North American Free Trade Agreement (NAFTA) passed in Congress, despite an organized labor campaign to block its approval.

1970's–1980's Hundreds of unionized factories in the United States closed, as manufacturers moved their production facilities to countries where labor costs were low.

1992 The United Auto Workers abandoned a major strike against Caterpillar, Incorporated, in Peoria, Ill., fearing that the company would hire replacement workers.

1965   1970   1975   1980   1985   1990   1993

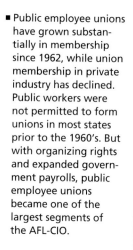

■ Public employee unions have grown substantially in membership since 1962, while union membership in private industry has declined. Public workers were not permitted to form unions in most states prior to the 1960's. But with organizing rights and expanded government payrolls, public employee unions became one of the largest segments of the AFL-CIO.

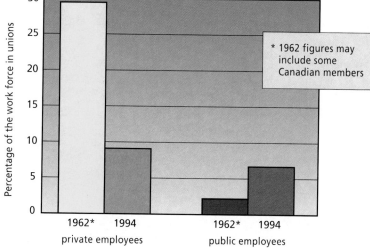

Changes in union membership in private and public industry

Percentage of the work force in unions

* 1962 figures may include some Canadian members

1962* 1994
private employees

1962* 1994
public employees

larly ordered strikers to return to work. The courts had also supported some employers' requirement that workers sign a pledge not to join a union. In 1935, Congress passed the National Labor Relations Act, also called the Wagner Act. This act guaranteed the right of workers to organize unions without restrictions from employers. The act also called for the creation of the National Labor Relations Board (NLRB) to investigate unfair labor practices by either employers or labor unions and to help settle labor disputes.

In this changing political and legal environment, a rival to the AFL emerged. Many labor leaders and workers had become dissatisfied with the AFL. They claimed that the AFL did not adequately represent the increasing number of unskilled workers employed in growing industries such as steel and automobile manufacturing. In 1935, John L. Lewis, president of the United Mine Workers (UMW), and the leaders of several other unions formed the Committee for Industrial Organization (CIO), but remained part of the AFL.

In a short period, the CIO won remarkable victories in the steel industry, and membership in CIO unions boomed. The committee also promoted a major organizing effort in the automobile industry. In 1936, the United Auto Workers (UAW)—a newly formed member of the CIO—called a sit-down strike in Flint, Mich., against the General Motors Corporation (GM), which had opposed the union. In response to the strike, GM recognized the UAW. This victory led to successful organizing campaigns at other automakers and in other mass-production industries.

As the CIO unions became more powerful, the AFL began to see them as a threat to its dominance over organized labor. In 1938, the AFL expelled the CIO unions, which immediately joined to form the Congress of Industrial Organizations. Lewis became its first president.

World War II (1939-1945) marked another period of change for the labor movement. Millions of workers flocked to join unions in industries boosted by the war effort. President Roosevelt and the federal government encouraged union membership, hoping that an organized and contented work force would speed production of American war supplies. In turn, labor leaders agreed to suspend strikes and other protests so that the production would not be interrupted.

By the end of the war, however, business leaders had convinced many legislators that labor had grown too powerful. Despite labor's agreement to suspend protests, John L. Lewis led the UMW in strikes during the war. These strikes brought on widespread accusations of labor's disloyalty to the nation's war efforts. In 1946, as the United States entered a period of soaring postwar prosperity, labor unions were determined to ensure greater benefits for their members. Strikes broke out against businesses across the nation, expanding labor's influence even as disapproval of unions grew.

By the mid-1940's, about 36 percent of the nation's nonagricultural workers belonged to unions. Faced with labor's mounting strength, employers went on the offensive and demanded new amendments to labor laws. In 1947, Congress passed the Labor-Management Relations Act, commonly called the Taft-Hartley Act, which banned many of the labor practices that had helped unions thrive during the 1930's.

The Taft-Hartley Act dramatically increased employers' rights in labor disputes. It prohibited certain strikes and other methods of protest and permitted states to pass right-to-work laws, which forbid unions from requiring that all employees of a company belong to the union.

The Taft-Hartley Act did not have an immediate, measurable impact on the labor movement, however, and union membership and influence continued to grow. As the nation continued to prosper, businesses tended to accommodate unions with generous wage increases and benefits. Unions secured dramatically increased buying power for their members, and many workers reached a comfortable standard of living.

By the mid-1950's, the AFL and CIO endorsed remarkably similar agendas. One of the traditional differences between the two organizations had been their attitude toward Communism. Unlike the anti-Communist AFL, the CIO had included some radical leftist leaders, whose beliefs added an element of social reform to the CIO agenda. But during the late 1940's, in response to the intense anti-Communist sentiment that was sweeping the nation, CIO leaders turned against the organization's radical left. In 1949 and 1950, the CIO expelled 11 unions for being Communist-led. In 1955, the two old rivals merged, forming the AFL-CIO.

The modern decline

The formation of the AFL-CIO may have seemed like a new beginning for organized labor. But the 1950's actually marked a period of decline that has continued through today. As the nation's population increased from 1955 to 1965, the unions' share of the work force thinned. During that period, the percentage of nonagricultural workers who belonged to unions dropped from 33 percent to 28 percent.

During the early 1970's, losses in organized labor's membership became more obvious, as the nation's economy shifted from a manufacturing to a service economy. As early as the 1950's, service industries had begun to employ a growing percentage of the work force. These industries produced white-collar jobs in areas such as government, technology, health care, and education. White-collar workers tended to avoid unions because they were usually well paid and did not want to be represented by a blue-collar movement.

Unions in manufacturing industries reflected this shift to a service economy, shrinking by about 1 million members—about 11 percent of their total membership—from 1974 to 1978. In manufacturing, American labor unions had become victims of their own success. From 1950 to 1965, average hourly earnings for production workers rose by as much as 100 percent, and many unions vastly expanded the benefits their members received. The dramatic wage increases were partly due to inflation, brought on by the nation's economic prosperity. But higher labor costs meant that foreign companies, with their low-wage work forces, could challenge the dominance of American manufacturers.

In response to foreign competition, American businesses began to relocate their production facilities to low-wage areas of the United States and to other nations where labor costs were low. During the 1970's and 1980's, manufacturers closed hundreds of factories in the United States and opened new plants in such countries as Mexico, South Korea, and Taiwan. These plant closings cost thousands of union jobs. And as unions failed to organize in growing industries, membership continued to slide.

Since 1983, total union membership has declined by about 2.2 million, recording losses in every industry except services. By the end of 1993, unions represented only about 16 percent of the nation's work force. Only public employee unions, which were not permitted to organize in much of the United States until the 1960's, showed any significant growth.

Behind the decline

Many labor scholars suggest that union leaders themselves carry much of the blame for the decline of organized labor. Unions suffer today, these experts argue, partly because of decisions that labor leaders made before the decline began. During the late 1940's, for example, the CIO failed in a major drive to organize workers in the South, where there were few unions. In the following decades, the Southern states became a safe haven for businesses avoiding unionization.

Even more serious, however, were charges of labor union corruption. In 1957, a Senate committee held hearings that produced sensational revelations of illegal activities among labor leaders. They found that officials of some labor organizations fixed union elections, stole union funds, and had connections with organized crime. In 1959, Congress passed the Labor-Management Reporting and Disclosure Act, also called the Landrum-Griffin Act, which regulated the activities of union officials.

■ Union workers and managers at an assembly plant for the Saturn automobile in Spring Hill, Tenn., hold a team meeting in which both groups influence company decisions. The cooperative agreement between Saturn management and the United Auto Workers union represents one of organized labor's new strategies for survival in a changing economy.

As the government's watchdog role increased, employers also began to oppose unions more aggressively. The growth of large, multinational corporations that control businesses in a variety of industries and countries helped further this trend. From 1960 to 1980, the number of manufacturing corporations with assets of $1 billion or more rose from 28 to 212. Such massive corporations were much less sensitive to the impact of a strike in one location or among one group of workers.

Employers recognized their growing leverage in labor relations. Beginning in the high-inflation period of the late 1960's, they increased their confrontation with unions. Business leaders sought and won concessions from unions on wages, benefits, work rules, and job security. Cost-of-living wage increases, once automatic, became rare.

The mounting resistance of employers to organized labor exposed what some see as weaknesses in labor law. According to union leaders and some labor scholars, labor law—and the way it is currently enforced—gives employers an unfair advantage in labor relations. For example, many employers have thwarted organizing efforts by firing workers who lead the drive. This is an illegal practice, but employers who do so are subject only to relatively mild penalties, which are much less expensive than the long-term costs of bargaining with a union. Moreover, the ability of unions to respond to such practices is limited by the provisions of the Taft-Hartley Act. Unions must appeal to the NLRB, and the conflict can take years to resolve.

The usefulness of a strike as an economic weapon against even small- or moderate-sized companies also dwindled as employers simply began to hire replacement workers. In 1981, newly elected President Ronald Reagan sent one of the strongest antiunion signals in the history of the labor movement. He fired about 12,000 unionized air traffic controllers, who were conducting an illegal strike, and his Administration hired new ones to take their place. Another large-scale union defeat occurred in 1992, when a UAW strike against Caterpillar Incorporated, based in Peoria, Ill., ended with nothing more than the promise of government mediation. Caterpillar had threatened to hire permanent replacements for the strikers.

The practice of hiring replacement workers is legal during economic strikes, which are called for better wages and benefits. Employers, however, cannot hire replacement workers during a union organizing drive. But many union activists believe the practice should be illegal in any situation. In 1994, President Clinton endorsed a bill that would ban employers from hiring permanent replacement workers. A filibuster led by Senate Republicans blocked passage of the bill.

As union leaders fight for their right to strike and organize, some evidence indicates that many workers are not even interested in union representation. Studies show that U.S. workers as a whole have mixed feelings toward unions, and distrust of unions runs high among many groups. Some labor scholars have suggested that the waning interest in unions is related to expanded legal rights and options for individual employees, including protection against arbitrary firings and against racial or sexual harassment.

In the search for answers to labor's dilemma, many labor leaders have begun to endorse a change in traditional union strategies. Some promote cooperation with employers in exchange for greater participation in company operations. Several manufacturers have established workplace teams, in which union officials and company managers work together to improve both production techniques and workers' job satisfaction. Critics of this approach, however, argue that unions are effective only because they fight openly with employers.

Many union leaders who believe the strike is an outdated approach

■ Union members demonstrate outside the White House in Washington, D.C., in support of the Workplace Fairness Bill, which would bar employers from hiring replacement workers during most strikes. The bill had President Bill Clinton's support but was blocked in Congress by a Republican-led filibuster.

have tried other methods of pressuring employers. These include carrying out public relations campaigns aimed at embarrassing large companies, filing environmental lawsuits against businesses that might be committing a violation, and calling in safety inspectors. In some cases, these pressure tactics have helped unions win concessions.

Role for the federal government?

The federal government may also play a role in helping regenerate the labor movement. President Clinton's Commission on the Future of Worker-Management Relations, called the Dunlop Commission, is expected to recommend measures that will make it easier for unions to organize, while also calling for greater labor-management cooperation. NLRB Chairman William B. Gould IV has also advocated changing labor laws to make it easier for unions to organize.

Many union supporters argue that the decline of organized labor has hurt the nation's economy. They say that unions boost the wages, benefits, and the standard of living of union employees and their nonunion colleagues. They point out that during the last 20 years, average wages have not kept pace with cost of living increases. Furthermore, the gap between the wealthy and the poor has steadily widened. Critics of organized labor agree that unions raise wages, but they claim that wages only go up for a small percentage of workers while reducing the total number of available jobs. Since the mid-1980's, they argue, the unemployment rate has dropped as unions have steadily lost their grip on the American workplace.

Labor scholars tend to agree that diminished unions and a transformed economy have created a much more flexible labor market. Workers have less protection from layoffs or wage cuts. But workers are also more likely to switch jobs, potentially for greater rewards, these experts say. The number of self-employed workers has been gradually rising as well. Those with desirable or more versatile skills are more likely to succeed.

During the course of its history, organized labor in America has risen and fallen with the cycles of economic growth and decline. And unions have recovered after periods of great weakness, such as the 1920's. But some labor scholars remain certain that as the economy continues to shift to service industries and more workers become self-employed, legislation rather than unions will protect workers' rights. Frances Perkins, secretary of labor under President Franklin D. Roosevelt, once declared, "I'd rather have a law than a union." That may be just what U.S. workers will get. ■ ■ ■

For further reading:

Bernstein, Aaron. "Why America Needs Unions, But Not the Kind It Has Now." *Business Week*, May 23, 1994, p. 70.

Dulles, Foster R., and Dubofsky, M. *Labor in America: A History.* 4th ed. Harlan Davidson, 1984.

Geoghegan, Thomas. *Which Side Are You On?* Farrar, Straus & Giroux, 1991.

Latin America

Political turmoil in Haiti and Mexico captured world attention during 1994. In Haiti, international determination combined with high-level diplomatic efforts by the United States and a show of U.S. military force allowed democracy a second chance. In Mexico, an Indian rebellion and political assassinations rocked the ruling establishment. For much of the year, thousands of Cubans and Haitians tried to escape tyranny and economic hardship in flimsy rafts bound for Florida, often with disastrous results.

Elections in Mexico and Brazil. Crucially important presidential elections took place in Mexico and Brazil in 1994. On August 21, Mexican voters elected Ernesto Zedillo Ponce de León, 42, of the incumbent Institutional Revolutionary Party (PRI), after the party's initial candidate, Luis Donaldo Colosio, was assassinated on March 23. Zedillo's selection as the PRI standardbearer caused deep divisions within the party over the wisdom of staking the country's economic future on the North American Free Trade Agreement (NAFTA), which took effect on January 1. On September 28, José Francisco Ruíz Massieu, the PRI secretary general, was assassinated. Two federal congressmen from the state of Tamaulipas and a former federal aide to Ruíz were charged on October 6 with conspiracy in the assassination.

On October 3, Brazilians elected Fernando Henrique Cardoso, 63, the self-styled "candidate of optimism." Cardoso pledged to push Brazil's economy into a new period of growth with the help of foreign investment. Cardoso won over a candidate who advocated protectionist policies.

Brazilian business leaders at home and abroad were euphoric over Cardoso's campaign promise to break up long-standing state monopolies in such important sectors as oil, mining, telecommunications, and highway and dam construction. As Cardoso maintained his lead in the polls during the third quarter of 1994, companies traded on Brazil's stock market increased in value by an incredible 77 percent, driven by the enthusiasm of foreign investors and the Brazilian business community.

Sons of presidents. Two sons of popular former presidents won presidential elections in 1994: José Maria Figueres Olsen in Costa Rica and Eduardo Frei Ruíz-Tagle in Chile. Figueres won the presidency on February 6. He was head of the National Liberation Party, which his father founded in the late 1940's to prevent what he said was a threatened Communist take-over. Frei's father was the last elected Chilean president to finish his term before Chile was engulfed in civil strife and nearly two decades of military dictatorship. Frei was elected in December 1993 and took office on March 11, 1994.

Old and new leaders. In the Dominican Republic, voters on May 16 elected 87-year-old Joaquín

Balaguer to his seventh term as president. He took office despite widespread allegations of election fraud. At a time of financial crisis brought on by corruption, Rafael Caldera Rodríguez became president of Venezuela on February 2. The 78-year-old leader had also served as the nation's president from 1969 to 1974. Among the newcomers to high office was Carlos Roberto Reina Idiáquez of the center-right Liberal Party in Honduras, who began his four-year presidential term on Jan. 27, 1994, with a pledge to target corruption and human rights abuses.

Monitoring of elections. The practice of international observers monitoring national elections in Latin America became common in 1994, even in Mexico, long known for its ardent opposition to the presence of foreigners at the polls. Within several small, strife-torn countries, such monitoring has become part of an elaborately scripted peace process, the result of accords between governments and rebels. The accords were often mediated by United Nations (UN) officials and prelates of the Roman

United States marines enter Port-au-Prince, Haiti, in September on a peaceful mission to restore Haitian President Jean-Bertrand Aristide to power.

Catholic Church. In El Salvador, for example, some 3,000 outsiders, including 900 UN officials, oversaw two rounds of presidential election balloting in March and April, the first national elections since a 1992 peace accord which put an end to a bitter 12-year civil war.

Largely as a result of the election monitoring, political parties that traced their origins to leftist insurrectionary movements appeared in many newly elected governments in Latin America. On the other end of the political spectrum, once-discredited, right wing military officers themselves openly entered politics in 1994. In Venezuela, Lieutenant Colonel Hugo Chávez Frías, who led an unsuccessful 1992 coup to topple the country's president and was subsequently jailed for corruption, was pardoned in March 1994 and immediately began organizing a political party. In Guatemala, the party of a discredited general, Efraín Ríos Montt, who had seized

power in 1982 only to be overthrown 18 months later, won nearly half the seats on Aug. 14, 1994, in the nation's newly elected Congress. The legislative victories positioned the general for a possible legitimate bid for power in 1995.

Strengthened commercial ties. The United States benefited in 1994 from the trend toward trade liberalization throughout Latin America. By mid-September, trade analysts calculated that U.S. exports to the region were growing at three times the pace of those to other regions of the world. If the trend continued, U.S. exports to Latin America would surpass those to Western Europe by the year 2000.

Mining rush. Foreign mining companies rushed to gain a foothold in Latin America in 1994. The region was "fast becoming the world's largest mining economy," according to Eul-Soo Pang, director of the International Institute of the Colorado School of

Facts in brief on Latin America

Country	Population	Government	Monetary unit*	Foreign trade (million U.S.$) Exports†	Imports†
Antigua and Barbuda	69,000	Governor General James B. Carlisle; Prime Minister Lester Bird	dollar (2.70 = $1)	22	225
Argentina	34,883,000	President Carlos Saúl Menem	peso (1.00 = $1)	12,235	14,872
Bahamas	277,000	Governor General Clifford Darling; Prime Minister Hubert Ingraham	dollar (1.00 = $1)	2,678	2,920
Barbados	261,000	Governor General Dame Nita Barrow; Prime Minister Owen Arthur	dollar (2.01 = $1)	189	521
Belize	205,000	Governor General Sir Colville Young; Prime Minister Manuel Esquivel	dollar (2.00 = $1)	132	280
Bolivia	8,074,000	President Gonzalo Sanchez de Lozada Bustamente	boliviano (4.68 = $1)	710	1,131
Brazil	161,382,000	President Fernando Henrique Cardoso	cruzeiro real (0.85 = $1)	38,701	27,740
Chile	14,237,000	President Eduardo Frei Ruíz-Tagle	peso (411.00 = $1)	9,202	11,125
Colombia	35,101,000	President Ernesto Samper Pizano	peso (837.25 = $1)	6,917	6,516
Costa Rica	3,424,000	President José Maria Figueres Olsen	colón (159.55 = $1)	2,085	2,907
Cuba	11,091,000	President Fidel Castro	peso (1.00 = $1)	3,585	3,690
Dominica	75,000	President Crispin Anselm Sorhaindo; Prime Minister Eugenia Charles	dollar (2.7 = $1)	56	111
Dominican Republic	7,915,000	President Joaquín Balaguer Ricardo	peso (13.92 = $1)	555	2,443
Ecuador	11,822,000	President Sixto Durán Ballén Cordovez	sucre (2,153.00 = $1)	3,007	2,501
El Salvador	5,768,000	President Armando Calderon Sol	colón (8.75 = $1)	555	1,544
Grenada	92,000	Governor General Reginald Palmer; Prime Minister Nicholas Brathwaite	dollar (2.7 = $1)	23	121
Guatemala	10,621,000	President Ramiro De León Carpio	quetzal (5.75 = $1)	1,291	2,599
Guyana	834,000	President Cheddi Jagan	dollar (141.30 = $1)	293	382
Haiti	7,180,000	President Jean-Bertrand Aristide; Prime Minister Smarck Michel	gourde (19.00 = $1)	103	374
Honduras	5,968,000	President Carlos Roberto Reina Idiáquez	lempira (8.91 = $1)	814	1,130
Jamaica	2,547,000	Governor General Howard Cooke; Prime Minister P. J. Patterson	dollar (33.20 = $1)	1,057	2,118
Mexico	93,670,000	President Ernesto Zedillo Ponce de León	new peso (3.43 = $1)	30,241	50,147
Nicaragua	4,433,000	President Violeta Barrios de Chamorro	gold córdoba (7.18 = $1)	218	892
Panama	2,659,000	President Ernesto Pérez Balladares	balboa (1 = $1)	508	2,187
Paraguay	4,465,000	President Juan Carlos Wasmosy	guaraní (1,910.00 = $1)	1,119	819
Peru	23,854,000	President Alberto Fujimori	new sol (2.19 = $1)	3,497	4,914
Puerto Rico	3,522,000	Governor Pedro Rosselló	U.S. dollar	21,800	14,800
St. Christopher and Nevis	44,000	Governor General Clement Athelston Arrindell; Prime Minister Kennedy Alphonse Simmonds	dollar (2.70 = $1)	28	111
St. Lucia	144,000	Governor General Sir Stanislaus James; Prime Minister John Compton	dollar (2.70 = $1)	123	313
St. Vincent and the Grenadines	112,000	Governor General David Jack; Prime Minister James F. Mitchell	dollar (2.70 = $1)	83	136
Suriname	463,000	President Ronald R. Venetiaan	guilder (285.55 = $1)	472	472
Trinidad and Tobago	1,305,000	President Noor Hassanali; Prime Minister Patrick Manning	dollar (5.59 = $1)	1,612	1,448
Uruguay	3,186,000	President Luis Alberto Lacalle	peso (5.50= $1)	1,647	2,289
Venezuela	20,108,000	President Rafael Caldera Rodríguez	bolívar (169.75 = $1)	14,378	10,979

*Exchange rates as of Oct. 28, 1994, or latest available data.
†Latest available data.

Mines in Golden, Colo. Pang said that Latin America's exports of metallic minerals could double from $25 billion to $50 billion by the year 2000.

According to Pang, U.S. mining companies spent more than half of their exploration dollars in Latin America in 1994, partly because environmental regulations and activists blocked their activities at home. Most of the area's governments had also rewritten mining codes to lure foreign mining firms.

Economic integration. On December 10, 34 nations of the Western Hemisphere signed an agreement to negotiate a free trade pact among themselves and implement it by 2005. The agreement, signed in Miami, Fla., would create the world's largest free trade zone. Negotiations were set to begin in January 1995 on the specifics of the agreement. On Dec. 11, 1994, the three members of NAFTA—Canada, Mexico, and the United States—invited Chile to join the group.

Spurred by Mexico's early positive results as a partner in NAFTA, the nations of South America and the Caribbean rushed to work out similar agreements. Contrary to its traditional protectionist trade policies, Brazil in 1994 supported the creation of a South American common market. On August 5, Argentina, Brazil, Uruguay, and Paraguay signed an agreement to reduce tariffs by an average 85 percent on goods traded among themselves. The agreement was set to begin on Jan. 1, 1995. Another sign of Latin-American economic integration occurred on June 13, 1994, when Colombia, Mexico, and Venezuela signed a free-trade agreement. César Gaviria Trujillo, Colombia's outgoing president, had concluded free-trade pacts with 22 nations.

New OAS chief. Mindful of this accomplishment, ambassadors and representatives of the Organization of American States (OAS) selected Gaviria to become the new OAS secretary-general on March 27, 1994. Even before commencing his five-year term on September 15, he pledged to work toward the creation of a single free-trade zone encompassing the entire Western Hemisphere—a goal championed by a majority of Latin America's leaders.

Corruption and profiteering. Despite the gains that democracy and free enterprise won in Latin America in 1994, corruption still flourished. In Venezuela, a scandal involving elected leaders and some of the nation's most prominent bankers rocked the nation's economy throughout much of the year. The nation's second-largest bank collapsed in January, and eight more banks failed in June, forcing the government to sink more than $6 billion into its banks to prevent more collapses. In Brazil, a corruption scandal involving the budget committee of the lower house of Brazil's Congress resulted in the expulsion of three members of Congress on April 13 and 14. A congressional investigative panel had recommended expelling 18 Congress members in January for allegedly taking kickbacks and stealing from

the public treasury. Nationally televised hearings detailed the extent of the scandal during the April expulsion proceedings. In Argentina, a handful of people reaped staggering profits from the privatization of several state-run businesses in 1994.

Growing poverty. Despite strong economic growth in much of the region, many Latin Americans remained poor in 1994. In September, the United Nations Economic Commission for Latin America and the Caribbean, headquartered in Santiago, Chile, warned that the disparity between rich and poor was deepening. By the year 2000, the UN commission estimated, 38 percent of Latin America's population of 192 million people would be mired in poverty.

According to the UN, some 46 million Latin Americans were homeless in 1994, and 85 million others lived in homes so dilapidated that they should be demolished. An additional 100 million Latin Americans lacked water and electricity.

Armed rebellion. In Mexico, such poverty resulted in an armed rebellion that began on January 1 in the poor, largely Indian state of Chiapas. A rebel group calling itself the Zapatista National Liberation Army seized four towns in the state of Chiapas and declared war against the federal government. The leader of the rebellion was the self-styled "Subcomandante Marcos." Although he hid his identity behind a ski mask, Marcos established himself as a hero of oppressed people throughout Latin America. The rebellion reawakened cries for social justice on a scale not heard in that country since the days of the Mexican Revolution (1910-1917).

Grisly finds. Evidence of torture and mass executions by death squads continued to surface in Latin America throughout 1994. On January 11, General Alfonso Ortega of Colombia touched off an investigation by reporting the finding of 65 bullet-marked corpses in a cave near the village of Landazuri, 105 miles (170 kilometers) north of Bogotá. On June 23, investigators unearthed four mass graves containing the charred remains of some 1,000 men, women, and children in Guatemala's Quiché province, about 100 miles (160 kilometers) north of Guatemala City. In Haiti, U.S. occupation forces in September found a mass grave just outside the walls of Fort Dimanche, a prison in the slums of Port-au-Prince, where police had beaten, electrocuted, dismembered, blinded, or castrated an estimated 3,000 dissidents in the late 1980's and early 1990's.

World Cup. For an unprecedented fourth time, Brazil won the coveted World Cup soccer tournament on July 17, 1994, with a tie-breaking shoot-out victory over Italy at the Rose Bowl in Pasadena, Calif. Argentine fans were bitterly disappointed when their team's star player, Diego Maradona, was removed from the roster after he failed a random drug test on June 26. On July 2, a gunman in Medellín, Colombia, murdered Andrés Escobar, 27, who

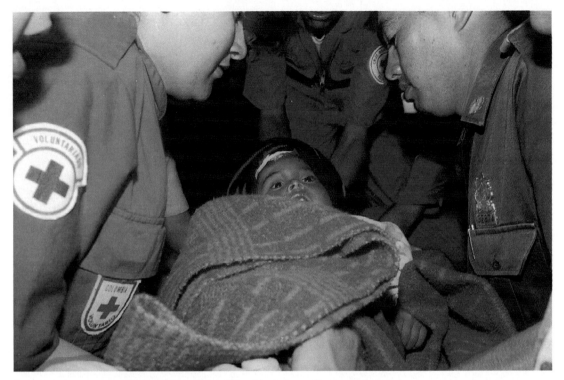

Rescue workers carry a child to safety in Neiva, Colombia, in June after an earthquake struck the area, killing at least 1,000 people.

had inadvertently scored a goal against his own team in a first-round loss to the United States.

Illegal immigration. Many voters in the United States were angry in 1994 over the high cost of providing social services for illegal immigrants, many of whom come from Latin America. On November 8, California voters passed Proposition 187—a measure that would deny all but emergency health care services to illegal immigrants. On September 30, a federal commission chaired by former Representative Barbara Jordan (D. Tex.) recommended a similar proposal at the federal level. (See also **Immigration.**)

Environmental concerns. Nature combined with the growing Latin-American population to raise new environmental concerns during 1994. Australian marine biologist Terence P. Hughes reported in September 1994 on the destruction of coral reefs in Jamaica. Hughes studied Jamaican reefs from the late 1970's to the early 1990's and reported that hurricanes, disease among marine organisms, and overfishing had combined to nearly destroy the island's reefs. A huge section of the Patagonia region of Argentina had become an ash-covered wasteland in 1994 after experiencing three successive years of drought and the August 1991 eruption of the Hudson volcano in Chile.   ☐ Nathan A. Haverstock

See also articles on the individual nations. In *World Book,* see **Latin America** and articles on the individual nations.

Latvia and Russia in 1994 remained in conflict over the treatment of Latvia's more than 900,000 ethnic Russians. The government passed a law in June making it extremely difficult for people who are not ethnic Latvians to become citizens. The law drew angry protests from the Russian government and criticism from other European nations. Latvian officials, eager to avoid setbacks in European relations, eased the restrictions on citizenship in July.

Despite the tensions, Latvia and Russia were able to reach an agreement over the withdrawal of the remaining Russian troops in Latvia. Russia withdrew all troops by August 31, but retained control of a key radar station at Skrunda under a four-year lease.

Five deputies, including Latvia's foreign minister, were charged in April with assisting the KGB, the secret intelligence agency of the Communist Party, while Latvia was under control of the former Soviet Union. By November, two deputies had been acquitted of the charges.

Latvia's ruling coalition broke apart in July, when the Farmer's Union ended its cooperation with Latvian Way, the dominant party. In September, parliament formed a new government, still primarily controlled by Latvian Way and headed by Prime Minister Maris Gailis.   ☐ Steven L. Solnick

See also **Europe** (Facts in brief table). In *World Book,* see **Latvia.**

Law. See **Courts; Supreme Court of the U.S.**

Lebanon. Political violence and rising crime in 1994 threatened the national reconciliation that followed Lebanon's civil war (1975-1991). Israel's continued occupation of a "security zone" in southern Lebanon and Israeli raids against the militant Hezbollah (Party of God) in Lebanon also threatened the peace.

Violence. In April, Pope John Paul II postponed a long-awaited May trip to Lebanon, which would have been his first Mideast trip. Concern had grown when a bomb killed 10 people and wounded 55 at a Maronite Catholic church near the capital, Beirut, on February 27. Although Muslims and Christians joined in national mourning the next day, attacks against other Christian targets in east Beirut and north Lebanon renewed fears of civil strife.

Samir Geagea, former head of the Christian militia Lebanese Forces (LF), and seven former LF members were charged on June 13 with plotting the February bombing. The motive was reportedly to split Lebanon along sectarian lines. Like other Christians, Geagea refused to participate in the postwar Lebanese political system because of diminished Christian influence and opposition to Syrian influence. Geagea was also charged with the 1990 murder of rival Christian warlord Dani Chamoun.

Israel. The United States pressured Lebanon in 1994 to curb the activities of Hezbollah, but Lebanese officials firmly restated that Israel's continued military influence over a 9-mile (14-kilometer) wide security zone in southern Lebanon encouraged guerrilla resistance. Israel attacked a Hezbollah camp in Lebanon's Bekaa Valley on June 2, killing more than 30 people.

On May 21, Israeli commandos kidnapped Mustafa Dirani, guerrilla leader of the pro-Iranian Faithful Resistance group, to question him about Israeli airman Ron Arad. Arad was one of six missing Israeli soldiers captured in Lebanon in 1986 and the only one believed to be still alive.

Israel's 27th and 28th raids into Lebanon in 1994 were launched on August 4 against guerrilla targets. Ten civilians died, eliciting a rare Israeli apology.

Assassinations. Foreign political figures became targets in 1994. A high-ranking Jordanian diplomat was slain in Beirut on January 29. Jordan blamed Iranian-linked Islamic militants for the death. Iraqi diplomats were expelled from Lebanon after they were alleged to be linked to the killing of an Iraqi opposition figure on April 12. (See **Jordan; Iraq.**)

Crime. Public outrage over violent crime led to the reinstatement of capital punishment in March. The first execution in 11 years occurred on April 23, and a week later two Syrian soldiers were executed. All three men had been convicted of murder. □ Christine Helms

See also **Middle East** (Facts in brief table). In *World Book,* see **Lebanon.**

Lesotho. See **Africa.**

Liberia. A peace agreement signed in July 1993 failed to end Liberia's civil war in 1994. Warring factions failed to abide by the pact, and new warring groups arose.

In September, Ghana's President Jerry John Rawlings hosted talks for the leaders of three major Liberian factions. Those attending were Charles Taylor, head of the National Patriotic Front of Liberia; Lieutenant General Alhaji Kromah, leader of one faction of the United Liberation Movement of Liberia for Democracy; and General Hezekiah Bowen, the top officer of the Armed Forces of Liberia, the former national army.

On September 12, the three men signed a new treaty, agreeing to share power in a Council of State until October 1995. They also said they would hold presidential and legislative elections within a year.

The power-sharing agreement angered many Liberians, and on September 15 a small group of rebels attempted to seize control of the government. The uprising was quickly put down by a Nigerian-led peacekeeping force that had been in Liberia since 1990. Taylor's troops also rebelled and declared a new leader, Tom Woeweiyu.

Fighting decreased late in the year, though factional conflict remained. In October, Nigeria began recalling its troops from Liberia. □ Mark DeLancey

See also **Africa** (Facts in brief table). In *World Book,* see **Liberia.**

Library. Using new technologies became a top item on librarians' agendas in 1994. While librarians worked to meet basic community needs, they also planned to be part of the *information superhighway,* the vast, growing network of computers and other electronic technologies. United States President Bill Clinton said in his January 1994 State of the Union address, "We must also work with the private sector to connect every classroom, every clinic, every library, every hospital in America into a national information superhighway by the year 2000."

On Jan. 11, 1994, Vice President Al Gore, Jr., outlined the Clinton Administration's plan for the superhighway. The plan included the development of one standardized system available to all with regulatory guidelines established by the Federal Communications Commission. Gore said that private industry would continue to lead in developing the superhighway, and he challenged telephone and cable television companies to provide free electronic links to every classroom and library. This access, he said, would keep the country from becoming divided into "information haves and have-nots." (See **Telecommunications: Regulating the Information Highway.**)

Internet. Librarians did not wait for federal policies to pave the way for access to the information superhighway. A 1994 study commissioned by the U.S. National Commission on Libraries and Information Science found that 21 percent of public libraries were already linked to the Internet, a collection of computer networks. Almost three out of four of the nation's larger libraries—those that serve a population of 250,000 or more—were connected. However, only about 13 percent of the connected libraries provided public access to the Internet.

Maryland's state library made it possible in 1994 for all state residents to have free Internet access either from a home computer or at public libraries. On July 27, Baltimore's Enoch Pratt Free Public Library became the first site to offer the service, and from then through August 8 received 90,253 calls. On one night, a library employee found that even at 3 a.m., 12 patrons were on the Internet.

The U.S. Library of Congress released a plan in September for the creation of a digital library. By the year 2000, 5 million items in the library's collection would be *digitized* (converted into binary codes for computers). Initially, the librarians will give priority to "unique and historically significant materials." The project will begin to make the resources of one of the world's largest libraries available over computer networks to people across the country and around the world. Through a combination of public and private funding, the National Digital Library project, as it was named, would become the most extensive source of content materials on the information superhighway.

California libraries both prospered and suffered in 1994. To jump-start the technological development of California's schools and libraries, Pacific Bell telephone company announced in February a donation of some $100 million in wiring to connect nearly 7,400 sites to the Internet by the end of 1996. However, severe funding cuts continued to plague many California libraries. An estimated $3 billion was needed to equip and support links to every school and library statewide. Educators and librarians hoped Pacific Bell's leadership would inspire the development of a state information infrastructure.

As California already dealt with the country's worst library funding crisis, many California libraries faced a natural disaster when the Los Angeles area was rocked with a severe earthquake on Jan. 17, 1994. Most Los Angeles libraries reopened within days of the quake, after workers reshelved thousands of books that had been thrown to the floor. Libraries closest to the epicenter of the quake, near Northridge in the San Fernando Valley, faced more serious structural problems.

The Oviatt Library at California State University, in Northridge, suffered serious damage. By September, the concrete center of the library, which was not expected to do well in an earthquake, had been reopened. The steel-frame wings of the library, meant to be more quake-resistant, remained badly damaged and were not expected to reopen until 1996. □ Peggy Barber

In *World Book*, see **Library**.

Libya. Libyan leader Muammar Muhammad al-Qadhafi celebrated 25 years in power on Sept. 1, 1994, with a massive military parade in Libya's capital, Tripoli. Qadhafi and 11 other military officers had won power in a coup on Sept. 1, 1969. All but 2 of the other officers have since died or retired. One officer remained in exile in 1994.

United Nations (UN) sanctions imposed in April 1992 took a heavy toll on the Libyan economy. The sanctions were intended to pressure Qadhafi into turning over for trial two Libyans suspected of bombing a United States airplane in 1988 and a French plane in 1989, killing a total of 441 people. The UN froze Libya's overseas assets and banned air traffic and sales of weapons and oil equipment to Libya. The nation's factories operated at half capacity in 1994. Government salaries were delayed, and payments to overseas contractors and membership fees to organizations were withheld. The oil industry, Libya's major revenue source, began to suffer in 1994 from a lack of parts and poor maintenance.

Libya withdrew from a contested border area, the Aozou Strip, on May 30, 1994. The International Court of Justice had ruled in February that the border region, believed to be rich in oil and uranium, belonged to Chad. □ Christine Helms

See also **Middle East** (Facts in brief table). In *World Book*, see **Libya**.

Liechtenstein. See Europe.

Limbaugh, Rush (1951-), was one of the top radio and TV personalities in the United States in 1994. His conservative commentaries poking fun at liberal politicians, feminists, and other targets on the political left won him millions of avid listeners.

Rush Hudson Limbaugh III was born on Jan. 12, 1951, in Cape Girardeau, Mo. He entered radio in 1971, after dropping out of college, working at stations in Pittsburgh, Pa., and Kansas City, Mo. In 1978, with his career stalled, he quit radio to do promotional work for the Kansas City Royals baseball team.

Limbaugh returned to the airwaves in 1983, taking a position at a Kansas City station. His irreverent comments on news stories won him a job at radio station KFBK in Sacramento, Calif. There, Limbaugh was encouraged to express himself freely, and he tripled the station's ratings in four years.

In 1988, Limbaugh was hired by the ABC radio network and given his own daily three-hour program, "The Rush Limbaugh Show," which aired from station WABC in New York City. By mid-1992, the show was carried by 600 stations and had 20 million listeners. In September 1992, he also began hosting a late-night syndicated television talk show.

Limbaugh is the author of two best-selling books, *The Way Things Ought to Be* (1992) and *See, I Told You So* (1993). In May 1994, Limbaugh married Marta Fitzgerald, a former aerobics instructor. It was the third marriage for both. □ David Dreier

Literature.

Literature. England exported important novels in 1994: Beryl Bainbridge's *The Birthday Boys*, based on Robert F. Scott's last trip to Antarctica; Kingsley Amis' *The Russian Girl,* a satire of Russian novels, and Irish-born Iris Murdoch's *The Green Knight.*

From Canada came the American-born Carol Shields's *The Stone Diaries*, a novel of 20th-century North America, and Alice Munro's *Open Secrets*, a collection of short stories. South Africa contributed two important novels, Andre Brink's *On the Contrary* and Nadine Gordimer's *None to Accompany Me.*

Memoirs. *Selected Letters of Philip Larkin, 1940-1985*, shed much light on the eccentric British poet. Irish writer William Trevor's *Excursions in the Real World* was a stylish memoir. Trinidad-born novelist V. S. Naipaul, who lives in England, offered *A Way in the World*, an autobiographical musing on empire and culture. Writer Doris Lessing produced the first volume of her autobiography, *Under My Skin.*

Translated novels included Ursula Hegi's *Stones from the River*, about small-town Germany between 1915 and 1952, and Reinaldo Arenas' *The Assault*, a counterrevolutionary novel of Cuba. Translated non-fiction included Ingmar Bergman's *Images: My Life in Film*. Teen-ager Zlata Filipovic's *Zlata's Diary* told of life in besieged Sarajevo, the capital of Bosnia-Herzegovina.   □ Henry Kisor

See also **Canadian literature; Literature, American; Literature for children.**

Novelist Kenzaburo Oe, known for his stories of postwar Japan, in October became the second Japanese writer to win the Nobel Prize for literature.

Literature, American.

Literature, American. The year 1994 was noteworthy for much that was good from mature masters of the American novel. These writers held their own against an outpouring of excellent fiction from younger writers.

William Gaddis' *A Frolic of His Own* stylishly satirized the American legal system. John Updike's *Brazil* explored love and class in the Amazon jungles. Thomas Flanagan's *The End of the Hunt* was a rich novel based on revolutionary and civil wars in Ireland from 1916 to 1923.

Henry Roth's *Mercy of a Rude Stream* was a fine second novel by the octogenarian who first won fame in 1934 for *Call It Sleep.* E. L. Doctorow's *The Waterworks* was a spellbinding novel of New York City in 1871. Ken Kesey's *Last Go Round* (written with Ken Babbs) told a story about rodeo cowboys based on the dime Westerns of 100 years ago.

Cormac McCarthy's *The Crossing* was the second novel in the *Border Trilogy* projected by the fine chronicler of the American West. John Gregory Dunne's *Playland* was a scorching satire of Hollywood. Gail Godwin's *The Good Husband* related a memorable tale of death.

Peter Taylor's *In the Tennessee Country* was an elegant novel of an academic's search for a long-lost kinsman. (Taylor died November 2.) Joseph Heller's *Closing Time,* a sequel to his classic 1961 novel *Catch-22,* was disappointing in the main but nevertheless contained long stetches of masterly prose.

Middle-aged writers also produced notable work. Joyce Carol Oates's *What I Lived For* showed that the prolific novelist had lost none of her talent. Paul Theroux's *Millroy the Magician* was a satiric tale of an itinerant conjurer and a 14-year-old runaway. Louise Erdrich's *The Bingo Palace* reconfirmed this Native-American novelist's considerable talent. Howard Norman's *The Bird Artist* was a stylishly bleak novel of Canada's harsh Newfoundland wilderness.

John Irving's *A Son of the Circus* was an ingenious tale of a Bombay physician living in Canada. Tim O'Brien's *In the Lake of the Woods* cast the long shadow of Vietnam on today's American politics.

Established younger writers published important novels, including Caryl Phillips' *Crossing the River*, Alice Hoffman's *Second Nature*, Carolyn Chute's *Merry Men*, Nicholson Baker's *The Fermata*, William T. Vollman's *The Rifles*, Doris Betts's *Souls Raised from the Dead*, Dennis McFarland's *School for the Blind*, A. G. Mojtabai's *Called Out*, Barry Gifford's *Arise and Walk*, James Carroll's *The City Below*, Paul Auster's *Mr. Vertigo*, Anna Quindlen's *One True Thing*, Bebe Moore Campbell's *Brothers and Sisters*, Jayne Anne Phillips' *Shelter*, Jane Hamilton's *A Map of the World*, and Lorrie Moore's *Who Will Run the Frog Hospital?*

Notable first novels came from Gwendolyn M. Parker (*These Same Long Bones*), John Dufresne

(*Louisiana Power & Light*), and Susan Power (*The Grass Dancer*).

Short stories. Ethan Canin's *The Palace Thief* offered four tales centered on the ancient Greek philosopher Heraclitus' observation that character is fate. Grace Paley's *Collected Stories* displayed the New York writer's distinctive command of the form. Other important collections were T. Coraghessan Boyle's *Without a Hero*, Ellen Currie's *Moses Supposes*, Richard Bausch's *Rare & Endangered Species*, and Alison Lurie's *Women and Ghosts*. Interesting books from American writers under 30 years old included Douglas Coupland's short-story collection *Life After God*.

Contemporary nonfiction. One of the year's most important books on race relations was Ellis Cose's *The Rage of a Privileged Class*, which explored the frustrations of middle-class African Americans.

Race was at the heart of four excellent memoirs. Brent Staples' *Parallel Time: Growing Up in Black and White* told of growing up black in a Pennsylvania industrial town. Nathan McCall's *Makes Me Wanna Holler* told how a bright young black man entered and escaped a life of crime. Henry Louis Gates, Jr., affectingly explored the segregated but exuberant West Virginia society of his youth in *Colored People: A Memoir*. *Warriors Don't Cry*, by Melba Pattillo Beals, was a compelling memoir of a young girl's participation in the 1957 battle to integrate Central High School in Little Rock, Ark.

In the Shadow of the Panther, by Hugh Pearson, was a powerful indictment of Huey Newton, a Black Panther leader of the 1960's and 1970's, as a criminal rather than a militant.

On the Real Side, by Mel Watkins, explored how black Americans have used humor as a survival strategy. John Edgar Wideman's *Fatheralong* was a searingly honest book on the meaning of race and racism to the black novelist's family.

Controversial nonfiction. Christopher Jencks' *The Homeless* contended that the number of homeless Americans is smaller than earlier believed and that homelessness is a problem so complex that conventional methods of solving it are bound to fail. Mark Danner's *The Massacre at El Mozote* was an engrossing, disturbing study of the 1981 attack on a Salvadoran village by U.S.-sponsored soldiers that left 750 unarmed villagers dead and precipitated an attempted U.S. cover-up.

The recovery of forgotten memories of child abuse came under attack in Lawrence Wright's *Remembering Satan* and Michael D. Yapko's *Suggestions of Abuse,* which charged that such memories often were suggested by therapists. Lenore Terr's *Unchained Memories* argued that many recollections indeed are true.

Autobiography and letters. Three renowned journalists published fine life stories: Peter Arnett's *Live from the Battlefield* was an engrossing memoir by a Vietnam War and Persian Gulf War correspondent. Pete Hamill's *A Drinking Life* was a stylish look back on the role of alcohol in the writer's life. Columnist Art Buchwald's *Leaving Home* was a fine reminiscence about growing up as a Jewish orphan during the Great Depression.

The Chinese immigrant Anchee Min's *Red Azalea* was a wrenching memoir of youth as a Red Guard during Mao Zedong's Cultural Revolution. *Shot in the Heart* was Mikal Gilmore's nightmarish chronicle of growing up in the troubled family that produced Gary Mark Gilmore, a killer executed in 1977. *Autobiography of a Face* was Lucy Grealy's affecting chronicle of life with disfigurement. *Family* was Ian Frazier's multigenerational memoir of his Midwestern ancestors, full of emotional nuance and artistry.

Two excellent books about deafness were Hannah Merker's *Listening*, an enlightening meditation by a woman who lost her hearing in adulthood, and Leah Hager Cohen's *Train Go Sorry*, a hearing woman's chronicle of growing up at a high school for the deaf where her father was superintendent.

Elizabeth Bishop's *One Art* was a deeply engrossing collection of the late poet's correspondence. Another important collection was *In Touch: The Letters of Paul Bowles*.

Biography. *Josephine: The Hungry Heart*, by Jean-Claude Baker and Chris Chase, was an irresistibly entertaining life of the black American singer who became a beloved institution in Paris. David Leeming's *James Baldwin* assessed the troubled yet brilliant career of the African-American writer. Neal Gabler's *Winchell* told the story of Walter Winchell, a powerful and feared American columnist and broadcaster who was at the height of his fame in the 1930's and 1940's. Peter Guralnick's sparkling *Last Train to Memphis* related the early life of Elvis Presley.

Among significant literary biographies were Joan D. Hedrick's magisterial *Harriet Beecher Stowe;* Janet Malcolm's *The Silent Woman*, a chronicle of the stormy relationship between the late poet Sylvia Plath and her husband, Ted Hughes, England's poet laureate in 1994; Joan Mellen's *Kay Boyle*, about an American novelist and short-story writer who published 45 volumes over her long career; and Jeffrey Meyers' *Scott Fitzgerald*, a measured assessment of the writer's tragic story, filled with a wealth of new detail.

Leading the political biographies was Stephen Lesher's *George Wallace*, a fine study of the former segregationist Alabama governor. Gerald Gunther's *Learned Hand* ably appraised the distinguished federal judge. Doris Kearns Goodwin's *No Ordinary Time* was a magisterial biography of Franklin D. and Eleanor Roosevelt during World War II (1939-1945).

The American Civil War (1861-1865) was the subject of several important historical biographies, among them Stephen B. Oates's *A Woman of Valor: Clara Barton and the Civil War*; Joseph T. Glatthaar's

Partners in Command: The Relationships Between Leaders in the Civil War; and Mark E. Neely, Jr.'s The Last Best Hope of Earth: Abraham Lincoln and the Promise of America.

The Catcher Was a Spy by Nicholas Dawidoff explored the bizarre life of Morris (Moe) Berg, a major league ballplayer who spied on Nazi Germany during World War II.

Essays and criticism. The distinguished novelist Saul Bellow published the collection It All Adds Up. Harold Bloom's The Western Canon was a brilliant and impassioned defense of teaching traditional European literature in universities.

History. Important history books were W. Bruce Lincoln's The Conquest of a Continent: Siberia and the Russians; Henry Kissinger's Diplomacy; Hugh Thomas' Conquest: Montezuma, Cortes and the Fall of Old Mexico; and John Boswell's Same-Sex Unions in Premodern Europe.

Leading the popular histories marking the 50th anniversary of the Allied landings in Normandy during World War II was Stephen Ambrose's D-Day, June 6, 1944, a collection of firsthand accounts of the invasion.

Medicine, science, and social science. Two books by physicians won wide notice. Sherwin Nuland's How We Die, which explored what happens to the human body at the moment of death, won the National Book Award for nonfiction. Richard Selzer's Raising the Dead chillingly told of his own near-death experience.

The Beak of the Finch, by Jonathan Weiner, was a fine chronicle about biologists who tracked evolution in a group of small birds over 20 years. The Coming Plague, by Laurie Garrett, contended that the world faces an onslaught of deadly viruses as rain forests disappear.

Andrew Chaikin's A Man on the Moon was a candid and detailed account of the Apollo 11 voyage. Stalin and the Bomb, by David Holloway, related the Soviet Union's int`ase effort to acquire nuclear weaponry and its effect on the Cold War.

The Bell Curve, by Richard J. Herrnstein and Charles Murray, provoked intense controversy with its contention that intelligence is inherited and linked to race. Also controversial was The Social Organization of Sexuality, by Edward O. Laumann, John H. Gagnon, Robert T. Michael, and Stuart Michaels, a massive study that contended that Americans are neither promiscuous nor obsessed with sex.

Best sellers. Among the year's best sellers were Michael Crichton's controversial novel of office sexual politics, Disclosure, and James Finn Garner's amusing Politically Correct Bedtime Stories, in which Mother Goose meets multiculturalism.　□ Henry Kisor

See also **Canadian literature; Literature; Literature for children; Poetry.** In *World Book,* see **American literature.**

Literature for children. Children's books published in 1994 were notably multicultural. There were picture books on many subjects, especially fantasy and folk tales. Books for preteen and teen-aged readers focused on problems of growing up, often under difficult circumstances. A variety of informational books were published, and there was less poetry than in some past years. Outstanding books of 1994 included the following:

Picture Books. Tucker Pfeffercorn: An Old Story Retold by Barry Moser (Little, Brown). Bessie must guess a stranger's name or lose her baby to him in a Southern-style Rumpelstiltskin tale. Ages 4 to 8.

The Bird, the Frog, and the Light by Avi, illustrated by Matthew Henry (Orchard Bks.). A pompous frog king demands that a bird bring light to his den. Ages 5 to 7.

Eugenio by Marianne Cockenpot, illustrated by Lorenzo Mattotti (Little, Brown). Eugenio, a famous clown, suddenly cannot laugh. No advice works until he goes to a fortuneteller. Ages 4 to 8.

Mole's Hill by Lois Ehlert (Harcourt Brace). Fox and friends want Mole to move her hill. Ages 4 to 7.

Imani in the Belly by Deborah Newton Chocolate, illustrated by Alex Boies (BridgeWater Bks.). When a lion eats her children, Imani hunts him. Ages 5 to 9.

Wind Says Good Night by Katy Rydell, illustrated by David Jorgensen (Houghton Mifflin). Wind helps a child fall asleep by solving a problem. Ages 2 to 8.

A Teeny Tiny Baby by Amy Schwartz (Orchard Bks.). A new baby tells what he likes and does. Ages 2 to 6.

Baby Crow by John A. Rowe (North-South Bks.). Baby crow's beeps worry his parents until he regains his voice. Then they are sorry! Ages 5 to 8.

The Boy Who Ate Around by Henrik Drescher (Hyperion). A boy dislikes his dinner, and his imagination runs riot as he eats everything. Ages 5 to 8.

Troll's Search for Summer by Nicolas van Pallandt (Farrar, Straus, Giroux). When Troll is carried off by the winter wind, he has many encounters looking for summer. Wonderful paintings. Ages 4 to 8.

How Georgie Radbourn Saved Baseball by David Shannon (Blue Sky/Scholastic). A Georgie is born when baseball is outlawed and it is always winter. Ages 5 and up.

Pigsty by Mark Teague (Scholastic). Wendell's room is such a pigsty that pigs begin to move in, and that is not much fun. Ages 5 to 8.

Jaguarundi by Virginia Hamilton, illustrated by Floyd Cooper (Blue Sky/Scholastic). When Rundi's homeland is taken by humans, he leaves for a safer place. All ages.

Time Flies by Eric Rohmann (Crown). A bird flies into a hall filled with dinosaur skeletons that take her back into their time. Wordless. All ages.

The story of a Japanese immigrant's travels to a new land, written and illustrated by Allen Say in *Grandfather's Journey* (1993), won a Caldecott Medal in January.

Looking for Atlantis by Colin Thompson (Knopf). Detailed paintings accent an imaginative tale of a boy's search using his grandfather's advice. All ages.

Rata-pata-scata-fata: A Caribbean Story by Phillis Gershator, illustrated by Holly Meade (Little, Brown). When Junjun is given tasks that he wishes into completion, is it really magic? Ages 4 to 8.

Swamp Angel by Anne Isaacs, illustrated by Paul O. Zelinsky (Dutton). In this tall tale, Angelica has great strength and gets her bearskin. Ages 5 and up.

The Book that Jack Wrote by Jon Scieszka, illustrated by Daniel Adel (Viking). A zany tale with odd events and unique paintings. All ages.

John Jeremy Colton by Bryan J. Leech, illustrated by Byron Glaser and Sandra Higashi (Hyperion). In humorous, rhymed verse, Jeremy baffles the villagers with his bright house and odd behavior. All ages.

Grandpa's House by Harvey Stevenson (Hyperion). Active, inventive, not-very-old Grandpa and Woody spend a weekend together. Ages 4 to 8.

The Moon Man by Gerda Marie Scheidl, translated by J. Alison James, illustrated by Josef Wilkon (North-South Bks.). Marion's picture of the Moon Man comes to life. Ages 4 to 8.

The Frog Princess retold by J. Patrick Lewis, illustrated by Gennady Spirin (Dial). A prince marries a frog princess. Ages 5 to 8.

288

When the Fly Flew In by Lisa Westberg Peters, illustrated by Brad Sneed (Dial). A messy room gets a cleaning in a zany fly-chasing tale. Ages 4 to 8.

Moving Days by Marc Harshman, illustrated by Wendy Popp (Cobblehill/Dutton). Tommy is unhappy about moving, but good things happen. Ages 4 to 8.

George Washington's Cows by David Small (Farrar, Straus & Giroux). A silly rhyme about Washington's animals has rollicking illustrations. All ages.

Rattlebang Picnic by Margaret Mahy, illustrated by Steven Kellogg (Dial). A family goes on a picnic in their old car. Ages 4 to 8.

Courtney by John Burningham (Crown). When the children select Courtney to be their pet, they discover his hidden talents. Ages 4 to 8.

How Night Came from the Sea retold by Mary-Joan Gerson, illustrated by Carla Golembe (Little, Brown). Three Brazilian servants are sent to get night so that Lemanja's daughter will be happy on land. Ages 4 to 8.

The Battle of Luke and Longnose by Barbara McClintock (Houghton Mifflin). Luke, tired after playing with his toy-soldiers theater, dreams an imaginative, dramatic plot as he combats the villain Long-nose. Ages 4 to 8.

Scared Silly! A Book for the Brave by Marc Brown (Little, Brown). Here are scary but often silly stories, riddles, and poems. Ages 4 to 8.

Baba Yaga & the Little Girl retold by Katya Arnold (North-South Bks.). A girl outwits Baba Yaga and the cruel stepmother. Ages 5 to 8.

Mama Is a Miner by George Ella Lyon, illustrated by Peter Catalanotto (Orchard Bks.). Mama works underground in a coal mine while her children go to school. Ages 5 to 8.

John Henry by Julius Lester, illustrated by Jerry Pinkney (Dial). The legend of black labor hero John Henry takes on new strength and drama through an interesting story and fine paintings. All ages.

Sleep Well, Little Bear by Quint Buchholz, translated from the German by Peter Neumeyer (Farrar, Straus & Giroux). Little bear thinks about tomorrow in this fine bedtime story with a surprise letter. Ages 3 to 8.

Poetry. *Never Take a Pig to Lunch and Other Poems About the Fun of Eating* selected by Nadine Bernard Westcott (Orchard Bks.). Humorous collection of rhymes. All ages.

The Dream Keeper and Other Poems by Langston Hughes, illustrated by Brian Pinkney (Knopf). Poems capture hopes, dreams, and feelings. All ages.

My Song Is Beautiful, selected by Mary Ann Hoberman (Little, Brown). Poems from various cultures. All ages.

Animal Fare by Jane Yolen, illustrated by Janet Street (Harcourt Brace). Nonsense poems to tickle the ear have equally comical illustrations. All ages.

Beast Feast by Douglas Florian (Harcourt Brace). A humorous look at a variety of creatures. All ages.

The Fat-Cats at Sea by J. Patrick Lewis, illustrated by Victoria Chess (Apple Soup/Knopf). Cats sail on the *Frisky Dog*, their adventures told in 12 funny poems. All ages.

Winter Poems selected by Barbara Rogasky, illustrated by Trina Schart Hyman (Scholastic). Poetry collection pays tribute to the season. All ages.

Over the Hills and Far Away by Alan Marks (North-South Books). These nursery rhymes have wonderful paintings and silhouettes. Ages 5 to 9.

Animal Vegetable Mineral: Poems About Small Things selected by Myra Cohn Livingston (HarperCollins). Poems look at small things. Ages 8 to 12.

Fiction. *Cezanne Pinto* by Mary Stoltz (Knopf). An old man, Cezanne, tells the vivid story of his boyhood escape from slavery and journey north to Canada. Ages 12 and up.

Donovan's Word Jar by Monalisa DeGross, illustrated by Cheryl Hanna (HarperCollins). Donovan collects words. When his jar fills up, he needs a new way to expand his collection. Ages 7 to 10.

Escape from Egypt by Sonia Levitin (Little, Brown). The riveting tale of Jesse and the Israelites' misery in Egypt and later in the wilderness where they have been led by Moses. Ages 12 and up.

Beyond the Burning Time by Kathryn Lasky (Blue Sky/Scholastic). The Salem witch trials erupt. Ages 12 and up.

The Glory Field by Walter Dean Myers (Scholastic). The strengths and difficulties of five generations of the Lewis family are revealed. Ages 12 and up.

Rites of Passage: Stories About Growing Up by Black Writers from Around the World, edited by Tonya Bolden (Hyperion). An excellent collection of coming-of-age tales. Ages 12 and up.

Flour Babies by Anne Fine (Little, Brown). Simon and all-male schoolmates must tend bags of flour for three weeks to learn about parenting. Funny events occur and Simon learns about himself. Ages 9 to 12.

Adam and Eve and Pinch-Me by Julie Johnston (Little, Brown). A foster child comes out of her shell with the help of her computer and caring people. Ages 12 and up.

Billy by Laura Roybal (Houghton Mifflin). Billy, kidnapped at age 10 by his father, is retaken suddenly at 16 by his adoptive parents. Ages 12 and up.

The Richest Kids in Town by Peg Kehret (Cobblehill/Dutton). Peter's hilarious attempts to earn plane-ticket money to visit an old friend have even better results. Ages 8 to 11.

Street Child by Berlie Doherty (Orchard Bks.). After his mom dies, Jim flees a workhouse but finds street life has unexpected hazards. Ages 8 to 12.

The Barn by Avi (Orchard Bks.). Ben and his siblings build a barn for Ben's dad after he has a bad stroke. Ages 9 to 11.

Fantasy. *Jacob and the Stranger* by Sally Derby, illustrated by Leonid Gore (Ticknor & Fields). Miniature wild animals come from a plant. Ages 6 to 8.

Wolf-Woman by Sherryl Jordan (Houghton Mifflin). Tanith, first raised by wolves, is not accepted by her human clan. Ages 12 and up.

The Girl Who Married the Moon retold by Joseph Bruchac and Gail Ross, illustrated by S. S. Burrus (BridgeWater Bks.). Native-American tales celebrate a girl's journey to womanhood. Ages 10 to 13.

Seven Spiders Spinning by Gregory Maguire (Clarion Bks.). Poisonous spiders from the Ice Age come to life in Vermont. Humorous. Ages 8 to 12.

The Ear, the Eye & the Arm by Nancy Farmer (Orchard Bks.). When Tendai, Rita, and Kuda are kidnapped in futuristic Zimbabwe, an unlikely trio of detectives tries to find them. Ages 12 and up.

The Tin Princess by Phillip Pullman (Knopf). Becky and Jim help Adelaide, a queen, survive plots against her life. Ages 12 and up.

Wonderful Alexander and the Catwings by Ursula Le Guin, illustrated by S. D. Schindler (Orchard Bks.). A lost kitten is rescued by the Catwings, and he repays them in a special way. Ages 5 to 8.

Diane Goode's Book of Scary Stories & Songs by Diane Goode (Dutton). This collection from around the world has comical illustrations for often silly tales and verses. Musical notes included. All ages.

Misoso: Once Upon a Time Tales from Africa retold by Verna Aardema, illustrated by Reynold Ruffins (Apple Soup/Knopf). Wonderful tales, each with a short glossary and an afterword. All ages.

Hob and the Goblins by William Mayne (Dorling Kindersley). Hob joins a family that has put themselves and others in terrible danger. Ages 8 to 12.

Here and Then by George Ella Lyon (Orchard Bks.). In a Civil War (1861-1865) reenactment, Abby's character talks to her through a diary. Ages 10 to 12.

Informational books. *Rosie: A Visiting Dog's Story* by Stephanie Calmenson, illustrated by Justin Sutcliffe (Clarion). A dog is specially trained to cheer people who are ill, sad, or lonely. Ages 4 to 7.

Kids at Work: Lewis Nine and the Crusade Against Child Labor by Russell Freedman (Clarion Bks.). Photographs and descriptions of child labor reveal earlier frightful conditions. Ages 10 and up.

Castle: Cross-Sections by Stephen Biesty (Dorling Kindersley). Everything connected with a castle is shown in an intriguing I Spy book. Ages 10 and up.

The Magic School Bus in the Time of the Dinosaurs by Joanna Cole, illustrated by Bruce Degen (Scholastic). Ms. Frizzle's class goes on another wild, informative adventure Ages 8 to 11.

Poisons in Our Path: Plants that Harm and Heal by Anne Ophelia Dowden (HarperCollins). Facts and fictions about many plants. All ages.

What Does the Crow Know? The Mysteries of Animal Intelligence by Margery Facklam, illustrated by Pamela Johnson (Sierra Club). Ages 7 and up.

War Game by Michael Foreman (Arcade Publishing). Some British and Germans exchange Christmas gifts during the war. All ages.

Water, Water Everywhere by Mark J. Rauzon and Cynthia Overbeck Bix (Sierra Club). Color photos show how water moves on Earth. Text explains why water is a precious resource. Ages 5 to 8.

A Time for Playing by Ron Hirschi, illustrated by Thomas D. Mangelsen (Cobblehill Bks./Dutton). Wonderful color photos capture a variety of animals at play, an important learning tool. Ages 3 to 6.

Blue Potatoes, Orange Tomatoes by Rosalind Creasy, illustrated by Ruth Heller (Sierra Club). Tells how to grow unusual fruits and vegetables.

Awards. Lois Lowry won the 1994 Newbery Medal for her novel *The Giver.* The medal is given by the American Library Association (ALA) for outstanding children's literature published the previous year. The ALA's Caldecott Medal for "the most distinguished American picture book for children" went to Allen Say, the illustrator and author of *Grandfather's Journey.*   □ Marilyn Fain Apseloff

In *World Book,* see **Caldecott Medal; Newbery Medal; Literature for Children.**

Lithuania on Jan. 27, 1994, joined the Partnership for Peace, a new North Atlantic Treaty Organization (NATO) program of cooperation with nations that had belonged to the Warsaw Pact, a military alliance led by the former Soviet Union. Lithuania had sought to establish ties with NATO since 1991, when the nation became independent. Lithuania continued to express concerns during the year over the threat of Russian military domination. Leaders protested Russia's reluctance to reduce its massive military presence in Kaliningrad, an isolated Russian city surrounded by Lithuania and Poland on the Baltic Sea. In April, Lithuania and Poland signed a "friendship treaty," symbolically ending territorial disputes that had soured their relations for decades.

To stabilize its sinking currency, Lithuania on March 30 linked the value of the litas to that of the United States dollar. Officials hoped the move would help control inflation and restore confidence in Lithuanian markets. In April, the United Nations' International Monetary Fund granted the Lithuanian government a loan of $36 million. The Democratic Labor Party (formerly the Communist Party) won a crucial parliamentary vote to retain power in June, despite complaints that President Algirdas Brazauskas had replaced half the cabinet ministers.

□ Steven L. Solnick

See also **Europe** (Facts in brief table). In *World Book,* see **Lithuania.**

A Los Angeles expressway lies in ruins after a severe earthquake shook the city on January 17, causing 57 deaths and about 7,000 injuries.

Los Angeles. A devastating earthquake rocked the Los Angeles area on Jan. 17, 1994, killing 57 people and injuring about 7,000 others. The property damage caused by the quake made it the costliest earthquake in United States history in terms of insured property losses.

The earthquake, which struck at 4:31 a.m., measured 6.7 on the Richter scale. It was centered in the suburban community of Northridge, about 25 miles (40 kilometers) northwest of downtown Los Angeles. The quake collapsed several freeway overpasses, caused severe damage to thousands of structures, and destroyed an apartment building in Northridge, where many of the deaths occurred. Property damage was estimated at $13 billion to $20 billion, including over $7 billion in insured property losses.

A strong aftershock, measuring 5.3 on the Richter scale, hit the Los Angeles area on March 20, the largest since the Northridge quake. Although there were no reports of additional major damage or injuries, new cracks were found in highway supports on at least two freeway overpasses.

O. J. Simpson trial. One of the most sensational murder cases in memory unfolded in Los Angeles in 1994 as former football star and sports broadcaster O. J. Simpson faced charges that he killed his second ex-wife and a male friend of hers. Simpson, 46, was arrested on June 17 after a nationally televised slow-speed pursuit by police officers over several freeways that ended at Simpson's home in Los Angeles.

Simpson was charged with killing Nicole Brown Simpson, 35, and Ronald L. Goldman, 25, a waiter at a local restaurant. The two were stabbed to death on the night of June 12 outside the doorway of Nicole Simpson's condominium in Los Angeles. Simpson pleaded not guilty to the crime.

Eight women and four men were sworn in on November 3 in Los Angeles Superior Court to serve as the jury in the Simpson trial. Eight of the jurors were African American, a factor that some observers thought might help the defense. Polls indicated that blacks were more likely than whites to think that Simpson was innocent. Superior Court Judge Lance A. Ito presided over the trial. (See also **Crime; Courts: Guilty or Not Guilty . . . by a Hair?**)

Transit strike. Employees of the Metropolitan Transportation Authority (MTA) walked off the job on July 25 in Los Angeles' first transit strike in 12 years. The work stoppage, which affected more than 500,000 passengers, was triggered by 1,900 mechanics involved in a contract dispute with MTA officials. Joining them in the walkout were 5,000 service attendants, clerks, and bus and train drivers.

The strike ended on August 2 after both sides agreed to a three-year contract. Under the settlement agreement, union members will be granted wage increases in the second year of the contract. Union members and the MTA also agreed to solve the controversial issue of subcontracting by establishing a joint committee to review any controversial bids or contracts that union members want to keep in-house.

City and county governments. On May 19, the Los Angeles City Council approved a $4.3-billion spending plan that included Mayor Richard J. Riordan's plan to expand the police department. The mayor's proposal, known as Project Safety Los Angeles, called for adding nearly 3,000 officers to the police department over five years. The additional officers would increase the force by almost 40 percent, from a 1994 level of 7,700 officers to a total of 10,455 by the end of the 1990's.

The city budget also made road repairs a high priority after a blue-ribbon business panel reported that poor maintenance would lead to higher construction costs in the future. A total of 200 miles (322 kilometers) of streets will be resurfaced under the new budget.

The Los Angeles County Board of Supervisors on July 14 approved a $14.5-billion budget that maintained essential public services but included $57 million in cuts. Among the cuts were reductions for mental health services, the district attorney's office, and the Department of Public Social Services. Most of the savings were to be achieved through reducing administrative costs. □ Victor Merina

See also **City.** In *World Book,* see **Los Angeles.**
Louisiana. See **State government.**
Luxembourg. See **Europe.**

Magazine. After four years of doldrums caused by declining advertising, the magazine industry began to spring back in 1994.

Face-lifts. Two venerable magazines, *Esquire* and *New York,* acquired new editors who brought vitality and a spruced-up look to the magazines. Edward Kosner was lured to *Esquire* from *New York,* which he edited for 13 years. At *Esquire,* Kosner introduced new writers in an attempt to revive the magazine's former literary glory. He also increased the amount of fashion and service journalism.

Kurt Andersen, who replaced Kosner at *New York,* tried to bring more bite to the magazine and make it at once more brash and more sophisticated. The new, irreverent tone can be traced to Andersen's days at *Spy* magazine, which he cofounded in 1986.

A third familiar magazine, *Mademoiselle,* received a face-lift in 1994. Under Elizabeth Crow, its third new editor in two years, *Mademoiselle* tried to turn around sagging newsstand sales by returning to a more traditional tone. It faced an uphill battle from competing magazines for young women, such as *Glamour* and *Cosmopolitan.*

Death and resurrection. *Spy* closed temporarily after printing its March issue but returned to the newsstands in August. The magazine—regarded by its admirers as satiric and hilarious and by its critics as unconscionably unfair in the way it savages people—takes aim at Establishment figures. It skewered the movers and shakers of the high-flying 1980's, and its clever, cutting-edge design has had a profound influence on many leading magazines.

A true 1994 casualty was *Lear's,* which closed in March. The magazine was started in 1988 by Frances Lear with settlement money after her divorce from television producer Norman Lear. The magazine was aimed at educated women over 30 years of age and reflected Frances Lear's belief that women should be addressed as intelligent and entrepreneurial people, as interested in business and finance as in beauty and fashion. The magazine reportedly failed because Lear wanted to move on to other projects and lost interest in the publication.

New titles. Sensing a turnaround in the economic climate for magazines, established publishers and young entrepreneurs alike took their chances at starting up new magazines. From Time Inc. came *In Style, Makeover,* and *Mouth2Mouth. In Style* and *Makeover* were offshoots of *People* magazine. *In Style* was a monthly magazine that looks at the homes and lifestyles of celebrities such as Barbra Streisand and Whoopi Goldberg. Prototype issues of *Makeover,* a magazine for women interested in how to make over anything from their looks to their lives, and *Mouth2Mouth,* a hip magazine for teen-agers, were put on newsstands to determine whether interest was sufficient to justify making them permanent Time Inc. publications.

A *Time* magazine cover in June, right, drew controversy when it became apparent that *Time* had darkened a police mug shot of O. J. Simpson.

A newly formed partnership, Meigher Communications, brought out *Garden Design,* a lush magazine for people who love to garden and have sophisticated tastes in food. Meigher also introduced *Saveur,* the American edition of *Saveurs,* a food magazine published in France. Taunton Press introduced a third new food magazine, *Fine Cooking.*

Three new computer magazines that try to eliminate confusing jargon and write about computers in language that everyone can understand were started up in 1994. From the Walt Disney Company and the Ziff-Davis Publishing Company came *Family PC,* aimed at parents and children who are trying to figure out computing together; from CMP Publications came *Home PC,* for any household that has a computer, regardless of whether children are involved; and from Ziff-Davis came *Computer Life,* for people without highly technical interests.

Also introduced in 1994 was *Civilization,* which is based on the 100 million items collected in the Library of Congress, including documents, photographs, motion pictures, music compositions, manuscripts, books, and periodicals. *Civilization* was to be published six times a year under a 20-year licensing agreement with the Library of Congress.

☐ Deirdre Carmody

In *World Book,* see **Magazine.**
Maine. See **State government.**
Malawi. See **Africa.**

Malaysia. Prime Minister Mahathir bin Mohamad spent much of 1994 preparing his United Malays National Organization (UMNO) for parliamentary elections, expected in early 1995. The UMNO has held power in the region since before Malaysia became a unified country in 1963. Over time, the party moved from its rural Islamic Malay origins to become associated with an urban elite tied to corporate wealth. The political opposition charged that the UMNO had become corrupt in its selection of party leaders, who automatically gained leadership positions in government. In response, the UMNO called for a special general assembly on June 19, 1994, that amended the party's constitution to stiffen penalties for bribery in party elections.

Competition quelled. Although the UMNO was expected to win the elections handily, it worried about a fundamentalist Islamic sect called Al Arqam. Mahathir described Al Arqam as a threat to national security, though his critics said he feared its appeal to the growing Muslim middle class. Founded in 1968 by a former government teacher, Ashaari Muhammad, the sect claimed as many as 100,000 followers in Malaysia. It ran communes with their own schools and medical clinics and owned prosperous companies at home and abroad.

On Aug. 26, 1994, the government outlawed Al Arqam, and on September 2, police in Thailand arrested Ashaari, who for six years had been living in

Maldives

self-imposed exile there. Thai police turned him over to Malaysian authorities. Upon his release in October, Ashaari officially disbanded Al Arqam, saying he had deviated from Islamic principles.

Another long-time foe of Mahathir, Joseph Pairin Kittingan, and his United Sabah Party (PBS) narrowly won February elections for the Sabah state assembly. Sabah had one of the few state governments not controlled by the UMNO. In March, Mahathir failed in his attempt to block Pairin from becoming chief minister. However, after Mahathir said he would not work with Pairin, some PBS members defected to other parties. Pairin lost power to a new coalition government led by a party allied with the UMNO.

New king. Under a system of rotating the king of Malaysia among the country's nine hereditary state sultans, Tuanku Ja'afar ibni Al-Marhum Tuanku Abdul Rahman was sworn in April 26 as chief of state. Ja'afar had been a Malaysian ambassador.

The economy grew by more than 8 percent in 1994, while inflation and unemployment remained low. Malaysia encouraged technologically advanced industries, and more than half of its manufactured exports were electronics products. □ Henry S. Bradsher

See also **Asia** (Facts in brief table). In *World Book*, see **Malaysia**.

Maldives. See Asia.
Mali. See Africa.
Malta. See Europe.

Mandela, Nelson R. (1918-　　), a prominent opponent of the former white-dominated government of South Africa, was inaugurated as South Africa's executive president on May 10, 1994. Mandela, that nation's first black head of state, said South Africans of all races must work together to create a just and prosperous new society.

Nelson Rolihlahla Mandela was born on July 18, 1918, in the Transkei area of South Africa. His father was a tribal chief. Mandela attended Fort Hare University in the Cape Province but was suspended for leading a protest. He continued his education by correspondence and later earned a law degree.

In 1944, Mandela joined the African National Congress (ANC), the largest black group opposing the South African government. His activities against the government led to his arrest. He was acquitted of treason in 1961 but was later arrested again on other charges. In 1964, he was convicted of sabotage and conspiracy and sentenced to life in prison.

In 1990, as the government—besieged by black protests and foreign pressures—prepared to end white rule, Mandela was released from prison. He was elected ANC president the next year. Mandela worked closely with State President Frederik Willem de Klerk to assure a smooth transition to black rule.

Mandela and his second wife, Winnie, are separated. They have two daughters. □ David Dreier
Manitoba. See Canadian provinces.

Manufacturing. For the third year in a row, the United States economy, led by manufacturing, expanded as consumers spent more and businesses invested in new plants and equipment. *Gross domestic product* (GDP), the total value of all goods and services produced in a country, was up 3.3 percent in the first quarter, raced ahead 4.0 percent in the second quarter, and continued on at a 3.9 percent pace in the third quarter, according to the U.S. Commerce Department. Economists even feared the economy was too strong and could bring rising prices and inflation. Thus, the U.S. Federal Reserve Board, also known as the *Fed*, raised short-term interest rates six times in 1994 to cool off the economy.

The manufacturing sector was almost too hot in 1994. Orders were plentiful. Consumer confidence was strong. Many people refinanced their home mortgages to take advantage of lower interest rates, and therefore had more cash to spend on such items as automobiles, furniture, appliances, and computers, purchases that they had put off making in previous years.

Output. Manufacturers started the first quarter of 1994 by posting production gains of about 0.5 percent. As home building roared ahead in the first half of the year because of low mortgage rates, the production of appliances, building materials, carpets, and furniture also raced ahead. However, after the Fed raised interest rates in the spring and summer, the housing market slowed and production of construction supplies began to fall.

Automakers were scheduled to produce 15.5 million cars and trucks in 1994 and the year saw continued strong demand for computers and office equipment. Production of technology equipment in October was up 12.1 percent over October 1993.

Factory orders started the year strong with a solid 2.4 percent gain in January, according to the Commerce Department, the sixth consecutive gain since August 1993. Orders for durable goods, items intended to last three or more years including appliances and machine tools, were up 4.4 percent.

Factory orders fell 4 percent in July, the largest drop since 1991, but some of that was due to automakers retooling their factories in advance of 1995 model year cars. A dramatic turnaround happened in August 1994 as new factory orders surged 4.4 percent, the largest gain in two years. Autos and heavy machinery, a big part of the July drop, accounted for more than half of the August jump.

Manufacturing survey. The National Association of Purchasing Management (NAPM) surveys 300 industrial companies each month on the status of orders, exports, employment, and confidence. An NAPM reading above 50 percent indicates growth in the manufacturing sector. In January, the NAPM index stood at a healthy 57.7 percent. It stayed close to that level for months before reaching a robust 61.2 percent in November, the highest since 1983.

Capital spending. Quarterly surveys by the Commerce Department indicated that businesses would spend 8.8 percent on new plants and equipment in 1994. Global competition and the inability to increase prices on their products prompted manufacturers to invest in computer hardware and software and other productivity-enhancing equipment to keep production costs down.

The production of computers and other office equipment soared by 26.2 percent from late 1993 through the fall of 1994. Because this equipment helps boost productivity and control labor costs, the growth was expected to continue. A market research firm said manufacturing software revenue would grow 15 percent annually through 1998.

Exports. Selling to foreign markets became a key strategy for American manufacturers in 1994. More than 80 percent of the NAPM members surveyed said they exported their products. The NAPM predicted U.S. manufacturing exports would grow by at least 8 to 9 percent in 1994 and 1995, due to the economic recovery in Europe and Japan and continued demand for goods from the emerging Latin-American and Pacific Rim (Southeast Asian) markets. United States exports overall were up 10.6 percent for the 12-month period ending July 1994. The low rate of the U.S. dollar helped make U.S. products more attractive to overseas buyers. The North American Free Trade Agreement (NAFTA), which was ratified in 1993, helped U.S. manufacturers in 1994 to

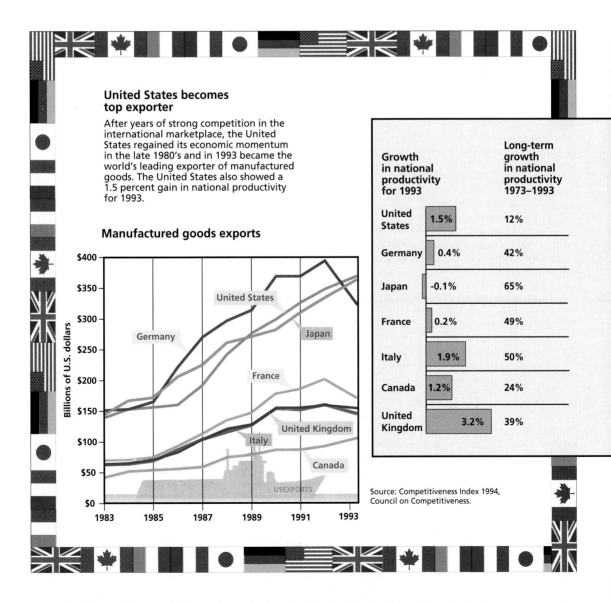

United States becomes top exporter

After years of strong competition in the international marketplace, the United States regained its economic momentum in the late 1980's and in 1993 became the world's leading exporter of manufactured goods. The United States also showed a 1.5 percent gain in national productivity for 1993.

Manufactured goods exports

Billions of U.S. dollars

$400 · $350 · $300 · $250 · $200 · $150 · $100 · $50 · $0

United States
Germany
Japan
France
Italy
United Kingdom
Canada

1983 1985 1987 1989 1991 1993

	Growth in national productivity for 1993	Long-term growth in national productivity 1973–1993
United States	1.5%	12%
Germany	0.4%	42%
Japan	-0.1%	65%
France	0.2%	49%
Italy	1.9%	50%
Canada	1.2%	24%
United Kingdom	3.2%	39%

Source: Competitiveness Index 1994, Council on Competitiveness.

increase their exports to Canada and Mexico, the other members of the free-trade zone.

Productivity. High productivity became important for manufacturers unable to pass their increased costs for materials on to consumers due to tough national and foreign competition. Plants operated at near full capacity, and the factory workweek increased to a record peak of more than 42 hours in April as people worked overtime to meet demand. After years of streamlining work forces and operations, manufacturers had become leaders in productivity. By reducing their work forces, using computers on the factory floor, and keeping wages in check, manufacturers had averaged 3 percent annual productivity growth over 10 years, compared with 1 percent for all businesses, the National Association of Manufacturers reported in 1994.

Employment. In 1994, the rise in exports along with the increase in new factory orders and production resulted in the creation of many new jobs. The national unemployment rate started the year at 6.7 percent before plummeting to a four-year low of 5.6 percent in November. Manufacturers added more than 225,000 workers through November. Employment in the auto industry was the highest since 1979, according to the U.S. Labor Department.

Machine tools, which cut and shape metal parts for other machines, mirrored the health of the manufacturing sector in 1994. Economists watch machine tool orders closely as an indicator of future economic activity.

In the first quarter of 1994, orders raced 24 percent ahead of the first quarter of 1993. This was the best first quarter since 1980, according to the Association of Manufacturing Technology. Orders jumped a huge 57 percent in September, the highest monthly level since 1979, due to a spate of new orders derived from the biennial International Manufacturing Technology trade show. Through October, orders were up 36 percent over 1993, at $3.71 billion.

New plants. In August, computer chip maker Intel Corp. announced plans for a $705-million expansion of a plant near Portland, Ore., to produce multiprocessor chips. Another chip maker, Micron Technology of Boise, Ida., announced in October its intention to build a $1.3-billion plant that would double Micron's chip-making capacity and employ 3,500 workers. German carmaker BMW began building its first cars in the United States in Spartanburg, S.C. Cimtek, a market research firm, found that in the first half of 1994, plans were filed to build 1,066 plants. This level was up 69 percent from the first six months of 1993. Plans to expand plants were also up 60 percent. □ Ronald Kolgraf

In *World Book,* see **Manufacturing.**
Maryland. See **State government.**
Massachusetts. See **State government.**
Mauritania. See **Africa.**
Mauritius. See **Africa.**

Medicine. A worldwide effort to isolate the gene that causes an inherited form of breast cancer culminated on Sept. 14, 1994, in an announcement of the gene's discovery. The gene, called BRCA1, is thought to cause half of all cases of hereditary breast cancer. Cancer experts estimate, however, that only about 5 percent of the 182,000 breast cancer cases diagnosed in the United States each year are hereditary. The remaining 95 percent occur for unknown reasons.

Experts had long suspected that the prevalence of breast cancer in some families involves an abnormal gene passed from mother to daughter. By 1990, researchers had traced the gene to chromosome 17, one of the 23 pairs of chromosomes that carry genes in human cells. The group that finally isolated the gene was led by Mark H. Skolnick, a geneticist at the University of Utah Medical Center in Salt Lake City. The team included 45 scientists from institutions in the United States, Canada, and Sweden.

Cancer experts predicted that the discovery could eventually lead to a laboratory test for identifying the estimated 600,000 American women who carry BRCA1. Harmon Eyre, chief medical officer of the American Cancer Society, said that the discovery of BRCA1 could help scientists understand the biochemical changes that underlie all forms of breast cancer.

Falsified data. The National Cancer Institute (NCI) in April 1994 reassured breast cancer patients that the findings of a major clinical trial remain valid despite the study's use of falsified data from a Canadian hospital. NCI said falsified data was submitted by a researcher at St. Luc's Hospital in Montreal, one of 484 medical centers that participated in the study.

The study had concluded that women with early-stage breast cancer need not undergo *mastectomy,* the surgical removal of the entire breast, to prevent the cancer from spreading. Less extensive surgery, involving the removal of the cancerous tumor and surrounding tissue, followed by radiation therapy was just as effective in preventing recurrence, the study found. The findings helped thousands of women with breast cancer decide on the breast-sparing treatment. NCI said that a reanalysis of the data, after the falsified entries had been removed, confirmed the original conclusion.

Vitamin supplements. A study published on April 14 did not support the idea that supplements of vitamin E and beta carotene (which the body converts to vitamin A) can reduce the risk of cancer and heart disease. The study tested the effects of vitamin supplements on 29,000 Finnish men who were long-time smokers. One group of men took vitamin E supplements, another group took beta carotene, a third received both supplements, and a control group took a *placebo* (inactive substance).

After five to eight years, the men who took beta carotene had an 18 percent higher incidence of lung cancer than those who did not take the vitamin, and men who took vitamin E had a slightly higher risk of

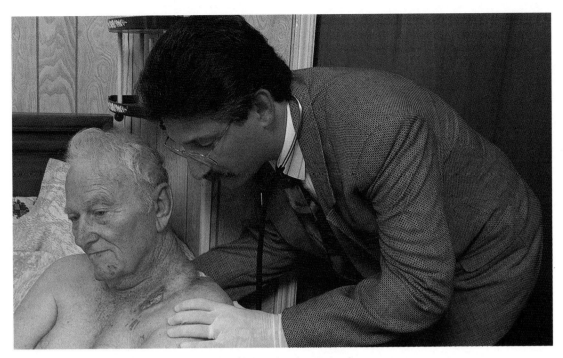

Quick treatment saves the life of a New York man infected with a strain of "flesh-eating" streptococcus bacteria that made lurid headlines in May.

stroke. Earlier studies had suggested that so-called antioxidants such as vitamin E and beta carotene could neutralize the effects within the body of damaging molecules called free radicals, which are thought to play a role in cancer and heart disease.

Fetal surgery. The success of a new technique for performing operations on unborn fetuses was announced on February 17 by surgeons at Wayne State University in Detroit. In the operation, the surgeons passed tiny instruments through a needle-sized hole in the abdomen of a woman who was 19 weeks pregnant with twins. One of the fetuses lacked both a heart and a brain. Although the other fetus was normal, its heart had to pump blood for itself and its twin. Without surgery, the normal fetus had a 75 percent chance of dying from heart failure prior to birth. Surgeons used the instruments to stop blood circulation to the defective fetus, so that the normal fetus was born healthy.

Roberto Romero of the National Institute of Child Health and Human Development in Bethesda, Md., said the procedure opened a new era in prenatal medicine, enabling surgeons to perform a variety of lifesaving operations on sick fetuses. These operations range from removing tumors to separating twins whose bodies are joined at major blood vessels. In the past, Romero said, such conditions often resulted in fetal death or the birth of a child with permanent disabilities.

Heart attack patients should be given clot-dissolving drugs within 30 minutes of arrival at a hospital emergency department, according to a report issued on February 7. A group of 39 medical organizations and government health agencies made the recommendation in an effort to improve the care of heart attack victims.

The report said that only about 39 percent of heart attack patients currently receive drugs to break up clots blocking arteries that supply blood to the heart. Such drugs can stop a heart attack and prevent permanent damage to heart tissue. The drugs work best when administered soon after a heart attack, usually within two hours of an attack. But in many cases, the drugs are given too late.

The report recommended a number of steps to speed care of heart attack victims. These include storing clot-dissolving drugs in the emergency room, rather than the hospital pharmacy; allowing nurses to order certain diagnostic tests for patients with heart attack symptoms; and authorizing emergency room physicians to administer clot-dissolving drugs without waiting for approval from the patient's personal physician.

Watchful waiting. Many men with symptoms of an enlarged prostate may not need treatment—or nonsurgical treatment at most—according to new guidelines issued February 8. The guidelines on the care of benign prostatic hyperplasia (BPH) were drafted by a panel of medical experts for an agency of the U.S. Public Health Service. The prostate is a walnut-sized gland encircling the urethra in men.

An estimated 10 million American men, including 50 percent of men over age 60, suffer from BPH. They may awaken several times at night to urinate, feel an urgent need to urinate, and have other symptoms. The panel sought to reassure men that mild or moderate BPH sometimes improves by itself. It advised men to consider a period of observation by their physician, rather than choosing immediate surgery or medication to shrink the prostate. The panel also said that some tests routinely given to men with BPH are unnecessary and waste millions of dollars each year. The panel said that such tests as kidney X rays, ultrasound imaging, and examination of the urinary tract with an instrument called an endoscope should be used only in special cases.

Ulcer treatment. An expert panel convened by the National Institutes of Health (NIH) in Bethesda in February advised physicians that many cases of stomach ulcers and chronic *gastritis* (stomach inflammation) result from a bacterial infection that should be treated with antibiotics. The panel noted, however, that some ulcers are caused by other factors, especially heavy use of aspirin or related drugs. But it said most patients would benefit from treatment with antibiotics in addition to the standard ulcer drugs that reduce the secretion of stomach acid.

Mysterious health problems occurring among some veterans of the 1991 Persian Gulf War cannot be traced to a single cause, NIH concluded on April 29, 1994. After reviewing information on the so-called Gulf War syndrome, NIH said the symptoms—including diarrhea, fatigue, muscle pain, depression, difficulty concentrating, and sensitivity to common chemicals—seemed to result from multiple illnesses with different causes. Veterans have blamed the illness on a variety of factors, including chemical or biological agents used by the enemy, parasites, smoke from burning oil wells, and side effects of vaccines.

A virulent strain of streptococcus bacteria aroused alarm in May, after newspapers in the United Kingdom reported on seven cases of infection with a "deadly flesh-eating bacteria." The bacteria, known as group A streptococcus, in their invasive form can penetrate deep into the body, destroy flesh or muscle, and trigger fatal complications. Infectious disease experts said the condition was not new and posed no widespread health threat. Public health officials in June estimated that as many as 15,000 cases of infection with group A streptococci occurred in the United States in 1993 and that 5 to 10 percent involved the tissue-destroying strain, which can be successfully treated with penicillin if caught early enough. □ Michael Woods

See also **AIDS: The Changing Face of AIDS; Drugs; Public Health: The Radiation Experiments.** In *World Book,* see **Medicine.**

Mental health. The American Psychological Association (APA) on Aug. 24, 1994, cautioned that a widely used procedure termed facilitated communication has no scientific basis. Facilitated communication has been adopted in educational programs throughout the United States and Canada for use with people who are severely retarded or have other conditions that prevent normal verbal communication. In the procedure, a person called a facilitator supports the impaired person's arm or hand over a keyboard, reportedly to enable the person to type out answers to questions. In some instances, facilitated communication has resulted in accusations of abuse against family members or caregivers.

In the August policy statement, the APA said scientific studies have repeatedly shown that facilitated communication is not a valid technique for people with profound mental disabilities. The APA said its use produces the illusion of communication from the impaired person when there is none. Unsubstantiated allegations of abuse made through facilitated communication have caused psychological distress, alienation, or financial hardship for family members and caregivers, the APA said. The APA is the largest professional organization of psychologists in the United States.

Poor mental health is experienced by about one out of three Americans at least one day every month, a study by the U.S. Centers for Disease Control and Prevention in Atlanta, Ga., reported in May. The study included data from about 45,000 people around the country who responded to a survey. Poor mental health days were defined as those when people were especially aware of feelings of depression, stress, or other emotional problems.

Researchers found that people aged 75 and over had fewer days of poor mental health (1.9) than people from ages 18 to 24 (3.4). Women reported an average of 3.4 such days a month, compared with 2.2 days for men.

Employment was a major factor in determining mental health. People unable to work because of health problems reported the highest number of poor mental health days (8.9), followed by unemployed people (5.2). People experiencing marital problems also had more poor days (5.4 for separated people and 3.9 for divorced people) than did the never married (3.0) and the currently married (2.4).

Preventing mental illness. A panel of mental health experts on January 25 recommended that the federal government fund more research on new ways of preventing mental disorders. The panel cited many important advances in treating mental illnesses once symptoms are severe enough to be apparent. But it said treatment will never solve the enormous economic and social problems associated with mental illness. The panel was organized by the Institute of Medicine, an agency that advises the government on health and technology.

The panel estimated that about one in three American adults will suffer a mental disorder at some point and that mental illnesses cost the U.S. economy more than $200 billion a year in treatment and lost productivity. Although treatment can alleviate symptoms and improve the quality of life for patients, it rarely results in permanent cures. Many mental illnesses are chronic or involve relapses in which symptoms recur after periods of improvement. The panel thus cited prevention as a clear first choice. The report added that new knowledge about the causes of mental illness has given researchers a stronger basis for seeking new prevention methods.

Chronic stress among teen-agers who feel frustrated in their efforts to succeed may more than double their risk of developing high blood pressure at an early age, a study conducted at Johns Hopkins University in Baltimore reported in April. Psychologists studied 240 ninth-graders at a science magnet school in Baltimore. They found frustration with life events to be linked more closely to increases in blood pressure than were moods such as anger. Girls tended to experience rises in blood pressure as they tried to assert themselves or compete. Among boys, blood pressure rose as they struggled with parents' expectations or parents' understanding of their problems. □ Michael Woods

See also **Psychology.** In *World Book,* see **Mental illness.**

Mexico. The Dec. 1, 1994, inauguration of Mexico's new president, Ernesto Zedillo Ponce de León of the Institutional Revolutionary Party (PRI), capped a tumultuous year in which rebellion and political assassination rocked Mexico's political system. Zedillo's August 21 election continued the unbroken hold on power that the PRI had enjoyed since 1929, but the party tallied a record low percentage of votes in 1994. (See **Zedillo Ponce de León, Ernesto.**)

New Year's Day rebellion. On January 1, a rebel group calling itself the Zapatista National Liberation Army seized four towns in the southern state of Chiapas. The rebels, mostly native Mayan Indians and peasants, issued a "declaration of war" against the federal government. The government deployed troops, and more than 100 rebels, soldiers, police, and civilians died in the fighting.

The rebels charged the government with discrimination against the region's predominantly Indian population and officially sanctioned evictions of Indians from communal farmlands. The rebels said they had launched their offensive on January 1 to oppose the implementation that day of the North American Free Trade Agreement (NAFTA) between Mexico, the United States, and Canada. The rebels said NAFTA was a plan to enrich well-to-do Mexicans while ignoring the plight of the nation's poor.

The Mexican government promised to address the social and political conditions that had prompt-

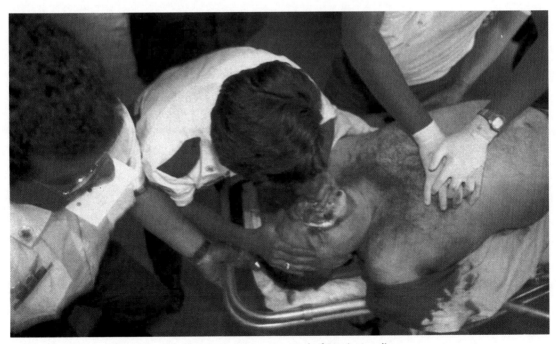

Medics attend to José Francisco Ruíz Massieu, secretary-general of Mexico's ruling party, after he was shot in Mexico City in September. Ruíz later died.

Rebellion in Chiapas

Mayan Indians and peasants in Mexico's state of Chiapas rose in armed rebellion against the federal government on Jan. 1, 1994. The rebels were protesting poor economic conditions and alleged discrimination.

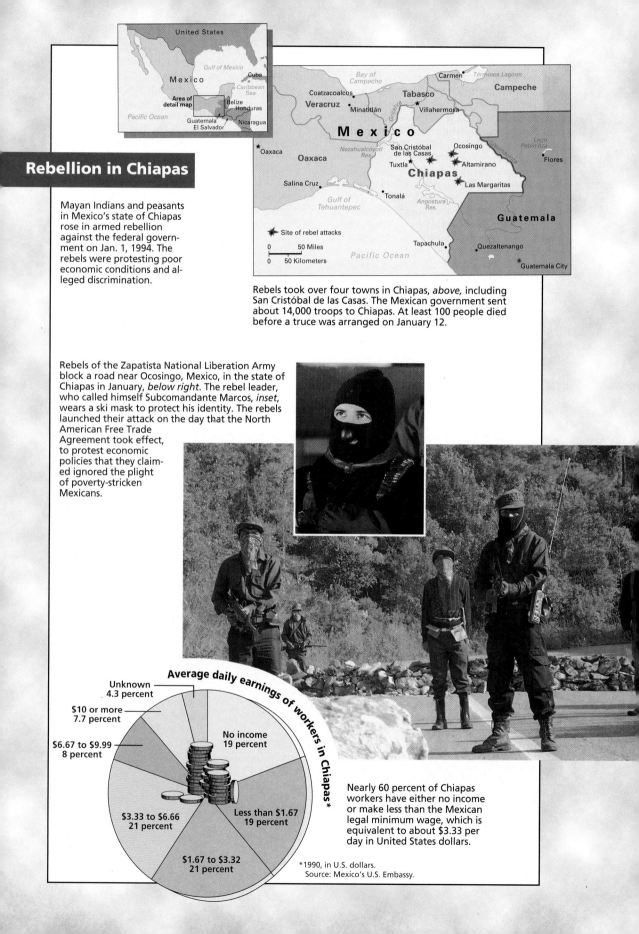

Rebels took over four towns in Chiapas, *above,* including San Cristóbal de las Casas. The Mexican government sent about 14,000 troops to Chiapas. At least 100 people died before a truce was arranged on January 12.

Rebels of the Zapatista National Liberation Army block a road near Ocosingo, Mexico, in the state of Chiapas in January, *below right.* The rebel leader, who called himself Subcomandante Marcos, *inset,* wears a ski mask to protect his identity. The rebels launched their attack on the day that the North American Free Trade Agreement took effect, to protest economic policies that they claimed ignored the plight of poverty-stricken Mexicans.

Average daily earnings of workers in Chiapas*

- Unknown — 4.3 percent
- $10 or more — 7.7 percent
- $6.67 to $9.99 — 8 percent
- No income — 19 percent
- $3.33 to $6.66 — 21 percent
- Less than $1.67 — 19 percent
- $1.67 to $3.32 — 21 percent

Nearly 60 percent of Chiapas workers have either no income or make less than the Mexican legal minimum wage, which is equivalent to about $3.33 per day in United States dollars.

*1990, in U.S. dollars.
Source: Mexico's U.S. Embassy.

ed the uprising, and a shaky peace held for most of the year. But in late December, the rebels again threatened armed rebellion to protest alleged fraud in August's race for governor of Chiapas. Rebels took over several towns in Chiapas but retreated peacefully when government troops moved in.

Assassination of Colosio. Most Mexicans were more interested in the plight of the Chiapas Indians than what seemed like a lackluster presidential campaign. But on March 23 in Tijuana, a gunman killed Luis Donaldo Colosio Murrieta, 44, the PRI presidential candidate. Mario Aburto Martínez, 23, a local factory worker, confessed to the killing, and a government investigation confirmed that he had acted alone. But public opinion polls showed that most Mexicans believed there had been a conspiracy, and on July 14, outgoing President Carlos Salinas de Gortari reopened the investigation.

On March 29, Salinas picked Zedillo as the new PRI presidential candidate. Zedillo had served as Mexico's secretary of planning and budget and subsequently as education minister. In November 1993, he had become Colosio's campaign manager.

Killing of a top PRI official. On Sept. 28, 1994, José Francisco Ruíz Massieu, secretary-general of the ruling PRI, was shot to death in Mexico City by a hired assassin. Police immediately arrested the suspect, identified as Daniel Aguilar Treviño. On October 6, police charged Abraham Rubio Canales, a former aide to Ruíz who was serving a prison sentence for fraud, and Manuel Muñoz Rocha, a federal congressman, with planning the murder.

Ruíz's brother, Assistant Attorney General Mario Ruíz Massieu, took over the investigation of the murder. But he resigned on November 23, claiming that top PRI officials were hindering the investigation to mask the party's involvement in the killing.

Kidnappings. On March 14, kidnappers abducted billionaire Alfredo Harp Helu, 50, chairman of Financiero Banamex-Accival S.A., Mexico's largest bank and brokerage firm. His captors did not release him until June 28, when they received a ransom estimated at between $30 million and $60 million. On April 25, Angel Losada Moreno, 38, vice chairman of the supermarket chain Grupo Gigante S.A., was also kidnapped. He was freed on August 5 after his family paid a ransom of an undisclosed amount.

Peso falls. Mexico's peso fell as much as 40 percent in value compared with the U.S. dollar in late December as the government announced a plan to focus more on reducing foreign debt than on economic growth. As the peso fell, many investors waited anxiously to see whether the Mexican currency's troubles would affect other financial markets in Latin America. □ Nathan A. Haverstock

See also **Latin America** (Facts in brief table). In *World Book,* see **Mexico.**

Michigan. See **Detroit; State government.**

Supporters of the leftist Democratic Revolutionary Party in Mexico City protest alleged election fraud in August following national elections.

Middle East

The Arab-Israeli peace process moved forward so rapidly and on so many fronts in 1994 that few observers could predict its economic and political impact on the Middle East. But hopes for peace were also tempered by some of the bloodiest acts of terrorism by Jews and Arabs since the Arab-Israeli Six-Day War of 1967.

Jordan-Israel peace. Palestine Liberation Organization (PLO) leader Yasir Arafat and Israeli Prime Minister Yitzhak Rabin had stunned the world in 1993 by accepting a declaration that could lead to an independent Palestinian state. But King Hussein I of Jordan in 1994 moved even further down the road of peace with Israel. On July 25, Hussein and Rabin agreed to end a 46-year-old state of belligerency between their countries when they signed a nonaggression pact in Washington, D.C. It was revealed afterwards that Hussein and Rabin had met secretly for 20 years.

On October 26, Hussein and Rabin met again and exchanged ratified copies of a peace treaty between their countries on the shore of the Sea of Galilee in Israel. Hussein thus became the second Arab head of state to sign a peace treaty with Israel. Egyptian President Anwar el-Sadat had signed a treaty with Israel in 1979.

Many experts believed that, mainly for economic reasons, peace between Jordan and Israel had a chance for lasting success. Even before the peace treaty was signed, Jordanian and Israeli officials had met to resolve water and border disagreements. The two countries opened telephone links and two border posts in 1994. Other joint projects being discussed included developing the Jordan River Valley bordering both countries, linking electrical grids, creating a financial organization to draw investors into development projects, and creating a free-trade zone.

Jerusalem. The Jordanian-Israeli pact also recognized Jordan's special role as administrator of Islamic shrines in Jerusalem, including one of Islam's holiest sites, the Dome of the Rock, built in 691. Hussein, whose family had acted as custodian of the sites for five decades, saw the recognition as a personal triumph. He had spent $6.5 million of his own money to refurbish the golden-domed building.

However, control of Islam's sites remained controversial. Arafat demanded that the status of Jerusalem be a priority topic in Arab-Israeli peace negotiation and that Palestinians have control over Islamic sites there. Although Rabin asserted that Jerusalem was open to all religions, he maintained that it would remain the capital of the Jewish state of Israel. The royal families of Morocco and Saudi Arabia were also believed to covet a special role in administering the Islamic holy sites.

The Palestinians. Many observers believed that the Palestinians were key to a broader Arab-Israeli peace. But on February 25, the peace process nearly derailed when a Jewish settler massacred at least 29 Muslims praying at a mosque in the West Bank town of Hebron. Increased violence between Arabs and Jews who opposed peace led to a ban on Arab workers entering Israel, worsening the economic plight of many Palestinians. Some estimates put Palestinian unemployment as high as 50 percent in 1994.

In spite of the tensions, the Palestinians began self-rule in the Gaza Strip and the West Bank town of Jericho on May 4. Their new status followed the signing of an agreement in Cairo, Egypt, between Israel and Arafat, who, as leader of the PLO, was recognized by Israel as the sole representative of the Palestinian people. By May 18, Israeli troops had

Israeli Prime Minister Yitzhak Rabin, left, and Jordan's King Hussein I, right, shake hands as United States President Bill Clinton looks on at the start of peace talks in July.

withdrawn from Gaza and Jericho, except from areas bordering Israel and buffer zones protecting about 4,500 Israeli settlers in Gaza. The troops were replaced by 4,000 Palestinian police, mainly former guerrillas who had been retrained.

Israel gave the new body, known as the Palestine National Authority, control over tourism and social services on August 15. The Authority took over educational affairs on September 1 and health issues and taxation in November.

Arafat as leader. On July 1, Arafat, as leader of the new Palestine National Authority, made a triumphant return to Gaza and Jericho after decades in exile. But after the euphoria of 1993, many Palestinians were somber in 1994. They believed that Arafat

had conceded too much to the Israelis, and Arafat became a focus of criticism in 1994. On November 18, the new Palestinian police force, loyal to Arafat, fired on Islamic militants in the Gaza Strip, killing 14 people and wounding about 200. The incident began when police tried to break up a protest outside a mosque in the city of Gaza. It was the most serious breach among several between Arafat and Islamic extremist groups, mainly Hamas and Islamic Jihad, that had opposed peace with Israel. Hamas was said by some experts to have sympathizers among 30 percent of the Palestinian population.

Earlier in November, mourners forced Arafat out of a mosque when he tried to attend the funeral of pro-Islamic figure Hani Abed, who had been killed by a car bomb inside Palestinian-controlled territory on November 2. Some Palestinians alleged that Israelis were responsible for the bombing, and they accused Arafat of being an Israeli "collaborator." Arafat had been under pressure from Israel to control Islamic extremists, and following his return to Gaza and Jericho, Palestinian police conducted mass roundups of suspected Islamic militants.

Arafat had trouble in delegating authority. Various nations and international organizations had pledged around $2.4 billion to aid the Palestinians, but they waited for the creation of a responsible financial agency to oversee the money. Elections for a planned 24-member Palestine National Council had not happened by the end of the year. But in late November, the donors did promise $58 million. Some Palestinians also complained that Arafat filled positions with formerly exiled Palestinians, while leaders of the *intifada* (uprising) were overlooked.

Economic summit. A three-day Middle East-North African Economic Summit on October 30 in Casablanca, Morocco, drew leaders from about 40 nations, including Israel, and more than 1,500 businesspeople. The premise of the conference was that Middle East peace depended upon economic development and regional integration.

Many businesspeople said that Middle East countries need to create a more favorable climate for investment. Necessary reforms included greater privatization, improved financial institutions, and protections for foreign investors. They also said regional integration would depend on improving transportation, communication, and electrical systems.

Arab nations in the Gulf applauded the steps taken in 1994 toward establishing Arab-Israeli peace, but many Gulf nations said the peace process was occurring too quickly. Some feared that Western investors would find the countries near the Mediterranean Sea more attractive for investment than the Persian Gulf states. Some also worried that their nations would be expected to pay for a planned U.S.-backed regional development bank to aid the peace process. Some of the oil-rich Gulf nations suffered a 20 percent drop in revenues due to low oil prices in late 1993 and early 1994.

Bahrain, Oman, and Qatar nonetheless said in 1994 that they were discussing the possibility of a diplomatic exchange with Israel. The Gulf Cooperation Council (GCC) also announced on September 30 that it was ending the "secondary" and "tertiary" aspects of an economic boycott against Israel that began in 1946. Under these aspects of the boycott, any companies or individuals doing business with Israel were blacklisted from trade with members of the Arab League. But the "primary" boycott—prohibition of direct trade between Arab states and Israel—still remained in force. GCC members were Bahrain, Kuwait, Oman, Qatar, Saudi Arabia, and the United Arab Emirates.

Events in Iraq and Yemen also alarmed the Gulf states in 1994. In early October, Iraqi troops massed on Iraq's border with Kuwait, renewing fears that as long as Iraqi President Saddam Hussein remained in power, Kuwait was vulnerable to attack. Iraqi forces later withdrew after the United States airlifted troops to the Gulf and threatened military action. However, some Gulf Arabs and even Western nations privately accused the United States of overreacting in order to gain a better foothold in the Gulf. The Gulf Arabs, some of whom feared a U.S. presence would heighten Islamic extremism, also had to bear the cost of the military action, estimated at $750 million.

The Gulf nations were reportedly pleased when

Yasir Arafat, head of the Palestine Liberation Organization, enters the Gaza Strip in July after decades of exile from the Israeli-occupied territory.

civil war erupted in Yemen on May 5. Kuwait and Saudi Arabia were said to have given money and weapons to southern Yemeni secessionist leaders. They also wanted to recognize the South as an independent state because they saw a united Yemen as threatening. However, pressure from the United States, which feared growing regional instability, kept the Gulf states from doing so. The secessionists were defeated in July.

Islam as a political force gained ground in 1994 even in countries that had relatively little political strife. Oman arrested as many as 200 people for *sedition* (creating rebellion) because they allegedly belonged to an underground Islamic group with foreign ties, according to an August report. Saudi Arabia in September announced the arrests of some 110 alleged Muslim "agitators." Arrests were also reported in Bahrain and Qatar during 1994. Egypt continued harsh measures to quell Islamic militants, while Algeria's conflict between the government and Islamic extremists had become a civil war, some experts said.

Naguib Mahfouz, Egyptian author and the only Arab to win the Nobel Prize for literature (1988), received serious stab wounds near his Cairo home on October 14. Police blamed Islamic fundamentalists, who reportedly oppose Mahfouz because of his book *Children of Gebelawi* (1959), which they view as heretical to Islam, and because of his support of peace with Israel.

Attacks on Jewish targets outside the Middle East during 1994 raised fear internationally. About 100 people died on July 18 in Buenos Aires, Argentina, in the bombing of a building that housed the country's two main Jewish organizations. The next day, a bomb destroyed a commuter plane in Panama, killing 21 people, many of whom were Jewish. At least 14 people were injured by a bomb outside the Israeli Embassy in London on July 26. Another five were hurt in a similar attack on a Jewish fundraising center in London a day later. Although no arrests were made in 1994, Israeli officials blamed Iran and pro-Iranian groups.

Guilty. Four Muslim fundamentalists were found guilty on March 4 of conspiracy to bomb New York City's World Trade Center. The February 1993 bombing killed six people and injured more than 1,000. It was called the worst act of terrorism on U.S. soil. The four men each received sentences of 240 years in prison. Two Iranians were convicted in Iran on Dec. 6, 1994, of killing former Iranian Prime Minister Shahpour Bakhtiar in Paris in 1991.

Natural resources. Delegates to multilateral peace talks in Oman agreed in April to establish in Oman a center to research how to *desalinate* (remove the salt from) seawater more cheaply. Although many oil-rich Arab states rely heavily on desalination for their water, the technology is too expensive for most countries. The World Bank, a

Israeli settlements

As Israel and the Palestine Liberation Organization implemented limited Palestinian self-rule in the Gaza Strip and the West Bank town of Jericho, below, the issue of what to do with Israeli settlements in Gaza and the West Bank was still being debated in 1994. An estimated 114,500 Israelis occupied the settlements.

West Bank population, 1994	
Israeli settlers	110,000
Palestinians	1,300,000

Gaza Strip population, 1994	
Israeli settlers	4,500
Palestinians	720,000

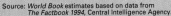

Source: *World Book* estimates based on data from *The Factbook 1994,* Central Intelligence Agency.

Facts in brief on Middle Eastern countries

Country	Population	Government	Monetary unit*	Foreign trade (million U.S.$)	
				Exports†	Imports†
Bahrain	578,000	Amir Isa bin Salman Al-Khalifa; Prime Minister Khalifa bin Salman Al-Khalifa	dinar (0.38 = $1)	3,689	3,825
Cyprus	736,000	President Glafcos Clerides (Turkish Republic of Northern Cyprus: President Rauf R. Denktas)	pound (0.46 = $1)	883	2,534
Egypt	58,519,000	President Hosni Mubarak; Prime Minister Atef Sedky	pound (3.38 = $1)	2,243	8,176
Iran	66,720,000	Leader of the Islamic Revolution Ali Hoseini Khamenei; President Ali Akbar Hashemi Rafsanjani	rial (1,749.00 = $1)	15,500	23,700
Iraq	21,224,000	President Saddam Hussein	dinar (0.55 = $1)	10,400	6,600
Israel	5,884,000	President Ezer Weizman; Prime Minister Yitzhak Rabin	new shekel (2.95 = $1)	14,770	22,619
Jordan	4,013,000	King Hussein I; Prime Minister Abd al-Salam al-Majali	dinar (0.69 = $1)	1,246	3,539
Kuwait	1,804,000	Amir Jabir al-Ahmad al-Jabir al-Sabah; Prime Minister & Crown Prince Saad al-Abdallah al-Salim al-Sabah	dinar (0.30 = $1)	10,494	6,584
Lebanon	3,028,000	President Ilyas Harawi; Prime Minister Rafik Hariri	pound (1,661.50 = $1)	925	4,100
Oman	1,822,000	Sultan Qaboos bin Said Al-Said	rial (0.39 = $1)	5,428	3,769
Qatar	490,000	Amir and Prime Minister Khalifa bin Hamad Al-Thani	riyal (3.64 = $1)	3,107	1,720
Saudi Arabia	17,608,000	King & Prime Minister Fahd bin Abd al-Aziz Al-Saud	riyal (3.75 = $1)	44,417	24,069
Sudan	28,960,000	President Umar Hasan Ahmad al-Bashir	pound (311.00 = $1)	509	1,060
Syria	14,775,000	President Hafiz al-Asad; Prime Minister Mahmud Zubi	pound (23.00 = $1)	3,147	4,140
Turkey	62,032,000	President Süleyman Demirel; Prime Minister Tansu Ciller	lira (35,859.00 = $1)	14,878	22,579
United Arab Emirates	1,785,000	President Zayid bin Sultan Al-Nuhayyan; Prime Minister Maktum bin Rashid Al-Maktum	dirham (3.67 = $1)	15,837	6,422
Yemen	13,897,000	President Ali Abdallah Salih; Acting Prime Minister Muhammad Said al-Attar	rial (12.00 = $1)	101	1,378

*Exchange rates as of Oct. 28,1994, or latest available data.
†Latest available data.

United Nations agency, predicted that by 2025 the Middle East would have only 23,555 cubic feet (667 cubic meters) per year of renewable water for each person if problems such as urban growth and sewage treatment are not resolved. An average person needs 63,531 cubic feet (1,799 cubic meters) of water a year. Many experts warned that competition for scarce water resources could lead to regional conflicts in the Middle East.

The World Bank said in December that environmental problems cost the Arab world over $10 billion a year. Health problems and reduced labor productivity made up half of that cost.

Population conference. The UN International Conference on Population and Development convened in Cairo on September 5. Islamic extremists, who accused the conference of encouraging promiscuity and degrading family values, threatened violence. Some Middle Eastern states refused to attend, and others sent a low-level delegation. But many Islamic nations, including Iran, came to discuss the social issues related to overpopulation. The conference ended without violence. ☐ Christine Helms

See also articles on the various Middle Eastern countries. In *World Book*, see **Middle East** and individual Middle Eastern country articles; **Palestine.**

Mining. The United States Department of the Interior on May 16, 1994, was forced to sell to a Canadian company the rights to mine billions of dollars in gold on federally owned land in Nevada for just $9,765. Interior Secretary Bruce Babbitt said the sale was required under a 1872 law enacted to encourage settlement of the West. The law gave companies the right to mine gold, silver, copper, and other materials on federal land without paying royalties. The law also stipulated that they could buy title to the land for no more than $5 per acre (0.4 hectare).

An attempt by the U.S. Congress to change the law in 1992 ended in deadlock. But it encouraged companies to file official land claims before the law was changed. American Barrick Resources Incorporated, based in Toronto, Ont., filed for title to a mine operating on 1,949 acres (789 hectares) of land near Elko, Nev. The mine contains an estimated 30 million ounces (850 million grams) of gold worth $8-billion to $10 billion. Babbitt tried to stall the sale, but a federal court in March 1994 ordered the government to comply with the law. Babbitt called the sale "the biggest gold heist since the days of [American outlaw] Butch Cassidy." Barrick officials noted that the mine is owned by a U.S. subsidiary. They said the company had invested $1 billion in the mine and that extracting the gold was costly.

The U.S. Bureau of Mines (BOM) in February reported that the total value of raw nonfuel minerals produced from American mines in 1993 declined by about 1 percent to $31.6 billion. Nonfuel minerals include all mine products except coal and petroleum. BOM attributed the drop to poor overall economic conditions that reduced demand for minerals. Steeper decreases occurred in exports. The value of raw metal exports dropped 16 percent in 1993 to $900-million, and mineral exports decreased about 16 percent to $1.1 billion.

Mine safety. A study conducted by the National Institute for Occupational Safety and Health on April 14, 1994, ranked mining as America's most dangerous occupation. The government agency found that mining had the highest average annual death rate, with 31.9 deaths per 100,000 workers.

Part of the roof of the largest salt mine in North America collapsed on March 12. The collapse at the Akzo Salt Incorporated mine, about 25 miles (40 kilometers) south of Rochester, N.Y., occurred after water from an underground aquifer flooded part of the mine. The water dissolved columns of salt left in place to support the roof.   □ Michael Woods

See also **Coal; Petroleum and gas.** In *World Book*, see **Mining.**

Minnesota. See **State government.**
Mississippi. See **State government.**
Missouri. See **State government.**
Moldova. See **Europe.**
Mongolia. See **Asia.**
Montana. See **State government.**

Montreal voters showed their dissatisfaction with how the city has been run the past few years by ousting two-term Mayor Jean Doré and most of his fellow Council members in the Nov. 6, 1994, municipal elections. Doré, who cruised to easy victories in 1986 and 1990, was handily defeated by former city civil servant Pierre Bourque, who formed his Vision Montreal Party only about six months before residents went to the polls. Bourque and his slate of candidates won 39 of the 51 Council seats, leaving Doré's Montreal Citizens' Movement with only 6 seats.

The Doré administration had come under fire in recent years for its extravagant spending, high property taxes, and for an unpopular business surtax. Bourque promised Montrealers he would cut spending by $100 million in 1995 and abolish half the $108-million surtax remaining in 1994 on commercial and industrial properties. (All monetary figures are in Canadian dollars.) Doré announced the day after the elections that he was quitting city politics.

Montreal beat out 25 Canadian cities to be selected on March 28, 1994, as the future site for a new environmental watchdog agency. The agency, known as the Secretariat of the North American Commission for Environmental Cooperation, will receive a $15-million budget for the first three years of operation. The agency was formed to monitor environmental problems resulting from the North American Free Trade Agreement between Canada, Mexico, and the United States.

Jarry Tennis Stadium received federal, provincial, and municipal funding in June for a $24-million face-lift. The two-year project, which started in the fall, will include new seating, an 8-court indoor facility, and 11 additional outdoor courts to complement the existing 4 outdoor courts. The stadium was to be home to two major tennis tournaments—the Players' International for men and the Matinee International for women—as well as a national training center and a public recreational facility.

The Montreal Expos finished the strike-shortened major league baseball season with the best overall record of 74 wins and 40 losses. A number of fans led an unsuccessful push to have the team recognized as the 1994 champions. But league officials decided in October that no team would be declared either division or league champion because the season had not been completed.

Via Rail, Canada's passenger railway company headquartered in Montreal, slashed 478 jobs nationwide—including 273 in Montreal—on October 13. The firings were reportedly made without warning, though many employees said that massive layoffs had been rumored for as long as six months.

A fraudulent cancer study submitted by Montreal surgeon Roger Poisson shook the public's faith in medical research in early 1994. The *Chicago Tribune* reported in March that Poisson had provided false data to the National Surgical Adjuvant Breast and Bowel Project, a cancer study conducted by the United States National Cancer Institute. The landmark study had concluded that removal of a cancerous breast lump, combined with radiation therapy, was just as effective as removal of the entire breast in treating breast cancer.

The Chicago newspaper had obtained information from a 1993 report by the Office of Research Integrity of the U.S. Department of Health and Human Services. The report had concluded that Poisson had enrolled ineligible patients in the cancer study and had falsified data on at least 100 patients he had treated for breast cancer.

Poisson was subsequently barred from participating in any U.S.-funded research for eight years. He also lost his job as a full-time professor at the Université de Montréal and was removed as chairman of the oncology department at St. Luc Hospital.

The first Canadian convicted of pirating computer software was a 41-year-old Beaconsfield man who had pleaded guilty on Aug. 22, 1994, to criminal copyright infringement. A federal court in Montreal fined Michael Solomon $20,000 for allowing subscribers to his bulletin-board service to download pirated copies of popular software packages.

□ Mike King

See also **Baseball; Canada; Medicine.** In *World Book,* see **Montreal.**

Allan Gosset, right, a former Montreal police officer, leaves the courtroom after he was acquitted in April of the shooting death of a black teen-ager.

Morocco. King Hassan II excluded opposition parties from a new government he formed in May when he appointed Abdellatif Filali prime minister. The king's promise to form a broader coalition government was delayed because of a politically sensitive vote slated for late 1994 among people of the Western Sahara to decide whether they will be independent or part of Morocco. But because Morocco and the rebel Polisario Front disagreed about voter eligibility, the vote was postponed until 1995.

King Hassan II granted amnesty to 424 prisoners on July 21, 1994. Most of those released were leftist and Islamic political detainees and people convicted of participating in riots in late 1990 over poor economic conditions. Morocco's parliament in 1994 also repealed a 1935 law that permitted people to be jailed for any "activity liable to disturb the peace."

Relations with Algeria soured after Aug. 28, 1994, when Morocco imposed visa restrictions on Algerians. Morocco reportedly feared that Algeria's turmoil might spill into Morocco. Algeria closed its border in retaliation. Morocco and Israel agreed on September 1 to open low-level diplomatic relations.

One of Morocco's national airliners crashed into the Atlas Mountains on August 21, killing all 44 people on board. The pilot, for unknown reasons, reportedly crashed on purpose.   □ Christine Helms

See also **Africa** (Facts in brief table); **Middle East.** In *World Book,* see **Morocco.**

Motion pictures. For movie audiences and the film industry, 1994 was a year of monumental achievements and notable disappointments. By the end of 1994, Walt Disney Pictures' animated film *The Lion King* and Paramount's *Forrest Gump* each looked poised to earn $300 million in the United States, with overseas grosses set to match. If the two films lived up to predictions, 1994 would be the first year in which two films grossed $300 million in the domestic market.

If the mood of the American film industry was optimistic, there was no discounting such expensive failures as *Wyatt Earp, I'll Do Anything, Ed Wood, I Love Trouble,* or *Love Affair.* Once again, the U.S. box-office boom seemed limited to winter and summer. Movie attendance slumped in spring and fall.

The Lion King extended Disney's animation renaissance, which began with 1989's *The Little Mermaid* and continued with 1991's *Beauty and the Beast* and 1992's *Aladdin. The Lion King* treated childhood emotions, including fear and guilt over the loss of a parent, with empathy. Its mix of hand-drawn and computerized animation was dazzling. Worldwide, animation enjoyed renewed popularity on television and in feature films.

Unexpected giant. *Forrest Gump* was expected to be a commercial success. It starred Tom Hanks, winner of 1993's best actor Oscar for *Philadelphia,* and was directed by Robert Zemeckis of the *Back to*

Tom Hanks won the Academy Award for best actor in March for his portrayal of an HIV-infected attorney in the motion picture *Philadelphia* (1993).

the *Future* trilogy. But no one anticipated the magnitude of its box-office take.

Hanks won praise for his performance as a kind-hearted, simple-minded Southerner whose endless optimism allows him to triumph over any temporary adversity. The movie's stunning special effects included the highly realistic depiction of a Vietnam amputee, portrayed by the fully limbed Gary Sinise, and the insertion of Hanks into newsreel footage featuring such real-life figures as Beatle John Lennon and U.S. Presidents John F. Kennedy, Lyndon B. Johnson, and Richard M. Nixon.

Computerized special effects also were used in *The Crow,* which completed filming after the March 31, 1993, death of its star Brandon Lee, son of the late Bruce Lee. Computers were used in seven different scenes, including 52 separate shots. Computers took Lee's image from one scene and put it in others, some filmed after his accidental death.

Monster movies. The casting of Tom Cruise—generally considered an apple-cheeked charmer—as an elegant, evil vampire in the movie version of Anne Rice's best seller *Interview With the Vampire* aroused much controversy. Yet initial response to the film was positive, with Cruise winning praise for his offbeat, sardonic portrayal. The lavish film was director Neil Jordan's first since 1992's *The Crying Game,* and his direction was widely praised.

Conversely, Robert De Niro's interpretation of the creature in the Kenneth Branagh adaptation of *Mary Shelley's Frankenstein* disappointed many filmgoers, who found De Niro more frightening in 1976's *Taxi Driver* and 1991's *Cape Fear.* Branagh, whose versions of Shakespeare's *Henry V* (1989) and *Much Ado About Nothing* (1993) had been embraced by critics, received some of the worst notices of his career as a director.

Box-office hits. Arnold Schwarzenegger, fresh from the high-profile 1993 flop *Last Action Hero,* regained momentum with his tongue-in-cheek action drama *True Lies.* Keanu Reeves, largely known as a teen star, was at the center of the critically praised and popular adult action drama *Speed,* in which he matched wits with a mad bomber who had placed explosives on a Los Angeles bus. *The Flintstones,* which industry insiders had pegged as a disappointment, emerged as one of the summer's big draws.

Harrison Ford again played reluctant CIA hero Jack Ryan in the hit *Clear and Present Danger.* That film was loosely adapted from a Tom Clancy novel. Writer John Grisham's *The Client* received a much more faithful adaptation. Susan Sarandon starred in the film of the same name.

Comic actor Jim Carrey emerged as the hottest new star of the year when his unexpected hit *Ace Ventura, Pet Detective* was followed by the summer smash *The Mask.* Both comedies used special effects to enhance Carrey's elastic features, and his glib de-

Steven Spielberg's *Schindler's List* (1993), starring Liam Neeson and Ben Kingsley, won Academy Awards in March for best picture and best director.

livery won fans. When Robin Williams turned down the role of The Riddler in *Batman Forever,* Carrey was chosen to play the comic villain. Carrey's *Dumb and Dumber,* released at year-end with an advertising campaign that spoofed *Forrest Gump's* bench-sitting pose, was expected to be another comedy hit.

Director Quentin Tarantino, whose violent and witty *Reservoir Dogs* became an art-house sensation in 1992, scored even more emphatically with 1994's *Pulp Fiction.* The film's multilayered plot, including overlapping time sequences, drew endorsements from critics and adventurous moviegoers.

Pulp Fiction brought fresh vitality to the careers of late-1970's star John Travolta, whose stardom faltered during the 1980's, and Bruce Willis, who had

been stuck in a series of unsuccessful action pictures. For example, Willis played an unbilled supporting role in *Nobody's Fool,* which featured Paul Newman as an older man trying to renew family ties after a life of heedlessness. He also appeared in the unsuccessful *Color of Night* and filled a supporting part in the disappointing *North.* The Tarantino movie won a stronger response than *Natural Born Killers,* Oliver Stone's mixture of comedy and violence.

The romantic *Four Weddings and a Funeral* became a crossover art-house hit. The British comedy starred Hugh Grant and Andie MacDowell as a couple whose romance is ignited when they keep meeting at the nuptials of others. The clever, glossily photographed film was a strong worldwide hit.

Unabashed romance proved less successful in other hands. Warren Beatty produced, co-scripted, and starred in *Love Affair,* featuring his wife, Annette Bening. The same story had been produced successfully in 1939's *Love Affair* and 1957's *An Affair to Remember.* Interest in the 1957 version had been revived by the 1993 hit *Sleepless in Seattle.* Yet the Beatty adaptation failed to attract more than a modest audience, despite featuring Katharine Hepburn's first big-screen appearance since 1984.

Two other old-fashioned romances also failed to win favor. Marisa Tomei and Robert Downey, Jr., did not ignite sparks in *Only You,* while Nicolas Cage and Bridget Fonda enjoyed only marginally warmer response in *It Could Happen to You.*

Flops. The public failed to respond as enthusiastically as expected to such sequels as *The Next Karate Kid, City Slickers II,* and *Beverly Hills Cop III.*

The popular Kevin Costner did not have any hits during 1994. *A Perfect World,* released late in 1993, won the actor strong personal notices but attracted small domestic audiences in 1994, though overseas response was more enthusiastic. *Wyatt Earp* was an instant flop in the United States, with some industry observers labeling it Hollywood's costliest failure. The Western epic, which presented a somber and complex view of the legendary frontier hero, had a modest reception overseas. *The War,* in which Costner took a supporting role as a Vietnam veteran trying to instill his children with ideals, was met with indifference by critics and audiences.

Nick Nolte also starred in highly publicized flops. *I'll Do Anything,* with Nolte as an aspiring actor trying to cope with single parenthood, was directed by James L. Brooks of *Terms of Endearment* and *Broadcast News* acclaim. *I'll Do Anything* originally was filmed as a musical but disastrous test responses prompted the removal of musical numbers. The film was released as a straight comedy-drama to indifferent reactions everywhere. Nolte starred opposite Julia Roberts in a romantic comedy, *I Love Trouble,* which was scorned by the press and ignored by audiences. A third Nolte film, *Blue Chips,* came and went.

Critics praise, viewers pass. Some films earned critical approval without striking a chord with the public. *Quiz Show,* directed by Robert Redford, was a striking examination of the personal and public trauma perpetrated by television scandals of the 1950's. Perhaps the era and the events were too remote for public enthusiasm. *The Shawshank Redemption,* based on a short novel by Stephen King, won praise for its depiction of friendship behind prison bars, but audiences stayed home.

Spike Lee's *Crooklyn,* a sensitive depiction of urban life told from a child's point of view, found only modest acceptance. Tim Burton's critically applauded *Ed Wood*—featuring Johnny Depp as the real-life director, Ed Wood, who was often considered the worst director of all time—played to empty theaters outside of major metropolitan areas. Woody Allen's warmly reviewed *Bullets Over Broadway,* with Dianne Wiest as a desperate, aging Broadway diva, did acceptable but unimpressive business.

Noteworthy debut. Darnell Martin became the first female African-American director to win major studio backing. Martin's *I Like It Like That,* about a woman's coming of age in the Bronx, a borough of New York City, and her relationship with a Latino couple in her neighborhood, won endorsements from many film critics.

Sexual harassment found its way into a mainstream movie but with a twist that disconcerted some. In the film of the Michael Crichton best seller *Disclosure,* Michael Douglas charges his employer Demi Moore with sexual harassment. The film had strong scenes of sexuality, and some felt it odd that one of the few Hollywood films to deal with harassment should portray a male character as the victim.

A strong documentary was *Hoop Dreams,* which followed the experiences of two African-American youths from inner-city Chicago whose dream is to play professional basketball. Directors Peter Gilbert, Steve James, and Frederick Marx shot 250 hours of footage over 5 years, which were edited to 171 minutes. The result was one of the most enthusiastically reviewed films of 1994.

Year-end releases. Iconoclastic director Robert Altman continued his irreverent ways with a sharp look at the fashion industry, *Ready to Wear.* The film's large international cast included Julia Roberts, Tim Robbins, Lyle Lovett, Lauren Bacall, Kim Basinger, Marcello Mastroianni, and Sophia Loren.

Alan Rudolf's inspection of the Algonquin round table, the legendary intellectual group that gathered at the Algonquin Hotel in New York City, was titled *Mrs. Parker and the Vicious Circle.* It starred Jennifer Jason Leigh as author and wit Dorothy Parker. Arnold Schwarzenegger's comic portrayal of a scientifically impregnated man in *Junior* opened in November to mixed reviews.

Jodie Foster played the title role in *Nell,* as a backwoods young woman who speaks an indecipherable language. Liam Neeson, fresh from his success in *Schindler's List,* and Natasha Richardson appeared as the doctor and psychologist who treat her.

Susan Sarandon played a strong New England mother in the third Hollywood movie version of Louisa May Alcott's *Little Women.* Considered a daring venture for sophisticated 1994 audiences, *Little Women* starred Winona Ryder.

New cinemas. Multiplex cinemas continued their stronghold on worldwide exhibition. The largest multiplex in the United States, called the AMC Grand and sporting 24 screens, was to open in Dallas in the spring of 1995.	□ Philip Wuntch

See also **Hanks, Tom; Hunter, Holly.** In *World Book,* see **Motion pictures.**

Mozambique. See Africa.

Murayama, Tomiichi (1924-   ), chairman of the Social Democratic Party (SDP), was named prime minister on June 29, 1994, in a 261 to 214 vote by members of the lower house of the Diet, Japan's parliament. Murayama became the nation's first Socialist premier since 1948. (See **Japan.**)

Murayama was born the seventh of 11 children on March 3, 1924, in Oita City on Japan's island of Kyushu. In 1946, the same year he joined the Japan Socialist Party, as the SDPJ was then known, he graduated from Meiji University in Tokyo with a degree in politics and economics. He entered politics in 1955 when he won his first election to the Oita City Assembly. In 1972, he won the first of seven terms to the Diet's lower house.

Murayama was a compromise candidate for prime minister whose victory was the result of a deal between the Socialists and their archrivals, the conservative Liberal Democratic Party (LDP). Murayama took over from reformist Tsutomu Hata, who had resigned on June 25, 1994. Murayama is regarded as an expert on welfare issues.

Murayama and his wife have two daughters.

□ Carol L. Hanson

Music. See Classical music; Popular music.
Myanmar. See Burma.
Namibia. See Africa.
Nebraska. See State government.
Nepal. See Asia.

Netherlands elected a new government on May 3, 1994. Willem Kok, leader of the Labor Party, became prime minister on August 22, at the head of an unusual, three-party coalition. Kok had been finance minister in the last coalition government, which was led by Prime Minister Ruud Lubbers.

In the May 3 elections, the Labor Party won the single largest bloc of seats in the 150-member National Assembly, or lower house of parliament. Its 39 seats were 10 fewer than it had held in the last parliament. The Christian Democratic Appeal lost even more ground, dropping to 34 seats from 54.

Lubbers, who had headed the government for 12 years, stepped down as leader of the Christian Democrats in an attempt to become the president of the European Commission, the executive branch of the European Union (EU), formerly the European Community. Belgian Prime Minister Jacques Santer was chosen for the post instead. Lubbers' successor as party leader was Elco Brinkman, whose more conservative views cost the party votes in the May elections. Brinkman resigned as party leader on August 16 because of the poor election showing.

Smaller fringe parties won key seats in the parliament. Their electoral gains reflected a number of politically sensitive issues difficult for the larger parties to handle. Seven seats went to the General Old People's Party, a group representing elderly people angry at a government plan to freeze the level of pension payments in order to cut government spending. The far-right Central Democrats won 4 seats, reflecting fears that too many refugees were being given political asylum in the Netherlands. The Green Left, an environmentalist party, won 5 seats, largely reflecting fears about the increasing use of nuclear power to generate electricity in Europe.

The new coalition government was made up of the left wing Labor Party; the right wing Liberal Party, with 31 seats in the assembly; and the left wing Democrats '66 bloc, which won 24 seats. Kok's priorities for the new government were to cut about $10 billion in government spending over the next four years, cut some individual taxes, and boost some social benefits. Kok said these measures would help private companies create more jobs and thus help reduce the country's high unemployment rate.

Nobel Prize winner dies. Jan Tinbergen, an economist who won the Nobel Prize in economics in 1969, died in Amsterdam, the capital, on June 9 at the age of 91. Tinbergen was famous for his work on unemployment. □ Philip Revzin

See also **Europe** (Facts in brief table). In *World Book,* see European Union; Netherlands.

Nevada. See State government.
New Brunswick. See Canadian provinces.
New Hampshire. See State government.
New Jersey. See State government.
New Mexico. See State government.

New York City. Mayor Rudolph W. Giuliani, New York City's first Republican mayor since 1965, stunned political observers on Oct. 24, 1994, by crossing party lines and endorsing the state's Democratic governor, Mario M. Cuomo, for reelection. Giuliani, who supported the rest of the Republican ticket in the November 8 election, said the three-term governor would be a better friend to the city than his opponent, Republican George E. Pataki. Pataki's tax-cut proposals, Giuliani said, would reduce state aid and lead to higher property taxes.

Despite Giuliani's endorsement of Cuomo, however, Pataki won. New Yorkers expected the new governor to show little sympathy for the city's needs and problems.

Police corruption scandal grows. Twenty-nine police officers in Harlem's 30th precinct were arrested on corruption charges in 1994, the worst scandal ever to involve a single New York City police precinct. The arrests marked the latest, and perhaps final, episode in a Police Department scandal that began in 1992 and led to the naming of a mayoral commission the next year. That group uncovered evidence of police corruption in several precincts, including reselling confiscated drugs, pocketing money found at the site of drug busts, and extorting payoffs from drug dealers. The commission made its final report on July 7, 1994. It recommended more than 100 changes in Police Department procedures and the creation of an independent body to investigate future reports of police abuses.

Bombing suspects convicted. Four Muslim fundamentalists charged with bombing the World Trade Center in February 1993 were convicted in a New York City federal court on March 4. On May 24, each man was sentenced to 240 years in prison, ensuring that none would ever be paroled.

Madison Square Garden, the nation's best-known sports and performance complex, was sold on August 28 to a partnership of Cablevision Systems Corporation and the ITT Corporation for $1.075 billion. The seller was Viacom Inc., a media conglomerate which had acquired the 20,000-seat arena just months earlier.

Times Square development. A long-term project to clean up seedy West 42nd Street in Times Square was bolstered in February when the Walt Disney Company announced that it would restore and modernize the landmark New Amsterdam Theater. The Disney company said it would stage live family fare at the theater beginning in 1996. In addition, Music Television said in September that it planned to lease three West 42nd Street theaters for a new TV studio and entertainment complex.

Subway bombing. A firebomb exploded on a crowded subway train in the New York City borough of Manhattan on December 21, injuring more than 40 people. One of the casualties, Edward J. Leary, 49, was arrested in his hospital bed and charged with the bombing. Police investigators said Leary had apparently been carrying the bomb with the intention of leaving it on the train with a timer when it went off. They said the man had planned to extort money from the city with the threat of more bombings.

Corporations look for greener pastures. The Swiss Bank Corporation of Basel, Switzerland, announced on September 21 that it would relocate its North American headquarters from Manhattan to Stamford, Conn. Connecticut lawmakers had agreed to provide the bank with a $120-million package of tax breaks. The announcement ended a three-year agreement between Connecticut, New Jersey, and New York not to steal businesses from one another.

Meanwhile, as the New York City Council considered an ordinance to further restrict smoking in public places, the Philip Morris Company, the nation's largest cigarette manufacturer, threatened on September 25 to move its headquarters out of the city if the bill passed. If Philip Morris were to leave, it would just be the latest in a long list of companies that have transferred their operations out of New York City. Since 1983, the number of corporate headquarters in the city has dwindled from 69 to fewer than 30. The companies' reasons for leaving have included the high cost of doing business in New York City and the deteriorating quality of life there. □ Owen Moritz

See also **City.** In *World Book,* see **New York City.**

New Zealand in 1994 enjoyed its fastest economic growth in more than a decade. The nation's *gross domestic product* (GDP)—the total value of all goods and services produced within a nation—rose 6.1 percent during the first six months of the year, making its growth rate the highest in the Organization for Economic Cooperation and Development, an association of 24 industrialized nations in Europe, North America, and the Pacific. In November, the government reported unemployment at 7.8 percent of the labor force, down from a 1991 peak of 11.6 percent. Agriculture grew by 5.5 percent, manufacturing by 5.8 percent, and construction by almost 17 percent. However, the growth spurred demand for loans, which caused interest rates to rise in the second half of the year to 9.4 percent.

New parties on the horizon. Several members of Parliament announced in 1994 that they would leave the ruling National Party or the Labour Party to form new parties in time for the 1996 election. A new system of proportional representation will then be in place whereby 56 of the 120 parliamentary seats will be filled according to the percentage of votes a party wins in national elections. The remaining seats will be elected by a simple majority. However, several breakaway members agreed to vote with the National Party on crucial issues in 1994.

Labor laws. Representatives from the International Labor Organization (ILO), a United Nations (UN) agency, visited New Zealand in April to investigate trade union complaints regarding provisions of New Zealand's 1991 employment legislation. An interim report upheld union charges that the laws opposed the right to collective bargaining. But Labour Minister Douglas Kidd told the ILO in June that New Zealand's labor reforms gave employees the right to bargain individually or collectively. A final report modified the ILO view, but reminded the government about the right to collective bargaining.

Water crisis. Auckland, New Zealand's largest urban area, endured a severe water shortage in the summer that threatened to close industries and bring on rationing to homes. But water savings in excess of 25 percent and rainfall that exceeded all expectation ended the five-month crisis.

International affairs. In May, Prime Minister James B. Bolger announced that New Zealand was sending 250 soldiers to Bosnia-Herzegovina to carry out UN peacekeeping duties there. It was the first time New Zealand combat forces served in Europe since World War II (1939-1945). In July 1994, the Royal New Zealand Air Force flew food relief missions into Rwanda. And New Zealand sent UN observers to Haiti in October, when, with the backing of the United States, President Jean-Bertrand Aristide was restored to power. □ Gavin Ellis

See also **Asia** (Facts in brief table). In *World Book,* see **New Zealand.**

Newfoundland. See Canadian provinces.

Newsmakers of 1994

Newsmakers of 1994 included the following people and events:

Alexander Solzhenitsyn, home again. Nobel Prize-winning author Alexander Solzhenitsyn returned to his native Russia in 1994, 20 years after being exiled from the Soviet Union for exposing the brutal Soviet labor camp system. Arriving by plane in Vladivostok on the windy, rainy evening of May 27, Solzhenitsyn was greeted by a large crowd of friends and admirers.

Solzhenitsyn, who had lived in rural Cavendish, Vt., since 1976, was the last well-known dissident to return to Russia after the demise of the Soviet Union in 1991. He had delayed his return to complete a multivolume work on the Russian Revolution, titled *The Red Wheel.* Solzhenitsyn said his 18 years in Vermont were the happiest and most creative period of his life.

Goldwater accused of liberal heresy. Former Arizona Senator Barry Goldwater, often called Mister Republican and the father of modern American conservatism, has been accused of sounding more like a liberal Democrat of late. In March, he said that Republican members of Congress should stop hounding President Bill Clinton about his past financial dealings in Arkansas and get on with the business of governing the nation. That remark was the last straw for many dyed-in-the-wool conservatives, who were already peeved at Goldwater for some of his earlier pronouncements, such as statements supporting homosexual rights.

But the rising chorus of condemnation from fellow Republicans did not faze the 85-year-old Goldwater. "You know something?" he said. "I don't give a damn."

Nessie photo declared a fake. For 60 years, a single photograph has been offered as tangible evidence that the alleged Loch Ness monster really exists. The grainy image supposedly shows a long-necked creature swimming in the loch, a body of water in the Scottish Highlands.

No it doesn't, said two British researchers, David Martin and Alastair Boyd, in March. After several years of research, Martin and Boyd reported that the "monster" in the image is actually a small model made and photographed by three hoaxers in 1934. They said the man long credited with taking the picture, a London physician named Robert Wilson, agreed on a lark to take part in the prank. But while the photo may be a fraud, Martin and Boyd said they think the Loch Ness monster itself is real. Martin pointed out that there have been "thousands of eyewitness accounts" of the storied monster over the years and those sightings could not be disregarded.

1994 Kennedy Center honorees. On September 7, the Kennedy Center for the Performing Arts in Washington, D.C., announced the recipients of the Kennedy Center Honors. The award is presented each year to five individuals who have had outstanding careers in the performing arts. The 1994 honorees were actor Kirk Douglas, soul singer Aretha Franklin, composer Morton Gould, Broadway producer Harold Prince, and folk singer Pete Seeger. The five were saluted at a performance at the Kennedy Center Opera House on December 4.

Alone to the North Pole. After dragging a heavy supply sledge across a frozen wasteland for more than seven weeks, Norwegian diver and explorer Boerge Ousland reached the North Pole on April 22. Ousland became the first person to make it to the pole alone and with no support—no airplanes dropping food, not even a dog team to pull his sledge. "This is an unmerciful place to be," the intrepid Norwegian said in a radio transmission on April 20 as he neared his goal. He said his face was so swollen from the cold that he had trouble op-

ening his eyes when he awoke each morning. But Ousland had been through it all before. In 1990, he and a companion became the first two-person team to make the trip unaided.

Proof that the world is getting wackier. We're living in weird times, and they're getting weirder by the day. At any rate, that was the conclusion reported in the February/March 1994 issue of the *Fortean Times,* a British magazine that chronicles 34 categories of bizarre events around the globe. The publication said 1993 was 3.5 percent stranger than 1992. In 1993, for example, a trash bin belonging to the London borough of Lewisham turned up on the shore of the Sea of Galilee in northern Israel, and Swedish doctors restored a man's hearing by extracting a 47-year-old bus ticket from his ear. Also noteworthy was a robber who taped two cucumbers together and tried to convince his victims—presumably without success—that he was brandishing a sawed-off shotgun. The *Fortean Times* said 1994 was showing signs of being even odder than 1993.

Pentagon doomsday plan is shelved. Oct. 1, 1994, could be considered the day when the Cold War between the United States and the former Soviet Union finally wheezed to an end. Even though the Cold War had been essentially over since 1991, when the Soviet Union ceased to exist, the Department of Defense kept working on a plan for the continuance of U.S. civilian and military leadership in the event of nuclear war. The so-called Doomsday Project, begun in the 1950's, was top secret, but some details became known. The plan called for high-ranking political and military leaders to be secluded in a number of underground bunkers and to communicate with one another by means of satellites.

In April 1994, Pentagon officials announced that because nuclear war was no longer thought to be a likely possibility, the plan would be termi-

Heather Whitestone, a junior at Jacksonville State University in Alabama, gives the sign for "I love you" in Atlantic City, N.J., in September after becoming the first deaf Miss America.

Peter Blake of New Zealand, left, and Robin Knox-Johnston of the United Kingdom exult in April after sailing around the world in just under 75 days—a new record.

315

nated. It set October 1 as the date for the Dooms-day Project's demise.

A controversial punishment in Singapore. Vandalism is considered a serious crime in the tiny Southeast Asian nation of Singapore, as teen-ager Michael P. Fay learned in 1994. Fay, an American living in Singapore with his mother and stepfather, had pleaded guilty in October 1993 to defacing cars with eggs and spray paint and tearing down traffic signs. The boy said later that he was innocent and had signed a confession only because he was punched and slapped by police in-vestigators. Nonetheless, he was sentenced in March 1994 to four months in jail and six lashes on the bare buttocks with a wet rattan cane. This punish-ment—used routinely in Singapore—is so harsh and painful that it can cause shock. The Sin-gapore government rejected President Clinton's appeal for clemency, but it did agree to reduce the number of lashes to four. The sentence was carried out on May 5, and Fay was released the follow-ing month after serving 83 days behind bars.

Bible Trek. To the ap-proximately 5,000 transla-tions of the Bible, a group of scholars with too much time on their hands were laboring in 1994 to add one more: a version in the Klingon lan-guage. The Klingons, as any-one versed in American popu-lar culture knows, are a warlike race of space aliens in the *Star Trek* motion pictures and television shows. In 1984, a linguist invented a 2,000-word language for the Kling-ons, and it soon became all the rage among *Star Trek* fol-lowers. The new Bible is a pro-ject of the Klingon Language Institute (KLI), based in Flour-town, Pa. The 10 translators are working from original scriptural sources in Greek and other ancient languages. But with only 2,000 Klingon words

to work with and no equivalents for many Earth terms, the going has not been easy. For example, the miracle of the loaves and fishes in the Book of Mark becomes the miracle of the blood pies and serpent worms. KLI is also working on a translation of the complete works of William Shakespeare.

Fragile treasure. Not all sunken treasure con-sists of gold, silver, or jewels. The *Diana*, a British sailing ship headed for India, was carrying a large cargo of Chinese porcelain in 1817 when it struck submerged rocks and went to the bottom of the Strait of Malacca, off the coast of present-day Ma-laysia. British treasure hunter Dorian Ball found the remains of the *Diana* in December 1993 after spending a decade re-searching the wreck. In a five-month salvaging operation, completed in June 1994, Ball recovered 24,000 pieces of blue-and-white porcelain, in perfect condition from be-ing buried in mud. It was one of the largest recov-eries ever made of china-ware from a sunken ves-sel. Experts predicted the porcelain would fetch several million dollars when auctioned.

A fabled tomb. A treasure far greater than was ever carried on any ship may lie within the tomb of Genghis Khan. By the time of his death in 1227, the Mongol conquer-or and his huge army of mounted soldiers had sub-dued a vast area of central Asia and had plundered cit-ies from China to Iran. His-torians think Genghis Khan may have been buried with fabulous riches, but the lo-cation of his tomb is a mys-tery. According to legend, the tomb's builders were put to death so no one would know the khan's resting place.

Maury Kravitz, an ama-teur historian from Chicago who has studied Genghis Khan's life for more than 30 years, thinks he knows where the tomb is located. In August 1994, Kravitz an-nounced that he had made

Pop singer Michael Jackson and his wife, Lisa Marie Presley-Jackson, the daughter of Elvis Presley, open the 11th annual MTV Video Music Awards in September in New York City. The couple were wed in May.

an agreement with a Mongolian research institution to search for the burial site. He said he hopes to raise $5 million for an expedition to find the tomb.

A family's grief, and grace, touches Italy. It would have been understandable if Reginald and Margaret Green of Bodega Bay, Calif., had expressed bitterness after their son, Nicholas, was killed by highway bandits in southern Italy on September 30. The 7-year-old boy, sleeping on the back seat of the Green's automobile with his sister, was struck in the head by a bullet fired by the bandits, who pursued the family as they drove toward Reggio di Calabria.

But the Greens, rather than condemning Italy for the tragedy, chose to make their son's death count for something by donating his organs to medicine. Within a few days, Nicholas' heart had been transplanted into a 14-year-old boy in Rome, and his liver had been given to a 19-year-old Sicilian woman. Commentators throughout Italy saluted the Greens for their action and condemned the rampant lawlessness on many Italian highways, which one newspaper called "our shame."

The envelope, please. In August 1993, *Sky & Telescope* magazine challenged its readers to come up with a new and better name for the explosion of matter and energy that most astronomers think gave birth to the universe some 15 billion years ago. That titanic event has long been called the big bang, a name coined in 1950 by British astronomer Fred Hoyle. But Hoyle, who did not accept the explosive-origin theory of the universe, had intended only sarcasm in suggesting the name.

The "Big Bang Challenge" elicited more than 13,000 responses. Proposed names included the Super Seed, the Grand Expansion, Space-Time Zero, MOM (Mother of Matter), and What Happens If I Press This Button? The final decision of the three judges—television personality Hugh Downs, astronomy writer Timothy Ferris, and astronomer Carl Sagan—was announced in the March 1994 issue of *Sky & Telescope*. They declared that the winner was . . . the big bang. None of the entries even came close to dethroning that time-tested name, said Sagan.

Michael and Lisa Marie tie the knot. After weeks of reports in the tabloid press that they had wed, pop singer Michael Jackson and Lisa Marie Presley, the daughter of rock-and-roll legend Elvis Presley, finally came clean on August 1. Jackson, 35, and Presley, 26, said they had exchanged vows in May "in a private ceremony outside the United States," reportedly in the Dominican Republic. They explained that they had waited almost three months to publicly announce their marriage in order to avoid "the distraction of a media circus."

As the couple settled down to domestic life, Jackson's image continued to be tainted by a 1993 accusation that he had sexually molested a teen-

American teen-ager Michael P. Fay crosses himself as he enters Singapore's High Court in March to appeal a sentence of six strokes with a rattan cane for vandalism. The sentence, later reduced to four strokes, was carried out in May.

age boy at his California estate. Although no criminal charges were filed against Jackson, he and his lawyers settled a civil case with the boy's parents in January 1994 for an amount said to be at least $15 million.

Another '60's radical stops running. One of the last remaining fugitives from the counterculture of the late 1960's, Jeffrey David Powell, gave himself up in Chicago on January 6. Powell was a onetime leader of the Weather Underground, one of the most radical student organizations of the time. During the October 1969 "Days of Rage" in Chicago, a violent protest against the Vietnam War (1957-1975), Powell, then 19, hit a police officer in the head with a lead pipe, causing a wound that required 70 stitches. He was convicted of aggravated assault, a felony. While out on bail, he fled and went into hiding.

In a court appearance after his surrender, Powell, who said he had spent much of his 24 years on the run working for social-service agencies, pleaded guilty to a reduced charge of mob action. He received a sentence of 18 months' probation and was fined $500.

Balloonists fail again to circle globe. The crew of the balloon Earthwinds had another go in 1994 at being the first balloonists to fly nonstop around the world, the last remaining major feat of lighter-than-air aviation. Their first attempt was a short one. Just seven hours after it took off from an airfield near Reno, Nev., on January 12, the huge balloon was forced down by mechanical problems. Three earlier attempts by the Earthwinds crew to circumnavigate the globe—two in 1993 and one in 1992—also ended in failure. The crew tried again on Dec. 31, 1994, but that effort also had to be aborted.

Capitalist theologian honored. Michael Novak, a Roman Catholic author and theologian noted for his spirited defense of capitalism, in March was named the recipient of the 1994 Templeton Prize for Progress in Religion. The prize was worth 650,000 British pounds—nearly $1 million. It was established in 1972 by Sir John Templeton, an American-born Wall Street investor who became a British subject.

Novak, 60, a liberal turned conservative, is considered the founder of a new discipline, the theology of economics. He has argued that democracy and free-market capitalism embody Christian principles and provide greater economic opportunities for the poor than socialism.

Promo boosts library's popularity. The staff of the Fort Worth, Tex., Central Library was dumbfounded on the evening of April 5, 1994, as people suddenly began running into the building and rampaging through the fiction department. Within a short time, a huge mob was grabbing novels off shelves, flipping through them frenziedly, and tossing them onto the floor. Library employees learned that a Dallas radio station, KYNG-FM, had told listeners it had placed $5 and $10 bills in some of the books in the fiction section as a promotion to encourage people to visit the library. KYNG said it would pay for replacing the many damaged books and would make a $1,000 donation to the library.

☐ David Dreier

Ben Cohen, left, and Jerry Greenfield, cofounders of Ben & Jerry's Ice Cream, show off a poster aimed at recruiting a new chief executive officer to replace Cohen, who is retiring. They said the CEO would be chosen in an essay contest.

Newspaper. Although 62 percent of adults in the United States read a newspaper each day in 1994, newspapers were still trying to appeal to a greater range and number of people. Newspapers said they were changing because the nation's population is changing.

To serve the many immigrants in its Florida city, for example, the *Miami Herald* published in four languages. In January, it began a weekly page of Brazilian news written in Portuguese, Brazil's native language, and in February added a page devoted to Haitian news written in Creole. Since 1987 the *Miami Herald* has published a complete Spanish-language paper called *El Nuevo Herald.*

To attract minority employees, dozens of newspapers sent recruiters to Unity '94 in July, the first joint convention of African-, Asian-, Hispanic-, and Native-American journalists. To serve an aging population that is having a harder time reading small print, some newspapers increased their type size, including *The New York Times* on September 15.

Civic journalism. In addition to simply covering news events, more newspapers in 1994 began encouraging readers to find solutions for community problems. This greater newspaper involvement in the community is known as *public* or *civic journalism.* For instance, *The Virginian-Pilot* and *The Ledger-Star* newspapers in Norfolk, Va., appointed a "public life editor" and in September sponsored a series of public meetings to talk about crime.

Merged and folded. Despite a good newspaper industry economy, the number of two-paper cities decreased again in 1994. The 143-year-old Sacramento, Calif., *Union* ran the front-page headline "We're history" in its final edition on January 14.

Shenandoah, Iowa, lost its distinction as the smallest American city with competing daily newspapers on May 1 when the *Valley News Today* bought the 112-year-old *Shenandoah Evening Sentinel.* The papers were merged into a single paper called the *Valley News Today-Daily Sentinel.*

The 95-year-old *Oxnard* (Calif.) *Press-Courier* ceased publication on June 16. The 90-year-old *Ypsilanti* (Mich.) *Press* folded on June 27.

Important sales. In the biggest newspaper sale of 1994, Morris Communications of Augusta, Ga., spent $275 million in July to buy another historic, family-owned chain, Stauffer Communications. Stauffer owned the *Topeka* (Kans.) *Capital-Journal,* other newspapers, all-advertising publications, and television and radio stations in 12 states.

On March 31, the *Chicago Sun-Times* sold for $180 million to American Publishing Co., a unit of Canadian press baron Conrad Black's Hollinger Inc. In February, Australian-born Rupert Murdoch's News Corp. Ltd. sold the *Boston Herald* for a reported $10-million to $20 million to the newspaper's publisher, Patrick Purcell. □ Mark Fitzgerald

In *World Book,* see **Newspaper.**

Nicaragua. On May 18, President Violeta Barrios de Chamorro presented a proposal to Nicaragua's National Assembly that would place the army under civilian control. She also said that Sandinista General Humberto Ortega Saavedra would be replaced as Army commander in chief in February 1995.

The steps were calculated to respond to critics in the United States Congress, who charged that the leftist Sandinistas had played too large a role in Chamorro's administration since she took office in 1990. Sandinista opponents in the U.S. Congress had held up millions of dollars in aid to Nicaragua.

Last contras give up. The last remaining band of contra rebels agreed to surrender their weapons to the army on Feb. 24, 1994. About 400 contras agreed to give up their weapons in exchange for amnesty and incorporation into the national police force. Right wing contras had fought a guerrilla war against the Sandinista government for much of the 1980's, but most contras had laid down their weapons when Chamorro took office.

Sandinista congress. At a party congress from May 20 to 22, 1994, the Sandinista Forces for National Liberation reelected former President Daniel Ortega Saavedra as secretary-general. Ortega is the brother of General Ortega. □ Nathan A. Haverstock

See also **Latin America** (Facts in brief table). In *World Book,* see **Nicaragua.**

Niger. See Africa.

Nigeria. Rather than moving toward democracy in 1994, Nigeria declined further into authoritarian rule. The economy of Africa's most heavily populated country also continued to sink.

Abacha v. Abiola. On June 12, Moshood Abiola, who was elected president in 1993 but was not allowed to take office, proclaimed that he was the rightful head of the government. Head of State Sani Abacha, the nation's military dictator since November 1993, had Abiola arrested on June 23, 1994.

Ethnic differences, always crucial in Nigeria, were a factor in the Abacha-Abiola conflict. Abacha is from the Muslim-dominated north, which has provided most of Nigeria's rulers since independence in 1960. Abiola, though also a Muslim, comes from the mostly Christian southwest, home of the large Yoruba ethnic group. Many Yoruba felt Abiola's inability to take office was a blow against them.

Attempting to calm the waters, Abacha gave his blessing to a constitutional conference to set a path for a transition to democracy. The conference began on June 27. Many Nigerians, however, were skeptical because other such conferences in the past had led to nothing but more military rule. Abacha added to public cynicism and anger on July 6 when the government charged Abiola with treason.

Abacha faces down strikers. On July 4, to apply pressure on the Abacha regime for true reform, the powerful National Union of Petroleum and Gas

Workers went on strike. The work stoppage cut off Nigeria's primary source of income, crude oil. Other unions joined the strike, and riots broke out in the south, raising fears of civil war.

On September 4, after two months of tension, the unions backed down. After that victory, the government cracked down hard, suppressing human rights, throttling the press, and removing a number of civilians and military officers from their posts. On September 6, Abacha issued a decree proclaiming that his regime had "absolute power" in Nigeria and that the courts had no jurisdiction over his actions.

Indicative of the sense of crisis, Abacha in October ordered many of Nigeria's troops home from Liberia. Nigerian units had been in that war-torn nation since 1990 as part of a peacekeeping force.

Nigeria's economy, already damaged by widespread corruption and a worldwide drop in petroleum prices declined still more in 1994 as a result of the government's bad management and the two-month strike. Inflation raged during the year, and the economy approached collapse.

A border dispute with Cameroon erupted on January 3 over the oil-rich Bakassi area. After much saber-rattling, the conflict went to the Organization of African Unity, an association of more than 50 African nations, for resolution. ☐ Mark DeLancey

See also **Africa** (Facts in brief table). In *World Book,* see **Nigeria.**

Nobel Prizes in literature, peace, sciences, and economics were awarded in October 1994 by the Norwegian Storting (parliament) in Oslo and by the Royal Swedish Academy of Sciences, the Karolinska Institute, and the Swedish Academy of Literature in Stockholm. The value of each prize was $930,000.

The literature prize went to Japanese writer Kenzaburo Oe, 59, whose novels and short stories express the anger and alienation that gripped his country after its defeat in World War II (1939-1945). Oe gained renown as a leading writer after his first work, *The Catch in the Shadow of the Sunrise,* was published in 1958 while he was a university student. The birth of Oe's brain-damaged first son, Hikari, influenced later novels, such as *A Personal Matter* (1964), *The Silent Cry* (1967), and *Teach Us to Outgrow Our Madness: Four Short Novels* (1969).

Oe is the second Japanese writer to receive the prize. Yasunari Kawabata won in 1968. The Nobel committee said that Oe's "poetic force creates an imagined world where life and myth condense to form a disconcerting picture of the human predicament today."

The peace prize for the first time was shared by three people: Palestine Liberation Organization (PLO) Chairman Yasir Arafat, Israeli Prime Minister Yitzhak Rabin, and Israeli Foreign Minister Shimon Peres. The prize recognized a 1993 accord between the PLO and Israel that allowed limited Palestinian self-rule in the Gaza Strip and the West Bank town of Jericho. The committee praised the three men's "great courage" in signing a pact that "has opened up opportunities for a new development toward fraternity in the Middle East."

The Oct. 14, 1994, announcement of the prize was overshadowed by news that an Israeli soldier kidnapped by the militant Palestinian group Hamas had been killed the same day, with four other people, during a failed rescue bid. Nahshon Waxman's abductors had demanded the release of 200 Palestinian prisoners. The kidnapping strained the peace process lauded by the prize committee: Israel broke off talks with the PLO, and the two parties traded recriminations over who was to blame for the incident. Rabin and Arafat separately said the prize was for their people rather than themselves.

The physics prize was shared by American Clifford G. Shull and Canadian Bertram N. Brockhouse, who in the 1940's and 1950's adapted beams of neutrons to explore atomic matter. A *neutron* is one of the subatomic particles that form the nucleus of an atom. Shull and Brockhouse realized that because neutrons behave like waves, they could be used to examine an atom's structure. The neutron probes they devised were more precise than other tools then used, such as X rays, and gave scientists a closer look at the atomic structure of matter. Shull, 78, is retired from the Massachusetts Institute of Technology (MIT) in Cambridge. Brockhouse, 76, is a professor at McMaster University in Hamilton, Canada.

The chemistry prize went to George A. Olah, a Hungarian-born professor at the University of Southern California in Los Angeles, who discovered how to split and rebuild compounds of carbon and hydrogen. Olah, 67, researched *carbocations,* positively charged fragments of hydrocarbon molecules that normally survive for only a split second. Olah used extremely strong acids called *superacids* to split hydrocarbon molecules and give the fragments a positive charge. He stabilized the resulting carbocations in ultracold solvents, allowing scientists to study the fragments for the first time. This ability enabled scientists to research the development of new fuels from carbon-based substances such as coal and petroleum.

The prize for physiology or medicine was won by Americans Alfred G. Gilman, 53, of the University of Texas Southwestern Medical Center in Dallas and Martin Rodbell, 68, who retired in June from the National Institute of Environmental Health Sciences, a federal agency near Durham, N.C. Their separate research explained how the body receives signals from outer or inner stimuli, such as light or hormones, and transmits those signals into its cells.

In the 1950's, scientists knew that hormones send messages to sites called *receptors* on the surface of cells. Rodbell showed that the signal reaches the interior of each cell with the help of three substances,

PLO Chairman Yasir Arafat, center, gestures to Israeli Prime Minister Yitzhak Rabin, right, as Foreign Minister Shimon Peres, left, looks on. The three men shared the Nobel Peace Prize in October.

rather than two as then believed. He called the third substance a *transducer.*

Gilman researched damaged cells that lacked transducers. He discovered a protein in normal cells that could restore the transducers of the damaged cells. This protein, called a *G-protein,* acts as a switch when messages reach the cell's receptors, thus stimulating the body's response. Its discovery has expanded understanding of diseases such as cancer, some types of which are associated with damaged or overactive G-proteins.

The economics prize was awarded to American John F. Nash of Princeton University in New Jersey, Hungarian-born John C. Harsanyi of the University of California at Berkeley, and German Reinhard Selten of the University of Bonn. The three men are pioneers of game theory, which examines how businesses act when they must predict how their rivals will react to their moves.

Game theory strives to explain behavior that is not explained by classical economics, such as hostile takeovers. Nash laid out the principles for economic "games" in which every "player" possesses the same information. Harsanyi and Selten adjusted the game theory to take into account other variables. ☐ Mary Feely

In *World Book,* see **Nobel Prizes.**

North Carolina. See **State government.**
North Dakota. See **State government.**

Northern Ireland. Efforts to achieve peace in Northern Ireland took a historic step forward when the Irish Republican Army (IRA) announced a "complete cessation of military operations" on Aug. 31, 1994. Demonstrations of relief and delight reverberated throughout Northern Ireland's Roman Catholic areas. But the British government pointed out that the IRA had not announced that the cease-fire was permanent. And it would not allow Sinn Fein, the political wing of the IRA, to join negotiations on the future of Northern Ireland until three months after it had become clear that the violence had stopped for good. The Irish government, however, accepted that the IRA had ended its campaign of violence, and then Irish Prime Minister Albert Reynolds shook hands with Sinn Fein leader Gerry Adams in Dublin on September 6. It was the first meeting between an Irish prime minister and the Sinn Fein since the Irish civil war period of the 1920's.

Reaction to truce. As the cease-fire continued to hold, the British government introduced measures to lower tension in the province. The British military presence on the streets was reduced, and soldiers on patrol exchanged their helmets for berets.

But fears of a backlash remained among Irish Protestants, who make up a majority of the population in Northern Ireland. Protestant paramilitary groups killed a Catholic man the day after the cease-fire announcement and detonated a bomb on

321

September 4 outside the Sinn Fein headquarters in Belfast. The Combined Loyalist Military Command hesitated for weeks before announcing on October 13 that it would accept the cease-fire.

Protestant political parties were also wary. Ian Paisley, leader of the more extreme Ulster Democratic Unionist Party, complained bitterly that the British government had made a secret deal with the IRA, a charge British Prime Minister John Major denied. However, the more moderate Ulster Unionist Party did not denounce the cease-fire as a trick.

On September 16, Major announced that any constitutional changes in Northern Ireland would be put to the people of Northern Ireland in a referendum. He also lifted the broadcasting ban on Sinn Fein. Later, he lifted a ban preventing Sinn Fein leaders from traveling to mainland Britain.

Peace talks begin. On December 9, after it appeared that the cease-fire was holding, the British government and Sinn Fein began a series of peace talks on Northern Ireland. Through the talks, the British government hoped to negotiate the surrender of the large IRA arsenal. Among Sinn Fein's priorities are an end to British military operations in Northern Ireland. □ Ian J. Mather

See also **Ireland.** In *World Book,* see **Northern Ireland.**

Northwest Territories. See Canadian territories.

Norway voted against joining the European Union (EU), formerly the European Community, in a national referendum held Nov. 28 to 29, 1994. About 52 percent of the voters opposed joining the EU, with most of the opposition coming from rural areas. Several of Norway's trading partners—Austria, Finland, and Sweden—within an organization called the European Free Trade Association, had approved membership in referendums held earlier in the year.

Norwegian Prime Minister Gro Harlem Brundtland had argued strongly for passage of the referendum, saying that Norway would suffer economically and politically if it stayed out of the EU while most of its neighbors and trading partners joined. But opponents of full EU membership felt that Norway was economically strong enough to remain independent. Some also feared that Norway would have to give up too much national decision-making power to the EU's central organizations, based in Brussels, Belgium. Norwegians were also concerned about giving up control over the country's natural resources, in particular its oil reserves and rich fishing waters.

Whaling ban defied. Norway continued to defy environmentalists who want to ban all commercial whaling. On June 7, 1994, the Norwegian government said it would allow its whalers to catch 301 minke whales, despite a general worldwide ban governed by the International Whaling Commission on whale hunting. Norway claimed the minke species

Gerry Adams, center, leader of the IRA's political wing, announces a truce in the 25-year-long fight against British rule in Northern Ireland in August.

favored by its whalers is not an endangered whale species.

The Scream stolen. One of Norway's most famous paintings, *The Scream,* by Norwegian artist Edvard Munch, was stolen on February 12 from the National Art Museum in Oslo. The theft was reportedly linked to antiabortion activists, who claimed they would return the painting either for ransom money or if an antiabortion television documentary was shown on state television. Authorities ignored both demands. Norwegian police recovered the painting on May 7. (See also **Art.**)

The Winter Olympics, held in Lillehammer, Norway, from February 12 to 27, were judged to be among the best organized in recent years. Norwegian athletes won more medals—26, including 10 gold medals—than all other competitors. (See also **Olympic Games.**)

Foreign minister dies. Johan Jorgen Holst, Norway's foreign minister, died on January 13 in Oslo, after a stroke at the age of 56. Holst was instrumental in secret negotiations that led to the Israeli-Palestinian self-rule agreement signed in Washington, D.C., in September 1993.   □ Philip Revzin

See also **Europe** (Facts in brief table). In *World Book,* see European Union; Norway.

Nova Scotia. See Canadian provinces.
Nuclear energy. See Energy supply.
Nutrition. See Food.

Ocean. After years of preparation, teams of scientists from the United States, Japan, and Europe embarked in June 1994 on a pioneering program to study an undersea vent and a growing mound of material around it. The mound was located 2,250 miles (3,620 kilometers) east of Florida in the Atlantic Ocean, about 2 miles (3.2 kilometers) below the ocean surface. The mound was from 40,000 to 50,000 years old, about 660 feet (200 meters) in diameter, 160 feet (50 meters) high, and still growing in late 1994, scientists said.

The mound is in the largest and deepest field of undersea vents in the world. Undersea vents form when gigantic pieces of Earth's crust pull apart, allowing *magma* (molten rock) below the crust to flow up toward the ocean floor. As the magma hardens and cracks, seawater enters the cracks and percolates back up, forming vents of sulfurous, mineral-laden waters. The minerals and sediment form mounds as they settle around the geyser. Sulfur and other chemicals in the vents support bacteria, which other life forms in turn feed upon. Such volcanic fissures exist in many areas among submerged undersea mountain chains.

In the first phase of the expedition, the U.S. research ship *Knorr* lowered robotic sonars, cameras, and lighting equipment to make a detailed survey. Next, the Japanese submersible *Shinkai* placed thermometers and other sensors on the mound. Re-

searchers on the ship *JOIDES Resolution* then drilled about 1,640 feet (500 meters) into the mound to take samples in October and November, marking the first time scientists had drilled into a deep vent.

Deepwater warming. Scientists studying the subtropical Atlantic Ocean announced in May that they had detected increases in deepwater temperatures that could be a signal of *global warming.* Global warming is a rapid increase in Earth's average temperature due to the build-up in the atmosphere of heat-trapping gases. The main heat-trapping gas is carbon dioxide, and the major source of this gas is the consumption of *fossil fuels* (coal, gasoline, and natural gas). Some scientists believe that if the build-up of carbon dioxide continues unchecked, it could cause temperature increases by the mid-2000's severe enough to melt some polar icecaps, shift croplands farther north, and cause widespread droughts.

Oceanographer Harry Bryden of the James Rennell Centre for Ocean Circulation at Southampton, England, and his colleagues said they had recorded temperature increases of as much as 0.6 Fahrenheit (0.33 Celsius) degree compared with readings taken in 1957 in the same area and depth. Bryden's team took temperature readings at depths from 2,300 to 8,200 feet (700 to 2,500 meters).

Bryden said that the magnitude of the deep ocean warming is broadly consistent with computer model predictions of ocean warming that would result from a doubling of carbon dioxide in Earth's atmosphere. But the increases did not match the computer models exactly. Most computer models show that global warming would produce the most dramatic ocean warming at the surface. Bryden said his measurements showed a combination of warming and cooling at the surface.

Depletion of the world's fisheries. More than 90 nations met at a United Nations (UN) conference in August 1994 to begin attempts to set limits on international fishing. Catches of most world fish populations have declined heavily since 1989. The declines have resulted from more fishing fleets, larger nets, fish-locating sonar, mechanized net-hauling gear, and the use of planes and helicopters to spot schools of fish. According to the UN's Food and Agricultural Organization, which tracks world fishing activity, overfishing has drastically reduced populations of more than 60 fish species.

***Achille Lauro* sinking.** The ill-fated Italian cruise ship *Achille Lauro* sank on Dec. 2, 1994, after a fire crippled its engines in the Indian Ocean about 150 miles (240 kilometers) off the coast of Somalia. Nearly 1,000 passengers and crew had to abandon the ship after the fire broke out on November 30. Three people died during the ordeal. The ship gained notoriety when Arab terrorists hijacked it in 1985, killing Leon Klinghoffer, a U.S. tourist who was confined to a wheelchair.   □ Arthur G. Alexiou

In *World Book,* see **Ocean.**

Olympic Games

Olympic Games. A new format for the Olympic Games took effect in 1994. Since 1924, the Winter and Summer Olympic Games had taken place in the same year, and both were held every four years. The International Olympic Committee, realizing that world attention and marketing were suffering because of the traditional time frame, in 1986 announced a new time frame. It decided to stage the Winter and Summer Olympics in alternating even-numbered years.

The new format started with the XVII Winter Olympic Games in Lillehammer and nearby sites in Norway. These games, from February 12 to 27, attracted 1,920 athletes, including former figure-skating professionals, from a record 80 nations and political units. There were 9 athletes from war-torn Bosnia-Herzegovina and 2 from South Africa, which was competing in its first Winter Olympics since 1960. There were athletes from 11 republics that had once been part of the Soviet Union. There were also athletes from Israel, which had never competed in a Winter Olympics before.

Several athletes with dual nationality seized an opportunity to become Olympians. They included two Greek lugers and a Greek bobsledder from Minnesota, a Chilean skier from Buffalo, N.Y., and a Puerto Rican bobsled driver from New Jersey.

Speed skaters. The star of stars was Johann Olav Koss, a 25-year-old medical student from Nor-

Tommy Moe of the United States, *above,* flies past a gate on the way to winning the gold medal in the downhill in February.

Bonnie Blair of the United States, *below,* skates to one of her two gold medals at the Winter Olympics in Lillehammer, Norway, in February. Blair won the 500- and 1,000-meter speed-skating events.

way. In the Olympic Hall, a building shaped like an upside-down Viking ship, Koss won the gold medals in world-record time in the three longest races for male speed skaters—the 1,500 meters in 1 minute 51.29 seconds, the 5,000 meters in 6 minutes 34.96 seconds, and the 10,000 meters in 13 minutes 30.55 seconds. He received a $33,000 bonus from Norwegian Olympic officials and donated it to the Olympic Aid relief fund for Sarajevo, the war-torn capital of Bosnia-Herzegovina and site of the 1984 Winter Olympics. He donated his skates to a charity auction, where they were sold for $85,000.

America's two best speed skaters triumphed as Dan Jansen of Greenfield, Wis., finally won a gold medal, and Bonnie Blair of Milwaukee, won two more. In Nordic skiing, Manuela Di Centa of Italy won five women's medals. Ljubov Egorova of Russia won four women's medals, and Bjorn Daehlie of Norway won four men's medals.

A major distraction involved the two leading U.S. female figure skaters—Nancy Kerrigan of Stoneham, Mass., and Tonya Harding of Portland, Ore. On January 6, Kerrigan was clubbed on the right knee in a conspiracy involving Harding's former husband and three of his associates. At first, Harding insisted she knew nothing of the clubbing, and United States officials, faced with a threatened lawsuit if they barred her from the Olympics, allowed her to compete. Kerrigan won the silver medal behind Oksana Baiul of Ukraine. Harding finished eighth.

Later, Harding pleaded guilty in a federal court to hindering prosecution, but her sentence did not include prison. (See **Crime; Ice Skating; Sports.**)

Medals. The host team from Norway led in total medals with 26, followed by Germany with 24, Russia with 23, Italy with 20, and the United States and Canada with 13 each. In gold medals, the leaders were Russia with 11, Norway with 10, Germany with 9, Italy with 7, and the United States with 6.

The 13 medals were the most the United States had ever won in a Winter Olympics. Although U.S. athletes won two gold and two silver medals in

Oksana Baiul of Ukraine performs during the technical program in figure skating in February. She won a gold medal.

Medal standings, Winter Olympics

Nation	Gold	Silver	Bronze	Total
Norway	10	11	5	26
Germany	9	7	8	24
Russia	11	8	4	23
Italy	7	5	8	20
United States	6	5	2	13
Canada	3	6	4	13
Switzerland	3	4	2	9
Austria	2	3	4	9
S. Korea	4	1	1	6
Finland	0	1	5	6

Alpine skiing, they won only one medal in figure skating, their poorest showing in that sport since 1972.

Canada did well with 13 medals. Biathlon racer Myriam Bedard won two of Canada's three gold medals. The United Kingdom was disappointed when it won only two medals, both bronze. Many observers felt that Britain's Jayne Torvill and Christopher Dean in ice dancing deserved the gold or silver, rather than the bronze. Australia won its first Winter Olympic medal, a bronze in the men's 5,000-meter short-track speed-skating relay.

Russia won five medals in figure skating and, surprisingly, five in speed skating. However, its hockey team failed to win a medal, the first time that had happened to a Soviet or Russian team.

U.S. stars. Few will forget Jansen's agony in the 1988 Winter Olympics, when he fell in both of his races, the first only hours after his sister, Jane Beres, died of leukemia. He did not win a medal in 1984, 1988, or 1992, but he entered his first race in 1994 as the favorite in his best event, the 500 meters. But bad luck still plagued him as he slipped on the final turn and finished eighth.

Four days later, the 28-year-old Jansen skated the 1,000 meters, his final Olympic race. He won, set a world record, and then skated a dramatic victory lap holding his 9-month-old daughter, Jane, named for his late sister. "Finally," he said, "I feel like I've made other people happy instead of having them feel sorry for me."

The 29-year-old Blair won the women's 500 and 1,000 meters for the fourth and fifth gold medals of her career, the most ever by a U.S. woman in Winter or Summer Olympics. Blair also finished fourth in the 1,500 meters, missing a medal by three-hundredths of a second.

Tommy Moe, 23, of Palmer, Alaska, turned in one of the most surprising performances when he won the gold medal in men's downhill skiing and the silver medal in the super giant slalom. In the downhill, he beat Kjetil Andre Aamodt of Norway by four-hundredths of a second, the closest Olympic downhill finish ever. In another upset, 26-year-old Diann Roffe-Steinrotter of Potsdam, N.Y., won the women's super giant slalom.

In short-track speed skating, 31-year-old Cathy Turner of Hilton, N.Y., won the 500-meter gold medal for her second consecutive Olympics. After Zhang Yanmei of China, the world record holder, had won the silver medal, she accused Turner of

Dan Jansen, *above,* takes a long-awaited Olympic victory lap with his daughter, Jane, after he won the 1,000-meter speed-skating gold medal in February.

Official results of the 1994 Winter Olympic Games

Winners of the Winter Olympics

Event	Winner	Country	Mark
Men's skiing			
Downhill	Tommy Moe	United States	1:45.75
Combined	Lasse Kjus	Norway	3:17.53
Super giant slalom	Markus Wasmeier	Germany	1:32.53
Giant slalom	Markus Wasmeier	Germany	2:52.46
Slalom	Thomas Stangassinger	Austria	2:02.02
Cross-country:			
10 kilometers	Bjorn Daehlie	Norway	24:20.1
15 kilometers	Bjorn Daehlie	Norway	1:00:08.8
30 kilometers	Thomas Alsgaard	Norway	1:12:26.4
50 kilometers	Vladimir Smirnov	Kazahkstan	2:07:20.3
40-kilometer relay	De Zolt, Albarello, Vanzetta, Fanner	Italy	1:41:15.0
Ski jumping			
90-meter jump	Espen Bredesen	Norway	282 pts.
120-meter jump	Jens Weissflog	Germany	274.5 pts.
Team	Jaekle, Duffner, Thoma, Weissflog	Germany	970.1 pts.
Nordic combined skiing			
Men's individual	Fred Borre Lundberg	Norway	
Men's team	Kono, Abe, Ogiwara	Japan	
Women's skiing			
Downhill	Katja Seizinger	Germany	1:35.93
Combined	Pernilla Wiberg	Sweden	3:05.16
Super giant slalom	Diann Roffe-Steinrotter	United States	1:22.15
Giant slalom	Deborah Compagnoni	Italy	2:30.97
Slalom	Vreni Schneider	Switzerland	1:56.01
Cross-country:			
5 kilometers	Ljubov Egorova	Russia	14:08.8
15-kilometer pursuit	Ljubov Egorova	Russia	41:38.1
15-kilometer freestyle	Manuela Di Centa	Italy	39:44.5
30 kilometers	Manuela Di Centa	Italy	1:25:41.6
20-kilometer relay	Vaelbe, Lazutina, Gavriluk, Egorova	Russia	57:12.5
Freestyle skiing			
Men's moguls	Jean-Luc Brassard	Canada	27.24 pts.
Men's aerials	Andreas Schoenbaechler	Switzerland	234.67 pts.
Women's moguls	Stine Lise Hattestad	Norway	25.97 pts.
Women's aerials	Lina Tcherjazova	Uzbekistan	166.84 pts.
Figure skating			
Men's singles	Aleksei Urmanov	Russia	1.5
Women's singles	Oksana Baiul	Ukraine	2.0
Pairs	Ekaterina Gordeeva Sergei Grinkov	Russia	1.5
Ice dancing	Oksana Grichtchuk Yevgeny Platov	Russia	3.4

American figure skating rivals Tonya Harding, left, and Nancy Kerrigan warm up during team practice in Hamar, Norway, in February, *right.*

grabbing her leg during the race, preventing her from winning. Turner responded that she had put her hand down on a turn to steady herself, and if her hand bumped Zhang, it was Zhang's fault because Turner was leading. After Zhang received her medal, she stalked off the ceremonial stand, took off the medal, and flung her flower bouquet to the ground.

There were also disappointments for the Americans. Donna Weinbrecht of West Milford, N.J., the gold medalist in 1992 when freestyle moguls skiing made its Olympic debut, finished seventh this time. Duncan Kennedy of Lake Placid, N.Y., perhaps seconds away from America's first-ever Olympic luge medal, suffered a bad crash instead. Four months

Norwegian speed skater Johann Olav Koss exults after winning the 1,500 meters in February. He won three gold medals and set three world records.

Event	Winner	Country	Mark
Men's speed skating			
Long track			
500 meters	Aleksandr Golubev	Russia	36.33
1,000 meters	Dan Jansen	United States	1:12.43*
1,500 meters	Johann Olav Koss	Norway	1:51.29*
5,000 meters	Johann Olav Koss	Norway	6:34.96*
10,000 meters	Johann Olav Koss	Norway	13:30.55*
Short track			
500 meters	Ji-Hoon Chae	S. Korea	43.45
1,000 meters	Ki-Hoon Kim	S. Korea	1:34.57
5,000-meter relay	Carnino, Fagone, Herrnhos, Vuillermin	Italy	7:11.74
Women's speed skating			
Long track			
500 meters	Bonnie Blair	United States	39.25
1,000 meters	Bonnie Blair	United States	1:18.74
1,500 meters	Emese Hunyady	Austria	2:02.19
3,000 meters	Svetlana Bazhanova	Russia	4:17.43
5,000 meters	Claudia Pechstein	Germany	7:14.37
Short track			
500 meters	Cathy Turner	United States	45.98†
1,000 meters	Lee-Kyung Chun	S. Korea	1:36.87
3,000-meter relay	Chun, Kim, Kim, Kyung	S. Korea	4:26.64
Men's biathlon			
10-kilometer event	Serguei Tchepikov	Russia	28:07.0
20-kilometer event	Serguei Tarasov	Russia	57:25.3
30-kilometer relay	Gross, Luck, Kirchner, Fischer	Germany	1:30:22.1
Women's biathlon			
7.5-kilometer event	Myriam Bedard	Canada	26:08.8
15-kilometer event	Myriam Bedard	Canada	52:06.6
30-kilometer relay	Talanova, Snytina, Noskova, Reztsova	Russia	1:47:19.5
Bobsledding			
Two-man	Gustav Weder Donat Acklin	Switzerland	3:30.81
Four-man	Czudaj, Brannasch, Hampel, Szelig	Germany	3:27.78
Men's luge			
Singles	Georg Hackl	Germany	3:21.571
Doubles	Kurt Brugger Wilfried Huber	Italy	1:36.720
Women's luge			
Singles	Gerda Weissensteiner	Italy	3:15.517
Ice hockey		Sweden	6 wins, 1 loss, 1 tie

*New world record   †New Olympic record.

were poor, contributing to overall losses of about $39 million.

As expected, Russia and the United States won the most medals. Russia won 171 medals (68 gold, 50 silver, 53 bronze), and the United States won 119 (37 gold, 39 silver, 43 bronze). Among the gold medalists were Dan O'Brien and Jackie Joyner-Kersee of the United States and Noureddine Morceli of Algeria in track and field, Aleksandr Popov of Russia in swimming, Shannon Miller of the United States in gymnastics, and Surya Bonaly of France in figure skating. Carl Lewis of the United States (100-meter dash) and Sergei Bubka of Ukraine (pole vault) were unexpectedly shut out of the medals, though Lewis later won a gold medal in a relay.

Other. Preparations continued in Atlanta, Ga., for the 1996 Olympics there. Organizers said they would offer 11 million tickets, an Olympic record, with prices ranging from $6 for baseball preliminaries to $600 for the best seats for the opening and closing ceremonies.   □ Frank Litsky

See also **Hockey; Ice skating; Kerrigan, Nancy; Skiing.** In *World Book,* see **Olympic Games.**

Oman. See **Middle East.**

Ontario. See **Canadian provinces.**

Opera. See **Classical music.**

Oregon. See **State government.**

before, in Oberhof, Germany, Kennedy was assaulted when he went to the aid of Robert Pipkins of Staten Island, N.Y., an African-American teammate, to protect him from an attack by neo-Nazi skinheads.

Goodwill Games. This quadrennial, Olympic-style competition began in 1986 as primarily the United States against the Soviet Union. The 1994 games, from July 22 through August 6, were in St. Petersburg, Russia, with 2,000 athletes from 60 nations participating.

Faulty filtration in the swimming pool left the water brownish black on one day and sickly green the next, and the two-day program was crammed into one day. Figure skating was delayed a day because with the temperatures above 90 °F (32 °C) outdoors and no air conditioning indoors, the indoor rink would not freeze. Foreign visitors were few, and ticket sales were so slow that organizers gave away tickets. American television ratings

Pacific Islands. The end of the Cold War had important repercussions for the Pacific in 1994. With the absence of a threat from the former Soviet Union, the strategic importance of the region declined. Aid to nations of the former Soviet bloc took priority over aid to the islands among traditional aid donors. For example, the United Kingdom withdrew from the South Pacific Commission, the oldest regional organization serving the islands. The United States ended much of its aid to the region and reduced its diplomatic presence. Australia began a reexamination of its Pacific commitments. But Japan emerged as an important source of assistance.

Papua New Guinea. Tumult touched the prime ministership during 1994. In September 1993, incumbent Paias Wingti had resigned after 15 months in office and was reelected in less than 24 hours. The maneuver was an attempt to avoid a no-confidence motion in Parliament. Under Papua New Guinea's Constitution, such a motion is not allowed until a new prime minister has served 18 months. Wingti's 18 months would have expired in December 1993, so his resignation and reelection reset the clock on any possible parliamentary ouster.

Wingti's opponents legally challenged the election, and in August 1994, the Supreme Court ruled that Wingti's resignation was proper, but not his reelection. Citing a constitutional provision that requires a one-day advance notice before an election, the court ordered another election. Wingti declined to stand, and on August 30, Parliament elected as the new prime minister, Sir Julius Chan, the deputy prime minister and minister of foreign affairs. Chan had also served as prime minister from 1980 to 1982.

Chan immediately intensified efforts he had begun earlier in the year to resolve his nation's long-standing crisis with Bougainville, an island that is part of Papua New Guinea and lies about 500 miles (800 kilometers) northeast of the Papua New Guinea capital of Port Moresby. Disputes over Bougainville's lucrative copper mine and other grievances had fueled an armed revolt by the Bougainville Revolutionary Army, which had tried since 1988 to gain independence from Papua New Guinea. Chan initiated talks with the rebels, and the two sides agreed on a cease-fire that began on September 10.

On September 28, Papua New Guinea and the rebels signed an agreement with Fiji, Tonga, and Vanuatu that formed a South Pacific Regional Peace Keeping Force made up of troops from the three nations. The peacekeeping force entered Bougainville in early October to help enforce the earlier peace agreement. Australia and New Zealand also provided financial and logistical support to the effort.

But in mid-October, the peace talks broke down between the rebels and the government. A breakaway faction of rebels signed an agreement on October 18 to negotiate a separate peace accord with the government.

Two volcanoes erupted near the port town of Rabaul in the East New Britain Province on September 19. The eruptions buried the town under a thick layer of ash and mud. Officials had evacuated almost all of the city's 30,000 residents, as well as people from nearby villages, before the Vulcan and Tavurvur volcanoes erupted. Local officials reported only two deaths.

Fiji. One of Fiji's most respected leaders, Ratu Sir Penaia Ganilau, died at age 75 in mid-December 1993 after a long illness and was buried on the island of Tuveui among his ancestors on Jan. 1, 1994. Sir Penaia was Fiji's third-highest ranking paramount chief and had a distinguished career as a soldier, administrator, and statesman. He was appointed as Fiji's governor-general in 1983 and president after the two military coups in 1987. Ganilau was credited with averting violence and bloodshed after the military takeover. Ratu Sir Kamisese Mara succeeded Sir Penaia as president. Mara had been prime minister most of the years since Fiji gained its independence from the United Kingdom in 1970.

In the meantime, Prime Minister Sitiveni Rabuka, the army major general who had orchestrated the 1987 coups, was having political troubles. In late 1993, a year and a half after assuming office, discord wracked Rabuka's government. A political scandal combined with the defeat of Rabuka's 1994 budget in Parliament weakened his stature.

To avoid a no-confidence vote, Rabuka asked President Mara to dissolve Parliament and hold new elections in February. Rabuka's Fijian Political Party won 31 seats in the 70-member House of Representatives, and he was sworn in for a second term as prime minister on February 28.

Palau. On Oct. 1, 1994, the Republic of Palau became a self-governing state in free association with the United States. Palau, an island republic in the western Pacific Ocean, saw some of the heaviest fighting between U.S. and Japanese military forces during World War II (1939-1945). Palau was the last remnant of the former U.S. Trust Territory of the Pacific Islands. The Commonwealth of the Northern Marianas Islands, the Federated States of Micronesia, and the Republic of the Marshall Islands had been the other trust members. The Trust Territory was the last of the 11 trusteeships established under the umbrella of the United Nations after World War II.

Residents of states in free association with America have free entry to the United States for purpose of residence and employment. During the first 15 years of the relationship, Palau's population of about 15,000 will receive more than half a billion dollars in assistance. The United States in turn will retain rights to use the islands for military purposes and will remain responsible for Palau's defense.

□ Robert C. Kiste

In *World Book,* see **Pacific Islands.**
Painting. See Art.

Facts in brief on Pacific Island countries

Country	Population	Government	Monetary unit*	Foreign trade (million U.S.$) Exports†	Imports†
Australia	17,820,000	Governor General Bill Hayden; Prime Minister Paul Keating	dollar (1.35 = $1)	42,710	45,556
Fiji	787,000	President Ratu Sir Kamisese Mara; Prime Minister Sitiveni Rabuka	dollar (1.42 = $1)	407	634
Kiribati	79,000	President Teburoro Tito	Australian dollar	3	27
Marshall Islands	43,000	President Amata Kabua	U.S. dollar	4	63
Micronesia, Federated States of	15,000	President Bailey Olter	U.S. dollar	2	68
Nauru	11,000	President Bernard Dowiyogo	Australian dollar	93	73
New Zealand	3,552,000	Governor General Dame Catherine Tizard; Prime Minister James B. Bolger	dollar (1.63 = $1)	10,537	9,636
Palau	15,000	President Kuniwo Nakamura	U.S. dollar	no statistics available	
Papua New Guinea	4,344,000	Governor General Sir Wiwa Korowi; Prime Minister Sir Julius Chan	kina (1.14 = $1)	2,452	1,297
Solomon Islands	378,000	Governor General Sir George Lepping; Prime Minister Francis Billy Hilly	dollar (3.26 = $1)	83	110
Tonga	99,000	King Taufa'ahau Tupou IV; Prime Minister Baron Vaea	pa'anga (1.35 = $1)	17	61
Tuvalu	13,000	Governor General Tomu Malaefono Sione; Prime Minister Kamuta Latasi	Australian dollar	1	4
Vanuatu	169,000	President Jean Marie Leye; Prime Minister Maxime Carlot Korman	vatu (114.50 = $1)	24	82
Western Samoa	170,000	Head of State Malietoa Tanumafili II; Prime Minister Tofilau Eti Alesana	tala (2.53 = $1)	6	105

*Exchange rates as of Oct. 28, 1994, or latest available data.   †Latest available data.

Pakistan. Confrontations between Prime Minister Benazir Bhutto and a former prime minister, Nawaz Sharif, kept Pakistani politics in turmoil in 1994. Bhutto's Pakistan People's Party (PPP) had defeated Sharif's Pakistan Moslem League (PML) in parliamentary elections in October 1993. Sharif sought to regain power, and the chaos that ensued damaged public confidence in the ability of politicians to govern the country.

Early in 1994, Bhutto began moves to capture political control of the North-West Frontier Province, where the PML dominated the provincial assembly. Her PPP took control on April 24, when the assembly elected a PPP member as its chief minister. The province became the third of Pakistan's four provinces to come under Bhutto's control.

Angered, Sharif tried to destabilize Bhutto's national government. In August, he said he could confirm that Pakistan had an atomic bomb, and any attack by India would trigger "a nuclear holocaust." The government denied Pakistan had the bomb, though it had long claimed the capability of making one. Also in August, Sharif accused Bhutto's ally President Farooq Leghari of corruption. Parliamentary debates led to fistfights. Then, after Bhutto and Leghari refused to resign, Sharif launched nationwide demonstrations against the government. In September, he called a general strike in what he said was a state of war against the government.

Observers believed Sharif was triggering unrest to force the army into ousting Bhutto. The army has often intervened in Pakistani politics, including in Sharif's own ouster in 1993. Observers said that Sharif believed he could win if new elections were called. But Sharif had alienated the army. He said in a taped interview in May that army generals had proposed a plan to him in 1991, when he was prime minister, in which the army would secretly sell heroin to fund its covert intelligence operations. When the interview was made public in September 1994, the angry commanders denied devising such a plan.

Family feud. Bhutto's mother, Nusrat Bhutto, supported Bhutto's brother Murtaza as the rightful leader of the PPP, which had been founded by Nusrat's late husband. On June 5, Murtaza was released on bail from prison, where he had been held since returning in 1993 from a 16-year, self-imposed exile. Once released, Murtaza spread reports that Benazir's husband, Asif Ali Zardari, was taking illegal kickbacks on government contracts. Benazir denied the rampant rumors, but they undermined her rule.

The economy. Bhutto tried to improve an ailing economy in 1994. The budget included measures to reduce the deficit and attract foreign investment. Some income taxes were raised, but only 1 percent of Pakistanis paid the tax.   □ Henry S. Bradsher

See also **Asia** (Facts in brief table). In *World Book,* see **Pakistan.**

Paleontology

Paleontology. Two discoveries of fossil whales in Pakistan provided new insight in 1994 into how aquatic mammals such as whales and dolphins evolved from their four-legged, land-dwelling ancestors.

Walking whale. In January, anatomist J. G. M. Thewissen of Northeastern Ohio Universities College of Medicine in Rootstown reported the discovery of a nearly complete whale skeleton in shallow marine deposits dated as approximately 50 million years old. The animal, named *Ambulocetus,* was about 10 feet (3 meters) long. Although the body was somewhat streamlined for swimming, it also had well-developed front and hind limbs. The pelvis was firmly anchored to the spine, unlike the pelvis of fully aquatic mammals.

The skeleton suggested that *Ambulocetus* was amphibious and could not only swim but also walk, at least in the clumsy fashion of sea lions. The structure of the backbone indicated that *Ambulocetus* could undulate up and down for a swimming style similar to that of modern whales and dolphins. The hind limbs may also have worked as propelling flippers. Other details of the skeleton helped support the hypothesis that whales descended from odd-toed ungulates, a group of grazing mammals such as modern cattle, sheep, pigs, and hippopotamuses.

A second important discovery, reported in April by a team of paleontologists led by Philip D. Gingerich of the University of Michigan in Ann Arbor,

described the fossils of a second whale buried in sediment about 3 million years later than the *Ambulocetus* fossils. This whale, called *Rodhocetus,* was a fully marine animal. The skeleton showed several adaptations for swimming: a shortened neck, reduced upper hind limb bones, and no connection between the pelvis and the spine. Such an animal could not have walked on land. The fossils were found in deep offshore marine deposits, indicating that the transition from land to water had been completed.

Antarctic dinosaur. In May, William R. Hammer and William J. Hickerson, paleontologists at Augustana College in Rock Island, Ill., reported the discovery of several dinosaur skeletal remains in the Transantarctic Mountains about 400 miles (640 kilometers) from the South Pole. The fossils were dated to the Early Jurassic Period, approximately 200 million years ago.

The most complete skeleton discovered was that of a theropod, a meat-eating dinosaur. This fossil dinosaur, which the scientists named *Cryolophosaurus,* is unique because it has a bony crest above the eyes. Near the theropod fossils, the paleontologists found the remains of several other animals *Cryolophosaurus* may have fed upon.

During the Jurassic, the fossil site was on the coast of Gondwanaland, an ancient southern land mass that incorporated Antarctica, South America, Africa, and Australia. The climate there would not

Fossils of a meat-eating dinosaur with an unusual bony crest on its forehead, *below,* were discovered in Antarctica by paleontologist William R. Hammer, *right,* and a colleague. The scientists reported in May that the dinosaur, named *Cryolophosaurus,* lived about 200 million years ago.

have been as harsh as in present-day Antarctica, but the temperature probably varied with the seasons. Finding evidence of large dinosaurs in the area indicated that much of Gondwanaland had a mild climate during the early Jurassic Period.

Earliest life on land. Discoveries of ancient fossil bacteria extend the probable record of life on land to more than 1.5 billion years, according to a January report. The oldest previously known land fossils date from approximately 450 million years ago. Paleontologist Robert J. Horodyski of Tulane University in New Orleans and geologist L. Paul Knauth of Arizona State University in Tempe found fossils of tiny filaments of blue-green algae, also called *cyanobacteria,* in flint from Arizona and Death Valley, California. The Arizona rocks were dated to almost 1.2 billion years ago, and the California rocks were dated to 800 million years ago.

At both sites, the rocks appear to have been deposited as sediments in some of the oldest terrestrial soils. If the researchers' dates are correct, the landscape 1 billion years ago may not have been a barren soil surface. Rather, it may have been covered with extensive green mats of cyanobacteria. For such organisms to survive, the ozone layer, which protects life from deadly ultraviolet solar radiation, must have existed in the upper atmosphere by about 1.5 billion years ago. □ Carlton E. Brett

In *World Book*, see **Paleontology.**

Panama. Ernesto Pérez Balladares, 48, of the Revolutionary Democratic Party (PRD) was sworn in for a five-year term as president on Sept. 1, 1994. Balladares had only the narrowest of mandates, having garnered just 33 percent of the popular vote in elections held May 8.

Balladares' rise represented the reemergence of the party of former dictator Manuel Noriega, who was toppled in 1989 by a United States invasion and who was serving a 40-year sentence in Florida for drug trafficking. During the campaign, Balladares had sought to distance himself from Noriega, calling him "a disgrace to the country." Shortly after his inauguration, Balladares sought U.S. favor by reversing the stand of his predecessor and approving the settlement of up to 10,000 Cuban refugees for six months at U.S. military bases in Panama. (See **Cuba.**)

But many Panamanians were fearful of the military's influence on the PRD. Their uneasiness increased when, on Sept. 23, 1994, Balladares pardoned some 200 people associated with Noriega's government. They had been jailed on a variety of charges, including corruption and murder.
□ Nathan A. Haverstock

See also **Latin America** (Facts in brief table). In *World Book,* see Panama.

Papua New Guinea. See Asia; Pacific Islands.
Paraguay. See Latin America.
Pennsylvania. See State government.

Perry, William J. (1927-), deputy secretary of defense since March 1993, was sworn in as secretary of defense on Feb. 3, 1994, after receiving unanimous confirmation from the United States Senate. Perry succeeded Defense Secretary Les Aspin, Jr., who resigned in December 1993 because of heavy criticism for his management of the Department of Defense. As secretary, Perry oversaw U.S. military operations in 1994 in Haiti and the Persian Gulf.

Perry was born on Oct. 11, 1927, in Vandergrift, Pa. He graduated from Stanford University in California in 1949 with a degree in mathematics. In 1950, he was commissioned a second lieutenant in the Army Reserves, and he served in the reserves until 1955. In 1957, he earned a doctorate in mathematics at Pennsylvania State University in University Park.

In 1964, Perry was a cofounder of ESL, Inc., a San Francisco-area military electronics company. He was president of ESL until 1977, when he became undersecretary of defense for research and engineering in the Administration of President Jimmy Carter. He received the Defense Department's Distinguished Service Medal in 1980 and 1981. Before returning to the Defense Department as deputy secretary, Perry taught engineering at Stanford and was codirector of Stanford's Center for International Security and Arms Control.

Perry and his wife, Lee, have five grown children and eight grandchildren. □ David Dreier

Peru. A soap opera unfolded during 1994 in Lima, Peru's capital, as Peruvians prepared to go to the polls in April 1995 to select a new president. The drama was played out in the presidential palace, where President Alberto Fujimori, 56, though credited with quelling a rebel insurgency and reducing inflation, faced a challenge in his quest for a second term from his wife, Susana Higuchi.

On Aug. 24, 1994, Fujimori announced that he was relieving his wife of her duties as first lady, because, as he said, she had become "unstable" and fallen under the influence of "unscrupulous" advisers. Higuchi, who had publicly accused her husband's sister, brother, and sister-in-law of profiting by selling clothing donated by Japan in 1992, was quick to counterattack. She criticized her husband's authoritarian policies and charged members of his family and administration with corruption.

Higuchi startled Peruvians by announcing on Sept. 12, 1994, that she would form her own party—the 21st Century Harmony Party—and run for president. Peru's National Election Board disallowed her candidacy on October 20, however, because she failed to collect enough valid signatures on qualifying petitions.

Presidential challenger. With the situation in the Fujimori household chaotic, Javier Pérez de Cuellar, former secretary-general of the United Nations, announced on September 22 that he would run for the presidency as an independent. The 74-year-old diplomat said he was troubled by Fujimori's authoritarian tendencies, which had included shutting down Congress in 1992, and his subsequent rewriting of the Constitution to permit his own reelection. No less urgent, Pérez de Cuellar said, was the need to attack chronic poverty.

Soldiers sentenced. On Feb. 22, 1994, the Supreme Court of Military Justice convicted nine members of the armed forces of complicity in the July 1992 murder of nine students and a professor at the Enrique Guzmán y Valle University east of Lima. The defendants received from 4 to 20 years in prison.

Telephones privatized. On March 1, 1994, a consortium led by Telefónica de España S.A. of Madrid, Spain, paid more than $2 billion for controlling interests in the Peruvian Telephone Company and National Telecommunications Enterprise, more than twice that offered by consortia led by Southwestern Bell and GTE of the United States.

Mining investments. A new probusiness mining code stimulated investments by some 20 foreign companies, as the Peruvian government privatized this key industry. For example, the Cyprus Amax Minerals Corporation of the United States paid $37-million for a Peruvian copper mine and pledged to invest nearly $500 million in it. □ Nathan A. Haverstock

See also **Latin America** (Facts in brief table). In *World Book,* see **Peru.**

Petroleum and gas.

Petroleum and gas. The world used more petroleum in 1994 as many nations recovered from an economic slump. Although the rise in world oil demand was only a little more than 1 percent, that was enough to push total consumption of petroleum products in 1994 to 68 million barrels a day. Until 1994, demand had been flat as a result of the rise of oil prices that developed during the 1991 war in the oil-rich Persian Gulf region. Much of the growth in oil demand in 1994 was accounted for by the United States, the leading consumer of petroleum, and by fast-growing nations in Asia.

Prices of petroleum products increased slightly as a result of the rise in consumption. Most fuels remained relatively cheap, however, and prices of natural gas fell in the United States.

U.S. oil consumption and production. An especially cold 1993-1994 winter and buoyant economic conditions led to the highest U.S. petroleum use in years. By the end of September, Americans were using more than 17.5 million barrels of petroleum products a day, nearly 3 percent more than in the first nine months of 1993. One barrel equals 42 gallons (159 liters).

Even as the United States used more oil, it produced less. The drop in production of crude oil, which had begun in 1986, appeared to slow up in 1994, however. Drilling activity remained sluggish, and U.S. oil companies continued to focus their ma-

jor exploration efforts in other countries. The U.S. crude oil output was down 3 percent from previous years to 6.6 million barrels a day for the first nine months of 1994. As a result of the fall in production and the rise in demand, the United States had to buy more oil from abroad. Before the year ended, the United States was importing almost half of the oil it consumed.

Total imports of crude oil and petroleum products by the United States averaged 9 million barrels a day for the first nine months of 1994, according to the American Petroleum Institute. "That's the highest level in history for the first three quarters, surpassing the period in 1977, when U.S. crude and products imports averaged 8.792 million barrels a day," the *Oil & Gas Journal* reported in October.

Petroleum imports factored into the nation's trade deficit. Even at relatively low prices in 1994, foreign oil cost the United States more than $50 billion a year. Also, a growing U.S. appetite for oil helped evaporate a petroleum glut that had periodically depressed oil markets for years.

World oil supplies remained ample in 1994. A surge in production from the North Sea reached a record 5 million barrels of oil a day. Oil production in Russia, formerly the world's biggest producer, continued to decline, but political and economic chaos in Russia also depressed its demand for oil. As a result, its oil exports remained fairly steady.

Although world oil supplies were plentiful, production capacities did not keep pace with rising demand in 1994. Some oil industry observers worried whether oil markets could be nearing a flash point because of a fragile supply-demand balance. At the end of the year, for example, only Saudi Arabia and Iraq had significant unused production capacity, and the latter country was banned from world oil markets by the United Nations (UN).

Barring a major disruption, however, oil supplies were expected to be sufficient to meet the demand for two or three more years. By then, the oil industry of the former Soviet Union, with its huge potential, was expected to recover.

OPEC. Among members of the Organization of Petroleum Exporting Countries (OPEC), the main group of oil-exporting nations, crude oil output averaged about 25 million barrels a day for the second consecutive year. That rate was close to the highest in a decade.

However, Iraq, one of the five founding members of OPEC, remained banned from world oil markets. The UN had imposed the embargo against Iraq for its 1990 invasion of Kuwait, another OPEC founder, which led to the Persian Gulf War. In October 1994, Iraqi President Saddam Hussein sent troops to Iraq's border with Kuwait, reportedly to focus world attention on the economic plight of the Iraqi people that resulted from the oil embargo. But Hussein drew a quick response from the United States, which sent

Factories and other buildings blaze as a result of a natural gas pipeline explosion in March in Edison, N.J. One person died and several were injured.

forces to the Gulf area, stationing some of them just inside Kuwait's border with Iraq. Hussein then moved his troops back toward Baghdad, Iraq's capital city.

World oil prices rose only briefly as a result of the perception that Iraq again was threatening Middle East oil fields. A strike by oil workers in Nigeria, from July to September, had a bigger impact on oil markets, helping prices to rise from their near-collapse of late 1993.

By early 1994, after a drop of some $5 a barrel in 1993, prices of crude oil reached a five-year low. But it soon became clear that the world oil glut was evaporating. Formerly huge petroleum inventories in tanks, tankers, and pipelines shrank. OPEC's production held steady despite growing demand for its oil, and evidence mounted that the world's economic recovery was spreading, triggering the need for more petroleum.

The higher demand for petroleum put a floor under the price of crude. West Texas Intermediate crude oil, the main U.S. grade, averaged slightly more than $17 a barrel in 1994. Oil economists predicted a range of $18 to $20 a barrel for West Texas Intermediate crude oil for 1995.

Gasoline prices. Partly due to the comparatively low price of crude oil, wholesale prices of gasoline reached record low levels in 1994, after adjustments for inflation. At the pump in the United States, after federal and state taxes were applied, gasoline averaged only slightly more than $1.20 a gallon by September.

But gasoline prices were expected to increase as petroleum refiners began stockpiling a variety of "reformulated," cleaner-burning motor fuels to meet requirements of the U.S. Clean Air Act of 1990. Producing and transporting the new fuels, to be available beginning January 1995, created an expensive and complex changeover for the gasoline companies. Consumers were expected to feel the cost.

Natural gas supplies were plentiful worldwide in 1994. Gas gained as a preferred fuel due to its abundance and its status as clean burning. American gas production reached about 11 trillion cubic feet (311 billion cubic meters) through July 1994, about 3 percent more than the same period in 1993.

American demand for gas continued to rise even faster than its production, with imports mainly from Canada making up the supply difference. According to the U.S. Department of Energy, the nation used about 12.9 trillion cubic feet of gas (366 billion cubic meters) through July 1994. That was a 5 percent increase from the 12.3 trillion cubic feet (349 billion cubic meters) consumed in the first seven months of 1993. With emphasis on the environment growing in the United States, forecasters predicted domestic consumption of natural gas to continue rising at annual rates of 2 percent to 3 percent. ☐ James Tanner

In *World Book,* see **Gas; Petroleum.**

Philadelphia. Mayor Edward G. Rendell said on October 28 that the city completed fiscal 1994, which ended on June 30, with a $15.3-million surplus in a budget of $2.3 billion. It was the second consecutive budget surplus. Not since the 1970's had Philadelphia posted surpluses two years in a row without enacting a tax increase. The news was particularly good for Philadelphians in light of the city's recent financial history—a total of $403 million in deficits between 1988 and 1992.

Public schools. David Hornbeck, known as a pioneering educational reformer in his job as Maryland state schools superintendent, in June 1994 was named superintendent of the Philadelphia public schools. Hornbeck, 52, faced the possibility of taking his post during a strike. The teachers' contract was due to expire in September, and the teachers union and the Board of Education were divided over the issue of health-care benefits. But the union and the board finally agreed on a new two-year contract, which the teachers approved on August 29. The teachers received a 5 percent salary increase over two years and agreed to pay an additional 10 percent of their health insurance premiums.

All was not well with the city's schools, however. On September 15, a judge and a seven-member panel of educators that had been studying the Philadelphia school system issued a dismal assessment. Their report concluded that the system fails to educate many of its students, particularly the poorest ones. The panel said the school system needed $300 million a year in additional money to carry out sweeping reforms, including radically reducing class size and extending the school year to 11 months.

On November 28, after presiding over hearings on the report's recommendations, Commonwealth Court Judge Doris A. Smith rejected many of the panel's recommendations as untested. She ordered the school district to come up with a new plan emphasizing "proven educational strategies," including increased parent involvement and better training of teachers.

Nightclub fires. Three arson fires in three months destroyed a South Philadelphia complex of buildings that had housed one of the city's leading nightclubs. The complex, Palumbo's Cafe-Restaurant, included the nightclub, a large banquet hall, and a restaurant. After the first blaze, on June 20, only the nightclub was still standing. A second fire, on August 25, destroyed the nightclub and six adjoining row houses and apartments. The remaining ruins went up in flames on September 10. Investigators were trying to learn who set the fires.

State senator removed. For the first time in Pennsylvania history, a judge in 1994 ordered the removal of a legislator in office. United States District Court Judge Clarence C. Newcomer ruled on February 18 that Democratic State Senator William G. Stinson of Philadelphia had to give up his seat in the legislature. The judge declared that massive vote fraud had helped put Stinson in office in an election in November 1993.

Judge Newcomer's ruling opened the way for Republican Bruce S. Marks, the loser in the election, to replace Stinson. But on March 11, 1994, a higher court blocked Marks from being seated. The court directed Newcomer to review the case and determine whether to seat Marks or order a new election.

On April 26, the judge said he found no evidence to support the assertions of Philadelphia Democratic leaders, who maintained that some ballot irregularities were traditional in the city and should be accepted. The judge ordered Marks to be seated, and the Republican was sworn in on April 28. Stinson was charged with violating several state election laws, but he was acquitted on June 22.

Avenue of the Arts. The Arts Bank, a small performance hall built in an abandoned bank, opened on January 18. The 238-seat facility became the first new theater to open along the Avenue of the Arts, a downtown thoroughfare that is being revitalized at the cost of about $270 million as a center for the performing arts. To celebrate its opening, the Arts Bank, owned by the local University of the Arts, presented several days and nights of free performances by Philadelphia-area dance and theater troupes and musical ensembles. ☐ Howard S. Shapiro

See also **City.** In *World Book,* see **Philadelphia.**

Philippines. Political parties in the Philippines moved in 1994 to consolidate into two or three major parties in preparation for 1995 congressional elections. Political parties had proliferated after President Ferdinand Marcos was deposed in 1986. He had ruled for more than 20 years, in which time he had severely restricted political activity. But in 1994, the nation seemed to be heading back to the two-party system it had before Marcos came to power.

On August 26, President Fidel V. Ramos announced the formation of a coalition between his Lakas-National Union of Christian Democrats party and the largest opposition party, Laban ng Demokratikong Pilipino (Struggle of Filipino Democrats) (LDP). Ramos feared that the LDP would continue to block his economic development program in the Congress. For its part, the LDP feared it would lose Senate seats to Ramos' party in the upcoming elections. Thus, the two parties decided to share equally a slate for the 12 Senate seats up for election in 1995. However, to oppose Ramos' coalition, two other parties, the Nationalist People's Coalition and the People's Reform Party, formed their own alliance on Sept. 21, 1994.

Tax problems. Ramos encountered strong resistance to higher taxes needed to fund social programs and to reduce the deficit. In September 1993, the government had imposed a tax of 16 to 28 percent on petroleum products. But on Feb. 9, 1994, the LDP and other groups opposed to the tax threatened to call for nationwide demonstrations and a general strike. Ramos immediately suspended the tax and two weeks later rescinded it altogether.

To replace that income, Ramos got Congress to approve in May a law extending the national 10 percent value-added tax (VAT) to a range of products and services. Some LDP senators who had voted for the law failed to support it when popular protests began, and the Supreme Court received petitions challenging the law's constitutionality. But on August 25, the Supreme Court ruled in favor of the VAT, and the law went into effect on October 1.

Insurgencies. Ramos worked in 1994 to end 25 years of fighting by a Muslim group, the Moro National Liberation Front (MNLF), which seeks a separate state in the southern Philippines. Secessionist fighting had taken some 50,000 lives. After signing an interim agreement in 1993, the government and MNLF leader Nur Misuari signed a cease-fire on Jan. 26, 1994, in Indonesia, and on September 5, the two sides agreed on certain issues, including that Islamic law would prevail in Muslim areas. But an MNLF faction refused to accept this arrangement and continued to fight the army and seize foreign hostages.

The Communist New People's Army (NPA) was another group in 1994 that had been fighting the Philippine government for 25 years. The NPA wanted to overthrow the government. But on January 10, government forces captured Arturo Tabara, a major NPA leader who had operated in the central islands. On May 26, the military captured NPA leader Filemon Lagman in Manila.

In an attempt to restore national stability, Ramos proclaimed on March 25 a general amnesty for all Communist, Muslim, and other dissidents, including police and soldiers accused of crimes in fighting the rebel groups. The NPA, weakened and torn by internal dissension in recent years, assassinated one of its former leaders who planned to accept the amnesty.

East Timor trouble. The Philippine government was indebted to Indonesia for helping with the MNLF talks in January. However, in May, the Indonesian government embarrassed Ramos by pressuring him to block a privately organized, international conference on East Timor from taking place in Manila. Indonesia had seized East Timor from Portugal in 1975 and since then had faced guerrilla resistance to its rule. The conference addressed Indonesia's human rights record on East Timor. Ramos said the Philippines recognized East Timor as an Indonesian territory, but it could not constitutionally ban a private meeting. Still, by preventing some well-known foreigners from attending, including Danielle Mitterrand, the wife of French President François Mitterrand, Ramos unintentionally drew worldwide attention to the conference. ☐ Henry S. Bradsher

See also **Asia** (Facts in brief table). In *World Book,* see **Philippines.**

Physics. The final missing piece in the puzzle of subatomic matter appeared to have been found, according to an April 1994 announcement by physicists at Fermi National Accelerator Laboratory (Fermilab) in Batavia, Ill. The scientists released evidence of the existence of the long-sought *top quark*, the heaviest of the 12 fundamental building blocks of matter.

Evidence of the top quark. The building blocks are six particles called *quarks* and six particles called *leptons*. The electron is a member of the lepton family, and quarks are found inside the atomic nucleus. Protons and neutrons are combinations of the two lightest quarks, designated *up* and *down*. The four other quarks are highly unstable and quickly break down into up quarks or down quarks.

Unstable particles like the top quark are not present in ordinary matter. They must be created by converting energy into matter in particle collisions. The researchers created such collisions in Fermilab's Tevatron, currently the world's most powerful particle accelerator. The Tevatron accelerates and stores two beams of particles moving in opposite directions. One beam consists of protons, the *nuclei* (cores) of ordinary hydrogen atoms, and the other beam contains antiprotons, particles that are equal to protons in mass but opposite in electric charge. Each particle carries an energy of 900 billion electronvolts. (An electronvolt is the amount of energy gained by a particle with one unit of electric charge moving across an electric potential difference of one volt.) Powerful electromagnets hold the beams on course. At one point along the race track, the beams are brought to a focus so that protons and antiprotons collide. Each collision produces many new particles traveling in various directions. Special detectors enable computers to reconstruct the particle paths.

Scientists found evidence of the top quark by searching for one of several tell-tale patterns produced by the quark's breakup. It took more than 10 billion collisions to produce 12 examples. From those examples, physicists determined that the mass of the top quark is approximately 185 atomic mass units, 40 times heavier than the bottom quark, the next heaviest quark.

Other reactions can produce similar patterns, but the experimenters estimated that those reactions would have produced only 3 or 4 examples, rather than the 12 observed. However, the presence of the other reactions made the scientists reluctant to claim that they had actually "discovered" the top quark. Between May and October, they produced as many collisions as had previously been studied—and were on their way to producing many times more—in the hope of eliminating all doubt that they were indeed seeing the traces of the top quark.

Laser fusion. In July 1994, the United States Department of Energy (DOE) released detailed information on government-sponsored research on laser fusion, in which powerful laser beams blast tiny fuel

Physicists Melvyn J. Shochet, left, and William Carithers, Jr., reported in April that their team of more than 400 scientists found evidence of the top quark.

pellets to produce nuclear reactions. The technique causes miniature explosions that may someday be harnessed as a source of energy. Details of the research had been kept secret because the work is closely related to the design of nuclear weapons.

The data came from the NOVA laser facility at the Lawrence Livermore Laboratory near Livermore, Calif. This facility boasts 10 of the world's most powerful lasers. The 10 beams are aimed at fuel pellets that contain a mixture of deuterium and tritium, the two heavy *isotopes* (forms) of hydrogen. Each pellet is a few millimeters in diameter and has an outer shell of plastic or glass. The beams hit each pellet from all sides at once to compress it to a tiny fraction of its original volume. The compression heats the pellet to temperatures measured in millions of degrees Celsius, high enough to kindle the fusion reaction. The nuclei fuse to become a helium nucleus and a neutron, and in the process energy is released.

The declassified data revealed that pellets have been compressed to as little as 1/34 of their original dimensions. Although experts say this is an impressive achievement, it was not clear whether the bigger pellets required to produce useful amounts of energy can be compressed to a similar extent. The DOE announced plans on October 21 to spend $1.8-billion on a new fusion device, the National Ignition Facility. (See also **Energy supply.**) □ Robert H. March

In *World Book,* see **Particle accelerator; Physics.**

Poetry. In his introduction to *The Best American Poetry 1994,* series editor David Lehman observed that the 75 poets represented write about sex and romance, as readers might expect, but also about "baseball, science, nature, alcoholism, AIDS, childbirth, snow, the human anatomy, Greek mythology, Leni Riefenstahl, and John Cage." In other words, American poetry in 1994 continued to strive for the timeless and the timely.

Douglas Messerli's *From the Other Side of the Century: The New American Poetry 1960-1990* and Paul Hoover's *Postmodern American Poetry* also provided two comprehensive overviews of recent poetic practice and achievement. Both anthologies presented themselves as successors to Donald Allen's epoch-making 1960 volume, *The New American Poetry.*

New collections. Many of the most admired poets in midcareer offered new collections this year. Jorie Graham's *Materialism* revealed "a mind in the act of finding itself," as she wrote about the Holocaust; the arrival of Columbus in America; and other complex matters while drawing on the testimony of writers as diverse and demanding as Plato, Ludwig Wittgenstein, and Jonathan Edwards.

In contrast to Graham's striving for grandeur, Mary Jo Salter in *Sunday Skaters* wrote frequently about home and family while skimming along with puns, wordplay, and considerable charm. In "The Hand of Thomas Jefferson," she discovers in the word *treason* the "reason" to "authorize a nation."

Rodney Jones's *Apocalyptic Narrative* follows on his 1989 National Book Critics Circle award for *Transparent Gesture*. The collection shows Jones to be, in critic David Barber's words, a marvel of "demonic energy and demotic bravura." Jones writes: "I took each rip and splinter as Baudelaire took his cripples and imbeciles,/As the true pessimist relishes the catastrophe that confirms his faith. . ./Most of my country abhors filth and denounces a ruin, but I want that heart that ripens in desolation."

Jones's intensity may recall the much honored, albeit more formal Philip Levine, who often memorializes working-class life. Levine's latest collection, *The Simple Truth*, may be his most elegiac, mixing memory and desire, mingling prayer and history: "Some things/You know all your life. They are so simple and true/they must be said without elegance, meter and rhyme,/they must be laid on the table beside the salt shaker,/the glass of water, the absence of light gathering/in the shadows of picture frames/they must be/naked alone, they must stand for themselves." Levine's collection of essays and memoirs, *The Bread of Time*, was also published in 1994.

Final work. Amy Clampitt published her first collection, *The Kingfisher* (1983), when she was 63; with it she rocketed into the front rank of contemporary poets. Just before she died in 1994, she brought out her fourth collection, *A Silence Opens*. It reconfirmed her mastery of formal verse, lavish with elaborate syntax and allusion but also laced with moral passion, as in "Matoaka," about Pocahontas. But Clampitt could be topical too, writing a poem for *The New York Times* to celebrate the winter solstice. "A Catalpa Tree on West Twelfth Street" opens: "While the sun stops, or/seems to, to define a term/for the interminable. . . ."

Other collections. Stephen Dobyns' *Velocities: New and Selected Poems 1966-1972* gathered the satirical, sometimes lurid verse of this multitalented writer. (Dobyns also writes serious novels and lighthearted mysteries.) One early poem opens with a kind of surrealistic hook: "The men with long faces have come after my knives."

Similar imagery has long characterized John Ashbery's sometimes controversial work, including 1994's *And The Stars Were Shining*. Ashbery's friend and fellow New York school poet Kenneth Koch also brought out a new volume, *One Train*, as well as *On the Great Atlantic Rainway: Selected Poems 1950-1988*. Koch displays his usual energy, skewed vision of the world, and humorous incongruity.

The Library of America published Ralph Waldo Emerson's *Collected Poems and Translation;* Princeton brought out W. H. Auden's *Juvenilia;* and Ronald Schuchard edited T. S. Eliot's previously unpublished lectures, *The Varieties of Metaphysical Poetry*.

☐ Michael Dirda

In *World Book,* see **Poetry.**

Poland. Poland's coalition government struggled in 1994 to sustain economic reform while easing the burden of those reforms on the population. The parliament, led by Prime Minister Waldemar Pawlak's Polish Peasant Party and the Democratic Left Alliance, passed a tight budget on March 5 to control the nation's deficit. A tighter budget was necessary to obtain a loan from the United Nations' International Monetary Fund (IMF), but it brought criticism from many workers. On February 9, about 30,000 workers gathered in Warsaw, the capital, to protest the new budget.

The push for a free market economy raised conflict within the coalition and between parliament and President Lech Walesa. Pawlak, who supported greater social spending, helped pass new laws increasing the pensions and wages of workers in service industries. Pawlak's government also adopted a number of policies to benefit agriculture in 1994, including an increase in social security for farmers. But parliament voted against Pawlak's wishes in May by approving wage controls for state employees.

Walesa continued to promote reform, but saw his popularity and political support crumble in 1994. In July, Walesa vetoed a proposed amendment to relax Poland's strict abortion laws. The veto fueled criticism of the president's commitment to the Roman Catholic Church, which opposes abortion. Walesa also campaigned to increase the powers of the presidency and argued that such powers should be written into the nation's new constitution, which was scheduled for completion in 1995. His appeals drew an official reprimand from parliament in October.

Strong economy. Despite political tensions, Poland's economy continued its steady growth in 1994. By October, industrial production had increased by about 13 percent. Foreign trade also showed promise, as the nation's total exports increased more than 20 percent by October. But many Poles continued to suffer during the year. Unemployment averaged about 16 percent. In some parts of the country, as much as 25 percent of the labor force was unemployed. The cost of living, along with the inflation rate, also grew during the year.

Poland's economic progress brought encouragement from international lending agencies in 1994. The London Club, a group of commercial banks, agreed in August to refinance Poland's loans, reducing the nation's debt by about one half. The IMF also continued to provide support during the year.

Privatization of large state enterprises moved very slowly in 1994. Disagreements among leaders over the pace and methods of privatization held up progress. In October, Pawlak finally approved a bill to launch a privatization plan for the nation's major enterprises.

☐ Sharon L. Wolchik

See also **Europe** (Facts in brief table). In *World Book,* see **Poland.**

Pollution. See Environmental pollution.

Popular music. A 25th anniversary concert commemorating the legendary Woodstock rock festival rivaled the original in 1994. The event drew an estimated 350,000 people to a field in Saugerties, N.Y., where performances were held from August 12 to 14. Another 250,000 people watched the concert on pay-per-view television.

Although scorned in some quarters for commercializing the "peace and love" nature of the first festival, the organizers, who charged a $135 admission price, pulled off a wild event that satisfied many. Among the highlights was the performance by Green Day, a punk-influenced group, whose set was barraged by mud from the crowd. Nine Inch Nails went one better by rolling about in the mud before going on stage. Other artists who participated in the festival included Aerosmith, Bob Dylan, Melissa Etheridge, and Cypress Hill. Crosby, Stills and Nash, who had performed at the original concert, returned for the anniversary.

Other acts from the first Woodstock appeared at its original site in nearby Bethel, N.Y. As many as 50,000 people came out for free concerts by Richie Havens, Melanie, Country Joe McDonald, and others.

Music business news. A United States Supreme Court decision on March 7 held that 2 Live Crew's rap parody of Roy Orbison's classic "Oh, Pretty Woman" was legal. The court ruled that written, visual, and musical parodies could be exempt from copyright law under certain circumstances.

A round of chief executive shakeups at the major record labels included the elevation in July of Atlantic's co-chairman Doug Morris as president/CEO of Warner Music-U.S., thereby controlling the Atlantic, Elektra, and Warner Brothers labels. Stepping down in Morris' wake was Mo Ostin, who had headed Warner Brothers for 25 years and was considered one of the founders of the modern record industry.

War on violent lyrics. A growing number of radio stations cut back on songs with violent, sexually explicit, or derogatory lyrics. In January, a demonstration against "gangsta" rap was staged at a Sam Goody's record store near the White House in Washington, D.C., by the National Political Congress of Black Women and the local chapter of the Coalition of Labor Union Women. Several federal government hearings focusing on the lyrics issue began in February. Music Television (MTV) began an antiviolence campaign in February as well.

Tributes. Tribute albums were all the rage in 1994. Eric Clapton, Whitney Houston, and Bruce Springsteen were among the artists gracing *All Men Are Brothers: A Tribute to Curtis Mayfield,* which honored the R&B giant, who was paralyzed after a freak accident in 1990. Other star-studded albums commemorated the music of such artists as The Carpenters, Leonard Cohen, George Gershwin, Merle Haggard, Kiss, and Richard Thompson.

Grammy Award winners in 1994

Record of the Year, "I Will Always Love You," Whitney Houston.

Album of the Year, *The Bodyguard,* Whitney Houston.

Song of the Year, "A Whole New World (Aladdin's Theme)," Alan Menken and Tim Rice, songwriters.

New Artist, Toni Braxton.

Pop Vocal Performance, Female, "I Will Always Love You," Whitney Houston.

Pop Vocal Performance, Male, "If I Ever Lose My Faith in You," Sting.

Pop Performance by a Duo or Group with Vocal, "A Whole New World (Aladdin's Theme)," Peabo Bryson and Regina Belle.

Traditional Pop Vocal Performance, *Steppin' Out,* Tony Bennett.

Pop Instrumental Performance, "Barcelona Mona," Bruce Hornsby and Branford Marsalis.

Rock Vocal Performance, Solo, "I'd Do Anything for Love (But I Won't Do That)," Meat Loaf.

Rock Performance by a Duo or Group with Vocal, "Livin' on the Edge," Aerosmith.

Hard Rock Performance, "Plush," Stone Temple Pilots.

Metal Performance with Vocal, "I Don't Want to Change the World," Ozzy Osbourne.

Rock Instrumental Performance, "Sofa," Zappa's Universe featuring Steve Vai.

Rock Song, "Runaway Train," David Pirner, songwriter.

Alternative Music Album, *Zooropa,* U2.

Rhythm-and-Blues Vocal Performance, Female, "Another Sad Love Song," Toni Braxton.

Rhythm-and-Blues Vocal Performance, Male, "A Song for You," Ray Charles.

Rhythm-and-Blues Performance by a Duo or Group with Vocal, "No Ordinary Love," Sade.

Rhythm-and-Blues Song, "That's the Way Love Goes," Janet Jackson, James Harris III, and Terry Lewis, songwriters.

Rap Solo Performance, "Let Me Ride," Dr. Dre.

Rap Performance by a Duo or Group, "Rebirth of Slick (Cool Like Dat)," Digable Planets.

New-Age Album, *Spanish Angel,* Paul Winter Consort.

Contemporary Jazz Performance, *The Road to You,* Pat Metheny Group.

Jazz Vocal Performance, *Take a Look,* Natalie Cole.

Jazz Instrumental Solo, "Miles Ahead," Joe Henderson.

Jazz Instrumental Performance, Individual or Group, *So Near, So Far (Musings for Miles),* Joe Henderson.

Large Jazz Ensemble Performance, *Miles and Quincy Live at Montreux,* Miles Davis and Quincy Jones.

Country Vocal Performance, Female, "Passionate Kisses," Mary-Chapin Carpenter.

Country Vocal Performance, Male, "Ain't That Lonely Yet," Dwight Yoakam.

Country Performance by a Duo or Group with Vocal, "Hard Workin' Man," Brooks & Dunn.

Country Vocal Collaboration, "Does He Love You," Reba McEntire and Linda Davis.

Country Instrumental Performance, "Red Wing," Asleep at the Wheel.

Bluegrass Album, *Waitin' for the Hard Times to Go,* The Nashville Bluegrass Band.

Country Song, "Passionate Kisses," Lucinda Williams, songwriter.

Rock Gospel Album, *Free at Last,* DC Talk.

Woodstock 1994 rocked a new generation in August. Some 350,000 people showed up to celebrate the 25th anniversary of the original rock festival.

Rockin' in cyberspace. Interactive formats kicked into high gear while artists and record companies tapped into computer networks in 1994. Subscribers to various online computer services could download Aerosmith's unreleased song "Head First" and Madonna's single and video for "Secret." Artists such as Meat Loaf, Peter Gabriel, and Ozzy Osbourne answered questions from fans via computer link. "Vid Grid," a CD-ROM game that allows players to manipulate videos by musicians, came out in 1994.

On November 18, the Rolling Stones performed the first ever live broadcast of a major rock concert on a computer network.

Rock. The rock world was shocked by the suicide of Nirvana's Kurt Cobain in Seattle on April 8. Cobain died from a self-inflicted gunshot wound shortly after an accidental drug-and-alcohol overdose in Rome. His death sparked music industry support for a musicians' drug and alcohol abuse referral service. A posthumous live Nirvana album, *MTV Unplugged in New York,* was released in early November.

Young "modern rock" artists, such as Counting Crows, Crash Test Dummies, Beck, Stone Temple Pilots, Smashing Pumpkins, the Breeders, Cracker, and The Cranberries achieved commercial success in 1994, as did a new wave of bold female rockers, including Liz Phair, Tori Amos, Juliana Hatfield, Sheryl Crow, Me'Shell NdegéOcello, Lisa Loeb, and Courtney Love.

Older rock powerhouses also made news in 1994. The Eagles, Traffic, the Rolling Stones, and Pink Floyd all returned to the music scene with albums and tours. John Mellencamp, Neil Young, and Eric Clapton released acclaimed albums in 1994, with Clapton surprisingly returning to his blues roots.

The annual Lollapalooza tour of alternative rock acts was headed in 1994 by Smashing Pumpkins. Absent from the touring scene was Pearl Jam, who canceled touring in a battle with the powerful ticket agency Ticketmaster over high ticket prices but ended the year with the number one album *Vitalogy*.

Country music. Newcomer Tim McGraw overcame controversy with his debut hit "Indian Outlaw," which offended some Native Americans who felt it portrayed negative stereotypes. Faith Hill broke through as well, aided by a number-one country version of Janis Joplin's "Piece of My Heart."

David Ball became country's newest "new traditionalist" with his classic-sounding hit "Thinkin' Problem." Martina McBride came to the fore with "Independence Day," her hit single and video about domestic violence.

Two legendary performers, Johnny Cash and Waylon Jennings, teamed up with younger rock producers in turning out their most critically acclaimed albums in years. And in March, the *Rhythm, Country & Blues* compilation featured legendary R&B greats duetting with top country singers.

339

The tragic suicide of Nirvana's Kurt Cobain on April 8 brought fans to the streets of Seattle, his hometown, to mourn his death.

Jazz vocalists enjoyed a banner year in 1994, with the ageless Tony Bennett solidifying his remarkable appeal with young audiences through an "MTV Unplugged" concert. Cassandra Wilson had her biggest year with her soul and blues inflected album "Blue Light 'Til Dawn." Diane Schuur teamed with bluesman B. B. King and topped the jazz album chart.

On the instrumental side, trumpeters Wallace Roney and Roy Hargrove, bassist Christian McBride, and pianist Jacky Terrason led a charge by a new generation of jazz players. The British "acid jazz"—a dance club style music, fusing elements of jazz, soul, reggae, and rap—grew in popularity via artists like Brand New Heavies, Galliano, and US3.

Pop comebacks. Michael Jackson returned from the brink of a public relations disaster with a January 25 agreement to pay a reported sum of at least $15 million to settle a civil suit on sexual molestation charges brought by a 13-year-old boy. On August 1, Jackson and Lisa Marie Presley, daughter of Elvis Presley, said that they had married in May.

Barbra Streisand's comeback was among the year's biggest milestones. Following the superstar's New Year's concert triumphs in Las Vegas, Nev., she set out in May on her first tour in 27 years. A two-disc CD captured the concert for posterity.

Rhythm and blues. Producer and performer R. Kelly shot to stardom with his pop smash "Bump N' Grind," and as writer and producer for new artists

Aaliya and Changing Faces. Toni Braxton maintained her presence as a top new female vocalist, while male vocalist Gerald Levert scored with his version of Boy Howdy's country hit "She'd Give Anything."

All-4-One, which had a huge pop hit version of John Michael Montgomery's country hit "I Swear," joined Blackgirl among several emerging vocal groups. And Boyz II Men topped the charts with the single "I'll Make Love to You" and the album *II*.

Rap artists of the year included Coolio, whose West Coast style shone on his big hit single "Fantastic Voyage," while Warren G. & Nate Dogg, brought a more raw East Coast touch to "Regulate." Nas and Wu-Tang Clan were also noteworthy East Coast rappers. The Jamaican dance-hall rap style, led by female artist Patra, also continued to increase its impact on the reggae scene.

New Beatles release. On December 6, Capitol Records released the *Beatles: Live at the BBC*, a two-disk compilation of radio performances from 1962 to 1965. It marked the first release of unissued Beatles material since 1977.

Tupac gets rap. Rapper Tupac Shakur was convicted on December 1 of felony sexual abuse charges for groping a 19-year-old woman in his hotel room in 1993. The conviction came one day after he was shot five times in a robbery.   □ Jim Bessman

In *World Book*, see **Country music; Jazz; Popular music.**

Population. The Second U.S. Circuit Court of Appeals in New York City ruled on Aug. 8, 1994, that the federal government under former President George Bush had failed to adequately defend its decision not to correct the tally on the 1990 national census. The Census Bureau estimated the tally was short by about 5 million people. The federal government uses census figures to determine legislative districts and the amount of federal funding given to state and local governments. Advocates of adjusting the census count argued that the Republican Bush Administration refused to adjust the census because most of the counting error occurred in urban areas where minorities live. Urban minorities typically vote Democratic. The ruling, which was returned to a lower court for further argument, could ultimately give large cities more money and more representation in Congress.

The fastest growing metropolitan areas, in decreasing order of growth, in 1994 were Las Vegas, Nev.; Laredo, Tex.; Yuma, Ariz.; McAllen-Edinburg-Mission, Tex.; Anchorage, Alaska; Naples, Fla.; Las Cruces, N. Mex.; Bakersfield, Calif.; Lawton, Okla.; and Boise, Ida., according to a Census Bureau report released on Feb. 7, 1994. Analysts believed much of the growth in the Western cities was due in part to migrations by Californians fleeing the economic recession in their home state.

The UN Population Conference. On September 5 to 13, an estimated 20,000 dignitaries, journalists, and other interested groups met in Cairo, Egypt, for the United Nations' third International Conference on Population and Development. After days of debate over abortion rights and other controversial topics, the delegations representing 179 nations agreed that the advancement of women is essential to containing world population growth.

Four important goals to come out of the conference were a commitment to the education of girls; to the reduction of infant, child, and maternal mortality; to creating universal access to family planning and reproductive health services; and to gender equality. The conference also developed a program of action to stabilize the world's population at about 7.27 billion by the year 2015, up from 5.66 billion in 1994. Analysts said that most of the population growth over the next 20 years would occur in developing countries.

Delegates agreed that the amount spent on stabilizing population growth should increase to an annual $17 billion, up from the current $5 billion, by the year 2000. By the year 2015, that amount would be increased to $22 billion.

The Vatican delegation, representing the Roman Catholic Church, and delegates from Muslim countries opposed early drafts of the program, arguing that parts of it undermined their religious beliefs.

☐ Patricia Ohlenroth

See also **Census.** In *World Book,* see **Population.**

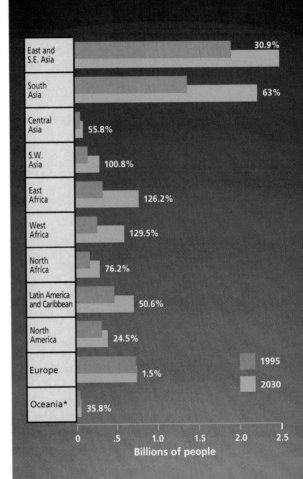

World population to soar

The World Bank estimates that from 1995 to 2030, most of the world's people will live in Asia but the highest growth rate will occur in African countries.

East and S.E. Asia — 30.9%
South Asia — 63%
Central Asia — 55.8%
S.W. Asia — 100.8%
East Africa — 126.2%
West Africa — 129.5%
North Africa — 76.2%
Latin America and Caribbean — 50.6%
North America — 24.5%
Europe — 1.5%
Oceania* — 35.8%

1995
2030

0   .5   1.0   1.5   2.0   2.5
Billions of people

* Australia, New Zealand, Western Pacific island nations.
Source: World Bank.

Portugal in 1994 emerged from a steep economic recession that had begun in 1992. The country's gross domestic product, the value of all goods and services produced within the country, rose 1 percent after two years of decline. Inflation, long a problem for Portugal, fell from more than 6 percent in late 1993 to about 5 percent in 1994. However, unemployment rose from 6.8 percent in 1993 to 8 percent in 1994.

The government continued plans to modernize Portugal's economy and align its political system with its partners in the European Union (EU), formerly the European Community. One of its goals is to meet the EU's economic standards by 1996, which would allow Portugal to join the single European currency, set to take effect in 1999. From 1994 to the year 2000, Portugal is slated to receive more than $20 billion in aid from the EU to improve its roads, telephone system, and other infrastructure facilities.

Prime Minister Aníbal Cavaço Silva privatized more of Portugal's state-owned industries in 1994. Among the companies sold were the power company, a steel company, and parts of the phone system.

Cultural celebration. Portugal's capital, Lisbon, was the EU's designated European Capital of Culture for 1994. The event was marked by dozens of special art exhibitions. ☐ Philip Revzin

See also **Europe** (Facts in brief table). In *World Book,* see European Union; Portugal.

Postal Service, United States. The Postal Service Board of Governors voted on March 7, 1994, to seek a 10.3 percent increase in postal rates, a request that was approved on November 30 by the independent Postal Rate Commission. The increase, which was to take effect on Jan. 1, 1995, was the first hike in postal rates since February 1991.

The increase raised the cost of a first-class letter from 29 cents to 32 cents and of a postcard from 19 cents to 21 cents. Postmaster General Marvin T. Runyon, Jr., said the increase was necessary because of a projected $1.3-billion deficit for fiscal year 1994.

The Postal Service was the target of mounting criticism in 1994 for slow service and even failure to deliver mail. Runyon went to Chicago in March after postal authorities there discovered thousands of letters in a burning pile. Similar problems were found in New York City and Washington, D.C.

In December, the Japanese government protested a Postal Service plan to issue a stamp in 1995 commemorating the dropping of atomic bombs on two Japanese cities in 1945. Within days, the Postal Service scrapped the stamp. ☐ William J. Eaton

In *World Book,* see Post office; Postal Service, United States.

President of the United States. See Clinton, Bill; United States, Government of the.

Prince Edward Island. See Canadian provinces.

Prison. State and federal prisons in the United States held 1,012,851 prisoners as of June 30, 1994, according to the Department of Justice's Bureau of Justice Statistics (BJS). It was the first time the U.S. prison population ever surpassed 1 million. The number had more than quadrupled since 1975, when U.S. prisons held 240,593 inmates.

As prison and jail populations grew, crime experts debated the wisdom of national anticrime policies. Throughout the 1980's, the public increasingly demanded tougher penalties for criminals, and few voices were raised in opposition, in part because elected officials feared their constituents would regard them as "soft on crime." More recently, officials in many states have begun to question whether too many people receive prison sentences. In 1994, the National Governors' Association, the National Conference of State Legislatures, and the Association of State Correctional Administrators, among other organizations, opposed the harsher sentencing provisions included in the federal anticrime bill signed into law in September.

Demographics. The Federal Bureau of Investigation reported that 44.8 percent of people arrested for committing a violent crime in America in 1992 (the latest available data) were African American. The rate differed little from 1979, when 44.1 percent of people arrested for violent crimes were black. But more blacks than whites went to prison in 1992.

More prison sentences for blacks than for whites was not the result of bias by police, prosecutors, or judges, according to major reviews of research by both African-American and white scholars. Instead, the increase in black inmates resulted from policy decisions to increase the use of imprisonment for nonviolent offenses and from carrying out the so-called "War on Drugs," which stiffened penalties for crimes involving illegal drugs. The drug war targeted inner-city minority areas and brought about vast increases in drug arrests of blacks living there.

The BJS reported that there were 55,365 women in state and federal prisons in 1993, far fewer than the 893,516 men in prison. But the rate at which women were sent to prison rose faster than that for men.

Dahmer killed. Convicted serial killer Jeffrey L. Dahmer was himself attacked and killed in the Columbia Correctional Institution in Portage, Wis., on Nov. 28, 1994. Dahmer died of massive head injuries as he was being taken to a hospital. He had been found in a staff bathroom of a recreation center, where he and another inmate, who was also killed, had been cleaning. Dahmer had confessed to murdering 17 young men and boys over a 13-year period. In February 1992, he was sentenced to serve 16 consecutive life terms in prison. ☐ Michael Tonry

See also **Crime: Fighting Crime in America.** In *World Book,* see Prison.

Prizes. See Nobel Prizes; Pulitzer Prizes.

Some of the 32 women to be ordained as the Anglican Church of England's first female priests arrive at Bristol Cathedral in Bristol, England, in March.

Protestantism. Controversies over abortion and sexuality dominated many Protestant denominations during 1994, as they had in recent years. On July 29, a former Presbyterian minister, Paul Hill, was arrested for shooting to death physician John Britton and another man outside a Pensacola, Fla., clinic, where Britton performed abortions. Prior to the shooting, Hill had publicly advocated the killing of doctors who perform abortions, calling such acts "justifiable homicide." He was convicted of murder on November 2 and sentenced to death December 6.

Homosexuality controversy. In late August 1994, delegates to the Episcopal Church's General Convention in Indianapolis debated a draft document on homosexuality and the celibacy of single people, the fifth draft since 1991, when a bishops' committee began working on the statement. A conservative group called Episcopalians United for Revelation, Renewal, and Reformation vehemently opposed the inclusion in the statement of a call for the church to develop moral guidelines for homosexual as well as heterosexual relationships. Unable to find a consensus, the delegates proposed that the committee continue its work with theologians, ethicists, and local parishes to produce another draft.

The American Baptist Churches (ABC) denomination has been less public in its debate over homosexuality than Lutherans, United Methodists, and others have in recent years. Since 1992, the ABC's top policy-making body has adopted conflicting resolutions on the issue. One declares homosexual practice to be incompatible with Christian teaching, and another calls for dialogue in recognition of the diversity of opinion on homosexuality within the ABC. In 1994, some conservative ABC congregations threatened to leave if homosexuality were officially sanctioned.

The Presbyterian Church (U.S.A.) in its June convention in Wichita, Kans., however, made progress toward promoting denominational unity over the issue of homosexuality. The delegates voted to bar clergy from blessing unions of people of the same sex, but the delegates left unresolved the issue of requiring gay or single clergy to remain celibate.

The Christian Reformed Church overturned in June 1994 its 1993 vote approving the ordination of women as ministers, elders, and evangelists. By a 95 to 89 margin, delegates to the synod meeting in Grand Rapids, Mich., disapproved the ordination of women, but approved the idea that women could "expound the Word of God." Delegates also voted to urge congregations that had already ordained women to "release them from office" by June 1, 1995. Local churches that had been ordaining women elders for some years announced that they would disregard the denominational prohibitions. The denomination has been losing moderate and ultraconservative congregations alike, both of them dissatisfied with conservative denominational actions.

Protestantism

The Southern Baptist Convention (SBC), the largest Protestant denomination in the United States, continued to favor a conservative direction in 1994. Thus, SBC members were shocked in March, when the board of Southwestern Baptist Theological Seminary in Fort Worth, Tex., fired conservative board president Russell Dilday after citing him for excellent administration. Dilday angered the board for publicly siding at times with moderate SBC members outside the seminary.

In July, the SBC directed its various institutions to refuse funds from the Cooperative Baptist Fellowship, the group of moderates that had been edged out of all positions of power in the SBC in recent years. Speculation continued in 1994 whether the fellowship would become an independent denomination or whether it would remain a protest movement within the SBC, advancing progressive causes.

Anglicanism in England. On March 12, 32 women became the Church of England's first female priests. In February, seven Anglican bishops had said they would resign if women were ordained. In July, the General Synod of the Church of England voted against ending Anglicanism as the official church in England. The Church's official status gives it certain legal and financial privileges. George Carey, archbishop of Canterbury, and John Habgood, archbishop of York, also opposed the move. □ Martin E. Marty

In *World Book,* see **Protestantism.**

Psychology. By 4½ months of age, babies can recognize their own names upon hearing them and prefer their names over similar-sounding names, psychologists reported in June 1994. Infants begin to build a mental vocabulary in their native language during the first months of life, though speech usually does not emerge until about 1 year of age, asserted Peter W. Jusczyk of the State University of New York College at Buffalo and his colleagues.

In their study, 24 mothers held their 4½-month-old babies on their laps in front of a three-sided enclosure. A flashing red light on either of the outer two panels attracted a baby's gaze. A loudspeaker in the panel then broadcast four names, including the infant's own, for about 20 seconds each or until the child turned away for more than 2 seconds.

Each baby heard two names that had little resemblance to their own, and one that was similar to theirs in rhythm and intonation. In a series of name presentations from both panels, infants listened substantially longer to their own names than to other names. This indicated that the babies had learned to recognize and pay special attention to their own names, Jusczyk said. Other words that babies hear repeatedly, such as "mommy," may also spark recognition by 4½ months of age, he noted.

Musical thinking. Preschool children who take music lessons experience a boost in spatial skills that may later improve their performance in related areas, such as mathematics, according to a study released in August by psychologist Frances H. Rauscher of the University of California in Irvine.

Rauscher and her co-workers provided 19 youngsters in a preschool with weekly keyboard lessons taught by a professional piano instructor and daily singing sessions directed by a professional vocal instructor. Another 15 preschoolers received no musical training. The children ranged in age from 3 to 5.

After eight months, preschoolers receiving music lessons dramatically outscored the others on a spatial task in which they had to arrange pieces of a puzzle to form a picture. This task required children to form a complete mental image of an entity, such as a dog, and then orient puzzle pieces to reproduce it, Rauscher said. The coordination of a number of brain areas that facilitate this spatial skill may improve after several months of music lessons, she proposed. Rauscher planned to examine whether keyboard or singing lessons alone strengthen spatial skills, how long such effects last, and whether elementary school children respond to music lessons in the same way as the preschoolers did.

Bilingual learning. Spanish-speaking people who immigrate to the United States would probably learn English faster and better in educational programs that immerse them in their new language, concluded researchers led by psychologist Harry P. Bahrick of Ohio Wesleyan University in Delaware, Ohio, in a September report. Most school systems place Spanish-speaking students in classes that balance English and Spanish because of concerns about preserving their native language and culture.

The researchers gave 801 Cuban and Mexican immigrants Spanish and English language tests. Most of the participants spoke English well after having lived in the United States for an average of 12 years. In addition, their understanding of Spanish held steady as many as 50 years after immigrating, and they still spoke Spanish about half the time.

Most participants in the study had immigrated between the ages of 10 and 26 and lived in one of three places: Miami, Fla.; El Paso, or small Midwestern communities in which Hispanic Americans were a minority. They had immigrated between 4 months and 50 years previous to the test.

Those who immigrated at age 18 or older demonstrated a firmer grasp of English vocabulary and other aspects of English knowledge than those who arrived before age 18, the researchers found. This contradicts the widespread belief that it inevitably becomes harder to learn a second language as people get older.

The similarities between English and Spanish words gave older immigrants a boost in learning English, Bahrick said. Their larger Spanish vocabularies gave them a foundation for understanding similar English words and phrases. □ Bruce Bower

In *World Book,* see **Psychology.**

Public health. Efforts to prevent lead poisoning have resulted in a major decline in levels of lead in the bloodstreams of Americans, the United States Centers for Disease Control and Prevention (CDC) in Atlanta, Ga., reported on July 27, 1994. Previous studies had found that high levels of lead can stunt mental and physical development and cause hyperactivity and other problems.

Researchers at the CDC compared measurements of blood lead levels from two nationwide surveys, one conducted from 1976 to 1980 and the other from 1988 to 1991. Lead levels fell by an average of 78 percent during the period. The CDC said most of the decline resulted from the removal of lead from gasoline and the virtual elimination of lead solder from food and soft-drink cans. *The Journal of the American Medical Association,* which reported the decline, described it as "one of the most remarkable public health achievements of the decade."

In addition to the overall decline, CDC detected a sharp drop in the percentage of children aged 5 and under with high blood lead levels, from 88.2 percent to 8.9 percent. Young children are especially vulnerable to lead poisoning because their nervous systems are developing rapidly. The CDC emphasized, however, that about 1.7 million children under age 5 still have high blood lead levels. Most are poor children who live in urban areas where soil and dust are contaminated by old lead-based paint and past emissions from leaded gasoline.

Obesity. The number of overweight Americans rose about 8 percent from 1980 to 1991, a government study reported on July 19, 1994. The study concluded that one-third of adults—26 million men and 32 million women—weigh at least 20 pounds (9 kilograms) over the recommended weight for their height and age. Researchers at the National Center for Health Statistics compared 1991 data on the body weight of 8,260 adults with data compiled in 1980. Over the 11-year period, the weight of an American adult increased on average by almost 8 pounds (3.6 kilograms). The researchers said their findings support the view that obesity is an increasingly serious public health problem.

Researchers at Rockefeller University on Dec. 1, 1994, announced they have found a gene that regulates appetite. A malfunctioning gene, they said, could leave a person feeling hungry all the time, thus leading to overeating. But they cautioned that a treatment based on the finding was still many years away.

Smoking ban. In one of a growing number of actions to curb cigarette smoking, the U.S. Department of Defense (DOD) on April 8 banned smoking in all military workplaces around the world. DOD is the nation's largest employer, with 1.7 million uniformed personnel and about 900,000 civilian employees. The ban, intended to protect nonsmokers from the health hazards of inhaled smoke, covered offices, hallways, stairwells, bathrooms, and areas just outside military facilities.

Polio, a viral disease that once paralyzed thousands of children each year, has been completely eliminated from North, Central, and South America, the Pan American Health Organization (PAHO) announced on September 29. PAHO, the Western Hemisphere office of the World Health Organization, said the last documented case of polio had occurred in 1991 in Peru.

Polio has declined in the Americas since 1985, when health officials began a $540-million program to vaccinate all children. PAHO said vaccination programs also reduced the incidence of polio elsewhere, though about 120,000 cases still occur each year.

An outbreak of plague began in August 1994 in Maharashtra, a state in western India. Panic erupted in September when pneumonic plague, a more deadly and far more contagious form of the bacterial disease, broke out in Surat, a city in the neighboring state of Gujarat. An estimated 400,000 people fled Surat to escape infection. Reports that the disease had spread to India's three largest cities added to fears. International agencies rushed supplies of antibiotics to India, and by November, the outbreak was under control. Health officials said the disease killed 56 people. ☐ Michael Woods

See also **AIDS: The Changing Face of AIDS; Medicine.** In *World Book,* see **Public health.**

The Lone Star tick, below left, and American dog tick are suspected of transmitting a potentially deadly new bacterial disease, ehrlichiosis, which public health investigators described in May.

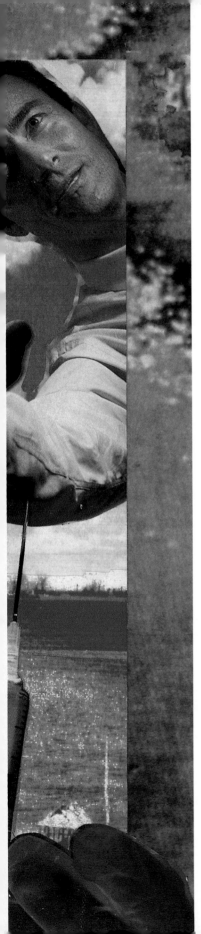

■ An atomic bomb explodes at Bikini Atoll in the Pacific Ocean in 1946, one of a series of bomb tests there. Witnesses say the giant water column that shot into the sky rained debris and radiation upon military ships and servicemen.

The Radiation Experiments

By Eileen Welsome

Revelations about government-sponsored radiation experiments on human subjects shocked Americans in 1994.

R evelations about human radiation experiments conducted during the Cold War came tumbling out of United States government files in 1993 and 1994. The disclosures showed that government-affiliated researchers had experimented with radioactive substances on terminally ill patients, pregnant women, mentally retarded children, prisoners, and others.

On Dec. 7, 1993, Hazel R. O'Leary, secretary of the U.S. Department of Energy (DOE), responded to a three-part series of articles in *The Albuquerque* (N. Mex.) *Tribune* that detailed the story of 18 people who received injections of plutonium, a highly toxic radioactive element, at the hands of government researchers in the late 1940's. O'Leary said she was appalled by the experiment and announced that the DOE would investigate that experiment and others like it. Many of the experiments appeared to be unethical, having violated the principle of *informed consent*, by which subjects of an experiment must be fully informed of the nature of the experiment and the risks it entails and must freely give their consent to taking these risks.

O'Leary promised to open DOE files and to declassify many formerly secret documents. Her candor drew strong support from the Administration of President Bill Clinton. In early 1994, President Clinton ordered other federal agencies to comb their files for similar ex-

347

periments, and he created the Advisory Committee on Human Radiation Experiments to study the information.

In the days and weeks following O'Leary's announcement, stories about other alleged human radiation experiments appeared in the nation's newspapers. The DOE established a hot line for victims to call, and within days the toll-free number logged thousands of calls. By June 1994, the DOE had spent $3.7 million, reviewed 97,000 documents, fielded 21,792 phone calls, received 5,011 letters, and responded to more than 414 inquiries from Congress. On June 27, O'Leary herself revealed new information about 48 other government-sponsored radiation experiments performed on human beings.

The plutonium experiment

The human radiation experiments began in the 1940's in conjunction with the development of the atomic bomb. Early in 1940, U.S. scientists began research to find a method of preparing enough plutonium or greatly enriched uranium for a bomb. After the United States entered World War II (1939-1945) in 1941, the government ordered an all-out effort to develop an atomic bomb and established the top-secret Manhattan Project to achieve this goal. The first atomic bomb was produced at Los Alamos, N. Mex., and exploded on July 16, 1945, near Alamogordo, N. Mex.

In the summer of 1944, in a crude chemistry laboratory in Los Alamos, a 22-year-old chemist with the Manhattan Project, Don Mastick, broke open a tiny glass vial filled with a material so secret it was known only as "the product." The material, partially converted to gas, shot out of the vial, bounced off a wall, and entered Mastick's mouth. He had just swallowed much of the world's supply of manufactured plutonium, an element that occurs in nature only in tiny amounts.

According to formerly secret memos written just after the accident, scientists at Los Alamos, concerned for the health and safety of thousands of workers on the Manhattan Project, decided that experiments on humans were needed to determine plutonium's effects on the body. Experiments had been done on animals that showed the rates at which their bodies excreted radioactive material and how much remained in the bones, but the scientists did not know if the results would be the same in people. The longer radioactive material remained in the body's tissues, the more harm it could cause.

The experiments were to be done at research hospitals associated with the Manhattan Project, using patients suffering from diseases that made their survival beyond 10 years unlikely. Doctors would inject a known quantity of plutonium into the patients, track the rate at which it left the body, and then use that data to calculate the risks to workers who were accidentally exposed. Between 1945 and 1947, 18 patients received plutonium injections. Three of the patients were at the hospital of the University of California in San Francisco; 3 received injections at the University of Chicago's Billings Hospital; 1 at the U.S. Army Hospital in Oak Ridge, Tenn., and 11 at the University of Rochester's Strong Memorial Hospital in upstate New York.

Glossary

Ground zero: The point on the ground directly below a nuclear explosion.

Informed consent: Subjects of an experiment are fully informed of the nature and risks of the experiment and freely give their consent.

Manhattan Project: The U.S. government's top-secret effort to produce an atomic bomb.

Nuclear radiation: High-energy particles and rays given off from the *nuclei* (cores) of certain types of atoms.

Plutonium: A radioactive metallic element.

Radioactivity: The process by which atoms emit radiation.

Rads: A measurement of the amount of radiation absorbed by tissues.

■ **The author**

Eileen Welsome is a reporter for *The Albuquerque* (N. Mex.) *Tribune.* She won the 1994 Pulitzer Prize for national reporting for her 1993 series, "The Plutonium Experiment."

Decades of radiation experiments

▪ 1940's

1945-1947—Scientists injected 18 terminally ill patients with radioactive plutonium in order to calculate how long the substance remained in the body. Doctors monitored some of the patients, including Elmer Allen, *right,* as late as the 1970's.
Late 1940's—Researchers at Vanderbilt University in Nashville gave about 800 pregnant women radioactive iron to measure their absorption of iron.
1940's-1950's—At the Fernald School in Waltham, Mass., scientists fed mentally retarded children cereal with milk dosed with radioactive minerals in it to test the rate of digestion of those minerals.

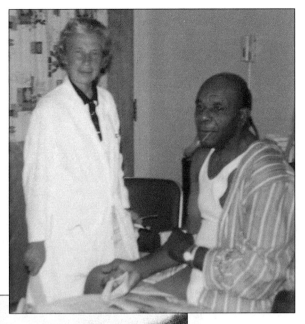

▪ 1950's

April 1953—Army troops take cover in a trench, *left,* only 4,000 yards (3,700 meters) from ground zero, the area directly below the center of an atomic explosion, at a test site in Nevada. Some veterans claim that they developed cancers or other illnesses because of the radiation they were exposed to during such tests.
1953—Government-sponsored scientists at the University of Iowa in Iowa City embarked on a top-secret, worldwide program aimed at studying the effects of fallout from nuclear explosions on plants, animals, and human beings. The program, called Operation Sunshine, included an experiment with pregnant women about to undergo abortions who were injected with radioactive iodine-131 to determine the effect on their fetuses.

One of the California patients was an African-American railroad porter named Elmer Allen, age 36. Allen had sought help at the hospital after falling from a train and injuring his knee. In July 1947, doctors injected the calf of his injured leg with a small amount of plutonium and amputated the leg three days later. Tissue samples from the severed limb were sent to a laboratory and analyzed for plutonium content. According to medical records, the doctors amputated because they discovered bone cancer in Allen's injured knee. Bone cancer is a rare disease that claims most victims within five years. But Allen lived 44 years after the surgery, leading scientists who reviewed the case in 1993 to speculate that Allen's condition had been misdiagnosed. Of the 18 patients, 7 survived for more than 10 years. Five of them lived for more than 20 years after the injections. Allen's medical records contain a memo stating that the experimental nature of the injection was explained to him and that he consented to it, but the records indicate only that the injection involved a radioactive material, which was unidentified. There are no records of consent among the other patients.

■ **1960's**

1960-1971—At the University of Cincinnati in Ohio, more than 85 cancer patients received high levels of radiation. About one-fourth of the patients may have died from the radiation, though doctors in the study contend that the radiation benefited some patients.
1963-1971—Sixty-seven prisoners at Oregon's state prison near Salem and 64 prisoners at the Washington state prison in Walla Walla had their testicles irradiated by X rays. The experiments were designed to study the effects of radiation on male fertility.
1965—The Atomic Energy Commission, a government agency responsible for atomic energy until 1974, created a nuclear "accident" that caused a low-level radioactive cloud to blow over Los Angeles and San Diego.

More experiments on humans

In 1976, *Science Trends*, a small publication in Washington, D.C., broke the first story describing the experiment. Nothing happened until 10 years later. In 1986, Representative Edward J. Markey (D., Mass.) issued a report entitled "American Nuclear Guinea Pigs: Three Decades of Radiation Experiments on U.S. Citizens." But even this attracted little attention. The account of the plutonium patients slipped back into unexplored history until November 1993, when *The Albuquerque Tribune* series sparked O'Leary's revelations. In the months following her statements, more than six congressional hearings were held, several lawsuits were filed, and numerous victims' organizations sprang up around the country. Some of the experiments that were disclosed included the following:

Nutritional studies were conducted in the 1940's and 1950's at the Fernald State School for mentally retarded people in Waltham, Mass. During the studies, scientists from Harvard University and Massachusetts Institute of Technology, both in Cambridge, Mass., gave about 70 mentally retarded children cereal with milk dosed with tiny amounts of radioactive iron or calcium. The tests were sponsored by the Atomic Energy Commission (AEC, an agency later absorbed by the DOE and the Nuclear Regulatory Commission) and the Quaker Oats Company. The radioactive tracers allowed the scientists to follow the path of the minerals through the body, similar to some procedures used routinely in medical diagnostics. The scientists sought to determine whether diets heavy in cereal slowed digestion of iron and calcium. A Massachusetts governmental task force investigated in early 1994 and found no evidence that the children at Fernald suffered physical harm from the experiment, but the experiment raised ethical questions about whether the mentally impaired could give "informed consent."

In the mid-1940's, more than 800 pregnant women ingested radioactive iron in a study aimed at measuring the absorption of iron during pregnancy. In the spring of 1994, some of the women and their children filed a class action lawsuit, claiming the experiment was harmful and unethical. The study occurred at Vanderbilt University in Nashville. Researchers in 1969 had concluded in the *American Journal of Epidemiology* that three of the children born to the nearly 800 women died of leukemia, soft tissue cancer, and bone cancer, cancers that are rare in children under the age of 15. Vanderbilt University officials have said that the radiation given the women was too small to cause harm, but they acknowledged that such testing would not be done today because of possible injury to the fetus.

Cancer patients and prisoners

High levels of radiation to the whole body were given to more than 85 cancer patients in studies that took place between 1960 and 1971 at the University of Cincinnati's hospital, then called Cincinnati General Hospital. Whole body radiation is used today in the treatment of some diseases, such as leukemia. In 1972, the studies, led by radiologist Eugene L. Saenger, came under fire when three faculty members at the university determined that as many as a fourth of the patients may have died from the radiation. Many of the patients were poor and African American. Records released by the university in 1994 indicate much internal debate over the experiment at the time it was performed.

Although Saenger has maintained that the primary purpose of the radiation was to treat the patients' cancers, critics have questioned its therapeutic purpose because the study was funded partly by the Department of Defense, which was interested in how much radiation a soldier in an atomic attack could withstand before becoming disoriented or disabled. At an April congressional hearing, relatives of the deceased patients accused researchers of falsifying the signatures of patients on consent forms.

Another group of experiments involved prisoners in Oregon and Washington. From 1963 to 1971, 67 prisoners at Oregon State Prison near Salem gave consent to have their testicles irradiated by X rays. The doses ranged from 8 to 640 rads (*rad*iation unit*s*, a measurement

■ **1970's and 1980's**

1972—Researchers ended a program in which airplanes were flown through radioactive exhaust from nuclear rockets and doses to aircrews were measured. The program began in the 1960's.

Mid-1970's—Nearly 200 patients with leukemia and other cancers were exposed to high levels of radiation at the Oak Ridge National Laboratory, in Oak Ridge, Tenn.

1978—From 1958 to 1978, at Vanderbilt University, researchers performed experiments using radioactive materials on patients, including a program in which test results were passed on to the Atomic Energy Commission.

1986—U.S. Representative Edward J. Markey (D., Mass.) chaired a congressional subcommittee that issued a report entitled "American Nuclear Guinea Pigs: Three Decades of Radiation Experiments on U.S. Citizens."

■ **1990's**

November 1993—*The Albuquerque* (N. Mex.) *Tribune* published a series of articles on the 18 plutonium experiment subjects.

January 1994—Hazel R. O'Leary, secretary of the United States Department of Energy (DOE), *above,* center, meets with other Cabinet officials after announcing in December 1993 that the DOE would investigate the plutonium experiment and any others like it. O'Leary promised to open up many secret DOE files.

January 1994—President Bill Clinton created the Advisory Committee on Human Radiation Experiments to study the experiments and recommend ethical guidelines.

June 1994—O'Leary disclosed previously secret information about 48 human radiation experiments, 95 underground nuclear bomb tests, uranium stockpile amounts, and radiation leaks from underground atomic explosions.

■ Testifying before a congressional committee in April 1994, Catherine Hager, *above,* displays a photograph of her father who died in 1965 while receiving experimental radiation therapy at the University of Cincinnati in Ohio.

of the amount of radiation absorbed by tissues). From 1963 to 1969, 64 prisoners at Washington State Prison in Walla Walla had their testicles irradiated by X rays, with doses ranging from 7 to 400 rads. According to Markey's report, the legal limit for occupational exposure to reproductive organs is 5 rads per year.

Both experiments were designed to obtain data on the effects of radiation on male fertility. The experiments at the Washington prison reportedly were prompted after a 1962 accident at the Hanford Nuclear Reservation, a nuclear weapons plant in Richland, Wash., where three men were exposed to high doses of radiation. Scientists, concerned about whether the workers would become sterile, designed the experiment to find a minimum dose that would interfere with the development of sperm, according to C. Alvin Paulsen, a reproductive physiologist at the University of Washington in Seattle. The researchers had the inmates agree to have vasectomies afterward "to avoid any possibility of contaminating the general population with irradiation-induced mutants," according to government documents.

Paulsen defended his work in 1994, saying he believed the experiments were ethical and scientifically important. But several former inmates claimed they were misled about the research. And experts on medical ethics argued that prisoners by their very circumstances are prone to coercion and are not in a position to give their consent freely. The experiments in Washington were halted in 1969 after a review board refused to authorize further irradiation of prisoners.

Ethical standards

A major question surrounding all of the revelations in 1994 was: Did the scientists who designed these experiments believe that they were following the ethical standards current at the time the experiments were performed? Although formal policies governing human experiments funded by the AEC did not exist until 1947, for centuries physicians had been guided by the principles of the Hippocratic oath, which instructed them to do no harm to their patients. And the notion that patients should give consent for any procedures performed on them had long been rooted in the tradition of English common law.

Some researchers have defended the early human radiation experiments, contending that standards of the time were not as stringent as today. However, a 1942 memo released in May 1994 by Clinton's Advisory Committee showed that a government Committee on Medical Research had recommended that only fully informed volunteers be used in research that put subjects at risk. In March 1947, the AEC's legal division had issued a memo saying clinical testing on human beings should include proof that the patient was in an understanding state of mind, that the nature and risks of the treatment were fully explained, and that the patient was willing to receive the treatment. A patient's signature was not required, but at least two doctors were to certify in writing that the patient understood the experiment and was willing to accept treatment. In April 1947, AEC officials said that testing on human patients could be conducted "only when there is expectation that it may have therapeutic effect."

In 1994, a formerly secret memo from 1953 surfaced, showing that the Pentagon had adopted the Nuremberg Code as its policy for protecting human test subjects. Viewed as the universal standard for human experiments, the Nuremberg Code requires full, informed, and voluntary consent for all experiments on humans.

On Oct. 21, 1994, the Advisory Committee, composed of ethicists, historians, lawyers, and scientists, reported on the first six months of their one-year term. They said that there may have been more than 1,000 experiments involving human subjects as well as hundreds of intentional radiation releases through the government's nuclear weapons program. The second phase of the committee's task will be to evaluate the ethics of the experiments. The committee was to conclude its work by April 1995 and then make recommendations to the Human Radiation Interagency Working Group. This group, consisting of the heads of eight major federal agencies, was created in January 1994. Its purpose was to determine if any actions should be taken, such as issuing a public apology or offering financial compensation to the participants in the experiments or their families, and to recommend those actions, if any, to Congress. ■ ■ ■

Puerto Rico

Puerto Rico. On Jan. 7, 1994, a barge carrying 1.5 million gallons (5.7 million liters) of heavy diesel oil struck a coral reef and spilled half its cargo along 3 miles (4.8 kilometers) of pristine beaches in San Juan, the capital of Puerto Rico. As the year progressed, the worst drought since the mid-1960's hit the island, withering crops and damaging the tourist industry, which provides 6 percent of the island's *gross domestic product* (the total value of goods and services produced within a country).

Beginning on May 7, 1994, the government began to ration water for more than half of the island's 3.5 million residents, mainly those in the metropolitan San Juan area. By mid-October, rationing had been relaxed in areas popular with tourists, but it remained in effect elsewhere.

Governor Pedro J. Rosselló declared three days of national mourning after José Jaime Pierluisi, 28, one of his economic advisers, was shot to death on June 7 during a carjacking. The killing occurred in front of Pierluisi's home and was part of a wave of carjackings in 1994, about 80 percent of which occurred in the San Juan area.

A referendum on the November 6 ballot would have amended the island's Constitution by prohibiting bail for those previously convicted of a violent crime. But the measure failed. □ Nathan A. Haverstock

See also **Latin America** (Facts in brief table). In *World Book*, see **Puerto Rico**.

Pulitzer Prizes in journalism, letters, drama, and music were awarded in April 1994 by Columbia University in New York City, on the recommendation of the Pulitzer Prize Board.

Journalism. The public service award went to the Akron *Beacon Journal* in Ohio, for stories on local racial attitudes. *The New York Times* took three prizes: spot news reporting, for staff stories on the 1993 World Trade Center bombing; feature photography, for free-lance photographer Kevin Carter's picture of a vulture waiting near a starving child in Sudan; and feature writing, for Isabel Wilkerson's profile of a fourth-grader from Chicago's South Side and her reports on the 1993 Midwest floods.

The *Chicago Tribune* received the editorial writing prize for R. Bruce Dold's editorials criticizing the Illinois child welfare system. The *Tribune*'s Ronald Kotulak earned the explanatory journalism award for stories on neurological science.

The beat reporting prize went to Eric Freedman and Jim Mitzelfeld of *The Detroit News,* who uncovered spending abuses by the Michigan House (of Representatives) Fiscal Agency. Eileen Welsome of *The Albuquerque* (N. Mex.) *Tribune* won the national reporting prize for stories about government radiation experiments on Americans during the late 1940's. *The Dallas Morning News* team received the international reporting prize for a series on violence against women around the world. Stories on corrup-

An image of a starving child in Sudan by free-lance photographer Kevin Carter won *The New York Times* a Pulitzer Prize in April.

tion in Rhode Island's court system earned the investigative prize for the staff of *The* (Providence) *Journal-Bulletin.*

The commentary prize was taken by William Raspberry of *The Washington Post* for columns on a variety of topics. The criticism award went to Lloyd Schwartz of *The Boston Phoenix* for writings on classical music. Michael P. Ramirez of *The Commercial Appeal* in Memphis received the editorial cartooning award. In spot news photography, Paul Watson of *The Toronto Star* in Canada won for a photograph of a United States soldier's body being dragged through the streets of Mogadishu, Somalia.

Letters and drama. The fiction award went to E. Annie Proulx for her novel *The Shipping News.* Playwright Edward Albee won the drama prize for *Three Tall Women.* The biography prize was awarded to David Levering Lewis for *W.E.B. Du Bois: Biography of a Race, 1868-1919.* Yusef Komunyakaa won the poetry award for *Neon Vernacular.* The general nonfiction prize was taken by David Remnick for *Lenin's Tomb: The Last Days of the Soviet Empire.* No history award was presented. The music award went to Gunther Schuller for *Of Reminiscences and Reflections,* an orchestral work composed in memory of his wife, Marjorie, who died in 1992. □ Mary Feely

See also **Public health: The Radiation Experiments.** In *World Book,* see **Pulitzer Prizes.**
Quebec. See Canadian provinces.

Religion. Various religious groups played key roles at the United Nations International Conference on Population and Development in Cairo, Egypt, in September 1994. The Roman Catholic Church objected to passages in conference documents that it regarded as supporting abortion. But the world also witnessed a diversity of opinion among Islamic nations on conference issues.

More than 20,000 participants from 179 nations addressed ways to deal with global population growth, hunger, and poverty outlined in a previously prepared draft document. Some Muslim moderate groups, including Al-Azhar University, a prestigious center of Islamic scholarship in Cairo, opposed the conference and charged that the draft document contradicted Islamic principles banning extramarital sex and abortion. Militant Muslim clerics called for Islamic nations to boycott the conference, and Saudi Arabia, Lebanon, and Sudan did so. However, other Islamic nations and individual Muslims resisted threats of violence by Muslim extremists and participated in the conference in large numbers. Egypt's chief Islamic cleric, Grand Mufti Muhammad Said Tantawy, said that the Cairo conference exemplified Islamic traditions of tolerance, diversity of opinion, and intellectualism.

The Vatican on January 19 named its first ambassador to Israel, after Israel and the Vatican extended official recognition to each other in 1993. It

Religious groups with 150,000 or more members in the United States*

African Methodist Episcopal Church	3,500,000
African Methodist Episcopal Zion Church	1,200,000
American Baptist Association	300,000
American Baptist Churches in the U.S.A.	1,534,078
Antiochian Orthodox Christian Archdiocese of North America	250,000
Armenian Apostolic Church of America	150,000
Armenian Church of America, Diocese of the	414,000
Assemblies of God	2,257,846
Bahá'í Faith	260,000
Baptist Bible Fellowship International	1,500,000
Baptist Missionary Association of America	236,604
Buddhists	240,000
Christian and Missionary Alliance	289,391
Christian Church (Disciples of Christ)	1,011,502
Christian Churches and Churches of Christ	1,088,000
Christian Methodist Episcopal Church	876,000
Christian Reformed Church in North America	223,617
Church of God (Anderson, Ind.)	214,743
Church of God (Cleveland, Tenn.)	672,008
Church of God in Christ	5,499,875
Church of God in Christ, International	200,000
Church of Jesus Christ of Latter-day Saints	4,430,000
Church of the Nazarene	573,834
Churches of Christ	1,684,872
Conservative Baptist Association of America	200,000
Coptic Orthodox Church	180,000
Episcopal Church	2,471,880
Evangelical Free Church of America	214,186
Evangelical Lutheran Church in America	5,234,568
General Association of Regular Baptist Churches	160,123
Greek Orthodox Archdiocese of North and South America	1,500,000
International Church of the Foursquare Gospel	207,455
Hindus	600,000
International Council of Community Churches	500,000
Jehovah's Witnesses	914,079
Jews	5,981,000
Liberty Baptist Fellowship	150,000
Lutheran Church—Missouri Synod	2,609,905
Muslims	4,600,000
National Association of Free Will Baptists	209,223
National Baptist Convention of America	3,500,000
National Baptist Convention, U.S.A., Inc.	8,200,000
National Missionary Baptist Convention of America	2,500,000
National Primitive Baptist Convention, Inc.	500,000
Orthodox Church in America	600,000
Pentecostal Assemblies of the World	500,000
Presbyterian Church in America	239,500
Presbyterian Church (U.S.A.)	3,758,085
Progressive National Baptist Convention, Inc.	2,500,000
Reformed Church in America	274,521
Reorganized Church of Jesus Christ of Latter Day Saints	150,143
Roman Catholic Church	59,220,723
Salvation Army	446,403
Seventh-Day Adventist Church	748,687
Southern Baptist Convention	15,358,866
United Church of Christ	1,555,382
United Methodist Church	8,789,101
United Pentecostal Church International	550,000
Wisconsin Evangelical Lutheran Synod	420,039

*A majority of the figures are for the years 1992 and 1993. Includes only groups with at least 150,000 members within the United States.
Sources: Representatives of individual organizations; David B. Barrett, Editor, *The World Christian Encyclopedia; Yearbook of American and Canadian Churches 1994.*

was the Vatican's first formal recognition of Israel since its founding in 1948. In Washington, D.C., the National Conference of Catholic Bishops and the Synagogue Council of America said in a joint statement that the 1993 accord "represents a revolution in the relations almost 2,000 years old between the Catholic Church and the Jewish people." The accord was expected to bring Vatican involvement in Middle East peace efforts. Observers also expected the Vatican role to influence the status of Jerusalem, a holy city of Jews, Christians, and Muslims.

New Pentecostal association. Black and white Pentecostal groups created a new association at a meeting in Memphis in October 1994 that they hoped would help end racial divisions in the denomination that have lasted 70 years. The new association brought to an end the Pentecostal Fellowship of North America, which had been made up of 21 white denominations, including the Assemblies of God. They joined with several black denominations, including the Church of God in Christ, to form the Pentecostal-Charismatic Churches of North America.

The congregations in the new organization trace their roots to a multiracial religious revival in Los Angeles, called the Azusa Street Mission Revival, that began in 1906 and lasted until 1909. By the mid-1920's, the movement had split into separate churches for blacks and whites. In 1994, there were an estimated 18 million Pentecostals in the United States. Of that number, the Church of God in Christ reported it had 5.5 million members.

The United States Supreme Court on June 27 ruled unconstitutional a 1989 New York state law that created a special public school district for the education of disabled Jewish children. The children lived in Kiryas Joel, a small town inhabited solely by members of the Satmar Hasidim, the most conservative sect of Orthodox Judaism. Most of the children of the town attended private religious schools, but the town could not afford to build a special facility for the disabled children, who, according to state and federal laws, must receive equal education. The New York law provided public funds for a school for the disabled children. The majority opinion said that the New York law violated the court's neutrality-toward-religion test because it "singles out a particular religious sect for special treatment."

Religious right. People for the American Way, a liberal group, said that 60 percent of the candidates supported by the religious right in local, state, and national contests won in the November 8 elections. But the most prominent candidate backed by the religious right, Republican Oliver North, lost. The religious right is a loose coalition of conservatives, who oppose abortion and gay rights and support school prayer, among other issues.   □ Leon Howell

See also **Eastern Orthodox Churches; Islam; Judaism; Protestantism; Roman Catholic Church.** In *World Book,* see **Religion.**

Republican Party. Republicans dealt Democrats an overwhelming defeat in the midterm election of Nov. 8, 1994, winning control of both the United States Senate and the House of Representatives for the first time since 1954 and scoring big gains in governors' races. Political analysts likened the outcome to a tidal wave in its benefit to the Grand Old Party (GOP), because not a single Republican incumbent running for congressional or gubernatorial reelection was defeated. In contrast, scores of Democrats lost office, including such key figures as Representative Thomas S. Foley of Washington, Speaker of the House and a 30-year veteran in Congress, and Senator James Sasser of Tennessee, chairman of the Budget Committee. The election raised GOP hopes of recapturing the White House in 1996.

The new political landscape. The Republicans picked up 52 seats in the House to gain a 230 to 204 advantage over the Democrats, with one independent completing the 435-seat total. In the Senate, Republicans gained eight seats in the election and a ninth when Democratic Senator Richard C. Shelby of Alabama decided to switch parties. As a result, Republicans will outnumber Democrats, 53 to 47, in the Senate. Even so, it may be possible for Democrats to block Republican measures in the Senate by *filibustering* (using extended debate to delay legislation), just as the Republicans often did in the first two years of President Bill Clinton's term. In that case, it would take 60 votes to overcome the talkathon and bring GOP legislation to a vote.

Republicans also did extremely well in statehouse races, with GOP governors gaining reelection in California, Illinois, Michigan, Ohio, and Massachusetts. In addition, Republicans were elected to replace Democrats in New York, Texas, Pennsylvania, and several other states. In Texas, George W. Bush, oldest son of former President George Bush, defeated a popular Democrat, Governor Ann W. Richards. Only in Florida did a Democratic governor hold on to office against a GOP challenger. Florida Governor Lawton M. Chiles, Jr., staved off a strong Republican challenge from Jeb Bush, another son of the former President. The election gave the GOP 30 governorships, up from 19.

Republicans also gained control of 19 more state legislative chambers. GOP gains were most visible in the South, where Democrats were once totally dominant. But the Republican trend was also apparent in other regions. In Washington state, for example, the GOP picked up six House seats. Three-term New York Governor Mario M. Cuomo was defeated by George E. Pataki, a close ally of Senator Alphonse M. D'Amato, who may be the new political power in the Empire State. New York City's Republican mayor, Rudolph W. Giuliani, broke with his party to endorse Cuomo.

The GOP landslide was interpreted by Republicans as a rebuke of President Bill Clinton, and it marked a victory for Republican efforts to make the off-year election a referendum on the policies of the Clinton Administration and the Democratic-controlled Congress. As part of that strategy, more than 300 Republican candidates for the House on September 27 signed a "Contract with America." The document pledged lower taxes, increased defense spending, term limits for members of Congress—though not for those serving in the 104th Congress—and several other measures.

Republicans also campaigned on an antigovernment theme, promising to get tough with criminals and welfare recipients. Conservative groups, such as the Christian Coalition and the National Rifle Association, helped many Republicans defeat Democrats who had offended the groups' interests.

Gingrich and Dole. One big winner in the election was House Republican leader Newt Gingrich of Georgia, who was in line to become Speaker of the House in the 104th Congress. Gingrich was a chief author of the "Contract" plan. Another beneficiary of the Republican surge was Senator Robert J. Dole of Kansas, who was due to become the next Senate majority leader, an elevation that could benefit his presidential ambitions. Haley Barbour, chairman of the Republican National Committee, and Representative William Paxon of New York emerged as leading GOP strategists after working together on the party's 1994 congressional races.

Gridlock fears. Despite Republican assurances of cooperation with the Clinton Administration, many political analysts expected an escalation of partisan warfare in the two years leading up to the 1996 presidential election. Some observers said the Republicans may suffer in 1996 if they overdo a confrontational approach in Congress while accomplishing little, if anything, of substance.

In the postelection euphoria, however, the GOP victors confidently talked of reducing taxes, axing many federal programs, and stepping up the investigation of Clinton's former financial and real estate dealings in Arkansas—the so-called Whitewater affair. Republicans in the 104th Congress, scheduled to convene on Jan. 4, 1995, would be setting the agenda for the first time since 1955.

Scattered GOP losses. Despite the favorable national trend, Republicans did not come out on top everywhere. In Virginia, where the nomination of former Marine Lieutenant Colonel Oliver L. North on the GOP ticket split the party, Democratic Senator Charles S. Robb eked out a narrow victory in a three-way race. And in Massachusetts, liberal Democratic Senator Edward M. (Ted) Kennedy won a sixth term, prevailing against a strong campaign by Republican candidate Mitt Romney, son of former Michigan Governor George W. Romney. ☐ William J. Eaton

See also **Democratic Party; Elections.** In *World Book,* see **Republican Party.**

Rhode Island. See State government.

Roman Catholic Church. On April 10, 1994, Roman Catholic bishops from Africa and other members of the hierarchy gathered at the Vatican to open a historic month-long meeting on the religious and social needs of African Roman Catholics. Pope John Paul II had called for the unprecedented Special Assembly for Africa of the Synod of Bishops.

The overall theme of the meeting was *evangelization,* the preaching of the Gospel in order to convert people to Christianity. The African bishops were especially concerned with *inculturalization,* the effort to accommodate local African customs within Roman Catholic religious practices. About 200 million of Africa's more than 700 million people practice local traditional religions. However, Catholicism has grown steadily, from about 2 million converts in 1900 to 92 million in 1991, according to official church figures.

Altar girls approved. In April 1994, Vatican spokesman Joaquin Navarro-Valls announced that the pope had approved the practice of girls assisting priests during mass, a role traditionally reserved only for boys. Archbishop William H. Keeler of Baltimore, president of the National Conference of Catholic Bishops, immediately welcomed the decision.

Bishops in the United States first petitioned Rome to open the practice to girls in the early 1980's, and some U.S. parishes have had female altar servers for years. Following the papal decision, the practice spread quickly throughout the United States.

Women as priests. On May 30, Pope John Paul II issued an *apostolic letter* (an important church statement) that reaffirmed the traditional church ban on women priests. He said his declaration was to be "definitively held" by all Catholics and that further discussion of the subject had to stop.

Many reform-minded Catholics have argued that until women are allowed to be priests they will remain "second-class citizens" within the church. Church officials, however, counter that tradition must stand and that Jesus gathered only men at the Last Supper, where, the church teaches, he commissioned his first apostles. Despite the pope's letter, discussion continued on the subject in a number of churches, especially among women's groups.

Population conference. In September, Vatican delegates attending the United Nations (UN) International Conference on Population and Development in Cairo, Egypt, harshly criticized the section of the conference's draft document regarding birth control. The document, Vatican delegates said, did not take a firm stand against abortion as a method of birth control. After several days of debate, however, the other delegates agreed to add an antiabortion clause to the final document.

But when the conference ended, Vatican delegates said they could only partially consent to the final document. The Vatican still opposed wording that dealt with human sexuality and the use of artificial contraceptives, which the church bans. The final document established guidelines for the next 20 years that signatory nations agreed to use in formulating policies for population control and economic development. About 179 nations were represented.

The pope's health caused considerable concern in 1994, especially after the Vatican announced on September 22 that because of an ailing hip he would not visit the United States in October as scheduled. Months earlier, on April 28, the 74-year-old pontiff had fallen getting out of his bath. After an X ray revealed a broken right thighbone, doctors surgically inserted metal replacements for the neck and head of the broken bone. It was the pope's second fall in six months. On Nov. 14, 1993, he dislocated his right shoulder in a fall down a stair.

While visiting the United States, the pope was to have addressed the UN concerning the church's position on the family. The Vatican postponed the speech until the fall of 1995 to coincide with the UN's 50th anniversary celebrations.

In October 1994, the pope announced the appointment of 30 new cardinals from 24 nations, including 2 from the United States, bringing the U.S. total to 12. The new U.S. cardinals were Archbishop Keeler of Baltimore and Archbishop Adam Joseph Maida of Detroit. □ Thomas C. Fox

See also **Religion.** In *World Book,* see **Roman Catholic Church.**

Romania. Romania's economic troubles grew worse in 1994, despite foreign financial aid. In May, the International Monetary Fund, a United Nations agency, granted Romania a $454-million loan requiring Romanian officials to pursue economic reforms. International lenders expressed concern when by late 1994 Romania had fallen far short of its pledge to privatize about 2,500 businesses. Romania's leaders also made little progress in attracting foreign investment, and the national debt expanded further.

Dissatisfaction among Romanian workers spread during 1994, as real wages continued to fall and unemployment rose to 11 percent. Economic hardship brought on a wave of labor protests.

In March, the legislature replaced the ministers of defense, justice, internal affairs, and transport. President Ion Iliescu's Democratic Party maintained its monopoly over government seats, but right wing nationalist parties continued to gain influence.

On January 26, Romania became the first post-Communist country to join the new Partnership for Peace, a North Atlantic Treaty Organization (NATO) program of cooperation with nations that had belonged to the Warsaw Pact. The pact was a military alliance led by the former Soviet Union.

□ Sharon L. Wolchik

See also **Europe** (Facts in brief table). In *World Book,* see **Romania.**

Rowing. See **Sports.**

Russia. Russia's advocates of Western-style reform were in a defensive position as 1994 began. Elections held on Dec. 12, 1993, had produced a parliament dominated by right wing nationalists and Communists, who were elected by a public that was weary of economic reform, angry about rising crime and corruption, and concerned about Russia's apparent weakness in the post-Communist world. Reformers regarded the threat of extremism in Russian politics with gloom and predicted that a reversal of reform would plunge the nation into economic chaos. By the end of January, the government had lost most of the original architects of reform.

First Deputy Prime Minister Yegor T. Gaidar, the chief creator of Russia's economic reform program, resigned on January 16. He explained that his economic policies no longer had support from the government and that a shift away from financial austerity was bound to bring on hyperinflation and other economic woes. Shortly afterward, Minister of Finance Boris Fedorov, regarded by many Western officials as Russia's strongest proponent of economic stabilization, also resigned. Fedorov protested President Boris Yeltsin's appointment of two conservatives to the cabinet and predicted that the nation's conservative course would bring on economic and social catastrophe. After Fedorov's departure, the cabinet contained only one prominent reformer—Anatolii Chubais, head of the State Property Committee and a leading advocate of privatization.

As the year progressed, however, the Russian political scene, so explosive in 1993, began to show signs of stability. On April 28, in a largely symbolic gesture, Yeltsin and other officials signed a "civic accord," declaring political peace until elections scheduled for 1996. Although the pact bore the signatures of ideologically diverse officials—including extreme nationalist leader Vladimir Zhirinovsky, one of Yeltsin's fiercest opponents—most observers agreed that it had little legal substance.

Strides toward economic stability. Contrary to many predictions, Russia's conservative government made progress in stabilizing the nation's economy in 1994. Inflation rates fell from more than 20 percent monthly in January to about 6 percent in August. A stronger financial market emerged in 1994, generating unexpected enthusiasm from Western investors. The ruble finally began to stabilize in relation to the United States dollar and the flow of capital out of Russia—estimated at more than $1 billion a month in January—began to slow.

Tight financial policies, initiated by liberal reformers and later adopted by Russia's new leaders, particularly Prime Minister Viktor Chernomyrdin, brought about many of the nation's economic gains. Officials took pains to control the growth of the budget deficit. Russia's central bank sharply reduced its issue of subsidized credits to struggling industries and collective farms, and interest rates were raised to levels above the rate of inflation to encourage increased savings.

In April, the International Monetary Fund, a United Nations agency, released a $1.5-million loan to Russia to support economic reform and stabilization. Russia also won a vote of confidence and an invitation to help address political issues from the Group of Seven (G-7), an organization of seven leading Western industrialized nations—Canada, France, Germany, Italy, Japan, the United Kingdom, and the United States. But the G-7 denied Russia's request for full membership in the group.

Privatization of state-owned businesses proceeded on schedule in 1994. By July, nearly all the 148 million privatization vouchers issued to Russian citizens had been invested, concluding the first stage of the program. The vouchers could be used to buy shares in enterprises released from state control. By the end of the first stage, about 70 percent of all state enterprises—about 20,000 businesses—had been transferred to private hands.

The second stage of privatization, which calls for the remaining state assets to be sold for cash, was launched by presidential decree on July 23 after several attempts by the State Duma (Russia's lower parliament) to halt the process. Opposition leaders claimed that privatization represented "the theft of national assets." Critics of the program also argued that in the vast majority of cases, privatization simply involved handing businesses over to the current managers and workers without creating any strong incentives for improving their operations.

Serious weaknesses remained in the Russian economy in 1994, despite the success of stabilization and privatization efforts. Industrial production plummeted by about 25 percent during the year, and unemployment continued to rise. Thousands of enterprises hung on the verge of bankruptcy. Unpaid debts among Russian enterprises reached the astonishing level of more than 30 trillion rubles by midyear. Employers owed an estimated 4 trillion rubles in back wages to workers, some of whom had not been paid for almost a year. Prices of many basic consumer goods soared during 1994.

Financial scandals and crises broke out repeatedly in 1994, calling further attention·to flaws in Russia's developing market economy. One of the most serious scandals erupted when one of the nation's largest investment funds, MMM, collapsed in late July. The stock fund, which had attracted millions of individual shareholders through popular television commercials, was a classic "pyramid," using the funds of new investors to pay absurdly high rates of return to early investors. As word of MMM's financial trouble spread, thousands of shareholders gathered in central Moscow to redeem virtually worthless shares and to demand compensation.

Nobel Prize-winning author Alexander Solzhenitsyn greets a crowd at Vladivostok airport in May, when he returned to Russia after 20 years of exile.

Russian tax authorities arrested MMM President Sergei Mavrodi in August. Mavrodi, claiming the government conspired against his company, gathered enough public support to win election to a vacant seat in the Duma on October 31, gaining legal immunity from prosecution for the scandal. The government warned that it had limited ability to prevent future corrupt investment schemes.

In late September, the value of the ruble began to drop as fears of rising inflation mounted and the central bank stopped intervening to support the ruble in the currency market. The ruble's fall accelerated into a collapse on October 11, when the currency lost more than 20 percent of its value. The central bank managed to boost the ruble's value in the next few days, but financial markets remained cautious.

Cabinet shakeup. The ruble's collapse led to accusations that currency speculators, commercial bankers, and government officials conspired to cause the collapse. On October 12, Yeltsin fired the acting minister of finance, Sergei Dubinin, and ordered the National Security Council to investigate the matter. Yeltsin also asked parliament to dismiss the chairman of the central bank, Viktor Gerashchenko, who resigned on October 14. The investigation reported no findings of illegal activity.

On October 18, Yeltsin replaced Gerashchenko with the former minister's close deputy, Tatiana Paramanova. Viktor Panskov, a conservative, Soviet-era economist, became minister of finance on November 4. Following Panskov's appointment, Minister of the Economy Aleksandr Shokhin and other liberal reformers resigned in protest of the cabinet's shift toward conservatism. The next day, in part to allay such fears, Yeltsin promoted Chubais, the government's most prominent reformer, to the position of first deputy prime minister for economy and finance. Yevgeny Yasin, another reformer, became minister of the economy on November 8.

Public concern over crime in Russia escalated in 1994. Violent crime rates increased dramatically throughout the year, and several prominent government officials, industrialists, and bankers were murdered. A wave of kidnappings in southern Russia made headlines during the year. Government reports in June confirmed that organized crime was growing and expanding its influence. The reports noted a tenfold increase in the number of gangs from 1990 to 1994. Public outrage peaked in mid-October after Dmitri Kholodov, a reporter for a Moscow newspaper, was killed when a bomb exploded in the newspaper's office. Kholodov had been investigating illegal arms sales and corruption in the Russian military. Yeltsin responded to Russia's growing crime problem by issuing a decree on June 14 giving police broad powers to make arrests and conduct searches with little evidence of crime. The decree was widely criticized as a violation of civil rights.

Chechnya. On December 11, about 40,000 Russian troops invaded the autonomous republic of Chechnya, an oil-rich region near Russia's border with Georgia, in an attempt to quell a separatist revolt. Heavy fighting reportedly claimed the lives of 1,000 Chechen fighters on December 24 and 25. On Jan. 1, 1995, Russia's Defense Minister Pavel Grachev said that Russian troops had taken control of the center of Grozny, the capital of Chechnya.

Foreign affairs. Russia became more involved in 1994 in the affairs of the former republics of the Soviet Union and increased its role as a regional peacekeeper. In May, Russian forces were sent to protect a cease-fire agreement between Armenia and Azerbaijan over the disputed territory of Nagorno-Karabakh. Russian peacekeeping forces were also deployed in May to mediate a conflict between Georgia and the separatist region of Abkhazia.

Yeltsin and Foreign Minister Andrei Kozyrev made separate public commitments in 1994 to defend the rights of the more than 25 million ethnic Russians living outside Russia. In July, Yeltsin delivered a strong protest against the treatment of ethnic Russians in Estonia and Latvia. But by the year's end, tensions had eased. On August 31, Russia completed its withdrawal of troops from Estonia, Latvia, and what had been East Germany.

Yeltsin and U.S. President Bill Clinton forged a security agreement on January 14 with Ukraine under

Car wreckage, grim evidence of Russia's growing criminal gang activity, blocks a Moscow street after a hidden bomb exploded, killing a driver.

Russian nationalist Vladimir Zhirinovsky hurls a plant at students protesting his views during his visit to Strasbourg, France, in April.

which all nuclear warheads from the former Soviet arsenal in Ukraine would be transferred to Russia over a seven-year period. In April, Russia and Belarus signed a treaty on economic unity, but the treaty was scrapped following elections in Belarus. (See **Belarus; Ukraine.**)

Environmental concerns. Reports in 1994 of Russia's negligence toward its environment raised fears about the long-term effects of the nation's policies. A major oil spill from a ruptured pipeline in the Russian arctic was reported in late October. Officials said the pipeline had been leaking for several weeks. Like many pipelines built under Soviet rule, it had been poorly maintained. Estimates of the quantity of oil spilled ranged widely—from about 4 million to 85 million gallons (15 million to 321 million liters).

In late November, a group of Russian scientists revealed that the former Soviet Union and, later, Russia had pumped billions of gallons of radioactive atomic waste directly into the Earth. The practice, which Russia continued to use at the time of the report, does not comply with international standards for the disposal of nuclear waste. The scientists reported that waste at one of three main disposal sites had already begun to spread beyond its intended boundaries.   □ Joel S. Hellman

See also **Europe** (Facts in brief table); **Zhirinovsky, Vladimir.** In *World Book,* see **Russia.**

Rwanda. The world recoiled in horror from the events in Rwanda in 1994. Mass murder, civil war, and enormous refugee movements made the year one of the worst that any African country has ever experienced.

The killing and strife occurred between Rwanda's two major ethnic groups: the majority Hutu and the minority Tutsi. The relationship between the two groups had often been violent, though it seemed to be improving. In August 1993, an exiled Tutsi rebel group, the Rwandan Patriotic Front (RPF), and the Hutu-led government signed a peace treaty to end a civil war.

Although there still were many difficulties to be ironed out between Hutus and Tutsis, both the RPF and Rwanda's President Juvénal Habyarimana, a Hutu, appeared sincere in their desire for peace. However, Habyarimana faced opposition from the Hutu elite, some of whom did not want peace and wished to see the Tutsis eliminated from Rwanda.

Plane crash sparks slaughter. On April 6, 1994, an airplane carrying Habyarimana and the Hutu president of neighboring Burundi, Cyprien Ntaryamira, crashed as it approached Kigali, Rwanda's capital. The plane had reportedly been hit by gunfire or a rocket, and the Rwandan government blamed the RPF. Gangs of government militia then went on a killing spree, murdering Tutsis as well as many Hutus who had wished to live in peace with the Tutsi.

The killings continued relentlessly. By the end of April, an estimated 200,000 people, mostly Tutsis, were dead. Another 500,000 had fled to Tanzania. United Nations (UN) troops who had been in Rwanda to oversee the cease-fire also left, their lives in danger and their numbers too small to stop the bloodshed. The carnage appeared to be a methodical slaughter of Tutsis instigated by radical elements of the Hutu military and civilian leadership. By June, estimates of the dead ranged as high as 500,000.

Tutsi forces strike back. RPF forces reacted as soon as the killings began in April. The rebels were better trained and more disciplined than the government troops. They captured the Kigali airport on May 22, setting off a second wave of refugees, this time mainly of Hutus fleeing to Zaire in fear of Tutsi retribution. On June 22, the UN Security Council authorized France to intervene in Rwanda in an effort to prevent further deaths and slow the refugee movement. The next day, French troops crossed the Zairian border into Rwanda to establish a safe zone in the southwest.

On July 4, the RPF overran Kigali. On July 18, it proclaimed victory and on July 19 announced the formation of a new coalition government headed by a new Hutu prime minister, Faustin Twagiramungu.

No end of woes. Despite the French intervention, the massive exodus of Hutus continued. From July 15 to 17, about 1 million Hutu refugees arrived in Goma, Zaire. Cholera broke out within a few days

Rwanda

The bodies of Rwandans killed by rampaging militia groups lie in heaps on a street in Kigali in April as the nation is engulfed by ethnic violence.

in the overcrowded refugee camps, adding to the suffering. On August 21, the French pulled out of Rwanda, causing still another Hutu exodus.

Among those jamming into the relief camps were thousands of troops from the defeated Hutu army. The soldiers terrorized the refugees, telling them that to return home was certain death. They also took control of the camps and even attacked some relief workers. Many Zairian soldiers were also tormentors, stealing from refugees and relief agencies.

An uncertain future. By November, there were growing fears that the displaced Hutu troops and exiled political leaders were organizing for an invasion in an effort to retake control of Rwanda. Further warfare and chaos seemed likely.

Meanwhile, the UN was making plans to conduct trials for people accused of being involved in the Rwandan massacres. The UN Security Council voted on November 8 to set up a tribunal for such trials. Some 7,000 suspects were in Rwandan jails at the time, but most of the leaders who had encouraged the killings were still at large.

At year-end, Rwanda was in desperate straits. In addition to facing the threat of further bloodshed, the nation was in ruins. The world's interest in the situation had ebbed, and Rwanda was receiving little foreign aid. □ Mark DeLancey

See also **Africa** (Facts in brief table). In *World Book,* see **Rwanda.**

Safety. A group of United States government and private health organizations on June 21, 1994, began a national campaign to persuade parents to put healthy babies to sleep on their back or side rather than on their stomach. The campaign, called Back to Sleep, is intended to reduce the risk of sudden infant death syndrome (SIDS). SIDS is the leading cause of death among infants aged 1 month to 1 year, killing about 6,000 infants each year. Although the cause of SIDS is unknown, risk for it has been linked with a variety of factors, including the mother's smoking during pregnancy and lack of regular prenatal care.

M. Joycelyn Elders, who was then the U.S. surgeon general, said in announcing the campaign that putting infants to sleep on their side or back may reduce their risk of suffocation. Duane Alexander, director of the National Institute of Child Health and Human Development (NICHD), a co-sponsor of the program, noted that a 50 percent decline in SIDS has occurred in countries that have advocated putting infants to sleep on their back or side. The American Academy of Pediatrics, another campaign sponsor, first recommended the sleeping position in 1992 but had not actively promoted the measure because experts wanted more time to evaluate it.

At present, an estimated 45 percent of American babies sleep face-down. NICHD noted that this position may still be safer for certain infants, including infants troubled by vomiting and infants who have breathing problems or certain birth defects. Parents should check with their physician if they have any question. Parents, grandparents, baby sitters, and others who care for young babies can receive more information from NICHD by calling 1-800-505-CRIB.

In-line skates. The U.S. Consumer Product Safety Commission (CPSC) on June 9 warned that the number of serious injuries from in-line skating would more than double in 1994. The CPSC estimated that about 83,000 people would require treatment in a hospital emergency room for in-line skating injuries in 1994, compared with 37,000 in 1993. About 60 percent of the injuries were expected to occur in children under age 16, the CPSC said, with a threefold increase expected in the number of head injuries and fractured bones.

A CPSC spokesperson said experts had been unable to identify any design flaw in in-line skates that could account for the injuries. Most of the injuries seemed to result from the actions of skaters, who often fail to wear protective gear, lack the necessary skills when beginning, and engage in dangerous stunts and other high-risk behavior. The CPSC urged in-line skaters to buy protective gear, including a helmet, elbow pads, knee pads, and wrist guards. Also, the agency advised beginning in-line skaters to take lessons to learn how to control speed, how to brake, turn, and stop. The agency added that in-line skating should be done in daylight, away from motor vehicle traffic, and only on smooth, paved surfaces free from water, gravel, sand, and debris.

Keyboarding risks. In an effort to help prevent hand and wrist injuries among computer users, the Compaq Computer Corporation and Microsoft Corporation announced in August 1994 that they would put warning labels on computer keyboards. The labels would be the first to state clearly that people who misuse keyboards or do too much typing face a risk of so-called repetitive strain injuries. Such injuries range from mild soreness to carpal tunnel syndrome, a potentially disabling nerve disorder that can restrict use of the wrist. The labels refer consumers to information in instruction booklets on how to position the arms and wrists properly while typing. To reduce the risk of injury, experts advise holding the hands, wrists, and arms in a level position, and taking frequent breaks.

Infant safety seats. The National Highway Traffic Safety Administration (NHTSA) on February 18 warned parents against placing infant safety seats in the front seat of the car. Danger arises because the safety seats face backward. In an accident, the passenger-side airbag may slam into the back of the infant seat with a force great enough to cause serious head or neck injury. NHTSA said the passenger-side airbag poses no danger for older children who have outgrown their infant seat.   □ Michael Woods

In *World Book,* see **Safety.**

Sailing. See **Boating.**

San Diego. The economy of San Diego continued to stagnate in 1994 as a result of corporate restructuring and military cutbacks. Several of the major defense contractors in the area announced plant closures during the year, forcing the layoff of thousands of workers. Employment figures for San Diego County showed that the number of workers in the aircraft and missile manufacturing industries had declined to 11,600 in April 1994, from a high of 27,800 in January 1990.

One of the biggest blows to the local economy came in July 1994, when the General Dynamics Corporation, for decades the region's largest private employer, announced that it would be closing its Convair Division in early 1996, putting 1,900 aerospace workers out of work.

In June 1994, the Martin Marietta Corporation announced that it was moving 1,800 jobs from San Diego to Denver, Colo. About 1,100 of those positions were gone by year-end.

Controlling illegal immigration. In September 1994, United States Attorney General Janet Reno announced a plan, called Operation Gatekeeper, aimed at reducing illegal immigration from Mexico into the San Diego area. San Diego has long been the major entry point for illegal immigrants from the south.

Operation Gatekeeper will beef up border patrols with hundreds of new and redeployed federal officers. The officers will use an automated fingerprinting system that will make it easier to identify illegal immigrants who make repeated attempts to enter the United States. The program also calls for improved fences and lighting along the border and faster deportation of illegal immigrants. In addition, Reno said the federal government would provide funds to pay for the incarceration of illegal immigrants who are awaiting deportation.

Animals in the news. Animal keepers at the San Diego Zoo helped bring a Galapagos tortoise into the world in May, the first Galapagos tortoise to be hatched successfully at the zoo since 1987. Zookeepers blamed the low birth rate on the inept mating behavior of the zoo's male tortoises. To enhance the chances of tortoise births, keepers retrieved eggs from female tortoises and incubated them. But fertilized eggs were rare. The new tortoise came from the only fertile egg among 14 from one female.

In August, Karen, a two-year-old orangutan at the San Diego Zoo, underwent open-heart surgery at the University of California at San Diego Medical Center. Doctors and zoo officials said the operation, for the correction of a heart defect, was apparently the first of its kind for an orangutan.

New performing arts center opens. The new California Center for the Performing Arts in the community of Escondido, a few miles north of San Diego, opened its inaugural season in September. A number of world-renowned artists and troupes, including violinist Itzhak Perlman, opera singer Cecilia

Bartoli, and the Kirov Orchestra of St. Petersburg, Russia, were scheduled to perform during the season. The center includes a 1,500-seat concert hall and a 400-seat theater as well as other facilities.

Lego park planned. On June 7, voters in Carlsbad, a coastal town north of San Diego, approved plans for the construction of Lego Family Park USA. The $100-million park would be the first American theme park constructed by the Danish makers of the multicolored plastic Lego building blocks.

Company and city officials estimated that the park would draw 1.8 million visitors a year after its opening in 1999. Lego chose Carlsbad over several competing U.S. cities. Many residents of Carlsbad, however, expressed strong opposition to the project and said they would try to stop it.

Anniversary for bridge. On Aug. 2, 1994, San Diegans celebrated the 25th anniversary of the San Diego-Coronado Bridge. The 11,179-foot (3,407-meter) structure carries about 65,000 cars daily over San Diego Bay between San Diego and Coronado.

Hotel-room tax rises. In June, the San Diego City Council approved an increase in the city's hotel-room tax, from 9 cents on the dollar to 10.5 cents, to help pay for the construction of a downtown sports arena and the expansion of the San Diego Convention Center. □ Caron Golden

See also **City.** In *World Book,* see **San Diego.**

Saskatchewan. See **Canadian provinces.**

Saudi Arabia. Economic problems and charges of human rights abuses tarnished Saudi Arabia's image in 1994. On August 24, the United States granted asylum to Mohammed al-Khilewi, former first secretary at the Saudi United Nations mission, who claimed that the government threatened his life. Khilewi said that he had 14,000 documents showing human rights abuses, corruption, and support of terrorism by the Saudi government. He also said the kingdom had given about $5 billion to Iraq in the 1980's for its nuclear weapons program in an effort to share Iraq's nuclear weapons technology.

Internal dissent. Saudi officials confirmed on September 26 that 110 dissident Islamic fundamentalists had been arrested as "agitators." Foreign embassies in Saudi Arabia warned their nationals to be careful after a group called the Battalions of Faith threatened violence toward Westerners and Saudi royalty if one of the fundamentalists, Sheik Salman al-Odeh, was not freed.

A human rights group called the Committee for the Defense of Legitimate Rights, made up of Sunni Muslims and banned by the Saudi government in 1993, opened an office in London in April 1994. The group accused Saudi rulers of corruption and repression. This was the first time that Sunnis, the dominant sect in Saudi Arabia, had set up an opposition group outside the country. By contrast, opposition Shiite Muslims had reportedly agreed to end their dissent against the Sunni-dominated government in 1993.

Mecca. Iran criticized the Saudis in 1994 for banning political activity during the annual *hajj* (pilgrimage) to Islam's holiest site, in Mecca, Saudi Arabia. The Saudis rejected Iran's demand to double its quota of 60,000 pilgrims. After a 1987 clash between Saudi security forces and Iranian pilgrims that caused 400 deaths, the Saudis had permitted countries to send only 1 pilgrim for each 1,000 Muslim citizens.

The 1994 hajj was generally peaceful. But 270 pilgrims died in a stampede during a symbolic ritual called *stoning the devil* near Mecca on May 23. A record 2.5 million pilgrims attended the 1994 hajj.

Economy. King Fahd announced in January that the 1994 budget would be cut by 20 percent to $42.6 billion, reflecting a decline in oil prices in late 1993 and early 1994. Oil exports have made up some 75 percent of Saudi revenues. Bankers praised Fahd's move because budget deficits since 1987 had caused concern. According to some estimates, the kingdom may have a debt of $60 billion. □ Christine Helms

See also **Middle East** (Facts in brief table). In *World Book,* see **Saudi Arabia.**

School. See **Education.**

Senegal. See **Africa.**

Sierra Leone. See **Africa.**

Singapore. See **Asia.**

Skating. See **Hockey; Ice skating; Sports.**

Skiing. United States Alpine skiers did better than expected in 1994, with two gold and two silver medals in the Winter Olympic Games in Lillehammer, Norway, and three race victories in the season-long World Cup series. Tommy Moe of Palmer, Alaska, and Diann Roffe-Steinrotter of Potsdam, N.Y., won Olympic gold medals, and they and Hilary Lindh of Juneau, Alaska, won World Cup races.

Winter Olympics. To watch the Winter Olympics from February 12 to 27, Tom Moe, Sr., traveled 46 hours from Alaska. He arrived minutes before his 24-year-old son won the downhill, beating Kjetil-Andre Aamodt of Norway by four-hundredths of a second in the closest downhill race in Olympic history.

In the next race, the 26-year-old Roffe-Steinrotter surprisingly won the women's super giant slalom. Silver medals went to Moe in the men's super giant slalom, eight-hundredths of a second behind Markus Wasmeier of Germany, and to Picabo (*PEEK-ah-boo*) Street of Sun Valley, Ida., in the women's downhill.

Other men's winners were Wasmeier in the giant slalom, Thomas Stangassinger of Austria in the slalom, and Lasse Kjus in the combined. Other women's winners were Katja Seizinger of Germany in the downhill, Deborah Compagnoni of Italy in the giant slalom, Vreni Schneider of Switzerland in the slalom, and Pernilla Wiberg of Sweden in the combined. Schneider's medal was her fifth, a career record for Alpine skiing.

Diann Roffe-Steinrotter of the United States races toward a gold medal in the super giant slalom at the Winter Olympics in Norway, in February.

World Cup. The series ran from October 1993 to March 1994 and was made up of 35 events for men and 34 for women, mostly in Europe. Aamodt and Schneider won the overall titles.

Aamodt totaled 1,392 points to 1,007 for Marc Girardelli of Luxembourg and 822 for Alberto Tomba of Italy. Moe was eighth. The discipline champions were Girardelli in downhill, Jan Einar Thorsen of Norway in super giant slalom, Christian Mayer of Austria in giant slalom, and Tomba in slalom.

Schneider won the women's overall title from Wiberg, 1,656 points to 1,343. Eva Twardokens of Santa Cruz., Calif., the leading American, was 23rd. Seizinger won the downhill and super giant slalom titles, with Kate Pace of Canada second in the downhill. Schneider also won the slalom title.

Ulrike Maier, a 26-year-old Austrian and twice a world champion, died on January 29 as a result of a skiing accident. She crashed at almost 65 miles (105 kilometers) per hour during a World Cup downhill race in Garmisch-Partenkirchen, Germany.

Other. In the World Cup cross-country series, Vladimir Smirnov of Kazakhstan won the men's title and Manuela Di Centa of Italy won the women's title. Kristean Porter of Greenland, N.H., won the women's overall World Cup freestyle series, and Sergei Shupletsov of Russia won the men's title.   □ Frank Litsky

See also **Olympics.** In *World Book,* see **Skiing.**

Slovakia endured political turbulence in 1994, the nation's second year of independence since splitting from the former Czechoslovak federation in January 1993. A parliamentary vote of no confidence on March 11, 1994, ousted Prime Minister Vladimir Mečiar from his position. Opponents accused Mečiar of corruption and poor management of the economy. A coalition of five politically diverse parties took control of the government from Mečiar's Movement for a Democratic Slovakia (HZDS). Slovak Foreign Minister Jozef Moravčik became the nation's new prime minister.

In parliamentary elections held on October 1 and 2, the HZDS in coalition with the Peasant Party won 35 percent of the votes—more than any other party—and Mečiar prepared to regain control of the government with a broader coalition. Two mainstream parties refused to join with Mečiar. But on December 11, he announced that he had formed a coalition government with two small parties, one on the far left and one on the far right. Many observers feared that Mečiar's return to power would bring an end to the limited progress that Moravčik's government had made.

Slovakia under Moravčik. The Moravčik-led coalition moved quickly to address problems that had grown during Mečiar's term as prime minister. Moravčik reestablished Slovakia's commitment to the creation of a market economy—which Mečiar had largely opposed—and instituted programs to accelerate privatization. The new government also enacted restrictive monetary and budgetary policies to stabilize the nation's economy.

Moravčik's government also took steps to improve Slovakia's relations with other nations and seek foreign investment and aid. On July 22, the International Monetary Fund (IMF), a United Nations agency, approved a $263-million loan for Slovakia. The IMF had committed $94 million of the funds to Slovakia in 1993. Under the terms of the loan, Slovak leaders will be required to follow economic guidelines set by the IMF. In September 1994, the European Investment Bank also agreed to aid Slovakia to improve telecommunications and air navigation.

In February, Slovakia joined the Partnership for Peace, a new North Atlantic Treaty Organization (NATO) program of cooperation with nations that had belonged to the Warsaw Pact, the military alliance led by the former Soviet Union.

The new government attempted in 1994 to reduce tensions between Slovaks and Slovakia's 600,000 ethnic Hungarians, which had grown severe under Mečiar's leadership. In June, parliament overturned a law that required married Hungarian women to use the Slovak suffix *ová* in their names. Parliament also adopted a law in July that allowed the use of bilingual road signs in areas where ethnic minorities make up at least 20 percent of the population. Mečiar had ordered the removal of Hungarian street signs in the predominantly Hungarian districts.

Economic improvement. Slovakia saw some relief in 1994 from the economic hardship that the nation has suffered since independence. Officials reported that the *gross domestic product* (the total of all goods and services produced within a country) grew by more than 4 percent during the first half of 1994. The rate of inflation decreased, and the nation's cash reserves increased from $318 million in early 1994 to about $1.3 billion in September. Slovakia's budget deficit also dropped sharply.

Slovakia's trade deficit decreased in 1994. The nation's main trading partner continued to be the Czech Republic, which took in two-fifths of Slovakia's exports. Slovakia's imports from the Czech Republic dropped an additional 10 percent in the first half of 1994, thus giving Slovakia a sizable trade surplus with that country. Slovak exports to other European countries, particularly Italy, Germany, and France, also expanded during 1994. Exports to the United States increased by more than 100 percent.

Other economic problems, however, continued to plague Slovakia in 1994. Growing shortages of food led the government in September to set price limits for meat and temporarily remove surcharges on imports of beef and potatoes. □ Sharon L. Wolchik

See also **Czech Republic; Europe** (Facts in brief table). In *World Book,* see **Slovakia.**

Slovenia. See Europe.

Soccer. The World Cup, the *quadrennial* (every four years) event with perhaps more international prestige than the Olympics, came to the United States in 1994 for the first time. For the organizers and for the sport itself, it was a major success. It was especially successful for Brazil, which defeated Italy in the final in the first tie-breaking shoot-off in cup history.

Preparations. The Federation Internationale de Football Association (FIFA), soccer's world governing body, had always wanted soccer to be more popular in the United States. Although FIFA felt that soccer could not displace baseball, basketball, and American football in popularity, it wanted greater television and marketing exposure. It also wanted the United States to create a major outdoor league.

To make World Cup games more attractive to spectators and television viewers, FIFA tried to encourage attacking and more scoring. It outlawed tackling from behind, with violators to be ejected. It told game officials to give the offense the benefit of the doubt in offside situations. It also banned back-passes to the goalkeeper. The changes helped create a competition filled with entertaining games, more goals, and less rough play.

The competition. Two teams qualified automatically for the World Cup—Germany as the defending champion and the United States as the host nation. The 22 other national teams survived two years of

eliminations. One notable nonqualifier was England, a perennial world power. Between June 17 and July 17, the 24 teams played 52 matches in 31 days at nine sites. The sites were Pasadena and Palo Alto, Calif.; Pontiac, Mich.; Foxboro, Mass.; East Rutherford, N.J.; Orlando, Fla.; Washington, D.C.; Chicago; and Dallas.

The United States was paired in Group A with Colombia, Switzerland, and Romania. The Americans tied Switzerland, 1-1, upset Colombia, 2-1, and lost to Romania, 1-0. They finished third in their group and advanced beyond the group matches for the first time since the inaugural World Cup in 1930.

In a dramatic twist, the United States played its second-round match on the Fourth of July in Palo Alto. However, the United States lost to Brazil, 1-0, even though the Brazilians played one man short for nearly the entire second half. Still, the Americans did better in the tournament than many expected.

In the quarterfinals, Bulgaria upset Germany, 2-1, eliminating a team that had played in the last three World Cup finals. In the semifinals on July 13, Brazil defeated Sweden, 1-0, in Pasadena, and Italy beat Bulgaria, 2-1, at East Rutherford.

The final on July 17 at the Rose Bowl in Pasadena attracted a sellout crowd of 94,194 and a worldwide television audience of nearly 2 billion people. The game was scoreless after the regulation 90 minutes and still scoreless after 30 minutes of extra time. That meant the game and the cup would be settled in a shoot-out in which five players from each team would alternate in taking penalty shots from 12 yards (11 meters) out. When Roberto Baggio, Italy's star and final shooter, sailed the potential tying shot high above the crossbar, Brazil won the shoot-out, and the cup, 3-2. With the win, Brazil became the only country to win the World Cup four times.

The Brazilian forward Romário (Brazilian players are generally known by one name) was voted the Most Valuable Player in the cup competition. Baggio was second in the voting. Two weeks after the final, the Brazilian coach, Carlos Alberto Parreira, resigned to coach Valencia in the Spanish League. Before and during the World Cup, Parreira had been second-guessed by the media, the public, President Itamar Franco of Brazil, and even his mother.

Highs and lows. One low moment occured during the Brazil-United States match, when Leonardo of Brazil elbowed Tab Ramos of the United States and fractured his skull. FIFA suspended Leonardo for the rest of the tournament.

In Colombia's loss to the United States, the first U.S. goal came when Andrés Escobar of Colombia, trying to deflect a pass by a U.S. attacker, accidentally kicked the ball into his own net. Ten days later, on July 2, three irate supporters of the Colombian team

United States defender Alexi Lalas, *above,* leaps for joy after the United States defeated Colombia, 2-1, on June 22 at the Rose Bowl in Pasadena, Calif.

shot Escobar to death near Medellín, Colombia.

Diego Maradona, the 33-year-old Argentine superstar, failed a random drug test after a cup game on June 26. When the testing laboratory reported that Maradona's urine sample contained ephedrine and four other banned stimulants, the Argentine soccer federation suspended him, and two months later FIFA suspended him for 15 months. FIFA had also suspended Maradona from April 1991 to June 1992 for cocaine use.

For the organizers, the tournament did well. The total attendance of 3,567,415 was more than 1 million more than the previous record for a 52-match World Cup. Organizers estimated that ticketholders spent $4 billion in and around the nine sites. Tele-

Brazilian team members parade triumphantly across the Rose Bowl after defeating Italy to win the World Cup on July 17, *below.* Italy's Franco Baresi collapses in disappointment after missing his penalty kick during the match-ending shoot-out, *right.*

vision ratings were higher than expected, and police made only 400 arrests.

U.S. league. FIFA awarded the World Cup to the United States on the condition that the Americans form a first-division league before the tournament. The projected league, the Major Soccer League, did not form in 1994, but organizers at first said that it would begin play in April 1995 with 12 teams. Some of the $60-million World Cup profits would be used to help finance the league. Only seven cities had been awarded franchises as of early November, however, and on November 16, the league postponed the debut until 1996 and said the number of teams would probably be reduced to 10.

Other. AC Milan became the first team in 45 years to win three successive Italian League titles, then routed Barcelona, 4-0, in the final of the European Champions Cup. AC Milan's crosstown rival, Internazionale, won the UEFA Cup, and Arsenal of London won the European Cup Winners' Cup. Man- chester United won the English League's premier division and the Football Association Cup, then lost to Aston Villa, 3-1, in the final of the English League Cup. The United States women's team defeated Canada, 6-0, in the final of the North American and Caribbean qualifying tournament, with both advancing to the 1995 world championships. □ Frank Litsky

See also **Sports.** In *World Book,* see **Soccer.**

Social security. President Bill Clinton on Aug. 15, 1994, signed a bill making the Social Security Administration (SSA) an independent agency. The bill, passed unanimously by Congress earlier in the month, calls for the SSA to be separated from the Department of Health and Human Services (HHS) by March 31, 1995. The agency will be run by a commissioner and deputy commissioner appointed by the President and confirmed by the Senate for six-year terms.

Advocates of the change argued that social security services had declined since the 1980's. In addition, they said, independence would assure that the agency would be free of political control. The law also put new restrictions on disability benefits for drug addicts and alcoholics. They will be required to get treatment or lose their benefits.

On April 11, 1994, the trustees of the social security system warned that funds for the payment of benefits would run out in 2029—seven years earlier than projected in 1993—unless Congress takes action. On April 18, Representative Dan Rostenkowski (D., Ill.) proposed a long-range plan to assure the financial health of the system. His recommendations included hiking social security payroll taxes starting in 2020 and raising the age at which benefits can be received from 65 to 67. But Congress took no action on the proposal in 1994. □ William J. Eaton

In *World Book,* see **Social security.**

Somalia. Hopes rose in 1994 for the possibility of bringing peace to Somalia, but at year-end the outlook did not look bright. The United Nations (UN), even though it had failed to achieve its objective of ending strife in the east African nation and overseeing the founding of a new government, planned to withdraw its peacekeeping force in March 1995. A return to civil war and mass starvation—the very conditions that prompted the United States to intervene in Somalia in December 1992—seemed imminent. Somalis appeared to face either that prospect or the military triumph of one of the competing clan warlords and the imposition of a dictatorship.

U.S. leaves field to UNISOM. On March 25, 1994, the last major contingent of U.S. troops left Somalia. With their departure, the peacekeeping mission was completely in the hands of about 19,000 UNISOM (UN Operation in Somalia) troops.

During the remainder of the year, UNISOM's mission shifted from peacekeeping to survival as violence escalated throughout the country. The warring clans attacked UNISOM forces and abducted several UNISOM soldiers and relief organization employees. Meanwhile, the various factions continued to fight one another and terrorize the populace.

Abortive peace movement. On January 16, representatives of the two major clan leaders, Mohamed Farah Aideed and Ali Mahdi Mohammed, signed a peace agreement. Follow-up talks in Nairobi, Kenya, resulted in the signing of another pact on March 24, in which the two sides renounced violence and promised to work together to establish a new government. The treaty called for a meeting on April 15 to lay the groundwork for a peace conference and the creation of a national legislature.

The April meeting, however, was postponed by bickering between the rival factions. UN officials, who were aiding in the peace negotiations, rescheduled the meeting several times but were unsuccessful in bringing the clan leaders together again.

Part of the difficulty in restoring stability to Somalia was that many of the competing factions opposed the UN peace efforts. Many clan leaders argued that all UNISOM wanted was an agreement between the warlords that would allow the UN to get out of Somalia. In an effort to get that agreement, they complained, UN negotiators were concentrating their efforts on two clan leaders—Aideed and Mohammed—while ignoring the needs and desires of other Somali factions.

UNISOM was also accused of ignoring perhaps the most difficult question: how to reunite the so-called Republic of Somaliland, which had declared independence in May 1991, with Somalia. The government of the self-proclaimed republic declared on May 28, 1994, that it would "never form a federal state with Somalia." □ Mark DeLancey

See also **Africa** (Facts in brief table). In *World Book,* see **Somalia.**

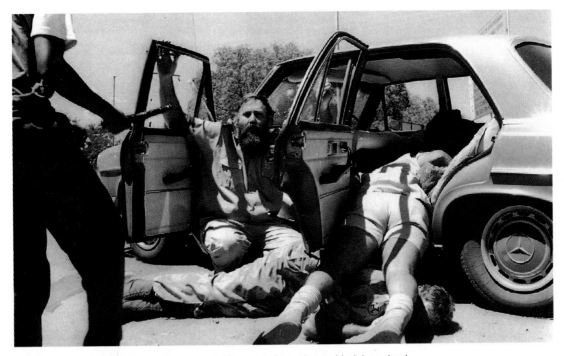

A member of a neo-Nazi group who was part of an armed assault on a black homeland in South Africa begs for his life before being shot dead by a black soldier, in March.

South Africa. The democratic reforms of recent years in South Africa reached fruition in 1994 with the country's first all-race elections in April and the installation of a new government in May. On May 9, the newly seated National Assembly chose Nelson R. Mandela as the nation's first black head of state. Mandela, who had been a leader in the long struggle to end *apartheid* (racial separation) in South Africa, was inaugurated on May 10. (See also **Mandela, Nelson R.**)

The elections. Violence increased as the elections approached, perpetuated by those wishing to derail the electoral process. Much of the violence was the work of right wing white extremists, who set off many bombs, killing more than 20 people.

A major impediment to the electoral process was the refusal of Chief Mangosuthu Buthelezi's Inkatha Freedom Party, a Zulu-based organization, to participate in the election. That impasse was finally resolved on April 19. The elections, which were held from April 26 to 29, took place peacefully and were widely regarded as fair. Mandela's African National Congress (ANC), the oldest and largest antiapartheid organization, was the big winner in the balloting, collecting 62.6 percent of the vote. (See **South Africa Special Report: New Era for South Africa.**)

Addressing the nation's needs. The initial actions of the new government were viewed by most South Africans as positive and reassuring. A Reconstruction and Development Program (RDP), which Mandela announced on May 24, promised new-home construction, jobs, school improvements, and numerous other benefits. In June, Finance Minister Derek Keys presented a budget that allocated 2.5 billion rand (about $525 million) for RDP projects.

But many people thought the pace of reform was too slow, and strikes by frustrated workers disrupted a number of industries during the year. Mandela urged employers and workers to seek arbitration.

Land controversy. In late May, a furor erupted over a secret agreement in April between the previous government and the Zulu King, Goodwill Zwelithini, that placed millions of acres of KwaZulu-Natal land under the king's control. Revelation of the deal raised questions about whether it had been an incentive to win Zwelithini's support for the election. Mandela said he had been unaware of the land transfer, and officials of the ANC and other political organizations questioned its legality.

No longer isolated. South Africa, long shunned by the world because of its racial policies, on June 6 was admitted to the Organization of African Unity, an association of African nations. On June 1, South Africa rejoined the British Commonwealth of Nations. It had withdrawn in 1961. ☐ Mark DeLancey

See also **Africa** (Facts in brief table). In the World Book Supplement section, see **South Africa.** In *World Book,* see **South Africa.**

New Era

South Africa's first free multiracial elections in
April 1994 finally ended the system of *apartheid*
(racial segregation), but the new government faced
the difficult task of raising the living standards of
the largely impoverished black majority.

for South Africa

By Janice Love

O
n April 26, 1994, the people of South Africa experienced a day
like no other in their history. It was the opening day of their
country's first all-race parliamentary elections. The election,
to choose members of the new National Assembly, was the culmination of a long, hard-fought struggle by South Africa's black majority to
end the nation's policy of *apartheid* (racial separation) and to establish a democracy in which all races could participate. More than 86
percent of those eligible to do so voted during the four days of polling,
a turnout most established democracies do not achieve.

To no one's surprise, the African National Congress (ANC), the oldest and largest black organization in the fight against apartheid, won a
resounding victory, collecting 62.6 percent of the vote. To almost everyone's surprise, considering the amount of conflict that South Africa has seen over the years, the voting took place with few incidents
of violence or fraud. All parties agreed that the election, presided over
by an Independent Electoral Commission, was free and fair.

On May 9, at its first meeting, the newly seated Assembly chose
ANC President Nelson R. Mandela as South Africa's first black head of
state. It was a proud day for Mandela, who had been jailed for more
than 27 years for his activities against apartheid.

Since his release from prison in 1990, Mandela had worked with
State President Frederik Willem de Klerk to dismantle apartheid in a

■ African National Congress (ANC) President Nelson R. Mandela
is surrounded by well-wishers as he arrives at a polling place
near Durban, South Africa, on April 27, 1994, to vote in the
nation's first all-race election.

371

■ **The author**

Janice Love is an associate professor in the Department of Government and International Studies at the University of South Carolina in Columbia.

way that would assure majority rule while protecting minority rights. At his inauguration as executive president on May 10 in Pretoria, the administrative capital, Mandela gripped de Klerk's hand and held it aloft, proclaiming his predecessor "one of the greatest reformers" in South Africa. De Klerk was sworn in as one of two deputy presidents in a five-year Transitional Government of National Unity.

Mandela had often tried to assure South Africa's whites that they had nothing to fear from black rule, and now he did so again. In his inaugural address, he said, "Out of the experience of an extraordinary human disaster that lasted too long must be born a society of which all humanity will be proud." In that society, Mandela pledged, "all South Africans, both black and white, will be able to walk tall, without any fear in their hearts, assured of their inalienable right to human dignity."

Creating this shining new South Africa will be no easy task. Mandela's government faced a number of challenges, including writing a new, permanent constitution as a prelude to the next general elections in 1999, defusing still-simmering racial and ethnic hostilities, and reforming the military and police forces. And perhaps most important, it had to find a way of addressing the enormous imbalance in wealth between black and white South Africans. Many observers feared that if political power does not lead to a better standard of living for South Africa's blacks—or Africans, as they are often called—the country might once again be plunged into violence.

But as Mandela took the oath of office, hope reigned. The very fact that an African had become president of a country that had been dominated so long, and so completely, by its white minority made almost anything seem possible.

The beginnings of white rule

White control of South Africa began with the founding of the Cape Colony, at the southern tip of the continent, by Dutch traders in 1652. The descendants of those Dutch settlers—together with some German and French immigrants—came to be known as *Boers* (farmers) and later as Afrikaners. In 1814, the Netherlands, which claimed ownership of the Cape Colony, ceded the colony to Britain. Within a few years, the Afrikaners were joined by new, English-speaking settlers.

For decades, the Afrikaners and British vied for control of the region. In the late 1830's, most of the Afrikaners left the Cape Colony and moved inland, where they later established two Boer republics. But friction with the British continued, finally erupting into war. In 1880 and 1881 and again from 1899 to 1902, the Afrikaners and British fought two wars, known as the Boer Wars to the British and the Wars of Freedom to the Afrikaners. The Afrikaners won the first war but were decisively defeated in the second, after which all of South Africa came under British rule.

By that time, the Afrikaners and the British army had subjugated all of South Africa's native peoples. Some groups of Africans, including the Zulu, the largest of South Africa's ethnic groups, struggled fiercely to maintain their independence. The Africans won some victories. In

The new South Africa

Zimbabwe

Botswana

Mozambique

Limpopo River

Northern Transvaal
★ Pietersburg

Eastern Transvaal
★ Nelspruit

★ Mmabatho   ⊛ **Pretoria**
Soweto ● ★ **Johannesburg**
P W V

North West
Klerksdorp ●

Swaziland

Namibia

Upington ●

Kimberley ★

Vaal River

● Kroonstad

● Welkom

Orange Free State

● Ladysmith

Richards Bay ●

KwaZulu-Natal

Pietermaritzburg
★

Umlazi ● ● **Durban**

Orange River

Bloemfontein ★

Lesotho

Indian Ocean

Northern Cape

Orange River

● Queenstown

Atlantic Ocean

Eastern Cape

King William's Town ★
East London ●

Western Cape

Saldanha ●

● Worcester

Port Elizabeth ●

Cape Town ★
● Stellenbosch

Africa

Equator

Atlantic Ocean   *Indian Ocean*

South Africa

Transvaal

⊛ Pretoria

Johannesburg ●

Orange
Free State

Natal

● Durban

Cape Province

● Cape Town

▨ Homelands

0 ———— 200 Miles
0 ———— 200 Kilometers

one well-known engagement in January 1879, an army of some 20,000 Zulu warriors decimated a British force of 1,700 men. But in the end, the force of British firearms was too strong for the blacks, who had only primitive weapons.

Soon after the second South African war, sentiment grew in Britain in favor of granting South Africa its independence. In 1910, the British Parliament passed an act establishing the independent Union of South Africa, part of the British Commonwealth of Nations. (In 1961, South Africa would withdraw from the Commonwealth and become the Republic of South Africa.) But even though South Africa had broken free of British rule, its government and economy continued to be dominated by white English-speaking people.

The new nation's Constitution, adopted in 1910, legalized the monopoly on power already held by the white minority. The government soon extended that power with a series of laws that enforced the segregation of the races and controlled the daily lives of Africans. The best jobs, at higher pay scales, were officially reserved for whites. Africans were required to live in "native reserves." Black men could work and travel outside the reserves, which made up about 13 percent of South Africa's land, but only if employed by whites. All African

■ In 1994, the political landscape of South Africa underwent significant change. Prior to the April 1994 election, South Africa was divided into four provinces and 10 black homelands. After the election, the homelands ceased to exist, and the country was reorganized into nine provinces.

GENERAL WAITING ROOM – WHITES ONLY
ALGEMENEWAGKAMER – NET BLANKES
IZINDLU ZANGASESE YOKULINDELA
ABAMHLOPHE BODWA

■ Life under apartheid

Racial segregation, which had existed in South Africa through-out the 1900's, was established as the official policy of apar-theid after 1948, when the Afrikaner-dominated National Party (NP) came to power. Under apartheid, Africans were denied access to many white facilities, *above,* and black adults were required to carry identity passes, *above right,* wherever they went. Africans holding jobs in cities had to live in "townships," *below,* impoverished shanty-towns on the urban fringe—where many blacks still live.

adults were required to carry identity passes that made it easier for the government to monitor their movements. Other segregation measures were aimed at people of Asian (mainly Indian) origin, who were descended from laborers imported by the British in the 1800's.

Many blacks began to resist the discriminatory government policies. In 1912, a group of African intellectuals founded the South African Native National Congress, the organization that became the ANC. But such efforts did little to stem the tide of segregation.

Apartheid becomes the law of the land

Life got even worse for Africans and other nonwhites after 1948, when the Afrikaner-dominated National Party (NP) won control of the government. The NP government established apartheid as official policy and proceeded over the next 20 years to pass one law after another segregating the races and increasing white power. The Mixed Marriages Act of 1949 prohibited marriage between people of different racial groups. The Population Registration Act of 1950 categorized South Africans as white (13 percent of the present population of about 43 million); African (76 percent); Asian, primarily Indian (2 percent); and Colored, or mixed ancestry (9 percent). Other acts prescribed separate public facilities for whites and other races and formalized the native reserves as black "homelands."

The objective of the homelands policy was to permanently separate South Africa's blacks from the white population. The 10 homelands were governed by Africans chosen and financed by the white government. Four homelands were declared to be independent nations. That distinction, however, did not receive formal recognition

■ At a country club in Vereeniging, white South Africans relax on a lawn-bowling green. Within their affluent communities, most whites were long isolated from the black majority and from the rage that often seethed just a few miles away in the townships.

▪ A system under siege

Resistance to apartheid escalated in the 1950's and early 1960's, subsided for a decade, and then erupted again with fury in 1976. In June of that year, thousands of black high school students clashed with the police in the Johannesburg township of Soweto, *right,* after the students protested a government order requiring that they be taught some courses in the Afrikaner language. The violence spread to other cities, and by year-end at least 600 people—nearly all of them blacks—had been killed.

from the United Nations (UN) or any other countries, because the homelands were dependent on the white government rather than being truly independent nations.

Moreover, it proved impossible to confine all of the country's Africans in homelands—the nation's economy was too dependent on black labor. Many Africans who held jobs in urban areas took up residence in so-called townships on the outskirts of major cities. These impoverished shantytowns, a world away from the affluent suburbs where South Africa's urban-dwelling whites lived, became hotbeds of black unrest and opposition to apartheid.

Mounting pressure against apartheid

Protests against the government's segregationist policies began to escalate in the 1950's. Although many liberal whites, as well as Coloreds and Asians, raised their voices against apartheid, the main impetus for change came from Africans. Mandela was one of the most visible leaders of the ANC at that time. In 1956, he and 155 other black leaders working against the government were arrested and charged with treason. All were acquitted after a trial that lasted until 1961.

While the trial was in progress, a state of war had been developing between the government and South Africa's blacks. In March 1960, at a rally in the township of Sharpeville, outside Johannesburg, the police opened fire on a crowd of demonstrators, killing 69 people. The next month, the government banned the ANC and an offshoot of the ANC, the Pan Africanist Congress (PAC), which had organized the Sharpeville protest. In response, both organizations launched guerrilla campaigns against the government, bombing rail lines, utilities,

■ In the 1980's, antiapartheid activists in the United States, *left,* and elsewhere denounced South Africa's racial policies. In response, the governments of the United States and a number of other nations in 1986 imposed economic *sanctions* (bans) against South Africa. Meanwhile, South African government forces battled almost constantly with black dissidents, *below.*

and public buildings and attacking police stations. In 1962, Mandela was jailed again, and the following year he was charged with sabotage and plotting to overthrow the government. He was convicted in 1964 and sentenced to life in prison.

The outburst of violence was suppressed, but guerrilla warfare continued. Military wings of the ANC and PAC established bases in nearby countries and trained recruits for infiltration and sabotage.

The black protest movement simmered for a decade and then roared back to life in 1976. In June of that year, African high school students in the Johannesburg township of Soweto, angry about a government order that they be taught some courses in the Afrikaner language, marched in protest. Rioting broke out, and the police shot several students. Riots and other disturbances spread to other townships and later to other cities as blacks gave voice to a host of grievances. The government responded with force. By year-end, at least 600 people, nearly all of them blacks, had been killed in the unrest.

Through the rest of the 1970's and into the 1980's, South Africa was rocked by hundreds of demonstrations, riots, boycotts, and strikes. The government also faced intensified guerrilla activities by the ANC, the PAC, and other black liberation movements. Additional pressure came from antiapartheid activists abroad, who in 1986 finally convinced a number of nations, including the United States, to impose economic *sanctions* (bans) against South Africa.

The South African government tried to quell the crisis by declaring a state of emergency, an action by which it assumed even greater power to deal with dissent. It also made a number of small-scale reforms aimed at restoring calm without ending the white monopoly on power. But the halfway measures being enacted or proposed were too little, too late. As the 1980's drew to a close, it was clear that if apartheid was not ended, the nation faced either civil war or anarchy.

Change comes, and with it new conflicts

The winds of true reform began to blow in 1989 with the election of Frederik de Klerk as president. Turning his back on the failed policies of his NP predecessor, Pieter W. Botha, de Klerk immediately set about dismantling apartheid. In 1990, he declared, "Our goal is a new South Africa . . . free of domination or oppression in whatever form." That same year, he released Mandela from prison and lifted the bans on the ANC and PAC and about 30 other outlawed opposition groups. He also desegregated all public facilities, including beaches, parks, and hospitals. Further reforms, including revocation of the Population Registration Act and other pillars of apartheid, followed in the coming months.

There was widespread skepticism in South Africa and elsewhere that de Klerk and the NP-dominated Parliament would actually go so far as to end white rule, but they did. In February 1993, the government and the ANC agreed on a plan by which whites and other large minority groups would participate in a transitional government for five years. And in June, a national convention in Johannesburg that was writing an interim constitution (a document approved in December by the Parliament) set all-race parliamentary elections for April 1994. The stage was thus set for the black majority to take command of the government. It seemed certain that the ANC would win a large majority in the coming election and that Mandela would be South Africa's next president.

But as April 1994 approached, the nation was still dangerously fragmented. Many white people, even those who had supported de Klerk's policies, had misgivings about the ANC. Not only did the ANC have a tradition of militancy, it also had strong ties to the South African Communist Party (SACP), which had long opposed apartheid. The SACP had allied itself with the ANC for the election, and many ANC candidates for the new Parliament were members of the SACP.

If some white people were worried about the coming transition to black rule, others, on the far-right end of the political spectrum, were outraged. An organization calling itself the Afrikaner Volksfront (AVF, the Afrikaner People's Front) said it would not submit to black rule and demanded the creation of a separate Afrikaner state. The AVF was formed in 1993 from several right wing groups, including the Conservative Party—established in 1982 by a faction that split from the NP—and a neofascist organization called the Afrikaner Resistance Movement (AWB). During the months leading up to the election, right wing conservatives organized commando units and threatened to create vi-

■ Competing for power

In the 1990's, the NP government began to dismantle apartheid. The ANC was the leading contender for power once white rule ended. After his 1990 release from prison, where he had spent more than 27 years for his activities against apartheid, Mandela appeared with South African Communist Party (SACP) leader Joe Slovo, *left.* The SACP had long supported the ANC, and the two organizations were allied as the nation moved toward the 1994 election.

■ Many South Africans opposed reform. The most militant white group, the neofascist Afrikaner Resistance Movement, *above,* vowed to wage war on a black-led government. Opposition also came from the Inkatha Freedom Party, a Zulu organization, whose leaders— King Goodwill Zwelithini and Chief Mangosuthu Buthelezi, *left,* left and right—feared that an ANC government would be dominated by Mandela's Xhosa ethnic group.

olent disruptions at polling places, perhaps even to launch a civil war. In April 1994, right wing extremists set off bombs across South Africa, killing more than 20 people.

Not all opponents of the impending new order were whites. For several years, a major obstacle to reform had been the Inkatha Freedom Party, an organization made up mostly of Zulus. Inkatha and its leader, Chief Mangosuthu Buthelezi, the top minister of the KwaZulu homeland, feared that Zulus would lose their homeland and that an ANC-led government would be dominated by Mandela's Xhosa ethnic group. In addition, Buthelezi was afraid Inkatha would not receive enough votes in the election to ensure him a prominent role in the new government. Throughout the early 1990's, Inkatha engaged in bloody clashes with supporters of the ANC that resulted in thousands of deaths. There were persistent reports that Inkatha was being supported by white security forces and right wing groups, charges that were confirmed in early 1994 by a special investigating commission.

By that time, Inkatha had joined with the AVF to form a coalition called the Freedom Alliance (FA). The FA insisted on the creation of homelands for each racial and ethnic group in South Africa and called for a boycott of the election if that demand was not agreed to. Although the coalition soon fell apart, Buthelezi continued to withhold his support for the election. In mid-April, however, after de Klerk's government and the ANC made a deal with the Zulu king, Goodwill Zwelithini, Buthelezi agreed to participate in the balloting. The king was guaranteed that even though KwaZulu and the other homelands were to be dissolved under the interim constitution, he could reign as a constitutional monarch in KwaZulu-Natal, one of nine provinces in the reorganized nation.

After the collapse of the Freedom Alliance, some members of the AVF founded another organization, the Freedom Front, to field candidates for Parliament. In the end, despite all the violence and threats, only two factions—the AWB and a highly militant black group called the Azanian People's Organization—boycotted the election. The AWB vowed to wage war on the new government.

The ANC won 252 of the 400 seats in the National Assembly, the lower house of the new Parliament, and the lion's share of seats in the president's Cabinet. The NP came in second, with 20.4 percent of the vote and 82 seats in the Assembly, and Inkatha was third with 10.5 percent and 43 seats. The Freedom Front, the PAC, and two other parties (out of a total of 19 contending) split up the remaining 23 seats. The 90 members of the Senate, the upper house, were selected later by lawmakers in the nation's nine provincial legislatures.

■ A prime mover in the reform process was State President Frederik Willem de Klerk, shown with Mandela at a conference in Johannesburg in 1991. De Klerk worked closely with Mandela to ensure a smooth transition to black rule. After the April 1994 election, de Klerk became one of two deputy presidents in a five-year Transitional Government of National Unity.

One of the first orders of business for the Parliament was to begin drafting a permanent constitution. The constitutional debate focused mainly on how much power the national government should have. The ANC favored a unitary system—one in which the national government holds most of the political power in the country. Historically, South Africa has had a unitary system, and the ANC argued that only a strong central government would be able to address the country's enormous social and economic inequalities.

The NP, the Freedom Front, and Inkatha all wanted to limit the authority of the national government. The NP favored a federal system, in which many powers would be allocated to the provinces. Under such an arrangement, the NP and other secondary political parties would have more control over local affairs. Inkatha and the Freedom

Front advocated the establishment of virtually autonomous ethnic enclaves, with even less power allowed to the national government.

The new constitution would also have to be written to protect the rights of whites and other minority groups. The transitional constitution contains a strong, detailed bill of rights, a number of assurances for protection of minorities, and a Constitutional Court to enforce those provisions. Presumably, those guarantees would be incorporated into the permanent constitution as well.

Confronting social and economic ills

The new government also had to find a way to defuse the serious racial and ethnic hostilities that could flare up in renewed violence at any time. Some of the threat from the white right wing had been neutralized by the time the new government took office. Several hundred white extremists were jailed between mid-1993 and mid-1994, including 32 accused of taking part in the preelection bombings. Still, the Afrikaner Resistance Movement did not back away from its vow to make war on the ANC government, so right wing terrorism remained a threat. Prior to the election, the ANC agreed to establish a council to consider the possibility of creating a white homeland. After the Freedom Front's poor showing at the polls, however, that idea did not gain momentum.

The predominantly white South African defense and police forces, which had long enjoyed state sanction to crush all opposition to apartheid, were another possible source of instability. But again, the danger may have been lessened by government action. In 1992, after repeated military and police efforts to sabotage his reform policies, de Klerk fired or suspended dozens of senior officers, including six generals in the armed forces. Nevertheless, the top posts in the military and police forces in 1994 were still held mostly by whites. So the ANC government faced the task of creating a new national defense and police force with no political agenda, devoted wholly to promoting peace, order, and security.

Ethnic tensions within the black population were a major concern as the new South Africa took shape. The territorial agreement with King Zwelithini calmed the waters a bit with the Zulu, but the ANC raised new anxieties among Zulus and other non-Xhosas as well. Although the ANC received strong support from all of South Africa's black ethnic groups, including the Zulu, it gave most of the choicest government positions to Xhosas. Many observers were watching closely to see whether the new regime would live up to its promise of promoting ethnic diversity in the government.

Finally, there was the challenge of providing a decent standard of living for all of South Africa's people. Despite the nation's image of wealth, the economic disparities in South Africa in the 1990's were among the worst in the world. A study by the World Bank, an agency of the UN, estimated that the average yearly income of the nation's whites was 9.5 times that of blacks and up to 4.5 times that of other racial groups. More than 50 percent of South African families live in

▪ A new day, but old problems

From April 26 to 29, 1994, South Africans in great numbers went to the polls to vote, *right.* As expected, the ANC won a decisive victory, and on May 9 the new National Assembly chose Mandela as South Africa's first black president. As 1994 ended, Mandela's government faced difficult challenges.

The political factions in South Africa

Although 19 political parties took part in South Africa's April 1994 election, 7 parties attracted more than 99 per cent of the vote. Two other groups—the white supremacist Afrikaner Resistance Movement and the Azanian People's Organization, a black organization that opposes any white role in the South African government—boycotted the election. In addition, the South African Communist Party (SACP), rather than competing in the election as a separate party, was allied with the African National Congress (ANC), the largest black group that worked to end white minority rule and apartheid in South Africa. A number of ANC parliamentary candidates were members of the SACP. The 400 seats in the National Assembly, the lower house of the new Parliament, were divided proportionally among the winning parties, based on each party's percentage of the vote. (The Senate, the upper house of the Parliament, consists of 90 members, 10 from each province, who were chosen on a proportional basis by provincial lawmakers.)

Party	Type of Organization	Percent of 1994 vote	Seats in National Assembly
African National Congress	Oldest and largest black liberation movement—diverse membership	62.6	252
National Party	Largest white political party—moderately conservative	20.4	82
Inkatha Freedom Party	Conservative black nationalist	10.5	43
Freedom Front	Far right wing white nationalist	2.2	9
Democratic Party	Liberal white	1.7	7
Pan Africanist Congress	Militantly antiwhite black nationalist	1.3	5
African Christian Democratic Party	Conservative black homeland-based Christian	0.5	2

▪ Africans demanding jobs are a reminder to the new government that many poor blacks seek a quick improvement in their living standards. Observers believe that the huge disparity of wealth between whites and blacks is just one of several problems that must be addressed as South Africa faces the future.

extreme poverty, earning less than $170 a month, and 61 percent of infant deaths among black families are caused by malnutrition. Illiteracy and homelessness are also rampant among the black population, and many Africans do not have even the most basic of services, such as sewage systems, running water, or electricity.

Boosting blacks and other racial groups into the economic mainstream, while protecting the property rights of nervous whites, presented a difficult chore for Mandela and the ANC. In their campaign platforms, both the ANC and the NP said South Africa must combine economic growth with a redistribution of wealth. The parties deeply disagreed, however, on how to achieve that goal. The NP argued in favor of free-market forces and the private ownership of most industries. The ANC put forward a pragmatic Reconstruction and Development Program (RDP) designed to address the needs of the poor while reassuring investors and financial institutions. The RDP called for significant public investment in jobs, housing, electrification, health, and education. But finding the money for those priorities could be difficult. The nation's economy has declined since the early 1980's as a result of an inefficient government bureaucracy, a worldwide economic slowdown, and the stiff trade and financial sanctions against South Africa, which lasted until 1991. South Africa's per capita income declined yearly throughout most of the 1980's and into the 1990's, and the average annual growth rate of the economy during the same period was barely 1 percent.

After the election, the white population, while giving up political power, continued to hold tremendous economic power. But black militants and South Africa's vast, hungry masses possessed a different kind of power. They could make the country ungovernable, as they did in the turbulent 1980's, if they feel they are not getting their fair share in the new society. The future political fortunes of Nelson Mandela and the ANC will depend largely on how well they can walk the tightrope of reaching compromise with their adversaries, both black and white, while satisfying the needs of supporters impatient for a taste of prosperity.

The May 10, 1994, inaugural ceremonies and festivities repeatedly rang out with the new South African national anthem, "Nkosi Sikelele Afrika"—"God Bless Africa." Although they sang with great joy and thanksgiving for the remarkable transformation they had achieved, the people of South Africa were at the same time mindful of the difficult days that lie ahead. ■ ■ ■

Space exploration

Space exploration. Astronauts on the seven space shuttle missions flown in 1994 carried out a variety of scientific experiments, took spacewalks and measured how human activity has changed the surface of Earth. The first flight of the year began on February 3, when the shuttle Discovery went into orbit with a crew of six. The crew included Sergei K. Krikalev, the first Russian to fly on a United States space shuttle.

Discovery carried a 12-foot (3.7-meter) disk called the Wake Shield Facility (WSF), which was designed to be placed in the shuttle's wake for an experiment in growing ultrapure films for electronic devices. A faulty guidance system on the WSF prevented its launch, so the experiment had to be done with the disk suspended from the shuttle's robot arm. The crew also performed several other materials-processing and biotechnology experiments in Spacehab-2, a laboratory carried in the shuttle's cargo bay. The flight ended on February 11 with a landing at the Kennedy Space Center (KSC) in Florida.

Columbia and Endeavour flights. Columbia blasted into space on March 4 with a crew of five. It carried the United States Microgravity Payload, a package of experiments on various materials that could not be conducted in Earth's gravity. The experiments were controlled by ground-based computers. Columbia completed the 14-day mission with a landing at KSC on March 18.

Endeavour went into space on April 9 with six astronauts aboard. It carried the Space Radar Laboratory, an advanced radar system that produced three-dimensional images of Earth's surface. The radar images taken on the flight were expected to enable scientists to detect changes on Earth caused both by nature and by human activities. An orbit that took Endeavour as far north as Alaska and as far south as the tip of South America enabled the crew to scan 25 percent of the planet's land area. The astronauts came down at Edwards Air Force Base (EAFB) in California on April 20.

Longest mission. Columbia took off on July 8 with thousands of aquatic animals and a crew of seven, including Chiaki Naito-Mukai, the first Japanese woman to fly in space. A main goal of the mission was to determine how newts, goldfish, jellyfish, toad eggs, flies, and other living things hatch and develop in the reduced gravity of space.

Because of a one-day landing delay, the flight lasted 14 days, 18 hours, making it the longest mission in the history of the shuttle program.

Untethered spacewalk. Discovery took six astronauts into orbit on September 9. They launched a small satellite called Spartan that observed the sun's atmosphere and the solar wind, an outflow of charged particles from the sun. After two days of measurements, astronauts retrieved Spartan with the robot arm. Later in the mission, astronauts Mark C. Lee and Carl J. Meade used a jet pack to fly free of Discovery, maneuvering 150 miles (240 kilometers) above Earth without a lifeline. The flight ended on September 20 with a landing at EAFB.

Delayed mission. Endeavour was scheduled to go into orbit on August 18, but computers shut off the shuttle's three main engines less than two seconds before liftoff. Investigators determined that a faulty fuel pump caused the problem.

On September 30, Endeavour carried six astronauts on a mission to observe changes on Earth with the Space Radar Laboratory. The crew made radar scans of oceans, forests, deserts, erupting volcanoes, and an oil spill off Denmark. By flying the same orbits for three days, the astronauts captured three-dimensional images that revealed changes in terrain, including those that had occurred since the April flight of Endeavour. The shuttle landed on October 11 at EAFB.

The shuttle Atlantis went into orbit on November 3 with six astronauts and a cargo that included 10 pregnant rats. During the flight, the crew launched and then retrieved a German-made satellite equipped with sensors to measure changes in Earth's protective ozone layer. The rats were orbited to determine the effects of weightlessness on unborn fetuses, an experiment that anticipates a time when pregnant women will fly in space. Atlantis landed at EAFB on November 14.

Mapping the moon. On January 25 at Vandenberg Air Force Base in California, a Titan 2G rocket launched a small military spacecraft called Clementine 1. The unmanned spacecraft went into lunar orbit on February 19. During the next two months, onboard cameras mapped the entire lunar surface and surveyed its mineral content.

On May 3, Clementine headed for a rendezvous with an asteroid called Geographos. On May 7, however, the probe malfunctioned, and the rendezvous was canceled. Nonetheless, the flight demonstrated the feasibility of inexpensive missions using small spacecraft and simplified launch and control systems.

Tense moments on Mir. Three cosmonauts on the Russian Mir space station almost had to abandon the station and return to Earth on August 30, when Mir failed to dock with an unmanned supply ship. On September 2, cosmonaut Yuri Malenchenko took control from the automatic docking system and brought the two spacecraft together.

On October 6, a Russian spacecraft docked with Mir, bringing a new three-man crew to the space station. The crew included a German scientist.

International space station. A program to build a multinational space station survived attempts by Congress in 1994 to eliminate funding for U.S. participation in the project. The United States, Canada, Japan, Russia, and the European Space Agency (ESA) have agreed to share in building and manning the space base, now called Alpha. Construction of the station is scheduled to begin in late 1997.

Delta Clipper. Tests of a small, reusable rocket called the Delta Clipper (DC-X) continued in 1994. The inexpensive 42-foot (12.8-meter) tall experimental rocket takes off and lands vertically and can be launched by only 10 people. On June 27, the DC-X flew 17 seconds at the White Sands Missile Range in New Mexico before an on-board explosion forced it to land. Originally a project of the Department of Defense and McDonnell Douglas Corporation, the DC-X was transferred in 1994 to the National Aeronautics and Space Administration. Plans call for constructing a 132-foot (40-meter) tall Delta Clipper to carry payloads into low-Earth orbit.

Ulysses reaches sun's pole. On September 13, the Ulysses spacecraft became the first space probe to pass beneath the south pole of the sun. Built by the ESA, Ulysses was deployed from the shuttle Discovery in 1990. After completing a study of the sun's south pole, the craft looped out into space on a path that will take it over the sun's north pole in 1995.

Projects in Japan and China. Japan launched its first large rocket, called the H-2, on February 4. China used its Long March 3A rocket for the first time on February 8 to orbit a research satellite. An attempt by the Chinese to launch a weather satellite ended on April 2 when the craft exploded during fueling operations.   □ William J. Cromie

See also **Astronomy.** In *World Book,* see **Space travel.**

Spain. Spanish Prime Minister Felipe González Márquez plunged in political popularity polls as his government was rocked by scandal in 1994. On April 30, Interior Minister Antoni Asunción resigned, reportedly to spare the government further embarrassment, after Luis Roldán, the former head of the Spanish Civil Guard, a police force, had fled into hiding. Roldán had been charged with stealing government funds and taking bribes. On May 3, Agriculture Minister Vincente Albero Silla resigned because he had failed to pay income tax on certain investment earnings. Two Socialist Party members of parliament also quit in May over other corruption charges.

The wave of resignations weakened González' Socialist government but did not tip the balance of power in parliament. Opponents of González called for his resignation, but the prime minister declined, saying that the scandals did not warrant his resignation. On May 5 and May 10, respectively, the nationalist Catalán Convergence and Union Party and the Basque Nationalist Party announced their support of the González government, thus ensuring that González would not be voted out of office.

Losses in European Parliament. González' Socialist Workers' Party suffered a poor showing in the June 12 elections for the 567-member European Parliament, an advisory institution of the European Union (EU), formerly the European Community. The Socialists won only about 31 percent of the votes and 22 seats in the parliament, down from about 40 percent of the votes and 27 seats in the last election in 1989. The conservative Popular Party made big gains in the European vote, winning 40 percent of the vote and 28 seats, up from 15 seats. The United Left, a coalition of left wing groups led by the Communist Party, won 9 seats, up from 4.

Economic recovery. In 1994, Spain's economy slowly recovered from a recession that had sent unemployment above 20 percent in 1993. Spain's gross domestic product, the value of all goods and services produced in a country in a given period, grew an estimated 1.5 percent, after two years of declines.

Business news. Telefonica de Espana SA, the telephone company that is partially owned by the Spanish government, expanded overseas in 1994. In April, it bought 35 percent of Peru's telephone company for $2 billion and on July 3 joined Unisource NV, a pan-European telecommunications alliance with close ties to AT&T Corp. The moves will help prepare Telefonica for greater competition from foreign telephone companies in Spain.

Theater fire. The Liceo Theater in Barcelona, a historic, 145-year-old opera house, was gutted by fire on January 31. The regional government of Catalonia said it planned to rebuild the theater.   □ Philip Revzin

See also **Europe** (Facts in brief table). In *World Book,* see **European Union; Spain.**

Spielberg, Steven (1947-   ), won his first Academy Award for best director in 1994 for the motion picture *Schindler's List (*1993). He had been nominated previously for best director for *Close Encounters of the Third Kind* (1977), *Raiders of the Lost Ark* (1981), and *E.T.: The Extra-Terrestrial* (1982).

Spielberg was born on Dec. 18, 1947, in Cincinnati, Ohio. He was the only son in a family with three daughters. Spielberg became interested in filmmaking as a youngster. At age 12, after his family moved to Phoenix, he began making films with actors. At age 13, he won a contest with his 40-minute war movie, *Escape to Nowhere.*

In the 1960's, while enrolled in the film department of California State College, now California State University, in Long Beach, his film *Amblin'* (1969) won prizes at the Atlanta (Ga.) Film Festival and Venice Film Festival in Italy. This movie earned him, at age 21, a seven-year contract with Universal Studios in Los Angeles as a director of television series and films. He formed his own production company, Amblin Entertainment, in 1984.

Spielberg's first major box-office success was *Jaws* (1975). *Jurassic Park,* which he directed in 1993, became the biggest money-maker in the history of motion pictures.

Spielberg and his wife, actress Kate Capshaw, have a son, a daughter, and an adopted son. He also has a son by a previous marriage.   □ Carol L. Hanson

Sports. There were spectacular athletic displays in 1994 at the Winter Olympics and soccer's World Cup. But in many ways, the year in sports was a troubled one. The most serious difficulties occurred when collective-bargaining disputes shut down the major leagues in two of the four largest professional team sports. And athletes who had been heroes found themselves in prison, in court, or in trouble with the people who ran their sports.

Labor woes. Because club owners and players could not agree on a salary cap or other restrictions on salaries, the major league baseball season was cut short, and the start of the National Hockey League's (NHL) 1994-1995 season was delayed. In addition to a salary cap, the baseball owners wanted to end contract arbitration. On August 12, the players struck. On September 14, the owners called off the rest of the season, the play-offs, and the World Series. (See also **Baseball.**)

The hockey owners wanted to tax themselves 5 percent of payrolls and 5 percent of gate receipts, with the money to help teams that were struggling financially. The players said that would, in effect, be a salary cap. On September 30, the owners postponed the start of the season for up to 15 days. On October 11, they postponed it again indefinitely, and on December 12, the NHL board of governors authorized Commissioner Gary Bettman to cancel the season if a 50-game schedule and four rounds of play-offs could not be played by July 1, 1995. (See also **Hockey.**)

The National Basketball Association (NBA) had a salary cap that the players wanted to end and the owners wanted to tighten. On October 27, despite no collective-bargaining agreement, the owners and players reached a no-strike, no-lockout accord that allowed the 1994-1995 season to be played on schedule. The National Football League was unaffected as it played its first season under a salary cap.

Tainted heroes. It was a bad year for many sports figures, notably skater Tonya Harding and former football star O. J. Simpson. Harding's former husband and three other men admitted their roles in the January 1994 clubbing of Nancy Kerrigan, Harding's main rival for U.S. figure-skating supremacy. The four men went to prison for their actions. Harding said she knew nothing about the attack before it happened, then pleaded guilty to obstructing justice. But she avoided a prison term.

Simpson, a Hall of Fame football star, went on trial in September for the brutal June 12 murders of his former wife and her friend in Los Angeles. He denied the charges. (See **Courts.**)

Former baseball star Mickey Mantle, current baseball players Darryl Strawberry and Dwight Gooden, and 18-year-old tennis player Jennifer Capriati entered programs for drug or alcohol abuse. John Daly was suspended from the profes-

sional golf tour for irresponsible behavior, and Mike Tyson, once boxing's hero of heroes, remained in an Indiana prison on a rape conviction.

NCAA. Colleges, trying to assure themselves of a good share of television rights money, played musical chairs with conferences. As part of the fallout, the Southwest Conference, a powerful league since its founding in 1914, would become extinct on June 30, 1996. In February 1994, Texas, Texas A&M, Texas Tech, and Baylor announced that they would join the Big Eight, which would become the Big 12. Rice, Southern Methodist, and Texas Christian later said that they would join the Western Athletic Conference. In November, Houston joined Southern Mississippi, Louisville, Tulane, Memphis, and Cincinnati to form an all-sports conference that was to begin play in 1995.

FBI probe. The Federal Bureau of Investigation (FBI) arrested the former head basketball coach at Baylor University, three of his former assistants, and four others on Nov. 17, 1994, on charges of postal and mail fraud and conspiracy. The FBI alleged that the Baylor coaches, along with junior-college officials, helped prospective Baylor recruits cheat on junior-college exams.

LeMond retires. Star American cyclist Greg LeMond, 33, retired from racing on December 3. LeMond won the Tour de France, the world's most prestigious bicycle race, three times. His Tour de France victory in 1989 came just two years after he nearly died from gunshot wounds he suffered in a hunting accident.

Little League World Series. A team from Maracaibo, Venezuela, won the Little League World Series on August 27 in Williamsport, Pa., with a 4-3 victory over Northridge, Calif. The Northridge team had been known throughout the tournament as the "Earthquake Kids" for the earthquake that struck the town on Jan. 17, 1994.

Soap Box Derby. Danielle Del Ferraro, 13, of Stow, Ohio, on August 6 became the first two-time champion in the All-American Soap Box Derby's 57-year history. She won four of six races she entered before the Derby in Akron, Ohio.

English Channel record. Californian Chad Hundeby, 23, set a record on September 27, swimming the English Channel in 7 hours 17 minutes, 23 minutes faster than the previous mark. He beat American Penny Lee Dean's standard for the 21-mile (34-kilometer) swim set in 1978.

Awards. In March 1994, Charlie Ward, the Florida State quarterback, was voted the James E. Sullivan Award as America's outstanding amateur athlete in 1993. He was the first football player honored since 1946. The United States Olympic Committee in March 1994 named Michael Johnson and Gail Devers, 1992 Olympic gold medalists and 1993 world champions in track and field, as its 1993 Sportsman and Sportswoman of the Year.

Among the winners in 1994 were:

Cycling. Miguel Indurain of Spain won the Tour de France, the world's premier race, on July 24 for the fourth consecutive year. Martin Nothstein of Trexlertown, Pa., became the first American in 82 years to win a world sprint title. He also won the Keirin final to become the first American to win two world track titles in the same year since 1893.

Cricket. Brian Lara, a 25-year-old left-hander from Trinidad, established two world batting records for one innings. In April, playing for the West Indies against England, he scored 375 runs, the most ever in a test match. In June, playing for Warwickshire against Durham in an English county match, he scored 501 runs, the most ever in a first-class match.

Diving. China won four of the six titles and 9 of the 18 medals in the world championships in September in Rome. The best U.S. finish was a third place by Brian Earley of Mission Viejo, Calif., in the men's 1 meter. Evan Stewart, a University of Tennessee student from Zimbabwe, won the men's 1-meter title. Mary Ellen Clark swept the three women's titles in the United States indoor championships.

Gymnastics. In April, at the world individual championships in Brisbane, Australia, 17-year-old Shannon Miller of Edmond, Okla., won the all-around title for the second consecutive year. Ivan Ivankov of Belarus won the men's title. His celebrated teammate, Vitali Scherbo, won the bronze medal and three of the six individual titles. In the world team championships in November in Dortmund, Germany, the winners were the men from China and the women from Romania.

Rowing. The American men and the German women won the eight-oared titles in the world championships in September. Americans won four of the five eight-oared titles in the Henley Royal Regatta in England in June, with the U.S. national open eight taking the Grand Challenge Cup. The College Boat Club of Philadelphia won the lightweight-eight Ladies' Challenge Plate. The best American college crews were the Brown men and Princeton women.

Wrestling. American men won one silver and one bronze medal in the world freestyle championships in August in Istanbul, Turkey, their fewest number of medals in 19 years. American women won two silver medals at the world freestyle championships in Sofia, Bulgaria, in August. American men won one medal, a bronze, in the world Greco-Roman championships. The world team champions were Turkey (men's freestyle), Russia (men's Greco-Roman), and Japan (women).

Other champions

Archery, world Olympic-bow field champions: men, Andrea Parenti, Italy; women, Jenny Sjouall, Sweden.

Badminton, All-England champions: men, Heryanto Arbi, Indonesia; women, Susi Susanti, Indonesia.

Figure skater Tonya Harding and her former husband, Jeff Gillooly, speak to reporters after Gillooly was implicated in January in an assault on Harding's main rival.

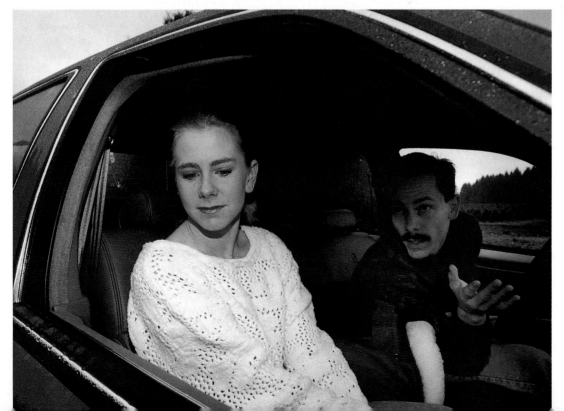

Sports

Biathlon, World Cup overall champions: men, Patrice Bailly-Salins, France; women, Svetlana Paramygina, Belarus.

Billiards, world three-cushion champion: Sang Chun Lee, New York City.

Bobsledding, World Cup champions: two-man sled, Pierre Leuders, Canada; four-man sled, Hubert Schosser, Austria.

Canoeing, world champions: men's 500-meter canoe, Nikolai Buchalov, Bulgaria; men's 500-meter kayak, Zsombor Borhi, Hungary; women's 500-meter kayak, Birgit Schmidt, Germany.

Court tennis, world champion: Bob Fahey, Australia.

Cross-country, world champions: men, William Sigei, Kenya; women, Helen Chepngeno, Kenya.

Curling, world champions: men, Rick Folk, Canada; women, Sandra Paterson, Canada.

Equestrian, world champions: jumping, Franke Sloothaak, Germany; freestyle dressage, Anky Van Grunsven, the Netherlands; three-day, Vaughn Jefferis, New Zealand.

Fencing, world foil champions: men, Rolando Tucker Leon, Cuba; women, Reka Szabo-Lazar, Romania.

Handball, world four-wall champions: men, David Chapman, Long Beach, Calif.; women, Lisa Fraiser, Canada.

Luge, World Cup champions: men, Markus Prock, Austria; women, Gabi Kolish, Germany.

Modern pentathlon, world champions: men, Dmitri Svatkovsky, Russia; women, Eva Fjellerup, Denmark.

Motorcycle racing, world 500-cc champion: Michael Doohan, Australia.

Racquetball, world amateur champions: men, Herman Greenfeld, Canada; women, Michelle Gould, Boise, Ida.

Rodeo, world all-around champion: Ty Murray, Stephenville, Tex.

Roller skating, world freestyle champions: men, Heath Medeiros, Westport, Mass.; women, Dezera Salas, Golta, Calif.

Shooting, world three-position rifle champions: men, Petr Kurka, Czech Republic; women, Anna Maloukhina, Russia.

Softball, women's world champion: United States.

Synchronized swimming, world champion: Becky Dyroen-Lancer, Campbell, Calif.

Table tennis, U.S. open champions: men, Kong Linghui, China; women, Gao Jun, China.

Triathlon, Ironman champions: men, Greg Welch, Australia; women, Paula Newby-Fraser, Australia.

Volleyball, world champions: men, Italy; women, Cuba.

Water polo, world champions: men, Italy; women, Hungary.

Water skiing, world junior overall champions: men, Javier Julio, Argentina; women, Brandi Hunt, Clermont, Fla. ☐ Frank Litsky
See also articles on the various sports. In *World Book,* see articles on the sports.

Sri Lanka. President Dingiri Banda Wijetunga called parliamentary elections for Aug. 16, 1994, six months ahead of schedule. In March elections for the Southern Provincial Council, Wijetunga's United National Party (UNP) had been defeated by the Sri Lanka Freedom Party (SLFP) and its allies in a coalition called the People's Alliance (PA). Wijetunga hoped a UNP parliamentary victory would strengthen his own candidacy in the upcoming November presidential elections.

Instead, after 17 years in power, the UNP lost the parliamentary elections, and SLFP leader Chandrika Kumaratunga became prime minister on August 19. She went on to win the more powerful position of president on November 9, running against Srima Dissanayake, the wife of the UNP presidential candidate who was killed in a bomb blast a few weeks before the election. Wijetunga had decided not to run.

The SLFP had governed Sri Lanka much of the time since its leader, S. W. R. D. Bandaranaike, became prime minister in 1956. After Bandaranaike was assassinated in 1959, his widow, Sirimavo, became prime minister several times. She was the formal head of the SLFP, but active leadership of the party was contested between her son, Anura, and daughter, Chandrika Kumaratunga, a leftist who had been educated in France. When Sirimavo indicated she favored Kumaratunga over Anura, he joined the UNP. Kumaratunga appointed her mother prime minister after winning the presidency.

Kumaratunga and her PA coalition won 105 of the new Parliament's 225 seats. The UNP took 94 seats. As the new president, Kumaratunga promised efforts to alleviate poverty, especially among people who had not benefited from the UNP's free enterprise policies. She reassured those who were apprehensive of her leftist background that she was "committed to free-market policies."

Tamil Tigers. Kumaratunga also promised unconditional peace talks with the Liberation Tigers of Tamil Eelam in an effort to end their 11-year guerrilla war. The Tigers' fight for independence for the Tamil ethnic minority living in northeast Sri Lanka had cost an estimated 35,000 lives. Tiger leader Veluppillai Prabhakaran agreed to begin negotiations, but on September 20 two Tiger boats loaded with explosives rammed a naval patrol boat, sinking it and killing 25 sailors along with five Tigers in the suicide boats. In October, a second round of talks was called off when a bomb blast, suspected to be the work of Tigers, killed 54 people, including the UNP presidential candidate. But Kumaratunga initiated more peace talks in November.

Economic growth, which in 1993 had been the highest in 16 years at 6.9 percent, slowed in 1994. Seeking votes, Wijetunga cut taxes on May 1. Inflation rose above 10 percent. ☐ Henry S. Bradsher
See also **Asia** (Facts in brief table). In *World Book,* see **Sri Lanka.**

Republican George E. Pataki beams while declaring victory over incumbent Mario M. Cuomo in New York's November 8 gubernatorial election.

State government. The political makeup of state governments in the United States moved to the right in 1994, as November 8 elections put 30 of the 50 governorships in Republican hands. Before the elections, the nation had only 19 Republican governors. The Republican Party had not held a majority of governors' seats since 1970.

Among the Democrats defeated were New York's Mario M. Cuomo, who lost to George E. Pataki, and Texas governor Ann W. Richards, defeated by George W. Bush, son of the former President. Republican governors returned to office included Pete Wilson of California, Jim Edgar of Illinois, William F. Weld of Massachusetts, and George V. Voinovich of Ohio. Florida Governor Lawton M. Chiles, Jr., a Democrat, retained his post by a narrow margin.

Conservative ballot initiatives generally found favor with voters in 1994 as well. Measures to limit the number of terms of elected officials passed in eight states. Victim's rights or crime initiatives succeeded in nine states. And voters in California backed a controversial measure to deny nearly all state services to illegal immigrants. (See also **Elections.**)

Crime and punishment. State legislators and governors sought to show voters that they were tough on crime by beefing up penalties for criminals and building more prisons. Crimes committed by young people were a target in Colorado, which followed up its 1993 special session on juvenile justice

by funding new programs in 1994 to pay for community crime prevention programs for at-risk youth. Programs aimed at keeping youths off the streets and away from a life of crime were funded in several other states.

States also passed measures to punish violent juveniles more severely. Legislators in Kansas, Kentucky, South Dakota, and Tennessee made it a crime for a minor to possess a gun, and by year-end, more than half the states had laws to ban juveniles from having handguns. In Arizona, California, Delaware, North Carolina, and Utah, lawmakers increased penalties for selling or giving a weapon to a minor.

Many states considered "three-time loser" laws, which typically mandate life without *parole* (early conditional release from prison) for conviction of a third serious violent offense. After voters in Washington state in November 1993 approved such a law, at least 16 state legislatures enacted their own versions to put repeat offenders behind bars. Georgia voters in 1994 supported an especially tough measure that mandates life in prison without parole for felons convicted of a second serious offense.

Also popular were so-called "truth-in-sentencing" laws, which require violent criminals to serve most of their sentences rather than being given parole. In an extreme example, Virginia abolished parole for offenses committed on or after Jan. 1, 1995. More states were expected to follow suit, because

Selected statistics on state governments

State	Resident population*	Governor†	Legislature† House (D)	(R)	Senate (D)	(R)	State tax revenue‡	Tax revenue per capita‡	Public school expenditures per pupil§
Alabama	4,062,608	Fob James, Jr. (R)	74	31	23	12	$ 4,218,000,000	$1,020	$4,060
Alaska	551,947	Tony Knowles (D)	16	22**	8	12	1,590,000,000	2,710	9,810
Arizona	3,677,985	Fife Symington (R)	22	38	11	19	4,827,000,000	1,260	4,290
Arkansas	2,362,239	Jim Guy Tucker (D)	88	12	28	7	2,746,000,000	1,140	3,950
California	29,839,250	Pete Wilson (R)	31	41	21	17††	46,128,000,000	1,490	4,620
Colorado	3,307,912	Roy Romer (D)	24	41	16	19	3,521,000,000	1,010	5,580
Connecticut	3,295,699	John G. Rowland (R)	90	61	17	19	6,060,000,000	1,650	8,430
Delaware	688,696	Tom Carper (D)	14	27	12	9	1,341,000,000	1,950	6,590
Florida	13,003,362	Lawton Chiles (D)	63	57	19	21	14,504,000,000	1,080	5,340
Georgia	6,508,419	Zell Miller (D)	114	66	35	20‡‡	7,267,000,000	1,080	4,470
Hawaii	1,115,274	Ben Cayetano (D)	44	7	23	2	2,710,000,000	2,340	5,940
Idaho	1,011,986	Phil Batt (R)	13	57	8	27	1,402,000,000	1,310	4,210
Illinois	11,466,682	Jim Edgar (R)	54	64	26	33	13,463,000,000	1,160	5,520
Indiana	5,564,228	Evan Bayh (D)	44	56	20	30	6,476,000,000	1,140	5,890
Iowa	2,787,424	Terry E. Branstad (R)	36	64	27	23	3,602,000,000	1,280	5,630
Kansas	2,485,600	Bill Graves (R)	44	81	14	26	2,802,000,000	1,110	5,650
Kentucky	3,698,969	Brereton C. Jones (D)	63	37	23	17	5,081,000,000	1,350	5,170
Louisiana	4,238,216	Edwin W. Edwards (D)	87	16	31	6	4,250,000,000	990	4,810
Maine	1,233,223	Angus King (I)	77	74	16	18§§	1,664,000,000	1,350	6,050
Maryland	4,798,622	Parris Glendening (D)#	100	41	32	15	6,502,000,000	1,320	6,500
Massachusetts	6,029,051	William F. Weld (R)	125	34§§	30	10	9,903,000,000	1,650	6,610
Michigan	9,328,784	John Engler (R)	54	56	16	22	11,279,000,000	1,200	6,570
Minnesota	4,387,029	Arne H. Carlson (R)	71	63	44	23	7,450,000,000	1,660	5,770
Mississippi	2,586,443	Kirk Fordice (R)	89	30	37	15	2,494,000,000	950	3,430
Missouri	5,137,804	Mel Carnahan (D)	87	76	19	15	5,131,000,000	990	4,640
Montana	803,655	Marc Racicot (R)	33	67	19	31	1,035,000,000	1,260	5,280
Nebraska	1,584,617	E. Benjamin Nelson (D)	unicameral (49 nonpartisan)				1,890,000,000	1,180	5,190
Nevada	1,206,152	Bob Miller (D)	21	21	8	13	1,823,000,000	1,370	4,960
New Hampshire	1,113,915	Steve Merrill (R)	112	286##	6	18	829,000,000	750	5,990
New Jersey	7,748,634	Christine Todd Whitman (R)	28	52	16	24	12,803,000,000	1,640	10,060
New Mexico	1,521,779	Gary E. Johnson (R)	46	24	27	15	2,243,000,000	1,420	4,970
New York	18,044,505	George E. Pataki (R)	94	56	25	36	30,113,000,000	1,660	8,600
North Carolina	6,657,630	James B. Hunt, Jr. (D)	52	67‡‡	26	24	9,010,000,000	1,320	4,970
North Dakota	641,364	Edward T. Shafer (R)	23	75	20	29	755,000,000	1,190	4,450
Ohio	10,887,325	George V. Voinovich (R)	43	55	14	19	12,115,000,000	1,100	6,270
Oklahoma	3,157,604	Frank Keating (R)	65	36	35	13	3,882,000,000	1,210	4,160
Oregon	2,853,733	John Kitzhaber (D)	26	34	11	19	3,313,000,000	1,110	6,070
Pennsylvania	11,924,710	Tom J. Ridge (R)	103	100	20	29	16,270,000,000	1,350	8,220
Rhode Island	1,005,984	Lincoln C. Almond (R)	84	16	40	10	1,307,000,000	1,300	6,760
South Carolina	3,505,707	David Beasley (R)	58	62***	29	17	3,936,000,000	1,090	4,550
South Dakota	699,999	William J. Janklow (R)	24	46	16	19	565,000,000	790	4,730
Tennessee	4,896,641	Don Sundquist (R)	59	40	19	14	4,526,000,000	900	4,200
Texas	17,059,805	George W. Bush (R)	89	61	17	14	17,031,000,000	960	5,070
Utah	1,727,784	Michael O. Leavitt (R)	55	20	10	19	1,988,000,000	1,100	3,420
Vermont	564,964	Howard Dean (D)	86	61†††	12	18	763,000,000	1,340	7,720
Virginia	6,216,568	George Allen (R)	52	47§§	22	19	7,025,000,000	1,100	5,560
Washington	4,887,941	Mike Lowry (D)	38	60	25	24	8,477,000,000	1,650	5,760
West Virginia	1,801,625	Gaston Caperton (D)	69	31	26	8	2,352,000,000	1,300	5,790
Wisconsin	4,906,745	Tommy G. Thompson (R)	48	51	16	17	7,389,000,000	1,480	7,000
Wyoming	455,975	Jim Geringer (R)	14	45	10	20	646,000,000	1,390	5,920

*1990 Census (source: U.S. Bureau of the Census).
†As of December 1994 (source: state government officials).
‡1992 figures (source: U.S. Bureau of the Census).
§1993-1994 figures for elementary and secondary students in average daily attendance (source: National Education Association).
#Declared winner by official election results.
**One independent; one rural Alaskan.

††Two independents.
‡‡One vacancy.
§§One independent.
##Two libertarians.
***Four independents.
†††Two independents; one progressive.

the federal crime bill passed in 1994 provides additional funding for states that require violent offenders to serve at least 85 percent of their sentences.

Rhode Island lawmakers established a special "gun court" in Providence to hear cases of gun-law violation. The new court, which opened on September 1, was expected to deal quickly with such cases, avoiding the long wait for a trial in regular criminal court. In New York, lawmakers required police to make arrests in domestic violence cases in an attempt to drive home the seriousness of those crimes.

Tough new drunk driving laws passed in New York and Virginia. And California legislators passed a bill to take away the cars of those caught driving without a license. (See also **Crime: Fighting Crime in America.**)

State health care reform. Congressional gridlock on a federal health care reform package left it up to states to move ahead on their own. But one of the biggest stumbling blocks for states was how to fund expanded health care for their citizens.

After years of planning, Oregon in February began putting into place a comprehensive health care reform plan. With federal government permission, the state limited Medicaid services to 587 medical procedures so that it could afford to expand Medicaid eligibility to some 120,000 low-income, uninsured residents. Florida got federal approval for a managed-care system for Medicaid, allowing the state to subsidize insurance premiums for working low-income Floridians. California voters in November turned down a single-payer initiative for health care.

Several states passed laws establishing tax-free medical savings accounts that encourage citizens to set aside funds for routine medical care. Other legislatures agreed to plans guaranteeing health coverage to all state residents. The difficulty of finding ways to pay for health care slowed efforts to ensure universal health care in Vermont and Florida.

Three states filed lawsuits against tobacco companies to recover taxpayer dollars spent on tobacco-related illnesses under Medicaid and other public health programs. The suits, filed by Florida, Mississippi, and Minnesota, sought to recover expenses for the treatment of lung cancer, emphysema, and heart disease caused by tobacco use.

Welfare reforms. Many states requested federal waivers to make changes in federal-state welfare programs, particularly Aid to Families with Dependent Children (AFDC). Late in 1993, Wisconsin lawmakers resolved to end the state's participation in AFDC by 1999. Other states passed laws requiring aid recipients to work, to keep their children in school, or to obtain health care services for their children. Some states began extending benefits, including health care and child care, to former welfare recipients who took jobs or job training.

Also popular were "family caps," which deny increases in payments to women who conceive a child while on welfare. Such caps on payments were approved by several states following a pioneering law enacted in New Jersey. In addition, several legislatures adopted time limits—typically of two years—on how long people can receive welfare.

California and Pennsylvania sought to curb welfare fraud by fingerprinting welfare recipients, and New York expanded its welfare fingerprinting statewide. (See also **Welfare: Time to Reform Welfare?**)

Adoption laws. Highly publicized fights over the custody of adopted children led to new adoption laws in Michigan and Iowa. When the Illinois Supreme Court in June 1994 nullified the adoption of an Illinois boy known as Baby Richard, Governor Edgar called a special legislative session, which established more clearly the rights of adoptive parents in that state.

Gay rights. The Colorado Supreme Court on October 12 struck down a measure adopted by voters in 1992 that tried to limit constitutional protection for gays and lesbians. The court said the voter initiative, which was never allowed to take effect, violated the state and federal constitutions. The measure sought to overturn local laws that prohibited job and housing discrimination due to a person's sexual orientation.

Education. A survey by the National Conference of State Legislatures released in August 1994 found that states spend the largest portion of their general-fund budgets paying for kindergarten through 12th-grade education. Still, heavy reliance on local property taxes for school funding resulted in unequal spending among school districts in many states. Because of such inequities, courts ruled that school funding systems in Arizona and New Jersey were not constitutional.

In other education news, charter public schools run by parents or teachers were approved in Kansas and Arizona in 1994, bringing the total number of states with such schools to 10. And Georgia designated state lottery proceeds to pay for college educations for the state's high school graduates. Georgia students who have a B average and a family income of $100,000 or less are eligible for free tuition at the state's public four-year colleges and universities.

Taxes and finance. Most states finished the fiscal year ending June 30 with no deficits, and few took major tax actions. However, Michigan voters in March approved a legislative plan to raise the sales tax from 4 cents to 6 cents in return for lowering school property taxes. Another exception was New Jersey, where first-year Republican Governor Christine Todd Whitman and the Republican state legislature laid out a plan to reduce income taxes by 10 percent by January 1995 and 30 percent over Whitman's four-year term. □ Elaine Stuart

In *World Book,* see **State government** and the articles on the individual states.

Stocks and bonds

Stocks and bonds. Good news in the economy at large brought bad news to the world of stocks and bonds in 1994. The United States economy grew more strongly than expected, prompting the Federal Reserve Board to push short-term interest rates up and causing a historic slide in bond prices. In turn, stock prices suffered as the higher interest rates drew investors to money-market funds and bank certificates of deposit. Higher interest rates clouded the outlook for 1995 corporate profits.

These factors produced a disappointing year for stock market investors, but greater damage occurred in the bond market. Bond prices move in the opposite direction of bond yields. The yield on the closely watched 30-year U.S. Treasury bond rose steadily for most of 1994 to 8.16 percent in early November. Bond prices fell by the same proportion. On December 31, the 30-year yield stood at 7.87 percent.

Interest rates on short-term investments soared. The rate on three-month U.S. Treasury bills climbed from 2.99 percent at the end of 1993 to 5.54 percent on December 31. As a result, investors fled from *mutual funds* (publicly sold pools of stocks and bonds) that invested in bonds. By late 1994, even mutual funds with stock investments reported net outflows.

Highs and lows. After a fairly calm trading pattern in 1993, volatility returned to the stock market with a vengeance in 1994. The New York Stock Exchange imposes a limit on certain computer-driven trades whenever the Dow Jones Industrial Average, a composite of the stock prices of 30 major companies, rises or falls by 50 points in a day. That limit was imposed 30 times in 1994, compared with 9 times in 1993. The biggest market slide occurred around Easter, when the Dow lost 302 points in 10 trading days from March 21, 1994, to April 4.

From early July to mid-September, a summer rally took the Dow from 3,646 to 3,954. But the closely watched index never closed at or above the 4,000 mark. On January 31, though, an all-time high for the Dow was posted during the trading day at 4,002.84. The Dow closed at 3,834.44 on December 31, up 2.14 percent for the year. The all-time high for Standard & Poor's 500-Stock Index, a broader measure of the U.S. market, was set on February 2 at 482.00. The S&P 500 Index on December 31 closed at 459.27, down 1.5 percent since the end of 1993.

Winners and losers. Computer-related stocks gained in 1994. Software development leader Microsoft Corporation closed at $61.12 on December 31, up 52 percent for the year. International Business Machines Corporation (IBM) climbed 30 percent for the year to $73.50 on December 31. Despite the strength in technology stocks, prices on the National Association of Securities Dealers Automated Quotation (NASDAQ) system, where many computer-related stocks trade, closed at 751.96 on December 31, down 3.2 percent from the end of 1993. Among the worst-performing sectors was the casino gambling

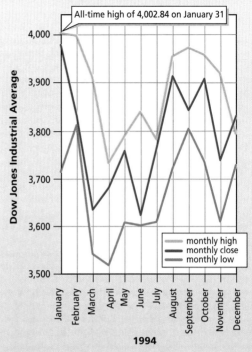

Volatile year on the stock market

All-time high of 4,002.84 on January 31

The Dow Jones Industrial Average rose or fell by 50 points or more 30 days during 1994 in what was a volatile year in the stock market.

industry, which suffered from declining casino patronage. International Game Technology, the leading maker of slot machines, closed on December 31 at $15.75, down 47 percent from 1993 year's end.

International stock markets. The hottest markets in 1994 were in South America. Brazil's Bovespa Stock Index was up nearly tenfold in 1994. The Chile Stock Market general index rose 39 percent in the same period. Emerging capitalist economies and prospects of greater trade, especially with North America, encouraged investment in South America. In Europe, higher interest rates took their toll on stock prices. The London Financial Times-Stock Exchange Index of 100 stocks (FT-SE 100) closed on December 31 at 3,065.5, down 10 percent after a 20 percent gain in 1993. In Canada, the Toronto Stock Exchange's 300-Stock Index closed December 31 at 4,231.61, down 8 percent for 1994.

Japan's fragile coalition government and continued troubles in the nation's banking system caused considerable unease on the Tokyo Stock Exchange. But after a rally in the first half of 1994, the Nikkei Index of 225 major Japanese companies closed on December 31 at 19,723.06, up 13 percent for the year. After more than doubling in 1993, the Hang Seng Index of major companies on the Hong Kong Stock Exchange fell to 8,191.04 on Dec. 31, 1994, down 31 percent for the year.   □ Bill Barnhart

In *World Book,* see **Bond; Investment; Stock.**

392

Streisand, Barbra (1942-), an American singer, actress, director, and producer, made her first on-stage commercial appearance in more than 20 years in a 1994 six-city concert tour. Her opening performances in Las Vegas, Nev., on Dec. 31, 1993, and Jan. 1, 1994, grossed a record $12 million, with tickets running as high as $1,000 apiece. In August, *Barbra: The Concert* became the highest-rated HBO television special, seen in about 5 million homes.

Streisand was born April 24, 1942, in New York City. Her father died when she was a baby and the family struggled. Streisand's career began in 1961 with a nightclub gig that she won in a talent contest. She made her Broadway debut in the musical *I Can Get It for You Wholesale* (1962) and became famous with the musical *Funny Girl* (1964). Streisand's record albums, which reflected a variety of musical styles, became best-sellers and earned many Grammy Awards.

Streisand's first motion picture was *Funny Girl* (1968) for which she won an Academy Award as best actress. She starred in the films *Hello, Dolly!* (1969), *The Way We Were* (1973), *Funny Lady* (1975), *A Star Is Born* (1976), and *Nuts* (1987). In 1983, she cowrote, coproduced, directed, and starred in the musical film *Yentl*. In 1991, she directed, coproduced, and starred in *The Prince of Tides*.

Streisand married actor Elliott Gould in 1963. They later divorced. □ Mary Carvlin

Sudan. Sudanese authorities arrested international terrorist Illich Ramirez Sanchez, known as Carlos the Jackal, on Aug. 14, 1994. He was flown to France the next day to await trial there on charges of murder and kidnapping. The action surprised observers because Sudan had been known to harbor terrorist groups. Some observers speculated that Sudan may have been motivated to improve its image abroad, or France may have offered Sudan satellite intelligence on the movements of southern rebels in exchange for Carlos.

Fighting between Sudan's Muslim-Arab north and its largely non-Muslim, African south, which raged from 1955 to 1972 and then began again in 1983, continued in 1994. In February, Sudan's President Umar Hasan Ahmad al-Bashir launched an offensive against the rebels to end the civil war. His attempt failed, and 100,000 refugees fled to Zaire and Uganda. The fighting halted relief aid to another 2 million people. In addition to more than 1 million war-related deaths since 1983, some 392,000 Sudanese were refugees in other countries, and about 2.5 million were displaced within Sudan.

The war, which cost about $1 million a day, led to rising inflation, a shortage of basic food supplies, and fuel rationing. In 1993, more than 100,000 Sudanese died of malaria. AIDS surpassed malaria as the leading cause of death in 1994. □ Christine Helms

In *World Book*, see **Sudan**.

Supreme Court of the United States.

The Supreme Court of the United States lost its senior member when Associate Justice Harry A. Blackmun, 85, retired at the end of the 1993-1994 term on June 30. Blackmun was appointed to the high court by President Richard M. Nixon in 1970. He is best known for writing a 1973 Supreme Court ruling in *Roe v. Wade* that said states may not prohibit a woman's right to an abortion, except under certain conditions, during the first six months of pregnancy.

As Blackmun's replacement, President Bill Clinton nominated Judge Stephen G. Breyer of Massachusetts. In 1980, President Jimmy Carter appointed Breyer to the U.S. Court of Appeals for the First Circuit in Boston, and Breyer became chief judge of that court in 1990. Before his appointment to that court, Breyer taught at Harvard Law School in Cambridge, Mass., and served as counsel to the Judiciary Committee of the U.S. Senate. Breyer, who is considered a political moderate, has specialized in government regulations and business law. He won Senate confirmation by a vote of 87 to 9 and was formally sworn in on Aug. 12, 1994. (See **Breyer, Stephen G.**)

Abortion rights. On June 30, the Supreme Court ruled that a federal court can create a buffer zone to prevent antiabortion protesters from getting too close to abortion clinics. In a 6-to-3 decision, the court upheld a judge's order that kept demonstrators at least 36 feet (11 meters) away from a Florida abortion clinic. But the justices said larger buffer zones would violate protesters' rights of free speech, guaranteed under the First Amendment to the Constitution of the United States. The June ruling came shortly after President Clinton signed a new federal law making it a crime to block access to abortion clinics or to intimidate clinic patients or employees.

In an earlier ruling, the court voted 9 to 0 on January 24 that abortion-rights groups can sue violent antiabortion protesters for damages under a federal law against *racketeering* (organized criminal acts). The National Organization for Women had sued several antiabortion groups for allegedly conspiring to drive abortion clinics out of business by means of acts of violence. The high court ruling gave lower courts the go-ahead to hear lawsuits contending that such tactics constitute racketeering.

Discrimination. A unanimous 9-to-0 Supreme Court decision on Nov. 9, 1993, made it easier for workers who complain of sexual harassment on the job to win lawsuits. Some lower courts had required workers to show that the harassment had caused "severe psychological injury." The high court said that such evidence was not necessary to prove sexual harassment under the Civil Rights Act of 1964.

On April 19, 1994, the justices ruled that lawyers cannot exclude people from juries solely on the basis of gender. In a 6-to-3 vote, the court overturned the verdict of an all-female Alabama jury that required a man to pay support for a child he fathered. In the

Supreme Court of the United States

Alabama case, the prosecutors had kept nine men off the jury, presumably in the belief that women would be more likely to rule against the father. The April ruling was the latest in a series of court decisions that prevent unfair discrimination against potential jurors, based upon constitutional guarantees of equal protection under the law.

The Supreme Court limited the application of the Civil Rights Act of 1991 in two 8-to-1 votes on April 26. The 1991 law made it possible for workers to collect monetary awards from employers if the workers experienced job discrimination based on their sex, religion, or national origin. In both April rulings, the justices said the Civil Rights Act did not cover the thousands of lawsuits already in the courts when the act took effect on Nov. 21, 1991.

Voting rights. In two rulings on June 30, 1994, the court limited the scope of the Voting Rights Act, a law that bars state and local governments from actions that would limit the voting rights of racial or ethnic minorities. In a case from Florida, the court ruled 7 to 2 that when drawing new voting districts, a state legislature does not have to create the maximum possible number of minority districts. In a Georgia case, the justices voted 5 to 4 that minorities cannot use the Voting Rights Act to challenge the size of city councils and other governing bodies. The court said the act did not require a county to expand its single-member governing commission just so the commission could have minority members.

Free speech. The court unanimously ruled on June 13 that a city may not bar residents from posting signs on their own property. Margaret Gilleo, a resident of Ladue, Mo., had been cited in 1991 for violating a local law that banned all signs on private property except "for sale" and small identification signs. Gilleo had placed an 8-by-11-inch (20-by-28-centimeter) sign in her bedroom window that read, "For Peace in the Gulf." The court's ruling said the law violated residents' free-speech rights under the Constitution. The suburban St. Louis community had passed the law to prevent "visual blight" and to maintain high property values.

In another case protecting speech rights, the court on March 7, 1994, unanimously ruled that comics, musicians, and others who parody copyrighted material do not necessarily violate copyright laws. A lower court had found the rap group 2 Live Crew guilty of copyright infringement when it recorded an off-color parody of the rock song "Oh, Pretty Woman." The justices told the lower court to take another look at the lawsuit filed by the music company holding the copyright.

Religion. On June 27, the court ruled that by creating a special school district for a village of Hasidic Jews, New York state had violated constitutional prohibitions against government preference for a religious doctrine. In a 6-to-3 vote, the justices ruled that the school district amounted to government fa-

Federal Judge Stephen G. Breyer appears before the U.S. Senate in July, before winning confirmation to the Supreme Court by a vote of 87 to 9.

voritism toward one religion. The school district was set up to provide special-education classes for children with disabilities. The state, which is required by law to provide special education, created the district after Hasidic parents expressed fears that their children would be ridiculed for dressing differently and for speaking Yiddish, if they attended public schools.

Criminal law. The court on June 17 said that a state seeking the death penalty in a murder case must inform the jury if a life sentence without parole is an alternative. The 7-to-2 ruling struck down a South Carolina law that prevented jurors from learning that a convicted murderer had no chance of parole. The ruling may help some convicted murderers avoid the death penalty, because jurors sometimes vote for death if they believe a life sentence does not really mean that a convicted murderer will spend a lifetime in prison.

On June 6, the court said states cannot require drug offenders to pay a tax on illegal drugs in addition to criminal fines for drug possession. The court's 5-to-4 ruling in a Montana case said drug-possession taxes, on the books in many states, violate the Constitution's ban on punishing a person twice for the same crime.

Property rights. The court on June 24 made it more difficult for the government to require property developers to set aside part of land under development for public use, such as parks and sidewalks.

An Oregon city council had told the owner of a hardware store she could get permission to build a larger store only if she gave the city land for a bike path and open space by a creek. Voting 5 to 4, the court said the amount of land to be set aside should be based upon the impact the development would have, such as increased traffic.

Garbage disposal. In a 6-to-3 ruling on May 16, the justices said local governments cannot require that all trash generated within their borders be sent to designated plants for recycling. Such requirements had become a common way for local governments to pay for costly recycling plants. The court said the laws interfere with interstate commerce by excluding others from the business of trash collection and waste disposal.

In a 7-2 ruling issued May 2, the court said that the ash created by burning solid waste is hazardous material and cannot be dumped in ordinary landfills. The decision, based on federal environmental law, was important to many communities because, by requiring special landfills, it could make municipal incinerators too expensive to operate.

□ Geoffrey A. Campbell and Linda P. Campbell
See also **Courts.** In *World Book,* see **Supreme Court of the United States.**

Surgery. See Medicine.

Suriname. See Latin America.

Swaziland. See Africa.

Sweden voted to join the European Union (EU) in a national referendum held on Nov. 13, 1994. The vote was 52.2 percent in favor of membership. Sweden joined Austria and Finland in becoming members of the EU, formerly known as the European Community, on Jan. 1, 1995, bringing the total EU membership to 15. Other EU members are Belgium, Denmark, France, Germany, Greece, Ireland, Italy, Luxembourg, the Netherlands, Spain, Portugal, and the United Kingdom. Norway had also considered joining the EU, but a majority of Norwegians voted against membership in a November 28 referendum.

Most politicians in Sweden campaigned in favor of joining the EU, arguing that the country would lose out economically if it remained outside the trade bloc while its neighbors, Norway and Finland, joined. Opponents argued that relatively wealthy Swedish taxpayers would have to subsidize poorer EU members, such as Greece and Portugal, and perhaps eventually Eastern European nations.

Parliamentary elections. Swedish voters returned to power Social Democratic Party Prime Minister Ingvar Carlsson in national elections held September 18. Carlsson, who had been prime minister from 1986 to 1991, succeeded Prime Minister Carl Bildt, leader of the Moderate Party, whose conservative coalition government had ruled since 1991. The Social Democrats jumped to 45 percent of the vote, up 8 percent from the 1991 election, and gained 24 new seats in the 349-seat Riksdag (parliament), for a total of 162. Bildt's coalition won 41 percent of the popular vote and 147 seats, down from 170 seats in the previous parliament.

In part because of its minority status, Carlsson's government adopted policies that could win broad support from parties to its right. He proposed over the next four years a package of tax increases and spending cuts of about $8.5 billion, or about 4 percent of Sweden's gross national product, the total value of goods and services produced by a nation. This was necessary, Carlsson said, because of Sweden's huge public debt, large government deficit, and high interest rates, which were making it difficult for businesses to borrow money and create new jobs. The shift toward creating jobs in the private sector was a major change for Swedes, who since 1960 had seen most of the country's growth in government-controlled companies.

Economic news. Swedish exports grew in 1994 by almost 13 percent from 1993, aided by the 20 percent devaluation since 1992 of the Swedish currency, the krona, against most foreign currencies. The marked devaluation made Swedish products cheaper to buy abroad. The surge in exports helped Sweden's economy grow in 1994 for the first time in three years. □ Philip Revzin
See also **Europe** (Facts in brief table). In *World Book,* see **Europe; European Union; Sweden.**

Swimming. Ten Chinese swimmers tested positive in 1994 for the use of illegal body building drugs. Six of the swimmers were women, confirming the suspicions of many observers that banned substances had contributed to the recent rise of Chinese women to the top of world swimming ranks.

Chinese women dominated the 1994 world championships held from September 5 to 11 in Rome. They won 12 of the 16 gold medals for women and 19 of a possible 29 medals. Although they won 4 gold medals in the 1991 world championships and 4 in the 1992 Olympics, their overwhelming success in Rome led to widespread accusations that the Chinese were using banned drugs.

The Chinese attributed their success to hard training and charged that jealousy and racism had caused the uproar. Furthermore, swimming's international federation said that all 169 drug tests it had administered in Rome were negative. A handful of Chinese swimmers tested positive for illegal drug use during the year, but there had been no evidence of systematic drug use.

But in September, 11 Chinese athletes, 7 of them swimmers, tested positive for steroid use before the Asian Games in Hiroshima, Japan. By the end of the year, 10 Chinese swimmers had been banned for two years from international competition, including the 1996 Summer Olympics. Two female world champions—Lu Bin (200-meter individual medley) and Yang

Australia's Kieren Perkins reacts after breaking his own world records in the 800- and 1,500-meter freestyle events in August.

Aihua (400 meters)—were among those banned.

World championships. The United States, with 4 gold medals, 10 silver and 7 bronze, led in total medals with 21. Next were China with 19 (all by women), Russia with 11, and Australia with 9.

The only Americans to win individual gold medals were Janet Evans of Placentia, Calif., in the women's 800-meter freestyle and Tom Dolan of Arlington, Va., in the men's 400-meter individual medley. Dolan set a world record in 4 minutes 12.30 seconds.

Four women won two individual titles each at Rome—Le Jingyi, He Cihong, and Liu Limin of China, and Samantha Riley of Australia. Three men scored doubles—Kieren Perkins of Australia, Aleksandr Popov of Russia, and Norbert Rosza of Hungary.

Other. During the year, Perkins set world records for the three longest freestyle races—3 minutes 43.80 seconds for 400 meters, 7 minutes 46.00 seconds for 800 meters, and 14 minutes 41.66 seconds for 1,500 meters. The 800 and 1,500 records came in the same race in the Commonwealth Games on August 24 in Victoria, Canada.

Evans, with three national titles in the spring championships and three in the summer championships, raised her career total to 42, only 6 behind Tracy Caulkins' record. Dolan became only the second man to win four titles in the spring championships. Mark Spitz did it in 1971. □ Frank Litsky

In *World Book,* see **Swimming.**

Switzerland. In a national referendum held on Feb. 20, 1994, Swiss voters approved banning truck traffic through the Swiss Alps by the year 2004 and called for all foreign freight to travel by rail through the Alps because it is less damaging to the environment. Switzerland's neighbors protested that the ban would have disastrous economic consequences for them and Switzerland because the quickest route between northern and southern Europe is a road that cuts through the Swiss Alps.

Renewed interest in EU. Swiss politicians and businessmen began efforts in 1994 to revive Switzerland's application to join the European Union (EU), formerly the European Community. This action came after Austria, Finland, and Sweden voted during 1994 to join the EU on Jan. 1, 1995. Swiss advocates of EU membership argued that the country would suffer economically by staying out of the union.

Cult members found dead. Forty-eight members of the Order of the Solar Temple, a religious cult, were found dead in two Swiss villages on October 5. Another 5 people related to the cult were found dead in Canada. Authorities said the people died in what may have been a mass suicide or execution. The leader of the cult, the charismatic Luc Jouret, died along with the others. Authorities have linked the cult to arms trafficking. □ Philip Revzin

See also **Europe** (Facts in brief table). In *World Book,* see **Switzerland.**

Syria. Peace talks between Syria and Israel, which began in October 1991, remained stalemated in 1994. Hopes for peace had been raised by a rare meeting between Syrian President Hafiz al-Asad and United States President Bill Clinton on January 16 after Syria said it would return to the peace table. But Syria refused to define peace terms unless Israel left the Golan Heights, a region on the Syrian-Israeli border captured by Israel in the Six-Day War (1967). Israel, in turn, refused to discuss withdrawal unless Syria first agreed to peace terms. Israel also preferred a phased withdrawal over a period of some years to ensure Syria's commitment to peace, rather than an immediate, one-time withdrawal.

Some observers said Asad's refusal to define peace terms was meant to secure concessions from the United States. Asad had agreed to discuss Syrian human rights issues with the United States, and by February he had also granted exit visas to a remaining 1,000 Jewish Syrians, an issue of U.S. concern.

Another setback to peace talks occurred after a Jewish settler killed 29 Muslim worshipers in the West Bank town of Hebron on February 25. Asad, who did not want to negotiate a separate peace, was further irritated when Jordan and Israel moved swiftly to conclude a peace treaty in July 1994. Syria had been stunned by the 1993 announcement that the Palestine Liberation Organization had been secretly negotiating a declaration of peace in principle with Israel. The Syrian government reacted angrily on May 9 when the United States named Syria as one of seven countries sponsoring terrorism. The listing came a week before U.S. Secretary of State Warren Christopher was due in Damascus, the capital, to try to break the peace impasse. Syria was also on a U.S. list of countries, released April 1, accused of involvement in drug trade. Nations on that list were ineligible for foreign aid without a presidential waiver.

Defense was the largest single item in Syria's $3.4-billion budget, which Asad approved on June 12, 1994. Syria and Russia had signed a military cooperation agreement on April 27. The deal, the first that Russia agreed to since the Soviet Union collapsed in 1991, meant that Russia might begin selling weapons and providing military training to Syria. The former Soviet Union was once Syria's largest arms supplier. Syria's debt to Russia was expected to reach $10 billion by 2010.

Elections for Syria's 250-member People's Assembly began on Aug. 24, 1994. The National Progressive Front, a group of at least six parties led by Asad's own Baath Party, won a majority, as they had in five previous elections. Asad's son Basil, presumed to be Asad's political heir, died in a car crash on January 21.   □ Christine Helms

See also **Middle East** (Facts in brief table). In *World Book*, see **Syria**.

Taiwan. The Justice Ministry tried in 1994 to reform Taiwan's political system. In 1989, opposition to the ruling Kuomintang (KMT) party had become legal, and thereafter, elections had become frequent. But the buying of votes for as much as $190 apiece was common, and a councilor in a county council seeking the speaker's job could pay as much as $113,000 for a fellow member's vote.

The Justice Ministry began a crackdown in March 1994. It indicted 436 local politicians for accepting bribes and got convictions for more than half of them. But the campaign stirred widespread cynicism. The KMT was probably the world's richest non-Communist political party, receiving large sums from corporations in return for favorable laws. The main opposition party, the Democratic Progressive Party (DPP), also had considerable corporate financial support. Politicians all the way up to the national level received payment from construction companies, criminals, and others who wanted official favors.

In local elections, the DPP slowly made gains on the KMT in 1994. Independent candidates also won some offices long held by KMT members. A test of the opposition's strength and the effectiveness of the vote-buying cleanup came in December 3 elections for governor and for mayors and city councilors of the two main cities, Taipei and Kaohsiung. The KMT governor, Sung Chu-yu, was reelected. The DPP captured Taipei, and the KMT won Kaohsiung.

Syrian President Hafiz al-Asad, left, meets with U.S. President Bill Clinton, right, in Geneva, Switzerland, in January to discuss Middle East peace.

Tajikistan

A scandal developed over arms purchases in the aftermath of the murder on Dec. 8, 1993, of the navy's procurement chief, Captain Yin Ching-feng. Authorities believed he was killed because he was about to reveal details of bribery by arms dealers to get weapons contracts from the military. The murder remained unsolved, but the attention brought about investigations into military procurement procedures. On June 2, 1994, the Control Yuan, a branch of the national government, impeached eight generals for wasting weapons money. In October, the Yuan censured the Defense Ministry because more than a dozen officers were involved in the scandal.

Foreign relations. The United States announced expanded contacts with Taiwan on September 7. But it continued to withhold official recognition as a nation separate from China. China continued to claim Taiwan as part of the mainland.

Taiwan and China, which had begun high-level talks in April 1993, reached their first major agreements on Aug. 8, 1994. They agreed on ways to deal with fishing disputes, the repatriation of airplane hijackers from China to Taiwan, and the return of illegal Chinese immigrants in Taiwan. ☐ Henry S. Bradsher

See also **Asia** (Facts in brief table). In *World Book,* see **Taiwan.**

Tajikistan. See **Commonwealth of Independent States.**

Tanzania. See **Africa.**

Taxation. In the wake of the November 1994 midterm elections, which many political analysts saw as an expression of middle-class anger, both the triumphant Republicans and the shaken Democrats began floating proposals for a middle-class tax cut. President Bill Clinton went on national television on December 15 to present his own plan.

Clinton offered a "middle-class bill of rights." His plan would provide a $500 tax credit for every child 12 and under for families making up to $60,000 a year and a declining credit for families making up to $75,000 a year. It would also provide a tax deduction of up to $10,000 a year for college tuition for families earning as much as $120,000 a year.

Republican plans were even more generous, offering tax relief to families with incomes as high as $200,000. Both Democratic and Republican plans promised to balance the tax cuts with spending cuts so as not to increase the budget deficit, but they were short on specifics. The plans would cost up to $20 billion a year.

Avoiding a tax increase. Clinton and Congress avoided any broad-based tax increases in 1994, aware of a possible political backlash in the midterm elections. Clinton, who put through a large income tax increase in his 1993 budget—though only for the top 1.2 percent of taxpayers—proposed only one tax hike in 1994. That was a 75-cent-a-pack increase in cigarette taxes to help finance universal health care.

The growing tax bite

Taxes are the largest single expense for most Americans, far exceeding outlays for food and housing. Taxes averaged $7,927 per person in 1994, up from $6,586 in 1984.

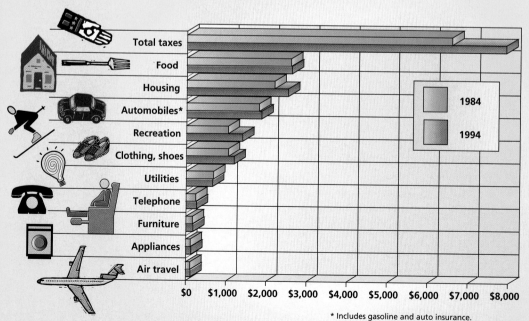

Total taxes
Food
Housing
Automobiles*
Recreation
Clothing, shoes
Utilities
Telephone
Furniture
Appliances
Air travel

1984
1994

$0 $1,000 $2,000 $3,000 $4,000 $5,000 $6,000 $7,000 $8,000

* Includes gasoline and auto insurance.
Sources: Department of Commerce, Tax Foundation.

The cigarette-tax proposal died when Congress was unable to agree on a health bill.

Supreme Court tax rulings. The Supreme Court of the United States made several important rulings in tax cases in 1994. The justices decided unanimously on June 13 that Congress could pass retroactive tax increases, resolving a dispute that had erupted over parts of the 1993 tax law. In another case that generated political controversy, the Supreme Court ruled 7 to 2 on April 4 that states could not impose a higher tax on garbage imported from other states to waste disposal sites. At issue was the commerce clause of the Constitution, which bars states from hindering interstate trade.

The high court on June 20 upheld a California law by which the state had taxed local subsidiaries of multinational corporations. Although the law was in effect repealed in 1993, an adverse ruling by the Supreme Court would have required the state to rebate more than $2 billion in taxes previously collected. In a 5-to-4 decision on June 6, the court declared that a defendant convicted of a narcotics violation cannot then be taxed on the value of the illegal drugs. Twenty-seven states had imposed such a tax.

Estimated revenues. The federal government estimated in 1994 that it would collect $1.353 trillion in taxes and fees in fiscal 1995, which runs from Oct. 1, 1994, to Sept. 30, 1995. ☐ William J. Eaton

In *World Book,* see **Taxation.**

Telecommunications.
The communications landscape became more diverse in 1994 as telephone, cable, and entertainment companies expanded aggressively through mergers and alliances. The lengthy battle for control of Paramount Communications Incorporated came to symbolize the marriage of technologies sought by many companies seeking new markets and financial security. On February 15, Viacom Incorporated won the five-month long battle for Paramount by outbidding QVC Network Incorporated with an offer of about $10 billion. The merger created an entertainment goliath, folding Paramount's film, studio, and publishing resources with Viacom's cable holdings, which include cable channels Music Television and Nickelodeon. Viacom also merged with video king Blockbuster Entertainment Corporation, which added a strong video component to the merger.

Government affairs. Much of the year's merger activity was built on the hope that the U.S. Congress would approve a massive restructuring of telecommunications laws. The proposed reform bill would have allowed phone companies to venture into the cable television business and cable operators to launch telephone services. But competing telephone and cable interests, concerned about the risks of too much competition in a wide open marketplace, could not reconcile their differences. On September 23, the bill was declared dead for the year.

Preparing for the information highway. Visions of a vast information superhighway led to announced mergers linking phone companies with cable operators in 1994. However, a number of the deals fell through. A $33 billion Bell Atlantic Corporation/TeleCommunications Incorporated merger collapsed February 24, shortly after the Federal Communications Commission (FCC) moved to re-regulate cable television rates. A planned $4.9 billion partnership linking Southwestern Bell Corporation with Cox Cable Communications fell apart April 5.

Although the FCC was blamed by some for the cancellation of these deals, others noted that massive mergers may not be the smartest way to build for the evolving and still uncertain technological future. As a result, many companies narrowed the scope of their ventures. Bell Atlantic, the East Coast regional Bell telephone company, sought and won FCC approval on July 19 to offer video programming. On October 31, Bell Atlantic Corporation, Nynex, and Pacific Telesis Group announced the formation of a new media company to deliver home entertainment, information, and interactive services.

On September 19, the purchase of McCaw Cellular Communications, the world's largest wireless service, by AT&T Corp., the world's largest long-distance carrier, spurred moves by other carriers to forge alliances for personal communications services, or PCS's. Sprint Corporation, the third largest long-distance carrier, allied itself with the cable firms TCI, Comcast Corporation, and Cox Enterprises Incorporated. And two East Coast telephone companies, Bell Atlantic and Nynex, merged their cellular units with US West Incorporated and a cellular spin-off of Pacific Telesis, AirTouch Communications Incorporated.

Upheaval in television. Rupert Murdoch's Fox Broadcasting Company shook the network television landscape on May 23 with a $500 million alliance with New World Communications Group Incorporated. The alliance would result in 12 local affiliates of ABC, CBS, and NBC switching their affiliation to Fox, sending a clear message that Murdoch would continue to be an aggressive competitor.

On July 13, a deal that would have merged QVC Network Incorporated, the home shopping network, with CBS collapsed when Comcast submitted a higher bid. The deal gave CBS a foothold in cable TV.

The CBS moves sparked renewed interest in TV networks from entertainment companies looking for a distribution arm for their programming. Walt Disney Company, Time Warner Incorporated, Turner Broadcasting Company, and ITT Corporation each explored buying or merging with NBC. The November 1995 expiration of regulations that had prevented networks from producing, owning, and profiting from syndicated programming, such as situation comedies, was the moving force behind these entertainment companies seeking alliances. ☐ Tim Jones

In *World Book,* see **Cable; Telecommunication.**

Regulating the Information Highway

By Mark Lewyn

A new era in telecommunications raises questions about who will have access to the coming information highway.

Whithin Federal Communications Commission Chairman Reed E. Hundt peers out the windows of his eighth-floor corner office, his view of the Washington, D.C., skyline is spoiled by a jarring sight: Almost every large office building is crowned with antennas resembling white snare drums tilted on their sides. What Hundt is witnessing is a new era in telecommunications, one in which the traditional lines delineating cable, telephone, wireless, and other communications markets are blurring.

The drums that dot the Washington skyline are microwave antennas that businesses use to send phone calls across town and to long-distance carriers. By using the antennas, businesses can bypass the local phone company and the high rates associated with its use.

The antennas were set up by companies that have invaded the lucrative local telephone market, which for years was controlled largely by the seven regional Bell operating companies spun off by AT&T Corp. in 1984. But it is not just the local telephone market that is under attack. Cable television businesses and phone companies are also beginning to invade each other's turf. And cellular phone companies, which operate mobile telephones, are scrambling to protect themselves against new wireless start-ups. Long-distance companies are

■ In the late 1800's, workers began building the infrastructure of the telephone system, *right,* through a network of telephone poles and wires. Because the benefits of telephones were great, the nation wanted to ensure that the service became available to everyone, a concept known as *universal service.* Through inflated rates, businesses helped subsidize the cost of running telephone service to poor and rural customers.

■ A worker lays fiber-optic cable across a remote region of Idaho, *above.* Experts believe much of the information superhighway will operate through fiber-optic cable, *left,* a single strand of which, *left,* can transmit the same amount of information as a bundle of copper wires, right. Congress is considering a new subsidy system to help fund fiber-optic service to the poor and to those living in remote areas.

eyeing new communications markets for the first time as well.

These companies are all anticipating the development of the *information superhighway*, a far-reaching system of computer networks capable of carrying vast amounts of information to homes, workplaces, schools, and government institutions. As currently envisioned, the superhighway will be interactive, offering users the opportunity both to transmit and receive video, voice, and data communications.

In an effort to usher in the new era in telecommunications, the United States Congress in 1994 considered a major revision of the nation's 60-year-old communications law, the Federal Communications Act of 1934. In June 1994, the House of Representatives passed legislation removing barriers that restrict phone companies from offering cable television and vice versa. But a companion measure in the U.S. Senate died in committee, and legislators were expected to take up the issue anew in 1995.

As of 1994, the information superhighway, also known as the National Information Infrastructure, remained more concept than reality. Exactly what information would travel on the highway and how and when it would be delivered had yet to be determined. However, industry analysts believed people would be able to use this highway for a vast array of electronic services and entertainment, including ordering motion pictures in their home through the touch of a button on a remote control device. Through this new network, a child in Boston might be able to play a video game with a cousin in Seattle, or a student might access a tremendous collection of databases and libraries. And home shopping might become internationalized.

Communications experts believe that much of the system will operate through *optical fibers*, hair-thin strands of glass that carry data as pulses of light. Compared with a pair of copper wires, which can carry just one telephone conversation, a pair of optical fibers can handle more than 15,000 conversations at once. Such high-capacity lines will be necessary if the system is to offer extensive interactive services.

Models for the information highway

The concept of a high-capacity electronic network is not altogether new. In the 1980's, the National Science Foundation (NSF) launched the *Internet*, a global web of computer networks that operate over telephone lines. It offers such services as electronic mail (E-mail), video conferencing, and complex information searches through vast libraries of data. By 1994, an estimated 15 million people in 50 countries around the world were users of the Internet.

The Internet is not the only model for the National Information Infrastructure. According to a July 1994 report from the National Governors Association, more than a dozen states have local information highway projects in various stages of development. The governors of these states believe that to attract industry and jobs, they must invest in sophisticated communication networks.

For example, planning for a fiber-optic network in Iowa began in the 1980's during a farm crisis that threatened many rural areas with

■ **The author**
Mark Lewyn is a Washington, D.C., correspondent for *Business Week* magazine.

economic ruin. The electronic network was designed to link all the public schools in the state to the resources of state universities. The hope was that improved school systems and a better-educated work force would attract new industry.

Already some of the benefits of the Iowa network are visible. In April 1994, for example, a group of eighth-graders in Mount Ayr used Iowa's new electronic network to teleconference with James Van Allen, the astrophysicist who discovered Earth's radiation belt, at the University of Iowa in Iowa City, 200 miles (320 kilometers) away. The one-hour interview session cost the school only $10.

Education is not the only use for these networks. The state of North Carolina has linked Central Prison in Raleigh to East Carolina University Medical School in Greenville, more than 100 miles (160 kilometers) away. With this link, doctors at the hospital can remotely monitor a prisoner's heartbeat through a digital stethoscope that a nurse uses at the jail. When the nurse points a video camera into the prisoner's ear, the physician can peer deeply via video into the patient's ear canal. The cost of such consultations is $70, compared with the $750 cost of transporting the prisoner and two guards to Greenville. Since the start of the pilot program in 1990, North Carolina has saved $211,000 on treatment while spending only $100,000 on the network.

Who will build the highway?

Who will provide the data, the software, and the hardware for the coming information superhighway, however, is one of the major questions yet to be answered. A blizzard of mergers, strategic al-

■ **Investing in the future**

Major companies have announced plans to invest billions of dollars over the next 5 to 15 years to construct the information superhighway.

Company	Time commitment (in years)	Investment (in billions)
Ameritech Corp.	15	$33
Bell Atlantic Corp.	5	$11
MCI Communications	6	$20
Pacific Telesis Group	7	$16
Time Warner Inc.	6	$5

Source: Mark Lewyn.

liances, and joint ventures by large and small companies alike in the early 1990's all involved jockeying for position on the superhighway. For example, Microsoft Corp. of Redmond, Wash., one of the world's largest computer software companies, wants to play a leading role in developing the software for the highway. General Instrument Corp. of Chicago, manufacturer of cable and satellite television equipment, wants to supply some of the equipment, such as a cable box that would be attached to a TV and would send and receive electronic data. The AT&T Corp., the largest long-distance carrier in the United States, in September 1994 acquired McCaw Cellular Communications Inc. of Kirkland, Wash., the nation's largest cellular telephone company, so that it might extend its network to include airwaves. Viacom Inc. of Dedham, Mass., the owner of cable channels MTV and Nickelodeon, merged with Paramount Communications Inc. of New York in July 1994, because it wanted to have more programs to pipe through its network of cable systems. The list goes on and on.

Many companies have already announced a monetary commitment to the highway. Over the next 15 years, AT&T will invest as much as $33 billion. Pacific Telesis Group Inc., a regional phone company serving California and Nevada, has set aside $16 billion over the next 7 years. Bell Atlantic Corp., the phone company that serves the Pennsylvania-Virginia area, has committed itself to $11 billion over the next 5 years. During the next 6 years, MCI Communications Corp. of Washington, D.C., the nation's second largest long-distance company, and Time Warner Inc. of New York City, one of the world's largest information and entertainment conglomerates, plan to invest $20 billion and $5 billion, respectively.

The role of the government

The upheaval in communications has raised many perplexing questions. What role, if any, should the government play in building this vast information network? And who should build it: government, industry, or some combination of both? What can be done to ensure that those least able to afford riding on the highway will not be left out in the cold? And how can the government ensure that the information superhighway will be an interactive network with public roads in two directions, rather than a complex jumble of private one-way roads?

■ **Major players shaping telecommunications reform**

While legislators considered a major revision of the nation's communications law in 1994, industry groups sought to protect their own interests as the reform took shape.

- ■ **Congress and the White House** want to allow communications carriers to compete in each other's markets while guaranteeing all citizens fair access to those services.

- ■ **Local phone companies** want the right to offer long-distance and cable television services and to manufacture phone equipment.

- ■ **Long-distance companies** want local phone companies kept out of the long-distance market until they face true competition in their own market first.

- ■ **Cable television companies** want to provide local and long-distance phone services.

- ■ **Computer and software companies** want to play leading roles in developing the software and equipment that will make up the highway.

- ■ **Media and entertainment companies** want to be able to use the superhighway to expand their markets.

Officials of the Administration of President Bill Clinton have agreed that the information superhighway should be built by private companies because these companies have the billions of dollars it will take to build the highway, whereas the government does not. Administration officials and most members of the U.S. Congress also appear to be in agreement that many existing restrictions on phone companies should be scrapped, or at least revised, so that the telephone companies can compete in the new telecommunications era.

Accordingly, work on a new telecommunications law began in early 1994. When the proposed legislation emerged from the House of Representatives, it promised to fling open the gates of competition. The regional Bell companies would be allowed to manufacture phone equipment and provide long-distance telephone and cable television services. Meanwhile, cable television companies would be allowed to provide telephone service, but only in areas where they did not also provide cable TV service. The House did not want one

■ A world of information

The information superhighway will provide people with access to a vast array of electronic services, entertainment, and databases. As currently envisioned, this expansive system of computer networks will offer users the opportunity both to transmit and receive video, voice, and data communications.

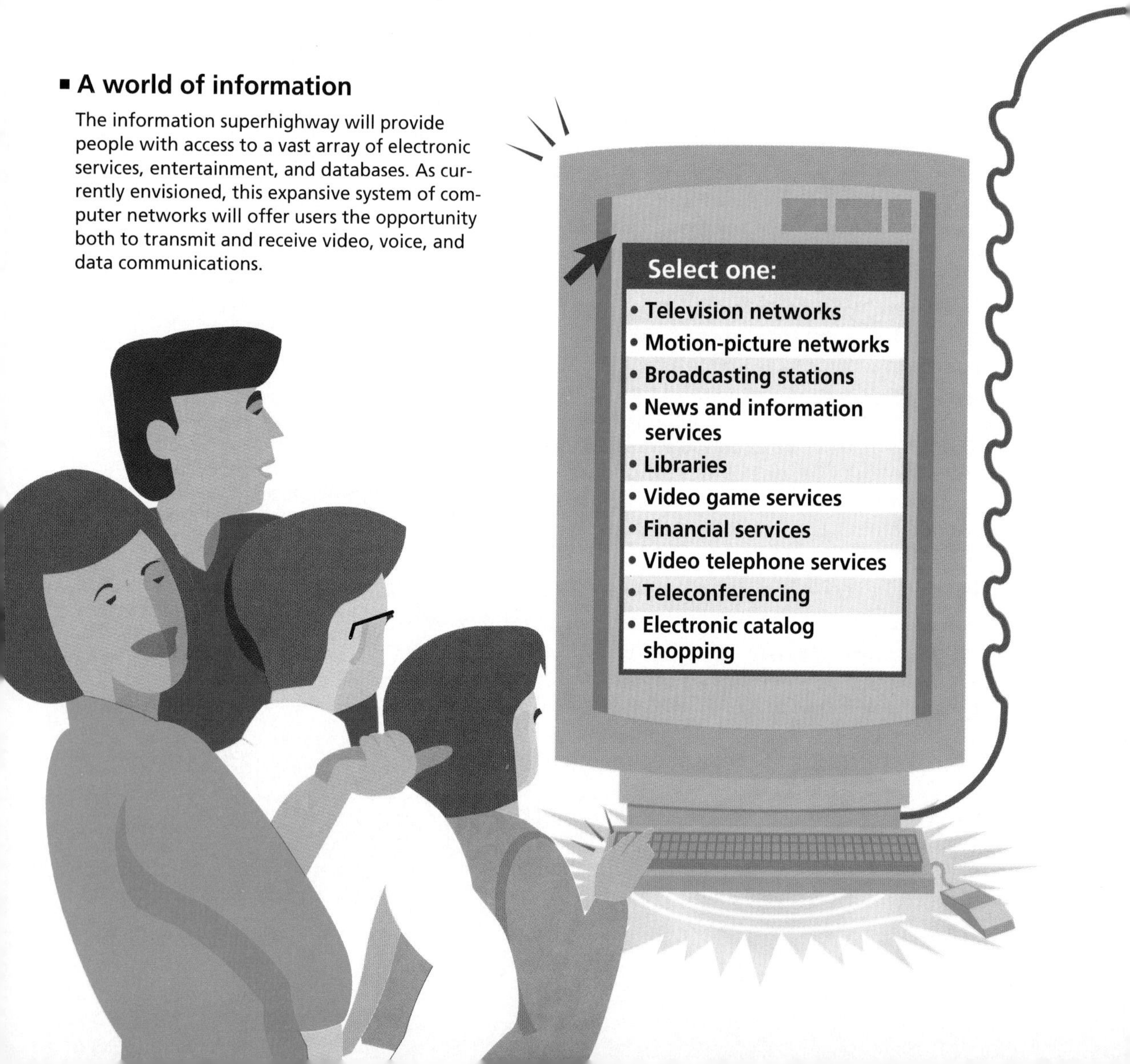

Select one:

- Television networks
- Motion-picture networks
- Broadcasting stations
- News and information services
- Libraries
- Video game services
- Financial services
- Video telephone services
- Teleconferencing
- Electronic catalog shopping

company controlling both the cable and telephone wiring going into a home, thus potentially choking off competition.

The new thinking behind communications law reform represents a fundamental shift away from restrictions of the past. However, the federal government still maintains an interest in regulating the development of the information superhighway so that a number of broad social and economic goals will be upheld. Among these goals are ensuring universal service so that the poor and people living in rural areas are able to link up with the information superhighway; providing open access so that small businesses can compete with large corporations in offering services on the highway; and safeguarding privacy so that electronic transactions are as secure as today's telephone conversations.

Establishing universal service

The first goal, universal service, has been a mainstay of communications regulation since the early days of telephones. FCC Chairman Hundt and others, however, worry that unless there is equal access to the fruits of the communications revolution, some people could be left at an economic disadvantage. Hundt has cited past efforts to ensure universal telephone service, noting that while these efforts have been generally successful, they have not been without problems.

■ Vice President Al Gore, Jr., holds a live interactive news conference with people in the United States and abroad in January on the Internet, a global computer network. It was the first on-line news conference conducted from the White House.

■ Milestones in communications history

Although early federal legislation restricted communications carriers to their own market segments, recent proposals would open up the industry to competition.

■ **1934:** The Federal Communications Act established the Federal Communications Commission (FCC) to centralize the regulation of U.S. interstate and foreign communication by radio, wire, and cable. It restricted individual communications carriers, such as telephone and wireless, from competing in markets outside their own.

■ **1984:** A federal court broke the monopoly of the American Telephone and Telegraph Company (AT&T) after long-standing charges of anticompetitive practices. AT&T was forced to spin off its local telephone companies, creating the seven regional phone companies known as "Baby Bells." This breakup launched the beginning of competition in the long-distance market and helped lower long-distance prices for consumers.

■ **1992:** The Cable Television Consumer Protection and Competition Act regulated cable rates, forced cable companies to pay television networks for their programming, and guaranteed all programmers access to cable lines. Regulations were imposed in response to consumer complaints of sharply rising cable television charges and poor service.

■ **1995?** Proposed communications law reform would allow local phone companies to offer long-distance service, and cable and utility companies, such as power companies, to offer local and long-distance phone service. It would also allow local phone companies to offer cable service and to manufacture electronic equipment. Finally, it would ensure that all citizens have fair access to the information superhighway.

Hundt said that although 97 percent of the nation is currently wired for phone service, the percentage of telephones among the African-American and Hispanic-American minority groups is much lower, only around 85 percent.

As Congress considered new legislation in 1994, many members recognized that a more fundamental change in the concept of universal service was required to reflect new market realities. In the past, the government attempted to ensure universal phone service through a complex series of cross-subsidies. Business customers would pay their local phone company inflated prices for phone service. The inflated prices would then help subsidize the cost of maintaining service to poor and rural customers, typically a money-losing proposition. For example, it costs a lot more to string a single phone wire to a remote rural area, where there are few customers, than it does to a densely populated city like New York, where many customers can use the same line.

The system of cross-subsidies worked well before the 1984 AT&T divestiture and in the era of local phone monopolies. But the monopoly of the local phone service is eroding. New players in telecommunications are becoming providers in local phone business, which generates annual revenues of about $90 billion. For example, Teleport Communications Group in New York City and MFS Telecom Inc. in Oakbrook Terrace, Ill., now offer business customers the ability to bypass the local phone network when they make long-distance calls. Such services are beneficial for customers that can afford them—they can save as much as 40 percent off their telephone bills—but are detrimental to the system of cross-subsidies that has been built over the years. If companies such as Teleport and MFS are allowed to siphon big-spending customers from the local phone monopolies, it will become more difficult for the local phone companies to subsidize poor and rural customers.

To address the universal-service problem, some members of Congress have suggested improving the nation's infrastructure. Improvements could include wiring houses with such high-capacity digital lines as fiber optics. Currently, most homes have only copper wiring, which has much less capacity to send and receive electronic data than fiber-optic lines. The Federal Communications Commission (FCC), the agency that regulates interstate communication, would be mandated to determine just how this could be done. Many communications experts predict that it will not be technically or financially feasible until after the year 2000.

Congress has also suggested implementing a new system of cross-subsidies. Because competition will make it more difficult over time for local phone companies to continue subsidies, every new player in the local phone market would have to pay a portion of its revenues into a pool. The money in the pool, which would be administered by a federal-state board, would go toward paying the cost of basic service for those least able to afford it.

Determining basic service

A major issue yet to be settled, however, is what is meant by *basic service*. In the past, basic service was generally defined as access to a telephone at a fairly low price. That way, if a customer needed to, he or she could, for example, make emergency phone calls to the police or fire department. But in a multimedia world, the definition of basic service becomes much more difficult. Should cellular phone service and interactive TV be considered basic service? Some people say that proposition is ridiculous because it is too expensive and because cellular phones and interactive TV's are not necessities. But others argue that such services will be essential for the poor if they are to compete in an economy in which access to information is critical to success.

Providing open access

In addressing the second goal—open access—some members of Congress seek a so-called "level playing field" so that small businesses can compete with large corporations. Then, anyone who wanted to provide a service on a computer network—a stock-quote service, for example—or to market their goods over someone else's information

■ Key regulatory issues

Some of the key issues of communications law reform that were debated in Congress in 1994 included how to guarantee universal service, open access, and privacy on the proposed information superhighway, and what to include in everyone's basic service.

UNIVERSAL SERVICE

The government wants to guarantee every citizen fair access to the superhighway. To finance this service, each carrier on the highway may be mandated to pay a portion of its revenues to help subsidize services for those least able to afford them.

OPEN ACCESS

To ensure that the superhighway is open to competition, the government may mandate that anyone who wants to provide a service on the information highway can do so by paying the network operator a fair price. The Federal Communications Commission (FCC) will likely be the agency to determine that fair price.

BASIC SERVICE

The information superhighway will offer a tremendous array of multimedia services, including interactive TV and cellular phone services. The FCC will likely determine just what should be included in the basic service package that everyone gets.

PRIVACY

Every transaction on the information highway will leave an electronic record. If such records are easily available, anyone could use the information for their own purposes. Congress is searching for an electronic means of protecting privacy without interfering with law-enforcement efforts.

network would be able to do so by paying the network operator a fair price. Under this proposal, the FCC would determine what that fair price is. The FCC would also require that all service providers have compatible equipment where two networks intersect so that the superhighway is a true two-way highway.

Ensuring privacy

Finally, safeguarding privacy was a goal that was debated in 1994 but without resolution. Communications experts say every transaction on the highway will leave an electronic trail. By monitoring those transactions, businesses, the government, and others could collect massive amounts of information on a person's habits, tastes, and activities. To protect the privacy of individuals, some industry analysts say people should have the right to send coded transmissions. However, such a system would make it difficult for law-enforcement agencies to carry out wiretaps on suspected criminals.

The Clinton Administration has advocated use of the so-called "Clipper Chip." This device, installed in telecommunications equipment, would let the federal government eavesdrop on electronic communications once a court order for a wiretap was secured. The Clipper Chip, however, has run into strong opposition from the American Civil Liberties Union and other privacy advocates, who fear that the government might abuse such power.

Congress's failure to reform telecommunications law in 1994 left most of these issues unresolved. The nation's communications laws have not been fundamentally changed since 1934. The opportunity and the risks are great. What the federal government does ultimately will not only shape the information superhighway but will also likely have an enormous impact on the U.S. economy through the year 2000 and beyond. ■ ■ ■

For further reading:

Antonoff, Michael, and others. "The Complete Survival Guide to the Information Superhighway." *Popular Science,* May 1994, pp. 97-126.

Auletta, Ken. "Under the Wire." *The New Yorker,* Jan. 17, 1994, pp. 49-53.

Bogart, Leo. "Shaping a New Media Policy." *The Nation,* July 12, 1993, pp. 57-60.

Gore, Al. "Infrastructure for the Global Village." *Scientific American,* September 1991, pp. 150-153.

Schiller, Herbert I. "Public Way or Private Road?" *The Nation,* July 12, 1993, pp. 64-66.

Television

Television. In February, record numbers of viewers tuned in to the Winter Olympics, which were broadcast from Lillehammer, Norway, by CBS Inc. and Turner Network Television (TNT). Viewers were particularly interested in the rivalry between United States figure-skaters Nancy Kerrigan and Tonya Harding. Kerrigan had been clubbed above the knee on January 6 by an associate of Harding's ex-husband. Kerrigan nevertheless took a silver medal in women's figure skating, while Harding received relatively low marks.

The American TV audience cheered speed-skater Dan Jansen, who won a gold medal and set a world record in winning the 1,000-meter race in 1 minute 12.43 seconds. They also witnessed the gold and silver medal-winning performances of the U.S. ski team.

Cut to the chase. On June 17, regular programming was interrupted on CBS Inc., the American Broadcasting Companies (ABC), the National Broadcasting Company (NBC), and Cable News Network (CNN) to show the flight of football player-turned-actor O. J. Simpson. Simpson was wanted by Los Angeles police on suspicion of murdering his second ex-wife Nicole Brown Simpson and her friend Ronald Goldman. Instead of surrendering to the authorities as agreed, Simpson and a friend drove for hours along a California freeway, followed by police cars and TV vans. The chase ended peacefully at Simpson's Los Angeles home, where he surrendered to police.

The coverage did not end with the chase. During the summer, the massive attention paid to the Simpson case by print and electronic media led to concern that Simpson would be unable to receive a fair trial. But the media blitz continued when jury selection began in October, with daily reporting by networks and gavel-to-gavel coverage by cable channel Court TV.

Detour for information superhighway. There was drama behind the scenes as well as on the screens for communications companies. In late February, the merger of Bell Atlantic Corporation and TeleCommunications Incorporated (TCI) was called off. The deal had been seen as heralding the arrival of the information superhighway, which would combine video, telephone, cable, and computer technologies to provide TV viewers with new channels, databanks, and services. The merger collapsed shortly after the Federal Communications Commission (FCC) announced rules on February 22 to reduce cable TV prices by an average of 7 percent. Bell Atlantic, which had offered $22 billion for TCI, believed the cable company's cash flow would be drastically cut by the price rollbacks.

Shopping for channels. Merger news also surrounded the networks. In July, five months after it lost a bid to buy Paramount Communications, the home shopping cable channel company QVC agreed

In May, the Fox Broadcasting Company announced that 12 television stations, located in some of the nation's largest markets, had switched to Fox.

TV stations moving to the Fox network	Networks TV stations are moving from	National market rank
KDFW Dallas	CBS	8
WJBK Detroit	CBS	9
WJW Cleveland	CBS	13
WTVT Tampa, Fla.	CBS	15
WAGA Atlanta	CBS	10
KSAZ Phoenix	CBS	19
KTVI St. Louis, Mo.	ABC	20
WITI Milwaukee	CBS	29
WDAF Kansas City, Mo.	NBC	31
WGHP High Point, N.C.	ABC	48
WBRC Birmingham, Ala.	ABC	51
KTBC Austin, Tex.	CBS	65

Source: Nielsen Media Research.

to be acquired by CBS. But the new, combined cable-and-broadcast-TV corporation never materialized. Angered by the $7-billion deal, a rival group composed of Liberty Media and Comcast Corporation, the nation's third largest cable company and a minority shareholder in QVC, began bidding for QVC. The group's offer of $46 per share, higher than CBS's $38 per share bid, was accepted by the QVC board in August.

NBC for sale? In the fall, rumors began circulating that General Electric Corporation was putting up NBC for sale. Walt Disney Inc., Time Warner, and Turner Broadcasting were among companies expected to join in the bidding for a stake in the network.

Network gains. In business terms, the three major networks (ABC, NBC, and CBS), once rumored to be near extinction, proved surprisingly healthy. After five years of losing viewers to cable, the networks' combined audience share rose slightly, to about 61 percent of the prime-time market. Advertising revenues exceeded $4 billion, a record high. Regulatory changes by the FCC and federal courts also allowed the networks to be the sole producers of their programs. More than one-third of the "Big Three's" fall season consisted of shows owned or co-owned by ABC, NBC, and CBS. The number of cable subscribers, meanwhile, had flattened out.

Fox proves feisty. The networks faced competition in the form of the increasingly aggressive Fox Broadcasting Company, which hopes to become the fourth major network. In December 1993, Fox owner Rupert Murdoch had announced that a bid of $1.6 billion had bought Fox the broadcast rights to National Football League games, which for 38 years had been a Sunday afternoon staple on CBS. In late May 1994, he persuaded 12 television stations around the country to switch from network affiliation to Fox affiliation by investing $500 million in their parent company, New World Communications Group Inc. Overall, Fox gained 50 new stations in 1994, bringing its total to 188 affiliates.

New network? A potential fifth network, called United Paramount, announced plans to begin broadcasting in January 1995. Its president, Lucie Salhany, was formerly president of Fox Broadcasting's television division. United Paramount will aim for the same 18- to 34-year-old audience that Fox targets.

Cable debuts, complaints. Although cable system operators complained that the regulatory atmosphere lessened their ability to offer new programming, several new cable channels did debut in 1994. Fox launched fx, which featured reruns, talk shows, and service shows. NBC offered America's Talking, consisting entirely of talk shows. Turner Broadcasting introduced Turner Classic Movies, showing vintage films from the golden days of MGM and Warner Brothers.

Heeding the cable industry's complaints, the FCC in October began studying proposals to give compa-

nies more flexibility in setting rates by letting them establish new packages of programming that would be exempt from any price regulation.

More home shopping. Although QVC failed to complete any of its attempted mergers, its bids attracted attention to the growing world of shopping via cable TV. QVC, run by Chief Executive Officer Barry Diller, sold $1 billion of merchandise ranging from costume jewelry to designer sportswear. QVC launched a second, more upscale channel called Q2 in New York City in the summer. QVC's archrival, Home Shopping Network, also launched a second channel, devoted to specialty store goods.

Two new shopping networks, TV Macy's and Catalog 1, debuted in the autumn. Catalog 1 featured expensive merchandise from catalogue companies such as The Sharper Image, Williams-Sonoma, and the Nature Company.

A mix of miniseries. A variety of miniseries were shown throughout the year. The six-part *Middlemarch*, an intelligent costume drama from British television, revived interest in the 19th-century novel by George Eliot when it aired on PBS stations in April and May. *The Stand* was a four-part adaptation of a long but more contemporary work—a 1,000-page novel by Stephen King. Airing on ABC the week of May 15, its story of a deadly virus that escapes from a government laboratory was eerily echoed in real life. In September, a Yale University

Top-rated U.S. television series

The following were the most-watched television series for the 31-week regular season—Sept. 20, 1993, through April 17, 1994—as determined by Nielsen Media Research.

1. "Home Improvement" (ABC)
2. "60 Minutes" (CBS)
3. "Seinfeld" (NBC)
4. "Roseanne" (ABC)
5. "These Friends of Mine" (ABC)
6. "Grace Under Fire" (ABC)
7. "Frasier" (NBC)
8. "Coach" (ABC)
9. "Murder, She Wrote" (CBS)
10. "NFL Monday Night Football" (ABC)
11. "Murphy Brown" (CBS)
12. "CBS Sunday Movie" (CBS)
13. "Thunder Alley" (ABC)
14. "20/20" (ABC)
15. "Love & War" (CBS)
16. "Northern Exposure" (CBS)
17. "Wings" (NBC)
18. (tie) "Full House" (ABC)
        "Primetime Live" (ABC)
20. "Dave's World" (CBS)
21. (tie) "Dr. Quinn, Medicine Woman" (CBS)
        "NYPD Blue" (ABC)
        "Rescue: 911" (CBS)
24. "Turning Point" (ABC)
25. "Fresh Prince of Bel Air" (NBC)

Emmy Award winners in 1994

Comedy
Best Series: "Frasier"
Lead Actress: Candice Bergen, "Murphy Brown"
Lead Actor: Kelsey Grammer, "Frasier"
Supporting Actress: Laurie Metcalf, "Roseanne"
Supporting Actor: Michael Richards, "Seinfeld"

Drama
Best Series: "Picket Fences"
Lead Actress: Sela Ward, "Sisters"
Lead Actor: Dennis Franz, "NYPD Blue"
Supporting Actress: Leigh Taylor-Young, "Picket Fences"
Supporting Actor: Fyvush Finkel, "Picket Fences"

Other awards
Drama or Comedy Miniseries or Special: *Mystery: Prime Suspect 3*
Variety, Music, or Comedy Series: "Late Show with David Letterman"
Made for Television Movie: *And the Band Played On*
Lead Actress in a Miniseries or Special: Kirstie Alley, *David's Mother*
Lead Actor in a Miniseries or Special: Hume Cronyn, *Hallmark Hall of Fame: To Dance with the White Dog*
Supporting Actress in a Miniseries or Special: Cicely Tyson, *Oldest Living Confederate Widow Tells All, Parts One and Two*
Supporting Actor in a Miniseries or Special: Michael Goorjian, *David's Mother*

School of Medicine researcher in New Haven, Conn., was infected by a mysterious Brazilian virus while conducting lab experiments with it.

In August, the Discovery Channel aired a five-part British series examining Watergate, the scandal that led to the late Richard Nixon's resignation from the U.S. presidency. Baseball fans, deprived of their season by the players' strike, took some consolation in watching *Baseball,* presented on public TV in nine two-hour "innings" from September 18 through September 28. This leisurely history of the game was directed and written by Ken Burns, the creator of a highly popular documentary on the American Civil War four years earlier.

Fresh shows. Among the new programs for the fall 1994-1995 season, one early critical success was ABC's "My So-Called Life." Developed by the creators of the long-running "thirtysomething," it focused on the adolescent angst of a 15-year-old girl.

Two medical shows went scalpel to scalpel in the same time slot on Thursday nights: "ER" on NBC and "Chicago Hope" on CBS. "Chicago Hope" had better-known stars, including E. G. Marshall and Mandy Patinkin. But "ER," done in the psuedodocumentary style of the mid-1980's doctor show "St Elsewhere," was the early winner in the ratings war. □ Troy Segal

See also **Telecommunications.** In *World Book,* see **Television.**

Tennessee. See State government.

Tennis. Pete Sampras of the United States and Arantxa Sánchez Vicario of Spain won two titles each in 1994 grand-slam tournaments. The separate men's and women's tours were more lucrative than ever, with the men's purses reaching $58.6 million and the women's $35 million.

Young stars. However, the continuing off-court problems of young female stars tarnished some of the sport's successes. Among the young stars who had difficulties in 1994 were 20-year-old Monica Seles and 18-year-old Jennifer Capriati.

Seles, born in Yugoslavia and raised in the United States, was the dominant women's player until April 1993, when she was stabbed in the back during a match by a fanatic follower of Steffi Graf, the German star. Seles was said to be physically fit, but she did not compete in 1994.

Capriati, an American, turned pro at age 13 and became an instant millionaire through endorsements. She had not played in a tournament since August 1993. On May 16, 1994, she was arrested in Coral Gables, Fla., on a misdemeanor charge of possessing marijuana. She entered a drug-rehabilitation program and later began a comeback.

The Women's Tennis Association was troubled by these problems and by the burnout in recent years of such teen-age stars as Capriati, Tracy Austin, and Andrea Jaeger. It introduced a new eligibility rule to discourage 14- and 15-year-olds from turning professional and to limit the number of tournaments they could play. Before the rule took effect in January 1995, two 14-year-old prodigies turned pro—Martina Hingis, a Czech-born resident of Switzerland, and Venus Williams, an American.

Grand slam. The four grand-slam tournaments were the Australian Open on hard courts ending Jan. 30, 1994, in Melbourne, the French Open on clay ending June 4 in Paris, the Wimbledon championships on grass ending July 3 in Wimbledon, England, and the United States Open on hard courts ending September 11 in Flushing Meadow, N.Y.

Graf defeated Sánchez Vicario, 6-0, 6-2, in the Australian women's final for her fourth consecutive grand-slam title. Sánchez Vicario beat Mary Pierce by 6-4, 6-4 in the French final and Graf by 1-6, 7-6, 6-4 in the U.S. Open final. Graf lost to Pierce in the French semifinals and Lori McNeil in the first round at Wimbledon, the first defender in Wimbledon's 108-year history to be eliminated in the first round. Conchita Martinez of Spain won the Wimbledon final from Martina Navratilova of the United States, 6-4, 3-6, 6-3.

Sampras beat fellow American Todd Martin in the Australian men's final, 7-6, 6-4, 6-4. At Wimbledon, Sampras defeated Goran Ivanisevic of Croatia, 7-6, 7-6, 6-0, for the title. But slowed by tendinitis in his left ankle, Sampras lost in the fourth round of the French and U.S. Opens. He had won four of the five slam titles before his defeat in the U.S. Open.

In the U.S. Open final, Andre Agassi, a 24-year-old American, defeated Michael Stich of Germany, 6-1, 7-6, 7-5. Agassi became the first unseeded player in the 114-year history of the United States championship to win the title. In the all-Spanish final of the French Open, Sergi Bruguera defeated Alberto Berasategui, 6-3, 7-5, 2-6, 6-1.

International. In the Davis Cup competition for men, the United States eliminated India, 5-0, and the Netherlands, 3-2. Then Sweden beat the Americans, 3-2, in the semifinals from September 23 to 25 in Göteborg, Sweden. In the final December 2 to 4 in Moscow, Sweden defeated Russia, 4-1. Spain won the Federation Cup for women by defeating the United States, 3-0, on July 24 in Frankfurt, Germany.

Navratilova, Lendl retire. Navratilova, 38, regarded by many as the best woman ever to play the game, retired on November 15. She had won 167 titles, including 18 grand slam titles, in her 21-year career. Ivan Lendl, 34, retired on December 20, citing back problems. He was ranked number one in the world for a record 270 total weeks from 1983 to 1990 and won eight grand slam titles.

Death of Gerulaitis. Former tennis star Vitas Gerulaitis, 40, died of accidental carbon monoxide poisoning on September 18 in Southampton, N.Y. His highest ranking was number four in the world in 1984. □ Frank Litsky

In *World Book,* see **Tennis.**

Pete Sampras of the United States reaches for a volley during his Wimbledon singles title win over Goran Ivanisevic of Croatia in July.

Thailand. Scandals involving drugs and stolen gems flared during 1994. First, on May 10, United States officials said Thanong Siripreechapong, a member of the main opposition party, Chat Thai, had been indicted in 1991 in California on charges of smuggling tons of marijuana into the United States from 1973 to 1987. He denied the charge, but resigned from parliament. Then, on July 1, 1994, it was reported that the deputy leader of Chat Thai, Watthana Atsawahem, had been denied a U.S. visa for similar reasons. In addition, Foreign Minister Prasong Soonsiri said that U.S. officials had reportedly identified at least 17 current and past members of opposition parties in parliament as drug traffickers.

The Chat Thai charged that Prasong's allegations were made for political purposes. The government had wanted to make the Constitution more democratic, mainly by reducing the power of the armed forces to appoint members of parliament's upper house. The upper house had frequently obstructed government-sponsored legislation. But the military and opposition groups defeated the government's efforts at constitutional reform and by so doing raised the possibility that the government might have to resign and call new elections. The drug trafficking revelations discredited the opposition and postponed the necessity of new elections.

A second scandal involved more than $20 million worth of jewels stolen in 1989 from a prince's palace in Saudi Arabia by a Thai servant, who fled back to Thailand, where he was imprisoned. Thai police recovered the gems in 1990, but Saudi diplomats claimed, when the collection was returned, that most of the gems were fake and more than 80 percent of the jewelry was still missing. The Saudis accused Thai police of keeping the gems.

At least eight unsolved murders, including those of three Saudi diplomats and the wife and son of a Thai jeweler, were believed to be connected to the case. Two Thai police generals were dismissed, and 16 other police officers also were implicated. In November 1994, Thai police said some of the gems had been returned anonymously in response to a televised appeal. But the case continued to strain Saudi-Thai relations.

Cambodian connections. Thailand angrily denied various reports that some of its generals and businessmen were still helping the radical Communist Khmer Rouge (KR) in Cambodia. In the 1980's, Thailand and China had aided the KR in its attempts to prevent Vietnam from overrunning Cambodia. In 1994, the KR was leading a revolt in Cambodia. The reports said the KR was sending timber and gems to Thailand in return for arms and other supplies.

The economy grew about 8 percent in 1994, one of the world's higher rates. Most of the growth centered around Bangkok. □ Henry S. Bradsher

See also **AIDS: The Changing Face of AIDS; Asia** (Facts in brief table). In *World Book,* see **Thailand.**

A revival of *Carousel* (1945) opens at the Vivian Beaumont Theater at Lincoln Center in New York City in March for what appeared to be a long run.

Theater. The American theater could no longer deny in 1994 that the curtain was being forcibly rung down on live drama, due in part to the high cost of mounting new productions and the public's apparent preference for electronic entertainment.

Broadway. "You know Broadway is dead as a showcase for American drama," wrote theater critic Frank Rich in *The New York Times* in October, "when (a) there are no new plays running there; (b) Neil Simon announces he would rather be in Greenwich Village; (c) New York's Attorney General is closing in on its box offices, or (d) the theater industry's leaders are fighting in public, like passengers on the *Titanic* shoving each other out of the lifeboats. The answer is, (e) all of the above."

No less a figure than Arthur Miller, one of the best-known and most revered living American playwrights, found Broadway hostile to his new work. Miller's *Broken Glass*—a courageous study of a Jewish American's denial of his heritage—closed on June 26 after only 73 performances. Another influential American playwright, Sam Shepard, watched as funding for his new Broadway work *Simpatico* fell apart. The show reopened on November 13 at the Joseph Papp Public Theater in Greenwich Village—a nonprofit off-Broadway house.

One compelling example of plays as an endangered species on Broadway was the mighty $2.2-million *Angels in America,* Tony Kushner's two-play epic subtitled *A Gay Fantasia on National Themes.* Having won the 1993 Tony Award for its first part, *Millennium Approaches,* Kushner picked up the 1994 Tony for the second, *Perestroika.* But, Rich wrote, "*Angels in America* was scheduled to close in early 1995 without recouping its investment." *Angels in America* actually closed on Dec. 4, 1994.

Following a limited run of the British import *Medea* with Diana Rigg, there were only two other nonmusicals on Broadway at year's end: the Tony-winning *An Inspector Calls* (1945) and a revival of Tennessee Williams' *The Glass Menagerie* (1945) with Julie Harris playing Amanda Wingfield. The Williams play was staged by artistic director Todd Haimes's nonprofit Roundabout Theatre Company. *An Inspector Calls,* a British import, revived J. B. Priestley's indictment of an upper-class English family's callous devastation of a working woman. The success of *An Inspector Calls* was attributable to Stephen Daldry's enlightened direction and to the production's rain-soaked surreal set by Ian MacNeil.

Musicals. In February, multimillion-dollar revivals of *Damn Yankees* (1955) and *Carousel* (1945) settled in for what looked to be runs of a year or more. The next month, Disney's stage version of *Beauty and the Beast* joined the pack, only to be largely snubbed by Tony voters who saw it as an invasion by Hollywood money of cash-strapped legitimate theater.

In April, *The Best Little Whorehouse Goes Public* started previews but closed after only 15 performances. *Cyrano* closed after only 137 performances. (By comparison, in the 1960's *Hello, Dolly!* racked up 2,844 performances and *Fiddler on the Roof* 3,242 performances.) A lavish revival of Andrew Lloyd Webber's *Joseph and the Amazing Technicolor Dreamcoat* (1968) survived only 231 performances and the Richard Chamberlain revival of *My Fair Lady* (1956) went down after just 165 performances.

Grease (1972) joined Broadway's revivals and extended its run by adding Brooke Shields to the cast in November. Only *Passion,* Stephen Sondheim's dark work about an ugly woman's obsession with a handsome young man, survived as a new musical on Broadway.

Broadway had only two major openings as 1994 drew to a close. *Show Boat,* a sumptuous revival of the 1927 "Old Man River" musical, came to Broadway in Harold Prince's staging. Lloyd Webber's *Sunset Boulevard,* based on the 1950 Billy Wilder film classic, made its opulent Broadway debut with Glenn Close in the lead.

The two megamusicals arrived freighted with controversy. Producer Garth Drabinsky's *Show Boat* cost more than $10 million to stage, brought Broadway its highest ticket price yet ($75 per seat), and spent $1.5 million on advertising alone, only to draw protests to its pre-Broadway mounting in Toronto, Canada, from African Americans who felt its depiction of blacks on the Mississippi River in the 1800's needed no revival. *Sunset Boulevard* might have been retitled "Diva Drive" when Patti LuPone, who premiered the show in London, signed a contract to play on Broadway but was dumped by Lloyd Webber. Close, who opened the show in Los Angeles and was an instant hit, received the Broadway role. Close was to be replaced in Los Angeles by Faye Dunaway, but Lloyd Webber decided that Dunaway's singing was inadequate and closed the production.

Touring theater. The national touring circuit of professional shows continued to be the one aggressively growing segment of theater. The League of American Theatres and Producers reported gross ticket sales of $621 million in 1993, up from $503-million in 1992 and $450 million in 1991.

Regional theater. If Broadway was too expensive a risk for new plays, the logical shelter was the nation's highly touted $349-million regional theater circuit of some 300 professional nonprofit theaters. But Theatre Communications Group (TCG), the national organization of the regional theaters, had only unhappy news to report from its annual survey.

The survey indicated that while TCG's sample 67 theaters ranged in budget from $53,000 to $12 million and played to more than 16.5 million people some 45,000 performances of 2,300 productions in the 1992-1993 season, many of those theaters were not making ends meet. The theaters' aggregate

Tony Award winners in 1994

Best Play, *Angels in America: Perestroika,* Tony Kushner.
Best Musical, *Passion.*
Best Play Revival, *An Inspector Calls.*
Best Musical Revival, *Carousel.*
Leading Actor in a Play, Stephen Spinella, *Angels in America: Perestroika.*
Leading Actress in a Play, Diana Rigg, *Medea.*
Leading Actor in a Musical, Boyd Gaines, *She Loves Me.*
Leading Actress in a Musical, Donna Murphy, *Passion.*
Featured Actor in a Play, Jeffrey Wright, *Angels in America: Perestroika.*
Featured Actress in a Play, Jane Adams, *An Inspector Calls.*
Featured Actor in a Musical, Jarrod Emick, *Damn Yankees.*
Featured Actress in a Musical, Audra Ann McDonald, *Carousel.*
Direction of a Play, Stephen Daldry, *An Inspector Calls.*
Direction of a Musical, Nicholas Hytner, *Carousel.*
Book of a Musical, James Lapine, *Passion.*
Original Musical Score, Stephen Sondheim, *Passion.*
Scenic Design, Bob Crowley, *Carousel.*
Costume Design, Ann Hould-Ward, *Beauty and the Beast.*
Lighting, Rick Fisher, *An Inspector Calls.*
Choreography, Sir Kenneth MacMillan, *Carousel.*
Regional Theater, McCarter Theater, Princeton, N.J.

deficit increased 14 percent over the previous year. In five years, the theaters went from an aggregate budget surplus of $1.2 million to a combined deficit of more than $5 million.

Federal grants dropped 8 percent in one year, and local grants dropped 13 percent. Chicago's Body Politic Theatre closed, as did Theater Factory Saint Louis in Missouri, Players Theatre Columbus in Ohio, Fairfield County Stage Company in Connecticut, and the New Mexico Repertory Theatre in Santa Fe.

Most alarming was the news that new-play development had declined 65.7 percent since 1989. Two major centers for new plays continued: the Actors Theatre of Louisville's (Ky.) Humana Festival of New American Plays and the Eugene O'Neill Theater Center's National Playwrights Conference in Waterford, Conn. Most regional theaters turned to revivals of classics and tried-and-true light comedy in a bid to attract as many ticket buyers as possible.

One penetrating response to the take-over of the public's fancy by electronic entertainment was Anne Bogart's treatment of the writings of media commentator Marshall McLuhan. Titled *The Medium,* the movement-theater work explored the rush to television, film, virtual reality, home-computer on-line entertainment, and CD-ROM. *The Medium* was born in Bogart's Saratoga International Theater Institute at Skidmore College. In January 1995, it would be staged at Actors Theatre of Louisville.

For some regional theaters, the only salvation was sending a show to Broadway to earn some commercial revenue. The *Damn Yankees* revival, for example, came from San Diego's Old Globe Theatre.

Off-Broadway proved the country's most supportive ground for new American theater. Anna Deavere Smith's journalistic theater was a greatly praised success when her *Twilight: Los Angeles, 1992* premiered at the off-Broadway Public Theater. When it moved to the Broadway district's Cort Theatre, it closed after only 72 performances.

Off-Broadway continued to shelter some of the nation's most gifted younger playwrights. Circle Rep mounted a rewritten version of Craig Lucas' play with music, *Three Postcards.* Manhattan Theatre Club premiered Terrence McNally's *Love! Valour! Compassion!* Wendy Wasserstein's *Uncommon Women and Others* was revived at the Lucille Lortell Theatre, and the 1994 Pulitzer Prize-winning play, Edward Albee's *Three Tall Women,* settled into a long run at the Promenade Theatre. Under artistic director Andre Bishop, Lincoln Center Theatre's Mitzi E. Newhouse Theatre became a site of adventurous programming with new plays, including *SubUrbia* by Eric Bogosian; *The Lights* by Howard Korder; and *Hello Again,* a new treatment by Michael John LaChiusa. □ Porter Anderson

In *World Book,* see **Theater.**

Togo. See Africa.

Toronto. In the biggest surprise of 1994 municipal elections, Councillor Barbara Hall was elected mayor of Toronto, defeating incumbent June Rowlands. Hall became just the second member of the socialist New Democratic Party to head the city. William Dennison, elected in 1969, was the first.

The Nov. 14, 1994, elections also brought new mayors to three other municipalities of Metropolitan Toronto. Councillor Frances Nunziata was elected mayor of York after a hard fought campaign against political veteran Fergy Brown, the incumbent. The voters of Scarborough chose Frank Faubert to replace retiring Mayor Joyce Trimmer. And Councillor Doug Holyday unseated Bruce Sinclair to become mayor of Etobicoke.

Through a referendum on the November ballot, 58 percent of Toronto city voters indicated that they would abolish the Metropolitan federation, the system of government that has linked Toronto and its suburbs since 1954. The referendum carried no legal weight, however, because the government of Ontario controls the status of its municipalities.

The Raptors are coming! An agreement between the National Basketball Association (NBA) and the Ontario government in 1994 cleared a final path for professional basketball in Toronto. The news gave some comfort to Toronto fans discouraged during the year by major league baseball and National Hockey League strikes. Labor disputes suspended play of their two-time World Series champion Blue Jays and recently successful Maple Leafs.

The NBA had awarded a franchise to a group of Toronto businessmen in November 1993, but the NBA, according to its official policy, insisted that Ontario withdraw basketball betting from its sports lottery. Ontario officials argued that such a move would cost millions of dollars in tax revenues. In February, however, the province agreed to lift basketball betting from the lottery in exchange for substantial donations from the NBA to local charities.

Based on a public contest held in May, the owners named the team the Raptors. T-shirts, sports caps, and other Raptors souvenirs went on sale almost immediately. The team will begin play at Toronto's SkyDome for the 1995-1996 season.

Public works suggest recovery. Three major development projects for Metropolitan Toronto gained final funding in 1994, indicating that the city was headed toward recovery from recent years of economic recession. In March, the Metropolitan Council approved the construction of two new subway lines. The subways were part of "Let's Move," a provincial transportation program introduced in early 1993. According to the program, Ontario will fund 75 percent of construction costs, an estimated $1.9-billion for the two lines. (All monetary figures are in Canadian dollars.) One will travel along Eglinton Ave. The second will run from the Yonge Subway to Don Mills Road.

The provincial government also proposed two additional lines, costing about $1 billion, to extend the Spadina Subway and the Scarborough elevated train. At the end of the year, the additional lines were still under the Council's consideration.

In August, as part of a jobs creation program initiated by Canadian Prime Minister Jean Chrétien, the Metropolitan Council approved construction of a $180-million trade center along the lakefront on the Canadian National Exhibition fairgrounds. In October, the provincial government gave final approval for a $180-million expansion to the Metropolitan Toronto Convention Center.

Scandal concluded. The final chapter of a local political scandal was played out in September, when Mario Gentile, a metropolitan councillor from North York, was sentenced to two years in prison for accepting bribes from developer Louis Charles. The scandal began in the summer of 1990 when police investigated a York council decision to sell a public swimming pool to Charles. The investigation ultimately revealed that Charles had issued bribes to three government officials from 1988 to 1991. In May 1994, Charles was sentenced to nine months in prison. Two former York councillors, Jim Fera and Tony Mandarano, were also convicted and received prison sentences for accepting the bribes.

□ David Lewis Stein

In *World Book,* see **Toronto.**

Toys and games. Retail toy sales in the United States increased about 5 percent in 1994 from 1993. Price-conscious consumers again favored discount stores as their preferred toy outlets. Discount stores captured more than 40 percent of total dollar sales of toys in 1994, and Toys "R" Us Incorporated of Paramus, N.J., remained the single largest toy retailer in terms of dollar sales.

Power Rangers conquer the market. The Mighty Morphin Power Rangers continued to be the most sought after toys of 1994, after becoming one of the biggest hits of the 1993 holiday toy-buying season. These action figures, manufactured by Bandai America Incorporated of Cerritos, Calif., are licensed characters from the syndicated television series of the same name. The series is based on six American teen-agers who *morph* (transform) into martial arts warriors known as Power Rangers by calling upon the spirits of dead dinosaurs. The spirits supply the warriors with super powers to fight Rita Repulsa, an evil sorceress.

The television show became an instant hit shortly after its premiere in August 1993. Heavy demand for the program's licensed toy items followed soon after the show's debut, causing a shortage of products for the 1993 holiday season and into 1994. The shortage of Power Ranger products continued through much of 1994. Parents and children across the country waited in long lines at retail stores to purchase the toys as soon as shipments arrived.

More than 90 different Power Ranger products are on the market. By December, sales of Power Ranger products approached an estimated $1 billion.

A magic year. Magic was the theme for some of 1994's new products and toy hits. Nature's Nursery, manufactured by Toy Biz Incorporated of New York City, is a line of necklace lockets and play sets, such as greenhouses, in which plants can grow without soil. Each locket and play set holds special Magic Grow Gel, which is derived from the same water-based substance that the National Aeronautics and Space Administration (NASA) uses in high technology farming. The sprouting seedlings are clearly visible in the nontoxic gel.

Magic: The Gathering is a fantasy card game that enjoyed great success in 1994. In the game, each player becomes a mighty magician, whose various powers come from cards with such titles as the Icy Manipulator, Black Lotus, and Keldon Warlord. The cards are beautifully illustrated and have become collectibles among players. Magic: The Gathering was created by Richard Garfield, a math professor, and is manufactured by Wizards of the Coast of Renton, Wash.

Science gone mad. Children can play mad scientist with Dr. Dreadful Food Lab and Dr. Dreadful Drink Lab, both new for 1994 from Tyco Toys, Incorporated of Mt. Laurel, N.J. The lab sets include beakers, test tubes, recipes, and ingredients for making lemon-flavored Monster Warts, solid eyes that taste like strawberry, cotton-candy Monster Brains, and other concoctions.

New craze in old game. A Hawaiian children's game called POG in 1994 gained widespread popularity across the United States and around the world. The game employs cardboard disks, which are placed face down in a stack. A larger disk, known as a kini or slammer, is then thrown at the stack. The thrower keeps every disk that flips over. The name of the game comes from the name on the bottle cap of a juice drink made of passion fruit, orange, and guava juices, that was once used to play the game.

The World POG Federation of Costa Mesa, Calif., is the major manufacturer of the disks. More than 30 other companies also market the products under names that include milk caps, jots, and trovs. The caps feature various television, motion picture, comic book, or sports figures and other designs. In 1994, collectors bought more than 2 billion of the caps, worth an estimated $500 million.

According to the World POG Federation, the game started in Hawaii in the early 1920's, when children began flipping milk or juice bottle caps as an inexpensive pastime. The game's popularity faded and then resurged for a short time after World War II (1939-1945), when toys were scarce. In the early 1970's, the Haleakala Dairy of Maui, the original distributor of the beverage POG, resurrected the game by bringing the caps back into print and selling tubes of the caps to children on Maui. In the early 1990's, a Hawaiian schoolteacher reintroduced POG caps and the game to her students on the Hawaiian island of Oahu, and its popularity spread around the world.

Happy 35th, Barbie! A special 35th Anniversary Barbie was one of the top-selling toys of 1994. The anniversary doll is a re-creation of the original Barbie introduced in 1959. It features the late 50's style of blond hair swept back into a ponytail, black-and-white striped bathing suit, open-toe shoes, and a replica of the original 1959 Barbie "shoe-box" package. The queen of fashion dolls celebrated her 35th anniversary on March 9, 1994. Barbie and her clothing, accessories, doll friends, and licensed merchandise now generate roughly $1 billion in annual sales for manufacturer Mattel Toys of El Segundo, Calif.

Several new looks for the 1994 line of Barbie dolls reflected the American focus on fitness. Bicyclin' Barbie, with flexible joints, pumps her legs up and down when placed on her special mountain bike and comes dressed in a shiny bicycle shorts set. Gymnast Barbie is a specially designed doll whose arms and knees flex and whose back bends at the waist. Battery-operated Swim 'N Dive Barbie, complete with scuba suit and matching scuba gear, is the first Barbie ever that actually kicks and swims when placed in water. □ Diane P. Cardinale

In *World Book*, see **Doll; Game; Toy.**

Track and field

Track and field. In a two-month span during the summer of 1994, African men broke the world records for three long runs—3,000, 5,000, and 10,000 meters. In that period, the men's world records also fell in the 100-meter dash and the pole vault, two of the sport's showcase events.

Sonia O'Sullivan of Ireland set the only world record in a standard running or field event for women. That seemed to revert to a women's drought in which those events produced one world record in 1989, one in 1990, one in 1991, and none in 1992.

There were five women's world records in 1993, three by Chinese women who ran such amazing times that many people suggested they had used illegal bodybuilding drugs. But Wang Junxia and Qu Yunxia, the Chinese record-breakers, passed every international drug test. They did not compete internationally for most of 1994, supposedly because of injuries and high-altitude training. When they did run in the Asian Games from October 2 to 16 in Hiroshima, Japan, they won, but their times were slower than their world records.

Records. Haile Gebreselasie, a 21-year-old Ethiopian policeman, trained for two months to break the 5,000-meter record on June 4 at Hengelo, the Netherlands. He was disappointed when the day was rainy and cold, but his time of 12 minutes 56.96 seconds broke Said Aouita's 1987 world record.

Leroy Burrell of the United States sets a world record in the 100-meter dash on July 6 in Lausanne, Switzerland. Burrell's time was 9.85 seconds.

World outdoor track and field records established in 1994

Men

Event	Holder	Country	Where set	Date	Record
100 meters	Leroy Burrell	U.S.A.	Lausanne, Switzerland	July 6	9.85
4 x 200 meters	Mike Marsh Leroy Burrell Floyd Heard Carl Lewis	U.S.A.	Walnut, Calif.	April 17	1:18.68
3,000 meters	Noureddine Morceli	Algeria	Monte Carlo, Monaco	Aug. 2	7:25.11
5,000 meters	Haile Gebreselasie	Ethiopia	Hengelo, Netherlands	June 4	12:56.96
10,000 meters	William Sigei	Kenya	Oslo, Norway	July 22	26:52.23
20 km walk	Bernardo Segura	Mexico	Fana, Norway	May 7	1:17:25.5
50 km walk	Rene Piller	France	Fana, Norway	May 7	3:41:28.2
Pole vault	Sergei Bubka	Ukraine	Sestriere, Italy	July 31	20 ft. 1¾ in. (6.14 m)

Women

Event	Holder	Country	Where set	Date	Record
2,000 meters	Sonia O'Sullivan	Ireland	Edinburgh, Scotland	July 9	5:25.36
10 km walk	Gao Hongmiao	China	Beijing	April 7	41:37.9

Km = kilometers   m = meters

Scotland, when she won the rarely run 2,000 meters in 5 minutes 25.36 seconds. She also ran the year's fastest times for 1,500 meters (3 minutes 59.10 seconds) and the mile (4 minutes 17.25 seconds).

Near misses. Dan O'Brien, the American who held the world record and world championship in the decathlon, endured a frustrating year. In the U.S. championships in mid-June in Knoxville, Tenn., O'Brien entered the final event, the 1,500 meters, on world-record pace. In the Goodwill Games in St. Petersburg, Russia, in July, he entered the 1,500 only 7 points short of world-record pace. Although he won, he ran out of energy and missed the record.

The 41-year-old Eamonn Coghlan, an Irishman who dominated indoor mile races in the United States during the 1980's, became the first runner older than 40 to run a mile in less than four minutes. On February 20 in Boston, he ran a mile in 3 minutes 58.15 seconds, then retired from the sport.

It was another year of dominance for two British men—34-year-old Linford Christie in the 100 meters and Colin Jackson in the 110-meter hurdles. Among the best Americans were Jackie Joyner-Kersee in the women's long jump and heptathlon, Gwen Torrence in the women's 100 and 200 meters, Michael Johnson in the men's 200 and 400 meters, and Lance Deal in the men's hammer throw. □ Frank Litsky

In *World Book*, see **Track and field**.

Transit. See **Transportation**.

Transportation. A bidding war broke out in October 1994 for control of the Atchinson, Topeka, and Santa Fe railroad, the sixth largest railroad in the United States. On June 30, the Burlington Northern Railroad of Fort Worth, Tex., and the Santa Fe Pacific Corporation of Schaumburg, Ill., which operates the Santa Fe railroad, announced plans to merge. Burlington Northern was the second largest railroad in the United States.

The merger would have created the largest railroad in the country, with more than $7.1 billion in revenues and 31,000 miles (50,000 kilometers) of track throughout the Midwest and West. The two railroads planned to continue operating separately until the Interstate Commerce Commission approved the merger.

But on October 5, the Union Pacific Corporation of Bethlehem, Pa., operator of the nation's largest railroad, offered about $3.2 billion for the Santa Fe, about $200 million more than Burlington's bid. Santa Fe professed loyalty to Burlington on grounds that federal regulators would not approve a merger with Union Pacific. But Union Pacific's bid appeared to gain strength in November as Santa Fe postponed a shareholders' vote to decide the matter, while seeking a better offer from Union Pacific.

The Channel Tunnel, the 31-mile (50-kilometer) Eurotunnel railway beneath the English Channel, opened for freight traffic on May 6. Queen Elizabeth

On July 22, in the Bislett Games in Oslo, Norway, William Sigei of Kenya won the 10,000 in 26 minutes 52.23 seconds, chopping more than 6 seconds off Yobes Ondieki's world record a year earlier. Sigei had finished second in Ondieki's record race.

Noureddine Morceli of Algeria, who held the world records at 1,500 meters and a mile, added the 3,000-meter record. On August 2 in Monte Carlo, Monaco, his time of 7 minutes 25.11 seconds took almost 4 seconds off Moses Kiptanui's record. Morceli also ran the year's fastest times for the 1,500 (3 minutes 30.61 seconds) and the mile (3 minutes 48.67 seconds).

For the second time in three years, Leroy Burrell broke the 100-meter record held by his fellow American and training partner, Carl Lewis. On July 6 in Lausanne, Switzerland, Burrell ran the 100 in 9.85 seconds, bettering Lewis's time at the 1991 world championships by a hundredth of a second. Burrell and Lewis also helped the Santa Monica, Calif., Track Club set a world record of 1 minute 18.68 seconds for the 800-meter relay on April 17 in Walnut, Calif.

The 30-year-old Sergei Bubka of Ukraine had ruled the pole vault since 1983, breaking the world record 18 times indoors and 17 times outdoors. His latest record came outdoors on July 31 in Sestriere, Italy, where he cleared 20 feet 1¾ inches (6.14 meters).

O'Sullivan's record came on July 9 in Edinburgh,

II of the United Kingdom and President François Mit-terrand of France participated in opening cere-monies. The railway opened almost two years be-hind schedule and at a cost between $15 billion and $16 billion, nearly twice the original cost estimates.

The tunnel is regarded as one of the outstand-ing engineering feats of the 1900's. It will enable passengers to travel from Folkestone, England, to Calais, France, in about 35 minutes and from London to Paris in about 3 hours. Passenger service began on November 14.

End of truck regulation. SIxty years of govern-ment regulation of the trucking industry ended on Dec. 31, 1994. In August 1994, the U.S. Congress vot-ed to eliminate state and local regulations on the trucking industry that affected trucking rates and services when shipping within a state. Goods that move across state lines have been deregulated since 1980. States were permitted to regulate only house-hold moving companies. (See **Consumerism.**)

New rail services. On October 7, Denver, Colo., joined the growing number of cities with a mass-transit system when a 5.3-mile (8.5-kilometer) light-rail line opened in the downtown area. Many cities, including Portland, Ore., and Toronto, Canada, had extensions to their existing systems under construc-tion during 1994.

The most powerful diesel locomotives built in recent times began operation on several railroads in 1994. On September 12, the Morrison Knudsen Corporation of Boise, Ida., delivered three 5,000-horsepower locomotives to the Southern Pacific Rail-road. Previously, the largest locomotives commonly in use in the United States were 4,000 horsepower. The new locomotives enable railroads to save oper-ating expenses by reducing the number of locomo-tives on trains. Union Pacific railroad was scheduled to take delivery of three more 5,000-horsepower lo-comotives in late 1994.

Earthquake commuters. Damage to freeways as a result of the earthquake 25 miles (40 kilometers) north of Los Angeles on January 17 forced many people who otherwise drove automobiles to work to commute by train. Ridership on the Metrolink Santa Clarita line temporarily rose from 1,000 people a day to more than 20,000.

Meeting clean air regulations. States had to file plans by Nov. 15, 1994, for complying with the Clean Air Act of 1990. The act calls for a reduction of air pollutants from many sources, including automo-biles, electric power plants, and factories. One sec-tion of the act requires companies with more than 100 employees in nine areas of the country with the worst air quality to reduce by 25 percent the number of people who drive to work alone.   □ Ian Savage

See also **Automobile; Aviation.** In *World Book,* see **Bus; Electric railroad; Subway; Transportation.**
Trinidad and Tobago. See **Latin America.**
Tunisia. See **Middle East.**

Turkey suffered a financial crisis in 1994 when at least three banks failed in April and $9 billion of Turkey's $60-billion debt fell due. Inflation soared in May by nearly 30 percent, and the Turkish lira fell in value by 58 percent.

In response to the crisis, Prime Minister Tansu Ciller on April 5 announced austerity measures that included spending cuts and new taxes. The govern-ment also lifted subsidies, increasing the prices of sugar, alcohol, gasoline, and tobacco by as much as 100 percent. Ciller also pledged to sell off state-owned companies, a plan that met legal obstacles but won approval in September. Ciller's reforms al-lowed Turkey to qualify for loans from the Inter-national Monetary Fund, an agency of the United Nations (UN), but many feared the crisis would recur unless Turkey reduced its debt.

The crisis deepened Turkey's bitterness about UN trade sanctions against Iraq, formerly Turkey's third largest trading partner. Turkey claimed that it had lost $20 billion in revenue since the sanctions began in 1990 when Iraq invaded Kuwait. Turkey proposed in 1994 that Iraq be allowed to sell oil stranded in an idle pipeline that crosses Turkey. No agreement had been reached by the end of 1994. In August, 70 top Turkish businessmen openly visited Iraq to explore trade possibilities.

Kurds. Turkey blamed the sanctions for inflam-ing the independence drive by the militant Kurdish Workers' Party (PKK). In 1994, the government in-tensified attacks against PKK rebel positions, com-mitting about 300,000 troops to fight the PKK. More than 13,000 people have been killed since Kurdish rebels began fighting in 1984 to establish an inde-pendent homeland in the Kurdish region of Turkey and Iraq.

On Dec. 8, 1994, in a trial that began in August, eight Kurdish members of Turkey's parliament were found guilty of supporting the outlawed PKK. The parliamentarians received prison terms ranging from 3 to 15 years.

Two Kurdish women set themselves on fire and died in Germany on March 21, the Kurdish New Year, to protest German arms sales to Turkey and Turkey's treatment of Kurds. At least seven more Kurds immolated themselves during what became a violent week of protests. Although Germany threat-ened to deport Kurdish activists, they suspended arms shipments to Turkey in April. The European Parliament later condemned both Turkey for de-stroying 120 Kurdish villages and the PKK for terror-ist attacks in Istanbul in 1994.

Elections. The pro-Islamic Refah, or Welfare, Party, stunned observers by winning more than 18 percent of the vote during municipal elections in March, barely behind Ciller's leading True Path Party and the opposition Motherland Party. Refah won the mayorships of some 26 cities, including Ankara, the capital, and Istanbul, Turkey's largest city.

Turkey's Prime Minister Tansu Ciller, left (foreground), and Pakistan's Prime Minister Benazir Bhutto, center, visit war-torn Bosnia-Herzegovina in February.

Dev-Sol. On September 11, French police captured Dursun Karatas, fugitive leader of the extreme left wing guerrilla group Dev-Sol, or Revolutionary Left. Turkey sought his extradition from France after his capture. Karatas, accused of killing 37 people, had escaped from an Istanbul prison in 1989.

Environment. Turkey issued new safety regulations on July 1, 1994, for ships transiting the Bosporus strait in an effort to prevent an environmental disaster in the congested international waterway that connects the Black Sea to the Mediterranean Sea. A crisis had nearly occurred on March 13 when an oil tanker collided with a freighter.

Istanbul, already home to 40 percent of Turkey's heavy industry, incurred more pollution and congestion as 700 new vehicles a day were added in 1994. Many Istanbulis heat their homes with lignite coal, which adds sulfur and ash to the city's air.

Greek-Turkish relations worsened when a Turkish diplomat was slain on July 4 in Athens, Greece, the fourth diplomat to be killed since 1980. A Greek guerrilla group claimed responsibility for the slaying, saying it had avenged crimes "against Cyprus and the Kurds." UN-led talks between Turkish and Greek Cypriots had collapsed in April. Cyprus was divided in 1974 when Turkey invaded after a coup led by Greece. □ Christine Helms

Turkmenistan. See Asia.
Uganda. See Africa.

Ukraine began to show signs of stability in 1994, after approaching the brink of economic and political collapse in the final months of 1993. In presidential elections held in July, former Prime Minister Leonid Kuchma, a proponent of reform, defeated incumbent Leonid Kravchuk, who had failed to improve the nation's situation. Kuchma quickly announced a bold program of economic reforms supported by leaders of Western nations and the United Nations' International Monetary Fund (IMF).

But economic troubles still plagued Ukraine in 1994. Production fell by more than 30 percent during the year, and the majority of Ukrainians continued to live in poverty. Although a tight monetary policy from Ukraine's central bank brought some improvement, high inflation remained a problem. Meanwhile, foreign and domestic investment declined, and the nation's debt continued to grow.

Election results in 1994 indicated a desire among Ukrainians for reform, but underlined serious ethnic and political divisions. Kuchma, a proponent of closer economic ties with Russia, won the presidency with about 52 percent of the vote. His support came mainly from the nation's eastern and southern regions, heavily populated with ethnic Russians. Kravchuk, who campaigned on Ukrainian nationalist themes, won about 45 percent of the vote with strong support in western Ukraine among people who fear a Russian threat to Ukrainian sovereignty.

Ukraine

The geographical and ethnic split among the electorate fueled growing fears that the nation might eventually break apart. In response to these fears, Kuchma moved quickly to strengthen his power over the central government and to bring local government councils under presidential control.

Elections for the 450 seat *Rada* (parliament), held in several rounds beginning in March 1994, also reflected Ukraine's political ambivalence. Low voter turnout and new electoral laws resulted in a Rada dominated by independent candidates, but weakened by unfilled seats. A 50 percent voter turnout is required for a candidate to claim a seat. After the last round of elections was held in November, about 45 seats remained unfilled. Independents controlled more than half of the seats, and Communists and Socialists made up the second largest bloc with about 150 seats. Nationalists and reformers lost ground. But some observers argued that the weakening of the Rada, which had stifled reform efforts in the past, might actually enhance the nation's progress.

Economic reform became a top priority under Kuchma, who took immediate and decisive measures to implement a stabilization plan. In July, he met with leaders of the Group of Seven (G-7), an organization of seven leading Western industrialized nations. The G-7 leaders promised a package of more than $4 billion in aid, under conditions that call for Ukraine to introduce significant economic reforms.

On October 11, Kuchma submitted to the Rada a comprehensive reform program, which was backed by $365 million in support from the IMF. The program called for elimination of price controls, privatization of state-owned firms, land reform, an overhaul of the tax system, reduced trade restrictions, drastic cuts in subsidies, and reduction of the budget deficit. The Rada approved most of the plan, but denied support for privatization, charging that the process was riddled with corruption.

Parliamentary approval of Kuchma's reform plan generated optimism that Ukraine would avoid economic collapse. But opposition to reforms that might bring on temporary hardship remained high among officials and threatened Kuchma's chances of carrying out the program.

Tensions in Crimea, an autonomous region within Ukraine, heightened in early 1994. The Crimean Peninsula was placed under Ukrainian jurisdiction by the Soviet Union in 1954. Since Ukraine became independent in 1991, many Crimeans have called for independence or union with Russia. In elections held in January 1994, Yurii Meshkov, a lawyer and politician who advocated union with Russia, became the Crimea's first president. Meshkov announced that Crimea would hold a referendum in March to determine the region's status. Ukrainian officials immediately denied Crimea's authority to make such a determination. In May, Crimea adopted its own Constitution, which included a declaration of sovereignty. Kravchuk, Ukraine's president at the time, sent troops to the area and opened negotiations with Russia to defuse the crisis.

Russia expressed little interest in absorbing the region. As Crimeans faced a possible civil war, support for separation diminished. On June 3, Ukrainian and Crimean officials issued a statement recognizing Crimea as a part of Ukraine. In October, the Crimean parliament appointed Anatolii Franchuk, an ally of President Kuchma and strong supporter of economic reform, as prime minister. An angry Meshkov then attempted to shut down parliament, leading officials to strip most of his constitutional powers.

Arms control agreement. On January 14, Ukraine signed a security agreement with the United States and Russia calling for the transfer of all remaining long-range nuclear weapons from Ukraine to Russia, where they would be destroyed. The treaty provided security guarantees to Ukraine as well as compensation from Russia for the returned nuclear material. In November, the Ukrainian parliament ratified the Nuclear Nonproliferation Treaty, pledging the elimination of all its nuclear weapons. The United States offered Ukraine about $350 million in aid in 1994 to support the nation's nuclear disarmament.   □ Joel S. Hellman

See also **Commonwealth of Independent States.** In *World Book,* see **Ukraine.**

Unemployment. See Economics; Labor.

United Kingdom. The year 1994 began with a succession of scandals involving members of the ruling Conservative Party. As the year continued, Conservatives fared poorly in elections and dropped lower in opinion polls. Yet at year's end, the Conservatives, in power since 1979, still headed the government. And Prime Minister John Major, who had become increasingly unpopular both with the public and within his own Conservative Party, retained his premiership.

Scandals rock Conservatives. On Jan. 5, 1994, Tim Yeo, the minister for the environment, resigned after admitting that he had fathered a child outside his marriage. On January 9, Transport Minister Lord Caithness resigned after his wife shot and killed herself, reportedly because of his alleged affair with another woman. Several other sexually related scandals involving Conservative Party Members of Parliament (MP's) followed. The scandals were particularly embarrassing to Major and the Conservative Party because in October 1993, Major had announced a "back to basics" campaign, which was widely understood as promoting family values.

Conservative slump. The government's popularity slumped to an all-time low of 21.5 percent in 1994. Opinion polls showed that most people no longer believed the Conservatives to be the party of morality. To add to the government's unpopularity, tax increases introduced in the 1993 budget were felt for the first time when the new financial year began on April 6.

In local council elections on May 5, the Conservatives suffered their worst defeat since World War II (1939-1945), losing 429 seats, a third of what they had held. In elections to the 567-seat European Parliament on June 9, they suffered their worst performance in history when they won only 18 of the 32 seats they had held. The Labour Party took 62 seats, up from 45.

Problems continued to plague Major as a number of Conservatives, popularly known as "Euroskeptics" because they oppose moves toward a more centralized Europe, accused Major of failing to stand up for British interests.

British veto at Corfu summit. Major improved his standing with the Euroskeptics following a summit meeting of the European Union (EU), formerly the European Community, in Corfu, Greece, on June 25. At the summit, Major vetoed the choice of Jean-Luc Dehaene, the Belgian prime minister, to succeed Jacques Delors as president of the European Commission, the EU's top executive post. Major objected to Dehaene on the grounds that he represented big government and interventionism. Jacques Santer, prime minister of Luxembourg, was eventually chosen as president on July 21.

New Labour leader. On May 12, John Smith, Labour Party leader, died suddenly of a heart attack at the age of 55. Tony Blair, a charismatic Oxford-educated lawyer, succeeded Smith. Blair immediately began reforming the party's unpopular left wing platforms. He announced that Labour was no longer the "tax and spend" party, and that only the very wealthy would pay high taxes. He further pledged that Labour would not give the trade unions any special privileges. At Labour's annual conference at Blackpool on October 6, Blair risked an internal row by proposing to delete "Clause Four" of the party's constitution, which for 76 years had committed Labour to state ownership of all industry.

Economic news. The economy, which had been in deep recession for two years, began to recover in 1994. In June, the unemployment rate fell for the fifth straight month to 9.4 percent, the lowest in two years.

D-Day remembered. In May 1994, the government scrapped plans for fireworks, street parties, and cooking contests and decided instead to hold commemorative religious events to mark the 50th anniversary of D-Day, the 1944 landing of Allied troops on the Normandy beaches of Nazi-occupied France. The invasion led to the liberation of Western Europe. Veterans' organizations protested that the memory of the 37,000 people killed in the Normandy battle would be trivialized by the originally planned street parties. Such festivities, they said, should be reserved for V-E Day, or Victory in Europe Day, the end of World War II in Europe. On June 6, Queen Elizabeth II and members of the royal family joined other heads of state and more than 30,000 veterans at commemorations held on the beaches and at the cemeteries of Normandy. (See **Armed Forces: Remembering D-Day.**)

Law and order issues divided the country in 1994. On July 28, Home Secretary Michael Howard decided to almost double the minimum sentences to be served by two 10-year-old boys convicted in 1993 of kidnapping and murdering a 2-year-old toddler, James Bulger. The trial judge had recommended that the two boys serve at least 8 years before being considered for release. But Howard increased the minimum sentences to 15 years.

On April 12, Howard agreed to introduce stricter controls on the rental of video motion pictures that depict violence and to impose stiffer penalties, including imprisonment, on dealers who supplied extremely violent or pornographic videos to children. The agreement represented a compromise with MP's who had proposed an amendment to a pending criminal justice bill. The amendment would have outlawed the home viewing of any videotape regarded as unsuitable for children. The proposed amendment followed claims that violent videos had played a part in the Bulger murder case.

Parliament voted on February 21 to lower the age of legal consent for homosexual relations between men from 21 to 18. Some groups declared the

Prince Charles, right, calmly views the man who fired two blank shots at him and then fell at an Australia Day celebration in Sydney in January.

Tony Blair receives a hug from his wife, Cherie, after he was elected leader of the Labour Party at a special party meeting in London in July.

vote discriminatory because the age of consent for heterosexuals is 16.

The Child Support Agency, set up to force absent parents to pay more child support, provoked widespread criticism in 1994. In early July, reports showed that only 1.4 percent of the money collected to date had gone to needy families. Most of the remaining funds had gone into the Treasury, where, according to a government spokesperson, it was used to offset money already spent on single-parent families. Critics also said the agency's pursuit of absent fathers and the high child support bills they sent them was wrecking their second families, and even causing suicides. Absent fathers and second families took to the streets in protest. On July 4, in its first annual report, the agency's chief executive, Ros Hepplewhite, apologized for the agency's shortcomings and said it had not reached key targets. On September 2, Hepplewhite resigned.

Women priests? The Church of England was scarred by a theological battle over whether women should be ordained as priests. After a bitter and lengthy feud, the General Synod, the church's ruling body, voted on February 22 to allow women priests. The first ordinations of 32 women priests took place in Bristol Cathedral on March 12, and many celebrated communion for the first time the following day, Mothering Sunday. Hundreds of male priests and lay worshipers quit the church in protest, and seven An-

glican bishops said they would become Roman Catholics. (See also **Protestantism**.)

Channel Tunnel opens. Britain and France were officially linked by land on May 6, when Queen Elizabeth II and French President François Mitterrand traveled through the Channel Tunnel under the English Channel and formally declared it open. Hailed as one of the great engineering feats of modern times, the 31-mile (50-kilometer) tunnel cost between 10 billion and 10.7 billion pounds (U.S. $15 billion and $16 billion). (See also **Transportation**.)

National lottery begins. Camelot, a business consortium, won a competition to run a national lottery. The first drawing was held on November 19. The weekly lottery offered a possible jackpot of 2 million pounds (U.S. $1.22 million) in addition to other prizes. About 30 percent of the money raised will go to the arts, charities, sports, and a fund for celebrations of the year 2000.

Royal troubles. The difficult estrangement between Prince Charles and his wife, Diana, continued. And a series of leaks to the press about their respective lives was considered part of a damaging public relations battle between them.

On May 18, reports revealed that Diana spent 160,000 pounds (U.S. $97,600) a year on clothes and beauty treatments. It was widely believed that these reports were leaked by Charles' public relations agents in order to undermine his estranged wife's popularity.

In a TV documentary broadcast on June 29, Charles openly agonized over his role as king-in-waiting and admitted adultery after his marriage with Diana had "irretrievably broken down." He said he was not contemplating an early divorce from Diana, but insisted that even if he did divorce, it would not prevent him from succeeding to the throne.

Diana publicly denied making a barrage of telephone calls to Oliver Hoare, a wealthy art dealer and friend of Diana and Charles. The *London Daily Mail* disclosed on August 22 that Diana believed the media were trying to portray her as having a "fatal attraction" for Hoare. Newspapers reported that Hoare had received up to 20 calls a week and that each time the caller had been silent. Hoare alerted police because he thought that the calls might be the work of terrorists since he dealt in Islamic art. He withdrew his complaint after British Telecom traced the source.

On October 3, a book by Anna Pasternak, called *Princess in Love*, detailed Diana's alleged romantic affair from 1986 to 1991 with Major James Hewitt, a 36-year-old former cavalry officer. Although written in the style of romantic fiction, the book was apparently based on conversations with Hewitt, who had reportedly shown the author letters he had received from Diana. □ Ian J. Mather

See also **Ireland; Northern Ireland**. In *World Book*, see **European Union; United Kingdom**.

United Nations. The prestige of the United Nations (UN) suffered as a result of its inability to contain aggression by Bosnian Serbs in Bosnia-Herzegovina in late 1994. The UN had taken decisive steps in early 1994 to deal with violations of UN resolutions regarding a demilitarized zone around Sarajevo, the capital of Bosnia-Herzegovina (often called simply Bosnia). UN Secretary-General Boutros Boutros-Ghali asked the North Atlantic Treaty Organization (NATO) to work out a process for air strikes against those violating the zone after a single mortar shell struck an open-air market in Sarajevo on February 5, killing 68 people and wounding some 200. Bosnian Serbs were told to withdraw their military equipment by February 21 or face NATO air strikes. On February 21, the chief of the UN Protection Force, Yasushi Akashi, announced that Bosnian Serb troops had withdrawn.

Bosnian Serbs continued to fire on other Muslim-inhabited towns in Bosnia that the UN Security Council had declared "safe areas," meaning Serb forces were not to attack them. On April 10 and 11, NATO ordered air strikes on Serbian targets near the town of Gorazde. The bombing came after Bosnian Serbs had refused UN demands to withdraw from the vicinity of Gorazde, where some 65,000 people, mostly Muslims, had suffered months of deprivation and intense attacks. Bosnian Serbs withdrew after NATO issued a third air strike warning on April 24.

Akashi negotiated a one-month cease-fire beginning June 10 with Bosnian Serbs, Bosnian Muslims, and Bosnian Croats. But on August 5 and September 22, NATO again launched air strikes against Bosnian Serb targets after they attacked a UN weapons depot and a French armored personnel carrier.

A diplomatic group composed of France, Germany, Russia, the United Kingdom, and the United States devised a peace plan that included a new territorial map for the warring parties. The Muslim-led Bosnian government accepted the plan on July 8, but the Bosnian Serbs rejected it because it made them relinquish about a third of the territory they had gained after three years of war.

Disappointed by the rejection of the peace plan, Serbian President Slobodan Milosevic on August 4 severed political and economic ties with Serbian nationalists in Bosnia. Milosevic closed the Serbian border to areas under control of Bosnian Serbs to all traffic except vehicles carrying humanitarian aid.

In recognition of Serbia's severance of economic and political ties to the Bosnian Serbs, the UN Security Council eased economic sanctions on Serbia and Montenegro, the two remaining republics of Yugoslavia, beginning October 3 for 100 days. The Council also allowed Serbia and Montenegro to take part in international sports events and cultural exchanges. But the Council imposed a new series of economic sanctions against the Bosnian Serbs in response to their rejection of the peace plan.

On November 3, the UN General Assembly adopted a resolution that called for an end to the arms embargo on the Bosnian government. The arms embargo had been imposed on all of Yugoslavia and its former republics in 1991. In late November, Bosnian Serb advances and the kidnappings of UN soldiers raised doubts about the viability of the UN mission.

Rwandan refugees fleeing a civil war overwhelmed the humanitarian resources of international relief agencies in the summer of 1994. The crisis began when Rwandan President Juvénal Habyarimana and Burundi's President Cyprien Ntaryamira were killed as their plane attempted to land at Rwanda's Kigali airport on April 6. Rwandan sources said the plane was shot down. The incident set off a campaign by Rwanda's Hutu majority to kill ethnic Tutsis to avenge the death of Habyarimana, who was a Hutu. The attacks set off a military offensive by the Tutsi-led Rwandan Patriotic Front. An estimated 500,000 people were killed in the ensuing civil war.

On April 21, the Security Council decided to withdraw most of its peacekeeping force from Rwanda, an action that several African countries denounced. On May 13, the Council reversed itself and agreed to deploy 5,500 troops. However, difficulties in obtaining the necessary manpower and equipment delayed the deployment of a scaled-down UN force until October. In the meantime, the Rwandan Patriotic Front proclaimed a military victory on July 18 and set up a new government the next day. The Tutsi-led victory caused widespread panic among Hutus fearing repression. Within weeks, more than a million Rwandans, mostly Hutus, fled to Zaire. In July and August, UN officials estimated that there were also at least 460,000 Rwandan refugees in Tanzania and 150,000 in Burundi. As the violence in Rwanda subsided, some refugees began to return home.

Haiti's military leader, Lieutenant General Raoul Cédras, remained in power for most of 1994 despite repeated calls for his resignation. Cédras led a military coup in 1991 that ousted democratically elected President Jean-Bertrand Aristide. On May 6, the UN renewed efforts to oust Cédras when the Security Council imposed wide-ranging economic sanctions that took effect on May 21. The sanctions included a trade ban and a freeze on overseas assets belonging to Haitian military officers and their families.

On July 31, the Council voted 12-0 to allow a U.S.-led multinational military alliance to remove Cédras by force. China and Brazil abstained, and Rwanda, because of the change in government in that country, was not present. The decision marked the first time the UN had approved the invasion of a country in the Western Hemisphere. The Council said the multinational force would disarm the military and help Aristide to regain constitutional power and train a new police force and army.

However, under a negotiated settlement conducted by former United States President Jimmy

Carter, Cédras accepted a peaceful landing of American troops, who began to arrive in Haiti on September 19. Cédras also agreed to resign. On October 13, Cédras left Haiti for exile in Panama, and two days later, Aristide returned as president. Economic sanctions ended on October 16.

Iraq. On October 15, the Security Council demanded the immediate and complete withdrawal of Iraqi forces from the border area of Kuwait after Iraq deployed five army divisions, 700 tanks, and 900 armored personnel carriers there in early October. Iraq staged the military action because the UN had failed to set a time limit on economic sanctions that had been imposed on Iraq in August 1990. In response to the Iraqi show of force, the United States rushed troops to Kuwait on Oct. 9, 1994. By October 20, Iraq had withdrawn most of its troops. In 1990, Iraqi troops had overrun Kuwait and claimed it as Iraq's 19th province, but the troops were expelled during the 1991 Persian Gulf War.

The government of Iraq, suffering from the continued UN economic sanctions, demanded a clear timetable for the lifting of sanctions. But the Council, which reviewed the sanctions every two months, demanded that Iraq first comply with UN resolutions. On November 10, Iraq recognized Kuwait's sovereignty and border, but this did not prompt the Council to ease the sanctions.

Somalia. On October 26, a seven-member mission of the Security Council arrived in Mogadishu, the capital of Somalia, to assess the usefulness of its peacekeeping mission there. The group came after a series of attacks on UN peacekeeping staff and failure by Somali clans to reach a political settlement to their long-running rivalry.

Human rights. The UN General Assembly on February 14 appointed Ecuadorean diplomat Jose Ayala Lasso to a five-year term as the first High Commissioner for Human Rights. The post was created in response to increased demands by the international community to combat human rights abuses around the world.

Population. The UN's International Conference on Population and Development took place in Cairo, Egypt, from September 5 to 13 to draw up a 20-year plan of action on issues of population, economic development, and empowerment of women. A total of 179 governments and some 1,500 nongovernmental organizations took part in the conference. The plan recognized that improving the health, rights, and education of women was essential to effectively controlling the world's population. It called for the universal availability of family planning methods by the year 2015. The program also called for governments around the world to spend an annual collective total of $17 billion on family planning until the year 2000, at which time the budget would increase.

The Vatican and several Islamic countries protested discussions on reproductive rights because they feared such rights would include abortion, to which they are opposed. The conference agreed on a compromise under which abortion would not be promoted as a method of family planning. The compromise removed a major stumbling block at the conference and permitted the adoption of resolutions on reproductive health and rights, family planning, and improving prenatal care.

The General Assembly began its 49th session on September 20 and elected Ivory Coast Foreign Minister Amara Essy as president of the 184-member organization. Discussions at the 49th session turned to the question of reforming the world organization as it prepares to celebrate its 50th anniversary in 1995. Among the key concerns is funding for UN peacekeeping operations and for social and humanitarian programs. The UN said it was owed an overall total of $2.1 billion on November 15. Of this amount, $559 million was for the regular administrative budget and $1.6 billion for peacekeeping operations. UN officials estimate that 1994 peacekeeping operations around the world cost about $3.5 billion.

On October 20, the Assembly elected Germany, Italy, Honduras, Indonesia, and Botswana to serve as nonpermanent members in the 15-member Security Council for a two-year term beginning in 1995.

□ J. Tuyet Nguyen

See also **Bosnia-Herzegovina; Haiti; Iraq; Rwanda; Somalia.** In *World Book,* see **United Nations.**

United States, Government of the.

Democratic Party candidates were swamped by a Republican tidal wave in the Nov. 8, 1994, midterm elections, losing control of Congress for the first time since 1955. The catastrophic Democratic defeat was expected to severely limit President Bill Clinton's ability to carry out his policies in the final two years of his term. The election outcome was widely interpreted as a vote of no confidence in Clinton and his party despite an improving economy. As they prepared to take charge of the Senate and House of Representatives in January 1995, Republican congressional leaders initially pledged cooperation with the President while vowing also to pursue their conservative agenda.

The November upset came after Clinton and Democratic members of Congress failed to achieve any progress in 1994 on the President's top priority—health care reform. Clinton also was bedeviled by personal problems, ranging from congressional hearings into an Arkansas real estate investment he made in the 1980's—the so-called Whitewater affair—to a sexual harassment suit filed against him by a former state employee in Arkansas.

Whitewater investigation. With public concern mounting over the Whitewater affair, Attorney General Janet Reno on Jan. 20, 1994, named an independent counsel, New York lawyer Robert B. Fiske, Jr., to direct a special criminal inquiry into the mat-

Selected agencies and bureaus of the U.S. government*

Executive Office of the President
President, Bill Clinton
Vice President, Albert Gore, Jr.
White House Chief of Staff, Leon E. Panetta
Presidential Press Secretary, Dee Dee Myers†
Assistant to the President for Domestic Policy, Carol H. Rasco
Assistant to the President for National Security Affairs, W. Anthony Lake
Assistant to the President for Science and Technology, John H. Gibbons
Council of Economic Advisers—Laura D'Andrea Tyson, Chairman
Office of Management and Budget—Alice M. Rivlin, Director
Office of National Drug Control Policy—Lee P. Brown, Director
U.S. Trade Representative, Mickey Kantor

Department of Agriculture
Secretary of Agriculture, Mike Espy‡

Department of Commerce
Secretary of Commerce, Ronald H. Brown
Bureau of Economic Analysis—Carol S. Carson, Director
Bureau of the Census—Martha F. Riche, Director

Department of Defense
Secretary of Defense, William J. Perry
Secretary of the Air Force, Sheila E. Widnall
Secretary of the Army, Togo D. West, Jr.
Secretary of the Navy, John H. Dalton
Joint Chiefs of Staff—
General John Shalikashvili, Chairman
General Merrill A. McPeak, Chief of Staff, Air Force
General Gordon R. Sullivan, Chief of Staff, Army
Admiral Jeremy M. Boorda, Chief of Naval Operations
General Carl E. Mundy, Jr., Commandant, Marine Corps

Department of Education
Secretary of Education, Richard W. Riley

Department of Energy
Secretary of Energy, Hazel R. O'Leary

Department of Health and Human Services
Secretary of Health and Human Services, Donna E. Shalala
Public Health Service—Philip R. Lee, Assistant Secretary
Centers for Disease Control and Prevention—David Satcher, Director
Food and Drug Administration—David A. Kessler, Commissioner
National Institutes of Health—Harold Varmus, Director
Surgeon General of the United States, M. Joycelyn Elders§
Social Security Administration—Shirley S. Chater, Commissioner

Department of Housing and Urban Development
Secretary of Housing and Urban Development, Henry G. Cisneros

Department of the Interior
Secretary of the Interior, Bruce Babbitt

Department of Justice
Attorney General, Janet Reno
Bureau of Prisons—Kathleen M. Hawk, Director
Drug Enforcement Administration—Thomas A. Constantine, Administrator
Federal Bureau of Investigation—Louis J. Freeh, Director
Immigration and Naturalization Service—Doris M. Meissner, Commissioner
Solicitor General, Drew S. Days III

Department of Labor
Secretary of Labor, Robert B. Reich

Department of State
Secretary of State, Warren Christopher
U.S. Ambassador to the United Nations, Madeleine K. Albright

Department of Transportation
Secretary of Transportation, Federico F. Peña
Federal Aviation Administration—David R. Hinson, Administrator
U.S. Coast Guard—Admiral Robert E. Kramek, Commandant

*As of Dec. 31, 1994. †Resigned Dec. 22 ‡Resigned Dec. 31.
§Resigned Dec. 9

Department of the Treasury
Secretary of the Treasury, Lloyd M. Bentsen, Jr.†
Internal Revenue Service—Margaret Milner Richardson, Commissioner
Treasurer of the United States, Mary Ellen Withrow
U.S. Secret Service—Eljay B. Bowron, Director
Office of Thrift Supervision—Jonathan L. Fiechter, Acting Director

Department of Veterans Affairs
Secretary of Veterans Affairs, Jesse Brown

Supreme Court of the United States
Chief Justice of the United States, William H. Rehnquist
Associate Justices—
John Paul Stevens
Sandra Day O'Connor
Antonin Scalia
Anthony M. Kennedy
David H. Souter
Clarence Thomas
Ruth Bader Ginsburg
Stephen G. Breyer

Congressional officials
President of the Senate pro tempore, Robert C. Byrd
Senate Majority Leader, George J. Mitchell
Senate Minority Leader, Robert J. Dole
Speaker of the House, Thomas S. Foley
House Majority Leader, Richard A. Gephardt
House Minority Leader, Robert H. Michel
Congressional Budget Office—Robert D. Reischauer, Director
General Accounting Office—Charles A. Bowsher, Comptroller General of the United States
Library of Congress—James H. Billington, Librarian of Congress
Office of Technology Assessment—Roger C. Herdman, Director

Independent agencies
Central Intelligence Agency—R. James Woolsey, Director‡
Commission on Civil Rights—Mary Frances Berry, Chairperson
Commission of Fine Arts—J. Carter Brown, Chairman
Consumer Product Safety Commission—Ann Winkelman Brown, Chairman
Corporation for National and Community Service—Eli J. Segal, Chief Executive Officer
Environmental Protection Agency—Carol M. Browner, Administrator
Equal Employment Opportunity Commission—Gilbert F. Casellas, Chairman
Federal Communications Commission—Reed E. Hundt, Chairman
Federal Deposit Insurance Corporation—Ricki Rhodarmer Tigert, Chairman
Federal Election Commission—Trevor Potter, Chairman
Federal Emergency Management Agency—James Lee Witt, Director
Federal Reserve System Board of Governors—Alan Greenspan, Chairman
Federal Trade Commission—Janet D. Steiger, Chairman
General Services Administration—Roger W. Johnson, Administrator
International Development Cooperation Agency—J. Brian Atwood, Acting Director
Interstate Commerce Commission—Gail C. McDonald, Chairman
National Aeronautics and Space Administration—Daniel S. Goldin, Administrator
National Endowment for the Arts—Jane Alexander, Chairman
National Endowment for the Humanities—Sheldon Hackney, Chairman
National Labor Relations Board—William B. Gould IV, Chairman
National Railroad Passenger Corporation (Amtrak)—Thomas M. Downs, Chairman
National Science Foundation—Neal F. Lane, Director
National Transportation Safety Board—James E. Hall, Chairman
Nuclear Regulatory Commission—Ivan Selin, Chairman
Peace Corps—Carol Bellamy, Director
Securities and Exchange Commission—Arthur Levitt, Jr., Chairman
Selective Service System—Gil Coronado, Director
Small Business Administration—Phillip Lader, Administrator
Smithsonian Institution—I. Michael Heyman, Secretary
U.S. Arms Control and Disarmament Agency—John D. Holum, Director
U.S. Information Agency—Joseph D. Duffey, Director
U.S. Postal Service—Marvin T. Runyon, Jr., Postmaster General

A huge headquarters complex for a U.S. spy agency drew controversy in August when U.S. senators charged that its $350-million cost had been hidden from them.

ter. Later, after Clinton signed a law giving federal courts the power to appoint such special prosecutors, a panel of federal judges on August 5 replaced Fiske. Their choice to succeed him was Kenneth W. Starr, a former federal appeals court judge and a senior lawyer in the Administration of President George Bush. The move came on the final day of Senate and House hearings into the controversy.

Administration changes. On March 5, White House Counsel Bernard W. Nussbaum resigned as a result of the Whitewater controversy. Nussbaum had played a key role in a number of Whitewater-related events that critics said gave the appearance of a White House cover-up.

On June 27, the President replaced his chief of staff, Thomas F. (Mack) McLarty III, with a Washington insider, Leon E. Panetta, director of the Office of Management and Budget (OMB). Panetta's deputy, Alice M. Rivlin, was named to head the OMB.

Three Cabinet officers left in 1994. Les Aspin departed as secretary of defense in January and was succeeded by his deputy, William J. Perry. Secretary of Agriculture Mike Espy, who was under fire on ethics charges, announced on October 3 that he would step down at the end of 1994. On December 6, Secretary of the Treasury Lloyd M. Bentsen, Jr., announced his resignation, effective December 22. Clinton chose Robert Rubin, the White House adviser on economic policy to succeed him. (See **Cabinet**.)

A close friend of Clinton's from Arkansas, Associate Attorney General Webster L. Hubbell, resigned on March 14. He said he was leaving because of controversy over his allegedly fraudulent billing practices at a Little Rock, Ark., law firm. On December 6, Hubbell pleaded guilty in a Little Rock federal court.

On December 9, Clinton fired controversial Surgeon General M. Joycelyn Elders after she suggested the teaching of masturbation in schools.

Foreign policy. Clinton announced on August 19 that the United States would end its policy of accepting all Cuban refugees who land on U.S. territory or are rescued in American waters. The President responded to the prospect of a massive influx of Cubans to the United States as Cuba's leader, Fidel Castro, said his government would not interfere with Cubans wishing to leave the island. As thousands of Cubans boarded small craft to undertake the journey to Florida, Clinton acted to divert the immigrants to camps at the U.S. naval base in Guantánamo, Cuba, and in Panama. On September 9, the United States and Cuba signed an agreement to allow 20,000 Cubans to enter the United States legally each year if Cuba would halt the exodus by sea.

There were two other foreign-policy switches during the year. On February 3, the United States ended its trade embargo against Vietnam, paving the way for normal business relations. And in May, Clinton decided not to continue linking trade benefits for China with human rights concerns. On May 26, he signed an executive order extending most-favored-nation (MFN) status to China for another year. MFN status allows China to export goods to the United States under the lowest U.S. tariff rate.

Relations with Congress. At home, Clinton frequently was checked by Republican opponents in Congress. In the Senate, Republicans used delaying tactics to block passage of Administration-backed bills. And in both the Senate and House late in the year, Republicans adopted a tactic of opposing any legislation favored by the White House—even bills that they had initially supported.

But Congress did pass a comprehensive anticrime measure on August 25, allocating $30.2 billion over six years for additional police officers for U.S. cities, more prisons, and a wide variety of crime prevention programs. And Clinton's $1.51-trillion budget for the 1995 fiscal year, with increased spending on education, job training, and other social programs, went through Congress without major changes. The budget received final congressional approval on May 12.

Clinton was also able to advance part of his plan for "reinventing government"—a proposal to reduce the federal bureaucracy and simplify the way the government conducts its business. In March, Congress passed and the President signed into law a bill to offer cash payments to government workers who voluntarily resign or retire early.

New Supreme Court justice. During the year, the President had the opportunity to name a second justice to the Supreme Court of the United States to fill a vacancy created by the retirement of Justice Harry A. Blackmun, 85. Clinton selected federal appeals court judge Stephen G. Breyer, 55, and the Senate confirmed him easily on July 29.

CIA traitor exposed. The U.S. government was shaken on February 21 when a top-level official of the Central Intelligence Agency (CIA) and his wife were arrested on charges of selling secrets to the Soviet Union and Russia over a period of at least nine years. The suspect, Aldrich Hazen Ames, 52, was the highest-ranking intelligence official ever accused of spying for a foreign power. His wife, Colombian-born Maria del Rosario Casas Ames, was accused of helping her husband betray U.S. agents to Moscow.

Ames, the son of a career CIA officer, avoided suspicion for years even though he had lived far beyond his means on at least $2 million he received from Soviet authorities. After pleading guilty to spying and tax evasion on April 28, he was sentenced to life in prison. His wife was sentenced to five years in prison after pleading guilty to a lesser charge.

CIA Director R. James Woolsey, Jr., reprimanded 11 senior active or retired CIA officials for failing to discover Ames's traitorous activities earlier. A Senate Intelligence committee report, however, said a mere reprimand was too lenient in view of Ames's betrayal of dozens of Soviet citizens working for the CIA or allied intelligence agencies, who were executed or imprisoned when found out. The Senate committee said Ames had caused more damage to national security than any other spy in U.S. history. Woolsey resigned on December 31. (See **Espionage: Why Spy?**)

Health and medicine. In a follow-up to Clinton's 1993 decision to end a five-year ban on federal research using tissue from aborted fetuses, a U.S. agency in 1994 authorized such research. On January 4, the National Institute of Neurological Disorders and Stroke in Bethesda, Md., approved a $4.5-million grant to three institutions to study whether implanting fetal tissue into the brains of patients with Parkinson's disease, a disorder of the nervous system, would be an effective treatment.

On March 10, the Centers for Disease Control and Prevention (CDC) in Atlanta, Ga., announced that the number of new AIDS cases in the United States in 1993 had more than doubled from the year before. It said the number of new cases shot up 111 percent to 103,500, with the sharpest increases among teen-agers and young adults. The CDC attributed the dramatic increase to a broader definition of AIDS that was adopted in January 1993. Earlier in the year, on Jan. 4, 1994, the CDC announced a new radio and television advertising campaign aimed at limiting the spread of AIDS as well as other sexually transmitted diseases. Clinton's chief AIDS policy coordinator, Kristine M. Gebbie, was replaced in November by her deputy, Patricia S. Fleming. (See **AIDS: The Changing Face of AIDS.**)

Tailhook scandal. Admiral Frank B. Kelso II, chief of naval operations, announced his retirement on February 15 and stepped down on April 23. Kelso claimed that he had been made a scapegoat for the Tailhook sex harassment scandal and he denounced a Navy judge's finding that he had manipulated the early stages of the investigation. The scandal resulted from allegations of sexual assaults on female naval personnel at a 1991 Las Vegas, Nev., convention of the Tailhook Association, an organization of naval aviators. On March 14, 1994, Clinton named Admiral Jeremy M. Boorda to succeed Kelso.

Military procurement fraud. A seven-year investigation of fraud in military purchases ended on January 14 after the conviction of 54 people, including former senior government officials, and 10 corporations. The inquiry, known as Operation Ill Wind, exposed a pattern of bid-rigging and bribery in Defense Department procurement.

The last case closed with a guilty plea by a unit of Litton Industries Inc. to charges of conspiracy and wire fraud to obtain information for bidding on three Navy contracts. Litton agreed to pay $3.9 million in fines, civil claims, and prosecution costs.

Final Iran-contra report. Another lengthy investigation was brought to a close on January 18 when Lawrence E. Walsh, the independent counsel who led the investigation of the Iran-contra affair, released his final report. The Iran-contra affair concerned the secret and illegal sale of arms to Iran during the Administration of President Ronald Reagan and the diversion of money from those arms sales to *contra* rebels in Nicaragua.

Walsh's report, which ended a 6½-year inquiry, criticized former Presidents Reagan and Bush for taking part in a cover-up of the scandal. Walsh said, however, that he had found no credible evidence of criminal activities by either Reagan or Bush.

Appointments. Clinton on April 22 made his first two appointments to the Board of Governors of the Federal Reserve System, selecting Alan S. Blinder, a member of the Administration's Council of Economic Advisers, for the vice chairman's post and naming Janet L. Yellen, an economist at the University of California at Berkeley, as a member of the seven-member board. The two appointees were regarded as advocates of a monetary policy that encourages economic growth.

William B. Gould IV, whom Clinton had nominated in June 1993 to head the National Labor Relations Board, an independent agency that works to prevent or correct unfair labor practices, was confirmed by the Senate on March 2, 1994, by a vote of 58 to 38. Conservative Republicans in Congress had accused Gould, a law professor at Stanford University in Stanford, Calif., of being too prounion.

On January 13, the President chose Thomas A. Constantine, former superintendent of the New York state police, to be administrator of the Drug Enforcement Administration. Constantine was confirmed on March 10.

Morton H. Halperin, whom Clinton had nominated to a new post of assistant secretary of defense for democracy and peacekeeping, withdrew his name on January 19. Halperin, a former senior official of the American Civil Liberties Union, had become a target of conservative Senate Republicans.

The White House under assault. In a bizarre episode that raised security concerns, a jobless truckdriver crashed a small plane on the South Lawn of the White House in the early morning hours of September 12, slightly damaging one of the walls. The pilot, Frank E. Corder, 38, of Aberdeen, Md., was killed in the crash. The President was not in the White House when the incident occurred.

On the afternoon of October 29, a man fired 27 bullets at the north side of the White House. Clinton was in the White House at the time but was not harmed. The alleged assailant, Francisco Martin Duran, 26, a maintenance worker at a Colorado resort, was taken into custody by Secret Service agents. On November 17, Duran was charged with attempting to assassinate the President.   □ William J. Eaton

See also **Clinton, Bill; Congress of the United States.** In *World Book,* see **United States, Government of the.**

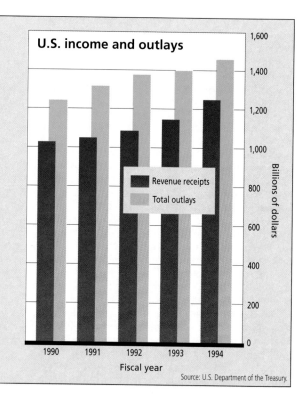

Federal spending
United States budget for fiscal 1994*

	Billions of dollars
National defense	281.5
International affairs	17.2
General science, space, technology	17.6
Energy	5.9
Natural resources and environment	20.9
Agriculture	15.1
Commerce and housing credit	– 4.9
Transportation	36.8
Community and regional development	11.9
Education, training, employment, and social services	44.7
Health	106.5
Social security	319.6
Medicare	144.7
Income security	214.0
Veterans' benefits and services	37.6
Administration of justice	15.3
General government	11.3
Interest	203.0
Undistributed offsetting receipts	– 37.8
Total budget outlays	**1,460.9**

*Oct. 1, 1993, to Sept. 30, 1994.
Source: U.S. Department of the Treasury.

U.S. income and outlays

Billions of dollars

Revenue receipts
Total outlays

1990   1991   1992   1993   1994
Fiscal year

Source: U.S. Department of the Treasury.

Uruguay. In the closest national elections in Uruguay's history, Julio María Sanguinetti, 58, of the Colorado Party won the presidency on Nov. 27, 1994, by a single percentage point. Sanguinetti served as president from 1985 to 1990 and will take office for another five-year term on March 1, 1995.

Sanguinetti set about trying to forge a coalition to carry out his legislative agenda in the General Assembly, whose seats were divided about equally among representatives of three parties. The three parties included the incumbent Blanco Party, which came in second at the polls, and the left wing Broad Front Party, made up of Communists, socialists, and former Tupamaro guerrillas. The Broad Front ran third in the national elections by less than a percentage point and retained its hold on the mayor's office of the capital city of Montevideo—home to half of Uruguay's voters.

New highway. Feasibility studies began in April on a $1-billion, 30-mile (48-kilometer) bridge joining Colonia, Uruguay, and Buenos Aires, Argentina. The bridge would be a vital link in a planned 1,500-mile (2,400-kilometer) highway between São Paulo, Brazil, and Buenos Aires. ☐ Nathan A. Haverstock

See also **Latin America** (Facts in brief table). In *World Book,* see Uruguay.

Utah. See State government.

Uzbekistan. See Asia.

Vanuatu. See Pacific Islands.

Venezuela. Rafael Caldera Rodríguez took the oath of office for a five-year term as president of Venezuela on Feb. 2, 1994. The 78-year-old leader, who was the nation's president from 1969 to 1974, quickly sought to defuse public anger over a growing banking scandal and corruption in government.

On March 26, 1994, Caldera pardoned Lieutenant Colonel Hugo Chaves Frías, leader of a February 1992 coup attempt against former President Carlos Andrés Pérez, who was removed from office in May 1993 on charges of embezzling public funds. The Supreme Court of Justice of Venezuela on May 18, 1994, ordered Pérez jailed during his trial.

Caldera took office in the middle of a financial panic caused by the January failure of Venezuela's second largest bank. On June 14, the government closed eight more banks. Economists estimated that it would cost Venezuelan taxpayers $6.1 billion to bail out the banks.

The Caldera administration adopted extraordinary powers on June 28 to deal with the financial crisis. Caldera imposed currency and price controls and limited civil liberties guaranteed by Venezuela's Constitution. ☐ Nathan A. Haverstock

See also **Latin America** (Facts in brief table). In *World Book,* see Venezuela.

Vermont. See State government.

Vice President of the U.S. See Gore, Albert, Jr.

Vietnam. The last international restriction placed on Vietnam since the end of the Vietnam War (1957-1975) was lifted on Feb. 3, 1994, when United States President Bill Clinton removed a U.S. embargo on trade. Clinton's decision, which followed earlier steps toward establishing normal relations between the two countries, led to an agreement to open liaison offices in Washington, D.C., and Hanoi, Vietnam's capital.

The Clinton Administration said the decision to lift the embargo was based on Vietnam's continued cooperation in locating American military personnel still officially listed as missing in action (MIA's). On October 26, the U.S. military commander for the Pacific, Admiral Richard C. Macke, praised Vietnam's cooperation in accounting for MIA's, but some Defense Department officers and congressmen thought Vietnam was still hiding the remains of many MIA's.

The economy. Vietnam's economy grew at a rate of 10.5 percent in the first half of 1994, spurred in part by good harvests. But summer floods in the Mekong River Delta—which killed 300 people—and in northern Vietnam in September sharply reduced the rice crop, the nation's most important.

Expatriated Vietnamese brought business skills and money to invest, as they returned home in increasing numbers in 1994. They had fled after the Communist takeover in 1975. Foreign investors, too, particularly from Taiwan and Hong Kong, began to

Excavation teams in January search a crash site in central Vietnam for traces of U.S. servicemen still listed as missing since the end of the Vietnam War (1957-1975).

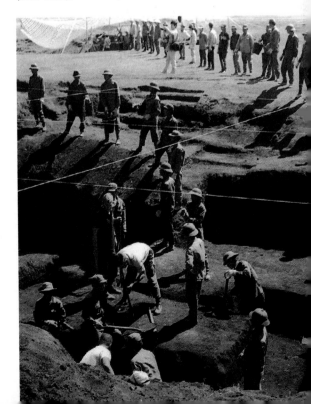

build factories, but inadequate electrical power generation and other infrastructure problems limited such construction. Vietnam's laws also complicated foreign investment. Designed for a controlled, centrally planned economy, the laws were inconsistent and inadequate when applied to a free market, which many government officials now see as the key to producing wealth.

The Communist Party of Vietnam warned the nation on January 25 that official corruption and smuggling were eroding the people's confidence in the party and the state. In August, the party said Vietnam faced "acute difficulties" from low economic growth, poor control of inflation, and increased competition from other countries for export markets and foreign investments. The party noted a widening gap between the poverty of rural areas and the growing prosperity of industrial regions.

ASEAN membership. The Association of Southeast Asian Nations (ASEAN), an organization of six anti-Communist countries in Southeast Asia that was created during the Vietnam War, said on July 24 that Vietnam would be admitted to ASEAN at its summit conference in mid-1995. ASEAN promotes cooperation among its member nations. ☐ Henry S. Bradsher

See also **Asia** (Facts in brief table). In *World Book,* see Vietnam.

Virginia. See State government.

Vital statistics. See Census; Population.

Washington, D.C.

Former Washington, D.C. Mayor Marion S. Barry, Jr., who left office in disgrace after his 1990 conviction for cocaine possession, completed a remarkable political comeback in 1994. In the November 8 general election, after conducting a bold campaign emphasizing the theme of his redemption from alcohol and drug abuse, Barry reclaimed his old job. He gathered 55 percent of the vote to defeat Republican candidate Carol Schwartz, who collected 41 percent.

Barry, a former member of the D.C. Board of Education and the D.C. Council, had dominated politics as mayor from 1979 through 1990. He decided not to seek reelection to a fourth term in 1990 after his drug arrest. Barry served six months in prison on the drug charge, from October 1991 to April 1992.

Barry won a decisive victory in the city's critical Sept. 13, 1994, Democratic mayoral primary with 47 percent of the vote. (A plurality of votes is sufficient to win nomination in District primaries.) Barry's total gave him a solid margin over D.C. Council member John Ray, who won 37 percent of the vote in his fourth try for mayor, and incumbent Mayor Sharon Pratt Kelly, who earned 13 percent. In the heavily Democratic District, the Democratic nomination is generally equivalent to final victory, so Barry's triumph in November was widely expected.

Another winner in the November election was Eleanor Holmes Norton, a Democrat, who was re-elected to a third term as the city's nonvoting delegate to the United States House of Representatives. D.C. Council Chairman David A. Clarke and all but one incumbent on the 13-member City Council also won reelection.

Troubled finances and management. The District government struggled throughout the year with budget problems and a loss of authority over some key municipal functions. In August, a D.C. Superior Court judge ordered the city's Department of Public Housing, ranked the worst in the country in a federal index, to be placed under the control of a court-appointed receiver. Mayor Kelly appealed the decision. In September, in a move also resisted by the mayor, a U.S. District Court judge ordered a part of the District's foster care system into receivership. Another Superior Court judge delayed the opening of the D.C. public schools for three days in September until the city repaired potentially life-threatening fire code violations in school buildings.

In September, the U.S. Congress, concerned about reports that the District was suffering a cash crunch, ordered the mayor and council to cut the city's $3.4-billion operating budget for 1995 by $140-million. It also instructed the District to eliminate 2,000 full-time positions on the city payroll.

Murder rate declines. The number of murders in the District declined in 1994 compared with the year before, and it appeared that the city would record fewer than 400 homicides for the first time since 1988. By Dec. 2, 1994, a total of 378 murders had been reported, compared with 463 by the same date in 1993. Homicides for all of 1993 totaled 467.

Nonetheless, widespread violence in 1994, including a shooting at Eastern High School in March, drove city leaders to increase the number of police officers patrolling the public schools. The police were given permission to search students and students' lockers for weapons.

Winter woes. The city endured 16 snow, sleet, or ice storms in 1994, which hurt business, snarled roads, and forced the cancellation of four days of school. On January 20, as the result of a storm that strained power sources across the mid-Atlantic region, both the federal and District governments were closed for the day. At the request of electrical and natural gas utility companies, Mayor Kelly declared a state of emergency that day, requiring all nonessential businesses to close. Hospitals, grocery stores, and other operations related to health and safety continued to operate.

Domingo named opera director. Spanish tenor Placido Domingo, one of the world's leading opera singers, was named artistic director of the Washington Opera in June. His appointment takes effect in 1996. ☐ Nell Henderson

See also **City.** In *World Book,* see **Washington, D.C.**

Washington. See State government.

Water. The magnitude 6.7-earthquake that struck the San Fernando Valley about 25 miles (40 kilometers) north of Los Angeles on Jan. 17, 1994, caused significant damage to the area's water supply facilities. The greatest damage occurred to the water distribution system. The quake's force affected water treatment plants and local distribution pipelines in the immediate area of the earthquake, cutting water supply to two-thirds of the densely populated valley. However, the Los Angeles Department of Water and Power restored water service to most customers by January 26.

The quake also damaged a major aqueduct serving Los Angeles. Los Angeles receives its water from groundwater, surface water reservoirs, and three major aqueducts, which import water from the Colorado River, Owens Valley in eastern California, and northern California. The earthquake damaged the Los Angeles Aqueduct, which carries water from the Owens Valley, but left the other two aqueducts unharmed. Engineers also inspected 108 dams in southern California following the earthquake but reported no substantial changes.

Some Sarajevo water restored. An international relief effort partially restored by mid-1994 the water supply of the besieged city of Sarajevo, capital of Bosnia-Herzegovina. The city's water supply had been disrupted since the summer of 1992, when ethnic Serbian armed forces blocked the flow of water and power into the city. As a result, residents of Sarajevo had to obtain water from the Miljacka River, wells, or public water distribution points. Many water sources exposed city residents to sniper fire and shelling.

However, in January 1994, under the direction of the New York City-based International Rescue Committee, Canadian and United States Air Force aircraft transported two self-contained water treatment plants containing pumps and purification equipment to Sarajevo. To provide shelter from shelling, engineers installed one plant in a tunnel. Engineers planned to install the remaining plant in a fortified building. The new equipment will filter local river water to remove sediment and kill organisms that could cause disease. By November, one plant was in operation. When both plants are working, they will supply 60,000 people in eastern Sarajevo with safe drinking water.

Mono Lake rescue plan. For years, scenic Mono Lake in eastern California has been threatened with falling water levels because the city of Los Angeles diverts water from streams that feed the lake. On September 28, the California State Water Resources Control Board ordered Los Angeles to reduce its diversions by one-third. Los Angeles began diverting water from the lake in 1941. The order raised expectations that the lake would rise to its pre-1941 level.

☐ Iris Priestaf

In *World Book*, see **Water.**

Weather. Extreme weather battered many areas of the United States and the world in 1994. Severe cold and heavy snow descended on the Great Plains, the Midwest, and the Northeast in January, followed by record heat in many areas of the Southwest and the East in June. Flooding caused extensive damage in Georgia and Texas. In China, a typhoon created disastrous flooding that led to about 1,000 deaths in Zhejiang province.

On January 4, heavy snow, falling at up to 5 inches (12.7 centimeters) per hour, moved through eastern Kentucky and into Pennsylvania and New York. In Waynesburg, Pa., 28 inches (71 centimeters) of snow fell during the first week of January. As cold air swooped southward behind this storm, a 24-hour record of 10.1 inches (25.7 centimeters) of snow was set at Williston, S. Dak., on January 4 and 5.

Biting cold followed in the ensuing two weeks, capped on January 17 by one of the coldest outbreaks of the 1900's. From January 19 to 21, at least 18 low-temperature records were set in the Midwest and the East. Among the cities that set new records were Indianapolis (-27 °F [-33 °C]); Akron, Ohio (-25 °F [-32 °C]); Clarksburg, W. Va., (-25 °F); and Allentown, Pa. (-15 °F [-9 °C]). On January 18, Tyler, Minn., registered a low temperature of -44 °F (-42 °C), and on January 19, Amasa, Mich., recorded a low of -52 °F (-47 °C). According to the Climate Analysis Center of the National Oceanic and Atmospheric Administration, in the Northeast January was the third coldest January in the 100 years that weather records have been kept.

January produced mild temperatures throughout the West. Rain returned to California during the last week of the month, and by February 20, excessive rains caused mud slides on hills that had been stripped of vegetation by fires around Los Angeles and Malibu. Despite the rainy February, the winter was generally dry in the West. Rainfall since Oct. 1, 1993, averaged 75 percent of normal over the entire Western United States, according to the Climate Analysis Center, and only 50 percent of normal in the Northwest and southern California. The California snowpack stood at only 50 to 80 percent of normal at the end of February 1994.

On March 1, a fierce storm came out of the Gulf of Mexico and moved up the East Coast. Heavy snow fell from central Pennsylvania through central New York to the Atlantic Coast. Boston received 10 inches (25 centimeters), raising its season total to a record 90.55 inches (230 centimeters). Authorities said the storm contributed to the deaths of seven people and left more than 500,000 customers without electricity. Another storm wreaked havoc from the Gulf Coastal Plains to New England from March 8 to 10, leaving snow, ice, and rain that contributed to many traffic accidents, closed schools, and disrupted power.

Seasonal snowfall records also fell in Elkins, W. Va., with 124.5 inches (316.3 centimeters) and Scran-

The Flint River deluges Montezuma, Ga., in July. Torrential rain from the remains of Tropical Storm Alberto caused severe flooding in central Georgia.

ton, Pa., with 88.7 inches (225.3 centimeters). On March 16, a cold front brought more snowfall, surpassing previous season records at Binghamton, N.Y.; State College, Pa.; and Boston.

Spring brings tornadoes. On March 27, from 20 to 30 tornadoes struck five states from Alabama to North Carolina, resulting in at least 43 deaths. In Alabama, 20 people died when a tornado hit the crowded Goshen Methodist Church outside Piedmont. A tornado swept through Pickens County, Georgia, on the same day, resulting in the deaths of 11 people. State officials described the Palm Sunday outbreak as the worst to hit Georgia since the early 1970's. More tornadoes took 6 lives in Missouri, Oklahoma, and Illinois from April 10 to 12. On April 15 and 16, a second wave of storms spawned nearly 48 tornadoes from the Mississippi Valley to the Atlantic coast, taking 7 lives.

During the week of April 24 to 30, more than 80 tornadoes and 450 severe storms occurred throughout the country. On April 25, storms took 3 lives and injured 48 people at De Soto and Lancaster, Tex. On April 26, a tornado struck Lafayette, Ind., killing 3 people and injuring 60 more. On April 29, 12 more tornadoes hit Texas, and President Bill Clinton declared Dallas, Cooke, and Lamar counties federal disaster areas.

Hot and dry. The average temperature for June over the lower 48 states was 2.7 Fahrenheit degrees

(1.5 Celsius degrees) above normal, due largely to two heat waves. The first heat wave occurred in the central Mississippi Valley and mid-Atlantic states and lasted about a week. Baltimore had a high temperature record of 101 °F (38 °C) on June 15 and joined Philadelphia; Portland, Me.; and Denver, Colo., as cities where the average June temperature was the highest on record.

The second heat wave stifled the Southwest, which also had its hottest June on record. From June 26 to July 1, more than 50 new high-temperature records were set from southern California east to the Central Plains.

For most of the West, the heat and dryness of June and July were the most extreme since 1895. The arid conditions contributed to widespread forest fires. By early July, thousands of acres of forestland were burning in seven Western states. On July 21, lightning started 300 new fires across Oregon and northern California and another 150 on July 28. According to the National Fire Coordinating Center in Boise, Ida., a federal office that coordinates forest fire control efforts, the July wildfires consumed more than 3 million acres (1.2 million hectares).

Floods hit the Gulf states. Tropical Storm Alberto moved north out of the Gulf of Mexico on July 3 near Fort Walton Beach, Fla., and stalled in northwest Georgia on July 5. The remains of the storm produced up to 24 inches (61 centimeters) of rain in some locations in Georgia. Through July 25, flooding had resulted in the deaths of 31 people in Georgia, left more than 150,000 people without drinking water, and damaged 1 million acres (400,000 hectares) of planted crops. On July 11, the Flint River crested at Albany, Ga., at 42.6 feet (12.9 meters) above flood stage—4.8 feet (1.5 meters) higher than the previous record. Three other rivers also had record crest levels. Clinton pledged $66.1 million of federal aid to portions of Georgia, Alabama, and Florida hardest hit by flooding.

On October 15, an intense, slow-moving cyclone developed over the central Rocky Mountains, where as much as 4 feet (1.2 meters) of snow accumulated. The vast circulation from this storm pushed a flood of warm, humid air across the central Gulf Coast. From October 16 to 20, as much as 30 inches (76 centimeters) of rain fell on Conroe, Tex., and neighboring areas in southeast Texas. Clinton granted federal disaster relief to 37 Texas counties. At least 22 deaths were caused by the storm, and 10,000 people fled their homes because of floods.

Gordon brings trouble. Tropical Storm Gordon formed off Nicaragua on November 5. On November 12, Gordon dumped heavy rain on Haiti, causing floods and mud slides that killed about 800 people. From November 14 through 16, Gordon drifted through southern Florida, bringing 10 to 15 inches (25 to 38 centimeters) of rain and floods that caused about $300 million of damage to winter vegetable crops. Eight Florida deaths were associated with the storm. Gordon traveled north and gained strength, and on November 17, it reached hurricane force. After brushing North Carolina, Gordon turned south again but weakened and died out in Florida.

Tropical cyclones. During the first three months of 1994, five tropical cyclones battered the island of Madagascar off the southeast coast of Africa. Cyclone Daisy hit the island on January 13 with sustained winds of 103 miles per hour (mph) or 166 kilometers per hour (kph); Geralda, with winds of 128 mph (206 kph), hit on February 2; Julita, with winds of 97 mph (156 kph), hit on February 17; Litanne, with winds of 128 mph, hit on March 17; and Nadia, with winds of 116 mph (187 kph), hit on March 23. Nadia took 12 lives and destroyed about 80 percent of the town of Vohemar. Geralda's winds, measured over the ocean, were 161 mph (259 kph), making it the most powerful cyclone on record in the South Indian Ocean.

On August 21 and 22, Typhoon Fred moved into coastal Zhejiang province of China. Winds gusting to 161 mph and floods from heavy rain and high tides killed about 700 people, destroyed or damaged about 700,000 homes, and closed 90,000 businesses. Local officials described Fred as the worst storm since the late 1800's. □ Alfred K. Blackadar

See also **Disasters.** In *World Book*, see **Weather.**
Weightlifting. See Sports.

Welfare. A major overhaul of the federal welfare system seemed likely to occur in 1995 after the Republican Party swept midterm elections on Nov. 8, 1994, and captured control of both houses of Congress for the first time since 1954. The Republicans said they would make welfare reform one of their first legislative priorities. Earlier, on June 14, 1994, President Bill Clinton had unveiled his long-delayed plan to reform the federal welfare system, but it was immediately caught in a cross fire of criticism. Many liberals charged that Clinton's proposals were too harsh, but conservatives regarded them as too lenient to achieve the President's goal to "end welfare as we know it."

Representative Newt Gingrich (R., Ga.), the Speaker-designate after the November elections, said he favored eliminating many current federal welfare programs and replacing them with cash grants to be given to the 50 states to disperse as they see fit. Congress, however, did not consider any welfare reform bill in 1994, because it was preoccupied with health care reform.

The central issue in the welfare debate was how to cut back on the estimated $23-billion annual cost of the Aid to Families with Dependent Children (AFDC) program. The median AFDC benefit per family in 1994 was $367 a month. Most advocates of change had hoped that the 14 million AFDC recipients—mostly young single mothers and their children—could become less dependent on government assistance.

Clinton's plan. The President proposed a two-year lifetime limit on AFDC payments for women born after 1971. The government would provide educational programs, vocational training, and job placement assistance to help mothers on AFDC find work. Recipients who remained unemployed after two years would be required either to do community service work or take a government-subsidized job with a private employer. Both kinds of work would pay the prevailing minimum wage.

Under the plan, no benefits would be paid to anyone who failed to attend school, look for work, or take part in a training program. Clinton's plan would also require the fathers of children born out of wedlock to pay child support.

Critics open fire. The proposals unveiled by the President were considerably less ambitious than many advocates of welfare reform had hoped for. Republicans and conservative Democrats alike favored a faster phase-in of changes and more stringent measures to reduce welfare costs. More than 300 Republican candidates for the House of Representatives, for example, demanded a cutoff of benefits for mothers under the age of 21 or in cases where a child's paternity had not been established. □ William J. Eaton

See also **Welfare** Special Report: **Time to Reform Welfare?** In *World Book,* see **Welfare.**

■ Most welfare recipients, such as this family residing in the south Bronx area of New York City, live in poverty despite government assistance.

Time to Reform Welfare?

America's welfare system is the target of criticism, but efforts to end long-term dependency face political battles and carry a high price tag.

By Saul D. Hoffman

Glossary

Aid to Families with Dependent Children (AFDC): A welfare program that provides income to poor families. AFDC families usually are headed by divorced, separated, or never-married women.

Dependency: The condition of relying on others for support.

Food stamps: Vouchers that look like cash but can buy only food.

Medicaid: A welfare program that provides free health care to poor people.

Poverty line: An income level determined by the federal government. People living under the poverty line are regarded as poor.

Welfare: A number of government programs designed to assist needy people.

W elfare reform became one of the foremost political issues in 1994. United States President Bill Clinton on June 14 unveiled legislation to reform America's welfare system, making good on his campaign pledge "to end welfare as we know it." Under his plan, single mothers born since 1971 who qualify for welfare would receive cash payments for up to two years. Then they would be required to find work in the private sector or enroll in a public works program. In November 1994, members of the Republican Party, after winning control of the U.S. Congress, also made welfare reform a priority. The Republican plan would not only limit cash payments to two years, but would deny cash benefits to unmarried mothers under the age of 18 and in cases when a child's father is unknown.

Welfare has long been a target of criticism. Some critics believe that it is costly, complex, and does little to eradicate poverty. Others think it discourages work and family stability. Any change made to the welfare system will affect millions of lives and likely carry a high price tag. Among members of the public, many questions remain. For a start, what exactly is the welfare system? What does it do? And—perhaps most importantly—how can welfare be ended?

The welfare system consists of government programs designed to assist needy people. People who receive welfare include the blind, the disabled, and those who live below the *poverty line,* an income level determined by the federal government. In 1993, about one in seven Americans lived in poverty. The federal government regarded an individual as poor if he or she earned less than $7,356 in 1993; a family of four, if it earned less than $14,763. Poor Americans include nearly one in four children and almost half of all African-American children. The welfare system provides poor families with cash, goods, and services.

Welfare: legacy of the Great Depression

Before the 1930's, no federal welfare system existed in the United States. The need for federal assistance became apparent during the Great Depression of the 1930's, the worst economic slump in the nation's history. President Franklin D. Roosevelt offered government help as part of his New Deal program to fight the depression. Called General Relief, it was intended to end once the economy recovered.

Today's welfare system originated as part of the landmark Social Security Act of 1935, which also set up an old-age insurance program. The legislation created Aid to Dependent Children (ADC), a program to provide income primarily to mothers whose husbands had died before becoming eligible for the new social security benefits. In 1935, mothers were not expected to work, so it seemed appropriate for society to support them. Because it was assumed that fathers should support their families, married couples were ineligible for assistance.

The ADC program was later renamed Aid to Families with Dependent Children (AFDC) and is now the largest source of income for welfare families and the primary focus of reform efforts. In 1994, most families receiving AFDC were headed by divorced, separated, or never-married women. Although poor families headed by married cou-

■ **The author**

Saul D. Hoffman is a professor of economics at the University of Delaware in Newark.

Social Welfare Spending

Type of program	Number of recipients	Cost
Medicaid	32 million people	$118 billion
Food Stamps	27 million people*	$25 billion*
Aid to Families with Dependent Children	14 million people*	$23 billion*
Supplemental Security Income	5.6 million people	$22 billion
Housing	5.5 million people	$18 billion
School Lunch and Breakfast Program	24.5 million people	$5 billion
Supplemental Food Program for Women, Infants, and Children	1.2 million people	$3 billion
Low Income Home Energy Assistance Program	5.8 million families	$2 billion

*1993 data.
Source: *Overview of Entitlement Programs;* U.S. House of Representatives Committee on Ways and Means, 1992 data (1993 edition).

ples are now eligible to receive welfare, they have a harder time getting assistance than families headed by single parents.

Other welfare programs were added later, many during the War on Poverty launched by President Lyndon B. Johnson in the mid-1960's. These included food stamps, vouchers that look like cash but can buy only food; and Medicaid, which provides free health care to poor people. Several programs provide shelter, either in public projects or by subsidizing rent for private housing. The School Lunch and Breakfast Program; the Low Income Home Energy Assistance Program; and the Supplemental Food Program for Women, Infants, and Children also are considered welfare. During the mid-1970's, Supplemental Security Income (SSI) was established for low-income people who cannot support themselves because they are aged, blind, or physically or mentally disabled.

The most expensive program by far is Medicaid, which cost nearly $120 billion in 1992. (By contrast, AFDC cost $22 billion that year.) Spending on Medicaid has grown quickly—up from $72 billion in 1990—because of rising health-care costs. The number of people on the Medicaid rolls has also risen, from 28.3 million in 1991 to 31.6 million in 1992. Most Medicaid spending, however, does not go to AFDC families. They account for about 30 percent of Medicaid costs. Most of the money spent goes to people receiving SSI, who often have substantial medical needs, and to low-income elderly Americans living in nursing homes.

The AFDC and food stamp programs each cost between $23 bil-

■ **Who receives AFDC?**
About 14 million people—including 9.5 million children—received Aid to Families with Dependent Children (AFDC) in 1993, usually as a result of single parenthood, divorce, or separation. Educated women tend to leave the system quickly; teen-age mothers are more likely to remain there long term.

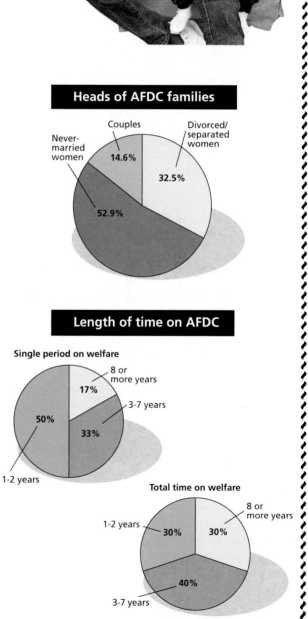

Age of AFDC mothers

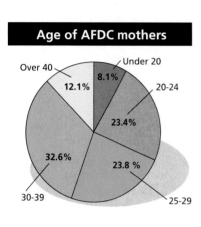

Under 20 8.1%
20-24 23.4%
25-29 23.8 %
30-39 32.6%
Over 40 12.1%

Race of AFDC mothers

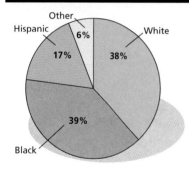

Other 6%
Hispanic 17%
White 38%
Black 39%

Education of AFDC mothers

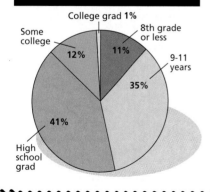

College grad 1%
8th grade or less 11%
9-11 years 35%
High school grad 41%
Some college 12%

Heads of AFDC families

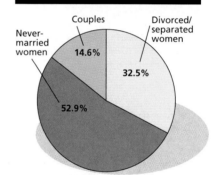

Never-married women 52.9%
Couples 14.6%
Divorced/separated women 32.5%

Length of time on AFDC

Single period on welfare

8 or more years 17%
3-7 years 33%
1-2 years 50%

Total time on welfare

8 or more years 30%
1-2 years 30%
3-7 years 40%

lion and $25 billion a year. About 14 million people received AFDC benefits in 1993; more than 27 million people—a record number—received food stamps in 1993. Participation in each program has risen by about 25 percent since 1985.

These programs are mandated by the federal government, which regulates how they should run, and are operated by the states. Funding usually comes from both state and federal governments. Under some programs, people receive approximately the same benefits no matter where they live. This is true of food stamps and SSI. Under other programs, such as Medicaid and AFDC, benefits vary widely.

Most states also provide cash to low-income individuals ineligible for other assistance, usually through a program called General Assistance. In 1990, 1.2 million people received General Assistance, at a cost of $4.6 billion.

Who gets welfare, and how much?

Not every poor family can avail itself of all welfare programs. Each program has its own rules and may not be available in every state or city. Families that receive AFDC, however, almost always receive food stamps and Medicaid. These three programs sometimes are regarded as the core of the welfare system. In 1992, about 24 percent of American families and 73 percent of poor families had incomes low enough to receive some kind of assistance.

The amount of assistance that goes to a family depends on its size, the state it lives in, and its income. Each state decides the amount AFDC should provide and the medical services Medicaid should cover within its borders. The allotments differ enormously from state to state. In 1993, a family of three received less than $200 a month under AFDC in Alabama, Louisiana, Mississippi, Tennessee, and Texas. The same family would receive more than $600 a month in Alaska, Hawaii, California, Connecticut, New York, and Vermont. In Illinois—the median state, which pays more than half the states and less than the other half—a family of three would receive a maximum of $367 a month.

Food stamps are more uniform. A family that has no income beyond AFDC would qualify for food stamps worth about $275 a month. A family of three receiving both AFDC and food stamps would collect about $7,800 a year, approximately 70 percent of the income needed to rise above the poverty line. This means that most families receiving welfare are living in poverty.

After adjusting for inflation, a family on welfare in 1994 received less money than it would have received in 1970. AFDC benefits fell by 45 percent from 1970 to 1993 because most states did not increase them to keep up with inflation. Even adding in food stamps and Medicaid, which have increased in value, total benefits have fallen about 20 percent since 1970.

More than 9 million children and about 5 million women received AFDC in 1993. Nearly 40 percent of the women were white, 40 percent were African American, and most of the rest were Hispanic American. African Americans and Hispanic Americans are overrepresented in

A woman on welfare in Illinois with two children

Receives: Maximum of $367 per month in AFDC
$275 per month in food stamps
Free health care under Medicaid

Annual income: $7,704, plus free health care
Weekly income: $148.15

A working woman in Illinois with two children

Who receives: Annual salary of $9,360 ($4.50 per
hour 40 hours a week)
Earned Income Tax Credit of $2,528
$45 per month in food stamps
Medicaid benefits reduced or eliminated

Deductions: Social security $716.04 per year
Illinois income tax $160.80 per year
Federal income tax $0 per year
Total: $876.84 per year

Annual income after deductions: $11,551.16
Weekly income: $222.14

Expenses
Full-time day care for 2-year-old and 4-year-old:
$125 per week*

Weekly income after child care: $97.14

*Average cost of unsubsidized full-time child care in
provider's home on the South Side of Chicago.
Sources: Internal Revenue Service, Social Security Administration, Illinois Department of Public Aid, Illinois
Department of Revenue, Day Care Action Council.

■ **Work or welfare?**
A mother of two living in Illinois could receive a maximum of $367 in welfare benefits per month. This amount is the median welfare payment in the United States—half of the states pay less and the other half pay more. With food stamps, a mother of two children on welfare in Illinois receives a weekly income of $148.15 and free health care. This compares with a weekly income of $97.14 for a single mother with two children working at slightly above the minimum wage and paying average day care costs. Critics argue that the welfare system thus discourages people from seeking work.

the AFDC population. Blacks make up about 11 percent of the U.S. population and Hispanics 9 percent.

Most women on AFDC were young—nearly one-third were less than 25 years old and an additional one-fourth were in their late 20's. Nearly half had less than a high school education. More than half entered the welfare system after becoming unmarried mothers, and about a third after a divorce or separation.

Many people think that the major problem of the welfare system is dependency—families receiving welfare benefits year after year. The many studies of this topic all lead to the same conclusion: Most families that receive welfare do not depend on it for a long time. About half of families who receive welfare become self-supporting within two years of their first payment. About one-third receive benefits for between three and seven consecutive years, and about one-sixth for eight or more years in a row. This last group tends to pile up on the welfare rolls. Because of that, on any particular date, roughly half of welfare recipients are likely to be long-term recipients.

Different segments of the welfare population are dependent to substantially different degrees. High-school graduates who apply following a divorce or separation tend to stay on welfare for a relatively short time. In contrast, never-married women who did not graduate from high school tend to stay on welfare much longer. Teen-age mothers are especially likely to become long-term recipients.

Although most families leave the welfare rolls relatively quickly, many are unable to remain self-sufficient. Researchers estimate that more than 40 percent of women who ever receive welfare do so for two or more separate periods. When this additional time on welfare is factored in, roughly one-third of all welfare recipients receive benefits for two years or less, one-third for between three and seven years, and one-third for eight years or more.

Many people assume that daughters who grow up in welfare families are more likely to receive welfare themselves. But whether this is true is unclear. One study found that 3 percent of daughters from families that never received welfare became heavily dependent on welfare as adults, compared with 20 percent of daughters from families that did receive welfare. This suggests that welfare receipt is linked across generations, but it does not tell us why. It might be a sign that welfare breeds a "welfare culture," an acceptance of dependency. Or, it might be a sign that children in poor families face obstacles that others do not, and therefore have more economic difficulties as adults. It is important to note the study found that 80 percent of daughters from welfare families did not become recipients as adults.

A deeply flawed welfare system

Most experts agree that the welfare system has many flaws. AFDC is often cited as the most flawed, but many other programs work in a similar way. One problem is that families receiving welfare have little incentive to seek work. When a family on welfare earns income, its welfare benefits drop. A welfare recipient who starts work loses $2 of AFDC money for every $3 she earns. That means that she is just $1 better off. This rule applies only to the first four months of work. After that, an AFDC mother loses $1 of welfare for every $1 she earns.

It is not hard to see the problem this creates. The economic gain of work is reduced sharply. Suppose a welfare recipient found a job paying $4.50 an hour. If she worked 10 hours a week, she would earn $45. But even under the more attractive "$2 lost for $3 earned" rule, her welfare payments would be cut by $30 (two-thirds of $45), leaving her just $15 better off after 10 hours of work. It would be as if her wage were $1.50 an hour instead of $4.50. After four months, when she would lose a dollar in welfare for every dollar earned, work would make her no better off at all—as if her wage were $0 an hour. To make matters worse, she might lose some food stamps and, if she earned too much, all her Medicaid benefits.

Another problem is that welfare benefits have long been more easily available and more generous to single-parent families than married-couple families. Many researchers think the welfare system therefore encourages the breakup of a married-couple family. If a father cannot find work, his mere presence in the household may stand in the way of the family receiving AFDC benefits. According to these researchers, welfare deserves some blame for the rise in divorce since 1970 and the rise of births to single women, especially teen-agers. The United States has one of the highest teen birth rates in the developed world. In 1991, about 6.2 percent of American teen-age women gave birth. This is about twice as high as the teen birth rate in the United Kingdom and about seven times as high as that in France. About two-thirds of such births are to unmarried teen-agers, most of whom later receive welfare.

Finally, welfare does too little to help poor families. Most families and children who receive welfare still live in poverty. The rate of child poverty in the United States has risen from 15 percent of children in 1970 to 22 percent in 1990 and is among the highest in the developed world. About 10 percent of Canadian children are poor, for example,

■ Welfare recipients in Cleveland learn to remove lead and asbestos from buildings—training that has led to jobs with a starting hourly wage of $7.32. The Cleveland Works program teaches such skills so that parents can support their families through work rather than welfare.

and about 5 percent of Swedish children.

Most experts view welfare reform as a four-part task, consisting of (1) strengthening the child support system, (2) making work economically rewarding, (3) widening the availability of health care, and (4) reforming AFDC. The first two are partly in place, but in 1994 action on the last—and most difficult—two lay ahead.

Child support is considered an important part of welfare reform, because the failure of absent fathers to pay adequate child support is a large cause of poverty. Fathers are responsible for supporting their children, whether they live with the children or not. Yet, only 4 out of 10 absent fathers provide child support to their children.

The Family Support Act was passed in 1988 to help mothers, especially unmarried mothers, obtain child support. The legislation required states to determine how much child support should be paid and to withhold such payments from the wages of delinquent fathers. Some experts hope that men will act more responsibly if they know they have a financial obligation toward any children they

447

father. This may lower the number of children born to unmarried women, many of whom end up on welfare, but this result has not yet been shown.

Making low-wage work pay

Making work economically rewarding, especially low-wage work, also is considered crucial to welfare reform. In 1993, Congress expanded a program called the Earned Income Tax Credit (EITC). Under EITC, for every $1,000 that a low-income family earned (up to about $8,000) in 1994, it received an additional $300 from the government. That is exactly like receiving a 30 percent wage increase. By 1996, a low-income family could get as much as $400 for each $1,000 earned, receiving a maximum of $3,370. A family with a full-time worker earning the minimum wage of $4.25 an hour would have an income of $11,870.

The EITC is administered by the Internal Revenue Service (IRS) as part of the tax return that most families fill out each spring. If the tax credit due to a family under the EITC is greater than the taxes it owes, it gets a rebate from the IRS. If not, the family's taxes are cut by the amount of the credit. Either way, the family ends up better off. Only families with children are eligible for the EITC now, but in 1996, childless low-income families will qualify.

A major barrier to leaving welfare is the fact that low-wage jobs rarely provide health insurance. Families on AFDC, however, automatically receive free health care under Medicaid. If some kind of health-care reform is passed, it will likely enable low-income workers to buy health insurance at reduced cost. This ought to help low-wage workers move from welfare to work.

Limiting time on welfare

To redeem his pledge "to end welfare as we know it," most experts agreed that President Clinton had to reform AFDC. The key element of both the Clinton and the Republican plan was a strict two-year limit for a family to remain on welfare. This limit came, in part, from the fact that about half the women on welfare leave the system within two years. Under the Clinton plan, welfare recipients would receive job training during those two years. With the expanded EITC, which increases the income of low-wage workers, job training might make a difference. If welfare were limited, recipients would need work skills.

After two years, welfare recipients would have to find a job or enroll in a public works program, probably earning the minimum wage. Anyone who refused to work would lose all benefits. Child care would be provided for working mothers, and only women with children younger than age 1 would be exempt from the two-year limit.

Still undecided was what would happen to people in the subsidized work program who could not find a regular job. Would the work program have a time limit, just as AFDC benefits would? It is possible that at some point, welfare recipients would be cut off entirely, with no support at all.

The Republican plan went further than the Clinton plan in denying cash benefits to unmarried teen-age mothers and to those who fail to name their babies' fathers. In addition, and perhaps most significantly, the Republican plan would eliminate many federal programs. The programs would be replaced with cash grants for the 50 states to use as they saw fit. Welfare would no longer be an *entitlement,* under which all eligible individuals must receive benefits. Instead, the states would determine who receives benefits and how much. That would indeed "end welfare as we know it."

The President's plan contains two other parts. One would expand efforts to identify fathers and collect child support from them. The second provision would increase funding for programs aimed at reducing teen pregnancy.

President Clinton's welfare reform would cost money, at least in the near future. Providing training and jobs is costly. His proposal called for $9.3 billion of new spending over the first five years, and many experts think that is insufficient. Unlike most spending on AFDC, however, these costs could be regarded as an investment that will pay off over time. If the programs are effective and efficient, the AFDC rolls should shrink as more and more recipients find work.

States strive to lower welfare costs

As the federal government pondered welfare reform, states experimented with reforms of their own. New Jersey eliminated increased benefits for women who gave birth while on welfare. California required teens on welfare who have dropped out of high school to attend classes or receive job training. Oklahoma was planning a similar program. Georgia and Maryland penalized welfare families who failed to immunize preschool children. In all, more than 20 state initiatives were either underway or awaiting approval.

The final shape of welfare reform is uncertain, but its general direction is clear: The welfare system will no longer simply assist all who qualify. It will try to reduce poverty and dependency. It certainly will demand more from the mothers heading welfare families—and from fathers of the children in those families—than the welfare system does today. It will insist that parents accept more responsibility for the well-being of their families, and it will help parents do so. It eventually may do more for poor families than the current system has.

For further reading:
Bane, Mary Jo, and Ellwood, David T. *Welfare Realities: From Rhetoric to Reform.* Harvard University Press, 1994.
Ellwood, David T. *Poor Support.* Basic Books, 1988.
Murray, Charles. *Losing Ground.* Basic Books, 1984.
Wilson, William Julius. *The Truly Disadvantaged.* University of Chicago Press, 1987.

West Indies. Nations of the Caribbean region signed a trade agreement on July 24, 1994. The agreement created a new regional organization, the Association of Caribbean States (ACS), which combines the 13 member nations of the Caribbean Community and Common Market with 12 other nations in the Caribbean region. With a potential market of 200 million people, the ACS constitutes the world's fourth-largest trading bloc.

In a victory for its faltering economy, Cuba won membership in the ACS. Most ACS members were sympathetic to Cuban President Fidel Castro's call for lifting the U.S. trade embargo against Cuba.

British troops leave Belize. On January 1, the United Kingdom began withdrawing about 1,350 troops from Belize, formerly the colony of British Honduras. As in the case of other former colonial possessions, British troops had remained in Belize after the nation gained its independence in 1981. The troops' main mission was to discourage a threat from neighboring Guatemala, which had claimed Belize as part of its own territory.

The rising incidence of crime throughout the Caribbean posed a threat to the important tourism industry. On January 24, the government of Trinidad and Tobago announced that its military forces would patrol high crime areas to reassure tourists. The government of Dominica imposed a state of emergency on April 26, which included an 8 p.m. to 6 a.m. curfew, to control crime.

Dominican elections. Joaquín Balaguer of the conservative Social Christian Reform Party began a seventh term as president of the Dominican Republic on August 16. Responding to claims of vote-rigging during the election, the 87-year-old Balaguer agreed to serve a reduced term of two years rather than the customary four.

But Balaguer's principal opponent, Francisco Peña Gómez of the Dominican Revolutionary Party, remained unsatisfied. He continued to claim victory and to charge that 200,000 of his followers had been deprived of their votes. Demonstrations and political turbulence occurred even after the nation's election commission certified Balaguer's win by a narrow margin of 22,000 votes.

Elections elsewhere. On February 21, Prime Minister James F. Mitchell of the New Democratic Party won his third consecutive, five-year term in Saint Vincent and the Grenadines. On March 8, Lester Bird, 56, won the right to succeed his father, Vere, as prime minister of Antigua and Barbuda. On September 6, Owen Arthur of the Labor Party, an economist, won election to a five-year term as prime minister of Barbados. □ Nathan A. Haverstock

See also **Latin America** (Facts in brief table). In *World Book,* see West Indies.

West Virginia. See State government.
Wisconsin. See State government.
Wyoming. See State government.

Yemen. Tensions between North and South Yemen erupted into civil war on May 5, 1994. The war nearly divided Yemen again into two separate states. But the North claimed victory on July 7, and President Ali Abdallah Salih declared the country reunited. Yemen (Sana), also called North Yemen, and Yemen (Aden), also called South Yemen, had united into a single country on May 22, 1990.

The war had its roots in historical and ideological differences between the more conservative and tribal North and the South, which had been ruled by the Arab world's only Marxist leaders. Yemen's 1990 merger created power-sharing problems. The military forces of North and South remained segregated, and a dispute grew over oil resources. Yemen's major oil fields lie in the South, but most of Yemen's people live in the North.

Secession. Before the war broke out, tensions had mounted between Yemen's two leaders, President Salih and Vice President Ali Salem al-Baidh, who led South Yemen prior to 1990. Several Northern and Southern officials were assassinated. In August 1993, Baidh retired to Aden, the former capital of South Yemen. Fighting began in early May 1994. The South attacked the Northern capital of Sana with surface-to-surface missiles called Scuds, reportedly killing at least 23 civilians in the first Scud explosion on May 11. Airports and oil fields were also damaged in the fighting.

Baidh declared the South an independent state on May 21. Saudi Arabia and Kuwait, which have feared a united Yemen, reportedly sent arms and money to aid the South. The United Nations, the United States, and other Arab countries tried to mediate a cease-fire, but failed.

Although the South was better armed and trained, the North captured the Southern military base of Ataq and the nearby Shabwah oil fields in late May. Northern forces then began a slow advance, capturing the South's second largest city, Al Mukalla, in the first week of July. The South's main city, Aden, besieged and suffering heavy damage, fell on July 7. Baidh was granted asylum in Oman, and hundreds of Southern troops fled there and to neighboring Saudi Arabia and Djibouti.

Estimates of war deaths varied widely, reaching as high as 12,000. Although many foreigners had fled Yemen during the fighting, hundreds of Somali refugees, who had escaped their country's violence, died in May when their refugee camp was caught between rival Yemeni forces.

Aftermath. After Aden fell, Salih began efforts to quell looting, repair damage to water and electrical facilities, and supply badly needed food, medicine, and water to Aden. Salih also issued an amnesty for all but the main Southern secessionists. Observers estimated that the country suffered billions of dollars of damage. □ Christine Helms

In *World Book,* see Yemen.

Yugoslavia continued to play a crucial role during 1994 in the war in Bosnia-Herzegovina (often called Bosnia), which declared its independence from Yugoslavia in March 1992. Serbia and Montenegro—the two republics that now make up Yugoslavia—began the year under an international trade embargo imposed by the United Nations (UN) Security Council in May 1992. The embargo was aimed at ending Yugoslav support of Bosnian Serbs fighting against the Bosnian government. UN officials reported in early 1994 that Yugoslavia was providing military, as well as economic, support to the Bosnian Serbs.

Diplomatic progress. On August 4, Serbian President Slobodan Milošević, Yugoslavia's most powerful leader, announced that his government would cut off most of its support to the Bosnian Serbs in response to their rejection of an international peace plan. Yugoslav leaders accepted international observers stationed along their Bosnian border to ensure enforcement of the blockade.

The UN Security Council on September 23 voted 11 to 2, with two abstentions, to lift certain sanctions against Yugoslavia for 100 days. Some observers criticized the easement of sanctions, charging that Yugoslavia continued to supply Bosnian Serbs.

Serbian-Croatian ties. Tensions also relaxed between Serbia and Croatia. On January 19, the two sides agreed to establish low-level diplomatic relations. Croatian and Serbian forces had fought over territory since Croatia split from Yugoslavia in June 1991.

Party politics. Opposition parties fought for parliamentary control in early 1994, after Milošević's Socialist Party of Serbia (SPS) failed to retain a majority of seats in December 1993 elections. In February, however, six members of New Democracy, formerly part of an opposition party, joined with the SPS to form a majority in parliament.

Economic stability became a chief concern in 1994 among Yugoslav officials, who enacted several measures to stem the nation's runaway rate of inflation. One of the most controversial was the introduction in January of the so-called *superdinar,* a new currency whose value was linked to the German mark. Officials also stopped printing large amounts of money to cover national expenses. These measures helped slow inflation, but prices on many basic consumer goods continued to rise.

Yugoslavia's economy continued to feel the impact of the UN embargo and years of international conflict. Widespread poverty and severe shortages of goods plagued the nation, and production levels remained extremely low.   ☐ Sharon L. Wolchik

See also **Bosnia-Herzegovina; Croatia; Europe** (Facts in brief table); **United Nations.** In *World Book,* see Yugoslavia.

Yukon Territory. See **Canadian territories.**

Troops from Southern Yemen take up positions in May in sand dunes east of the Southern port of Aden as Yemen erupted into full-scale civil war.

Zaire continued to be disrupted by an ongoing political crisis in 1994 as forces opposed to President Mobutu Sese Seko fought to bring about democratic reform and oust Mobutu. But Mobutu held on.

The year began with a general strike on January 19 to protest Mobutu's refusal to recognize Etienne Tshisekedi as prime minister and his dissolution of the legislature on January 14. Mobutu and Tshisekedi were heading rival governments. In late January, Mobutu merged the two governments into one, and in June he named a new prime minister, Kengo wa Dondo. Tshisekedi's supporters boycotted the new government, but Mobutu won over enough of the opposition to return Zaire to a single government.

As political turmoil continued, Zaire was on the verge of collapse. The economy continued a steep decline. Most exports stopped, the mining industry came close to shutting down, most cities lacked electricity, and public works deteriorated. Inflation ran at an annual rate estimated at up to 12,000 percent. Widespread malnutrition and a substantial increase in AIDS cases added to the general misery.

Despite this chaotic state of affairs, Mobutu's hold on power seemed to be substantially greater at year-end. He was helped by his control of the military and the treasury. □ Mark DeLancey

See also **Africa** (Facts in brief table). In *World Book,* see Zaire.

Zambia. See Africa.

Zedillo Ponce de León, Ernesto (1951-),

was elected president of Mexico on Aug. 21, 1994. Zedillo was a member of the Institutional Revolutionary Party (PRI), and his election continued the PRI's unbroken history of rule in Mexico since 1929.

Zedillo was born on Dec. 27, 1951, in Mexico City, the second of six children. His father was an electrician, and his mother was a nurse. The family moved to Mexicali on the California border when Zedillo was 3 years old.

Zedillo earned a bachelor's degree in economics from the Advanced School of Economics of the National Polytechnic Institute in Mexico City in 1972. He also attended Yale University in New Haven, Conn., earning a master's degree in economics in 1976 and a doctorate in 1981. In 1978, he took a job at Banco de México, Mexico's central bank, and rose to assistant director of economic research in 1982.

In 1988, Mexican President Carlos Salinas de Gortari appointed Zedillo secretary of planning and budget. In 1992, Zedillo served as Mexico's secretary of education. In November 1993, he became campaign director for PRI presidential candidate Luis Donaldo Colosio Murrieta. After Colosio was assassinated on March 23, 1994, Salinas chose Zedillo as the PRI presidential candidate.

Zedillo is married and has five children. His wife, Nilda Patricia Velasco Núñez, is also an economist. □ Mark Dunbar

Zhirinovsky, Vladimir (1946-), a Russian

nationalist, was reelected leader of Russia's Liberal Democratic Party at the party's fifth annual congress in April 1994. The election gave Zhirinovsky absolute power over all party matters for 10 years. One of Russia's most controversial figures, Zhirinovsky has been cited for advocating the restoration of Russia to its imperial borders, the annexation of Alaska, and the build-up of the Russian military.

Zhirinovsky was born on April 26, 1946, in Alma-Ata, Kazakhstan. In 1970, he graduated from the Institute of Oriental Languages at Moscow M. V. Lomonosov State University in Moscow, where he specialized in Turkish. He later earned a law degree from the same university. After serving in the army for two years, Zhirinovsky worked for a state legal agency and a large publishing house.

In 1990, Zhirinovsky founded the Liberal Democratic Party. In June 1991, before the Soviet Union dissolved, he finished third to Boris Yeltsin in the Russian republic's first free presidential elections. In 1993, in Russia's first parliamentary elections since the collapse of the Soviet Union, his party scored a major victory, winning the most seats of any single party and capturing nearly 23 percent of the vote. In 1994, Zhirinovsky's party controlled about one-fifth of the seats in the State Duma, the lower house of Russia's legislative assembly. □ Patricia Ohlenroth

Zimbabwe. See Africa.

Zoology. Dutch biologists in March 1994 demonstrated an important link between the chemical composition of soil and the populations of snails and birds in forests in the Netherlands. Since the late 1980's, bird watchers had seen fewer birds in the forests, and one common species, the great tit, had begun laying eggs with unusually thin eggshells.

Biologist Jaap Graveland and his colleagues with the Institute for Forestry and Nature Research in Wageningen, the Netherlands, discovered that the problem was caused by *acid rain* (rain that contains acids from burning fossil fuels), which had removed calcium from the forest soil. The number of snails then declined, because there was not enough calcium for their shells. With fewer snails to eat, the birds failed to get enough calcium, which caused the thin eggshells. Other scientists found that adding lime, a powdered substance containing calcium, to the soil boosted snail populations. Birds fed a diet supplement of ground shells laid stronger eggshells.

Deadly epidemics. In February 1994, African lions in the Serengeti National Park in Tanzania began to sicken with a deadly disease. By mid-June, 60 of the park's 3,000 lions had died. Virologist Max J. G. Appel of Cornell University in Ithaca, N.Y., confirmed that canine distemper virus had made the lions sick. The virus, which causes convulsions and uncontrollable twitching, usually infects dogs. Until 1993, the disease was not known to strike felines, and biologists were unsure why the virus had become deadly to them.

Distemper viruses have been implicated in outbreaks of disease among dolphins and other marine mammals since 1986. Biologist Albert D. M. E. Osterhaus of Erasmus University in Rotterdam, the Netherlands, reported in March 1994 that pollution may make seals and other marine mammals more susceptible to infection. Dutch researchers raised 11 seals on herring from relatively unpolluted water and 11 seals on fish from the polluted Baltic Sea. After two years, the blood of seals eating the contaminated fish contained 20 to 40 percent less vitamin A and far fewer infection-fighting white blood cells than did the blood of seals fed fish from cleaner waters.

Colorful coot coats. Most baby birds have dull brown feathers, but American coots hatch with bright orange feathers and a patch of bare red skin on top of the head. The bright colors, which soon fade, help the birds catch the attention of their parents, according to a September 1994 report by biologists with the University of Toronto in Ontario and the University of Calgary in Alberta, both in Canada. The scientists found that parents gave the colorful coot chicks more food than they fed chicks whose bright feathers had been trimmed. The well-fed and brighter birds grew faster than the shorn chicks, the researchers reported. □ Elizabeth Pennisi

In *World Book,* see **Zoology.**

Zoos and aquariums across the United States presented new exhibits depicting an array of habitats in 1994. Aquatic themes were especially popular.

Hawaii aquarium modernized. After a 19-month, $3-million renovation, the Waikiki Aquarium in Honolulu reopened in May with many new displays as well as updated older ones. Founded in 1904, the United States' third oldest aquarium now focuses primarily on Hawaiian and South Pacific waters, taking a regional approach similar to that of the newest aquariums. (See **Zoos** Special Report: **The New Aquariums.**)

The centerpiece at Waikiki features endangered Hawaiian monk seals. An 85,000-gallon (320,000-liter) tank and surrounding artificial shore duplicate the rocky atolls and coral shoals that are the seals' natural home. In addition, the "Hunters of the Reef" gallery stars sharks and other coral reef predators, and "Hawaiian Marine Communities" explores unique features of the islands' ecology. A gallery devoted to diversity and adaptations showcases the creatures that emerge from reef caves at night; the camouflage mechanisms developed by some sea animals for protection; and the defensive strategies (such as armor, spines, and toxic skin) evolved by other beasts, including many visitors' favorite fish, the humuhumunukunukuapuaa.

North America in North Carolina. Major additions to the North American section of the North Carolina Zoological Park in Asheboro opened on August 4, also displaying a strong aquatic orientation. Visitors follow a boardwalk into an exhibit called the "Cypress Swamp," a thicket of lush rhododendrons, American holly, and bald cypress trees. As alligators warm themselves on electrically heated artificial rocks, turtles paddle along a quiet stream, and cougars prowl the damp forest nearby. In the swamp is a carnivorous garden, with insect-eating Venus's-flytraps and pitcher plants. The path meanders into a marsh where the vegetation changes to wild rice, cattails, bulrushes, yellow water lilies, and dune grass amid a watery complex of lagoons and sand dunes. The site is a typical nesting habitat for waterfowl such as green-winged and blue-winged teal and hooded mergansers.

In the "Rocky Coast" exhibit, the scene shifts to the colder waters of the Arctic and Pacific Northwest. Surrounded by a jagged, rocky shoreline, rushing streams, and tumbling waterfalls, polar bears dive and swim in a pool of chilly water. Arctic foxes skulk among rocks nearby, and sea lions swoop through the water in another pool.

West Coast hip-hop. The San Diego Wild Animal Park in Escondido, Calif., acquired a new bounce with the premiere of "Kangaroo Encounter" on May 28. On a grassy, partially wooded hillside, visitors enter an enclosure and come face-to-face with Australian wildlife: 75 kangaroos and their relatives, wallabies and wallaroos, plus emus, which are large, flightless birds similar, but unrelated, to ostriches.

Jungle adventures. The Indonesian Rain Forest, which opened June 18 at the Fort Wayne (Ind.) Children's Zoo, focuses on the exceptionally diverse array of animal species in Indonesia, an island nation in the Indian Ocean northwest of Australia. After an introduction to the country's geography and culture, visitors walk through the entrance of a ruined temple and into Dr. Diversity's Rain Forest Research Station. This replica of an imaginary scientist's field outpost contains a variety of living "specimens," among them insects called walking sticks, archerfish that shoot insects from the air with jets of water, and a 20-foot (6-meter) python.

Next stop is a steamy geodesic dome, where brilliantly colored butterflies, birds, and fruit bats flit amid bamboo, palms, and fig trees. At ground level are Komodo dragons, and, in a cave behind a waterfall, tropical frogs. Outside, young and old can ride a carousel whose carvings are of endangered Asian animals instead of horses. The path continues by elevated boardwalk along a forest inhabited by a colorful Prevost's squirrel, little muntjacs (also called barking deer), and a binturong, a large bushy-tailed tree dweller from the civet family. The final segment reveals big-beaked birds called hornbills, long-armed apes called gibbons, and their noisy cousins called siamangs. □ Eugene J. Walter, Jr.

In *World Book,* see **Zoo.**

The New Aquariums

By Eugene J. Walter, Jr.

Innovative technologies have allowed aquariums in the United States and around the world to provide more realistic views of the underwater world.

E xploring a coral reef can be a nearly mystical experience. Stately French and queen angelfish flash a rainbow of color as they glide through branches of coral. Sea fans, barrel sponges, and other animals abound, seemingly transforming the ocean floor into a garden with their plantlike appearances. A wild-eyed moray eel appears with its mouth agape, revealing menacing needle-sharp teeth. A large shadow clouds the scene, and smaller fish dart for shelter as a shark moves into view and then slowly disappears. A bulky sea turtle pauses to peer at the viewer, then drifts on.

Although the fish on this reef are real, the coral itself is artificial. The human spectators wear street clothes, not wet suits, as they walk along a ramp that circles a giant acrylic cylinder four stories tall and filled with 187,000 gallons (708,000 liters) of salt water. This is not the Caribbean Sea but Boston, and the reef is the central exhibit of the New England Aquarium.

In June 1994, the New England Aquarium celebrated its 25th anniversary, a major milestone for what many regard as the first "modern" aquarium. The New England Aquarium's success has been an important influence on the design and operation of many new aquariums in the United States in the 1980's and into the 1990's. From 1990 through 1992, five major aquariums opened in the United States, all of them dedicated to a relatively new concept that started in Boston—presenting marine life in the most authentic possible re-creation of their natural habitats. Still more aquariums incorporating this type of display have premiered in Europe and Asia, particularly Japan, and others are in the works. Ten new aquariums plan to open between 1995 and 2000, including the lavish $84-million Florida Aquarium in Tampa, set to open in March 1995.

Public aquariums as we know them originated in 1851, when a small "Aqua-vivarium" opened at the Regents Park Zoo in London. Fish and marine invertebrates in small, plate glass "water cages" enchanted the public. Aquariums—the word was coined in 1854—soon sprouted throughout Europe. In the United States, the famous showman P. T. Barnum introduced a collection of aquatic curiosities in New York City in 1861. Part of his collection became the basis for the first major U.S. aquarium, the New York Aquarium (now called the Aquarium for Wildlife Conservation), which opened in 1896. The manner in which aquariums displayed marine life changed little in the century following Barnum's inaugural exhibition. Visitors viewed fish and other marine life through windows, as though they were pieces in a stamp collection.

■ **The author**

Eugene J. Walter, Jr., is a free-lance writer.

The first "modern" aquarium

But the opening of the New England Aquarium in 1969 offered a different view of marine life. With the help of advanced plastics and other new technologies, the aquarium displayed an entire *ecosystem* (the living and nonliving things in a given area and the relationships between them). Using similar technologies, the next generation of aquariums were larger and more technologically sophisticated than

■ Economic booster

Visitors to Baltimore Harbor relax near the Baltimore Aquarium. The aquarium helped revitalize a run-down harbor area by attracting other businesses and spurring tourism.

traditional aquariums. And architects designed many new displays to make viewers feel immersed in water, almost as if they were swimming with the marine life.

Beyond their focus on marine ecosystems, the new aquariums have helped revitalize run-down urban areas. Boston's busy waterfront had deteriorated into a dreary mix of rotting wharves, rusting barges, and abandoned warehouses. Several business and civic leaders believed that an aquarium could be the cornerstone for a revival of the harbor. They committed money and held a design competition. The winner, architect Peter Chermayeff, a partner in the firm of Cambridge Seven Associates, drew upon a variety of advanced technologies, the expertise of marine biologists, and his own talent for theatrical illusion to create this new kind of aquarium. For example, his use of low, indirect light levels in the visitor areas with primary illumination coming from inside the exhibits immersed visitors in the habitats without getting them wet.

The new facility lured people back to the harbor area in droves (about 1.3 million people visit annually) and sparked an abundance of other development. It also inspired officials in Baltimore, another city that formerly had a shabby, economically unproductive waterfront. Those officials hired Chermayeff to design an aquarium as the anchor for a development scheme that included shops, restaurants, theaters, and other attractions. Since its 1981 opening, Baltimore's National Aquarium has drawn 1.5 million people a year, and the whole harbor project is now a long-running hit.

About 3,000 miles (4,800 kilometers) to the west in California, a similar idea took hold. Several marine biologists affiliated with Stanford University's Hopkins Marine Station in Monterey conceived of an aquarium with a theme based on Monterey Bay's ecosystem, which is incredibly rich in marine life. Two of the group were daughters of David Packard, cofounder of the Hewlett-Packard electronics firm. After a feasibility study indicated that such a facility would draw a million people a year, Packard and his wife, Lucille, committed $55-million to its construction and helped form a foundation to build it.

Monterey's Cannery Row, made famous by the novels of John Steinbeck, had become a graveyard of aging, decrepit sardine processing plants put out of business by severe declines in the sardine population. Using the site of a defunct factory, Chuck Davis of the San Francisco architectural firm of Esherick, Homsey, Dodge, and Davis designed the exterior of the aquarium to resemble a cannery—complete with tall, artificial smokestacks—thereby blending with neighborhood history and culture. Inside, the architect, biologists, and exhibit designers collaborated to create an array of innovative exhibits based on Monterey Bay ecology. The best-known of those exhibits is the kelp forest, a duplicate of the vast groves of giant seaweed that grow underwater along America's Pacific Coast. When the Monterey Bay Aquarium opened in 1984, it attracted 2.35 million visitors the first year, and since then has averaged 1.7 million visitors annually.

The combined success of the new East and West Coast aquariums created a model that stimulated other communities. Typically, each of the newest U.S. aquariums has a signature, or "blockbuster," exhibit, sometimes several. The Aquarium of the Americas, which opened in 1990 along the Mississippi River in New Orleans, adopted a broad regional scope: waters of the Western Hemisphere. In a 400,000-gallon (1,500,000-liter) simulation of the Gulf of Mexico, several shark species, stingrays, barracudas, tarpons, and groupers prowl through a jumble of metal beams designed to resemble the supporting structure of a typical oil rig in the Gulf of Mexico. Other large exhibits include a Caribbean coral reef and an Amazon rain forest.

At the New Jersey State Aquarium in Camden, which opened in February 1992, the Open Ocean exhibit replicates New Jersey's offshore waters, including Hudson Canyon, an underwater canyon 1,500 feet (460 meters) deep at the edge of the continental shelf. Within the exhibit's 760,000 gallons (2,900,000 liters), some 400 species of fish (among them various sharks, cownose stingrays, striped bass, and sea robins) cruise about. Human divers also speak over special underwater phones and answer questions from visitors.

The Oregon Coast Aquarium, which opened in May 1992 on a 32-acre (13-hectare) site off Yaquina Bay in Newport, presents its larger habitats in outdoor exhibits, including rock-bound pools with sandy beaches and underwater canyons where visitors can observe seals, sea lions, and sea otters from both above and below the surface. An aviary features tufted puffins, rhinoceros auklets, and other sea birds that dive from tall, craggy cliffs. A large, rocky cave is inhabited by a giant octopus.

Most expensive aquarium

In Japan, the Osaka Ring of Fire Aquarium laid claim to the biggest region of all: the Pacific Ocean and locales around its edge that are part of the "Ring of Fire," a region noted for active volcanoes and frequent earthquakes. It also set the record for most expensive aquarium so far: $133 million. The Osaka exhibits depict ecosystems off the coasts of Japan, North and South America, New Zealand, and Australia. The culmination is a 1.4-million-gallon (5.3-million-liter) tank, 90 feet (27 meters) tall and shaped like a cross. It contains thousands of fish, the most impressive of which are 20-foot (6-meter) whale sharks, the world's largest fish species.

The Tennessee Aquarium in Chattanooga opened in May 1992 and marked another significant departure from the past. It is the world's first and largest aquarium devoted to freshwater ecosystems. It is also an especially good example of a total ecosystem, blending terrestrial and aquatic habitats. The aquarium exhibits are designed as a tour along the Tennessee River, starting in an Appalachian mountain forest where pools among rock crevices depict the source of the river's beginning. Other exhibits feature a "bowl" in the stream bed 15 feet (4.6 meters) deep where rainbow and brook trout swim and a pool where river otters frolic.

■ Views above and below

A worker at the Oregon Coast Aquarium in Newport, *right,* feeds seals in an outdoor exhibit designed to replicate the rocky coastline of the Pacific Northwest. Visitors to the exhibit, *below,* can also watch marine life from windows beneath the water line.

■ A freshwater aquarium

Visitors to the Tennessee Aquarium in Chattanooga view a combination of marine and terrestrial wildlife in an exhibit depicting the ecosystems of the Tennessee River, *above.* An alligator rests in one of the Tennessee Aquarium's exhibits, *left.* The facility is the world's largest aquarium devoted to freshwater ecosystems.

Another feature that characterizes all these new institutions is a reliance on modern equipment and materials. Most critical are life-support systems that keep aquatic animals alive. Older aquariums depended on cast iron, concrete, and asbestos for piping and other equipment. But those materials crack and corrode, especially when subjected to salt water. Those substances often created toxic environments for animals as well. Advanced plastics literally gave aquariums new life. Polyvinyl chloride pipes, pumps, valves, ladders, walkways, and other devices are strong, durable, and rarely cause problems.

Plastic has also greatly aided exhibit designers. Fabricators pour latex over real rocks and coral formations to create molds that they can use to cast duplicates in concrete, reinforced with plastic fiberglass. The molds are hollow and thus lighter and easier to maneuver than the originals, which often are massive.

The Monterey Bay Aquarium is a leader in special effects that mimic nature and involve visitors. Nowhere is this more evident than in the kelp forest. Stalks of the giant seaweed 28 feet (8.5 meters) tall sway gracefully, apparently propelled by ocean currents in the exhibit's 335,000-gallon (1.3-million-liter) tank. Schools of sardines and anchovies weave amid the kelp fronds, which move up and down with their waving trunks. Surveys show that the kelp forest exhibit is so convincing that a high percentage of aquarium visitors believe they are looking into Monterey Bay itself.

Creating this illusion required considerable ingenuity. To survive, kelp needs wave motion to sweep the stalks back and forth so the plants can extract nutrients from

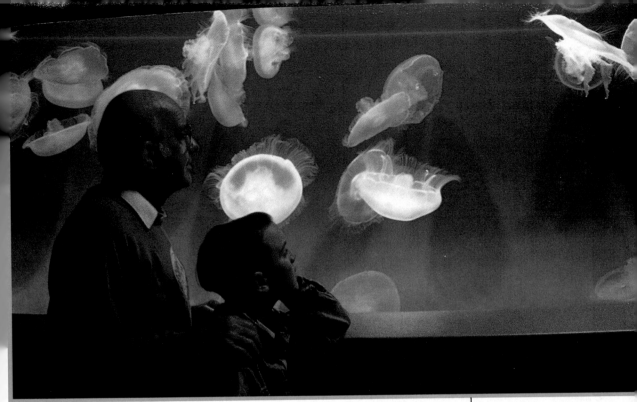

The jellyfish exhibit at the Monterey Bay Aquarium enchants two visitors. Aquarium architects designed the exhibit with no corners and a constant current to push the jellyfish away from the exhibit wall in order to prevent the animals from puncturing themselves or scraping their delicate bodies.

the water. A surge machine—a hidden piston 7 feet (2 meters) long plunges repeatedly in and out of the water, creating waves. Water jets hidden in rocks also generate motion around the giant plants. The kelp grows so vigorously that workers must prune it regularly.

To simulate the underwater forest floor, David Powell, director of animal husbandry at the aquarium, and other scuba-diving staff members toted rocks made of concrete and fiberglass into the bay and left them for four years while the exhibit was under construction. When it was time to lay the floor, they retrieved the fakes, by then encrusted with living barnacles, sea anemones, and other organisms.

The ability of technicians to build large viewing tanks and walkways of acrylic plastic accounts for the impact of many aquariums' blockbuster exhibits. Glass is too brittle to withstand the enormous water pressure behind giant windows, and the deeper the tank, the higher the pressure. Sheets of acrylic can be laminated together to gain extra strength, and technicians can weld large, thick sheets together to produce even vaster vistas. Aquarium-sized windows of glass would be far heavier and many times more expensive than acrylics of the same size. Acrylic also has greater optical purity than glass, which distorts form and color.

The biggest acrylic windows are yet to come. Monterey Bay may reach the limit of this technology in 1996 when it adds an exhibit depicting the outer reaches of the bay where it joins the open ocean. In a tank 34 feet (10.4 meters) tall, holding 1 million gallons (3.8 million liters) of water, some 7,000 fish, most of which have never been exhibited by aquariums, will be viewed through an acrylic window 15 feet (4.6 meters) tall and 54 feet (16.5 meters) long.

■ An aquarium education

Many new aquariums offer broad educational programs on regional ecosystems. A marine biologist at the Monterey Bay Aquarium, *right,* narrates an educational video featuring an image of a mushroom coral found in the depths of Monterey Bay. In the aquarium's wet lab, *below,* a child can touch a live crab.

The virtues of acrylic go beyond size. Acrylic's flexibility also means that it can be made into a variety of shapes. At the Aquarium of the Americas, visitors experience a 132,000-gallon (500,000-liter) display of a Caribbean reef by walking through an acrylic tunnel 30 feet (9 meters) long. Several aquariums have also added acrylic bubble windows that project into habitats, allowing visitors to lean in and gain a fish-eye perspective.

Improved technology has allowed aquarium technicians to display certain creatures that were once impossible to keep in artificial environments. For example, jellyfish are extremely fragile, poor candidates for exhibition. Their soft, exposed bodies are susceptible to abrasions and punctures from sharp points or corners in most traditional aquarium exhibit spaces. So Monterey Bay's aquarium specialists devised a circular acrylic tank with no life-threatening corners. Pumps combine with the flow of water through the whole aquarium to generate a constant current of water around the walls. The current gently nudges the jellyfish away from walls and drains. To highlight the animal's beauty, designers colored the rear of the tank deep blue and backlighted it. Against this background, the jellyfish resemble a multicolored glass menagerie exploring outer space. Other institutions copied the system. Virtually undisplayed in the early 1980's, jellyfish are one of the most popular aquarium exhibits today.

Aquariums of the 1990's have exceeded expectations for attendance and economic impact. The Aquarium of the Americas, for instance, had projected that 870,000 people would visit the facility in the first year. The actual attendance was 2.3 million. After drawing heavy crowds the first year, aquariums tend to level off at very healthy numbers. The Louisiana facility has averaged 1.4 million people annually since its first year, making it the most-visited paid attraction in the city. By the end of 1993, it had contributed nearly $400 million to the local economy through jobs, gift-shop purchases, tax revenues, and expenditures by visitors on hotels, restaurants, and public transportation, according to aquarium officials. Similar economic benefits have occurred in Tennessee, Oregon, California, and New Jersey.

Aquarium boom continuing

There is no sign of the aquarium boom slowing down, and the taste for regional displays remains dominant. The Florida Aquarium will trace fresh water as it flows from a subterranean limestone spring to the open ocean. Visitors will be able to view four main exhibits featuring wetlands, beaches, and the open ocean. In all, 4,300 plants and animals representing 550 species native to Florida will be on display. The aquarium's signature exhibit is a 500,000-gallon (1.9-million-liter) Florida Keys coral reef display that visitors view by walking through an acrylic tunnel.

Different approaches to regional exhibits also are evolving. The Alaska Sea Life Center, scheduled to open in 1997 in Seward, will include displays on the decline of Bering Sea wildlife populations and rehabilitation of stranded, injured, or orphaned animals. Other facilities merge aquarium and museum techniques. The Oregon Rivers Museum, due to open in 1997 on a 75-acre (30-hectare) site in Eugene, will interpret the diversity of Pacific Northwest rivers, streams, and lakes, covering not only biological aspects but also the waterways' cultural, historic, and recreational values.

Other aquariums due by the year 2000 include the Orange County Marine Institute in Dana Point, Calif.; the Pennsylvania Aquarium and Science Center in Erie; the South Carolina Aquarium in Charleston; the Wisconsin Aquarium in Sheboygan; and Taiwan's National Institute for Marine Biology, which will be the largest aquarium in the world. Worldwide, 60 to 70 cities have aquariums on the drawing board.

Assuming they match the high standards set by their predecessors, virtually all of the planned aquariums seem likely to succeed. But the real payoff will not be at the box office. As Julie Packard, executive director of Monterey Bay Aquarium, noted, "The measure of our success is not solely how many people come, but how many leave with a greater awareness of the wealth of life our oceans hold. For only through this awareness will the oceans rise to the forefront of world conservation efforts, where they belong." ■ ■ ■

1994

DICTIONARY SUPPLEMENT

A list of new words added to the 1995 edition of **The World Book Dictionary** because they have been used enough to become a permanent part of our ever-changing language.

word

(wėrd), *n., v.* –*n.* ...nd or a group of ...that has meaning ...an independent ...speech; vocable: ...ak words when ... A free form which ...phrase is a word. ...then, is a free form which does not consist entirely of... lesser free forms; in brief, a word is a minimum free form (Leonard Bloomfield).

spell | ing

dictionary

dic|tion|ar|y (dik´shə ner´ē), *n., pl.* –ar ies. 1. a book that explains the words of a language, or some special kind of words. It is usually arranged alphabetically. One can use a dictionary to find out the meaning, pronunciation, or spelling of a word.

1. a way of pronouncing:
pro|nun|ci|a|tion
a foreign pronunciation.

sup||ple|ment

(sup´lə mənt), *n.* 1. Something added to complete a thing, or to make it larger or better.

definition

A a

air guitar, an imaginary guitar played in imitation of a rock musician: *I have fond memories of shooting pool . . . and playing air guitar with my cue stick* (Rolling Stone).

air|strike (âr′strīk′), *v.t.* **-struck, -struck** or **-strick|en, -strik|ing**. to attack with aircraft: *Our President's refusal . . . to airstrike the Serbian artillery is dismaying* (William Safire).

as|sist|ed suicide (ə sis′təd), the act of giving assistance or advice to a terminally ill person in order to commit suicide: *Voters turned down initiatives that would have legalized assisted suicide if a patient wrote out a "death directive"* (Nancy Gibbs).

B b

bat|tered-wom|an syndrome (bat′ərd wùm′ən), a condition in which a woman's ability to act reasonably is impaired by experiencing repeated physical violence: *Evidence about battered-woman syndrome may be the only way to persuade a jury to identify with a killer* (Time).

bhan|gra (bäng′grä′), *n.* a traditional form of Punjabi music, now often played with a rap or Latin rhythm for dancing: *A lot of parents didn't like this pumped-up bhangra . . . they thought the old sound was being lost* (New York Magazine). [< Hindi]

buck|y|tube (buk′ē tüb′, -tyüb′), *n.* a microscopic carbon tube with a molecular structure similar to the buckyball; channel: *Ever since chemists discovered buckytubes, they've speculated that these hollow, nanometer-size carbon cylinders . . . could prove the strongest fibers known* (Science News).

C c

ca|ble-ac|cess (kā′bəl ak′ses), *adj.* of or having to do with cable-television channels reserved for local public use: *Wayne and Garth, a couple . . . who do a cable-access show from Wayne's basement* (Rolling Stone).

cam|cord|ing (kam′kôr ding), *n.* the act or process of using a camcorder: *Camcording can get expensive, but there is a growing "garage video" movement whose members buy much of their equipment at discount stores* (Philip Elmer-DeWitt).

cam|mer (kam′ər), *n.* a person who uses a camcorder: *Among . . . cammers, [there are] . . . dedicated . . . enthusiasts who are not content simply to point and shoot* (Time).

carbon tax, a tax on fossil fuels that is based on the amount of carbon emitted when the fuel is burned: *A carbon tax would add roughly four cents to the price of coal for every penny it added to the price of oil* (New York Times).

car|cer|and (kär′sər and), *n.* a hollow molecule which encloses but does not bond to a smaller molecule: *Cram envisions using . . . carcerands to shuttle drugs to diseased cells* (Science News). [< Latin *carcer* prison + *-and* abstracted from *operand*]

cav|i|tand (kav′ə tand), *n.* a hollow molecule with one open end: *Cram can also combine a pair of his cavitands to form a closed hollow shell . . . a "carcerand"* (Science News). [< English *cavit*(y) + *-and*, as in *operand*]

chan|nel-surf (chan′əl sėrf′), *v.i.* to switch among several television channels, only briefly watching each program.

co-hous|ing (kō hou′zing), *n.* a housing complex for many families in which units are individually owned by residents who share responsibility for its management and the provision of services: *Cohousing differs from traditional housing in . . . that the residents decide in advance what the complex should look like and how it should function* (New York Times).

community po|lic|ing (pə lē′sing), the practice of using police officers to patrol a beat on foot and maintain public order in an area: *The new chief is promoting community policing, which encourages contact between officers and the neighborhoods they patrol* (Richard Lacayo).

control gene, any of a group of genes that determine cell specialization and development: *Control genes . . . set the paths of development of cells from egg to adulthood in . . . the common fruit fly* (New York Times).

cor|rect|ness (kə rekt′nis), *n.* **1** the quality or condition of being free from mistakes or faults or of agreeing with a standard of good taste: *He denied the correctness of the assertion* (H. H. Wilson). **2** the fact or condition of being politically correct: *The incident has sent the Globe into spasms . . . of correctness . . . Management quickly posted a stern memo saying that sexist remarks "will not be tolerated here"* (New Yorker).

cy|ber|punk (sī′bər pungk′), *n.* **1** = hacker (def. 2). **2** a type of science fiction involving human interaction with supercomputers.

D d

data glove, a glove, fitted with electronic sensors connected to a computer, that enables the user to experience virtual reality: *Virtual reality gives the user you-are-there sensations with data gloves, . . . [and] video display screens set into goggles or visors* (Joel Engel).

data superhighway, a computer network, such as a bulletin board, linking many users: *The action this spring is on what the Clinton Administration likes to call the data superhighway* (Time).

digital compression, a technique for digitally recording and consolidating a broadcast signal: *A company . . . announced in October that it would use . . . digital compression to squeeze 20 channels into a single satellite . . . making it the equivalent of 'a video shop in the sky'* (Annual Register).

drive-by shooting, a act or instance of shooting a person from a moving motor vehicle: *The low point was a drive-by shooting, in which rival gang members . . . exchanged gunfire* (New York Times).

E e

economic migrant or **refugee**, a person who leaves a country to improve his or her economic opportunities: *A strict separation must be made between . . . those fleeing wars or political or religious persecution—and so-called economic refugees* (Wall Street Journal).

edge city, a suburb that has the businesses and services usually found in a city: *The larger suburbs have become what . . . Joel Garreau calls "edge cities"—places where jobs have migrated to follow the population* (William Schneider).

eth|no|med|i|cine (eth′nō med′ə sən), *n.* **1** the traditional medical maxims, remedies, and methods prevalent among the people of a particular culture: *Joe brought his background in ethnomedicine and his understanding of conventional medicine* (New York Times). **2** the study of ethnomedicine.

eth|no|na|tion|al|ism (eth′nō nash′ə nə liz′əm, nash′nə liz-), *n.* the desire and plans for national independence of a particular ethnic group: *Defensive ethnonationalism . . . is now becoming the dominant political principle throughout Eastern Europe and beyond* (London Review of Books).

eth|no|vi|o|lent (eth′nō vī′ə lənt), *adj.* displaying abuse or violence toward a member or members of an ethnic group: *According to sociologist Howard Ehrlich, each year one minority student in five experiences ethnoviolent attack* (Newsweek).

Pronunciation Key: hat, āge, cãre, fär; let, ēqual, tėrm; it, īce; hot, ōpen, ôrder; oil, out; cup, pùt, rüle; child; long; thin; ᴛHen; zh, measure; ə represents **a** in about, **e** in taken, **i** in pencil, **o** in lemon, **u** in circus.

F f

focus group, a group of people brought together to give their opinion about a particular issue, product, policy, or the like: *Advisors have headed focus groups that show voters are uncomfortable with excessively negative ads* (Richard Zoglin).

food court, a section of a mall or other enclosed shopping area where fast-food shops or stands and tables for eating are located: *Inside the mall the atmosphere is enlivened by families eating lunch in the food court* (Atlantic Monthly).

Fourth Reich, the unified state of East and West Germany, especially as considered to exhibit the expansionist and totalitarian tendencies of the Third Reich (used in an unfriendly way): *But loyal comrades . . . considered the trial a "witch hunt" and an example of the "class justice of the Fourth Reich"* (Manchester Guardian Weekly).

G g

gang|sta (gang'stə), *n., adj.* —*n.* = gangster: *Kevin had noticed already, it was the "gangstas" who always had money, guns, girls* (John Skow). —*adj.* of or like a gangster; brutal; criminal: *The current "gangsta" genre in rap . . . [revels] in crimes and misdemeanors, drive-bys and lootings* (C. J. Farley).

gangsta rap or **gangster rap**, rap music that celebrates urban violence: *The brutal rhymes of West Coast gangsta rap weren't just macho posturing; they expressed the hard truths of real life* (Rolling Stone). —**gangsta rapper** or **gangster rapper**.

gap junction, a cluster of protein channels between cells that allows molecules to pass from one cell directly to another: *Because of the intricate network of gap junctions, molecules can spread through whole organs or parts of organs* (Lawrence K. Altman).

gene gun, a device for injecting genetic material into cells: *Genes can be transferred into plant cells with . . . a "gene gun" that shoots DNA into leaves* (Sandra Blakeslee).

H h

home shopping, the act of looking at or buying goods displayed on television and then purchasing by telephone: *Home shopping . . . is just the first of a vast array of things people will be able to do over the TV of the future* (Time). —**home'shop'per**, *n.* —**home'shop'ping**, *adj.*

ho|mo|so|cial (hō'mō sō'shəl), *adj.* having or showing a preference for the company of members of the same sex: *She was cut off by the "homosocial" traditions of her [political] party . . . It was a chaps' party* (Atlantic).

hot vent, a crack in the sea floor from which superheated water rich in minerals escapes, forming a mound of deposits around the opening: *Hot vents occur along the midocean ridges, where the sea floor is expanding* (World Book Year Book).

I i

image ad, an advertisement intended to alter or improve the public's impression of a person or thing: *Agencies such as Mingo help clients ranging from AT&T . . . to President George Bush . . . They create image ads* (Newsday).

in|clu|siv|ist (in klü'sə vist), *n.* a person who believes that Christianity best communicates the redemptive power of God, while conceding such power is also expressed in most other religions: *Inclusivists ardently favor interreligious dialogue . . . [but] Christ remains . . . the mediator of salvation* (Peter Steinfels).

J j

job-lock (job'lok'), *n.* commitment to a job in order to keep the health insurance and other benefits that go with it: *One spreading phenomenon is known as "job-lock" . . . those with chronic diseases are most vulnerable* (New York Times). —**job'locked'**, *adj.*

K k

keystone species, a plant or animal species necessary to the survival of an ecosystem: *So interdependent are the creatures in an ecosystem that even the temporary extinction of a single "keystone" species can create powerful ripples* (Richard Maybe).

L l

let|ter|boxed (let'ər bokst'), *adj.* (of an image on film or tape) reduced in size to fit on a television screen, usually appearing with black bands at the top and bottom of the picture: *Jaws (MCA/Universal) has finally arrived, remastered and letterboxed* (Rolling Stone).

leu|me|din (lü mē'din), *n.* a drug which is thought to prevent the passage of white blood cells through the walls of the circulatory system: *Scientists have evidence . . . that leumedins somehow

keep a set of receptor molecules from jutting out of the leucocyte's surface* (Wall Street Journal). [< *leu*(cocyte) + *med*(iator) + *-in*[2]]

local bubble, a bubble of hot, thin interstellar gas located near the solar system: *The "local bubble" . . . is believed to be 320 to 490 light years long* (New York Times).

M m

mall doll, a young woman who spends a great deal of time shopping in malls: *. . .a comic romance about a mall doll who finds more to life than shopping* (Peter Travers).

mall|ing (môl'ing, mal'-), *n.* **1** the practice of spending time shopping or socializing at a mall. **2** the excessive construction of shopping malls.

massively parallel, of or having many computer chips that simultaneously perform calculations related to a particular problem: *Massively parallel processing . . . will team hundreds or thousands of independent processors . . . to solve problems far too imposing for even the most powerful computers today* (John Markoff).

merit pay, wages paid on the basis of the merit or effective performance of an employee: *The outcry by teachers' organizations against merit pay may puzzle . . . Americans brought up on the idea that merit should be rewarded* (Fred Hechinger).

mi|cro|sat (mī'krō sat) or **mi|cro|sat|el|lite** (mī'krō sat'ə līt), *n.* a small artificial satellite: *The satellites, called "microsats," will weigh only 20 pounds each and will occupy a volume of about one gallon* (New York Times).

mor|phing (môr'fing), *n.* the manipulation of film images by means of a computer to create special effects: *It is now technically possible, through the magic of morphing, to show Ms. Streep with her head twisted on backward* (Janet Maslin). [< (meta)*morph*osis + *-ing*[1]]

mosh (mosh), *v.i.* to dance in a violent manner to rock music; slam-dance: *In the front of the stage, a herd of boys and girls . . . have commenced "moshing": hurling themselves about . . . , slamming into one another and falling down* (The Independent). —**mosh'ing**, *n.* —**mosh'er**, *n.*

mosh pit, the area near a stage where fans engage in moshing: *There was no moshing in the mosh pit . . . The band's doughnut-shaped stage was filled with attentive listeners* (Don McLeese).

mountain bike, a sturdy bicycle specially designed for off-road use: *A heavier mountain bike . . . is great on bumpy dirt trails, but sluggish and heavy when it comes to longer road rides* (New York Times).

mul|ti|cul|tur|al|ist (mul′ti kul′chər ə-list), *n.* a person who studies or advocates the study of the different cultures that contribute to a society: *Thanks to the proddings and scholarship of the multiculturalists, histories of the U.S. have grown remarkably more inclusive* (Time).

N n

na|no|phase (nan′ō fāz, nan′ə-), *adj.* only a few nanometers in size; ultrafine; subminiature: *The new nanophase form of pure copper . . . could find important structural uses* (New York Times).

no-brain|er (nō′brā′nər), *n., adj.* —*n.* something requiring little thought or effort: *As issues go, infant mortality should be a no-brainer for a politician* (Priscilla Painton).
—*adj.* requiring little thought or effort: *The Fed would be forced to think twice about making the no-brainer kinds of loans it is now making* (Donald W. Riegle).

O o

o|ver-the-top (ō′vər ᵺə top′), *adj.* beyond the ordinary, often in a way that is excessive or overdone: *Inside, the décor is as over-the-top as the maestro himself, with sconces, faux marble, muralled walls and over-padded barber's chairs* (The Independent).
go over the top, a go to an extreme: *It takes a genius like Kevin to go over the top and take the audience with him* (Ross Wetzsteon). **b** go mad: *Nick has gone over the top; he's dead inside* (New York Magazine).

P p

plant|i|bod|y (plan′tə bod′ē, plän′-), *n., pl.* **-bod|ies.** an antibody produced in a plant by means of genetic engineering: *To further the cancer-fighting prospects of plantibodies, the researchers now are working . . . in an attempt to put genes for human-tumor-attacking antibodies into plant cells* (Science News). [< *pl*(ant) + *antibody*]

pro|te|o|gly|can (prō′tē ə glī′kən), *n.* a molecule that maintains the growth pattern of optic nerve cells: *These molecular guardrails, called proteoglycans, consist of a core protein encrusted with sulfur-containing sugars that repel the growing neurons* (New York Times).

R r

ran|che|ra (ran chär′ə, rän-) *n.* a traditional form of Mexican country music:

Ranchera remains a major influence in today's Mexican pop, and its melodramatic style is a perfect foil for rock and roll (Daisann McLane). [American English < American Spanish *ranchera* < *rancho;* see etym. under **ranch**]

red-shirt|ing (red′shėr′ting), *n.* the practice of delaying entry into kindergarten in order to improve the child's performance in school: *Parents, fearful that their child might be labeled slow, are holding them back a year (a practice called red-shirting)* (Redbook). [< *red-shirt*]

re|en|ac|tor or **re-en|ac|tor** (rē′en ak′-tər), *n.* a person who participates in the reenactment of a historical event: *Almost all the cavalry are played by "re-enactors"* (Jonathan Storm).

re|pet|i|tive-mo|tion disorder (ri-pet′ə tiv mō′shən), an injury or condition resulting from frequently repeating the same movement: *In terms of repetitive-motion disorders . . . 1 in 3 chicken workers was found to have a work-related muscular-skeletal disorder resulting in moderate or extreme pain* (Richard Behar).

re|writ|a|ble (rē rī′tə bəl), *adj.* allowing a computer user to insert and delete data: *Rewritable disk technology . . . has innumerable uses beyond music. The most important may be in computing* (David E. Sanger).

S s

sell-by date (sel′bī′), date after which a perishable product cannot be sold in a store: *(Figurative.) Anyway, he is long past his sell-by date and will be retiring soon* (John Harlow).

shell company, a business, existing usually only in legal form, used to conceal funds or illegal activities: *Virtually anyone can still establish his or her own shell company for a few thousand dollars in legal fees* (Steve Lohr).

slam-dance (slam′ dans′, -däns′), *v.i.,* **-danced, -danc|ing.** to dance to rock music by whirling about and deliberately colliding with other dancers: *Anthrax draws a crowd that likes to slam-dance . . . dancing in which kids stomp around together, flailing and bouncing off each other* (Rolling Stone). —**slam dancing.**

social audit, 1 a systematic evaluation of the social consequences of a company's business policies and operations. **2** a statement of the findings of such a systematic evaluation: *The social audit . . . in general commends the company, which gives 7.5% of pre-tax profits to charity* (Suzanne Alexander).

su|per|de|formed (sü′pər di fôrmd′), *adj.* (of an atomic nucleus) having an unusual ellipsoid shape, the result of stress from being in an excited state: *Twin is being cited for his pioneering work in discovering the first superdeformed nucleus* (Drexel University News).

T t

tough love or **tough|love** (tuf′luv′), *n.* any of various means that seek to remedy a person's distress by seemingly unsympathetic attitudes or harsh actions: *Gates was warned . . . that he was showing Scott too much understanding. Steve advised him [Gates] to practice . . . "tough love"* (Frederic Dannen).

V v

vic|tim-im|pact statement (vik′təm im′pakt), a review of the consequences of a crime on its victim: *47 states now allow some form of . . . victim-impact statements to be included among the evidence weighed during the sentencing phase of criminal trials* (Time).

virtual office, an office that exists solely as a location in a computer network: *Rather than a suite in a skyscraper, . . . proponents of the virtual office see it as a bubble of information created by new technologies* (New York Times).

W w

whole language, a method of teaching language arts, based on language skills already acquired by a pupil: *Many teachers are experimenting with the "whole language" approach, which says that reading, writing and vocabulary are best taught together* (Lynda Richardson).

world music, popular music which blends a variety of folk influences from different cultures: *It's hardly surprising that the album's view of world music is catholic enough to encompass American Soul music* (David Wild).

Z z

ze|ro-e|mis|sion vehicle (zir′ō i mish′ən), a motor vehicle which produces no exhaust, especially an electrically powered car: *By 1998, 2 percent of all new cars sold . . . will have to be . . . zero-emission vehicles* (Lesley Hazleton).

AFRICA ▪ AIDS ▪ ALBANIA ▪ ALBERTA ▪ ALGERIA ▪ ANTHROPOLOGY ▪ ARC

SIA ▪ ASTRONOMY ▪ AUSTRALIA ▪ AUSTRIA ▪ AUTOMOBILE ▪ AUTOMOBILE

ELGIUM ▪ BIOLOGY ▪ BOATIN

BULGARIA ▪ BURMA ▪ CAB

CITY ▪ CIVIL RIGHTS ▪ CLAS

ONSERVATION ▪ CONSUMERISM

▪ DENMA

GYPT ▪

FASHION

SUES ▪ HOCKEY

1994

WORLD BOOK
SUPPLEMENT

To help World Book owners keep their
encyclopedias up to date, the following
articles are reprinted from the 1995 edition
of the encyclopedia.

EW BRUNS

NIGERIA

ACIFIC ISL

▪ PHY

PSY

RUSSIA

AIN ▪ SPORTS ▪ SRI LANKA ▪ S   VERNMENT ▪ TOCKS AND BONDS ▪ SU

IMMING ▪ SWITZERLAND ▪ SYRIA ▪ TAIWAN ▪ TAXATION ▪ TELECOMMUNICA

D GAMES ▪ TRACK AND FIELD ▪ TRANSPORTATION ▪ TUNISIA ▪ TURKEY ▪ U

NEZUELA ▪ VIETNAM ▪ WASHINGTON, D.C. ▪ WATER ▪ WEATHER ▪ WELFARE

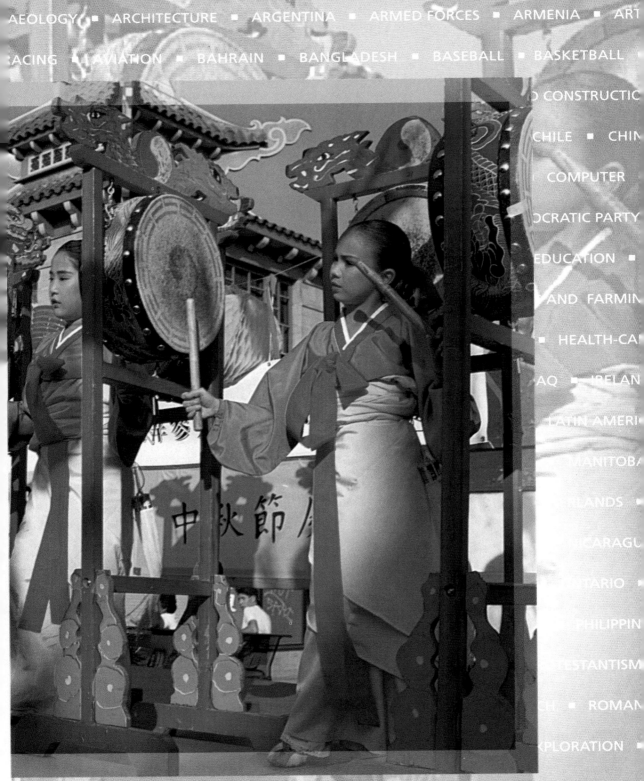

Rudi Von Briel

Asian neighborhoods are part of many American cities.

Michael Newman, Photo Edit

A Vietnamese American family enjoy a meal together.

Asian Americans add their many different ethnic and cultural groups to the blend of American life. They make up the country's third largest and fastest growing minority group.

Asian Americans

Asian Americans are Americans of Asian descent. They or their ancestors came from Asian countries, particularly Cambodia, China, India, Indonesia, Japan, Korea, Laos, Pakistan, the Philippines, Thailand, and Vietnam. More than 7 million people of Asian descent live in the United States. They make up the country's third largest minority group, after African Americans and Hispanic Americans.

The first Asian immigrants who arrived in large numbers in the United States came from southeastern China. They immigrated to California in 1849, after gold was discovered there. In 1882, however, the U.S. government began placing restrictions on Asian immigration because of pressure from native-born Americans. Many Americans feared job competition from the newcomers and resented their "foreign" customs. It was not until 1965 that all restrictions against Asian immigration were lifted. Today, their high rate of immigration makes Asians the country's fastest growing minority group.

Who Asian Americans are

According to the 1990 U.S. census, about 3 percent of the United States population is of Asian descent. Asia, the world's largest continent, has 49 countries, so the Asian American population consists of many different ethnic and cultural groups. Chinese Americans form the largest Asian group, making up about 1.6 million of the 7 million Asian Americans. Filipino Americans are the second largest group, with about 1.4 million people. The next largest groups are Americans of Japanese, Asian Indian, Korean, and Vietnamese ancestry.

The contributor of this article is Hyung-chan Kim, Professor of Education and Asian American Studies at Western Washington University and editor of the Dictionary of Asian American History.

The languages of the many Asian American groups include Chinese, Hindi, Japanese, Javanese, Korean, Tagalog, Thai, and Vietnamese. Asian Americans practice several major religions, including Buddhism, Christianity, Confucianism, Hinduism, Islam, and Shintoism.

Asian American groups differ in physical appearance, language, and culture from one another as well as from other Americans. But Asian Americans have many of the same values most other Americans cherish. For example, most strongly believe in the importance of family. Many Asian Americans, particularly the most recent immigrants, uphold a family value called *xiao.* The Chinese character for the word combines the word *lao,* meaning old age or old man, with *zi,* which means son. In practicing xiao, the young honor the old, and the old respect and protect the young.

Success through hard work and self-discipline is another value emphasized in most Asian American families. Children are encouraged to work hard in and out of school to be worthy of the sacrifices their parents make for them. Self-control is also an important value. Children are taught that mature people do not show their feelings too readily.

Where Asian Americans live

Most Asian Americans live in the Western United States. According to the 1990 census, only about a fifth of the total U.S. population lives in the West, but more than half of the Asian population resides there. Almost 4 out of 10 Asian Americans live in California.

More than 95 percent of Asian Americans live in urban areas. About half of them have homes in cities, and about half live in suburbs. In cities, Asian Americans are often concentrated in their ethnic neighborhoods, which are usually known by such names as Chinatown or Little Tokyo.

Asian American accomplishments

Asians have been in the United States for only about 150 years. In spite of their short history, they have influenced many areas of American culture. Asian Americans also have distinguished themselves in many fields.

Asian influences on American culture are reflected in many areas of life. *Tai chi chuan* is a form of exercise that the Chinese have practiced for centuries. It has become especially popular among older Americans, who find that its slow, gentle movements provide good exercise for aging bodies. *Tae kwon do* is a traditional Korean *martial art* (fighting art). It has been popularized by Korean immigrants who have established gyms across the country to teach it to American youth. *Judo* is a traditional Japanese form of wrestling. Many colleges in the United States offer judo as part of their physical education program.

Chow mein and other Chinese foods are familiar to most Americans. Chow mein is a steamed dish of vegetables topped with chicken, beef, or seafood and served with fried noodles. A favorite for some Americans is *sushi,* a Japanese dish of rice and fish. Restaurants that serve spicy Thai or Indian food are popular. The Korean dish *kimchi,* a highly seasoned mixture of Chinese cabbage, white radishes, and other vegetables, can be found in many American groceries.

Acupuncture is an ancient Chinese method of relieving pain and treating disease by inserting needles in the body. It has become accepted by the American medical profession as a way to treat certain ailments.

Individual achievements. Nuclear physicist Samuel Chao Chung Ting is among several Asian Americans who have won the Nobel Prize. He shared the 1976 Nobel Prize for physics for helping to discover a subatomic particle known as the *psi particle.* Subrahmanyan Chandrasekhar, an Indian-born astrophysicist, shared the 1983 Nobel Prize for physics for research on the evolution and death of stars. Chandrasekhar's work contributed to the theory of invisible astronomical objects called *black holes.*

Award-winning Asian American athletes include Sammy Lee and Kristi Yamaguchi. Lee was the first non-white American to win an Olympic gold medal in high diving. He received the medal in 1948 and again in 1952. In 1992, Yamaguchi became the first Asian American to win an Olympic gold medal in figure skating.

The first Asian American to serve in the U.S. Congress was Dalip Singh Saund. In 1956, he won election to the House of Representatives as a Democrat from California. He served from 1957 to 1963. Hiram L. Fong became the first Asian American to win a seat in the Senate. He represented Hawaii from 1959 until he retired from politics in 1977. Daniel K. Inouye became the first Asian American to serve in both the House and Senate. He was elected as a representative from Hawaii in 1959 and won election as a senator from that state in 1962. The first Asian American woman in Congress was Patsy T. Mink, who represented Hawaii from 1965 to 1977 and was elected again in 1990.

Ellison S. Onizuka was the first American astronaut of Asian descent. Onizuka and his fellow crew members died in January 1986 when their space shuttle Challenger was destroyed in an accident that took place shortly after launch.

A number of other Asian Americans have achieved success in their chosen professions. They include architects I. M. Pei and Minoru Yamasaki; authors Maxine

John Neubauer, Photo Edit

A Japanese American lawyer argues a case.

Gary Conner, Photo Edit

Korean American drummers perform at a festival.

David Weintraub, Photo Researchers

Ancient Chinese exercises called *t'ai chi chuan* are performed by large numbers of people throughout the United States. Many people practice t'ai chi outdoors early in the morning.

Where Asian Americans live

This map shows the state-by-state distribution of the U.S. Asian population according to the 1990 census. The numbers on the map indicate the percentage of Asians in the total population of each state.

Percent of total population by state

- More than 5.0
- 2.5 to 5.0
- 1.5 to 2.4
- 1.0 to 1.4
- Less than 1.0

WORLD BOOK map

[Map of the United States with state percentages:]
Wash. 4.0 · Oregon 2.3 · Montana 0.5 · N. Dak. 0.5 · Idaho 0.8 · Minn. 1.8 · Wis. 1.1 · Mich. 1.1 · N.H. 0.8 · Me. 0.5 · Vt. 0.6 · Mass. 2.4 · N.Y. 3.8 · R.I. 1.8 · Conn. 1.5 · Nevada 2.9 · Utah 1.5 · Wyoming 0.6 · S. Dak. 0.4 · Nebraska 0.8 · Iowa 0.9 · Illinois 2.5 · Ind. 0.7 · Ohio 0.8 · Penn. 1.1 · N.J. 3.5 · Del. 1.3 · California 9.2 · Colorado 1.7 · Kansas 1.2 · Missouri 0.8 · W.Va. 0.4 · D.C. 1.8 · Va. 2.5 · Md. 2.9 · Ken. 0.5 · Arizona 1.4 · New Mexico 0.9 · Oklahoma 1.0 · Arkansas 0.5 · Tenn. 0.6 · N.C. 0.8 · S.C. 0.6 · Miss. 0.5 · Ala. 0.5 · Georgia 1.1 · Texas 1.8 · La. 1.0 · Florida 1.2 · Alaska 3.2 · Hawaii 46.9

Hong Kingston and Amy Tan; broadcast journalist Connie Chung; composer and video artist Nam June Paik; and orchestra conductors Zubin Mehta and Seiji Ozawa.

History of Asian immigration

Asian immigration to the United States did not begin until the mid-1800's, more than 200 years after the first wave of European immigration. One reason for the slower start is that the rulers of many Asian countries prohibited their subjects from going abroad. In some cases, people who were caught attempting to leave were put to death.

Another reason that Asians did not leave their homelands was that their societies were relatively stable. Asia did not experience the revolutions that brought political, economic, and social changes to Europe. The people had little reason to leave in search of a better life. But by the mid-1800's, the traditional Asian systems began to prove ineffective in the face of increasing social problems.

The first major social crises erupted in China. The government began to weaken under repeated foreign invasions, domestic revolts, and problems caused by overpopulation. The rulers could no longer control people who wanted to leave the country.

The first wave of Asian immigration. The news in 1848 that gold had been discovered on John Sutter's California property attracted many people to the state. In 1849, about 700 Chinese arrived hoping to find work mining gold. They were poor peasants from southeastern China. Most of them had not even been able to pay their fare to the United States. They received loans from merchants in their own country and made promises to pay off their debts after they found work in America. By the end of 1850, there were 4,000 Chinese in California. By 1860, the United States had a Chinese population of about 35,000, most of whom lived in California. Many newcomers who could not find work in the California mines obtained jobs building railroads.

California civic leaders and industrialists greeted the first arrivals of Chinese laborers with enthusiasm. But

Ethnic background of Asian Americans

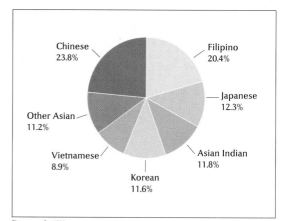

Chinese 23.8%
Filipino 20.4%
Japanese 12.3%
Asian Indian 11.8%
Korean 11.6%
Vietnamese 8.9%
Other Asian 11.2%

Figures are for 1990.
Source: U.S. Bureau of the Census.

soon, competition for jobs became intense between white workers and the increasing number of Chinese workers. In some instances, mobs attacked Chinese immigrants. In 1882, Congress passed the Chinese Exclusion Act, which prohibited all Chinese laborers from immigrating to the United States. The act permitted only merchants, teachers, and certain other groups from China to come to the United States.

The act was the first of numerous restrictions the U.S. government was to place on Asian immigration. The restrictions resulted in part because many American workers feared job competition from Asians, many of whom would work for low wages. In addition, some Americans argued that Asians could not be *assimilated* (incorporated) into American society because of their physical and cultural differences.

The second wave. Hawaii did not become a state until 1959. But in the late 1800's and early 1900's, it was the destination for several Asian immigrant groups. The first group was made up of Japanese workers. Between

1885 and 1894, an association of owners of Hawaiian sugar plantations recruited almost 29,000 Japanese as *contract laborers,* workers imported under an agreement to work for a particular employer.

After the Japanese fulfilled their contracts, most of them settled in Hawaii or in the Pacific Coast States of California, Oregon, and Washington. They worked first as farm hands and later grew vegetables on land they purchased or rented.

In the early 1900's, the Japanese population in the Pacific Coast States began to face the same opposition that had arisen against Chinese workers. In 1905, an organization that later became the Asiatic Exclusion League was established in California to work toward halting the immigration of Japanese people and other Asians. In 1908, the United States and Japan reached an understanding that became known as the *gentlemen's agreement.* The agreement restricted new Japanese immigration to the relatives of immigrants who had already settled in the United States. The gentlemen's agreement was not a law, and it was never put into writing. Japan cooperated voluntarily.

Arrivals of the early 1900's. The Hawaiian plantation owners began looking for other sources of labor in the early 1900's. Their Japanese workers had organized labor unions and frequently went on strike, demanding higher wages and better living conditions. The plantation owners turned to Korea, where the people had recently suffered through war and famine. During the early 1900's, the Hawaiians recruited more than 7,000 Korean laborers. But Korean immigration halted in 1905. Japanese workers had complained to their government that Korean workers were being used as strikebreakers. Japan, then in the process of taking control of Korea, put pressure on the Korean government to stop immigration to Hawaii. Most Koreans in Hawaii remained there. A small group migrated to the U.S. Pacific Coast.

In 1906, the plantation owners began bringing in workers from the Philippines. By 1931, about 110,000 Fil-

ipino laborers had arrived. During the early 1900's, a small number of Filipinos went to Alaska for seasonal work in the fishing industry. Others found agricultural work in such states as California and Oregon.

Groups of immigrants from India began arriving in the United States in the early 1900's. Most of the immigrants were young men from farm households in search of job opportunities. They arrived by ship in British Columbia, Canada, and then many made their way south into the United States. Most of them found work in lumber mills in Washington state or on farms in central California. Like other Asians before them, they faced opposition from local citizens. In 1907, a mob in Bellingham, Wash., rioted against Asian Indian sawmill workers. The mob attacked the homes of the Asians and drove the immigrants out of town. Most of the immigrants fled to Canada.

Asian immigration halted. In 1917, Congress passed one of the country's most restrictive immigration laws. The law prohibited immigrants from an area known as the Asiatic Barred Zone from coming to the United States. This area included most of Asia and a majority of islands in the Pacific Ocean.

The Immigration Act of 1924, which took effect in 1929, excluded any Asians who had not been barred by the 1917 law. The legislation closed the doors of the country to Asians—with one exception. People from the Philippines were allowed entry. At that time, the Philippines was a U.S. possession, so Filipinos were not considered foreigners. However, the Tydings-McDuffie Act of 1934 limited immigration from the Philippines to an annual quota of 50.

Japanese internment. Japan's surprise attack on the U.S. military base at Pearl Harbor, Hawaii, on Dec. 7, 1941, caused the United States to enter World War II. It also stirred hostility against Japanese people in the United States. Many Americans associated Japanese Americans with the Japanese pilots who had destroyed U.S. Navy ships.

Visual Communications

Filipino farm laborers, *above,* were among Asian immigrants of the early 1900's. During that period, thousands of Filipinos arrived to do agricultural work.

AP/Wide World

A Japanese American family is confined in a detention camp. In the early 1940's, during World War II, all West Coast residents of Japanese ancestry were forced into such camps.

In February 1942, President Franklin D. Roosevelt issued Executive Order 9066, which authorized military commanders to designate military areas from which "any or all persons may be excluded." The military chose to remove all people of Japanese ancestry from the West Coast and southern Arizona. About 110,000 Japanese were confined in 10 detention camps scattered over seven states: Arizona, Arkansas, California, Colorado, Idaho, Utah, and Wyoming. They lost their homes and their jobs as a result. In 1944, the Supreme Court of the United States ruled that it was unlawful to confine U.S. citizens whose loyalty was not in question.

About 1,500 young Japanese Americans from the camps volunteered to serve in the U.S. Army during the war. The 442nd Regimental Combat Unit was made up solely of Japanese American soldiers. The unit fought bravely in Europe and suffered many casualties. Public opinion changed as Japanese Americans showed their loyalty to the nation.

In 1948, Congress passed the Japanese American Evacuation Claims Act. The law authorized a maximum payment of $2,500 to individual Japanese Americans as compensation for what they had lost while confined.

In 1980, Representative Norman Y. Mineta of California and Senator Daniel Inouye of Hawaii sponsored a bill that resulted in the establishment of the Commission on Wartime Relocation and Internment of Civilians. After holding numerous hearings across the country, the commission recommended that the President offer a national apology to Japanese Americans. It also called for a compensatory payment of $20,000 to surviving Japanese Americans who had been in the camps. These and other commission recommendations became law under the Civil Liberties Act of 1988.

Restrictions lifted. Although World War II brought suffering to many Japanese Americans, it also brought about the first easing of U.S. restrictions on Asian immigration. Because China was fighting as an ally of the United States, many people felt that Chinese immigrants should no longer be barred from the country. In 1943, the government lifted the ban on Chinese immigration and also allowed Chinese immigrants to become citizens. This was the first time that foreign-born Asians were granted the right to U.S. citizenship. In 1946, the government extended similar rights to Filipino and Asian Indian immigrants.

In 1952, Congress passed the Immigration and Nationality Act, also called the McCarran-Walter Act. This law essentially retained the Asiatic Barred Zone provision, but it did allow very limited immigration from the countries within the zone. It extended to all Asian immigrants the right to become U.S. citizens.

The Immigration Act of 1965 eliminated the Asiatic Barred Zone. After 1965, large numbers of Asians started moving to the United States, particularly from China, South Korea, and the Philippines.

Arrivals of the late 1900's. Millions of Southeast Asians have come to the United States since the mid-1970's. Most of them fled their homelands as a result of the Vietnam War (1957-1975). The first wave to arrive were Vietnamese political refugees who had worked for the U.S. government or U.S. companies. For the most part, they were educated, skilled workers. Most of the second wave were rural people from Cambodia and Laos, who had less education and fewer job skills.

About three-fourths of the Southeast Asian immigrants settled in 10 states: California, Florida, Massachusetts, Minnesota, New York, Pennsylvania, Texas, Virginia, Washington, and Wisconsin. The initial response in most communities where the refugees settled was one of sympathy. But in some cases, conflicts arose with local residents when the newcomers began to move into the labor force. Many Vietnamese refugees, for example, found jobs in the shrimp fishing industry in Texas, Mississippi, and other Gulf Coast States. Local fishing crews accused the Southeast Asians of setting too many traps, fishing in areas claimed by American crews, and other offenses. Fighting often broke out, and vandals on both sides damaged their rivals' boats and fishing nets.

Asian Americans today

Asian Americans are the fastest growing minority group in the United States. Between 1980 and 1990, the number of Asian Americans almost doubled. During that period, the percentage of increase in the Asian American population was seven times greater than that of the African American population and more than twice that of Hispanic Americans. In spite of their growth, however, Asian Americans still make up less than 3 percent of the population.

Like other minorities, Asians face problems of acceptance in American society. Also like other minorities, Asians struggle against inaccurate images that many people have of them. On one hand, for example, many books and motion pictures portray Asians as either sinister villains or meek servants. On the other hand, sociologists have referred to Asians as the "model minority." The label implies that all Asians have achieved success through discipline and hard work and thus other minorities should imitate them. However, although many Asian Americans are successful, many are not.

Education levels of Asian Americans vary widely, for example. A higher percentage of Asian Americans receive doctorates every year than either blacks or Hispanics. Yet many recent Southeast Asian immigrants have little or no formal education and few job skills.

Income levels also differ greatly. The median household income among Asian Americans is higher than that for the U.S. population as a whole. But it is also true that a higher percentage of Asians than whites live in poverty. And Asian American household income often includes the wages of several people. Many Asian Americans operate small businesses, primarily restaurants, grocery stores, and dry cleaners. Often, the whole family is involved in the business, and some members may work 12 to 14 hours a day.

Lack of English language skills is a major problem facing recent Asian immigrants. Until Asian Americans are able to speak English well, limited job opportunities will be available to them.

The efforts to learn English and to become a part of American culture have led to another problem, particularly for young Asians in families of recent immigrants. In becoming part of American culture, these young Asians often put aside the language and traditions of their ancestors. As a result, they find themselves in conflict with their parents' generation. And they do not find

An Indian restaurant, *left,* is an example of the many small businesses owned and operated by Asian Americans today. Often, several members of a family work long hours to keep the business running.

Joseph Nettis, Tony Stone Images

complete acceptance in American society. They are left feeling that they are on the fringes of two societies and do not belong to either. This conflict eases over time as families become more Americanized, with more generations born in the United States. But it is something every immigrant group experiences upon coming to a new country.   Hyung-chan Kim

Related articles in *World Book* include:

Biographies

Chandrasekhar,
  Subrahmanyan
Hayakawa, S. I.
Lee, Tsung Dao
Mehta, Zubin

Noguchi, Isamu
Ozawa, Seiji
Pei, I. M.
Wu, Chien-shiung
Yang, Chen Ning

History

California (Early
  statehood)
Gentlemen's agreement
Hawaii (World War II)
Immigration (Immigration
  to the United States)

Oriental exclusion acts
Riot (During the 1800's)
Roosevelt, Theodore (Friction
  with Japan)
World War II (Treatment of
  enemy aliens)

Other related articles

City (Neighborhoods)
Hmong
Judo
Karate
Martial arts

Minority group (Asian
  Americans)
Nisei
Racism

Outline

I. **Who Asian Americans are**
II. **Where Asian Americans live**
III. **Asian American accomplishments**
  A. Asian influences on American culture
  B. Individual achievements
IV. **History of Asian immigration**
  A. The first wave of Asian immigration
  B. The second wave
  C. Arrivals of the early 1900's

D. Asian immigration halted
E. Japanese internment
F. Restrictions lifted
G. Arrivals of the late 1900's
V. **Asian Americans today**

Questions

Why was Korean immigration to Hawaii halted in 1905?
When were foreign-born Asians residing in the United States first allowed the right to become citizens?
What is *kimchi?*
In what part of the United States do most Asian Americans live?
What problem do many young Asian Americans face?
Who was the first American astronaut of Asian descent?
What happened as a result of President Franklin D. Roosevelt's Executive Order 9066?
Which Asian group entered the United States by way of Canada in the early 1900's?
What does the word *xiao* mean?
What is one reason Asian immigration to the United States began so much later than European immigration?

Additional resources

Level I
Morey, Janet N., and Dunn, Wendy. *Famous Asian Americans.* Cobblehill, 1992.
Peoples of North America. 47 vols. Chelsea Hse., 1987. Each of the books in this series focuses on a different immigrant group, including Asian immigrants.

Level II
Aguilar-San Juan, Karin. *The State of Asian America: Activism and Resistance in the 1990s.* South End, 1994.
Asian Women United of California, ed. *Making Waves: An Anthology of Writings by and About Asian American Women.* Beacon Pr., 1989.
Chan, Sucheng. *Asian Americans.* Twayne, 1991.
Kim, Hyung-chan, ed. *Dictionary of Asian American History.* Greenwood, 1986.
Kitano, Harry H., and Daniels, Roger. *Asian Americans.* Prentice-Hall, 1988.
Takaki, Ronald T. *Strangers from a Different Shore: A History of Asian Americans.* Little, Brown, 1989.

© Vic Bider, Tony Stone Images

Two Americans shake hands in greeting.

© Van Bucher, Photo Researchers

Two Europeans greet with a kiss on the cheek.

Customs differ from culture to culture. The photographs above and on the next page illustrate some of the different ways that people greet each other in various parts of the world.

Culture

Culture is a term used by social scientists for a way of life. Every human society has a culture. Culture includes a society's arts, beliefs, customs, institutions, inventions, language, technology, and values. A culture produces similar behavior and thought among most people in a particular society. To learn about a culture, one may ask such questions as these: What language do the people speak? What do the people of the society wear? How do they prepare their food? What kind of dwellings do they live in? What kind of work do they do? How do they govern themselves? How do they judge right from wrong?

People are not born with any knowledge of a culture. They generally learn a culture by growing up in a particular society. They learn mainly through the use of language, especially by talking and listening to other members of the society. They also learn by watching and imitating various behaviors in the society. The process by which people—especially children—learn their society's culture is called *enculturation*. Through enculturation, a culture is shared with members of a society and passed from one generation to the next. Enculturation unifies people of a society by providing them with common experiences.

The term *culture* has been defined in many ways. It often is used in a narrow sense to refer to activities in such fields as art, literature, and music. In that sense, a

Conrad Phillip Kottak, the contributor of this article, is a Professor of Anthropology at the University of Michigan. He is the author of several books, including Anthropology: The Exploration of Human Diversity *and* Assault on Paradise: Social Change in a Brazilian Village.

cultured person is someone who has knowledge of and appreciation for the fine arts. But under the broader definition used by social scientists, culture includes all areas of life, and all human beings have a culture.

Social scientists identify certain aspects of culture as *pop culture* or *popular culture*. Pop culture includes such elements of a society's arts and entertainment as television, radio, recordings, advertising, sports, hobbies, fads, and fashions.

The term *civilization* is similar to culture, but it refers mostly to cultures that have complex economic, governmental, and social systems. A civilization is technologically more advanced than other cultures of its time. A culture is any way of life, be it simple or complex, advanced or not advanced.

For hundreds of thousands of years, human beings have had at least some of the biological abilities on which culture depends. These abilities are to learn, to use language and other symbols, and to employ tools to organize their lives and adapt to their environments. Besides human beings, other animals also have such elements of culture as the ability to make and use tools and the ability to communicate. For example, elephants break off tree branches and wave them with their trunks to brush off flies. Dolphins communicate with one another by means of barks, whistles, and other sounds. But no other animals have developed language and other symbols as complex as those of human beings. Thus, no other animal possesses to the same extent the abilities to learn, to communicate, and to store, process, and use information. The rest of this article focuses on the main aspects of human culture.

Characteristics of culture

There are several important characteristics of culture. The main ones are these: (1) A culture satisfies human needs in particular ways. (2) A culture is acquired

Two Asians greet each other with a bow.

through learning. (3) A culture is based on the use of symbols. (4) A culture consists of individual *traits* and groups of traits called *patterns*.

Satisfying basic needs. All cultures serve to meet the basic needs shared by human beings. For example, every culture has methods of obtaining food and shelter. Every culture also has family relationships, economic and governmental systems, religious practices, and forms of artistic expression.

Each culture shapes the way its members satisfy human needs. Human beings have to eat, but their culture teaches them what, when, and how to eat. For example, many British people eat smoked fish for breakfast, but many Americans prefer cold cereals. In the Midwestern United States, people generally eat dinner at 5 or 6 p.m. However, most Spaniards dine at 10 p.m. Many Turks prefer strong coffee with the grounds left in the cup, but most Australians filter out the grounds for a weaker brew. Many Japanese eat their meals from low tables while sitting on mats on the floor. Canadians usually sit on chairs at higher tables.

Learning. Culture is acquired through learning, not through biological inheritance. That is, no person is born with a culture. Children take on the culture in which they are raised through enculturation.

Children learn much of their culture through imitation and experience. They also acquire culture through observation, paying attention to what goes on around them and seeing examples of what their society considers right and wrong. Children also may absorb certain aspects of culture unconsciously. For example, Arabs tend to stand closer together when speaking to one another than most Europeans do. No one instructs them to do so, but they learn the behavior as part of their culture.

Children also learn their culture by being told what to do. For example, a parent tells a son or daughter, "Say

thank you" or "Don't talk to strangers." Individual members of a particular culture also share many memories, beliefs, values, expectations, and ways of thinking. In fact, most cultural learning results from verbal communication. Culture is passed from generation to generation chiefly through language.

Using symbols. Cultural learning is based on the ability to use symbols. A symbol is something that stands for something else. The most important types of symbols are the words of a language. There is no obvious or necessary connection between a symbol and what it stands for. The English word *dog* is a symbol for a specific animal that barks. But other cultures have a different word that stands for the same animal—the French word *chien,* for example, or the Swahili word *mbwa.*

There are many other kinds of symbols besides the words in a language. A flag, for example, stands for a country. Colors have symbolic meaning, and the meanings vary from culture to culture. For Chinese people, white is a color of mourning. In Western societies, black is the color of mourning. White is a symbol of purity, and brides wear white. All human societies use symbols to create and maintain culture.

Forming patterns. Cultures are made up of individual elements called *cultural traits.* A group of related traits is a *cultural pattern.*

Cultural traits may be divided into *material culture* and *nonmaterial culture.* Material culture consists of all the things that are made by the members of a society. It includes such objects as buildings, jewelry, machines, and paintings. Nonmaterial culture refers to a society's behaviors and beliefs. A handshake, a marriage ceremony, and a system of justice are examples of nonmaterial culture.

Cultural patterns may include numerous traits, both material and nonmaterial. The pattern for agriculture, for example, includes the time when crops are harvested (nonmaterial), the methods (nonmaterial) and machinery (material) used in harvesting, and the structures for storing the crops (material).

Most traits that make up a cultural pattern are connected to one another. If one custom, institution, or value that helps form a cultural pattern changes, other parts of the pattern will probably change, too. For example, until the 1950's, the career pattern for most women in Western societies was to work full-time as homemakers and mothers. By the late 1900's, the pattern was for most women to get jobs outside the home. As part of the new pattern, attitudes about marriage, family, and children also changed. The new pattern includes marriage at a later age than ever before, a dependence on alternative child-care systems, and more frequent divorce.

The boundaries of cultures

Every human society has a culture. People who grow up in the same nation can be said to share a *national culture.* But they may be part of other societies within the nation that have separate cultural traditions.

Social scientists sometimes use the term *subculture* to describe variations within a culture. Social groups often develop some cultural patterns of their own that set them apart from the larger society they are part of.

Subcultures may develop in businesses, ethnic groups, occupational groups, regional groups, religious groups, and other groups within a larger culture. For example, Amish people in Pennyslvania and several Midwestern States make up a subculture, as do members of a teen-age street gang.

Many cultural traits and patterns are limited to a particular culture, but many others are common to more than one culture. For example, cultures in the same part of the world often have similar patterns. A geographical region in which two or more cultures share cultural traits and patterns is called a *culture area.* Northern Europe is an example of a culture area.

Some cultural traits have spread throughout the world. For example, some clothing, music, sports, and industrial processes are the same in many areas of the world. Cultural traditions that extend beyond national boundaries form what is called *international culture.* For example, countries that share an international culture include Australia, Canada, the United Kingdom, and the United States. Their common cultural traditions include the English language and a heritage of British founders.

Culture and society

Multiculturalism. Some societies—such as those of Tibetans in Tibet and various peoples of the Pacific Islands—have traditionally been associated with a single culture. Other societies—such as those of the United States and Canada—are multicultural societies. They include many distinct cultures.

A shared cultural background makes people feel more comfortable with other people from their own culture. Many people initially may feel confused and uneasy when they deal with people of another culture. The discomfort that people often feel when they have contact with an unfamiliar culture is called *culture shock.* Culture shock usually passes if a person stays in a new culture long enough to understand it and get used to its ways.

People of one culture who move to a country where another culture dominates may give up their old ways and become part of the dominant culture. The process by which they do this is called *assimilation.* Through assimilation, a minority group eventually disappears because its members lose the cultural characteristics that set them apart. In a multicultural society, however, assimilation does not always occur.

A multicultural society supports the view that many distinct cultures are good and desirable. The multicultural view encourages such diversity. Thus, in the United States, millions of people speak both English and the language of their own culture. They eat both American food (apple pie and hamburgers) and ethnic food. They celebrate both national holidays (Fourth of July and Thanksgiving) and their ethnic holidays. For example, many Mexican Americans celebrate Mexican Independence Day on September 16. In Chinese communities across the country, parades and other festivities mark the Chinese New Year.

Multiculturalism succeeds best in a society that has many different ethnic groups and a political system that promotes freedom of expression and awareness and understanding of cultural differences. Ethnic groups can bring variety and richness to a society by introducing their own ideas and customs. However, ethnic groups that keep their own values and traditions can also threaten national unity. In many parts of the world, neighboring ethnic groups dislike and distrust one another. In some cases, these feelings have even led to war. In Bosnia-Herzegovina, for example, a civil war broke out in the early 1990's between Serbs and non-Serbs, who included Bosnian Muslims and Croats.

Ethnocentrism and cultural relativism. Many people in all cultures think that their own culture is right, proper, and moral. They tend to use their own cultural standards and values to judge the behavior and beliefs of people from different cultures. They regard the behavior and beliefs of people from other cultures as strange or savage.

The attitude that one's culture is best is called *ethnocentrism.* Ethnocentrism is harmful if carried to extremes. It may cause prejudice, automatic rejection of

Soccer, the world's most popular sport, is played by millions of people from many different cultures. Some cultural traits are common to one or a few cultures, but others—like soccer—have spread beyond such boundaries and have become part of what is called *international culture.*

ideas from other cultures, and even persecution of other groups.

The opposite view of ethnocentrism is called *cultural relativism.* It contends that no culture should be judged by the standards of another. This view can also present problems if carried to extremes. An extreme cultural relativist would say there is no such thing as a universal morality. An extreme cultural relativist would argue that the rules of all cultures deserve equal respect, even rules that allow such practices as cannibalism and torture. But many social scientists would reply that certain values are common to all societies—a prohibition against incest, for example, and support for marriage. They would argue that international standards of justice and morality should not be ignored.

How cultures change

Every culture changes. But all parts of a culture do not change at the same time. For example, science and technology may sometimes change so rapidly that they lessen the importance of customs, ideas, and other nonmaterial parts of a culture. At other times, changes in ideas and social systems may occur before changes in technology. The failure of certain parts of a culture to keep up with other, related parts is referred to as *cultural lag.*

A number of factors may cause a culture to change. The two main ones are (1) contact with other cultures and (2) invention.

Contact with other cultures. No society is so isolated that it does not come in contact with other societies. When contact occurs, societies borrow cultural traits from one another. As a result, cultural traits and patterns tend to spread from the society in which they originated. This spreading process is called *diffusion.* Corn growing, for example, began in what is now Mexico thousands of years ago and eventually spread throughout the world.

Diffusion can occur without firsthand contact between cultures. Products or patterns may move from group A to group C through group B without any contact between group A and group C. Today, diffusion is rapid and widespread because many cultures of the world are linked through advanced means of transportation and communication.

When two cultures have continuous, firsthand contact with each other, the exchange of cultural traits is called *acculturation.* Acculturation has often occurred when one culture has colonized or conquered another, or as a result of trade. In addition to adopting each other's traits, the two cultures may blend traits. For example, if the people of the cultures speak different languages, they may develop a mixed language called *pidgin* in order to communicate. The cultures may also exchange or blend such traits as clothing, dances, music, recipes, and tools. Through acculturation, parts of the culture of one or both groups change, but the groups remain distinct. In this way, acculturation differs from assimilation. Through assimilation, one group becomes part of another group and loses its separate identity.

Invention is the creation of a new device, process, or product. Inventions provide a new solution to an old or new problem. Without inventions, human beings would be at the mercy of the climate and the land. Inventions

Young students use a computer as an educational tool. The invention of the computer has had enormous impact on modern life. Inventions are a major cause of cultural change.

have given people much control over their environment and enabled them to lead easier lives.

Inventions have led to many changes in a culture. The invention of agriculture, for example, made it possible for people to settle in farm villages. Their values and social organization changed. They placed importance on using land and animals to produce crops. They began to build permanent housing. They developed systems of irrigation and a number of tools.

The invention of spinning and weaving machines and an improved steam engine in the 1700's produced another great change in the way people lived. These inventions led to the opening of factories. Many people who had worked at home in rural areas flocked to the cities to work in the new factories. As cities became more crowded, new kinds of political, economic, and social systems developed.

The invention of the electronic computer in the mid-1900's has had enormous impact. It has brought far-reaching changes in communication, education, entertainment, and numerous other areas of modern life.

How people study culture

The scientific study of human beings is called *anthropology.* One of the main branches of anthropology is cultural anthropology, which studies human cultures. The work of cultural anthropologists is *comparative* and *cross-cultural*—that is, cultural anthropologists study various societies to determine their cultural similarities and differences.

Cultural anthropologists study the artwork, houses, tools, and other material products of contemporary cultures. They also investigate the nonmaterial creations, including social groups, religious beliefs, symbols, and values. They gather information primarily by living for a time among the people they are studying and by observing them and talking with them. They organize the information into a scientific description called an *ethnography.*

Another main branch of anthropology is archaeology. It focuses on cultures of the past. Archaeologists study the remains of these cultures, including buildings, clothing, pottery, tools, and artwork. They trace the development of cultures by examining the things the people made and used. Archaeologists work at a specific site. They dig carefully for buried objects in a process called *excavation*. They describe whatever they find in academic publications and take photographs of representative samples.

Archaeological research is the chief method available for learning about societies that existed before the invention of writing about 5,500 years ago. However, some archaeologists study later cultures, even contemporary cultures. For example, an archaeological project begun in 1973 in Tucson, Arizona, has provided information about contemporary American life through a study of people's garbage. The archaeologists made their study by digging in landfills.

Other social scientists who study aspects of culture include sociologists and political scientists. They work mainly in a single urban, industrial society, and they make cross-cultural comparisons less often than anthropologists.   Conrad Phillip Kottak

Related articles in *World Book.* See **Anthropology** and its list of *Related articles.* See also:

Acculturation	Etiquette
Assimilation	Folklore
City (Cultural variety in cities)	Language
Civilization	Mores
Communication (Cultural	Multiculturalism
studies)	Prehistoric people (The cul-
Cultural lag	tural development of human
Custom	beings)
Ethnic group	Social change
Ethnocentrism	Socialization

Outline

I. Characteristics of culture
   A. Satisfying basic needs
   B. Learning
   C. Using symbols
   D. Forming patterns
II. The boundaries of cultures
III. Culture and society
   A. Multiculturalism
   B. Ethnocentrism and cultural relativism
IV. How cultures change
   A. Contact with other cultures
   B. Invention
V. How people study culture

Questions

What is enculturation?
What are the two main causes of cultural change?
How does the use of the term *culture* in a narrow sense differ from the broader definition used by social scientists?
What is a culture area?
Under what conditions does multiculturalism succeed best?
What are the most important types of symbols?
How can one deal with culture shock?
What is the difference between a cultural trait and a cultural pattern?
In what ways can ethnocentrism be harmful?
How does acculturation differ from assimilation?

Additional resources

Auerbach, Susan, ed. *Encyclopedia of Multiculturalism.* 6 vols. Cavendish, 1993.
Encyclopedia of World Cultures. 10 vols. G. K. Hall, 1991-1994.
Great Ages of Man. 21 vols. Time-Life Bks., 1965-1968. Each volume focuses on one of the world's great culture areas.
Harris, Marvin. *Culture, People, Nature.* 5th ed. 1988. Reprint. HarperCollins, 1990.
Inge, M. Thomas, ed. *Concise Histories of American Popular Culture.* Greenwood, 1982.
Liptak, Karen. *Coming of Age: Traditions and Rituals Around the World.* Millbrook, 1994.
Panati, Charles. *Panati's Parade of Fads, Follies, and Manias.* HarperPerennial, 1991.
Reader, John. *Man on Earth.* Univ. of Texas Pr., 1988.

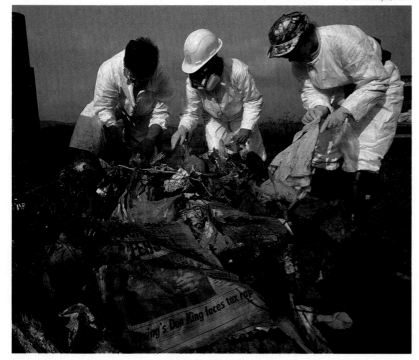

© Louie Psihoyos, Matrix

Archaeologists analyze a mound of garbage to learn about contemporary American life. Social scientists use a variety of methods to study past and present human cultures.

Downtown Dallas lies on the Trinity River. The city's landmarks include the 72-story NationsBank Plaza—the tallest building in Dallas—and the domed Reunion Tower, *left.*

Dallas

Dallas is the second largest city in Texas and is located in the heart of one of the fastest growing metropolitan areas in the United States. Houston is the only Texas city with more people. Nicknamed "Big D," Dallas ranks as one of the nation's major financial, insurance, manufacturing, and transportation centers. The city serves as the seat of Dallas County.

Dallas lies on the rolling prairies of north-central Texas, about 30 miles (50 kilometers) east of Fort Worth. John Neely Bryan, a lawyer and trader, founded Dallas in 1841 on the banks of the Trinity River. The city's rapid growth began when railroad companies built tracks through the city in the 1870's. Today, the city's financial success still depends on its transportation links. The Dallas/Fort Worth International Airport, which serves the two cities, is the second busiest airport in the world. Only Chicago's O'Hare International Airport serves more passengers. Convenient air service has helped the Dallas area become the national headquarters for many important U.S. companies.

The city

Layout of Dallas. The Trinity River divides the city of Dallas. North and east of the river is the downtown business district. Oak Cliff, a residential area, lies south and west of the Trinity. Outside the downtown area are sections of the city known as East Dallas, West Dallas, North Dallas, and South Dallas. Dallas covers 378 square miles (979 square kilometers). Most of the city lies in Dallas County, but small sections of Dallas extend into Denton

and Collin counties. Three independent communities, each with its own government—Cockrell Hill, Highland Park, and University Park—lie within the Dallas city limits.

Landmarks. The tallest building in downtown Dallas is the 72-story NationsBank Plaza, which opened in 1985. The West End Historic District, at the west edge of downtown, includes several historic sites. One is the Old Dallas County Courthouse, known as "Old Red," which was built of red sandstone in 1892. Also in the historic district is a restored log cabin that may include parts of a home built by the founder of Dallas, John Neely Bryan. Besides the historic sites, the district also features shops and restaurants in restored warehouses. These warehouses were once owned by early Dallas merchants.

In the West End Historic District are Dealey Plaza and the Texas School Book Depository (now the Dallas County Administration Building). In 1963, President John F. Kennedy was killed in Dealey Plaza by a bullet fired from the sixth floor of the building. The depository's sixth floor is now a museum depicting the events of Kennedy's life and death. Near Dealey Plaza is a memorial honoring the late President.

Shoppers flock to the famous Neiman-Marcus store in downtown Dallas. The Dallas City Hall, designed by American architect I. M. Pei, stands at the south end of downtown. A large sculpture, *The Dallas Piece* by English sculptor Henry Moore, decorates the City Hall plaza. Next to the City Hall is the Dallas Convention Center,

Facts in brief

Population: *City*—1,006,877. *Metropolitan area*—2,676,248. *Consolidated metropolitan area*—4,037,282.

Area: *City*—378 sq. mi. (979 km²). *Metropolitan area*—6,491 sq. mi. (16,812 km²). *Consolidated metropolitan area*—9,470 sq. mi. (24,527 km²).

Altitude: 512 ft. (156 m) above sea level.

Climate: *Average temperature*—January, 43 °F (6 °C); July, 85 °F (30 °C). *Average annual rainfall*—33.7 in. (85.6 cm). For the monthly weather in Dallas, see **Texas** (Climate).

Government: Council-manager. *Terms*—Two years for City Council members; four years for the mayor. City manager is appointed by the council.

Founded: 1841. Incorporated as a town, 1856; as a city, 1871.

Largest communities in the Dallas area

Name	Population	Name	Population
Dallas	1,006,877	Grand Prairie	99,616
Garland	180,650	Carrollton	82,169
Irving	155,037	Richardson	74,840
Plano	128,713	Duncanville	35,748
Mesquite	101,484	Farmers Branch	24,250

Symbols of Dallas. The red, white, and blue in the flag of Dallas, *left,* represent the United States and Texas, which use these colors in their flags. The star is the chief symbol of Texas, the Lone Star State. The flag, which was adopted in 1967, also bears the city seal, *right.*

with about 800,000 square feet (74,000 square meters) of exhibition space.

The beautiful Majestic Theatre serves as home to various arts organizations. Just west of the downtown business district is Reunion Arena, used for sporting events. Near the arena is the 50-story Reunion Tower. The tower's observation deck offers spectacular 360-degree views of the city and suburbs.

On the north side of downtown is the 60-acre (24-hectare) Dallas Arts District, site of the Dallas Museum of Art and the Morton H. Meyerson Symphony Center. The Dallas Market Center, a major wholesale buying center, lies along Stemmons Freeway northwest of downtown. It also offers major exhibition space for trade shows. The Dallas Zoo in Oak Cliff features a monorail that gives visitors good views of its African animals collection.

The Biblical Arts Center lies about 6 miles (10 kilometers) north of downtown. It has an international collection of religious art. The Dallas Farmer's Market on the southeast side of downtown offers fresh produce, flow-

ers, and other goods from throughout Texas.

The Dallas metropolitan area includes Collin, Dallas, Denton, Ellis, Henderson, Hunt, Kaufman, and Rockwall counties. It covers 6,491 square miles (16,812 square kilometers). From 1980 until 1990, the area's population increased 35 percent. Among the largest cities in the Dallas area are Carrollton, Garland, Grand Prairie, Irving, Mesquite, Plano, and Richardson. These suburban cities have many landmarks. The Heritage Farmstead in Plano is a museum of farm life from 1890 to the 1930's. Williams Square in Irving features a popular bronze sculpture of nine mustangs galloping across a stream.

People

Ethnic groups. Approximately 55 percent of Dallasites are white, and about 30 percent are African American. About 20 percent of the city's people are Hispanic, who may be white, black, or of mixed ancestry. The city's population also includes many people of Arab, Native American, and Southeast Asian ancestry. Although Dallas no longer is segregated, the greatest number of African Americans live in South Dallas. There are large Hispanic neighborhoods in Oak Cliff and just north of downtown. Many refugees from Southeast Asia have settled in older residential neighborhoods east of downtown. Most of the people who live in Dallas suburbs are white.

Housing. Housing in Dallas is relatively new compared to other large cities. More than 40 percent of the housing units in Dallas have been built since 1970.

There are many different types of housing in the city and suburbs. Many of the biggest homes are in North Dallas neighborhoods such as Preston Hollow, in the "island cities" of Highland Park and University Park, and in such higher-income suburbs as Addison, Irving, and Plano. The Swiss Avenue Historic District in East Dallas features many mansions built by the city's turn-of-the-century business leaders. Homes along Swiss Avenue began to be restored in the early 1970's.

Some of the lowest-income housing is in West Dallas, an area the city did not annex until the early 1950's. Before annexation, there were no construction guidelines in West Dallas to ensure that new structures were sturdily built and met other requirements. Today, the area has many run-down homes.

Social problems. Like other large cities, Dallas has experienced crime, unemployment, and urban decay. However, the city has tried to reduce these problems by promoting job creation, downtown and inner-city construction, and other activities.

Dallas has also experienced some racial problems. For example, minority groups have lacked political and job opportunities in the city. But community organizations, such as the Dallas Together Forum, work to improve the prospects of minorities.

Another problem facing Dallas is air pollution, created primarily by vehicle traffic. The city government encourages motorists to carpool or use buses to reduce air pollution.

Education. The Dallas Independent School District is one of the largest U.S. public school systems. It includes about 200 elementary and high schools with an enrollment of about 140,000 students. About 110 private schools provide education for approximately 27,000 stu-

City of Dallas

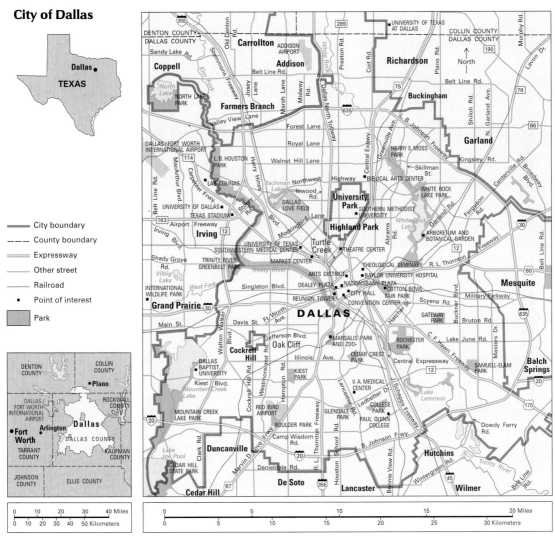

TEXAS
Dallas

City boundary
County boundary
Expressway
Other street
Railroad
■ Point of interest
Park

DENTON COUNTY | COLLIN COUNTY
● Plano
DALLAS FORT WORTH INTERNATIONAL AIRPORT | ROCKWALL COUNTY
● Fort Worth | Arlington | Dallas
TARRANT COUNTY | DALLAS COUNTY | KAUFMAN COUNTY
JOHNSON COUNTY | ELLIS COUNTY

0 10 20 30 40 Miles
0 10 20 30 40 50 Kilometers

0   5   10   15   20 Miles
0   5   10   15   20   25   30 Kilometers

WORLD BOOK maps

Dallas Convention and Visitors Bureau

The Dallas Black Dance Theatre is one of many performing arts groups in Dallas. Such groups make Dallas a cultural center.

dents in Dallas and the surrounding area. Greenhill School, Hockaday School, the Jesuit Preparatory School, and St. Mark's School of Texas are among the city's best-known private schools. In addition, the Dallas suburbs have many excellent public schools.

Southern Methodist University, in University Park, is the oldest and best-known university in the Dallas area. Founded in 1911, it has an enrollment of 9,000 students and offers strong programs in liberal arts and business administration. The University of Texas Southwestern Medical Center at Dallas has become a major facility for scientific research. Paul Quinn College, in South Dallas, is an African-American college associated with the African Methodist Episcopal Church. The Baylor College of Dentistry, Dallas Baptist University, and the Dallas Theological Seminary are also in the city. Other schools of higher education in the Dallas area include the University of Texas at Dallas, located in Richardson, and the University of Dallas, a Roman Catholic-affiliated school in Irving. In addition, the Dallas County Community Col-

The State Fair of Texas is held each October on the grounds of Fair Park in Dallas. The fair, which includes various amusement rides and activities, attracts about 3 million people each year.

Dallas Convention and Visitors Bureau

lege District consists of seven two-year community colleges in the Dallas area.

Cultural life

The arts. Dallas is an important cultural center of the Southwest. The Dallas Opera performs at the Music Hall at Fair Park, and the Dallas Symphony Orchestra plays at the Morton H. Meyerson Symphony Center. Touring Broadway productions appear in the Majestic Theatre. The Majestic is also home to such performing arts groups as the Dallas Black Dance Theatre, the Dallas Classic Guitar Society, Ballet Dallas, and the Anita M. Martinez Ballet Folklorico. Summer musicals at Fair Park and the Shakespeare Festival of Dallas attract thousands of people each year.

The Dallas Theatre Center has two facilities for stage performances—the Arts District Theater downtown and the Kalita Humphreys Theatre in the Turtle Creek area of North Dallas. American architect Frank Lloyd Wright designed the Kalita Humphreys Theatre. Smaller theater companies include Teatro Dallas, Pegasus Theatre, Undermain Theatre, and Theatre Three.

Museums and libraries. The Dallas Museum of Art is in downtown Dallas. It is noted for its collections of art from Africa, the Americas, and Europe.

Fair Park, 2 miles (3.2 kilometers) east of downtown, contains buildings in the streamlined art deco style of architecture. Many of the buildings were constructed for the 1936 Texas Centennial Exposition, which celebrated 100 years of Texas independence. Fair Park features several museums and cultural institutions. The Science Place there includes robotic dinosaurs and a planetarium. The Dallas Museum of Natural History at Fair Park exhibits dinosaur skeletons and rare fossils found in Texas. The park's Age of Steam Railroad Museum offers tours of antique railroad locomotives, freight cars, and passenger cars. The Texas Hall of State is run by the Dallas Historical Society. It displays historical documents as well as photographs, costumes, and other items from everyday life during the early days of Texas. Every October, about 3 million people attend the State Fair of Texas in the park's fairgrounds.

The Dallas Public Library System includes the J. Erik Jonsson Central Library downtown and many branch libraries throughout the city. The Dallas suburbs also have excellent libraries.

Recreation. Dallas has 335 public parks that cover 46,581 acres (18,851 hectares). More than two-thirds of the city's parkland is in the Trinity River Greenbelt, which is preserved as open space with few roads or buildings. White Rock Lake in East Dallas is a popular park for sailing, fishing, jogging, and biking. The Dallas Arboretum and Botanical Garden at White Rock Lake displays thousands of flowers and trees in an attractive lakeside setting. Six Flags over Texas, in Arlington, is a theme park that offers amusement rides and shows.

The Dallas area has teams in all four major professional sports. The Dallas Cowboys of the National Football League play in Texas Stadium, in Irving. The Texas Rangers major league baseball team meets opponents in the Ballpark in Arlington. The Dallas Mavericks of the National Basketball Association and the Dallas Stars of the National Hockey League play in Reunion Arena in

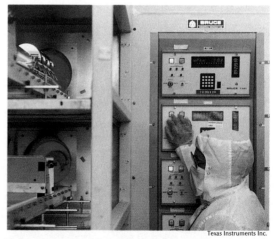

Texas Instruments Inc.

Electronics is one of the most important industries in the Dallas area. The area is home to several major producers of electronic equipment, including Texas Instruments, *above*.

downtown Dallas. Every New Year's Day, the Cotton Bowl football game, in Fair Park's Cotton Bowl stadium, features two of the nation's outstanding college teams.

Economy

The Dallas area's economy consists of a wide variety of industries. During the 1980's, the area shifted from a manufacturing to a service-based economy.

Service industries. Dallas depends heavily on convention business and tourism. Millions of people attend conventions in Dallas each year, adding billions of dollars to the economy. The city's many banks, including the Eleventh District Federal Reserve Bank, make Dallas an important financial center for the Southwestern United States. Dallas is the home of a great number of insurance companies. Dallas is also an important cotton market because Texas ranks as the nation's top cotton-producing state.

Manufacturing. The Dallas area is a major center for the manufacture of clothing, electronics and *telecommunications* (electronic communications) equipment, food products, machinery, and printed material. About 1,900 industrial facilities provide jobs for the city's labor force. The Dallas area also serves as the headquarters of many oil firms. Among the largest oil companies in the area are Exxon Corporation in Irving, and the Dallas-based companies Fina Incorporated, Maxus Energy Corporation, and Oryx Energy Company.

Transportation and communication. Dallas/Fort Worth International Airport and Dallas Love Field have helped make Dallas a vital transportation hub of the Southwest. Both international and domestic airlines serve the Dallas area. Railroad companies provide freight and passenger service to the city. Several interstate highways link Dallas with the rest of the nation. The city has one daily newspaper, *The Dallas Morning News.*

Government

Dallas has a council-manager form of government. The City Council consists of a mayor and 14 council members. Dallas voters elect the mayor to a four-year term and the council members to two-year terms.

The council sets general policies for governing. It hires the city manager, who is the administrative head of the government. The manager carries out the policies of the council, prepares the annual city budget, and appoints department heads. The city's chief sources of revenue include property taxes, sales taxes, and charges for services. Revenue bonds and federal grants also provide funds. The Dallas suburbs have their own independent local governments.

History

Early settlement. In 1841, John Neely Bryan, a lawyer from Tennessee, dug a rough shelter in a hillside along the Trinity River, at the site of what is now Dallas. Bryan laid claim to 640 acres (260 hectares) of land, and later built a log cabin home on the property. Dallas was made the temporary seat of Dallas County in 1846, while the town was still an obscure frontier village. It became the permanent seat in 1850. Bryan named the town Dallas, possibly after George Mifflin Dallas, Vice President of the United States from 1845 to 1849.

Bryan sold and gave away lots to new settlers, and he laid out the streets of the town. Dallas began to grow. In 1855, a group of European scientists, writers, artists, and musicians settled near Dallas. The Europeans, most of whom came from France, Belgium, and Switzerland, formed a cooperative community known as La Reunion. The members of the community farmed a tract of land that they owned in common. But La Reunion failed, and many of its residents moved to Dallas, where they helped promote the arts.

Dallas was incorporated as a town in 1856. The town became a stop for stagecoaches. During the American Civil War (1861-1865), Dallas served as a camp and an administrative center for the Confederate Army, which fought the Union Army.

Commercial growth. Dallas was incorporated as a city in 1871. The city's financial growth began in the 1870's, when two railroad lines—the Houston and Texas Central and the Texas and Pacific—reached Dallas and formed a junction. Farm tool manufacturers then began opening branches in Dallas. Cotton production boomed after rail shipment of the crop became possible. Dallas got its first telegraph line in 1872. By 1890, Dallas was the largest city in Texas, with 38,067 people.

By 1930, the Dallas population had grown to 260,475, but Houston had replaced it as the state's largest city. Discovery of the great East Texas oil field 100 miles (160 kilometers) east of Dallas in 1930 helped boost the city's economy and growth.

World War II (1939-1945) brought aircraft plants and other defense industries to the city. After the war, Dallas became a leading U.S. center for the manufacture of electrical and electronics equipment and aircraft and missile parts. Many large companies, including Chance Vought Aircraft (now part of LTV Corporation), moved to Dallas. Companies founded in Dallas, such as the electronics manufacturer Texas Instruments Incorporated and the computer services company Electronic Data Systems, also expanded rapidly. Industrial growth helped the city's population increase from 294,734 in 1940 to 844,401 in 1970. During this time, many Dallas-ites, like Americans elsewhere, moved from the city to the suburbs.

On Nov. 22, 1963, Dallas was the site of President John F. Kennedy's assassination. Vice President Lyndon B. Johnson was sworn in as President later that day aboard the presidential plane at Dallas Love Field airport.

During the early 1960's, the population and economy of Dallas continued to expand. Mayor Erik Jonsson and city leaders turned to the "Goals for Dallas" program to plan for the city's future. In 1967, Dallas voters passed a $175-million bond issue—the largest in the city's history—to fulfill some of these goals. The plans helped promote the construction of the Dallas/Fort Worth International Airport, which opened in 1974. Dallas also built a new city hall and the Martin Luther King, Jr., Community Center. The center provides many social services, such as rent assistance for poor people.

Recent developments. Large companies continued to move their headquarters to Dallas during the 1970's. New construction continued until the mid-1980's, when oil prices fell, the real estate market declined, and Dallas experienced serious economic problems. The city began a financial recovery in the early 1990's. At that time, its population exceeded 1 million.   Henry K. Tatum

Peter Cade, Tony Stone Images

Solid waste in France

Sergio Dorantes, Sygma

Air pollution in Mexico City

Bob Stern, Gamma/Liaison

Water pollution in Estonia

Environmental pollution is one of the most serious problems facing the world today. It threatens the health of all living things and damages the natural beauty of the earth.

Environmental pollution

Environmental pollution is a term that refers to all the ways that human activity harms the natural environment. Most people have witnessed environmental pollution in the form of an open garbage dump or a factory pouring out black smoke. However, pollution can also be invisible, odorless, and tasteless. Some kinds of pollution do not actually dirty the land, air, or water, but they reduce the quality of life for people and other living things. For example, noise from traffic and machinery can be considered forms of pollution.

Environmental pollution is one of the most serious problems facing humanity and other life forms today. Badly polluted air can harm crops and cause life-threatening illnesses. Some air pollutants have reduced the capacity of the atmosphere to filter out the sun's harmful ultraviolet radiation. Many scientists believe that these and other air pollutants have begun to change climates around the world. Water and soil pollution threaten the ability of farmers to grow enough food. Ocean pollution endangers many marine organisms.

Marian R. Chertow, the contributor of this article, is Director of the Partnership for Environmental Management at the Yale School of Forestry and Environmental Studies.

Many people think of air, water, and soil pollution as distinct forms of pollution. However, each of the parts of an environment—air, water, and soil—depends upon the others and upon the plants and animals living within the environment. The relationships among all the living and nonliving things in an environment make up an ecological system, called an *ecosystem*. All the ecosystems of the earth are connected. Thus, pollution that seems to affect only one part of the environment may also affect other parts. For example, sooty smoke from a power plant might appear to harm only the atmosphere. But rain can wash some harmful chemicals in the smoke out of the sky and onto land or into waterways.

Some pollution comes from one specific point or location, such as a sewage pipe spilling dirty water into a river. Such pollution is called *point source pollution*. Other pollution comes from large areas. Water can run off farmland and carry pesticides and fertilizers into rivers. Rain water can wash gasoline, oil, and salt from highways and parking lots into the wells that supply drinking water. Pollution that comes from such large areas is called *nonpoint source pollution*.

Nearly everyone would like to have pollution reduced. Unfortunately, most of the pollution that now threatens the health of our planet comes from products that many people want and need. For example, automobiles provide the convenience of personal transportation, but they create a large percentage of the world's air pollution. Factories make products that people use and enjoy, but industrial processes can also pollute. Pesticides and fertilizers aid in growing large quantities of food, but they also poison the soil and waterways.

To end or greatly decrease pollution, people would have to reduce use of cars and other modern conveniences, and some factories would have to close or change production methods. Because most people's jobs are dependent on industries that contribute to environmental pollution, shutting down these industries would increase unemployment. In addition, if farmers suddenly stopped using chemical fertilizers and pesticides, there would be less food to feed the people of the world.

Over time, however, pollution can be reduced in many ways without seriously disrupting people's lives. For example, governments can pass laws that encourage businesses to adopt less polluting methods of operation. Scientists and engineers can develop products and processes that are cleaner and safer for the environment. And individuals around the world can themselves find ways to reduce environmental pollution.

Types of pollution

The chief types of environmental pollution include air pollution, water pollution, soil pollution, pollution caused by solid waste and hazardous waste, and noise pollution.

Air pollution is the contamination of the air by such substances as fuel exhaust and smoke. It can harm the health of plants and animals and damage buildings and other structures. According to the World Health Organization, about one-fifth of the world's people are exposed to hazardous levels of air pollutants.

The atmosphere normally consists of nitrogen, oxygen, and small amounts of carbon dioxide and other gases and *particulates* (tiny particles of liquid or solid matter). A number of natural processes work to keep the parts of the atmosphere in balance. For example, plants use carbon dioxide and produce oxygen. Animals, in turn, use up oxygen and produce carbon dioxide through respiration. Forest fires and volcanic eruptions shoot gases and particulates into the atmosphere, and rain and wind wash them out or scatter them.

Air pollution occurs when industries and vehicles release such large amounts of gas and particulates into the air that natural processes can no longer keep the atmosphere in balance. There are two chief types of air pollution: (1) outdoor and (2) indoor.

Outdoor air pollution. Each year, hundreds of millions of tons of gases and particulates pour into the atmosphere. Most of this pollution results from the burning of fuel to power motor vehicles and heat buildings. Some air pollution also comes from business and industrial processes. For example, many dry cleaning plants remove dirt from clothing with a chemical called perchloroethylene, a hazardous air pollutant. The burning of garbage may discharge smoke and heavy metals, such as lead and mercury, into the atmosphere. Most heavy metals are highly poisonous.

One of the most common types of outdoor air pollution is *smog.* Smog is a brown, hazy mixture of gases and particulates. It develops when certain gases released by the combustion of gasoline and other petroleum products react with sunlight in the atmosphere.

This reaction creates hundreds of harmful chemicals that make up smog.

One of the chemicals in smog is a toxic form of oxygen called *ozone.* Exposure to high concentrations of ozone causes headaches, burning eyes, and irritation of the respiratory tract in many individuals. In some cases, ozone in the lower atmosphere can cause death. Ozone can also damage plant life and even kill trees.

Acid rain is a term for rain and other precipitation that is polluted mainly by sulfuric acid and nitric acid. These acids form when gases called sulfur dioxide and nitrogen oxides react with water vapor in the air. These gases come chiefly from the burning of coal, gas, and oil by cars, factories, and power plants. The acids in acid rain move through the air and water and harm the environment over large areas. Acid rain has killed entire fish populations in a number of lakes. It also damages buildings, bridges, and statues. Scientists believe high concentrations of acid rain can harm forests and soil. Regions affected by acid rain include large parts of eastern North America, Scandinavia, and central Europe.

Chemicals called *chlorofluorocarbons* (CFC's) are pollutants that destroy the ozone layer in the upper atmosphere. CFC's are used in refrigerators and air conditioners and to make plastic foam insulation. Ozone, the same gas that is a harmful pollutant in smog, forms a protective layer in the upper atmosphere. It shields the earth's surface from more than 95 percent of the sun's ultraviolet radiation. As CFC's thin the ozone layer, more ultraviolet radiation reaches the surface of the earth. Overexposure to such radiation damages plants and greatly increases people's risk of skin cancer.

The *greenhouse effect* is the warming that results when the earth's atmosphere traps the sun's heat. It is created by carbon dioxide, methane, and other atmospheric gases, which allow sunlight to reach the earth but prevent heat from leaving the atmosphere. These heat-trapping gases are often called *greenhouse gases.*

Fuel burning and other human activities are increasing the amount of greenhouse gases in the atmosphere. Many scientists believe such an increase is intensifying the greenhouse effect and raising temperatures worldwide. This increase in temperature, called *global warming,* may cause many problems. A strong greenhouse effect could melt glaciers and polar icecaps, flooding coastal areas. It could also shift rainfall patterns, creating more droughts and severe tropical storms.

Indoor air pollution occurs when buildings with poorly designed ventilation systems trap pollutants inside. The main types of indoor pollutants are tobacco smoke, gases from stoves and furnaces, household chemicals, small fiber particles, and hazardous fumes given off by building materials, including insulation, glue, and paint. In some office buildings, high amounts of these substances cause headaches, eye irritation, and other health problems in workers. Such health problems are sometimes called *sick building syndrome.*

Radon, a radioactive gas given off through the decay of uranium in rocks within the earth, is another harmful indoor pollutant. It can cause lung cancer if inhaled in large quantities. People can be exposed to radon when the gas leaks into basements of homes built over radioactive soil or rock. Energy-efficient buildings, which keep in heated or cooled air, can trap radon indoors

Kinds of environmental pollution

There are many kinds of environmental pollution that harm our planet in a wide variety of ways. Because all the parts of the environment are connected with one another, a pollutant that chiefly damages one natural system may also affect others.

WORLD BOOK illustration by Michael Yurkovic

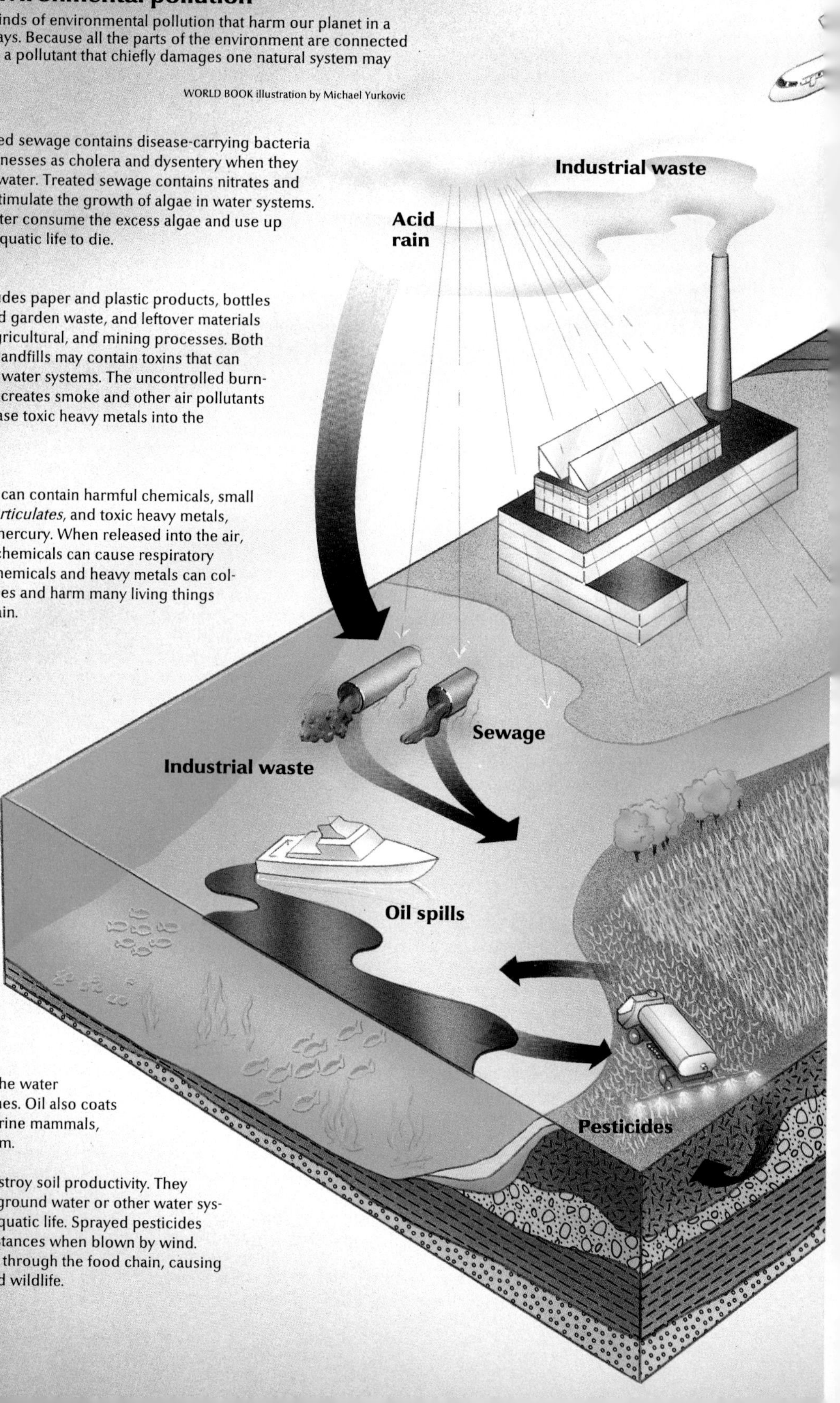

Sewage. Untreated sewage contains disease-carrying bacteria that cause such illnesses as cholera and dysentery when they get into drinking water. Treated sewage contains nitrates and phosphates that stimulate the growth of algae in water systems. Bacteria in the water consume the excess algae and use up oxygen, causing aquatic life to die.

Solid waste includes paper and plastic products, bottles and cans, food and garden waste, and leftover materials from industrial, agricultural, and mining processes. Both open dumps and landfills may contain toxins that can seep into soil and water systems. The uncontrolled burning of solid waste creates smoke and other air pollutants and may also release toxic heavy metals into the environment.

Industrial waste can contain harmful chemicals, small particles called *particulates*, and toxic heavy metals, such as lead and mercury. When released into the air, certain industrial chemicals can cause respiratory problems. Toxic chemicals and heavy metals can collect in animal tissues and harm many living things along the food chain.

Industrial waste

Acid rain

Industrial waste

Sewage

Oil spills

Pesticides

Oil spills pollute the water and damage beaches. Oil also coats fish, birds, and marine mammals, killing many of them.

Pesticides can destroy soil productivity. They can also flow into ground water or other water systems and poison aquatic life. Sprayed pesticides can travel great distances when blown by wind. They can also pass through the food chain, causing harm to people and wildlife.

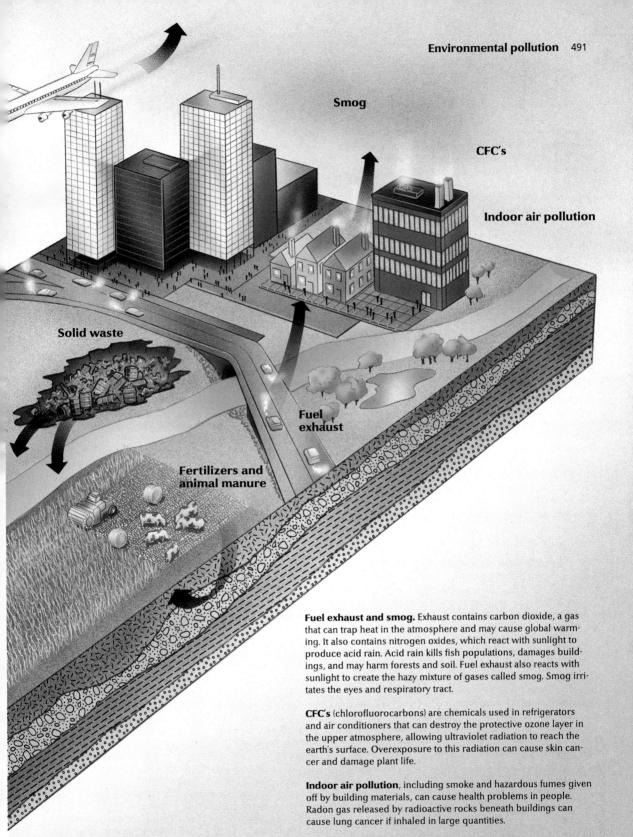

Smog

CFC's

Indoor air pollution

Solid waste

Fuel exhaust

Fertilizers and animal manure

Fuel exhaust and smog. Exhaust contains carbon dioxide, a gas that can trap heat in the atmosphere and may cause global warming. It also contains nitrogen oxides, which react with sunlight to produce acid rain. Acid rain kills fish populations, damages buildings, and may harm forests and soil. Fuel exhaust also reacts with sunlight to create the hazy mixture of gases called smog. Smog irritates the eyes and respiratory tract.

CFC's (chlorofluorocarbons) are chemicals used in refrigerators and air conditioners that can destroy the protective ozone layer in the upper atmosphere, allowing ultraviolet radiation to reach the earth's surface. Overexposure to this radiation can cause skin cancer and damage plant life.

Indoor air pollution, including smoke and hazardous fumes given off by building materials, can cause health problems in people. Radon gas released by radioactive rocks beneath buildings can cause lung cancer if inhaled in large quantities.

Fertilizers and animal manure can run off into water systems and supply nutrients that stimulate excess algae growth.

and lead to high concentrations of the gas.

Water pollution is the contamination of water by sewage, toxic chemicals, metals, oils, or other substances. It can affect such surface waters as rivers, lakes, and oceans, as well as the water beneath the earth's surface, called *ground water*. Water pollution can harm many species of plants and animals. According to the World Health Organization, about 5 million people die every year from drinking polluted water.

In a healthy water system, a cycle of natural processes turns wastes into useful or harmless substances. The cycle begins when organisms called *aerobic bacteria* use the oxygen dissolved in water to digest wastes. This digestion process releases nitrates, phosphates, and other *nutrients* (chemical elements that living things need for growth). Algae and aquatic green plants absorb these nutrients. Microscopic animals called *zooplankton* eat the algae, and fish eat the zooplankton. The fish, in turn, may be eaten by larger fish, birds, or other animals. These larger animals produce body wastes and eventually die. Bacteria break down dead animals and animal wastes, and the cycle begins again.

Water pollution occurs when people put so much waste into a water system that its natural cleansing processes cannot function properly. Some waste, such as oil, industrial acids, or farm pesticides, poisons aquatic plants and animals. Other waste, such as phosphate detergents, chemical fertilizers, and animal manure, pollutes by supplying excess nutrients for aquatic life. This pollution process is called *eutrophication*. The process begins when large amounts of nutrients flow into a water system. These nutrients stimulate excessive growth of algae. As more algae grow, more also die. Bacteria in the water use up large amounts of oxygen consuming the excess dead algae. The oxygen level of the water then drops, causing many aquatic plants and animals to die.

Water pollution comes from businesses, farms, homes, industries, and other sources. It includes sewage, industrial chemicals, agricultural chemicals, and livestock wastes. Another form of water pollution is the clean but heated water discharged by power plants into waterways. This heated water, called *thermal pollution,* harms fish and aquatic plants by reducing the amount of oxygen in the water. Chemical and oil spills can also cause devastating water pollution that kills water birds, shellfish, and other wildlife.

Some water pollution occurs when there is improper separation of sewer wastewater from clean drinking water. In parts of the world that lack modern sewage treatment plants, water carrying human waste can flow into drinking water supplies. Disease-carrying bacteria in the waste can then contaminate the drinking water and cause such illnesses as cholera and dysentery. In areas with good sanitation, most human waste flows through underground pipes to special treatment plants that kill the harmful bacteria and remove the solid waste.

Soil pollution is the destruction of the earth's thin layer of healthy, productive soil, where much of our food is grown. Without fertile soil, farmers could not grow enough food to support the world's people.

Healthy soil depends on bacteria, fungi, and small animals to break down wastes in the soil and release nutrients. These nutrients help plants grow. Fertilizers and pesticides can limit the ability of soil organisms to process wastes. As a result, farmers who overuse fertilizers and pesticides can destroy their soil's productivity.

A number of other human activities can also damage soil. The irrigation of soil in dry areas with poor drainage can leave water standing in fields. When this standing water evaporates, it leaves salt deposits behind, making the soil too salty for growing crops. Mining operations and smelters contaminate soil with toxic heavy metals. Many scientists believe acid rain can also reduce soil fertility.

Solid waste is probably the most visible form of pollution. Every year, people dispose of billions of tons of solid garbage. Industrial wastes account for the majority of the discarded material. Solid waste from homes, offices, and stores is called *municipal solid waste*. It includes paper, plastic, bottles and cans, food scraps, and yard trimmings. Other waste consists of junked automobiles, scrap metal, leftover materials from agricultural processes, and mining wastes known as *spoil.*

The handling of solid waste is a problem because most disposal methods damage the environment. Open dumps ruin the natural beauty of the land and provide a home for rats and other disease-carrying animals. Both open dumps and *landfills* (areas of buried wastes) may contain toxins that seep into ground water or flow into streams and lakes. The uncontrolled burning of solid waste creates smoke and other air pollution. Even burning waste in incinerators can release toxic chemicals, ash, and harmful metals into the air.

Hazardous waste is composed of discarded substances that can threaten human health and the environment. A waste is hazardous if it *corrodes* (wears away) other materials; explodes; ignites easily; reacts strongly with water; or is poisonous. Sources of hazardous waste include industries, hospitals, and laboratories. Such waste can cause immediate injury when people breathe, swallow, or touch it. When buried in the ground or left in open dumps, some hazardous waste can pollute ground water and contaminate food crops.

The mishandling or accidental release of hazardous waste has caused a number of disasters around the world. For example, in 1978, hazardous chemicals leaking from a waste disposal site in the Love Canal area of western New York threatened the health of nearby residents. Hundreds of people were forced to abandon their homes. In 1984, a leak of poisonous gas from a pesticide plant in Bhopal, India, killed more than 2,800 people and caused eye and respiratory damage to more than 20,000.

Some hazardous waste can seriously harm the health of people, wildlife, and plants. These pollutants include radiation, pesticides, and heavy metals.

Radiation is an invisible pollutant that can contaminate any part of the environment. Most radiation comes from natural sources, such as minerals and the sun's rays. Scientists can also produce radioactive elements in their laboratories. Exposure to large amounts of radiation can harm cells and result in cancer.

Radioactive waste produced by nuclear reactors and weapons factories pose a potentially serious environmental problem. Some of this waste will remain radioactive for thousands of years. The safe storage of radioactive waste is both difficult and expensive.

Pesticides can travel great distances through the environment. When sprayed on crops or in gardens, pesticides can be blown by the wind to other areas. They can also flow with rain water into nearby streams or can seep through the soil into ground water. Some pesticides can remain in the environment for many years and pass from one organism to another. For example, when pesticides are present in a stream, small fish and other organisms can absorb them. Larger fish who eat these contaminated organisms build up even larger amounts of pesticides in their flesh.

Heavy metals include mercury and lead. Mining operations, solid waste incinerators, industrial processes, and motor vehicles can all release heavy metals into the environment. Like pesticides, they are long lasting and can spread through the environment. Also, like pesticides, they can collect in the bones and other tissues of animals. In human beings, heavy metals can damage various internal organs, bones, and the nervous system. Many can also cause cancer.

Noise pollution comes from such machines as airplanes, motor vehicles, construction machinery, and industrial equipment. Noise does not dirty the air, water, or land, but it can cause discomfort and hearing loss in human beings and other animals.

Controlling pollution

Controlling pollution depends on the efforts of governments, scientists, business and industry, agriculture, environmental organizations, and individuals.

Government action. In many countries around the world, governments work to help clean up the pollution spoiling the earth's land, air, and water. Such environmental efforts come from both local and national governments. In addition, a number of international efforts have been made to protect the earth's resources.

Local efforts. Many local governments have enacted laws to help clean up the environment. For example, in 1989, California adopted a 20-year plan to reduce air pollution in the Los Angeles area, which had the worst air quality in the United States. The plan includes measures to restrict the use of gasoline-powered vehicles and to encourage the use of mass transportation.

Local governments can also pass recycling laws. Recycling is a process designed to recover and reuse materials instead of throwing them away. In Vienna, Austria, for example, citizens must separate their trash into containers for paper, plastic, metal, aluminum cans, clear glass, colored glass, and food and yard waste. Some cities ban the disposal of yard trimmings in landfills because they take up much space. These cities collect yard trimmings separately and deposit them in compost centers, where the materials decay into a substance used to improve the quality of the soil. Several states in the United States and a number of European countries encourage the reuse of bottles by charging a deposit that is refunded upon return of the bottle.

National efforts. Many national governments also pass legislation to help clean up pollution. In 1980, for example, the U.S. Congress enacted the Comprehensive Environmental Response, Compensation, and Liability Act. This act, also called "Superfund," began a government cleanup of hazardous waste dumps in the United States. This law and others hold polluters responsible

A government cleanup project called Superfund works to eliminate unsafe toxic waste dumps in the United States. Inspectors from the Environmental Protection Agency collect mud samples, *above,* to check for chemical contamination.

for repairing the environmental damage they create.

In the United States, the Environmental Protection Agency (EPA) sets and enforces pollution control standards. It also assists state and local governments in pollution control. Most other industrial countries, including Canada, Japan, and many European countries, also have pollution control agencies.

One of the most effective ways a government can control specific kinds of pollution is by banning the pollutant. In 1972, the U.S. government began a gradual ban on all uses of DDT, a pesticide found to harm wild birds and fish. Unfortunately, some countries still permit use of DDT and other banned pesticides. As a result, imported foods, migratory birds, and even the wind may carry toxic chemicals into the United States.

A government may also ban certain uses of a dangerous substance while permitting others. For example, lead is a poisonous metal that can damage the brain, kidneys, and other organs. The U.S. government bans leaded gasoline and lead-based household paint, but it permits lead in batteries, building materials, and industrial paint. Despite the continued use of lead in some products, restrictions on the metal in paints and gasoline have reduced the health problems it causes.

Still other pollution-control laws limit rather than ban the release of pollutants into the environment. In the United States, the Clean Air Act of 1970 and its amendments have limited the amount of air pollution that cars, power plants, and certain businesses may release. The Clean Water Act of 1972 and its amendments have reduced the discharge of untreated water and harmful chemicals into rivers and other waterways.

Another government strategy to help control pollution is to fine companies for polluting. Australia and a number of European countries fine businesses that pollute waterways. Such fines encourage companies to invest in pollution control equipment or to develop less polluting methods of operation. Governments may also place taxes on products that pollute. For example, most Scandinavian countries tax nonreturnable bottles. Some government regulations simply require businesses to tell the public how many pollutants they release into the environment. This regulation has caused some companies to find ways to reduce pollution so that consumers do not develop an unfavorable impression of them and perhaps refuse to purchase their products.

Governments also regulate the disposal of solid and hazardous wastes. According to U.S. regulations, landfills must have a double lining of nonporous substances, such as clay and plastic, which helps prevent the escape of toxic chemicals into water supplies. Waste incinerators must have devices that keep harmful gases and particulates from entering the atmosphere.

Global efforts. Many types of environmental pollution have been difficult to control because no single person or nation owns the earth's global resources—that is, its oceans and atmosphere. To control pollution, the people of the world must work together.

Since the 1970's, representatives of many nations have met to discuss ways of limiting the pollution that affects the earth's air and water. These nations have created environmental treaties to help control such problems as acid rain, the thinning of the ozone layer, and the dumping of waste into the oceans. In a treaty called the Montreal Protocol on Substances That Deplete the Ozone Layer, which took effect in 1989, the major CFC-producing nations agreed to gradually stop producing the chemicals. A 1991 amendment to the treaty called for a total ban on CFC's by the year 2000. In 1992, many European nations agreed to end their CFC production even earlier—by 1996. Also in 1992, representatives of 178 nations met in Rio de Janeiro, Brazil, for the United Nations (UN) Conference on Environment and Development. This meeting, known as the Earth Summit, was one of the most important global environmental conferences ever held. The UN members signed agreements on the prevention of global warming, the preservation of forests and endangered species, and other issues.

Scientific efforts. Increasing concern over the environment has caused scientists and engineers to look for technological solutions. Some research seeks ways to clean up or manage pollution. The goal of other research is to prevent pollution. Many industrial researchers are finding more economical ways to use fuels and other raw materials. As a result of their research, some European cities now use waste heat from power plants or trash incinerators to warm homes. New automobile engines burn gasoline much more cleanly and efficiently than older engines. Researchers have also developed automobiles that use such clean-burning fuels·as *methanol* (a type of alcohol) and natural gas. In Brazil, some cars use another type of alcohol, called *ethanol,* as fuel. Scientists are also developing cars that can use hydrogen gas as fuel. Hydrogen creates almost no pollution when it is burned.

Scientists and engineers are also researching ways to generate electricity more cheaply from such renewable energy sources as the wind and sun, causing little or no pollution. Large fields of windmills, known as *wind farms,* already supply about 1 percent of California's electricity and more than 2 percent of Denmark's. Devices called *photovoltaic cells* convert sunlight directly into electricity. Using such cells, a photovoltaic power plant in Sacramento, Calif., produces enough electricity for 1,000 homes.

Business and industry. Many companies have discovered that it makes good business sense to pollute less. Some have found that reducing pollution gives them a better public image and saves money. Others have developed environmentally safe products or packaging to satisfy consumer demands. Still others develop pollution control systems because they believe that laws will soon force them to do so anyway. And some companies limit pollution because the people running them choose to do so.

In the past, the disposal of wastes was relatively inexpensive for most businesses. Today, legal waste disposal sites have become increasingly scarce and more

Recycling helps prevent pollution by reducing the amount of solid waste that must be dumped or burned. These children are sorting trash for a school recycling program.

Environmental do's and don'ts

Reducing environmental pollution will require the efforts of people all over the world. The following illustrations show some of the ways individuals can help protect the environment.

WORLD BOOK illustrations by Yoshi Miyake

Buy sensibly, choosing products with minimal packaging to help reduce solid waste.

Insulate windows and use efficient appliances to conserve energy and reduce air pollution.

Ride a bike or use public transportation to avoid polluting the air with auto exhaust.

Don't use toxic pesticides. Use natural pest enemies or plant pest-resistant varieties.

Recycle as many different materials as possible instead of throwing them away.

Compost yard trimmings and food waste to keep garbage out of landfills and improve the soil.

Don't pour harmful chemicals down the drain. Take toxic materials to a drop-off center instead.

Don't use disposables, such as plastic foam containers. Buy products that can be used many times.

expensive to use. As a result, many businesses have found ways to produce less waste. For example, manufacturers may use a minimum of packaging and choose packing materials that can be recycled. Lighter packaging means distributors use less fuel transporting the products. In addition, the consumer throws out less packaging and creates less garbage.

Many businesses specialize in different types of pollution management. The business of reducing and cleaning up pollution is expected to be one of the fastest growing industries of the future. For example, some pollution management firms develop devices that remove harmful particulates from smokestack emissions. Particulates can be captured by filters, by traps that use static electricity, or by devices called *scrubbers* that wash out particulates with chemical sprays.

Other businesses assist companies in following government orders to clean up pollution. Some firms manage recycling or energy conservation programs. Still others help businesses develop less polluting processes.

Regardless of why or how industries begin to clean up pollution, it will be a slow, expensive process. Many businesses rely on the cheapest production methods available, even though such methods pollute. For example, power plants often burn oil and coal to generate electricity because it is generally the most economical method. Manufacturers use cadmium, lead, and mercury in batteries because those metals, though toxic, make batteries work well. When the cost of cleaning up the pollution created by current production methods is added to manufacturing costs, however, less polluting methods may prove more economical.

Agriculture. Scientists and farmers are developing ways to grow food that require less fertilizer and pesticides. Many farmers rotate their crops from year to year to reduce the need for chemical fertilizers. The rotation of corn, wheat, and other crops with legumes, such as alfalfa and soybeans, helps replace nitrogen lost from the soil. Crop rotation also helps control pests and plant diseases. Some farmers use compost and other fertilizers that are less harmful to the soil. Instead of spraying their crops with harmful pesticides, some farmers combat damaging insects by releasing certain other insects or bacteria that prey upon the pests. Scientists are also developing genetically engineered plants that are resistant to certain pests.

The rotation of crops and the use of natural pest enemies are called *natural pest control.* Combining a limited use of chemical pesticides with natural controls is known as *integrated pest management* (IPM). Farmers using IPM apply chemical pesticides in smaller amounts and only when they will have the most effect.

Environmental organizations work to help control pollution by trying to influence lawmakers and to elect political leaders who care about the environment. Some groups raise money to buy land and protect it from development. Other groups study the effects of pollution on the environment and develop pollution prevention and management systems. Such groups use their findings to persuade government and industry to prevent or reduce pollution. Environmental organizations also publish magazines and other materials to persuade people to prevent pollution.

Political parties representing environmental concerns have formed in many industrial nations. These organizations, often known as *Green parties,* have had a growing influence on environmental policies. Countries with Green parties include Australia, Austria, Germany, Finland, France, New Zealand, Spain, and Sweden.

Individual efforts. One of the most important ways an individual can reduce pollution is by conserving energy. Conserving energy reduces the air pollution created by power plants. A reduced demand for oil and coal could also result in fewer oil spills and less destruction of coal-bearing lands. Driving less is one of the best ways to save energy and avoid polluting the air.

People can save electricity by buying more efficient light bulbs and home appliances. For example, compact fluorescent light bulbs use only 25 percent as much electricity as traditional incandescent bulbs. People can also conserve by using appliances less often, by turning off appliances and lights when not in use, and by setting home thermostats at or below 68 °F (20 °C) in winter and at or above 78 °F (26 °C) in summer. In addition, buildings with specially treated windows and good insulation need far less fuel or electricity to heat or cool than buildings without such materials.

People can also buy products that are safe for the environment. For example, households can help reduce water pollution by using fewer toxic cleaning products and by properly disposing of any toxic products they do use. If consumers refuse to purchase harmful products, manufacturers will stop making them.

People can also help reduce pollution by eating less meat. Farmers use large quantities of fertilizer and pesticides to raise the grain on which cattle, hogs, and poultry feed. Farmers would use much less fertilizer and pesticides if people chose to eat less meat and more grains, beans, and vegetables. People have also come to expect the perfectly shaped, unmarked fruits and vegetables that most farmers achieve by using large amounts of pesticides. If consumers would accept produce with slight blemishes or imperfections, farmers could reduce their use of chemicals.

One of the simplest ways individuals can prevent pollution is by reusing products. For example, some milk suppliers use glass bottles instead of paper cartons. The bottles may be refilled and used again. People can reuse old paper or plastic bags to carry groceries or to hold garbage. When people reuse products, they avoid both the pollution associated with the creation of a new product and the pollution caused when the product is thrown out.

Recycling is another way of reusing materials. Many cities and towns have recycling programs. Recycling saves energy and raw materials, and it prevents pollution. Many different waste products can be recycled. Commonly recycled wastes include metal cans, glass, paper, plastic containers, and old tires. Cans can be melted down and used to make new ones. Glass can be ground up and made into new containers or used as a substitute for sand in road pavement. Paper can be reprocessed into different paper products. Plastics can be melted down and re-formed into plastic lumber for such uses as fences, decks, benches, and carpeting. Old tires can be burned to produce energy, shredded and added to asphalt, or melted down and molded into such products as floor mats and playground equipment.

The most important way people can fight pollution is to learn as much as possible about how their actions affect the environment. Then they can make intelligent choices that will reduce damage to the planet.

History

Human beings have always caused some environmental pollution. Since prehistoric times, people have created waste. Like garbage today, this waste was either burned, tossed into waterways, buried, or dumped aboveground. However, the waste of early peoples was mostly food scraps and other substances that broke down easily by natural decay processes. Prehistoric populations were also much smaller and were spread out over large areas. As a result, pollution was less concentrated and caused few problems.

The growth of pollution started during ancient times when large numbers of people began living together in cities. As cities grew, pollution grew with them. Poor sanitation practices and contaminated water supplies unleashed massive epidemics in early cities. Environmental problems became even more serious and widespread in the 1700's and early 1800's, during a period called the Industrial Revolution. This period was characterized by the development of factories and the overcrowding of cities with factory workers.

During the Industrial Revolution, coal powered most factories. Most city homes also relied on coal as a heating fuel. The burning of coal filled the air of London and other industrial cities with smoke and soot. Poor sanitation facilities also allowed raw sewage to get into water supplies in some cities. The polluted water caused typhoid fever and other illnesses.

In the United States, air pollution problems became particularly serious in the early 1900's. By the 1930's, smoke and soot from steel mills, power plants, railroads, and heating plants filled the air over many Eastern and Midwestern cities. In some industrial cities, such as Pittsburgh, Pa., and St. Louis, Mo., pollution frequently became so thick that drivers needed streetlights and headlights to see during the day.

Progress in controlling pollution has gained speed since the 1960's. Nearly all the railroads, industries, and homes of western Europe and the United States have switched from coal to cleaner-burning fuels, such as oil and natural gas. In many other places, pollution controls effectively limit the air pollution created by coal burning. Today, cities in many parts of the world also treat their water and process their sewage, thus greatly reducing the problems caused by harmful bacteria.

Important progress has been made in other areas of pollution management. Industrial waste, sewage, fertilizers, and other contaminants have polluted the Great Lakes since the mid-1800's. By the early 1970's, Lake Erie, Lake Ontario, and shallow regions of Lake Huron and Lake Michigan were so polluted that the waters had turned green and smelled foul, and huge fish kills were common. In 1972, Canada and the United States signed the Great Lakes Water Quality Agreement. Since then, local governments around the lakes have improved sewage treatment plants, controlled the runoff of chemical fertilizers from farms, and worked to reduce the use of phosphate detergents. They have also forced industries

Paul Fusco, Magnum

The first Earth Day was celebrated in April 1970. Its purpose was to increase public awareness of environmental problems.

to reduce the pollutants they dump into the lakes. Today, the Great Lakes are much cleaner.

Current environmental issues

Current environmental issues include the need to weigh the benefits and risks of pollution controls, and the effects of population growth.

Weighing benefits and risks. Increased concern about the environment has caused people to protest many products and practices. Some of the disputed products and processes provide benefits to society. For example, people have argued against the use of disposable diapers because they take up space in landfills and decay slowly. But cloth diapers must be washed, and washing pollutes water and consumes energy. Nuclear power plants generate energy without creating air pollution. But such plants produce radioactive waste, which is difficult to dispose of. Business, environmental groups, and scientists work to determine which products, materials, and processes produce the most pollution. However, few choices are clear cut. It is often difficult to determine the relative risks and benefits to the environment of various products and practices.

When creating pollution laws, government officials must consider both the dangers of the pollutant and the possible financial effects of regulation. Regulations often require that an industry purchase expensive pollution control devices, make costly production changes, or discontinue manufacturing certain products. Such sudden expenses can cause some industries to go out of business, which creates unemployment. As a result, the effects of certain proposed pollution laws could harm people more than the pollutant would.

Effect of population growth. Despite progress in protecting the environment, the problem of pollution has become increasingly widespread and potentially more harmful. The main cause for the increase in pollu-

tion is that the earth's population grows larger every day. More people means more waste of every kind. As a result, one of the most important ways to begin controlling environmental pollution is to slow population growth. A reduction in population growth would slow the destruction and give people more time to develop effective pollution control systems.

Most of the world's population growth occurs in the poorest parts of the world, including certain nations in Africa, Asia, and Latin America. In these areas, people use what little resources they have just trying to keep alive. Governments in developing countries struggle to build modern industries and agricultural systems to provide a basic standard of living for their citizens. However, many developing countries use old technology that tends to pollute because they cannot afford modern, efficient machinery. Even if they could afford pollution controls, pollution in the developing world would continue to rise simply because these nations are industrializing. And more industry means more pollution.

Wastefulness in the industrialized world. Many people in Japan and wealthier nations in North America and Europe have become accustomed to comfortable lifestyles that consume large amounts of energy and raw materials and produce many wastes. A person living in an industrialized nation uses about 10 times the amount of fossil fuels and electricity and produces 2 to 3 times as much municipal waste as a person in a developing country. For a true reduction in pollution, people in the industrialized world would probably have to accept less convenience and luxury in their lives. Solving the problems of global environmental pollution will require the cooperation of governments and industry in all countries, rich and poor, as well as the efforts of individuals all over the world.   Marian R. Chertow

Related articles. See **Air pollution** and **Water pollution** and their lists of *Related articles.* See also:

Acid rain	Fallout	Pesticide
Chlorofluorocarbon	Green party	Plastics (Plastics
Conservation	Hazardous wastes	and
Ecology	Insecticide	the environment)
Environment	Nitrogen (Nitrogen	Radiation
Environmental De-	and pollution)	Radon
fense Fund	Nuclear energy	Recycling
Environmental im-	Nuclear winter	Sound (Noises)
pact statement	Ocean (Ocean	Thermal pollution
Environmental Pro-	pollution)	Waste disposal
tection Agency	Ozone	

Outline

I. Types of pollution
   A. Air pollution   D. Solid waste
   B. Water pollution   E. Hazardous waste
   C. Soil pollution   F. Noise pollution

II. Controlling pollution
   A. Government action   D. Agriculture
   B. Scientific efforts   E. Environmental organiza-
   C. Business and industry   tions
                              F. Individual efforts

III. History
IV. Current environmental issues
   A. Weighing benefits and risks
   B. Effect of population growth
   C. Wastefulness in the industrialized world

Questions

How can consumers encourage manufacturers to produce less polluting products?
What causes most air pollution?

Gerald Cubitt

Cape Town, South Africa's legislative capital and oldest city, lies at the foot of the Cape Mountains in a setting of striking natural beauty. The city's location on the country's southwest coast and its excellent harbor make Cape Town an important shipping and trading center.

South Africa

South Africa is a country that lies at the southern tip of the continent of Africa. The country has a wealth of natural resources, especially minerals, and it is the most highly industrialized country in Africa. South Africa also has great natural beauty and geographical variety.

Despite South Africa's abundant resources and beautiful landscape, it has been troubled by violence and isolated from other countries because of its racial policies. It was the last nation in Africa ruled by a white minority. From the late 1940's until the early 1990's, the white-controlled government enforced a policy of rigid racial segregation called *apartheid* (pronounced *ah PAHRT hayt*). It denied voting rights and other rights to the black majority.

In 1990 and 1991, South Africa repealed the last of the laws on which apartheid was based. In 1993, the country extended voting rights to all races, and democratic elections were held the following year. After the 1994 elections, South Africa's white leaders handed over power to the country's first multiracial government. Nelson Mandela, a civil rights leader who had spent 27 years in prison, became South Africa's first black president.

South Africa's great riches are distributed unevenly among the country's population. White people, who are

The contributor of this article is Bruce Fetter, Professor of History at the University of Wisconsin—Milwaukee and the editor of Colonial Rule in Africa.

a minority of South Africa's population, own most of the wealth. Black people, people of mixed race, and people of Asian ancestry—who together make up a majority of the population—own very little. The new multiracial government has vowed to improve the economic status of nonwhites.

Government

South Africa has three capitals. Parliament meets in Cape Town, the legislative capital. All government departments have their headquarters in Pretoria, the administrative capital. The highest court meets in Bloemfontein, the country's judicial capital.

The structure of South Africa's government is based on a temporary constitution adopted in December 1993. The Constitution provided for a new government that took office in May 1994 following the country's first all-race elections. The new government is to serve until 1999. Its duties include writing a permanent constitution that will take effect in 1999. This section describes the government under the 1993 Constitution.

National government. South Africa's Parliament consists of two houses, the 400-seat National Assembly and the 90-seat Senate. Parliament writes the country's laws, which must be signed by the president to take effect. Parliament will also write the new constitution.

An advisory council of so-called *traditional leaders* makes recommendations to Parliament. These advisers are leaders from various black ethnic groups in South Africa, including the Xhosa and the Zulu. Parliament considers the recommendations of these leaders when it drafts legislation.

In the 1994 election for the National Assembly, voters selected parties, which had compiled lists of candidates before the election. The percentage of the total vote each party received determined the number of Assembly seats it was allowed to fill. The more votes a party received, the greater number of members each party could choose from its list to serve in the Assembly. Members of the Senate were chosen by the legislatures of the country's nine provinces. Each provincial legislature chose 10 senators.

An executive president, elected by the National Assembly, heads South Africa's government. Any party that wins at least 80 seats in the Assembly is entitled to choose a deputy president. If only one party wins that many seats, the two parties with the largest number of votes each choose a deputy president. The president determines the duties of the deputy presidents.

The Cabinet advises the executive president on major issues. The Cabinet consists of the deputy presidents and the heads of government departments. Cabinet members are chosen from the members of Parliament according to party. The president chooses at least one Cabinet member from each party that wins 20 or more seats in the National Assembly. The more votes a party wins, the more of its members are chosen to serve in the Cabinet. The methods of choosing the deputy presidents and Cabinet members are designed to protect the interests of minority groups.

South Africa's highest court is the Constitutional Court. This court settles disputes between national, provincial, and local governments that involve the Constitution. It also determines whether constitutional amendments and laws passed by Parliament are legal. Members of the court serve seven-year terms.

South Africa also has a Supreme Court, which hears appeals from its provincial and local divisions. The Supreme Court handles cases involving human rights violations and disputes between local and provincial governments that do not involve the Constitution. The country's lowest courts are local courts run by magistrates and traditional leaders.

Provincial government. Before 1994, South Africa was divided into 4 provinces and 10 areas called *homelands*. The provinces were (1) Cape Province, (2) Natal, (3) Orange Free State, and (4) Transvaal. The homelands, which were reserved for blacks, were self-governing in name but had no real power.

The 1993 Constitution dissolved the 4 provinces and 10 homelands, effective after the 1994 elections. In their place, 9 new provinces were created: (1) Eastern Cape, (2) Eastern Transvaal, (3) KwaZulu-Natal, (4) Northern Cape, (5) Northern Transvaal, (6) North-West, (7) Orange Free State, (8) Pretoria-Witwatersrand-Vereeniging, and (9) Western Cape. Each province is headed by a premier and an executive council of no more than 10 members. A provincial legislature elects the premier, and the premier appoints the executive council. Members of the provincial legislature are chosen from lists compiled by political parties according to the number of votes the parties receive in provincial elections.

The provincial legislatures can pass bills on many of the same matters as the national Parliament, but their powers are more limited. They receive some revenue from the national government and also can collect provincial taxes. Each provincial legislature is advised by a council of traditional leaders.

Local governments, such as those of cities and towns, can pass local laws and levy local taxes. Some local governments are advised by traditional leaders.

Political parties. The largest political parties in South Africa are the African National Congress (ANC), the National Party, and the Inkatha Freedom Party (IFP). The ANC was founded in 1912 to promote the rights of blacks. Although illegal from 1960 until 1990, the ANC became the main political voice for blacks, who were not allowed to vote during that period. Its supporters include people from all of South Africa's ethnic groups. The National Party controlled the South African government from 1948 until 1994. Formerly all white, its members now include many *Coloreds* (people of mixed race) and Asians. Most members of the Inkatha Freedom Party are Zulu. The IFP supports the formation of an independent Zulu state.

Armed forces. South Africa's 74,000-member armed forces include an army, navy, and air force. In addition, 706,000 people serve in reserve and volunteer units, and 110,000 people are in the national police. Members of all racial and ethnic groups serve in the armed forces. Before 1994, most of the officers were white. The number of black officers increased when armies of some of the black homelands were incorporated into the national armed forces. South Africa's armed forces also absorbed the military wing of the ANC.

People

South Africa has about 43 million people. More than half the people live in urban areas. The country has five cities with over 500,000 people. These cities are Cape Town, Durban, Johannesburg, Soweto, and Pretoria.

Population and ancestry. The ancestors of South Africa's population include people from Africa, Asia, and Europe. From the late 1940's to the early 1990's, South Africa's government enforced a policy of rigid racial segregation called *apartheid. Apartheid* means *separateness* in Afrikaans, a language spoken in South Africa. Under apartheid, the government officially categorized the people into four main racial groups: (1) black, (2) white, (3) Colored, and (4) Asian. The government segregated the groups from one another in housing, education, and employment, and in the use of transportation and other public facilities. Even after apartheid ended, the four groups remained generally separated from one another and followed different ways of life.

Blacks, also called Africans, number about 32 million people, or about three-fourths of South Africa's total population. Their ancestors moved into what is now eastern South Africa from the north between about A.D. 300 and 1000. The Zulu form the largest black ethnic group, and the Xhosa make up the second largest. Many Zulu live in KwaZulu-Natal, and the Xhosa live mostly in Eastern Cape. The Sotho and the Tswana are the third and fourth largest black ethnic groups. The South Sotho live in eastern Orange Free State. The North Sotho make their homes in Northern Transvaal. The Tswana, related to the people of Botswana, live near the border of that country.

Whites total about 6 million of South Africa's people. People who call themselves *Afrikaners* make up about

South Africa in brief

Capitals: Cape Town (legislative), Pretoria (administrative), Bloemfontein (judicial).

Official languages: South Africa's 11 official languages are (1) Afrikaans, (2) English, (3) Ndebele, (4) North Sesotho, (5) South Sesotho, (6) Swazi, (7) Tsonga, (8) Tswana, (9) Venda, (10) Xhosa, and (11) Zulu.

Official name: Republic of South Africa.

National anthems: "Die Stem van Suid-Afrika" ("The Call of South Africa") and "Nkosi Sikelele Afrika" ("God Bless Africa").

Largest cities: (1991 census)

Cape Town	854,616	Soweto	596,632
Durban	715,669	Pretoria	525,583
Johannesburg	712,507		

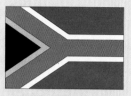

South Africa's flag, adopted in 1994, represents the country's peoples coming together in unity.

Coat of arms represents South Africa's four original provinces. *Ex Unitate Vires* means *Unity Is Strength.*

Land and climate

Land: South Africa lies at the southern tip of Africa, with a coastline on the Indian and Atlantic oceans. The country borders Namibia, Botswana, Zimbabwe, Mozambique, and Swaziland, and it completely surrounds the country of Lesotho. South Africa's interior is mostly plateau. Coastal lowlands lie in the east. The Cape Mountains are in the far south. The Namib Desert stretches along the west coast. The Kalahari Desert covers much of the northwest interior. South Africa's main rivers include the Orange and its branch, the Vaal.

Area: 471,445 sq. mi. (1,221,037 km²). *Greatest distances*—east-west 1,010 mi. (1,625 km); north-south, 875 mi. (1,408 km). *Coastline*—about 1,836 mi. (2,954 km).

Elevation: *Highest*—Champagne Castle, 11,072 ft. (3,375 m). *Lowest*—sea level.

Climate: South Africa's climate is generally mild and sunny. The Cape Mountains Region has warm, dry summers and cool, wet winters. Much of the Coastal Strip has hot, humid summers and dry, sunny winters. In the Plateau, summer days are hot, but the nights are cool. The winter is cold. The deserts are hot and dry. Only about a fourth of South Africa receives more than 25 inches (64 centimeters) of rain yearly. More rain falls in the east than in the west.

Government

Form of government: Parliamentary republic.

Head of government: Executive president.

Legislature: Parliament of two houses: 400-member National Assembly; 90-member Senate.

Executive: Executive president (elected by the National Assembly) and multiparty Cabinet.

Judiciary: Constitutional Court is highest court.

Political subdivisions: Nine provinces.

People

Population: *1995 estimate*—42,741,000. *1991 census*—30,986,920 (excluding the black homelands Bophuthatswana, Ciskei, Transkei, and Venda). *2000 estimate*—47,912,000.

Population density: 91 persons per sq. mi. (35 per km²).

Distribution: 51 percent urban, 49 percent rural.

Major ethnic/national groups: 76 percent black (mainly Zulu, Xhosa, Sotho, and Tswana); 13 percent white; 9 percent Colored people of mixed background; 2 percent Asian.

Major religions: 39 percent Protestant; 17 percent African indigenous churches; 15 percent traditional African religions; 8 percent Roman Catholic.

Population trend

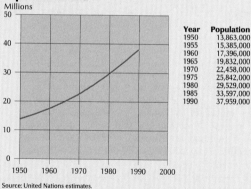

Year	Population
1950	13,863,000
1955	15,385,000
1960	17,396,000
1965	19,832,000
1970	22,458,000
1975	25,842,000
1980	29,529,000
1985	33,597,000
1990	37,959,000

Source: United Nations estimates.

Economy

Chief products: *Agriculture*—corn, chickens and eggs, beef cattle, wheat, sugar cane, sheep, wool, apples. *Manufacturing*—chemicals, processed foods and beverages, transportation equipment, iron and steel, fabricated metal products, machinery, paper products, textiles. *Mining*—gold, coal, diamonds, copper, iron ore, uranium, manganese, chromite, platinum, vanadium.

Money: *Basic unit*—rand. For value in U.S. dollars, see Money (table: Exchange rates).

Gross domestic product: *1991 total GDP*—$108,076,000,000. *1991 GDP per capita*—$2,670.

International trade: *Major exports*—gold, diamonds, metals and minerals, wool, corn, sugar. *Major imports*—machinery, petroleum and petroleum products, transportation equipment, electrical equipment, computers. *Major trading partners*—Germany, United States, Japan, United Kingdom, Switzerland.

Gerald Cubitt   Gerald Cubitt

Contrasting ways of life characterize South Africa's multiracial population. Many poor blacks in
rural areas live in traditional round houses called *rondavels, left.* South Africans of all races live
and work in modern cities, such as Cape Town, *right.*

three-fifths of the white population. Their ancestors
came chiefly from the Netherlands in the late 1600's,
though some came from Germany and France. Until the
1900's, most Afrikaners lived on farms and were called
Boers. Boer is a Dutch word that means *farmer.* Today,
most Afrikaners live in cities, but they still make up most
of the white population in rural areas.

English-speaking whites account for about two-fifths
of the white population. Their ancestors came chiefly
from England, Ireland, and Scotland beginning in the
1800's.

Colored people total about 4 million. Their ancestors
include the Khoikhoi and San peoples—black hunters
and herders who lived in western South Africa when the
first white settlers arrived in the 1600's. Some ancestors
of Colored people were black and Southeast Asian
slaves brought to the country by whites. Other ancestors
include early white settlers and passing sailors, soldiers,
and travelers. Most Colored people live in Western
Cape and Northern Cape provinces.

Asians. About 1 million Asians live in South Africa.
The ancestors of most of them came from India between
1860 and 1911 to work on sugar plantations in Natal
(now KwaZulu-Natal). Plantation owners recruited them
as *contract laborers,* workers imported under an agreement to work for a particular employer.

Languages. South Africa has 11 official languages.
They are (1) Afrikaans, (2) English, (3) Ndebele, (4) North
Sesotho, (5) South Sesotho, (6) Swazi, (7) Tsonga, (8)
Tswana, (9) Venda, (10) Xhosa, and (11) Zulu.

Afrikaans developed from Dutch, but it also has
words from other European languages and from Asian
and African languages. South African English resembles
American and British English with the addition of many
Afrikaans words. The other languages belong to the
Bantu group, a large group of black African languages.

About 60 percent of South Africa's white people use
Afrikaans as their first language, as do about 90 percent
of the Colored population. The other whites and Coloreds speak English as their first language. Blacks speak

a variety of Bantu languages. Many also speak English or
Afrikaans. Asians speak various Asian languages, though
most also know English.

For many years, English and Afrikaans were South Africa's only two official languages, and the only two used
in government. English was the chief language used in
business and industry. Under the 1993 Constitution, government documents are printed in each of the country's
11 official languages. Spoken government transactions
occur in any official language the speakers choose.

Ways of life. The differing cultural backgrounds of
South Africa's people have helped create contrasting
ways of life. In addition, the inequalities created by
apartheid and by earlier oppression of nonwhites have
profoundly affected how people live.

Since the end of apartheid in 1991, South Africa's racial groups have no longer been segregated by law.
However, nonwhites still face much unofficial discrimination. Some public elementary and high schools and
some housing remain segregated in practice. Most
high-paying jobs are still held by whites.

Economic differences exist within each racial group
as well as between the groups. In each group, some
people have better jobs and make more money than
others. Even in the black, Asian, and Colored
communities—which have many poor people—there are
successful executives and professional people.

Blacks. Because of years of oppression, many of
South Africa's blacks are poor. In 1990, the average *per
capita* (per person) income of blacks was about one-
tenth that of whites. Large numbers of blacks are unemployed, and many blacks lack adequate housing.

Many of South Africa's blacks live in areas that were
formerly black homelands. For many years, blacks were
assigned to permanent residency in the homelands. The
farms in the homelands were smaller than the farms
owned by whites. In addition, the soil on homeland
farms was poor. On some grazing lands, previous white
owners had damaged the soil by overgrazing their
herds. As a result, many black men and women had to

seek jobs in the cities to support their families. Only blacks who had jobs with white, urban employers were permitted to live temporarily in cities. Even then, they were restricted to segregated neighborhoods, far from the center of town.

In the mid-1980's, the government began to repeal the laws that kept blacks out of the cities. In 1994, the government ended the homelands system. Today, nearly 50 percent of blacks live in urban areas. Many urban blacks still live in segregated neighborhoods. Others have moved into formerly all-white neighborhoods. Still others have built makeshift shelters on empty land inside the city limits and on land along major roads leading into the cities.

Whites. About 90 percent of all white South Africans live in urban areas. Most whites have a high standard of living. Their clothing, homes, and social customs resemble those of middle-class North Americans and Europeans. Many whites live in luxurious suburban areas of Cape Town, Durban, Johannesburg, and Pretoria. Most white families live in single-family homes, and many have at least one servant who is not white.

Afrikaners and English-speaking whites generally lead separate lives. They live in different sections of cities, go to different schools, and belong to different churches and social and professional organizations. Until the new government took power in 1994, Afrikaners held many governmental jobs in South Africa. They continue to control most of the nation's agriculture. English-speaking whites dominate business and industry.

Colored people. About 85 percent of South Africa's Coloreds live in cities. The Colored community began in what is now Western Cape, and many Coloreds still live there. Colored people have worked for whites for many generations. In cities, many Coloreds have jobs as servants, factory laborers, or craftworkers. In rural areas, many work in vineyards or orchards.

The term *Colored* is controversial in South Africa. Many Colored people refer to themselves as *so-called Colored, classified Colored,* or *black.*

Asians. About 95 percent of South Africa's Asians live in cities. Indians make up almost all the Asian population. The majority of Indians live in KwaZulu-Natal. Some have kept many of their old social customs. Many Indian women wear the traditional *sari*—a long piece of cloth draped around the body. However, young people and most men wear Western-style clothing. Most Indians are poor and work in factories or grow vegetables for city markets. But a few are prosperous doctors, industrialists, lawyers, and merchants.

Food and drink vary among the people of South Africa according to their wealth and customs. Whites enjoy foods similar to those eaten by Americans and Europeans. They also eat local specialties, such as *boerewors,* an Afrikaner sausage dish, and *curry,* an Indian dish of eggs, fish, meat, or vegetables cooked in a spicy sauce. The diet of Colored people resembles that of whites but is less costly. The basic food of most blacks is *mealies* (corn), which they eat as a porridge. Wealthier blacks eat many of the same foods as the whites and Coloreds. A large number of poor blacks suffer from a shortage of protein and vitamins.

Popular beverages include coffee, tea, beer, and soft drinks. Wealthy people drink fine wines from Western Cape.

Recreation. South Africans love sports, and the country's mild climate enables them to spend much of their leisure time outdoors. White South Africans like to play rugby football—South Africa's national sport—and cricket, association football (soccer), tennis, and golf. Nonwhite South Africans have favored association football and track-and-field events. Some blacks have become world champions in long-distance running. On weekends and holidays, many city dwellers flock to the beaches or tour their country's national parks and game reserves.

For many years, such facilities as restaurants and theaters were allowed to serve only either whites or nonwhites. Also, sports events involving more than one race were outlawed. In the 1970's and 1980's, new regulations permitted restaurants and theaters to serve all races. Sports competition involving more than one race was also legalized. But segregation still occurs in private sports clubs, even though it is illegal.

Gerald Cubitt

A Sotho family gathers in front of its brightly painted home in the Orange Free State. The Sotho are a Bantu-speaking people whose ancestors began to arrive in South Africa about A.D. 300.

Gerald Cubitt

A soccer game provides recreation for a group of young South Africans. Soccer, called *association football* in South Africa, is one of the country's most popular sports.

South Africa political map

South Africa political map	Provincial boundary
	Road
	Railroad
	⊛ National capital
National park (N.P.)	★ Provincial capital
International boundary	• Other city or town
	WORLD BOOK map

South Africa map index

Provinces

Eastern Cape	6,436,790 .E 4
Eastern Transvaal	2,921,559 .B 6
KwaZulu-Natal	8,505,338 .D 6
Northern Cape	737,306 .D 2
Northern Transvaal	5,201,630 .A 6
North-West	3,252,991 .C 4
Orange Free State	2,726,840 .D 4
Pretoria-Witwatersrand-Vereeniging	6,869,103 .C 5
Western Cape	3,633,077 .F 2

Cities and towns

Alberton*	76,642 .C 5
Alexandra*	124,586 .C 5
Amanzimtoti‡	13,600 .D 6
Atteridgeville*	92,008 .D 5
Beaufort West‡	16,560 .E 3
Bellville*	78,822 .F 1
Benoni*	113,501 .C 6
Bethlehem‡	12,080 .C 5
Bisho	E 5
Bloemfontein	126,867 †300,150 .D 5
Boksburg*	119,890 .C 5
Brakpan*	53,522 .C 5
Cape Town	854,616 †1,869,144 .F 1
Carletonville*	118,699 .C 5
Ceres‡	12,260 .E 2
Cradock‡	11,320 .E 4
Daveyton*	151,659 .C 6
De Aar‡	14,940 .D 3
Diepmeadow*	241,099 .C 5
Dobsonville*	53,091 .C 5
Dundee‡	9,000 .C 6
Durban	715,669 †1,106,971 .D 7
East London‡	102,325 .E 4
Elsies River*	82,045 .F 2
Empangeni‡	12,180 .D 7
Ermelo‡	10,860 .C 6
Estcourt‡	10,340 .D 6
Evaton	201,026 .C 5
Fort Beaufort‡	6,080 .E 5
Galeshewe*	72,118 .D 4
George‡	34,940 .F 3
Germiston	134,005 .C 5
Giyani	A 6
Graaff-Reinet‡	14,700 .E 4
Grahamstown‡	25,120 .F 4
Grassy Park*	52,675 .F 1
Howick‡	10,560 .D 6
Johannesburg	712,507 †1,907,229 .C 5
Joubertina*	74,377 .F 4
Kathlehong*	201,785 .C 5
Kempton Park*	106,606 .C 5
Kimberley	80,082 †167,060 .D 4
King William's Town‡	14,260 .E 5
Klerksdorp‡	58,923 .C 5
Knysna‡	12,440 .F 3
Kroonstad‡	20,900 .C 5
Krugersdorp*	81,584 .C 5
Kuruman‡	8,320 .C 3
Kwa Nobuhle*	92,381 .F 4
Ladysmith‡	21,880 .D 6
Lebowakgomo	B 6
Lekoa*	217,582 .C 5
Lichtenburg‡	10,700 .C 5
Madadeni‡	60,940 .C 6
Mafikeng‡	6,500 .B 4
Mahwelereng‡	14,500 .B 6
Mamelodi	154,845 .B 6
Manguang	125,545 .D 5
Mariannhill‡	27,940 .D 6
Mdantsane‡	159,360 .E 5
Middelburg‡	18,600 .B 6
Mmabatho	B 4
Mossel Bay‡	17,600 .F 3
Motherwell*	72,999 .F 4
Namakgale‡	20,040 .B 7
Nelspruit‡	14,660 .B 7
Newcastle‡	34,120 .C 6
Nigel*‡	24,520 .C 6
Nyanga*	92,896 .F 2
Orkney*	18,500 .C 5
Oudtshoorn‡	33,480 .E 3
Paarl	73,415 .F 2
Parow	68,081 .F 2
Pietermaritzburg	156,473 †211,473 .D 6
Pietersburg‡	25,500 .B 6
Pinetown	70,001 .D 6
Port Alfred‡	8,920 .E 5
Port Elizabeth	303,353 †825,799 .F 4
Potchefstroom‡	38,920 .C 5
Pretoria	525,583 †1,025,790 .B 5
Prieska‡	22,280 .D 3
Queenstown‡	15,060 .E 5
Randburg*	90,557 .C 5
Randfontein*	51,940 .C 5
Roodepoort*	162,632 .C 5
Rustenburg‡	30,420 .B 5
Saldanha	E 1
Sandton*	101,197 .C 5
Seshego‡	28,880 .B 6
Somerset West*‡	16,500 .F 2
Soweto	596,632 .C 5
Springbok‡	8,180 .D 1
Springs	72,647 .C 6
Standerton‡	11,960 .C 6
Stanger‡	14,840 .D 7
Stellenbosch‡	37,680 .F 2
Strand‡	25,260 .F 2
Stutterheim‡	11,480 .E 5
Thabong*	88,547 .C 5
Thohoyandou	A 6
Tongaat*‡	24,640 .D 7
Uitenhage	67,581 .E 4
Ulundi	7
Umlazi*	177,100 .D 6
Upington‡	25,880 .C 3
Vanderbijlpark	67,291 †447,526 .C 5
Vereeniging	71,255 .C 5
Verwoerdburg*	80,552 .B 5
Virginia‡	14,080 .C 5
Vosloorus*	76,015 .C 5
Vredenburg‡	27,460 .E 1
Vryburg‡	8,980 .C 4
Vryheid‡	11,260 .C 6
Welkom	68,111 .C 5
Wellington‡	21,660 .E 2
Westonaria*	57,177 .C 5
Witbank‡	38,600 .C 6
Worcester‡	41,880 .E 2
Zwelitsha‡	29,260 .E 5

*Does not appear on map; key shows general location.
†Population of metropolitan area, including suburbs.

Sources: 1994 official estimates for provinces; 1991 census; 1980 census where indicated by ‡. Data not available for places without figures.

E. S. Ross

A group of schoolchildren reflect the mixed ancestry of South Africa's so-called Colored community. Almost all of the country's Colored people live in the province of Western Cape.

Education. Until 1991, students in each racial group were required by law to attend separate public schools. Since then, many black children have begun to attend previously all-white public schools. In large cities, schools that were formerly all white have become integrated or have become all black. South Africa's private schools are integrated.

Under apartheid, far more money per child was spent on the education of white children than on that of black children. About 90 percent of whites, 85 percent of Asians, 75 percent of Coloreds, and 65 percent of blacks can read and write.

White, Asian, and Colored children ages 7 through 16 must attend school. Until 1981, the law did not require any black children to go to school. That year, the government began to phase in schooling requirements for black children. Today, most black children attend the early elementary grades, but many drop out after four or five years. Many areas—especially black areas—have a shortage of schools.

South Africa has 10 universities originally established for whites, 4 established for blacks, 1 each for Coloreds and Asians, and a correspondence school that never had any racial requirements. Since the mid-1980's, qualified students of any race may attend any university that will accept them. An increasing number of nonwhites attend formerly all-white universities. Students enrolled at the universities include about 166,000 whites, 146,000 blacks, 27,000 Coloreds, and 23,000 Asians.

Religion. South Africa does not have an *established* (national) church. Most Afrikaners belong to the Dutch Reformed Church or to its sister churches. Most English-speaking whites belong to Anglican, Congregational, Methodist, or Roman Catholic churches, or to Jewish congregations. White religious groups played an important role in persuading the government to end apartheid.

Most Colored people belong to Anglican, Congrega-

tional, Dutch Reformed, Methodist, or Roman Catholic churches. The majority of Asians are Hindus or Muslims.

Nearly 45 percent of black people belong to Christian churches, chiefly Anglican, Dutch Reformed, Lutheran, Methodist, and Roman Catholic churches. About 25 percent of blacks follow traditional African religions. About 20 percent of blacks belong to *African indigenous churches,* which combine Christian and traditional African beliefs. Of these churches, the Zion Christian Church is the largest.

The arts. The South African government supports a performing arts council in each province. The councils sponsor artistic companies that present ballets, concerts, operas, and plays in small towns as well as in big cities. Private black, Asian, Colored, and white companies also perform throughout the country.

South Africa has produced outstanding artists in ballet, music, painting, sculpture, and other fields. One of the best-known performing groups is the black vocal and instrumental group Ladysmith Black Mambazo. The singers perform in a humming style called *mbube,* which is influenced by European harmonies and vocal traditions but retains black African rhythms.

South Africa has made an important contribution to world literature. Much of the country's literature reflects its political and social tensions. After the Boer War of 1899-1902, such Afrikaner writers as Jan Celliers, C. L. Leipoldt, and C. J. Langenhoven expressed their sorrow over Britain's conquest of land occupied by the Afrikaners. Eugene Marais gained critical praise for his poetry and his writings on nature.

Since the 1920's, many South African writers have dealt with racial themes. They include the black writers Es'Kia Mphahlele, Oswald Mtshali, Mbulelo Mzamane, Njabulo Ndebele, Sipho Sepamla, and Mongane Serote; the Colored novelist Peter Abrahams; and the white authors Breyten Breytenbach, André Brink, Athol Fugard, Nadine Gordimer, and Alan Paton. Gordimer won the 1991 Nobel Prize in literature.

Land

South Africa has five land regions: (1) the Plateau, (2) the Coastal Strip, (3) the Cape Mountains Region, (4) the Namib Desert, and (5) the Kalahari Desert.

The Plateau covers most of the interior of South Africa. The Great Escarpment, a semicircular series of cliffs and mountains, rims the Plateau and separates it from the coastal regions. The escarpment reaches its greatest heights—over 11,000 feet (3,350 meters) above sea level—in the Drakensberg mountain range in the east. The country's highest point, Champagne Castle, is in the Drakensberg. It stands 11,072 feet (3,375 meters) high.

The Plateau slopes gradually downward from the Great Escarpment. It has three chief subregions: (1) the Highveld, (2) the Middleveld, and (3) the Transvaal Basin. The Highveld occupies all the Plateau except for the northwestern and northeastern corners. It lies mostly between 4,000 and 6,000 feet (1,200 and 1,800 meters) above sea level and consists largely of flat, grass-covered land. In places, flat-topped mountains rise above the plain. The area of the Highveld around Johannesburg is called the *Witwatersrand* or *Rand.* It covers more than 1,000 square miles (2,600 square kilometers) and is the world's largest and richest gold field. This area is the nation's chief industrial and business center. Farmers in the Highveld raise cattle, corn, fruits, potatoes, and wheat.

The Middleveld, in the northwestern Plateau, averages less than 4,000 feet (1,200 meters) above sea level. It is a dry, flat area and serves largely as ranch country.

The Transvaal Basin forms the Plateau's northeastern part. It averages less than 4,000 feet above sea level but has mountain ranges more than 6,000 feet (1,800 meters) high. The area is largely a rolling grassland with scattered thorn trees. Farmers raise citrus and other fruits, corn, and tobacco. Kruger National Park, a world-famous game reserve, lies in the area. Elephants, leopards, lions, rhinoceroses, zebras, and other wild animals roam freely in the park, which is South Africa's most popular tourist attraction.

The Coastal Strip extends along the southeast coast from Mozambique to the Cape Mountains Region. Except in the northeast, the region has little low-lying land. In the Durban area, for example, the land rises to 2,000 feet (610 meters) within 20 miles (32 kilometers) of the sea. Chief crops include bananas, citrus fruits, sugar cane, and vegetables. Durban is a major industrial center, port, and resort area.

The Cape Mountains Region stretches from the Coastal Strip to the Namib Desert. Mountain ranges in the west and south meet northeast of the great port city of Cape Town. Between the mountains and the Great Escarpment lie two dry plateaus—the Little Karoo and the Great Karoo. There, farmers grow wine grapes and other fruits on irrigated land. They also raise wheat, sheep, and ostriches.

The Namib and Kalahari deserts. The Namib lies along the Atlantic Ocean north of the Cape Mountains Region and extends into Namibia. The Kalahari lies north of the Middleveld and extends into the country of Bot-

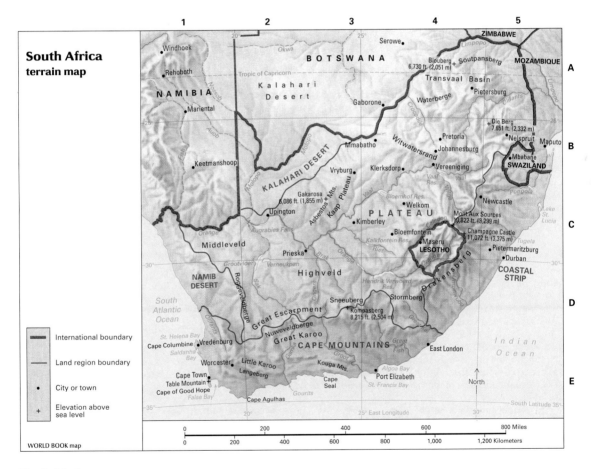

South Africa
terrain map

International boundary

Land region boundary

• City or town

+ Elevation above
sea level

WORLD BOOK map

| 0 | 200 | 400 | 600 | 800 Miles |
| 0 | 200 | 400 | 600 | 800 | 1,000 | 1,200 Kilometers |

Physical features

Algoa Bay	E 3	Crocodile River	A 4	Grootvloer (salt flat)	D 2	Middleveld (plateau)	C 1	St. Francis Bay	E 3
Asbestos Mountains	C 3	Die Berg (mountain)	B 5	Hendrik Verwoerd		Molopo River	B 2	St. Helena Bay	D 1
Augrabies Falls	C 2	Drakensberg		Reservoir	D 3	Mont Aux Sources		Sneeuberg (range)	D 3
Bloemhof Reservoir	C 3	(mountains)	D 3	Highveld (plateau)	D 3	(mountain)	C 4	Table Mountain	E 1
Blouberg (mountain)	A 4	False Bay	E 1	Kaap Plateau	C 3	Namib Desert	D 1	Transvaal Basin	A 4
Caledon River	C 4	Gakarosa		Kalahari Desert	B 2	Nuweveldberge (range)	D 2	Tugela River	C 5
Cape Agulhas	E 2	(mountain)	C 3	Kompasberg		Olifants River	A 5	Vaal River	B 4
Cape Columbine	E 1	Great Escarpment	D 2	(mountain)	D 3	Orange River	C 1	Vaal Reservoir	B 4
Cape Mountains	E 3	Great Fish River	E 4	Kouga Mountains	E 3	Pongola River	C 5	Verneukpan	
Cape of Good Hope	E 1	Great Karoo (plateau)	D 2	Lake St. Lucia	C 5	Rand, see		(salt flat)	C 2
Champagne Castle		Great Kei River	D 4	Limpopo River	A 4	Witwatersrand		Wilge River	C 4
(mountain)	C 4	Groot River	E 3	Little Karoo (plateau)	E 2	Saldanha Bay	E 1	Witwatersrand (ridge)	B 4

Martin Harvey, The Wildlife Collection

Zebras graze in Kalahari Gemsbok National Park in Northern Cape. The park lies in the Kalahari Desert, which is home to hyenas, lions, antelope, and much other wildlife.

swana. Small bands of hunters roam the deserts, living on the plants and animals they find.

Rivers. South Africa's longest river is the Orange River. It begins in Lesotho and flows westward about 1,300 miles (2,100 kilometers) into the Atlantic. The Vaal River, the Orange's largest branch, rises in Eastern Transvaal. It flows about 750 miles (1,210 kilometers) before joining the Orange in Northern Cape. The Limpopo River begins near Johannesburg and winds about 1,000 miles (1,600 kilometers) across eastern South Africa and Mozambique before emptying into the Indian Ocean. South Africa also has many shorter rivers. Waterfalls, sand bars, and shallow water make even the longest rivers useless for shipping.

Climate

South Africa lies south of the equator, and so its seasons occur at times opposite to when those same seasons occur in the Northern Hemisphere. Most of South Africa enjoys a mild, sunny climate. But differences in elevation, wind systems, and ocean currents create various climatic areas. For example, the Cape Mountains Region has warm, dry summers and cool, wet winters. Much of the Coastal Strip has hot, humid summers and dry, sunny winters. In the eastern Plateau, summer days are hot, but the nights are cool. In winter, the days are crisp and clear, and the nights are cold. Winter temperatures throughout most of the Plateau often drop below freezing.

Only about a fourth of South Africa receives more than 25 inches (64 centimeters) of rain a year. Most rain falls in summer, except in the Cape Mountains Region. In general, rainfall is greater in the east than in the west. Parts of the east coast get more than 40 inches (100 centimeters) annually. In the west, the Namib Desert gets almost no rain.

Economy

South Africa is the richest and most economically developed country in Africa. It occupies only about 4 percent of the continent's area and has only about 6 percent of Africa's people. Yet South Africa produces two-fifths

of Africa's manufactured goods, nearly half its minerals, and a fifth of its farm products.

In the late 1800's, diamonds and gold were discovered in South Africa. Mining quickly became the basis of the country's economy. Today, manufacturing is the single most important economic activity. It produces nearly a fourth of South Africa's *gross domestic product* (GDP), the value of all goods and services produced within the country. The various service industries together produce an even larger portion of the GDP.

From the 1950's through the 1970's, South Africa experienced spectacular economic growth. Many people from other countries invested in South African businesses. In the 1980's, a slowdown in economic growth and opposition to South Africa's policy of apartheid led to the withdrawal of some foreign investments. Some countries that opposed apartheid reduced or ended trade with South Africa. Since the repeal of the last apartheid laws in 1991, foreign trade and investment have increased.

South Africa's gross domestic product

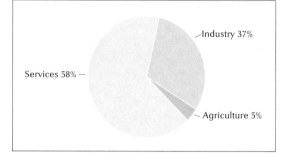

The gross domestic product (GDP) of South Africa was $108,076,000,000 in 1991. The GDP is the total value of goods and services produced within a country in a year. *Services* include community, government, and personal services; finance, insurance, and real estate; trade, restaurants, and hotels; transportation and communication; and utilities. *Industry* includes construction, manufacturing, and mining. *Agriculture* includes agriculture, forestry, and fishing.

Production and workers by economic activities

Economic activities	Percent of GDP produced	Employed workers Number of persons	Employed workers Percent of total
Manufacturing	24	1,417,000	12
Community, government, & personal services	18	5,153,000	44
Finance, insurance, real estate, & business services	15	504,000	4
Trade, restaurants, & hotels	13	1,358,000	12
Mining	10	841,000	7
Transportation & communication	8	497,000	4
Agriculture, forestry, & fishing	5	1,225,000	11
Utilities	4	103,000	1
Construction	3	526,000	5
Total	100	11,624,000	100

Figures are for 1991. Figures do not include totals for the former black homelands Bophuthatswana, Ciskei, Transkei, and Venda because data are not available for those areas. Source: International Labor Organization.

For many years, South Africa's apartheid government owned many businesses and appointed white South Africans to run them. It also passed laws that reserved the best positions in both industry and government for white employees. Today, whites still hold nearly all the executive, professional, and technical jobs. Black workers are generally less educated than whites and receive far lower wages. In 1979, the government for the first time allowed black workers to form labor unions, which have since won them higher salaries.

Natural resources. South Africa has long been famous for its fabulous deposits of gold and diamonds. It also has large supplies of chromite, coal, copper, iron ore, manganese, platinum, silver, and uranium (as a byproduct of gold). In fact, the country has nearly every useful mineral except oil. Offshore waters provide plentiful fish and lobsters and help make South Africa a leading fishing country.

South Africa is less fortunate in some other natural resources. Only a third of the farmland receives enough rain to grow crops easily. South Africa also has poor forest resources.

Service industries are economic activities that produce services rather than goods. Such industries account for 58 percent of South Africa's GDP. Community, government, and personal services employ more people than any other industry in South Africa. Other important services include banking, trade, transportation, and utilities.

Manufacturing. South Africa's factories produce almost all the country's manufactured goods. The chief products include chemicals, clothing and textiles, iron and steel and other metals, machinery, metal products, motor vehicles, and processed foods. South African factories manufacture gasoline and other fuels from coal. Most factories are in the Cape Town, Durban, Johannesburg, Port Elizabeth, and Pretoria areas.

Mining. South Africa produces more gold than any other country, supplying about a third of the gold mined in the world each year. South Africa is also a major producer of chromite, coal, copper, diamonds, iron ore, limestone, manganese, phosphate, platinum, uranium, and vanadium. South African miners also take dozens of other minerals from the earth.

Ever since gold was first discovered in South Africa in the 1880's, it has been the main force behind the country's growth. Gold mining has attracted huge foreign investments and has led to the development of the transportation and manufacturing facilities in South Africa.

Agriculture. South Africa's farmers produce almost all the food needed by its people. The leading crops include apples, corn, grapes, oranges, pineapples, potatoes, sugar cane, tobacco, and wheat. South Africa is one of the world's chief sheep-raising countries, and wool is its main agricultural export. Other leading farm products include beef and dairy cattle, chickens, eggs, milk, and wine.

South Africa has two main types of farming—that practiced by whites and that practiced by blacks. White farmers use modern methods and raise products chiefly for the market. The average size of white-owned farms is about 2,300 acres (931 hectares). Black farm families produce food mainly for their own needs. Black farms average about 52 acres (21 hectares). Production on black farms has been extremely low because, for many years, blacks were confined to areas where the land was of poor quality. In addition, most black farmers could not afford modern equipment. The government that was elected in 1994 promised to redistribute about one-third of the country's farmland.

Fishing industry. South Africa's coastal waters yield about 550,000 short tons (500,000 metric tons) of fish and shellfish a year. Important catches include anchovies, hake, and lobster.

Energy sources. Most of South Africa's electric power comes from plants that burn coal or petroleum. Nuclear power plants produce a small amount of the electricity. The country also purchases electricity from Mozambique and Zimbabwe. South Africa does not produce enough petroleum to support its needs, so it must import oil.

International trade. South Africa's chief trade partners—besides other African countries—include Germany, Japan, Switzerland, the United Kingdom, and the United States. Chief exports include gold, diamonds, metals and minerals, wool, corn, sugar, and fruits. Machinery and transportation equipment make up nearly half the value of the country's imports. Other imports include chemicals, manufactured goods, and petroleum.

Transportation. South Africa has the best transportation system in Africa. Paved roads crisscross the sections of the country populated by whites. Most roads in the former black homelands are unpaved. Most white families own at least one automobile. Most blacks rely on buses and trains. The country's railroads are operated by the government-owned South African Railways. South African Airways, the government-owned national airline, provides domestic and international service. Johannesburg, Cape Town, and Durban have major airports. South Africa has six large, well-equipped seaports—Cape Town, Durban, East London, Port Elizabeth, Richards Bay, and Saldanha.

Communication. South Africa has 20 daily newspapers, of which 14 are published in English, 5 in Afrikaans, and 1 in both English and Afrikaans. The *Sowetan,* an English-language paper for blacks, has the largest cir-

Mark Peters, Sipa

Gold brought wealth to South Africa, the world's leading gold producer. Hundreds of thousands of people, mostly blacks, work in the country's gold mines and smelting plants, *above.*

J. Kuus, Sipa

Blacks and whites work together in many businesses as the racial segregation produced by South Africa's former policy of apartheid gradually disappears.

culation of any paper in the country. Other large English-language dailies are *The Citizen* and *The Star,* both of Johannesburg. *Beeld,* also published in Johannesburg, is the largest Afrikaans daily.

Radio and television broadcasting in South Africa are controlled by the South African Broadcasting Corporation (SABC), which is licensed by the government but receives no government funds. The SABC offers 19 radio program services and four TV channels. Radio and TV shows are broadcast in English, Afrikaans, and a number of black languages. The government runs postal, telegraph, and telephone systems.

History

Early days. At least 2,000 years ago, a people called the Khoisan lived throughout much of the South Africa region. They hunted animals and gathered wild plants for food.

By A.D. 1500, great changes had occurred in western and eastern South Africa. The west was thinly occupied by two groups descended from the Khoisan. One of the groups, who called themselves the Khoikhoi, raised cattle and sheep. The other lived by hunting. The hunters had no general name for themselves, but the Khoikhoi called them the San. When Europeans arrived in the 1600's, they called the San *Bushmen* and the Khoikhoi *Hottentots.* Both of these European terms were considered derogatory by the Africans.

Meanwhile, eastern South Africa had become populated by peoples who spoke various Bantu languages. These groups began to enter the region from the north about A.D. 300. They lived in chiefdoms, raised cattle and sheep, and grew grain. They made tools and weapons out of iron.

Arrival of Europeans. Portuguese sailors were the first Europeans to see South Africa. They sighted it in 1488, when they rounded the Cape of Good Hope in their search for a water route east to India.

The first European settlers arrived in 1652. They worked for the Dutch East India Company, a powerful Dutch trading company. The company sent the settlers, headed by Jan van Riebeeck, to set up a supply base at the present site of Cape Town. The base was to serve as a halfway station where company ships could pick up food and water on the way to and from the East Indies. Soon after the base was set up, the company imported slaves—mostly from Southeast Asia—to work on its farms.

In 1657, the Dutch East India Company began to allow some employees to leave the firm and start their own farms. These people became known as *Boers* (farmers). In 1679, the company also began to offer free passage and land to new settlers from Europe. More Dutch farmers, as well as French and German settlers, joined what became known as the Cape Colony. By 1700, whites occupied most of the good farmland around Cape Town. Then they moved into drier areas and became sheep and cattle ranchers. As the white territory expanded, the Khoikhoi and San population declined. The whites killed some Khoikhoi and San, and many others died of smallpox. Most survivors became servants of the whites.

During this period, Dutch became the dominant language in the settlement. The language began to change as it incorporated words and sounds from the languages of other European settlers, and from Southeast Asian slaves and San and Khoikhoi servants. A new language, called *Afrikaans,* developed.

About 1770, the whites began to take land from the black Xhosa, a Bantu-speaking people. Between 1770 and 1870, the settlers and the Xhosa fought several wars in which the settlers took land from the Xhosa.

By 1795, the whites had spread about 300 miles (480 kilometers) north and more than 500 miles (800 kilometers) east of Cape Town. The colony had a total population of about 60,000. Nearly 20,000 were whites. The rest consisted mostly of Khoikhoi, San, and slaves.

British rule. In 1795, France conquered the Netherlands. British troops then occupied the Cape Colony to keep it out of French hands. Britain returned the colony to the Dutch in 1803 but reoccupied it in 1806. In 1814, the Netherlands formally gave the Cape to Britain. The first British settlers arrived in 1820. They expanded the amount of territory occupied by the colony, taking more land from the Xhosa.

The Boers soon came to resent British colonial rule. The government made English the colony's only official language in 1828. That same year, the Khoikhoi and Colored people received equal legal rights with whites. In 1833, Britain abolished slavery throughout its empire, ruining a number of Boer farmers who depended on slave labor to work their fields.

Many Boers decided to leave the Cape Colony to get away from British rule. Beginning in 1836, several thousand of them made a historic journey called the Great Trek. They loaded their belongings into ox-drawn covered wagons and headed inland. Their trek took them across the Orange River into lands occupied by black African peoples. The most powerful black kingdom was Zululand, established between 1818 and 1828 by the Zulu leader Shaka. Shaka's kingdom covered most of what is now the province of KwaZulu-Natal. The Boers defeated the Zulu and the other groups and settled in what became Natal, the Orange Free State, and the Transvaal. Britain annexed Natal in 1843. But it recognized the independence of the Transvaal in 1852 and the Orange Free State in 1854.

Discovery of diamonds and gold. In 1867, a rich diamond field was found near where Kimberley now stands. Miners, fortune seekers, and other people from Britain and other countries flocked to the area. Both the British and the Boers claimed the Kimberley area. In 1871, Britain annexed it, and it became part of the Cape Colony. Britain annexed the Transvaal (then known as the South African Republic) in 1877. Three years later, the Transvaal Boers rose in revolt in the First Boer War. They defeated the British in 1881.

In 1886, the fabulous Witwatersrand gold field was discovered where Johannesburg now stands. Miners and other people rushed to the Transvaal. By 1895, these *Uitlanders* (foreigners) made up about half the Transvaal's white male population. To keep control of the Transvaal, the Boers restricted the political rights of the Uitlanders, most of whom were British. As a result, tension grew between Britain and the Transvaal.

In 1895, Cecil Rhodes, the prime minister of the Cape Colony, plotted to overthrow the Transvaal government. He sent a force under Leander Jameson to invade the country. But the Boers captured the invaders, and the so-called Jameson Raid failed. Relations between Britain and the Transvaal then grew more strained. In 1899, the Transvaal and the Orange Free State declared war on Britain. The Boers fought bravely against huge odds before they finally surrendered in 1902. These Boer republics then became British colonies.

Meanwhile, whites extended their control over the black Africans in the region. Some groups surrendered to the whites without fighting. But other groups, especially the Zulu, resisted. In January 1879, the Zulu army destroyed a British regiment at a mountain called Isandhlwana before a small British force turned them back at Rorke's Drift, near Dundee. Later in 1879, the British defeated the Zulu. By 1898, all the blacks in South Africa had lost their independence.

The Union of South Africa. Britain gave colonial self-government to the Transvaal in 1906 and to the Orange Free State in 1907. The Cape Colony and Natal already had self-rule. In 1910, the four colonies formed the Union of South Africa, a self-governing country within the British Empire. The country's Constitution gave whites almost complete power.

Several nonwhite groups tried to defend themselves against repression by the white minority government. A lawyer from India named Mohandas K. Gandhi worked for greater rights for Indians in South Africa. Gandhi urged the Indians to defy laws that he considered unjust, such as a law requiring all Indians to register and be fingerprinted. Gandhi's efforts, called *civil disobedience,* resulted in the Indians gaining some additional rights, including a law declaring Hindu and Muslim marriages as valid as Christian ones.

Gandhi returned to India in 1914 and became a leader of the nationalist movement there. But his example helped inspire black South Africans to found the South African Native National Congress (SANNC) in 1912. The SANNC's purpose was to work for black rights in South Africa. In 1923, the SANNC shortened its name to the African National Congress (ANC).

During World War I (1914-1918), Britain, Russia, and the other Allies fought the Central Powers, including Austria-Hungary and Germany. Two Boer generals—Louis Botha and Jan Christiaan Smuts—led South African forces against Germany. Botha seized German Southwest Africa (now Namibia) from Germany in 1915, and Smuts drove the Germans from German East Africa (now Tanzania) in 1917. In 1920, the League of Nations, a forerunner of the United Nations, gave South Africa control of Namibia.

Botha and Smuts also were the first two prime ministers of the Union of South Africa. Botha served from 1910 to 1919. Smuts governed from 1919 to 1924, and from 1939 to 1948.

The rise of Afrikaner nationalism. Botha and Smuts had fought the British in the Boer War of 1899-1902. But as prime ministers, they tried to unite Afrikaners (as the Boers came to be called) and English-speaking whites. Many Afrikaner authors and religious leaders, however, urged their people to believe they were a nation to themselves. They said Afrikaners had a heroic history, a rich culture, and a God-given mission to rule South Africa. In 1914, James Barry Munnik Hertzog, another Boer general who had fought the British, founded the National Party to promote these nationalistic ideas.

In 1924, the National Party and the Labour Party joined forces and won control of the government. Hertzog became prime minister. During the next 15 years, he achieved many Afrikaner goals. Afrikaans became an official language in addition to English. Industries were developed to reduce dependence on British imports. In 1931, Britain gave South Africa full independence as a member of the Commonwealth of Nations, an association consisting of Britain and some of its former colonies.

Important dates in South Africa

c. A.D. 300 Bantu-speaking farmers began to enter eastern South Africa from the north. They were the ancestors of present-day South Africa's black population.

1652 The first Dutch settlers arrived at the site of Cape Town.

1814 The Netherlands gave the Cape Colony to Britain.

1818-1828 The Zulu leader Shaka built a powerful kingdom called Zululand in Natal (now KwaZulu-Natal).

1836 Boers left Cape Colony on the Great Trek to Natal, the Orange Free State, and the Transvaal.

1852 The Transvaal became a Boer republic.

1854 The Orange Free State became a Boer republic.

1867 Diamonds were discovered near what is now Kimberley.

1877 Britain annexed the Transvaal.

1879 Britain defeated the Zulu kingdom.

1880-1881 The Transvaal Boers defeated the British in the First Boer War.

1886 Gold was discovered near Johannesburg.

1893-1914 Mohandas K. Gandhi worked for Indian rights in South Africa.

1899-1902 Britain defeated the Boers in the Second Boer War.

1910 The Union of South Africa was formed.

1912 Blacks founded the African National Congress.

1948 The National Party came to power.

1961 South Africa became a republic.

1976 Blacks began widespread protests against the South African government.

1985 Protests followed the adoption of a new constitution that continued to exclude blacks from government.

1990-1991 The South African government repealed the last of the laws that had formed the legal basis of apartheid.

1994 South Africa held its first all-race elections. Nelson Mandela was elected as the nation's first black president.

Hertzog's government favored whites over blacks. At that time, blacks who owned a certain amount of property were permitted to vote in Cape Province. Hertzog's government reduced the blacks' voting rights. The government also passed laws that made it difficult for black Africans to live in cities. In contrast, it made city jobs available for poor Afrikaners, who were leaving their farms in search of work in the cities.

Afrikaner nationalism suffered a setback at the start of World War II (1939-1945). Hertzog wanted South Africa to be neutral. But Smuts wanted the country to join Britain and the other Allies—who eventually included Canada, the United States, and the Soviet Union—against Germany and the other Axis Powers. Smuts won the bitter debate in Parliament and became prime minister again in 1939. During the war, South Africans fought in Ethiopia, northern Africa, and Europe. In 1946, the United Nations (UN) rejected South Africa's request to annex Namibia.

Apartheid. During World War II, Daniel François Malan, a strong supporter of Afrikaner nationalism, reorganized the National Party. The party came to power, under Malan, in 1948. It began the apartheid program. It passed laws that segregated the racial groups and gave the government extensive police powers. In defense of apartheid, the government claimed that black ethnic groups hated each other and would fight a bloody civil war if whites did not keep control.

Opposition to the Nationalists' racial policies grew. The ANC played a main role in this opposition. In the 1950's, the ANC joined other nonwhite groups and white liberals to demand reforms through boycotts, rallies, and strikes. The government crushed each campaign. In 1959, some members left the ANC and formed the Pan-Africanist Congress (PAC) because they opposed the ANC's alliances with white groups. They wanted an all-black government instead. PAC first targeted the laws that required blacks to carry *passes* (identity papers). These laws restricted blacks from moving freely around the country. PAC leaders told blacks to appear on March 21, 1960, at police stations without their passes—and so invite arrest. In most places, the police broke up the crowd without incident. But at Sharpeville, near Johannesburg, the police opened fire and killed 69 blacks. The government then banned both the ANC and PAC.

Opposition to South Africa's system of apartheid also came from outside South Africa. The government especially resented criticism from Britain and other members of the Commonwealth of Nations. On May 31, 1961, South Africa became a republic and left the Commonwealth. (South Africa rejoined the Commonwealth in 1994.) In 1966, the UN voted to end the country's control over Namibia. South Africa called the UN action illegal.

While blacks were being stripped of their political rights in South Africa, they were gaining power in most other parts of Africa. Most European colonies in Africa became independent countries during the 1950's and 1960's.

Since 1958, South Africa's government had been headed by Prime Minister Hendrik F. Verwoerd, a man determined to carry out apartheid. In 1966, a messenger killed Verwoerd as he addressed Parliament. The assassin was mentally ill and apparently had no political motive. Balthazar J. Vorster then became prime minister.

During the 1970's, opposition to white rule of South Africa increased both inside and outside the country. In 1976, blacks in Soweto rioted to protest a policy that required some classes in schools for blacks to be taught in the Afrikaans language. Disturbances followed in many parts of the country, and clashes between blacks and the police took place. About 600 people, most of them blacks, were killed.

In 1978, Vorster resigned as prime minister. Pieter Willem Botha succeeded him.

The dismantling of apartheid. In the late 1970's, the government repealed some apartheid laws. It lifted many restrictions against multiracial sports. It also repealed the *job reservation system,* which had reserved certain jobs for certain races.

South Africa adopted a new constitution in 1984. The Constitution set up a three-house Parliament, with one house each for whites, Colored people, and Asians. The Constitution combined the offices and powers of the prime minister and state president under the office of state president. Prime Minister Botha became state president.

The new Constitution, like the one it replaced, made no provision for black representation in Parliament or in other parts of the national government. Also, like the old Constitution, it excluded blacks from voting in national elections. Many blacks staged demonstrations, and some rioted, to protest their exclusion from the government. Clashes between blacks and the police broke out again. Many people, mostly blacks, were killed in the conflicts. Some blacks accused other blacks of collaborating with the government. They attacked many of those they accused, resulting in deaths, injuries, and property damage.

In 1985, the government declared states of emergency in numerous areas. It declared a national state of emergency in 1986. Under the state of emergency, the government was allowed to arrest and hold people without a charge. The state of emergency ended in 1990.

Many countries expressed opposition to apartheid by reducing economic ties with South Africa. In 1986, the European Community, the Commonwealth of Nations, and the United States enacted *sanctions* (bans) on certain kinds of trade with South Africa. Some companies

Mike Persson, Gamma/Liaison

Nelson Mandela, *left,* takes the oath of office for the presidency of South Africa in May 1994. Mandela was elected president in the country's first elections open to all races.

announced that they would end or limit their business in South Africa.

In 1986, the South African government repealed more apartheid laws. It permitted nonwhites to attend "white" universities that were willing to admit them. The government also permitted interracial marriages, which apartheid laws had forbidden. In addition, it repealed the laws requiring blacks to carry passes. The government also made it legal for blacks to live in cities without special permission. As a result, more than 1 million blacks moved to the cities. But many apartheid regulations continued. Some public schools and neighborhoods remained segregated. Blacks were still excluded from participation in government.

In the late 1970's and in the 1980's, representatives of the South African government and the United Nations discussed plans for independence for Namibia. In 1990, Namibia gained full independence from South Africa.

In 1989, F. W. de Klerk became state president. De Klerk realized that minority rule could not continue in South Africa without great risk of civil war.

In February 1990, de Klerk released Nelson Mandela, the most famous member of the ANC, from prison. Mandela had been sentenced to life in prison in 1964 for sabotage and conspiracy against the South African government. The government had kept Mandela in prison since 1962. While in prison, Mandela had become a symbol of the black struggle for racial justice. Shortly before Mandela's release, the government lifted its bans on political organizations, including the ANC and PAC. In May 1990, the South African government held its first formal talks with the ANC. Mandela met with President de Klerk several times after that to discuss political change in South Africa.

In the early 1990's, much fighting occurred among rival groups in South Africa. Some of the fighting was between blacks who wanted majority rule immediately and whites who wanted to keep their power. Other fighting was among blacks. The Zulu-based Inkatha Freedom Party, which had made peace with the white-led government, did not want the government to be run by the ANC, which was dominated by the Xhosa. Thousands of people were killed in the conflicts.

In 1990 and 1991, the South African government repealed the remaining laws that had formed the legal basis of apartheid. In December 1991, the South African government, the ANC, and other groups began holding talks on a new constitution. In December 1993, the government adopted an interim constitution that gave South Africa's blacks full voting rights. The country held its first elections open to all races in April 1994. The ANC won nearly two-thirds of the seats in the National Assembly, and the Assembly then elected Nelson Mandela president. An ANC leader named Thabo Mbeki became first deputy president, and de Klerk became second deputy president.

The chief task of the new government, which would serve until 1999, was to write a permanent constitution. The government pledged to address the problems brought on by apartheid. It promised to improve education, housing, public utilities, and health care for nonwhites. It also vowed to increase the employment rate and to redistribute land so that nonwhites would have a larger share. Bruce Fetter

Related articles in *World Book* include:

Biographies

Barnard, Christiaan N.	Fugard, Athol	Mandela, Winnie
Biko, Steve	Gandhi, Mohandas K.	Rhodes, Cecil J.
Botha, Louis	Gordimer, Nadine	Smuts, Jan Christiaan
Botha, Pieter W.	Kruger, Paulus	Tutu, Desmond
Broom, Robert	Luthuli, Albert J.	Vorster, Balthazar
De Klerk, Frederik Willem	Mandela, Nelson	

Cities

Bloemfontein	Kimberley
Cape Town	Pietermaritzburg
Durban	Port Elizabeth
Johannesburg	Pretoria

Other related articles

Africa	Cape Province	San
African National Congress	Kalahari Desert	Transvaal
Afrikaans language	Khoikhoi	United Nations
Apartheid	Lesotho	(Problems in
Bantu	Limpopo River	southern
Boer War	Namibia	Africa)
Boers	Natal	Walvis Bay
Cape of Good Hope	Orange Free State	Xhosa
	Orange River	Zulu

Outline

I. Government
    A. National government   C. Political parties
    B. Provincial government   D. Armed forces
II. People
    A. Population and ancestry   E. Recreation
    B. Languages   F. Education
    C. Ways of life   G. Religion
    D. Food and drink   H. The arts
III. Land
    A. The Plateau
    B. The Coastal Strip
    C. The Cape Mountains Region
    D. The Namib and Kalahari deserts
    E. Rivers
IV. Climate
V. Economy
    A. Natural resources   F. Fishing industry
    B. Service industries   G. Energy sources
    C. Manufacturing   H. International trade
    D. Mining   I. Transportation
    E. Agriculture   J. Communication
VI. History

Questions

How did South Africa achieve spectacular industrial growth?
What land region covers most of South Africa's interior?
What was apartheid? How did it affect blacks in South Africa?
Who were the Boers?
How does South Africa rank economically in Africa?
How does life differ among South Africa's racial groups?
What was the Great Trek?
What are some of the black ethnic groups in South Africa?
When was the African National Congress founded?
How did the government elected in 1994 plan to address some of the problems facing South Africa?

Additional resources

Everist, Richard, and Murray, Jon. *South Africa, Lesotho & Swaziland: A Travel Survival Kit.* Lonely Planet Pubns., 1993.
Ottaway, David. *Chained Together: Mandela, De Klerk, and the Struggle to Remake South Africa.* Random Hse., 1993.
Ottaway, Marina. *South Africa: The Struggle for a New Order.* Brookings, 1993.
Rosmarin, Ike. *South Africa.* Cavendish, 1993. Younger readers.
Thompson, Leonard M. *A History of South Africa.* Yale, 1990.

Robert Frerck, Odyssey Productions

Bangkok, a booming metropolis on the Chao Praya River, is Thailand's capital and largest city. Its landmarks include the ornate towers of the Grand Palace, *above.*

Thailand

Thailand, *TY land,* is a tropical country in Southeast Asia. The people of Thailand are called Thai. Most are farmers and live in small, rural villages. However, Thailand has one of the fastest growing economies in the world, and its urban centers have expanded rapidly. Almost 6 million people live in Bangkok, Thailand's capital and largest city.

Thailand is the only nation in Southeast Asia that has never been ruled by a Western power. The Thai people date their history from A.D. 1238, when the Sukhothai Kingdom was founded in what is now Thailand. For most of its history, the country was called Siam. In 1939, it officially adopted the name Thailand.

Government

National government. Thailand is a constitutional monarchy, a form of government in which the constitution limits the power of the king or queen. The nation's Constitution provides for a monarch, a prime minister, and a legislature called the National Assembly. The monarch has an advisory role as head of state, and the prime minister heads the government.

The National Assembly consists of the House of Representatives with 360 members and the Senate with 270 members. The House members are elected by the people of Thailand and serve four-year terms. The senators

The contributors of this article are Charles Keyes, Professor of Anthropology and Director of Southeast Asian Studies at the University of Washington, and Jane Keyes, a writer and editor on Southeast Asia.

are chosen by the ruling parties in the House and are formally appointed by the monarch. Senators serve six-year terms. The National Assembly selects the prime minister, who is then formally appointed by the monarch. The prime minister selects the Cabinet, which has a maximum of 48 members.

Local government. Thailand is divided into 73 provinces. The provinces, in turn, are subdivided into 655 districts, 6,600 units of local government called *tambons,* and almost 60,000 villages. Each province has a governor, and every district has a district officer. These officials are appointed by the minister of the interior.

Facts in brief

Capital: Bangkok.
Official language: Thai (Central dialect).
Official name: Pratet Thai.
Area: 198,115 sq. mi. (513,115 km²). *Greatest distances*—north-south, 1,100 mi. (1,770 km); east-west, 480 mi. (772 km). *Coastline*—1,625 mi. (2,615 km).
Elevation: *Highest*—Inthanon Mountain, 8,514 ft. (2,595 m). *Lowest*—sea level.
Population: *Estimated 1995 population*—58,265,000; density, 294 persons per sq. mi. (114 per km²); distribution, 75 percent rural, 25 percent urban. *1990 census*—54,532,300. *Estimated 2000 population*—61,202,000.
Chief products: *Agriculture*—cassava, corn, pineapples, rice, rubber, sugar cane. *Manufacturing*—automobiles, cement, electronic goods, food products, plastics, textiles. *Fishing*—herring, tuna, shrimp and other shellfish. *Mining*—copper, iron ore, lead, natural gas, precious stones, tin, zinc.
Money: *Basic unit*—baht. For its price in U.S. dollars, see **Money** (table: Exchange rates).

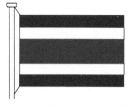

Thailand's flag was adopted in 1917. The red represents the nation; the white, purity; and the blue, the monarchy.

The national emblem, adopted in 1910, shows the *garuda,* a birdlike creature of Southeast Asian mythology.

Tourism Authority of Thailand

Wat Phrathat Doi Suthep is a Buddhist temple near Chiang Mai. Its gilded tower dates from the 1300's.

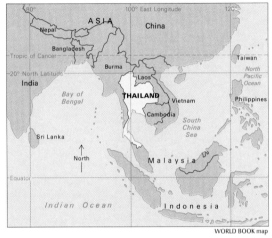

WORLD BOOK map

Thailand is a country that lies mostly in mainland Southeast Asia. Southern Thailand extends down the Malay Peninsula.

Thai villages range in size from a few hundred to a few thousand people. Each village elects a *headman* to be its leader. The people within each tambon then select from among the village headmen a *kamnan,* or chief administrator, for their tambon.

Politics. Thai citizens 20 years old or older have the right to vote. Thai political parties, however, have most often come to power through a military *coup* (revolt against the ruling party) rather than through popular elections. Traditionally, Thai political parties have been organized around leaders rather than common political philosophies, and few parties have had lasting strength.

Courts. The Supreme Court, the highest court, consists of a chief justice and 21 judges. The entire court meets only for special cases. The Court of Appeals, the second highest court, reviews decisions made by lower courts. A panel called the Judicial Commission chooses all Thai judges. The judges are approved by the prime minister and formally appointed by the king.

The armed forces of Thailand consist of an army, a navy, and an air force. The forces have a total membership of about 283,000. Men from 21 to 30 years old may be drafted for at least two years of military duty. Women may serve on a voluntary basis.

The people

Population and ancestry. Thailand has about 58 million people. About 75 percent of the people live in rural

areas, and only about 25 percent live in towns and cities. In addition to Bangkok, which has almost 6 million people, Thailand's largest cities include Khon-kaen, Nakhon Ratchasima, Nanthanburi, and Songkhla, each with a population over 200,000.

Most of Thailand's people belong to the Thai ethnic group. Chinese people make up the second largest population group. The next largest groups consist of Malays and Khmers. Small ethnic groups include the Hmong, the Karen, and other isolated hill peoples in the far north and northwest, and a number of Indians and Vietnamese.

Way of life. Each Thai village has a *wat* (Buddhist temple-monastery), which serves as the religious and social center of the community. Village life in Thailand traditionally has been organized around religious and agricultural rituals and festivals. But now radio and television also have a strong influence.

Since the early 1960's, large numbers of Thai—especially young adults—have moved from rural areas to cities in search of jobs and educational opportunities. As a result, a large educated middle class has emerged in Bangkok and other cities. But Thai cities have had to cope with serious problems caused by rapid population growth. Such problems include crowded living conditions, traffic jams, pollution, the growth of prostitution, and the spread of AIDS.

Most Thai people wear the same clothing styles worn in Western countries. For special or formal occasions, however, they often wear traditional Thai clothing made of such fabrics as Thai silk, Hmong embroidery, and *batik* (a special dye process).

Housing. Most Thai villagers live in traditional wood houses that are on stilts. The houses are built 7 to 10 feet (2 to 3 meters) above the ground mainly for protection against floods. In towns and cities, houses are typically made of stucco or concrete and are not on stilts. Middle-class Thai, especially in Bangkok, live in apartments,

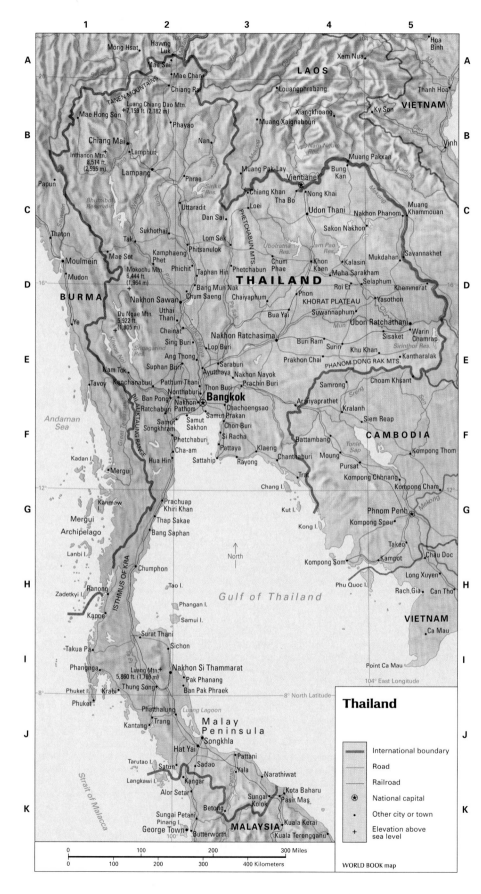

Thailand map index

Cities and towns

Ayutthaya	........51,628..E	2
Ban Pak		
Phraek	.........22,625..I	2
Ban Pong	.....25,047..E	2
Bangkok	...5,876,000..E	2
Buri Ram	.....25,899..E	4
Chachoengsao	....37,931..F	3
Chaiyaphum	...20,932..D	3
Chanthaburi	....30,242..F	3
Chiang Mai	....167,000..B	1
Chiang Rai	....40,641..A	2
Chon Buri	......50,070..F	3
Hat Yai	.........98,091..J	2
Hua Hin	.......30,415..F	2
Kalasin	.........22,152..D	4
Kamphaeng		
Phet	.........20,200..D	2
Kanchanaburi	...29,502..E	2
Khon Kaen	...206,000..D	4
Lampang	.......43,112..B	2
Lop Buri	......36,928..E	3
Mae Sot	.......18,719..D	1
Maha		
Sarakham	....32,989..D	4
Mukdahan*	...........D	5
Nakhon		
Pathom	.....45,242..F	2
Nakhon		
Phanom	....33,237..C	5
Nakhon		
Ratchasima	..278,000..E	3
Nakhon Sawan	..152,000..D	2
Nakhon Si		
Thammarat	...112,000..I	2
Nan	.............22,564..B	3
Narathiwat	....32,146..K	3
Nong Khai	....25,032..C	4
Nonthaburi	...233,000..E	2
Pattani	.........32,020..J	3
Pattaya*	............F	3
Phatthalung	...29,948..J	2
Phayao	.......24,400..B	2
Phetchabun	...23,763..D	3
Phetchaburi	...34,597..F	2
Phichit	.........18,675..D	2
Phitsanulok	...73,240..C	2
Phrae	.........19,872..B	2
Phuket	.........45,155..J	1
Prachin Buri	...20,330..E	3
Ratchaburi	....43,316..F	2
Rayong	.......37,305..F	3
Roi Et	.........31,223..D	4
Sakon Nakhon	..24,491..C	4
Samut Prakan	..48,960..F	3
Samut Sakhon	..47,697..F	2
Samut		
Songkhram	...30,419..F	2
Saraburi	.....107,000..E	3
Si Racha	.....21,651..F	3
Sisaket	.........19,823..E	5
Songkhla	....243,000..J	2
Sukhothai	....21,931..C	2
Sungai Kolok	..21,917..K	3
Suphan Buri	...22,903..E	2
Surat Thani	....35,678..I	2
Surin	.............33,737..E	4
Tak	.............20,039..C	2
Trang	.............44,102..J	2
Ubon		
Ratchathani	..137,000..D	5
Udon Thani	....81,060..C	4
Uttaradit	......33,311..C	3
Warin		
Chamrap	....29,586..D	5
Yala	.............49,283..J	3
Yasothon	....19,007..D	5

Physical features

Bhumibol Reservoir	C	1
Bilauktaung Range	.......F	2
Chang Island	...........G	3
Chao Phraya (river)	......E	2
Chi (river)	...........D	5
Du Ngae Mountain	......E	1
Gulf of Thailand	..........H	3
Inthanon Mountain	......B	1
Isthmus of Kra	...........H	1
Khorat Plateau	..........D	4
Khwae Noi (river)	........E	1
Kut Island	...............G	3
Luang Mountain	I	2
Luang Chiang Dao		
Mountain	...........B	1
Luang Lagoon	...........J	2
Malay Peninsula	.........J	2
Mekong (river)	C	5
Mokochu Mountain	......D	2
Mun (river)	...........D	4
Nan (river)	...........B	3
Pa Sak (river)	...........D	3
Phangan Island	.........H	2
Phanom Dong		
Rak Mountains	.........E	4
Phetchabun		
Mountains	C	3
Phuket Island	I	1
Ping (river)	.............B	1
Samui Island	.............H	2
Srinagarind		
Reservoir	...............E	2
Ta Pi (river)	I	2
Tanen Mountains	........A	2
Wang (river)	C	2
Yom (river)	C	2

*Population figure unavailable.
Source: 1990 census for the 10 largest cities; 1980 census for all other places.

condominiums, or large developments of single-family homes. Some shop owners reside above their shops. The government provides limited housing for the urban poor, many of whom end up living in slums.

Food. Thai people eat rice with almost every meal. Favorite foods to accompany the rice include hot, spicy stews called curries; salads of meat, fish, and vegetables; stir-fried dishes; and broiled or fried fish with sauces. Flavorful, spicy Thai food has become popular in many parts of the world.

Recreation. Thai people prize the art of *sanuk,* or having fun. The national sport is *muay Thai* (Thai boxing), also known as kickboxing, in which opponents fight with their feet as well as their hands. In another popular sport, called *takraw,* the players try to keep a ball made of *rattan* (woven palm stems) in the air by using their heads, legs, and feet. Many Thai enjoy gambling on the lottery, cockfights, and fightingfish contests.

Languages. Thai, the language spoken by almost all people in Thailand, has four main dialects. The Central Thai dialect is the official language and is taught in the schools. Many people in Thailand speak the Central Thai dialect in addition to their own regional or ethnic dialect. Many people also speak Malay or Chinese. English is taught in many schools and is often used in business and government affairs.

Religion. About 95 percent of the Thai people are Buddhists. Generally, Buddhists believe that people can obtain perfect peace and happiness by freeing themselves from worldly desires. Most Thai people follow the *Theravada* (Way of the Elders) tradition, an ancient form of Buddhism that emphasizes the virtues of monastic life. According to custom, many Thai men become monks for at least a short period, from about one week to several months. They wear yellow robes and lead lives of poverty, meditation, and study.

Most Chinese in Thailand follow Confucianism in addition to practicing other religions. The majority of Thailand's Malays are Muslims. Hinduism is the main religion among Indians in Thailand. Only about 1 percent of the nation's people are Christians.

Education. More than 85 percent of Thailand's people 15 and older can read and write. Thai law requires

© Horst Gossler, The Stock House

Thai boxing, known as *muay Thai* or *kickboxing,* is the national sport. Opponents fight with their feet as well as their hands.

children to attend school from age 7 to 14. The government provides free public education, but some students attend private schools. Only a small percentage of Thai students continue schooling beyond the required years. Thailand has 15 universities, several large institutes of technology, dozens of teachers' colleges, and numerous vocational colleges.

The arts in Thailand are greatly influenced by Buddhism. The country's Buddhist temples display some of the finest Thai architecture. The image of Buddha appears in many Thai paintings and sculptures. Modern Thai painting includes traditional religious themes and international styles.

Traditional Thai literature was written and performed for royalty and consisted of classical dramas and epic poems. Today, Thai classical dancers wear spectacular costumes and act out such traditional legends in performances called *khon* drama.

The land

Thailand covers 198,115 square miles (513,115 square kilometers). The country has four main land regions: (1) the Mountainous North, (2) the Khorat Plateau, (3) the Central Plain, and (4) the Southern Peninsula.

Saul Lockhardt, Advertasia Co., Ltd.

Middle-class housing in Thailand consists mainly of small, single-family dwellings. These houses belong to a housing development in a suburb of Bangkok.

Saul Lockhardt, Advertasia Co., Ltd.
Thai classical dancers act out traditional stories with religious themes. Jewels and embroidery decorate their costumes.

The Mountainous North. Mountains occupy part of northern Thailand and extend along the country's western border to the Malay Peninsula. Inthanon Mountain, Thailand's highest peak, is in this region. The mountain rises 8,514 feet (2,595 meters) above sea level. Forests of evergreen trees and some broadleaf trees, such as teak, cover most of the region. The mountains are broken by rivers running south. These rivers form narrow, fertile valleys where farmers grow rice and other crops.

The Khorat Plateau, also known as Isan, lies in the northeastern part of Thailand and makes up about one-third of the country's land area. Mountain ranges separate the plateau from central Thailand to the west and Cambodia to the south. The Mekong River forms the region's northern and eastern boundaries. Two other rivers, the Chi and the Mun, also run through the region.

Edward S. Ross
The Mountainous North region includes Thailand's highest peak, 8,514-foot (2,595-meter) Inthanon Mountain, *background.* In the foreground is a dwelling of the region's Hmong people.

But generally, the area is dry with sandy soil that makes poor farmland.

The Central Plain extends from the foothills of the north to the Gulf of Thailand. Its soil is so fertile that farmers raise more rice there than anywhere else in Thailand. Four rivers—the Nan, Ping, Wang, and Yom—unite in the plain and become the Chao Phraya River. The Chao Phraya, Thailand's main river, provides both irrigation and transportation.

The Southern Peninsula shares its northwestern border with Burma and extends south to Malaysia. This region of Thailand consists mainly of jungle and mountains. Narrow plains run along the coast. Fishing, rubber production, and tin mining in the region contribute much to the Thai economy.

Animal life. Thailand's forests once abounded with elephants, tigers, wild pigs, deer, crocodiles, king cobras and other snakes, and many varieties of birds. But since the mid-1900's, many species of wildlife in Thailand have become endangered. These animals are threatened with extinction, in part because thousands have been killed for profit. In addition, agriculture and industry have destroyed many of Thailand's forests. Some Thai families make pets of such wild animals as monkeys, catlike mammals called civets, and squirrels.

Climate

Thailand has a tropical climate. Most of the country has three seasons—a hot, dry season from March to May; a hot, wet period from June to October; and a cool, dry season from November to February. Bangkok has an average temperature of 77 °F (25 °C) in December and 86 °F (30 °C) in April. The mountain areas are cooler.

From late May to October, winds called *monsoons* cause heavy rains throughout Thailand. The Southern Peninsula region may receive more than 100 inches (254 centimeters) of rain in one year. Bangkok has an average annual rainfall of 55 inches (140 centimeters).

Economy

Thailand's economy developed rapidly in the 1980's and early 1990's. Today, Thailand has one of the fastest growing economies in the world.

The Thai economy is based on free enterprise, in which businesses operate largely free of government control. About 65 percent of the nation's workers make their living by farming or fishing, and only about 10 percent work in manufacturing. However, manufactured goods contribute more to the national income than agricultural products do. Government, education, trade, transportation, and other service industries employ large numbers of people in Thailand. Other Thai people work in construction and mining. Forestry, especially the harvesting of teak, was formerly important to Thailand's economy. But the government banned logging in 1988 because too many trees had been removed.

Agriculture. Farmland makes up about 45 percent of the nation's land. The chief crop is rice. Other leading farm products include *cassava* (a potatolike plant used to make tapioca), corn, cotton, *jute* (a fiber plant used in making rope and gunnysacks), pineapples, rubber, silk, soybeans, sugar cane, and tobacco. Farms in Thailand average about 10 acres (4 hectares), and about 75 percent of the farmers own their land.

Manufacturing first gained importance in Thailand in the 1970's, when the Thai government began expanding industries that would increase international trade, particularly with Japan. Thailand's main manufactured products include automobiles, cement, electronic goods, food products, plastics, and textiles.

Fishing has always been a mainstay of the Thai economy. Many farmers raise fish in ponds. Commercial fisheries in the south and southeast fish by *trawling,* pulling a funnel-shaped net through the sea. Fisheries also raise shrimp and other shellfish for sale worldwide.

Mining. Tin and zinc are Thailand's most important minerals. The nation ranks among the world's leading tin producers. Thailand also has copper, iron ore, and lead. Large amounts of natural gas lie under the Gulf of Thailand. Rubies and sapphires are mined in central Thailand, and many other precious stones are brought in from Cambodia and Burma.

Tourism contributes greatly to Thailand's national income. Millions of tourists visit each year to see the country's magnificent temples, interesting historical sites, beaches, and exciting night life.

International trade. Chief exports of Thailand include electronic goods, fish products, precious stones, rice, rubber, sugar, tapioca products, textiles, and tin. The nation's major imports include automobile parts, chemicals, fertilizers, fuels, iron and steel, and machinery. In the past, Thailand relied on the United States for much economic support. But today, Thailand carries on brisk trade with other Asian nations as well. Germany, Japan, Singapore, and the United States rank as its main trading partners.

Transportation in Thailand includes extensive road and railroad systems. Bus lines reach nearly every part of the country, and the state-owned railroads fan out in all directions from Bangkok. Rivers and canals in Thailand provide local transportation for passengers and cargo. Bangkok is the country's largest and busiest port. The city struggles with major traffic problems caused by rapid population growth.

Bangkok International Airport provides daily flights

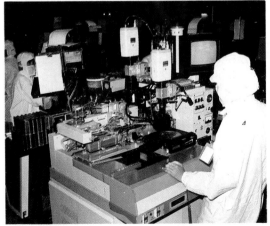

Chinteik Electronic Industries Co., Ltd.

Electronic equipment is manufactured in Thailand. Above, a worker operates machinery that produces integrated circuits—devices used in such equipment as computers and televisions.

between Thailand and other Asian nations, the United States, various European countries, and Australia. Several other Thai cities have international as well as domestic air service.

Communication. Thailand has dozens of daily newspapers, many of which are published in Bangkok. Most of the newspapers are published in the Thai language. Several are in Chinese, and a few are in English. The newspapers are privately owned. However, the government runs nearly all of the television and radio stations. Telephone services link most cities and towns, but many rural residents still lack phones.

History

People have lived in what is now Thailand for thousands of years. By the A.D. 1000's, people known as the Tai had begun migrating from what is now southern China into mainland Southeast Asia. There, the Tai came in contact with Mon and Khmer peoples who had long lived in the region. The Tai adopted Buddhism from the Mon and many Hindu practices from the Khmer. Foreigners began calling this region Syam as early as the 1000's. Later, the area became known as Siam and its people Siamese, still hundreds of years before the country officially adopted that name.

Early kingdoms. The people of Thailand date their history from the founding of a kingdom called Sukhothai (pronounced *soo KOH ty*) in 1238. The Tai people who had established the kingdom began calling themselves the Thai, meaning *free.* Sukhothai's most famous ruler, King Ramkhamhaeng (*rahm kahm HANG*), reigned from about 1279 to 1317 and greatly expanded the Thai territory. Historians also credit Ramkhamhaeng with developing a writing system for the Thai language. A form of his alphabet is still used today.

In 1350, the Thai kingdom of Ayutthaya (*ah YOOT tah yah*) was established. The capital, also called Ayutthaya, sat on an island in the Chao Phraya River, an ideal place for trade and defense. Within a century, Ayutthaya became more powerful than the kingdom of Sukhothai.

European contact began for the Thai in 1511, when Portuguese traders settled in Ayutthaya. During the next century, Dutch, English, Spanish, and French traders and missionaries entered the area. Ayutthayan kings also allowed settlements of Chinese and Japanese and sent government representatives to countries as distant as France and the Netherlands. However, many Thai became alarmed at the foreigners' growing influence in their kingdom. Partly as a result, Ayutthaya began to limit its relations with the West after 1688.

Throughout much of its over 400-year rule, Ayutthaya was at war with its neighbors—the Khmer to the east and the Burmese to the west. The Burmese, Ayutthaya's chief enemy, destroyed the capital in early 1767.

The Bangkok era. In late 1767, a military commander named Taksin drove out the Burmese and established a new Thai capital at Thon Buri, on the west bank of the Chao Phraya River. Taksin brought to the region many Chinese traders who helped rebuild the country's economy. After Taksin was overthrown in 1782, a general known as Chaophraya Chakri became king and ruled for 27 years. The new king took the name Rama I and established the Chakri *dynasty* (line of rulers), which still reigns today. During his reign, the capital was moved across the Chao Phraya River to Bangkok.

Modernization gained speed under two of the Chakri dynasty's most influential monarchs, King Mongkut (*mawng KOOT*) and King Chulalongkorn (*chu lah LAWNG kawn*). Mongkut, also known as Rama IV, ruled from 1851 to 1868. Before taking the throne, Mongkut had served as a monk for 27 years and had led a movement to reform Thai Buddhism. He also studied Western languages and science and, as king, appointed Western advisers to his court. The musical comedy *The King and I* is based on the journals of a British governess whom Mongkut hired to teach his children. The musical portrays Mongkut as a comic figure, and most Thai people consider it a distortion of history.

Mongkut signed many treaties with Western powers, greatly expanding trade and other relations that had been severely limited for over 100 years. The Western powers established several colonies in Southeast Asia. Siam was never colonized, but Mongkut was forced to grant the Western countries *extraterritorial rights*. These rights allowed them to set up courts of law for their people in Siam.

King Chulalongkorn (Rama V), who reigned from 1868 to 1910, is regarded as one of Thailand's greatest kings. With the help of several of his brothers in key government positions, Chulalongkorn furthered Thai modernization. He oversaw a complete reorganization of the government, which included establishing a cabinet to help the monarch rule. He also abolished slavery in Siam, introduced a modern school system, and built railroads and telegraphs linking the country.

King Vajiravudh (*wah jee rah WOOT*), or Rama VI, succeeded Chulalongkorn in 1910. Under him, Siam entered World War I in 1917 to help France, Britain, and the other Allies against Germany and Austria-Hungary. In return for Siam's support, Western powers gradually agreed to give up their extraterritorial rights. When King Vajiravudh died in 1925, the throne passed to his brother Prajadhipok (*prah JAH tee pohk*), or Rama VII.

Changes in government. In mid-1932, a group of Thai, many of whom had been educated in Europe, revolted against King Prajadhipok. Pridi Phanomyong (*pree dee pah nawm yawng*), a lawyer, and Phibun Songkhram (*pee boon sawng krahm*), an artillery officer, led the revolt. They forced the king to change the government from an absolute monarchy to a constitutional monarchy in late 1932, thus limiting the power of the king.

After the coup, a civilian government initially ruled Thailand. But from 1933 to 1938, the military increased its power. King Prajadhipok gave up the throne in 1935 to his nephew, Ananda Mahidol (*ah NAHN dah mah hee dawn*), Rama VIII. Phibun became prime minister in 1938 and ran a military government. The country's name was changed to Thailand in 1939.

In World War II (1939-1945), Germany, Japan, and other Axis powers fought the Allies, who included Britain, China, the Soviet Union, and the United States. In 1941, Japan invaded Thailand. Japan planned to use Thailand as a base to attack Burma, Malaya (now part of Malaysia), and Singapore, three countries then under British rule. At first, Thailand resisted. But Phibun decided to cooperate, and Japan took over Thailand's harbors, airports, and railroads.

As the war progressed, the Thai people began to resent Japanese control. Thailand's external trade halted, and the Thai economy suffered. In 1942, some Thai officials began a Free Thai Movement to work against the Japanese. With the support of Allied countries, the Free Thai gained influence within the Thai government. The National Assembly forced Phibun out of office in 1944.

Opposition to Communism. From 1944 to 1947, Thailand had civilian-led governments. The country's name was changed back to Siam for a few years after World War II ended. In 1946, King Ananda Mahidol was found dead of a gunshot wound. Some people believe his death was an accident, and others believe he was assassinated. His brother Bhumibol Adulyadej (*poo mee PAWN ah dool YAH deh*) became king.

Thailand came under military dictatorship from 1948 to 1973. During this time, Phibun and a series of other military leaders ruled. Worldwide, this period marked the height of the Cold War, an intense rivalry between Communist and non-Communist nations. Under military rule, Thailand increased its opposition to Communism and strengthened its alliance with the United States. The United States provided Thailand with much economic and military aid, and Thailand allowed the United States to use military bases on Thai territory. The United States used these bases to attack Communist forces in North Vietnam, Cambodia, and Laos during the Vietnam War (1957-1975).

In 1967, Thailand, Indonesia, Malaysia, the Philippines, and Singapore formed the Association of Southeast Asian Nations (ASEAN). ASEAN promotes economic, cultural, and social cooperation.

Democracy gains strength. In 1973, university students in Thailand led a successful revolt against the Thai government. They demanded democratic rights and an end to military dictatorship. For the next three years, Thailand experimented with parliamentary democracy. However, in October 1976, the military again seized power after violent student demonstrations took place in Bangkok. Numerous students were killed, and many others fled to the jungle, where they joined Communist forces. From 1976 through 1979, the military ruled Thailand, but with more openness to democratic policies.

From 1980 to 1991, Thailand's governments were democratically elected, but the military maintained much power. General Prem Tinsulanonda (*praym TIHN soo lah nawn*) became prime minister in 1980 and continued Thailand's openness to democracy. About a million refugees had fled to Thailand from Cambodia, Laos, and Vietnam after the Vietnam War ended in 1975. Prem's government provided Thailand with the political stability it needed to temporarily shelter these newcomers until many of them returned to their homes in the early 1990's. Political stability also helped Thailand develop a strong economy. In the late 1980's, the Thai economy grew an average of 12 percent per year.

In February 1991, the military took control of the government, dissolved the National Assembly, and suspended the Constitution. Thailand adopted a new constitution later that year. In March 1992, a group of promilitary parties won control of the National Assembly in parliamentary elections, and a general was appointed prime minister. Many Thai protested this appointment. A civilian leader became prime minister in September.   Charles Keyes and Jane Keyes

Index

How to use the index

This index covers the contents of the 1993, 1994, and 1995 editions of *The World Book Year Book*.

Each index entry gives the edition year and the page number or numbers—for example, **Slovenia, 95:** 170. This means that information on this country may be found on page 170 of the 1995 *Year Book*.

When there are many references to a topic, they are grouped alphabetically by clue words under the main topic. For example, the clue words under **Smoking** group the references to that topic under numerous subtopics.

When a topic such as **SOCIAL SECURITY** appears in all capital letters, this means that there is a *Year Book* Update article entitled Social Security in at least one of the three volumes covered by this index. References to the topic in other articles may also appear after the topic name.

When only the first letter of a topic, such as **Solar energy**, is capitalized, this means that there is no article entitled Solar energy, but that information on this topic may be found in the edition and on the pages listed.

The indication (il.) means that the reference is to an illustration only, as in the **Solzhenitsyn, Alexander** picture on page 359 of the 1995 edition.

An index entry followed by *WBE* refers to a new or revised *World Book Encyclopedia* article in the supplement section, as in **SOUTH AFRICA, 95:** 498. This means that a *World Book Encyclopedia* article on South Africa begins on page 498 of the 1995 *Year Book*.

The "see" and "see also" cross references—for example, **South Korea.** See **Korea, South**,—refer the reader to other entries in the index.

Index

A

Aamodt, Kjetil-Andre, 95: 364, 365, **94:** 378
Abacha, Sani, 95: 40, 319-320, **94:** 318
ABC. See **American Broadcasting Companies**
Abdel Rahman, Omar, 94: 123, 158, 191, 244, 313
Abdic, Fikret, 94: 100
Abiola, Moshood, 95: 40, 319, **94:** 318
Abkhazia, 95: 235, **94:** 214, **93:** 251
Aborigines, 94: 82
Abortion: advertising, **93:** 38; Australia, **93:** 92; clinic murders, **95:** 151, 159, 343; Clinton policy, **95:** 431, 94: 142, 337; Ireland, **94:** 244, **93:** 284; Islam, **95:** 253; laws and court cases, **95:** 151, 393, **94:** 153, 389, 404, **93:** 159, 430, 432; pill, **95:** 193-194; Poland, **95:** 337; Protestantism, **95:** 343, **94:** 339, **93:** 402; Republican Party, **95:** 411; Roman Catholic Church, **93:** 413
Abouhalima, Mahmud, 95: 151
Abu Musa (island), 95: 251, **93:** 282, 334
Aburto Martínez, Mario, 95: 301
Academy Awards, 95: 309, **94:** 300, **93:** 339
Acadians, 95: 118
Accidents. See **Disasters; Safety**
ACE inhibitors, 93: 200
Ace Ventura, Pet Detective (film), **95:** 309-310
Achille Lauro (ship), **95:** 323
Achtenberg, Roberta, 94: 428
Acid rain, 95: 452
Acquired immunodeficiency syndrome. See **AIDS**
Adams, Gerry, 95: 321, **94:** 320
Adams, John, 95: 134
Addiction. See **Alcoholism; Drug abuse; Smoking**
Addis Ababa, Ethiopia, 94: 380, 381
Aden. See **Yemen**
Adhikari, Mana Mohan, 95: 80
Adolescents, 95: 50, 299, 446, **94:** 133, 184, 340
Adoption, 95: 391, **94:** 156, 227
ADVERTISING, 93: 38
Advisory Committee on Human Radiation Experiments, 95: 348, 353
Aegean Sea (tanker), **93:** 219
Aerospace industry. See **Aviation; Space exploration**
AFDC. See **Aid to Families with Dependent Children**
Afeworke, Issaias, 94: 197
Affirmative action. See **Civil rights**
AFGHANISTAN, 93: 39; civil war, **95:** 76, 80 (il.), **94:** 64, **93:** 84; Pakistan, **94:** 64, **93:** 39; refugees, **94:** 63; tables, **95:** 78, **94:** 62, **93:** 86
AFL-CIO. See **American Federation of Labor and Congress of Industrial Organizations**
AFRICA, 95: 38-45, **94:** 38-44, **93:** 40-45; AIDS, **95:** 44-45, 50-51, 55, 393, **94:** 40, 46, **93:** 45; canine distemper virus, **95:** 452-453; conservation, **95:** 149; human origins, **93:** 48; Roman Catholic conference, **95:** 357
African Americans: African Summit, **94:** 40; Anderson, Marian, **94:** 175-177; census, **94:** 115; colonial burial ground, **93:** 49-50; disability benefits, **93:** 420; gangs, **94:** 136; imprisonment, **95:** 342, **94:** 339; Judaism, **95:** 259; literature, **94:** 278, **93:** 315; Postal Service, **94:** 338; race-based scholarships, **95:** 198; radiation experiments, **95:** 350, 351; religion, **94:** 356; welfare, **95:** 443-444, **94:** 449. See also **Aborigines; Civil rights; Race relations**
African Financial Community, 95: 44, **94:** 41-44
African National Congress, 95: 294, 369, 371, 375-383, **94:** 381-382, **93:** 44, 421
Afrikaner Resistance Movement, 95: 378-381, **94:** 382
Afrikaner Volksfront, 95: 378-380
Afrikaners, 95: 372-383
Agassi, Andre, 95: 415, **94:** 440-441
Agenda for Peace (plan), 93: 464
Agriculture. See **Farm and farming**
Agriculture, U.S. Department of, 95: 143, 223-225, **94:** 197, 204, 205
Aguilar Treviño, Daniel, 95: 301
Ahtisaari, Martii, 95: 227
Aid to Families with Dependent Children, 95: 391, 437, 440-449
Aideed, Mohamed Farah, 95: 368, **94:** 38, 53-54, 380-381, 403, 426, **93:** 421
AIDS, 95: 45-55, **94:** 44-46, **93:** 46; concert, **93:** 388; drugs, **94:** 185; French scandal, **93:** 248-249; German scandal, **94:** 215; heterosexual transmission, **94:** 47-55; immigration ban, **94:** 224; prisons, **94:** 339; stamp, **94:** 338 (il.). See also **Africa**
AIDS-like illness, 94: 45
Air Force, U.S. See **Armed forces**

Air Line Pilots Association, 95: 264-265, **94:** 267
Air pollution. See **Environmental pollution**
Air traffic controllers, 95: 275-276, **94:** 269, 428
Aircraft crashes. See **Aviation disasters**
Airlines. See **Aviation**
Ajaj, Ahmad, 95: 151
Akashi, Yasushi, 95: 427, **94:** 107, **93:** 118
Akebono, 94: 317
Akihito, 93: 289
Akzo Salt Inc., 95: 307
Alabama, 95: 393-394, **94:** 188, 387, 389; tables, **95:** 390, **94:** 388, **93:** 429
Alabama, University of, 93: 246
Al Arqam (sect), 95: 253, 293-294
Alaska, 95: 465; tables, **95:** 390, **94:** 388, **93:** 429
Alaska Airlines, 95: 265
Alaska Highway, 93: 476
ALBANIA, 95: 56, **94:** 46, **93:** 46-47; Eastern Orthodox Churches, **95:** 194, **94:** 185; Serbia, **93:** 476; tables, **95:** 220, **94:** 200, **93:** 236. See also **Berisha, Sali**
Al-Bashir, Umar Hasan Ahmad, 93: 393, **94:** 403, **93:** 408-409, 431
Albert II, 94: 96
ALBERTA, 95: 116-117, **94:** 46, **93:** 47
ALBRIGHT, MADELEINE K., 94: 47
Alcohol, Tobacco, and Firearms, Bureau of, 94: 158, 340, 431
Alcohol consumption, 94: 184, **93:** 199
Alcoholism, 94: 183. See also **Drunken driving**
Aleve (drug), 95: 193
Alexander, Jane, 94: 58, 413
Alexei II, 95: 194, **94:** 185
Algae, 93: 376-377
ALGERIA, 95: 56-57, **94:** 47, **93:** 47; Iran, **94:** 242; Islamic movements, **95:** 253, **93:** 285, 408; Morocco, **95:** 56-57, 308; nuclear weapons, **93:** 66; plane hijacking, **95:** 233; tables, **95:** 42, **94:** 42, **93:** 42
Ali Araki, Mohammad, 95: 251
Alia, Ramiz, 95: 56
Aliens. See **Immigration**
Aliyev, Heydar A., 95: 90, **94:** 88
Alkaisi, Bilal, 95: 151
Allen, Elmer, 95: 350
Allen, Woody, 94: 316, **93:** 339, 347
Alliance of Young Democrats (Hungary), 95: 244
Alligators, 95: 205
Al Nahyan family, 93: 334-335
Alps, 95: 396
Al-Sabah, Jabir al-Ahmad al-Jabir, 93: 294
Al-Sulh, Rashid, 93: 311
Altman, Robert A., 94: 90, **93:** 99, 178
Altman, Roger C., 95: 107
Al-Turabi, Hasan, 93: 408-409, 431
Aluminum Co. of America, 94: 267, **93:** 296
Álvarez Machaín, Humberto, 93: 329, 433
Alzheimer's disease, 94: 184
Amalgamated Transit Union, 94: 268
Amato, Giuliano, 94: 247, **93:** 287
Amazon region, 95: 103. See also **Rain forest**
Amber, 94: 305, 310, 326
Ambulocetus (animal), **95:** 330
AMC Grand (cinema), 95: 311
America Online, 95: 140
America West Airlines, 94: 86
American Airlines, 94: 86-87, 267, **93:** 95, 96
American Association for the Advancement of Science, 94: 188
American Ballet Theatre, 95: 173, **94:** 162-163, **93:** 181-182
American Barrick Resources Inc., 95: 307
American Broadcasting Companies, 95: 399, 412-414, **94:** 93, 409, **93:** 439
American Center (Paris), 95: 61
American Federation of Labor, 95: 269-273
American Federation of Labor and Congress of Industrial Organizations, 95: 273, **94:** 269
American Health Security Act, 94: 156, 218
American Hospital Association, 93: 268-269, 274-275
American Indian. See **Indian, American**
American League. See **Baseball**
American Library Association. See **Library; Literature for children**
American Medical Association, 93: 268-269
American Psychological Association, 95: 298
American Telephone & Telegraph Company. See **AT&T Corp.**
Americans with Disabilities Act (1990), 95: 188, **94:** 180, **93:** 196
America's Cup. See **Boating**
Ames, Aldrich Hazen and Maria del Rosario Casas, 95: 207-208, 216, 431

Ammons, R. A., 94: 333
Amnesty International, 95: 133, **94:** 139, **93:** 149, 449
Amtrak, 94: 420
Amyotrophic lateral sclerosis, 94: 290
Anabolic steroids, 95: 395-396
Anand, Viswanathan, 95: 123
Anastasios, 95: 194
ANC. See **African National Congress**
Andersen, Kurt, 95: 292
Anderson, Marian, 94: 175-177
Andorra, tables, **95:** 220, **94:** 200, **93:** 236
Andreotti, Giulio, 94: 246, **93:** 287
Andretti, Mario, 95: 88
Andretti, Michael, 94: 86, **93:** 94-95
Andrew, Prince, 94: 426
Andromeda Galaxy, 94: 80-81
Angelou, Maya, 94: 332
Angels in America (Kushner), **95:** 416, **94:** 414
Angiosperms, 94: 327
Anglicans. See **England, Church of**
Angola, 95: 40-41, **94:** 39, **93:** 41; tables, **95:** 42, **94:** 42, **93:** 42
Anheuser-Busch Cos., 95: 264
Animals: fur protests, **95:** 226; pollution and gender, **95:** 204-205; religious sacrifice, **94:** 404; *WBE*, **94:** 458. See also **Biology; Fossils; Paleontology; Zoology**
Animated film, 95: 308, **94:** 418, **93:** 337
Anne, Princess, 93: 254-255
Annenberg, Walter, 95: 189
Antall, Jozsef, 95: 244, **94:** 222, **93:** 276
Antarctica, 95: 204, 330-331, **93:** 218
ANTHROPOLOGY, 95: 57-59, **94:** 47-48, **93:** 48-49
Antigua and Barbuda, 95: 450; tables, **95:** 280, **94:** 273, **93:** 309
Antimatter, 93: 384
Anti-Semitism, 95: 255, 259
Anwar Ibrahim, 94: 285
Aozou Strip, 95: 44, 284
Apartheid. See **South Africa**
Apple Computer, Inc., 95: 140-141, **94:** 146, 147, 192, **93:** 155-156
Aptidon, Hassan Gouled, 94: 40
Aptiva (computer), 95: 141
Aquarium of the Americas, 95: 454-455 (il.), 459, 464, 465
Aquariums. See **Zoos**
Aquino, Corazon C., 93: 382, 408
Arab League, 95: 264, **93:** 311
Arabs. See **Islam; Middle East; Palestinians**
Arad, Ron, 95: 283
ARAFAT, YASIR, 95: 59, 254, 302-304, 320, **94:** 245, 292-293, 406, **93:** 334, 457
Aramis, Ethiopia, 95: 57-58
ARCHAEOLOGY, 95: 59-60, **94:** 49-50, **93:** 49-50; Dead Sea Scrolls, **94:** 358-367
Archer, Dennis W., 95: 187, **94:** 179
Archery, 95: 387, **94:** 386, **93:** 425
ARCHITECTURE, 95: 61-62, **94:** 51-52, **93:** 50-52; Holocaust Memorial Museum, **94:** 438-441. See also **Building and construction**
Arctic exploration, 95: 120
Arctic Ocean, 93: 359
Arctic ozone hole, 93: 218-219
ARGENTINA, 95: 62-63, **94:** 53, **93:** 52; anti-Jewish terrorism, **95:** 251, 305; corruption, **93:** 306; Iran terrorism, **93:** 282; Latin American trade, **95:** 281; nuclear weapons, **94:** 53; tables, **95:** 280, **94:** 273, **93:** 309. See also **Menem, Carlos Saúl**
ARISTIDE, JEAN-BERTRAND, 95: 239, 427-428, **94:** 217-218, 271-272, 427, **93:** 258
Arizona, 95: 151, 389, 391, **94:** 215; tables, **95:** 390, **94:** 388, **93:** 429
Arkansas, 94: 389; tables, **95:** 390, **94:** 388, **93:** 429
Arkansas, University of, 95: 95-96
ARMED FORCES, 95: 63-71, **94:** 53-56, **93:** 53-67; aircraft crashes, **95:** 252, **93:** 468; European army, **93:** 238; Germany, **94:** 215; Haiti invasion, **95:** 63, 138, 240, 279 (il.); manufacturing, **93:** 325; married individuals, **94:** 430; military base closings, **95:** 65, **94:** 55, 428-430; Navy scandals, **95:** 64, 65, 431, **94:** 430; procurement fraud, **95:** 431; radiation experiments, **95:** 349 (il.); San Diego naval training center, **94:** 376. See also **Defense, U.S. Department of; Homosexuals; Persian Gulf War; Women;** and specific country articles
Armed Islamic Group, 94: 47
ARMENIA, 95: 72, **94:** 56, **93:** 68; tables, **95:** 78, **94:** 62, **93:** 86; *WBE*, **93:** 489
Armey, Richard K., 95: 146
Arms control. See **Nuclear weapons; Weapons**
Army, U.S. See **Armed forces**

Index

Index

Index

Index

Index

Index

538

Acknowledgments

The publishers acknowledge the following sources for illustrations. Credits read from top to bottom, left to right, on their respective pages. An asterisk (*) denotes illustrations and photographs that are the exclusive property of *The Year Book*. All maps, charts, and diagrams were prepared by *The Year Book* staff unless otherwise noted.

6 Reuters/Bettmann; AP/Wide World
7 Peter Chermayeff; Boyes Kelvin, Gamma/Liaison
8 AP/Wide World; Allan Tannenbaum, Sygma; Reuters/Bettmann
9 Christopher Morris, Black Star; Reuters/Bettmann; David Butow, Black Star
10 Allan Tannenbaum, Sygma
12 Reuters/Bettmann; Intersport Television
14 Thierry Orban, Sygma
16 AP/Wide World; Alyx Kellington, Gamma/Liaison
17 Jacques M. Chenet, Gamma/Liaison
18 AP/Wide World
19 Charles Caratini, Sygma
20 AP/Wide World
21 Reuters/Bettmann
22 Richard Hartog
23 Larry Downing, Sygma
24 AP/Wide World
25 AP/Wide World
26 Andrew Moore, Saba
27 B. Swersey, Gamma/Liaison; Lori Grinker, Contact
28 AP/Wide World
30 Jon Jones, Sygma
31 Hartwell, SABA; AP/Wide World
32 AP/Wide World
33 Terry Ashe, Gamma/Liaison
34 AP/Wide World
35 Reuters/Bettmann
36 Christopher Morris, Black Star
39 Allan Tannenbaum, Sygma
41 Reuters/Bettmann
44 AP/Wide World
46 Christopher Loviny, Gamma/Liaison; Centers for Disease Control
47 Chiasson, Gamma/Liaison
51 Swapan Parekh, Black Star; Peter Charlesworth, JB Pictures
52 Mark Edwards, JB Pictures
53 Richard Falco, Black Star
54 Centers for Disease Control
57 Agence France-Presse
58 Tim White, Sipa Press; Sarah Figlio*
60 Jeffrey Newbury ©The Walt Disney Co. Reprinted with permission of *Discover* Magazine.
61 ©Erich Koyama
62 AP/Wide World
64 AP/Wide World
66 AP/Wide World
70 Robert Capa, Magnum; UPI Bettmann
73 *Composition* (1912), an oil painting on canvas by Marc Chagall; Kreeger Museum, Washington, D.C.; Franko Khoury
74 AP/Wide World
76 Reuters/Bettmann
80 AP/Wide World
81 Max-Planck-Institute fuer Astronomie, Heidelberg, Germany
82 Christopher Burrows, ESA/STScI and NASA
84 Reuters/Hulton
86 Reuters/Hulton

87 Reuters/Hulton
89 Walter Urbina, Gamma/Liaison
91 Sarah Figlio*
94 AP/Wide World
96 John Biever, *Sports Illustrated*
99 Reuters/Bettmann
100 AP/Wide World
102 Agence France-Presse
103 Reuters/Bettmann
105 Michael Schumann, SABA
107 Reuters/Bettmann
108 Reuters/Hulton
110 Canapress
112 Canapress
117 Agence France-Presse
118 Canapress
123 Claus Dyrlund
125 Reuters/Hulton
126 Agence France-Presse
128 Office of the Mayor, Chicago
132 AP/Wide World
135 Chris Delmas, Gamma/Liaison
137 Agence France-Presse
140 Frank C. Dougherty, NYT Pictures
146 AP/Wide World
148 Larry Lee, West Light
150 Todd Bigelow, Black Star
152 Jeffrey MacMillian, *U.S. News & World Report*
154 Peter Menzel
156 Kristine Larson
157 Reuters/Bettmann
158 Chavez, Gamma/Liaison
160 Greg Smith, SABA
166 UPI/Bettmann; Greg Smith, SABA
167 Yvonne Hemsey, Gamma/Liaison
171 Reuters/Bettmann
174 Archive Photos; UPI/Bettmann; Archive Photos; AP/Wide World
175 Barry King, Gamma/Liaison; Department of Energy; Charles B. Hoselton, Retna; UPI/Bettmann
176 Archive Photos; UPI/Bettmann; UPI/Bettmann; Bettmann Archive
177 Bill Wisser, Gamma/Liaison; UPI/Bettmann; Archive Photos; Bettmann Archive
178 Archive Photos; JFK Library from Sygma; AP/Wide World; Archive Photos
179 UPI/Bettmann; Douglas Kirkland, Sygma; UPI/Bettmann; Archive Photos
180 Jeanne Strongin
183 UPI/Bettmann; AP/Wide World; UPI/Bettmann; AP/Wide World
185 Wally McNamee, Woodfin Camp, Inc.
188 Agence France-Presse
190 Reuters/Bettmann
192 AP/Wide World
195 Walker, Gamma/Liaison
199 Marri-Beth Serritella*
204 AP/Wide World
206 Reuters/Bettmann
212 Gamma/Liaison; Roger Ressmeyer, Starlight; AP/Wide World

Index

A Preview of 1995

JANUARY

Sun	Mon	Tue	Wed	Thur	Fri	Sat
1	2	3	4	5	6	7
8	9	10	11	12	13	14
15	16	17	18	19	20	21
22	23	24	25	26	27	28
29	30	31				

1 **New Year's Day**
2 **Rose Bowl and other bowl games** played by top college football teams.
5 **Twelfth Night,** marking the traditional end of Christmas celebrations.
6 **Epiphany,** 12th day after Christmas celebrates visit of the Three Wise Men.
16 **Martin Luther King, Jr., Day**
   Tu B'Shebat, a Jewish arbor day; Jews throughout the world celebrate the day by donating funds to plant trees in Israel.
19 **Robert E. Lee's Birthday,** celebrated as a legal holiday in most Southern states.
21 **Senior Bowl,** featuring the best college seniors.
22 **Hula Bowl,** featuring college all-star football players.
29 **Super Bowl XXIX**
30 **Holiday of the Three Hierarchs,** Eastern Orthodox holy day.
31 **Chinese New Year,** the year 4693 of the ancient Chinese calendar (The Year of the Pig).

FEBRUARY

Sun	Mon	Tue	Wed	Thur	Fri	Sat
			1	2	3	4
5	6	7	8	9	10	11
12	13	14	15	16	17	18
19	20	21	22	23	24	25
26	27	28				

1 **Ramadan,** a Muslim holiday, beginning a month of fasting.
  African-American History Month, also known as Black History Month, begins.
2 **Ground-Hog Day;** according to legend, if the ground hog emerges and sees its shadow, six weeks of winter weather will follow.
5 **Boy Scouts of America Anniversary**

Week begins.
  National Crime Prevention Week begins.
  NFL Pro Bowl '95
6 **100th anniversary** of the birthday of baseball Hall of Famer Babe Ruth.
12 **Abraham Lincoln's Birthday,** celebrated in many states.
14 **Valentine's Day**
20 **Presidents' Day,** honoring Lincoln, Washington, and other past U.S. Presidents.
21 **30th anniversary** of the assassination of U.S. black leader Malcolm X.
22 **George Washington's Birthday**
28 **Mardi Gras,** last celebration before Lent, observed in New Orleans and many Roman Catholic countries.

MARCH

Sun	Mon	Tue	Wed	Thur	Fri	Sat
			1	2	3	4
5	6	7	8	9	10	11
12	13	14	15	16	17	18
19	20	21	22	23	24	25
26	27	28	29	30	31	

1 **Ash Wednesday,** first day of Lent, the penitential period that precedes Easter.
  National Women's History Month begins, to celebrate the contributions and achievements of women.
2 **World's Largest Concert,** on PBS stations nationwide, to draw attention to Music in Our Schools Month.
3 **World Day of Prayer**
5 **Girl Scout Week** begins.
  National PTA Drug and Alcohol Awareness Week begins.
  National Volunteers of America Week begins.
  Save Your Vision Week begins, to promote awareness of the importance of eye health.
8 **United Nations' International Women's Day**
13 **Commonwealth Day in Canada**
16 **Purim,** commemorates the saving of ancient Persian Jews from a plot to kill them.
17 **St. Patrick's Day,** honoring the patron saint of Ireland.
19 **American Chocolate Week** begins.
  National Poison Prevention Week begins.
20 **Spring begins** with the Vernal Equinox at 9:14 p.m. (E.S.T.).
  Earth Day, observed in some areas.

541

APRIL

Sun	Mon	Tue	Wed	Thur	Fri	Sat
						1
2	3	4	5	6	7	8
9	10	11	12	13	14	15
16	17	18	19	20	21	22
23	24	25	26	27	28	29
30						

1 April Fools' Day

2 Daylight-Saving Time begins at 2:00 a.m. in most areas of the United States.

7 United Nations' World Health Day

9 Palm Sunday, marking Jesus' final entry into Jerusalem along streets covered with palm leaves.
National Library Week begins.

13 Maundy Thursday

14 Good Friday, marks the death of Jesus.

15 Passover, or Pesah, begins, celebrating deliverance of the ancient Israelites from Egypt.
Partial eclipse of the moon, visible over parts of western North America and Mexico as well as Antarctica, Australia, and eastern Asia.

16 Easter Sunday
Boys and Girls Club Week begins.

22 25th Anniversary of the first Earth Day observance in 1970.

23 Eastern Orthodox Easter

27 Take Our Daughters to Work Day

26 Professional Secretaries Day

28 National Day of Mourning in Canada for workers killed or injured on the job.
National Arbor Day in the United States.

MAY

Sun	Mon	Tue	Wed	Thur	Fri	Sat
	1	2	3	4	5	6
7	8	9	10	11	12	13
14	15	16	17	18	19	20
21	22	23	24	25	26	27
28	29	30	31			

1 May Day; Law Day in the United States.

3 United Nations' World Press Freedom Day

4 National Day of Prayer

5 Cinco de Mayo, commemorating an 1862 battle in which Mexican forces defeated invading French troops.

Independence Day in Israel, commemorating proclamation of independence from British rule in 1948.

6 National Nurses' Week begins.
Kentucky Derby, famed horse race.

7 Be Kind to Animals Week begins.

8 50th Anniversary of V-E Day (Victory in Europe, World War II).
Basketball Hall of Fame Enshrinement Ceremonies

9 National Teacher's Day, to honor the contributions of American educators.

14 Mother's Day

15 Peace Officer Memorial Day

22 Armed Forces Day
Victoria Day in Canada.

25 African Freedom Day in Organization of African Unity countries.

29 Memorial Day celebrated.

30 Islamic New Year, the year 1416 of the Islamic era, begins at sundown.

JUNE

Sun	Mon	Tue	Wed	Thur	Fri	Sat
				1	2	3
4	5	6	7	8	9	10
11	12	13	14	15	16	17
18	19	20	21	22	23	24
25	26	27	28	29	30	

2 Donut Day, on which the Salvation Army raises funds by selling paper donuts.

3 Shavuot, a Jewish celebration commemorating Moses receiving the Torah, or Law, begins at sundown.

4 Pentecost, or Whitsunday, commemorates the descent of the Holy Spirit onto the Apostles.
National Safe Boating Week begins.

9 Red Earth Native American Cultural Festival, one of the largest intertribal gatherings, begins in Oklahoma City, Okla.

11 Children's Sunday, observed by many Christian congregations.

12 National Little League Baseball Week begins.

14 Flag Day, commemorates the adoption in 1777 of the Stars and Stripes as the U.S. flag.

18 Father's Day

21 Summer begins in the Northern Hemisphere with the summer solstice at 4:34 p.m. (E.D.T.).

24 100th Anniversary of the birth of heavyweight boxing champion Jack Dempsey.

JULY

Sun	Mon	Tue	Wed	Thur	Fri	Sat
						1
2	3	4	5	6	7	8
9	10	11	12	13	14	15
16	17	18	19	20	21	22
23	24	25	26	27	28	29
30	31					

1 Canada Day, commemorates the confederation of Upper and Lower Canada with certain Maritime provinces to form the Dominion of Canada in 1867.

4 Independence Day in the United States. 100th Anniversary of the publication of "America the Beautiful."

5 60th Anniversary of the signing of the National Labor Relations Act, giving workers the right to organize and bargain collectively.

6 Quebec International Summer Festival begins in Quebec City, Canada, and continues through July 16, with entertainment in streets and parks.

11 United Nations' World Population Day, calling attention to issues involving population growth.

14 Bastille Day, France's Independence Day.

16 50th Anniversary of the first atomic bomb test at Alamogordo Air Base in New Mexico.

21 Pro Football Hall of Fame Festival begins, to honor new inductees.

30 20th Anniversary of the disappearance of former Teamsters Union leader James R. Hoffa.

AUGUST

Sun	Mon	Tue	Wed	Thur	Fri	Sat
		1	2	3	4	5
6	7	8	9	10	11	12
13	14	15	16	17	18	19
20	21	22	23	24	25	26
27	28	29	30	31		

4 Coast Guard Day, celebrates the founding of the U.S. Coast Guard in 1790.

6 50th Anniversary of the dropping of an atomic bomb on Hiroshima, Japan, the first use of an atomic weapon in war. A second atomic bomb was dropped on Nagasaki on August 9.
30th Anniversary of the Voting Rights Act of 1965, designed to eliminate discrimination against minorities at the polls.

7 Canadian Civic Holiday observed in Alberta, British Columbia, Manitoba, New Brunswick, Ontario, Saskatchewan, and the Northwest Territories.

8 Intertribal Indian Ceremonial, a major festival, begins in Gallup, N. Mex., and continues through August 13.

9 Mulid al-Nabi, a Muslim festival, celebrates the birth of the Prophet Muhammad.

19 National Aviation Day, commemorating the Wright brothers' first flight.

20 Little League Baseball World Series begins in Williamsport, Pa., and continues through August 26.

26 Women's Equality Day, celebrating the 19th Amendment to the U.S. Constitution, granting women the right to vote.
75th Anniversary of the 19th Amendment

SEPTEMBER

Sun	Mon	Tue	Wed	Thur	Fri	Sat
					1	2
3	4	5	6	7	8	9
10	11	12	13	14	15	16
17	18	19	20	21	22	23
24	25	26	27	28	29	30

2 50th Anniversary of V-J Day (Victory over Japan), when Japan officially surrendered to the Allies aboard the battleship USS *Missouri,* ending World War II.

4 Labor Day in the United States and Canada.

9 Chinese Moon, or Mid-Autumn, Festival, celebrating the harvest.

10 National Grandparents Day

15 National Hispanic Heritage Month begins and continues through October 15.
105th Anniversary of the birth of mystery writer Agatha Christie.

17 National Constitution Day commemorates signing of the U.S. Constitution in 1787.

23 Autumn begins with the autumnal equinox at 8:14 a.m. (E.D.T.).
Banned Books Week begins, emphasizing the right to read and the importance of freedom from censorship.

25 Rosh Ha-Shanah, celebrating the Jewish New Year, 5756.

OCTOBER

Sun	Mon	Tue	Wed	Thur	Fri	Sat
1	2	3	4	5	6	7
8	9	10	11	12	13	14
15	16	17	18	19	20	21
22	23	24	25	26	27	28
29	30	31				

2 **Child Health Day** in the United States.

4 **Yom Kippur,** the Jewish Day of Atonement.

8 **Fire Prevention Week** begins.
Penumbral Eclipse of the Moon
Sukkot, Jewish Feast of Tabernacles, begins.

9 **Columbus Day** in the United States.
Leif Ericson Day
Canadian Thanksgiving Day

11 **General Pulaski Memorial Day,** recognizing the role of Polish cavalry officer Casimir Pulaski in the American Revolutionary War.

18 **Canadian Persons' Day** commemorates a 1929 court ruling that women in Canada are persons with rights and privileges.

23 **Total Solar Eclipse** visible over parts of Africa, Asia, Australia, and the Indian and Pacific oceans.

24 **United Nations' Day** and 50th Anniversary of the founding of the United Nations.

29 **Daylight Savings Time ends** and Standard Time resumes at 2:00 a.m.

31 **Halloween**
National UNICEF Day to raise awareness about the lives of children in the developing world.

NOVEMBER

Sun	Mon	Tue	Wed	Thur	Fri	Sat
			1	2	3	4
5	6	7	8	9	10	11
12	13	14	15	16	17	18
19	20	21	22	23	24	25
26	27	28	29	30		

1 **All Saints' Day**
National Alzheimer's Disease Month begins.
National Diabetes Month begins.
National Epilepsy Awareness Month begins.
200th Anniversary of the birth of James Knox Polk, 11th President of the United States.
All Souls' Day

5 **Guy Fawkes Day** in England commemorates the foiling of a plot in 1605 to blow up the Houses of Parliament.

7 **Election Day**

8 **95th Anniversary of the birth of Margaret Mitchell,** author of *Gone with the Wind* (1936).

11 **Veterans Day** in the United States.
Remembrance Day in Canada.

12 **American Education Week** begins, calling attention to the importance of public education in the United States.

13 **National Children's Book Week** begins.

16 **Great American Smokeout,** urging smokers to quit for at least a day.

22 **John F. Kennedy,** 35th President of the United States, assassinated in Dallas in 1963.

23 **Thanksgiving Day**

DECEMBER

Sun	Mon	Tue	Wed	Thur	Fri	Sat
					1	2
3	4	5	6	7	8	9
10	11	12	13	14	15	16
17	18	19	20	21	22	23
24	25	26	27	28	29	30
31						

1 **United Nations' World AIDS Day,** focusing on efforts to prevent and control AIDS.

3 **Advent** begins.

6 **St. Nicholas Day,** when children in parts of Europe receive gifts.

7 **Pearl Harbor Day,** commemorating the 1941 bombing of the U.S. fleet in Hawaii by the Japanese.

16 **225th Anniversary** of the birth of German composer Ludwig van Beethoven.

18 **Hanukkah,** the eight-day Jewish Feast of Lights, begins.

19 **Lailat al Miraj,** Muslim holy day commemorating the ascent of the Prophet Muhammad into heaven.

22 **Winter begins** in the Northern Hemisphere with the winter solstice at 3:18 a.m. (E.S.T.).

25 **Christmas Day**

26 **Kwanzaa,** an African-American family observance based on African harvest festivals, begins and continues through Jan. 1, 1996.
Boxing Day, observed in England, Canada, and other Commonwealth nations.

29 **150th Anniversary** of the admission of Texas to statehood.

31 **New Year's Eve**